T0190055

Lecture Notes in Computer Science 12373

More information about this series at http://www.springer.com/series/7412

Andrea Vedaldi · Horst Bischof ·
Thomas Brox · Jan-Michael Frahm (Eds.)

Computer Vision – ECCV 2020

16th European Conference
Glasgow, UK, August 23–28, 2020
Proceedings, Part XXVIII

 Springer

Editors
Andrea Vedaldi (iD)
University of Oxford
Oxford, UK

Horst Bischof (iD)
Graz University of Technology
Graz, Austria

Thomas Brox (iD)
University of Freiburg
Freiburg im Breisgau, Germany

Jan-Michael Frahm
University of North Carolina at Chapel Hill
Chapel Hill, NC, USA

ISSN 0302-9743   ISSN 1611-3349 (electronic)
Lecture Notes in Computer Science
ISBN 978-3-030-58603-4   ISBN 978-3-030-58604-1 (eBook)
https://doi.org/10.1007/978-3-030-58604-1

LNCS Sublibrary: SL6 – Image Processing, Computer Vision, Pattern Recognition, and Graphics

This Springer imprint is published by the registered company Springer Nature Switzerland AG
The registered company address is: Gewerbestrasse 11, 6330 Cham, Switzerland

Foreword

Hosting the European Conference on Computer Vision (ECCV 2020) was certainly an exciting journey. From the 2016 plan to hold it at the Edinburgh International Conference Centre (hosting 1,800 delegates) to the 2018 plan to hold it at Glasgow's Scottish Exhibition Centre (up to 6,000 delegates), we finally ended with moving online because of the COVID-19 outbreak. While possibly having fewer delegates than expected because of the online format, ECCV 2020 still had over 3,100 registered participants.

Although online, the conference delivered most of the activities expected at a face-to-face conference: peer-reviewed papers, industrial exhibitors, demonstrations, and messaging between delegates. In addition to the main technical sessions, the conference included a strong program of satellite events with 16 tutorials and 44 workshops.

Furthermore, the online conference format enabled new conference features. Every paper had an associated teaser video and a longer full presentation video. Along with the papers and slides from the videos, all these materials were available the week before the conference. This allowed delegates to become familiar with the paper content and be ready for the live interaction with the authors during the conference week. The live event consisted of brief presentations by the oral and spotlight authors and industrial sponsors. Question and answer sessions for all papers were timed to occur twice so delegates from around the world had convenient access to the authors.

As with ECCV 2018, authors' draft versions of the papers appeared online with open access, now on both the Computer Vision Foundation (CVF) and the European Computer Vision Association (ECVA) websites. An archival publication arrangement was put in place with the cooperation of Springer. SpringerLink hosts the final version of the papers with further improvements, such as activating reference links and supplementary materials. These two approaches benefit all potential readers: a version available freely for all researchers, and an authoritative and citable version with additional benefits for SpringerLink subscribers. We thank Alfred Hofmann and Aliaksandr Birukou from Springer for helping to negotiate this agreement, which we expect will continue for future versions of ECCV.

August 2020

Vittorio Ferrari
Bob Fisher
Cordelia Schmid
Emanuele Trucco

Preface

Welcome to the proceedings of the European Conference on Computer Vision (ECCV 2020). This is a unique edition of ECCV in many ways. Due to the COVID-19 pandemic, this is the first time the conference was held online, in a virtual format. This was also the first time the conference relied exclusively on the Open Review platform to manage the review process. Despite these challenges ECCV is thriving. The conference received 5,150 valid paper submissions, of which 1,360 were accepted for publication (27%) and, of those, 160 were presented as spotlights (3%) and 104 as orals (2%). This amounts to more than twice the number of submissions to ECCV 2018 (2,439). Furthermore, CVPR, the largest conference on computer vision, received 5,850 submissions this year, meaning that ECCV is now 87% the size of CVPR in terms of submissions. By comparison, in 2018 the size of ECCV was only 73% of CVPR.

The review model was similar to previous editions of ECCV; in particular, it was double blind in the sense that the authors did not know the name of the reviewers and vice versa. Furthermore, each conference submission was held confidentially, and was only publicly revealed if and once accepted for publication. Each paper received at least three reviews, totalling more than 15,000 reviews. Handling the review process at this scale was a significant challenge. In order to ensure that each submission received as fair and high-quality reviews as possible, we recruited 2,830 reviewers (a 130% increase with reference to 2018) and 207 area chairs (a 60% increase). The area chairs were selected based on their technical expertise and reputation, largely among people that served as area chair in previous top computer vision and machine learning conferences (ECCV, ICCV, CVPR, NeurIPS, etc.). Reviewers were similarly invited from previous conferences. We also encouraged experienced area chairs to suggest additional chairs and reviewers in the initial phase of recruiting.

Despite doubling the number of submissions, the reviewer load was slightly reduced from 2018, from a maximum of 8 papers down to 7 (with some reviewers offering to handle 6 papers plus an emergency review). The area chair load increased slightly, from 18 papers on average to 22 papers on average.

Conflicts of interest between authors, area chairs, and reviewers were handled largely automatically by the Open Review platform via their curated list of user profiles. Many authors submitting to ECCV already had a profile in Open Review. We set a paper registration deadline one week before the paper submission deadline in order to encourage all missing authors to register and create their Open Review profiles well on time (in practice, we allowed authors to create/change papers arbitrarily until the submission deadline). Except for minor issues with users creating duplicate profiles, this allowed us to easily and quickly identify institutional conflicts, and avoid them, while matching papers to area chairs and reviewers.

Papers were matched to area chairs based on: an affinity score computed by the Open Review platform, which is based on paper titles and abstracts, and an affinity score computed by the Toronto Paper Matching System (TPMS), which is based on the paper's full text, the area chair bids for individual papers, load balancing, and conflict avoidance. Open Review provides the program chairs a convenient web interface to experiment with different configurations of the matching algorithm. The chosen configuration resulted in about 50% of the assigned papers to be highly ranked by the area chair bids, and 50% to be ranked in the middle, with very few low bids assigned.

Assignments to reviewers were similar, with two differences. First, there was a maximum of 7 papers assigned to each reviewer. Second, area chairs recommended up to seven reviewers per paper, providing another highly-weighed term to the affinity scores used for matching.

The assignment of papers to area chairs was smooth. However, it was more difficult to find suitable reviewers for all papers. Having a ratio of 5.6 papers per reviewer with a maximum load of 7 (due to emergency reviewer commitment), which did not allow for much wiggle room in order to also satisfy conflict and expertise constraints. We received some complaints from reviewers who did not feel qualified to review specific papers and we reassigned them wherever possible. However, the large scale of the conference, the many constraints, and the fact that a large fraction of such complaints arrived very late in the review process made this process very difficult and not all complaints could be addressed.

Reviewers had six weeks to complete their assignments. Possibly due to COVID-19 or the fact that the NeurIPS deadline was moved closer to the review deadline, a record 30% of the reviews were still missing after the deadline. By comparison, ECCV 2018 experienced only 10% missing reviews at this stage of the process. In the subsequent week, area chairs chased the missing reviews intensely, found replacement reviewers in their own team, and managed to reach 10% missing reviews. Eventually, we could provide almost all reviews (more than 99.9%) with a delay of only a couple of days on the initial schedule by a significant use of emergency reviews. If this trend is confirmed, it might be a major challenge to run a smooth review process in future editions of ECCV. The community must reconsider prioritization of the time spent on paper writing (the number of submissions increased a lot despite COVID-19) and time spent on paper reviewing (the number of reviews delivered in time decreased a lot presumably due to COVID-19 or NeurIPS deadline). With this imbalance the peer-review system that ensures the quality of our top conferences may break soon.

Reviewers submitted their reviews independently. In the reviews, they had the opportunity to ask questions to the authors to be addressed in the rebuttal. However, reviewers were told not to request any significant new experiment. Using the Open Review interface, authors could provide an answer to each individual review, but were also allowed to cross-reference reviews and responses in their answers. Rather than PDF files, we allowed the use of formatted text for the rebuttal. The rebuttal and initial reviews were then made visible to all reviewers and the primary area chair for a given paper. The area chair encouraged and moderated the reviewer discussion. During the discussions, reviewers were invited to reach a consensus and possibly adjust their ratings as a result of the discussion and of the evidence in the rebuttal.

After the discussion period ended, most reviewers entered a final rating and recommendation, although in many cases this did not differ from their initial recommendation. Based on the updated reviews and discussion, the primary area chair then made a preliminary decision to accept or reject the paper and wrote a justification for it (meta-review). Except for cases where the outcome of this process was absolutely clear (as indicated by the three reviewers and primary area chairs all recommending clear rejection), the decision was then examined and potentially challenged by a secondary area chair. This led to further discussion and overturning a small number of preliminary decisions. Needless to say, there was no in-person area chair meeting, which would have been impossible due to COVID-19.

Area chairs were invited to observe the consensus of the reviewers whenever possible and use extreme caution in overturning a clear consensus to accept or reject a paper. If an area chair still decided to do so, she/he was asked to clearly justify it in the meta-review and to explicitly obtain the agreement of the secondary area chair. In practice, very few papers were rejected after being confidently accepted by the reviewers.

This was the first time Open Review was used as the main platform to run ECCV. In 2018, the program chairs used CMT3 for the user-facing interface and Open Review internally, for matching and conflict resolution. Since it is clearly preferable to only use a single platform, this year we switched to using Open Review in full. The experience was largely positive. The platform is highly-configurable, scalable, and open source. Being written in Python, it is easy to write scripts to extract data programmatically. The paper matching and conflict resolution algorithms and interfaces are top-notch, also due to the excellent author profiles in the platform. Naturally, there were a few kinks along the way due to the fact that the ECCV Open Review configuration was created from scratch for this event and it differs in substantial ways from many other Open Review conferences. However, the Open Review development and support team did a fantastic job in helping us to get the configuration right and to address issues in a timely manner as they unavoidably occurred. We cannot thank them enough for the tremendous effort they put into this project.

Finally, we would like to thank everyone involved in making ECCV 2020 possible in these very strange and difficult times. This starts with our authors, followed by the area chairs and reviewers, who ran the review process at an unprecedented scale. The whole Open Review team (and in particular Melisa Bok, Mohit Unyal, Carlos Mondragon Chapa, and Celeste Martinez Gomez) worked incredibly hard for the entire duration of the process. We would also like to thank René Vidal for contributing to the adoption of Open Review. Our thanks also go to Laurent Charling for TPMS and to the program chairs of ICML, ICLR, and NeurIPS for cross checking double submissions. We thank the website chair, Giovanni Farinella, and the CPI team (in particular Ashley Cook, Miriam Verdon, Nicola McGrane, and Sharon Kerr) for promptly adding material to the website as needed in the various phases of the process. Finally, we thank the publication chairs, Albert Ali Salah, Hamdi Dibeklioglu, Metehan Doyran, Henry Howard-Jenkins, Victor Prisacariu, Siyu Tang, and Gul Varol, who managed to compile these substantial proceedings in an exceedingly compressed schedule. We express our thanks to the ECVA team, in particular Kristina Scherbaum for allowing open access of the proceedings. We thank Alfred Hofmann from Springer who again serve as the publisher. Finally, we thank the other chairs of ECCV 2020, including in particular the general chairs for very useful feedback with the handling of the program.

August 2020   Andrea Vedaldi
                                                                    Horst Bischof
                                                                    Thomas Brox
                                                              Jan-Michael Frahm

Organization

General Chairs

Vittorio Ferrari	Google Research, Switzerland
Bob Fisher	University of Edinburgh, UK
Cordelia Schmid	Google and Inria, France
Emanuele Trucco	University of Dundee, UK

Program Chairs

Andrea Vedaldi	University of Oxford, UK
Horst Bischof	Graz University of Technology, Austria
Thomas Brox	University of Freiburg, Germany
Jan-Michael Frahm	University of North Carolina, USA

Industrial Liaison Chairs

Jim Ashe	University of Edinburgh, UK
Helmut Grabner	Zurich University of Applied Sciences, Switzerland
Diane Larlus	NAVER LABS Europe, France
Cristian Novotny	University of Edinburgh, UK

Local Arrangement Chairs

Yvan Petillot	Heriot-Watt University, UK
Paul Siebert	University of Glasgow, UK

Academic Demonstration Chair

Thomas Mensink	Google Research and University of Amsterdam, The Netherlands

Poster Chair

Stephen Mckenna	University of Dundee, UK

Technology Chair

Gerardo Aragon Camarasa	University of Glasgow, UK

Tutorial Chairs

Carlo Colombo   University of Florence, Italy
Sotirios Tsaftaris   University of Edinburgh, UK

Publication Chairs

Albert Ali Salah   Utrecht University, The Netherlands
Hamdi Dibeklioglu   Bilkent University, Turkey
Metehan Doyran   Utrecht University, The Netherlands
Henry Howard-Jenkins   University of Oxford, UK
Victor Adrian Prisacariu   University of Oxford, UK
Siyu Tang   ETH Zurich, Switzerland
Gul Varol   University of Oxford, UK

Website Chair

Giovanni Maria Farinella   University of Catania, Italy

Workshops Chairs

Adrien Bartoli   University of Clermont Auvergne, France
Andrea Fusiello   University of Udine, Italy

Area Chairs

Lourdes Agapito   University College London, UK
Zeynep Akata   University of Tübingen, Germany
Karteek Alahari   Inria, France
Antonis Argyros   University of Crete, Greece
Hossein Azizpour   KTH Royal Institute of Technology, Sweden
Joao P. Barreto   Universidade de Coimbra, Portugal
Alexander C. Berg   University of North Carolina at Chapel Hill, USA
Matthew B. Blaschko   KU Leuven, Belgium
Lubomir D. Bourdev   WaveOne, Inc., USA
Edmond Boyer   Inria, France
Yuri Boykov   University of Waterloo, Canada
Gabriel Brostow   University College London, UK
Michael S. Brown   National University of Singapore, Singapore
Jianfei Cai   Monash University, Australia
Barbara Caputo   Politecnico di Torino, Italy
Ayan Chakrabarti   Washington University, St. Louis, USA
Tat-Jen Cham   Nanyang Technological University, Singapore
Manmohan Chandraker   University of California, San Diego, USA
Rama Chellappa   Johns Hopkins University, USA
Liang-Chieh Chen   Google, USA

Timothy Hospedales	University of Edinburgh and Samsung, UK
Gang Hua	Wormpex AI Research, USA
Slobodan Ilic	Siemens AG, Germany
Hiroshi Ishikawa	Waseda University, Japan
Jiaya Jia	The Chinese University of Hong Kong, SAR China
Hailin Jin	Adobe Research, USA
Justin Johnson	University of Michigan, USA
Frederic Jurie	University of Caen Normandie, France
Fredrik Kahl	Chalmers University, Sweden
Sing Bing Kang	Zillow, USA
Gunhee Kim	Seoul National University, South Korea
Junmo Kim	Korea Advanced Institute of Science and Technology, South Korea
Tae-Kyun Kim	Imperial College London, UK
Ron Kimmel	Technion-Israel Institute of Technology, Israel
Alexander Kirillov	Facebook AI Research, USA
Kris Kitani	Carnegie Mellon University, USA
Iasonas Kokkinos	Ariel AI, UK
Vladlen Koltun	Intel Labs, USA
Nikos Komodakis	Ecole des Ponts ParisTech, France
Piotr Koniusz	Australian National University, Australia
M. Pawan Kumar	University of Oxford, UK
Kyros Kutulakos	University of Toronto, Canada
Christoph Lampert	IST Austria, Austria
Ivan Laptev	Inria, France
Diane Larlus	NAVER LABS Europe, France
Laura Leal-Taixe	Technical University Munich, Germany
Honglak Lee	Google and University of Michigan, USA
Joon-Young Lee	Adobe Research, USA
Kyoung Mu Lee	Seoul National University, South Korea
Seungyong Lee	POSTECH, South Korea
Yong Jae Lee	University of California, Davis, USA
Bastian Leibe	RWTH Aachen University, Germany
Victor Lempitsky	Samsung, Russia
Ales Leonardis	University of Birmingham, UK
Marius Leordeanu	Institute of Mathematics of the Romanian Academy, Romania
Vincent Lepetit	ENPC ParisTech, France
Hongdong Li	The Australian National University, Australia
Xi Li	Zhejiang University, China
Yin Li	University of Wisconsin-Madison, USA
Zicheng Liao	Zhejiang University, China
Jongwoo Lim	Hanyang University, South Korea
Stephen Lin	Microsoft Research Asia, China
Yen-Yu Lin	National Chiao Tung University, Taiwan, China
Zhe Lin	Adobe Research, USA

Haibin Ling	Stony Brooks, State University of New York, USA
Jiaying Liu	Peking University, China
Ming-Yu Liu	NVIDIA, USA
Si Liu	Beihang University, China
Xiaoming Liu	Michigan State University, USA
Huchuan Lu	Dalian University of Technology, China
Simon Lucey	Carnegie Mellon University, USA
Jiebo Luo	University of Rochester, USA
Julien Mairal	Inria, France
Michael Maire	University of Chicago, USA
Subhransu Maji	University of Massachusetts, Amherst, USA
Yasushi Makihara	Osaka University, Japan
Jiri Matas	Czech Technical University in Prague, Czech Republic
Yasuyuki Matsushita	Osaka University, Japan
Philippos Mordohai	Stevens Institute of Technology, USA
Vittorio Murino	University of Verona, Italy
Naila Murray	NAVER LABS Europe, France
Hajime Nagahara	Osaka University, Japan
P. J. Narayanan	International Institute of Information Technology (IIIT), Hyderabad, India
Nassir Navab	Technical University of Munich, Germany
Natalia Neverova	Facebook AI Research, France
Matthias Niessner	Technical University of Munich, Germany
Jean-Marc Odobez	Idiap Research Institute and Swiss Federal Institute of Technology Lausanne, Switzerland
Francesca Odone	Università di Genova, Italy
Takeshi Oishi	The University of Tokyo, Tokyo Institute of Technology, Japan
Vicente Ordonez	University of Virginia, USA
Manohar Paluri	Facebook AI Research, USA
Maja Pantic	Imperial College London, UK
In Kyu Park	Inha University, South Korea
Ioannis Patras	Queen Mary University of London, UK
Patrick Perez	Valeo, France
Bryan A. Plummer	Boston University, USA
Thomas Pock	Graz University of Technology, Austria
Marc Pollefeys	ETH Zurich and Microsoft MR & AI Zurich Lab, Switzerland
Jean Ponce	Inria, France
Gerard Pons-Moll	MPII, Saarland Informatics Campus, Germany
Jordi Pont-Tuset	Google, Switzerland
James Matthew Rehg	Georgia Institute of Technology, USA
Ian Reid	University of Adelaide, Australia
Olaf Ronneberger	DeepMind London, UK
Stefan Roth	TU Darmstadt, Germany
Bryan Russell	Adobe Research, USA

Kwang Moo Yi   University of Victoria, Canada
Zhaozheng Yin   Stony Brook, State University of New York, USA
Chang D. Yoo   Korea Advanced Institute of Science and Technology,
                             South Korea
Shaodi You   University of Amsterdam, The Netherlands
Jingyi Yu   ShanghaiTech University, China
Stella Yu   University of California, Berkeley, and ICSI, USA
Stefanos Zafeiriou   Imperial College London, UK
Hongbin Zha   Peking University, China
Tianzhu Zhang   University of Science and Technology of China, China
Liang Zheng   Australian National University, Australia
Todd E. Zickler   Harvard University, USA
Andrew Zisserman   University of Oxford, UK

Technical Program Committee

Sathyanarayanan N. Aakur	Samuel Albanie	Pablo Arbelaez
Wael Abd Almgaeed	Shadi Albarqouni	Shervin Ardeshir
Abdelrahman Abdelhamed	Cenek Albl	Sercan O. Arik
Abdullah Abuolaim	Hassan Abu Alhaija	Anil Armagan
Supreeth Achar	Daniel Aliaga	Anurag Arnab
Hanno Ackermann	Mohammad S. Aliakbarian	Chetan Arora
Ehsan Adeli	Rahaf Aljundi	Federica Arrigoni
Triantafyllos Afouras	Thiemo Alldieck	Mathieu Aubry
Sameer Agarwal	Jon Almazan	Shai Avidan
Aishwarya Agrawal	Jose M. Alvarez	Angelica I. Aviles-Rivero
Harsh Agrawal	Senjian An	Yannis Avrithis
Pulkit Agrawal	Saket Anand	Ismail Ben Ayed
Antonio Agudo	Codruta Ancuti	Shekoofeh Azizi
Eirikur Agustsson	Cosmin Ancuti	Ioan Andrei Bârsan
Karim Ahmed	Peter Anderson	Artem Babenko
Byeongjoo Ahn	Juan Andrade-Cetto	Deepak Babu Sam
Unaiza Ahsan	Alexander Andreopoulos	Seung-Hwan Baek
Thalaiyasingam Ajanthan	Misha Andriluka	Seungryul Baek
Kenan E. Ak	Dragomir Anguelov	Andrew D. Bagdanov
Emre Akbas	Rushil Anirudh	Shai Bagon
Naveed Akhtar	Michel Antunes	Yuval Bahat
Derya Akkaynak	Oisin Mac Aodha	Junjie Bai
Yagiz Aksoy	Srikar Appalaraju	Song Bai
Ziad Al-Halah	Relja Arandjelovic	Xiang Bai
Xavier Alameda-Pineda	Nikita Araslanov	Yalong Bai
Jean-Baptiste Alayrac	Andre Araujo	Yancheng Bai
	Helder Araujo	Peter Bajcsy
		Slawomir Bak

Mahsa Baktashmotlagh
Kavita Bala
Yogesh Balaji
Guha Balakrishnan
V. N. Balasubramanian
Federico Baldassarre
Vassileios Balntas
Shurjo Banerjee
Aayush Bansal
Ankan Bansal
Jianmin Bao
Linchao Bao
Wenbo Bao
Yingze Bao
Akash Bapat
Md Jawadul Hasan Bappy
Fabien Baradel
Lorenzo Baraldi
Daniel Barath
Adrian Barbu
Kobus Barnard
Nick Barnes
Francisco Barranco
Jonathan T. Barron
Arslan Basharat
Chaim Baskin
Anil S. Baslamisli
Jorge Batista
Kayhan Batmanghelich
Konstantinos Batsos
David Bau
Luis Baumela
Christoph Baur
Eduardo
   Bayro-Corrochano
Paul Beardsley
Jan Bednavr'ik
Oscar Beijbom
Philippe Bekaert
Esube Bekele
Vasileios Belagiannis
Ohad Ben-Shahar
Abhijit Bendale
Róger Bermúdez-Chacón
Maxim Berman
Jesus Bermudez-cameo

Florian Bernard
Stefano Berretti
Marcelo Bertalmio
Gedas Bertasius
Cigdem Beyan
Lucas Beyer
Vijayakumar Bhagavatula
Arjun Nitin Bhagoji
Apratim Bhattacharyya
Binod Bhattarai
Sai Bi
Jia-Wang Bian
Simone Bianco
Adel Bibi
Tolga Birdal
Tom Bishop
Soma Biswas
Mårten Björkman
Volker Blanz
Vishnu Boddeti
Navaneeth Bodla
Simion-Vlad Bogolin
Xavier Boix
Piotr Bojanowski
Timo Bolkart
Guido Borghi
Larbi Boubchir
Guillaume Bourmaud
Adrien Bousseau
Thierry Bouwmans
Richard Bowden
Hakan Boyraz
Mathieu Brédif
Samarth Brahmbhatt
Steve Branson
Nikolas Brasch
Biagio Brattoli
Ernesto Brau
Toby P. Breckon
Francois Bremond
Jesus Briales
Sofia Broomé
Marcus A. Brubaker
Luc Brun
Silvia Bucci
Shyamal Buch

Pradeep Buddharaju
Uta Buechler
Mai Bui
Tu Bui
Adrian Bulat
Giedrius T. Burachas
Elena Burceanu
Xavier P. Burgos-Artizzu
Kaylee Burns
Andrei Bursuc
Benjamin Busam
Wonmin Byeon
Zoya Bylinskii
Sergi Caelles
Jianrui Cai
Minjie Cai
Yujun Cai
Zhaowei Cai
Zhipeng Cai
Juan C. Caicedo
Simone Calderara
Necati Cihan Camgoz
Dylan Campbell
Octavia Camps
Jiale Cao
Kaidi Cao
Liangliang Cao
Xiangyong Cao
Xiaochun Cao
Yang Cao
Yu Cao
Yue Cao
Zhangjie Cao
Luca Carlone
Mathilde Caron
Dan Casas
Thomas J. Cashman
Umberto Castellani
Lluis Castrejon
Jacopo Cavazza
Fabio Cermelli
Hakan Cevikalp
Menglei Chai
Ishani Chakraborty
Rudrasis Chakraborty
Antoni B. Chan

Kwok-Ping Chan
Siddhartha Chandra
Sharat Chandran
Arjun Chandrasekaran
Angel X. Chang
Che-Han Chang
Hong Chang
Hyun Sung Chang
Hyung Jin Chang
Jianlong Chang
Ju Yong Chang
Ming-Ching Chang
Simyung Chang
Xiaojun Chang
Yu-Wei Chao
Devendra S. Chaplot
Arslan Chaudhry
Rizwan A. Chaudhry
Can Chen
Chang Chen
Chao Chen
Chen Chen
Chu-Song Chen
Dapeng Chen
Dong Chen
Dongdong Chen
Guanying Chen
Hongge Chen
Hsin-yi Chen
Huaijin Chen
Hwann-Tzong Chen
Jianbo Chen
Jianhui Chen
Jiansheng Chen
Jiaxin Chen
Jie Chen
Jun-Cheng Chen
Kan Chen
Kevin Chen
Lin Chen
Long Chen
Min-Hung Chen
Qifeng Chen
Shi Chen
Shixing Chen
Tianshui Chen

Weifeng Chen
Weikai Chen
Xi Chen
Xiaohan Chen
Xiaozhi Chen
Xilin Chen
Xingyu Chen
Xinlei Chen
Xinyun Chen
Yi-Ting Chen
Yilun Chen
Ying-Cong Chen
Yinpeng Chen
Yiran Chen
Yu Chen
Yu-Sheng Chen
Yuhua Chen
Yun-Chun Chen
Yunpeng Chen
Yuntao Chen
Zhuoyuan Chen
Zitian Chen
Anchieh Cheng
Bowen Cheng
Erkang Cheng
Gong Cheng
Guangliang Cheng
Jingchun Cheng
Jun Cheng
Li Cheng
Ming-Ming Cheng
Yu Cheng
Ziang Cheng
Anoop Cherian
Dmitry Chetverikov
Ngai-man Cheung
William Cheung
Ajad Chhatkuli
Naoki Chiba
Benjamin Chidester
Han-pang Chiu
Mang Tik Chiu
Wei-Chen Chiu
Donghyeon Cho
Hojin Cho
Minsu Cho

Nam Ik Cho
Tim Cho
Tae Eun Choe
Chiho Choi
Edward Choi
Inchang Choi
Jinsoo Choi
Jonghyun Choi
Jongwon Choi
Yukyung Choi
Hisham Cholakkal
Eunji Chong
Jaegul Choo
Christopher Choy
Hang Chu
Peng Chu
Wen-Sheng Chu
Albert Chung
Joon Son Chung
Hai Ci
Safa Cicek
Ramazan G. Cinbis
Arridhana Ciptadi
Javier Civera
James J. Clark
Ronald Clark
Felipe Codevilla
Michael Cogswell
Andrea Cohen
Maxwell D. Collins
Carlo Colombo
Yang Cong
Adria R. Continente
Marcella Cornia
John Richard Corring
Darren Cosker
Dragos Costea
Garrison W. Cottrell
Florent Couzinie-Devy
Marco Cristani
Ioana Croitoru
James L. Crowley
Jiequan Cui
Zhaopeng Cui
Ross Cutler
Antonio D'Innocente

Rozenn Dahyot
Bo Dai
Dengxin Dai
Hang Dai
Longquan Dai
Shuyang Dai
Xiyang Dai
Yuchao Dai
Adrian V. Dalca
Dima Damen
Bharath B. Damodaran
Kristin Dana
Martin Danelljan
Zheng Dang
Zachary Alan Daniels
Donald G. Dansereau
Abhishek Das
Samyak Datta
Achal Dave
Titas De
Rodrigo de Bem
Teo de Campos
Raoul de Charette
Shalini De Mello
Joseph DeGol
Herve Delingette
Haowen Deng
Jiankang Deng
Weijian Deng
Zhiwei Deng
Joachim Denzler
Konstantinos G. Derpanis
Aditya Deshpande
Frederic Devernay
Somdip Dey
Arturo Deza
Abhinav Dhall
Helisa Dhamo
Vikas Dhiman
Fillipe Dias Moreira
   de Souza
Ali Diba
Ferran Diego
Guiguang Ding
Henghui Ding
Jian Ding

Mingyu Ding
Xinghao Ding
Zhengming Ding
Robert DiPietro
Cosimo Distante
Ajay Divakaran
Mandar Dixit
Abdelaziz Djelouah
Thanh-Toan Do
Jose Dolz
Bo Dong
Chao Dong
Jiangxin Dong
Weiming Dong
Weisheng Dong
Xingping Dong
Xuanyi Dong
Yinpeng Dong
Gianfranco Doretto
Hazel Doughty
Hassen Drira
Bertram Drost
Dawei Du
Ye Duan
Yueqi Duan
Abhimanyu Dubey
Anastasia Dubrovina
Stefan Duffner
Chi Nhan Duong
Thibaut Durand
Zoran Duric
Iulia Duta
Debidatta Dwibedi
Benjamin Eckart
Marc Eder
Marzieh Edraki
Alexei A. Efros
Kiana Ehsani
Hazm Kemal Ekenel
James H. Elder
Mohamed Elgharib
Shireen Elhabian
Ehsan Elhamifar
Mohamed Elhoseiny
Ian Endres
N. Benjamin Erichson

Jan Ernst
Sergio Escalera
Francisco Escolano
Victor Escorcia
Carlos Esteves
Francisco J. Estrada
Bin Fan
Chenyou Fan
Deng-Ping Fan
Haoqi Fan
Hehe Fan
Heng Fan
Kai Fan
Lijie Fan
Linxi Fan
Quanfu Fan
Shaojing Fan
Xiaochuan Fan
Xin Fan
Yuchen Fan
Sean Fanello
Hao-Shu Fang
Haoyang Fang
Kuan Fang
Yi Fang
Yuming Fang
Azade Farshad
Alireza Fathi
Raanan Fattal
Joao Fayad
Xiaohan Fei
Christoph Feichtenhofer
Michael Felsberg
Chen Feng
Jiashi Feng
Junyi Feng
Mengyang Feng
Qianli Feng
Zhenhua Feng
Michele Fenzi
Andras Ferencz
Martin Fergie
Basura Fernando
Ethan Fetaya
Michael Firman
John W. Fisher

Matthew Fisher
Boris Flach
Corneliu Florea
Wolfgang Foerstner
David Fofi
Gian Luca Foresti
Per-Erik Forssen
David Fouhey
Katerina Fragkiadaki
Victor Fragoso
Jean-Sébastien Franco
Ohad Fried
Iuri Frosio
Cheng-Yang Fu
Huazhu Fu
Jianlong Fu
Jingjing Fu
Xueyang Fu
Yanwei Fu
Ying Fu
Yun Fu
Olac Fuentes
Kent Fujiwara
Takuya Funatomi
Christopher Funk
Thomas Funkhouser
Antonino Furnari
Ryo Furukawa
Erik Gärtner
Raghudeep Gadde
Matheus Gadelha
Vandit Gajjar
Trevor Gale
Juergen Gall
Mathias Gallardo
Guillermo Gallego
Orazio Gallo
Chuang Gan
Zhe Gan
Madan Ravi Ganesh
Aditya Ganeshan
Siddha Ganju
Bin-Bin Gao
Changxin Gao
Feng Gao
Hongchang Gao

Jin Gao
Jiyang Gao
Junbin Gao
Katelyn Gao
Lin Gao
Mingfei Gao
Ruiqi Gao
Ruohan Gao
Shenghua Gao
Yuan Gao
Yue Gao
Noa Garcia
Alberto Garcia-Garcia
Guillermo
    Garcia-Hernando
Jacob R. Gardner
Animesh Garg
Kshitiz Garg
Rahul Garg
Ravi Garg
Philip N. Garner
Kirill Gavrilyuk
Paul Gay
Shiming Ge
Weifeng Ge
Baris Gecer
Xin Geng
Kyle Genova
Stamatios Georgoulis
Bernard Ghanem
Michael Gharbi
Kamran Ghasedi
Golnaz Ghiasi
Arnab Ghosh
Partha Ghosh
Silvio Giancola
Andrew Gilbert
Rohit Girdhar
Xavier Giro-i-Nieto
Thomas Gittings
Ioannis Gkioulekas
Clement Godard
Vaibhava Goel
Bastian Goldluecke
Lluis Gomez
Nuno Gonçalves

Dong Gong
Ke Gong
Mingming Gong
Abel Gonzalez-Garcia
Ariel Gordon
Daniel Gordon
Paulo Gotardo
Venu Madhav Govindu
Ankit Goyal
Priya Goyal
Raghav Goyal
Benjamin Graham
Douglas Gray
Brent A. Griffin
Etienne Grossmann
David Gu
Jiayuan Gu
Jiuxiang Gu
Lin Gu
Qiao Gu
Shuhang Gu
Jose J. Guerrero
Paul Guerrero
Jie Gui
Jean-Yves Guillemaut
Riza Alp Guler
Erhan Gundogdu
Fatma Guney
Guodong Guo
Kaiwen Guo
Qi Guo
Sheng Guo
Shi Guo
Tiantong Guo
Xiaojie Guo
Yijie Guo
Yiluan Guo
Yuanfang Guo
Yulan Guo
Agrim Gupta
Ankush Gupta
Mohit Gupta
Saurabh Gupta
Tanmay Gupta
Danna Gurari
Abner Guzman-Rivera

JunYoung Gwak
Michael Gygli
Jung-Woo Ha
Simon Hadfield
Isma Hadji
Bjoern Haefner
Taeyoung Hahn
Levente Hajder
Peter Hall
Emanuela Haller
Stefan Haller
Bumsub Ham
Abdullah Hamdi
Dongyoon Han
Hu Han
Jungong Han
Junwei Han
Kai Han
Tian Han
Xiaoguang Han
Xintong Han
Yahong Han
Ankur Handa
Zekun Hao
Albert Haque
Tatsuya Harada
Mehrtash Harandi
Adam W. Harley
Mahmudul Hasan
Atsushi Hashimoto
Ali Hatamizadeh
Munawar Hayat
Dongliang He
Jingrui He
Junfeng He
Kaiming He
Kun He
Lei He
Pan He
Ran He
Shengfeng He
Tong He
Weipeng He
Xuming He
Yang He
Yihui He

Zhihai He
Chinmay Hegde
Janne Heikkila
Mattias P. Heinrich
Stéphane Herbin
Alexander Hermans
Luis Herranz
John R. Hershey
Aaron Hertzmann
Roei Herzig
Anders Heyden
Steven Hickson
Otmar Hilliges
Tomas Hodan
Judy Hoffman
Michael Hofmann
Yannick Hold-Geoffroy
Namdar Homayounfar
Sina Honari
Richang Hong
Seunghoon Hong
Xiaopeng Hong
Yi Hong
Hidekata Hontani
Anthony Hoogs
Yedid Hoshen
Mir Rayat Imtiaz Hossain
Junhui Hou
Le Hou
Lu Hou
Tingbo Hou
Wei-Lin Hsiao
Cheng-Chun Hsu
Gee-Sern Jison Hsu
Kuang-jui Hsu
Changbo Hu
Di Hu
Guosheng Hu
Han Hu
Hao Hu
Hexiang Hu
Hou-Ning Hu
Jie Hu
Junlin Hu
Nan Hu
Ping Hu

Ronghang Hu
Xiaowei Hu
Yinlin Hu
Yuan-Ting Hu
Zhe Hu
Binh-Son Hua
Yang Hua
Bingyao Huang
Di Huang
Dong Huang
Fay Huang
Haibin Huang
Haozhi Huang
Heng Huang
Huaibo Huang
Jia-Bin Huang
Jing Huang
Jingwei Huang
Kaizhu Huang
Lei Huang
Qiangui Huang
Qiaoying Huang
Qingqiu Huang
Qixing Huang
Shaoli Huang
Sheng Huang
Siyuan Huang
Weilin Huang
Wenbing Huang
Xiangru Huang
Xun Huang
Yan Huang
Yifei Huang
Yue Huang
Zhiwu Huang
Zilong Huang
Minyoung Huh
Zhuo Hui
Matthias B. Hullin
Martin Humenberger
Wei-Chih Hung
Zhouyuan Huo
Junhwa Hur
Noureldien Hussein
Jyh-Jing Hwang
Seong Jae Hwang

Sung Ju Hwang
Ichiro Ide
Ivo Ihrke
Daiki Ikami
Satoshi Ikehata
Nazli Ikizler-Cinbis
Sunghoon Im
Yani Ioannou
Radu Tudor Ionescu
Umar Iqbal
Go Irie
Ahmet Iscen
Md Amirul Islam
Vamsi Ithapu
Nathan Jacobs
Arpit Jain
Himalaya Jain
Suyog Jain
Stuart James
Won-Dong Jang
Yunseok Jang
Ronnachai Jaroensri
Dinesh Jayaraman
Sadeep Jayasumana
Suren Jayasuriya
Herve Jegou
Simon Jenni
Hae-Gon Jeon
Yunho Jeon
Koteswar R. Jerripothula
Hueihan Jhuang
I-hong Jhuo
Dinghuang Ji
Hui Ji
Jingwei Ji
Pan Ji
Yanli Ji
Baoxiong Jia
Kui Jia
Xu Jia
Chiyu Max Jiang
Haiyong Jiang
Hao Jiang
Huaizu Jiang
Huajie Jiang
Ke Jiang

Lai Jiang
Li Jiang
Lu Jiang
Ming Jiang
Peng Jiang
Shuqiang Jiang
Wei Jiang
Xudong Jiang
Zhuolin Jiang
Jianbo Jiao
Zequn Jie
Dakai Jin
Kyong Hwan Jin
Lianwen Jin
SouYoung Jin
Xiaojie Jin
Xin Jin
Nebojsa Jojic
Alexis Joly
Michael Jeffrey Jones
Hanbyul Joo
Jungseock Joo
Kyungdon Joo
Ajjen Joshi
Shantanu H. Joshi
Da-Cheng Juan
Marco Körner
Kevin Köser
Asim Kadav
Christine Kaeser-Chen
Kushal Kafle
Dagmar Kainmueller
Ioannis A. Kakadiaris
Zdenek Kalal
Nima Kalantari
Yannis Kalantidis
Mahdi M. Kalayeh
Anmol Kalia
Sinan Kalkan
Vicky Kalogeiton
Ashwin Kalyan
Joni-kristian Kamarainen
Gerda Kamberova
Chandra Kambhamettu
Martin Kampel
Meina Kan

Christopher Kanan
Kenichi Kanatani
Angjoo Kanazawa
Atsushi Kanehira
Takuhiro Kaneko
Asako Kanezaki
Bingyi Kang
Di Kang
Sunghun Kang
Zhao Kang
Vadim Kantorov
Abhishek Kar
Amlan Kar
Theofanis Karaletsos
Leonid Karlinsky
Kevin Karsch
Angelos Katharopoulos
Isinsu Katircioglu
Hiroharu Kato
Zoltan Kato
Dotan Kaufman
Jan Kautz
Rei Kawakami
Qiuhong Ke
Wadim Kehl
Petr Kellnhofer
Aniruddha Kembhavi
Cem Keskin
Margret Keuper
Daniel Keysers
Ashkan Khakzar
Fahad Khan
Naeemullah Khan
Salman Khan
Siddhesh Khandelwal
Rawal Khirodkar
Anna Khoreva
Tejas Khot
Parmeshwar Khurd
Hadi Kiapour
Joe Kileel
Chanho Kim
Dahun Kim
Edward Kim
Eunwoo Kim
Han-ul Kim

Hansung Kim
Heewon Kim
Hyo Jin Kim
Hyunwoo J. Kim
Jinkyu Kim
Jiwon Kim
Jongmin Kim
Junsik Kim
Junyeong Kim
Min H. Kim
Namil Kim
Pyojin Kim
Seon Joo Kim
Seong Tae Kim
Seungryong Kim
Sungwoong Kim
Tae Hyun Kim
Vladimir Kim
Won Hwa Kim
Yonghyun Kim
Benjamin Kimia
Akisato Kimura
Pieter-Jan Kindermans
Zsolt Kira
Itaru Kitahara
Hedvig Kjellstrom
Jan Knopp
Takumi Kobayashi
Erich Kobler
Parker Koch
Reinhard Koch
Elyor Kodirov
Amir Kolaman
Nicholas Kolkin
Dimitrios Kollias
Stefanos Kollias
Soheil Kolouri
Adams Wai-Kin Kong
Naejin Kong
Shu Kong
Tao Kong
Yu Kong
Yoshinori Konishi
Daniil Kononenko
Theodora Kontogianni
Simon Korman

Adam Kortylewski
Jana Kosecka
Jean Kossaifi
Satwik Kottur
Rigas Kouskouridas
Adriana Kovashka
Rama Kovvuri
Adarsh Kowdle
Jedrzej Kozerawski
Mateusz Kozinski
Philipp Kraehenbuehl
Gregory Kramida
Josip Krapac
Dmitry Kravchenko
Ranjay Krishna
Pavel Krsek
Alexander Krull
Jakob Kruse
Hiroyuki Kubo
Hilde Kuehne
Jason Kuen
Andreas Kuhn
Arjan Kuijper
Zuzana Kukelova
Ajay Kumar
Amit Kumar
Avinash Kumar
Suryansh Kumar
Vijay Kumar
Kaustav Kundu
Weicheng Kuo
Nojun Kwak
Suha Kwak
Junseok Kwon
Nikolaos Kyriazis
Zorah Lähner
Ankit Laddha
Florent Lafarge
Jean Lahoud
Kevin Lai
Shang-Hong Lai
Wei-Sheng Lai
Yu-Kun Lai
Iro Laina
Antony Lam
John Wheatley Lambert

Xiangyuan lan
Xu Lan
Charis Lanaras
Georg Langs
Oswald Lanz
Dong Lao
Yizhen Lao
Agata Lapedriza
Gustav Larsson
Viktor Larsson
Katrin Lasinger
Christoph Lassner
Longin Jan Latecki
Stéphane Lathuilière
Rynson Lau
Hei Law
Justin Lazarow
Svetlana Lazebnik
Hieu Le
Huu Le
Ngan Hoang Le
Trung-Nghia Le
Vuong Le
Colin Lea
Erik Learned-Miller
Chen-Yu Lee
Gim Hee Lee
Hsin-Ying Lee
Hyungtae Lee
Jae-Han Lee
Jimmy Addison Lee
Joonseok Lee
Kibok Lee
Kuang-Huei Lee
Kwonjoon Lee
Minsik Lee
Sang-chul Lee
Seungkyu Lee
Soochan Lee
Stefan Lee
Taehee Lee
Andreas Lehrmann
Jie Lei
Peng Lei
Matthew Joseph Leotta
Wee Kheng Leow

Gil Levi
Evgeny Levinkov
Aviad Levis
Jose Lezama
Ang Li
Bin Li
Bing Li
Boyi Li
Changsheng Li
Chao Li
Chen Li
Cheng Li
Chenglong Li
Chi Li
Chun-Guang Li
Chun-Liang Li
Chunyuan Li
Dong Li
Guanbin Li
Hao Li
Haoxiang Li
Hongsheng Li
Hongyang Li
Houqiang Li
Huibin Li
Jia Li
Jianan Li
Jianguo Li
Junnan Li
Junxuan Li
Kai Li
Ke Li
Kejie Li
Kunpeng Li
Lerenhan Li
Li Erran Li
Mengtian Li
Mu Li
Peihua Li
Peiyi Li
Ping Li
Qi Li
Qing Li
Ruiyu Li
Ruoteng Li
Shaozi Li

Sheng Li
Shiwei Li
Shuang Li
Siyang Li
Stan Z. Li
Tianye Li
Wei Li
Weixin Li
Wen Li
Wenbo Li
Xiaomeng Li
Xin Li
Xiu Li
Xuelong Li
Xueting Li
Yan Li
Yandong Li
Yanghao Li
Yehao Li
Yi Li
Yijun Li
Yikang LI
Yining Li
Yongjie Li
Yu Li
Yu-Jhe Li
Yunpeng Li
Yunsheng Li
Yunzhu Li
Zhe Li
Zhen Li
Zhengqi Li
Zhenyang Li
Zhuwen Li
Dongze Lian
Xiaochen Lian
Zhouhui Lian
Chen Liang
Jie Liang
Ming Liang
Paul Pu Liang
Pengpeng Liang
Shu Liang
Wei Liang
Jing Liao
Minghui Liao

Renjie Liao
Shengcai Liao
Shuai Liao
Yiyi Liao
Ser-Nam Lim
Chen-Hsuan Lin
Chung-Ching Lin
Dahua Lin
Ji Lin
Kevin Lin
Tianwei Lin
Tsung-Yi Lin
Tsung-Yu Lin
Wei-An Lin
Weiyao Lin
Yen-Chen Lin
Yuewei Lin
David B. Lindell
Drew Linsley
Krzysztof Lis
Roee Litman
Jim Little
An-An Liu
Bo Liu
Buyu Liu
Chao Liu
Chen Liu
Cheng-lin Liu
Chenxi Liu
Dong Liu
Feng Liu
Guilin Liu
Haomiao Liu
Heshan Liu
Hong Liu
Ji Liu
Jingen Liu
Jun Liu
Lanlan Liu
Li Liu
Liu Liu
Mengyuan Liu
Miaomiao Liu
Nian Liu
Ping Liu
Risheng Liu

Sheng Liu
Shu Liu
Shuaicheng Liu
Sifei Liu
Siqi Liu
Siying Liu
Songtao Liu
Ting Liu
Tongliang Liu
Tyng-Luh Liu
Wanquan Liu
Wei Liu
Weiyang Liu
Weizhe Liu
Wenyu Liu
Wu Liu
Xialei Liu
Xianglong Liu
Xiaodong Liu
Xiaofeng Liu
Xihui Liu
Xingyu Liu
Xinwang Liu
Xuanqing Liu
Xuebo Liu
Yang Liu
Yaojie Liu
Yebin Liu
Yen-Cheng Liu
Yiming Liu
Yu Liu
Yu-Shen Liu
Yufan Liu
Yun Liu
Zheng Liu
Zhijian Liu
Zhuang Liu
Zichuan Liu
Ziwei Liu
Zongyi Liu
Stephan Liwicki
Liliana Lo Presti
Chengjiang Long
Fuchen Long
Mingsheng Long
Xiang Long

Yang Long
Charles T. Loop
Antonio Lopez
Roberto J. Lopez-Sastre
Javier Lorenzo-Navarro
Manolis Lourakis
Boyu Lu
Canyi Lu
Feng Lu
Guoyu Lu
Hongtao Lu
Jiajun Lu
Jiasen Lu
Jiwen Lu
Kaiyue Lu
Le Lu
Shao-Ping Lu
Shijian Lu
Xiankai Lu
Xin Lu
Yao Lu
Yiping Lu
Yongxi Lu
Yongyi Lu
Zhiwu Lu
Fujun Luan
Benjamin E. Lundell
Hao Luo
Jian-Hao Luo
Ruotian Luo
Weixin Luo
Wenhan Luo
Wenjie Luo
Yan Luo
Zelun Luo
Zixin Luo
Khoa Luu
Zhaoyang Lv
Pengyuan Lyu
Thomas Möllenhoff
Matthias Müller
Bingpeng Ma
Chih-Yao Ma
Chongyang Ma
Huimin Ma
Jiayi Ma

K. T. Ma
Ke Ma
Lin Ma
Liqian Ma
Shugao Ma
Wei-Chiu Ma
Xiaojian Ma
Xingjun Ma
Zhanyu Ma
Zheng Ma
Radek Jakob Mackowiak
Ludovic Magerand
Shweta Mahajan
Siddharth Mahendran
Long Mai
Ameesh Makadia
Oscar Mendez Maldonado
Mateusz Malinowski
Yury Malkov
Arun Mallya
Dipu Manandhar
Massimiliano Mancini
Fabian Manhardt
Kevis-kokitsi Maninis
Varun Manjunatha
Junhua Mao
Xudong Mao
Alina Marcu
Edgar Margffoy-Tuay
Dmitrii Marin
Manuel J. Marin-Jimenez
Kenneth Marino
Niki Martinel
Julieta Martinez
Jonathan Masci
Tomohiro Mashita
Iacopo Masi
David Masip
Daniela Massiceti
Stefan Mathe
Yusuke Matsui
Tetsu Matsukawa
Iain A. Matthews
Kevin James Matzen
Bruce Allen Maxwell
Stephen Maybank

Helmut Mayer
Amir Mazaheri
David McAllester
Steven McDonagh
Stephen J. Mckenna
Roey Mechrez
Prakhar Mehrotra
Christopher Mei
Xue Mei
Paulo R. S. Mendonca
Lili Meng
Zibo Meng
Thomas Mensink
Bjoern Menze
Michele Merler
Kourosh Meshgi
Pascal Mettes
Christopher Metzler
Liang Mi
Qiguang Miao
Xin Miao
Tomer Michaeli
Frank Michel
Antoine Miech
Krystian Mikolajczyk
Peyman Milanfar
Ben Mildenhall
Gregor Miller
Fausto Milletari
Dongbo Min
Kyle Min
Pedro Miraldo
Dmytro Mishkin
Anand Mishra
Ashish Mishra
Ishan Misra
Niluthpol C. Mithun
Kaushik Mitra
Niloy Mitra
Anton Mitrokhin
Ikuhisa Mitsugami
Anurag Mittal
Kaichun Mo
Zhipeng Mo
Davide Modolo
Michael Moeller

Pritish Mohapatra
Pavlo Molchanov
Davide Moltisanti
Pascal Monasse
Mathew Monfort
Aron Monszpart
Sean Moran
Vlad I. Morariu
Francesc Moreno-Noguer
Pietro Morerio
Stylianos Moschoglou
Yael Moses
Roozbeh Mottaghi
Pierre Moulon
Arsalan Mousavian
Yadong Mu
Yasuhiro Mukaigawa
Lopamudra Mukherjee
Yusuke Mukuta
Ravi Teja Mullapudi
Mario Enrique Munich
Zachary Murez
Ana C. Murillo
J. Krishna Murthy
Damien Muselet
Armin Mustafa
Siva Karthik Mustikovela
Carlo Dal Mutto
Moin Nabi
Varun K. Nagaraja
Tushar Nagarajan
Arsha Nagrani
Seungjun Nah
Nikhil Naik
Yoshikatsu Nakajima
Yuta Nakashima
Atsushi Nakazawa
Seonghyeon Nam
Vinay P. Namboodiri
Medhini Narasimhan
Srinivasa Narasimhan
Sanath Narayan
Erickson Rangel
    Nascimento
Jacinto Nascimento
Tayyab Naseer

Lakshmanan Nataraj
Neda Nategh
Nelson Isao Nauata
Fernando Navarro
Shah Nawaz
Lukas Neumann
Ram Nevatia
Alejandro Newell
Shawn Newsam
Joe Yue-Hei Ng
Trung Thanh Ngo
Duc Thanh Nguyen
Lam M. Nguyen
Phuc Xuan Nguyen
Thuong Nguyen Canh
Mihalis Nicolaou
Andrei Liviu Nicolicioiu
Xuecheng Nie
Michael Niemeyer
Simon Niklaus
Christophoros Nikou
David Nilsson
Jifeng Ning
Yuval Nirkin
Li Niu
Yuzhen Niu
Zhenxing Niu
Shohei Nobuhara
Nicoletta Noceti
Hyeonwoo Noh
Junhyug Noh
Mehdi Noroozi
Sotiris Nousias
Valsamis Ntouskos
Matthew O'Toole
Peter Ochs
Ferda Ofli
Seong Joon Oh
Seoung Wug Oh
Iason Oikonomidis
Utkarsh Ojha
Takahiro Okabe
Takayuki Okatani
Fumio Okura
Aude Oliva
Kyle Olszewski

Björn Ommer
Mohamed Omran
Elisabeta Oneata
Michael Opitz
Jose Oramas
Tribhuvanesh Orekondy
Shaul Oron
Sergio Orts-Escolano
Ivan Oseledets
Aljosa Osep
Magnus Oskarsson
Anton Osokin
Martin R. Oswald
Wanli Ouyang
Andrew Owens
Mete Ozay
Mustafa Ozuysal
Eduardo Pérez-Pellitero
Gautam Pai
Dipan Kumar Pal
P. H. Pamplona Savarese
Jinshan Pan
Junting Pan
Xingang Pan
Yingwei Pan
Yannis Panagakis
Rameswar Panda
Guan Pang
Jiahao Pang
Jiangmiao Pang
Tianyu Pang
Sharath Pankanti
Nicolas Papadakis
Dim Papadopoulos
George Papandreou
Toufiq Parag
Shaifali Parashar
Sarah Parisot
Eunhyeok Park
Hyun Soo Park
Jaesik Park
Min-Gyu Park
Taesung Park
Alvaro Parra
C. Alejandro Parraga
Despoina Paschalidou

Nikolaos Passalis
Vishal Patel
Viorica Patraucean
Badri Narayana Patro
Danda Pani Paudel
Sujoy Paul
Georgios Pavlakos
Ioannis Pavlidis
Vladimir Pavlovic
Nick Pears
Kim Steenstrup Pedersen
Selen Pehlivan
Shmuel Peleg
Chao Peng
Houwen Peng
Wen-Hsiao Peng
Xi Peng
Xiaojiang Peng
Xingchao Peng
Yuxin Peng
Federico Perazzi
Juan Camilo Perez
Vishwanath Peri
Federico Pernici
Luca Del Pero
Florent Perronnin
Stavros Petridis
Henning Petzka
Patrick Peursum
Michael Pfeiffer
Hanspeter Pfister
Roman Pflugfelder
Minh Tri Pham
Yongri Piao
David Picard
Tomasz Pieciak
A. J. Piergiovanni
Andrea Pilzer
Pedro O. Pinheiro
Silvia Laura Pintea
Lerrel Pinto
Axel Pinz
Robinson Piramuthu
Fiora Pirri
Leonid Pishchulin
Francesco Pittaluga

Daniel Pizarro
Tobias Plötz
Mirco Planamente
Matteo Poggi
Moacir A. Ponti
Parita Pooj
Fatih Porikli
Horst Possegger
Omid Poursaeed
Ameya Prabhu
Viraj Uday Prabhu
Dilip Prasad
Brian L. Price
True Price
Maria Priisalu
Veronique Prinet
Victor Adrian Prisacariu
Jan Prokaj
Sergey Prokudin
Nicolas Pugeault
Xavier Puig
Albert Pumarola
Pulak Purkait
Senthil Purushwalkam
Charles R. Qi
Hang Qi
Haozhi Qi
Lu Qi
Mengshi Qi
Siyuan Qi
Xiaojuan Qi
Yuankai Qi
Shengju Qian
Xuelin Qian
Siyuan Qiao
Yu Qiao
Jie Qin
Qiang Qiu
Weichao Qiu
Zhaofan Qiu
Kha Gia Quach
Yuhui Quan
Yvain Queau
Julian Quiroga
Faisal Qureshi
Mahdi Rad

Filip Radenovic
Petia Radeva
Venkatesh
   B. Radhakrishnan
Ilija Radosavovic
Noha Radwan
Rahul Raguram
Tanzila Rahman
Amit Raj
Ajit Rajwade
Kandan Ramakrishnan
Santhosh
   K. Ramakrishnan
Srikumar Ramalingam
Ravi Ramamoorthi
Vasili Ramanishka
Ramprasaath R. Selvaraju
Francois Rameau
Visvanathan Ramesh
Santu Rana
Rene Ranftl
Anand Rangarajan
Anurag Ranjan
Viresh Ranjan
Yongming Rao
Carolina Raposo
Vivek Rathod
Sathya N. Ravi
Avinash Ravichandran
Tammy Riklin Raviv
Daniel Rebain
Sylvestre-Alvise Rebuffi
N. Dinesh Reddy
Timo Rehfeld
Paolo Remagnino
Konstantinos Rematas
Edoardo Remelli
Dongwei Ren
Haibing Ren
Jian Ren
Jimmy Ren
Mengye Ren
Weihong Ren
Wenqi Ren
Zhile Ren
Zhongzheng Ren

Zhou Ren
Vijay Rengarajan
Md A. Reza
Farzaneh Rezaeianaran
Hamed R. Tavakoli
Nicholas Rhinehart
Helge Rhodin
Elisa Ricci
Alexander Richard
Eitan Richardson
Elad Richardson
Christian Richardt
Stephan Richter
Gernot Riegler
Daniel Ritchie
Tobias Ritschel
Samuel Rivera
Yong Man Ro
Richard Roberts
Joseph Robinson
Ignacio Rocco
Mrigank Rochan
Emanuele Rodolà
Mikel D. Rodriguez
Giorgio Roffo
Grégory Rogez
Gemma Roig
Javier Romero
Xuejian Rong
Yu Rong
Amir Rosenfeld
Bodo Rosenhahn
Guy Rosman
Arun Ross
Paolo Rota
Peter M. Roth
Anastasios Roussos
Anirban Roy
Sebastien Roy
Aruni RoyChowdhury
Artem Rozantsev
Ognjen Rudovic
Daniel Rueckert
Adria Ruiz
Javier Ruiz-del-solar
Christian Rupprecht

Chris Russell
Dan Ruta
Jongbin Ryu
Ömer Sümer
Alexandre Sablayrolles
Faraz Saeedan
Ryusuke Sagawa
Christos Sagonas
Tonmoy Saikia
Hideo Saito
Kuniaki Saito
Shunsuke Saito
Shunta Saito
Ken Sakurada
Joaquin Salas
Fatemeh Sadat Saleh
Mahdi Saleh
Pouya Samangouei
Leo Sampaio
   Ferraz Ribeiro
Artsiom Olegovich
   Sanakoyeu
Enrique Sanchez
Patsorn Sangkloy
Anush Sankaran
Aswin Sankaranarayanan
Swami Sankaranarayanan
Rodrigo Santa Cruz
Amartya Sanyal
Archana Sapkota
Nikolaos Sarafianos
Jun Sato
Shin'ichi Satoh
Hosnieh Sattar
Arman Savran
Manolis Savva
Alexander Sax
Hanno Scharr
Simone Schaub-Meyer
Konrad Schindler
Dmitrij Schlesinger
Uwe Schmidt
Dirk Schnieders
Björn Schuller
Samuel Schulter
Idan Schwartz

William Robson Schwartz
Alex Schwing
Sinisa Segvic
Lorenzo Seidenari
Pradeep Sen
Ozan Sener
Soumyadip Sengupta
Arda Senocak
Mojtaba Seyedhosseini
Shishir Shah
Shital Shah
Sohil Atul Shah
Tamar Rott Shaham
Huasong Shan
Qi Shan
Shiguang Shan
Jing Shao
Roman Shapovalov
Gaurav Sharma
Vivek Sharma
Viktoriia Sharmanska
Dongyu She
Sumit Shekhar
Evan Shelhamer
Chengyao Shen
Chunhua Shen
Falong Shen
Jie Shen
Li Shen
Liyue Shen
Shuhan Shen
Tianwei Shen
Wei Shen
William B. Shen
Yantao Shen
Ying Shen
Yiru Shen
Yujun Shen
Yuming Shen
Zhiqiang Shen
Ziyi Shen
Lu Sheng
Yu Sheng
Rakshith Shetty
Baoguang Shi
Guangming Shi

Hailin Shi
Miaojing Shi
Yemin Shi
Zhenmei Shi
Zhiyuan Shi
Kevin Jonathan Shih
Shiliang Shiliang
Hyunjung Shim
Atsushi Shimada
Nobutaka Shimada
Daeyun Shin
Young Min Shin
Koichi Shinoda
Konstantin Shmelkov
Michael Zheng Shou
Abhinav Shrivastava
Tianmin Shu
Zhixin Shu
Hong-Han Shuai
Pushkar Shukla
Christian Siagian
Mennatullah M. Siam
Kaleem Siddiqi
Karan Sikka
Jae-Young Sim
Christian Simon
Martin Simonovsky
Dheeraj Singaraju
Bharat Singh
Gurkirt Singh
Krishna Kumar Singh
Maneesh Kumar Singh
Richa Singh
Saurabh Singh
Suriya Singh
Vikas Singh
Sudipta N. Sinha
Vincent Sitzmann
Josef Sivic
Gregory Slabaugh
Miroslava Slavcheva
Ron Slossberg
Brandon Smith
Kevin Smith
Vladimir Smutny
Noah Snavely

Roger
   D. Soberanis-Mukul
Kihyuk Sohn
Francesco Solera
Eric Sommerlade
Sanghyun Son
Byung Cheol Song
Chunfeng Song
Dongjin Song
Jiaming Song
Jie Song
Jifei Song
Jingkuan Song
Mingli Song
Shiyu Song
Shuran Song
Xiao Song
Yafei Song
Yale Song
Yang Song
Yi-Zhe Song
Yibing Song
Humberto Sossa
Cesar de Souza
Adrian Spurr
Srinath Sridhar
Suraj Srinivas
Pratul P. Srinivasan
Anuj Srivastava
Tania Stathaki
Christopher Stauffer
Simon Stent
Rainer Stiefelhagen
Pierre Stock
Julian Straub
Jonathan C. Stroud
Joerg Stueckler
Jan Stuehmer
David Stutz
Chi Su
Hang Su
Jong-Chyi Su
Shuochen Su
Yu-Chuan Su
Ramanathan Subramanian
Yusuke Sugano

Masanori Suganuma
Yumin Suh
Mohammed Suhail
Yao Sui
Heung-Il Suk
Josephine Sullivan
Baochen Sun
Chen Sun
Chong Sun
Deqing Sun
Jin Sun
Liang Sun
Lin Sun
Qianru Sun
Shao-Hua Sun
Shuyang Sun
Weiwei Sun
Wenxiu Sun
Xiaoshuai Sun
Xiaoxiao Sun
Xingyuan Sun
Yifan Sun
Zhun Sun
Sabine Susstrunk
David Suter
Supasorn Suwajanakorn
Tomas Svoboda
Eran Swears
Paul Swoboda
Attila Szabo
Richard Szeliski
Duy-Nguyen Ta
Andrea Tagliasacchi
Yuichi Taguchi
Ying Tai
Keita Takahashi
Kouske Takahashi
Jun Takamatsu
Hugues Talbot
Toru Tamaki
Chaowei Tan
Fuwen Tan
Mingkui Tan
Mingxing Tan
Qingyang Tan
Robby T. Tan

Xiaoyang Tan
Kenichiro Tanaka
Masayuki Tanaka
Chang Tang
Chengzhou Tang
Danhang Tang
Ming Tang
Peng Tang
Qingming Tang
Wei Tang
Xu Tang
Yansong Tang
Youbao Tang
Yuxing Tang
Zhiqiang Tang
Tatsunori Taniai
Junli Tao
Xin Tao
Makarand Tapaswi
Jean-Philippe Tarel
Lyne Tchapmi
Zachary Teed
Bugra Tekin
Damien Teney
Ayush Tewari
Christian Theobalt
Christopher Thomas
Diego Thomas
Jim Thomas
Rajat Mani Thomas
Xinmei Tian
Yapeng Tian
Yingli Tian
Yonglong Tian
Zhi Tian
Zhuotao Tian
Kinh Tieu
Joseph Tighe
Massimo Tistarelli
Matthew Toews
Carl Toft
Pavel Tokmakov
Federico Tombari
Chetan Tonde
Yan Tong
Alessio Tonioni

Andrea Torsello
Fabio Tosi
Du Tran
Luan Tran
Ngoc-Trung Tran
Quan Hung Tran
Truyen Tran
Rudolph Triebel
Martin Trimmel
Shashank Tripathi
Subarna Tripathi
Leonardo Trujillo
Eduard Trulls
Tomasz Trzcinski
Sam Tsai
Yi-Hsuan Tsai
Hung-Yu Tseng
Stavros Tsogkas
Aggeliki Tsoli
Devis Tuia
Shubham Tulsiani
Sergey Tulyakov
Frederick Tung
Tony Tung
Daniyar Turmukhambetov
Ambrish Tyagi
Radim Tylecek
Christos Tzelepis
Georgios Tzimiropoulos
Dimitrios Tzionas
Seiichi Uchida
Norimichi Ukita
Dmitry Ulyanov
Martin Urschler
Yoshitaka Ushiku
Ben Usman
Alexander Vakhitov
Julien P. C. Valentin
Jack Valmadre
Ernest Valveny
Joost van de Weijer
Jan van Gemert
Koen Van Leemput
Gul Varol
Sebastiano Vascon
M. Alex O. Vasilescu

Subeesh Vasu
Mayank Vatsa
David Vazquez
Javier Vazquez-Corral
Ashok Veeraraghavan
Erik Velasco-Salido
Raviteja Vemulapalli
Jonathan Ventura
Manisha Verma
Roberto Vezzani
Ruben Villegas
Minh Vo
MinhDuc Vo
Nam Vo
Michele Volpi
Riccardo Volpi
Carl Vondrick
Konstantinos Vougioukas
Tuan-Hung Vu
Sven Wachsmuth
Neal Wadhwa
Catherine Wah
Jacob C. Walker
Thomas S. A. Wallis
Chengde Wan
Jun Wan
Liang Wan
Renjie Wan
Baoyuan Wang
Boyu Wang
Cheng Wang
Chu Wang
Chuan Wang
Chunyu Wang
Dequan Wang
Di Wang
Dilin Wang
Dong Wang
Fang Wang
Guanzhi Wang
Guoyin Wang
Hanzi Wang
Hao Wang
He Wang
Heng Wang
Hongcheng Wang

Hongxing Wang
Hua Wang
Jian Wang
Jingbo Wang
Jinglu Wang
Jingya Wang
Jinjun Wang
Jinqiao Wang
Jue Wang
Ke Wang
Keze Wang
Le Wang
Lei Wang
Lezi Wang
Li Wang
Liang Wang
Lijun Wang
Limin Wang
Linwei Wang
Lizhi Wang
Mengjiao Wang
Mingzhe Wang
Minsi Wang
Naiyan Wang
Nannan Wang
Ning Wang
Oliver Wang
Pei Wang
Peng Wang
Pichao Wang
Qi Wang
Qian Wang
Qiaosong Wang
Qifei Wang
Qilong Wang
Qing Wang
Qingzhong Wang
Quan Wang
Rui Wang
Ruiping Wang
Ruixing Wang
Shangfei Wang
Shenlong Wang
Shiyao Wang
Shuhui Wang
Song Wang

Tao Wang
Tianlu Wang
Tiantian Wang
Ting-chun Wang
Tingwu Wang
Wei Wang
Weiyue Wang
Wenguan Wang
Wenlin Wang
Wenqi Wang
Xiang Wang
Xiaobo Wang
Xiaofang Wang
Xiaoling Wang
Xiaolong Wang
Xiaosong Wang
Xiaoyu Wang
Xin Eric Wang
Xinchao Wang
Xinggang Wang
Xintao Wang
Yali Wang
Yan Wang
Yang Wang
Yangang Wang
Yaxing Wang
Yi Wang
Yida Wang
Yilin Wang
Yiming Wang
Yisen Wang
Yongtao Wang
Yu-Xiong Wang
Yue Wang
Yujiang Wang
Yunbo Wang
Yunhe Wang
Zengmao Wang
Zhangyang Wang
Zhaowen Wang
Zhe Wang
Zhecan Wang
Zheng Wang
Zhixiang Wang
Zilei Wang
Jianqiao Wangni

Anne S. Wannenwetsch
Jan Dirk Wegner
Scott Wehrwein
Donglai Wei
Kaixuan Wei
Longhui Wei
Pengxu Wei
Ping Wei
Qi Wei
Shih-En Wei
Xing Wei
Yunchao Wei
Zijun Wei
Jerod Weinman
Michael Weinmann
Philippe Weinzaepfel
Yair Weiss
Bihan Wen
Longyin Wen
Wei Wen
Junwu Weng
Tsui-Wei Weng
Xinshuo Weng
Eric Wengrowski
Tomas Werner
Gordon Wetzstein
Tobias Weyand
Patrick Wieschollek
Maggie Wigness
Erik Wijmans
Richard Wildes
Olivia Wiles
Chris Williams
Williem Williem
Kyle Wilson
Calden Wloka
Nicolai Wojke
Christian Wolf
Yongkang Wong
Sanghyun Woo
Scott Workman
Baoyuan Wu
Bichen Wu
Chao-Yuan Wu
Huikai Wu
Jiajun Wu

Jialin Wu
Jiaxiang Wu
Jiqing Wu
Jonathan Wu
Lifang Wu
Qi Wu
Qiang Wu
Ruizheng Wu
Shangzhe Wu
Shun-Cheng Wu
Tianfu Wu
Wayne Wu
Wenxuan Wu
Xiao Wu
Xiaohe Wu
Xinxiao Wu
Yang Wu
Yi Wu
Yiming Wu
Ying Nian Wu
Yue Wu
Zheng Wu
Zhenyu Wu
Zhirong Wu
Zuxuan Wu
Stefanie Wuhrer
Jonas Wulff
Changqun Xia
Fangting Xia
Fei Xia
Gui-Song Xia
Lu Xia
Xide Xia
Yin Xia
Yingce Xia
Yongqin Xian
Lei Xiang
Shiming Xiang
Bin Xiao
Fanyi Xiao
Guobao Xiao
Huaxin Xiao
Taihong Xiao
Tete Xiao
Tong Xiao
Wang Xiao

Yang Xiao
Cihang Xie
Guosen Xie
Jianwen Xie
Lingxi Xie
Sirui Xie
Weidi Xie
Wenxuan Xie
Xiaohua Xie
Fuyong Xing
Jun Xing
Junliang Xing
Bo Xiong
Peixi Xiong
Yu Xiong
Yuanjun Xiong
Zhiwei Xiong
Chang Xu
Chenliang Xu
Dan Xu
Danfei Xu
Hang Xu
Hongteng Xu
Huijuan Xu
Jingwei Xu
Jun Xu
Kai Xu
Mengmeng Xu
Mingze Xu
Qianqian Xu
Ran Xu
Weijian Xu
Xiangyu Xu
Xiaogang Xu
Xing Xu
Xun Xu
Yanyu Xu
Yichao Xu
Yong Xu
Yongchao Xu
Yuanlu Xu
Zenglin Xu
Zheng Xu
Chuhui Xue
Jia Xue
Nan Xue

Tianfan Xue
Xiangyang Xue
Abhay Yadav
Yasushi Yagi
I. Zeki Yalniz
Kota Yamaguchi
Toshihiko Yamasaki
Takayoshi Yamashita
Junchi Yan
Ke Yan
Qingan Yan
Sijie Yan
Xinchen Yan
Yan Yan
Yichao Yan
Zhicheng Yan
Keiji Yanai
Bin Yang
Ceyuan Yang
Dawei Yang
Dong Yang
Fan Yang
Guandao Yang
Guorun Yang
Haichuan Yang
Hao Yang
Jianwei Yang
Jiaolong Yang
Jie Yang
Jing Yang
Kaiyu Yang
Linjie Yang
Meng Yang
Michael Ying Yang
Nan Yang
Shuai Yang
Shuo Yang
Tianyu Yang
Tien-Ju Yang
Tsun-Yi Yang
Wei Yang
Wenhan Yang
Xiao Yang
Xiaodong Yang
Xin Yang
Yan Yang

Yanchao Yang
Yee Hong Yang
Yezhou Yang
Zhenheng Yang
Anbang Yao
Angela Yao
Cong Yao
Jian Yao
Li Yao
Ting Yao
Yao Yao
Zhewei Yao
Chengxi Ye
Jianbo Ye
Keren Ye
Linwei Ye
Mang Ye
Mao Ye
Qi Ye
Qixiang Ye
Mei-Chen Yeh
Raymond Yeh
Yu-Ying Yeh
Sai-Kit Yeung
Serena Yeung
Kwang Moo Yi
Li Yi
Renjiao Yi
Alper Yilmaz
Junho Yim
Lijun Yin
Weidong Yin
Xi Yin
Zhichao Yin
Tatsuya Yokota
Ryo Yonetani
Donggeun Yoo
Jae Shin Yoon
Ju Hong Yoon
Sung-eui Yoon
Laurent Younes
Changqian Yu
Fisher Yu
Gang Yu
Jiahui Yu
Kaicheng Yu

Ke Yu
Lequan Yu
Ning Yu
Qian Yu
Ronald Yu
Ruichi Yu
Shoou-I Yu
Tao Yu
Tianshu Yu
Xiang Yu
Xin Yu
Xiyu Yu
Youngjae Yu
Yu Yu
Zhiding Yu
Chunfeng Yuan
Ganzhao Yuan
Jinwei Yuan
Lu Yuan
Quan Yuan
Shanxin Yuan
Tongtong Yuan
Wenjia Yuan
Ye Yuan
Yuan Yuan
Yuhui Yuan
Huanjing Yue
Xiangyu Yue
Ersin Yumer
Sergey Zagoruyko
Egor Zakharov
Amir Zamir
Andrei Zanfir
Mihai Zanfir
Pablo Zegers
Bernhard Zeisl
John S. Zelek
Niclas Zeller
Huayi Zeng
Jiabei Zeng
Wenjun Zeng
Yu Zeng
Xiaohua Zhai
Fangneng Zhan
Huangying Zhan
Kun Zhan

Xiaohang Zhan
Baochang Zhang
Bowen Zhang
Cecilia Zhang
Changqing Zhang
Chao Zhang
Chengquan Zhang
Chi Zhang
Chongyang Zhang
Dingwen Zhang
Dong Zhang
Feihu Zhang
Hang Zhang
Hanwang Zhang
Hao Zhang
He Zhang
Hongguang Zhang
Hua Zhang
Ji Zhang
Jianguo Zhang
Jianming Zhang
Jiawei Zhang
Jie Zhang
Jing Zhang
Juyong Zhang
Kai Zhang
Kaipeng Zhang
Ke Zhang
Le Zhang
Lei Zhang
Li Zhang
Lihe Zhang
Linguang Zhang
Lu Zhang
Mi Zhang
Mingda Zhang
Peng Zhang
Pingping Zhang
Qian Zhang
Qilin Zhang
Quanshi Zhang
Richard Zhang
Rui Zhang
Runze Zhang
Shengping Zhang
Shifeng Zhang

Shuai Zhang
Songyang Zhang
Tao Zhang
Ting Zhang
Tong Zhang
Wayne Zhang
Wei Zhang
Weizhong Zhang
Wenwei Zhang
Xiangyu Zhang
Xiaolin Zhang
Xiaopeng Zhang
Xiaoqin Zhang
Xiuming Zhang
Ya Zhang
Yang Zhang
Yimin Zhang
Yinda Zhang
Ying Zhang
Yongfei Zhang
Yu Zhang
Yulun Zhang
Yunhua Zhang
Yuting Zhang
Zhanpeng Zhang
Zhao Zhang
Zhaoxiang Zhang
Zhen Zhang
Zheng Zhang
Zhifei Zhang
Zhijin Zhang
Zhishuai Zhang
Ziming Zhang
Bo Zhao
Chen Zhao
Fang Zhao
Haiyu Zhao
Han Zhao
Hang Zhao
Hengshuang Zhao
Jian Zhao
Kai Zhao
Liang Zhao
Long Zhao
Qian Zhao
Qibin Zhao

Qijun Zhao
Rui Zhao
Shenglin Zhao
Sicheng Zhao
Tianyi Zhao
Wenda Zhao
Xiangyun Zhao
Xin Zhao
Yang Zhao
Yue Zhao
Zhichen Zhao
Zijing Zhao
Xiantong Zhen
Chuanxia Zheng
Feng Zheng
Haiyong Zheng
Jia Zheng
Kang Zheng
Shuai Kyle Zheng
Wei-Shi Zheng
Yinqiang Zheng
Zerong Zheng
Zhedong Zheng
Zilong Zheng
Bineng Zhong
Fangwei Zhong
Guangyu Zhong
Yiran Zhong
Yujie Zhong
Zhun Zhong
Chunluan Zhou
Huiyu Zhou
Jiahuan Zhou
Jun Zhou
Lei Zhou
Luowei Zhou
Luping Zhou
Mo Zhou
Ning Zhou
Pan Zhou
Peng Zhou
Qianyi Zhou
S. Kevin Zhou
Sanping Zhou
Wengang Zhou
Xingyi Zhou

Yanzhao Zhou
Yi Zhou
Yin Zhou
Yipin Zhou
Yuyin Zhou
Zihan Zhou
Alex Zihao Zhu
Chenchen Zhu
Feng Zhu
Guangming Zhu
Ji Zhu
Jun-Yan Zhu
Lei Zhu
Linchao Zhu
Rui Zhu
Shizhan Zhu
Tyler Lixuan Zhu

Wei Zhu
Xiangyu Zhu
Xinge Zhu
Xizhou Zhu
Yanjun Zhu
Yi Zhu
Yixin Zhu
Yizhe Zhu
Yousong Zhu
Zhe Zhu
Zhen Zhu
Zheng Zhu
Zhenyao Zhu
Zhihui Zhu
Zhuotun Zhu
Bingbing Zhuang
Wei Zhuo

Christian Zimmermann
Karel Zimmermann
Larry Zitnick
Mohammadreza
   Zolfaghari
Maria Zontak
Daniel Zoran
Changqing Zou
Chuhang Zou
Danping Zou
Qi Zou
Yang Zou
Yuliang Zou
Georgios Zoumpourlis
Wangmeng Zuo
Xinxin Zuo

Additional Reviewers

Victoria Fernandez
   Abrevaya
Maya Aghaei
Allam Allam
Christine
   Allen-Blanchette
Nicolas Aziere
Assia Benbihi
Neha Bhargava
Bharat Lal Bhatnagar
Joanna Bitton
Judy Borowski
Amine Bourki
Romain Brégier
Tali Brayer
Sebastian Bujwid
Andrea Burns
Yun-Hao Cao
Yuning Chai
Xiaojun Chang
Bo Chen
Shuo Chen
Zhixiang Chen
Junsuk Choe
Hung-Kuo Chu

Jonathan P. Crall
Kenan Dai
Lucas Deecke
Karan Desai
Prithviraj Dhar
Jing Dong
Wei Dong
Turan Kaan Elgin
Francis Engelmann
Erik Englesson
Fartash Faghri
Zicong Fan
Yang Fu
Risheek Garrepalli
Yifan Ge
Marco Godi
Helmut Grabner
Shuxuan Guo
Jianfeng He
Zhezhi He
Samitha Herath
Chih-Hui Ho
Yicong Hong
Vincent Tao Hu
Julio Hurtado

Jaedong Hwang
Andrey Ignatov
Muhammad
   Abdullah Jamal
Saumya Jetley
Meiguang Jin
Jeff Johnson
Minsoo Kang
Saeed Khorram
Mohammad Rami Koujan
Nilesh Kulkarni
Sudhakar Kumawat
Abdelhak Lemkhenter
Alexander Levine
Jiachen Li
Jing Li
Jun Li
Yi Li
Liang Liao
Ruochen Liao
Tzu-Heng Lin
Phillip Lippe
Bao-di Liu
Bo Liu
Fangchen Liu

Hanxiao Liu
Hongyu Liu
Huidong Liu
Miao Liu
Xinxin Liu
Yongfei Liu
Yu-Lun Liu
Amir Livne
Tiange Luo
Wei Ma
Xiaoxuan Ma
Ioannis Marras
Georg Martius
Effrosyni Mavroudi
Tim Meinhardt
Givi Meishvili
Meng Meng
Zihang Meng
Zhongqi Miao
Gyeongsik Moon
Khoi Nguyen
Yung-Kyun Noh
Antonio Norelli
Jaeyoo Park
Alexander Pashevich
Mandela Patrick
Mary Phuong
Bingqiao Qian
Yu Qiao
Zhen Qiao
Sai Saketh Rambhatla
Aniket Roy
Amelie Royer
Parikshit Vishwas
    Sakurikar
Mark Sandler
Mert Bülent Sarıyıldız
Tanner Schmidt
Anshul B. Shah

Ketul Shah
Rajvi Shah
Hengcan Shi
Xiangxi Shi
Yujiao Shi
William A. P. Smith
Guoxian Song
Robin Strudel
Abby Stylianou
Xinwei Sun
Reuben Tan
Qingyi Tao
Kedar S. Tatwawadi
Anh Tuan Tran
Son Dinh Tran
Eleni Triantafillou
Aristeidis Tsitiridis
Md Zasim Uddin
Andrea Vedaldi
Evangelos Ververas
Vidit Vidit
Paul Voigtlaender
Bo Wan
Huanyu Wang
Huiyu Wang
Junqiu Wang
Pengxiao Wang
Tai Wang
Xinyao Wang
Tomoki Watanabe
Mark Weber
Xi Wei
Botong Wu
James Wu
Jiamin Wu
Rujie Wu
Yu Wu
Rongchang Xie
Wei Xiong

Yunyang Xiong
An Xu
Chi Xu
Yinghao Xu
Fei Xue
Tingyun Yan
Zike Yan
Chao Yang
Heran Yang
Ren Yang
Wenfei Yang
Xu Yang
Rajeev Yasarla
Shaokai Ye
Yufei Ye
Kun Yi
Haichao Yu
Hanchao Yu
Ruixuan Yu
Liangzhe Yuan
Chen-Lin Zhang
Fandong Zhang
Tianyi Zhang
Yang Zhang
Yiyi Zhang
Yongshun Zhang
Yu Zhang
Zhiwei Zhang
Jiaojiao Zhao
Yipu Zhao
Xingjian Zhen
Haizhong Zheng
Tiancheng Zhi
Chengju Zhou
Hao Zhou
Hao Zhu
Alexander Zimin

Contents – Part XXVIII

SqueezeSegV3: Spatially-Adaptive Convolution for Efficient Point-Cloud Segmentation

Chenfeng Xu[1(✉)], Bichen Wu[2], Zining Wang[1], Wei Zhan[1], Peter Vajda[2], Kurt Keutzer[1], and Masayoshi Tomizuka[1]

[1] University of California, Berkeley, USA
{xuchenfeng,wangzining,wzhan,keutzer}@berkeley.edu,
tomizuka@me.berkeley.edu
[2] Facebook Inc., Menlo Park, USA
{wbc,vajdap}@fb.com

Abstract. LiDAR point-cloud segmentation is an important problem for many applications. For large-scale point cloud segmentation, the *de facto* method is to project a 3D point cloud to get a 2D LiDAR image and use convolutions to process it. Despite the similarity between regular RGB and LiDAR images, we are the first to discover that the feature distribution of LiDAR images changes drastically at different image locations. Using standard convolutions to process such LiDAR images is problematic, as convolution filters pick up local features that are only active in specific regions in the image. As a result, the capacity of the network is under-utilized and the segmentation performance decreases. To fix this, we propose Spatially-Adaptive Convolution (SAC) to adopt different filters for different locations according to the input image. SAC can be computed efficiently since it can be implemented as a series of element-wise multiplications, im2col, and standard convolution. It is a general framework such that several previous methods can be seen as special cases of SAC. Using SAC, we build SqueezeSegV3 for LiDAR point-cloud segmentation and outperform all previous published methods by at least 2.0% mIoU on the SemanticKITTI benchmark. Code and pretrained model are available at https://github.com/chenfengxu714/SqueezeSegV3.

Keywords: Point-cloud segmentation · Spatially-adaptive convolution

1 Introduction

LiDAR sensors are widely used in many applications [59], especially autonomous driving [1,9,56]. For level 4 & 5 autonomous vehicles, most of the solutions rely on LiDAR to obtain a point-cloud representation of the environment. LiDAR

Electronic supplementary material The online version of this chapter (https://doi.org/10.1007/978-3-030-58604-1_1) contains supplementary material, which is available to authorized users.

point clouds can be used in many ways to understand the environment, such as 2D/3D object detection [3,34,41,65], multi-modal fusion [17,64], simultaneous localization and mapping [2,4] and point-cloud segmentation [35,56,58]. This paper is focused on point-cloud segmentation. This task takes a point-cloud as input and aims to assign each point a label corresponding to its object category. For autonomous driving, point-cloud segmentation can be used to recognize objects such as pedestrians and cars, identify drivable areas, detecting lanes, and so on. More applications of point-cloud segmentation are discussed in [59].

Recent work on point-cloud segmentation is mainly divided into two categories, focusing on small-scale or large-scale point-clouds. For small-scale problems, ranging from object parsing to indoor scene understanding, most of the recent methods are based on PointNet [35,36]. Although PointNet-based methods have achieved competitive performance in many 3D tasks, they have limited processing speed, especially for large-scale point clouds. For outdoor scenes and applications such as autonomous driving, typical LiDAR sensors, such as Velodyne HDL-64E LiDAR, can scan about $64 \times 3000 = 192,000$ points for each frame, covering an area of $160 \times 160 \times 20$ m. Processing point clouds at such scale efficiently or even in real time is far beyond the capability of PointNet-based methods. Hence, much of the recent work follows the method based on spherical projection proposed by Wu et al. [56,58]. Instead of processing 3D points directly, these methods first transform a 3D LiDAR point cloud into a 2D LiDAR image and use 2D ConvNets to segment the point cloud, as shown in Fig. 1. In this paper, we follow this method based on spherical projection.

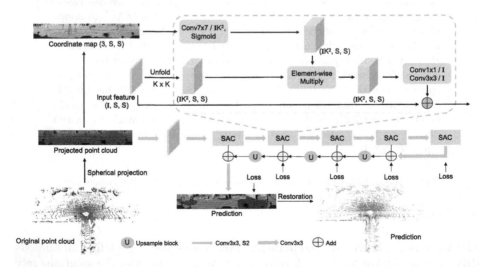

Fig. 1. The framework of SqueezeSegV3. A LiDAR point cloud is projected to generate a LiDAR image, which is then processed by spatially adaptive convolutions (SAC). The network outputs a point-wise prediction that can be restored to label the 3D point cloud. Other variants of SAC can be found in Fig. 4.

To transform a 3D point-cloud into a 2D grid representation, each point in the 3D space is projected to a spherical surface. The projection angles of each point are quantized and used to denote the location of the pixel. Each point's original 3D coordinates are treated as features. Such representations of LiDAR are very similar to RGB images, therefore, it seems straightforward to adopt 2D convolution to process "LiDAR images". This pipeline is illustrated in Fig. 1.

However, we discovered that an important difference exists between LiDAR images and regular images. For a regular image, the feature distribution is largely invariant to spatial locations, as visualized in Fig. 2. For a LiDAR image, its features are converted by spherical projection, which introduces very strong spatial priors. As a result, the feature distribution of LiDAR images varies drastically at different locations, as illustrated in Fig. 2 and Fig. 3 (top). When we train a ConvNet to process LiDAR images, convolution filters may fit local features and become only active in some regions and are not used in other parts, as confirmed in Fig. 3 (bottom). As a result, the capacity of the model is under-utilized, leading to decreased performance in point-cloud segmentation.

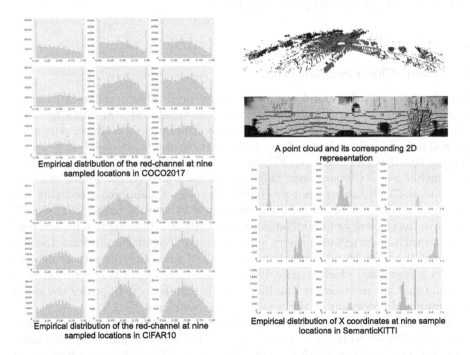

Empirical distribution of the red-channel at nine sampled locations in COCO2017

A point cloud and its corresponding 2D representation

Empirical distribution of the red-channel at nine sampled locations in CIFAR10

Empirical distribution of X coordinates at nine sample locations in SemanticKITTI

Fig. 2. Pixel-wise distribution at nine sampled locations from COCO2017 [25], CIFAR10 [21] and SemanticKITTI [1]. The left shows the distribution of the red channel across all images in COCO2017 and CIFAR10. The right shows the distribution of the X coordinates across all LiDAR images in SemanticKITTI.

To tackle this problem, we propose Spatially-Adaptive Convolution (SAC), as shown in Fig. 1. SAC is designed to be spatially-adaptive and content-aware. Based on the input, it adapts its filters to process different parts of the image. To ensure efficiency, we factorize the adaptive filter into a product of a static convolution weight and an attention map. The attention map is computed by a one-layer convolution, whose output at each pixel location is used to adapt the static weight. By carefully scheduling the computation, SAC can be implemented as a series of widely supported and optimized operations including element-wise multiplication, im2col, and reshaping, which ensures the efficiency of SAC.

SAC is formulated as a general framework such that previous methods such as squeeze-and-excitation (SE) [14], convolutional block attention module (CBAM) [51], context-aggregation module (CAM) [58], and pixel-adaptive convolution (PAC) [42] can be seen as special cases of SAC, and experiments show that the more general SAC variants proposed in this paper outperform previous ones.

Using spatially-adaptive convolution, we build SqueezeSegV3 for LiDAR point-cloud segmentation. On the SemanticKITTI benchmark, SqueezeSegV3 outperforms state-of-the art methods by at least 2.0 mIoU, demonstrating the effectiveness of spatially-adaptive convolution.

2   Related Work

2.1   Point-Cloud Segmentation

Recent papers on point-cloud segmentation can be divided into two categories - those that deal with small-scale point-clouds, and those that deal with large-scale point clouds. For small-scale point-cloud segmentation such as object part parsing and indoor scene understanding, mainstream methods are based on PointNet [35,36]. DGCNN [50] and Deep-KdNet [20] extend the hierarchical architecture of PointNet++ [36] by grouping neighbor points. Based on the PointNet architecture, [8,23,24] further improve the effectiveness of sampling, reordering and grouping to obtain a better representation for downstream tasks. PVCNN [27] improves the efficiency of PointNet-based methods [27,50] using voxel-based convolution with a contiguous memory access pattern. Despite these efforts, the efficiency of PointNet-based methods is still limited since they inherently need to process sparse data, which is more difficult to accelerate [27]. It is noteworthy to mention that the most recent RandLA-Net [15] significantly improves the speed of point cloud processing in the novel use of random sampling.

Large-scale point-cloud segmentation is challenging since 1) large-scale point-clouds are difficult to annotate and 2) many applications require real-time inference. A typical outdoor LiDAR (such as Velodyne HDL-64E) can collect about $200K$ points per scan, it is difficult for previous methods [22,26,29,31,37,38,47] to satisfy a real-time latency constraint. To address the data challenge, [48,56] proposed tools to label 3D bounding boxes and convert to point-wise segmentation labels. [56,58,62] proposed to train with simulated data. Recently, Behley et al. proposed SemanticKITTI [1], a densely annotated dataset for large-scale point-cloud segmentation. For efficiency, Wu et al. [56] proposed to project 3D point clouds to 2D and transform point-cloud segmentation to image segmentation. Later work [1,30,58] continued to improve the projection-based method, making it a popular choice for a large-scale point-cloud segmentation.

2.2 Adaptive Convolution

Standard convolutions use the same weights to process input features at all spatial locations regardless of the input. Adaptive convolutions may change the weights according to the input and the location in the image. Squeeze-and-excitation and its variants [13,14,51] compute channel-wise or spatial attention to adapt the output feature map. Pixel-adaptive convolution (PAC) [42] changes the convolution weight along the kernel dimension with a Gaussian function. Wang et al. [49] propose to directly re-weight the standard convolution with a depth-aware Gaussian kernel. 3DNConv [5] further extends [49] by estimating depth through an RGB image and using it to improve image segmentation. In our work, we propose a more general framework such that channel-wise attention [13,14], spatial attention [51,58] and PAC [42] can be considered as special cases of spatially-adaptive convolution. In addition to adapting weights, deformable convolutions [6,66] adapt the location to pull features to convolution. DKN [19] combines both deformable convolution and adaptive convolution for joint-image filtering. However, deformable convolution is orthogonal to our proposed method.

2.3 Efficient Neural Networks

Many applications that involve point-cloud segmentation require real-time inference. To meet this requirement, we not only need to design efficient segmentation pipelines [58], but also efficient neural networks which optimize the parameter size, FLOPs, latency, power, and so on [52].

Many neural nets target to achieve efficiency, including SqueezeNet [10,16, 54], MobileNets [11,12,39], ShiftNet [55,61], ShuffleNet [28,63], FBNet [53,57], ChamNet [7], MnasNet [44], and EfficientNet [45]. Previous work shows that using a more efficient backbone network can effectively improve efficiency in downstream tasks. In this paper, however, in order to rigorously evaluate the performance of spatially-adaptive convolution (SAC), we use the same backbone as RangeNet++ [30].

3 Spherical Projection of LiDAR Point-Cloud

To process a LiDAR point-cloud efficiently, Wu et al. [56] proposed a pipeline (shown in Fig. 1) to project a sparse 3D point cloud to a 2D LiDAR image as

$$\begin{bmatrix} p \\ q \end{bmatrix} = \begin{bmatrix} \frac{1}{2}(1 - arctan(y,x)/\pi) \cdot w \\ (1 - (arcsin(z \cdot r^{-1}) + f_{up}) \cdot f^{-1}) \cdot h \end{bmatrix}, \tag{1}$$

where (x,y,z) are 3D coordinates, (p,q) are angular coordinates, (h,w) are the height and width of the desired projected 2D map, $f = f_{up} + f_{down}$ is the vertical field-of-view of the LiDAR sensor, and $r = \sqrt{x^2 + y^2 + z^2}$ is the range of each point. For each point projected to (p, q), we use its measurement of (x, y, z, r) and remission as features and stack them along the channel dimension. This way, we can represent a LiDAR point cloud as a LiDAR image with the shape of $(h, w, 5)$. Point-cloud segmentation can then be reduced to image segmentation, which is typically solved using ConvNets.

Despite the apparent similarity between LiDAR and RGB images, we discover that the spatial distribution of RGB features are quite different from (x, y, z, r) features. In Fig. 2, we sample nine pixels on images from COCO [25], CIFAR10 [21] and SemanticKITTI [1] and compare their feature distribution. In COCO and CIFAR10, the feature distribution at different locations are rather similar. For SemanticKITTI, however, feature distribution at each locations are drastically different. Such spatially-varying distribution is caused by the spherical projection in Eq. (1). In Fig. 3 (top), we plot the mean of x, y, and z channels of LiDAR images. Along the width dimension, we can see the sinusoidal change of x and y channels. Along the height dimension, points projected to the top of the image have higher z-values than the ones projected to the bottom. As we will discuss later, such spatially varying distribution can degrade the performance of convolutions.

4   Spatially-Adaptive Convolution

4.1   Standard Convolution

Previous methods based on spherical projection [30,56,58] treat projected LiDAR images as RGB images and process them with standard convolution as

$$Y[m, p, q] = \sigma(\sum_{i,j,n} W[m, n, i, j] \times X[n, p + \hat{i}, q + \hat{j}]), \qquad (2)$$

where $Y \in \mathbf{R}^{O \times S \times S}$ is the output tensor, $X \in \mathbf{R}^{I \times S \times S}$ denotes the input tensor, and $W \in \mathbf{R}^{O \times I \times K \times K}$ is the convolution weight. O, I, S, K are the output channel size, input channel size, image size, and kernel size of the weight, respectively. $\hat{i} = i - \lfloor K/2 \rfloor$, $\hat{j} = j - \lfloor K/2 \rfloor$. $\sigma(\cdot)$ is a non-linear activation function.

Convolution is based on a strong inductive bias that the distribution of visual features is invariant to image locations. For RGB images, this is a somewhat valid assumption, as illustrated in Fig. 2. Therefore, regardless of the location, a convolution use the same weight W to process the input. This design makes the convolution operation very computationally efficient: First, convolutional layers are efficient in parameter size. Regardless of the input resolution S, a convolutional layer's parameter size remains the same as $O \times I \times K \times K$. Second, convolution is efficient to compute. In modern computer architectures, loading parameters into memory costs orders-of-magnitude higher energy and latency than floating point operations such as multiplications and additions [33]. For convolutions, we can load the parameter once and re-use for all the input pixels, which significantly improves the latency and power efficiency.

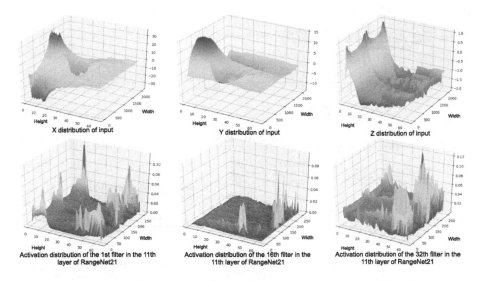

Fig. 3. Channel and filter activation visualization on the SemanticKITTI dataset. Top: we visualize the mean value of x, y, and z channels of the projected LiDAR images at different locations. Along the width dimension, we can see the sinusoidal change of the x and y channels. Along the height dimension, we can see z values are higher at the top of the image. Bottom: We visualize the mean activation value of three filters at the 11th layer of a pre-trained RangeNet21 [30]. We can see that those filters are sparsely activated only in certain areas.

However, for LiDAR images, the feature distribution across the image are no longer identical, as illustrated in Fig. 2 and 3 (top). Many features may only exist in local regions of the image, so the filters that are trained to process them are only active in the corresponding regions and are not useful elsewhere. To confirm this, we analyze a trained RangeNet21 [30] by calculating the average filter activation across the image. We can see in Fig. 3 (bottom) that convolutional filters are sparsely activated and remain zero in many regions. This validates that convolution filters are spatially under-utilized.

4.2 Spatially-Adaptive Convolution

To better process LiDAR images with spatially-varying feature distributions, we re-design convolution to achieve two goals: 1) It should be spatially-adaptive and content-aware. The new operator should process different parts of the image with different filters, and the filters should adapt to feature variations. 2) The new operator should be efficient to compute.

To achieve these goals, we propose Spatially-Adaptive Convolution (SAC), which can be described as the following:

$$Y[m, p, q] = \sigma(\sum_{i,j,n} W(X_0)[m, n, p, q, i, j] \times X[n, p + \hat{i}, q + \hat{j}]). \qquad (3)$$

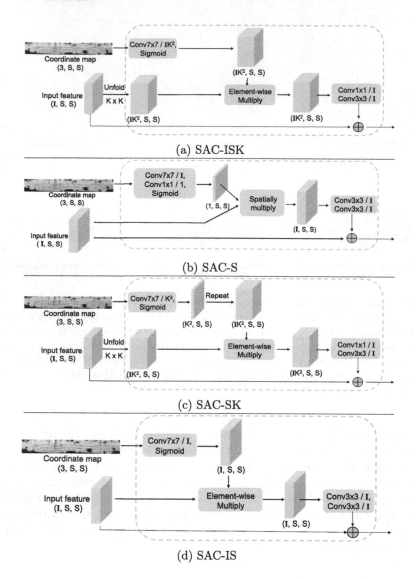

Fig. 4. Variants of spatially-adaptive convolution used in Fig. 1.

$W(\cdot) \in \mathbf{R}^{O \times I \times S \times S \times K \times K}$ is a function of the raw input X_0. It is spatially-adaptive, since W depends on the location (p, q). It is content-aware since W is a function of the raw input X_0. Computing W in this general form is very expensive since W contains too many elements to compute.

To reduce the computational cost, we factorize W as the product of a standard convolution weight and a spatially-adaptive attention map as:

$$W[m, n, p, q, i, j] = \hat{W}[m, n, i, j] \times A(X_0)[m, n, p, q, i, j]. \tag{4}$$

$\hat{W} \in \mathbf{R}^{O \times I \times S \times S}$ is a standard convolution weight, and $A \in \mathbf{R}^{O \times I \times S \times S \times K \times K}$ is the attention map. To reduce the complexity, we collapse several dimensions of A to obtain a smaller attention map to make it computationally tractable.

We denote the first dimension of A as the output channel dimension (O), the second as the input channel dimension (I), the 3rd and 4th dimensions as spatial dimensions (S), and the last two dimensions as kernel dimensions (K).

Starting from Eq. (4), we name this form of SAC as SAC-OISK, and we re-write A as A_{OISK}, where the subscripts denote the dimensions that are not collapsed to 1. If we collapse the output dimension, we name the variant as SAC-ISK, and the attention map as $A_{ISK} \in \mathbf{R}^{1 \times I \times S \times S \times K \times K}$. SAC-ISK adapts a convolution weight spatially as well as across the kernel and input channel dimensions, as shown in Fig. 4a. We can further compress the kernel dimensions to obtain SAC-IS with $A_{IS} \in \mathbf{R}^{1 \times I \times S \times S \times 1 \times 1}$, (Fig. 4d) and SAC-S with pixel-wise attention as $A_S \in \mathbf{R}^{1 \times 1 \times S \times S \times 1 \times 1}$ (Fig. 4b).

As long as we retain the spatial dimension A, SAC is able to spatially adapt a standard convolution. Experiments show that all variants of SAC effectively improve the performance on the SemanticKITTI dataset.

4.3   Efficient Computation of SAC

To efficiently compute an attention map, we feed the raw LiDAR image X_0 into a 7×7 convolution followed by a sigmoid activation. The convolution computes the values of the attention map at each location. The more dimensions to adapt, the more FLOPs and parameter size SAC requires. However, most of the variants of SAC are very efficient. Taking SqueezeSegV3-21 as an example, the cost of adding different SAC variants is summarized in Table 1. The extra FLOPs (2.4%–24.8%) and parameters (1.1%–14.9%) needed by SAC is quite small.

Table 1. Extra parameters and MACs for different SAC variants

Method	O	I	S	K	Extra params (%)	Extra MACs (%)
SAC-S	✗	✗	✓	✗	1.1	2.4
SAC-IS	✗	✓	✓	✗	2.2	6.2
SAC-SK	✗	✗	✓	✓	1.9	3.1
SAC-ISK	✗	✓	✓	✓	14.9	24.8

After obtaining the attention map, we need to efficiently compute the product of the convolution weight $\hat{W}$, attention map A, and the input X. One choice is to first compute the adaptive weight as Eq. (4) and then process the input X. However, the adaptive weight varies per pixel, so we are no longer able to re-use the weight spatially to retain the efficiency of standard convolution.

So, instead, we first combine the attention map A with the input tensor X. For attention maps without kernel dimensions, such as A_S or A_{IS}, we directly perform element-wise multiplication (with broadcasting) between A and X. Then, we apply a standard convolution with weight W on the adapted input. The examples of SAC-S and SAC-IS are illustrated in Figs. 4b and 4d respectively. Pseudo-code implementation is provided in the supplementary material.

For attention maps with kernel dimensions, such as A_{ISK} and A_{SK}, we first perform an unfolding (im2col) operation on X. At each location, we collect nearby K-by-K features and stack them along the channel dimension to get $\tilde{X} \in \mathbf{R}^{K^2 I \times S \times S}$. Then, we can apply element-wise multiplication to combine the attention map A and input X. Next, we reshape weight $W \in \mathbf{R}^{O \times I \times K \times K}$ as $\tilde{W} \in \mathbf{R}^{O \times K^2 I \times 1 \times 1}$. Finally, the output of Y can be obtained by applying a 1-by-1 convolution with $\tilde{W}$ on $\tilde{X}$. The computation of SAC-ISK and SAC-SK is shown in Figs. 4a and 4c respectively, and the pseudo-code implementation is provided in the supplementary material.

Overall, SAC can be implemented as a series of element-wise multiplications, im2col, reshaping, and standard convolution operations, which are widely supported and well optimized. This ensures that SAC can be computed efficiently.

4.4   Relationship with Prior Work

Several prior works can be seen as variants of a spatially-adaptive convolution, as described by Eqs. 3 and 4. Squeeze-and-Excitation (SE) [13,14] uses global average pooling and fully-connected layers to compute channel-wise attention to adapt the feature map, as illustrated in Fig. 5. It can be seen as the variant of SAC-I with a attention map of $A_I \in \mathbf{R}^{1 \times I \times 1 \times 1 \times 1 \times 1}$. The convolutional block attention module (CBAM) [51] can be see as applying A_I followed by an A_S to adapt the feature map. SqueezeSegV2 [58] uses the context-aggregation module (CAM) to combat dropout noises in LiDAR images. At each position, it uses a 7×7 max pooling followed by 1×1 convolutions to compute a channel-wise attention map. It can be seen as the variant SAC-IS with the attention map of $A_{IS} \in \mathbf{R}^{1 \times I \times S \times S \times 1 \times 1}$. Pixel-adaptive convolution (PAC) [42] uses a Gaussian function to compute kernel-wise attention for each pixel. It can be seen as the variant of SAC-SK, with the attention map of $A_{SK} \in \mathbf{R}^{1 \times 1 \times S \times S \times K \times K}$. All the detail figures of prior works are presented in the supplementary. Our ablation studies compare variants of SAC, including ones proposed in our paper and in prior work. Experiments show our proposed SAC variants outperform previous baselines.

5   SqueezeSegV3

Using the spatially-adaptive convolution, we build SqueezeSegV3 for LiDAR point-cloud segmentation. The overview of the model is shown in Fig. 1.

5.1   The Architecture of SqueezeSegV3

To facilitate rigorous comparison, SqueezeSegV3's backbone architecture is based on RangeNet [30]. RangeNet contains five stages of convolution, each stage contains several blocks. At the beginning of the stage, it performs downsampling.

The output is then upsampled to recover the resolution. Each block of RangeNet contains two stacked convolutions. We replace the first one with SAC-ISK as in Fig. 4a. We remove the last two downsampling. To keep the similar FLOPs, we reduce the channels of last two stages. The output channel sizes from $Stage1$ to $Stage5$ are 64, 128, 256, 256 and 256 respectively, while the output channel sizes in RangeNet [30] are 64, 128, 256, 512 and 1024. Due to the removal of the last two downsampling operations, we only adopt 3 upsample blocks using transposed convolution and convolution.

5.2   Loss Function

We introduce a multi-layer cross entropy loss to train the proposed network, which is also used in [18,32,40,60]. During training, from $stage1$ to $stage5$, we add a prediction layer at each stage's output. For each output, we respectively downsample the groundtruth label map by 1x, 2x, 4x, 8x and 8x, and use them to train the output of $stage1$ to $stage5$. The loss function can be described as

$$L = \sum_{i=1}^{5} \frac{-\sum_{H_i,W_i} \sum_{c=1}^{C} w_c \cdot y_c \cdot log(\hat{y}_c)}{H_i \times W_i}. \tag{5}$$

In the equation, $w_c = \frac{1}{log(f_c+\epsilon)}$ is a normalization factor and f_c is the frequency of class c. H_i, W_i are the height and width of the output in i-th stage, y_c is the prediction for the c-th class in each pixel and $\hat{y}_c$ is the label. Compared to the single-stage cross-entropy loss used for the final output, the intermediate supervisions guide the model to form features with more semantic meaning. In addition, they help mitigate the vanishing gradient problem in training.

6   Experiments

6.1   Dataset and Evaluation Metrics

We conduct our experiments on the SemanticKITTI dataset [1], a large-scale dataset for LiDAR point-cloud segmentation. The dataset contains 21 sequences of point-cloud data with 43,442 densely annotated scans and total 4549 millions points. Following [1], sequences-{0–7} and {9, 10} (19130 scans) are used for training, sequence-08 (4071 scans) is for validation, and sequences-{11–21} (20351 scans) are for test. Following previous work [30], we use mIoU over 19 categories to evaluate the accuracy.

6.2   Implementation Details

We pre-process all the points by spherical projection following Eq. (1). The 2D LiDAR images are then processed by SqueezeSegV3 to get a 2D predicted label map, which is then restored back to the 3D space. Following previous work [30,56,58], we project all points in a scan to a 64 × 2048 image. If multiple points are projected to the same pixel on the 2D image, we keep the point with the largest distance. Following RangeNet21 and RangeNet53 in [30], we propose SqueezeSegV3-21 (SSGV3-21) and SqueezeSegV3-53 (SSGV3-53). The model architecture of SSGV3-21 and SSGV3-53 are similar to RangeNet21 and RangNet53 [30], except that we replace regular convolution blocks with SAC blocks. Both models contain 5 stages, each of them has a different input resolution. In SSGV3-21, the 5 stages respectively contain 1, 1, 2, 2, 1 blocks and in SSGV3-53, the 5 stages contain 1, 2, 8, 8, 4 blocks, which are also same as RangeNet21 and RangeNet53, respectively.

We use the SGD optimizer to end-to-end train the whole model. During training, SSGV3-21 and SSGV3-53 are trained with an initial learning rate of 0.01 and 0.005, respectively. We use the warming up strategy to change the learning rate for 1 epoch. During inference, the original points will be projected and fed into SqueezeSegV3 to get a 2D prediction. Then we adopt the restoration operation to obtain the 3D prediction, as previous work [30,56,58].

6.3   Comparing with Prior Methods

We compare two proposed models, SSGV3-21 and SSGV3-53, with previous published work [22,30,35,36,43,46,56,58]. From Table 2, we can see that the proposed SqueezeSegV3 models outperforms all the baselines. Compared with the previous state-of-the-art RangeNet53 [30], SSGV3-53 improves the accuracy by 3.0 mIoU. Moreover, when we apply post-processing KNN refinement following [30] (indicated as *), the proposed SSGV3-53* outperforms RangeNet53* by 3.7 mIoU and achieves the best accuracy in 14 out of 19 categories. Meanwhile, the proposed SSGV3-21 also surpasses RangeNet21 by 1.4 mIoU and the performance is close to RangeNet53* with post-processing. The advantages are more significant for smaller objects, as SSGV3-53* significantly outperforms RangeNet53* by 13.0 IoU, 10.0 IoU, 7.4 IoU and 15.3 IoU in categories of bicycle, other-vehicle, bicyclist and Motorcyclist respectively.

In terms of speed, SSGV3-21 (16 FPS) is closet RangeNet21 (20 FPS). Even though SSGV3-53 (7 FPS) is slower than RangeNet53 (12 FPS), note that our implementation of SAC is primitive and it can be optimized to achieve further speedup. In comparison, PointNet-based methods [22,35,36,43,46] do not perform well in either accuracy and speed except RandLA-Net [15] which is a new efficient and effective work.

6.4   Ablation Study

We conduct ablation studies to analyze the performance of SAC with different configurations. Also, we compare it with other related operators to show its effectiveness. To facilitate fast training and experiments, we shrink the LiDAR images to 64 × 512, and use the shallower model of SSGV3-21 as the starting point. We evaluate the accuracy directly on the projected 2D image, instead of the original 3D points, to make the evaluation faster. We train the models in this section on the training set of SemanticKITTI and report the accuracy on

Table 2. IoU [%] on test set (sequences 11 to 21). SSGV3-21 and SSGV3-53 are the proposed method. Their complexity corresponds to RangeNet21 and RangeNet53 respectively. * means KNN post-processing from RangeNet++ [30], and ‡ means the CRF post-processing from SqueezeSegV2 used [58]. The first group reports PointNet-based methods. The second reports projection-based methods. The third include our results

Method	car	bicycle	motorcycle	truck	other-vehicle	person	bicyclist	Motorcyclist	road	parking	sidewalk	other-ground	building	fence	vegetation	trunk	terrain	pole	traffic-sign	mean IoU	Scans/sec
PNet [35]	46.3	1.3	0.3	0.1	0.8	0.2	0.2	0.0	61.6	15.8	35.7	1.4	41.4	12.9	31.0	4.6	17.6	2.4	3.7	14.6	2
PNet++ [36]	53.7	1.9	0.2	0.9	0.2	0.9	1.0	0.0	72.0	18.7	41.8	5.6	62.3	16.9	46.5	13.8	30.0	6.0	8.9	20.1	0.1
SPGraph [22]	68.3	0.9	4.5	0.9	0.8	1.0	6.0	0.0	49.5	1.7	24.2	0.3	68.2	22.5	59.2	27.2	17.0	18.3	10.5	20.0	0.2
SPLAT [43]	66.6	0.0	0.0	0.0	0.0	0.0	0.0	0.0	70.4	0.8	41.5	0.0	68.7	27.8	72.3	35.9	35.8	13.8	0.0	22.8	1
TgConv [46]	86.8	1.3	12.7	11.6	10.2	17.1	20.2	0.5	82.9	15.2	61.7	9.0	82.8	44.2	75.5	42.5	55.5	30.2	22.2	35.9	0.3
RLNet [15]	94.2	26.0	25.8	40.1	38.9	49.2	48.2	7.2	90.7	60.3	73.7	20.4	86.9	56.3	81.4	61.3	66.8	49.2	47.7	53.9	22
SSG [56]	68.8	16.0	4.1	3.3	3.6	12.9	13.1	0.9	85.4	26.9	54.3	4.5	57.4	29.0	60.0	24.3	53.7	17.5	24.5	29.5	65
SSG‡ [56]	68.3	18.1	5.1	4.1	4.8	16.5	17.3	1.2	84.9	28.4	54.7	4.6	61.5	29.2	59.6	25.5	54.7	11.2	36.3	30.8	53
SSGV2 [58]	81.8	18.5	17.9	13.4	14.0	20.1	25.1	3.9	88.6	45.8	67.6	17.7	73.7	41.1	71.8	35.8	60.2	20.2	36.3	39.7	50
SSGV2‡ [58]	82.7	21.0	22.6	14.5	15.9	20.2	24.3	2.9	88.5	42.4	65.5	18.7	73.8	41.0	68.5	36.9	58.9	12.9	41.0	39.6	39
RGN21 [30]	85.4	26.2	26.5	18.6	15.6	31.8	33.6	4.0	91.4	57.0	74.0	26.4	81.9	52.3	77.6	48.4	63.6	36.0	50.0	47.4	20
RGN53 [30]	86.4	24.5	32.7	25.5	22.6	36.2	33.6	4.7	91.8	64.8	74.6	27.9	84.1	55.0	78.3	50.1	64.0	38.9	52.2	49.9	12
RGN53* [30]	91.4	25.7	34.4	25.7	23.0	38.3	38.8	4.8	91.8	65.0	75.2	27.8	87.4	58.6	80.5	55.1	64.6	47.9	55.9	52.2	11
SSGV3-21	84.6	31.5	32.4	11.3	20.9	39.4	36.1	21.3	90.8	54.1	72.9	23.9	81.1	50.3	77.6	47.7	63.9	36.1	51.7	48.8	16
SSGV3-53	87.4	35.2	33.7	29.0	31.9	41.8	39.1	20.1	91.8	63.5	74.4	27.2	85.3	55.8	79.4	52.1	64.7	38.6	53.4	52.9	7
SSGV3-21*	89.4	33.7	34.9	11.3	21.5	42.6	44.9	21.2	90.8	54.1	73.3	23.2	84.8	53.6	80.2	53.3	64.5	46.4	57.6	51.6	15
SSGV3-53*	92.5	38.7	36.5	29.6	33.0	45.6	46.2	20.1	91.7	63.4	74.8	26.4	89.0	59.4	82.0	58.7	65.4	49.6	58.9	55.9	6

the validation set. We study different variations of SAC, input kernel sizes, and other techniques used in SqueezeSegV3.

Table 3. mIoU [%], Accuracy [%] and Latency [$e^{-4}s$] for variants of spatially-adaptive convolution

Method	Baseline	SAC-S	SAC-IS	SAC-SK	SAC-ISK	PAC [42]	SE [14]	CBAM [51]	CAM [58]
mIoU	44.0	44.9	44.0	45.4	46.3	45.2	44.2	44.8	42.1
Accuracy	86.8	87.6	86.9	88.2	88.6	88.2	87.0	87.5	85.8
Latency	3.0	5.3	4.6	15.0	5.2	18.4	54.5	15.8	10.6

Variants of Spatially-Adaptive Convolution: As shown in Figs. 4 and 5, spatially-adaptive convolution can have many variation. Some variants are equivalent to or similar with methods proposed by previous papers, including squeeze-and-excitation (SE) [14], convolutional block attention maps (CBAM) [51], pixel-adaptive convolution (PAC) [42], and context-aggregation module (CAM) [58]. To understand the effectiveness of SAC variants and previous methods, we swap them into SqueezeSegV3-21. For simple comparison, we evaluate the latency of one block for each variant, all of which are fed by an input with the size of $32 \times 64 \times 512$ and output a feature with the size of $64 \times 64 \times 512$. The results are reported in Table 3.

It can be seen that SAC-ISK significantly outperforms all the other settings in term of mIoU with few latency increments. CAM and SAC-IS have the worst performance, which demonstrates the importance of the attention on the kernel dimension. Squeeze-and-excitation (SE) also does not perform well, since SE is not spatially-adaptive, and the global average pooling used in SE ignores the feature distribution shift across the LiDAR image. In comparison, CBAM [51] improves the baseline by 0.8 mIoU. Unlike SE, it also adapts the input feature spatially. This comparison shows that being spatially-adaptive is crucial for processing LiDAR images. Pixel-adaptive convolution (PAC) is similar to the SAC variant of SAC-SK, except that PAC uses a Gaussian function to compute the kernel-wise attention. Experiments show that the proposed SAC-ISK slightly outperforms SAC-SK, possibly because SAC-SK adopts a more general and learnable convolution to compute the attention map. Comparing SAC-S and SAC-IS, adding the input channel dimension does not improve the performance.

Table 4. mIoU [%] and Accuracy [%] for different convolution kernel sizes for coordinate map

Kernel size	baseline	1×1	3×3	5×5	7×7
mIoU	44.0	45.5	44.5	45.4	46.3
Accuracy	86.8	88.4	87.6	88.2	88.6

Kernel Sizes of SAC: We use a one-layer convolution to compute the attention map for SAC. However, what should be the kernel size for this convolution? A larger kernel size makes sure that it can capture spatial information around, but it also costs more parameters and MACs. To examine the influence of kernel size, we use different kernel sizes in the SAC convolution. As we can see in Table 4, a 1×1 convolution provides a very strong result that is better than its 3×3 and 5×5 counterparts. 7×7 convolution performs the best.

The Effectiveness of Other Techniques: In addition to SAC, we also introduce several new techniques to SqueezeSegV3, including removing the last two downsample layers and multi-layer loss (Table 4). We start from the baseline of RangeNet21. First, we remove downsampling layers and reduce the channel sizes of the last two stages to 256 to keep the MACS the same. The performance improves by 3.9 mIoU. After adding the multi-layer loss, the mIoU increases by another 1.5%. Based on the above techniques, adding SAC-ISK further boost mIoU by 2.3%.

Table 5. mIoU [%] and Accuracy [%] with downsampling removal, multi-layer loss, and spatially-adaptive convolution

method	Baseline	+DS removal	+Multi-layer loss	+SAC-ISK
mIoU	38.6	42.5 (+3.9)	44.0 (+1.5)	46.3 (+2.3)
Accuracy	84.7	86.2 (+1.5)	86.8 (+1.4)	88.6 (+1.8)

7   Conclusion

In this paper, we are the first to explore the issue of spatially-varying feature distribution of LiDAR images and design efficient Spatially-Adaptive Convolution to mitigate it. Experiments show that SAC significantly improves the state-of-the-art methods by more than 2.0%.

Acknowledgement. Co-authors from UC Berkeley are sponsored by Berkeley Deep Drive (BDD). We would like to thank Ravi Krishna for his constructive feedback.

References

1. Behley, J., et al.: SemanticKITTI: a dataset for semantic scene understanding of LiDAR sequences. In: Proceedings of the IEEE/CVF International Conference on Computer Vision (ICCV) (2019)
2. Behley, J., Stachniss, C.: Efficient surfel-based SLAM using 3D laser range data in urban environments. In: Robotics: Science and Systems (2018)
3. Chen, X., Ma, H., Wan, J., Li, B., Xia, T.: Multi-view 3D object detection network for autonomous driving. In: Proceedings of the IEEE Conference on Computer Vision and Pattern Recognition, pp. 1907–1915 (2017)

4. Chen, X., Milioto, A., Palazzolo, E., Giguère, P., Behley, J., Stachniss, C.: SuMa++: efficient LiDAR-based semantic SLAM. In: 2019 IEEE/RSJ International Conference on Intelligent Robots and Systems (IROS), pp. 4530–4537. IEEE (2019)
5. Chen, Y., Mensink, T., Gavves, E.: 3D neighborhood convolution: learning depth-aware features for RGB-D and RGB semantic segmentation. In: 2019 International Conference on 3D Vision (3DV), pp. 173–182. IEEE (2019)
6. Dai, J., et al.: Deformable convolutional networks. In: Proceedings of the IEEE International Conference on Computer Vision, pp. 764–773 (2017)
7. Dai, X., et al.: ChamNet: towards efficient network design through platform-aware model adaptation. In: Proceedings of the IEEE Conference on Computer Vision and Pattern Recognition, pp. 11398–11407 (2019)
8. Dovrat, O., Lang, I., Avidan, S.: Learning to sample. In: Proceedings of the IEEE Conference on Computer Vision and Pattern Recognition, pp. 2760–2769 (2019)
9. Geiger, A., Lenz, P., Stiller, C., Urtasun, R.: Vision meets robotics: the KITTI dataset. Int. J. Robot. Res. **32**(11), 1231–1237 (2013)
10. Gholami, A., et al.: SqueezeNext: hardware-aware neural network design. In: Proceedings of the IEEE Conference on Computer Vision and Pattern Recognition Workshops, pp. 1638–1647 (2018)
11. Howard, A., et al.: Searching for MobileNetV3. In: Proceedings of the IEEE International Conference on Computer Vision, pp. 1314–1324 (2019)
12. Howard, A.G., et al.: MobileNets: Efficient convolutional neural networks for mobile vision applications. arXiv preprint arXiv:1704.04861 (2017)
13. Hu, J., Shen, L., Albanie, S., Sun, G., Vedaldi, A.: Gather-excite: exploiting feature context in convolutional neural networks. In: Advances in Neural Information Processing Systems, pp. 9401–9411 (2018)
14. Hu, J., Shen, L., Sun, G.: Squeeze-and-excitation networks. In: Proceedings of the IEEE Conference on Computer Vision and Pattern Recognition, pp. 7132–7141 (2018)
15. Hu, Q., et al.: RandLA-Net: Efficient semantic segmentation of large-scale point clouds. arXiv preprint arXiv:1911.11236 (2019)
16. Iandola, F.N., Han, S., Moskewicz, M.W., Ashraf, K., Dally, W.J., Keutzer, K.: SqueezeNet: Alexnet-level accuracy with 50x fewer parameters and <0.5 mb model size. arXiv preprint arXiv:1602.07360 (2016)
17. Jaritz, M., Vu, T.H., de Charette, R., Émilie Wirbel, Pérez, P.: xMUDA: Cross-modal unsupervised domain adaptation for 3D semantic segmentation (2019)
18. Johnson, J., Alahi, A., Fei-Fei, L.: Perceptual losses for real-time style transfer and super-resolution. In: Leibe, B., Matas, J., Sebe, N., Welling, M. (eds.) ECCV 2016. LNCS, vol. 9906, pp. 694–711. Springer, Cham (2016). https://doi.org/10.1007/978-3-319-46475-6_43
19. Kim, B., Ponce, J., Ham, B.: Deformable kernel networks for joint image filtering. arXiv preprint arXiv:1910.08373 (2019)
20. Klokov, R., Lempitsky, V.: Escape from cells: deep Kd-networks for the recognition of 3D point cloud models. In: Proceedings of the IEEE International Conference on Computer Vision, pp. 863–872 (2017)
21. Krizhevsky, A., Hinton, G., et al.: Learning multiple layers of features from tiny images (2009)
22. Landrieu, L., Simonovsky, M.: Large-scale point cloud semantic segmentation with superpoint graphs. In: Proceedings of the IEEE Conference on Computer Vision and Pattern Recognition, pp. 4558–4567 (2018)

23. Li, J., Chen, B.M., Hee Lee, G.: SO-Net: self-organizing network for point cloud analysis. In: Proceedings of the IEEE Conference on Computer Vision and Pattern Recognition, pp. 9397–9406 (2018)

24. Li, Y., Bu, R., Sun, M., Wu, W., Di, X., Chen, B.: PointCNN: convolution on X-transformed points. In: Advances in Neural Information Processing Systems, pp. 820–830 (2018)

25. Lin, T.Y., et al.: Microsoft COCO: common objects in context. In: Fleet, D., Pajdla, T., Schiele, B., Tuytelaars, T. (eds.) ECCV 2014. LNCS, vol. 8693, pp. 740–755. Springer, Cham (2014). https://doi.org/10.1007/978-3-319-10602-1_48

26. Liu, F., Li, S., Zhang, L., Zhou, C., Ye, R., Wang, Y., Lu, J.: 3DCNN-DQN-RNN: a deep reinforcement learning framework for semantic parsing of large-scale 3D point clouds. In: Proceedings of the IEEE International Conference on Computer Vision, pp. 5678–5687 (2017)

27. Liu, Z., Tang, H., Lin, Y., Han, S.: Point-voxel CNN for efficient 3D deep learning. In: Advances in Neural Information Processing Systems, pp. 963–973 (2019)

28. Ma, N., Zhang, X., Zheng, H.-T., Sun, J.: ShuffleNet V2: practical guidelines for efficient CNN architecture design. In: Ferrari, V., Hebert, M., Sminchisescu, C., Weiss, Y. (eds.) Computer Vision – ECCV 2018. LNCS, vol. 11218, pp. 122–138. Springer, Cham (2018). https://doi.org/10.1007/978-3-030-01264-9_8

29. Meng, H.Y., Gao, L., Lai, Y.K., Manocha, D.: VV-Net: Voxel VAE Net with group convolutions for point cloud segmentation. In: Proceedings of the IEEE International Conference on Computer Vision, pp. 8500–8508 (2019)

30. Milioto, A., Vizzo, I., Behley, J., Stachniss, C.: RangeNet++: fast and accurate LiDAR semantic segmentation. In: Proceedings of the IEEE/RSJ International Conference on Intelligent Robots and Systems (IROS) (2019)

31. Mo, K., et al.: PartNet: a large-scale benchmark for fine-grained and hierarchical part-level 3D object understanding. In: Proceedings of the IEEE Conference on Computer Vision and Pattern Recognition, pp. 909–918 (2019)

32. Newell, A., Yang, K., Deng, J.: Stacked hourglass networks for human pose estimation. In: Leibe, B., Matas, J., Sebe, N., Welling, M. (eds.) ECCV 2016. LNCS, vol. 9912, pp. 483–499. Springer, Cham (2016). https://doi.org/10.1007/978-3-319-46484-8_29

33. Pedram, A., Richardson, S., Horowitz, M., Galal, S., Kvatinsky, S.: Dark memory and accelerator-rich system optimization in the dark silicon era. IEEE Des. Test **34**(2), 39–50 (2016)

34. Qi, C.R., Liu, W., Wu, C., Su, H., Guibas, L.J.: Frustum PointNets for 3D object detection from RGB-D data. In: Proceedings of the IEEE Conference on Computer Vision and Pattern Recognition, pp. 918–927 (2018)

35. Qi, C.R., Su, H., Mo, K., Guibas, L.J.: PointNet: deep learning on point sets for 3D classification and segmentation. In: Proceedings of the IEEE Conference on Computer Vision and Pattern Recognition, pp. 652–660 (2017)

36. Qi, C.R., Yi, L., Su, H., Guibas, L.J.: PointNet++: deep hierarchical feature learning on point sets in a metric space. In: Advances in Neural Information Processing Systems, pp. 5099–5108 (2017)

37. Rethage, D., Wald, J., Sturm, J., Navab, N., Tombari, F.: Fully-convolutional point networks for large-scale point clouds. In: Ferrari, V., Hebert, M., Sminchisescu, C., Weiss, Y. (eds.) ECCV 2018. LNCS, vol. 11208, pp. 625–640. Springer, Cham (2018). https://doi.org/10.1007/978-3-030-01225-0_37

38. Riegler, G., Osman Ulusoy, A., Geiger, A.: OctNet: learning deep 3D representations at high resolutions. In: Proceedings of the IEEE Conference on Computer Vision and Pattern Recognition, pp. 3577–3586 (2017)

39. Sandler, M., Howard, A., Zhu, M., Zhmoginov, A., Chen, L.C.: MobileNetV2: inverted residuals and linear bottlenecks. In: Proceedings of the IEEE Conference on Computer Vision and Pattern Recognition, pp. 4510–4520 (2018)
40. Shen, W., Wang, B., Jiang, Y., Wang, Y., Yuille, A.: Multi-stage multi-recursive-input fully convolutional networks for neuronal boundary detection. In: Proceedings of the IEEE International Conference on Computer Vision, pp. 2391–2400 (2017)
41. Song, S., Xiao, J.: Deep sliding shapes for amodal 3D object detection in GB-D images. In: Proceedings of the IEEE Conference on Computer Vision and Pattern Recognition, pp. 808–816 (2016)
42. Su, H., Jampani, V., Sun, D., Gallo, O., Learned-Miller, E., Kautz, J.: Pixel-adaptive convolutional neural networks. In: Proceedings of the IEEE Conference on Computer Vision and Pattern Recognition, pp. 11166–11175 (2019)
43. Su, H., et al.: SPLATNet: sparse lattice networks for point cloud processing. In: Proceedings of the IEEE Conference on Computer Vision and Pattern Recognition, pp. 2530–2539 (2018)
44. Tan, M., et al.: MnasNet: platform-aware neural architecture search for mobile. In: Proceedings of the IEEE Conference on Computer Vision and Pattern Recognition, pp. 2820–2828 (2019)
45. Tan, M., Le, Q.V.: EfficientNet: Rethinking model scaling for convolutional neural networks. arXiv preprint arXiv:1905.11946 (2019)
46. Tatarchenko, M., Park, J., Koltun, V., Zhou, Q.Y.: Tangent convolutions for dense prediction in 3D. In: Proceedings of the IEEE Conference on Computer Vision and Pattern Recognition, pp. 3887–3896 (2018)
47. Tchapmi, L., Choy, C., Armeni, I., Gwak, J., Savarese, S.: SEGCloud: semantic segmentation of 3D point clouds. In: 2017 International Conference on 3D Vision (3DV), pp. 537–547. IEEE (2017)
48. Wang, B., Wu, V., Wu, B., Keutzer, K.: LATTE: accelerating LiDAR point cloud annotation via sensor fusion, one-click annotation, and tracking. In: 2019 IEEE Intelligent Transportation Systems Conference (ITSC), pp. 265–272. IEEE (2019)
49. Wang, W., Neumann, U.: Depth-aware CNN for RGB-D segmentation. In: Ferrari, V., Hebert, M., Sminchisescu, C., Weiss, Y. (eds.) ECCV 2018. LNCS, vol. 11215, pp. 144–161. Springer, Cham (2018). https://doi.org/10.1007/978-3-030-01252-6_9
50. Wang, Y., Sun, Y., Liu, Z., Sarma, S.E., Bronstein, M.M., Solomon, J.M.: Dynamic graph CNN for learning on point clouds. ACM Trans. Graph. (TOG) $38(5)$, 1–12 (2019)
51. Woo, S., Park, J., Lee, J.-Y., Kweon, I.S.: CBAM: convolutional block attention module. In: Ferrari, V., Hebert, M., Sminchisescu, C., Weiss, Y. (eds.) ECCV 2018. LNCS, vol. 11211, pp. 3–19. Springer, Cham (2018). https://doi.org/10.1007/978-3-030-01234-2_1
52. Wu, B.: Efficient deep neural networks. arXiv preprint arXiv:1908.08926 (2019)
53. Wu, B., et al.: FBNet: hardware-aware efficient ConvNet design via differentiable neural architecture search. In: Proceedings of the IEEE Conference on Computer Vision and Pattern Recognition, pp. 10734–10742 (2019)
54. Wu, B., Iandola, F., Jin, P.H., Keutzer, K.: SqueezeDet: unified, small, low power fully convolutional neural networks for real-time object detection for autonomous driving. In: Proceedings of the IEEE Conference on Computer Vision and Pattern Recognition Workshops, pp. 129–137 (2017)
55. Wu, B., et al.: Shift: A zero FLOP, zero parameter alternative to spatial convolutions. In: Proceedings of the IEEE Conference on Computer Vision and Pattern Recognition, pp. 9127–9135 (2018)

56. Wu, B., Wan, A., Yue, X., Keutzer, K.: SqueezeSeg: convolutional neural nets with recurrent CRF for real-time road-object segmentation from 3D LiDAR Point Cloud. In: ICRA (2018)
57. Wu, B., Wang, Y., Zhang, P., Tian, Y., Vajda, P., Keutzer, K.: Mixed precision quantization of convnets via differentiable neural architecture search. arXiv preprint arXiv:1812.00090 (2018)
58. Wu, B., Zhou, X., Zhao, S., Yue, X., Keutzer, K.: SqueezeSegV2: improved model structure and unsupervised domain adaptation for road-object segmentation from a LiDAR point cloud. In: ICRA (2019)
59. Xie, Y., Tian, J., Zhu, X.X.: A review of point cloud semantic segmentation. arXiv preprint arXiv:1908.08854 (2019)
60. Xu, C., Qiu, K., Fu, J., Bai, S., Xu, Y., Bai, X.: Learn to scale: generating multipolar normalized density maps for crowd counting. In: Proceedings of the IEEE International Conference on Computer Vision, pp. 8382–8390 (2019)
61. Yang, Y., et al.: Synetgy: algorithm-hardware co-design for ConvNet accelerators on embedded FPGAs. In: Proceedings of the 2019 ACM/SIGDA International Symposium on Field-Programmable Gate Arrays, pp. 23–32 (2019)
62. Yue, X., Wu, B., Seshia, S.A., Keutzer, K., Sangiovanni-Vincentelli, A.L.: A LiDAR point cloud generator: from a virtual world to autonomous driving. In: Proceedings of the 2018 ACM on International Conference on Multimedia Retrieval, pp. 458–464 (2018)
63. Zhang, X., Zhou, X., Lin, M., Sun, J.: ShuffleNet: an extremely efficient convolutional neural network for mobile devices. In: Proceedings of the IEEE Conference on Computer Vision and Pattern Recognition, pp. 6848–6856 (2018)
64. Zhou, Y., et al.: End-to-end multi-view fusion for 3D object detection in LiDAR point clouds. arXiv preprint arXiv:1910.06528 (2019)
65. Zhou, Y., Tuzel, O.: VoxelNet: end-to-end learning for point cloud based 3D object detection. In: Proceedings of the IEEE Conference on Computer Vision and Pattern Recognition, pp. 4490–4499 (2018)
66. Zhu, X., Hu, H., Lin, S., Dai, J.: Deformable ConvNets v2: more deformable, better results. In: Proceedings of the IEEE Conference on Computer Vision and Pattern Recognition, pp. 9308–9316 (2019)

An Attention-Driven Two-Stage Clustering Method for Unsupervised Person Re-identification

Zilong Ji[1], Xiaolong Zou[2], Xiaohan Lin[2], Xiao Liu[3], Tiejun Huang[2], and Si Wu[2,3(✉)]

[1] State Key Laboratory of Cognitive Neuroscience and Learning,
Beijing Normal University, Beijing, China
jizilong@mail.bnu.edu.cn
[2] School of Electronics Engineering and Computer Science, Peking University,
Beijing, China
{xiaolz,Lin.xiaohan,tjhuang,siwu}@pku.edu.cn
[3] IDG/McGovern Institute for Brain Research, Peking-Tsinghua Center for Life
Sciences, Academy for Advanced Interdisciplinary Studies,
Peking University, Beijing, China
xiaoliu23@pku.edu.cn

Abstract. The progressive clustering method and its variants, which iteratively generate pseudo labels for unlabeled data and per form feature learning, have shown great process in unsupervised person re-identification (re-id). However, they have an intrinsic problem of modeling the in-camera variability of images successfully, that is, pedestrian features extracted from the same camera tend to be clustered into the same class. This often results in a non-convergent model in the real world application of clustering based re-id models, leading to degenerated performance. In the present study, we propose an attention-driven two-stage clustering (ADTC) method to solve this problem. Specifically, our method consists of two strategies. Firstly, we use an unsupervised attention kernel to shift the learned features from the image background to the pedestrian foreground, which results in more informative clusters. Secondly, to aid the learning of the attention driven clustering model, we separate the clustering process into two stages. We first use kmeans to generate the centroids of clusters (stage 1) and then apply the k-reciprocal Jaccard distance (KRJD) metric to re-assign data points to each cluster (stage 2). By iteratively learning with the two strategies, the attentive regions are gradually shifted from the background to the foreground and the features become more discriminative. Using two benchmark datasets Market1501 and DukeMTMC, we demonstrate that our model outperforms other state-of-the-art unsupervised approaches for person re-id.

Electronic supplementary material The online version of this chapter (https://doi.org/10.1007/978-3-030-58604-1_2) contains supplementary material, which is available to authorized users.

Keywords: Attention · Clustering · Unsupervised learning · Person re-id

1 Introduction

The difficulties faced by supervised learning have motivated people to develop unsupervised person re-id models which is more applicable in the real world setting. One promising approach is the clustering-based method. The idea is to train a clustering model for the unlabeled data points and a feature learning model from the pseudo-labeled dataset in a iterative manner. However, in a real world re-id system, pedestrian images detected in the same camera often share similar background. This results in a clustering model which assigns pedestrian features extracted from the same camera into the same cluster. Such model shows great attention to the image background and fails to capture the in-camera variability of images (Fig. 1). Therefore, it is necessary to shift the foci from the background to the foreground during the implementation of the clustering based model. Under the setting of supervised person re-id, it is often done by introducing an attention kernel to highlight the informative features of pedestrians (e.g., logos on clothes, backpacks) and suppresses uninformative ones (e.g., the background) [14,23,38,41]. However, due to the lack of supervisory signals under the setting of unsupervised person re-id, it is hard for the attention model to learn correct attentive regions. An alternative way is to use the off-the-shelf pose estimation model to propose hard attentive local regions [34], but this introduces local network branches which increases computational complexity of the model.

In the present study, to solve the aforementioned challenges, we propose an Attention-Driven, Two-Stage Clustering method, referred to as ADTC hereafter (Fig. 2A), for unsupervised person re-id task. Specifically, we adopt a voxel attention kernel to highlight the features of images that are informative for pedestrian

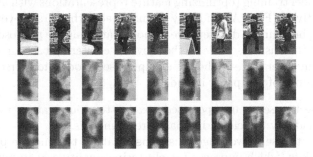

Fig. 1. Examples of class activation maps (CAMs) of pedestrians extracted from the same camera. From top to bottom are the original images, the CAMs without attention, and the CAMs with attention (the attention mechanism is described in Sect. 3.1). Without attention, the CAMs highlight more on the background, leading to that images from the same camera are likely to be assigned to the same cluster. With attention, the CAMs focus more on the informative features of pedestrians.

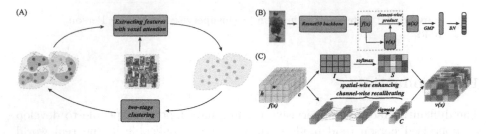

Fig. 2. The scheme of our method ADTC. (A) Our model consists of two iterative operations, the voxel attention and the two-stage clustering. The gray shadow denotes the manifold of feature representations at the current round, and different colors represent different clusters. (B) The feature extractor of our model. GMP denotes global max-pooling and BN batch normalization. (C) The detail of the attention kernel in the red dotted box in (B). (Color figure online)

discrimination. This attention mechanism enhances the informative spatial regions for pedestrians and recalibrates the channel-wise feature information adaptively according to the inter-dependencies between channels. As a result, it enlarges the separations between the negative and positive image pairs with respect to a query. Moreover, this voxel attention kernel only has a small number of trainable parameters, avoiding the overfitting problem during the iterative training. Furthermore, to improve the training of the attention-related parameters under the unsupervised setting, we adopt a two-stage clustering process to generate pseudo-labels for data points. We first use kmeans++ [1] to generate the centroids of clusters and then apply the k-reciprocal Jaccard distance (KRJD) metric [45] to re-assign data points to each cluster. Due to the appealing property of KRJD, data points belonging to the same class are more likely to be aggregated together, and the clustering quality of images is significantly improved, which in return facilitates the training of the model parameters. Overall, in our model, data clustering (generating pseudo-labels) and model training (optimizing feature representations with attention) are executed iteratively (Fig. 2A), and they promote each other to achieve good performances. Using benchmark datasets, we demonstrate that the proposed model can largely correct the mistakes made by the previous clustering based models (Fig. 4) and outperform other state-of-the-art unsupervised models for person re-id. The main contributions of this paper include:

- We propose to use an unsupervised voxel attention strategy to correct the mistakes made by the clustering based re-id models.
- We propose to use a two-stage clustering strategy to generate pseudo-labels for data points, which improves the clustering quality and stabilizes the progressive training.
- Our model achieves the state-of-the-art performances under the unsupervised setting for person re-id on a number of benchmark datasets.

2   Related Work

2.1   Unsupervised Person Re-ID

Traditional unsupervised person re-id studies have mainly focused on feature engineering [7,9,13,42], which created hand-craft features using human prior knowledge that can be applied directly to the unsupervised learning paradigm. These methods are efficient for a small dataset, but often fail to deal with a large dataset, since they can not fully exploit the data distribution to extract the appropriate semantic features. Recently, the domain adaptation strategy has been widely used for unsupervised person re-id [18,24,25,32,33], which attempts to reduce the discrepancy between the source and target data domains. During training, the knowledge learned from the source domain is continuously transferred to the target domain to facilitate the learning process. For example, Lin et al. [20] developed a feature alignment method to align the source and target data in the feature space by jointly optimizing the classification and alignment losses. Deng et al. [5] proposed a SPGAN model to preserve the similarity between two domains and integrate image translation and model learning. However, these approaches rely heavily on the assumption that the two domains have similar distributions. When the discrepancy between two domains is large, there is no guarantee that these methods will work well. Another direction for unsupervised person re-id is the clustering-based method [6,8,21,28,39,40], which generates pseudo-labels by clustering data points in the feature space and then use these pseudo-labels to train the model as if in the supervised manner. Fan et al. [6] proposed a progressive clustering method to transfer the pre-learned deep representations to an unseen domain, where feature clustering and representation learning are performed iteratively like the EM-style algorithm. Lin et al. [21] proposed a bottom-up clustering approach to jointly optimize a convolutional neural network and the relationship between the individual samples. Recently, Yang et al. [39] introduced the asymmetric co-teaching strategy in the clustering based method. For a clustering-based unsupervised model, the clustering quality of data is crucial. Compared to the existing clustering-based models, our method has two differences: 1) we use an attention mechanism to drive the clustering process, and 2) we cluster data points in two stages using a more appropriate distance metric. It turns out that our method improves the clustering quality significantly, which further leverages the model performances (see the details in Sects. 3.1 and 3.2).

2.2   Attention in Person Re-ID

The attention in a person re-id model aims to highlight the informative features of images to avoid the mis-alignments due to pose variance, occlusion, or body parts missing in a bounding box [3,4,27,36,49]. The attention mechanisms proposed in the literature can be divided into two main categories: hard-attention and soft-attention. The former typically uses a pose estimation model to locate coarse regions and then exploit these local features for discrimination [15,30,34,43]. However, these hard region-level attentions rely heavily on the pose estimation, which is often inaccurate and does not consider the pixel-level information within the selected regions that are potentially important for the identification task. A soft-attention mechanism typically inserts trainable layers into the main body of the model to mask the convolutional feature maps, so that the informative regions are highlighted [2,16,31,38]. Two main soft-attention mechanisms are widely used: the spatial attention and the channel attention. The former enables the model to pay attention to the valuable features at different spatial locations, and the latter enables the model to improve the representational power by performing channel-wise recalibration. There are also works combining the two soft-attention mechanisms. For example, Li et al. [17] proposed a Harmonious Attention Convolutional Neural Network (HA-CNN) which combines the pixel-level spatial information and the scale-level channel information to jointly learn the attentive regions and feature representations. Notably, so far the attention mechanism has only been used under the supervised setting; here we apply it under the unsupervised setting which is much harder to optimize.

3   Our Approach

3.1   Voxel Attention (VA)

We first introduce the voxel attention strategy[1]. Given an input image x in the unlabeled dataset X, denote the output of the backbone model as the corresponding feature map $f^{w \times h \times c}$, where w, h, c are the values of width and height, and the number of channels, respectively. The attention feature map $a^{w \times h \times c}$ is defined as (for clearance, we omit the superscript hereafter),

$$a = v \odot f, \tag{1}$$

where v is the voxel attention kernel having the same size as f, and $\odot$ denotes the element-wise product. v is composed of two complementary parts: the spatial and the channel attentions (Fig. 2C). For the spatial attention part, we first calculate the mean intensity of activation at each spatial location along the corresponding channel, which is given by $I(i,j) = \sum_{l=1}^{c} \frac{f(i,j,l)}{c}$; afterwards we apply softmax to calculate the probability of $I(i,j)$, which is $S(i,j) = e^{I(i,j)} / \left[\sum_{i,j} e^{I(i,j)} \right]$. Here, the divisive normalization makes the spatial filters competitive (acts like global inhibition) to highlight the most active (informative) ones. Note that no trainable parameter is introduced for the spatial attention branch. For the channel attention branch, we adopt the idea of [11] and apply a squeeze-and-excitation block to improve the quality of representations. Firstly, we perform global average pooling on f to squeeze the global spatial information into a

---

[1] The term of voxel attention comes from that it is a 3D attention mask combining the spatial and channel attentions.

channel descriptor C_{in}^c, with each element $c_{in}^l = \sum_{i=1,j=1}^{h,w} \frac{f(i,j,l)}{(h \times w)}$ aggregating the feature information distributed across the spatial space in channel l. Secondly, to capture the inter-dependencies between different channels in f, we employ a gating function on C_{in}^c by forming a bottleneck with two fully connected layers, i.e.,

$$C = \sigma\left[W_2 ReLU(W_1 C_{in})\right], \tag{2}$$

where σ represents the sigmoid function, $W_1 \in D^{d \times c}$, $W_2 \in D^{c \times d}$, $C \in D^c$, with $d \ll c$. The total number of parameters in the channel attention part is only $2cd$, which is computationally efficient. Eventually, the voxel attention kernel v can be written as tensor multiplication between S and C,

$$v = S \times C, \tag{3}$$

i.e., each voxel v_i in v at the location (i, j, l) is calculated as $S(i,j) \times C(l)$ (see Fig. 2C).

The above voxel attention kernel can be regarded as a self-attention function, which not only enhances the quality of spatial encoding by attending to active spatial locations in the feature map f, but also recalibrates the channel-wise feature responses adaptively by capturing the inter-dependencies between channels. Compared to the harmonious attention (HA) [17], the voxel attention has a few differences: 1) it has a much simpler form with a much smaller number of trainable parameters; 2) it is only applied after the backbone model, while HA is inserted between several building blocks; 3) it includes a normalization operation in the spatial attention to highlight the informative spatial locations. It turns out that these differences contribute to improve the model performances significantly (see Sects. 4.3 and 4.7).

3.2   Two-Stage Clustering (TC)

We now introduce the two-stage clustering strategy. The choice of the distance metric is crucial for clustering. Although an off-the-shelf clustering algorithm operating in the feature space, rather than in the raw pixel space, can alleviate the problem of "curse of dimensionality" [29] to some extent, it may still lead to an unsatisfactory clustering quality. Here we adopt a two-stage procedure to improve the clustering performance. Firstly, we use the conventional kmeans++ to get the centroids of clusters, denoted as $\{c_m\}_{m=1}^M$, with M the predefined number of clusters. Secondly, we re-assign data points to each cluster according to their k-reciprocal Jaccard distances (KRJDs) [45] to the cluster centroids. The k-reciprocal nearest neighbours of a feature point are defined as,

$$R(g,k) = \{g_j \mid (g_j \in N(g,k)) \cap (g \in N(g_j,k))\}, \tag{4}$$

where g is a feature point for clustering, which is obtained by performing max-pooling and 1-D batch normalization on the re-weighted attention feature map a. $N(g,k)$ denotes the k nearest neighbours of g. $R(g,k)$ indicates that g and each element in its neighbourhood are the mutually k nearest neighbours of each other. The KRJD distance between two feature points is then defined as

$$J(g_i, g_j) = 1 - \frac{|R(g_i, k) \cap R(g_j, k)|}{|R(g_i, k) \cup R(g_j, k)|}. \tag{5}$$

Compared to Euclidean distance, KRJD takes into account the reciprocal relationship between data points, and is a stricter rule measuring whether two feature points match or not (see Fig. 5 and more examples in SI.6). KRJD can also be seen as a refinement of the k-nearest neighbour in the Euclidean space which is more accurate for sorting feature points. Then we obtain a refined cluster C_m^p by selecting the top p closest feature points to c_m with the KRJD metric. Some of the refined clusters may share some data points due to noises or variances of input images, especially when feature points are intertwined with each other at the first few rounds of training. To alleviate this problem, we remove data points having ambiguous pseudo-labels, and obtain the final pseudo-labeled training set $\{(x_j, y_j)\}_{j=1}^{N_r}, y_j \in [1, 2, \ldots, M]$, where N_r is the number of remaining data.

3.3   Progressive Training

In our model, the voxel attention (in combination with model training and feature extraction) and two-stage clustering (generating pseudo-labels) are performed iteratively. At each training round t, we optimize the model parameters using the pseudo-labelled train set. When choosing the loss function, we note that the clustering assignments of two adjacent training rounds can be completely different, even if the same set of training samples are used. We therefore adopt the metric learning loss, rather than the softmax loss, as the latter will lead to the failure of model learning. In other words, we only impose that the difference of (dis-)similarities between the positive and negative pairs with respect to a query is larger than a predefined margin, such that the absolute values of assignments are irrelevant. Specifically, we adopt the triplet loss with in-batch hard example mining [10] to optimize the model parameters, which is written as

$$L_{tri}^m \left(g, g^+, g^-; \theta \right) = \max(0, \| g - g^+ \|_2^2 - \| g - g^- \|_2^2 + m),$$
$$\text{where} \quad g^+ = \arg\max_{\{g^p\}} \| g - g^p \|_2^2, \text{and} \quad g^- = \arg\min_{\{g^n\}} \| g - g^n \|_2^2. \tag{6}$$

Here $\{g^p\}$ and $\{g^n\}$ denote the positive and negative sets with respect to g in the mini-batch, respectively, m is the margin between feature pairs, θ denotes the model parameters. In order to avoid overfitting on the current pseudo labeled set, we only train $\mathcal{M}^t$ in each round for a few gradient update steps to get $\mathcal{M}^{t+1}$. $\mathcal{M}^T$ denotes the final model when the stopping criterion is reached. The two steps of attention-driven clustering and feature learning are performed iteratively, and they facilitate each other to achieve the final well-performing model. The detail of our method ADTC is summarized in Algorithm 1.

Algorithm 1. Attention-driven Two-stage Clustering (ADTC) method for unsupervised person re-id

---

Input: The unlabeled dataset X, the model $\mathcal{M}^0$.
Output: Final model $\mathcal{M}^T$.
 1: t=0.
 2: **repeat**
 3:    **Attention Step:**
 4:      Extracting feature point f_i of each data point $x_i \in X$ before the global max-pooling layer.
 5:      Applying the voxel attention kernel v_i on f_i to get the attention feature point a_i.
 6:      Applying global max-pooling and 1-D batch normalization on a_i to get the final feature point g_i.
 7:    **Clustering Step:**
 8:      Performing kmeans++ clustering on $\{g_i\}_{i=1}^N$ and obtaining centroids $\{c_m\}_{m=1}^M$.
 9:      For each centroid c_m, computing its p-nearest neighbours $\mathcal{C}_m^p$ based on the KRJD metric, and assigning the pseudo-label m to all data points in $\mathcal{C}_m^p$.
10:      Removing ambiguous data points belonging to more than one clusters and obtaining the pseudo-labelled train set $\{(x_j, y_j)\}_{j=1}^{N_r}$.
11:    **Parameter Updating Step:**
12:      Training $\mathcal{M}^t$ with the triplet loss on $\{(x_j, y_j)\}_{j=1}^{N_r}$ to get $\mathcal{M}^{t+1}$.
13:      t = t+1;
14: **until** $t = T$

---

4 Experiments

4.1 Datasets

Market-1501 is a dataset containing 32668 images with 1501 identities captured from 6 cameras [44]. The dataset is split into three parts: 12936 images with 751 identities forming the training data, 19732 images with 750 identities forming the testing gallery, and another 3368 images from the testing gallery forming the query data.

DukeMTMC contains 36411 images with 1812 identities captured from 8 cameras [26]. The dataset is split into three parts: 16522 images with 702 identities forming the training data, 17661 images with 1110 identities forming the testing gallery, and another 2228 images with 702 identities from the testing gallery forming the query data. Note that the evaluation protocol on two dataset are the same.

4.2 Implementation Details

We use a Resnet-50 pretrained on Imagenet as the backbone model. Following [37], we add a batch normalization layer after the global pooling layer to prevent overfitting and directly use the batch-normalized global pooling features to execute identity classification (for the performance of the model architecture on supervised dataset, see SI.4). The output channels are set as 800 in the voxel attention kernel. During clustering, we set the number of clusters M to be 1000 (for the effect of M, see SI.2) and the neighbour size p is 20. All input images are resized to 256×128. Except random horizontal flipping, no other data augmentation strategy is used. 32 pseudo-classes and 4 examples per class are randomly sampled to form a mini-batch. The margin m between negative pairs and positive pairs is 0.3. The total training rounds is set to be 20. To prevent overfitting, the model is fine-tuned for 10 epochs in each round. The Adam optimizer is used for optimization with an initial learning rate of 0.0001 which exponentially decays after epoch 5 (for more detailed setting of hyper-parameters, see SI.1).

4.3   Model Performances on Benchmark Datasets

We compare our model with other state-of-the-art unsupervised person re-id methods on two benchmark datasets Market1501 and DukeMTMC. These methods include: 1) two hand-crafted features: LOMO [19], BoW [44]; 2) four feature alignment methods, MMFA [20], TJ-AIDL [32], ARN [18], and EANet [12]; 3) four GAN-based domain adaptation methods, IPGAN [22], eSPGAN+LMP [5], CamStyle [47], and HHL [46]; 4) two clustering-based methods, PUL [6] and DAR [28]. Note that when training on Market1501, we first initialize our model on DukeMTMC and vice versa (domain adaptation).

The results are summarized in Table 1. We observe that: 1) our model achieves 59.7%/79.3% on Market1501 and 52.5%/71.9% on DukeMTMC on the mAP/rank1 accuracy, which is one of the state-of-the-art (SOTA) models. Note that we only initialized the model on the source labeled domain and then trained it without any auxiliary label information in the unlabeled domain; whereas most of the aforementioned methods keep using the auxiliary label information in the source domain during the domain transfer learning. 2) Compared to the feature alignment methods which implicitly make an assumption that the data distributions of the source and target domains are similar, our model learns directly from the unlabeled target dataset and achieves better performances. 3) Compared to the GAN-based models which aim at translating the style of labeled images from the source domain to the target domain, our model achieves better performances even without the voxel attention or two-stage clustering (see Table 2). 4) Although the clustering-based SSG model achieves a slightly better performance on DukeMTMC (mAP/rank1) than ours, they use multi learning branches and the DBSCAN clustering method while our model only consists of only one learning branch and adopts the simple kmeans clustering method. Notably, the main concern in our paper is to enhance the in-camera variability so as to improve the accuracy of unsupervised person ReID model rather than introduce other strategies to boost the performance. Overall, our model achieves the state-of-art performances on the two benchmark datasets. In below, we inspect how different elements of the model contribute to its superior performances.

Table 1. Comparison of different unsupervised learning methods. DukeMTMC to MarKet1501 means model initialized on DukeMTMC and trained on Market1501. Market1501 to DukeMTMC means model initialized on Market1501 and trained on DukeMTMC. ADTC w/o DA means we trained our model directly on the unlabeled dataset without initialization on the source domain dataset. Note that the LOMO, BoW and PUL also don't use the source domain data to initialize models.

Source to target	DukeMTMC to Market1501				Market1501 to DukeMTMC			
	mAP	rank1	rank5	rank10	mAP	rank1	rank5	rank10
Directly transfer	18.8	44.0	62.1	69.4	18.2	34.0	49.1	55.9
LOMO [19]	8.0	27.2	-	-	4.8	12.3	–	–
BoW [44]	14.8	35.8	-	-	8.3	17.2	–	–
MMFA [20]	24.7	45.3	59.8	66.3	27.4	56.7	75.0	81.8
TJ-AIDL [32]	26.5	58.2	74.8	81.1	23.0	44.3	59.6	65.0
ARN [18]	39.4	70.3	80.4	86.3	33.4	60.2	73.9	79.5
EANet [12]	51.6	78.0	-	-	48.0	67.7	–	–
IPGAN [22]	25.6	56.4	76.0	82.5	26.7	46.8	62.0	67.9
eSPGAN+LMP [5]	30.4	52.6	66.3	71.7	31.7	63.6	80.1	86.1
CamStyle [47]	27.4	58.8	78.2	84.3	25.1	48.4	62.5	68.9
HHL [46]	31.4	62.2	78.8	84.0	27.2	46.9	61.0	66.7
PUL [6]	20.1	44.7	59.1	65.6	16.4	30.4	44.5	50.7
DAR [28]	53.7	75.8	89.5	93.2	49.0	68.4	80.1	83.5
SSG [8]	58.3	**80.0**	90.0	92.4	**53.4**	**73.0**	80.6	83.2
ADTC w/o DA	38.8	59.5	71.6	76.9	37.9	59.4	70.0	74.1
ADTC (Ours)	**59.7**	79.3	**90.8**	**94.1**	52.5	71.9	**84.1**	**87.5**

4.4 Contribution of the Voxel Attention

Figure 3A and B present the class activation maps (CAMs) [48] of a few example images, which display the spatial regions where the model pays attention to. We see that without the voxel attention, the model pays more attention to the background than to the foreground, resulting in wrong cluster assignments. Indeed, such a degenerate performance often occurs in a clustering-based method without attention, since pedestrian images extracted from the same camera, especially those from the same location, tend to have less variability than those from different cameras (also see Fig. 1). Consequently, the model will assign clusters based on the overall image appearances, rather than the details of pedestrians, and thus fail to capture the in-camera variability of images crucial for the re-id task. Figure 3A and B also show that the voxel attention helps to increase the margin of the negative pair (g, g^-) and decrease the margin of the positive pair (g, g^+) in a triplet. We calculate the margin difference $\delta = \|g - g^-\|_2^2 - \|g - g^+\|_2^2$ of 10000 triplets randomly sampled from DukeMTMC, and find that by applying the voxel attention, δ increases significantly across the whole dataset (Fig. 3C).

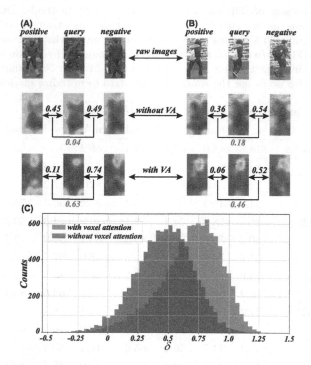

Fig. 3. The voxel attention highlights the informative parts of images and makes them more discriminatable. (A–B) Two examples from DukeMTMC with/without the voxel attention. From top to bottom are the raw images, the CAMs without the voxel attention, and the CAMs with the voxel attention. The value in black stands for the euclidean distance between two feature maps, and the value in red for the margin difference defined in Sect. 4.4. (C) The statistical result of the margin difference δ from 10000 triplets randomly sampled from DukeMTMC. (Color figure online)

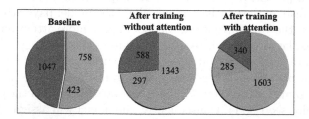

Fig. 4. The voxel attention enhances the in-camera discrimination. From left to right are the results of the initialized model without training (baseline), the model with progressive clustering but no attention, and the model with progressive clustering and attention. The total number of query images is 2228. Blue, red, and orange: the number of query images having the correct rank1, the number of in-camera error (ICE), and the number of cross-camera errors (CCE). DukeMTMC is used. (Color figure online)

This implies that the images belonging to the same identity have a more compact aggregation in the feature space, which makes the retrieval task easier than that without the voxel attention (see SI.5).

To further unveil the role of the voxel attention, we differentiate the wrongly retrieved rank1 images to a query into the in-camera errors (ICE), i.e., those in the same camera as the query, and the cross-camera errors (CCE), i.e., those in different cameras with the query. Figure 4 compares the results of our model with that of the progressive clustering method without attention. It shows that without attention, the progressive clustering method can improve the rank1 accuracy from 34.0% to 60.3% compared to the baseline (i.e., the result of the model initialized via the label data); but our model can improve the rank1 accuracy further to 71.9%. Notably, this further improvement is mainly attributed to the decrease of ICE, from 588 to 340 out of 2228 queries. This supports our idea that the voxel attention helps to capture the in-camera variability of images; whereas the progressive clustering method without attention is lack of this capability and hence makes more mistakes in-camera identifications.

4.5   Contribution of Two-Stage Clustering

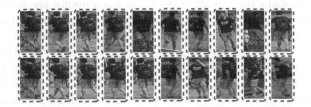

Fig. 5. Example clusters with top 10 nearest neighbours after training with/without two-stage clustering. Market1501 is used. Upper: ranking by the Euclidean distance to the cluster centroid. Lower: ranking by KRJD to the cluster centroid with two-stage clustering. Blue, Red: the correctly, the wrongly assigned images.

We continue to inspect the contribution of two-stage clustering. Figure 5 shows that when two-stage clustering is used during training, more positive (correct) examples appear in the neighbourhood of a given cluster centroid, compared to that of using only the Euclidean distance based Kmeans++ algorithm. This indicates that KRJD indeed serve as a better metric to compute the neighbourhood relationship between feature points, which improves the clustering quality and leverage the model performances (see SI.6 for more examples).

4.6   Contribution of Progressive Training

We further inspect how the voxel attention and two-stage clustering are executed iteratively to generate good feature representations. To measure the clustering

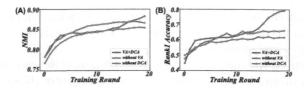

Fig. 6. (A) The clustering performance NMI vs. the training round. (B) The rank1 accuracy vs. the training round.

quality, we adopt the normalized mutual information (NMI), which is given by

$$NMI\,(\mathcal{C},\mathcal{L}) = \frac{I(\mathcal{C},\mathcal{L})}{\sqrt{H(\mathcal{C})H(\mathcal{L})}}, \tag{7}$$

where $\mathcal{C} = \{\mathcal{C}_1^p, \mathcal{C}_2^p, \ldots, \mathcal{C}_M^p\}$ denote M clusters, $\mathcal{L}$ the corresponding ground truth label set, and I the mutual information between $\mathcal{C}$ and $\mathcal{L}$. $H(\mathcal{C})$ and $H(\mathcal{L})$ are the entropies of $\mathcal{C}$ and $\mathcal{L}$, respectively. The value of NMI is between 0 and 1, with 1 standing for the perfect labeling of data points. The larger the NMI, the closer the pseudo-labels to the ground truth[2]. Figure 6A shows how the clustering performance increases along with the training round. Initially, the assignment of clusters is unsatisfactory (NMI ≈ 0.77), as data points are intertwined with each other. Along with the training, data points belonging to the same class are gradually grouped together, and the assigned pseudo-clusters become more similar to the ground truth (NMI ≈ 0.90). Figure 6B further shows that the rank1 accuracy of the model increases in the same pace as the clustering performance. This suggests that in our model, data clustering and model training promote each other during progressive training, in the sense that the improved assignments by two-stage clustering will select more reliable samples to facilitate the learning of the voxel attention, which in return will highlight more informative features to further improve cluster assignments.

4.7   Component Analysis of ADTC

We carry out component analysis of our method. Table 2 shows that both the voxel attention and two-stage clustering are indispensable to our model, in the sense that when either of them is ablated, the model performance is degraded. Moreover, we check that for the voxel attention, both the channel attention and the spatial attention are indispensable, in the sense that when either of them is ablated, the model performance is degraded. We also replace the proposed voxel attention module with the Harmonious Attention (HA) kernel [17] and the CABM attention kernel [35] (Table 2). It shows that the proposed attention kernel is superior and leads to better performance under the unsupervised setting. Besides, we also carry out robustness analysis of our model to hyper-parameters,

---

[2] Note that NMI is independent of the absolute values of labels, in term of that a permutation of cluster labels does not change its value.

Table 2. Component analysis of the performances of our model. Except the ablating part, all other hyper-parameters are fixed.

Source to target	DukeMTMC to Market1501				Market1501 to DukeMTMC			
	mAP	rank1	rank5	rank10	mAP	rank1	rank5	rank10
Only TC	41.1	66.2	84.2	88.9	28.2	49.8	68.2	74.2
Only VA	35.5	61.7	74.3	79.1	32.6	52.0	65.3	69.4
TC + channel attention	42.8	68.9	87.1	91.2	30.1	52.2	71.5	78.9
TC + spatial attention	41.3	66.6	85.0	89.2	28.8	50.7	69.1	75.2
TC + HA	50.6	76.2	88.1	92.0	48.9	69.2	81.5	85.1
TC + CABM	55.2	77.3	88.8	93.5	49.1	69.8	82.0	85.9
Full model	**59.7**	**79.3**	**90.8**	**94.1**	**52.5**	**71.9**	**84.1**	**87.5**

e.g., the number of clusters, the margin m the updating epochs in each training round (see SI.2) and the balance level of the original dataset (SI.3). All these results indicate that our model is potentially feasible in real-world applications.

5   Conclusion

In this study, we have proposed an Attention-Driven Two-stage Clustering (ADTC) method for learning an unsupervised model for person re-id. It captures the in-camera variability of images and reduce the noisy labels when clustering(which has been ignored in current unsupervised ReID methods). The method has two indispensable components. Firstly, we use the voxel attention strategy to highlight the informative parts of pedestrian images, which captures the in-camera variability of images crucial for the re-id task. Secondly, we adopts a two-stage clustering strategy, which uses the KRJD metric to improve the clustering quality and stabilizes the progressive training. Through progressive training, the two strategies facilitate with each and enables our model to outperform other unsupervised approaches for person re-ID and achieve the state-of-the-art performances on two benchmark datasets. We also empirically show that our model is robust to a number of varying conditions, making it potentially feasible in real-world applications.

Acknowledgments. ZLJ designed the study and carried out the experiments. XLZ, XHL and XL helped with integrating algorithms and conducting experiments. TJH and SW contributed to the conception and design of the study and revision. ZLJ and SW wrote the manuscript. This work was supported by Huawei Technology Co., Ltd. (YBN2019105137) and Guangdong Province with grant (No. 2018B030338001, SW). This work was also supported by BMSTC(Beijing municipal science and technology commission) with grant (No. Z161100000216143, SW) and the National Natural Science Foundation of China (No. 61425025, T.J. Huang).

References

1. Arthur, D., Vassilvitskii, S.: k-means++: the advantages of careful seeding. In: Proceedings of the 18th Annual ACM-SIAM Symposium on Discrete Algorithms, pp. 1027–1035. Society for Industrial and Applied Mathematics (2007)
2. Chen, B., Deng, W., Hu, J.: Mixed high-order attention network for person re-identification. In: Proceedings of the IEEE International Conference on Computer Vision (ICCV) (2019)
3. Chen, G., Lin, C., Ren, L., Lu, J., Zhou, J.: Self-critical attention learning for person re-identification. In: Proceedings of the IEEE International Conference on Computer Vision, pp. 9637–9646 (2019)
4. Dai, Z., Chen, M., Gu, X., Zhu, S., Tan, P.: Batch dropblock network for person re-identification and beyond. In: Proceedings of the IEEE International Conference on Computer Vision, pp. 3691–3701 (2019)
5. Deng, W., Zheng, L., Ye, Q., Kang, G., Yang, Y., Jiao, J.: Image-image domain adaptation with preserved self-similarity and domain-dissimilarity for person re-identification. In: Proceedings of the IEEE Conference on Computer Vision and Pattern Recognition, pp. 994–1003 (2018)
6. Fan, H., Zheng, L., Yan, C., Yang, Y.: Unsupervised person re-identification: clustering and fine-tuning. ACM Trans. Multimed. Comput. Commun. Appl. (TOMM) **14**(4), 83 (2018)
7. Farenzena, M., Bazzani, L., Perina, A., Murino, V., Cristani, M.: Person re-identification by symmetry-driven accumulation of local features. In: 2010 IEEE Computer Society Conference on Computer Vision and Pattern Recognition, pp. 2360–2367. IEEE (2010)
8. Fu, Y., Wei, Y., Wang, G., Zhou, Y., Shi, H., Huang, T.S.: Self-similarity grouping: a simple unsupervised cross domain adaptation approach for person re-identification. In: Proceedings of the IEEE International Conference on Computer Vision, pp. 6112–6121 (2019)
9. Gray, D., Tao, H.: Viewpoint invariant pedestrian recognition with an ensemble of localized features. In: Forsyth, D., Torr, P., Zisserman, A. (eds.) ECCV 2008. LNCS, vol. 5302, pp. 262–275. Springer, Heidelberg (2008). https://doi.org/10.1007/978-3-540-88682-2_21
10. Hermans, A., Beyer, L., Leibe, B.: In defense of the triplet loss for person re-identification. arXiv preprint arXiv:1703.07737 (2017)
11. Hu, J., Shen, L., Sun, G.: Squeeze-and-excitation networks. In: Proceedings of the IEEE Conference on Computer Vision and Pattern Recognition, pp. 7132–7141 (2018)
12. Huang, H., et al.: EANet: Enhancing alignment for cross-domain person re-identification. arXiv preprint arXiv:1812.11369 (2018)
13. Kodirov, E., Xiang, T., Gong, S.: Dictionary learning with iterative laplacian regularisation for unsupervised person re-identification. In: BMVC, vol. 3, p. 8 (2015)
14. Lan, X., Wang, H., Gong, S., Zhu, X.: Deep reinforcement learning attention selection for person re-identification. In: BMVC (2017)
15. Li, D., Chen, X., Zhang, Z., Huang, K.: Learning deep context-aware features over body and latent parts for person re-identification. In: Proceedings of the IEEE Conference on Computer Vision and Pattern Recognition, pp. 384–393 (2017)
16. Li, S., Bak, S., Carr, P., Wang, X.: Diversity regularized spatiotemporal attention for video-based person re-identification. In: Proceedings of the IEEE Conference on Computer Vision and Pattern Recognition, pp. 369–378 (2018)

17. Li, W., Zhu, X., Gong, S.: Harmonious attention network for person re-identification. In: Proceedings of the IEEE Conference on Computer Vision and Pattern Recognition, pp. 2285–2294 (2018)
18. Li, Y.J., Yang, F.E., Liu, Y.C., Yeh, Y.Y., Du, X., Frank Wang, Y.C.: Adaptation and re-identification network: an unsupervised deep transfer learning approach to person re-identification. In: Proceedings of the IEEE Conference on Computer Vision and Pattern Recognition Workshops, pp. 172–178 (2018)
19. Liao, S., Hu, Y., Zhu, X., Li, S.Z.: Person re-identification by local maximal occurrence representation and metric learning. In: The IEEE Conference on Computer Vision and Pattern Recognition (CVPR) (June 2015)
20. Lin, S., Li, H., Li, C.T., Kot, A.C.: Multi-task mid-level feature alignment network for unsupervised cross-dataset person re-identification. arXiv preprint arXiv:1807.01440 (2018)
21. Lin, Y., Dong, X., Zheng, L., Yan, Y., Yang, Y.: A bottom-up clustering approach to unsupervised person re-identification. Proc. AAAI Conf. Artif. Intell. **33**, 8738–8745 (2019)
22. Liu, J.: Identity preserving generative adversarial network for cross-domain person re-identification. arXiv preprint arXiv:1811.11510 (2018)
23. Liu, X., et al.: HydraPlus-Net: attentive deep features for pedestrian analysis. In: Proceedings of the IEEE International Conference on Computer Vision, pp. 350–359 (2017)
24. Peng, P., et al.: Unsupervised cross-dataset transfer learning for person re-identification. In: The IEEE Conference on Computer Vision and Pattern Recognition (CVPR) (June 2016)
25. Peng, P., et al.: Unsupervised cross-dataset transfer learning for person re-identification. In: Proceedings of the IEEE Conference on Computer Vision and Pattern Recognition, pp. 1306–1315 (2016)
26. Ristani, E., Solera, F., Zou, R., Cucchiara, R., Tomasi, C.: Performance measures and a data set for multi-target, multi-camera tracking. In: Hua, G., Jégou, H. (eds.) ECCV 2016. LNCS, vol. 9914, pp. 17–35. Springer, Cham (2016). https://doi.org/10.1007/978-3-319-48881-3_2
27. Song, C., Huang, Y., Ouyang, W., Wang, L.: Mask-guided contrastive attention model for person re-identification. In: Proceedings of the IEEE Conference on Computer Vision and Pattern Recognition, pp. 1179–1188 (2018)
28. Song, L., et al.: Unsupervised domain adaptive re-identification: Theory and practice. arXiv preprint arXiv:1807.11334 (2018)
29. Steinbach, M., Ertöz, L., Kumar, V.: The challenges of clustering high dimensional data. In: Wille, L.T. (ed.) New Directions in Statistical Physics, pp. 273–309. Springer, Heidelberg (2004). https://doi.org/10.1007/978-3-662-08968-2_16
30. Su, C., Li, J., Zhang, S., Xing, J., Gao, W., Tian, Q.: Pose-driven deep convolutional model for person re-identification. In: Proceedings of the IEEE International Conference on Computer Vision, pp. 3960–3969 (2017)
31. Wang, H., Fan, Y., Wang, Z., Jiao, L., Schiele, B.: Parameter-free spatial attention network for person re-identification. arXiv preprint arXiv:1811.12150 (2018)
32. Wang, J., Zhu, X., Gong, S., Li, W.: Transferable joint attribute-identity deep learning for unsupervised person re-identification. In: Proceedings of the IEEE Conference on Computer Vision and Pattern Recognition, pp. 2275–2284 (2018)
33. Wei, L., Zhang, S., Gao, W., Tian, Q.: Person transfer GAN to bridge domain gap for person re-identification. In: Proceedings of the IEEE Conference on Computer Vision and Pattern Recognition, pp. 79–88 (2018)

34. Wei, L., Zhang, S., Yao, H., Gao, W., Tian, Q.: GLAD: global-local-alignment descriptor for pedestrian retrieval. In: Proceedings of the 25th ACM International Conference on Multimedia, pp. 420–428. ACM (2017)

35. Woo, S., Park, J., Lee, J.-Y., Kweon, I.S.: CBAM: convolutional block attention module. In: Ferrari, V., Hebert, M., Sminchisescu, C., Weiss, Y. (eds.) ECCV 2018. LNCS, vol. 11211, pp. 3–19. Springer, Cham (2018). https://doi.org/10.1007/978-3-030-01234-2_1

36. Xia, B.N., Gong, Y., Zhang, Y., Poellabauer, C.: Second-order non-local attention networks for person re-identification. In: Proceedings of the IEEE International Conference on Computer Vision, pp. 3760–3769 (2019)

37. Xiong, F., Xiao, Y., Cao, Z., Gong, K., Fang, Z., Zhou, J.T.: Towards good practices on building effective cnn baseline model for person re-identification. arXiv preprint arXiv:1807.11042 (2018)

38. Xu, J., Zhao, R., Zhu, F., Wang, H., Ouyang, W.: Attention-aware compositional network for person re-identification. In: Proceedings of the IEEE Conference on Computer Vision and Pattern Recognition, pp. 2119–2128 (2018)

39. Yang, F., et al.: Asymmetric co-teaching for unsupervised cross-domain person re-identification. In: AAAI, pp. 12597–12604 (2020)

40. Zhang, X., Cao, J., Shen, C., You, M.: Self-training with progressive augmentation for unsupervised cross-domain person re-identification. arXiv preprint arXiv:1907.13315 (2019)

41. Zhao, H., et al.: Spindle Net: person re-identification with human body region guided feature decomposition and fusion. In: Proceedings of the IEEE Conference on Computer Vision and Pattern Recognition, pp. 1077–1085 (2017)

42. Zhao, R., Ouyang, W., Wang, X.: Unsupervised salience learning for person re-identification. In: Proceedings of the IEEE Conference on Computer Vision and Pattern Recognition, pp. 3586–3593 (2013)

43. Zheng, L., Huang, Y., Lu, H., Yang, Y.: Pose invariant embedding for deep person re-identification. IEEE Trans. Image Process. **28**, 4500–4509 (2019)

44. Zheng, L., Shen, L., Tian, L., Wang, S., Wang, J., Tian, Q.: Scalable person re-identification: a benchmark. In: The IEEE International Conference on Computer Vision (ICCV) (December 2015)

45. Zhong, Z., Zheng, L., Cao, D., Li, S.: Re-ranking person re-identification with k-reciprocal encoding. In: Proceedings of the IEEE Conference on Computer Vision and Pattern Recognition, pp. 1318–1327 (2017)

46. Zhong, Z., Zheng, L., Li, S., Yang, Y.: Generalizing a person retrieval model hetero- and homogeneously. In: Ferrari, V., Hebert, M., Sminchisescu, C., Weiss, Y. (eds.) ECCV 2018. LNCS, vol. 11217, pp. 176–192. Springer, Cham (2018). https://doi.org/10.1007/978-3-030-01261-8_11

47. Zhong, Z., Zheng, L., Zheng, Z., Li, S., Yang, Y.: CamStyle: a novel data augmentation method for person re-identification. IEEE Trans. Image Process. **28**(3), 1176–1190 (2018)

48. Zhou, B., Khosla, A., Lapedriza, A., Oliva, A., Torralba, A.: Learning deep features for discriminative localization. In: Proceedings of the IEEE Conference on Computer Vision and Pattern Recognition, pp. 2921–2929 (2016)

49. Zhou, S., Wang, F., Huang, Z., Wang, J.: Discriminative feature learning with consistent attention regularization for person re-identification. In: Proceedings of the IEEE International Conference on Computer Vision, pp. 8040–8049 (2019)

Toward Fine-Grained Facial Expression Manipulation

Jun Ling[1], Han Xue[1], Li Song[1,2(✉)], Shuhui Yang[1], Rong Xie[1], and Xiao Gu[1]

[1] Institutet of Image Communication and Network Engineering,
Shanghai Jiao Tong University, Shanghai, China
[2] MoE Key Lab of Artificial Intelligence, AI Institute, Shanghai Jiao Tong
University, Shanghai, China
{lingjun,xue_han,song_li,louisxiii,xierong,gugu97}@sjtu.edu.cn

Abstract. Facial expression manipulation aims at editing facial expression with a given condition. Previous methods edit an input image under the guidance of a discrete emotion label or absolute condition (e.g., facial action units) to possess the desired expression. However, these methods either suffer from changing condition-irrelevant regions or are inefficient for fine-grained editing. In this study, we take these two objectives into consideration and propose a novel method. First, we replace continuous absolute condition with relative condition, specifically, relative action units. With relative action units, the generator learns to only transform regions of interest which are specified by non-zero-valued relative AUs. Second, our generator is built on U-Net but strengthened by multi-scale feature fusion (MSF) mechanism for high-quality expression editing purposes. Extensive experiments on both quantitative and qualitative evaluation demonstrate the improvements of our proposed approach compared to the state-of-the-art expression editing methods. Code is available at https://github.com/junleen/Expression-manipulator.

Keywords: GANs · Expression editing · Image-to-image translation

1 Introduction

Over the years, facial expression synthesis has been drawing considerable attention in the field of both computer vision and computer graphics. However, synthesizing easy-to-use and fine-grained facial images with desired expression remains challenging because of the complexity of this task. Recently, the proposal of generative adversarial networks [9,20] sheds light on image synthesis, introducing significant advances with well-known architectures like [5,11,17,35]. However, these work suffer from fine-grained expression editing because they either rely on several binary emotion labels (e.g., smiling, mouth open) to synthesize target expressions, or suffer from limited naturalness and low quality (Fig. 1).

As one of the most successful generative models, GANimation [26] pushes the limits of facial expression manipulation by building a conditional GAN which

© Springer Nature Switzerland AG 2020
A. Vedaldi et al. (Eds.): ECCV 2020, LNCS 12373, pp. 37–53, 2020.
https://doi.org/10.1007/978-3-030-58604-1_3

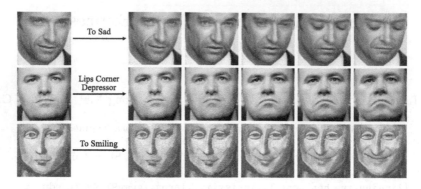

Fig. 1. Arbitrary Facial Expression Manipulation. Our model can 1) perform continuous editing between two expressions (*top*); 2) learn to only modify one facial component (*middle*); 3) transform expression in paintings (*bottom*). From left to right, the emotion intensity is set to 0, 0.5, 0.75, 1, and 1.25.

relies on attention-based generator and discrete facial action units activation (action units [7] (AUs), a kind embedding which indicates the facial muscles movement). As a novel expression editing method, GANimation is able to edit an image in a continuous manner and outperforms other popular multi-domain image-to-image translation methods [5, 16, 25, 37].

Despite the novelty and generality, GANimation suffers from two drawbacks. First, by taking absolute AUs as input condition, the generator needs to estimate the current facial muscles state so that it can apply a desired expression change to the input image. This is insufficient for the model to reserve its facial part corresponding to unchanged AUs. Besides, from the perspective of model testing, exploiting the entire set of AUs as conditional input imposes a restriction on fine-grained expression editing because a user always needs to acquire accurate underlying real value of each AU in the input image, even though he does not intend to to modify these facial regions. Second, the attention mechanism which is introduced for learning desirable change from expression of input image to desired expression, virtually applies a learned weighted sum between the input image and the generated one. This kind of operation, as pointed out in [26], brings about overlap artifacts around face deformation regions. Furthermore, spatial attention networks for attribute-specific region editing [35] are effective only for local attributes and not designed for arbitrary attribute editing [17].

To address these limitations, this work investigates arbitrary facial expression editing on the basis of relative condition. In terms of *relative*, which is defined as the difference between target AUs and source AUs, our model is capable of (i) only considering the facial components to be modified while keeping the remaining parts unchanged, and (ii) freely strengthening or suppressing the intensity of specified AUs or arbitrary emotions by user-input real numbers. This brings several benefits. First, by using relative AUs, the generator is not required to compare the current AUs with desired AUs before applying image transformation. Second, the values of the relative AUs indicate the desired change to facial

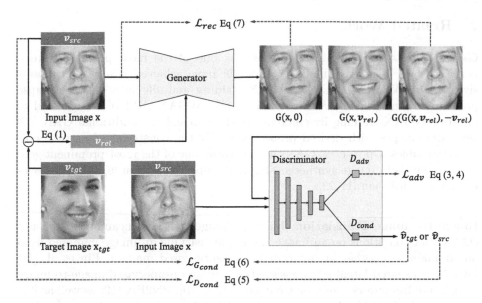

Fig. 2. An overview of proposed approach. Our model consists of a single generator (G) and two discriminators (D_{adv} and D_{cond}). (*top*) G conditions on an input image and relative action units to generate image with target expression. (*bottom right*) D_{adv} tries to distinguish between the input image **x** and generated image $G(\mathbf{x}, \mathbf{v}_{rel})$. Conditional discriminator D_{cond} aims at evaluating generated image in condition fulfillment.

muscles. In particular, non-zero values correspond to AUs of interest and zero values correspond to unchanged AUs. Hence, our generator can learn to manipulate single AU with scalable one-hot vector, eliminating the demand for all other AUs intensities.

For the purpose of higher image quality and better expression manipulation ability, we start from U-Net-based generator and analyze its limitations. Note that the features from encoder are directly concatenated with decoder features in U-Net structure. This often produces overlap artifacts when dealing with facial deformation. eIn this work, we resort to learn the model by simultaneously fusing and transforming image features at different spatial size. Particularly, we propose to introduce multi-resolution feature fusion mechanism and involve several multi-scale feature fusion (MSF) modules in basic U-Net architecture for image transformation. Taking relative AUs as conditional input, our MSF module adaptively fuse and modify both the features from the encoder and all lower resolution, and output fusion features with multi-resolution representation. The fusion features are further concatenated with decoder features for image decoding. Experimental results in Table 1 and Fig. 9 reveal the better expression manipulation ability and higher image quality brought by MSF mechanism and relative setting. Table 2 and Fig. 4, 6, and 7 demonstrate the superiority of our method compared to baseline model. An overview of our approach is provided in Fig. 2.

2 Related Work

Generative Adversarial Networks. As one of the most promising unsupervised deep generative models, GANs [9] have achieved a series of impressive results. WGAN [1] stabilizes GAN training and alleviates model collapse problems by introducing Wasserstein distance. WGAN-GP [10] is suggested to improve WGAN training by enforcing gradient penalty. Conditional GAN [20] generates images with desired properties under the constraint of extra conditional variables. Up to now, GANs have become one of the most prominent generative models in image synthesis [14, 24, 36], super-resolution [6, 32] and image-to-image translation [11, 22].

Image-to-Image Translation. Image-to-image translation can be treated as a cGAN that conditions on an image, aiming at learning an image mapping from one domain to another in supervised or unsupervised manner. Liu et al. [18] introduce a shared-latent space assumption and an unsupervised image-to-image translation framework based on Coupled GANs [19]. Pix2Pix [12] as well as [22] is a supervised cGANs based approach which relies on an abundance of paired images. However, the absence of adequate paired data limits the performance of conditional GAN. To alleviate the dependency on paired images, Zhu et al. [37] propose a cycle consistent framework for unpaired image-to-image translation. GANimation [26] utilizes an encoder-decoder network to take images and entire action units as input to generate animated images but suffers from undesired artifacts in generated images.

Facial Expression Manipulation. Facial expression manipulation is an interesting image-to-image translation problem, which has drawn prevalent attention recently. Some popular works tackle this task with multiple facial attributes editing [5, 11, 17, 34], modifying attribute categories such as to smiling, mouth open, mouth closed, adding beard, swapping gender and changing hair color, etc. However, these methods cannot simply generalize to an arbitrary human facial expression synthesizing tasks due to the limitations of discrete emotion categories (e.g., *happy, neutral, surprised, contempt, anger, disgust, and sad*). Several studies, aiming at manipulating human facial expression from facial geometric representation [27, 29], conditioning on face fiducial points to synthesize animated faces but suffers from fine-grained details. Geng et al. [8] proposes a 3D parametric face guided model to manipulate the geometry of facial components, while requiring real existent target face images rather than a simple vector.

3 Methodology

In this section, we present the components of our approach. We consider an input image as $\mathbf{x}$ with arbitrary facial expression. The expression is characterized by a one-dimensional AUs vector $\mathbf{v} = (v^1, \ldots, v^n)$, where each AU is normalized between 0 and 1 and v^i indicates the intensity of the i-th AU. With the goal of translating $\mathbf{x}$ into a photo-realistic image, our generator takes relative AUs $\mathbf{v}_{rel}$ as condition to renders with target expression. In the following parts, relative action units, MSF module, network structure, and loss functions are presented.

3.1 Relative Action Units (AUs)

Previous methods [26] take both absolute target AUs vector $\mathbf{v}_{src}$ and source image $\mathbf{x}$ as input to the generator. However, this input setting is flawed in that the generator needs to estimate the real AUs of input image to determine whether to edit image. From an application perspective, we are required to provide a value that must be strictly equal to the corresponding AU in the source image (i.e., $v_{tgt}^i = v_{src}^i$, where $i = 1, 2, \ldots, n$) even if we do not want to change it. Otherwise, the generator will probably introduce unintended modifications to editing results.

Compared to absolute AUs, relative AUs describe the desired change in selected action units. This is in accordance with the definition of action units [7] that indicates the activation state of facial muscles. Denote the source AUs and target AUs as $\mathbf{v}_{src}$ and $\mathbf{v}_{tgt}$. Therefore, the difference between target and source AUs can be defined as:

$$\mathbf{v}_{rel} \triangleq \mathbf{v}_{tgt} - \mathbf{v}_{src} \tag{1}$$

Introducing relative AUs as input brings several benefits. First, the relative AUs represented by the difference between the source and target images are intuitive and user friendly. For example, if we only intend to suppress AU10 (Upper Lip Raiser), we could assign an arbitrary real negative value to v_{10}, while making the other values zero. Second, in comparison to entire target AUs, the values in $\mathbf{v}_{rel}$ are zero-centered and can provide more expressive information for guiding expression editing and stabilize the training process. Moreover, with relative AUs, the generator learns to edit and reconstruct facial parts with respect to non-zero and zero values, which alleviates the cost for action units preserving. In our experiments, $\mathbf{v}_{rel}$ with zero values hardly introduces artifacts and errors.

Additionally, we propose to edit interpolated expressions $\mathbf{v}_{inter}$ among two different expressions $\mathbf{v}_1$ and $\mathbf{v}_2$. The interpolated AUs is denoted as Eq. 2.

$$\mathbf{v}_{inter} = \mathbf{v}_1 + \alpha(\mathbf{v}_2 - \mathbf{v}_1) - \mathbf{v}_{src}, \ 0 \leq \alpha \leq 1 \tag{2}$$

3.2 Network Structure

As presented in Fig. 3 (left), our generator is built on U-Net structure but replace several skip connections by our MSF modules in both high and low-resolution representation. The encoder consists of four convolutional layers with stride 2 for down-sampling, while the decoder is composed of four transposed convolutional layers with stride 2 for up-sampling. Furthermore, MSF module is applied as skip unit to fuse features from both higher and lower resolution in our generator. The kernel sizes are all 4×4 in down-sampling and up-sampling layers, while 5×5 in the rest convolutional layers.

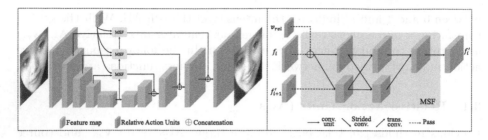

Fig. 3. Left: the structure of our generator, incorporating several MSF modules which render the encoder features in different feature level. Right: details of the proposed MSF module. The bottom legend on the right figure: conv. = convolution, trans. = transposed.

Our discriminator D is the same as which in [26], which is trained to evaluate the generated images both in realism score and desired expression fulfillment. Two branches of the discriminator, namely D_{adv} and D_{cond}, share a fully convolutional sub-network comprised of six convolutional layers with kernel size 4 and stride 2. On top of D_{adv}, we add a convolutional layer with kernel size 3, padding 1 and stride 1. For conditional critic D_{cond}, we add an auxiliary regression head to predict target AUs.

3.3   Multi-scale Feature Fusion

Encoder-decoder architecture is insufficient to manipulate the image with high quality but U-Net based architectures support the rise of generating quality, according to [17]. Taking these basics into consideration, we propose to modify the image features in different spatial resolution, simultaneously. To this end, we alter the structure in [30] and then build a learnable sub-network, namely our multi-scale feature fusion (MSF) module, to manipulate features in multi-scale level. In Fig. 3 (right), we show the overall architecture of multi-scale feature fusion module.

Our MSF module is different from [30] in two aspects. First, in MSF module, we fuse features from low-to-high, and the two kinds of conv streams noted above. In our approach, the MSF module takes the features across the encoder and the MSF modules as well as relative AUs as input and learns to manipulate image features at different spatial sizes. Second, we inject the condition at each MSF module. Such fusion mechanism helps MSF to learn the consistency of expressions of features with different resolutions, especially between encoder features and decoder features.

Without the loss of generality, we take the MSF module in i-th layer for example. Denote the input encoder features as f_i from i-th layer of encoder, and fusion feature as f'_{i+1} from the $i + 1$-th MSF module. Firstly, the encoder features are concatenated with relative AU $\mathbf{v}_{rel}$ in depth-wise fashion. Then a convolutional unit and a down-sample layer are applied to acquire two feature maps in different spatial size. The down-sampled features are then concatenated with higher-level features f'_{i+1} from $i + 1$-th MSF module. One more parallel feature fusion unit is applied across high and low-resolution representation, and then formulated into the output f'_i. The fusion feature f'_i will be one the input of decoder and $i - 1$-th MSF module. In this way, our generator learns and transforms the image features collaboratively in a multi-scale manner.

3.4 Loss Functions

Denote the conditional generated image as $\mathbf{x}' = G(\mathbf{x}, \mathbf{v}_{rel})$, where input image $\mathbf{x}$ and relative attributes $\mathbf{v}_{rel}$ are considered as inputs of the generator. In the following, we will introduce the loss functions employed in our framework.

Adversarial Loss. To synthesize photo-realistic images with GANs, we use the improved divergence criterion of standard GAN [9] proposed by WGAN-GP [10]. The adversarial loss can be written as:

$$\max_{D_{adv}} \mathcal{L}_{D_{adv}} = \mathbb{E}_{\mathbf{x}} D_{adv}(\mathbf{x}) - \mathbb{E}_{\mathbf{x}'} D_{adv}(\mathbf{x}') - \lambda_{gp} \mathbb{E}_{\hat{\mathbf{x}}}[(\| \nabla_{\hat{\mathbf{x}}} D_{adv}(\hat{\mathbf{x}}) \|_2 - 1)^2] \quad (3)$$

$$\max_{G} \mathcal{L}_{G_{adv}} = \mathbb{E}_{\mathbf{x}, \mathbf{v}_{rel}} D_{adv}(G(\mathbf{x}, \mathbf{v}_{rel})) \quad (4)$$

where λ_{gp} is a penalty coefficient and $\hat{\mathbf{x}}$ is randomly interpolated between $\mathbf{x}$ and generated image $\mathbf{x}'$. The discriminator D is unsupervised and aims to distinguish between real images and the generated fake images. The generator G tries to generate images which look realistic as the real.

Conditional Fulfillment. We require not only that the image synthesized by our model should look realistic, but also possess desired AUs. To this end, we adopt the core idea of conditional GANs [20] and employ an action units regressor D_{cond} which shares convolutional weights with D_{adv}, and define the following manipulation loss for training D_{cond} and G:

$$\min_{D_{cond}} \mathcal{L}_{D_{cond}} = \mathbb{E}_{\mathbf{x}, \mathbf{v}_{src}} \| D_{cond}(\mathbf{x}) - \mathbf{v}_{src} \|_2^2 \quad (5)$$

$$\min_{G} \mathcal{L}_{G_{cond}} = \mathbb{E}_{\mathbf{x}', \mathbf{v}_{tgt}} \| D_{cond}(\mathbf{x}') - \mathbf{v}_{tgt} \|_2^2 \quad (6)$$

where the AUs regression loss of real images $\mathbf{x}$ is used to optimize D_{cond}, thus G can learn to generate images $\mathbf{x}'$ which minimize the AUs regression loss $\mathcal{L}_{G_{cond}}$.

Reconstruction Regularization. Our generator G is trained to generate an output image $G(\mathbf{x}, \mathbf{v}_{rel})$ which not only looks realistic but also possesses desired facial action units. However, there is no ground-truth supervision provided in the dataset for our model to modify facial components while preserving identity information. To this end, we add extra constraints to guarantee the faces in both input and output images are from the same person in appearance.

On one hand, we utilize a *self-reconstruction* loss to enforce the generator to manipulate nothing when fed with zero-value relative AUs (i.e., $\mathbf{v}_{rel} = \mathbf{0}$). On the other hand, we adopt the concept of cycle consistency [37] and formulate the *cycle-reconstruction* loss which penalizes the difference between

$G(G(\mathbf{x}, \mathbf{v}_{rel}), -\mathbf{v}_{rel})$ and the input source $\mathbf{x}$. Hence, these two reconstruction losses can be written as:

$$\min_G \mathcal{L}_{rec} = \mathbb{E}_{\mathbf{x}}[\|\mathbf{x} - G(\mathbf{x}, \mathbf{0})\|_1] + \mathbb{E}_{\mathbf{x}, \mathbf{v}_{rel}}[\|G(G(\mathbf{x}, \mathbf{v}_{rel}), -\mathbf{v}_{rel}) - \mathbf{x}\|_1] \tag{7}$$

where $\mathbf{0}$ denotes a zero-padded vector with the same shape of $\mathbf{v}_{rel}$.

Total Variation Regularization. To ensure smooth spatial transformation and naturalness of output images in RGB color space, we follow the prior work [13,26] and perform a regularization $\mathcal{L}_{tv}$ over the synthesized fake samples $G(x, \mathbf{v}_{rel})$.

Model Objective. Taking the above losses into account, we finally build our total loss functions for D and G by combining all previous partial losses, respectively, as:

$$\min_D \mathcal{L}_D = -\mathcal{L}_{D_{adv}} + \lambda_1 \mathcal{L}_{D_{cond}} \tag{8}$$

$$\min_G \mathcal{L}_G = -\mathcal{L}_{G_{adv}} + \lambda_2 \mathcal{L}_{G_{cond}} + \lambda_3 \mathcal{L}_{rec} + \lambda_4 \mathcal{L}_{tv} \tag{9}$$

where λ_1, λ_2, λ_3, and λ_4 are tradeoff parameters that control the impact of each loss.

4 Experiments

4.1 Implementation Details

Dataset and Preprocessing. We randomly choose a subset of 200,000 samples from AffectNet [21] dataset. Besides, we remove some repeated images or cartoon faces in the validation set and take 3234 images as our testing samples to assess the training process. The images are centered cropped and resized to 128×128 by bicubic interpolation. All continuous AUs annotations are extracted by [2].

Baseline. As the current state-of-the-art method, GANimation [26], outperforming plenty of representative facial expression synthesis models [5,16,25,37], is taken as our baseline model. For fair comparison, we use the code[1] released by the authors and train the model on AffectNet [21] with default hyper-parameters.

Experiment Settings. We train the model by Adam [15] optimizer with settings of $\beta_1 = 0.5$, $\beta_2 = 0.999$ for 30 epochs at initial learning rate of 1×10^{-4}, and then linearly decay the rate to 1×10^{-5} for fine-tuning. We perform every single optimization step of the generator with four optimization steps of the discriminator. The weight coefficients for Eq. 8 and 9 are set to $\lambda_1 = \lambda_2 = 150, \lambda_3 = 30, \lambda_4 = 5 \times 10^{-6}$. All experiments are conducted in PyTorch [23] environment.

---

[1] https://github.com/albertpumarola/GANimation.

4.2   Evaluation Metrics

Evaluating a GAN model with respect to one criterion does not reliably reveal its convincing performance. In this work, we conduct model evaluation from two perspectives, which are network-based and human-based evaluation. Both methods measure the performance in three aspects, namely expression fulfillment, relative realism and identity preserving ability.

Network-Based Metrics. We evaluate 3234 images from AffectNet testing-set, each of which is transformed to 7 randomly selected expressions. Therefore, we get 22638 image pairs and then perform our quantitative evaluation.

- *Inception Score (IS).* IS [28] utilizes an Inception network to extract image representation and calculates the KL divergence between the conditional distribution and marginal distribution. Although previous work [3] has revealed the limitations of IS in intra-class images, it is still widely used to evaluate the model performance in image quality [4,26]. Following the evaluating method in [26], we calculate IS of images synthesized by our approach and GANimation [26].
- *Average Content Distance (ACD).* ACD [31] measures l_2-distance between embedded features of the input and generated images. We employ a famous facial recognition network[2], as GANimation did in [26], to extract face code for each individual and calculate the distance for each expression editing result. The lower value indicates the better identity similarity between images before and after editing.
- *Expression Distance (ED).* To consistently evaluate the ability of our model in expression editing, we reuse OpenFace2.0 [2] to acquire the AUs of edited images, and calculate l_2-distance between the generated and target AUs (the lower, the better). Performing such objective evaluation is not trivial, as a categorized expression often related to two different AU intensity [7].

Human-Based Metrics. For each metric in human-based evaluation, we asked 20 volunteers to evaluate 100 pairs of images which are generated by baseline and our method. During the test, we randomly display the images and ensure that the users do not know which image is edited by our model.

- *Relative realism.* In each comparison, we randomly select two images which are generated by GANimation and our model, respectively. The user is asked to pick the more realistic image they think.
- *Identity preserving.* One more user study for identity similarity metric is conducted to verify if humans agree that the given two images are from the same person. The display order of synthesized images from GANimation or our model is random.

---

[2] https://github.com/ageitgey/face_recognition.

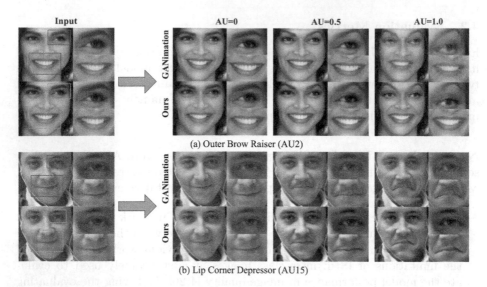

(a) Outer Brow Raiser (AU2)

(b) Lip Corner Depressor (AU15)

Fig. 4. Comparisons for single AU editing. Each time, we manipulate the face with only one AU activated, leaving the rest part of face unchanged. The values upon images denote the relative AUs value in our test.

- *Expression fulfillment.* Due to the complex distribution of human facial expressions, it is not very reasonable to classify expression into a specific category. To this end, we alleviate these limitations by asking the users to rate the similarity of two facial expressions instead of reporting the emotion labels. In every trail of human preference study, two images (one with target expression and the other one is edited by GANimation or our method) are displayed randomly. The users have to examine and rate the similarity of facial expressions in the two images. If the given two images are considered to be different in their opinion, the user is allowed to rate 0. When the user thinks the images are totally the same expression, 2 will be given. If the user is not sure about the similarity of two expressions or these expressions are partly the same (e.g., same AUs for mouth but different for eyebrows), 1 will be noted.

4.3 Qualitative Evaluation

We first qualitatively compare our model with GANimation in edition of single or multiple AUs. Figure 4 shows two typical examples of AU2 (Outer Brow Raiser) and AU15 (Lip Corner Depressor). From sample results of (a) in Fig. 4, it can be observed that GANimation fails to focus on Outer Brow and wrinkles the mouth, yielding less satisfying results than ours. In sample results of sub-figure (b), our model produces more plausible and better-manipulated results, especially in regions around the lip corner.

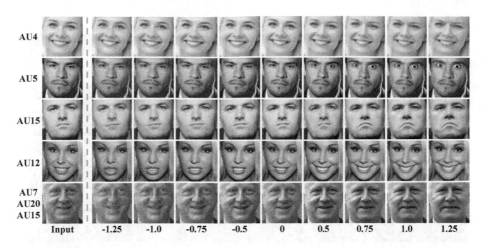

Fig. 5. Sample results in single/multiple AUs editing. AU4: Brow Lowerer; AU5: Upper Lid Raiser; AU7: Lid Tightener; AU12: Lip Corner Puller; AU15: Lip Corner Depressor; AU20: Lip Stretcher. The legend below the images are relative AUs intensity. The higher (lower) AUs value means to strengthen (weaken) the corresponding facial action unit in input image. Please zoom in for better observation.

Figure 5 shows more results in single/multiple AUs editing. By adopting relative action units as conditional input, our model convincingly learns to edit a single or multiple AUs instead of entire action units of the input image.

We proceed to compare our model against GANimation. From the observation in Fig. 6, we can find that our model successfully transforms source image in accordance with desired AUs, with fewer artifacts and manipulation cues. While the baseline model is less likely to generate high-quality details or preserve the facial regions corresponding to unchanged AUs, especially for eyes and mouth.

We next evaluate our network and discuss the model performance when dealing with extreme situations, which includes but not limited to image occlusions, portraits, drawings, and non-human faces. In Fig. 7, for instance, the first image shows occlusions created by a finger. To edit the expression for this kind of image, GANimation requires the entire set of AUs, including the activation status of Lip Corner and Chin, which imposes an extra burden on the user and brings an undesirable increase of visual artifacts. On the contrary, our method is able to edit expression without the need for source AUs. In the third and fourth row of Fig. 7, we present face editing examples from paintings and drawings, respectively. GANimation is either fails to efficiently manipulate input image with fully the same expression (the third row, left and the fourth row, right) or introduces unnatural artifacts and deformation (third row, right and fourth row, left). We can easily find the improvements of our method when compared to GANimation, although GANimation achieves plausible results on these images.

To better understand the benefits of continuous editing, we exploit AUs interpolation between different expressions and present results in Fig. 8. The plausible results verify the continuity in the action units space and demonstrate the generalization performance of our model.

48   J. Ling et al.

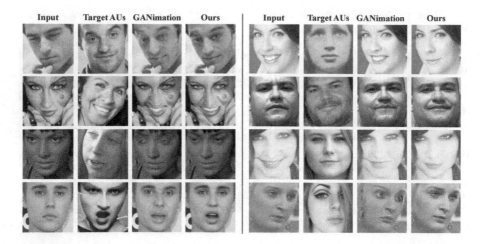

Fig. 6. Qualitative comparison. Images are taken from AffectNet dataset.

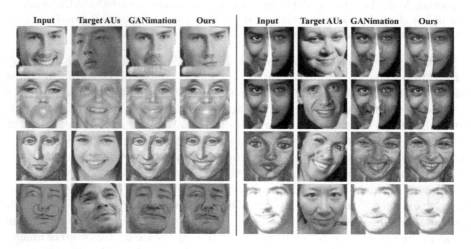

Fig. 7. Testing in difficult cases. We compare our model to GANimation in several difficult cases, covering occlusions, paintings and drawings.

Fig. 8. Expression interpolation. Example results of linear expression interpolation between two AUs vectors.

4.4   Quantitative Evaluation

Here we will conduct quantitative evaluations to verify the qualitative comparisons above. As described in Sect. 4.2, we resort to three alternative measures for quantitative evaluation of our method. First, we calculate metrics of IS, ACD and ED for both GANimation and the proposed approach. The comparison results are given in Table 1. It can be observed that our approach consistently achieves competitive results against GANimation for IS and ED. Our generator without MSF module attains the lowest score on ACD but the highest score in ED. This is reasonable because the accuracy of a facial recognition network inevitably suffers from expression variation.

Table 1. Network-based evaluation. Better results are in bold.

Method	IS $\uparrow$	ACD $\downarrow$	ED $\downarrow$
Real Images	3.024 ± 0.157	–	–
GANimation	2.861 ± 0.054	0.395	0.313
GANimation w/v_{rel}	2.901 ± 0.043	0.352	0.661
Ours, $k_{MSF} = 0$	2.809 ± 0.058	**0.335**	0.636
Ours, $k_{MSF} = 1$	2.864 ± 0.042	0.349	0.609
Ours, $k_{MSF} = 2$	2.899 ± 0.038	0.345	0.422
Ours	$\mathbf{2.940 \pm 0.039}$	0.375	**0.275**
Ours w/o v_{rel}	2.808 ± 0.050	0.426	0.290

Table 2. Human-based evaluation. We present the proportion of user subjective evaluation on edited expression fulfillment and human preference. Better results are in bold.

Method	Expression similarity			Human preference	
	0 $\downarrow$	1 $\uparrow$	2 $\uparrow$	Realism $\uparrow$	Identity $\uparrow$
GANimation	25.04	**43.25**	31.71	34.43	**90.59**
Ours	**17.66**	35.22	**47.12**	**65.57**	90.56

Table 2, as a supplement to metric ED, offers a human-based evaluation on expression editing ability. Benefiting from MSF modules which serve as skip connections from encoder to decoder, our approach outperforms GANimation by a large margin. Nearly a quarter of test samples transformed by GANimation are considered failures. The proposed model is slightly favorable to the baseline in terms of identity preservation and our model performs better in image realism score, according to human preference results in Table 2 (right part).

4.5   Ablation Study

In this section, we exploit the importance of each component within the proposed method. To begin with, we investigate the improvement brought by relative AUs. We compare our model with baseline model in action units preserving from reconstruction perspective. To perform facial image reconstruction, we respectively apply GANimation by taking source AUs as absolute condition, and apply our model by taking a zero-valued vector as relative condition. We present results of L1 norm, PSNR, and SSIM [33] between input and generated images in Table 3. From the second and third row, it can be seen that GANimation trained with relative AUs is slightly better than our approach without using relative AUs. When trained with our full approach (fourth row), we achieve the best reconstruction results.

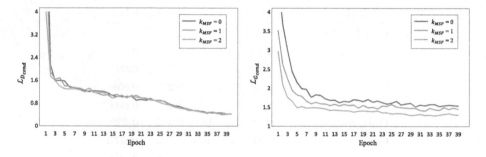

Fig. 9. Conditional loss convergence. Left (right) figure: the learning curves of condition loss in discriminator (generator). We use the same discriminator during ablation study.

Table 3. Reconstruction comparison. We measure the reconstruction error using L1 distance (lower is better), PSNR and SSIM [33] (higher is better).

Method	L1 ↓	PSNR ↑	SSIM ↑
GANimation	0.049	23.76	0.901
GANimation w/v_{rel}	0.022	29.11	0.954
Ours w/o v_{rel}	0.025	28.83	0.972
Ours	0.018	31.89	0.986

We next examine the importance of MSF module based on IS/ACD/ED metrics. Note that our model is built on U-Net, we carefully replace the skip connection with our MSF module and gradually train these generators separately. Quantitative comparison results are shown in Table 1. The first case is our model without MSF module (fourth row), which reduces to U-Net architecture. U-Net-based model acquires the best ACD result and the worst expression distance, which implies inefficient performance in expression editing. A conclusion can be drawn from the comparison results that a model has a greater potential to attain lower ACD if the ED gets higher. One proper explanation is that the expression editing intensity inevitably change the face features for facial recognition network. Figure 9 shows the loss optimization process in our experiments. As can be found, the trend of loss curves are almost the same during the period of training discriminator (left figure). From the right figure, we can find that the generator that has two MSF modules converges faster than those with less MSF modules, which implies the definite improvements are brought by our MSF mechanism.

5   Conclusion

In this study, we propose a novel approach by incorporating multi-scale fusion mechanism in U-Net based architecture for arbitrary facial expression editing. As a simple but competitive method, relative condition setting is proved to improve our model performance by a large margin, especially for action units preserving, reconstruction quality and identity preserving. We achieve better experimental results in visual quality, manipulation ability, and human preference compared to state-of-the-art methods.

Acknowledgements. This work was supported by NSFC (61671296, U1611461), National Key R&D Project of China (2019YFB1802701), MoE-China Mobile Research Fund Project (MCM20180702) and the Shanghai Key Laboratory of Digital Media Processing and Transmissions.

References

1. Arjovsky, M., Chintala, S., Bottou, L.: Wasserstein generative adversarial networks. In: Proceedings of the 34th International Conference on Machine Learning, pp. 214–223 (2017)
2. Baltrusaitis, T., Zadeh, A., Lim, Y.C., Morency, L.P.: Openface 2.0: facial behavior analysis toolkit. In: 2018 13th IEEE International Conference on Automatic Face & Gesture Recognition, FG 2018, pp. 59–66. IEEE (2018)
3. Barratt, S., Sharma, R.: A note on the inception score. arXiv preprint arXiv:1801.01973 (2018)
4. Brock, A., Donahue, J., Simonyan, K.: Large scale GAN training for high fidelity natural image synthesis. arXiv preprint arXiv:1809.11096 (2018)
5. Choi, Y., Choi, M., Kim, M., Ha, J.W., Kim, S., Choo, J.: StarGAN: unified generative adversarial networks for multi-domain image-to-image translation. In: Proceedings of the IEEE Conference on Computer Vision and Pattern Recognition, pp. 8789–8797 (2018)
6. Chu, M., Xie, Y., Leal-Taixé, L., Thuerey, N.: Temporally coherent GANs for video super-resolution (TecoGAN). arXiv preprint arXiv:1811.09393 (2018)
7. Friesen, E., Ekman, P.: Facial action coding system: a technique for the measurement of facial movement. Consulting Psychologists Press, Palo Alto (1978)
8. Geng, Z., Cao, C., Tulyakov, S.: 3D guided fine-grained face manipulation. In: Proceedings of the IEEE Conference on Computer Vision and Pattern Recognition, pp. 9821–9830 (2019)

9. Goodfellow, I., et al.: Generative adversarial nets. In: Advances in Neural Information Processing Systems, pp. 2672–2680 (2014)
10. Gulrajani, I., Ahmed, F., Arjovsky, M., Dumoulin, V., Courville, A.C.: Improved training of Wasserstein GAN. In: Advances in Neural Information Processing Systems, pp. 5767–5777 (2017)
11. He, Z., Zuo, W., Kan, M., Shan, S., Chen, X.: AttGAN: facial attribute editing by only changing what you want. IEEE Trans. Image Process. **28**, 5464–5478 (2019)
12. Isola, P., Zhu, J.Y., Zhou, T., Efros, A.A.: Image-to-image translation with conditional adversarial networks. In: Proceedings of the IEEE Conference on Computer Vision and Pattern Recognition, pp. 1125–1134 (2017)
13. Johnson, J., Alahi, A., Fei-Fei, L.: Perceptual losses for real-time style transfer and super-resolution. In: Leibe, B., Matas, J., Sebe, N., Welling, M. (eds.) ECCV 2016. LNCS, vol. 9906. Springer, Cham (2016). https://doi.org/10.1007/978-3-319-46475-6_43
14. Karras, T., Laine, S., Aila, T.: A style-based generator architecture for generative adversarial networks. In: Proceedings of the IEEE Conference on Computer Vision and Pattern Recognition, pp. 4401–4410 (2019)
15. Kingma, D.P., Ba, J.: Adam: A method for stochastic optimization. arXiv: Learning (2014)
16. Li, M., Zuo, W., Zhang, D.: Deep identity-aware transfer of facial attributes. arXiv preprint arXiv:1610.05586 (2016)
17. Liu, M., et al.: STGAN: a unified selective transfer network for arbitrary image attribute editing, pp. 3673–3682 (2019)
18. Liu, M.Y., Breuel, T., Kautz, J.: Unsupervised image-to-image translation networks. In: Advances in Neural Information Processing Systems, pp. 700–708 (2017)
19. Liu, M.Y., Tuzel, O.: Coupled generative adversarial networks. In: Advances in Neural Information Processing Systems, pp. 469–477 (2016)
20. Mirza, M., Osindero, S.: Conditional generative adversarial nets. Computer Science, pp. 2672–2680 (2014)
21. Mollahosseini, A., Hasani, B., Mahoor, M.H.: AffectNet: a database for facial expression, valence, and arousal computing in the wild. IEEE Trans. Affect. Comput. **10**(1), 18–31 (2017)
22. Park, T., Liu, M.Y., Wang, T.C., Zhu, J.Y.: Semantic image synthesis with spatially-adaptive normalization. In: Proceedings of the IEEE Conference on Computer Vision and Pattern Recognition, pp. 2337–2346 (2019)
23. Paszke, A., et al.: Automatic differentiation in PyTorch (2017)
24. Peng, X.B., Kanazawa, A., Toyer, S., Abbeel, P., Levine, S.: Variational discriminator bottleneck: improving imitation learning, inverse RL, and GANs by constraining information flow. arXiv preprint arXiv:1810.00821 (2018)
25. Perarnau, G., Van De Weijer, J., Raducanu, B., Álvarez, J.M.: Invertible conditional GANs for image editing. arXiv preprint arXiv:1611.06355 (2016)
26. Pumarola, A., Agudo, A., Martinez, A.M., et al.: GANimation: one-shot anatomically consistent facial animation. Int. J. Comput. Vis. **128**, 698–713 (2020). https://doi.org/10.1007/s11263-019-01210-3
27. Qiao, F., Yao, N., Jiao, Z., Li, Z., Chen, H., Wang, H.: Geometry-contrastive GAN for facial expression transfer. arXiv preprint arXiv:1802.01822 (2018)
28. Salimans, T., Goodfellow, I., Zaremba, W., Cheung, V., Radford, A., Chen, X.: Improved techniques for training GANs. In: Advances in Neural Information Processing Systems, pp. 2234–2242 (2016)

29. Song, L., Lu, Z., He, R., Sun, Z., Tan, T.: Geometry guided adversarial facial expression synthesis. In: 2018 ACM Multimedia Conference on Multimedia Conference, pp. 627–635. ACM (2018)
30. Sun, K., Xiao, B., Liu, D., Wang, J.: Deep high-resolution representation learning for human pose estimation. In: CVPR (2019)
31. Tulyakov, S., Liu, M.Y., Yang, X., Kautz, J.: MoCoGAN: decomposing motion and content for video generation. In: IEEE Conference on Computer Vision and Pattern Recognition (CVPR), pp. 1526–1535 (2018)
32. Wang, X., et al.: ESRGAN: enhanced super-resolution generative adversarial networks. In: Leal-Taixé, L., Roth, S. (eds.) ECCV 2018. LNCS, vol. 11133. Springer, Cham (2019). https://doi.org/10.1007/978-3-030-11021-5_5
33. Wang, Z., Bovik, A.C., Sheikh, H.R., Simoncelli, E.P.: Image quality assessment: from error visibility to structural similarity. IEEE Trans. Image Process. **13**(4), 600–612 (2004)
34. Wu, P.W., Lin, Y.J., Chang, C.H., Chang, E.Y., Liao, S.W.: RelGAN: Multi-domain image-to-image translation via relative attributes. arXiv preprint arXiv:1908.07269 (2019)
35. Zhang, G., Kan, M., Shan, S., Chen, X.: Generative adversarial network with spatial attention for face attribute editing. In: Ferrari, V., Hebert, M., Sminchisescu, C., Weiss, Y. (eds.) ECCV 2018. LNCS, vol. 11210. Springer, Cham (2018). https://doi.org/10.1007/978-3-030-01231-1_26
36. Zhang, H., et al.: StackGAN:: text to photo-realistic image synthesis with stacked generative adversarial networks. In: Proceedings of the IEEE International Conference on Computer Vision, pp. 5907–5915 (2017)
37. Zhu, J.Y., Park, T., Isola, P., Efros, A.A.: Unpaired image-to-image translation using cycle-consistent adversarial networks. In: Proceedings of the IEEE International Conference on Computer Vision, pp. 2223–2232 (2017)

Adaptive Object Detection with Dual Multi-label Prediction

Zhen Zhao[1], Yuhong Guo[1,2($\boxtimes$)], Haifeng Shen[1], and Jieping Ye[1]

[1] DiDi Chuxing, Beijing, China
{alexzhaozhen,shenhaifeng,yejieping}@didiglobal.com
[2] Carleton University, Ottawa, Canada
yuhong.guo@carleton.ca

Abstract. In this paper, we propose a novel end-to-end unsupervised deep domain adaptation model for adaptive object detection by exploiting multi-label object recognition as a dual auxiliary task. The model exploits multi-label prediction to reveal the object category information in each image and then uses the prediction results to perform conditional adversarial global feature alignment, such that the multimodal structure of image features can be tackled to bridge the domain divergence at the global feature level while preserving the discriminability of the features. Moreover, we introduce a prediction consistency regularization mechanism to assist object detection, which uses the multi-label prediction results as an auxiliary regularization information to ensure consistent object category discoveries between the object recognition task and the object detection task. Experiments are conducted on a few benchmark datasets and the results show the proposed model outperforms the state-of-the-art comparison methods.

Keywords: Cross-domain object detection · Auxiliary task

1 Introduction

The success of deep learning models has led to great advances for many computer vision tasks, including image classification [16,35,36], image segmentation [24,43] and object detection [11,23,28,29]. The smooth deployment of the deep models typically assumes a standard supervised learning setting, where a sufficient amount of labeled data is available for model training and the training and test images come from the same data source and distribution. However, in practical applications, the training and test images can come from different domains that exhibit obvious deviations. For example, Fig. 1 demonstrates images from domains with different image styles, which obviously present different visual appearances and data distributions. The violation of the i.i.d sampling principle across training and test data prevents effective deployment of supervised learning techniques, while acquiring new labeled data in each test domain is costly and impractical. To address this problem, unsupervised domain adaptation has recently received increasing attention [4,10,25,39].

© Springer Nature Switzerland AG 2020
A. Vedaldi et al. (Eds.): ECCV 2020, LNCS 12373, pp. 54–69, 2020.
https://doi.org/10.1007/978-3-030-58604-1_4

(a)   **(b)**

Fig. 1. (a) and (b) are images from real scenes and virtual scenes respectively. It is obvious that the visual appearances of the images from different domains are very different, even if they contain the same categories of objects.

Unsupervised domain adaptation aims to adapt information from a label-rich source domain to learn prediction models in a target domain that only has unlabeled instances. Although many unsupervised domain adaptation methods have been developed for simpler image classification and segmentation tasks [4,10,25,37,38,42], much fewer domain adaptation works have been done on the more complex object detection task, which requires recognizing both the objects and their specific locations. The authors of [2] propose a domain adaptive faster R-CNN model for cross-domain object detection, which employs the adversarial domain adaptation technique [10] to align cross-domain features at both the image-level and instance-level to bridge data distribution gaps. This adaptive faster R-CNN method presents some promising good results. However, due to the typical presence of multiple objects in each image, as shown in Fig. 1, both the image-level and instance-level feature alignments can be problematic without considering the specific objects contained. The more recent work [31] proposes to address the problem of global (image-level) feature alignment by incorporating an additional local feature alignment under a strong-weak alignment framework for cross-domain object detection, which effectively improved the performance of the domain adaptive faster R-CNN. Nevertheless, this work still fails to take the latent object category information into account for cross-domain feature alignment. With noisy background and various objects, a whole image can contain very complex information and the overall features of an image can have complex multimodal structures. Aiming to learn an accurate object detector in the target domain, it is important to induce feature representations that minimize the cross-domain feature distribution gaps, while preserving the cross-category feature distribution gaps.

In light of the problem analysis above, in this paper we propose a novel end-to-end unsupervised deep domain adaptation model, Multi-label Conditional distribution Alignment and detection Regularization model (MCAR), for multi-object detection, where the images in the target domain are entirely unannotated. The model exploits multi-label prediction as an auxiliary dual task to reveal the object category information in each image and then uses this information as an additional input to perform conditional adversarial cross-domain feature alignment. Such a conditional feature alignment is expected to improve the discriminability of the induced features while bridging the cross-domain representation gaps to increase the transferability and domain invariance of features. Moreover, as object recognition is typically easier to solve and can yield higher accuracy than the more complex object detection task, we introduce a consistency regularization mechanism to assist object detection, which uses the multi-label prediction results as auxiliary regularization information for the object detection part to ensure consistent object category discoveries between the object recognition task and the object detection task.

The contribution of this work can be summarized as follows: (1) This is the first work that exploits multi-label prediction as an auxiliary dual task for the multi-object detection task. (2) We deploy a novel multi-label conditional adversarial cross-domain feature alignment methodology to bridge domain divergence while preserving the discriminability of the features. (3) We introduce a novel prediction consistency regularization mechanism to improve the detection accuracy. (4) We conduct extensive experiments on multiple adaptive multi-object detection tasks by comparing the proposed model with existing methods, and demonstrate effective empirical results for the proposed model.

2   Related Work

Object Detection. Detection models have benefited from using advanced convolutional neural networks as feature extractors. Many widely used detection methods are two-stage methods based on the region of interest (ROI) [11,12,29]. The RCNN in [12] is the first detection model that deploys the ROI for object detection. It extracts features independently from each region of interest in the image, instead of using the sliding window and manual feature design in traditional object detection methods. Later, the author of [11] proposed a Fast-RCNN detection model, which adopts a ROI pooling operation to share the convolution layers between all ROIs and improve the detection speed and accuracy. The work in [29] made further improvements and proposed the Faster-RCNN, which combines Region Proposal Network (RPN) with Fast-RCNN to replace selective search and further improve detection performance. Faster-RCNN provides a foundation for many subsequent research studies [6,15,21,23,28]. In this work and many related unsupervised domain adaptation methods, the widely used two-stage method, Faster-RCNN, is adopted as the backbone detection model.

Unsupervised Domain Adaptation. Unsupervised domain adaptation has attracted a lot of attention in computer vision research community and made great progress [7,10,20,25,30,33]. The main idea employed in these works is to learn feature representations that align distributions across domains. For example, the work in [10] adopts the principle of generative adversarial networks

(GANs) [14] through a gradient reversal layer (GRL) [9] to achieve cross-domain feature alignment. The work in [25] further extends adversarial adaptation into conditional adversarial domain adaptation by taking the classifier's prediction into account. The works in [3, 30] use image generation to realize cross-domain feature transformation and align the source and target domains. Moreover, some other works adopt distance metric learning methods, such as asymmetric metric learning [20], maximum mean discrepancy (MMD) minimization [7] and Wasserstein distance minimization [33], to achieve domain alignment. Nevertheless, these studies focus on the simpler image classification and segmentation tasks.

Adaptive Object Detection. Recently domain adaptation for object detection has started drawing attention. The work in [2] proposes an adaptive Faster-RCNN method that uses adversarial gradient reversal to achieve image-level and instance-level feature alignment for adaptive cross-domain object detection. [18] adopts image transformation and exploits pseudo labels to realize a weakly supervised cross-domain detection. The work in [19] leverages multi-style image generation between multiple domains to achieve cross-domain object detection. The authors of [31] propose a strong and weak alignment of local and global features to improve cross-domain object detection performance. [44] focuses on relevant areas for selective cross-domain alignment. [17] adopts hierarchical domain feature alignment while adding a scale reduction module and a weighted gradient reversal layer to achieve domain invariance. [1] advances the Mean Teacher paradigm with object relations for cross-domain detection. [34] uses a gradient detach based multi-level feature alignment strategy for cross-domain detection. [40] adopts multi-level feature adversary to achieve domain adaptation. Nevertheless, these methods are limited to cross-domain feature alignment, while failing to take the latent object category information into account when performing feature alignment. Our proposed model employs multi-label object recognition as an auxiliary task and uses it to achieve conditional feature alignment and detection regularization.

3   Method

In this section, we present the proposed Multi-label Conditional distribution Alignment and detection Regularization model (MCAR) for cross-domain adaptive object detection. We assume there are two domains from different sources and with different distributions. The source domain is fully annotated for object detection and the target domain is entirely unannotated. Let $X_s = \{(x_i^s, \mathbf{b}_i^s, \mathbf{c}_i^s)\}_{i=1}^{n_s}$ denote the annotated images from the source domain, where x_i^s denotes the i-th image, $\mathbf{b}_i^s$ and $\mathbf{c}_i^s$ denote the bounding boxes' coordinates and the category labels of the corresponding objects contained in the image respectively. Let $X_t = \{x_i^t\}_{i=1}^{n_t}$ denote the unannotated images from the target domain. We assume in total K classes of objects are presented in images of both the source and target domains. We aim to train an object detection model by exploiting the available data from both domains such that the model can have good detection performance in the target domain.

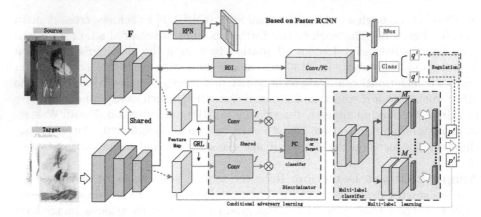

Fig. 2. The structure of the proposed MCAR model. Conditional adversarial global feature alignment is conducted through a domain discriminator by using multi-label prediction results as object category input. Meanwhile, multi-label prediction results are also used to provide a prediction consistency regularization mechanism on object detection after the RPN.

The main idea of the proposed MCAR model is to exploit multi-label prediction (for multi-object recognition) as an auxiliary task and use it to perform both conditional adversarial cross-domain feature alignment and prediction consistency regularization for the target object detection task. This end-to-end deep learning model adopts the widely used Faster-RCNN as the backbone detection network. Its structure is presented in Fig. 2. Following this structure, we present the model in detail below.

3.1 Multi-label Prediction

The major difference between object recognition and object detection lies in that the former task only needs to recognize the presence of any object category in the given image, while the latter task needs to identify each specific object and its location in the image. The cross-domain divergence in image features that impacts the object recognition task can also consequently degrade the detection performance, since it will affect the region proposal network and the regional local object classification. Therefore we propose to deploy a simpler task of object recognition to help extract suitable image-level features that can bridge the distribution gap between the source and target domains, while being discriminative for recognizing objects.

In particular, we treat the object recognition task as a multi-label prediction problem [13,41]. It takes the global image-level features produced by the feature extraction network F of the Faster-RCNN model as input, and predicts the presence of K object category using K binary classifier networks, $M_1, \cdots, M_K$. These classifiers can be learned on the annotated images in the source domain, where the global object category label indicator vector $\mathbf{y}_i^s \in \{0,1\}^K$ for the i-th image can be gathered from its bounding boxes' labels $\mathbf{c}_i^s$ through a fixed transformation operation function $\varphi : \mathbf{c}_i^s \rightarrow \mathbf{y}_i^s$, which simply finds all the existing object categories in $\mathbf{c}_i^s$ and represents their presence using $\mathbf{y}_i^s$. The multi-label classifiers can then be learned by minimizing the following cross-entropy loss:

$$\mathcal{L}_{multi} = -\frac{1}{n_s} \sum_{i=1}^{n_s} \left[\mathbf{y}_i^{s\top} \log(\mathbf{p}_i^s) + (1 - \mathbf{y}_i^s)^\top \log(1 - \mathbf{p}_i^s) \right] \tag{1}$$

where each k-th entry of the prediction output vector $\mathbf{p}_i^s$ is produced from the k-th binary classifier:

$$\mathbf{p}_{ik}^s = M_k(F(x_i^s)) \tag{2}$$

which indicates the probability of the presence of objects from the k-th class.

The multi-label classifiers work on the global features extracted before the RPN of the Faster-RCNN. For Faster-RCNN based object detection, these global features will be used through RPNs to extract region proposals and then perform object classification and bounding box regression on the proposed regions. In the source domain, supervision information such as bounding boxes and the object labels are provided for training the detector, while in the target domain, the detection is purely based on the global features extracted and the detection model parameters (for RPN, region classifiers and regressors) obtained in the source domain. Hence it is very important to bridge the domain gap at the global feature level. Moreover, image features that led to good global object recognition performance are also expected to be informative for the local object classification on proposed regions. Therefore we will exploit multi-label prediction for global feature alignment and regional object prediction regularization.

3.2 Conditional Adversarial Feature Alignment

The popular generative adversarial network (GAN) [14] has shown that two distributions can be aligned by using a discriminator as an adversary to play a minimax two-player game. Following the same principle, conditional adversary is designed to take label category information into account. It has been suggested in [25,27] that the cross-covariance of the predicted category information and the global image features can be helpful for avoiding partial alignment and achieving multimodal feature distribution alignment. We propose to integrate the multi-label prediction results together with the global image features extracted by F to perform conditional adversarial feature alignment at the global image level. The key component network introduced is the domain discriminator D, which predicts the domain of the input image instance, with label 1 indicating the source domain and 0 indicating the target domain. As shown in Fig. 2, the discriminator consists of a convolution filter layer f, which reduces the dimension of the input features, and a fully connected layer FC, which integrates the inputs to perform classification. It takes features $F(x_i)$ and the multi-label prediction probability vector $\mathbf{p}_i$ as input, and uses softmax activation function to produce probabilistic prediction output. For the conditional adversarial training, we adopted a focal loss [22,31], which uses the prediction confidence deficiency score to weight each instance in order to give more weights to hard-to-classify examples. The loss of conditional adversarial training, $\mathcal{L}_{adv}$, is as below:

$$\min_{F}\max_{D}\quad \mathcal{L}_{adv} = -\frac{1}{2}(\mathcal{L}_{adv}^s + \mathcal{L}_{adv}^t) \tag{3}$$

$$\mathcal{L}_{adv}^s = -\frac{1}{n_s}\sum_{i=1}^{n_s}(1-D(F(x_i^s),\mathbf{p}_i^s))^\gamma \log(D(F(x_i^s),\mathbf{p}_i^s))$$

$$\mathcal{L}_{adv}^t = -\frac{1}{n_t}\sum_{i=1}^{n_t}D(F(x_i^t),\mathbf{p}_i^t)^\gamma \log(1-D(F(x_i^t),\mathbf{p}_i^t))$$

where γ is a modulation factor that controls how much to focus on the hard-to-classify example; the global features $F(x_i)$ and the multi-label prediction probability vector $\mathbf{p}_i$ are integrated through a multi-linear mapping function such that $D(F(x_i),\mathbf{p}_i) = FC(f(F(x_i)) \otimes \mathbf{p}_i)$. With this adversary loss, the feature extractor F will be adjusted to try to confuse the domain discriminator D, while D aims to maximumly separate the two domains.

This multi-label prediction conditioned adversarial feature alignment is expected to bridge the domain distribution gaps while preserving the discriminability for object recognition, which will improve the adaptation of the consequent region proposal, object classification on each proposed region and its location identification in the target domain.

3.3   Category Prediction Based Regularization

The detection task involves recognizing both the objects and their locations, which is relatively more difficult than object recognition [8]. The multi-label classifiers we applied can produce more accurate recognition results as the region proposal mistakes can be accumulated to objection classification on the proposed regions in the detection task. Based on such an observation, we propose a novel category prediction consistency regularization mechanism for object detection by exploiting multi-label prediction results.

Assume N region proposals are generated through the region proposal network (RPN) for an input image x. Each proposal will be classified into one of the K object classes using an object classifier C, while its location coordinates will be produced using a regressor R. The multi-class object classifier produces a length K prediction vector $\hat{\mathbf{q}}$ on each proposal that indicates the probability of the proposed region belonging to one of the K object classes. The object prediction on the total N proposals can form a prediction matrix $Q \in [0,1]^{K \times N}$. We can then compute an overall multi-object prediction probability vector $\mathbf{q}$ by taking the row-wise maximum over Q, such that $\mathbf{q}_k = \max(Q(k,:))$, and use $\mathbf{q}_k$ as the prediction probability of the image x containing the k-th object category. To enforce consistency between the prediction produced by the detector and the prediction produced by the multi-label object recognition, we propose to minimize the KL divergence between their prediction probability vectors $\mathbf{p}$ and $\mathbf{q}$ after renormalizing each vector with softmax function. As KL divergence is an asymmetric measure, we define the consistency regularization loss as:

$$\mathcal{L}_{kl} = \mathcal{L}_{kl}^s + \mathcal{L}_{kl}^t \tag{4}$$

$$\mathcal{L}_{kl}^s = \frac{1}{2n_s} \sum_{i=1}^{n_s} (KL(\mathbf{p}_i^s, \mathbf{q}_i^s) + KL(\mathbf{q}_i^s, \mathbf{p}_i^s)) \tag{5}$$

$$\mathcal{L}_{kl}^t = \frac{1}{2n_t} \sum_{i=1}^{n_t} (KL(\mathbf{p}_i^t, \mathbf{q}_i^t) + KL(\mathbf{q}_i^t, \mathbf{p}_i^t)) \tag{6}$$

With this regularization loss, we expect the multi-label prediction results can assist object detection through unified mutual learning.

3.4 Overall End-to-End Learning

The detection loss of the base Faster-RCNN model, denoted as $\mathcal{L}_{det}$, is computed on the annotated source domain data under supervised classification and regression. It has two components, the proposal classification loss and the bounding box regression loss. We combine the detection loss, the multi-label prediction loss, the conditional adversarial feature alignment loss, and the prediction consistency regularization loss together for end-to-end deep learning. The total loss can be written as:

$$\begin{cases} \mathcal{L}_{all} = \mathcal{L}_{det} + \lambda \mathcal{L}_{adv} + \mu \mathcal{L}_{multi} + \varepsilon \mathcal{L}_{kl} \\ \\ \quad\quad \min_{F} \max_{D} \quad \mathcal{L}_{all} \end{cases} \tag{7}$$

where λ, μ, and ε are trade-off parameters that balance the multiple loss terms. We use SGD optimization algorithm to perform training, while GRL [9] is adopted to implement the gradient sign flip for the domain discriminator part.

4 Experiments

We conducted experiments with multiple cross-domain multi-object detection tasks under different adaptation scenarios: (1) Domain adaptation from real to virtual image scenarios, where we used cross-domain detection tasks from PASCAL VOC [8] to Watercolor2K [18] and Comic2K [18] respectively. (2) Domain adaption from normal/clear images to foggy image scenarios, where we used object detection tasks that adapt from Cityscapes [5] to Foggy Cityscapes [32]. In each adaptive object detection task, the images in the source domain are fully annotated and the images in the target domain are entirely unannotated. We present our experimental results and discussions in this section.

Table 1. Test results of domain adaptation for object detection from PASCAL VOC to Watercolor in terms of mean average precision (%). MC and PR indicate Multilabel-Conditional adversary and Prediction based Regularization, respectively.

Method	MC	PR	Bike	Bird	Car	Cat	Dog	Person	mAP
Source-only			68.8	46.8	37.2	32.7	21.3	60.7	44.6
BDC-Faster [31]			68.6	48.3	47.2	26.5	21.7	60.5	45.5
DA-Faster [2]			75.2	40.6	48.0	31.5	20.6	60.0	46.0
SW-DA [31]			82.3	**55.9**	46.5	32.7	35.5	66.7	53.3
SCL [34]			82.2	55.1	**51.8**	39.6	**38.4**	64.0	55.2
MCAR (Ours)	✓		**92.5**	52.2	43.9	**46.5**	28.8	62.5	54.4
	✓	✓	87.9	52.1	**51.8**	41.6	33.8	**68.8**	**56.0**
Train-on-Target			83.6	59.4	50.7	43.7	39.5	74.5	58.6

Table 2. Test results of domain adaptation for object detection from PASCAL VOC to Comic, The definition of MC and PR is same as in Table 1.

Method	MC	PR	Bike	Bird	Car	Cat	Dog	Person	mAP
Source-only			32.5	12.0	21.1	10.4	12.4	29.9	19.7
DA-Faster			31.1	10.3	15.5	12.4	19.3	39.0	21.2
SW-DA			36.4	21.8	29.8	15.1	23.5	49.6	29.4
MCAR (Ours)	✓		40.9	**22.5**	30.3	**23.7**	**24.7**	**53.6**	32.6
	✓	✓	**47.9**	20.5	**37.4**	20.6	24.5	50.2	**33.5**

4.1 Implementation Details

In the experiments, we followed the setting of [31] by using the Faster-RCNN as the backbone detection network, pretraining the model weights on the ImageNet, and using the same 600 pixels of images' shortest side. We set the training epoch as 25, and set λ, μ, ε, and γ as 0.5, 0.01, 0.1, and 5 respectively. The momentum is set as 0.9 and weight decay as 0.0005. For all experiments, we evaluated different methods using mean average precision (mAP) with a threshold of 0.5. By default, in the multi-label learning, all the convolutional layers have 3×3 convolution kernels and 512 channels. The convolution layer in conditional adversarial learning also has 3×3 convolution kernel and 512 channels. These convolution parameters can be adjusted to suit different tasks, but our experiments all adopt the default setting, which yield good results.

4.2 Domain Adaptation from Real to Virtual Scenes

In this set of experiments, we used the PASCAL VOC [8] dataset as the source domain, and used the Watercolor2k and Comic2k [18] as the target domains. PASCAL VOC contains realistic images, while Watercolor2k and Comic2k contain virtual scene images. There are significant differences between the source

Table 3. Test results of domain adaptation for object detection from Cityscapes to Foggy Cityscapes in terms of mAP (%). MC and PR are same as in Table 1.

Method	MC	PR	Person	Rider	Car	Truck	Bus	Train	Motorbike	Bicycle	mAP
Source-only			25.1	32.7	31.0	12.5	23.9	9.1	23.7	29.1	23.4
BDC-Faster [31]			26.4	37.2	42.4	21.2	29.2	12.3	22.6	28.9	27.5
DA-Faster [2]			25.0	31.0	40.5	22.1	35.3	20.2	20.0	27.1	27.6
SC-DA [44]			33.5	38.0	**48.5**	26.5	39.0	23.3	28.0	33.6	33.8
MAF [17]			28.2	39.5	43.9	23.8	39.9	33.3	29.2	33.9	34.0
SW-DA [31]			**36.2**	35.3	43.5	30.0	29.9	42.3	32.6	24.5	34.3
DD-MRL [19]			30.8	40.5	44.3	27.2	38.4	34.5	28.4	32.2	34.6
MTOR [1]			30.6	41.4	44.0	21.9	38.6	40.6	28.3	35.6	35.1
Dense-DA [40]			33.2	**44.2**	44.8	28.2	41.8	28.7	30.5	36.5	36.0
SCL [34]			31.6	44.0	44.8	30.4	41.8	40.7	33.6	36.2	37.9
MCAR (Ours)	✓		31.2	42.5	43.8	**32.3**	41.1	33.0	32.4	36.5	36.6
	✓	✓	32.0	42.1	43.9	31.3	**44.1**	**43.4**	**37.4**	**36.6**	**38.8**
Train-on-Target			50.0	36.2	49.7	34.7	33.2	45.9	37.4	35.6	40.3

and target domains. The training set of PASCAL VOC (Trainval of PASCAL VOC 2007 and PASCAL VOC 2012) includes 20 different object labels and a total of 16,551 images. Watercolor2k and Comic2k contain 6 different classes ('bicycle', 'bird', 'car', 'cat', 'Dog', 'person'), each providing 2K images, and splitting equally into training and test sets. These 6 categories are included in the 20 categories of PASCAL VOC. We used the 1K training set in each target domain for training the domain adaptation model, while evaluating the model and report results with the 1K test set. In this experiment, we used resnet101 [16] as the backbone network of the detection model.

PASCAL VOC to Watercolor. The test detection results yield by adaptation from PASCAL VOC to Watercolor are reported in Table 1. Our proposed MCAR model is compared with the source-only baseline and the state-of-the-art adaptive object detection methods, including BDC-Faster [31], DA-Faster [2], SW-DA [31], and SCL [34]. The Train-on-Target results, obtained by training on labeled data in the target domain, are provided as upperbound reference values. We can see under the same experimental conditions, our proposed method achieves the best overall result, while only underpeforming the Train-on-Target by 2.6%. Comparing to source only, our method achieves a remarkable overall performance improvement of 9.8%. Although SW-DA [31] confirmed the validity of local and global feature alignment and showed a significant performance improvement over other methods, our method surpasses SW-DA by 2.7%. Meanwhile, our method also outperforms SCL [34] which relies on stacked multi-level feature alignment. The results suggest the proposed multi-label learning based feature alignment and prediction regularization are effective.

PASCAL VOC to Comic. The results of adaptation from PASCAL VOC to Comic are reported in Table 2. Again, the proposed MCAR method achieved the best adaptive detection result. It outperforms the baseline, source-only (trained on source domain data without any adaptation), by 13.8%, and outperforms the best comparison method, SW-DA, by 4.1%, These results again show that our model is very suitable for adaptive multi-object detection.

4.3   Adaptation from Clear to Foggy Scenes

In this experiment, we perform adaptive object detection from normal clear images to foggy images. We use the Cityscapes dataset as the source domain. Its images came from 27 different urban scenes, where the annotated bounding boxes are generated by the original pixel annotations. We use the Foggy Cityscapes dataset as the target domain. Its images have been rendered by Cityscapes, which can simulate fog in real road conditions with deep rendering. They contain 8 categories: 'person', 'rider', 'car', 'truck', 'bus', 'train', 'motorcycle' and 'bicycle'. In this experiment, we used vgg16 [35] as the backbone of the detection model. We recorded the test results on the validation set of Foggy Cityscapes.

The results are reported in the Table 3. We can see the proposed MCAR method achieved the best adaptive detection result. It outperforms source-only by 15.4%, and outperforms the two best comparison methods, Dense-DA [40] and SCL [34], by 2.8% and 0.9%. Moreover, it is worth noting that the performance of the proposed approach is very close to the Train-on-Target; the result of the Train-on-Target is only 1.5% higher than ours. Due to the very complex road conditions in this task, although the multi-label classifier is more capable of category judgment than the detection model, its accuracy is not much higher. Hence in this experiment, we used the combination of the multi-label category prediction and the object detection level category prediction. That is, we used $softmax(\mathbf{p}+\mathbf{q})$ as the label category information for the conditional adversarial feature alignment. This experiment presents and validates a natural variant of the proposed model.

4.4   Ablation Study

The proposed MCAR model has two major mechanisms, Multilabel-conditional adversary (MC) and Prediction based Regularization (PR), which are incorporated into the learning process through the three auxiliary loss terms in Eq. (7): the conditional adversary loss $\mathcal{L}_{adv}$, the multi-label prediction loss $\mathcal{L}_{multi}$, and the prediction regularization loss $\mathcal{L}_{kl}$. The conditional adversary loss uses the multi-label prediction outputs as its conditions, and hence the two loss terms, $\mathcal{L}_{adv}$ and $\mathcal{L}_{multi}$, together form the multilabel-conditional adversary (MC), while the prediction regularization (PR) is also built on the multi-label prediction outputs through the regularization loss $\mathcal{L}_{kl}$. To investigate the impact of these loss components, we conducted a more comprehensive ablation study on the adaptive detection task from Cityscapes to Foggy Cityscapes by comparing MCAR with its multiple variants. The variant methods and results are reported in Table 4.

We can see that dropping the conditional adversary loss ($MCAR$-w/o-adv) leads to large performance degradation. This makes sense since the adversarial

Table 4. The ablation study results in terms of mAP(%) on the adaptive detection task of Cityscapes → Foggy Cityscapes. "w/o-adv" indicates dropping the conditional adversary loss; "uadv" indicates replacing the conditional adversary loss with an unconditional adversary loss; "w/o-PR" indicates dropping the prediction regularization loss; and "w/o-MP-PR" indicates dropping both the multilabel prediction loss and the prediction regularization loss.

Method	Person	Rider	Car	Truck	Bus	Train	Motorbike	Bicycle	mAP
MCAR	32.0	42.1	43.9	31.3	44.1	43.4	37.4	36.6	**38.8**
MCAR-w/o-PR	31.2	42.5	43.8	32.3	41.1	33.0	32.4	36.5	36.6
MCAR-uadv	31.7	42.0	45.7	30.4	39.7	14.9	28.6	36.5	33.7
MCAR-uadv-w/o-PR	32.8	40.1	43.8	23.0	30.9	14.3	30.3	33.1	31.0
MCAR-uadv-w/o-MP-PR	30.5	43.2	41.4	21.7	31.4	13.7	29.8	32.6	30.5
MCAR-w/o-adv	25.0	34.9	34.2	13.9	29.9	10.0	22.5	30.2	25.1

Table 5. Parameter sensitivity analysis on the adaptation task from PASCAL VOC to watercolor.

λ	0.5					γ	5				
γ	1	3	5	7	9	λ	0.1	0.25	0.5	0.75	1
mAP	44.0	46.1	**54.4**	49.1	44.8	mAP	49.1	50.2	**54.4**	50.1	49.3

loss is the foundation for cross-domain feature alignment. By replacing the conditional adversary loss with an unconditional adversary loss, *MCAR-uadv* loses the multilabel-conditional adversary (MC) component, which leads to remarkable performance degradation and verifies the usefulness of the multi-label prediction based cross-domain multi-modal feature alignment. Dropping the prediction regularization loss from either *MCAR*, which leads to *MCAR-w/o-PR*, or *MCAR-uadv*, which leads to *MCAR-uadv-w/o-PR*, induces additional performance degradation. This verifies the effectiveness of the prediction regularization strategy, which is built on the multi-label prediction outputs as well. Moreover, by further dropping the multi-label prediction loss from *MCAR-uadv-w/o-PR*, the variant *MCAR-uadv-w/o-MP-PR*'s performance also drops slightly. Overall these results validated the effectiveness of the proposed MC and PR mechanisms, as well as the multiple auxiliary loss terms in the proposed learning objective.

4.5   Further Analysis

Feature Visualization. On the task of adaptation from Cityscapes to Foggy Cityscapes, we used t-SNE [26] to compare the distribution of induced features between our model and the Source-only model (clear to fogg scenes). The results are shown in Fig. 3. We can see that with the feature distribution obtained by source-only (Fig. 3(a)), the source domain and target domain are obviously separated, which shows the existence of domain divergence. By contrast, our proposed method produced features that can well confuse the domain discriminators. This

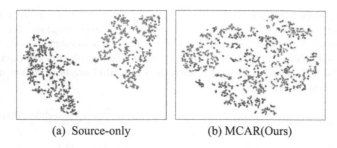

(a) Source-only   (b) MCAR(Ours)

Fig. 3. Feature visualization results. (a) and (b) respectively represent the feature distribution results of the Source-only model and our model in the clear (Cityscapes) and foggy (Foggy Cityscapes) scenes. Red indicates from the source domain and blue indicates from the target domain (Color figure online)

suggests that our proposed model has the capacity to bridge the domain distribution divergence and induce domain invariant features.

Parameters Sensitivity Analysis. We conducted sensitivity analysis on the two hyperparameters, λ and γ using the adaption task from PASCAL VOC to Watercolor. λ controls the weight of adversarial feature alignment, while γ controls the degree of focusing on hard-to-classify examples. Other hyperparameters are set to their default values. We conducted the experiment by fixing the value of γ to adjust λ, and then fixing λ to adjust γ. Table 5 presents the results. We can see with the decrease of parameter γ from its default value 5, the test performance degrades as the influence of domain classifier on difficult samples is weakened and the contribution of easy samples is increased. When $\gamma = 1$, it leads to the same result as the basic model, suggesting the domain regulation ability basically fails to play its role. On the other hand, a very large γ value is not good either, as the most difficult samples will dominate. For λ, we find that $\lambda = 0.5$ leads to the best performance. As detection is still the main task, it makes sense to have the $\lambda < 1$. When $\lambda = 0$, it degrades to a basic model without feature alignment. Therefore, some value in the middle would be a proper choice.

Qualitative Results. Object detection results are suitable to be qualitatively judged through visualization. Hence we present some qualitative adaptive detection results in the target domain in Fig. 4. The top row of Fig. 4 presents the qualitative detection result of three state-of-the-art adaptive detection methods, DA-Faster, SW-DA, and MCAR (ours), and the ground-truth on an image from Watercolor. We can see both 'DA-Faster' and 'SW-DA' have some false positives, while failing to detect the object of 'dog'. Our model correctly detected both the 'person' and the 'dog'. The bottom row of Fig. 4 presents the detection results of the DA methods and the ground-truth on an image from Foggy Cityscapes. We can see it is obvious that the cars in the distance are very blurred and difficult to detect due to the fog. The DA-Faster and SW-DA fail to find these cars, while our model successfully detected them.

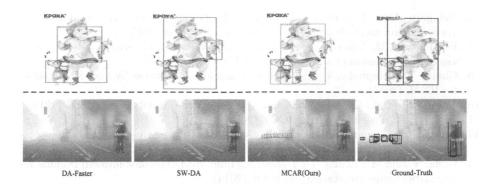

Fig. 4. Qualitative results on adaptive detection. The top row presents examples of domain adaptive detection from PASCAL VOC to Watercolor. The bottom row shows examples of adaptive detection from Cityscapes to Foggy Cityscapes. The green box represents the results obtained by the detection models, and the blue box represents the ground-truth annotation. (Color figure online)

5   Conclusion

In this paper, we propose an unsupervised multi-object cross-domain detection method. We exploit multi-label object recognition as a dual auxiliary task to reveal the category information of images from the global features. The cross-domain feature alignment is conducted by performing conditional adversarial distribution alignment with the combination input of global features and multi-label prediction outputs. We also use the idea of mutual learning to improve the detection performance by enforcing consistent object category predictions between the multi-label prediction over global features and the object classification over detection region proposals. We conducted experiments on multiple cross-domain multi-objective detection datasets. The results show the proposed model achieved the state-of-the-art performance.

References

1. Cai, Q., Pan, Y., Ngo, C.W., Tian, X., Duan, L., Yao, T.: Exploring object relation in mean teacher for cross-domain detection. In: CVPR (2019)
2. Chen, Y., Li, W., Sakaridis, C., Dai, D., Van Gool, L.: Domain adaptive faster R-CNN for object detection in the wild. In: CVPR (2018)
3. Choi, J., Kim, T., Kim, C.: Self-ensembling with GAN-based data augmentation for domain adaptation in semantic segmentation. In: ICCV (2019)
4. Cicek, S., Soatto, S.: Unsupervised domain adaptation via regularized conditional alignment. arXiv preprint arXiv:1905.10885 (2019)
5. Cordts, M., et al.: The cityscapes dataset for semantic urban scene understanding. In: CVPR (2016)
6. Dai, J., Li, Y., He, K., Sun, J.: R-FCN: object detection via region-based fully convolutional networks. In: NIPS (2016)

7. Dziugaite, G.K., Roy, D.M., Ghahramani, Z.: Training generative neural networks via maximum mean discrepancy optimization. In: UAI (2015)
8. Everingham, M., Van Gool, L., Williams, C.K., Winn, J., Zisserman, A.: The pascal visual object classes (voc) challenge. IJCV (2010)
9. Ganin, Y., Lempitsky, V.: Unsupervised domain adaptation by backpropagation. In: ICML (2015)
10. Ganin, Y., et al.: Domain-adversarial training of neural networks. JMLR (2016)
11. Girshick, R.: Fast R-CNN. In: ICCV (2015)
12. Girshick, R., Donahue, J., Darrell, T., Malik, J.: Rich feature hierarchies for accurate object detection and semantic segmentation. In: CVPR (2014)
13. Gong, Y., Jia, Y., Leung, T., Toshev, A., Ioffe, S.: Deep convolutional ranking for multilabel image annotation. In: ICLR (2014)
14. Goodfellow, I., et al.: Generative adversarial nets. In: NIPS (2014)
15. He, K., Gkioxari, G., Dollár, P., Girshick, R.: Mask R-CNN. In: ICCV (2017)
16. He, K., Zhang, X., Ren, S., Sun, J.: Deep residual learning for image recognition. In: CVPR (2016)
17. He, Z., Zhang, L.: Multi-adversarial faster-RCNN for unrestricted object detection. In: ICCV (2019)
18. Inoue, N., Furuta, R., Yamasaki, T., Aizawa, K.: Cross-domain weakly-supervised object detection through progressive domain adaptation. In: CVPR (2018)
19. Kim, T., Jeong, M., Kim, S., Choi, S., Kim, C.: Diversify and match: a domain adaptive representation learning paradigm for object detection. In: CVPR (2019)
20. Kulis, B., Saenko, K., Darrell, T.: What you saw is not what you get: Domain adaptation using asymmetric kernel transforms. In: CVPR (2011)
21. Lin, T.Y., Dollár, P., Girshick, R., He, K., Hariharan, B., Belongie, S.: Feature pyramid networks for object detection. In: CVPR (2017)
22. Lin, T.Y., Goyal, P., Girshick, R., He, K., Dollár, P.: Focal loss for dense object detection. In: ICCV (2017)
23. Liu, W., et al.: SSD: single shot multibox detector. In: Leibe, B., Matas, J., Sebe, N., Welling, M. (eds.) ECCV 2016. LNCS, vol. 9905, pp. 21–37. Springer, Cham (2016). https://doi.org/10.1007/978-3-319-46448-0_2
24. Long, J., Shelhamer, E., Darrell, T.: Fully convolutional networks for semantic segmentation. In: CVPR (2015)
25. Long, M., Cao, Z., Wang, J., Jordan, M.I.: Conditional adversarial domain adaptation. In: NIPS (2018)
26. van der Maaten, L., Hinton, G.: Visualizing data using t-SNE. JMLR (2008)
27. Mirza, M., Osindero, S.: Conditional generative adversarial nets. arXiv preprint arXiv:1411.1784 (2014)
28. Redmon, J., Farhadi, A.: Yolov3: an incremental improvement. arXiv preprint arXiv:1804.02767 (2018)
29. Ren, S., He, K., Girshick, R., Sun, J.: Faster R-CNN: towards real-time object detection with region proposal networks. In: NIPS (2015)
30. Russo, P., Carlucci, F.M., Tommasi, T., Caputo, B.: From source to target and back: symmetric bi-directional adaptive GAN. In: CVPR (2018)
31. Saito, K., Ushiku, Y., Harada, T., Saenko, K.: Strong-weak distribution alignment for adaptive object detection. In: CVPR (2019)
32. Sakaridis, C., Dai, D., Van Gool, L.: Semantic foggy scene understanding with synthetic data. IJCV (2018)
33. Shen, J., Qu, Y., Zhang, W., Yu, Y.: Wasserstein distance guided representation learning for domain adaptation. In: AAAI (2018)

34. Shen, Z., Maheshwari, H., Yao, W., Savvides, M.: SCL: towards accurate domain adaptive object detection via gradient detach based stacked complementary losses. arXiv preprint arXiv:1911.02559 (2019)
35. Simonyan, K., Zisserman, A.: Very deep convolutional networks for large-scale image recognition. arXiv preprint arXiv:1409.1556 (2014)
36. Szegedy, C., et al.: Going deeper with convolutions. In: CVPR (2015)
37. Tsai, Y.H., Hung, W.C., Schulter, S., Sohn, K., Yang, M.H., Chandraker, M.: Learning to adapt structured output space for semantic segmentation. In: CVPR (2018)
38. Tsai, Y.H., Sohn, K., Schulter, S., Chandraker, M.: Domain adaptation for structured output via discriminative representations. In: ICCV (2019)
39. Tzeng, E., Hoffman, J., Saenko, K., Darrell, T.: Adversarial discriminative domain adaptation. In: CVPR (2017)
40. Xie, R., Yu, F., Wang, J., Wang, Y., Zhang, L.: Multi-level domain adaptive learning for cross-domain detection. In: ICCV (2019)
41. Zhang, M.L., Zhou, Z.H.: Multilabel neural networks with applications to functional genomics and text categorization. TKDE (2006)
42. Zhang, Y., David, P., Gong, B.: Curriculum domain adaptation for semantic segmentation of urban scenes. In: ICCV (2017)
43. Zhao, H., Shi, J., Qi, X., Wang, X., Jia, J.: Pyramid scene parsing network. In: CVPR (2017)
44. Zhu, X., Pang, J., Yang, C., Shi, J., Lin, D.: Adapting object detectors via selective cross-domain alignment. In: CVPR (2019)

Table Structure Recognition Using Top-Down and Bottom-Up Cues

Sachin Raja(✉), Ajoy Mondal, and C. V. Jawahar

Center for Visual Information Technology, International Institute of Information Technology, Hyderabad, India
sachinraja13@gmail.com, {ajoy.mondal,jawahar}@iiit.ac.in

Abstract. Tables are information-rich structured objects in document images. While significant work has been done in localizing tables as graphic objects in document images, only limited attempts exist on table structure recognition. Most existing literature on structure recognition depends on extraction of meta-features from the PDF document or on the optical character recognition (OCR) models to extract low-level layout features from the image. However, these methods fail to generalize well because of the absence of meta-features or errors made by the OCR when there is a significant variance in table layouts and text organization. In our work, we focus on tables that have complex structures, dense content, and varying layouts with no dependency on meta-features and/or OCR.

We present an approach for table structure recognition that combines cell detection and interaction modules to localize the cells and predict their row and column associations with other detected cells. We incorporate structural constraints as additional differential components to the loss function for cell detection. We empirically validate our method on the publicly available real-world datasets - ICDAR-2013, ICDAR-2019 (cTDaR) archival, UNLV, SciTSR, SciTSR-COMP, TableBank, and PubTabNet. Our attempt opens up a new direction for table structure recognition by combining top-down (table cells detection) and bottom-up (structure recognition) cues in visually understanding the tables.

Keywords: Document image · Table detection · Table cell detection · Row and column association · Table structure recognition

1 Introduction

Deep neural networks have shown promising results in understanding document layouts [1–3]. However, more needs to be done for structural and semantic understanding. Among these, the problem of table structure recognition has been of

Electronic supplementary material The online version of this chapter (https://doi.org/10.1007/978-3-030-58604-1_5) contains supplementary material, which is available to authorized users.

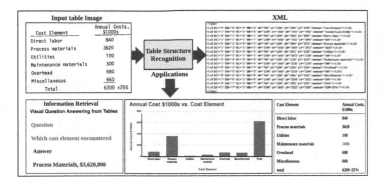

Fig. 1. The figure depicts the problem of recognizing table structure from it's image. This opens up many applications including information retrieval, graphical representation and digitizing for editing.

high interest in the community [4–20]. Table structure recognition refers to representation of a table in a machine-readable format, where its layout is encoded according to a pre-defined standard [10–14,17]. It can be represented in the form of either physical [10,12,14,17] or logical formats [11,13]. While logical structure contains every cells' row and column spanning information, physical structure additionally contains bounding box coordinates. Table structure recognition is a precursor to contextual table understanding, which has a myriad of applications in business document analysis, information retrieval, visualization, and human-document interactions, as motivated in Fig. 1.

Table structure recognition is a challenging problem due to complex structures and high variability in table layouts [4–17]. Early attempts in this space are dependent on extraction of hand-crafted features and meta-data extracted from the PDFs on top of heuristic/rule-based algorithms [21–24] to locate tables and understanding tables by predicting/recognizing structures. These methods, however, fail to extend to scanned documents as they rely on meta-data information contained in the PDFs. They also make strong assumptions about the structure of the tables. Some of these methods are also dependent on textual information analysis which make them domain dependent. While textual features are useful, visual analysis becomes imperative for analysis of complex page objects. Inconsistency of size and density of tables, presence and location of table cell borders, variation in table cells' shapes and sizes, table cells spanning multiple rows and/or columns and multi-line content are some challenges (refer Fig. 2 for some examples) that need to be addressed to solve the problem using visual cues [4,5,21–24].

We pose the table structure recognition problem as the generation of XML containing table's physical structure in terms of bounding boxes along with spanning information and, additionally, digitized content for every cell (see Fig. 1). Since our method aims to predict this table structure given the table image only (without using any meta-information), we employ a two-step process—(a)

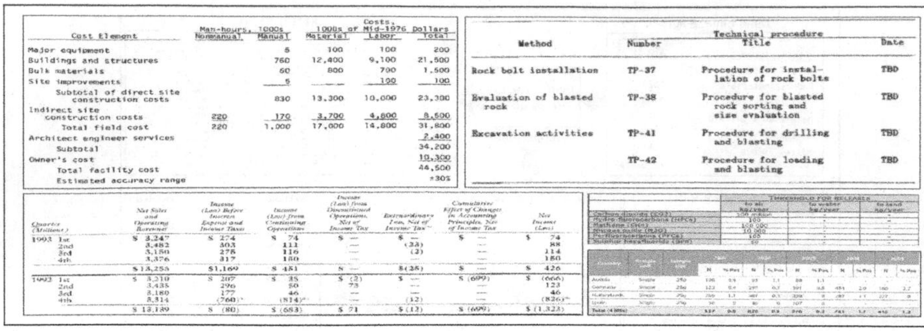

Cost Element	Man-hours, 1000s Nonmanual	Manual	Costs, 1000s of Mid-1976 Dollars Material	Labor	Total
Major equipment		5	100	100	200
Buildings and structures		760	12,400	9,100	21,500
Bulk materials		60	800	700	1,500
Site improvements		5		100	100
Subtotal of direct site construction costs		830	13,300	10,000	23,300
Indirect site construction costs	220	170	3,700	4,800	8,500
Total field cost	220	1,000	17,000	14,800	31,800
Architect engineer services					2,400
Subtotal					34,200
Owner's cost					10,300
Total facility cost					44,500
Estimated accuracy range					±30%

Method	Technical procedure Number	Title	Date
Rock bolt installation	TP-37	Procedure for installation of rock bolts	TBD
Evaluation of blasted rock	TP-38	Procedure for blasted rock sorting and size evaluation	TBD
Excavation activities	TP-41	Procedure for drilling and blasting	TBD
	TP-42	Procedure for loading and blasting	TBD

Quarter (Millions)		Net Sales and Operating Revenues	Income (Loss) Before Interest Expense and Income Taxes	Income (Loss) from Continuing Operations	Income (Loss) from Discontinued Operations, Net of Income Tax	Extraordinary Loss, Net of Income Tax	Cumulative Effect of Changes in Accounting Principles, Net of Income Tax	Net Income (Loss)
1993	1st	$ 3,247	$ 274	$ 74	$ —	$ —	$ —	$ 74
	2nd	3,482	303	111	—	(23)	—	88
	3rd	3,150	275	116	—	(2)	—	114
	4th	3,376	317	180	—	—	—	180
		$ 13,255	$1,169	$ 481	$ —	$(25)	$ —	$ 426
1992	1st	$ 3,210	$ 207	$ 35	$ (2)	$ —	$ (699)	$ (666)
	2nd	3,435	296	50	73	—	—	123
	3rd	3,180	177	46	—	—	—	46
	4th	3,314	(760)	(814)	—	(12)	—	(826)
		$ 13,139	$ (80)	$ (683)	$ 71	$ (12)	$ (699)	$ (1,323)

Fig. 2. Examples of complex table images from UNLV and ICDAR-2013 datasets. Complex tables are ones which contain partial or no ruling lines, multi-row/column spanning cells, multi-line content, many empty dense cells.

top-down: where we decompose the table image into fundamental table objects, which are table cells using a cell detection network and (b) *bottom-up:* where we re-build the entire table as a collection of all the table cells localized from the top-down process, along with their row and column associations with every other cell. We represent row and column associations of table cells using row and column adjacency matrices.

Though table detection has observed significant success [11,25–28], detection of table cells remains a challenging problem. This is because of (i) large variation in sizes and aspect ratios of different cells present in the same table, (ii) cells' inherent alignment despite high variance in text amount and text justification, (iii) lack of linguistic context in cells' content, (iv) presence of empty cells and (v) presence of cells with multi-line content. To overcome these challenges, we introduce a novel loss function that models the inherent alignment of cells in the cell detection network; and a graph-based problem formulation to build associations between the detected cells. Moreover, as detection of cells and building associations between them depend highly on one another, we present a novel end-to-end trainable architecture, termed as TabStruct-Net, for cell detection and structure recognition. We evaluate our model for physical structure recognition on benchmark datasets: SciTSR [14], SciTSR-COMP [14], ICDAR-2013 table recognition [18], ICDAR-2019 (cTDaR) archival [19], and UNLV [29]. Further, we extend the comparative analysis of the proposed work for logical structure recognition on TableBank [11] dataset. Our method sets up a new direction for table structure recognition as a collaboration of cell detection, establishing an association between localized cells and, additionally, cells' content extraction.

Our main contributions can be summarised as follows:

- We demonstrate how the top-down (cell detection) and bottom-up (structure recognition) cues can be combined visually to recognize table structures in document images.
- We present an end-to-end trainable network, termed as TabStruct-Net for training cell detection and structure recognition networks in a joint manner.

- We formulate a novel loss function (i.e., alignment loss) to incorporate structural constraints between every pair of table cells and modify Feature Pyramid Network (FPN) to capture better low-level and long-range features for cell detection.
- We enhance the visual features representation for structure recognition (built on top of model [9]) through LSTM.
- We unify results from previously published methods on table structure recognition for a thorough comparison study.

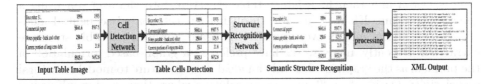

Fig. 3. Block diagram of our approach. Table detection is a precursor to table structure recognition and our method assumes that table is already localized from the input document image. The end-to-end architecture predicts cell bounding boxes and their associations jointly. From the outputs of cell detection and association predictions, XML is generated using a post-processing heuristic.

2   Related Work

In the space of document images, researchers have been working on understanding equations [30,31], figures [32,33] and tables [6–17]. Diverse table layouts, tables with many empty cells and multi-row/column spanning cells are some challenges that make table structure recognition difficult. Research in the domain of table understanding through its structure recognition from document images dated back to the early 1990s when algorithms based on heuristics were proposed [21–24,34–36]. These methods were primarily dependent on hand-crafted features and heuristics (horizontal and vertical ruling lines, spacing and geometric analysis). To avoid heuristics, Wang et al. [5] proposed a method for table structure analysis using optimization methods similar to the X-Y cut algorithm. Another technique based on column segmentation, header detection, and row segmentation to identify the table structure was proposed by Hu et al. [4]. These methods make strong assumptions about table layouts for a domain agnostic algorithm.

Many cognitive methods [6–12,14–16,37–43] have also been presented to understand table structures as they are robust to the input type (whether being scanned images or native digital). These also do not make any assumptions about the layouts, are data-driven, and are easy to fine-tune across different domains. Minghao et al. [11] proposed one class of deep learning methods to directly predict an XML from the table image using the image-to-markup model. Though this method worked well for small tables, it was not robust enough to dense and complex tables. Another set of methods is invoice specific table extraction [39,40], which were not competent for a more generic use-cases. To overcome this challenge, a combination of heuristics and cognitive methods has also been presented in [12]. Chris et al. [10] presented another interesting deep model, called SPLERGE, which is based on the fundamental idea of first splitting the table into sub-cells, and then merging semantically connected sub-cells to preserve the complete table structure. Though this algorithm showed considerable improvements over earlier methods, it was still not robust to skew present in the table images. Another interesting direction was presented by Vine et al. [42], where they used conditional generative adversarial networks to obtain table skeleton and then fit a latent table structure into the skeleton using a genetic algorithm. Khan et al. [15], through their GRU based sequential models, showed improvements over several CNN based methods for table structure extraction. Recently, many works have preferred a graph-based formulation of the problem as the graph is inherently an ideal data structure to model structural associativity. Qasim et al. [9] proposed a solution where they used graph neural networks to model table-level associativity between words. The authors validate their method on synthetic table images. Chi et al. [14] proposed another graph-based problem formulation and solution using a graph attention mechanism. While these methods made significant progress towards understanding complex structured tables, they made certain assumptions like availability of accurate word bounding boxes, accurate document text, etc. as additional inputs [6,9,14]. Our method does not make any such assumptions. We use the table image as the input and produce XML output without any other information. We demonstrate results on complex tables present in UNLV, ICDAR-2013, ICDAR-2019 cTDaR archival, SciTSR, SciTSR-COMP TableBank, and PubTabNet datasets.

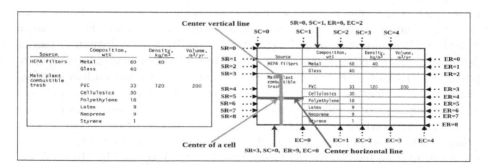

Fig. 4. Visual illustration of cell spanning information along rows and columns of a table from UNLV dataset. **Left Image:** shows original table image in UNLV and **Right Image:** illustrates ground-truth cell spanning information.

3   TabStruct-Net

Our solution for table structure recognition progresses in three steps—(a) detection of table cells; (b) establishing row/column relationships between the detected cells, and (c) post-processing step to produce the XML output as desired. Figure 3 depicts the block diagram of our approach.

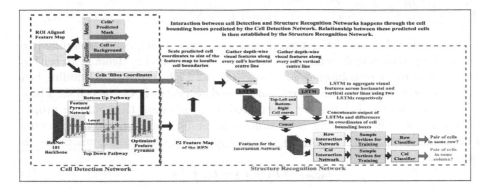

Fig. 5. Our TabStruct-Net. Modified RPN in cell detection network, which consists of both top-down and bottom-up pathways to better capture low-level visual features. P2 layer of the optimized feature pyramid is used in the structure recognition network to extract visual features.

3.1 Top-Down: Cell Detection

The first step of our solution for table structure recognition is localization of individual cells in a table image, for which we use the popular object detection paradigm. The difference from natural scene images, however, is an inherent association between table cells. Recent success of R-CNNs [44] and its improved modifications (Fast R-CNN [45], Faster R-CNN [46], Mask R-CNN [47]) have shown significant success in object detection in natural scene images. Hence, we employ Mask R-CNN [47] for our solution with additional enhancements—(a) we augment the Region Proposal Network (RPN) with dilated convolutions [48,49] to better capture long-range row and column visual features of the table. This improves detection of multi-row/column spanning and multi-line cells; (b) inspired by [50], we append the feature pyramid network with a top-down pathway, which propagates high-level semantic information to low-level feature maps. This allows the network to work better for cells with varying scales; and (c) we append additional losses during the training phase in order to model the inherent structural constraints. We formulate two ways of incorporating this information—(i) through an end-to-end training of cell detection and the structure recognition networks (explained next), and (ii) through a novel alignment loss function. For the latter, we make use of the fact that every pair of cells is aligned horizontally if they span the same row and aligned vertically if they span the same column. For the ground truth, where tight bounding boxes around the cells' content are provided [13,14,18], we employ an additional ground truth pre-processing step to ensure that bounding boxes of cells in the same row and same column are aligned vertically and horizontally, respectively. We model these constraints during the training in the following manner:

$$L_1 = \sum_{r \in SR} \sum_{c_i, c_j \in r} ||y1_{c_i} - y1_{c_j}||_2^2, \; L_2 = \sum_{r \in ER} \sum_{c_i, c_j \in r} ||y2_{c_i} - y2_{c_j}||_2^2$$
$$L_3 = \sum_{c \in SC} \sum_{c_i, c_j \in c} ||x1_{c_i} - x1_{c_j}||_2^2 \text{ and } L_4 = \sum_{c \in EC} \sum_{c_i, c_j \in c} ||x2_{c_i} - x2_{c_j}||_2^2$$

Here, SR, SC, ER and EC represent starting row, starting column, ending row and ending column indices as shown in Fig. 4. Also, c_i and c_j denote two cells in a particular row r or column c; $x1_{c_i}$, $y1_{c_i}$, $x2_{c_i}$ and $y2_{c_i}$ represent bounding box coordinates X-start, Y-start, X-end and Y-end respectively of the cell c_i. These losses (L_1, L_2, L_3, L_4) can be interpreted as constraints that enforce proper alignment of cells beginning from same row, ending on same row, beginning from same column and ending on same column respectively. Alignment loss is defined as

$$L_{align} = L_1 + L_2 + L_3 + L_4. \tag{1}$$

3.2   Bottom-Up: Structure Recognition

We formulate the table structure recognition using graphs similar to [9]. We consider each cell of the table as a vertex and construct two adjacency matrices - a row matrix M_{row} and a column matrix M_{col} which describe the association between cells with respect to rows and columns. $M_{row}, M_{col} \in \mathbb{R}^{N_{cells} \times N_{cells}}$. $M_{row_{i,j}} = 1$ or $M_{col_{i,j}} = 1$ if cells i, j belong to the same row or column, else 0.

The structure recognition network aims to predict row and column relationships between the cells predicted by the cell detection module during training and testing. During training, only those predicted table cells are used for structure recognition which overlap with the ground truth table cells having an IoU greater than or equal to 0.5. This network has three components:

- *Visual Component:* We use visual features from P2 layer (refer Fig. 5) of the feature pyramid based on the linear interpolation of cell bounding boxes predicted by the cell detection module. In order to encode cells' visual characteristics across their entire height and width, we pass the gathered P2 features for every cell along their centre horizontal and centre vertical lines using LSTM [51] to obtain the final visual features (refer Fig. 5) (as opposed to visual features corresponding to cells' centroids only as in [52]).
- *Interaction Component:* We use the DGCNN architecture based on graph neural networks used in [52] to model the interaction between geometrically neighboring detected cells. It's output, termed as interaction features, is a fixed dimensional vector for every cell that has information aggregated from its neighbouring table cells.
- *Classification Component:* For a pair of table cells, the interaction features are concatenated and appended with difference between cells' bounding box coordinates. This is fed as an input to the row/column classifiers to predict row/column associations. Please note that we use the same [52] Monte Carlo based sampling to ensure efficient training and class balancing. During testing time, however, predictions are made for every unique pair of table cells.

We train the cell detection and structure recognition networks in a joint manner (termed as TabStruct-Net) to collectively predict cell bounding boxes along with row and column adjacency matrices. Further, the two structure recognition pathways for row and column adjacency matrices are put together in parallel. The visual features prepared using LSTMs for every vertex are duplicated for both the pathways, after which they work in a parallel manner. The overall empirical loss of TabStruct-Net is given by:

$$L = L_{box} + L_{cls} + L_{mask} + L_{align} + L_{gnn}, \qquad (2)$$

where L_{box}, L_{cls} and L_{mask} are bounding box regression loss, classification loss and mask loss, respectively defined in Mask R-CNN [47], L_{align} is alignment loss which is modeled as a regularizer (defined in Eq. 1) and L_{gnn} is the cross-entropy loss back propagated from the structure recognition module of TabStruct-Net. The additional loss components help the model in better alignment of cells belonging to same rows/columns during training, and in a sense fine-tunes the predicted bounding boxes that makes it easier for post-processing and structure recognition in the subsequent step.

3.3   Post-Processing

Once all the cells and their row/column adjacency matrices are predicted, we create the XML interpretable output as a post-processing step. From the cell coordinates along with row and column adjacency matrix, SR, SC, ER and EC indexes are assigned to each cell, which indicate spanning of that cell along rows and columns. We use Tesseract [53] to extract the content of every predicted cell. The XML output for every table image finally contains coordinates of predicted cell bounding boxes and along with cell spanning information and its content.

4   Experiments

4.1   Datasets

We use various benchmark datasets—SciTSR [14], SciTSR-COMP [14], ICDAR-2013 table recognition [18], ICDAR-2019 (cTDaR) archival [19], UNLV [29], Marmot extended [12], TableBank [11] and PubTabNet [13] datasets for extracting structure information of tables. Statistics of these datasets are listed in Table 1.

Table 1. Statistics of the datasets used for our experiments.

	SciTSR	SciTSR COMP	ICDAR 2013	ICDAR-2013 -partial	ICDAR 2019	UNLV	UNLV- partial	Marmot extended	Table Bank	PubTabNet
Train	12000	12000	-	124	600	-	446	1016	145K	339K
Test	3000	716	158	34	150	558	112	-	1000	114K

4.2 Baseline Methods

We compare the performance of our TabStruct-Net against seven benchmark methods—DeepDeSRT [7], TableNet [12], GraphTSR [14], SPLERGE [10], DGCNN [9], Bi-directional GRU [15] and Image-to-Text [11].

4.3 Implementation Details

TabStruct-Net[1] has been trained and evaluated with table images scaled to a fixed size of 1536×1536 while maintaining the original aspect ratio as the input. While training, cell-level bounding boxes along with row and column adjacency matrices (prepared from start-row, start-column, end-row and end-column indices) are used as the ground truth. We use NVIDIA TITAN X GPU with 12 GB memory for our experiments and a batch-size of 1. Instead of using 3×3 convolution on the output feature maps from the FPN, we use a dilated convolution with filter size of 2×2 and dilation parameter of 2. Also, we use the ResNet-101 backbone that is pre-trained on MS-COCO [54] dataset. Dilated convolution blocks of filter size 7 are used in the FPN. To compute region proposals, we use 0.5, 1 and 2 as the anchor scale and anchor box sizes of 8, 16, 32, 64 and 128. LSTMs used to gather visual features have a depth of 128. The final memory state of the LSTM layers is concatenated with the cell's coordinates to prepare features for the interaction network. Further, for generation of the row/column adjacency matrices, we use 2400 as the maximum number of vertices keeping in mind dense tables. Next, features from 40 neighboring vertices are aggregated using an edge convolution layer followed by a dense layer of size 64 with ReLu activation. Since every input table may contain hundreds of table cells, training can be a time consuming process. To achieve faster training, we employ a two-stage training process. In the first stage, we use 2014 anchors and 512 RoIs, and in the second stage, we use with 3072 anchors and 2048 RoIs. During both the stages, we use 0.001 as the learning rate, 0.9 as the momentum and 0.0001 as the weight decay regularisation.

Table 2. Shows the performance of our TabStruct-Net for physical table structure recognition on various benchmark datasets.

Test dataset	Train dataset	S-A			S-B		
		P↑	R↑	F1↑	P↑	R↑	F1↑
ICDAR-2013	SciTSR	0.915	0.897	0.906	0.976	0.985	0.981
ICDAR-2013-partial	SciTSR	0.930	0.908	0.919	0.991	0.993	0.992
SciTSR	SciTSR	0.927	0.913	0.920	0.989	0.993	0.991
SciTSR-comp	SciTSR	0.909	0.882	0.895	0.981	0.987	0.984
UNLV-partial	SciTSR	0.849	0.828	0.839	0.992	0.994	0.993
ICDAR-2019	SciTSR	0.595	0.572	0.583	0.924	0.899	0.911
ICDAR-2019	ICDAR-2019	0.803	0.768	0.785	0.975	0.957	0.966
ICDAR-2019	SciTSR+ICDAR-2019	0.822	0.787	0.804	0.975	0.958	0.966

---

[1] Our code is available at https://github.com/sachinraja13/TabStructNet.git.

Table 3. Shows the performance of our TabStruct-Net for logical table structure recognition on various benchmark datasets.

Test dataset	Train dataset	Metric	Score
TableBank-Word	SciTSR	BLEU	0.914
TableBank-LaTeX	SciTSR	BLEU	0.937
TableBank-Word+LaTeX	SciTSR	BLEU	0.916
PubTabNet	SciTSR	TEDS	0.901

4.4 Evaluation Measures

We use various existing measures—precision, recall and F1 [14,18,29] to evaluate the performance of our model for recognition of physical structure of tables. For recognition of logical structure of tables, we use BLEU [55] score as used in [11] and Tree-Edit-Distance-based similarity (TEDS) [13]. Since XML is our final output for table structure recognition, we also use BLEU [55], CIDEr [56] and ROUGE [57] scores to compare generated XML and ground truth XML on spanning information and content of every cell. We first calculate these scores separately on each table and then compute both micro-averaged score and macro-averaged score as the final result. We consistently use an IoU threshold of 0.6 to compute the confusion matrix. Please note that only non-empty table cells are considered similar to [18] for the evaluation.

4.5 Experimental Setup

One major challenge in the comparison study with the existing methods is the inconsistent use of additional information (e.g., meta-features extracted from the PDFs [10], content-level bounding boxes from ground truths [12,14] and cell's location features generated from synthetic dataset [9]). Hence, we do experiments in two different setups

- **Setup-A (S-A):** using only table image as the input
- **Setup-B (S-B):** using table image along with additional information (e.g., cell bounding boxes) as the input. For this, instead of removing the cell detection component from the network, we ignore the predicted boxes and use the ground truth ones as input for structure recognition.

5 Results on Table Structure Recognition

Tables 2 and 3 summarize the performance of our model on standard datasets used in the space of table structure recognition.

5.1   Analysis of Results

Table 4 presents results on ICDAR-2013 dataset. In S-A, we observe that our model outperforms DeepDeSRT [7] method by a 27.5% F1 score. This is because cell coordinates for the latter are obtained by row and column intersections, making it unable to recognize cells that span multiple rows/columns. For dense tables (small inter-row spacing), row segmentation results of DeepDeSRT combined multiple rows into one in several instances. split+Heuristic [10] method outperforms TabStruct-Net by a small margin, however, it requires ICDAR-2013 dataset-specific cell merging heuristics and is trained on a considerably larger set of images. Therefore, a direct comparison of (split+Heuristic) with our method is not fair. Nevertheless, comparable results of TabStruct-Net indicates its robustness to ICDAR-2013 dataset, without using any kind of dataset-specific postprocessing. However, if compared under the same training environment and no post-processing, our model outperforms SPLERGE with a 3% average F1 score. SPLERGE works well for datasets where ground truth bounding boxes are annotated at the content-level instead of cell-level. This is because it allows for a wider area for a prospective prediction of a row/column separator. Further, since it is based on cell detection through the row and column separators, it is not agnostic to input image noise such as skew and rotations. This method is susceptible to dataset-specific post-processing as opposed to ours, where no post-processing is needed.

Table 4. Comparison of results for physical structure recognition on ICDAR-2013 dataset. **#Images:** indicates number of table images in the training set. **Heuristic:** indicates dataset specific cell merging rules for various models in [10].

Method	Training		Experimental	P↑	R↑	F1↑
	Dataset	#Images	Setup			
DeepDeSRT [7]	SciTSR	12K	S-A	0.631	0.619	0.625
SPLERGE [10]	SciTSR	12K	S-A	0.883	0.875	0.879
split+Heuristic [10]	Private [10]	83K	S-A	**0.938**	**0.922**	**0.930**
TabStruct-Net (our)	SciTSR	12K	S-A	0.915	0.897	0.906
TableNet [12]	Marmot Extended	1K	S-B	0.922	0.899	0.910
GraphTSR [14]	SciTSR	12K	S-B	0.885	0.860	0.872
split-PDF [10]	Private [10]	83K	S-B	0.920	0.913	0.916
split-PDF+Heuristic [10]	Private [10]	83K	S-B	0.959	0.946	0.953
DGCNN [9]	SciTSR	12K	S-B	0.972	0.983	0.977
TabStruct-Net (our)	SciTSR	12K	S-B	**0.976**	**0.985**	**0.981**

In S-B, TabStruct-Net sets up a state-of-the-art benchmark on the ICDAR-2013 dataset, outperforming all the existing methods [9,10,12,14]. It is further interesting to note that our technique outperforms split-PDF+Heuristic model also without needing any post-processing. It is because our enhancements to the DGCNN [9] model can capture the visual characteristics of a cell across a larger span through LSTMs. We observe that our model achieves significantly improved performance when content-level bounding boxes are used instead of cell-level, which are much easier to obtain with the help of OCR tools and PDF meta-information.

Table 5. Physical structure recognition results on ICDAR-2013 dataset for varying IoU thresholds to demonstrate TabStruct-Net's robustness. **ES:** Experimental Setup, **CD:** Cell Detection, **TH:** IoU threshold value, **SR:** Structure Recognition, **P2:** using visual features from P2 layer of the FPN instead of using separate convolution blocks, **LSTM:** use of LSTMs to model visual features along center-horizontal and center-vertical lines for every cell, **TD+BU:** use of Top-Down and Bottom-Up pathways in the FPN, **AL:** addition of alignment loss as a regularizer to TabStruct-Net.

CD Network	SR Network	IoU	CD Scores			SR Scores		
		TH	P↑	R↑	F1↑	P↑	R↑	F1↑
Mask R-CNN+TD+BU+AL	DGCNN+P2+LSTM	0.5	**0.935**	**0.942**	**0.938**	**0.927**	**0.911**	**0.919**
		0.6	0.921	0.926	0.923	0.915	0.897	0.906
		0.7	0.815	0.820	0.817	0.797	0.785	0.791
		0.8	0.638	0.653	0.645	0.629	0.615	0.622
		0.9	0.275	0.312	0.292	0.247	0.236	0.241

Table 5 shows the performance of our technique under the varying IoU thresholds. It can be inferred from the table that our model achieves an F1 score of 79.1% on structure recognition with an IoU threshold value of as high as 0.7. For the IoU values of 0.5 and 0.6, our model's performance is 91.9% and 90.6%, respectively. It demonstrates the robustness of our model. Figures 6 and 7 display some qualitative outputs of our method on the datasets discussed in Sect. 4.1. Figure 8 shows some of the failure cases of cell detection by our method. It can be seen that our model fails for table images that have large amounts of empty spaces. Supplementary material has (i) more quantitative results, (ii) more qualitative examples, (iii) specific implementation details, (iv) detailed comparative analysis, IoU variation results, and ablation study on all the datasets.

5.2   Ablation Study

Table 6 shows the outcome of our enhancements to Mask R-CNN [47] and DGCNN [9] models for both cell detection and structure recognition networks under S-A and S-B. From the table, it can be observed that our additions to the networks result in a significant increase of 4% average F1 scores on cell detection and structure recognition tasks. The novel alignment loss, along with the use of top-down and bottom-up pathways in the FPN results in an improvement of 2.3% F1 score for cell detection and 2.4% on structure recognition. Use of LSTMs and P2 layer output to prepare visual features for structure recognition results in a 2.1% improvement of F1 scores. Interestingly, because both models are trained together in an end-to-end fashion, cell detection's effect is also observed in the form of a 1.5% average F1 score. This empirically bolsters our claim of using an end-to-end architecture for cell detection and, in turn, structure recognition.

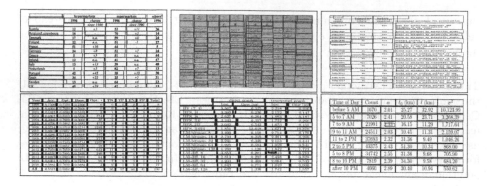

Fig. 6. Sample intermediate cell detection results of TabStruct-Net on table images of ICDAR-2013, ICDAR-2019 cTDaR and UNLV, SciTSR, SciTSR-COMP and TableBank datasets.

Table 6. Ablation study for physical structure recognition on ICDAR-2013 dataset. **ES:** Experimental Setup, **CD:** Cell Detection, **SR:** Structure Recognition, **P2:** using visual features from P2 layer of the FPN instead of using separate convolution blocks, LSTM: use of LSTMs to model visual features along center-horizontal and center-vertical lines for every cell, TD+BU: use of Top-Down and Bottom-Up pathways in the FPN, **AL:** addition of alignment loss as a regularizer to TabStruct-Net.

ES	CD Network	SR Network	CD Scores			SR Scores		
			P↑	R↑	F1↑	P↑	R↑	F1↑
S-A	Mask R-CNN	DGCNN	0.885	0.890	0.887	0.871	0.860	0.865
	Mask R-CNN	DGCNN+P2	0.886	0.892	0.889	0.877	0.863	0.870
	Mask R-CNN	DGCNN+P2+LSTM	0.898	0.904	0.901	0.885	0.879	0.882
	Mask R-CNN+TD+BU	DGCNN	0.895	0.899	0.897	0.883	0.867	0.875
	Mask R-CNN+TD+BU	DGCNN+P2	0.895	0.901	0.898	0.886	0.870	0.878
	Mask R-CNN+TD+BU	DGCNN+P2+LSTM	0.904	0.910	0.907	0.892	0.884	0.888
	Mask R-CNN+TD+BU+AL	DGCNN	0.905	0.911	0.908	0.891	0.879	0.885
	Mask R-CNN+TD+BU+AL	DGCNN+P2	0.914	0.920	0.917	0.906	0.885	0.895
	Mask R-CNN+TD+BU+AL	DGCNN+P2+LSTM	**0.921**	**0.926**	**0.924**	**0.915**	**0.897**	**0.906**
S-B	-NA-	DGCNN	-NA-	-NA-	-NA-	0.972	0.983	0.977
	-NA-	DGCNN+P2	-NA-	-NA-	-NA-	0.973	0.983	0.978
	-NA-	DGCNN+P2+LSTM	-NA-	-NA-	-NA-	**0.976**	**0.985**	**0.981**

Fig. 7. Sample structure recognition output of Tabstruct-Net on table images of ICDAR-2013, ICDAR-2019 CTDaR archival and UNLV datasets. **First Row:** prediction of cells which belong to the same row. **Second Row:** prediction of cells which belong to the same column. Cells marked with orange colour represent the examine cells and cells marked with green colour represent those which belong to the same row/column of the examined cell. (Color figure online)

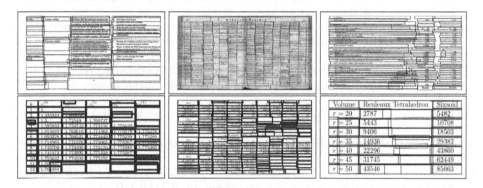

Fig. 8. Sample intermediate cell detection results of Tabstruct-Net on table images of ICDAR-2013, ICDAR-2019 CTDaR, UNLV, SciTSR, SciTSR-COMP and TableBank datasets illustrate failure of Tabstruct-Net.

6   Summary

We formulate the problem of table structure recognition as a combination of cell detection (top-down) and structure recognition (bottom-up) tasks. For cell detection, we make a modification to the RPN of original Mask R-CNN and introduce a novel alignment loss function (formulated for every pair of table cells) to enforce structural constraints. For structure recognition, we improve input representation for the DGCNN network by using LSTM, pre-trained ResNet-101 backbone and RPN of cell detection network. Further, we propose an end-to-end trainable architecture to collectively predict cell bounding boxes along with their row and column adjacency matrices to predict structure. We demonstrate our results on multiple public datasets on both digital scanned as well as archival handwritten table images. We observe that our approach fails to handle tables containing a large number of empty cells along both horizontal and vertical directions. In conclusion, we encourage further research in this direction.

Acknowledgment. This work is partly supported by MEITY, Government of India.

References

1. Yang, X., Yumer, E., Asente, P., Kraley, M., Kifer, D., Lee Giles, C.: Learning to extract semantic structure from documents using multimodal fully convolutional neural networks. In: CVPR (2017)
2. Augusto Borges Oliveira, D., Palhares Viana, M.: Fast CNN-based document layout analysis. In: ICCV (2017)
3. Yi, X., Gao, L., Liao, Y., Zhang, X., Liu, R., Jiang, Z.: CNN based page object detection in document images. In: ICDAR (2017)
4. Hu, J., Kashi, R.S., Lopresti, D.P., Wilfong, G.: Medium-independent table detection. In: Document Recognition and Retrieval VII (1999)
5. Wang, Y., Phillips, I.T., Haralick, R.M.: Table structure understanding and its performance evaluation. Pattern Recogn. (2004)
6. Nishida, K., Sadamitsu, K., Higashinaka, R., Matsuo, Y.: Understanding the semantic structures of tables with a hybrid deep neural network architecture. In: AAAI (2017)
7. Schreiber, S., Agne, S., Wolf, I., Dengel, A., Ahmed, S.: DeepDeSRT: deep learning for detection and structure recognition of tables in document images. In: ICDAR (2017)
8. Bao, J., et al.: Table-to-text: describing table region with natural language. In: AAAI (2018)
9. Qasim, S.R., Mahmood, H., Shafait, F.: Rethinking table parsing using graph neural networks. In: ICDAR (2019)
10. Tensmeyer, C., Morariu, V., Price, B., Cohen, S., Martinezp, T.: Deep splitting and merging for table structure decomposition. In: ICDAR (2019)
11. Li, M., Cui, L., Huang, S., Wei, F., Zhou, M., Li, Z.: TableBank: table benchmark for image-based table detection and recognition. In: ICDAR (2019)
12. Paliwal, S.S., Vishwanath, D., Rahul, R., Sharma, M., Vig, L.: TableNet: deep learning model for end-to-end table detection and tabular data extraction from scanned document images. In: ICDAR (2019)
13. Zhong, X., ShafieiBavani, E., Yepes, A.J.: Image-based table recognition: data, model, and evaluation. arXiv (2019)
14. Chi, Z., Huang, H., Xu, H.D., Yu, H., Yin, W., Mao, X.L.: Complicated table structure recognition. arXiv (2019)
15. Khan, S.A., Khalid, S.M.D., Shahzad, M.A., Shafait, F.: Table structure extraction with Bi-directional Gated Recurrent Unit networks. In: ICDAR (2019)
16. Siddiqui, S.A., Khan, P.I., Dengel, A., Ahmed, S.: Rethinking semantic segmentation for table structure recognition in documents. In: ICDAR (2019)
17. Xue, W., Li, Q., Tao, D.: ReS2TIM: reconstruct syntactic structures from table images. In: ICDAR (2019)
18. Göbel, M., Hassan, T., Oro, E., Orsi, G.: ICDAR 2013 table competition. In: ICDAR (2013)

19. Gao, L., et al.: ICDAR 2019 competition on table detection and recognition (cTDaR). In: ICDAR (2019)
20. Mondal, A., Lipps, P., Jawahar, C.V.: IIIT-AR-13K: a new dataset for graphical object detection in documents. In: DAS (2020)
21. Itonori, K.: Table structure recognition based on textblock arrangement and ruled line position. In: ICDAR (1993)
22. Green, E., Krishnamoorthy, M.: Recognition of tables using table grammars. In: Annual Symposium on Document Analysis and Information Retrieval (1995)
23. Kieninger, T.G.: Table structure recognition based on robust block segmentation. In: Document Recognition V (1998)
24. Tupaj, S., Shi, Z., Chang, C.H., Alam, H.: Extracting Tabular Information from Text Files. Tufts University, Medford, USA, EECS Department (1996)
25. Gilani, A., Qasim, S.R., Malik, I., Shafait, F.: Table detection using deep learning. In: ICDAR (2017)
26. Dong, H., Liu, S., Han, S., Fu, Z., Zhang, D.: TableSense: spreadsheet table detection with convolutional neural networks. In: AAAI (2019)
27. Kavasidis, I., et al.: A saliency-based convolutional neural network for table and chart detection in digitized documents. In: Ricci, E., Rota Bulò, S., Snoek, C., Lanz, O., Messelodi, S., Sebe, N. (eds.) ICIAP 2019. LNCS, vol. 11752, pp. 292–302. Springer, Cham (2019). https://doi.org/10.1007/978-3-030-30645-8_27
28. Saha, R., Mondal, A., Jawahar, C.V.: Graphical object detection in document images. In: ICDAR (2019)
29. Shahab, A., Shafait, F., Kieninger, T., Dengel, A.: An open approach towards the benchmarking of table structure recognition systems. In: DAS (2010)
30. Zanibbi, R., Blostein, D., Cordy, J.R.: Recognizing mathematical expressions using tree transformation. IEEE Trans. PAMI (2002)
31. Zhang, J., Du, J., Dai, L.: Multi-scale attention with dense encoder for handwritten mathematical expression recognition. In: ICDAR (2018)
32. Siegel, N., Horvitz, Z., Levin, R., Divvala, S., Farhadi, A.: FigureSeer: parsing result-figures in research papers. In: Leibe, B., Matas, J., Sebe, N., Welling, M. (eds.) ECCV 2016. LNCS, vol. 9911, pp. 664–680. Springer, Cham (2016). https://doi.org/10.1007/978-3-319-46478-7_41
33. Tang, B., et al.: DeepChart: combining deep convolutional networks and deep belief networks in chart classification. Sig. Process. (2015)
34. Harit, G., Bansal, A.: Table detection in document images using header and trailer patterns. In: ICVGIP (2012)
35. Gatos, B., Danatsas, D., Pratikakis, I., Perantonis, S.J.: Automatic table detection in document images. In: CVPR (2005)
36. Ohta, M., Yamada, R., Kanazawa, T., Takasu, A.: A cell-detection-based table-structure recognition method. In: ACM Symposium on Document Engineering (2019)
37. Deng, Y., Rosenberg, D., Mann, G.: Challenges in end-to-end neural scientific table recognition. In: ICDAR (2019)
38. Adiga, D., Bhat, S.A., Shah, M.B., Vyeth, V.: Table structure recognition based on cell relationship, a bottom-up approach. In: RANLP (2019)
39. Riba, P., Dutta, A., Goldmann, L., Fornes, A., Ramos, O., Llados, J.: Table detection in invoice documents by graph neural networks. In: ICDAR (2019)
40. Holeček, M., Hoskovec, A., Baudiš, P., Klinger, P.: Line-items and table understanding in structured documents. arXiv (2019)
41. Deng, L., Zhang, S., Balog, K.: Table2Vec: neural word and entity embeddings for table population and retrieval. In: SIGIR (2019)

42. Le Vine, N., Zeigenfuse, M., Rowan, M.: Extracting tables from documents using conditional generative adversarial networks and genetic algorithms. In: IJCNN (2019)
43. Sage, C., Aussem, A., Elghazel, H., Eglin, V., Espinas, J.: Recurrent neural network approach for table field extraction in business documents. In: ICDAR (2019)
44. Girshick, R., Donahue, J., Darrell, T., Malik, J.: Rich feature hierarchies for accurate object detection and semantic segmentation. In: CVPR (2014)
45. Girshick, R.: Fast R-CNN. In: ICCV (2015)
46. Ren, S., He, K., Girshick, R., Sun, J.: Faster R-CNN: towards real-time object detection with region proposal networks. In: NIPS (2015)
47. He, K., Gkioxari, G., Dollár, P., Girshick, R.: Mask R-CNN. In: CVPR (2017)
48. Yu, F., Koltun, V.: Multi-scale context aggregation by dilated convolutions. arXiv (2015)
49. Chen, L.C., Papandreou, G., Kokkinos, I., Murphy, K., Yuille, A.L.: Deeplab: Semantic image segmentation with deep convolutional nets, atrous convolution, and fully connected CRFs. IEEE Trans. PAMI (2017)
50. Woo, S., Hwang, S., Jang, H.D., Kweon, I.S.: Gated bidirectional feature pyramid network for accurate one-shot detection. Mach. Vis. Appl. (2019)
51. Hochreiter, S., Schmidhuber, J.: Long short-term memory. Neural Comput. (1997)
52. Qasim, S.R., Kieseler, J., Iiyama, Y., Pierini, M.: Learning representations of irregular particle-detector geometry with distance-weighted graph networks. arXiv (2019)
53. Smith, R.: An overview of the Tesseract OCR engine. In: ICDAR (2007)
54. Lin, T., et al.: Microsoft COCO: common objects in context. CoRR (2014)
55. Papineni, K., Roukos, S., Ward, T., Zhu, W.J.: BLEU: a method for automatic evaluation of machine translation. In: AMACL (2002)
56. Vedantam, R., Lawrence Zitnick, C., Parikh, D.: CIDEr: consensus-based image description evaluation. In: CVPR (2015)
57. Lin, C.Y.: ROUGE: a package for automatic evaluation of summaries. In: Text Summarization Branches Out (2004)

Novel View Synthesis on Unpaired Data by Conditional Deformable Variational Auto-Encoder

Mingyu Yin[1], Li Sun[1,2](✉)[iD], and Qingli Li[1][iD]

[1] Shanghai Key Laboratory of Multidimensional Information Processing,
East China Normal University, Shanghai 200241, China
sunli@ee.ecnu.edu.cn
[2] Key Laboratory of Advanced Theory and Application in Statistics
and Data Science, East China Normal University, Shanghai 200241, China

Abstract. Novel view synthesis often needs the paired data from both the source and target views. This paper proposes a view translation model under cVAE-GAN framework without requiring the paired data. We design a conditional deformable module (CDM) which uses the view condition vectors as the filters to convolve the feature maps of the main branch in VAE. It generates several pairs of displacement maps to deform the features, like the 2D optical flows. The results are fed into the deformed feature based normalization module (DFNM), which scales and offsets the main branch feature, given its deformed one as the input from the side branch. Taking the advantage of the CDM and DFNM, the encoder outputs a view-irrelevant posterior, while the decoder takes the code drawn from it to synthesize the reconstructed and the view-translated images. To further ensure the disentanglement between the views and other factors, we add adversarial training on the code. The results and ablation studies on MultiPIE and 3D chair datasets validate the effectiveness of the framework in cVAE and the designed module.

Keywords: View synthesis · cVAE · GAN

1 Introduction

Based on only a few sample images of a certain object with different poses, humans have the strong ability to infer and depict 2D images of the same object in arbitrary poses [27]. This paper focuses on a similar task, known as the novel view synthesis, which aims to make computer render a novel target view image

L. Sun—Supported by the the Science and Technology Commission of Shanghai Municipality (No.19511120800).

Electronic supplementary material The online version of this chapter (https://doi.org/10.1007/978-3-030-58604-1_6) contains supplementary material, which is available to authorized users.

© Springer Nature Switzerland AG 2020
A. Vedaldi et al. (Eds.): ECCV 2020, LNCS 12373, pp. 87–103, 2020.
https://doi.org/10.1007/978-3-030-58604-1_6

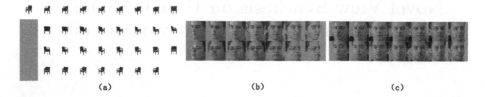

Fig. 1. We use unpaired data to realize view synthesis. In (a), given the first source view image, the chair rotates with a span of 360° . In (b), faces are synthesized into existing predefined views in the dataset. In (c), we are able to interpolate the face into unseen views in the training data. Details are given in the result Subsects. 4.2 and 4.3.

of an object given its current source view input. Obviously, this task requires the computer to understand the relationship between the 3D object and its pose. It has many potential applications in computer vision and graphic such as action recognition [32], 3D object recognition [26], modeling and editing [17] *etc.* Traditional approaches [2,13] for this task are mainly based on 3D projection geometry. They first construct the 3D shape model of the object from the cues in the image. Then the model is projected onto a 2D image plane of the target view. Actually, if 3D model can be perfectly built, object in arbitrary poses can be rendered precisely. However, building 3D object model from a single 2D image is an ill-posed problem. Therefore, it needs a large amount of close viewpoint images to capture the full object structure. Since structures of various objects are quite different, 3D geometry model for a particularly object may not generalize to other. Moreover, rendering a high quality image not only depends on the object model, but also other conditions such as the lighting and the background, but they need to be modeled independently.

Learning based approaches [25,36] begin to show the advantages with the help of deep convolutional neural network (CNN). This type of methods directly learn the mapping network from the source view to the target without building the 3D model and knowing the camera pose. The mapping network is modeled by a huge number of parameters determined in the data-driven manner. Hence it is large enough to accommodate not just the geometry projection function, but the background and lighting conditions. Recently, employing the image generation technique like generative adversarial notwork (GAN) has drawn researchers' attention. *E.g.*, novel synthesis can be modeled by a conditional GAN (cGAN) just like image-to-image translation [12].

Disadvantages of such methods lie in two aspects. First, the model dose not consider the prior knowledge about the projection geometry, though, previous works [31] already achieve the promising results given both the pose and identity labels as conditions. The works in [21,29,34] improves this by either designing differentiable 3D to 2D projection unit [21], predicting the warping flow between two different views [29], or using a specific pose matrix rather than one hot vector as the input conditions [34]. Training such a view translation model often requires the paired data, with one being used as the source view and the other as the target. The paired data essentially provide the important constraining loss function for minimization. Nonetheless, the ground truth data from target view are not easy to obtain in real applications. Lately, with the recent synthesis technique [3, 37], building a translation model by unpaired data becomes possible, which can greatly release the constraint of novel view synthesis.

This paper proposes a novel view synthesis algorithm using the conditional deformable flow in cVAE-GAN framework, and it designs for training with the unpaired data, although it still achieves the better results if the target view image can be further exploited in the loss functions. The key idea is to perform the view translation by deforming the latent feature map with the optical flows, computed from by the image feature and the view condition vectors together. We find that cVAE is able to disentangle the view-relevant and irrelevant factors, by mapping different source view images into posteriors, and making them close to a common prior. It greatly increases the performance on the unpaired data. To further improve the synthesis results, we incorporate the adversarial training in the pixel and latent feature domain, and the reconstruction loss on the sampling code from the view-irrelevant posterior.

Specifically, we built the generator with a pair of connected encoder and decoder. The source and target view conditions are added into them by our proposed conditional deformable module (CDM), in which the one-hot view vector is first mapped into two latent codes, and then they are used as two filters to convolve the features, giving the displacements on x and y directions. Note that instead of one flows, we actually get 3×3 flows for each location like in [4]. To achieve this, the features are divided into 9 channel groups and the two filters convolve each group to output a pair of displacement maps. Each 3×3 results then deform the corresponding location in its 3×3 neighbourhood, naturally followed by an ordinary conv layer to refine feature maps after the deformation. Rather than directly giving the deformed features into the later layers, we also design a deformed feature based normalization module (DFNM), which learns the scale and offset given the deformed feature as its input. With the help of the CDM and DFNM, the encoder maps the source into a posterior, while the decoder transforms the code, sampled from either the posterior or the prior, back into a target view image. Besides the reconstructed and prior-sampled image in traditional cVAE-GAN, our model also synthesizes a view-translated image to guide the generator for the view synthesis task.

The contributions of this paper lie in following aspects. First, we build a model in cVAE-GAN for novel view synthesis based on the unpaired data. With the traditional and the extra added constraining loss, the model maps the source image into a latent code, which does not reflect the view conditions. The target view then complements the code in the decoder. Second, we propose two modules named the CDM and DFNM for view translation. They fits in our model to improve the synthesis results. Third, extensive experiments are performed on two datasets to validate the effectiveness of the proposed method.

2   Related Works

Image Generation by VAE and GAN. GAN [6] and Variational Auto-Encoder (VAE) [15] are two powerful tools for generating high dimensional structured data. Both of them map the random code drawn from the prior into the image domain data. GAN introduces a discriminator D to evaluate the results from the generator G. D and G are training in the adversarial manner, and finally G is able to synthesize high quality images. However, GAN's training is unstable, and mode collapse often happens. Therefore, extra tricks are often added to limit the ability of D [8,9]. VAE has a pair of encoder and decoder. In VAE, the input image is first mapped into the latent probabilistic space by the encoder. The decoder takes the random code drawn from the posterior to reconstruct the input image. VAE can be easily trained by the reconstruction loss together with KL loss as its regularization. But it tends to give the blurry image. So it usually works with a discriminator to form a GAN [16]. Originally, both GAN and VAE perform unconditional generation. To better control the generated results, cGAN [12,18,20] and cVAE [3,28] are proposed. In these works, the conditional label is given to the network as the input. So it controls the generation results to fulfill the required condition. D in cGAN not only evaluates the image quality, but also the condition conformity. GAN and VAE become popular tool in novel view synthesis. Particularly, the latent code is disentangled into different dimensions in the unsupervised way [10,21], with some of them naturally controlling the pose, which shows their great potential on view synthesis.

Novel View Synthesis. Novel view synthesis is a classical topic in both computer vision and graphics. Traditional approaches are built by the 3D projection geometry [2,13,24,26,35]. These approaches estimate the 3D representation of the object, including the depth and camera pose [2], 3D meshes [35] and 3D model parameters [13,24,26]. Learning based method becomes increasingly popular with the help of CNN. Since all types of 3D representations can now be estimated by CNN, it is the main building blocks of the view synthesis algorithm. Dosovitskiy *et al.* [5] learn a CNN which takes the low dimensional code including the shape and camera pose as the input, and maps it into a high dimensional image. Zhou *et al.* [36] employ a CNN to predict the appearance flow to warp source view pixels directly. However, without the adversarial training, these works tend to give low quality images.

Since GAN and VAE is able to generate high quality images, GAN-based method becomes dominant recently [22,29–31,34]. Park *et al.* [22] predict the flow and the occlusion map to warp pixels first, and then the deformed image is given to the following network for refinement. The work [29] fully exploits a sequence of source images by giving them to an RNN-based network, which predicts a series of warping flows from sources to the current target view. In DR-GAN [31], a connected encoder-decoder based generator is proposed. The encoder transforms the image into a latent code. Together with the target view condition, the code is applied by the decoder to synthesize the image. The discriminator in DR-GAN takes advantage of the ID labels to ensure the view translation not to change the source ID. CR-GAN [30] extends the encoder-decoder based structure by adding an extra path beginning from the decoder, which gives an extra reconstruction constraint in the image domain. VI-GAN [34] employs the estimated camera pose matrix as the input condition for both source and target views, which replaces the one-hot condition vector. It also feeds back the view-translated image into the encoder, and requires its latent code to be close with the code from the source view, hence building the view-independent space. Note that in the above works, most of them [22,29,30,34] ask for the paired data to form the loss function. Although, DR-GAN do not have this constraint, it still requires the ID label for training the discriminator. Our work is totally based on the unpaired data and it dose not need any ID label during training.

3 Method

3.1 Overview Framework

This paper regards the novel view synthesis as the condition translation task in cVAE-GAN. To achieve the view translation based on the unpaired data, we propose a conditional deformable module (CDM) and a deformed feature based normalization module (DFNM) in our designed network. To enhance the separation between the view-relevant and irrelevant factors, a disentanglement adversarial classifier (DAC) is also incorporated. As is shown in the Fig. 2, our network consists of three major components, an encoder E, a decoder G and a discriminator D. Ψ_{EX}, Ψ_{EY} and Ψ_{GX}, Ψ_{GY} are four different MLPs in E and G, respectively. These MLPs maps the view label into conv filters, which are responsible for generating the optical flow. Given a source input image X_a and its view label Y_a, the algorithm synthesizes a view-translated image $\bar{X}_b$ under the target view Y_b. Note that we do not have the ground truth X_b to constrain the model during training.

In Fig. 2, E maps X into a posterior $E(Z|X,Y) = N(\mu, \Sigma)$, from which a random code $Z \sim E(Z|X,Y)$ can be sampled. With Z as its input, G renders the fake images, and they are given to D to evaluate the realness and view conformity. cVAE constrains $E(Z|X,Y)$ for all X with the common prior $N(0, I)$ by reducing the KL divergence between them. In cVAE, E removes Y_a from the source X_a, while G adds Y_b into the synthesized image. To fit the task of novel view synthesis, G generates three kinds images: the reconstructed, prior-sampled images and the view-translated image. Note that, our model employs Y as the input for E and G. Instead of directly concatenation, we propose the modules CDM and DFNM, which make the whole network suitable for view translation. Moreover, we follow the idea of BicycleGAN [38] to reconstruct Z from the prior-sampled image, and it ensures G to take effective information from the code Z.

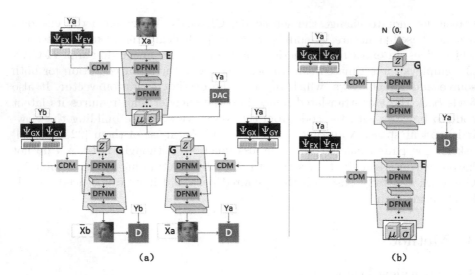

Fig. 2. Overview framework of the proposed network structure. (a) the source image X_a with its label viewpoint Y_a is translated into $\bar{X}_b$ in the target view Y_b. $\bar{X}_a$ is the reconstructed image with the same Y_a given at both E and G. (b) demonstrates that the code $Z \sim N(0, I)$ is synthesizing into a prior-sampled image, which is given back to E to reconstruct the code Z.

3.2   Conditional Deformable Module (CDM)

We now give the details about the proposed CDM, applied in both E and G. Our motivation is to change the source view Y_a to the target Y_b by warping X_a with the optical flow. Therefore, the CDM actually learns to generate the 2D flows for the features. Note that the warping is particularly useful when Y_a and Y_b are close. However, if they are far from each other, the deformed feature needs to be refined and complemented by the later layers.

Here, we argue that the flows are mainly determined by Y, but they are also influenced by the content in X. Therefore, they should be computed from both of them. As the view label Y has no spatial dimensions, Y is first mapped into a latent code, and then the code convolves the feature to get the offsets. Specifically, two sets of MLPs, Ψ_{EX}, Ψ_{EY} and Ψ_{GX}, Ψ_{GY}, first map Y_a and Y_b to the latent codes W (W_{EX}, W_{EY} in E and W_{GX}, W_{GY} in G). Here, we separate the filters for x and y directions, and for E and G. Detailed discussions are given in the experiments. Then, W are used as the filters to convolve on the feature maps, resulting several pairs of feature maps indicating the displacement dx and dy on x and y directions.

Figure 3 shows the details about CDM. It mainly composed of the conditional flow computation (CFC) and the deformable conv module, as is shown in Fig. 3 (a). Supposed the input $F^i \in \mathbb{R}^{H \times W \times C}$, of ith layer, CDM outputs the deformed F_d^i of the same size. W are also inputs, which are two latent vectors, computed from the view condition label Y by MLP. Particularly, F^i is given to a conv layer with C' filters to produce $F' \in \mathbb{R}^{H \times W \times C'}$. F' is split into different groups along the channel, then given to the CFC. Figure 3 (b) and (c) are two options for CFC. In practice, we choose the design in Fig. 3 (b), in which the layer of Kernel Given convolution ($KGconv$) uses $W_X, W_Y \in \mathbb{R}^{1 \times 1 \times \frac{C'}{9}}$ as a pair of filters to convolve on each $\frac{C'}{9}$ intervals, leading to a pair of $dx, dy \in \mathbb{R}^{H \times W \times 9}$. Note that dx, dy are composed of 9 groups of flows. Using 9 groups of flows is proposed by [4] to introduce adaptive receptive fields in conv layer, 9 sets flows correspond to the offsets of a 3×3 conv kernels, and it finally gives the deformed feature F_d^i. We follow it but the flows are redundant and correlated to some extend, since they are the offsets of adjacent 3×3 elements. However, the 9 sets of flows could sometimes be different, depending on the data.

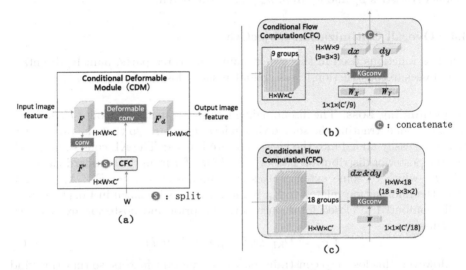

Fig. 3. The details for CDM. (a) Given the $F \in \mathbb{R}^{H \times W \times C}$ before the deformation, its output F_d is the deformed feature with the same size as F. (b) CFC also has two separated input latent codes W_X and W_Y, and they are used as the filters to convolve on a number (usually 9) of groups in F'. (c) Another design for CFC. Only one filter is provided, and it convolves on 18 groups.

3.3 Deformed Feature Based Normalization Module (DFNM)

The deformed feature maps F_d^i need to be further processed by $(i + 1)$th layers in E and G. One intuitive way is to directly use F_d^i as the input. However, recent advances in GAN and cGAN show the advantage of the conditional normalization like AdaIN [11] and SPADE [23]. Different from BN or IN, such layers do not learn the scale γ and offset β as trainable model parameters. Instead, they are the features from the side branch. In other words, the conditional adaptive normalization module learns to scale and offset based on the conditional input.

Inspired by SPADE, we propose a new conditional normalization way named DFNM, which uses F_d^i as the conditional input from the side branch. DFNM performs the de-normalization, which means to determine the appropriate values on β and γ. To be specific, it employs F_d^i as its input, and specifies β and γ by two conv layers. Note that DFNM has distinct internal parameters for different layers, hence it progressively adjusts the features in the main branch based on its current input. In practice, we can have different choices on the dimensions of β and γ. Here we simply follow the setting in SPADE, which outputs the unique $\gamma_{y,x,c}^i$ and $\beta_{y,x,c}^i$ at different 3D sites, where the subscripts are the indexes along the height, width and channel dimensions, respectively. Before the de-normalization, the features in the main branch should be normalized first by subtracting μ and dividing σ. Here we follow the way in BN to compute per-channel statistics μ_c^i and σ_c^i from $h_{n,y,x,c}^i$ in the batch.

3.4   Overall Optimization Objective

The loss functions used in this paper mainly are three parts, namely, disentangling losses, reconstruction losses and adversarial loss.

Disentangling Loss. The disentangling loss constrains the encoder E, and prevents it from extracting the source view-relevant feature, so that the target view Y_b can be easily added into the view-translated image. The KL constraint penalizes the posterior distribution $E(Z|X_a, Y_a)$ being far from the standard Gaussian $N(0, I)$, which to some extent makes the random code $Z \sim E(Z|X_a, Y_a)$ not carry the information related to Y_a. KL loss L_{KL}, as is shown in Eq. (1), can be easily computed in closed form since both the prior and posterior are assumed as Gaussians.

$$L_{KL} = D_{\mathrm{KL}}[E(Z|X_a, Y_a)||N(0, I)] \tag{1}$$

However, this loss also constrains on view-irrelevant factors, so that this kind of information in Z may lose because of the penalty from it. To cope with this issue, the paper proposes the DAC which mainly aims to reduce view-relevant factors in Z. With the help of DAC, the KL loss weight can be reduced so that the view-irrelevant factors remain in Z to a greater extent. In practice, we implement the DAC as two FC-layers with the purpose of classifying the view based on Z. DAC is trained in the adversarial manner. Hence it has two training stages, D and G stages. In D stage, the DAC is provided with the output Z from E and the correct source view label as well, while in G stage, DAC is fixed and E get trained with the adversarial loss from DAC. In this stage, we give an all-equal one-hot label to DAC with the same degree of confidence on each view. The cross entropy loss are defined as Eq. (2) and Eq. (3), respectively.

$$L_E^{cls} = -\mathbb{E}_{Z \sim E(Z|X_a, Y_a)} \sum_c \frac{1}{C} \log DAC(c|Z) \tag{2}$$

$$L_{DAC}^{cls} = -\mathbb{E}_{Z \sim E(Z|X_a, Y_a)} \sum_c \mathbb{I}(c = Y_a) \log DAC(c|Z) \tag{3}$$

where $\mathbb{I}(c = Y_a)$ is the indicator function, and $DAC(c|Z)$ is softmax probability output by the disentanglement adversarial classifier.

Reconstruction Losses. Reconstruction losses are important regularizations which also ensure that the view-irrelevant factors remain unchanged during view translation. Without extra supervisions, cVAE wants the synthesized image $\hat{X}_a$ to be close to the input when E and G are provided the same view label Y_a. In addition, the constraints of the middle layer features of the classification network is also employed in our work. As shown in Eq. (4) and Eq. (5), ϕ^i indicates ith of a pre-trained VGG network, and $Gram$ means to compute the Gram matrix, which is a typical second order features.

$$L_{E,G}^{pixel} = ||X_a - \bar{X}_a||_1, \quad L_{E,G}^{content} = \quad ||\phi^i(X_a) - \phi^i(\bar{X}_a)||_1 \tag{4}$$

$$L_{E,G}^{style} = ||Gram(\phi^i(X_a)) - Gram(\phi^i(\bar{X}_a))||_1 \tag{5}$$

When $Z \sim N(0, I)$ for the prior-sampled image $G(Z, Y_a)$, we cannot constrain it directly in the image domain, so we extract the feature from the image $G(Z, Y_a)$ with E, and to reconstruct Z. So that the information in Z is kept. The reconstruction loss expressed in Eq. (6)

$$L_G^{rec_z} = \mathbb{E}_{Z \sim N(0,I)}||Z - E(G(Z, Y_a), Y_a)||_1 \tag{6}$$

Adversarial Loss. In this paper, the projection discriminator [20] is adopted. Given the real image X_a, constraints are made for three types of fake images, reconstructed $G(E(X_a, Y_a), Y_a)$, view-translated $G(E(X_a, Y_a), Y_b)$ and prior-sampled image $G(Z, Y_a)$, as shown in Eq. (7) and Eq. (8).

$$\begin{aligned} L_D^{adv} = &\mathbb{E}_{X \sim p_{data}}[\max(0, 1 - D(X, Y_a))] \\ &+ \mathbb{E}_{Z \sim E(Z|X_a, Y_a)}[\max(0, 1 + D(G(Z, Y_a)), Y_a)] \\ &+ \mathbb{E}_{Z \sim E(Z|X_a, Y_a)}[\max(0, 1 + D(G(Z, Y_b)), Y_b)] \\ &+ \mathbb{E}_{Z \sim N(0,I)}[\max(0, 1 + D(G(Z, Y_a)), Y_a)] \end{aligned} \tag{7}$$

$$\begin{aligned} L_{E,G}^{adv} = &\mathbb{E}_{Z \sim E(Z|X_a, Y_a)}[\max(0, 1 - D(G(Z, Y_a)), Y_a)] \\ &+ \mathbb{E}_{Z \sim E(Z|X_a, Y_a)}[\max(0, 1 - D(G(Z, Y_b)), Y_b)] \\ &+ \mathbb{E}_{Z \sim N(0,I)}[\max(0, 1 - D(G(z, Y_a)), Y_a)] \end{aligned} \tag{8}$$

The total loss for E, G, D and DAC can be written as following.

$$L_{E,G} = L_{KL} + L_{E,G}^{adv} + \alpha_1 L_{E,G}^{style} + \alpha_2 L_{E,G}^{content} + \alpha_3 L_E^{pixel} + L_E^{cls} + L_G^{rec_z} \tag{9}$$

$$L_D = L_D^{adv}, \quad L_{DAC} = L_{DAC}^{cls} \tag{10}$$

We set the loss weight $\alpha_1 = 0.001$, $\alpha_2 = 10$, $\alpha_3 = 100$ for all experiments.

4   Experiments

4.1   Dataset and Implementation Details

Dataset. We validate the proposed method on the 3D chair [1] and the MultiPIE face datasets [7]. The 3D chair contains $86,304$ images with a span of $360°$ at azimuth and $30°$ at pitch, respectively, covering a total of 62 angles. There are 1,392 different types of chairs. The multiPIE contains about 130,000 images, with a total span of $180°$ and a spacing of $15°$ in azimuth dimension. A total of 13 angles are used for training and testing. Meanwhile, it also contains images of 250 identities under different lights. For all the datasets, 80% are used for model training and the rest 20% for testing.

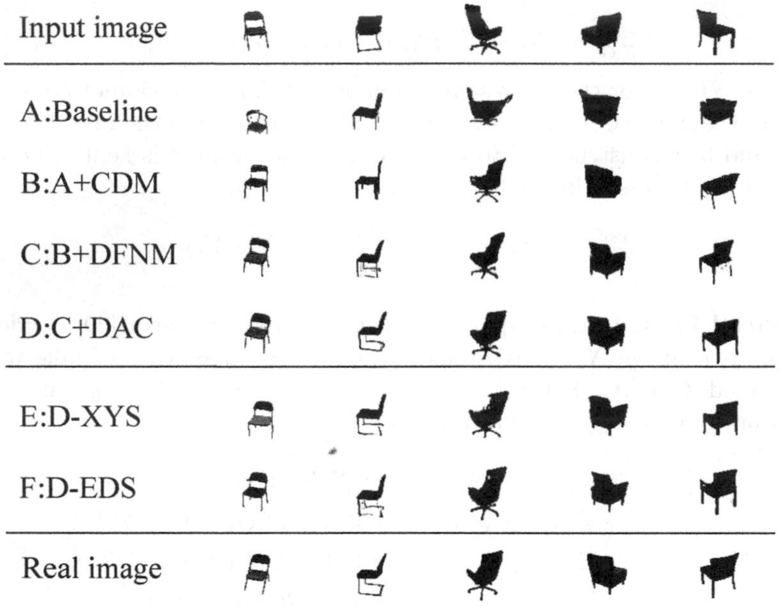

Fig. 4. Ablation study on 3D chair dataset.

Implementation Details. In E and G, all layers adopt instance normalization, except those replaced by DFNM. The spectral norm [19] is applied to all layers in D. All learning rates are set to 0.0002. We use the ADAM [14] and set $\beta_1 = 0$, $\beta_2 = 0.9$. Details are given in the supplementary materials.

4.2   Results and Ablation Studies on 3D Chair and MultiPIE

Extensive ablation studies is conducted to verify the effectiveness of each module. We have 6 different settings for it. View-translated images in different settings are presented in the corresponding rows in Fig. 4 and the quantitative metrics are given in Table 1.

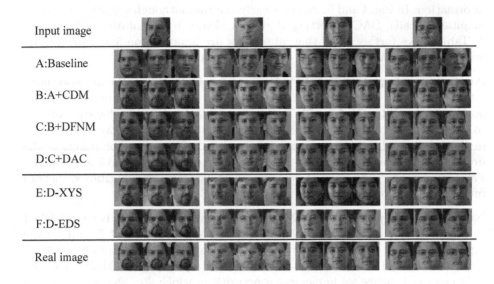

Input image	
A:Baseline	
B:A+CDM	
C:B+DFNM	
D:C+DAC	
E:D-XYS	
F:D-EDS	
Real image	

Fig. 5. Ablation study on multiPIE dataset.

Baseline. To verify the effectiveness of our proposed method, we use a general framework cVAE-GAN [3] as the baseline. To make the comparison fair, we introduce the view-translated image in it, and use all the loss functions that is presented. The result is indicated as "A: baseline" in Table 1 and Fig. 4 and 5.

Validity of CDM. To validate CDM, setting B is modified based on A. The only difference is we introduce the label through CDM, thus the setting is indicated by "B: A+CDM" in Table 1 and Fig. 4 and 5. Comparing the results between A and B in Fig. 4, we find that both can translate images to the given view. But when the difference between the target and input view is large, it is difficult for A to maintain the attributes and local details of the source image. While the CDM in B has the advantage of maintaining the representative details. In both the visual fidelity and similarity, B has a greater improvement on A.

Validity of DFNM. We validate the DFNM in setting C based on B. The only difference between B and C is that we apply DFNM in C, while the deformed features are directly given to the later layers in the main branch in B. This setting is written as "C: B+DFNM" in Table 1 and Fig. 4 and 5. As is shown in Fig. 4, for some of the complex chair types, the synthesized image keep the chair style, indicating that DFNM helps catching the detail features in the source image. The quantitative results in Table 1 indicate that DFNM refines the results compared with the setting B.

Validity of DAC. To demonstrate the effectiveness of DAC loss, we experiment in setting D based on C. In setting D, DAC is employed to provide the loss for encoder by Eq. (2) . By introducing DAC, it enables G to get more view-irrelevant information. In Fig. 4 and 5, we can clearly see that although setting C basically maintain details, DAC in setting D gives a clearer representation. The results in Table 1 give further proof that all metrics are improved on 3D chair, and L1 error and FID have only negligible decreasing on MultiPIE.

Necessity of Separating MLPs for x and y Directions. We are also interested in the way that CFC is implemented in CDM. There are at least two options for the filters W from MLPs. One possible way is to employ the same W to generate both dx and dy, as is shown in Fig. 3(c). The other way is illustrated in the conditional flow computation sub-module in Fig. 3(b). The results of the first option are specified as "E: D-XYS", as is shown in Fig. 4 and 5 and Table 1. We can see that the image is defective. The declines in quantitative metrics further illustrate the necessity of our design in CDM.

Necessity of Separating the MLPs in E and G. E and G both use CDM to warp the features. But considering the different purposes of E and G, the input conditional filters are different, coming from Ψ_{EX}, Ψ_{EY}, and Ψ_{GX}, Ψ_{GY}, as is shown in Fig. 2. We are wondering whether separating the MLPs in E and G is necessary, hence we implement a network in which Ψ_X, Ψ_Y are sharing in E and G. The results are presented as "F: D-EDS", which are worse than D, as is shown in Fig. 4 and 5 and Table 1. It shows the necessity of separating MLPs.

Table 1. Quantitative ablation study on the MultiPIE and the 3D chair dataset. The pixel-wise mean L1 error and the structural similarity index measure (SSIM) [33] are computed between the view-translated images and the ground truths. Besides, the FID is also reported.

	Method	MultiPIE			3D chair		
		L1	SSIM	FID	L1	SSIM	FID
A:	Baseline	31.37	0.49	44.84	8.39	0.86	104.78
B:	CDM	23.43	0.55	26.79	7.88	0.87	88.23
C:	B + DFNM	**21.53**	0.56	**23.59**	6.68	0.88	93.11
D:	C + DAC	21.90	**0.57**	23.95	**6.37**	**0.89**	**86.34**
E:	D - XYS	24.48	0.54	31.02	7.18	0.88	90.31
F:	D - EDS	23.59	0.54	28.40	6.94	0.88	89.56

4.3   Results and Analysis on MultiPIE

View-Translation Among Discrete Angles. Qualitative comparisons are performed among our proposed method and the existing works like cVAE-GAN [3], VI-GAN [34] and CR-GAN [30]. The results are listed in Fig. 6. Note that

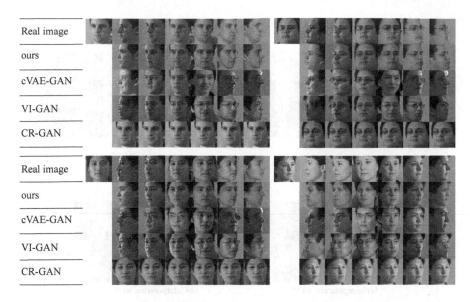

Fig. 6. Comparison on Multi-PIE. For each image, the top row is the ground truth while the second row is generated by ours. The third , fourth and fifth rows are the output of cVAE-GAN [3] ,VI-GAN [34] and CR-GAN [30] respectively.

in this study, we do not use paired data for all experiments during training. The results of the quantitative metrics on each method are shown in the Table 2. After removing the constraint from the paired data, CR-GAN can hardly realize the view translation. The image qualities of VI-GAN significantly deteriorate under the condition of large angle translation. Although cVAE-GAN can still work, the converted image can not keep the view-irrelevant details from the source.

Table 2. Quantitative metrics comparisons. Results from CR-GAN, VI-GAN and cVAE-GAN are provided on MultiPIE and the 3D chair datasets, respectively.

Method	MultiPIE			3D chair		
	L1	SSIM	FID	L1	SSIM	FID
CR-GAN [30]	39.80	0.397	48.87	13.45	0.696	111.34
VI-GAN [34]	38.18	0.464	47.02	10.54	0.802	105.78
cVAE-GAN [3]	31.37	0.493	44.84	8.39	0.859	104.78
Ours	**21.90**	**0.571**	**23.95**	**6.37**	**0.885**	**86.34**

Continuous View Synthesis by Interpolation. Synthesizing images at continuously varying angles is important in real applications. In our implementation, this can be achieved by interpolating between two adjacent labels. Meanwhile, we realize that the filter W, computed from the discrete view labels through the

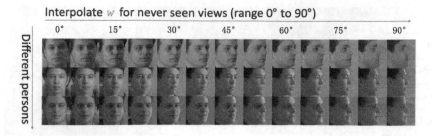

Fig. 7. Interpolating W to synthesis unseen view images.

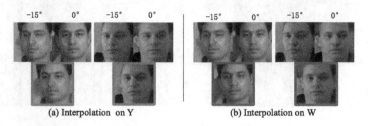

(a) Interpolation on Y   (b) Interpolation on W

Fig. 8. Comparisons on different interpolation schemes for synthesizing an unseen view image on MultiPIE. (Color figure online)

MLPs Ψ, can help synthesizing the image at an unseen angle. Therefore, we can also directly interpolate on W.

The minimum angle interval in MultiPIE is 15°, and we choose to interpolate at every 7.5°. As is shown in Fig. 7, we visualize all the images by interpolating W from 0° to 90° and find that the face realized smooth transformation.

For comparison, zooming-in results by interpolating on both W and Y are given in Fig. 8. Note that all these images are the outputs from our model with the source view at 0°. The image marked with the red box is the obtained by interpolating W, while the green box is the result from interpolating Y. The results show that interpolation on W gives the more accurate images. This also demonstrates that we have learned good representation W for the angle since it directly relates to the optical flow on the feature. The above results can be verified by the quantitative metric of FID. By interpolation on W, FID achieves 30.70, while it is 32.04 if the interpolation is implemented on Y.

5 Conclusions

This paper proposes the conditional deformable VAE for the novel view synthesis based on unpaired training data. We design the CDM and DFNM which are utilized in both the encoder and decoder. The CDM employs the latent code mapping from the conditional view label as the filters to convolve the feature, so that a set of optical flows can be obtained to deform the features. The output from CDM are not directly given to the later layers, instead, they take effect through DFNM, which actually performs the conditional normalization according to its input. The experiments on 3D chair and MultiPIE show the effectiveness of our method particularly for unpaired training.

References

1. Aubry, M., Maturana, D., Efros, A.A., Russell, B.C., Sivic, J.: Seeing 3D chairs: exemplar part-based 2D–3D alignment using a large dataset of cad models. In: Proceedings of the IEEE Conference on Computer Vision and Pattern Recognition, pp. 3762–3769 (2014)
2. Avidan, S., Shashua, A.: Novel view synthesis in tensor space. In: Proceedings of IEEE Computer Society Conference on Computer Vision and Pattern Recognition, pp. 1034–1040. IEEE (1997)
3. Bao, J., Chen, D., Wen, F., Li, H., Hua, G.: cVAE-GAN: fine-grained image generation through asymmetric training. In: Proceedings of the IEEE International Conference on Computer Vision, pp. 2745–2754 (2017)
4. Dai, J., et al.: Deformable convolutional networks. In: Proceedings of the IEEE International Conference on Computer Vision, pp. 764–773 (2017)
5. Dosovitskiy, A., Tobias Springenberg, J., Brox, T.: Learning to generate chairs with convolutional neural networks. In: Proceedings of the IEEE Conference on Computer Vision and Pattern Recognition, pp. 1538–1546 (2015)
6. Goodfellow, I., et al.: Generative adversarial nets. In: Advances in Neural Information Processing Systems, pp. 2672–2680 (2014)
7. Gross, R., Matthews, I., Cohn, J., Kanade, T., Baker, S.: Multi-pie. Image Vis. Comput. 28(5), 807–813 (2010)
8. Gulrajani, I., Ahmed, F., Arjovsky, M., Dumoulin, V., Courville, A.C.: Improved training of Wasserstein GANs. In: Advances in Neural Information Processing Systems, pp. 5767–5777 (2017)
9. Heusel, M., Ramsauer, H., Unterthiner, T., Nessler, B., Hochreiter, S.: GANs trained by a two time-scale update rule converge to a local Nash equilibrium. In: Advances in Neural Information Processing Systems, pp. 6626–6637 (2017)
10. Higgins, I., et al.: beta-VAE: Learning basic visual concepts with a constrained variational framework. ICLR 2(5), 6 (2017)
11. Huang, X., Belongie, S.: Arbitrary style transfer in real-time with adaptive instance normalization. In: Proceedings of the IEEE International Conference on Computer Vision, pp. 1501–1510 (2017)
12. Isola, P., Zhu, J.-Y., Zhou, T., Efros, A.A.: Image-to-image translation with conditional adversarial networks. In: Proceedings of the IEEE Conference on Computer Vision and Pattern Recognition, pp. 1125–1134 (2017)
13. Kholgade, N., Simon, T., Efros, A., Sheikh, Y.: 3D object manipulation in a single photograph using stock 3D models. ACM Trans. Graph. (TOG) 33(4), 1–12 (2014)
14. Kingma, D.P., Adam, J.Ba.: A method for stochastic optimization. arXiv preprint arXiv:1412.6980 (2014)
15. Kingma, D.P., Welling, M.: Auto-encoding variational bayes. arXiv preprint arXiv:1312.6114 (2013)
16. Larsen, A.B.L., Sønderby, S.K., Larochelle, H., Winther, O.: Autoencoding beyond pixels using a learned similarity metric. arXiv preprint arXiv:1512.09300 (2015)
17. Massa, F., Russell, B.C., Aubry, M.: Deep exemplar 2D–3D detection by adapting from real to rendered views. In: Proceedings of the IEEE Conference on Computer Vision and Pattern Recognition, pp. 6024–6033 (2016)

18. Mirza, M., Osindero, S.: Conditional generative adversarial nets. arXiv preprint arXiv:1411.1784 (2014)
19. Miyato, T., Kataoka, T., Koyama, M., Yoshida, Y.: Spectral normalization for generative adversarial networks. arXiv preprint arXiv:1802.05957 (2018)
20. Miyato, T., Koyama, M.: cGANs with projection discriminator. arXiv preprint arXiv:1802.05637 (2018)
21. Nguyen-Phuoc, T., Li, C., Theis, L., Richardt, C., Yang, Y.-L.: Hologan: unsupervised learning of 3D representations from natural images. In: Proceedings of the IEEE International Conference on Computer Vision, pp. 7588–7597 (2019)
22. Park, E., Yang, J., Yumer, E., Ceylan, D., Berg, A.C.: Transformation-grounded image generation network for novel 3D view synthesis. In: Proceedings of the IEEE Conference on Computer Vision and Pattern Recognition, pp. 3500–3509 (2017)
23. Park, T., Liu, M.-Y., Wang, T.-C., Zhu, J.-Y.: Semantic image synthesis with spatially-adaptive normalization. In: Proceedings of the IEEE Conference on Computer Vision and Pattern Recognition, pp. 2337–2346 (2019)
24. Rematas, K., Nguyen, C.H., Ritschel, T., Fritz, M., Tuytelaars, T.: Novel views of objects from a single image. IEEE Trans. Pattern Anal. Mach. Intell. **39**(8), 1576–1590 (2016)
25. Rematas, K., Ritschel, T., Fritz, M., Tuytelaars, T.: Image-based synthesis and re-synthesis of viewpoints guided by 3D models. In: Proceedings of the IEEE Conference on Computer Vision and Pattern Recognition, pp. 3898–3905 (2014)
26. Savarese, S., Fei-Fei, L.: View synthesis for recognizing unseen poses of object classes. In: Forsyth, D., Torr, P., Zisserman, A. (eds.) ECCV 2008. LNCS, vol. 5304, pp. 602–615. Springer, Heidelberg (2008). https://doi.org/10.1007/978-3-540-88690-7_45
27. Shepard, R.N., Metzler, J.: Mental rotation of three-dimensional objects. Science **171**(3972), 701–703 (1971)
28. Sohn, K., Lee, H., Yan, X.: Learning structured output representation using deep conditional generative models. In: Advances in Neural Information Processing Systems, pp. 3483–3491 (2015)
29. Sun, S.-H., Huh, M., Liao, Y.-H., Zhang, N., Lim, J.J.: Multi-view to novel view: synthesizing novel views with self-learned confidence. In: Ferrari, V., Hebert, M., Sminchisescu, C., Weiss, Y. (eds.) ECCV 2018. LNCS, vol. 11207, pp. 162–178. Springer, Cham (2018). https://doi.org/10.1007/978-3-030-01219-9_10
30. Tian, Y., Peng, X., Zhao, L., Zhang, S., Metaxas, D.N.: CR-GAN: learning complete representations for multi-view generation. arXiv preprint arXiv:1806.11191 (2018)
31. Tran, L., Yin, X., Liu, X.: Disentangled representation learning GAN for pose-invariant face recognition. In: Proceedings of the IEEE Conference on Computer Vision and Pattern Recognition, pp. 1415–1424 (2017)
32. Wang, J., Nie, X., Xia, Y., Wu, Y., Zhu, S.-C.: Cross-view action modeling, learning and recognition. In: Proceedings of the IEEE Conference on Computer Vision and Pattern Recognition, pp. 2649–2656 (2014)
33. Wang, Z., Bovik, A.C., Sheikh, H.R., Simoncelli, E.P.: Image quality assessment: from error visibility to structural similarity. IEEE Trans. Image Process. **13**(4), 600–612 (2004)
34. Xu, X., Chen, Y.-C., Jia, J.: View independent generative adversarial network for novel view synthesis. In: Proceedings of the IEEE International Conference on Computer Vision, pp. 7791–7800 (2019)

35. Zhang, C., Li, Z., Cheng, Y., Cai, R., Chao, H., Rui, Y.: Meshstereo: a global stereo model with mesh alignment regularization for view interpolation. In: Proceedings of the IEEE International Conference on Computer Vision, pp. 2057–2065 (2015)
36. Zhou, T., Tulsiani, S., Sun, W., Malik, J., Efros, A.A.: View synthesis by appearance flow. In: Leibe, B., Matas, J., Sebe, N., Welling, M. (eds.) ECCV 2016. LNCS, vol. 9908, pp. 286–301. Springer, Cham (2016). https://doi.org/10.1007/978-3-319-46493-0_18
37. Zhu, J.-Y., Park, T., Isola, P., Efros, A.A.: Unpaired image-to-image translation using cycle-consistent adversarial networks. In: Proceedings of the IEEE International Conference on Computer Vision, pp. 2223–2232 (2017)
38. Zhu, J.-Y., et al.: Toward multimodal image-to-image translation. In: Advances in Neural Information Processing Systems, pp. 465–476 (2017)

Beyond the Nav-Graph: Vision-and-Language Navigation in Continuous Environments

Jacob Krantz[1(✉)], Erik Wijmans[2,3], Arjun Majumdar[2], Dhruv Batra[2,3], and Stefan Lee[1]

[1] Oregon State University, Corvallis, USA
krantzja@oregonstate.edu
[2] Georgia Institute of Technology, Atlanta, USA
[3] Facebook AI Research, Menlo Park, USA

Abstract. We develop a language-guided navigation task set in a continuous 3D environment where agents must execute low-level actions to follow natural language navigation directions. By being situated in continuous environments, this setting lifts a number of assumptions implicit in prior work that represents environments as a sparse graph of panoramas with edges corresponding to navigability. Specifically, our setting drops the presumptions of known environment topologies, short-range oracle navigation, and perfect agent localization. To contextualize this new task, we develop models that mirror many of the advances made in prior settings as well as single-modality baselines. While some transfer, we find significantly lower absolute performance in the continuous setting – suggesting that performance in prior 'navigation-graph' settings may be inflated by the strong implicit assumptions. Code at jacobkrantz.github.io/vlnce.

Keywords: Vision-and-Language Navigation · Embodied agents

1 Introduction

Springing forth from the pages of science fiction and capturing the daydreams of weary chore-doers everywhere, the promise and potential of general-purpose robotic assistants that follow natural language instructions has been long understood. Taking a small step towards this goal, recent work has begun developing artificial agents that follow natural language navigation instructions in perceptually-rich, simulated environments [4,6]. An example instruction might be *"Go down the hall and turn left at the wooden desk. Continue until you reach the kitchen and then stop by the kettle."* and agents are evaluated by their ability to follow the described path in (potentially novel) simulated environments.

Electronic supplementary material The online version of this chapter (https://doi.org/10.1007/978-3-030-58604-1_7) contains supplementary material, which is available to authorized users.

© Springer Nature Switzerland AG 2020
A. Vedaldi et al. (Eds.): ECCV 2020, LNCS 12373, pp. 104–120, 2020.
https://doi.org/10.1007/978-3-030-58604-1_7

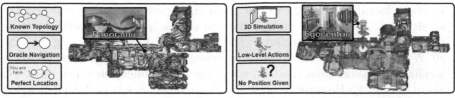

(a) Vision-and-Language Navigation (VLN)   (b) VLN in Continuous Environments (VLN-CE)

Fig. 1. The VLN setting **(a)** operates on a fixed topology of panoramic images (shown in blue) – assuming perfect navigation between nodes (often meters apart) and precise localization. Our VLN-CE setting **(b)** lifts these assumptions by instantiating the task in continuous environments with low-level actions – providing a more realistic testbed for robot instruction following.

Many of these tasks have been developed from datasets of panoramic images captured in real scenes – e.g. Google StreetView images in Touchdown [6] or Matterport3D panoramas captured in homes in Vision-and-Language Navigation (VLN) [4]. This paradigm enables efficient data collection and high visual fidelity compared to 3D scanning or creating synthetic environments; however, scenes are only observed from a sparse set of points relative to the full 3D environment (~117 viewpoints per environment in VLN). As a consequence, environments in these tasks are defined in terms of a navigation graph (or nav-graph for short) – a static topological representation of 3D space. As shown in Fig. 1(a), nodes in the nav-graph correspond to 360° panoramic images taken at fixed locations and edges between nodes indicate navigability. This nav-graph based formulation introduces a number of assumptions that make it a poor proxy for what a robotic agent would encounter while navigating the real world.

Focusing our discussion on Vision-and-Language Navigation (VLN), the existence and common usage of the nav-graph imply the following assumptions:

- **Known topology.** Rather than continuous environments in which agents can move freely, agents operate on a fixed topology of traversable nodes (shown in blue in Fig. 1(a)). Aside from being a poor match to robot control, this also provides prior information about environment layout to agents – even in "unseen" test settings. For example, it is common practice to define agent actions by selecting directions in the current panorama and 'snapping' to the nearest adjacent nav-graph node in that direction. How an actual agent might acquire and update such a topology in new environments is an open question.
- **Oracle navigation.** Movement between adjacent nodes in the nav-graph is deterministic, implying the existence of an oracle navigator capable of accurately traversing multiple meters in the presence of obstacles – abstracting away the problem of visual navigation. Further, this movement between nodes is perceptually akin to teleportation – the current panorama is simply replaced by the panorama at the new location meters away. This is in contrast to the continuous stream of observations a real agent would encounter while moving.

– **Perfect localization.** Agents are given their precise location and heading at all times. Most works use this data to encode precise geometry between nodes in the nav-graph as part of the decision making process, e.g. moving 30°W and 1.12 m forward from the previous node. Others use precise agent localization to construct spatial maps of the environment on which to reason about paths [3]. However, precise localization indoors is still a challenging problem.

Taken together, these assumptions make current settings poor reflections of the real world both in terms of control (ignoring actuation, navigation, and localization error) and visual stimuli (lacking the poor framing and long observation-sequences agents will encounter). In essence, the problem is reduced to that of visually-guided graph search. As such, closing the loop by transferring these trained agents to physical robotic platforms has not been examined.

These assumptions are often justified by invoking existing technologies as potential oracles. For example, simultaneous localization and mapping (SLAM) or odometry systems can offer strong localization in appropriate conditions [16,21]. Likewise, algorithms for path planning and control can navigate short distances in the presence of obstacles [11,25,31]. Further, it is reasonable to suggest that issuing commands at the level of relative waypoints (in analogy to nav-graph nodes) is the proper interface between language-guided AI navigators and lower-level agent control. However, these techniques are each independently far from perfect and such an agent would need to learn the limitations of these lower-level control systems – facing consequences when proposed waypoints cannot be reached effectively. Integrative studies that combine and evaluate techniques for control and mapping with learned AI agents are not possible in current nav-graph based problem settings. In this work, we develop a continuous setting that enables such studies and take a first step towards integrating VLN agents with control.

Vision-and-Language Navigation in Continuous Environments. In this work, we focus in on the Vision-and-Language Navigation (VLN) [4] task and lift these implicit assumptions by instantiating it in continuous 3D environments [5,19]. Consequently, we call this task Vision-and-Language Navigation in Continuous Environments (VLN-CE). Agents in our task are free to navigate to any unobstructed point through a set of low-level actions (e.g. move `forward` 0.25 m, `turn-left` 15°) rather than teleporting between fixed nodes. This setting introduces many challenges ignored in prior work. Agents in VLN-CE face significantly longer time horizons; the average number of actions along a path in VLN-CE is ~55 compared to the 4–6 node hops in VLN (as illustrated in Fig. 1). Moreover, the views the agent receives along the way are not well-posed by careful human operators as in the panoramas, but rather a consequence of the agent's actions. Agents must also learn to avoid getting stuck on obstacles, something that is structurally impossible in VLN's navigability defined nav-graph. Further, agents are not provided their location or heading while navigating.

We develop agent architectures for this task and explore how popular mechanisms for VLN transfer to the VLN-CE setting. Specifically, we develop a simple

Table 1. Comparison of language-guided visual navigation tasks. Ours is the only to provide unconstrained navigation in real environments for crowdsourced instructions.

Task	Instructions	Environment	Navigation
LANI [20]	Crowdsourced	Synthetic	Unconstrained
StreetNav [13]	Templated	Real	Nav-Graph Based
Touchdown [6]	Crowdsourced	Real	Nav-Graph Based
VLN [4]	Crowdsourced	Real	Nav-Graph Based
VLN-CE (ours)	Crowdsourced	Real	Unconstrained

sequence-to-sequence baseline architecture as well as a cross-modal attention-based model. We perform a number of input-modality ablations to assess the biases and baselines in this new setting (including models without perception or instructions as suggested in [27]). Unlike in VLN where depth is rarely used, our analysis reveals depth to be an integral signal for learning embodied navigation – echoing similar findings in point-goal navigation tasks [19,31]. We also apply existing training augmentations [17,24,26] popular in VLN to our setting, finding mixed results. Overall, our best performing agent successfully navigates to the goal in approximately a third of episodes in unseen environments.

To further examine the relationship between the nav-graph-based VLN task and VLN-CE, we also transfer paths from agents trained in continuous environments back to the nav-graph to provide a direct comparison. We find significant gaps in performance between these settings indicative of the strong prior provided by the nav-graph. This suggests prior results in VLN may be overly optimistic in terms of progress towards instruction-following robots functioning in the wild.

Contributions. To summarize our contributions, we:

- Lift the VLN task to continuous 3D environments – removing many unrealistic assumptions imposed by the nav-graph-based representation.
- Develop model architectures for the VLN-CE task and evaluate a suite of single-input ablations to assess the biases and baselines of the setting.
- Investigate how a number of popular techniques in VLN transfer to this more challenging long-horizon setting – identifying significant gaps in performance.

2   Related Work

Language-Guided Visual Navigation Tasks. Language-guided visual navigation tasks require agents to follow navigation directions in simulated environments. There have been a number of recent tasks proposed in this space [4,6,13,20]. Chen et al. [6] introduce the Touchdown task which studies outdoor language-guided navigation in Google Street View panoramas. Hermann et al. [13] investigates the same setting; however, the instructions are automatically generated from Google Map directions rather than being crowdsourced from human annotators. Both adopt a nav-graph setting due to the source data being panoramic images – constraining agent navigation to fixed points. Misra et al. [20] introduce a simulated environment with unconstrained navigation and a dataset of crowdsourced instructions; however, the environments are unrealistic, synthetic scenes. Most related to our work is the Vision-and-Language Navigation (VLN) task of Anderson et al. [4]. VLN provides nav-graph trajectories and crowdsourced instructions in Matterport3D [5] environments as the Room-to-Room (R2R) dataset. We build VLN-CE directly on these annotations – converting R2R panorama-based trajectories to fine-grained paths in continuous Matterport3D environments (Fig. 1(a) to Fig. 1(b)). This shift to continuous environments with unconstrained agent navigation lifts a number of unrealistic assumptions.

The variation in these tasks is primarily in the source of navigation instructions (crowdsourced from human annotators vs. generated via template), environment realism (hand-designed synthetic worlds vs. captures from real locations), and constraints on agent navigation (nav-graph based navigation vs. unconstrained agent motion). Table 1 provides a comparison between tasks along these axes. Our proposed VLN-CE task provides the first setting with crowdsourced instructions in realistic environments with unconstrained agent navigation.

Approaches to Vision-and-Language Navigation. VLN has seen considerable progress. Multimodal attention mechanisms have become popular to provide better grounding between instructions and the observations [29]. Orthogonal to new modeling architectures, improvements have also come from new training approaches and data augmentation methods. One prevalent technique is to utilize inverse "speaker" models to re-rank candidate trajectories or augment the available training data by generating instructions for novel trajectories [9]. Tan et al. [26] improve upon this idea by improving the diversity of the generated instructions. Ma et al. [17] show that an additional training signal can be gained by explicitly estimating progress toward the goal (referred to as self-monitoring). We adapt these methods to VLN-CE and examine their impact.

Other Language-Based Embodied AI. A number of other embodied tasks have considered language-conditioned navigation. For instance, referring to specific rooms or objects that agents must then navigate to [7,10,30]. However, these settings use language to specify end-goals or query agent knowledge rather than to provide navigational directions. For example, specifying *"lamp"* or *"What color is the lamp in the living room?"* rather than multi-step, grounded navigation instructions. This loose coupling of intermediate agent action with the language instruction differentiates these tasks from language-guided navigation settings.

3   VLN in Continuous Environments (VLN-CE)

We consider a continuous setting for the vision-and-language navigation task which we refer to as Vision-and-Language Navigation in Continuous Environments (VLN-CE). Given a natural language navigation instruction, an agent must navigate from a start position to the described goal in a continuous 3D environment by executing a sequence of low-level actions based on egocentric perception alone. In overview, we develop this setting by transferring nav-graph-based Room-to-Room (R2R) [4] trajectories to reconstructed continuous Matterport3D environments in the Habitat simulator [19]. We discuss these details below.

Continuous Matterport3D Environments in Habitat. We set our problem in the Matterport3D (MP3D) [5] dataset, a collection of 90 environments captured through over 10,800 high-definition RGB-D panoramas. In addition to the panoramic images, MP3D also provides corresponding mesh-based 3D environment reconstructions. To enable agent interaction with these meshes, we develop the VLN-CE task on top of the Habitat Simulator [19], a high-throughput simulator that supports basic movement and collision checking for 3D environments including MP3D. In contrast to the simulator used in VLN [4], Habitat allows agents to navigate freely in the continuous environments.

Observations and Actions. We select observation and action spaces to emulate a ground-based, zero-turning radius robot with a single, forward-mounted RGBD camera, similar to a LoCoBot [1]. Agents perceive the world through egocentric RGBD images from the simulator with a resolution of 256×256 and a horizontal field-of-view of $90°$. Note that this is similar to the egocentric RGB perception in the original VLN task [4] but differs from the panoramic observation space adopted by nearly all follow-up work [9,17,26,29].

While the simulator is quite flexible in terms of agent actions, we consider four simple, low-level actions for agents in VLN-CE – move `forward` 0.25 m, `turn-left` or `turn-right` $15°$, or `stop` to declare that the goal position has been reached. These actions can easily be implemented on robotic agents with standard motion controllers. In contrast, actions to move between panoramas in [4] traverse 2.25 m on average and can include avoiding obstacles.

3.1   Transferring Nav-Graph Trajectories

Rather than collecting a new dataset of trajectories and instructions, we instead transfer those from the nav-graph-based Room-to-Room dataset to our continuous setting. Doing so enables us to compare existing nav-graph-based techniques with our methods that operate in continuous environments on the same instructions.

Matterport3D Simulator and the Room-to-Room Dataset. The original VLN task is based on panoramas from Matterport3D (MP3D) [5]. To enable agent interaction with these panoramas, Anderson et al. [4] developed the Matterport3D Simulator. Environments in this simulator are defined as nav-graphs

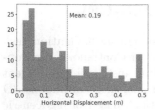

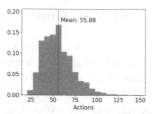

(a) Node Location Displacement   (b) Discontinuities   (c) Trajectory Length in Actions

Fig. 2. We successfully transfer 77% of the R2R trajectories. (a) Most panorama nodes transfer directly, but 3% require horizontal adjustment – with an average displacement of 0.19 m. (b) Some trajectories are not navigable due to differences between the panoramas and reconstructed environments, e.g. holes in the 3D mesh (top) or objects like chairs being moved between panorama captures (bottom). (c) Optimal paths in our setting require 10x more agent actions per trajectory – 55.88 compared to 5 in R2R.

$E = \{\mathcal{V}, \mathcal{E}\}$. Each node $v \in \mathcal{V}$ corresponds to a panoramic image I captured by a Matterport camera at location x, y, z – i.e. $v = \{I, x, y, z\}$. Edges in the graph correspond to navigability between nodes. Navigability was defined by ray-tracing between node locations at varying heights to check for obstacles in the reconstructed MP3D scene and then manually inspected. Edges were manually added or removed based on judgement whether an agent could navigate between nodes – including by avoiding minor obstacles[1]. Agents act by teleporting between adjacent nodes in this graph. Based on this simulator, Anderson et al. [4] collect the Room-to-Room (R2R) dataset containing 7189 trajectories each with three human-generated instructions on average. These trajectories consist of a sequence of nodes $\tau = [v_1, \ldots, v_T]$ with length T averaging between 4 and 6 nodes.

Converting Room-to-Room Trajectories to Habitat. Given a mapping between the coordinate frames of Matterport3D Simulator and MP3D in Habitat, it is seemingly simple to transfer the Room-to-Room trajectories – after all, each node has a corresponding xyz location. However, node locations often do not correspond to reachable locations for a ground-based agent – existing at variable height depending on tripod configuration or placed on top of flat furniture like tables. Further, the reconstructions and panoramas may differ if objects are moved between camera captures.

For each node, $v = \{I, x, y, z\}$, we would like to identify the nearest, navigable point on the reconstructed mesh – i.e. the closest point that can be occupied by a ground-based agent represented by a 1.5 m tall cylinder of diameter of 0.2 m. Directly projecting to the nearest mesh location fails for 73% of nodes where failure is projecting to distant (>0.5 m) or non-navigable points. Many of these points project to surfaces other than the floor due to camera height. Instead, we cast a ray up to 2 m directly downward from the node. At small, fixed intervals along this ray, we project to the nearest mesh point. If multiple navigable

---

[1] Details included from correspondence with the author of [4].

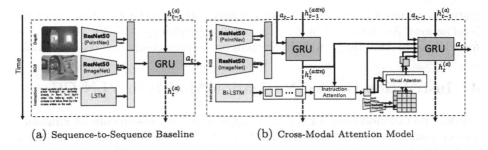

(a) Sequence-to-Sequence Baseline   (b) Cross-Modal Attention Model

Fig. 3. We develop a simple baseline agent (a) as well as an attentional agent (b) comparable to that in [29]. Both receive RGB and depth frames represented by pretrained networks for image classification [8] and point-goal navigation [31], respectively.

points are identified, we take the one with minimal horizontal displacement from the original location. If no navigable point is found with less than a 0.5 m displacement, we consider this MP3D node unmappable to the 3D mesh and thus invalid. We manually reviewed invalid nodes and made corrections if possible, e.g. shifting nodes around furniture. After these steps, 98.3% of nodes transferred successfully. We refer to these transferred nodes as waypoint locations. In Fig. 2(a), points needing adjustment (3% of points) require small displacement, averaging 0.19 m.

Given a trajectory of converted waypoints $\tau = [w_1, \ldots, w_T]$, we verify that an agent can actually navigate between each location. We employ an A*-based search algorithm to compute an approximate shortest path to a goal. We run this algorithm between each waypoint in a trajectory to the next (e.g. w_i to w_{i+1}). A trajectory is considered navigable if for each pairwise navigation, an agent can follow the shortest path to within 0.5 m of the next waypoint (w_{i+1}). In total, we find 77% of the R2R trajectories navigable in the continuous environment.

Non-Navigable Trajectories. Among the 23% of trajectories that were not navigable, we observed two primary failure modes. First and most simply, 22% included one of the 1.7% of invalid nodes that could not be projected to MP3D 3D meshes. The remaining unnavigable trajectories spanned disjoint regions of the reconstruction – i.e. lacking a valid path from some waypoint w_i to w_{i+1}. As shown in Fig. 2(b), this may be due to holes or other mesh errors dividing the space. Alternatively, objects like chairs may be moved in between panorama captures – possibly resulting in a reconstruction that places the object mesh on top of individual panorama locations. Nodes in the R2R nav-graph were manually connected if there appeared to be a path between them, even if most other panoramas (and thus the reconstruction) showed blocking objects.

3.2   VLN-CE Dataset

In total, the VLN-CE dataset consists of 4475 trajectories converted from R2R train and validation splits. For each trajectory, we provide the multiple R2R instructions and a pre-computed shortest path following the waypoints via low-level actions. As shown in Fig. 2(c), the low-level action space of VLN-CE makes for a longer horizon task – with 55.88 steps on average compared to 4–6 in R2R.

4 Instruction-Guided Navigation Models in VLN-CE

We develop two models for VLN-CE. A simple sequence-to-sequence baseline and a more powerful cross-modal attentional model. While there are many differences in the details, these models are conceptually similar to early [4] and more recent [29] work in the nav-graph based VLN task. Exploring these gives insight into the difficulty of this setting in isolation and by comparison relative to VLN. Further, these models allow us to test whether improvements from early to later architectures carry over to a more realistic setting. Both of our models make use of the same observation and instruction encodings described below.

Instruction Representation. We convert tokenized instructions to GLoVE [23] embeddings which are processed by recurrent encoders for each model. We denote these encoded tokens as $\mathbf{w}_1, \ldots, \mathbf{w}_T$ for a length T instruction.

Observation Encoding. For RGB, we apply a ResNet50 [12] pretrained on ImageNet [8] to collect semantic visual features. We denote the final spatial features of this model as $\mathcal{V} = \{\mathbf{v}_i\}$ where i indexes over spatial locations. Likewise for depth, we use a modified ResNet50 that was trained to perform point-goal navigation (i.e. to navigate to a location given in relative coordinates) [31] and denote these as $\mathcal{D} = \{\mathbf{d}_i\}$.

4.1 Sequence-to-Sequence Baseline

We consider a simple sequence-to-sequence model shown in Fig. 3(a). This model consists of a recurrent policy that takes visual observations (depth and RGB) and instructions at time step t to predict an action a. We can write the agent as

$$\bar{\mathbf{v}}_t = \text{mean-pool}\,(\mathcal{V}_t)\,, \quad \bar{\mathbf{d}}_t = [\mathbf{d}_1, \ldots, \mathbf{d}_{wh}]\,, \quad \mathbf{s} = \text{LSTM}\,(\mathbf{w}_1, \ldots, \mathbf{w}_T) \quad (1)$$

$$\mathbf{h}_t^{(a)} = \text{GRU}\left([\bar{\mathbf{v}}_t, \bar{\mathbf{d}}_t, \mathbf{s}], \mathbf{h}_{t-1}^{(a)}\right), a_t = \underset{a}{\text{argmax}} \; \text{softmax}\left(W_a \mathbf{h}_t^{(a)} + \mathbf{b}_a\right) \quad (2)$$

where $[\cdot]$ denotes concatenation and $\mathbf{s}$ is the final hidden state of an LSTM instruction encoder. This model enables straight-forward input-modality ablations.

4.2 Cross-Modal Attention Model

The previous model lacks powerful inductive biases common to vision-and-language tasks including cross-modal attention and spatial reasoning which are intuitively important for language-guided visual navigation. In Fig. 3(b) we consider a model incorporating these mechanisms. This model consists of two recurrent networks – one tracking visual history and the other tracking attended instruction and visual features. We write the first recurrent network as:

$$\mathbf{h}_t^{(attn)} = \text{GRU}\left(\left[\bar{\mathbf{v}}_t, \bar{\mathbf{d}}_t, \mathbf{a}_{t-1}\right], \mathbf{h}_{t-1}^{(attn)}\right) \qquad (3)$$

where $\mathbf{a}_{t-1} \in \mathbb{R}^{32}$ and is a learned linear embedding of the previous action. We encode instructions with a bi-directional LSTM and reserve all hidden states:

$$\mathcal{S} = \{\mathbf{s}_1, \ldots, \mathbf{s_T}\} = \text{BiLSTM}\left(\mathbf{w}_1, \ldots, \mathbf{w}_T\right) \qquad (4)$$

We then compute an attended instruction feature $\hat{\mathbf{s}}_t$ over these representations which is then used to attend to visual ($\hat{\mathbf{v}}_t$) and depth ($\hat{\mathbf{d}}_t$) features. Concretely,

$$\hat{\mathbf{s}}_t = \text{Attn}\left(\mathcal{S}, \mathbf{h}_t^{(attn)}\right), \quad \hat{\mathbf{v}}_t = \text{Attn}\left(\mathcal{V}_t, \hat{\mathbf{s}}_t\right), \quad \hat{\mathbf{d}}_t = \text{Attn}\left(\mathcal{D}_t, \hat{\mathbf{s}}_t\right) \qquad (5)$$

where Attn is a scaled dot-product attention [28]. For a query $\mathbf{q} \in \mathbb{R}^{1 \times d_q}$, $\hat{\mathbf{x}} = \text{Attn}(\{\mathbf{x}_i\}, \mathbf{q})$ is computed as $\hat{\mathbf{x}} = \sum_i \alpha_i \mathbf{x}_i$ for $\alpha_i = \text{softmax}_i((W_K\mathbf{x}_i)^T \mathbf{q} / \sqrt{d_q})$. The second recurrent network then takes a concatenation of these features including $\mathbf{a}_{t-1}$ and $\mathbf{h}_t^{(attn)}$ and predicts an action.

$$\mathbf{h}_t^{(a)} = \text{GRU}\left(\left[\hat{\mathbf{s}}_t, \hat{\mathbf{v}}_t, \hat{\mathbf{d}}_t, \mathbf{a}_{t-1}, \mathbf{h}_t^{(attn)}\right], \mathbf{h}_{t-1}^{(a)}\right) \qquad (6)$$

$$a_t = \underset{a}{\text{argmax}} \ \text{softmax}\left(W_a\mathbf{h}_t^{(a)} + \mathbf{b}_a\right) \qquad (7)$$

4.3   Auxiliary Losses and Training Regimes

Aside from modeling details, much of the remaining progress in VLN has come from adjusting the training regime – adding auxiliary losses / rewards [17,29], mitigating exposure bias during training [4,29], or incorporating synthetic data augmentation [9,26]. We explore some common variants of these directions in VLN-CE. We suspect addressing exposure bias and data sparsity will be important in VLN-CE where these issues may be amplified by lengthy action sequences.

Imitation Learning. A natural starting point for training is maximizing the likelihood of the ground truth trajectories. To do so, we perform teacher-forcing training with inflection weighting (IW). As described in [30], IW places emphasis on time-steps where actions change (i.e. $a_{t-1} \neq a_t$), adjusting loss weight proportionally to the rarity of such events. This was found to be helpful for navigation problems with long sequences of repeated actions. We observe a positive effect in early experiments and apply IW in all our experiments.

Coping with Exposure Bias. Imitation learning in auto-regressive settings suffers from a disconnect between training and test – agents are not exposed to the consequences of their actions during training. Prior work has shown significant gains by addressing this issue for VLN through scheduled sampling [4]

Table 2. No-learning baselines and input modality ablations for our baseline sequence-to-sequence model. Given the long trajectories involved, we find both random agents and single-modality ablations to perform quite poorly in VLN-CE.

Model	Vision	Instr.	History	Val-Seen						Val-Unseen					
				TL ↓	NE ↓	nDTW ↑	OS ↑	SR ↑	SPL ↑	TL ↓	NE ↓	nDTW ↑	OS ↑	SR ↑	SPL ↑
Random	-	-	-	3.54	10.20	0.28	0.04	0.02	0.02	3.74	9.51	0.30	0.04	0.03	0.02
Hand-Crafted	-	-	-	3.83	9.56	0.33	0.05	0.04	0.04	3.71	10.34	0.30	0.04	0.03	0.02
Seq2Seq	RGBD	✓	✓	8.40	8.54	0.45	0.35	0.25	0.24	7.67	8.94	0.43	0.25	0.20	0.18
– No Image	D	✓	✓	7.77	8.55	0.46	0.31	0.24	0.23	7.87	9.09	0.41	0.23	0.17	0.15
– No Depth	RGB	✓	✓	4.93	10.76	0.29	0.10	0.03	0.03	5.54	9.89	0.31	0.11	0.04	0.04
– No Vision	-	✓	✓	4.26	11.07	0.26	0.03	0.00	0.00	4.68	10.06	0.30	0.07	0.00	0.00
– No Instruction	RGBD	-	✓	7.86	9.09	0.42	0.26	0.18	0.17	7.27	9.03	0.42	0.22	0.17	0.16

or reinforcement learning fine-tuning [26,29]. In this work, we apply Dataset Aggregation (DAgger) [24] towards the same end. While DAgger and scheduled sampling share many similarities, DAgger trains on the aggregated set of trajectories from all iterations 1 to n. Thus, the resulting policy after iteration n is optimized over all past experiences and not just those collected from iteration n.

Synthetic Data Augmentation. Another popular strategy is to learn a 'speaker' model that produces instructions given a trajectory. Both [26] and [9] use these models to generate new trajectory-instruction pairs and many following works have leveraged these additional trajectories. We convert ~150k synthetic trajectories generated this way from [26] to our continuous environments.

Progress Monitor. An important aspect of success is identifying where to stop. Prior work [17] found improvements from explicitly supervising the agent with a progress-toward-goal signal. Specifically, agents are trained to predict their fraction through the trajectory at each time step. We apply progress estimation during training with a mean squared error loss term akin to [17].

5   Experiments

Setting and Metrics. We train and evaluate our models in VLN-CE. We perform early stopping based on val-unseen performance. We report standard metrics for visual navigation defined in [2,4,18] – trajectory length in meters (TL), navigation error in meters from goal at termination (NE), oracle success rate (OS), success rate (SR), success weighted by inverse path length (SPL), and normalized dynamic-time warping (nDTW). For full details on metrics, see [2,4,18].

Implementation Details. We utilize the Adam optimizer [15] with a learning rate of 2.5×10^{-4} and a batch size of 5 full trajectories. We set the inflection weighting coefficient [30] to 3.2 (inverse frequency of inflections in our ground-truth paths). We train on all ground-truth paths until convergence on val-unseen (at most 30 epochs). For DAgger [24], we collect the nth set by taking the oracle

Table 3. Performance in VLN-CE. We find that popular techniques in VLN have mixed benefit in VLN-CE; however, our best performing model combining all examined techniques succeeds nearly 1/3rd of the time in new environments. * denotes fine-tuning.

#	Model	PM [17]	DA [24]	Aug. [26]	Val-Seen						Val-Unseen					
					TL ↓	NE ↓	nDTW ↑	OS ↑	SR ↑	SPL ↑	TL ↓	NE ↓	nDTW ↑	OS ↑	SR ↑	SPL ↑
1	Seq2Seq Baseline	-	-	-	8.40	8.54	0.45	0.35	0.25	0.24	7.67	8.94	0.43	0.25	0.20	0.18
2		✓	-	-	8.34	8.48	0.47	0.32	0.22	0.21	8.93	9.28	0.40	0.28	0.17	0.15
3		-	✓	-	9.32	7.09	0.53	0.44	0.34	0.32	8.46	7.92	0.48	0.35	0.26	0.23
4		-	-	✓	8.23	7.76	0.51	0.34	0.26	0.25	7.22	8.70	0.44	0.26	0.19	0.17
5		✓	✓*	✓	9.37	7.02	0.54	0.46	0.33	0.31	9.32	7.77	0.47	0.37	0.25	0.22
6	Cross-Modal Attention	-	-	-	8.26	7.81	0.49	0.38	0.27	0.25	7.71	8.14	0.47	0.31	0.23	0.22
7		✓	-	-	8.51	8.17	0.47	0.35	0.28	0.26	7.87	8.72	0.44	0.28	0.21	0.19
8		-	✓	-	8.90	7.40	0.52	0.42	0.33	0.31	8.12	8.00	0.48	0.33	0.27	0.25
9		-	-	✓	8.50	8.05	0.49	0.36	0.26	0.24	7.58	8.65	0.45	0.28	0.21	0.19
10		✓	✓*	✓	9.26	7.12	0.54	0.46	**0.37**	**0.35**	8.64	**7.37**	**0.51**	**0.40**	**0.32**	**0.30**
11		✓	-	✓	8.49	8.29	0.47	0.36	0.27	0.25	7.68	8.42	0.46	0.30	0.24	0.22
12		-	✓*	✓	9.32	**6.76**	**0.55**	**0.47**	**0.37**	0.33	8.27	7.76	0.50	0.37	0.29	0.26

action with probability $\beta = 0.75^n$ and the current policy action otherwise. We collect $5,000$ trajectories at each stage and then perform 4 epochs of imitation learning (with inflection weighting) over all collected trajectories. Once again, we train to convergence on val-unseen (6 to 10 dataset collections, depending on the model). We implement our agents in PyTorch [22] and on top of Habitat [19].

5.1 Establishing Baseline Performance for VLN-CE

No-Learning Baselines. To establish context for our results, we consider random and hand-crafted agents in Table 2 (top two rows). The random agent selects actions according to the action distribution in train.[2] The hand-crafted agent picks a random heading and takes 37 forward actions (dataset average) before calling stop. Both these agents achieve a ~3% success rate in val-unseen despite no learned components or input processing. A similar hand-crafted model in VLN yields a 16.3% success rate [4]. Though not directly comparable, this gap illustrates the strong structural prior provided by the nav-graph in VLN.

Seq2Seq and Single-Modality Ablations. Table 2 also shows performance for the baseline Seq2Seq model along with input ablations. All models are trained with imitation learning without data augmentation or any auxiliary losses. Our baseline Seq2Seq model significantly outperforms the random and hand-crafted baselines, successfully reaching the goal in 20% of val-unseen episodes.

As illustrated in [27], single modality models can be strong baselines in embodied tasks. We train models without access to the instruction (No Instruction) and with ablated visual input (No Vision/Depth/Image). All of these ablations under-perform the Seq2Seq baseline. We find depth is a very strong signal for learning – models lacking it (No Depth and No Vision) fail to outperform chance (≤1% success rates). We believe depth enables agents to

---

[2] 68% forward, 15% turn-left, 15% turn-right, and 2% stop.

Fig. 4. Example of our Cross Modal Attention model taken in an unseen environment.

quickly begin traversing environments effectively (e.g. without collisions) and without this it is very difficult to bootstrap to instruction following. The No Instruction model achieves 17% success, similarly to a hand-crafted agent in VLN, suggesting shared trajectory regularities between VLN and VLN-CE. While these regularities can be manually exploited in VLN via the nav-graph, they are implicit in VLN-CE as evidenced by the significantly lower performance of our random and hand crafted agents which collide with and get stuck on obstacles. The No Image model also achieves 17% success, similarly failing to reason about instructions. This hints at the importance of grounding visual referents (through RGB) for navigation.

5.2   Model Performance in VLN-CE

Table 3 shows a comparison of our models (Seq2Seq and Cross-Modal) under three training augmentations (Progress Monitor, DAgger, Data Augmentation).

Cross-Modal Attention vs. Seq2Seq. We find the cross-modal attention model outperforms Seq2Seq under all settings for new environments. For example, in teacher-forcing training (row 1 vs. 6), the cross-modal attention model improves from 0.18 to 0.22 SPL on val-unseen, an improvement of 0.04 SPL (22% relative). When applying all three augmentations (row 5 vs. 10), the cross-modal model improves from 0.22 to 0.30 SPL, an improvement of 0.08 SPL (36% relative).

Training Augmentation. We find DAgger-based training impactful for both the Seq2Seq (row 1 vs. 3) and Cross-Modal (row 6 vs. 8) models – improving by 0.03-0.05 SPL in val-unseen. Contrary to findings in prior work, we observe negative effects from progress monitor auxiliary loss or data augmentation for both models (rows 2/4 and 7/9) – dropping 0.01-0.03 SPL from standard training (rows 1/6). Despite this, we find combining all three techniques to lead to significant performance gains for the cross-modal attention model (row 10). Specifically, we pretrain with imitation learning, data augmentation, and the progress monitoring loss, then finetune using DAgger (with $\beta=0.75^{n+1}$) on the original data. This Cross-Modal Attention PM+DA*+Aug model achieves an

Table 4. Comparison on the VLN validation and test sets with existing models. Note there is a significant gap between techniques that leverage the oracle nav-graph at train and inference (top set) and our best method in continuous environments.

Model	Val-Seen (VLN)					Val-Unseen (VLN)					Test (VLN)				
	TL↓	NE↓	OS↑	SR↑	SPL↑	TL↓	NE↓	OS↑	SR↑	SPL↑	TL↓	NE↓	OS↑	SR↑	SPL↑
VLN Task VLN-Seq2Seq [4]	11.33	6.01	0.52	0.38	-	8.39	7.81	0.28	0.21	-	8.13	7.85	0.27	0.20	0.18
Self-Monitoring [17]	-	3.18	0.77	0.68	0.58	-	5.41	0.68	0.47	0.34	18.04	5.67	0.59	0.48	0.35
RCM [29]	10.65	3.53	0.75	0.66	-	11.46	6.09	0.50	0.42	-	11.97	6.12	0.495	0.43	0.38
Back-Translation [26]	10.1	4.71	-	0.55	0.53	9.37	5.49	-	0.46	0.43	11.7	-	-	0.51	0.47
Cross-Modal (PM+DA*+Aug.)	6.92	7.77	0.30	0.25	0.23	7.42	8.17	0.28	0.22	0.20	9.47	8.55	0.32	0.24	0.21

SPL of 0.35 on val-seen and 0.30 on val-unseen – succeeding on 32% of episodes in new environments.

We explore this trend further for the Cross-Modal model. We examine the validation performance of PM+Aug (row 11) and find it to outperform Aug or PM alone (by 0.02–0.03 SPL). Next, we examine progress monitor loss on val-unseen for both PM and PM+Aug. We find that without data augmentation, the progress monitor over-fits considerably more (validation loss of 0.67 vs. 0.47) – indicating that the progress monitor can be effective in our continuous setting but tends to over-fit on the non-augmented training data, negatively affecting generalization. Finally, we examine the performance of DA*+Aug (row 12) and find that this outperforms DA (by 0.01–0.02 SPL), but is unable to match pre-training with the progress monitor and augmented data (row 10).

Example. We examine our Cross-Modal Attention PM+DA*+Aug model in an unseen environment (Fig. 4). The example demonstrates the increased difficultly of VLN-CE (37 actions vs. 4 hops in VLN). It also shows a failure of the agent – the agent navigates towards the wrong windows and fails to first *"pass the kitchen"* – stopping instead at the nearest couch. We observe failures when the agent never sees the instruction referent(s) – with a limited egocentric field-of-view, the agent must actively choose to observe the surrounding scene.

5.3   Examining the Impact of the Nav-Graph in VLN

To draw a direct comparison between the VLN and VLN-CE settings, we convert trajectories taken by our Cross-Modal Attention (PM+DA*+Aug.) model in continuous environments to nav-graph trajectories (details in the supplement) and then evaluate these paths on the VLN leaderboard.[3] We emphasize that the point of this comparison is not to outperform existing approaches for VLN, but rather to highlight how important the nav-graph is to the performance of existing VLN systems by contrasting them with our model. Unlike the approaches shown, our model does not benefit from the nav-graph during training or inference.

As shown in Table 4, we find significant gaps between our model and prior work in the VLN setting. Despite having similar cross-modal attention architectures, RCM [29] achieves an SPL of 0.38 in test environments while our model

---

[3] Note that the VLN test set is not publicly available except through this leaderboard.

yields 0.21. Further, state-of-the-art on the test set is near 0.47 SPL, over 2x what we report. However, it is unclear if these gains could be realized on a real system given the strong assumptions set by the nav-graph. In contrast, our approach does not rely on external information and recent work has shown promising sim2real transferability for navigation agents trained in continuous simulations [14].

Caveats. Direct comparisons between drastically different settings are challenging, we note some caveats. About 20% of VLN trajectories are non-navigable in VLN-CE and thus our models cannot succeed on these. Further, continuous VLN-CE paths can translate poorly to nav-graph trajectories when traversing areas of the environment not well-covered by the sparse panoramas. Comparing VLN-CE val results in Table 3 with the same in Table 4 shows these effects account for a drop of ~0.10 SPL. Even compensating for this possible underestimation, nav-graph-based approaches still outperform our continuous models significantly.

6   Discussion

In this work, we explore the problem of following navigation instructions in continuous environments with low-level actions – lifting many of the unrealistic assumptions in prior nav-graph-based settings. Our work lays the groundwork for future research into reducing the gap between simulation and reality for VLN agents. Crucially, setting our VLN-CE task in continuous environments (rather than a nav-graph) provides the community a testbed where integrative experiments studying the interface of high- and low-level control are possible. This includes studying the effect of imperfect actuation by leveraging recent features in the Habitat simulator [19], reasoning about (potentially dynamic) objects inserted in the 3D environment, or developing modular planner-controller architectures that leverage existing robot path planning algorithms.

Acknowledgements. We thank Anand Koshy for his implementation of nDTW. The GT effort was supported in part by NSF, AFRL, DARPA, ONR YIPs, ARO PECASE, Amazon. The OSU effort was supported in part by DARPA. The views and conclusions contained herein are those of the authors and should not be interpreted as necessarily representing the official policies or endorsements, either expressed or implied, of the U.S. Government, or any sponsor.

References

1. Locobot: an open source low cost robot (2019). https://locobot-website.netlify.com/
2. Anderson, P., et al.: On evaluation of embodied navigation agents. arXiv preprint arXiv:1807.06757 (2018)
3. Anderson, P., Shrivastava, A., Parikh, D., Batra, D., Lee, S.: Chasing ghosts: instruction following as Bayesian state tracking. In: NeurIPS (2019)

4. Anderson, P., et al.: Vision-and-language navigation: Interpreting visually-grounded navigation instructions in real environments. In: CVPR (2018)
5. Chang, A., et al.: Matterport3D: learning from RGB-D data in indoor environments. In: 3DV (2017). MatterPort3D dataset license available at: http://kaldir.vc.in.tum.de/matterport/MP_TOS.pdf
6. Chen, H., Suhr, A., Misra, D., Snavely, N., Artzi, Y.: Touchdown: natural language navigation and spatial reasoning in visual street environments. In: CVPR (2019)
7. Das, A., Datta, S., Gkioxari, G., Lee, S., Parikh, D., Batra, D.: Embodied question answering. In: CVPR (2018)
8. Deng, J., Dong, W., Socher, R., Li, L.J., Li, K., Fei-Fei, L.: ImageNet: a large-scale hierarchical image database. In: CVPR (2009)
9. Fried, D., et al.: Speaker-follower models for vision-and-language navigation. In: NeurIPS (2018)
10. Gordon, D., Kembhavi, A., Rastegari, M., Redmon, J., Fox, D., Farhadi, A.: IQA: visual question answering in interactive environments. In: CVPR (2018)
11. Gupta, S., Davidson, J., Levine, S., Sukthankar, R., Malik, J.: Cognitive mapping and planning for visual navigation. In: CVPR (2017)
12. He, K., Zhang, X., Ren, S., Sun, J.: Deep residual learning for image recognition. In: CVPR (2016)
13. Hermann, K.M., Malinowski, M., Mirowski, P., Banki-Horvath, A., Anderson, K., Hadsell, R.: Learning to follow directions in street view. In: AAAI (2020)
14. Kadian, A., et al.: Are we making real progress in simulated environments? Measuring the sim2real gap in embodied visual navigation. In: IROS (2020)
15. Kingma, D., Ba, J.: Adam: a method for stochastic optimization. In: ICLR (2015)
16. Kohlbrecher, S., Meyer, J., von Stryk, O., Klingauf, U.: A flexible and scalable slam system with full 3D motion estimation. In: SSRR. IEEE, November 2011
17. Ma, C.Y., et al.: Self-monitoring navigation agent via auxiliary progress estimation. In: ICLR (2019)
18. Magalhaes, G., Jain, V., Ku, A., Ie, E., Baldridge, J.: Effective and general evaluation for instruction conditioned navigation using dynamic time warping. arXiv preprint arXiv:1907.05446 (2019)
19. Savva, M., et al.: Habitat: a platform for embodied AI research. In: ICCV (2019)
20. Misra, D., Bennett, A., Blukis, V., Niklasson, E., Shatkhin, M., Artzi, Y.: Mapping instructions to actions in 3D environments with visual goal prediction. In: EMNLP (2018)
21. Mur-Artal, R., Montiel, J.M.M., Tardos, J.D.: ORB-SLAM: a versatile and accurate monocular slam system. IEEE Trans. Robot. **31**(5), 1147–1163 (2015)
22. Paszke, A., et al.: Pytorch: an imperative style, high-performance deep learning library. In: NeurIPS (2019)
23. Pennington, J., Socher, R., Manning, C.D.: GloVe: global vectors for word representation. In: EMNLP (2014)
24. Ross, S., Gordon, G., Bagnell, D.: A reduction of imitation learning and structured prediction to no-regret online learning. In: AISTATS (2011) 3, 10, 12
25. Stentz, A.: Optimal and efficient path planning for partially known environments. In: Hebert, M.H., Thorpe, C., Stentz, A. (eds.) Intelligent Unmanned Ground Vehicles. SECS, vol. 388, pp. 203–220. Springer, Boston (1997). https://doi.org/10.1007/978-1-4615-6325-9_11
26. Tan, H., Yu, L., Bansal, M.: Learning to navigate unseen environments: back translation with environmental dropout. In: NAACL HLT (2019)
27. Thomason, J., Gordon, D., Bisk, Y.: Shifting the baseline: single modality performance on visual navigation & QA. In: NAACL HLT (2019)

28. Vaswani, A., et al.: Attention is all you need. In: NeurIPS (2017)
29. Wang, X., et al.: Reinforced cross-modal matching and self-supervised imitation learning for vision-language navigation. In: CVPR (2019)
30. Wijmans, E., et al.: Embodied question answering in photorealistic environments with point cloud perception. In: CVPR (2019)
31. Wijmans, E., et al.: DD-PPO: learning near-perfect pointgoal navigators from 2.5 billion frames. In: ICLR (2020)

Boundary Content Graph Neural Network for Temporal Action Proposal Generation

Yueran Bai[1], Yingying Wang[2], Yunhai Tong[1(✉)], Yang Yang[2], Qiyue Liu[2], and Junhui Liu[2(✉)]

[1] Key Laboratory of Machine Perception (MOE), School of EECS,
Peking University, Beijing, China
{baiyueran,yhtong}@pku.edu.cn
[2] iQIYI, Inc., Beijing, China
{wangyingying02,andyang,liuqiyue,liujunhui}@qiyi.com

Abstract. Temporal action proposal generation plays an important role in video action understanding, which requires localizing high-quality action content precisely. However, generating temporal proposals with both precise boundaries and high-quality action content is extremely challenging. To address this issue, we propose a novel Boundary Content Graph Neural Network (BC-GNN) to model the insightful relations between the boundary and action content of temporal proposals by the graph neural networks. In BC-GNN, the boundaries and content of temporal proposals are taken as the nodes and edges of the graph neural network, respectively, where they are spontaneously linked. Then a novel graph computation operation is proposed to update features of edges and nodes. After that, one updated edge and two nodes it connects are used to predict boundary probabilities and content confidence score, which will be combined to generate a final high-quality proposal. Experiments are conducted on two mainstream datasets: ActivityNet-1.3 and THU-MOS14. Without the bells and whistles, BC-GNN outperforms previous state-of-the-art methods in both temporal action proposal and temporal action detection tasks.

Keywords: Temporal action proposal generation · Graph Neural Network · Temporal action detection

1 Introduction

Temporal action proposal generation becomes an active research topic in recent years, as it is a fundamental step for untrimmed video understanding tasks,

---

Y. Bai and Y. Wang—Equal contributions.
Y. Bai—Work was done during an internship in iQIYI, Inc.

Electronic supplementary material The online version of this chapter (https://doi.org/10.1007/978-3-030-58604-1_8) contains supplementary material, which is available to authorized users.

© Springer Nature Switzerland AG 2020
A. Vedaldi et al. (Eds.): ECCV 2020, LNCS 12373, pp. 121–137, 2020.
https://doi.org/10.1007/978-3-030-58604-1_8

such as temporal action detection and video analysis. A useful action proposal method could distinguish the activities we are interested in, so that only intervals containing visual information indicating activity categories can be retrieved. Although extensive studies have been carried out in the past, generating temporal proposals with both precise boundaries and rich action content remains a challenge[1, 2, 5, 11–13, 15, 26].

Some existing methods [1, 2, 5, 12, 15, 26] are proposed to generate candidate proposals by sliding multi-scale temporal windows in videos with regular interval or designing multiple temporal anchor instances for temporal feature maps. Since the lengths of windows and anchors are fixed and set previously, these methods cannot generate proposals with precise boundaries and lack flexibility to retrieve action instances of varies temporal durations.

Recent works [11, 13] aim to generate higher quality proposals. [13] adopts a "local to global" fashion to retrieve proposals. In the first, temporal boundaries are achieved by evaluating boundary confidence of every location of the video feature sequence. Then, content feature between boundaries of each proposal is used to generate content confidence score of proposal. [11] proposes an end-to-end pipeline, in which confidence score of boundaries and content of densely distributed proposals are generated simultaneously. Although these works can generate proposals with higher quality, they ignore to make explicit use of interaction between boundaries and content.

To address this drawback, we propose Boundary Content Graph Neural Network (BC-GNN), which uses a graph neural network to model interaction between boundaries and content of proposals. As shown in Fig. 1, a graph neural network links boundaries and content into a whole. For the graph of each video, the nodes denote temporal locations, while the edges between nodes are defined based on content between these locations. This graph enables information exchanging between nodes and edges to generate more dependable boundary probabilities and content confidence scores. In our proposed framework, a graph neural network is constructed to link boundaries and content of temporal proposals firstly. Then a novel graph computation operation is proposed to update features of edges and nodes. After that, one updated edge and two nodes it connects are used to product boundary probabilities and content confidence score, which are combined to generate a candidate proposal.

In summary, the main contributions of our work are three folds:

(1) We propose a new approach named Boundary Content Graph Neural Network (BC-GNN) based on the graph neural network to enable the relationship between boundary probability predictions and confidence evaluation procedures.
(2) We introduce a novel graph reasoning operation in BC-GNN to update attributes of the edges and nodes in the boundary content graph.
(3) Experiments in different datasets demonstrate that our method outperforms other existing state-of-the-art methods in both temporal action proposal generation task and temporal action detection task.

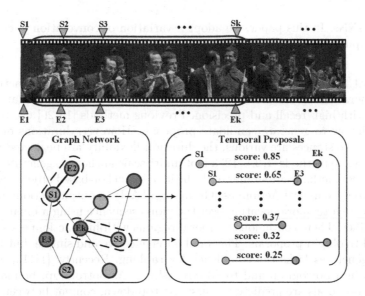

Fig. 1. Schematic depiction of the proposed approach. The red box denotes an action instance in a video. We regard temporal locations with regular interval as start locations and end locations for video segments. Start locations S and end locations E are regarded as nodes. Only when the location of S is before E, we define the content between them as an edge to connect them. Then, a novel graph reasoning operation is applied to enable the relationship between nodes and edges. Finally, two nodes and the edge connected them form a temporal proposal. (Color figure online)

2   Related Work

Action Recognition. Recognizing action classes in trimmed videos is a both basic and significant task for the purpose of video understanding. Traditional approaches are mostly based on hand-crafted feature [4,10,18,25]. As the progress of Convolutional Neural Networks (CNN) in recent years, CNN based methods are widely adopted in action recognition and achieve superior performance. One type of these methods [6,27] focus on combining multiple data modalities. Furthermore, other methods attempt to exploit the spatial-temporal feature by using 3D convolution operation [3,16,23]. The feature sequence extracted by action recognition models can be used as the input feature sequence of our network framework to analyze long and untrimmed video.

Graph Neural Network. Graph Neural Networks (GNNs) are proposed to handle graph-structured data with deep learning. With the development of deep learning, different kinds of GNNs appear one after another. [17] proposes the Graph Convolutional Networks (GCNs), which defines convolutions on the non-grid structures. [24] adopts attention mechanism in GNNs. [9] proposes an effective way to exploit features of edges in GNNs. Methods [19,29,31] based on GNNs are also applied to many areas in computer vision, since the effectiveness of these GNNs. In this paper, we adopt a variation of convolution operation in [9] to compute feature of nodes in our graph neural network.

Temporal Action Proposal Generation. The goal of temporal action proposal generation task is to retrieve temporal segments that contain action instance with high recall and precision. Previous methods [15,26] use temporal sliding window to generate candidate proposals. However, durations of ground truth action instances are various, the duration flexibility are neglected in these methods. Some methods [1,2,5,12] adopt multi-scale anchors to generate proposals, and these methods are similar with the idea in anchor-based object detection. [32] proposes Temporal Actionness Grouping (TAG) to output actionness probability for each temporal location over the video sequence using a binary actionness classifier. Then, continuous temporal regions with high actionness score are combined to obtain proposals. This method is effective and simple, but the proposal it generates lacks the confidence for ranking. Recently, [11,13] generate proposals in a bottom-up and top-down fashion. As bottom-up, boundaries of temporal proposals are predicted at first. As top-down, content between boundaries is evaluated as a confidence score. While the relations between boundaries and content is not utilized explicitly, which is quite important we believe. In this paper, we combine boundary probability predictions and confidence evaluation procedures into a whole by graph neural network. It facilitates information exchanging through these two branches, and brings strong quality improvement in temporal action proposal generation and temporal action detection.

3   Our Approach

In this section, we will introduce the details of our approach illustrated in Fig. 2. In Feature Encoding, visual contents of input video are encoded into feature sequence by a spatial and temporal action recognition network, then this sequence of features is fed into our proposed Boundary Content Graph Neural Network (BC-GNN) framework. There are four modules in BC-GNN: Base Module, Graph Construction Module (GCM), Graph Reasoning Module (GRM) and Output Module. The Base Module is the backbone which is used to exploit local semantic information of input feature sequence. GCM takes feature sequences from Base Module as input and construct a graph neural network. In the GRM module, a new graph computation operation is proposed to update attributes of edges and nodes. Output Module takes the updated edges and nodes as input to predict boundary and content confidence scores. At last, proposals are generated by score fusion and Soft-NMS.

3.1   Problem Definition

One untrimmed video consists of a sequence of l_v frames, and this sequence can be denoted as $X = \{x_n\}_{n=1}^{l_v}$. Action instances in the video content compose a set named $\Psi_g = \{\psi_n = (t_s^n, t_e^n)\}_{n=1}^{N_g}$, where t_s^n and t_e^n denote the start and end temporal points of the n_{th} action instance respectively, and N_g denotes the total number of action instances in this video. Classes of these action instances are not considered in temporal action proposal generation task.

3.2   Feature Encoding

Two-stream network [22] is adopted in our framework as visual encoder, since this encoder shows good performance in video action recognition task. This two-stream network consists of spatial and temporal branches. Spatial one is used to encode RGB frames and temporal one is adopted for encoding flow frames. They are designed to capture information from appearance and motion separately.

More specifically, an input video X with l_v frames is downsampled to a sequence of l_s snippets $S = \{s_n\}_{n=1}^{l_s}$ in a regular temporal interval τ. Thus, the length of snippet sequence l_s is calculated as $l_s = l_v/\tau$. Every snippet s_n in sequence S is composed of a RGB frame x_n and several optical frames o_n.

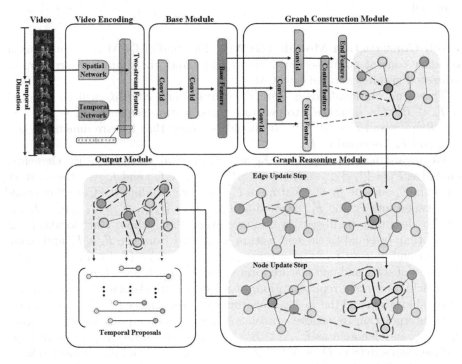

Fig. 2. The framework of BC-GNN. Feature Encoding encodes the video into sequence of feature. Base Module expands the receptive field. GCM constructs boundary content graph network in which start nodes and end nodes are denoted as green circles and yellow circles separately. GRM updates edges and nodes, to relate information between edges and nodes. Finally, Output Module generates every candidate proposal with each edge and its connected nodes.

After feeding S into two-stream network, two sequences of action class scores are predicted from top layers of both branches. Then, these two sequences of scores are concatenated together at feature dimension to generate a feature sequence $F = \{f_n\}_{n=1}^{l_s}$.

3.3   Boundary Content Graph Network

Base Module. On one hand, Base Module expands the receptive field, thus it serves as the backbone of whole network. On the other hand, because of the uncertainty of untrimmed videos' length, Base Module applies temporal observation window with fixed length l_w to normalize length of input sequences for the whole framework. The length of observation windows depends on type of datasets. We denote input feature sequence in one window as $F_i \in R^{D_i \times l_w}$, where D_i is the input feature dimension size.

We use two stacked 1D convolution to design our Base Module since local features are needed in sequential parts, written by $F_b = conv1d_2(conv1d_1(f_i))$. After feeding feature sequence F_i into convolutional layers, $F_b \in R^{D_b \times l_w}$ is generated.

Graph Construction Module (GCM). The goal of GCM is to construct a boundary content graph network. Figure 3(a) shows the simplified structure of undirected graph generated by GCM.

Three convolutional layers $conv1d_s$, $conv1d_e$ and $conv1d_c$ will be adopted for $F_b \in R^{D_b \times l_w}$ separately to generate three feature sequence $F_s \in R^{D_g \times l_w}$, $F_e \in R^{D_g \times l_w}$ and $F_c \in R^{D_c \times l_w}$. It should be noted that feature dimension size of F_s and F_e are equal to D_g.

We regard feature sequences F_s and F_e as two sets of feature elements, denoted as $F_s = \{f_{s,i}\}_{i=1}^{l_w}$ and $F_e = \{f_{e,j}\}_{j=1}^{l_w}$, where $f_{s,j}$ and $f_{e,j}$ are the i_{th} start feature in F_s and the j_{th} end feature in F_e. Then we conduct the Cartesian product between sets F_s and F_e, denoted as $F_s \times F_e = \{(f_{s,i}, f_{s,j}) | f_{s,i} \in F_s \wedge f_{e,j} \in F_e\}$. To clear out the illegals, we remove every tuple whose start location i is greater than or equal to the end feature location j from the $F_s \times F_e$ and name the start-end pair set to $M_{SE} = \{(f_{s,i}, f_{s,j}) | (f_{s,i} \in F_s) \wedge (f_{e,j} \in F_e) \wedge (i < j)\}$. The pairs of start and end feature form a start-end pair set M_{SE}.

To achieve content representation, we select feature elements between the i_{th} temporal location and the j_{th} location from F_c as a sequence $\{f_{c,n}\}_{n=i}^{j}$. We adopt linear interpolation to achieve constant N vectors at temporal dimension from $\{f_{c,n}\}_{n=i}^{j}$, and denote it as $f_{c,(i,j)} \in R^{D_c \times N}$. After generating $f_{c,(i,j)}$, we reshape its dimension size from $D_c \times N$ to $(D_c \cdot N) \times 1$, and apply a fully connected layer fc_1 to make dimension size of $f_{c,(i,j)}$ same with $f_{s,i}$ and $f_{e,j}$, denoted as $f_{c,(i,j)} \in R^{D_g}$. Thus, we achieve a content set $M_C = \{f_{c,(i,j)} | i < j\}$. Content between the i_{th} temporal location and the j_{th} temporal location composes content set M_C.

Then, the start-end pair set M_{SE} and content set M_C make up a undirected graph. Since the tuple $(f_{s,i}, f_{e,j}) \in M_{SE}$ corresponds to the video segment that starts at the i_{th} temporal location and ends at the j_{th} temporal location. If elements in F_s and F_e are regarded as the nodes of a graph, tuples in M_{SE} identify the connection relationship between these nodes. Meanwhile the tuples in M_{SE} and elements in M_C are mapped one by one. Therefore, elements in M_C can be regarded as the edges of this graph. Formally, graphs can be denoted as $G = (V, E, I)$, where V, E and I are their nodes, edges and incidence functions respectively. In our graph, we define nodes as $V = F_s \cup F_e$, edges as $E = M_C$ and incidence function as $I = M_c \leftrightarrow M_{SE}$, where $M_{SE} \subset V \times V$. We call $f_{s,i}$ start node, and call $f_{e,i}$ end node.

In summary, we build a restricted undirected bipartite graph in which start nodes are only connected to end nodes whose temporal locations are behind them. It should be noted edge feature in our boundary content graph is not scalars but multi-dimensional feature vectors.

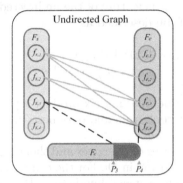
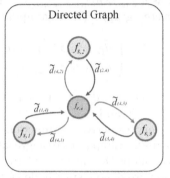

(a) Undirected Graph in GCM   (b) Directed Graph in GRM

Fig. 3. (a) Construction of undirected graph in GCM. Yellow circle denotes the start node $f_{s,i}$ sampled from feature F_s, green circle denotes the end node $f_{e,i}$ sampled from feature F_e, and blue line denotes the undirected edge which is generated from feature vectors between temporal locations P_i and P_j in F_c. The translucent circles denote the nodes without edge connection. (b) Structure of directed graph in GRM. For convenience of description, this digraph only contains one end node and three start nodes. Red curves denote the start to end edge which point from start node to end node, and the grey curves denote the end to start edge which point from end node to start node.

Graph Reasoning Module (GRM). In order to enable information exchanging between nodes and edges, we propose a new graph computation operation. One time of graph reasoning operation is applied in a block named Graph Reasoning Block (GRB). GRM consists of two stacked GRBs.

Our graph computation operation is divided into edge update and node update step. Edge update step is intended to aggregate the attributes of the two nodes connected by the edge. As mentioned above, we construct an undirected bipartite graph, in which edges are not directed and start nodes only connect with end nodes. Since the feature required from start nodes to end nodes is different from information from end nodes to start nodes. We converse the undirected graph into a directed graph or a bi-directed edge. This conversion is shown in Fig. 3(b), every undirected edge is split into two opposite directed edges. In detail, we divide an undirected edge in this graph into two directed edges with the same nodes connection and opposite direction. In other words, one undirected edge turns into two directed edges, which are start to end directed edge and end to start directed edge. We define one directed edge from the i_{th} start feature $f_{s,i} \in F_s$ to the j_{th} end feature $f_{e,j} \in F_e$ as $d_{(i,j)}$, and define directed edge from end feature $f_{e,j}$ to start feature $f_{s,i}$ as $d_{(j,i)}$, where subscript i is only used for start node, j is only used for end node, and (i,j) identifies the direction of the directed edge which points from the i_{th} start node to the j_{th} end node.

Features of directed edges $d_{(i,j)}$ and $d_{(j,i)}$ are same before the edge updating, denoted as $d_{(i,j)} = d_{(j,i)} = f_{c,(i,j)}$, where $f_{c,(i,j)}$ is feature of the undirected edge in undirected graph. The edge updating can be described as

$$\begin{cases} \tilde{d}_{(i,j)} = \sigma(\theta_{s2e} \times (d_{(i,j)} * f_{s,i} * f_{e,j})) + d_{(i,j)}) \\ \tilde{d}_{(j,i)} = \sigma(\theta_{e2s} \times (d_{(j,i)} * f_{s,i} * f_{e,j}) + d_{(j,i)}) \end{cases}, \tag{1}$$

where "$*$" and "$\times$" denote element-wise product and matrix product separately. $\theta_{s2e} \in R^{D_g \times D_g}$ and $\theta_{e2s} \in R^{D_g \times D_g}$ are different trainable parameter matrices, and "σ" denotes activation function ReLU.

Node update step aims to aggregate attributes of the edges and their adjacent nodes. We adopt the variation of graph convolution in [9]. For the convenience of description, we denote start node and end node as general node $n_k \in R^{D_g}$, where k denotes the k_{th} node in the graph. The total number of these nodes is $l_N = l_w \cdot 2$, and these general nodes form a set as $N = \{n_k\}_{k=1}^{l_N}$. Meanwhile, we treat updated start to end edge $\tilde{d}_{(i,j)}$ and updated end to start edge $\tilde{d}_{(j,i)}$ as general edge $e_{(h,t)} \in R^{D_g}$. These general edges form a set as $E = \{e_{(h,t)} | n_h \in N \wedge n_t \in N\}$. As usual, the node pointed by the directed edge is called the tail node, and the node where the edge starts is called the head node. It is defined that $e_{(h,t)}$ is from head node n_h to tail node n_t. Considering that the number of nodes connected to each other is different, and to avoid increasing the scale of output features through multiplication, we first normalize the features of edges before the graph convolution operation. This normalization operation is described as

$$\tilde{e}_{(h,t)}^p = \frac{e_{(h,t)}^p}{\sum_{k=1}^K e_{(h,k)}^p}, \tag{2}$$

where p is the p_{th} feature in feature vectors $e_{(h,t)}$ and $\tilde{e}_{(h,t)}$, and K is the number of tail nodes. Note that all elements in $e_{(h,t)}$ are nonnegative. Then the convolution process of node features is described as

$$\tilde{n}_t = \sigma(\theta_{node} \times (\sum_{h=1}^H (\tilde{e}_{(h,t)} * n_h)) + n_t), \tag{3}$$

where trainable matrix $\theta_{node} \in R^{D_g \times D_g}$ is divided into θ_{start} and θ_{end} depending on type of node n_t, and H is the number of head nodes. This convolution operation gathers the information of head nodes to the tail nodes through the directed edges.

After performing the above two steps, there are a new node feature set $\tilde{N} = \{\tilde{n}_k\}_{k=1}^{l_N}$ and an edge feature set $\tilde{E} = \{\tilde{e}_{(h,t)} | \tilde{n}_h \in \tilde{N} \wedge \tilde{n}_t \in \tilde{N}\}$ generated in one GRB. These two sets become input of the second GRB.

Output Module. As shown in Fig. 1, a candidate proposal is generated using a pair of opposite directed edges and their connected nodes. Boundaries and content confidence scores of the candidate proposals are generated based on their nodes and edges, respectively. The details are described as following.

Before fed into Output Module, directed edge feature set $\tilde{E}$ is divided into a start to end edge feature set and an end to start edge feature set, which are denoted as $\tilde{E}_{s2e} = \{\tilde{e}_{s2e,(i,j)} | i < j \wedge \tilde{e}_{s2e} \in \tilde{E}\}$ and $\tilde{E}_{e2s} = \{\tilde{e}_{e2s,(j,i)}, | i < j \wedge \tilde{e}_{e2s,(j,i)} \in \tilde{E}\}$. Meanwhile, node feature set $\tilde{N}$ is divided into a start node feature set $\tilde{N}_s = \{\tilde{n}_{s,i}\}_{i=1}^{l_w}$ and an end node feature set $\tilde{N}_e = \{\tilde{n}_{e,j}\}_{j=1}^{l_w}$. Based on this divided feature sets, we build a candidate proposal feature set $M_{SCE} = \{(\tilde{n}_{s,i}, \tilde{n}_{e,j}, \tilde{e}_{s2e,(i,j)}, \tilde{e}_{e2s,(j,i)}) | i < j\}$, where $\tilde{n}_{s,i} \in \tilde{N}_s$ is the i_{th} start node feature , $\tilde{n}_{e,j} \in \tilde{N}_e$ is the j_{th} end node feature, $\tilde{e}_{s2e,(i,j)} \in \tilde{E}_{s2e}$ is directed edge feature from the i_{th} start node to the j_{th} end node and $\tilde{e}_{e2s,(j,i)} \in \tilde{E}_{e2s}$ is directed edge feature from the j_{th} end node to the i_{th} start node. The elements in M_{SCE} are mapped to M_{SE} one by one.

Output Module generates one proposal set $\Psi_p = \{\psi_n\}_{n=1}^{l_\psi}$, where $\psi_n = (t_s, p_s, t_e, p_e, p_c)$. t_s and t_e are start and end temporal locations of ψ_n separately. p_s, p_e and p_c are the confidence scores of boundary locations t_s, t_e and confidence score of content between boundaries t_s and t_e.

Each element in M_{SCE} is computed to get a ψ_n, and the computation operation is described as

$$\psi_n = \begin{cases} t_s = i, \\ t_e = j, \\ p_s = \sigma(\theta_{SO} \times \tilde{n}_{s,i}), \\ p_e = \sigma(\theta_{EO} \times \tilde{n}_{e,j}), \\ p_c = \sigma(\theta_{CO} \times (\tilde{e}_{s2e,(i,j)} \| \tilde{e}_{s2e,(j,i)})) \end{cases}, \tag{4}$$

where "σ" denotes activation function sigmoid, "$\times$" denotes matrix multiplication, and "$\|$" denotes concatenating operation at feature dimension between vectors. θ_{SO}, θ_{EO} and θ_{CO} denote trainable vectors.

3.4   Training of BC-GNN

Label Assignment. Given a video, we first extract feature sequence by two-stream network [22]. Then, we use sliding observation windows with length l_w in feature sequence to get a series of feature sequences with length of l_w.

The ground-truth action instances in this window compose an instance set $\Psi_g = \{\psi_g^n = (t_{g,s}^n, t_{g,e}^n)\}_{n=1}^{l_g}$, where l_g is the size of Ψ_g. ψ_g^n starts at the temporal position $t_{g,s}^n$ and ends at $t_{g,e}^n$. For each ground truth action instance ψ_n^g, we define its start interval $r_s^n = [t_{g,s}^n - d_g^n/10, t_{g,s}^n + d_g^n/10]$ and end interval $r_{g,e}^n = [t_{g,s}^n - d_g^n/10, t_{g,s}^n + d_g^n/10]$ separately, where $d_g^n = t_{g,e}^n - t_{g,s}^n$. After that, the start region and end region are defined as following

$$
\begin{cases}
r_{g,s} = \overset{l_g}{\underset{n=1}{\cup}} r_{g,s}^n \\
r_{g,e} = \overset{l_g}{\underset{n-1}{\cup}} r_{g,e}^n
\end{cases}
. \tag{5}
$$

Extracted features in observation window are denoted as F_i. Taking F_i as the input, BC-GNN outputs a set $\Psi_p = \{\psi_n = (t_s, p_s, t_e, p_e, p_c)\}_{n=1}^{l_p}$, where l_p is the size of Ψ_p. Because a plenty of temporal proposals share boundaries, boundary locations t_s and t_e are duplicated in Ψ_p. We select a start set $S = \{s_n = (t_s, p_s, b_s)|\}_{n=1}^{l_s}$, an end set $E = \{e_n = (t_e, p_e, b_e)\}_{n=1}^{l_e}$ and a content set $C = \{c_n = (t_s, t_e, p_c, b_c)\}_{n=1}^{l_c}$ from Ψ_P. In these three sets, b_s, b_e and b_c are assigned labels for s_n, e_n and c_n based on Ψ_g. If t_s locates in the scope of $r_{g,s}$, label b_s in start tuple s_n is set to constant 1, otherwise it is set to 0. In the same way we can get the label of e_n. If b_c of content tuple c_n is set to 1, two conditions need to be satisfied. One is that t_s and t_e of content tuple c_n located in the regions of $r_{g,s}$ and $r_{g,e}$ respectively. The other is that IoU between $[t_s, t_e]$ and any ground-truth action instances $\psi_g = (t_{g,s}, t_{g,e})$ is larger than 0.5.

Training Objective. We train BC-GNN in the form of a multi-task loss function. It can be denoted as

$$
L_{objective} = L_{bl}(S) + L_{bl}(E) + L_{bl}(C). \tag{6}
$$

We adopt weighted binary logistic regression loss function L_{bl} for start, end and content losses, where L_{bi} is denoted as

$$
L_{bl}(X) = \sum_{n=1}^{N} (\alpha^+ \cdot bi \cdot \log p_n + \alpha^- \cdot (1 - bi)) \cdot \log(1 - p_n)), \tag{7}
$$

where $\alpha^+ = \frac{N}{\sum(b_i)}$, $\alpha^- = \frac{N}{\sum(1-b_i)}$ and N is the size of set X.

3.5   Inference of BC-GNN

During inference, we conduct BC-GNN with same procedures described in training to generation proposals set $\Psi_p = \{\psi_n = (t_s, t_e, p_s, p_e, p_c)\}_{n=l}^{l_p}$. To get final results, BC-GNN undergoes score fusion and redundant proposals suppression steps.

Score Fusion. To generate a confidence score for each proposal ψ_n, we fuse its boundary probabilities and content confidence score by multiplication. This procedure can be described as

$$p_f = p_s * p_e * p_c. \qquad (8)$$

Thus, the proposals set can be denoted as $\Psi_p = \{\psi_n = (t_s, t_e, p_f)\}_{n=l}^{l_p}$.

Redundant Proposals Suppression. After generating a confidence score for each proposal, it is necessary to remove redundant proposals which highly overlap with each other. In BC-GNN, we adopt Soft-NMS algorithm to remove redundant proposals. Candidate proposal set Ψ_P turns to be $\Psi'_P = \psi_n = (ts, te, p'_f)_{n=1}^{l'_P}$, where l'_P is the number of final proposals.

4 Experiment

We present details of experimental settings and evaluation metrics in this section. Then we compare the performance of our proposed method with previous state-of-the-art methods on benchmark datasets.

4.1 Dataset and Setup

ActivityNet-1.3. This dataset is a large-scale dataset for temporal action proposal generation and temporal action detection tasks. ActivityNet-1.3 contains 19,994 annotated videos with 200 action classes, and it is divided into three sets by ratio of 2:1:1 for training, validation and testing separately.

THUMOS-14. This dataset includes 1,010 videos and 1,574 videos in the validation and testing sets with 20 classes. And it contains action recognition, temporal action proposal generation and temporal action detection tasks. For the action proposal generation and detection tasks, there are 200 and 212 videos with temporal annotations in the validation and testing sets.

Evaluation Metrics. Average Recall (AR) with Average Number (AN) of proposals per video calculated under different temporal intersection over union (tIoU) is used to evaluate the quality of proposals. AR calculated at different AN is donated as AR@AN. tIoU thresholds $[0.5 : 0.05 : 0.95]$ is used for ActivityNet-1.3 and tIoU thresholds $[0.5 : 0.05 : 1.0]$ is used for THUMOS-14. Specially, the area under the AR vs. AN curve named AUC is also used as an evaluation metric in ActivityNet-1.3 dataset.

Mean Average Precision (mAP) is used to evaluate the results of action detector. Average Precision (AP) of each class is calculated individually. On ActivityNet-1.3 dataset, a set of tIoU thresholds $[0.5 : 0.05 : 0.95]$ is used for calculating average mAP and tIoU thresholds $\{0.5, 0.75, 0.95\}$ for mAP. On THUMOS-14, mAP with tIoU thresholds $\{0.3, 0.4, 0.5, 0.6, 0.7\}$ is used.

Implement Details. We adopt two-stream network [22] for feature encoding, which pre-trained on training set of ActivityNet-1.3. The frame interval τ is set to 5 in THUMOS-14 and 16 in ActivityNet-1.3. In Base Module, we set the length of observation window l_w to 128 on THUMOS-14. And in GCM, we get rid of the segments more than 64 snippets, which can cover 98% of all action instances. We linearly interpolate feature sequence of each video to 100 at the temporal dimension in ActivityNet-1.3, which means $lw = 100$ in this dataset. The learning rate of training BC-GNN is set to 0.0001, and weight decay is set to 0.005 on both datasets. We conduct 20 epoch of model training with the strategy of early stopping.

4.2 Temporal Action Proposal Generation

Temporal action proposal generation method aims to find segments in videos which highly overlap with ground-truth action instances. We compare BC-GNN with state-of-the-art methods to verify the effectiveness of our method in this section.

Comparison with State-of-the-Art Methods. Comparative experiments are conducted on two widely used benchmarks ActivityNet-1.3 and THUMOS-14.

The results of comparison on validation of ActivityNet-1.3 dataset between our method and other state-of-the-art temporal action proposal generation approaches are shown in Table 1. Our method BC-GNN outperforms other leading methods by a large margin, and our method performs particularly well in aspect of AR@100.

Table 1. Comparison between our approach and other state-of-the-art methods on validation set of ActivityNet-1.3 dataset in terms of AR@AN and AUC.

Method	Prop-SSAD [12]	CTAP [7]	BSN [13]	MGG [14]	BMN [11]	BC-GNN
AR@100(val)	73.01	73.17	74.16	74.54	75.01	**76.73**
AUC(val)	64.40	65.72	66.17	66.43	67.10	**68.05**

Comparison between our method and other state-of-the-art proposal generation methods on testing set of THUMOS-14 dataset in terms of AR@AN is demonstrate in Table 2. Flow feature, 2Stream feature and C3D feature are adopt as the input of these methods for ensuring a fair comparison. In this experiment, BC-GNN outperforms other state-of-the-art methods in a large margin.

These experiments verify the effectiveness of our BC-GNN. BC-GNN achieves the significant performance improvement since it makes explicit use of interaction between boundaries and content.

Table 2. Comparison between our approach with other state-of-the-art methods on testing set of THUMOS-14 in terms of AR@AN.

Feature	Method	@50	@100	@200	@500	@1000
C3D	SCNN-prop [21]	17.22	26.17	37.01	51.57	58.20
C3D	SST [1]	19.90	28.36	37.90	51.58	60.27
C3D	BSN [13] + NMS	27.19	35.38	43.61	53.77	59.50
C3D	BSN + Soft-NMS	29.58	37.38	45.55	54.67	59.48
C3D	MGG [14]	29.11	36.31	44.32	54.95	**60.98**
C3D	BMN [11] + NMS	29.04	37.72	46.79	56.07	60.96
C3D	BMN + Soft-NMS	32.73	40.68	47.86	56.42	60.44
C3D	BC-GNN + NMS	**33.56**	**41.20**	**48.23**	56.54	59.76
C3D	BC-GNN + Soft-NMS	33.31	40.93	48.15	**56.62**	60.41
2Stream	TAG [32]	18.55	29.00	39.61	-	-
Flow	TURN [8]	21.86	31.89	43.02	57.63	64.17
2Stream	CTAP [7]	32.49	42.61	51.97	-	-
2Stream	BSN [13] + NMS	35.41	43.55	52.23	61.35	65.10
2Stream	BSN + Soft-NMS	37.46	46.06	53.21	60.64	64.52
2Stream	MGG [14]	39.93	47.75	54.65	61.36	64.06
2Stream	BMN [11] + NMS	37.15	46.75	54.84	62.19	65.22
2Stream	BMN + Soft-NMS	39.36	47.72	54.70	62.07	65.49
2Stream	BC-GNN + NMS	**41.15**	**50.35**	56.23	61.45	66.00
2Stream	BC-GNN + Soft-NMS	40.50	49.60	**56.33**	**62.80**	**66.57**

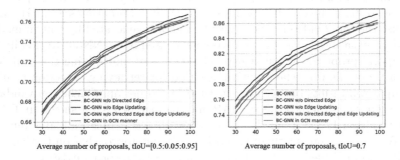

Fig. 4. Ablation study for our BC-GNN is verified the effectiveness of its modules.

Ablation Study. In GRM module, we convert an undirected graph into a directed graph and propose an edge feature updating operation. To evaluate the effectiveness of these strategies, we study ablation experiments in two control groups. We study the models in two control groups. In the first group, we study three types of the graphs: model with Graph Convolutional Network (GCN) manner in which edges are formed by cosine distance between nodes features, and model with directed or undirected edges. Since GCNs does not update edges, the models in the first group do not apply edge updating for the fair. In the second group, we study the effectiveness of directed edge in BC-GNN. The experimental results are listed in Table 3 and the average recall against average number of proposals at different tIoU thresholds are shown in Fig. 4. The comparison results show that both of strategies are effective and essential.

Table 3. Ablation study for model with GCN, edge update step and directed edge.

Method	Directed	Edge updating	AR@100	AUC(val)
GCN	-	-	75.57	66.88
BC-GNN	×	×	76.18	67.36
BC-GNN	✓	×	76.15	67.53
BC-GNN	×	✓	76.40	67.79
BC-GNN	✓	✓	76.73	68.05

4.3   Temporal Action Detection with Our Proposals

Temporal action detection is another aspect of evaluating the quality of proposals. On ActivityNet-1.3, we adopt a two-stage framework that detects action instances by classifying proposals. Proposals are generated by our proposal generator firstly and the top-100 temporal proposals per video are retained by ranking. Then, for each video in validation set, its top-1 video-level classification result will be obtained by using two-stream network [33] and all the proposals of this video share the classification result as their action classes. On THUMOS-14, we use the top-2 video-level classification scores generated by UntrimmedNet [28] and proposal-level classification score generated by SCNN-cls to classify first 200 temporal proposals for one video. The results of multiplying the confidence scores of proposals with classification are used for retrieving detection results.

Comparison results between our method and other approaches on validation set of ActivityNet-1.3 in terms of mAP and average mAP are shown in Table 4. Our method reaches state-of-the-art on this dataset which validates our approach. We compare our method with other existing approaches on testing set of THUMOS-14 in Table 5. Our approach is superior to the other existing two-stage methods on the evaluation metrics mAP, which confirms the effectiveness of our proposed proposal generator.

Table 4. Action detection results on validation set of ActivityNet-1.3 dataset in terms of mAP and average mAP.

Method	0.5	0.75	0.95	Average
CDC [20]	43.83	25.88	0.21	22.77
SSN [30]	39.12	23.48	5.49	23.98
BSN [13] + [33]	46.45	29.96	8.02	30.03
BMN [11] + [33]	50.07	**34.78**	8.29	33.85
BC-GNN + [33]	**50.56**	34.75	**9.37**	**34.26**

Table 5. Comparison between our approach and other temporal action detection methods on THUMOS-14.

Method	Classifier	0.7	0.6	0.5	0.4	0.3
TURN [8]	SCNN-cls	7.7	14.6	25.6	33.2	44.1
BSN [13]	SCNN-cls	15.0	22.4	29.4	36.6	43.1
MGG [14]	SCNN-cls	15.8	23.6	29.9	37.8	44.9
BMN [11]	SCNN-cls	17.0	24.5	32.2	40.2	45.7
BC-GNN	SCNN-cls	**19.1**	**26.3**	**34.2**	**41.2**	**46.3**
TURN [8]	UNet	6.3	14.1	24.5	35.3	46.3
BSN [13]	UNet	20.0	28.4	36.9	45.0	53.5
MGG [14]	UNet	21.3	29.5	37.4	46.8	53.9
BMN [11]	UNet	20.5	29.7	38.8	47.4	56.0
BC-GNN	UNet	**23.1**	**31.2**	**40.4**	**49.1**	**57.1**

5   Conclusion

In this paper, a new method of temporal action proposal generation named Boundary Content Graph Network (BC-GNN) is proposed. A boundary content graph is proposed to exploit the interaction between boundary probability generation and confidence evaluation. A new graph reasoning operation is also introduced to update the features of nodes and edges in the boundary content graph. In the meantime, an output module is designed to generate proposals using the strengthened features. The experimental results on popular datasets show that our proposed BC-GNN method achieves promising performance in both temporal proposal generation and temporal action detection tasks.

References

1. Buch, S., Escorcia, V., Shen, C., Ghanem, B., Carlos Niebles, J.: SST: single-stream temporal action proposals. In: Proceedings of the IEEE Conference on Computer Vision and Pattern Recognition, pp. 2911–2920 (2017)

2. Caba Heilbron, F., Carlos Niebles, J., Ghanem, B.: Fast temporal activity proposals for efficient detection of human actions in untrimmed videos. In: Proceedings of the IEEE Conference on Computer Vision and Pattern Recognition, pp. 1914–1923 (2016)

3. Carreira, J., Zisserman, A.: Quo vadis, action recognition? A new model and the kinetics dataset. In: Proceedings of the IEEE Conference on Computer Vision and Pattern Recognition, pp. 6299–6308 (2017)

4. Dalal, N., Triggs, B., Schmid, C.: Human detection using oriented histograms of flow and appearance. In: Leonardis, A., Bischof, H., Pinz, A. (eds.) ECCV 2006. LNCS, vol. 3952, pp. 428–441. Springer, Heidelberg (2006). https://doi.org/10.1007/11744047_33

5. Escorcia, V., Caba Heilbron, F., Niebles, J.C., Ghanem, B.: DAPs: deep action proposals for action understanding. In: Leibe, B., Matas, J., Sebe, N., Welling, M. (eds.) ECCV 2016. LNCS, vol. 9907, pp. 768–784. Springer, Cham (2016). https://doi.org/10.1007/978-3-319-46487-9_47

6. Feichtenhofer, C., Pinz, A., Zisserman, A.: Convolutional two-stream network fusion for video action recognition. In: Proceedings of the IEEE Conference on Computer Vision and Pattern Recognition, pp. 1933–1941 (2016)

7. Gao, J., Chen, K., Nevatia, R.: CTAP: complementary temporal action proposal generation. In: Ferrari, V., Hebert, M., Sminchisescu, C., Weiss, Y. (eds.) ECCV 2018. LNCS, vol. 11206, pp. 70–85. Springer, Cham (2018). https://doi.org/10.1007/978-3-030-01216-8_5

8. Gao, J., Yang, Z., Chen, K., Sun, C., Nevatia, R.: TURN TAP: temporal unit regression network for temporal action proposals. In: Proceedings of the IEEE International Conference on Computer Vision, pp. 3628–3636 (2017)

9. Gong, L., Cheng, Q.: Exploiting edge features for graph neural networks. In: Proceedings of the IEEE Conference on Computer Vision and Pattern Recognition, pp. 9211–9219 (2019)

10. Klaser, A., Marszałek, M., Schmid, C.: A spatio-temporal descriptor based on 3D-gradients (2008)

11. Lin, T., Liu, X., Li, X., Ding, E., Wen, S.: BMN: boundary-matching network for temporal action proposal generation. In: Proceedings of the IEEE International Conference on Computer Vision, pp. 3889–3898 (2019)

12. Lin, T., Zhao, X., Shou, Z.: Temporal convolution based action proposal: submission to activitynet 2017. arXiv preprint arXiv:1707.06750 (2017)

13. Lin, T., Zhao, X., Su, H., Wang, C., Yang, M.: BSN: boundary sensitive network for temporal action proposal generation. In: Ferrari, V., Hebert, M., Sminchisescu, C., Weiss, Y. (eds.) ECCV 2018. LNCS, vol. 11208, pp. 3–21. Springer, Cham (2018). https://doi.org/10.1007/978-3-030-01225-0_1

14. Liu, Y., Ma, L., Zhang, Y., Liu, W., Chang, S.: Multi-granularity generator for temporal action proposal. In: Proceedings of the IEEE Conference on Computer Vision and Pattern Recognition, pp. 3604–3613 (2019)

15. Oneata, D., Verbeek, J., Schmid, C.: The LEAR submission at Thumos 2014 (2014)

16. Qiu, Z., Yao, T., Mei, T.: Learning spatio-temporal representation with pseudo-3D residual networks. In: Proceedings of the IEEE International Conference on Computer Vision, pp. 5533–5541 (2017)

17. Schlichtkrull, M., Kipf, T.N., Bloem, P., van den Berg, R., Titov, I., Welling, M.: Modeling relational data with graph convolutional networks. In: Gangemi, A., et al. (eds.) ESWC 2018. LNCS, vol. 10843, pp. 593–607. Springer, Cham (2018). https://doi.org/10.1007/978-3-319-93417-4_38

18. Scovanner, P., Ali, S., Shah, M.: A 3-dimensional sift descriptor and its application to action recognition. In: Proceedings of the 15th ACM International Conference on Multimedia, pp. 357–360. ACM (2007)
19. Shen, Y., Li, H., Yi, S., Chen, D., Wang, X.: Person re-identification with deep similarity-guided graph neural network. In: Ferrari, V., Hebert, M., Sminchisescu, C., Weiss, Y. (eds.) ECCV 2018. LNCS, vol. 11219, pp. 508–526. Springer, Cham (2018). https://doi.org/10.1007/978-3-030-01267-0_30
20. Shou, Z., Chan, J., Zareian, A., Miyazawa, K., Chang, S.: CDC: convolutional-de-convolutional networks for precise temporal action localization in untrimmed videos. In: Proceedings of the IEEE Conference on Computer Vision and Pattern Recognition, pp. 5734–5743 (2017)
21. Shou, Z., Wang, D., Chang, S.: Temporal action localization in untrimmed videos via multi-stage CNNs. In: Proceedings of the IEEE Conference on Computer Vision and Pattern Recognition, pp. 1049–1058 (2016)
22. Simonyan, K., Zisserman, A.: Two-stream convolutional networks for action recognition in videos. In: Advances in Neural Information Processing Systems, pp. 568–576 (2014)
23. Tran, D., Bourdev, L., Fergus, R., Torresani, L., Paluri, M.: Learning spatiotemporal features with 3D convolutional networks. In: Proceedings of the IEEE International Conference on Computer Vision, pp. 4489–4497 (2015)
24. Veličković, P., Cucurull, G., Casanova, A., Romero, A., Lio, P., Bengio, Y.: Graph attention networks. arXiv preprint arXiv:1710.10903 (2017)
25. Wang, H., Schmid, C.: Action recognition with improved trajectories. In: Proceedings of the IEEE International Conference on Computer Vision, pp. 3551–3558 (2013)
26. Wang, L., Qiao, Y., Tang, X.: Action recognition and detection by combining motion and appearance features. THUMOS14 Action Recognition Challenge 1(2), 2 (2014)
27. Wang, L., Xiong, Y., Wang, Z., Qiao, Y.: Towards good practices for very deep two-stream convnets. arXiv preprint arXiv:1507.02159 (2015)
28. Wang, L., Xiong, Y., Lin, D., Van Gool, L.: UntrimmedNets for weakly supervised action recognition and detection. In: Proceedings of the IEEE Conference on Computer Vision and Pattern Recognition, pp. 4325–4334 (2017)
29. Wang, X., Gupta, A.: Videos as space-time region graphs. In: Ferrari, V., Hebert, M., Sminchisescu, C., Weiss, Y. (eds.) ECCV 2018. LNCS, vol. 11209, pp. 413–431. Springer, Cham (2018). https://doi.org/10.1007/978-3-030-01228-1_25
30. Xiong, Y., Zhao, Y., Wang, L., Lin, D., Tang, X.: A pursuit of temporal accuracy in general activity detection. arXiv preprint arXiv:1703.02716 (2017)
31. Yan, S., Xiong, Y., Lin, D.: Spatial temporal graph convolutional networks for skeleton-based action recognition. In: Thirty-second AAAI Conference on Artificial Intelligence (2018)
32. Zhao, Y., Xiong, Y., Wang, L., Wu, Z., Tang, X., Lin, D.: Temporal action detection with structured segment networks. In: Proceedings of the IEEE International Conference on Computer Vision, pp. 2914–2923 (2017)
33. Zhao, Y., et al.: CUHK & ETHZ & SIAT submission to activitynet challenge 2017. arXiv preprint arXiv:1710.08011 (2017)

Pose Augmentation: Class-Agnostic Object Pose Transformation for Object Recognition

Yunhao Ge[1]($\boxtimes$) (iD), Jiaping Zhao[2], and Laurent Itti[1] (iD)

[1] University of Southern California, Los Angeles, USA
{yunhaoge,itti}@usc.edu
[2] Google Research, Los Angeles, USA
jiapingz@google.com

Abstract. Object pose increases intraclass object variance which makes object recognition from 2D images harder. To render a classifier robust to pose variations, most deep neural networks try to eliminate the influence of pose by using large datasets with many poses for each class. Here, we propose a different approach: a class-agnostic object pose transformation network (OPT-Net) can transform an image along 3D yaw and pitch axes to synthesize additional poses continuously. Synthesized images lead to better training of an object classifier. We design a novel eliminate-add structure to explicitly disentangle pose from object identity: first 'eliminate' pose information of the input image and then 'add' target pose information (regularized as continuous variables) to synthesize any target pose. We trained OPT-Net on images of toy vehicles shot on a turntable from the iLab-20M dataset. After training on unbalanced discrete poses (5 classes with 6 poses per object instance, plus 5 classes with only 2 poses), we show that OPT-Net can synthesize balanced continuous new poses along yaw and pitch axes with high quality. Training a ResNet-18 classifier with original plus synthesized poses improves mAP accuracy by 9% over training on original poses only. Further, the pre-trained OPT-Net can generalize to new object classes, which we demonstrate on both iLab-20M and RGB-D. We also show that the learned features can generalize to ImageNet. (The code is released at this github url).

Keywords: Pose transform · Data augmentation · Disentangled representation learning · Object recognition · GANs

1 Introduction and Related Work

In object recognition from 2D images, object pose has a significant influence on performance. An image depends on geometry (shape), photometry (illumination

Electronic supplementary material The online version of this chapter (https://doi.org/10.1007/978-3-030-58604-1_9) contains supplementary material, which is available to authorized users.

and material properties of objects) and dynamics (as objects move) of the scene. Thus, every image is a mixture of instance-specific information and nuisance factors [27], such as 3D viewpoint, illumination, occlusions, shadows, etc. Nuisance factors often depend on the task itself. Specifically, in object recognition from 2D images, we care for instance-specific information like shape, while the dynamics of pose is a nuisance that often degrades classification accuracy [27].

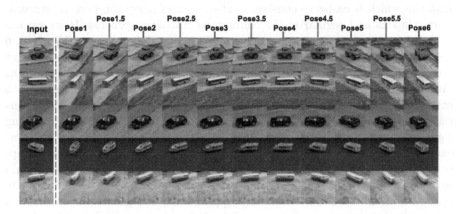

Fig. 1. Object pose transformation with OPT-Net. The first column shows input images from the test dataset, and the remaining columns show target pose images transformed by OPT-Net. Integer poses (1, 2, 3, 4, 5, 6 in red) are defined in the training dataset, while decimal poses (1.5, 2.5, 3.5, 4.5, 5.5 in green) are new poses, which shows OPT-Net can achieve continuous pose transformation.

Deep convolution neural networks (CNNs) have achieved great success in object recognition [15,17,23,35,38] and many other tasks, such as object detection [10,11,31,32], image segmentation [14,28,33], etc. Most research tries to discount pose, by eliminating pose information or improving pose robustness of a classifier. Typical CNN architectures, such as LeNet [25] AlexNet [23] and VGG [35] use convolution layers and pooling layers to make the high-level feature representations invariant to object pose over some limited range [43]. In contrast, recent results have shown that explicitly modeling pose information can help an object recognition task [2,3,40,43]. Some approaches use multi-task learning where pose information can be an auxiliary task or regularization to improve the main object recognition task [18,37,41,42]. These neural networks have the potential to disentangle content from their instantiation attributes [13,30,44]. Training on multiple views of the object can improve recognition accuracy [36]. A common method is collecting all poses of the object and creating a pose-balanced dataset, with the hope that pose variations will average out. However, collecting pose-balanced datasets is hard and expensive. One notable such dataset is iLab-20M which comprises 22 million images of 704 toy vehicles captured by 11 cameras while rotating on a turntable [5]. Here, we use a subset of this data to learn about pose transformations, then transferring this knowledge to new datasets (RGB-D [24], ImageNet [9]).

2D images can be seen as samples of 3D poses along yaw and pitch axes (Fig. 2(a)). We want our OPT-Net to imitate the 3D pose transformation along these two axes. Thus given any single pose image, we can 'rotate' the object along yaw and pitch axes to any target pose. Instead of directly training a transformation model to continuously 'rotate' images, we start with a discrete transform, which is easier to constrain. Then we can make the pose representation continuous and regularize the continuous transform process. Here, we use sampled discrete poses along yaw and pitch as our predefined poses (Fig. 2(b), 6 poses along the yaw axis and 3 poses along pitch axis). We treat different object poses as different domains so that discrete pose transformation can be seen as an image-to-image translation task, where a generative model can be used to synthesize any target pose given any input pose. Recently, Generative Adversarial Networks (GAN) [12] have shown a significant advantage in transforming images from one modality into another modality [19,22,29,34,45]. GANs show great performance in various tasks, such as style transfer [6,21], domain adaptation [16,39], etc. However, there is a high cost in our task, because we should train specific GANs for all pairs of poses [4]. StarGAN [8] and CollaGAN [26] proposed a method for multi-domain mapping with one generator and showed great results in appearance changes such as hair color, age, and emotion transform. However, pose transform creates a large, nonlinear spatial change between input and output images. The traditional structure of the generators (Unet [33], Vnet [28]) has few shared structures which satisfy all randomly paired pose transformation. It makes StarGAN training hard to converge (see Exp 4.1).

Learning a better representation could also reduce variance due to pose. [46] tried to learn better representation features to disentangle identity rotation and view features. InfoGAN [7] learns disentangled representations in an unsupervised manner. [20] seeks a view-invariant representation shared by views.

To combine the idea of better representation and multi-domain image transformation, we propose a class-agnostic object pose transformation neural network (OPT-Net), which first transforms the input image into a canonical space with pose-invariant representation and then transform it to the target domain. We design a novel eliminate-add structure of the OPT-Net and explicitly disentangle pose from object identity: OPT-Net first 'eliminates' the pose information of the input image and then 'adds' target pose information to synthesize any target pose. Convolutional regularization is first used to implicitly regularize the representation to keep only the key identification information that may be useful to any target pose. Then, our proposed pose-eliminate module can explicitly eliminate the pose information contained in the canonical representation by adversarial learning. We also add a discriminator leveraging pose classification and image quality classification to supervise the optimization of transforming.

Overall our contributions are multifold: (1) developed OPT-Net, a novel class-agnostic object pose transformation network with an eliminate-add structure generator that learns the class-agnostic transformation among object poses by turning the input into a pose-invariant canonical representation. (2) design a continuous representation of 3D object pose and achieve continuous pose transforming in 3D, which can be learned from limited discrete sampled poses and adversarial regularization. (3) demonstrated the generative OPT-Net significantly boosts the performance of discriminative object recognition models. (4) showed OPT-Net learns class-agnostic pose transformations, generalizes to out-of-class categories and transfers well to other datasets like RGB-D and ImageNet.

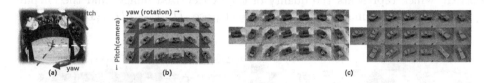

Fig. 2. (a) Discrete predefined pose images sample. (b) Predefined sample poses and pose change along pitch and yaw axes. (c) Given any pose (1st and 8th columns), OPT-Net can transform it along pitch and yaw axes to target poses (remaining columns)

2 Object Pose Transforming Network

As shown in Fig. 3, the proposed OPT-Net has an eliminate-add structure generator, a discriminator and a pose-eliminate module.

2.1 Eliminate-Add Structure of the Generator

The generator (G) of OPT-Net transforms an input object pose image x into a target object pose y conditioned on the target pose label c, $G(x, c) \rightarrow$ y. Different from the hair color, gender and age transform, which have more appearance transfer with smaller shape changes, object pose transformation creates large shape differences. Our eliminate-add structure generator (Fig. 3(a)) first turns the input pose image into a pose-invariant canonical representation by 'eliminating' pose information, and then 'adds' target pose information to turn the representation into the target pose. As shown in Fig. 3(b), given an input image, we randomly select the target pose domain. We do not input target pose along with the input image. Instead, in the 'eliminate' part, the first several convolution layers with stride $s > 2$ are used to implicitly regularize the preserved representation features. This implicit regularization makes the representation features contain only key information for the transformation (appearance, color, shape), and eliminates useless information which may hinder transformation (pose). At the same time (Fig. 3(b)), the 'pose-eliminate module' (P_{elim}) explicitly forces the representation to contain as little pose information as possible, by predicting equal probability for every pose. After both implicit and explicit elimination of pose information, the input image is turned to a pose-invariant canonical representation space. We then 'add' the target pose information by concatenating it with the representation feature map. The remaining layers in the generative model transform the concatenated features into the target pose image. This eliminate-add structure is shared and can be used for any pose transformation. This shared structure makes the generator easy to converge. To control the translation direction, as shown in Fig. 3(b), we use an auxiliary classifier as discriminator D to guide the image quality and pose transform. Given one image, the discriminator has two outputs, the probability that the input image is real, which represents the quality of the synthesized image, and the output pose, which should match the desired target pose, $D : x \rightarrow \{D_{src}(x), D_{cls}(x)\}$.

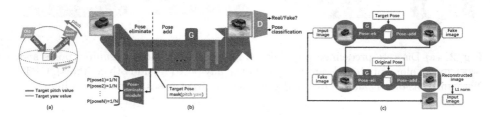

Fig. 3. Flow of OPT-Net, consisting of three modules: eliminate-add structure generator G, discriminator D, and pose-eliminate module. (a) Pose transformation sketch (b) Origin to target pose transformation. In the pose 'eliminate' part, G takes in the original pose image and first uses both implicit regularization and the explicit pose-eliminate module to eliminate pose information of the input, yielding a pose-invariant canonical representation. Then, in the pose 'add' part, the representation features are concatenated with a target pose mask and the target pose image is synthesized. D learns to distinguish between real and fake images and to classify real images to their correct pose. (c) Training OPT-Net: G first maps the original pose image to target pose and synthesizes a fake image, then G tries to reconstruct the original pose image from the fake image given the original pose information.

2.2   Pose-Eliminate Module

The pose-eliminate module (P_{elim}) takes the preserved representation feature x_r as input and outputs pose classification $\{P_{elim}(x_r)\}$. P_{elim} can be treated as a discriminator which forms an adversarial learning framework with the 'eliminate' part of the generator (G_{elim}). The canonical representation features of real images with pose labels are used to train P_{elim}. We use Cross-Entropy loss to make P_{elim} predict the correct pose from the pose-invariant feature after G_{elim}. Different from traditional adversarial training, when using P_{elim} to train G_{elim}, we want the generator to eliminate all pose information in the pose-invariant feature, which makes P_{elim} produce equal output probability for every pose. We use the uniform probability ($1/N$) as the ground truth label to compute the pose-eliminate loss, which is used to optimize the G_{elim}.

2.3   Continuous Pose Transforming Training

We design a 2-dimension linear space to represent pitch and yaw values, in which we could interpolate and achieve continuous pose representation (Fig. 1). The yaw and pitch values can be duplicated as a matrix with same h and w dimension as the canonical representation features and N (totally 6, 3 for yaw and 3 for pitch) channel dimension, which is easy to be concatenated and can be adjusted depending on the canonical features channel. We start the training on discrete sampled poses (which can be represented as integer in linear space). After the network has converged, we randomly sample decimal poses as target poses and use a style consistency loss to regularize the synthesized images, which keeps pose representation consistent along yaw and pitch axes.

2.4   Loss Function

Our goal is to train a generator G that learns object pose transformations along yaw and pitch axes. The overall loss is formed by adversarial loss, domain classification loss, reconstruction loss, pose-eliminate loss and style consistency loss.

Adversarial Loss. The adversarial loss is used to make the synthesized image indistinguishable from real images.

$$L_{adv} = E_x[log D_{src}(x)] + E_{x,c}[log(1 - D_{src}(G(x,c)))] \tag{1}$$

$D_{src}(x)$ represent the probability that input x belongs to the real images given by D. The generator G tries to minimize the loss, while the discriminator D tries to maximize it.

Pose Classification Loss. The pose classification loss is used to guide the pose transformation which makes the synthesized image y belong to the target pose c. This pose classification loss is used to optimize both D and G. The pose classification loss of D is defined as

$$L^r_{cls} = E_{x,c'}[-log D_{cls}(c'|x)] \tag{2}$$

The loss for D is similar to a traditional Cross-Entropy loss for classification, where $D_{cls}(c'|x)$ means the predicted probability of real image x belongs to the ground truth pose label c'. The pose classification loss of G is defined as

$$L^f_{cls} = E_{x,c}[-log D_{cls}(c|G(x,c))] \tag{3}$$

G tries to minimize this loss to make the synthesized fake image $G(x,c)$ be classified as the target pose c.

Reconstruction Loss. To make the synthesized image preserve the content information and change only the object pose, as shown in Fig. 3(c), we use the cycle consistency loss [45] to optimize G.

$$L_{rec} = E_{x,c,c'}[\|x - G(G(x,c),c')\|_1] \tag{4}$$

where G can reconstruct the original image x by transforming the synthesized fake target pose image $G(x,c)$ back to the original pose c'. $L1$ norm is used as reconstruction loss.

Pose-eliminate Loss. In the eliminate-add structure of G, to eliminate the pose information in preserved canonical representation features, we designed pose-eliminate loss to optimize the pose eliminate module (P_{elim}) and the eliminate part of G,(G_{elim}). The pose eliminate loss is

$$L_{pose}^P = E_{x,c'}[-log P_{elim}(c'|G_{elim}(x))] \tag{5}$$

where $P_{elim}(c'|G_{elim}(x))$ means the predicted probability of the canonical representation features of a real image belongs to the ground truth pose label c'. The pose eliminate loss for G_{elim} is defined as

$$L_{pose}^G = -E_x \sum_{c_i=1}^{N} 1/N \cdot log(P_{elim}(c_i|G_{elim}(x))) \tag{6}$$

where N is the number of pose classes we defined, c_i represent the pose label, $c_i \in [0,N)$, $P_{elim}(c_i|G_{elim}(x))$ represent the probability of the synthesized canonical representation belongs to the c_i pose. In ideal situations, the P_{elim} can hardly predict the correct pose from canonical representation features and output equal probability for every pose, which means the pose information is eliminated in preserved canonical features. We use equal prediction of every pose to optimize G_{elim} instead of minimizing the pose classification accuracy of to avoid a 'cheated optimize' that P_{elim} tries to predict all input to a fixed pose class.

Style Consistency Loss. After the converge of the previous loss, we randomly sample decimal target pose instead of all integers to make continuous pose transforming, the style consistency loss can regularize the synthesized images. The equation of style consistency loss is same as adversarial loss above, but the target pose is randomly sampled decimal value along yaw and pitch axes.

Full Loss Function. Finally, we optimize:

$$L_G = L_{adv} + \lambda_{cls}L_{cls}^f + \lambda_{rec}L_{rec} + \lambda_{pose}L_{pose}^G \tag{7}$$

$$L_D = -L_{adv} + \lambda_{cls}L_{cls}^r \tag{8}$$

$$L_{P_{elim}} = L_{pose}^P \tag{9}$$

where λ_{cls}, λ_{rec} and λ_{pose} are hyper-parameters that control the relative importance of classification, reconstruction, and pose-eliminate losses.

3   Experimental Methods

3.1   Datasets

iLab-20M Dataset [5]. The iLab-20M dataset is a controlled, parametric dataset collected by shooting images of toy vehicles placed on a turntable using 11 cameras at different viewing points. There are in total 15 object categories with each object having 25 160 instances. Each object instance was shot on more than 14 backgrounds (printed satellite images), in a relevant context (e.g., cars on roads, trains on rail tracks, boats on water). In total, 1,320 images were captured for each instance and background combinations: 11 azimuth angles (from the 11 cameras), 8 turntable rotation angles, 5 lighting conditions, and 3 focus values (-3, 0, and $+3$ from the default focus value of each camera). The complete dataset consists of 704 object instances, with 1,320 images per object-instance/background combination, almost 22M images (18 times of ImageNet).

RGB-D Dataset. The RGB-D Object Dataset consists of 300 common household objects organized into 51 categories. This dataset was recorded using a Kinect style 3D camera. Each object was placed on a turntable and video sequences were captured for one whole rotation. For each object, there are 3 video sequences, each recorded with the camera mounted at a different height so that the object is shot from different viewpoints.

3.2   Network Implementation

OPT-Net consists of two parts, pose 'eliminate', (including G_{elim} and P_{elim}) and pose 'add', (including G_{add} and D). As shown in Fig. 3(b), G_{elim} first has 3 convolution layers, 2 of them with stride size of 2 to down-sample the input image. Then, 3 Residual blocks [15] form the backbone of G_{elim}. The output $G_{elim}(x)$ is the pose-invariant canonical representation feature. The canonical feature is copied to different streams, one concatenates with the target pose mask, forming the input of G_{add} to synthesize the target pose image. The other one is treated as the input of P_{elim} to predict the pose class. G_{add} uses first layer merge the target pose information, then has 5 Residual blocks as a backbone and ends with 3 convolution layers (2 of them perform up-sampling) to transform the canonical representation features to a target pose image, given a target pose information mask. For discriminator D, we adopt the PatchGAN [19] network.

P_{elim} has a traditional classification network structure, which has the first 3 convolution layers with stride size of 2 to down-sample the input features, followed with 1 Residual block and another 3 down-sampling convolution layers. In the end, the output layer turns the feature to a N-dimensional (N poses) vector and we use Softmax to obtain the prediction of pose class.

We use Wasserstein GAN objective with a gradient penalty [1] to stabilize the training process. We adjust the λ_{pose} during training the generator, at the beginning epochs of training, improving the value of λ_{pose} can accelerate the convergence of generator, which makes the synthesized fake pose image have meaningful corresponding spacial structure. We gradually reduce the value of λ_{pose}. At the last ending part of the training, λ_{pose} can be very small to make the optimization concentrate on improving the image quality. (More network architecture and training details are in supplementary materials)

4   Experiments and Results

We have five main experiments: in Subsect. 4.1 on object pose transformation task, we compare OPT-Net with baseline StarGAN [8] by quantitatively and qualitatively comparing the synthesized object pose image quality. In Subsect. 4.2, we use the OPT-Net as a generative model to help the training of a discriminative model for object recognition, by synthesizing missing poses and balancing a pose bias in the training dataset. In Subsect. 4.3, we further show the class-agnostic transformation property of OPT-Net by generalizing the pretrained OPT-Net to new datasets. In Subsect. 4.4, we study the influence of object pose information for objects which are mainly distinguishable by shape, as opposed to other features like color. Finally, in Subsect. 4.5, we further demonstrate how the learned pose features in OPT-Net and object recognition model with the iLab-20M dataset can generalize to other datasets like ImageNet.

4.1   Object Pose Transformation Experiments

Because the baseline models can only do discrete pose transform, we fix the pitch value and use 6 different yaw viewpoints among the 88 different views of iLab-20M as our predefined pose to implement our OPT-Net. As is shown in Fig. 2, the selected 6 viewpoints have big spatial variance which can better represent the general object pose transformation task. In training set, each pose has nearly 26k images with 10 vehicle classes (Table 2). Each class contains 20~80 different instances. The test set has the same 10 vehicle categories, but different instances than the training set. Both training and test datasets are 256×256 RGB images. The training dataset is used to train our OPT-Net and the baseline models, StarGAN. Our OPT-Net has one generator, one discriminator and one pose-eliminate module; StarGAN has one generator and one discriminator.

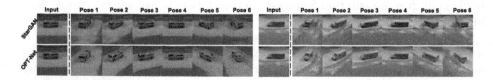

Fig. 4. Object pose transform comparison for StarGAN and OPT-Net.

Qualitative Evaluation. The experiment results are shown in Fig. 4. Compared with StarGAN, which struggles with large pose variations, the synthesized target pose images by OPT-Net are high quality with enough details. One possible reason is that eliminate-add structure decrease the conflicts between different directions on pose transformation. Figure 1 shows more results of OPT-Net.

Quantitative Evaluation. Real target pose images of input are used as ground truth. To reduce background influence, we segment the foreground vehicle with the Graph-Based Image Segmentation method and only compute mean squared error (MSE) and peak signal to noise ratio (PSNR) of foreground between the synthesized image and ground truth (Table 1). The result is the mean MSE and PSNR computed by 200 different instances, the MSE and PSNR for each instance is the average of 6 synthesized fake pose images. Table 1 shows that the quality of synthesized images by OPT-Net is better than StarGAN.

Table 1. Average Mean squared error (MSE; lower is better) and peak-signal-to-noise ratio (PSNR; higher is better) for different methods

	StarGAN	OPT-Net
Mean MSE	502.51	**374.76**
Mean PSNR	21.95	**23.04**

4.2 Object Recognition Experiment

We design an object recognition experiment to explore the performance of OPT-Net as a generative model to help the training of a discriminative model. Two different training datasets are tailored from iLab-20M, pose-unbalanced (P-UB) and pose-balanced (P-B). In P-UB (Table 2), 5 classes of vehicles (boat, car, semi, tank, and van) have all 6 pose images (same poses as 4.1), while the other 5 classes (bus, military car, monster, pickup, and train) have only two poses (pose2 and pose5), which has significant pose bias. In P-B, each category among 10 classes of vehicles has all 6 pose images (no pose bias). The test dataset is a pose-balanced dataset which contains different instances of the 10 classes of vehicles that were not in either training dataset (P-UB and P-B). The classification neural network we used is Resnet-18 [15] (no pre-training).

We first train the classification model on P-UB and P-B, calculating the test accuracy of each class of vehicles on the test dataset. To evaluate the performance of OPT-Net, we first train it on P-UB to learn the object transformation ability. After training, for each category in P-UB which have only pose2 and pose5 (bus, military car, monster, pickup, and train), we use the trained OPT-Net to synthesize the missing 4 poses (pose1, pose3, pose4, pose6). We combine the synthesized images with P-UB and form a synthesized-pose-balanced (S-P-B)

148   Y. Ge et al.

Table 2. Poses used in the pose-unbalanced (P-UB) training dataset to train OPT-Net

	Pose1	Pose2	Pose3	Pose4	Pose5	Pose6
Boat	✓	✓	✓	✓	✓	✓
Bus		✓			✓	
Car	✓	✓	✓	✓	✓	✓
Mil		✓			✓	
Monster		✓			✓	
Pickup		✓			✓	
Semi	✓	✓	✓	✓	✓	✓
Tank	✓	✓	✓	✓	✓	✓
Train		✓			✓	
Van	✓	✓	✓	✓	✓	✓

training dataset. To show continuous transforms, we also interpolate pose values and synthesize 5 new poses beyond the predefined ones, and form a synthesized-additional-pose-balanced (SA-P-B) training dataset. S-P-B and SA-P-B were used to train the same resnet-18 classification model from scratch and to calculate test accuracy of each class of vehicles in the test dataset. We also use common data augmentation methods (random crop, horizontal flip, scale resize, etc.) to augment the P-UB dataset to the same number of images as P-B, called A-P-UB (Table 3).

The test accuracy of each class is shown in Table 4. From P-UB to S-P-B, the overall accuracy improved from 52.26% to 59.15%, which shows the synthesized missing pose images by OPT-Net can improve the performance of object recognition. It is also shown that OPT-Net, as a generative model, can help the discriminative model. Specifically, the vacant pose categories show significant improvement in accuracy: military improved by 11.68%, monster improved by 14.97%, pickup and train improved by 8.74% and 16.12% respectively. The comparison of S-P-B and A-P-UB shows that synthesized images by OPT-Net are better than traditional augmented images in helping object recognition. Because of the continuous pose transformation ability, our OPT-Net can synthesize additional poses different from the 6 poses in P-B. With these additional poses, SA-P-B (61.23%) performs even better than the P-B (59.20%), achieve 9% improvement compared with P-UB.

Table 3. Different training and testing datasets for object recognition

Dataset	P-UB	P-B	S-P-B	SA-P-B	A-P-UB	Test
Source	Real	Real	Synthesized	Synthesized	Augmented	Real
Size	25166	37423	37423	66041	37423	4137

Table 4. Testing object recognition accuracy (%) of each class after trained on different training dataset. Comparing S-P-B and SA-P-B with P-UB shows how much classification improves thanks to adding synthesized images for missing poses in the training set, reaching or surpassing the level of when all real poses are available (P-B). Our synthesized poses yield better learning than traditional data augmentation (A-P-UB)

Category	P-UB	P-B	S-P-B	SA-P-B	A-P-UB
Boat	54.0	61.6	65.4	57.7	51.3
Bus	35.2	42.5	38.1	47.8	37.2
Car	85.1	76.3	79.8	64.0	78.9
Mil	73.8	84.2	85.4	86.4	70.7
Monster	45.3	67.4	60.2	66.0	52.9
Pickup	17.8	26.7	26.6	36.5	18.7
Semi	83.9	79.8	79.0	83.5	86.1
Tank	78.1	69.4	78.6	77.0	72.5
Train	41.1	65.1	57.2	58.1	43.1
Van	23.6	18.6	24.2	20.7	21.0
Overall	52.3	59.2	59.2	**61.2**	52.3

4.3   Class-Agnostic Object Transformation Experiment

Our proposed OPT-Net can simultaneously make pose transformation on different classes of vehicles, which demonstrate that the learned object pose transformation has not fixed with object classes, it is a class-agnostic object pose transformation. To further explore the class-agnostic property of OPT-Net, we design experiments that generalize OPT-Net's ability for object pose transformation from one dataset to other datasets.

15 categories of objects from RGB-D are used. They are both common household objects with big spatial variance between different object poses. Similar poses of objects in RGB-D are selected and defined as the same pose as iLab-20M. For each pose, RGB-D contains only about 100 images which cannot train our OPT-Net from scratch, thus we use RGB-D to finetune OPT-Net pre-trained on iLab-20M. We can see (Fig. 5) that our pre-trained OPT-Net can generalize well to other datasets, which demonstrates that OPT-Net is a class-agnostic object pose transformation framework.

To further explore the performance of OPT-Net as a generative model to help a discriminative model of object recognition, we split RGB-D into a pose-unbalanced (P-UB) training dataset, where each category randomly takes 3 poses among all 6 poses; pose-balanced (P-B), and test dataset similar to 4.2.

We first use P-UB to finetune the pretrained OPT-Net, and then use the trained OPT-Net to synthesize missing poses of household objects in RGB-D. The synthesized images and the original pose-unbalanced images form the

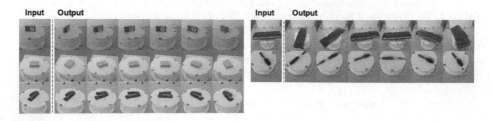

Fig. 5. Generalization results of OPT-Net on RGB-D dataset pretrained on iLab-20M.

synthesized pose balanced (S-P-B) training dataset. Similarly, to eliminate the influence of the number of training images, we created A-P-UB using common data augmentation methods. We trained Alexnet [23] on the 4 training datasets separately, and showed the test accuracy for each category in Table 5.

Table 5. Overall object recognition accuracy for different training dataset in RGB-D

Dataset	P-UB	P-B	S-P-B	A-P-UB
Accuracy(%)	99.1	99.9	**99.7**	99.2

The (small) accuracy improvement in S-P-B compared with P-UB demonstrates that our pretrained OPT-Net can be generalized to different datasets after finetune, which can help the discriminative model in object recognition. While the overall improvement is small, below we show that this is not the case uniformly across all object categories.

4.4   Object Pose Significance on Different Object Recognition Tasks

Because the accuracy improvement in RGB-D is smaller than in iLab-20M, we tested whether this was the case across all object categories, or whether those which look more alike would benefit more from synthesized images from OPT-Net. Indeed, maybe classifying a black keyboard vs. a blue stapler can easily be achieved by size or color even without pose-dependent shape analysis. To verify our hypothesis, we use the confusion matrix of classification to select categories which are more confused by classifier: marker, comb, toothbrush, stapler, lightbulb, and sponge. We then assign different fixed poses to each category to improve overall pose variance and form P-UB-1 (randomly fix 1 pose for each category), P-UB-2 (randomly fix 2 poses for each category), and P-UB-3 (randomly fix 3 poses for each category) pose-unbalanced datasets (suppl. material). Similarly, we create 3 other training datasets using the same method as in 4.2 and 4.3: (S-P-B: use pretrained OPT-Net to synthesize the missing poses; P-B, and A-P-UB for each unbalanced datasets), and report the object recognition performance on the test dataset in Table 6.

Table 6. Object recognition overall accuracy for different datasets

Dataset	P-UB-1	A-P-UB-1	S-P-B-1	P-UB-2	A-P-UB-2	S-P-B-2
Accuracy(%)	75.1	77.6	**83.2**	90.4	91.2	**94.2**
Dataset	P-UB-3	A-P-UB-3	S-P-B-3	P-B		
Accuracy(%)	99.3	99.2	**99.4**	99.8		

The results in Table 6 demonstrate that object pose information has different degrees of impact on the object recognition task. Compared with the results in 4.3, where the improvement between P-UB and S-P-B is less than 1%, here, when the class variance is small, OPT-Net can improve more accuracy after synthesizing the missing poses in the unbalanced dataset. The accuracy improvement in experiment group 1 (P-UB-1 and S-P-B-1) is 8.1%. This result verified our hypothesis that pose balance is more important in small interclass variance object cognition tasks. Meanwhile, comparing the different accuracy improvements in different experimental groups, group 2 (P-UB-2 and S-P-B-2) is 3.8%, while group 3 (P-UB-3 and S-P-B-3) is 0.1%. This demonstrates that when class-variance is fixed, the more pose bias we have, the more accuracy improvement we will get with the help of our OPT-Net pose transformation.

4.5 Generalization to Imagenet

We directly use the pretrained OPT-Net on iLab-20M to synthesize images of different poses on ImageNet (Shown in suppl. material). Results are not as good and might be improved using domain adaptation in future work. However, the discriminator of OPT-Net makes decent prediction of image poses: Fig. 6 shows the top 8 ImageNet images for each of our 6 poses. To test object recognition in ImageNet, we replace real images by OPT-Net synthesized images in S-P-B (4.2) and form a S-P-B (OPT-Net) dataset (all synthesized images). Similarly, we use StarGAN synthesized images form S-P-B (StarGAN). We use a resnet18 10-class vehicles classifier pretrained with this two synthesized datasets and predict 4 classes of vehicles in ImageNet which have similar meanings as iLab-20M, with good results on some classes like car (Shown in suppl. material). To further explore generalization, we pretrian an AlexNet on S-P-B which synthesized pose images by StarGAN and OPT-Net respectively and then finetune it on ImageNet. Results in suppl. material shows significantly better accuracy compared to training from scratch when using only a small number of images per class, demonstrating generalization from iLab-20M to ImageNet.

Fig. 6. Top 8 ImageNet images for each pose predicted by discriminator in OPT-Net without finetune.

5   Conclusions

We proposed OPT-Net, a class-agnostic object pose transformation network (OPT-Net) to synthesize any target poses continuously given a single pose image. The proposed eliminate-add structure generator can first eliminate pose information and turn the input to a pose-invariant canonical representation, then adding the target pose information to synthesize the target pose image. OPT-Net also gives a more common framework to solve big variance continuous transformation problems. OPT-Net generated images have higher visual quality compared to existing methods. We also demonstrate that the OPT-Net, as a generative model can help the discriminative model in the object recognition task, which achieve a 9% accuracy improvement. We design experiments to demonstrate that pose balance is more important in small between-class variance object cognition tasks. Finally, we demonstrate the learned pose features in OPT-Net with the iLab-20M dataset can better generalize to other datasets like ImageNet.

Acknowledgements. This work was supported by C-BRIC (one of six centers in JUMP, a Semiconductor Research Corporation (SRC) program sponsored by DARPA), and the Intel and CISCO Corporations. The authors affirm that the views expressed herein are solely their own, and do not represent the views of the United States government or any agency thereof.

References

1. Arjovsky, M., Chintala, S., Bottou, L.: Wasserstein generative adversarial networks. In: Proceedings of the 34th International Conference on Machine Learning (ICML), pp. 214–223 (2017)
2. Bakry, A., Elgammal, A.: Untangling object-view manifold for multiview recognition and pose estimation. In: Fleet, D., Pajdla, T., Schiele, B., Tuytelaars, T. (eds.) ECCV 2014. LNCS, vol. 8692, pp. 434–449. Springer, Cham (2014). https://doi.org/10.1007/978-3-319-10593-2_29
3. Bengio, Y., Courville, A., Vincent, P.: Representation learning: a review and new perspectives. IEEE Trans. Pattern Anal. Mach. Intell. **35**(8), 1798–1828 (2013)

4. Bhattacharjee, A., Banerjee, S., Das, S.: PosIX-GAN: generating multiple poses using GAN for pose-invariant face recognition. In: Leal-Taixé, L., Roth, S. (eds.) ECCV 2018. LNCS, vol. 11131, pp. 427–443. Springer, Cham (2019). https://doi. org/10.1007/978-3-030-11015-4_31
5. Borji, A., Izadi, S., Itti, L.: iLAB-20M: a large-scale controlled object dataset to investigate deep learning. In: Proceedings of the IEEE Conference on Computer Vision and Pattern Recognition, pp. 2221–2230 (2016)
6. Chang, H., Lu, J., Yu, F., Finkelstein, A.: PairedCycleGAN: asymmetric style transfer for applying and removing makeup. In: Proceedings of the IEEE Conference on Computer Vision and Pattern Recognition, pp. 40–48 (2018)
7. Chen, X., Duan, Y., Houthooft, R., Schulman, J., Sutskever, I., Abbeel, P.: Info-GAN: interpretable representation learning by information maximizing generative adversarial nets. In: Advances in Neural Information Processing Systems, pp. 2172–2180 (2016)
8. Choi, Y., Choi, M., Kim, M., Ha, J.W., Kim, S., Choo, J.: StarGAN: unified generative adversarial networks for multi-domain image-to-image translation. In: Proceedings of the IEEE Conference on Computer Vision and Pattern Recognition, pp. 8789–8797 (2018)
9. Deng, J., Dong, W., Socher, R., Li, L.J., Li, K., Fei-Fei, L.: ImageNet: a large-scale hierarchical image database. In: 2009 IEEE Conference on Computer Vision and Pattern Recognition, pp. 248–255. IEEE (2009)
10. Fang, H.S., Xie, S., Tai, Y.W., Lu, C.: RMPE: regional multi-person pose estimation. In: Proceedings of the IEEE International Conference on Computer Vision, pp. 2334–2343 (2017)
11. Girshick, R., Donahue, J., Darrell, T., Malik, J.: Rich feature hierarchies for accurate object detection and semantic segmentation. In: Proceedings of the IEEE Conference on Computer Vision and Pattern Recognition, pp. 580–587 (2014)
12. Goodfellow, I., et al.: Generative adversarial nets. In: Advances in Neural Information Processing Systems, pp. 2672–2680 (2014)
13. Goroshin, R., Mathieu, M.F., LeCun, Y.: Learning to linearize under uncertainty. In: Advances in Neural Information Processing Systems, pp. 1234–1242 (2015)
14. He, K., Gkioxari, G., Dollár, P., Girshick, R.: Mask R-CNN. In: Proceedings of the IEEE International Conference on Computer Vision, pp. 2961–2969 (2017)
15. He, K., Zhang, X., Ren, S., Sun, J.: Deep residual learning for image recognition. In: Proceedings of the IEEE Conference on Computer Vision and Pattern Recognition, pp. 770–778 (2016)
16. Hoffman, J., et al.: CyCADA: cycle-consistent adversarial domain adaptation. arXiv preprint arXiv:1711.03213 (2017)
17. Huang, G., Liu, Z., Van Der Maaten, L., Weinberger, K.Q.: Densely connected convolutional networks. In: Proceedings of the IEEE Conference on Computer Vision and Pattern Recognition, pp. 4700–4708 (2017)
18. Huang, Y., Wang, W., Wang, L., Tan, T.: Multi-task deep neural network for multi-label learning. In: 2013 IEEE International Conference on Image Processing, pp. 2897–2900. IEEE (2013)
19. Isola, P., Zhu, J.Y., Zhou, T., Efros, A.A.: Image-to-image translation with conditional adversarial networks. In: Proceedings of the IEEE Conference on Computer Vision and Pattern Recognition, pp. 1125–1134 (2017)
20. Kan, M., Shan, S., Chen, X.: Multi-view deep network for cross-view classification. In: Proceedings of the IEEE Conference on Computer Vision and Pattern Recognition, pp. 4847–4855 (2016)

21. Karras, T., Laine, S., Aila, T.: A style-based generator architecture for generative adversarial networks. In: Proceedings of the IEEE Conference on Computer Vision and Pattern Recognition, pp. 4401–4410 (2019)
22. Kim, T., Cha, M., Kim, H., Lee, J.K., Kim, J.: Learning to discover cross-domain relations with generative adversarial networks. In: Proceedings of the 34th International Conference on Machine Learning, vol. 70, pp. 1857–1865. JMLR.org (2017)
23. Krizhevsky, A., Sutskever, I., Hinton, G.E.: ImageNet classification with deep convolutional neural networks. In: Advances in neural information processing systems, pp. 1097–1105 (2012)
24. Lai, K., Bo, L., Ren, X., Fox, D.: A large-scale hierarchical multi-view RGB-D object dataset. In: 2011 IEEE International Conference on Robotics and Automation, pp. 1817–1824. IEEE (2011)
25. LeCun, Y., et al.: LeNet-5, convolutional neural networks
26. Lee, D., Kim, J., Moon, W.J., Ye, J.C.: CollaGAN: collaborative GAN for missing image data imputation. In: Proceedings of the IEEE Conference on Computer Vision and Pattern Recognition, pp. 2487–2496 (2019)
27. Ma, Y., Soatto, S., Kosecka, J., Sastry, S.S.: An Invitation to 3-D Vision: From Images to Geometric Models, vol. 26. Springer, New York (2012)
28. Milletari, F., Navab, N., Ahmadi, S.A.: V-Net: fully convolutional neural networks for volumetric medical image segmentation. In: 2016 Fourth International Conference on 3D Vision (3DV), pp. 565–571. IEEE (2016)
29. Mirza, M., Osindero, S.: Conditional generative adversarial nets. arXiv preprint arXiv:1411.1784 (2014)
30. Ranzato, M., Huang, F.J., Boureau, Y.L., LeCun, Y.: Unsupervised learning of invariant feature hierarchies with applications to object recognition. In: 2007 IEEE Conference on Computer Vision and Pattern Recognition, pp. 1–8. IEEE (2007)
31. Redmon, J., Divvala, S., Girshick, R., Farhadi, A.: You only look once: unified, real-time object detection. In: Proceedings of the IEEE Conference on Computer Vision and Pattern Recognition, pp. 779–788 (2016)
32. Ren, S., He, K., Girshick, R., Sun, J.: Faster R-CNN: towards real-time object detection with region proposal networks. In: Advances in Neural Information Processing Systems, pp. 91–99 (2015)
33. Ronneberger, O., Fischer, P., Brox, T.: U-Net: convolutional networks for biomedical image segmentation. In: Navab, N., Hornegger, J., Wells, W.M., Frangi, A.F. (eds.) MICCAI 2015. LNCS, vol. 9351, pp. 234–241. Springer, Cham (2015). https://doi.org/10.1007/978-3-319-24574-4_28
34. Sangkloy, P., Lu, J., Fang, C., Yu, F., Hays, J.: Scribbler: controlling deep image synthesis with sketch and color. In: Proceedings of the IEEE Conference on Computer Vision and Pattern Recognition, pp. 5400–5409 (2017)
35. Simonyan, K., Zisserman, A.: Very deep convolutional networks for large-scale image recognition. arXiv preprint arXiv:1409.1556 (2014)
36. Su, H., Maji, S., Kalogerakis, E., Learned-Miller, E.: Multi-view convolutional neural networks for 3D shape recognition. In: Proceedings of the IEEE International Conference on Computer Vision, pp. 945–953 (2015)
37. Su, H., Qi, C.R., Li, Y., Guibas, L.J.: Render for CNN: viewpoint estimation in images using CNNs trained with rendered 3D model views. In: Proceedings of the IEEE International Conference on Computer Vision, pp. 2686–2694 (2015)
38. Szegedy, C., Ioffe, S., Vanhoucke, V., Alemi, A.A.: Inception-v4, inception-resnet and the impact of residual connections on learning. In: Thirty-First AAAI Conference on Artificial Intelligence (2017)

39. Tzeng, E., Hoffman, J., Saenko, K., Darrell, T.: Adversarial discriminative domain adaptation. In: Proceedings of the IEEE Conference on Computer Vision and Pattern Recognition, pp. 7167–7176 (2017)
40. Wohlhart, P., Lepetit, V.: Learning descriptors for object recognition and 3D pose estimation. In: Proceedings of the IEEE Conference on Computer Vision and Pattern Recognition, pp. 3109–3118 (2015)
41. Zhang, C., Zhang, Z.: Improving multiview face detection with multi-task deep convolutional neural networks. In: IEEE Winter Conference on Applications of Computer Vision, pp. 1036–1041. IEEE (2014)
42. Zhang, Z., Luo, P., Loy, C.C., Tang, X.: Facial landmark detection by deep multi-task learning. In: Fleet, D., Pajdla, T., Schiele, B., Tuytelaars, T. (eds.) ECCV 2014. LNCS, vol. 8694, pp. 94–108. Springer, Cham (2014). https://doi.org/10.1007/978-3-319-10599-4_7
43. Zhao, J., Chang, C.k., Itti, L.: Learning to recognize objects by retaining other factors of variation. In: 2017 IEEE Winter Conference on Applications of Computer Vision (WACV), pp. 560–568. IEEE (2017)
44. Zhao, J., Mathieu, M., Goroshin, R., Lecun, Y.: Stacked what-where auto-encoders. arXiv preprint arXiv:1506.02351 (2015)
45. Zhu, J.Y., Park, T., Isola, P., Efros, A.A.: Unpaired image-to-image translation using cycle-consistent adversarial networks. In: Proceedings of the IEEE International Conference on Computer Vision, pp. 2223–2232 (2017)
46. Zhu, Z., Luo, P., Wang, X., Tang, X.: Multi-view perceptron: a deep model for learning face identity and view representations. In: Advances in Neural Information Processing Systems, pp. 217–225 (2014)

VLANet: Video-Language Alignment Network for Weakly-Supervised Video Moment Retrieval

Minuk Ma, Sunjae Yoon, Junyeong Kim, Youngjoon Lee, Sunghun Kang, and Chang D. Yoo[✉]

Korea Advanced Institute of Science and Technology, Daejeon, Republic of Korea
{akalsdnr,dbstjswo505,junyeong.kim,yjlee22,sunghun.kang, cd_yoo}@kaist.ac.kr

Abstract. Video Moment Retrieval (VMR) is a task to localize the temporal moment in untrimmed video specified by natural language query. For VMR, several methods that require full supervision for training have been proposed. Unfortunately, acquiring a large number of training videos with labeled temporal boundaries for each query is a labor-intensive process. This paper explores a method for performing VMR in a weakly-supervised manner (wVMR): training is performed without temporal moment labels but only with the text query that describes a segment of the video. Existing methods on wVMR generate multi-scale proposals and apply query-guided attention mechanism to highlight the most relevant proposal. To leverage the weak supervision, contrastive learning is used which predicts higher scores for the correct video-query pairs than for the incorrect pairs. It has been observed that a large number of candidate proposals, coarse query representation, and one-way attention mechanism lead to blurry attention map which limits the localization performance. To address this issue, Video-Language Alignment Network (VLANet) is proposed that learns a sharper attention by pruning out spurious candidate proposals and applying a multi-directional attention mechanism with fine-grained query representation. The Surrogate Proposal Selection module selects a proposal based on the proximity to the query in the joint embedding space, and thus substantially reduces candidate proposals which leads to lower computation load and sharper attention. Next, the Cascaded Cross-modal Attention module considers dense feature interactions and multi-directional attention flows to learn the multi-modal alignment. VLANet is trained end-to-end using contrastive loss which enforces semantically similar videos and queries to cluster. The experiments show that the method achieves state-of-the-art performance on Charades-STA and DiDeMo datasets.

Keywords: Multi-modal learning · Weakly-supervised learning · Video moment retrieval

---

M. Ma and S. Yoon—Both authors have equally contributed.

A. Vedaldi et al. (Eds.): ECCV 2020, LNCS 12373, pp. 156–171, 2020.
https://doi.org/10.1007/978-3-030-58604-1_10

1   Introduction

Video moment retrieval (VMR) is a task to find a temporal moment in untrimmed video specified by a text description as illustrated in Fig. 1. With the rising number of videos along with the need for a more detailed and refined search capability that demand a better understanding of the video, the task of Video Moment Retrieval is drawing appreciable attention.

A number of fully-supervised methods that learn from a set of videos with ground-truth time stamps corresponding to a given query have been proposed [3,6,23,25]. For these methods, a large-scale video dataset that requires the laborious burden of temporally annotating the boundaries corresponding to each query is a sine qua non. In general, the performance of a fully-supervised method hinges on the quality of the dataset; however, for VMR, temporal boundaries are often ambiguous to annotate and may act as noise in the learning process.

Recently, weakly-supervised VMR (wVMR) [12,14] that does not require the temporal boundary annotation for each query has been studied. To leverage the weak supervision, contrastive learning is applied such that higher scores are predicted for the correct video-query pairs than for incorrect pairs. This learning process improves the accuracy of the attention mechanism which plays a vital role in wVMR. Inspired by recent methods [12,14], this paper addresses two critical challenges: (1) generating appropriate multi-scale video candidate proposals, and (2) learning the latent alignment between the text query and the retrieved video segment.

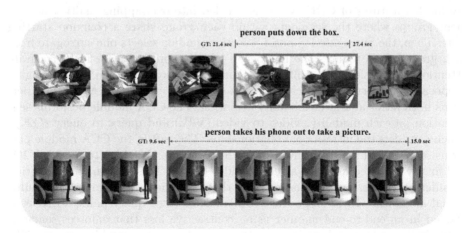

Fig. 1. Illustration of video moment retrieval task. The goal is to search the temporal boundary of the video moment that is most relevant to the given natural language query.

The first challenge is that the video segment proposals should be adequate in number to give high recall without excessive computational load, and the video segment should be of appropriate length to have high intersection-of-union (IoU) with ground truth. Previous methods [3,6,12,14] greedily generated video candidate proposals using a pre-defined set of multi-scale sliding windows. As a consequence, these methods generally produce large number of multi-scale proposals which increase the chance of achieving high recall at the expense of high computational cost. When an attention mechanism is used thereafter to weigh the proposals, the attention becomes blurry as there are too many proposals to attend.

The second challenge is to learn a similarity measure between video segment and text query without ground truth annotation. In [14], a text-to-video attention mechanism is incorporated to learn the joint embedding space of video and text query. More accurate multi-modal similarity could be attained with a text query representation that is more effective in interacting with video frame feature. Representing the text query as the last hidden feature of the Gated Recurrent Unit (GRU), as used in some previous methods [12,14], is overly simplistic. In addition, applying one-way attention from query to video is not sufficient to bring out the most prominent feature in the video and query. Recent studies in Visual Question Answering [5,9,24] have explored the possibility of applying multi-directional attention flows that include both inter- and intra-modality attention. This paper devises an analogous idea for the problem of wVMR, and validate its effectiveness in retrieving the moment using the weak labels.

To rise to the challenge, this paper proposes a Video-Language Alignment Network (VLANet) for weakly-supervised video moment retrieval. As a first step, the word-level query representation is obtained by stacking all intermediate hidden features of GRU. Video is divided into overlapping multi-scale segment groups where the segments within each group share a common starting time. Then, the Surrogate Proposal Selection module selects one surrogate from each group which reduces the number of effective proposals for more accurate attention. To consider the multi-directional interactions between each surrogate proposal and query, the Cascaded Cross-modal Attention (CCA) module performs both intra- and inter-modality attention. The CCA module performs self-attention on each modality: video to video (V2V) and query to query (Q2Q), which considers the intra-modal relationships. Thereafter, the CCA module performs cross-modal attention from query to video (Q2V), video to query (V2Q) and finally attended query to attended video (Q2V). This cross-modal attention considers the inter-modal relationships that is critical in learning the multi-modal alignment. To leverage the weak labels of video-query pairs, VLANet is trained in an end-to-end manner using contrastive loss that enforces semantically similar videos and queries to cluster in the joint embedding space. The experiment results show that the VLANet achieves state-of-the-art performance on Charades-STA and DiDeMo datasets. Extensive ablation study and qualitative analyses validate the effectiveness of the proposed method and provide interpretability.

2   Related Work

2.1   Temporal Action Detection

The goal of temporal action detection is to predict the temporal boundary and category for each action instance in untrimmed videos. Existing works are divided into two groups: the fully-supervised and weakly-supervised. Zhao *et al.* [26] proposed a structured segment network that models the temporal structure of each action instance by a structured temporal pyramid. Gao *et al.* [4] proposed Cascaded Boundary Regression which uses temporal coordinate regression to refine the temporal boundaries of the sliding windows. Lin *et al.* [11] proposed Boundary Sensitive Network that first classifies each frame as the start, middle, or end, then directly combines these boundaries as proposals.

In the weakly-supervised settings, however, only the coarse video-level labels are available instead of the exact temporal boundaries. Wang *et al.* [22] proposed UntrimmedNet that couples two components, the classification module, and the selection module, to learn the action models and reason about the temporal duration of action instances, respectively. Nguyen *et al.* [15] proposed a Sparse Temporal Pooling Network that identifies a sparse subset of key segments associated with the target actions in a video using an attention module and fuse the key segments using adaptive temporal pooling. Shou *et al.* [17] proposed AutoLoc that uses Outer-Inner-Contrastive loss to automatically discover the required segment-level supervision to train a boundary predictor. Liu *et al.* [13] proposed CleanNet that leverages an additional temporal contrast constraint so that the high-evaluation-score action proposals have a higher probability to overlap with the ground truth action instances.

2.2   Video Moment Retrieval

The VMR task is focused on localizing the temporal moment that is semantically aligned with the given natural language query. For this task, various supervised methods have been proposed [3,6,23,25]. In Gao *et al.* [3] and Hendricks *et al.* [6], candidate moments are sampled using sliding windows of various lengths, and multi-modal fusion is performed to estimate the correlation between the queries and video moments. Xu *et al.* [23] proposed a model that integrates vision and language features using attention mechanisms and leverages video captioning as an auxiliary task. Zhang *et al.* [25] proposed Moment Alignment Network (MAN) that considers the relationships between proposals as a structured graph, and devised an iterative algorithm to train a revised graph convolution network.

Recently, the task was studied under the weakly-supervised setting [2,12,14]. Duan *et al.* [2] proposed to decompose weakly-supervised dense event captioning in videos (WS-DEC) into a pair of dual problems: event captioning and sentence localization. They proposed a cycle system to train the model based on the assumption that each caption describes only one temporal segment. Mithun *et al.* [14] proposed Text-Guided-Attention (TGA) model that learns a joint representation between video and sentence. The attention weight is used to retrieve

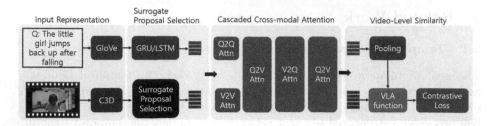

Fig. 2. Illustration of VLANet architecture. The Surrogate Proposal Selection module prunes out irrelevant proposals based on the similarity metric. Cascaded Cross-modal Attention considers various attention flows to learn multi-modal alignment. The network is trained end-to-end using contrastive loss.

the relevant moment at test time. Lin *et al.* [12] proposed Semantic Completion Network (SCN) that selects the top-K proposals considering exploration and exploitation, and measures the semantic similarity between the video and query. As an auxiliary task, SCN takes the masked sentence as input and predicts the masked words from visual representations.

3   Method

3.1   Method Overview

Figure 2 illustrates the overall VLANet architecture. The input text query is embedded using GloVe [16] after which each embedded representation is fed into a GRU [1]. In the meanwhile, the video is embedded based on C3D [21]. Video is divided into overlapping multi-scale segment groups where the proposals within each group share a common starting time. Given the video and query representations V and Q, the similarity c between video and query is evaluated by the Cascaded Cross-modal Attention (CCA) module. The learned attention weights by CCA are used to localize the relevant moment at test time. A video-query pair (V, Q) is positive if it is in the training data; otherwise, it is negative. The network is trained in an end-to-end manner using contrastive loss to enforce the scores of the positive pairs to be higher than those of the negative pairs. In practice, the negative pairs are randomly sampled in a batch.

3.2   Input Representation

Query Representation. Gated Recurrent Unit (GRU) [1] is used for encoding the sentences. Each word of the query is embedded using GloVe and sequentially fed into a GRU. Prior methods [14] use only the final hidden feature of GRU to represent the whole sentence, which leads to the loss of information by excluding the interactions between frame- and word-level features of video and query.

Motivated by recent works in visual question answering [5,24], this paper uses all intermediate hidden features of the GRU. The query Q is represented as:

$$Q = [\mathbf{w}_1\ \mathbf{w}_2\ \cdots\ \mathbf{w}_M] \tag{1}$$

where $\mathbf{w}_m \in \mathbb{R}^D$ denotes the m-th GRU hidden feature, and D is the dimension of the hidden feature. Each $\mathbf{w}_m$ is L2 normalized to output a unit vector.

Video Representation. Video is encoded using a C3D [21] model pre-trained on Sports-1M dataset [8] as in [3]. The feature was extracted at every 16 frames for Charades-STA. The VGG16 model [19] is used for frame-level feature extraction for DiDeMo dataset following [6]. Both C3D and VGG16 features were extracted from the penultimate fully-connected layer, which results in the feature dimension of 4096.

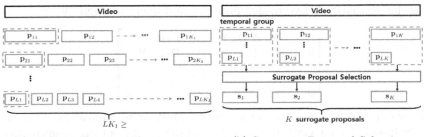

(a) Multi-scale proposal generation   (b) Surrogate Proposal Selection

Fig. 3. Comparison between the previous and the proposed proposal generation method. (a) generates large number of proposals of various lengths. (b) groups the proposals, and selects the surrogate proposals based on the proximity to the query.

Video Proposal Generation. As depicted in image Fig. 3(a) previous methods [12,14] generated proposals using multi-scale sliding windows. Meanwhile, as in Fig. 3(b), VLANet organizes the multi-scale windows in segment groups such that within a group, all windows start at the same time instance. Each group will have the same number of windows of fixed scales. The interval between the starting times of each segment group is regular. With K segment groups and L multi-scale proposals, the total number of proposals is $K \cdot L$. Then, the video V is represented by:

$$V = \begin{bmatrix} \mathbf{p}_{11} & \mathbf{p}_{12} & \cdots & \mathbf{p}_{1K} \\ \mathbf{p}_{21} & \mathbf{p}_{22} & \cdots & \mathbf{p}_{2K} \\ \vdots & & \cdots & \\ \mathbf{p}_{L1} & \mathbf{p}_{L2} & \cdots & \mathbf{p}_{LK} \end{bmatrix} \tag{2}$$

where each $\mathbf{p}_{lk} \in \mathbb{R}^D$ denotes the proposal feature of the l-th scale in the k-th segment group, which is the average of the C3D features of the frames participating in the proposal. Fully-connected layers are used to resize the feature dimension of Q and V to D. L2 normalization is performed to make each $\mathbf{p}_{lk}$ a unit vector.

3.3   Surrogate Proposal Selection Module

To reduce the large number of proposals, [12] proposed a sampling-based selection algorithm to prune out irrelevant proposals considering the exploration and exploitation. However, the method is trained using policy gradient algorithm [20] which suffers from high variance. Instead, as depicted in Fig. 3(b), the Surrogate Proposal Selection module selects the best-matched proposals from each segment group based on the cosine similarity to the final hidden feature of the query. A surrogate proposal of the k-th segment group is defined as the proposal that has the largest cosine similarity to the final hidden feature of the query. The cosine similarity between each proposal and query is given by

$$\begin{bmatrix} \mathbf{p}_{11} \cdot \mathbf{w}_M & \mathbf{p}_{12} \cdot \mathbf{w}_M & \cdots & \mathbf{p}_{1K} \cdot \mathbf{w}_M \\ \mathbf{p}_{21} \cdot \mathbf{w}_M & \mathbf{p}_{22} \cdot \mathbf{w}_M & \cdots & \mathbf{p}_{2K} \cdot \mathbf{w}_M \\ \vdots & & \cdots & \\ \mathbf{p}_{L1} \cdot \mathbf{w}_M & \mathbf{p}_{L2} \cdot \mathbf{w}_M & \cdots & \mathbf{p}_{LK} \cdot \mathbf{w}_M \end{bmatrix} \tag{3}$$

where $\mathbf{w}_M$ is the final hidden feature of the query. It is empirically determined that the final hidden query feature is sufficient in pruning out irrelevant proposals at a low computational cost. The Surrogate Proposal Selection module pick the l'-th scale from each k-th segment group which is given by,

$$l' = \operatorname{argmax} \begin{bmatrix} \mathbf{p}_{1k} \cdot \mathbf{w}_M & \mathbf{p}_{2k} \cdot \mathbf{w}_M & \cdots & \mathbf{p}_{Lk} \cdot \mathbf{w}_M \end{bmatrix}, \tag{4}$$

$$\mathbf{s}_k = \mathbf{p}_{l'k} \tag{5}$$

where $\mathbf{s}_k$ is the surrogate proposal feature of the k-th segment group. In backpropagation, only the surrogate proposals $\mathbf{s}_k$'s contribute to the weight update which allows end-to-end learning. Then the video is represented by K surrogate proposal features:

$$\mathcal{V} = \begin{bmatrix} \mathbf{s}_1 & \mathbf{s}_2 & \cdots & \mathbf{s}_K \end{bmatrix} \tag{6}$$

where $\mathcal{V}$ is the updated video representation composed of the surrogate proposals.

3.4   Cascaded Cross-Modal Attention Module

Cascaded Cross-modal Attention (CCA) module takes the video and query representations as inputs, and outputs a compact attended video representation. Compared to text-guided attention (TGA) [14], CCA module considers more diverse multi-modal feature interactions including V2V, Q2Q, V2Q, and Q2V where each has its own advantages as described below.

Dense Attention. The basic attention unit of CCA module is referred to as Dense Attention which calculates the attention between two multi-element features. Given $Y = [\mathbf{y}_1 \ldots \mathbf{y}_M]^T \in \mathbb{R}^{M \times D}$ and $X = [\mathbf{x}_1 \ldots \mathbf{x}_N]^T \in \mathbb{R}^{N \times D}$, the Dense Attention $A(X, Y) : \mathbb{R}^{N \times D} \times \mathbb{R}^{M \times D} \to \mathbb{R}^{N \times D}$ attends X using Y and is defined as follows:

$$\mathcal{E}(\mathbf{x}_n, Y) = \sum_{m=1}^{M} \tanh(W_1 \mathbf{x}_n \cdot W_2 \mathbf{y}_m), \tag{7}$$

$$A(X, Y) = \text{Softmax}([\mathcal{E}(\mathbf{x}_1, Y) \; \mathcal{E}(\mathbf{x}_2, Y) \; \cdots \; \mathcal{E}(\mathbf{x}_N, Y)])X, \tag{8}$$

where W_1, W_2 are learnable parameters. Here, $\mathcal{E} : \mathbb{R}^D \times \mathbb{R}^{M \times D} \to \mathbb{R}$ is referred to as the Video-Language Alignment (VLA) function that performs the multi-modal alignment.

Self-attention. Based on the Dense Attention defined above, the CCA module initially performs a type of self-attention that attends $\mathcal{V}$ and Q using $\mathcal{V}$ and Q respectively as given below,

$$\mathcal{V} \leftarrow A(\mathcal{V}, \mathcal{V}), \tag{9}$$

$$Q \leftarrow A(Q, Q). \tag{10}$$

The intra-attention allows each element of itself to be attended by its global contextual information. The attention from $\mathcal{V}$ to $\mathcal{V}$ is capable of highlighting the salient proposals by considering the innate temporal relationships. The attention from Q to Q updates the each word-level feature by considering the context of the whole sentence.

Cross Modal Attention. Following self-attention defined above, the CCA module is used to cross-attend $\mathcal{V}$ and Q using Q and $\mathcal{V}$ respectively such that cross-modal attention is defined as follows:

$$\mathcal{V} \leftarrow A(\mathcal{V}, Q), \tag{11}$$

$$Q \leftarrow A(Q, \mathcal{V}). \tag{12}$$

The above attention is critical in learning the latent multi-modal alignment. It has been empirically observed that cross-modal attention applied in series several times until near-saturation can be conducive in producing better performance. Finally, a compact attended video representation $\mathbf{v}_{comp}$ is obtained by taking the sum of all elements of $\mathcal{V}$, and video-level similarity c is obtained by the VLA function between $\mathbf{v}_{comp}$ and Q as given below:

$$c = \mathcal{E}(\mathbf{v}_{comp}, Q). \tag{13}$$

The network is trained using the following contrastive loss:

$$\mathcal{L}_{contrastive} = max[0, \Delta - \mathcal{E}(\mathbf{v}_{comp}, Q^+) + \mathcal{E}(\mathbf{v}_{comp}, Q^-)] \tag{14}$$

where $\mathcal{E}$ is the VLA function defined above in Sect. 3.4 and Δ is the margin. Q^+ and Q^- is positive and negative query features.

4   Experiment

4.1   Datasets

Charades-STA. The Charades dataset was originally introduced in [18]. It contains temporal activity annotation and multiple video-level descriptions for each video. Gao *et al.* [3] generated temporal boundary annotations for sentences using a semi-automatic way and released the Charades-STA dataset that is for video moment retrieval. The dataset includes 12,408 video-sentence pairs with temporal boundary annotations for training and 3,720 for testing. The average length of the query is 8.6 words, and the average duration of the video is 29.8 s.

DiDeMo. The Distinct Describable Moments (DiDeMo) dataset [6] consists of over 10,000 unedited, personal videos in diverse visual settings with pairs of localized video segments and referring expressions. The videos are collected from Flickr and each video is trimmed to a maximum of 30 s. The dataset includes 8,395, 1,065 and 1,004 videos for train, validation, and test, respectively. The videos are divided into 5-s segments to reduce the complexity of annotation, which results in 21 possible moments per video. The dataset contains a total of 26,892 moments with over 40,000 text descriptions. The descriptions in the DiDeMo dataset are natural language sentences that contain activities, camera movement, and temporal transition indicators. Moreover, the descriptions in DiDeMo are verified to refer to a single moment.

Evaluation Metric. For Charades-STA, the evaluation metric proposed by [3] is adopted to compute "R@n, IoU=m". For the test set predictions, the recall R@n calculates the percentage of samples for which the correct result resides in the top-n retrievals to the query. If the IoU between the prediction and the ground truth is greater than or equal to m, the prediction is correct. The overall performance is the average recall on the whole test set.

For DiDeMo, the evaluation metric proposed by [6] is adopted. The evaluation metric is also R@n with different criteria for correct prediction. If the ground truth moment is in the top-n predictions, the prediction for the sample is counted as correct. The mIoU metric is computed by taking the average of the IoU between the predicted moment and the ground truth moment.

4.2   Quantitative Result

Table 1 shows the performance comparison between VLANet and the related methods on Charades-STA. The first section indicates random baseline, the second section indicates fully-supervised methods, and the third section indicates weakly-supervised methods. VLANet achieves state-of-the-art performance on Charades-STA among weakly-supervised methods. It outperforms the random baseline, VSA-RNN, and VSA-STV by a large margin. Compared to the other

Table 1. Performance comparison of VLANet to the related methods on Charades-STA

Type	Method	R@1			R@5		
		IoU = 0.3	IoU = 0.5	IoU = 0.7	IoU = 0.3	IoU = 0.5	IoU = 0.7
Baseline	Random	19.78	11.96	4.81	73.62	52.79	21.53
Fully	VSA-RNN [3]	–	10.50	4.32	–	48.43	20.21
	VSA-STV [3]	–	16.91	5.81	–	53.89	23.58
	CTRL [3]	–	23.63	8.89	–	58.92	29.52
	EFRC [23]	53.00	33.80	15.00	94.60	77.30	43.90
	MAN [25]	–	46.53	22.72	–	86.23	53.72
Weakly	TGA [14]	32.14	19.94	8.84	86.58	65.52	33.51
	SCN [12]	42.96	23.58	9.97	95.56	71.80	**38.87**
	VLANet (ours)	**45.24**	**31.83**	**14.17**	**95.70**	**82.85**	33.09

Table 2. Performance comparison of VLANet to the related methods on DiDeMo

Type	Method	R@1	R@5	mIoU
Baseline	Upper bound	74.75	100	96.05
	Random	3.75	22.50	22.64
	LSTM-RGB-Local [6]	13.10	44.82	25.13
Fully	Txt-Obj-Retrieval [7]	16.20	43.94	27.18
	EFRC [23]	13.23	46.98	27.57
	CCA [10]	18.11	52.11	37.82
	MCN [6]	28.10	78.21	41.08
	MAN [25]	27.02	81.70	41.16
Weakly	TGA [14]	12.19	39.74	24.92
	VLANet (ours)	**19.32**	**65.68**	**25.33**

fully-supervised methods such as CTRL and EFRC, its performance is comparable. Besides, compared to the other weakly-supervised methods TGA and SCN, VLANet outperforms others by a large margin.

Table 2 shows the performance comparison on DiDeMo. The first section contains the baselines, the second section contains fully-supervised methods, and the third section contains weakly-supervised methods. VLANet achieves state-of-the-art performance among the weakly-supervised methods. In the R@5 based test, especially, its performance is 25.94 higher than the runner-up model TGA. It is comparable to some fully-supervised methods such as CCA[1] and Txt-Obj-Retrieval. These indicate that even without the full annotations of temporal boundary, VLANet has the potential to learn latent multi-modal alignment between video and query, and to localizing semantically relevant moments.

---

[1] Here, CCA refers to a previous method [10], but not Cascaded Cross-modal Attention proposed in this paper.

Table 3. Performance of model variants and ablation study of VLANet on Charades-STA. The unit of stride and window size is frame.

Method	R@1			R@5		
	IoU = 0.3	IoU = 0.5	IoU = 0.7	IoU = 0.3	IoU = 0.5	IoU = 0.7
stride 4, window(176, 208, 240)	44.76	31.53	14.78	77.04	63.17	31.80
stride 6, window(176, 208, 240)	42.17	28.60	12.98	88.76	74.91	**34.70**
stride 8, window(176, 208, 240)	45.03	31.82	14.19	95.72	82.82	33.33
stride 6, window(128, 256)	42.39	28.03	13.09	94.70	73.06	30.69
stride 6, window(176, 240)	42.92	30.24	13.57	95.72	82.80	33.46
w/o cross-attn	43.41	30.08	13.23	95.72	82.41	33.06
w/o self-attn	42.31	30.81	15.38	95.38	80.02	33.76
w/o surrogate	35.81	25.30	12.26	80.61	64.57	31.31
Full model	**45.03**	**31.82**	**14.19**	**95.72**	**82.82**	33.33

4.3   Model Variants and Ablation Study

Table 3 summarizes the performance of model variants and the ablation study conducted on VLANet. The first section shows the performance variation by varying stride and window sizes, and the second section shows the performance drop without core components. The strides and the sizes of the windows were determined by considering the average video length. The first three rows show that the network performs best with the stride of 8. While the proposals with stride 4 have finer granularity, the large number of proposals decreases the performance. The networks with three multi-scale proposals tend to achieve higher performance than the networks with two multi-scale proposals. This shows the importance of stride and the number of scales. After finding the best hyper-parameters of 'stride 8, window(176, 208, 240)' these values were fixed for the subsequent experiments and analyses. The network without cross-attention, self-attention show a decrease in performance, demonstrating the importance of the attention mechanisms. We generally notice a drop in performance with an increasing IoU metric. The drop is more drastic without cross-attention than without self-attention. This observation indicates that cross-modal attention has a larger influence on performance than self-attention. The performance of w/o surrogate is decreased significantly across all metrics. This indicates that selecting probable proposals in the early stage is critical to the performance.

4.4   Analysis of Multi-modal Similarity

Figure 4 shows similarity predicted by the network on the whole test set of Charades-STA while training. The x-axis indicates the epoch of training, and the y-axis indicates the similarity. It is observed that the similarity scores of the positive pairs (blue) increase and reach a high plateau of about 0.9, while those of the negative pairs (red) keep a low value of about 0.15. These demonstrate that contrastive learning was successfully conducted.

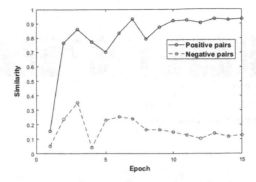

Fig. 4. The multi-modal similarity prediction by VLANet on the positive and negative pairs while training. The similarity gap increases as epoch increases. (Color figure online)

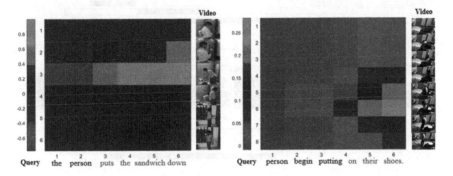

Fig. 5. Visualization of Cascaded Cross-modal Attention. The attention map is calculated by the outer-product of video and query features that are obtained after the Cascaded Cross-modal Attention module and before the pooling layer.

4.5 Visualization of Attention Map

Figure 5 visualizes the attention map of the proposed Cascaded Cross-modal Attention. The x-axis indicates the words in the query and the y-axis indicates the time. In the left example, the attention weight of the "put the sandwich down" is high when the person is putting the sandwich down. Similarly in the right example, important words such as action or object have high attention weight with the related moment of the video. The high attention weights are biased on the right side in Fig. 5 as the final GRU feature has the context information about the whole sentence. The above example demonstrates that VLANet can learn the latent multi-modal alignment.

4.6 Visualization of Inference

Figure 6 provides a visualization of the inference of VLANet. Only a subset of total proposals were depicted whose color indicates the attention strength. In the

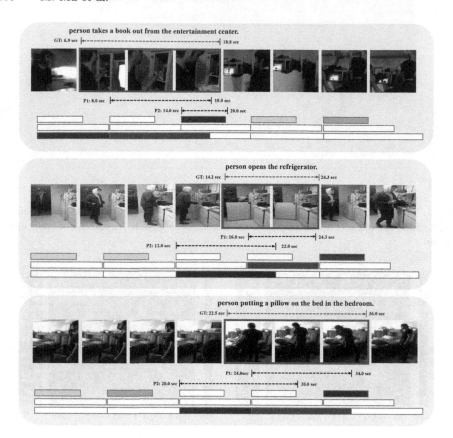

Fig. 6. At inference time, VLANet successfully retrieves the moment described by the query. Due to the limited space, only some proposals are visualized. The color indicates the attention strength. The top-2 predicted moments are visualized with the temporal boundaries. (Color figure online)

first example, both top-1 and top-2 predictions by VLANet have high overlaps with the ground truth moment. In the second example, the network localizes the moment when the person actually *opens* the refrigerator. Similarly in the third example, the network localizes the moment when person *puts* the pillow. This shows that the network successfully captures the moment when a certain action is taken or an event occurs. The inference visualization demonstrates the moment retrieval ability of VLANet and suggests its applicability to real-world scenarios.

5   Conclusions

This paper considers Video-Language Alignment Network (VLANet) for weakly-supervised video moment retrieval. VLANet is able to select appropriate candidate proposals using a more detailed query representation that include intermediate hidden features of the GRU. The Surrogate Proposal Selection module reduces the number of candidate proposals based on the similarity between each proposal and the query. The ablation study reveals that it has the largest influence on performance. The Cascaded Cross-modal Attention module performs a modified self-attention followed by a cascade of cross-attention based on the Dense Attention defined. It also has a significant influence on performance. VLANet is trained in an end-to-end manner using contrastive loss which enforces semantically similar videos and queries to cluster in the joint embedding space. The experiments shows that VLANet achieves state-of-the-art performance on Charades-STA and DiDeMo datasets.

Acknowledgement. This work was partly supported by Institute for Information & communications Technology Planning & Evaluation (IITP) grant funded by the Korea government (MSIT) (2017-0-01780, The technology development for event recognition/relational reasoning and learning knowledge based system for video understanding) and partly supported by Institute for Information & communications Technology Planning & Evaluation (IITP) grant funded by the Korea government (MSIT) (No. 2019-0-01396, Development of framework for analyzing, detecting, mitigating of bias in AI model and training data).

References

1. Cho, K., van Merrienboer, B., Bahdanau, D., Bengio, Y.: On the properties of neural machine translation: encoder-decoder approaches. In: Proceedings of SSST@EdMNLP 2014, pp. 103–111. Association for Computational Linguistics (2014)
2. Duan, X., Huang, W., Gan, C., Wang, J., Zhu, W., Huang, J.: Weakly supervised dense event captioning in videos. In: Advances in Neural Information Processing Systems 31: Annual Conference on Neural Information Processing Systems 2018, NeurIPS 2018, pp. 3063–3073 (2018)
3. Gao, J., Sun, C., Yang, Z., Nevatia, R.: TALL: temporal activity localization via language query. In: IEEE International Conference on Computer Vision, ICCV 2017, pp. 5277–5285. IEEE Computer Society (2017)
4. Gao, J., Yang, Z., Nevatia, R.: Cascaded boundary regression for temporal action detection. In: British Machine Vision Conference 2017, BMVC 2017. BMVA Press (2017)
5. Gao, P., et al.: Dynamic fusion with intra- and inter-modality attention flow for visual question answering. In: IEEE Conference on Computer Vision and Pattern Recognition, CVPR 2019, pp. 6639–6648. Computer Vision Foundation/IEEE (2019)
6. Hendricks, L.A., Wang, O., Shechtman, E., Sivic, J., Darrell, T., Russell, B.C.: Localizing moments in video with natural language. In: IEEE International Conference on Computer Vision, ICCV 2017, pp. 5804–5813. IEEE Computer Society (2017)
7. Hu, R., Xu, H., Rohrbach, M., Feng, J., Saenko, K., Darrell, T.: Natural language object retrieval. In: 2016 IEEE Conference on Computer Vision and Pattern Recognition (CVPR), pp. 4555–4564 (2016)

8. Karpathy, A., Toderici, G., Shetty, S., Leung, T., Sukthankar, R., Li, F.: Large-scale video classification with convolutional neural networks. In: 2014 IEEE Conference on Computer Vision and Pattern Recognition, CVPR 2014, pp. 1725–1732. IEEE Computer Society (2014)
9. Kim, J., Ma, M., Pham, T., Kim, K., Yoo, C.D.: Modality shifting attention network for multi-modal video question answering. In: IEEE/CVF Conference on Computer Vision and Pattern Recognition (CVPR) (2020)
10. Klein, B., Lev, G., Sadeh, G., Wolf, L.: Associating neural word embeddings with deep image representations using fisher vectors. In: 2015 IEEE Conference on Computer Vision and Pattern Recognition (CVPR), pp. 4437–4446 (2015)
11. Lin, T., Zhao, X., Su, H., Wang, C., Yang, M.: BSN: boundary sensitive network for temporal action proposal generation. In: Ferrari, V., Hebert, M., Sminchisescu, C., Weiss, Y. (eds.) ECCV 2018. LNCS, vol. 11208, pp. 3–21. Springer, Cham (2018). https://doi.org/10.1007/978-3-030-01225-0_1
12. Lin, Z., Zhao, Z., Zhang, Z., Wang, Q., Liu, H.: Weakly-supervised video moment retrieval via semantic completion network. CoRR abs/1911.08199 (2019). http://arxiv.org/abs/1911.08199
13. Liu, Z., et al.: Weakly supervised temporal action localization through contrast based evaluation networks. In: The IEEE International Conference on Computer Vision (ICCV) (2019)
14. Mithun, N.C., Paul, S., Roy-Chowdhury, A.K.: Weakly supervised video moment retrieval from text queries. In: IEEE Conference on Computer Vision and Pattern Recognition, CVPR 2019, pp. 11592–11601. Computer Vision Foundation/IEEE (2019)
15. Nguyen, P., Liu, T., Prasad, G., Han, B.: Weakly supervised action localization by sparse temporal pooling network. In: 2018 IEEE Conference on Computer Vision and Pattern Recognition, CVPR 2018, pp. 6752–6761. IEEE Computer Society (2018)
16. Pennington, J., Socher, R., Manning, C.D.: GloVe: global vectors for word representation. In: Moschitti, A., Pang, B., Daelemans, W. (eds.) Proceedings of the 2014 Conference on Empirical Methods in Natural Language Processing, EMNLP 2014, pp. 1532–1543. ACL (2014)
17. Shou, Z., Gao, H., Zhang, L., Miyazawa, K., Chang, S.-F.: AutoLoc: weakly-supervised temporal action localization in untrimmed videos. In: Ferrari, V., Hebert, M., Sminchisescu, C., Weiss, Y. (eds.) ECCV 2018. LNCS, vol. 11220, pp. 162–179. Springer, Cham (2018). https://doi.org/10.1007/978-3-030-01270-0_10
18. Sigurdsson, G.A., Varol, G., Wang, X., Farhadi, A., Laptev, I., Gupta, A.: Hollywood in homes: crowdsourcing data collection for activity understanding. In: Leibe, B., Matas, J., Sebe, N., Welling, M. (eds.) ECCV 2016. LNCS, vol. 9905, pp. 510–526. Springer, Cham (2016). https://doi.org/10.1007/978-3-319-46448-0_31
19. Simonyan, K., Zisserman, A.: Very deep convolutional networks for large-scale image recognition. In: Bengio, Y., LeCun, Y. (eds.) 3rd International Conference on Learning Representations, ICLR 2015 (2015)
20. Sutton, R.S., McAllester, D., Singh, S., Mansour, Y.: Policy gradient methods for reinforcement learning with function approximation. In: Proceedings of the 12th International Conference on Neural Information Processing Systems, pp. 1057–1063. MIT Press (1999)
21. Tran, D., Bourdev, L.D., Fergus, R., Torresani, L., Paluri, M.: Learning spatiotemporal features with 3D convolutional networks. In: 2015 IEEE International Conference on Computer Vision, ICCV 2015, pp. 4489–4497. IEEE Computer Society (2015)

22. Wang, L., Xiong, Y., Lin, D., Gool, L.V.: UntrimmedNets for weakly supervised action recognition and detection. In: 2017 IEEE Conference on Computer Vision and Pattern Recognition, CVPR 2017, pp. 6402–6411. IEEE Computer Society (2017)

23. Xu, H., He, K., Sigal, L., Sclaroff, S., Saenko, K.: Text-to-clip video retrieval with early fusion and re-captioning. ArXiv abs/1804.05113 (2018)

24. Yu, Z., Yu, J., Cui, Y., Tao, D., Tian, Q.: Deep modular co-attention networks for visual question answering. In: IEEE Conference on Computer Vision and Pattern Recognition, CVPR 2019, pp. 6281–6290. Computer Vision Foundation/IEEE (2019)

25. Zhang, D., Dai, X., Wang, X., Wang, Y., Davis, L.S.: MAN: moment alignment network for natural language moment retrieval via iterative graph adjustment. In: IEEE Conference on Computer Vision and Pattern Recognition, CVPR 2019, pp. 1247–1257. Computer Vision Foundation/IEEE (2019)

26. Zhao, Y., Xiong, Y., Wang, L., Wu, Z., Tang, X., Lin, D.: Temporal action detection with structured segment networks. Int. J. Comput. Vision **128**(1), 74–95 (2020)

Attention-Based Query Expansion Learning

Albert Gordo[(✉)] [iD], Filip Radenovic [iD], and Tamara Berg [iD]

Facebook AI, Menlo Park, USA
agordo@fb.com

Abstract. Query expansion is a technique widely used in image search consisting in combining highly ranked images from an original query into an expanded query that is then reissued, generally leading to increased recall and precision. An important aspect of query expansion is choosing an appropriate way to combine the images into a new query. Interestingly, despite the undeniable empirical success of query expansion, ad-hoc methods with different caveats have dominated the landscape, and not a lot of research has been done on *learning* how to do query expansion. In this paper we propose a more principled framework to query expansion, where one trains, *in a discriminative manner*, a model that learns how images should be aggregated to form the expanded query. Within this framework, we propose a model that leverages a self-attention mechanism to effectively learn how to transfer information between the different images before aggregating them. Our approach obtains higher accuracy than existing approaches on standard benchmarks. More importantly, our approach is the only one that consistently shows high accuracy under different regimes, overcoming caveats of existing methods.

Keywords: Image retrieval · Query expansion learning · Attention-based aggregation

1 Introduction

Image search is a fundamental task in computer vision, directly applied in a number of applications such as visual place localization [2,21,39], 3D reconstruction [16,24,40], content-based image browsing [1,27,50], *etc.* Image search is typically cast as a nearest neighbor search problem in the image representation space, originally using local feature matching and bag-of-words-like representations [43], and, more recently, CNN-based global image representations [13,33].

To increase the accuracy of image search systems, a robust representation of the query image is desirable. Query expansion (QE) is a commonly used technique to achieve this goal, where relevant candidates produced during an initial ranking are aggregated into an expanded query, which is then used to search more images in the database. Aggregating the candidates reinforces the information shared between them and injects new information not available in

© Springer Nature Switzerland AG 2020
A. Vedaldi et al. (Eds.): ECCV 2020, LNCS 12373, pp. 172–188, 2020.
https://doi.org/10.1007/978-3-030-58604-1_11

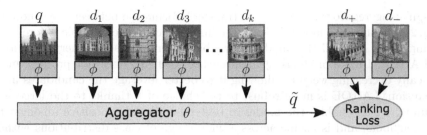

Fig. 1. Outline of our proposed approach. During training, we sample a query q and its nearest neighbors in the training dataset (where their features have been precomputed with the function ϕ, typically a CNN) and use our proposed attention-based model θ to aggregate them into an expanded query $\tilde{q}$. Given positive ($\mathbf{d}_+$) and/or negative ($\mathbf{d}_-$) samples, we use a ranking loss to optimize θ. Images with the **green** (**red**) border represent relevant (non-relevant) samples to the query. At inference, we construct the expanded $\tilde{\mathbf{q}}$ given $\mathbf{q}$ and its neighbors in the index, and use it to query the index again. (Color figure online)

the original query. This idea was originally exploited in the work of Chum *et al.* [7], introducing the first attempt at image retrieval QE. This averaging of query and top ranked results [7], or ad-hoc variations of it [3,6,13,33,45], are now used as a standard method of performance boosting in image retrieval.

Selecting which images from the initial ranking should be used in the QE procedure is however a challenging problem, since we do not have guarantees that they are actually relevant to the query. Early methods use strong geometrical verification of local features to select true positives [3,6,7,45]. As CNN-based global features lack this possibility, the most common approach is to use the k-nearest neighbors to the query [13,33], potentially including false positives. Yet, if k is larger than the number of relevant images, topic drift will degrade the results significantly. This leads to two unsatisfying alternatives: either use a very small k, potentially not leveraging relevant images, or use weighted average approaches with decreasing weights as a function of ranking [13] or image similarity [33], where setting the appropriate decay is a task just as challenging as choosing the optimal k. This has unfortunately led to many works tuning the k parameter directly on test, as well as to use different values of k for each dataset. Replacing k-nearest neighborhoods with similarity-based neighborhoods turn out to be just as unstable, as, unlike inlier count for local features, cosine similarity of CNN global features is not directly comparable between different query images [29].

We argue that existing QE approaches are generally not robust and use ad-hoc aggregation methods, and instead propose to cast QE as a discriminative learning problem. Similar to recent methods that learn embeddings suitable for image retrieval using large-scale datasets [13,33], we formulate the problem as a ranking one, where we train an aggregator that produces the expanded query, optimized to rank relevant samples ahead of non-relevant ones, *cf.* Fig. 1. We use a large-scale dataset, disjoint from the evaluation ones, to train and validate our model and its parameters. We then leverage a self-attention mechanism to design an aggregator model that can transfer information between the candidates (Fig. 2), enabling the model to learn the importance of each sample before aggregating them. We call this model Learnable Attention-based Query Expansion, or LAttQE. Unlike previous QE approaches, LAttQE does not produce monotonically decreasing weights, allowing it to better leverage the candidates in the expansion. LAttQE is more robust to the choice of k thanks to the large-scale training, which enables the model to better handle false positive amongst the top neighbors, and is usable across a wide range of class distributions without sacrificing the performance at any number of relevant images.

Our contributions are as follows: (i) We show that standard query expansion methods, albeit seemingly different, can be cast under the same mathematical framework, allowing one to compare their advantages and shortcomings in a principled way. (ii) We propose to treat query expansion as a discriminative learning problem, where an aggregation model is learned in a supervised manner. (iii) We propose LAttQE, an aggregation model designed to share information between the query and the top ranked items by means of self-attention. We extend this query expansion model to also be useful for database-side augmentation. (iv) We show that our proposed approach outperforms commonly-used query expansion methods in terms of both accuracy and robustness on standard benchmarks.

2   Related Work

Image Retrieval Query Expansion. Average query expansion (AQE) in image retrieval was originally proposed for representations based on local features [7], and tuned for the bag-of-words search model [43], where local features are aggregated after a strict filtering step, usually based on strong feature geometry [6,7] or Hamming embedding distance [45]. For CNN-based global image representation, AQE is implemented by mean-aggregating the top k retrieved images [13,33]. It has been argued that setting an optimal k for several datasets of different positive image distributions is a non-trivial task [33]. Instead, Gordo *et al.* [13] propose using a weighted average, where the weight is a monotonically decaying function over the rank of retrieved images. We denote this method as average query expansion with decay, or AQEwD. Likewise, Radenovic *et al.* [33] use a weighted average, where the weights are computed as a power-normalized similarity between the query and the top ranked images. This method, known as alpha query expansion (αQE), has proven to be fairly robust to the number of neighbors k, and is used as a *de facto* standard by a number of recent state-of-the-art image retrieval works [11,14,17,18,34,36]. Finally, Arandjelovic *et al.* [3] proposed discriminative query expansion (DQE) where they train a linear SVM using top ranked images as positives, and low ranking images as negatives, and use the resulting classifier as the expanded query. Note that this is very different from our method, as DQE trains independent classifiers for each query, while we train one single model using a large disjoint dataset.

Image Retrieval Database Pre-processing. If the database is fixed at indexing time, one can pre-process the database to refine the image representations and improve the accuracy. Database-side augmentation (DBA) [3] is a method that applies QE to each image of the database and replaces the original representation of the image by its expanded version. Although it increases the offline pre-processing time, it does not increase the memory requirements of the pipeline or the online search time. All aggregation-based QE methods described in the previous paragraph [3,7,13,33] can be applied as different flavors of DBA, including our proposed LAttQE. A different line of work [8,32,42] indexes local neighborhoods of database images together with their respective representations, in order to refine the search results based on the reciprocal neighborhood relations between the query and database images. Besides offline pre-processing, these approaches require additional storage and are slower at query time. Finally, some works [5,19] build a nearest neighbor graph using the database image representations and traverse it at query time, or, alternatively, encode graph information into image descriptors [23]. It increases the amount of required memory by storing the graph structure of the database, and increases online search complexity by orders of magnitude. Both reciprocal-nearest-neighbor and graph-based methods are complementary to our work, and can be applied after augmenting the database representations with our method. When dealing with dynamically-growing indexes, applying these methods becomes even more challenging, which makes them generally unappealing despite the accuracy gains.

Self-attention. The self-attention transformer [47] has established itself as the core component of strong language representation models such as BERT [10] or GPT-2 [35] due to its ability to capture complex interactions between tokens and due to how easy it is to increase the capacity of models simply by stacking more encoders. Self-attention has also shown applications outside of NLP. Wang *et al.* [48] leverage self-attention to aggregate descriptors from different parts of the image in order to capture interactions between them in a non-local manner. In a similar way, Girdhar and Ramanan [12] use self-attention as an approximation for second order pooling. In a different context, Lee *et al.* [22] use self-attention as a graph pooling mechanism to combine both node features and graph topology in the pooling. In this paper we use self-attention as a way to transfer information between the top k results so we can construct a more discriminative query. As we describe in Sect. 3, self-attention is an excellent mechanism to this end.

Query Expansion and Relevance Feedback in Information Retrieval. The information retrieval community has leveraged query expansion techniques for several decades [4,26,37]. Most interestingly, in the information retrieval community, query expansion methods expand or reformulate query terms independently of the query and results returned from it, via, *e.g.*, reformulation with a thesaurus [25]. What the image search community denotes as query expansion is generally known as relevance feedback (RF), and more precisely, pseudo-RF, as one generally does not have access to the true relevance of the neighbors – although a case could be made for geometrical verification methods [7] providing explicit feedback. Our focus in this work is not on information retrieval methods for two reasons: (i) they generally deal with explicit or implicit RF instead of pseudo-RF; (ii) they generally assume high-dimensional, sparse features (*e.g.* bags of terms), and learn some form of term weighting that is not applicable in our case.

3 Attention-Based Query Expansion Learning

We start this section by presenting a generalized form of query expansion, and by showing that well-known query expansion methods can be cast under this framework. We then propose a general framework for learning query expansion in a discriminative manner. Last, we propose LAttQE (Learnable Attention-Based Query Expansion), an aggregation model that leverages self attention to construct the augmented query and that can be trained within this framework.

3.1 Generalized Query Expansion

We assume that there exists a known function $\phi : \Omega \to \mathcal{R}^D$ that can embed items (*e.g.* images) into an l_2-normalized D-dimensional vectorial space. For example, ϕ could be a CNN trained to perform image embedding [13,33,36]. Let us denote with q a query item, and, following standard convention of using bold typeface for vectors, let us denote with $\mathbf{q} = \phi(q)$ its D-dimensional embedding. Similarly, let us denote with $\{\mathbf{d}\}^k = \mathbf{d}_1, \mathbf{d}_2, \ldots, \mathbf{d}_k$ the embeddings of the top k nearest neighbors of $\mathbf{q}$ in a dataset $\mathcal{D}$ according to some measure of similarity, *e.g.* the cosine similarity, and sorted in decreasing order. Let us also denote with $\{\mathbf{d}\}^-$ a collection of dataset items that are not close to the query, according to the same measure of similarity. Last, for convenience, let us alias $\mathbf{d}_0 := \mathbf{q}$.

We propose the following generalized form of query expansion:

$$\hat{\mathbf{q}} = \frac{1}{Z} \sum_{i=0}^{k} \theta(\mathbf{d}_i \mid \mathbf{q}, \{\mathbf{d}\}^k, \{\mathbf{d}\}^-, i), \tag{1}$$

where Z is a normalization factor, and θ is a learnable function that takes an individual sample and applies a transformation conditioned on the original query $\mathbf{q}$, the top k retrieved results $\{\mathbf{d}\}^k$, a collection of low-ranked samples $\{\mathbf{d}\}^-$, and its position i in the ranking. The final augmented query is computed by aggregating the transformed top k results, including the query, and applying a normalization Z (*e.g.* ℓ_2 normalization)[1].

Standard query expansion methods can be cast under this framework. In fact, they can be cast under a more constrained form: $\theta(\mathbf{d}_i \mid \mathbf{q}, \{\mathbf{d}\}^k, \{\mathbf{d}\}^-, i) = w_i \mathbf{d}_i$, where the value of w_i is method-dependent, see Table 1. Two things are worth noticing. First, for all methods, w_i depends either on positional information (*e.g.* the sample got ranked at position i out of k, as done by AQEwD), or on information about the content (*e.g.* the power-normalized similarity between the item and the query, as done by αQE). None of the methods leverage both the positional and the content information simultaneously. Second, except for DQE, all methods produce a monotonically decreasing $\mathbf{w}$, *i.e.*, if $i > j$, then $w_i \leq w_j$. The implication is that these methods do not have the capacity to uplift the samples amongst the top k retrieved results that are indeed relevant to the query

---

[1] Note that Eq. (1) does not aggregate over $\{\mathbf{d}\}^-$. This is just to ease the exposition; negative samples can also be aggregated if the specific method requires it, *e.g.*, DQE.

Table 1. Standard query expansion (QE) methods and their associated transformations. More details about the methods can be found in Sect. 2.

Method		$\theta(\mathbf{d}_i \mid \mathbf{q}, \{\mathbf{d}\}^k, \{\mathbf{d}\}^-, i) = w_i \mathbf{d}_i$
[7]	**AQE:** Average QE	$w_i = 1$
[13]	**AQEwD:** AQE with decay	$w_i = (k - i)/k$
[3]	**DQE:** Discriminative QE	$\mathbf{w}$ is the dual-form solution of an SVM optimization problem using $\{\mathbf{d}\}^k$ as positives and $\{\mathbf{d}\}^-$ as negatives
[33]	α**QE:** α-weighted QE	$w_i = \mathrm{sim}(\mathbf{q}, \mathbf{d}_i)^\alpha$, with α being a hyperparameter

but were ranked after some non-relevant samples. That is, any top-ranked, non-relevant item will contribute more to the construction of the expanded query than any relevant item ranked after it, with clear negative consequences.

3.2 Query Expansion Learning

We propose that, following recent approaches in representation learning [13,33], one can learn a differentiable θ transformation in a data-driven way (Fig. 1). This training is done in a supervised manner, and ensures that relevant items to the (expanded) query are closer to it than elements that are not relevant. This is achieved by means of losses such as the triplet loss [49] or the contrastive loss [15]. The approach requires access to an annotated dataset (*e.g.* rSfM120k [33]), but the training data and classes used to learn θ can be disjoint from the pool of index images that will be used during deployment, as long as the distributions are similar. From that point of view, the requirements are similar to other existing image embedding learning methods in the literature.

At training time, besides sampling queries, positive, and negative samples, one also has to consider the nearest neighbors of the query for the expansion. Sampling a different subset of neighbors each time, as a form of data augmentation, can be useful to improve the model robustness. We provide more details about the process in the experimental section. Finally, we note that this framework allows one to learn θ and ϕ jointly, as well as to learn how to perform QE and DBA jointly, but we consider those variations out of the scope of this work.

3.3 Learnable Attention-Based Query Expansion (LAttQE)

We propose a more principled θ function that overcomes the caveats of previous methods, and that can be trained using the framework described in the previous section. In particular, our θ function is designed to be capable of transferring information between the different retrieved items, giving all top-ranked relevant samples the opportunity to significantly contribute to the construction of the expanded query. To achieve this we rely on a self-attention mechanism.

We leverage the transformer-encoder module developed by Vaswani *et al.* [47], where, in a nutshell, a collection of inputs first share information through a multi-head attention mechanism, and later are reprojected into an embedding space using fully connected layers with layer normalization and residual connections – see Fig. 1 of Vaswani *et al.* [47] for a diagram of this module (left) and the decoder module (right), not used in this work. Stacking several of these encoders increases the capacity of the model and enables sharing more contextual information. The exact mechanism that the stack of self-attention encoders uses to transfer information is particularly suited for our problem:

1. The encoder's scaled dot-product attention [47] performs a weighted sum of the form $\sum_{j=0}^{k} \text{Softmax}(\mathbf{d}_i^T [\mathbf{d}_0, \mathbf{d}_1, \ldots, \mathbf{d}_k] / C)_j \mathbf{d}_j$, where C is a constant, in practice computing the similarity between $\mathbf{d}_i$ and all other inputs and using that as weights to aggregate all the inputs. Observing Eqs. (1) and (3), one can see self-attention as a way to perform expansion of the input samples, leading to richer representations that are then used to compute the weights.
2. The multihead attention enables focusing on different parts of the representations. This is important because computing similarities using only the original embedding will make it difficult to change the original ranking. By using multihead attention, we discover parts of the embeddings that are still similar between relevant items and dissimilar between non-relevant items, permitting the model to further upweight relevant items and downweight non-relevant ones.
3. Under this interpretation of the encoder, the stack of encoders allows the model to "refine" the expansion process in an iterative manner. One can see this as expanding the queries, making a first search, using the new neighbors to expand a better query, find new neighbors, etc. Although the pool of neighbors remains constant, we expect the expansion to become more and more accurate.

Aggregation. The stack of encoders takes the query $\mathbf{q}$ and the top results $\mathbf{d}_1 \ldots \mathbf{d}_k$ as input, and produces outputs $\tilde{\mathbf{q}}$ and $\tilde{\mathbf{d}}_1 \ldots \tilde{\mathbf{d}}_k$. To construct the expanded query, a direct solution consists in aggregating them (*e.g.* through average or weighted average) into a single vector that represents the expanded query. However, this is challenging in practice, as it requires the encoder to learn how to create outputs that lie in the same space as the original data, something particularly hard when the embedding function ϕ is not being simultaneously learned. We empirically verify that learning such a function leads to weak results. Although we speculate that learning a "direct" θ function jointly with ϕ could lead to superior results, the practical difficulties involved in doing so make this approach unappealing. Instead, to ensure that we stay in a similar space, we relax the problem and also construct the expanded query as a weighted sum of the top k results, where the weights $\mathbf{w}$ are predicted by our model. If we denote with M the stack of encoders, the transformed outputs can be represented as

$$\tilde{\mathbf{d}}_i = M(\{\mathbf{q}\} \cup \{\mathbf{d}\}^k)_i. \tag{2}$$

Then, inspired by other methods such as αQE, we can construct the weight w_i as the similarity between item $\mathbf{d}_i$ and the query $\mathbf{q}$ *in the transformed space, i.e.,* $w_i = \text{sim}(\tilde{\mathbf{q}}, \tilde{\mathbf{d}}_i)$. This leads to our proposed θ:

$$\theta(\mathbf{d}_i \mid \mathbf{q}, \{\mathbf{d}\}^k, \{\mathbf{d}\}^-, i) = \text{sim}(\tilde{\mathbf{q}}, \tilde{\mathbf{d}}_i)\mathbf{d}_i. \tag{3}$$

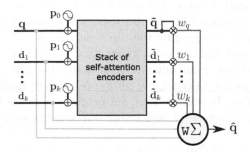

Fig. 2. Proposed aggregator. The output $\hat{\mathbf{q}}$ is constructed as the weighted sum ($w\Sigma$) of the query $\mathbf{q}$ and the nearest neighbors $\mathbf{d}_1 \dots \mathbf{d}_k$. The weights are computed by running the inputs through a stack of self-attention encoders after including positional information $\odot$ and computing the similarity (through a normalized dot product $\otimes$) between the transformed query $\tilde{\mathbf{q}}$ and all the transformed samples $\tilde{\mathbf{d}}_1 \dots \tilde{\mathbf{d}}_k$.

Including Rank Information. As presented, the proposed method does not leverage in any way the ranking of the results. Indeed, the encoders see the inputs as a set, and not as a sequence of results. This prevents the model from leveraging this information, *e.g.* by learning useful biases such as "top results tend to be correct, so pay more attention to them to learn the transformations". To enable the model to reason not only about the content of the results but also about their ranking, we follow standard practice when dealing with transformers and include a positional encoding that is added to the inputs before being consumed by the encoder, *i.e.*, $\text{pe}(\mathbf{d}_i) = \mathbf{d}_i + \mathbf{p}_i$, where each $\mathbf{p}_i \in \mathcal{R}^D$ is a learnable variable within our model. The full proposed aggregator that leverages θ with positional encoding is depicted in Fig. 2.

Auxiliary Classification Loss. Since, at training time, we have access to the annotations of the images, we know which of the top k results are relevant to the query and which ones are not. This enables us to have an auxiliary linear classifier that predicts whether $\tilde{\mathbf{d}}_i$ is relevant to the query or not. The role of this classifier, which is only used at train time and discarded at inference time, is to encourage the relevant and non-relevant outputs of the encoder to be linearly separable, inducing the relevant items to be more similar to the query than the non-relevant ones. Our empirical evaluation in Sect. 4 shows that the use of this auxiliary loss can noticeably increase the accuracy of the model.

3.4   Database-Side Augmentation

Database-side augmentation (DBA) is technique complementary to query expansion. Although different variations have been proposed [3,13,44,46], the main idea is that one can perform query expansion, *offline*, on the database images. This produces an expanded version of the database images, which are then indexed, instead of indexing the original ones. When issuing a new query, one searches on the expanded index, and not on the original one.

Our proposed approach can also be used to perform better database-side augmentation, using θ to aggregate the top k neighbors of each database image. However, this approach did not work in practice. We believe that the reason is that, on the database side, many images are actually distractors, unrelated to any query, and our model was assigning weights too high for unrelated images when using them as queries. To address this, we propose to use a tempered softmax over the weights, *i.e.*, instead of computing our weights as $w_i = \text{sim}(\tilde{\mathbf{q}}, \tilde{\mathbf{d}}_i)$, we compute it as

$$w_i = \text{Softmax}(\text{sim}(\tilde{\mathbf{q}}, [\tilde{\mathbf{d}}_0, \tilde{\mathbf{d}}_1, \dots, \tilde{\mathbf{d}}_k])/T)_i, \tag{4}$$

where $\text{sim}(\tilde{\mathbf{q}}, [\tilde{\mathbf{d}}_0, \tilde{\mathbf{d}}_1, \dots, \tilde{\mathbf{d}}_k])$ is a vector of similarities between $\tilde{\mathbf{q}}$ and all the $\tilde{\mathbf{d}}$s, and T is a learnable scalar.

To achieve the best results, we employ a curriculum learning strategy, where first we train our model without softmax, and then we freeze the parameters of the model, incorporate the tempered softmax, and continue training while updating only T. This strategy led to a DBA that not only gave the best results in terms of accuracy but that was also more stable than other variants.

4   Experiments

In this section we discuss implementation details of our training, evaluate different components of our method, and compare to the state of the art.

4.1   Training Setup and Implementation Details

Image Representation. For all experiments we use a publicly-available, state-of-the-art model for image retrieval [33][2] to extract the underlying features. We use the best-performing model from the project page (trained on Google Landmarks 2018 data [29]), consisting of a ResNet101 trunk followed by generalized-mean pooling and a whitening layer, which produces features of 2048 dimensions. Following [33], we extract features at 3 scales $(1, \sqrt{2}, 1/\sqrt{2})$, mean-aggregate them, and finally ℓ_2-normalize to form the final 2048D representation.

Training Dataset. We use the publicly available rSfM120k created by Radenovic *et al.* [33], which comprises images selected from 3D reconstructions of landmarks and urban scenes. These reconstructions are obtained from an

---

[2] github.com/filipradenovic/cnnimageretrieval-pytorch.

unordered image collection using a combined local-feature-based image retrieval and structure-from-motion pipeline. The 3D reconstruction cluster ids serve as a supervision for selecting positive and negative pairs. In total, 91642 images from 551 classes are used for training, while additional 6403 database images – 1691 of which are used as queries – from 162 classes, disjoint from the training ones, are set aside for validation. Performance on validation is measured as mean average precision (mAP) [30] over all 1691 queries.

Learning Configuration. To train LAttQE we follow [33] and use a contrastive loss of the form $yz^2 + (1-y)max(0, m-z)^2$, with m being the margin, $z = ||\hat{q}-d||$, and $y \in \{0, 1\}$ denotes whether d is relevant to q or not. We backpropagate through $\hat{q}$, which in turn optimizes the transformers (see Fig. 2). Other recent ranking losses [9,28,36] could also be used. Since the base representations are already strong, we use a margin of 0.1, which ensures that positives are pulled together while only pushing away negatives that are too close to the query. LAttQE consists of a stack of 3 transformer encoders, each one with 64 heads. We did not see any improvement after further increasing the capacity of the model. The self-attention and fully-connected layers within the encoders preserve the original dimensionality of the inputs, 2048D. We also follow [33] regarding the sampling strategy for positives and negatives: we select 5 negatives per positive, found in a pool of 20000 samples that gets refreshed every 2000 updates. When sampling neighbors to construct the augmented query, as a form of data augmentation, the exact number of neighbors is drawn randomly between 32 and 64, and neighbors are also randomly dropped according to a Bernoulli distribution (where the probability of dropping neighbors in each query is itself drawn from a uniform distribution between 0 and 0.6). The auxiliary classification head uses a binary cross-entropy loss. We use Adam to optimize the model, with a batch size of 64 samples, a weight decay of 1e-6, and an initial learning rate of 1e-4 with an exponential decay of 0.99. The optimal number of epochs (typically between 50 and 100) is decided based on the accuracy on the validation set, and is typically within 1% of the optimal iteration if it was validated directly on test.

4.2 Test Datasets and Evaluation Protocol

Revisited Oxford and Paris. Popular Oxford Buildings [30] and Paris [31] datasets have been revisited by Radenovic *et al.* [34], correcting and improving the annotation, adding new more difficult queries, and updating the evaluation protocol. Revisited Oxford ($\mathcal{R}$Oxford) and Revisited Paris ($\mathcal{R}$Paris) datasets contain 4,993 and 6,322 images respectively, with 70 held out images with regions of interest that are used as queries. Unlike the original datasets, where the full-size version of query images are present in the database side, this is not the case in revisited versions, making query expansion a more challenging task. For each query, the relevant database images were labeled according to the "difficulty" of the match. The labels are then used to define three evaluation protocols for $\mathcal{R}$Oxford and $\mathcal{R}$Paris: Easy (E), Medium (M), and Hard (H). As suggested by Radenovic *et al.* [34], which points out that the Easy protocol is saturated, we only report results on the Medium and Hard protocols. Note that Oxford and Paris landmarks are not present in rSfM120k training and validation datasets.

Distractors. A set of 1 million hard distractor images ($\mathcal{R}$1M) were collected in [34]. These distractors can, optionally, be added to both $\mathcal{R}$Oxford and $\mathcal{R}$Paris to evaluate performance on a more realistic large-scale setup.

We do not evaluate on INRIA Holidays [20], another common retrieval dataset, since performing query expansion on Holidays is not a standard practice.

4.3 Model Study

Table 2 displays the results of our proposed model, using all components (row ii), and compares it with the results without query expansion (row i). We use 64 neighbors for query expansion, as validated on the validation set of rSfM120k. Our model clearly improves results on $\mathcal{R}$Oxford and $\mathcal{R}$Paris, both on the M and H settings. We further study the impact of the components introduced in Sect. 3.

Table 2. Mean average precision (mAP) performance of the proposed model (ii) compared to the baseline without query expansion (i) and to variations where parts of the model have been removed (iii–vi).

		$\mathcal{R}$Oxford		$\mathcal{R}$Paris		Mean
		M	H	M	H	
(i)	No QE	67.3	44.3	80.6	61.5	63.4
(ii)	**Full model**	73.4	49.6	86.3	70.6	70.0
(iii)	Without self-attention	66.0	41.5	86.1	70.2	66.0
(iv)	Without positional encoding	58.6	33.2	87.8	73.4	63.2
(v)	Without visual embedding	67.1	42.9	83.8	66.7	65.1
(vi)	Without auxiliary loss	71.8	47.0	85.8	69.4	68.5

Self-attention: Replacing the stack of self-attention encoders with a stack of fully-connected layers leads to a very noticeable drop in accuracy (iii), highlighting how important the attention is for this model.

Positional Encoding (PE): Removing the PE (iv) leads to a very pronounced loss in accuracy for $\mathcal{R}$Oxford (which has very few relevant images per query). PE is necessary for queries with few relevant items because the model has to learn which images are important, and anchoring to the query (through the PE) enables it to do so. This is less important for queries with many relevant items, as in $\mathcal{R}$Paris. We additionally experiment with a position-only setup (v), where the self-attention computes the weights using only the positional encodings, not the actual image embeddings. This leads to a content-unaware weighting function, such as the AQE or AQEwD methods. The drop in accuracy is also remarkable, highlighting the need to combine both content and positional information.

Auxiliary Loss: Removing the auxiliary loss (vi) leads to a small but consistent drop in accuracy. Although the model is fully functional without this auxiliary loss, it helps the optimization process to find better representations.

Inference Time: When considering 64 neighbors for the expansion, our non-optimized PyTorch implementation can encode, on average, about 250 queries per second on a single Tesla M40 GPU. This does not include the time to extract the query embedding, which is orders of magnitude slower than our method (about 4 images per second on the same GPU) and the main bottleneck. Techniques such as distillation [38] and quantization [41], that have worked for transformer-based models, could further increase speed and reduce memory use.

4.4 Comparison with Existing Methods

Query Expansion (QE). We compare the performance of our proposed method with existing QE approaches. All methods and their associated transformations are given in Table 1. For LAttQE, hyper-parameters are tuned on the validation set of rSfM120k, that has no overlapping landmarks or images with the test datasets. For competing methods, we select their hyper-parameters on the mean performance over test datasets, giving them an advantage. We denote the number of neighbors used for QE as nQE. **AQE:** nQE = 2; **AQEwD:** nQE = 4; **αQE:** nQE = 72, α = 3; **DQE:** nQE = 4, neg = 5, C = 0.1; **LAttQE:** nQE = 64.

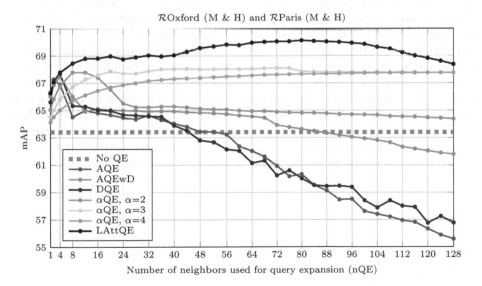

Fig. 3. Mean average precision over all queries of four protocols ($\mathcal{R}$Oxford (M & H) and $\mathcal{R}$Paris (M & H)) as a function of the number of neighbors used for query expansion.

Database-Side Augmentation (DBA). All of the before-mentioned methods can be combined with DBA. We separately tune all hyper-parameters in this combined scenario. We denote number of neighbors used for DBA as nDBA. **ADBA + AQE:** nDBA = 4, nQE = 4; **ADBAwD + AQEwD:** nDBA = 4, nQE = 6; **αDBA + αQE:** nDBA = 36, nQE = 10, α = 3; **DDBA + DQE:** nDBA = 4, nQE = 2, C = 0.1, neg = 5; **LAttDBA + LAttQE:** nDBA = 48, nQE = 64.

Sensitivity to the Number of Neighbors Used in the QE. Figure 3 shows the mean accuracy of LAttQE as well as other query expansion methods on $\mathcal{R}$Oxford and $\mathcal{R}$Paris, as a function of the number of neighbors used in the expansion. We highlight: (i) Unsurprisingly, methods that assume all samples are positive (*e.g.* AQE, DQE) degrade very fast when the number of neighbors is not trivially small. AQEwD degrades a bit more gracefully, but can still obtain very bad results if nQE is not chosen carefully. (ii) It is also unsurprising that αQE has become a standard, since the accuracy is high and results do not degrade when nQE is high. However, this only happens because of the weighting function is of the form r^{α}, with $r < 1$, *i.e.*, the weight rapidly converges to zero, and therefore most neighbors barely have any impact in the aggregation. (iii) Our proposed LAttQE consistently obtains the best results across the whole range of nQE. Our method is not limited by a weight that converges to zero, and therefore can still improve when αQE has essentially converged (nQE > 40).

Different "Number of Relevant Images" and "AP" Regimes. We evaluate query expansion impact at different regimes to showcase further differences between methods. In all cases we report the relative improvement in mAP introduced by using query expansion. In the first set of experiments, see Fig. 4 (top), we group queries based on the number of relevant images, using percentiles 33 and 66 as cut-off. AQE (with nQE = 4) works very well for queries with very few relevant samples, but leads to small improvements when the number of relevant is high, as they are not leveraged. On the other hand, αQE, with α = 3 and nQE = 72 obtains good results when the number of relevant is high, but really struggles when the number of relevant is low. LAttQE is the only method that is able to obtain high accuracy on all regimes. Figure 4 (bottom) groups queries based on their accuracy before query expansion. Similarly, LAttQE is the only method that consistently obtains high accuracy.

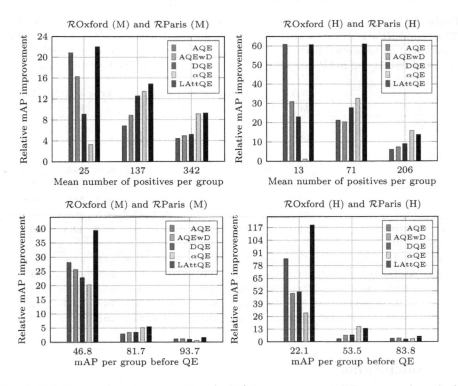

Fig. 4. Relative mean average precision (mAP) improvement at different number of relevant images (top) and AP regimes (bottom) split into 3 groups. Evaluation performed on $\mathcal{R}$Oxford and $\mathcal{R}$Paris at two difficulty setups, Medium (left) and Hard (right). Mean number of relevant images over all queries in the group (top) and mean average precision over all queries in the group (bottom) shown under respective group's bar plot.

State-of-the-Art Comparison. Table 3 reports the accuracy of different methods on $\mathcal{R}$Oxford and $\mathcal{R}$Paris, both with and without the $\mathcal{R}$1M distractor set. The optimal number of neighbors for our approach (64 for LAttQE and 48 for LAttDBA) was decided on the validation set of rSfM120k. On the other hand, the optimal number of neighbors for the remaining methods was adjusted on test to maximize their mean accuracy on $\mathcal{R}$Oxford and $\mathcal{R}$Paris, giving them an unfair edge. Our method is the only one that consistently obtains good results on both $\mathcal{R}$Oxford and $\mathcal{R}$Paris. Compare this to other methods, where, for example, αQE obtains the best results on $\mathcal{R}$Paris but the worst results on $\mathcal{R}$Oxford, while AQE obtains the best results on $\mathcal{R}$Oxford (excepting our method) but the worst results on $\mathcal{R}$Paris. Generally, this gap becomes even larger when including the $\mathcal{R}$1M distractors. When using DBA and QE we observe the same trends: although some method can be slightly more accurate on specific datasets, our approach is the only one that obtains consistently good results on all datasets.

Table 3. Performance evaluation via mean average precision (mAP) on $\mathcal{R}$Oxford ($\mathcal{R}$Oxf) and $\mathcal{R}$Paris ($\mathcal{R}$Par) with and without 1 million distractors ($\mathcal{R}$1M). Our method is validated on validation part of rSfM120k and is marked with $\star$. Other methods are validated directly on mAP over all queries of 4 protocols of $\mathcal{R}$Oxford and $\mathcal{R}$Paris.

		$\mathcal{R}$Oxf		$\mathcal{R}$Oxf + $\mathcal{R}$1M		$\mathcal{R}$Par		$\mathcal{R}$Par + $\mathcal{R}$1M		Mean
		M	H	M	H	M	H	M	H	
No QE										
—		67.3	44.3	49.5	25.7	80.6	61.5	57.3	29.8	52.0
QE										
[7]	AQE	72.3	49.0	57.3	30.5	82.7	65.1	62.3	36.5	56.9
[13]	AQEwD	72.0	48.7	56.9	30.0	83.3	65.9	63.0	37.1	57.1
[3]	DQE	72.7	48.8	54.5	26.3	83.7	66.5	64.2	38.0	56.8
[33]	αQE	69.3	44.5	52.5	26.1	**86.9**	**71.7**	66.5	41.6	57.4
$\star$	LAttQE	**73.4**	**49.6**	**58.3**	**31.0**	86.3	70.6	**67.3**	**42.4**	**59.8**
DBA + QE										
[7]	ADBA + AQE	71.9	53.6	55.3	32.8	83.9	68.0	65.0	39.6	58.8
[13]	ADBAwD + AQEwD	73.2	53.2	57.9	34.0	84.3	68.7	65.6	40.8	59.7
[3]	DDBA + DQE	72.0	50.7	56.9	32.9	83.2	66.7	65.4	39.1	58.4
[33]	αDBA + αQE	71.7	50.7	56.0	31.5	87.5	73.5	**70.6**	**48.5**	61.3
$\star$	LAttDBA + LAttQE	**74.0**	**54.1**	**60.0**	**36.3**	**87.8**	**74.1**	70.5	48.3	**63.1**

5   Conclusions

In this paper we have presented a novel framework to learn how to perform query expansion and database side augmentation for image retrieval tasks. Within this framework we have proposed LAttQE, an attention-based model that outperforms commonly used query expansion techniques on standard benchmark while being more robust on different regimes. Beyond LAttQE, we believe that the main idea of our method, tackling the aggregation for query expansion as a supervised task learned in a discriminative manner, is general and novel, and hope that more methods build on top of this idea, proposing new aggregation models that lead to more efficient and accurate search systems.

References

1. Alletto, S., Abati, D., Serra, G., Cucchiara, R.: Exploring architectural details through a wearable egocentric vision device. Sensors **16**, 237 (2016)
2. Arandjelovic, R., Gronat, P., Torii, A., Pajdla, T., Sivic, J.: NetVLAD: CNN architecture for weakly supervised place recognition. In: CVPR (2016)
3. Arandjelovic, R., Zisserman, A.: Three things everyone should know to improve object retrieval. In: CVPR (2012)
4. Azad, H.K., Deepak, A.: Query expansion techniques for information retrieval: a survey. IP&M **56**, 1698–1735 (2019)
5. Chang, C., Yu, G., Liu, C., Volkovs, M.: Explore-exploit graph traversal for image retrieval. In: CVPR (2019)

6. Chum, O., Mikulík, A., Perdoch, M., Matas, J.: Total recall II: query expansion revisited. In: CVPR (2011)
7. Chum, O., Philbin, J., Sivic, J., Isard, M., Zisserman, A.: Total recall: automatic query expansion with a generative feature model for object retrieval. In: CVPR (2007)
8. Delvinioti, A., Jégou, H., Amsaleg, L., Houle, M.E.: Image retrieval with reciprocal and shared nearest neighbors. In: VISAPP (2014)
9. Deng, J., Guo, J., Xue, N., Zafeiriou, S.: ArcFace: additive angular margin loss for deep face recognition. In: CVPR (2019)
10. Devlin, J., Chang, M.W., Lee, K., Toutanova, K.: BERT: pre-training of deep bidirectional transformers for language understanding. In: NAACL (2019)
11. Fan, L., Zhao, H., Zhao, H., Liu, P., Hu, H.: Image retrieval based on learning to rank and multiple loss. IJGI **8**, 393 (2019)
12. Girdhar, R., Ramanan, D.: Attentional pooling for action recognition. In: NeurIPS (2017)
13. Gordo, A., Almazan, J., Revaud, J., Larlus, D.: End-to-end learning of deep visual representations for image retrieval. IJCV **124**, 237–254 (2017)
14. Gu, Y., Li, C., Xie, J.: Attention-aware generalized mean pooling for image retrieval. arXiv:1811.00202 (2019)
15. Hadsell, R., Chopra, S., LeCun, Y.: Dimensionality reduction by learning an invariant mapping. In: CVPR (2006)
16. Heinly, J., Schonberger, J.L., Dunn, E., Frahm, J.M.: Reconstructing the world* in six days* (as captured by the Yahoo 100 million image dataset). In: CVPR (2015)
17. Husain, S.S., Bober, M.: REMAP: multi-layer entropy-guided pooling of dense CNN features for image retrieval. TIP **28**, 5201–5213 (2019)
18. Husain, S.S., Ong, E.J., Bober, M.: ACTNET: end-to-end learning of feature activations and multi-stream aggregation for effective instance image retrieval. arXiv:1907.05794 (2019)
19. Iscen, A., Tolias, G., Avrithis, Y., Furon, T., Chum, O.: Efficient diffusion on region manifolds: recovering small objects with compact CNN representations. In: CVPR (2017)
20. Jegou, H., Douze, M., Schmid, C.: Hamming embedding and weak geometric consistency for large scale image search. In: Forsyth, D., Torr, P., Zisserman, A. (eds.) ECCV 2008. LNCS, vol. 5302, pp. 304–317. Springer, Heidelberg (2008). https://doi.org/10.1007/978-3-540-88682-2_24
21. Kalantidis, Y., et al.: VIRaL: visual image retrieval and localization. Multimed. Tools Appl. **51**, 555–592 (2011)
22. Lee, J., Lee, I., Kang, J.: Self-attention graph pooling. In: ICML (2019)
23. Liu, C., et al.: Guided similarity separation for image retrieval. In: NIPS (2019)
24. Makantasis, K., Doulamis, A., Doulamis, N., Ioannides, M.: In the wild image retrieval and clustering for 3D cultural heritage landmarks reconstruction. Multimed. Tools Appl. **75**, 3593–3629 (2016)
25. Manning, C.D., Raghavan, P., Schütze, H.: Introduction to Information Retrieval. Cambridge University Press, Cambridge (2008)
26. Maron, M.E., Kuhns, J.L.: On relevance, probabilistic indexing and information retrieval. JACM **7**, 216–244 (1960)
27. Mikulik, A., Chum, O., Matas, J.: Image retrieval for online browsing in large image collections. In: Brisaboa, N., Pedreira, O., Zezula, P. (eds.) SISAP 2013. LNCS, vol. 8199, pp. 3–15. Springer, Heidelberg (2013). https://doi.org/10.1007/978-3-642-41062-8_2

28. Ng, T., Balntas, V., Tian, Y., Mikolajczyk, K.: SOLAR: second-order loss and attention for image retrieval. arXiv:2001.08972 (2020)
29. Noh, H., Araujo, A., Sim, J., Weyand, T., Han, B.: Large-scale image retrieval with attentive deep local features. In: ICCV (2017)
30. Philbin, J., Chum, O., Isard, M., Sivic, J., Zisserman, A.: Object retrieval with large vocabularies and fast spatial matching. In: CVPR (2007)
31. Philbin, J., Chum, O., Isard, M., Sivic, J., Zisserman, A.: Lost in quantization: improving particular object retrieval in large scale image databases. In: CVPR (2008)
32. Qin, D., Gammeter, S., Bossard, L., Quack, T., Van Gool, L.: Hello neighbor: accurate object retrieval with k-reciprocal nearest neighbors. In: CVPR (2011)
33. Radenovic, F., Tolias, G., Chum, O.: Fine-tuning CNN image retrieval with no human annotation. TPAMI 41, 1655–1668 (2018)
34. Radenović, F., Iscen, A., Tolias, G., Avrithis, Y., Chum, O.: Revisiting Oxford and Paris: large-scale image retrieval benchmarking. In: CVPR (2018)
35. Radford, A., Wu, J., Child, R., Luan, D., Amodei, D., Sutskever, I.: Language models are unsupervised multitask learners. OpenAI Blog 1, 9 (2019)
36. Revaud, J., Almazan, J., de Rezende, R.S., de Souza, C.R.: Learning with average precision: training image retrieval with a listwise loss. In: ICCV (2019)
37. Rocchio, J.: Relevance feedback in information retrieval. SMART Retrieval Syst. (1971)
38. Sanh, V., Debut, L., Chaumond, J., Wolf, T.: DistilBERT, a distilled version of BERT: smaller, faster, cheaper and lighter. In: NeurIPS Workshop (2019)
39. Sattler, T., Weyand, T., Leibe, B., Kobbelt, L.: Image retrieval for image-based localization revisited. In: BMVC (2012)
40. Schonberger, J.L., Frahm, J.M.: Structure-from-motion revisited. In: CVPR (2016)
41. Shen, S., et al.: Q-BERT: Hessian based ultra low precision quantization of BERT. In: AAAI (2020)
42. Shen, X., Lin, Z., Brandt, J., Wu, Y.: Spatially-constrained similarity measure for large-scale object retrieval. TPAMI 36, 1229–1241 (2013)
43. Sivic, J., Zisserman, A.: Video Google: a text retrieval approach to object matching in videos. In: ICCV (2003)
44. Tolias, G., Avrithis, Y., Jégou, H.: Image search with selective match kernels: aggregation across single and multiple images. IJCV 116, 247–261 (2015)
45. Tolias, G., Jégou, H.: Visual query expansion with or without geometry: refining local descriptors by feature aggregation. PR 47, 3466–3476 (2014)
46. Turcot, T., Lowe, D.G.: Better matching with fewer features: the selection of useful features in large database recognition problems. In: ICCV Workshop (2009)
47. Vaswani, A., et al.: Attention is all you need. In: NeurIPS (2017)
48. Wang, X., Girshick, R., Gupta, A., He, K.: Non-local neural networks. In: CVPR (2018)
49. Weinberger, K.Q., Saul, L.K.: Distance metric learning for large margin nearest neighbor classification. JMLR 10, 207–244 (2009)
50. Weyand, T., Leibe, B.: Discovering favorite views of popular places with iconoid shift. In: ICCV (2011)

Interpretable Foreground Object Search as Knowledge Distillation

Boren Li[✉], Po-Yu Zhuang, Jian Gu, Mingyang Li, and Ping Tan

Alibaba Group, Hangzhou, China
{boren.lbr,po-yu.zby,gujian.gj}@alibaba-inc.com, mingyangli009@gmail.com,
pingtan@sfu.ca

Abstract. This paper proposes a knowledge distillation method for foreground object search (FoS). Given a background and a rectangle specifying the foreground location and scale, FoS retrieves compatible foregrounds in a certain category for later image composition. Foregrounds within the same category can be grouped into a small number of patterns. Instances within each pattern are compatible with *any* query input interchangeably. These instances are referred to as *interchangeable foregrounds*. We first present a pipeline to build pattern-level FoS dataset containing labels of interchangeable foregrounds. We then establish a benchmark dataset for further training and testing following the pipeline. As for the proposed method, we first train a foreground encoder to learn representations of interchangeable foregrounds. We then train a query encoder to learn query-foreground compatibility following a knowledge distillation framework. It aims to transfer knowledge from interchangeable foregrounds to supervise representation learning of compatibility. The query feature representation is projected to the same latent space as interchangeable foregrounds, enabling very efficient and interpretable instance-level search. Furthermore, pattern-level search is feasible to retrieve more controllable, reasonable and diverse foregrounds. The proposed method outperforms the previous state-of-the-art by 10.42% in absolute difference and 24.06% in relative improvement evaluated by mean average precision (mAP). Extensive experimental results also demonstrate its efficacy from various aspects. The benchmark dataset and code will be release shortly.

1 Introduction

Foreground object search (FoS) retrieves compatible foregrounds in a certain category given a background and a rectangle as query input [25]. It is a core task in many image composition applications [21]. For object insertion in photo editing, users often find it challenging and time-consuming to acquire compatible foregrounds in a foreground pool. Object insertion can be used to fill a new foreground to a region comprising undesired objects in the background [26].

This work was partially supported by the National Key Research and Development Program of China (No. 2018YFB1005002).

In a larger sense, for text-to-image synthesis with multiple objects, recent researches [8,12] have shown insight to generate semantic layout at first. Then, one way to solve the follow-up task, layout to image, is multi-object retrieval and composition [1]. Directly retrieving multiple objects simultaneously suffers from combinatorial explosion that can be perfectly avoided by iteratively performing FoS with composition. Hence, FoS is also a significant underlying task (Fig. 1).

(a) Query input   (b) Pool of patterns to   (c) Search results by
                                    be retrieved   proposed method

Fig. 1. Foreground object search (FoS). Given a background and a rectangle specifying the foreground location and scale as query input, FoS is to find compatible foregrounds within a certain category. (a) illustrates the query input. (b) exemplifies patterns in the foreground pool. (c) demonstrates search results by the proposed method.

Two problems arise to solve FoS. The first problem is how to classify foreground instances and define what are similar foregrounds to be retrieved together. The second problem is that given a query input and a foreground instance, how to define and decide their compatibility. Most recent methods [25,26] jointly learned foreground similarity and query-foreground compatibility without decoupling the two problems. It makes the results difficult to interpret.

We notice that foregrounds in a certain category can be grouped to a small number of *patterns*. Instances within the same pattern are compatible with *any* query input interchangeably. These instances are referred to as *interchangeable foregrounds*. Then, the first question arises: how to define and label interchangeable foregrounds specifically?

Suppose we have answered the first question well, manually labelling compatibility for many pairs of query-foreground data is still extremely challenging, if not impossible. Since definition of interchangeable foregrounds relates to compatibility, the second question is: can we transfer knowledge from labelled interchangeable foregrounds to supervise representation learning of compatibility?

We answer these two questions in this work. For the first question, we propose a pipeline to build pattern-level FoS dataset comprising labels of interchangeable foregrounds. We exemplify 'person' as the foreground category to explain how to label and establish a benchmark dataset for further training and testing. We then train a foreground encoder to classify these patterns in order to learn feature representations for interchangeable foregrounds.

For the second question, we train a query encoder to learn query-foreground compatibility. It learns to transform query inputs into query features such that the feature similarities between query and compatible foregrounds are closer than those between query and incompatible ones. We follow a knowledge distillation scheme to transfer interchangeable foregrounds labelling to supervise compatibility learning. More specifically, we freeze the trained foreground encoder as the teacher network to generate embeddings as 'soft targets' to train the query encoder in the student network. As a result, the query inputs are projected to the same latent space as interchangeable foregrounds, enabling very efficient and interpretable instance-level search. Furthermore, as interchangeable foregrounds are grouped into patterns, pattern-level search is feasible to retrieve more controllable, reasonable and diverse foregrounds.

We first show effectiveness of the foreground encoder to represent interchangeable foregrounds. We then demonstrate efficacy of the query encoder to represent query-foreground compatibility. The proposed method outperforms the previous state-of-the-art by 10.42% in absolute difference and 24.06% in relative improvement evaluated by mean average precision (mAP).

The key contributions are summarized as follows:

- We introduce a novel concept called interchangeable foregrounds. It allows interpretable and direct learning of foreground similarity specifically for FoS. In addition, it makes pattern-level search feasible to retrieve more controllable, reasonable and diverse foregrounds.
- We propose a new pipeline to establish pattern-level FoS dataset containing labels of interchangeable foregrounds. We establish the first benchmarking dataset using this pipeline. This dataset will be released to the public.
- We propose a novel knowledge distillation framework to solve FoS. It enables fully interpretable learning and outperforms the previous state-of-the-art by a significant margin.

2 Related Works

2.1 Foreground Object Search

Early efforts on FoS, such as Photo Clip Art [11] and Sketch2Photo [1], applied handcrafted features to search foregrounds according to matching criterion as camera orientation, lighting, resolution, local context and so on. Manually designing either these matching criterion or handcrafted features is challenging. With the success of deep learning on image classification [17], deep features are involved to replace handcrafted ones. Tan et al. [19] employed local region retrieval using semantic features extracted from an off-the-shelf CNN model. The retrieved regions contain person segments which are further used for image composition. They assume the foregrounds have surrounding background context and therefore, not feasible when the foregrounds are just images with pure background. Zhu et al. [28] trained a discriminative network to decide the realism of a composite image. They couple the suitability of foreground selection, adjustment and composition into one realism score, making it difficult to interpret.

Zhao et al. [25] first formally defined the FoS task and focused on the foreground selection problem alone. They applied end-to-end feature learning to adapt for different object categories. This work is the closest to ours and serves as the baseline method for comparison purpose. More recently, Zhao et al. [26] proposed an unconstrained FoS task that aims to retrieve universal compatible foreground without specifying its category. We only focus on the constrained FoS problem with known foreground category in this work.

2.2   Knowledge Distillation

Knowledge distillation is a general purpose technique that is widely applied for neural network compression [16]. The key idea is to use soft probabilities of a larger teacher network to supervise a smaller student network, in addition to the available class labels. The soft probabilities reveal more information than the class labels alone that can purportedly help the student network learn better.

In addition to neural network compression, prior works has found knowledge distillation to be useful for sequence modelling [9], domain adaptation [15], semi-supervised learning [20] and so on. The closest work to ours is multi-modal learning [5]. They trained a CNN model for a depth map as a new modality by teaching the network to reproduce the mid-level semantic representations learned from a well-labelled RGB image with paired data. For our case, we learn query-foreground compatibility as a new modality by teaching the network to reproduce the mid-level foreground similarity representations learned from a well-labelled interchangeable foreground modality with paired data. Therefore, the proposed FoS method can be viewed as another knowledge distillation application.

3   Foreground Object Search Dataset

In this section, we describe the proposed pipeline to build pattern-level FoS dataset containing labels of interchangeable foregrounds. We exemplify 'person' as the foreground category to explain how to label and establish a benchmark dataset for further training and testing. Building a benchmark dataset is necessary for two reasons. First, there is no publicly available dataset for FoS. We do not have access to the one established by the baseline method [25]. Second, the previous dataset is instance-level and not sufficient to validate our method.

3.1   Pipeline to Establish Pattern-Level FoS Dataset

Figure 2 demonstrates the general pipeline to establish pattern-level FoS dataset. There exists publicly available datasets that contain instance segmentation masks, such as MS-COCO [13], PASCAL VOC 2012 [13] and ADE20K [27]. We can decompose an image into a background scene, a foreground and a rectangle using a mask. Since they are all from the same image, they are naturally compatible.

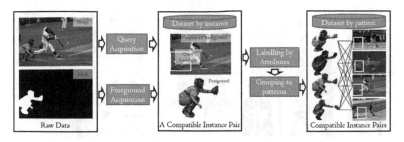

Fig. 2. The proposed pipeline to establish a pattern-level FoS dataset. The instance-level dataset is first established to obtain compatible instance pairs transformed from instance segmentation annotations. Through grouping interchangeable foregrounds to patterns, pattern-level dataset is finally built. A compatible instance pair in the instance-level dataset can be augmented to many pairs in the pattern-level dataset.

Previous methods [25,26] leave the original foreground in the background scene when building the dataset. They do so because they mask out the foreground by a rectangle filled with image mean values during training with an early-fusion strategy. By contrast, we apply a free-form image inpainting algorithm [23] to fill the foreground region in the background scene when building the dataset. This is because the deep inpainting algorithm trained on millions of images can perform reasonably well on this task. On the other hand, the early-fusion strategy by previous methods masks out too much background context, leaving the compatibility decision much more difficult. As for foreground samples in the dataset, we paste the foreground in the original image to the center location on a pure white square background.

With sufficient number of foregrounds in a certain category, the next goal is to group them into patterns of interchangeable foregrounds. Given many thousands of instances, this task is very challenging without supervision. Hence, we label foregrounds by attributes at first. We then group them into the same pattern if they have identical values in every attribute dimension. Finally, we establish a pattern-level dataset where much more compatible instance pairs can be extracted than its instance-level counterpart.

3.2 Interchangeable Foregrounds Labelling

We show how to label interchangeable foregrounds by using 'person' as the foreground category. 'person' is adopted because it is one of the most frequent categories for image composition. Furthermore, it is a non-rigid object with numerous different states. It is sufficiently representative to address the issues for interchangeable foregrounds labelling. We do not consider style issues in this work since all the raw images are photographs.

Fig. 3. An illustration of attributes for the 'person' foreground. It contains six attribute dimensions: orientation, truncation, sport, motion, viewpoint and state. For a particular foreground, orientation and truncation are mandatory dimensions to be assigned with the presented values while the others are optional.

Figure 3 illustrates the six attribute dimensions we defined to classify patterns of interchangeable foregrounds. For a particular foreground, *orientation* and *truncation* are two mandatory attribute dimensions to be assigned with the presented values. They are mandatory because they will largely determine most aspects of interchangeable foregrounds. The other four attribute dimensions are sport, motion, viewpoint and state. These dimensions can further distinguish various aspects of 'person'. Their values can be left as 'unspecified' when we cannot assign them with available values. Table 1 shows the number of available attribute values in each dimension.

Table 1. Number of available attribute values in each dimension

Orientation	Truncation	Sport	Motion	Viewpoint	State
8	6	12	31	4	3

We adopt images with mask annotations in the MS-COCO [13] dataset as raw data. Before labelling attribute values for each sample, we first exclude inappropriate samples that are heavily occluded, small or incomplete, resulting in 10154 foregrounds. We label 5468 samples from them with these attribute values, leading to 699 different patterns after grouping. Thus, we obtain 5468 pattern-level query-foreground compatibility pairs in total. Furthermore, the remaining 4686 unannotated foregrounds can be labelled automatically by a trained foreground encoder presented in Sect. 4. It leads to more pairs of pattern-level data to train query-foreground compatibility. In a larger sense, applying our trained foreground encoder with an instance segmentation model such as Mask-RCNN [6], we can automate the whole pipeline using internet images to learn query-foreground compatibility.

3.3   Evaluation Set and Metrics

The annotated foreground patterns follow a heavy-tailed distribution. Therefore, we only select those patterns with at least 20 interchangeable foregrounds for testing. This leads to 69 patterns in total. We randomly select 5 foreground instances from each of these patterns to obtain the foreground database at test time. These foregrounds can be also applied to evaluate the capability of the foreground encoder in classifying interchangeable foregrounds. We adopt top-1 and top-5 accuracies to evaluate the classifier with 699 classes altogether.

Simultaneously, we obtain the same number of corresponding query inputs. We select 100 query samples and prefer those with more 'person' in the query background intentionally to make the dataset more challenging. We then manually label their compatibility to each foreground pattern in the test-time foreground database. This is because one query input may have multiple other compatible foreground patterns except the corresponding one. On average, for each query input, we label 22.35 and 6.07 compatible foreground instances and patterns, respectively. These pairs are employed to evaluate query-foreground compatibility. We adopt mAP to evaluate the overall performance of FoS.

4   Proposed Approach

4.1   Overall Training Scheme

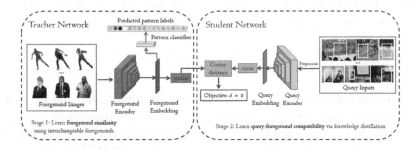

Fig. 4. The overall training scheme. The foreground encoder is first trained to classify patterns of interchangeable foregrounds. It then serves as the teacher network to generate foreground embeddings as soft targets to train the query encoder which encodes query-foreground compatibility.

Figure 4 presents the overall training scheme comprising two successive stages. The first stage trains the foreground encoder to classify patterns of interchangeable foregrounds in order to learn foreground feature representations. Feature similarities from the same pattern are closer than those from other patterns. Therefore, the learned features are fully interpretable.

The second stage trains the query encoder to learn *query-foreground compat-ibility*. This encoder transforms query inputs into embeddings such that embed-ding distances between query and compatible foregrounds are closer. We aim to transfer the knowledge of interchangeable foregrounds labelling to supervise compatibility learning. Hence, during training, we freeze the foreground encoder trained from the first stage as the teacher network. It generates foreground embeddings as 'soft targets' to train the query encoder in the student network. As a result, the query inputs are projected to the same latent space as interchange-able foregrounds, enabling very efficient and interpretable instance-level search. Cosine distance is applied to measure embedding distances between query and foreground. The embeddings are l_2 normalized before computing cosine distance.

4.2   Foreground Encoder

Training for the foreground encoder follows a typical image classification pipeline. The deeply learned embeddings need to be not only *separable* but also *discriminative*. These embeddings require to be well-classified by k-nearest neighbour algorithms without necessarily depend on label prediction.

Therefore, we adopt center loss [22] in addition to softmax loss to train more discriminative features. The center loss is used due to its proven success in the face recognition task that is very similar to ours. The loss function is given by

$$\mathcal{L}^f = \mathcal{L}^f_S + \lambda \mathcal{L}^f_C. \tag{1}$$

$\mathcal{L}^f$ denotes the total loss for foreground classification. The superscript f denotes *foreground* later on. $\mathcal{L}^f_S$ is the conventional softmax loss. $\mathcal{L}^f_C$ is the center loss and λ is the weight. $\mathcal{L}^f_C$ is given by

$$\mathcal{L}^f_C = \frac{1}{2} \sum_{i=1}^{m} \|\mathbf{x}^f_i - \mathbf{c}^f_{y_i}\|^2_2, \tag{2}$$

where m is the batch size, $\mathbf{x}^f_i \in \mathbb{R}^d$ denotes the ith embedding, and $\mathbf{c}^f_{y_i} \in \mathbb{R}^d$ is the embedding center of the y_i^{th} pattern. d is the feature dimension.

As for the foreground encoder architecture, we adopt ResNet50 [7] with 2048 dimensional feature embedding as feature extractor. We initialize the weights that were pre-trained for the ILSVRC-2014 competition [17]. A fully connected layer is further appended to the feature extractor for pattern classification.

4.3   Query Encoder

Compatibility is determined by three factors: the background context, the fore-ground context, and the foreground location and scale (i.e. layout). We do not consider style compatibility in this work, but our framework is fully adaptable to style encodings learned from [2]. We focus to retrieve compatible foregrounds in a certain category without considering the multi-class problem, since our work can be easily expanded using [25] to tackle this issue. It is still challenging to hand-design compatibility criterion, even considering only the three factors.

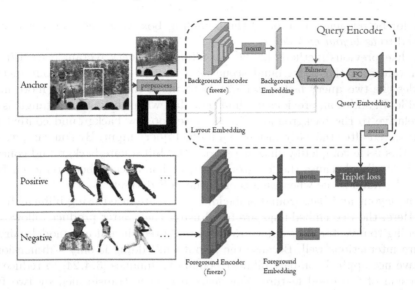

Fig. 5. The training scheme for the query encoder as knowledge distillation. The query encoder is trained to generate query embeddings using a triplet network. This network aims to distill compatibility information from the foreground encoder trained to represent patterns of interchangeable foregrounds.

Network Architecture Figure 5 demonstrates the training scheme for the query encoder as knowledge distillation. This encoder transforms query inputs into embeddings such that embedding distances between query and compatible foregrounds are closer. The general architecture follows a typical two-stream network. The bottom stream takes the square foreground image with pure white background as input. It encodes the image to feature embedding using the foreground encoder trained in the first stage. We freeze the weights in the foreground encoder during training for the query encoder.

The top stream takes a background scene and a rectangle specifying the desired foreground location and scale as query input. The background scene is first cropped to a square image, where the desired foreground location is placed as close to the image center as possible. This cropping also preserves as much context as possible for the square-background. Such cropping makes the background image more consistent so that the training is more stable. The square-background is encoded by a ResNet50 [7] backbone pre-trained on ImageNet [17] with 2048-dimensional features. This network serves as the background encoder to represent scene context. Since the pre-trained network can represent semantic context well, we freeze its weights during training for the query encoder.

The query rectangle is just a bounding box with four degrees of freedom (DoF). We adopt the centroid representation for the bounding box. The first two DoF are coordinates of the bounding box centroid. The other two DoF are width and height of the bounding box. These coordinates are then normalized by dividing the image side length. We only keep the first two digits after the decimal point for better generalization of the bounding box encoding. This encoding is referred to as *layout embedding*.

Unlike previous methods [25, 26] by filling the query rectangle with image mean values to the background scene as a unified query input, our method encodes the two query factors separately to make the embeddings more interpretable. In addition, previous methods may fail when the query rectangle is too big relative to the background scene because too few background context can be preserved after the early-fusion to a unified query input. By contrast, we can avoid this issue completely since we encode the full square-background context. This is feasible because the foreground object has already been removed from the background scene when we establish the FoS dataset.

The layout and background embeddings are late-fused using bilinear fusion [14]. Here, the two embeddings are fused using their outer product followed by flattening to a vector. The outer product is adopted since it can model pairwise feature interactions well. Because the layout embedding is only 4-dimensional, we have not applied compact bilinear pooling techniques [3, 4, 24] to reduce the dimension of the fused feature. This feature is then transformed by two fully connected (FC) layers with ReLU activation to obtain the query embedding. The output dimensions for the first and second FC are all 2048.

Loss Function. We construct triplets consisting of a query input as anchor, a compatible foreground as positive, and an incompatible foreground as negative to train the network. We adopt triplet loss [18] and enforce the embedding distance between anchor and positive to be closer than the one between anchor and negative. These embeddings are l_2 normalized before measuring distance using cosine function.

Formally, a fused feature after bilinear fusion is given by $\mathbf{u}^q \in \mathbb{R}^e$, where the superscript q denotes *query* later on and e is the dimension of the feature embedding. Denote the foreground embeddings for the positive and negative samples are $\mathbf{x}_p^f$ and $\mathbf{x}_n^f$, respectively. The operation of two FC layers with ReLU is denoted as $\mathcal{F}$. The triplet loss is then given by

$$\mathcal{L}^q = \max\left(0, \frac{\mathcal{F}(\mathbf{u}^q)^T \mathbf{x}_p^f}{\|\mathcal{F}(\mathbf{u}^q)\| \|\mathbf{x}_p^f\|} - \frac{\mathcal{F}(\mathbf{u}^q)^T \mathbf{x}_n^f}{\|\mathcal{F}(\mathbf{u}^q)\| \|\mathbf{x}_n^f\|} + M\right), \tag{3}$$

where M is a positive margin. The objective is to train $\mathcal{F}$ by minimizing $\mathcal{L}^q$ over all the sampled triplets.

Training Data. The pattern-level FoS dataset is used for training. The dataset contains pairs of query and compatible pattern containing interchangeable foreground instances. A query with these instances form positive pairs, whereas the query with the others are all negative ones. With pattern-level FoS dataset, we can largely alleviate the severe imbalance in the number of training samples, coupled with noise in the negative pair sampling where some compatible foregrounds are mistreated as negative ones.

We apply different data augmentation strategies for the three types of input. To augment the query rectangle, we relax its size and scale constraints by randomly resizing the rectangle with maximum possible space being half of the rectangle's width and height. To augment the query background, we add random zoom on the cropped square-background while keep the whole query rectangle within the field of view. This augmentation strategy cannot be applied by previous methods [25,26] since it will result in fewer background context in the early-fused query input. As for foreground augmentation, we adopt the same strategy when training the foreground encoder.

4.4   Pattern-Level Foreground Object Search

With the novel concept of interchangeable foregrounds, we can apply pattern-level FoS instead of instance-level. For each foreground instance in the query database, we can assign a pattern label on it. Having all foreground instances within a pattern, the pattern embedding is computed using the centroid of all the instance embeddings transformed by the trained foreground encoder. These pattern embeddings can be also indexed for retrieval. Pattern-level FoS can easily stratify the results, making it more feasible to retrieve controllable, reasonable and diverse foreground instances.

4.5   Implementation Details

To train the foreground encoder, we use the SGD optimizer with momentum and weight decay set to 0.9 and 0.0001, respectively. The learning rate for the softmax loss is 0.02 and the learning rate decay is 0.5 for every 10 epochs. The center loss weight, λ, is set to 0.005. The learning rate for the center loss is 0.5. Batch size is 32 during training. For offline augmentation, we add random padding to the foreground and fill in the padded region with white color. Each foreground is augmented to 20 samples. We then pad them to square images with pure white background. For online augmentation, we apply color jitter by randomly changing the brightness, saturation, contrast and hue by 0.4, 0.4, 0.4 and 0.2, respectively. These samples are resized to 256×256 before fed into the foreground encoder.

To train the query encoder, we use the Adam optimizer [10] with $\beta_1 = 0.5$, $\beta_2 = 0.99$ and $\epsilon = 10^{-9}$. The learning rate is 10^{-4} for the triplet loss. Batch size is 16 during training. The margin, M, is set to 0.1. The input size of the background encoder is 256×256. We perform offline augmentations as described. Each query-foreground pair is augmented to 20 samples. For online augmentation, we apply color jitter by randomly changing the brightness, saturation, contrast and hue by 0.4, 0.4, 0.4 and 0.2, respectively.

Fig. 6. Retrieval results comparison on similar foregrounds. The yellow box denotes the query foreground. The top-5 most similar foregrounds retrieved by the proposed method, the baseline method [25] and the pre-trained ResNet50 model are shown in the green, blue and orange boxes, respectively. (Color figure online)

5   Experiments

5.1   Foreground Encoder

We train foreground encoder in the first stage to classify patterns of interchange-able foregrounds. We use a foreground as query and search for its top-5 most sim-ilar foregrounds in a large database comprising 10154 samples. We first encode all the samples into embeddings using our trained foreground encoder. These embeddings are further l_2 normalized for query using cosine distance. We apply brute-force k-nearest neighbour matching to obtain the retrieval results. We compare results with the baseline method [25] and the pre-trained ResNet50 model on ImageNet as shown by Fig. 6. Clearly, similar instances retrieved by our method are much more interpretable. We can also apply pattern-level search to create interpretable and controllable diversity.

To further quantify the performance of foreground encoder as a pattern classifier, we test it on our evaluation set. The top-1 and top-5 accuracies are respectively 53.15% and 85.79% with 699 classes. The accuracy can be further improved with more labelled data, while the trained foreground encoder is suffi-cient to achieve much better performance over the baseline method in supervising query-foreground compatibility later.

5.2   Query Encoder

We compare our results with the baseline method [25]. We remove the MCB module in the baseline method since we only focus on FoS with one foreground category. Since their implementation is not publicly available, we implement it by strictly following all the settings in their paper. We train both methods on the newly established FoS dataset. We prepare 2 million triplets for each method and train for 2 epochs until convergence.

We first compare results from the two methods qualitatively in Fig. 7. Each row represents one query. The leftmost image shows the query input. Results from pattern- and instance-level search using our method are given in the red

Fig. 7. Retrieval results comparison with baseline method [25]. Each row represents one query. The leftmost image demonstrates the query input. The red box shows top-3 patterns from pattern-level search, each with top-2 instances shown in a column, using the proposed method. The top-5 instance-level search results by our method and the baseline method are shown in the green and blue boxes, respectively. (Color figure online)

and green boxes, respectively. The instance-level search results from the baseline method are shown in the blue box. As can be seen, pattern-level search can provide reasonable and diverse results in a more controllable fashion than instance-level search. As for instance-level search, our results are much more reasonable and interpretable as seen from the first to third row. When the query rectangle is big relative to the background image, the baseline method cannot work properly due to its early-fusion strategy in the query stream. The third row illustrates such a case where a skateboard appears in the background image but most parts of the skateboard are within the query rectangle. The baseline method masks out this crucial cue with early-fusion, resulting in the fatal errors. Our method uses late-fusion without losing any information from the query inputs and therefore, it easily captures the important cue within the query rectangle. Results in the forth and fifth row demonstrate a limitation of both the proposed and baseline method. This limitation originates from the preprocessing step that square-crops the background image. Take the case in the fifth row for example. After square-cropping the query background, the woman playing tennis on the opposite side to the query rectangle is completely cropped, resulting in the final confusion of the retrieval results.

Quantitatively, we test both methods on our evaluation set. The mAP is 43.30% using the baseline method whereas ours is 53.72%. It outperforms the baseline by 10.42% in absolute difference and 24.06% in relative improvement.

Ablation Study. Table 2 shows results in mAP of five ablation variants. The value in blue shows their respective absolute changes relative to the baseline method. We first investigate the significance to apply interchangeable

Table 2. Ablation study results with mAP in percentage. 'Baseline' denotes baseline method [25]. 'Early-fusion' denotes training using early-fused query inputs. 'No-aug' denotes late fusion without random zoom augmentation. 'No-bg-freeze' denotes training without freezing background context encoder. 'Multi-task' denotes training using a multi-task loss to jointly train the foreground and query encoder.

Baseline	Early-fusion	No-aug	No-bg-freeze	Multi-task	Ours
43.30	48.98 5.68↑	51.91 8.61↑	53.61 10.31↑	54.48 11.18↑	**53.72** 10.42↑

foregrounds. We employ early fusion strategy in the query stream similar to the baseline method, while we keep our pre-training for interchangeable foregrounds. With the newly introduced interchangeable foregrounds pre-training, the mAP is enhanced by 5.68%, contributing to 54.51% for the overall improvement. In the second variant, we apply our late fusion strategy in the query stream without random zoom augmentation. It further improves the mAP by 2.93%, contributing to 28.12% for the overall improvement. In the third experiment, we add random zoom augmentation. The baseline method [25] cannot perform this augmentation since in many cases, the zoomed background with masked query rectangle lacks background context. In this experiment, we do not freeze the background encoder. With this augmentation, the mAP is further enhanced by 1.7%, contributing to 16.31% for the overall improvement. In the fourth experiment, we freeze the background encoder and just train the two FC with ReLU layers. Results have shown that training for the background encoder simultaneously cannot help determining compatibility. It implies that the pre-trained model is sufficient to encode semantic context well for the background. In the final ablation experiment, we further fine-tune the foreground and query encoder with a multi-task loss without freezing the foreground encoder. It gives a gain of 0.76%. However, the gain will be less as we enlarge the interchangeable foreground dataset. By contrast, our knowledge distillation framework can modularize FoS into two sub-tasks whose dataset can be prepared separately.

6   Conclusions

This paper introduces a novel concept called interchangeable foregrounds for FoS. It enables interpretable and direct learning of foreground similarity. It also makes pattern-level search feasible to retrieve controllable, reasonable and diverse foregrounds. A new pipeline is proposed to build pattern-level FoS dataset with labelled interchangeable foregrounds. The first FoS benchmark dataset is established accordingly. A novel knowledge distillation framework is proposed to solve the FoS task. It provides fully interpretable results and enhances the absolute mAP by 10.42% and relative mAP by 24.06% over the previous state-of-the-art. It implies the knowledge from interchangeable foregrounds can be transferred to supervise compatibility learning for better performance.

References

1. Chen, T., Cheng, M.M., Tan, P., Shamir, A., Hu, S.M.: Sketch2photo: internet image montage. ACM Trans. Graph. (2009)
2. Collomosse, J., Bui, T., Wilber, M., Fang, C., Jin, H.: Sketching with style: visual search with sketches and aesthetic context. In: ICCV (2017)
3. Fukui, A., Park, D.H., Yang, D., Rohrbach, A., Darrell, T., Rohrbach, M.: Multimodal compact bilinear pooling for visual question answering and visual grounding. In: EMNLP (2016)
4. Gao, Y., Beijbom, O., Zhang, N., Darrell, T.: Compact bilinear pooling. In: CVPR (2016)
5. Gupta, S., Hoffman, J., Malik, J.: Cross modal distillation for supervision transfer. In: CVPR (2016)
6. He, K., Gkioxari, G., Dollár, P., Girshick, R.: Mask R-CNN. In: ICCV (2017)
7. He, K., Zhang, X., Ren, S., Sun, J.: Deep residual learning for image recognition. In: CVPR (2016)
8. Johnson, J., Gupta, A., Fei-Fei, L.: Image generation from scene graphs. In: CVPR, pp. 1219–1228 (2018)
9. Kim, Y., Rush, A.M.: Sequence-level knowledge distillation. In: EMNLP (2016)
10. Kingma, D.P., Ba, J.: Adam: a method for stochastic optimization. CoRR arXiv:1412.6980 (2014)
11. Lalonde, J.F., Hoiem, D., Efros, A.A., Rother, C., Winn, J., Criminisi, A.: Photo clip art. ACM Trans. Graph. (TOG) (2007)
12. Li, B., Zhuang, B., Li, M., Gu, J.: SEQ-SG2SL: inferring semantic layout from scene graph through sequence to sequence learning. In: ICCV (2019)
13. Lin, T.Y., et al.: Microsoft COCO: common objects in context. In: Fleet, D., Pajdla, T., Schiele, B., Tuytelaars, T. (eds.) Computer Vision – ECCV 2014. Lecture Notes in Computer Science, vol. 8693, pp. 740–755. Springer, Cham (2014). https://doi.org/10.1007/978-3-319-10602-1_48
14. Lin, T.Y., RoyChowdhury, A., Maji, S.: Bilinear CNN models for fine-grained visual recognition. In: ICCV (2015)
15. Meng, Z., Li, J., Gong, Y., Juang, B.H.: Adversarial teacher-student learning for unsupervised domain adaptation. In: ICASSP (2018)
16. Mishra, A., Marr, D.: Apprentice: using knowledge distillation techniques to improve low-precision network accuracy. In: ICLR (2018)
17. Russakovsky, O., et al.: ImageNet large scale visual recognition challenge. Int. J. Comput. Vis. **115**, 211–252 (2015)
18. Schroff, F., Kalenichenko, D., Philbin, J.: FaceNet: a unified embedding for face recognition and clustering. In: CVPR (2015)
19. Tan, F., Bernier, C., Cohen, B., Ordonez, V., Barnes, C.: Where and who? Automatic semantic-aware person composition. In: WACV (2017)
20. Tarvainen, A., Valpola, H.: Mean teachers are better role models: weight-averaged consistency targets improve semi-supervised deep learning results. In: NIPS (2017)
21. Tsai, Y., Shen, X., Lin, Z., Sunkavalli, K., Lu, X., Yang, M.: Deep image harmonization. In: CVPR (2017)
22. Wen, C., Zhang, K., Li, Z., Qiao, Y.: A discriminative feature learning approach for deep face recognition. In: Leibe, B., Matas, J., Sebe, N., Welling, M. (eds.) Computer Vision – ECCV 2016. Lecture Notes in Computer Science, vol. 9911, pp. 499–515. Springer, Cham (2016). https://doi.org/10.1007/978-3-319-46478-7_31

23. Yu, J., Lin, Z., Yang, J., Shen, X., Lu, X., Huang, T.S.: Free-form image inpainting with gated convolution. In: ICCV (2019)
24. Yu, Z., Yu, J., Fan, J., Tao, D.: Multi-modal factorized bilinear pooling with co-attentionlearning for visual question answering. In: ICCV (2017)
25. Zhao, H., Shen, X., Lin, Z., Sunkavalli, K., Price, B., Jia, J.: Compositing-aware image search. In: Ferrari, V., Hebert, M., Sminchisescu, C., Weiss, Y. (eds.) Computer Vision – ECCV 2018. Lecture Notes in Computer Science, vol. 11207, pp. 517–532. Springer, Cham (2018). https://doi.org/10.1007/978-3-030-01219-9_31
26. Zhao, Y., Price, B., Cohen, S., Gurari, D.: Unconstrained foreground object search. In: ICCV (2019)
27. Zhou, B., Zhao, H., Puig, X., Fidler, S., Barriuso, A., Torralba, A.: Scene parsing through ade20k dataset. In: CVPR (2017)
28. Zhu, J.Y., Krahenbuhl, P., Shechtman, E., Efros, A.A.: Learning a discriminative model for the perception of realism in composite images. In: ICCV (2015)

Improving Knowledge Distillation
via Category Structure

Zailiang Chen[1], Xianxian Zheng[1], Hailan Shen[1(✉)], Ziyang Zeng[1],
Yukun Zhou[2], and Rongchang Zhao[1]

[1] School of Computer Science and Engineering, Central South University,
Changsha 410083, Hunan, China
{xxxyczl,xxzheng,hailansh,zengziyang,zhaorc}@csu.edu.cn
[2] Centre for Medical Image Computing, University College London,
London WC1V 6LJ, UK
yukun.zhou.19@ucl.ac.uk

Abstract. Most previous knowledge distillation frameworks train the student to mimic the teacher's output of each sample or transfer cross-sample relations from the teacher to the student. Nevertheless, they neglect the structured relations at a category level. In this paper, a novel Category Structure is proposed to transfer category-level structured relations for knowledge distillation. It models two structured relations, including intra-category structure and inter-category structure, which are intrinsic natures in relations between samples. Intra-category structure penalizes the structured relations in samples from the same category and inter-category structure focuses on cross-category relations at a category level. Transferring category structure from the teacher to the student supplements category-level structured relations for training a better student. Extensive experiments show that our method groups samples from the same category tighter in the embedding space and the superiority of our method in comparison with closely related works are validated in different datasets and models.

Keywords: Knowledge distillation · Intra-category structure · Inter-category structure · Structured relation

1 Introduction

Recent developments of deep neural network (DNN) have achieved state-of-the-art performance in many tasks [1,21]. In several challenging datasets [3,11], well-designed networks can even perform better than humans. However, these networks typically have millions of parameters and consume large amounts of computation resources. Applications of these large networks are limited on embedded devices due to their high resource demands. Therefore, there is an urgency for training small networks with low resource demands, while keeping the performance of small networks as close as possible to large networks. Several methods,

© Springer Nature Switzerland AG 2020
A. Vedaldi et al. (Eds.): ECCV 2020, LNCS 12373, pp. 205–219, 2020.
https://doi.org/10.1007/978-3-030-58604-1_13

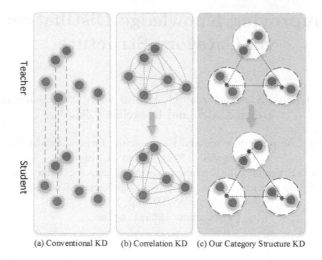

(a) Conventional KD   (b) Correlation KD   (c) Our Category Structure KD

Fig. 1. Differences in transferred knowledge between conventional knowledge distillation, correlation knowledge distillation and our Category Structure Knowledge Distillation (CSKD). In contrast to previous methods, CSKD considers intra-category structure and inter-category structure at a category level as profitable knowledge for knowledge distillation to better improve the performance of the student

such as low-rank factorization [4,10], network pruning [15,18], network quantization [13,17] and knowledge distillation [8,22], have been developed to solve this problem. Knowledge distillation has been proved to be an effective approach to improve the performance of small networks by transferring effective knowledge from a large model to a small model. Through additional regression constraints on outputs of teacher and student for input data, knowledge distillation forces the student model to imitate teacher's behaviors to obtain better performance.

The key problem of knowledge distillation is to extract effective, adequate and general knowledge from the teacher to the student. To handle this problem, conventional knowledge distillation transfers knowledge in a single-sample manner, keeping the student learning the consistency of each input sample as shown in Fig. 1(a). It focuses on extracting knowledge from the final and immediate outputs of the teacher and transferring them to the student. Recently, correlation congruence [20] has been proposed to add constraints on relations between multiple samples as shown in Fig. 1(b). However, these methods ignore the structured relations at a category level, which depict relations from a more abstract and high-level perspective.

We suppose that the category-level structured relations are also profitable knowledge for improving the performance of the student. In this paper, we further propose a novel general framework called Category Structure Knowledge Distillation (CSKD) which focuses on transferring category-level structured relations named category structure from the teacher to the student. Category structure consists of two types of structured relations: intra-category structure for each category and inter-category structure between different categories. Intra-category structure contains relations between samples from the same category and inter-category structure transfers relations between different categories. CSKD is easy to be implemented and the effectiveness of the proposed method is demonstrated by extensive empirical results on three datasets and different models.

Our contributions in this paper are summarized as follows:

1. We propose a new general distillation framework called Category Structure Knowledge Distillation (CSKD), which transfers structured relations from the teacher to the student at a category level. To the best of our knowledge, it is the first work to introduce category-level structured relations for knowledge distillation.
2. We define intra-category and inter-category structure to form the category structure. And two effective relation functions are introduced to better extract intra-category structure and inter-category structure from the embedding space of the teacher and the student.
3. Extensive experiments show that our method achieves state-of-the-art performance. We conduct experiments on different datasets and different teacher-student architecture settings to show the effectiveness of the proposed method in comparison with closely related works.

2   Related Work

In this paper, we focus on improving the performance of small networks. Therefore, we summarize recent methods in model compression and knowledge distillation in this section.

2.1   Model Compression

Model compression focuses on designing small networks with few parameters and high performance simultaneously. Sindhwani [24] proposed a unified framework to learn structured parameter matrices that are characterized by the notion of low displacement rank. Louizos [15] employed L_0 norm regularization in the training to prune the neural networks by encouraging weights to become exactly zero. Energy-aware pruning was utilized to construct energy-efficient convolutional neural networks [27]. Binary quantization with weights and activation constrained to $\{-1, +1\}$ at run-time were adopted in [13]. Adaptive quantization for finding optimal quantization bit-width for each layer was also explored in recent work [30].

2.2   Knowledge Distillation

The purpose of knowledge distillation is improving the performance of small models by transferring knowledge from large models to small models. Hinton [8] first proposed to distill teacher's knowledge to student by soft targets under a controlled temperature. Romero [22] proposed a two-stage training procedure and transferred not only final outputs but also intermediate outputs to student. In [29], a compact student network was improved by mimicking the attention maps of a powerful teacher network. Yim [28] proposed a flow of solution procedure (FSP) to inherit relations between two convolutional layers. In [16], neurons in the deeper hidden layers were used to transfer essential characteristics of the learned face representation for face recognition task. To obtain a promising improvement, noise regularization was added while training the student [23]. Huang [9] regarded knowledge transfer as a distribution matching problem and utilized neuron selectivity patterns between teacher and student models to solve the distribution matching problem. In [7], activation boundary, which meant the activations of neurons instead of their exact output values, was employed to transfer classification-friendly partitions of the hidden feature space.

Recent works also adopt generative adversarial network (GAN) and adversarial examples to obtain better performance. In [26], conditional generative adversarial network was used to learn a proper loss function to transfer effective knowledge from teacher to student. And in [25], a three-player game, consisting of a teacher, a student, and a discriminator, was proposed based on generative adversarial network to force teacher and student learning each other mutually. Heo [6] forced student to learn the decision boundary by adversarial examples.

In addition to the above methods that transfer knowledge in a single-sample manner, there are also a few methods to explore relations between multiple samples for knowledge distillation. Chen [2] used cross-sample similarities which could be naturally derived from deep metric models. In [19], distance-based and angle-based relations were proposed to penalize structural differences in relations. Similarly, Liu [14] utilized instance relationship graph to transfer a relation graph from teacher to student.

In this paper, we further take the category structure in feature space as profitable knowledge to transfer the intra-category structure and inter-category structure from teacher to student.

3   Category Structure Knowledge Distillation

In this section, we describe the details of our proposed category structure for knowledge distillation.

3.1   Knowledge Distillation

We start from conventional knowledge distillation in this section for a better understanding. The concept of knowledge distillation is first proposed in [8] to distill hint knowledge from teacher to the student using cross-entropy

$$\mathcal{L}_{KD-CE} = \frac{1}{n} \sum_{i=1}^{n} \mathcal{H}_{cross}(\boldsymbol{y}_i^t, \boldsymbol{y}_i^s), \tag{1}$$

where n is the number of samples and $\mathcal{H}_{cross}$ is cross-entropy loss function. $\boldsymbol{y}_i^t$ and $\boldsymbol{y}_i^s$ refer to teacher's and student's softmax outputs under distillation temperature τ

$$y_{ij} = \frac{e^{z_j/\tau}}{\sum_{k=1}^{c} e^{z_k/\tau}}, \tag{2}$$

where y_{ij} refers to the predicted probability belonging to the j-th class, z_j refers to the logits of teacher and student and c represents the number of classes. By minimizing the cross-entropy loss function, student mimics teacher's behaviors progressively. In several works [7,20], KL divergence is adopted to better match distributions of teacher and student.

$$\mathcal{L}_{KD-KL} = \frac{1}{n} \sum_{i=1}^{n} \mathcal{KL}(\boldsymbol{y}_i^t, \boldsymbol{y}_i^s). \tag{3}$$

Correlation constraints are utilized in [20] to transfer relations between multiple samples by computing cross sample correlations.

$$\mathcal{L}_{correlation} = \frac{1}{n^2} \|\Phi(\boldsymbol{F}^t) - \Phi(\boldsymbol{F}^s)\|_2^2, \tag{4}$$

where $\boldsymbol{F}^t$ and $\boldsymbol{F}^s$ represent feature maps of teacher and student, respectively. $\Phi(\cdot)$ is a mapping function, $\Phi : \boldsymbol{F} \to \boldsymbol{\Omega} \in \mathbb{R}^{n \times n}$, which maps feature representation $\boldsymbol{F}$ to a relational matrix $\boldsymbol{\Omega}$ by computing pairwise similarity or distance between any two samples in a mini-batch of training dataset. Correlation reflects relations between samples and transferring mutual correlation to student can improve the performance of student by providing extra beneficial information that can not be noticed in single sample manner.

Transferring pairwise relations between any two samples is straight-forward and it may contain some redundant and irrelevant information for knowledge distillation. For example, relations between samples from different classes are calculated for any pair in [20]. Samples from highly related classes may get high similarity and samples from irrelevant classes may get low similarity. However, most of these relations are redundant and unnecessary for classification task. Samples from the same class may have similar relations between themselves and samples from other classes. Transferring redundant information from teacher to student may confuse student to some extent. Inspired by this, we consider structured relations at a category level as principal and sparse knowledge. Beyond sample correlation, we further explore category structure for knowledge distillation.

3.2 Category Structure

In this section, we describe Category Structure Knowledge Distillation in detail. Category structure consists of two parts: intra-category structure and inter-category structure. Intra-category structure describes structured relations between samples from the same category, while inter-category structure represents structured relations between different categories at a category level.

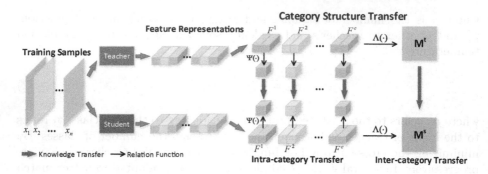

Fig. 2. The overview of our CSKD. Extract intra-category structure and inter-category structure by relation functions $\Psi(\cdot)$ and $\Lambda(\cdot)$ respectively, and transfer them from the teacher to the student

The overall framework of our proposed method is illustrated in Fig. 2. Given n training samples $\boldsymbol{X} = \{x_1, x_2, ..., x_n\}$, a pre-trained teacher model f^t and a random initialized student model f^s. Let feature representations $\boldsymbol{F}^{it} = f^t(\boldsymbol{X}^i; \boldsymbol{W}^t)$ and $\boldsymbol{F}^{is} = f^s(\boldsymbol{X}^i; \boldsymbol{W}^s)$, respectively. $\boldsymbol{W}^t$ and $\boldsymbol{W}^s$ are weights of teacher and student. $\boldsymbol{X}^i$ refers to samples belonging to the i-th class. We divide training samples into different categories by labels. Then category structure denoted as CS is constructed to represent relation structures across samples and can be expressed as

$$CS = (CS_{intra}, CS_{inter}) = (\{\Psi(\boldsymbol{F}^i)\}_{i=1}^c, \Lambda(\{\boldsymbol{F}^i\}_{i=1}^c)), \tag{5}$$

where $\Psi(\cdot)$ is the intra-category structure function constructing relations between samples from the same category and $\Lambda(\cdot)$ refers to the inter-category structure function representing relations between different categories. For each feature representation set $\boldsymbol{F}^i = f(\boldsymbol{X}^i; \boldsymbol{W})$ belonging to the i-th category, $\Psi(\boldsymbol{F}^i)$ formalise their structured relations to group a tight cluster in the embedding space. Correspondingly, $\Lambda(\{\boldsymbol{F}^i\}_{i=1}^c))$ is a mapping function: $\Lambda : \boldsymbol{F} \rightarrow \boldsymbol{M} \in \mathbb{R}^{c \times c}$, calculating similarities between different categories to separate samples from irrelevant categories from each other. $\boldsymbol{M}$ is a category relational matrix.

To construct relations at a category level, we define a category center as

$$\boldsymbol{C}^i = \frac{1}{m} \sum_{j=1}^m \boldsymbol{F}_j^i, \tag{6}$$

where $\boldsymbol{F}_j^i$ refers to the feature map belonging to the j-th sample from the i-th category, and m is the number of samples from the i-th category. Category center is calculated by the average feature map for samples from the same category and it represents the general category feature representation in high-level feature space to some extent.

Then the relation function of intra-category structure can be defined as

$$\Psi(\boldsymbol{F}^i) = \{\boldsymbol{F}_j^i - \boldsymbol{C}^i\}_{j=1}^m. \tag{7}$$

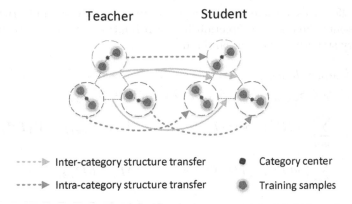

Fig. 3. **Fig. 3.** Illustration of category structure transfer. Yellow solid arrows indicate the inter-category structure transfer, and blue dotted arrows refer to intra-category structure transfer. Inter-category structure transfers cross-category similarity between any two categories and intra-category structure transfer relative structure formed by category center and training samples from the same category (Color figure online)

It preserves the structured information of relative distances between each sample and its category center. We assume that samples from the same category group tight in the embedding space and category center can represent samples from the same category in the embedding space. Based on category center, relations of samples from the same category are involved in the relation structure in a more efficient and sparse way. We further define the relation function of inter-category structure based on similarity:

$$M(i,j) = \Lambda(\boldsymbol{F}^i, \boldsymbol{F}^j) = \frac{\boldsymbol{C}^i \cdot \boldsymbol{C}^j}{\|\boldsymbol{C}^i\|_2 \|\boldsymbol{C}^j\|_2}, i,j = 1,2,...,c. \tag{8}$$

It reflects the structured relations between any two categories. Highly related categories have high similarity scores and irrelevant categories have low similarity scores.

Intra-category structure ignores redundant relations between cross-category samples and focuses on pairwise relations formed by relative distance to category center between samples from the same category. Correspondingly, inter-category structure maintains principal category-wise relations and it complements structured relations in a global sense. And our extensive experiments shows that intra-category structure and inter-category structure shows mutual positive effects to each other. Since we conduct structured relations at a category level, category structure constructs sparser relations than correlation that calculates relations between any two samples (see analysis in Sect. 4.6).

3.3   Loss for Category Structure Transfer

Figure 3 shows the illustration of category structure and its transfer process. To transfer category structure from teacher to student, we construct L_{CS} to measure differences between category structures of teacher and student. Let $D(\cdot)$ represents the distance function between relation structures, then the loss for category structure transfer can be defined as

$$
\begin{aligned}
L_{CS} &= L_{intra} + L_{inter} \\
&= \beta \cdot D(CS^t_{intra}, CS^s_{intra}) + \gamma \cdot D(CS^t_{inter}, CS^s_{inter}) \\
&= \frac{\beta}{c} \cdot \sum_{i=1}^{c} \|\Psi(F^{it}) - \Psi(\sigma(F^{is}))\|_2 + \gamma \cdot \|\Lambda(\{F^{it}\}_{i=1}^{c}) - \Lambda(\{F^{is}\}_{i=1}^{c})\|_2 \\
&= \frac{\beta}{c} \cdot \sum_{i=1}^{c} \|\Psi(F^{it}) - \Psi(\sigma(F^{is}))\|_2 + \gamma \cdot \|M^t - M^s\|_2,
\end{aligned}
\tag{9}
$$

where β and γ are hyper-parameters to control weights of intra-category structure and inter-category structure. $\sigma(\cdot)$ is a transformer with 1×1 convolution layer for matching student's channels to teacher's. Therefore, total loss for training student is

$$
L_{total} = \alpha L_{CE} + (1 - \alpha)L_{KD} + L_{CS},
\tag{10}
$$

where L_{CE} is the cross-entropy loss based on student's output and ground truth and L_{KD} is the mean square errors of teacher's and student's logits in our experiments. α is a trade-off between supervision from labels and single-sample based knowledge transfer. Our CSKD is summarized in Algorithm 1.

4   Experiments

We evaluate CSKD on three datasets: CIFAR-10, CIFAR-100 and Tiny ImageNet to show the effectiveness of our proposed method. And we compare CSKD with closely related works. Extensive experiments are conducted to explore category structure for knowledge distillation. Our codes for experiments and more results will be available at https://github.com/xeanzheng/CSKD.

4.1   Experimental Settings

We adopt ResNet [5] as the main architecture in our experiments. In the main experiments, the hyper-parameter α is set to 0.1, the weight of intra-category structure loss β is empirically set to 0.01, and $\gamma = 0.2$.

On CIFAR-10, CIFAR-100, and Tiny ImageNet, we compare CSKD with the student trained with only cross-entropy (CE), original knowledge distillation (KD) [8], Fitnet [22], KDGAN [25], activation boundary transfer (AB) [7], and correlation congruence knowledge distillation (CCKD) [20]. For fare comparisons, all methods are implemented and compared under the same architecture configurations.

Algorithm 1. Category structure knowledge distillation.

Input:

  Training samples, $X = \{x_1, x_2, ..., x_n\}$;

  Labels of training samples, $y = \{y_1, y_2, ..., y_n\}$;

  Teacher model f^t with pre-trained weights W^t;

  Student model $\hat{f}^s$ with random initialized weights $\hat{W}^s$;

  Transformer with 1×1 convolution layer, σ;

Output:

  Student model f^s with optimized weights W^s;

1: **while** not convergence **do**

2:    Choose a random batch $\hat{X}$ and their labels $\hat{y}$ from training samples X and labels y;

3:    Extract features from teacher and student model, $F^t = f^t(\hat{X}; W^t)$, $F^s = \hat{f}^s(\hat{X}; W^s)$;

4:    Group features into different groups by labels $\hat{y}$, $F^t = \{F^{it}\}_{i=1}^{c}$, $F^s = \{F^{is}\}_{i=1}^{c}$;

5:    Extract structured relations by Ψ and Λ relation functions, $\Psi(F^{it})$, $\Psi(\sigma(F^{is}))$, $\Lambda(\{F^{it}\}_{i=1}^{c})$, $\Lambda(\{F^{is}\}_{i=1}^{c})$;

6:    Transfer category structure to student model f^s by descending the stochastic gradient from L_{CS}:
$$\nabla_W s \frac{\beta}{c} \cdot \sum_{i=1}^{c} `\|\Psi(F^{it}) - \Psi(\sigma(F^{is}))\|_2 + \gamma \cdot \|\Lambda(\{F^{it}\}_{i=1}^{c}) - \Lambda(\{F^{is}\}_{i=1}^{c})\|_2,$$
and train the student model by supervision from labels and single-sample based knowledge distillation loss from the teacher:
$$\nabla_W s \alpha L_{CE} + (1 - \alpha) L_{KD};$$

7: **end while**

8: **return** f^s with its weights W^s;

4.2 Results on CIFAR-10

CIFAR-10 [12] consists of 60 K 32 × 32 images in 10 classes and each class contains 5000 images in training set and 1000 images in validation set. We first resize images to 40×40 by zero-padding, and then randomly crop images to original size 32 × 32. Meanwhile, random horizontal flip and normalization with channel means and standard deviations are adopted to augment the training data. We use a batch size 128 and a standard SGD optimizer with an initial learning rate 0.1 and momentum 0.9 to optimize our model and the weight decay is set to 1e−4. We train the model with 200 epochs and the learning rate is multiplied by a scale factor 0.1 when training epochs are at 80, 120, 160.

We conduct our CSKD on teacher networks ResNet152_0.5 (14.6 M) with a accuracy 93.22% and ResNet101_0.5 (10.7 M) with a accuracy 92.91% and student networks ResNet18_0.25 (0.7 M), ResNet34_0.25 (1.3 M) and ResNet50_0.25 (1.4 M). ResNet_x represents a ResNet with a channel reduction to a ratio of x. The first convolution kernel is changed to size 3 × 3 with a stride 1 and the stride of the first max-pooling is set to 1 to fit the image size.

We show our results on CIFAR-10 in Table 1. CSKD shows remarkable improvements under all evaluated teacher-student architecture settings. It obtains an average 1.52% improvement on different student networks and surpasses several closely related state-of-the-art methods with obvious margins. And

Table 1. Accuracy of different methods on CIFAR-10. We explore our CSKD on different teacher-student architecture settings and keep the same training configuration for all the methods for fair comparisons. The proposed method surpasses all other methods. R101_0.5: ResNet101 with a channel reduction to the ratio of 50%

Teacher/Student Model	CE	KD	Fitnet	KDGAN	AB	CCKD	Proposed	Teacher
R101_0.5/R18_0.25	90.14	91.01	91.05	91.54	91.42	91.07	**91.99**	92.91
R101_0.5/R34_0.25	91.25	91.48	91.61	92.09	91.94	91.87	**92.67**	92.91
R101_0.5/R50_0.25	92.16	92.18	92.37	92.65	92.49	92.34	**93.20**	92.91
R152_0.5/R18_0.25	90.14	91.11	91.37	91.50	91.44	91.56	**92.27**	93.22
R152_0.5/R34_0.25	91.25	91.81	92.14	92.38	92.16	92.10	**92.76**	93.22
R152_0.5/R50_0.25	92.16	92.29	92.53	93.01	92.79	92.75	**93.31**	93.22

it is noticed that our compression ratios are around 4.8%~13.1%, however, the performance of the student even can surpass the teacher in some teacher-student architecture settings, e.g., 92.91% of teacher ResNet101_0.5 versus 93.20% of student ResNet50_0.25.

Table 2. Accuracy of different methods on CIFAR-100. Our CSKD outperforms all other methods and even better than the teacher

Teacher/Student Model	CE	KD	Fitnet	KDGAN	AB	CCKD	Proposed	Teacher
R101_0.5/R18_0.25	65.64	67.43	68.04	68.35	68.17	68.96	**69.14**	71.77
R101_0.5/R34_0.25	66.86	69.30	69.76	69.81	69.91	70.14	**70.39**	71.77
R101_0.5/R50_0.25	68.79	70.57	71.39	71.24	71.05	71.32	**71.61**	71.77
R152_0.5/R18_0.25	65.64	67.99	68.41	68.34	68.73	69.15	**69.22**	72.15
R152_0.5/R34_0.25	66.86	70.08	70.48	70.70	70.75	70.98	**71.01**	72.15
R152_0.5/R50_0.25	68.79	71.24	71.92	71.52	72.25	72.19	**72.60**	72.15

Table 3. Top-1 accuracy and top-5 accuracy on Tiny ImageNet. The teacher is ResNet152 (58.5M) and the student is ResNet18_0.25 (0.7 M)

Method	Top-1 accuracy	Top-5 accuracy
Teacher	60.70	81.87
CE	45.21	71.03
KD	49.53	74.90
Fitnet	50.12	75.41
KDGAN	52.84	77.62
CCKD	53.14	78.14
AB	52.72	77.89
Proposed	**53.66**	**78.75**

4.3   Results on CIFAR-100

CIFAR-100 [12] is similar to CIFAR-10 dataset. But it is a more complicated dataset because it contains 100 classes rather than 10 classes in CIFAR-10. There are also 60 K 32×32 images in CIFAR-100 and 50K/10K images for training/validation. Each class contains 500 training images and 100 validation images and we adopt the same data augmentation scheme used in CIFAR-10 (resize/padding/crop/flip/normalization) for CIFAR-100. The same multi-step SGD optimizer is also adopted and we train our model with 200 epochs.

We show results on CIFAR-100 in Table 2. The same network architecture settings are used and CSKD outperforms other methods. In this dataset, there exists a relatively big margin (compression ratio around 2.98%~6.51%) between teacher and student and our CSKD improves the performance of the student by 2.82%~4.15%. And the student achieves a better accuracy 72.60% (ResNet50_0.25) than the teacher with an accuracy 72.15% (ResNet152_0.5) at the last entry in Table 2.

4.4   Results on Tiny ImageNet

Tiny ImageNet is a downsampled version of the ImageNet [3] for classification. It consists of 120 K images with 200 classes and each class contains 500 training images, 50 validating images, and 50 test images. The images are downsampled from 256×256 to 64×64. It is more difficult to classify these images in Tiny ImageNet than CIFAR datasets. We adopt Resnet152 (58.5 M) as the teacher model and Resnet18_0.25 (0.7 M) as the student model to explore the performance of CSKD when there is a big gap in capacity between the teacher and the student. The student only has around 1.2% of the teacher's parameters under this teacher-student architecture setting. We resize input images to 72×72 and then randomly crop them to 64×64. Random horizontal flip operation and channel normalization are also utilized to augment and normalize the training data. To better extract feature representations in the embedding space, the first convolutional kernel in original ResNet18 is changed to 3×3 with a stride 1 to fit the image size. The batch size is chosen as 200 and the student is trained with 200 epochs. A SGD optimizer with initial learning rate 0.1 and momentum 0.9 is utilized and the weight decay is set to $5e-4$. The learning rate is divided by a factor 10 at 50, 100, 150 epochs.

Table 3 shows the results of CSKD and related works on Tiny ImageNet. All models are evaluated on validation set and trained with the same epochs for fair comparisons. Our CSKD surpasses all other methods in Table 3 and gets a 53.66% top-1 accuracy and a 78.75% top-5 accuracy. Compared with original KD, CSKD surpasses by around 4% in both top-1 accuracy and top-5 accuracy.

Table 4. Ablation study of Category Structure Knowledge Distillation. It is observed that every part of our category structure takes effect. Intra-category structure and inter-category structure show mutual effects when both of them are used

Intra loss	Inter loss	Top-1 accuracy	Top-5 accuracy
✗	✗	49.53	74.90
✓	✗	52.51	78.36
✗	✓	52.48	78.45
✓	✓	**53.66**	**78.75**

4.5 Ablation Study

We conduct an ablation study on the setting of a teacher ResNet152 and a student ResNet18_0.25 to delve into two parts of category structure, i.e., intra-category structure and inter-category structure. The results are summarized in Table 4. Each part of category structure loss is stripped to show the effectiveness of two parts of our category structure. When applied only intra-category loss or inter-category loss, our method gets similar improvements. If unabridged category structure loss is used, intra-category loss and inter-category loss show mutual effects on each other and CSKD achieves better promotions. It is also noticed that our method gets a general higher top-5 accuracy when compared with all other methods in Table 3, which reveals that category structure groups similar categories tighter in the embedding space and separates irrelevant categories far away from each other.

4.6 Analysis

Since we construct relation structures at a category level, the relations are sparser than cross-sample correlation which penalizes relations between any two samples. We simply regard different kinds of relations as the same edges between different vertices (samples) and calculate the number of edges to compare the complexity between category structure and cross-sample correlation. Let a dataset consists of c categories and to simplify the calculation, each category is assumed to contain m images, then the number of edges in correlation is m^2c^2. In category structure, the number of edges is $mc + c^2$. Then the quantity ratio can be calculated as

$$m^2c^2/(mc + c^2) = m^2c/(m + c) \leq \frac{m}{2}\sqrt{mc}. \tag{11}$$

It is obvious that category structure compresses original correlation at most $\frac{m}{2}\sqrt{mc}$ times. Our CSKD helps reduce redundant relations between cross-category samples by focusing on relations between samples from the same category (intra-category relations) and using relations based on category center between different categories (inter-category relations).

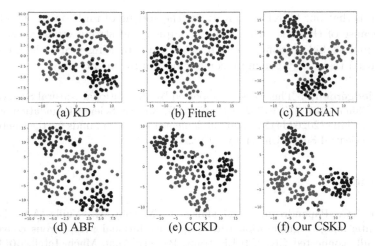

Fig. 4. Feature visualization of different methods. Each point represents a sample and each color represents a class. Our CSKD groups samples from the same category tighter than all other methods. Best viewed in color (Color figure online)

To better show the effect of our CSKD, we extract feature representations of the last layer in student ResNet18_0.25 and visualize them as shown in Fig. 4. A random batch of validation set in Tiny ImageNet is used and therefore, there are only four random classes for a clear comparison. It is observed that CSKD group samples from the same category tighter than all other methods (e.g., the green clusters in Fig. 4) and each cluster in CSKD has a relatively clear boundary to other clusters.

5   Conclusion

In this paper, we find that relation transfer for knowledge distillation can be further explored at a category level. For classification tasks, the concept of category can be easily defined by labels. So we construct intra-category structure and inter-category structure based on labels to transfer principal relational knowledge in a sparse but powerful way. Intra-category structure preserves the structured relations in samples from the same category, while inter-category structure reflects the cross-category relations at a category level.

Our CSKD is implemented in a mini-batch, which may be a limitation when the number of categories is close to batch size. In this case, our category structure may degrade to the cross-sample correlation that transfers relations between any two samples. We set batch size equal to or larger than the number of classes to ensure that our CSKD takes effect in our experiments. And for the sake of fair comparisons, we set the batch sizes of all other methods to the same as our CSKD. An alternative to address this issue is to construct a better sampler for training and we will explore this problem in future. Another issue worth exploring is that our CSKD naturally fits the setting of multi-label classification tasks because of the existence of more complex and strong cross-category relations in multi-label classification datasets. Implementing CSKD in multi-label classification tasks may get more convincing improvement.

Acknowledgements. This work is supported by the National Natural Science Foundation of China (61972419, 61702558, 61672542), Natural Science Foundation of Hunan Province of China (2020JJ4120), and Fundamental Research Funds for the Central Universities of Central South University (2019zzts963).

References

1. Chen, L.C., Papandreou, G., Kokkinos, I., Murphy, K., Yuille, A.L.: Deeplab: semantic image segmentation with deep convolutional nets, atrous convolution, and fully connected CRFs. IEEE Trans. Pattern Anal. Mach. Intell. **40**(4), 834–848 (2017)
2. Chen, Y., Wang, N., Zhang, Z.: Darkrank: accelerating deep metric learning via cross sample similarities transfer. In: Thirty-Second AAAI Conference on Artificial Intelligence (2018)
3. Deng, J., Dong, W., Socher, R., Li, L.J., Li, K., Fei-Fei, L.: Imagenet: a large-scale hierarchical image database. In: 2009 IEEE Conference on Computer Vision and Pattern Recognition, pp. 248–255. IEEE (2009)
4. Denton, E.L., Zaremba, W., Bruna, J., LeCun, Y., Fergus, R.: Exploiting linear structure within convolutional networks for efficient evaluation. In: Advances in Neural Information Processing Systems, pp. 1269–1277 (2014)
5. He, K., Zhang, X., Ren, S., Sun, J.: Deep residual learning for image recognition. In: Proceedings of the IEEE Conference on Computer Vision and Pattern Recognition, pp. 770–778 (2016)
6. Heo, B., Lee, M., Yun, S., Choi, J.Y.: Knowledge distillation with adversarial samples supporting decision boundary. Proc. AAAI Conf. Artif. Intell. **33**, 3771–3778 (2019)
7. Heo, B., Lee, M., Yun, S., Choi, J.Y.: Knowledge transfer via distillation of activation boundaries formed by hidden neurons. Proc. AAAI Conf. Artif. Intell. **33**, 3779–3787 (2019)
8. Hinton, G., Vinyals, O., Dean, J.: Distilling the knowledge in a neural network. arXiv preprint arXiv:1503.02531 (2015)
9. Huang, Z., Wang, N.: Like what you like: knowledge distill via neuron selectivity transfer. arXiv preprint arXiv:1707.01219 (2017)
10. Jaderberg, M., Vedaldi, A., Zisserman, A.: Speeding up convolutional neural networks with low rank expansions. arXiv preprint arXiv:1405.3866 (2014)
11. Johnson, J., Hariharan, B., van der Maaten, L., Fei-Fei, L., Lawrence Zitnick, C., Girshick, R.: CLEVR: a diagnostic dataset for compositional language and elementary visual reasoning. In: Proceedings of the IEEE Conference on Computer Vision and Pattern Recognition, pp. 2901–2910 (2017)
12. Krizhevsky, A., Hinton, G., et al.: Learning multiple layers of features from tiny images. Technical report. Citeseer (2009)
13. Lin, X., Zhao, C., Pan, W.: Towards accurate binary convolutional neural network. In: Advances in Neural Information Processing Systems, pp. 345–353 (2017)

14. Liu, Y., et al.: Knowledge distillation via instance relationship graph. In: Proceedings of the IEEE Conference on Computer Vision and Pattern Recognition, pp. 7096–7104 (2019)
15. Louizos, C., Welling, M., Kingma, D.P.: Learning sparse neural networks through l_0 regularization. arXiv preprint arXiv:1712.01312 (2017)
16. Luo, P., Zhu, Z., Liu, Z., Wang, X., Tang, X.: Face model compression by distilling knowledge from neurons. In: Thirtieth AAAI Conference on Artificial Intelligence (2016)
17. Micikevicius, P., et al.: Mixed precision training. arXiv preprint arXiv:1710.03740 (2017)
18. Molchanov, P., Tyree, S., Karras, T., Aila, T., Kautz, J.: Pruning convolutional neural networks for resource efficient inference. arXiv preprint arXiv:1611.06440 (2016)
19. Park, W., Kim, D., Lu, Y., Cho, M.: Relational knowledge distillation. In: Proceedings of the IEEE Conference on Computer Vision and Pattern Recognition, pp. 3967–3976 (2019)
20. Peng, B., et al.: Correlation congruence for knowledge distillation. In: Proceedings of the IEEE International Conference on Computer Vision, pp. 5007–5016 (2019)
21. Redmon, J., Farhadi, A.: YOLOV3: an incremental improvement. arXiv preprint arXiv:1804.02767 (2018)
22. Romero, A., Ballas, N., Kahou, S.E., Chassang, A., Gatta, C., Bengio, Y.: FitNets: hints for thin deep nets. arXiv preprint arXiv:1412.6550 (2014)
23. Sau, B.B., Balasubramanian, V.N.: Deep model compression: Distilling knowledge from noisy teachers. arXiv preprint arXiv:1610.09650 (2016)
24. Sindhwani, V., Sainath, T., Kumar, S.: Structured transforms for small-footprint deep learning. In: Advances in Neural Information Processing Systems, pp. 3088–3096 (2015)
25. Wang, X., Zhang, R., Sun, Y., Qi, J.: KDGAN: knowledge distillation with generative adversarial networks. In: Advances in Neural Information Processing Systems, pp. 775–786 (2018)
26. Xu, Z., Hsu, Y.C., Huang, J.: Training shallow and thin networks for acceleration via knowledge distillation with conditional adversarial networks. arXiv preprint arXiv:1709.00513 (2017)
27. Yang, T.J., Chen, Y.H., Sze, V.: Designing energy-efficient convolutional neural networks using energy-aware pruning. In: Proceedings of the IEEE Conference on Computer Vision and Pattern Recognition, pp. 5687–5695 (2017)
28. Yim, J., Joo, D., Bae, J., Kim, J.: A gift from knowledge distillation: Fast optimization, network minimization and transfer learning. In: Proceedings of the IEEE Conference on Computer Vision and Pattern Recognition, pp. 4133–4141 (2017)
29. Zagoruyko, S., Komodakis, N.: Paying more attention to attention: improving the performance of convolutional neural networks via attention transfer. arXiv preprint arXiv:1612.03928 (2016)
30. Zhou, Y., Moosavi-Dezfooli, S.M., Cheung, N.M., Frossard, P.: Adaptive quantization for deep neural network. In: Thirty-Second AAAI Conference on Artificial Intelligence (2018)

High Resolution Zero-Shot Domain Adaptation of Synthetically Rendered Face Images

Stephan J. Garbin$^{(\boxtimes)}$, Marek Kowalski, Matthew Johnson, and Jamie Shotton

Microsoft, Cambridge, UK
stephangarbin@outlook.com

Abstract. Generating photorealistic images of human faces at scale remains a prohibitively difficult task using computer graphics approaches. This is because these require the simulation of light to be photorealistic, which in turn requires physically accurate modelling of geometry, materials, and light sources, for both the head and the surrounding scene. Non-photorealistic renders however are increasingly easy to produce. In contrast to computer graphics approaches, generative models learned from more readily available 2D image data have been shown to produce samples of human faces that are hard to distinguish from real data. The process of learning usually corresponds to a loss of control over the shape and appearance of the generated images. For instance, even simple disentangling tasks such as modifying the hair independently of the face, which is trivial to accomplish in a computer graphics approach, remains an open research question. In this work, we propose an algorithm that matches a non-photorealistic, synthetically generated image to a latent vector of a pretrained StyleGAN2 model which, in turn, maps the vector to a photorealistic image of a person of the same pose, expression, hair, and lighting. In contrast to most previous work, we require no synthetic training data. To the best of our knowledge, this is the first algorithm of its kind to work at a resolution of 1K and represents a significant leap forward in visual realism.

1 Introduction

Generating photorealistic images of human faces remains a challenge in computer graphics. While we consider the arguably easier problem of still images as opposed to animated ones, we note that both pose unsolved research questions. This is because of the complicated and varied appearance of human tissue found in the hair, skin [45], eyes [7] and teeth of the face region. The problem is further complicated by the fact that humans are highly attuned to the appearance of faces and thus skilled at spotting any unnatural aspect of a synthetic render [36].

Electronic supplementary material The online version of this chapter (https://doi.org/10.1007/978-3-030-58604-1_14) contains supplementary material, which is available to authorized users.

© Springer Nature Switzerland AG 2020
A. Vedaldi et al. (Eds.): ECCV 2020, LNCS 12373, pp. 220–236, 2020.
https://doi.org/10.1007/978-3-030-58604-1_14

Synthetic	Our Result	Synthetic	Our Result	Synthetic	Our Result

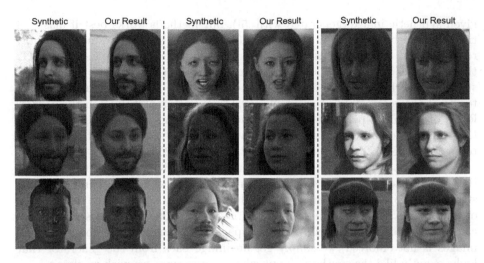

Fig. 1. Pairs of synthetic input images, and samples from our algorithm at 1K resolution. Best viewed zoomed in, and in colour. (Color figure online)

Machine learning has recently seen great success in generating still images of faces that are nearly indistinguishable from the domain of natural images to a non-expert observer. This gives methods like StyleGAN2 (SG2) [28] a clear advantage over computer graphics if the goal is to generate photorealistic image samples only. The limitation of models like SG2 is that we get RGB data only, and that such samples are often only useful if annotations such as head pose, UVs, or expression parameters are available for downstream tasks. The second major issue is that generative models necessarily inherit the bias of the data they were trained on. For large image collections, this may be hard to assess [48]. In computer graphics on the other hand, annotations such as UVs can be trivially obtained for an image. Since the assets that define the data input into the renderer need to be explicitly created, bias control becomes more feasible (Fig. 1).

In this paper, we propose to play to the strengths of both fields by using machine learning to change the appearance of non-photorealistic renders to be more natural, while keeping semantics such as the shape, the expression of the face, and the lighting as consistent as possible given constraints imposed by the training data. This means that the annotations obtained from the renders are still largely valid for the images after domain transfer. Because we do not require photo-realism from the synthetic renders, we can produce them at scale and with significant variety using a traditional graphics pipeline.

In contrast to other work using non-photorealistic renders to train models that map from one domain to another (e.g. [17] for faces, or [8]), we require no synthetic images for training at all, and thus no paired data. In fact, our method only requires a pre-trained StyleGAN2 model, and a small number of manual annotations from the data it was trained on as outlined below. For a given synthetic image (generated with [5]), our methods works best if masks of the hair and background are available. These can be easily obtained from any renderer. Our method works by finding an embedding in the latent space of SG2 that produces an image which is perceptually similar to a synthetic sample, but still has the characteristic features of the data the GAN was trained with. In terms of the scale space of an image [10,11], we attempt to match the coarser levels of an image pyramid to the synthetic data, and replace fine detail with that of a photorealistic image. Another way to interpret this is that we attempt to steer StyleGAN2 with the help of synthetic data [25].

While embedding images in the latent space of SG2 is not a new concept [1,2], the issue with using existing approaches is that they either do not, or struggle to, enforce constraints to keep the results belonging to the distribution of real images. In fact, the authors in [2] explicitly note that almost any image can be embedded in a StyleGAN latent space. If closeness to the domain of real images is not enforced, we simply get an image back from the generator that looks exactly like the synthetic input whose appearance we wish to change.

We make the observation that samples from the prior distribution usually *approximately* form a convex set, *i.e.* that convex combinations of any set of such points mapped through the generator are statistically similar to samples from the data distribution the GAN was trained on. We also note that showing interpolations between pairs of latent vectors is a common strategy of evaluating the quality of the latent embeddings of generative models [37]. As part of our method, we propose an algorithm, Convex Set Approximate Nearest Neighbour Search (CS-ANNS), which can be used to traverse the latent space of a generative model while ensuring that the reconstructed images closely adhere to the prior. This algorithm optimises for the combination of a set of samples from the SG2 prior by gradient descent, and is detailed in the method section below.

In summary, our contributions are:

1. The first zero-shot domain transfer method to work at 1K and with only limited annotations of the real data, and
2. a novel algorithm for approximate nearest neighbour search in the latent spaces of generative models.

2   Related Work

2.1   Generative Models

Generative models are of paramount importance to deep learning research. In this work, we care about those that map samples from a latent space to images. While many models have been proposed (such as Optimized MMD [40], Noise Contrastive Estimation [20], Mixture Density Networks [9], Neural Autoregressive Distribution Estimators [33,41], Diffusion Process Models [39], and flow-based models [13,14,32]), the most popular ones are the family of Variational Autoencoders (VAEs) [26,30], and Generative Adversarial Networks (GANs) [19].

Because GANs are (at the time of writing) capable of achieving the highest quality image samples, we focus on them in this work, and specifically on the current state of the art for face images, StyleGAN2 (SG2) [28]. In any GAN, a neural sampler called the generator is trained to map samples from a simple distribution to the true data distribution, defined by samples (the training set). A second network, called the discriminator, is trained to differentiate samples produced by the generator and those from the data space.

Our method takes as input only the pretrained *generator* of SG2, and while we backpropagate through it, we do not modify its weights as part of our algorithm. Since SG2 uses a variant of Adaptive Instance Normalisation (AdaIn)[22], its latent space is mapped directly to the AdaIn parameters at 18 different layers. We do not use the additional noise inputs at each layer. This way of controlling the generator output via the AdaIn inputs is the same methodology as used in the Image2StyleGAN work [2]. The authors in [2] also consider style transfer by blending two latent codes together, but choose very different image modalities such as cartoons and photographs. We build on their work by defining a process that finds a close nearest neighbour to blend with, thereby creating believable appearance transfer that preserves semantics.

2.2   Zero-Shot Domain Transfer

To the best of our knowledge, there are no zero-shot image domain transfer methods in the literature that require only one source domain operating at comparable resolution. By domain adaptation we mean the ability to make images from dataset A look like images from dataset B, while preserving content. While one-shot methods like [49] or [6] have been proposed, they work at significantly lower resolution than ours and still require one sample from the target domain. ZstGAN [34], the closest neighbour, requires many source domains (that could for example be extracted from image labels of one dataset). The highest resolution handled in that work is 128^2, which is signifantly lower than our method. The categories are used to bootstrap the appearance transfer problem, as if multiple datasets were available. Without labels for dividing the data into categories, we were unable to use it as a baseline.

2.3   Domain Adaptation

If paired training data from two domains is available, Pix2Pix [24] and its successors (e.g. Pix2Pix HD [43], which uses multiple discriminators at multiple scales to produce high resolution images) can be used effectively for domain adaptation.

CycleGAN does not require paired training data [50]. This brings it closer to the application we consider. However, it still requires a complete dataset of both image modalities. Many improvements have since been suggested to improve CycleGAN. HarmonicGAN adds an additional smoothness constraint to reduce artefacts in the outputs [47], Sem-GAN exploits additional information [12], as does [3], Discriminative Region Proposal Adversarial Networks (DRPAN) [42]

224   S. J. Garbin et al.

add steps to fix errors, Geometry-Consistent GANs (GcGAN) [15] use consistency under simple transformations as an additional constraint. Some methods also model a distribution of over possible outputs, such as MUNIT [23] or FUNIT [35].

However, none of these methods are capable of zero-shot domain adaptation.

3 Method

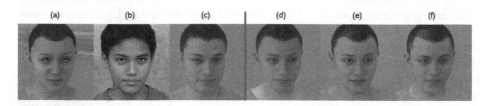

Fig. 2. Illustration of the different steps of our method. (a) is the input synthetic render, (b) the output of the sampling in step 1, (c) the result of Convex Set Approximate Nearest Neighbour Search in step 2, and (d–f) results from step 3.

In the following, any variable containing w refers to the 18×512 dimensional inputs of the pretrained SG2 generator, G. Any variable prefixed with I refers to an image, either given as input, or obtaining by passing a w through the generator G. The proposed method takes as input a synthetically rendered image I^s, and returns a series of ws that represent domain adapted versions of that input.

Our algorithm has four stages, each producing results more closely matching the input. In the first, we find the latent code, w^s, of an approximate nearest neighbour to a given synthetic input image, I^s, by sampling. This is the starting point of our method. For the second step, we propose Convex Set Approximate Nearest Neighbour Search (CS-ANNS), an algorithm to refine the initial sample by traversing the latent space while being strongly constrained to adhere to the prior. This gives us a refined latent code, w^n. Please note that additional details and results can be found in the supplementary material.

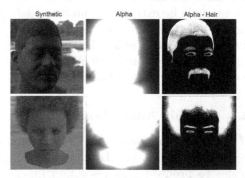

Fig. 3. Example tuples of renders and alpha masks, $\{I^s, I^a, I^{ahair}\}$, derived from synthetic images. Note that we apply a falloff at sharp boundaries to preserve them as described in the text.

In the third step, we fit SG2 to the synthetic image *without any constraint* to obtain another latent code w^f that matches I^s as closely as possible. We can then combine w^f and w^n with varying interpolation weights to obtain a set of final images that strongly resemble I^s, but which have the appearance of real photographs.

Because w^s, w^n and the results from step 3 are all valid proposals for the final result, we select the latent code that gives an image as semantically similar to I^s as possible from among them in the fourth and final step. An example of the different steps of our method can be seen in Fig. 2.

We note that the SG2 model used in this section was trained on the FFHQ dataset [27], a dataset of photographs at high resolution. We use the same pre-processing and face normalisation as the authors of that work.

Since we care about closely matching the face in this work, we construct floating-point alpha masks from the synthetic renders that de-emphasize the background and allow us to separate the hair. This gives us tuples of renders and alpha masks $\{I^s, I^a, I^{a_{hair}}\}$ for each input. We observe that in order to get accurate matching of face boundaries, the sharp opacity edges of I_a that come from the renderer need to be extended outwards from the face. We compute the distance transfer for the face boundary and produce a quickly decaying falloff by mapping the resulting values, remapped to be in the range $0 - 1$, by x^{10}, where x is the output of the distance transform at a pixel. This is illustrated in Fig. 3.

3.1 Step 1: Sampling

To find a good initialisation, we could sample from the prior of SG2 and take the best match as input to the other steps. However, we found that, for a finite number of samples, this could fail to produce convincing results for faces at an angle, under non frontal illumination etc. because our synthetic data is more varied in pose, lighting and ethnicity than FFHQ. To overcome this problem we annotate a small subset of 2000 samples from SG2 with a series of simple attributes to obtain a set of 33 control vectors, $v_{control}$. These are detailed in the supplementary material. The effect of adding some of these to the mean face of SG2 is shown in Fig. 4. We also select a set of centroids,

Fig. 4. Example of adding our control vectors to the 'mean' face of SG2: (a) face angle; (b) hair length (including headgear); (c) beard length; (d) hair curlyness. Note that these can be found by only rough annotations of a small number of samples.

$v_{centroid}$, to sample around. As can be seen in Fig. 5, these are selected to be

somewhat balanced in terms of sex, skin tone and age, and are chosen empirically. We are unable to prove conclusively that this leads to greater overall fairness [16], and acknowledge that this sensitive issue needs closer examination in future work.

The loss used in the sampling step is a combination of the LPIPS distance [46], an L1 loss with different weights for colour and luminance, and landmark loss based on 68 points computed with DLIB [29].

This loss is computed at a quarter resolution of 256^2 pixels after low pass filtering, and multiplication with the mask I^a. We do not compute the loss at full resolution because our synthetics do not exhibit fine-scale details, and we use a low-pass filter to not penalise their presence in the result. The entire loss function for the sampling step is thus:

$$
\begin{aligned}
L_{sampling} = & L_{LPIPS}(r(I^s * I^a), r(G(w^s) * I^a)) \\
& + \lambda_{lum} * \|y(r(I^s * I^a)) - y(r(G(w^s) * I^a))\|^1 \\
& + \lambda_{col} * \|u(r(I^s * I^a)) - u(r(G(w^s) * I^a))\|^1 \\
& + \lambda_{landm} * \|l(r(I^s * I^a)) - l(r(G(w^s) * I^a))\|^2,
\end{aligned}
\tag{1}
$$

where r is the resampling function that changes image size after Gaussian filtering, u separates out the colour channels in the YUV colour space, y the luminance channel, G is the pretrained SG2 generator, I^s a synthetic image, w^s a latent code sample, and l the landmark detector. λ_{lum} is set to 0.1, λ_{col} to 0.01, and λ_{landm} to $1e-5$.

For each sample at this stage of our method, we pick one of the centroids $v_{centroid}$ with uniform probability, and add Gaussian noise to it.

We then combine this with a random sample of our control vectors to vary pose, light, expression etc. The i'th sample is thus obtained as:

$$
\begin{aligned}
w_i^s = & s(v_{centroid}) + \mathcal{N}(0.0, \sigma^2) \\
& + v_{control} * N_{uniform} * 2.0,
\end{aligned}
\tag{2}
$$

where s is the random centroid selection function, $\sigma^2 = 0.25$, and $N_{uniform}$ is uniform noise to scale the control vectors.

Fig. 5. Our manually curated set of centroids for sampling.

The output of this stage is simply the best w^s under the loss in Eq. 1, for any of the 512 samples taken.

3.2   Step 2: Latent Code Refinement

In step 2, we refine the previously obtained w^s while keeping the results constrained to the set of photorealistic images the SG2 generator can produce. The intuition is that any convex combination of samples from the prior in the latent space also leads to realistic images when decoded through G. We highlight that w^n is the current point in the latent space, and updated at every iteration. It is initialised with the result from step 1.

At each step, we draw 512 samples using the same procedure as before. Each of these sample proposals w^p is obtained as:

$$w_i^p = s(v_{centroid}) + \mathcal{N}(0.0, \sigma^2). \tag{3}$$

To ensure samples are sufficiently close to the current w^n, we interpolate each w_i^p with w^n using a random weight drawn at uniform from the range $0.25 - 0.75$.

We then optimise for a set of weights, α, which determine how the w_i^ps and current w^n are combined. It is an important detail that we use sets of α for each of the 18 StyleGAN2 latent space inputs for this optimisation, i.e. α is a matrix of shape $[512 + 1, 18]$ (note how the current w^n is included).

We constrain the optimisation to make sure each row of α sums to 1 using the softmax function, ensuring a convex combination of the samples. In addition to α, we include the control vectors in the optimisation, which are scaled by a learnable parameter β. Because this last step could potentially lead to solutions far outside the space of plausible images, we clamp β to 2.0. The loss is the same as Eq. 1, just without the non-differentiable landmark term, i.e. with λ_{landm} set to 0.

We use 96 outer iterations for which the sample proposals w^p are redrawn, and α and β reset so that the current w^n is the starting point (i.e. β is set to zero, and $alpha$ to one only for the current w^n). For each of these outer loops, we optimise α and β using Adam [31] with a learning rate of 0.01 in an inner loop. We divide the initial learning rate by 10.0 for every 4 iterations in that inner loop, and return the best result at any point, which gives us the refined w^n. We name this algorithm Convex Set Approximate Nearest Neighbour Search (CS-ANN). More details can be found in the supplementary material.

3.3   Step 3: Synthetic Fit and Latent Code Interpolation

To fit SG2 to the synthetic image I^s, we use the method of [28] with minor modifications based on empirical observation. We set the number of total steps to 1000, the initial learning rate to 0.01, and the initial additive noise to 0.01. These changes are justified as we start from w^n and so have a much-improved initialisation compared to the original algorithm. We also mask the loss using the same I^a as above.

Having obtained a latent code w^s that closely resembles the synthetic input image I^s, and a latent code that describes that apprximate nearest neighbour I^n, we can combine them in such a way that preserves the overall facial geometry

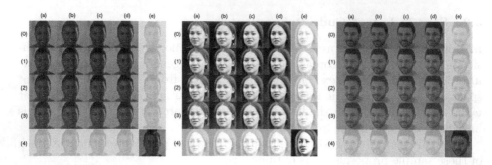

Fig. 6. Interpolating between the output of step 2 (a0) and the output of the exact fit to the synthetics (e4). $(a-e)$ represent the number of latent codes used for blending, and $(0-4)$ the floating point weights for them.

of I^s but has the fine detail of I^n. We use simple interpolation to do this, *i.e.* the final latent code is obtained as:

$$w^{final} = w_s * \sqrt{\alpha} + w_n * \sqrt{1.0 - \alpha}, \tag{4}$$

where w^{final} is a candidate for the final output of our method. We generate candidates by letting α retain the first $\{1, 3, 5, 7\}$ of the 18 latent codes with a floating point weight of $\{1.0, 0.9, 0.8, 0.7\}$ each. An example of the effect of this interpolation can be seen in Fig. 6.

3.4   Step 4: Result Sample Selection

Having obtained a sequence of proposals, from step 1–4, we simply select the one that matches input most using the Structural Similarity (SSIM) [44] metric at a resoluton of 368^2 pixels, which we empirically found to give better qualitative results than the LPIPS distance. We hypothesise that this is due to the fact that perceptual losses prioritise texture over shape [18], and alignment of facial features is important for effective domain adaptation. We note that step 1–3 are run ten times with different random seeds to ensure that even difficult samples are matched with good solutions.

4   Experiments

We want to establish how realistic the images generated by our method are, and how well they preserve the semantics of the synthetic images, specifically head pose and facial features. To do so, we obtain a diverse set of 1000 synthetic images, and process with them with our method, as well as two baselines.

We evaluate our algorithm quantitatively against the fitting method proposed in [28], wich was designed to provide a latent embedding constrained to the domain of valid images in a pretrained SG2 model, and also operates at 1K resolution. This method is referred to as the *StyleGAN2 Baseline*.

To assess how well we can match face pose and expression, we additionally compare facial landmark similarity as computed by OpenFace [4].

A qualitative comparison is made to the *StyleGAN2 Baseline*, and Cycle-GAN [50], with the latter trained on the entirety of our synthetic dataset. We conducted a user study to assess the perceived realism of our results compared to the *StyleGAN2 Baseline* as well as the input images, and to provide an initial assessment of loss of semantics.

We make use of two variants of our results throughout this section. For *Ours (only face)*, we replace the background and hair using the masks from the synthetic data by compositing them using a Laplacian Pyramid [11]. Because of the close alignment of our results with the input, this produces almost no visible artefacts. This allows us to ensure that the background does not impact the quantitative metrics., and to isolate just the appearance change of the face itself.

4.1 Qualitative Experiments

We train CycleGAN on FFHQ as well as a dataset of 12000 synthetic images, using the default training parameters suggested by the authors. Despite having access to the synthetic training data, and using a much tighter crop, we found the results after 50 epochs unconvincing. Even at 128^2, the images show artefacts, and lack texture detail. We show some results in Fig. 7, and more in the supplementary material. Because of the overall quality of the results and because this method has access to the entire synthetic dataset during training, we do not include it in our user study. Instead, we focus on the *StyleGAN2 Baseline* for extensive evaluation.

We show each annotator three images: The synthetic input, the baseline result and our result, in random order. We ask if our result or the baseline is more photorealistic, and which image is the overall most realistic looking, *i.e.* comparable to a real photograph. Finally, we ask if the synthetic image and our result could be the same image of the same person. In this case, we let each annotator answer {Definitely No, Slightly No, Slightly Yes, Definitely Yes}.

From the annotation of 326 images, our results are considered more photoreal than the *StyleGAN2 Baseline* in 94.48% of cases. In 95.1% of responses, our result was considered more realistic looking than the input or the baseline.

In terms of whether the annotators thought the input and our result could be a photograph of the same person, the responses to the options {Definitely No, Slightly No, Slightly Yes, Definitely Yes} were selected {18.71, 19.1, 30.67, 31.6} percent of the time. Despite the large gap in appearance, and the fact that our results are designed to alter aspects of the face like freckles which could be considered part of identity, roughly 60% still believed our results sufficiently similar to pass as photograph of the same person at the same moment in time.

Figure 8 shows some of our results compared to the input synthetic images and the baseline.

Synthetic   Ours (only face)   CycleGAN

Fig. 7. Representative comparison of results of our *zero-shot* method vs CycleGAN trained on the whole synthetic dataset. Note how CycleGAN is unable to change the input images enough to make them look realistic. We suggest viewing this figure zoomed in.

Synthetic	Ours (only face)	Ours	SG2 Baseline

Fig. 8. Representative comparison of results of our method vs the *StyleGAN2 Baseline*. Both variants of our method are able to produce substantially more realistic samples with much greater detail. We suggest viewing this figure zoomed in.

(a) IS and FID (to FFHQ) - large crop.

	IS	FID (to FFHQ)
SG2 Baseline	3.4965	90.342
Ours (only face)	3.3187	**78.728**
Ours	**3.653**	81.06

(b) IS and FID (to FFHQ) - tight crop.

	IS	FID (to FFHQ)
SG2 Baseline	3.398	78.185
Ours (only face)	**3.464**	**70.731**
Ours	3.435	76.947

Fig. 9. *Ours (only face)* uses the same background and hair as the renders, while *Ours* replaces the entire image with our fit. We hypothesise that the difference in FID between *Ours (only face)* and *Ours* is because the background HDRs are visible in the renders, and those backgrounds are photographs. Note that we resize the large crop to match CycleGAN resolution when calculating the IS.

4.2 Quantitative Experiments

The preservation of important facial features is also assessed quantitatively by examing the alignment of 68 landmarks [4]. On our 1024^2 images, the median absolute error in pixels is just 20.2 horizontally, and 14.2 vertically.

We illustrate alignment errors per landmark in Fig. 10. The results indicate that the biggest errors occur on the boundary of the face near the ears, and that in the face region the eyebrows and lips have the highest degree of misalignment. Since FFHQ contains mostly smiling subjects, or images of people with their mouth closed, it is unsurprising that the diverse facial expressions from the synthetic data would show the greatest discrepancy in these features. We emphasize however, that these errors are less than two percent of the effective image resolution on average.

Fig. 10. Standard deviation of the L_1 landmark error in our results (scaled 20× for figure). Blue/red = horizontal/vertical error. (Color figurre online)

We also compute both the FID [21] and IS [38] metrics. The results are shown in Fig. 9 for the large and small crops used throughout this paper. Our method improves the FID signifcantly compared to the baseline, and slightly in case of the IS. This backs up the user study in terms of the perceptual plausibility of our results, but a larger number of samples would be beneficial for a conclusive result.

The FID difference between *Ours* and *Ours (only face)* shows that the background can significantly impact this metric, which is not reflected in human assessment.

5   Conclusions

We have presented a novel zero-shot algorithm for improving the realism of non-photorealistic synthetic renders of human faces. The user study indicates that it produces images which look more photorealistic than the synthetic images themselves. It also shows that previous work on embedding images in the StyleGAN2 latent space produces results of inferior visual quality.

This result is reflected in quantitative terms in both the FID and IS metrics comparing our result to real images from FFHQ. CycleGAN, having access to a large dataset of synthetic images which our method never sees, and working on an inherently easier crop, is clearly not able to compare with our results qualitatively or quantitatively as well.

A downside of our method is that it requires substantial processing time per image. We hypothesise that this could be amortised by training a model that predicts the StyleGan2 embeddings directly from synthetic images once a large enough dataset has been collected. We leave temporal consistency for processing animations as future work, and show more results as well as failure cases (for which the algorithm can simply be repeated with a different random seed) in the supplementary material.

We would like to conclude by noting that our algorithm works across a wide range of synthetic styles (due to its zero-shot nature), and even with some non-photoreal images. Examples of this can be seen in Fig. 11.

Fig. 11. Our method applied to synthetic characters from popular culture. Left to right, row by row, these are: Nathan Drake from Uncharted, Geralt of Rivia from the Witcher, Flynn Rider from Tangled, Aloy from Horizon Zero Dawn, Grand Moff Tarkin from Rogue One, and Ellie from The Last of Us. We note that this is the output of only step 1 and 2 of our method. This indicates that we can find visually plausible nearest neighbours even with some exaggerated facial proportions.

References

1. Abdal, R., Qin, Y., Wonka, P.: Image2StyleGAN++: How to edit the embedded images? (2019)
2. Abdal, R., Qin, Y., Wonka, P.: Image2StyleGAN: How to embed images into the StyleGAN latent space? CoRR abs/1904.03189 (2019). http://arxiv.org/abs/1904.03189
3. AlBahar, B., Huang, J.B.: Guided image-to-image translation with bi-directional feature transformation (2019)
4. Baltrusaitis, T., Zadeh, A., Lim, Y.C., Morency, L.: OpenFace 2.0: facial behavior analysis toolkit. In: 2018 13th IEEE International Conference on Automatic Face Gesture Recognition (FG 2018), pp. 59–66, May 2018. https://doi.org/10.1109/FG.2018.00019
5. Baltrusaitis, T., et al.: A high fidelity synthetic face framework for computer vision. Technical Report MSR-TR-2020-24, Microsoft (July 2020). https://www.microsoft.com/en-us/research/publication/high-fidelity-face-synthetics/
6. Benaim, S., Wolf, L.: One-shot unsupervised cross domain translation. CoRR abs/1806.06029 (2018). http://arxiv.org/abs/1806.06029
7. Bérard, P., Bradley, D., Gross, M., Beeler, T.: Lightweight eye capture using a parametric model. ACM Trans. Graph. **35**(4), 1–12 (2016). https://doi.org/10.1145/2897824.2925962
8. Bi, S., Sunkavalli, K., Perazzi, F., Shechtman, E., Kim, V.G., Ramamoorthi, R.: Deep CG2Real: synthetic-to-real translation via image disentanglement. In: Proceedings of the IEEE/CVF International Conference on Computer Vision (ICCV), October 2019
9. Bishop, C.M.: Mixture density networks. Technical report, Citeseer (1994)
10. Burt, P.J.: Fast filter transform for image processing. Comput. Graph. Image Proc. **16**(1), 20–51 (1981). https://doi.org/10.1016/0146-664X(81)90092-7
11. Burt, P.J., Adelson, E.H.: The Laplacian pyramid as a compact image code. In: Fischler, M.A., Firschein, O. (eds.) Readings in Computer Vision, pp. 671–679. Morgan Kaufmann, San Francisco (1987). https://doi.org/10.1016/B978-0-08-051581-6.50065-9
12. Cherian, A., Sullivan, A.: Sem-GAN: semantically-consistent image-to-image translation. In: 2019 IEEE Winter Conference on Applications of Computer Vision (WACV), pp. 1797–1806, January 2019. https://doi.org/10.1109/WACV.2019.00196
13. Dinh, L., Krueger, D., Bengio, Y.: Nice: Non-linear independent components estimation (2014)
14. Dinh, L., Sohl-Dickstein, J., Bengio, S.: Density estimation using real NVP (2016)
15. Fu, H., Gong, M., Wang, C., Batmanghelich, K., Zhang, K., Tao, D.: Geometry-consistent adversarial networks for one-sided unsupervised domain mapping. CoRR abs/1809.05852 (2018). http://arxiv.org/abs/1809.05852
16. Gajane, P.: On formalizing fairness in prediction with machine learning. CoRR abs/1710.03184 (2017). http://arxiv.org/abs/1710.03184
17. Gecer, B., Bhattarai, B., Kittler, J., Kim, T.: Semi-supervised adversarial learning to generate photorealistic face images of new identities from 3D morphable model. CoRR abs/1804.03675 (2018). http://arxiv.org/abs/1804.03675
18. Geirhos, R., Rubisch, P., Michaelis, C., Bethge, M., Wichmann, F.A., Brendel, W.: ImageNet-trained CNNs are biased towards texture; increasing shape bias improves accuracy and robustness. CoRR abs/1811.12231 (2018). http://arxiv.org/abs/1811.12231

19. Goodfellow, I.J., et al.: Generative Adversarial Networks. ArXiv e-prints (June 2014)
20. Gutmann, M., Hyvärinen, A.: Noise-contrastive estimation: a new estimation principle for unnormalized statistical models. In: Teh, Y.W., Titterington, M. (eds.) Proceedings of the Thirteenth International Conference on Artificial Intelligence and Statistics. Proceedings of Machine Learning Research, vol. 9, pp. 297–304. PMLR, Chia Laguna Resort, Sardinia, Italy, 13–15 May 2010. http://proceedings.mlr.press/v9/gutmann10a.html
21. Heusel, M., Ramsauer, H., Unterthiner, T., Nessler, B., Klambauer, G., Hochreiter, S.: GANs trained by a two time-scale update rule converge to a nash equilibrium. CoRR abs/1706.08500 (2017). http://arxiv.org/abs/1706.08500
22. Huang, X., Belongie, S.: Arbitrary style transfer in real-time with adaptive instance normalization. In: International Conference on Computer Vision (ICCV), Venice, Italy (2017). https://vision.cornell.edu/se3/wp-content/uploads/2017/08/adain.pdf. oral
23. Huang, X., Liu, M.-Y., Belongie, S., Kautz, J.: Multimodal unsupervised image-to-image translation. In: Ferrari, V., Hebert, M., Sminchisescu, C., Weiss, Y. (eds.) ECCV 2018, Part III. LNCS, vol. 11207, pp. 179–196. Springer, Cham (2018). https://doi.org/10.1007/978-3-030-01219-9_11
24. Isola, P., Zhu, J., Zhou, T., Efros, A.A.: Image-to-image translation with conditional adversarial networks. CoRR abs/1611.07004 (2016). http://arxiv.org/abs/1611.07004
25. Jahanian, A., Chai, L., Isola, P.: On the "steerability" of generative adversarial networks. CoRR abs/1907.07171 (2019). http://arxiv.org/abs/1907.07171
26. Jimenez Rezende, D., Mohamed, S., Wierstra, D.: Stochastic Backpropagation and Approximate Inference in Deep Generative Models. ArXiv e-prints (January 2014)
27. Karras, T., Laine, S., Aila, T.: A style-based generator architecture for generative adversarial networks. CoRR abs/1812.04948 (2018). http://arxiv.org/abs/1812.04948
28. Karras, T., Laine, S., Aittala, M., Hellsten, J., Lehtinen, J., Aila, T.: Analyzing and improving the image quality of StyleGAN (2019)
29. Kazemi, V., Sullivan, J.: One millisecond face alignment with an ensemble of regression trees. In: 2014 IEEE Conference on Computer Vision and Pattern Recognition, pp. 1867–1874, June 2014. https://doi.org/10.1109/CVPR.2014.241
30. Kingma, D.P., Welling, M.: Auto-Encoding Variational Bayes. ArXiv e-prints (December 2013)
31. Kingma, D.P., Ba, J.: Adam: A method for stochastic optimization. arXiv preprint arXiv:1412.6980 (2014)
32. Kingma, D.P., Dhariwal, P.: Glow: Generative flow with invertible 1x1 convolutions (2018)
33. Larochelle, H., Murray, I.: The neural autoregressive distribution estimator. In: The Proceedings of the 14th International Conference on Artificial Intelligence and Statistics. JMLR: W and CP, vol. 15, pp. 29–37 (2011)
34. Lin, J., Xia, Y., Liu, S., Qin, T., Chen, Z.: Zstgan: An adversarial approach for unsupervised zero-shot image-to-image translation. CoRR abs/1906.00184 (2019). http://arxiv.org/abs/1906.00184
35. Liu, M.Y., et al.: Few-shot unsupervised image-to-image translation. In: The IEEE International Conference on Computer Vision (ICCV), October 2019
36. Mori, M., MacDorman, K., Kageki, N.: The uncanny valley. IEEE Robot. Autom. Mag. **19**, 98–100 (2012). https://doi.org/10.1109/MRA.2012.2192811

37. Radford, A., Metz, L., Chintala, S.: Unsupervised representation learning with deep convolutional generative adversarial networks. CoRR abs/1511.06434 (2015). http://arxiv.org/abs/1511.06434
38. Salimans, T., Goodfellow, I.J., Zaremba, W., Cheung, V., Radford, A., Chen, X.: Improved techniques for training GANs. CoRR abs/1606.03498 (2016). http:// arxiv.org/abs/1606.03498
39. Sohl-Dickstein, J., Weiss, E.A., Maheswaranathan, N., Ganguli, S.: Deep unsupervised learning using nonequilibrium thermodynamics. CoRR abs/1503.03585 (2015). http://arxiv.org/abs/1503.03585
40. Sutherland, D.J., et al.: Generative Models and Model Criticism via Optimized Maximum Mean Discrepancy. ArXiv e-prints (November 2016)
41. Uria, B., Murray, I., Larochelle, H.: RNADE: the real-valued neural autoregressive density-estimator. Adv. Neural Inf. Proc. Syst. **26**, 2175–2183 (2013)
42. Wang, C., Zheng, H., Yu, Z., Zheng, Z., Gu, Z., Zheng, B.: Discriminative region proposal adversarial networks for high-quality image-to-image translation. CoRR abs/1711.09554 (2017). http://arxiv.org/abs/1711.09554
43. Wang, T.C., Liu, M.Y., Zhu, J.Y., Tao, A., Kautz, J., Catanzaro, B.: High-resolution image synthesis and semantic manipulation with conditional GANs (2017)
44. Wang, Z., Simoncelli, E.P., Bovik, A.C.: Multiscale structural similarity for image quality assessment. In: The Thrity-Seventh Asilomar Conference on Signals, Systems Computers, 2003, vol. 2, pp. 1398–1402, November 2003. https://doi.org/10.1109/ACSSC.2003.1292216
45. Wrenninge, M., Villemin, R., Hery, C.: Path traced subsurface scattering using anisotropic phase functions and non-exponential free flights. Technical report
46. Zhang, R., Isola, P., Efros, A.A., Shechtman, E., Wang, O.: The unreasonable effectiveness of deep features as a perceptual metric. CoRR abs/1801.03924 (2018). http://arxiv.org/abs/1801.03924
47. Zhang, R., Pfister, T., Li, J.: Harmonic unpaired image-to-image translation. CoRR abs/1902.09727 (2019). http://arxiv.org/abs/1902.09727
48. Zhao, S., Ren, H., Yuan, A., Song, J., Goodman, N.D., Ermon, S.: Bias and generalization in deep generative models: An empirical study. CoRR abs/1811.03259 (2018). http://arxiv.org/abs/1811.03259
49. Zheng, Z., Yu, Z., Zheng, H., Yang, Y., Shen, H.T.: One-shot image-to-image translation via part-global learning with a multi-adversarial framework. CoRR abs/1905.04729 (2019). http://arxiv.org/abs/1905.04729
50. Zhu, J.Y., Park, T., Isola, P., Efros, A.A.: Unpaired image-to-image translation using cycle-consistent adversarial networks. In: Computer Vision (ICCV), 2017 IEEE International Conference on (2017)

Attentive Prototype Few-Shot Learning with Capsule Network-Based Embedding

Fangyu Wu[1,2] (iD), Jeremy S. Smith[2] (iD), Wenjin Lu[1] (iD), Chaoyi Pang[3],
and Bailing Zhang[3(✉)] (iD)

[1] Department of Computer Science and Software Engineering, Xi'an
Jiaotong-liverpool University, SuZhou, JiangSu Province, China
{fangyu.wu,wenjin.lu}@xjtlu.edu.cn
[2] Department of Electrical Engineering and Electronic, University of Liverpool,
Liverpool, UK
J.S.Smith@liverpool.ac.uk
[3] School of Computer and Data Engineering, Zhejiang University Ningbo Institute
of Technology, Ningbo, Zhejiang Province, China
{chaoyi.pang,bailing.zhang}@nit.zju.edu.cn

Abstract. Few-shot learning, namely recognizing novel categories with
a very small amount of training examples, is a challenging area of
machine learning research. Traditional deep learning methods require
massive training data to tune the huge number of parameters, which
is often impractical and prone to over-fitting. In this work, we further
research on the well-known few-shot learning method known as prototypical networks for better performance. Our contributions include (1) a
new embedding structure to encode relative spatial relationships between
features by applying a capsule network; (2) a new triplet loss designated
to enhance the semantic feature embedding where similar samples are
close to each other while dissimilar samples are farther apart; and (3) an
effective non-parametric classifier termed attentive prototypes in place of
the simple prototypes in current few-shot learning. The proposed attentive prototype aggregates all of the instances in a support class which
are weighted by their importance, defined by the reconstruction error for
a given query. The reconstruction error allows the classification posterior probability to be estimated, which corresponds to the classification
confidence score. Extensive experiments on three benchmark datasets
demonstrate that our approach is effective for the few-shot classification
task.

Keywords: Few-shot learning · Meta learning · Capsule network ·
Feature embedding · Attentive prototype learning

1 Introduction

Deep learning has been greatly advanced in recent years, with many successful
applications in image processing, speech processing, natural language processing

© Springer Nature Switzerland AG 2020
A. Vedaldi et al. (Eds.): ECCV 2020, LNCS 12373, pp. 237–253, 2020.
https://doi.org/10.1007/978-3-030-58604-1_15

and other fields. However, the successes usually rely on the condition to access a large dataset for training. If the amount of training data is not large enough, the deep neural network would not be sufficiently trained. Consequently, it is significant to develop deep learning for image recognition in the case of a small number of samples, and enhance the adaptability of deep learning models in different problem domains.

Few-shot learning is one of the most promising research areas targeting deep learning models for various tasks with a very small amount of training dataset [24,29,31,34,37,39], i.e., classifying unseen data instances (query examples) into a set of new categories, given just a small number of labeled instances in each class (support examples). The common scenario is a support set with only 1~10 labeled examples per class. As a stark contrast, general classification problems with deep learning models [15,38] often require thousands of examples per class. On the other hand, classes for training and testing sets are from two exclusive sets in few-shot learning, while in traditional classification problems they are the same. A key challenge, in few-shot learning, is to make best use of the limited data available in the support set in order to find the right generalizations as required by the task.

Few-shot learning is often elaborated as a meta-learning problem, with an emphasis on learning prior knowledge shared across a distribution of tasks [21, 34,39]. There are two sub-tasks for meta-learning: an embedding that maps the input into a feature space and a base learner that maps the feature space to task variables. As a simple, efficient and the most popularly used few-shot learning algorithm, the prototypical network [34] tries to solve the problem by learning the metric space to perform classification. A query point (new point) is classified based on the distance between the created prototypical representation of each class and the query point. While the approach is extensively applied, there are a number of limitations that we'd like to address and seek better solutions.

Firstly, the prototypical representations [34,39], generated by deep Convolutional Neural Networks, cannot account for the spatial relations between the parts of the image and are too sensitive to orientation. Secondly, a prototypical network [34] divides the output metric space into disjoint polygons where the nearest neighbor of any point inside a polygon is the pivot of the polygon. This is too rough to reflect various noise effects in the data, thus compromising the discrimination and expressiveness of the prototype. It has been well-known that the performance of such a simple distance-based classification is severely influenced by the existing outliers, especially in the situations of small training sample size [7].

From the aforementioned discussion, we intend to improve the prototype network by proposing a capsule network [32] based embedding model and reconstruction-based prototypical learning within the framework of meta-learning. There are two main components in the proposed scheme: a capsule network-based embedding module which create feature representations, and an improved non-parametric classification scheme with an attentive prototype for each class in the support set, which is obtained by attentive aggregation over the representations of its support instances, where the weights are calculated using the reconstruction error for the query instance.

The training of the proposed network is based on the metric learning algorithm with an improved triplet-like loss, which generalizes the triplet network [33] to allow joint comparison with K negative prototypes in each mini-batch. This makes the feature embedding learning process more tally with the few-shot classification problem. We further propose a semi-hard mining technique to sample informative hard triplets, thus speeding up the convergence and stabilize the training procedure.

In summary, we proposed a new embedding approach for few-shot learning based on a capsule network, which features the capability to encode the part-whole relationships between various visual entities. An improved routing procedure using the DeepCaps mechanism [27] is designed to implement the embedding. With a class-specific output capsule, the proposed network can better preserve the semantic feature representation, and reduce the disturbances from irrelevant noisy information. The proposed attentive prototype scheme is query-dependent, rather than just averaging the feature points of a class for the prototype as in the vanilla prototype network, which means all of the feature points from the support set are attentively weighted in advance, and then the weighting values completely depend on the affinity relations between two feature points from the support set and the query set. By using reconstruction as an efficient expression of the affinity relation, the training points near the query feature point acquire more attention in the calculation of the weighting values.

The proposed approach has been experimentally evaluated on few-shot image classification tasks using three benchmark datasets, i.e. the *mini*ImageNet, *tiered*ImageNet and Fewshot-CIFAR100 datasets. The empirical results verify the superiority of our method over the state-of-the-art approaches. The main contributions of our work are two-fold:

- We put forward a new few-shot classification approach with a capsule-based model, which combines a 3D convolution based on the dynamic routing procedure to obtain a semantic feature representation while preserving the spatial information between visual entities.
- We propose a novel attentive prototype concept to take account of all the instances in a given support class, with each instance being weighted by the reconstruction errors between the query and prototype candidates from the support set. The attentive prototype is robust to outliers by design and also allows the performance to be improved by refraining from making predictions in the absence of sufficient confidence.

2   Related Work

2.1   Few-Shot Learning

Few-shot learning aims to classify novel visual classes when very few labeled samples are available [3,4]. Current methods usually tackle the challenge using meta-learning approaches or metric-learning approaches, with the representative works elaborated below.

Metric learning methods aim to learn a task-invariant metric, which provide an embedding space for learning from few-shot examples. Vinyals et al. [39] introduced the concept of episode training in few-shot learning, where metric learning-based approaches learn a distance metric between a test example and the training examples. Prototypical networks [34] learn a metric space in which classification can be performed by computing distances to prototype representations of each class. The learned embedding model maps the images of the same class closer to each other while different classes are spaced far away. The mean of the embedded support samples are utilized as the prototype to represent the class. The work in [18] goes beyond this by incorporating the context of the entire support set available by looking between the classes and identifying task-relevant features.

There are also interesting works that explore different metrics for the embedding space to provide more complex comparisons between support and query features. For example, the relation module proposed in [37] calculates the relation score between query images to identify unlabeled images. Kim et al. [12] proposed an edge-labeling Graph Neural Network (EGNN) for few-shot classification. Metric-based task-specific feature representation learning has also been presented in many related works. Our work is a further exploration of the prototype based approaches [34,37], aiming to enhance the performance of learning an embedding space by encoding the spatial relationship between features. Then the embedding space generates attentive prototype representations in a query-dependent scheme.

2.2 Capsule Networks

The capsule network [11] is a new type of neural network architecture proposed by Geoffrey Hinton, with the main motivation to address some of the shortcomings of Convolutional Neural Networks (CNNs). For example, the pooling layers of CNNs lose the location information of relevant features, one of the so-called instantiation parameters that characterize the object. Other instanced parameters include scale and rotation, which are also poorly represented in CNNs. Capsule network handles these instantiation parameters explicitly by representing an object or a part of an object. More specifically, a capsule network replaces the mechanisms of the convolution kernel in CNNs by implementing a group of neurons to encode the spatial information and the probability of the existence of objects. The length of the capsule vector is the probability of the features in the image, and the orientation of the vector will represent its instantiation information.

Sabour et al. [32] first proposed a dynamic routing algorithm for capsule networks in 2017 for the bottom-up feature integration, the essence of which is the realization of a clustering algorithm for the information transmission in the model. In [32], a Gaussian mixture model (GMM) was integrated into the feature integration process to adjust network parameters through EM routing.

Since the seminal works [11,32], a number of approaches have been proposed to implement and improve the capsule architecture [13,17,27,43].

Many applications have been attempted by applying capsule networks, for example, intent detection [40], text classification [25] and computer vision [41, 42]. A sparse, unsupervised capsules network [28] was proposed showing that the network generalizes better than supervised masking, while potentially enabling deeper capsule networks. Rajasegaran et al. [27] proposed a deep capsule network architecture called DeepCaps that adapts the original routing algorithm for 3D convolutions and increases its performance on more complex datasets.

3   Method

3.1   Approach Details

In this section, we first revisit the DeepCaps network [27], which is designed for more complex image datasets. We then extend it to the scenario of few-shot learning and describe the proposed algorithm in detail.

DeepCaps Revisit. DeepCaps is a deep capsule network architecture proposed in [27] to improve the performance of the capsule networks for more complex image datasets. It extends the dynamic routing algorithm in [32] to stacked multiple layers, which essentially uses a 3D convolution to learn the spatial information between the capsules. The model consists of four main modules: skip connected CapsCells, 3D convolutional CapsCells, a fully-connected capsule layer and a decoder network. The skip-connected CapsCells have three ConvCaps layers, the first layer output is convolved and skip-connected to the last layer output. The motivation behind skipping connections is to borrow the idea from residual networks to sustain a sound gradient flow in a deep model. The element-wise layer is used to combine the outputs of the two capsule layers after skipping the connection.

DeepCaps has a unit with a ConvCaps3D layer, in which the number of route iterations is kept at 3. Then, before dynamic routing, the output of ConvCaps is flattened and connected with the output of the capsule, which is then followed by 3D routing (in CapsCell 3). Intuitively, this step helps to extend the model to a wide range of different datasets. For example, for a dataset composed of images with less rich information, such as MNIST, the low-level capsule from cell 1 or cell 2 is sufficient, while for a more complex dataset, we need the deeper 3D ConvCaps to capture rich information content. Once all capsules are collected and connected, they are routed to the class capsule through the fully-connected capsule layer.

Network Architecture. As explained in the Introduction, our proposed model has two parts: (1) a modified DeepCaps network with improved triplet-like loss that learns the deep embedding space, and (2) a non-parameter classification scheme that produces a prototype vector for each class candidate, which is

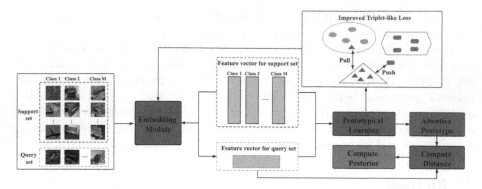

Fig. 1. Framework of the proposed method for few-shot learning. We perform joint end-to-end training of the Embedding Module (modified DeepCaps) together with the Prototypical Learning via an improved triplet-like loss from the training dataset. The well-learned embedding features are used to compute the distances among the query images and the attentive prototype generated from the support set. The final classification is performed by calculating the posterior probability for the query instance.

derived from the attentive aggregation over the representations of its support instances, where the weights are calculated using the reconstruction errors for the query instance from respective support instances in the embedding space. The final classification is performed by calculating the posterior probability for the query instance based on the distances between the embedding vectors of the query and the attentive prototype. Figure 1 schematically illustrates an overview of our approach to few-shot image classification. Each of the parts is described in detail below.

Embedding Module. We follow the practice of episodic training in [39] which is the most popular and effective meta learning methodology [34,37]. We construct support set S and query set Q from D_{train} in each episode to train the model.

$$
\begin{aligned}
S &= \{s_1, s_2, .., s_K\}, \\
Q &= \{q_1, s_2, ..., q_N\},
\end{aligned}
\tag{1}
$$

where K and N represent the number of samples in the support set and query set for each class, respectively. As shown in Fig. 2, we first feed the samples S and Q into the convolution layer and CapsCells, then the collected capsules are routed to the class capsules after the Flat Caps layer. Here, the decision making happens via L_2 and the input image is encoded into the final capsule vector. The length of the capsule's output vector represents the probability that the object represented by the capsule exists in the current input. We assume the class capsules as $P \in Y^{b \times d}$ which consists of the activity vectors for all classes, where b and d represents the number of classes in the final class capsule and capsule dimension, respectively. Then, we only feed the activity vector of predicted class $P_m \in Y^{1 \times d}$ into the final embedding space in our setting, where

$m = argmax_i(\||P_i\||_2^2)$. The embedding space acts as a better regularizer for the capsule networks, since it is forced to learn the activity vectors jointly within a constrained Y^d space. The function of margin loss used in DeepCaps enhances the class probability of the true class, while suppressing the class probabilities of the other classes. In this paper, we propose the improved triplet-like loss based on an attentive prototype to train the embedding module and learn more discriminative features.

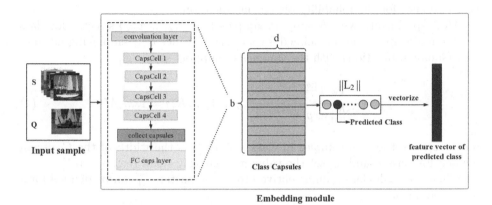

Fig. 2. The architecture of the embedding module in which obtains only the activity vectors of the predicted class.

Attentive Prototype. The prototypical network in [34] computes a D dimensional feature representation $p_i \in \mathbb{R}^D$, or prototype, of each class through an embedding function $f_\phi : \mathbb{R}^D \to \mathbb{R}^M$ with learnable parameters ϕ. Each prototype is the mean vector of the embedded support points belonging to its class:

$$p_i = \frac{1}{|s_i|} \sum_{(x_i, y_i) \in s_i} f_\phi(x_i) \tag{2}$$

where each $x_i \in s_i$ is the D-dimensional feature vector of an example from class i. Given a distance function $d : \mathbb{R}^D \times \mathbb{R}^D \to [0, +\infty)$, prototypical networks produce a distribution over classes for a query point x based on a softmax over distances to the prototypes in the embedding space:

$$p_\phi(y = t|x) = \frac{exp(-d(f_\phi(x), p_t))}{\sum_{t'} exp(-d(f_\phi(x), p_{t'}))} \tag{3}$$

Learning proceeds by minimizing the negative log-probability $J(\phi) = -logp_\phi(y = t|x)$ of the true class t via Stochastic Gradient Descent (SGD). Most prototypical networks for few-shot learning use some simple non-parametric classifiers, such as kNN. It is well known that non-parametric classifiers are usually affected by existing outliers [6], which is particularly serious when the number of samples is small, the scenario addressed by few-shot learning. A practical and reliable classifier should be robust to outliers. Motivated by this observation, we propose an improved algorithm based on the local mean classifier [22]. Given all prototype instances of a class, we calculate their reconstruction errors for the query instance, which are then used for the weighted average of prototype instances. The new prototype aggregates attentive contributions from all of the instances. The reconstruction error between the new prototype and the query instance not only provides a discrimination criteria for the classes, but also serves as a reference for the reliability of the classification.

More specifically, with K support samples $\{x_{i1}, x_{i2}, ..., x_{iK}\}$ selected for class i, a membership γ_{ij} can be defined for a query instance q by employing normalized Gaussian functions with the samples in support sets, e.g.,

$$\gamma_{ij} = \frac{exp(\frac{||q-x_{ij}||^2}{2\sigma_i^2})}{\sum_{l=1}^{K} exp(\frac{||q-x_{il}||^2}{2\sigma_i^2})}, j = 1, ..., K, i = 1, ..., M \tag{4}$$

where x_{ij} are the j-th samples in class i, and σ_i is the width of the Gaussian defined for class i, and we set the value σ_i relatively small (e.g., σ_i=0.1).

Then, for each class i, an attentive prototype pattern $\hat{q}_i$ can be defined for a query sample q

$$\hat{q}_i = \frac{\sum_{j=1}^{K} \gamma_{ij} x_{ij}}{\sum_{l=1}^{K} \gamma_{ij}}, i = 1, ..., M \tag{5}$$

where γ_{ij} is defined in Eq. 4 and $\hat{q}_i$ can be considered as the generalized support samples from class i for the query instance q. Here we want to ensure that an image q^a (anchor) of a specific class in the query set is closer to the attentive prototype of the positive class $\hat{q}^p$ (positive) than it is to multiple $\hat{q}^n$ (negative) attentive prototypes.

$$||q^a - \hat{q}^p||_2^2 + \alpha < ||q^a - \hat{q}^n||_2^2, \forall q^a \in Q. \tag{6}$$

f where α is a margin that is enforced between positive and negative pairs, Q is the query set cardinality MN. The loss that is being minimized is then:

$$\sum_{m=1}^{MN} \left[||f(q_m^a) - f(\hat{q}_m^p)||_2^2 - ||f(q_m^a) - f(\hat{q}_m^n)||_2^2 + \alpha \right]_+ \tag{7}$$

For image classification, a query image can be classified based on the comparison of the errors between the reconstructed vectors and the presented image. That is, a query image q is assigned to class m^* if

$$m^* = \underset{m}{argmin}\, err_m \tag{8}$$

where $err_m = ||q - \hat{q}_m||, m = 1, ..., M$.

Improved Triplet-Like Loss. In order to ensure fast convergence it is crucial to select triplets that violate the triplet constraint in Eq. 7. The traditional triplet loss interacts with only one negative sample (and equivalently one negative class) for each update in the network, while we actually need to compare the query image with multiple different classes in few-shot classification. Hence, the triplet loss may not be effective for the feature embedding learning, particularly when we have several classes to handle in the few-shot classification setting. Inspired by [1,35], we generalize the traditional triplet loss with E-negatives prototypes to allow simultaneous comparisons jointly with the E negative prototypes instead of just one negative prototype, in one mini-batch. This extension makes the feature comparison more effective and faithful to the few-shot learning procedure, since in each update, the network can compare a sample with multiple negative classes.

In particular, we randomly choose the E negative prototypes $\hat{q}^{n_e}, e = \{1, 2, ..., E\}$ to form into a triplet. Accordingly, the optimization objective evolves to:

$$\mathcal{L}(q_{m^a}, \hat{q}_{m^p}, \hat{x}_m^n) = \sum_{m=1}^{MN} \frac{1}{E} \sum_{e=1}^{E} \left[||f(q_{m^a}) - f(\hat{q}_{m^p}))||_2^2 \right. \tag{9}$$
$$\left. - ||f(q_{m^a}) - f(\hat{q}_{m^{n_e}})||_2^2 + \alpha \right]_+$$

For the sample q_m^a in the query set, the optimization shall maximize the distance to the negative prototype q_m^n to be larger than the distance to the positive prototypes q_m^p in the feature space. For each anchor sample q_m^a, we then learn the positive prototype q_m^p from the support set of the same class as q_m^a and further randomly select E other negative prototypes whose classes are different from q_m^a. Compared with the traditional triplet loss, each forward update in our improved Triplet-like loss includes more inter-class variations, thus making the learnt feature embedding more discriminative for samples from different classes.

Mining hard triplets is an important part of metric learning with the triplet loss, as otherwise training will soon stagnate [10]. This is because when the model begins to converge, the embedding space learns how to correctly map the triples relatively quickly. Thus most triples satisfying the margin will not contribute to the gradient in the learning process. To speed up the convergence and stabilize the training procedure, we propose a new hard-triplet mining strategy to sample more informative hard triplets in each episode. Specifically, triplets will be randomly selected in each episode as described above, we then check whether the sampled triplets satisfy the margin. The triplets that have already met the margin will be removed and the network training will proceed with the remaining triplets.

4 Experiments

Extensive experiments have been conducted to evaluate and compare the proposed method for few-shot classification using on three challenging few-shot learning benchmarks datasets, *mini*ImageNet [39], *tiered*ImageNet [29] and Fewshot-CIFAR100 (FC100) [24]. All the experiments are implemented based on PyTorch and run with NVIDIA 2080ti GPUs.

4.1 Datasets

*mini*ImageNet is the most popular few-shot learning benchmark proposed by [39] and derived from the original ILSVRC-12 dataset [30]. It contains 100 randomly sampled different categories, each with 600 images of size 84 × 84 pixels. The *tiered*ImageNet [29] is a larger subset of ILSVRC-12 [30] with 608 classes and 779,165 images in total. The classes in *tiered*ImageNet are grouped into 34 categories corresponding to higher-level nodes in the ImageNet hierarchy curated by humans [2]. Each hierarchical category contains 10 to 20 classes, which are divided into 20 training (351 classes), 6 validation (97 classes) and 8 test (160 classes) categories. **Fewshot-CIFAR100 (FC100)** is based on the popular object classification dataset CIFAR100 [14]. Oreshkin et al. [24] offer a more challenging class split of CIFAR100 for few-shot learning. The FC100 further groups the 100 classes into 20 superclasses. Thus the training set has 60 classes belonging to 12 superclasses, the validation and test data consist of 20 classes each belonging to 5 superclasses each.

4.2 Implementation Details

Following the general few-shot learning experiment settings [34,37], we conducted 5-way 5-shot and 5-way 1-shot classifications. The Adam optimizer is exploited with an initial learning rate of 0.001. The total training episodes on *mini*ImageNet, *tiered*ImageNet and FC100 are 600,000, 1,000,000 and 1,000,000, respectively. The learning rate is dropped by 10% every 100,000 episodes or when the loss enters a plateau. The weight decay is set to 0.0003. We report the mean accuracy (%) over 600 randomly generated episodes from the test set.

4.3 Results Evaluation

Comparison with the Baseline Model. Using the training/testing data split and the procedure described in Sect. 3, the baseline in Table 1, Table 2 and Table 3 evaluate a model with modified DeepCaps, without the attentive prototype. The accuracy is $75.21 \pm 0.43\%$, $78.41 \pm 0.34\%$ and $59.8 \pm 1.0\%$ and in the 5-way 5-shot setting on *mini*ImageNet, *tiered*ImageNet and FC100 respectively. Our baseline results are on a par with those reported in [34,37]. As shown in Table 1, Table 2 and Table 3, using the attentive prototype strategy in the model training with improved triplet-like loss, our method significantly improves the accuracy on all three datasets. There are obvious improvements of approximately +4.96% (from 75.21% to 80.17%), +4.83% (from 78.41% to 83.24%), +2.5% (from 57.3% to 59.8%) under the 5-way 5-shot setting for *mini*ImageNet, *tiered*ImageNet and FC100, respectively. These results indicate that the proposed approach is tolerant to large intra- and inter-class variations and produces marked improvements over the baseline.

Comparison with the State-of-the-Art Methods. We also compare our method with some state-of-the-art methods on *mini*ImageNet,*tiered*ImageNet in

Table 1. Few-shot classification accuracies (%) on *mini*ImageNet.

Few-shot learning method	5-Way 1-Shot	5-Way 5-Shot
Matching Networks [39]	43.56 ± 0.84	55.31 ± 0.73
MAML [5]	48.70 ± 1.84	63.11 ± 0.92
Relation Net [37]	50.44 ± 0.82	65.32 ± 0.70
REPTILE [23]	49.97 ± 0.32	65.99 ± 0.58
Prototypical Net [34]	49.42 ± 0.78	68.20 ± 0.66
Predict Params [26]	59.60 ± 0.41	73.74 ± 0.19
LwoF [8]	60.06 ± 0.14	76.39 ± 0.11
TADAM [24]	58.50 ± 0.30	76.70 ± 0.30
EGNN [12]	–	66.85
EGNN+Transduction [12]	–	76.37
CTM [18]	62.05 ± 0.55	78.63 ± 0.06
wDAE-GNN [9]	62.96 ± 0.15	78.85 ± 0.10
MetaOptNet-SVM-trainval [16]	64.09 ± 0.62	80.00 ± 0.45
CTM, data augment [18]	64.12 ± 0.82	80.51 ± 0.13
Baseline	59.71 ± 0.35	75.21 ± 0.43
Ours	63.23 ± 0.26	80.17 ± 0.33
Ours, data augment	**66.43 ± 0.26**	**82.13 ± 0.21**

Table 1 and Table 2, respectively. On *mini*ImageNet, we achieve a **5-way 1-shot accuracy = 63.23 ± 0.26, 5-way 5-shot accuracy =80.17 ± 0.33%** when using the proposed method, which has a highly competitive performance compared with the state-of-the-art. On *tiered*ImageNet, we arrive at **5-way 1-shot accuracy = 65.53 ± 0.21, 5-way 5-shot accuracy = 83.24 ± 0.18%** which is also very competitive. The previous best result was produced by introducing a Category Traversal Module [18] and data augmentation that can be inserted as a plug-and-play module into most metric-learning based few-shot learners. We further investigate whether the data augmention could work on our model. By training a version of our model with basic data augmentation, we obtain the improved results **5-way 5-shot accuracy = 82.13 ± 0.21%** on *mini*ImageNet. On *tiered*ImageNet, we also observe a performance **5-way 5-shot accuracy = 86.35 ± 0.41%**.

For the FC100 dataset, our proposed method is superior to all the other methods [5, 24, 36] in accuracy. The comparisons consistently confirm the competitiveness of the proposed method on few-shot image classification. In terms of size and computational cost, for the models trained on mini-ImageNet, the proposed model has only 7.22 million parameters, while the ResNet-18 used in the existing SOTA approach has 33.16 million parameters. We also tested both models' inference time, ResNet-18 takes 3.65 ms for a 64 × 64 ×3 image, while our model takes only 1.67 ms for a 64 × 64 ×3 image.

Table 2. Few-shot classification accuracies (%) on *tiered*ImageNet.

Few-shot learning method	5-Way 1-Shot	5-Way 5-Shot
MAML [5]	51.67 ± 1.81	70.30 ± 0.08
Meta-SGD [19], reported by [31]	62.95 ± 0.03	79.34 ± 0.06
LEO [31]	66.33 ± 0.05	81.44 ± 0.09
Relation Net [37]	54.48 ± 0.93	71.32 ± 0.78
Prototypical Net [34]	53.31 ± 0.89	72.69 ± 0.74
EGNN [12]	–	70.98
EGNN+Transduction [12]	–	80.15
CTM [18]	64.78 ± 0.11	81.05 ± 0.52
MetaOptNet-SVM-trainval [16]	65.81 ± 0.74	81.75 ± 0.53
CTM, data augmention [18]	68.41 ± 0.39	84.28 ± 1.73
Baseline	63.25 ± 0.31	78.41 ± 0.34
Ours	65.53 ± 0.21	83.24 ± 0.18
Ours, data augmention	$\mathbf{69.87 \pm 0.32}$	$\mathbf{86.35 \pm 0.41}$

In summary, our proposed attentive prototype learning scheme improve over the previous methods, mainly due to the better embedding space provided by the capsule network and the attentive prototyping scheme. The importance value is used as the weighting value for the support set instances, which is completely dependent on the affinity relationship between the two feature points from the support set and the query. The importance weighting values vary exponentially, with larger value reflecting nearby pairs of feature points and a smaller value for the distant pair. This conforms that the feature points from the support set that are nearer to the query feature point should be given more attention.

Table 3. Few-shot classification accuracies (%) on the FC100 dataset.

Few-shot learning method	5-Way 1-Shot	5-Way 5-Shot	5-Way 10-Shot
MAML [5]	38.1 ± 1.7	50.4 ± 1.0	56.2 ± 0.8
TADAM [24]	40.1 ± 0.4	56.1 ± 0.4	61.6 ± 0.5
MTL [36]	45.1 ± 1.8	57.6 ± 0.9	63.4 ± 0.8
Baseline	44.2 ± 1.3	57.3 ± 0.8	62.8 ± 0.6
Ours	$\mathbf{47.5 \pm 0.9}$	$\mathbf{59.8 \pm 1.0}$	$\mathbf{65.4 \pm 0.5}$

Ablation study: To verify the effectiveness of components in the proposed method, we conducted ablation experiments on the *mini*ImageNet and *tiered*ImageNet datasets. First, to investigate the contribution of the designed attentive prototype method, we compare the performance of the proposed method with vanilla prototypical networks [34]. Then, we verify the effectiveness of our proposed feature embedding module by embedding it into the metric-based algorithm Relation Net [37]. Table 4 summarizes the performance of the different variants of our method.

Table 4. Ablation study on the attentive prototype and embedding module.

Few-shot learning method	*mini*ImageNet		*tiered*ImageNet	
	5-Way 5 shot	10-Way 5 shot	5-Way 5-shot	10-Way 5-shot
Prototypical Net [34]	68.20	-	72.69	-
Ours (average mechanism)	76.32	58.41	80.31	62.17
Ours (attentive prototype)	80.17	63.12	83.24	66.33
Relation Net [37]	65.32	–	71.32	–
Relation Net [37] (our implementation)	80.91	64.34	83.98	67.86

1)*Attentive prototype:* In vanilla prototypical networks [34], the prototypes are defined as the averages the embed features of each class in the support set. Such a simple class-wise feature takes all instances into consideration equally. Our attentive prototype scheme is a better replacement. A variant of DeepCaps is applied with improved triplet-like loss to learn the feature embedding instead of a shallow CNN network. To further verify the effectiveness of our attentive prototype, we also compared the average-based prototypes created from our embedding framework. The experimental results on *mini*ImageNet and *tiered*ImageNet are summarized in Table 4. It can be observed that the attentive prototype gains an approximately 3%-4% increase after replacing the average mechanism. This shows that the attentive prototypes can be more 'typical' when compared to the original average vectors by giving different weights for different instances.

2)*Embedding module:* The embedding is switched from four convolutional blocks in Relation Net [37] to the modified DeepCaps model and the supervision loss is changed to the improved triplet-like loss. Table 4 shows the results obtained by the improvements over the Relation Net. We find that the improved Relation Net exceeds the original model by approximately +10%. This shows the ability of the proposed capsule network-based embedding network to improve the performance of the metric based method. Figure 3 visualizes the feature distribution using t-SNE [20] for the features computed in 5-way 5-shot setting and 10-way 5-shot setting. As can be clearly observed, the improved Relation Net model has more compact and separable clusters, indicating that features are more discriminative for the task. This is caused by the design of the embedding module.

3)*Improved Triplet-like loss:* To help analyze our model and show the benefit of improved Triplet-like loss, we design several comparison methods as follows:

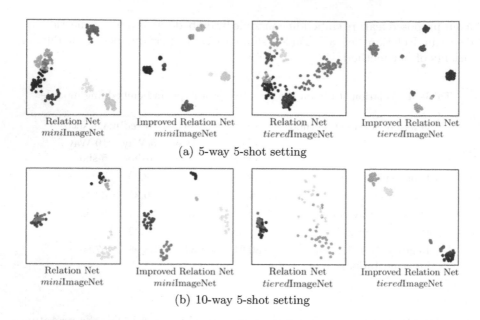

Relation Net
*mini*ImageNet

Improved Relation Net
*mini*ImageNet

Relation Net
*tiered*ImageNet

Improved Relation Net
*tiered*ImageNet

(a) 5-way 5-shot setting

Relation Net
*mini*ImageNet

Improved Relation Net
*mini*ImageNet

Relation Net
*tiered*ImageNet

Improved Relation Net
*tiered*ImageNet

(b) 10-way 5-shot setting

Fig. 3. The t-SNE visualization [20] of the improved feature embeddings learnt by our proposed approach.

Setting-1: Baseline model (modified DeepCaps); Setting-2: Using the attentive prototype strategy in the model training; Setting-3: Based on the Setting 2, we add the improved triplet-like loss to make the feature comparison more effective.

Table 5. Few-shot classification accuracies (%) on *mini*ImageNet.

Few-shot learning method	5-Way 1-Shot	5-Way 5-Shot
Setting-1	59.71 ± 0.35	75.21 ± 0.43
Setting-2	61.76 ± 0.12	78.45 ± 0.23
Setting-3	63.23 ± 0.26	80.17 ± 0.33

With the help of improved triplet-like loss, we observed an improvement of $+1.5\%$ as shown in Table 5. Thus making the learnt feature embedding more discriminative for samples from different classes.

5   Conclusion

In this paper, we proposed a new few-shot learning scheme aiming to improve the metric learning-based prototypical network. Our proposed scheme has the following novel characteristics: (1) a new embedding space created by a capsule network, which is unique in its capability to encode the relative spatial relationship between features. The network is trained with a novel triple-loss designed to learn the embedding space; (2) an effective and robust non-parameter classification scheme, named attentive prototypes, to replace the simple feature average for prototypes. The instances from the support set are taken into account to generate prototypes, with their importance being calculated by the reconstruction error for a given query. Experimental results showed that the proposed method outperforms the other few-shot learning algorithms on all of the miniImageNet, tieredImageNet and FC100 datasets.

References

1. Arik, S.O., Pfister, T.: Attention-based prototypical learning towards interpretable, confident and robust deep neural networks. arXiv preprint arXiv:1902.06292 (2019)
2. Deng, J., Dong, W., Socher, R., Li, L.J., Li, K., Fei-Fei, L.: Imagenet: a large-scale hierarchical image database. In: IEEE Conference on Computer Vision and Pattern Recognition (CVPR), pp. 248–255 (2009)
3. Fe-Fei, L., et al.: A Bayesian approach to unsupervised one-shot learning of object categories. In: IEEE International Conference on Computer Vision (ICCV), pp. 1134–1141 (2003)
4. Fei-Fei, L., Fergus, R., Perona, P.: One-shot learning of object categories. IEEE Trans. Pattern Anal. Mach. Intell. (TPAMI) **28**(4), 594–611 (2006)
5. Finn, C., Abbeel, P., Levine, S.: Model-agnostic meta-learning for fast adaptation of deep networks. In: Proceedings of the 34th International Conference on Machine Learning (ICML), pp. 1126–1135 (2017)
6. Fukunaga, K.: Introduction to Statistical Pattern Recognition. Elsevier, New York (2013)
7. Gao, T., Han, X., Liu, Z., Sun, M.: Hybrid attention-based prototypical networks for noisy few-shot relation classification. In: AAAI Conference on Artificial Intelligence (AAAI) (2019)
8. Gidaris, S., Komodakis, N.: Dynamic few-shot visual learning without forgetting. In: IEEE Conference on Computer Vision and Pattern Recognition (CVPR), pp. 4367–4375 (2018)
9. Gidaris, S., Komodakis, N.: Generating classification weights with GNN denoising autoencoders for few-shot learning. In: IEEE Conference on Computer Vision and Pattern Recognition (CVPR) (2019)
10. Hermans, A., Beyer, L., Leibe, B.: In defense of the triplet loss for person re-identification. arXiv preprint arXiv:1703.07737 (2017)
11. Hinton, G.E., Krizhevsky, A., Wang, S.D.: Transforming auto-encoders. In: Honkela, T., Duch, W., Girolami, M., Kaski, S. (eds.) ICANN 2011, vol. 6791, pp. 44–51. Springer, Berlin, Heidelberg (2011). https://doi.org/10.1007/978-3-642-21735-7_6
12. Kim, J., Kim, T., Kim, S., Yoo, C.D.: Edge-labeling graph neural network for few-shot learning. In: IEEE Conference on Computer Vision and Pattern Recognition (CVPR), pp. 11–20 (2019)
13. Kosiorek, A.R., Sabour, S., Teh, Y.W., Hinton, G.E.: Stacked capsule autoencoders. arXiv preprint arXiv:1906.06818 (2019)
14. Krizhevsky, A., Hinton, G., et al.: Learning multiple layers of features from tiny images. Technical report, Citeseer (2009)

15. Krizhevsky, A., Sutskever, I., Hinton, G.E.: Imagenet classification with deep convolutional neural networks. In: Advances in Neural Information Processing Systems (NIPS), pp. 1097–1105 (2012)
16. Lee, K., Maji, S., Ravichandran, A., Soatto, S.: Meta-learning with differentiable convex optimization. In: Proceedings of the IEEE/CVF Conference on Computer Vision and Pattern Recognition (CVPR), June 2019
17. Lenssen, J.E., Fey, M., Libuschewski, P.: Group equivariant capsule networks. In: Advances in Neural Information Processing Systems (NIPS), pp. 8844–8853 (2018)
18. Li, H., Eigen, D., Dodge, S., Zeiler, M., Wang, X.: Finding task-relevant features for few-shot learning by category traversal. In: IEEE Conference on Computer Vision and Pattern Recognition (CVPR), pp. 1–10 (2019)
19. Li, Z., Zhou, F., Chen, F., Li, H.: Meta-SQD: learning to learn quickly for few-shot learning. arXiv preprint arXiv:1707.09835 (2017)
20. Maaten, L., Hinton, G.: Visualizing data using t-SNE. J. Mach. Learn. Res. **9**, 2579–2605 (2008)
21. Mishra, N., Rohaninejad, M., Chen, X., Abbeel, P.: A simple neural attentive meta-learner. arXiv preprint arXiv:1707.03141 (2017)
22. Mitani, Y., Hamamoto, Y.: A local mean-based nonparametric classifier. Pattern Recogn. Lett. **27**(10), 1151–1159 (2006)
23. Nichol, A., Achiam, J., Schulman, J.: On first-order meta-learning algorithms. arXiv preprint arXiv:1803.02999 (2018)
24. Oreshkin, B., López, P.R., Lacoste, A.: Tadam: task dependent adaptive metric for improved few-shot learning. In: Advances in Neural Information Processing Systems (NIPS), pp. 721–731 (2018)
25. Peng, H., et al.: Hierarchical taxonomy-aware and attentional graph capsule RCNNs for large-scale multi-label text classification. arXiv preprint arXiv:1906.04898 (2019)
26. Qiao, S., Liu, C., Shen, W., Yuille, A.L.: Few-shot image recognition by predicting parameters from activations. In: IEEE Conference on Computer Vision and Pattern Recognition (CVPR), pp. 7229–7238 (2018)
27. Rajasegaran, J., Jayasundara, V., Jayasekara, S., Jayasekara, H., Seneviratne, S., Rodrigo, R.: Deepcaps: going deeper with capsule networks. In: IEEE Conference on Computer Vision and Pattern Recognition (CVPR), pp. 10725–10733 (2019)
28. Rawlinson, D., Ahmed, A., Kowadlo, G.: Sparse unsupervised capsules generalize better. arXiv preprint arXiv:1804.06094 (2018)
29. Ren, M., et al.: Meta-learning for semi-supervised few-shot classification. In: International Conference on Learning Representations (ICLR) (2018)
30. Russakovsky, O., et al.: Imagenet large scale visual recognition challenge. Int. J. Comput. Vis. **115**(3), 211–252 (2015)
31. Rusu, A.A., Rao, D., Sygnowski, J., Vinyals, O., Pascanu, R., Osindero, S., Hadsell, R.: Meta-learning with latent embedding optimization. In: International Conference on Learning Representations (ICLR) (2018)
32. Sabour, S., Frosst, N., Hinton, G.E.: Dynamic routing between capsules. In: Advances in Neural Information Processing Systems (NIPS), pp. 3856–3866 (2017)
33. Schroff, F., Kalenichenko, D., Philbin, J.: Facenet: a unified embedding for face recognition and clustering. In: IEEE Conference on Computer Vision and Pattern Recognition (CVPR), pp. 815–823 (2015)
34. Snell, J., Swersky, K., Zemel, R.: Prototypical networks for few-shot learning. In: Advances in Neural Information Processing Systems (NIPS), pp. 4077–4087 (2017)
35. Sohn, K.: Improved deep metric learning with multi-class n-pair loss objective. In: Advances in Neural Information Processing Systems (NIPS), pp. 1857–1865 (2016)

36. Sun, Q., Liu, Y., Chua, T.S., Schiele, B.: Meta-transfer learning for few-shot learning. In: IEEE Conference on Computer Vision and Pattern Recognition (CVPR), pp. 403–412 (2019)
37. Sung, F., Yang, Y., Zhang, L., Xiang, T., Torr, P.H., Hospedales, T.M.: Learning to compare: Relation network for few-shot learning. In: IEEE Conference on Computer Vision and Pattern Recognition (CVPR), pp. 1199–1208 (2018)
38. Szegedy, C., et al.: Going deeper with convolutions. In: IEEE Conference on Computer Vision and Pattern Recognition (CVPR), pp. 1–9 (2015)
39. Vinyals, O., Blundell, C., Lillicrap, T., Wierstra, D., et al.: Matching networks for one shot learning. In: Advances in Neural Information Processing Systems (NIPS), pp. 3630–3638 (2016)
40. Xia, C., Zhang, C., Yan, X., Chang, Y., Yu, P.S.: Zero-shot user intent detection via capsule neural networks. arXiv preprint arXiv:1809.00385 (2018)
41. Zhang, W., Tang, P., Zhao, L.: Remote sensing image scene classification using CNN-capsNET. Remote Sens. 11(5), 494 (2019)
42. Zhang, X., Zhao, S.G.: Cervical image classification based on image segmentation preprocessing and a CapsNET network model. Int. J. Imaging Syst. Technol. 29(1), 19–28 (2019)
43. Zhao, Y., Birdal, T., Deng, H., Tombari, F.: 3D point capsule networks. In: IEEE Conference on Computer Vision and Pattern Recognition (CVPR), pp. 1009–1018 (2019)

Weakly Supervised Instance Segmentation by Learning Annotation Consistent Instances

Aditya Arun[1(✉)], C.V. Jawahar[1], and M. Pawan Kumar[2]

[1] CVIT, KCIS, IIIT Hyderabad, Hyderabad, India
aditya.arun@research.iiit.ac.in
[2] OVAL, University of Oxford, Oxford, UK

Abstract. Recent approaches for weakly supervised instance segmentations depend on two components: (i) a pseudo label generation model which provides instances that are consistent with a given annotation; and (ii) an instance segmentation model, which is trained in a supervised manner using the pseudo labels as ground-truth. Unlike previous approaches, we explicitly model the uncertainty in the pseudo label generation process using a conditional distribution. The samples drawn from our conditional distribution provide accurate pseudo labels due to the use of semantic class aware unary terms, boundary aware pairwise smoothness terms, and annotation aware higher order terms. Furthermore, we represent the instance segmentation model as an annotation agnostic prediction distribution. In contrast to previous methods, our representation allows us to define a joint probabilistic learning objective that minimizes the dissimilarity between the two distributions. Our approach achieves state of the art results on the PASCAL VOC 2012 data set, outperforming the best baseline by 4.2% $mAP_{0.5}^r$ and 4.8% $mAP_{0.75}^r$.

1 Introduction

The instance segmentation task is to jointly estimate the class labels and segmentation masks of the individual objects in an image. Significant progress on instance segmentation has been made based on the convolutional neural networks (CNN) [9,17,24,26,28]. However, the traditional approach of learning CNN-based models requires a large number of training images with instance-level pixel-wise annotations. Due to the high cost of collecting these supervised labels, researchers have looked at training these instance segmentation models using weak annotations, ranging from bounding boxes [18,20] to image-level labels [1,10,13,23,42,43].

Many of the recent approaches for weakly supervised instance segmentation can be thought of as consisting of two components. First, a pseudo label generation model, which provides instance segmentations that are consistent with the

Electronic supplementary material The online version of this chapter (https:// doi.org/10.1007/978-3-030-58604-1_16) contains supplementary material, which is available to authorized users.

© Springer Nature Switzerland AG 2020
A. Vedaldi et al. (Eds.): ECCV 2020, LNCS 12373, pp. 254–270, 2020.
https://doi.org/10.1007/978-3-030-58604-1_16

weak annotations. Second, an instance segmentation model which is trained by treating the pseudo labels as ground-truth, and provides the desired output at test time.

Seen from the above viewpoint, the design of a weakly supervised instance segmentation approach boils down to three questions. First, how do we represent the instance segmentation model? Second, how do we represent the pseudo label generation model? And third, how do we learn the parameters of the two models using weakly supervised data? The answer to the first question is relatively clear: we should use a model that performs well when trained in a supervised manner, for example, Mask R-CNN [17]. However, we argue that the existing approaches fail to provide a satisfactory answer to the latter two questions.

Specifically, the current approaches do not take into account the inherent uncertainty in the pseudo label generation process [1,23]. Consider, for instance, a training image that has been annotated to indicate the presence of a person. There can be several instance segmentations that are consistent with this annotation, and thus, one should not rely on a single pseudo label to train the instance segmentation model. Furthermore, none of the existing approaches provide a coherent learning objective for the two models. Often they suggest a simple two-step learning approach, that is, generate one set of pseudo labels followed by a one time training of the instance segmentation model [1]. While some works consider an iterative training procedure [23], the lack of a learning objective makes it difficult to analyse and adapt them in varying settings.

In this work, we address the deficiencies of prior work by (i) proposing suitable representations for the two aforementioned components; and (ii) estimating their parameters using a principled learning objective. In more detail, we explicitly model the uncertainty in pseudo labels via a conditional distribution. The conditional distribution consists of three terms: (i) a semantic class aware unary term to predict the score of each segmentation proposal; (ii) a boundary aware pairwise term that encourages the segmentation proposal to completely cover the object; and (iii) an annotation consistent higher order term that enforces a global constraint on all segmentation proposals (for example, in the case of image-level labels, there exists at least one corresponding segmentation proposal for each class, or in the case of bounding boxes, there exists a segmentation proposal with sufficient overlap to each bounding box). All three terms combined enable the samples drawn from the conditional distribution to provide accurate annotation consistent instance segmentations. Furthermore, we represent the instance segmentation model as an annotation agnostic prediction distribution. This choice of representation allows us to define a joint probabilistic learning objective that minimizes the dissimilarity between the two distributions. The dissimilarity is measured using a task-specific loss function, thereby encouraging the models to produce high quality instance segmentations.

We test the efficacy of our approach on the Pascal VOC 2012 data set. We achieve 50.9% $mAP_{0.5}^r$, 28.5% $mAP_{0.75}^r$ for image-level annotations and 32.1% $mAP_{0.75}^r$ for bounding box annotations, resulting in an improvement of over 4% and 10% respectively over the state-of-the-art.

2   Related Work

Due to the taxing task of acquiring the expensive per-pixel annotations, many weakly supervised methods have emerged that can leverage cheaper labels. For the task of semantic segmentation various types of weak annotations, such as image-level [2,19,29,32], point [6], scribbles [25,39], and bounding boxes [11,31], have been utilized. However, for the instance segmentation, only image-level [1,10,13,23,42,43] and bounding box [18,20] supervision have been explored. Our setup considers both the image-level and the bounding box annotations as weak supervision. For the bounding box annotations, Hsu et al. [18] employs a bounding box tightness constraint and train their method by employing a multiple instance learning (MIL) based objective but they do not model the annotation consistency constraint for computational efficiency.

Most of the initial works [42,43] on weakly supervised instance segmentation using image-level supervision were based on the class activation maps (CAM) [30,35,40,41]. In their work, Zhou et al. [42] identify the heatmap as well as its peaks to represent the location of different objects. Although these methods are good at finding the spatial location of each object instance, they focus only on the most discriminative regions of the object and therefore, do not cover the entire object. Ge et al [13] uses the CAM output as the initial segmentation seed and refines it in a multi-task setting, which they train progressively. We use the output of [42] as the initial segmentation seed of our conditional distribution but the boundary aware pairwise term in our conditional distribution encourages pseudo labels to cover the entire object.

Most recent works on weakly supervised learning adopt a two-step process - generate pseudo labels and train a supervised model treating these pseudo labels as ground truth. Such an approach provides state-of-the-art results for various weakly supervised tasks like object detection [5,37,38], semantic segmentation [11,20], and instance segmentation [1,23]. Ahn et al. [1] synthesizes pseudo labels by learning the displacement fields and pairwise pixel affinities. These pseudo labels are then used to train a fully supervised Mask R-CNN [17], which is used at the test time. Laradji et al. [23] iteratively samples the pseudo segmentation label from MCG segmentation proposal set [3] and train a supervised Mask R-CNN [17]. This is similar in spirit to our approach of using the two distributions. However, they neither have a unified learning objective for the two distribution nor do they model the uncertainty in their pseudo label generation model. Regardless, the improvement in the results reported by these two methods advocates the importance of modeling two separate distributions. In our method, we explicitly model the two distributions and define a unified learning objective that minimizes the dissimilarity between them.

Our framework has been inspired by the work of Kumar et al. [22] who were the first to show the necessity of modeling uncertainty by employing two separate distributions in a latent variable model. This framework has been adopted for weakly supervised training of CNNs for learning human poses and object detection tasks [4,5]. While their framework provides an elegant formulation for weakly supervised learning, its various components need to be carefully constructed for each task. Our work can be viewed as designing conditional and prediction distributions, as well as the corresponding inference algorithms, which are suited to instance segmentation.

3   Method

3.1   Notation

We denote an input image as $\mathbf{x} \in \mathbb{R}^{(H \times W \times 3)}$, where H and W are the height and the width of the image respectively. For each image, a set of segmentation proposals $\mathcal{R} = \{r_1, \ldots, r_P\}$ are extracted from a class-agnostic object proposal algorithm. In this work, we use Multiscale Combinatorial Grouping (MCG) [3] to obtain the object proposals. For the sake of simplicity, we only consider image-level annotations in our description. However, our framework can be easily extended to other annotations such as bounding boxes. Indeed, we will use bounding box annotations in our experiments. Given an image and the segmentation proposals, our goal is to classify each of the segmentation proposals to one of the $C + 1$ categories from the set $\{0, 1, \ldots, C\}$. Here category 0 is the background and categories $\{1, \ldots, C\}$ are object classes.

We denote the image-level annotations by $\mathbf{a} = \{0, 1\}^C$, where $\mathbf{a}^{(j)} = 1$ if image x contains the $j-$th object. Furthermore, we denote the unknown instance-level (segmentation proposal) label as $\mathbf{y} = \{0, \ldots, C\}^P$, where $\mathbf{y}^{(i)} = j$ if the $i-$th segmentation proposal is of the $j-$th category. A weakly supervised data set $\mathcal{W} = \{(\mathbf{x}_n, \mathbf{a}_n) \mid n = 1, \ldots, N\}$ contains N pairs of images $\mathbf{x}_n$ and their corresponding image-level annotations $\mathbf{a}_n$.

3.2   Conditional Distribution

Given the weakly supervised data set $\mathcal{W}$, we wish to generate pseudo instance-level labels $\mathbf{y}$ such that they are annotation consistent. Specifically, given the segmentation proposals $\mathcal{R}$ for an image $\mathbf{x}$, there must exists at least one segmentation proposal for each image-level annotation $\mathbf{a}^{(j)} = 1$. Since the annotations are image-level, there is inherent uncertainty in the figure-ground separation of the objects. We model this uncertainty by defining a distribution $\Pr_c(\mathbf{y} \mid \mathbf{x}, \mathbf{a}; \boldsymbol{\theta}_c)$ over the pseudo labels conditioned on the image-level weak annotations. Here, $\boldsymbol{\theta}_c$ are the parameters of the distribution. We call this a *conditional distribution*.

The conditional distribution itself is not explicitly represented. Instead, we use a neural network with parameters $\boldsymbol{\theta}_c$ which generates samples that can be used as pseudo labels. For the generated samples to be accurate, we wish that they have the following three properties: (i) they should have high fidelity with the scores assigned by the neural network for each region proposal belonging to each class; (ii) they should cover as large a portion of an object instance as possible; and (iii) they should be consistent with the annotation.

Modeling: In order for the conditional distribution to be annotation consistent, the instance-level labels **y** need to be compatible with the image-level annotation **a**. This constraint cannot be trivially decomposed over each segmentation proposal. As a result, it would be prohibitively expensive to model the conditional distribution directly as one would be required to compute its partition function. Taking inspiration from Arun *et al.* [5], we instead draw representative samples from the conditional distribution using the Discrete DISCO Nets [7]. We will now describe how we model the conditional distribution through a Discrete DISCO Nets, which we will now call a *conditional network*.

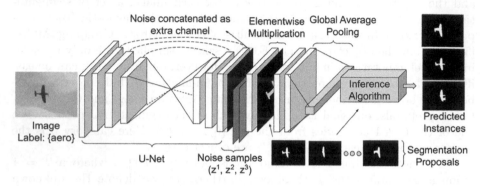

Fig. 1. The conditional network: a modified U-Net architecture is used to model the conditional network. For a single input image and three different noise samples $\{z^1, z^2, z^3\}$ (represented as red, green, and blue matrix) and a pool of segmentation proposals, three different instances are predicted for the given weak annotation (aeroplane in this example). Here the noise sample is concatenated as an extra channel to the final layer of the U-Net. The segmentation proposals are multiplied element-wise with the global feature to obtain the proposal specific feature. A global average pooling is applied to get class specific score. Finally, an inference algorithm generates the predicted samples. (Color figure online)

Consider the modified fully convolutional U-Net [34] architecture shown in Fig. 1 for the conditional distribution. The parameters of the conditional distribution $\boldsymbol{\theta}_c$ are modeled by the weights of the conditional network. Similar to [21], noise sampled from a uniform distribution is added after the U-Net block (depicted by the colored filter). Each forward pass through the network takes the image **x** and noise sample $\mathbf{z}^k$ as input and produces a score function $F_{u,\mathbf{y}_u}^k(\boldsymbol{\theta}_c)$ for each segmentation proposal u and the corresponding putative label $\mathbf{y}_u$. We generate K different score functions using K different noise samples. These score functions are then used to sample the segmentation region proposals $\mathbf{y}_c^k$ such that they are annotation consistent. This enables us to efficiently generate the samples from the underlying distribution.

Inference: Given the input pair $(\mathbf{x}, \mathbf{z}^k)$ the conditional network outputs K score functions for each of the segmentation proposal $F_{u,\mathbf{y}_u}^k(\boldsymbol{\theta}_c)$. We redefine these score functions to obtain a final score function such that it is then used to sample the segmentation region proposals $\mathbf{y}_c^k$. The final score function has the following three properties.

1. The score of the sampled segmentation region proposal should be consistent with the score function. This *semantic class aware unary term* ensures that the final score captures the class specific features of each segmentation proposal. Formally, $G_{u,\mathbf{y}_u}^k(\mathbf{y}_c) = F_{u,\mathbf{y}_u}^k(\boldsymbol{\theta}_c)$.

2. The unary term alone is biased towards segmentation proposals that are highly discriminative. This results in selecting a segmentation proposal which does not cover the object in its entirety. We argue that all the neighboring segmentation proposals must have the same score discounted by the edge weights between them. We call this condition *boundary aware pairwise term*. In order to make the score function $G_{u,\mathbf{y}_u}^k(\mathbf{y}_c)$ pairwise term aware, we employ a simple but efficient iterative algorithm. The algorithm proceeds by iteratively updating the scores $G_{u,\mathbf{y}_u}^k(\mathbf{y}_c)$ by adding the contribution of their neighbors discounted by the edge weights between them until convergence. In practice, we fix the number of iteration to 3. Note that, it is possible to backpropagate through the iterative algorithm by simply unrolling its iterations, similar to a recurrent neural networks (RNN). Formally,

$$G_{u,\mathbf{y}_u}^{k,n}(\mathbf{y}_c) = G_{u,\mathbf{y}_u}^{k,n-1}(\mathbf{y}_c) + \frac{1}{H_{u,v}^{k,n-1}(\mathbf{y}_c) + \delta} \exp\left(-I_{u,v}\right). \tag{1}$$

Here, n denotes the iteration step for the iterative algorithm and δ is a small positive constant added for numerical stability. In our experiments, we set $\delta = 0.1$. The term $H_{u,v}^{k,n-1}(\mathbf{y}_c)$ is the difference between the scores of the neighboring segmentation proposal. It helps encourage same label for the neighboring segmentation proposals that are not separated by the edge pixels. It is given as,

$$H_{u,v}^{k,n-1}(\mathbf{y}_c) = \sum_{u,v \in \mathcal{N}_u} \left(G_{u,\mathbf{y}_u}^{k,n-1}(\mathbf{y}_c) - G_{v,\mathbf{y}_u}^{k,n-1}(\mathbf{y}_c)\right)^2. \tag{2}$$

The term $I_{u,v}$ is the sum of the edge pixel values between the two neighboring segmentation regions. Note that the pairwise term is a decay function weighted by the edge pixel values. This ensures a high contribution to the pairwise term is only from the pair of segmentation proposals that does not share an edge.

3. In order to ensure that at there must exist at least one segmentation proposal for every image-level annotation,a higher order penalty is added to the score. We call this *annotation consistent higher order term*. Formally,

$$S^k(\mathbf{y}_c) = \sum_{u=1}^{P} G_{u,\mathbf{y}_u}^{k,n}(\mathbf{y}_c) + Q^k(\mathbf{y}_c). \tag{3}$$

Algorithm 1: Inference Algorithm for the Conditional Net

Input : Region masks: R, Image-level labels: a
Output: Predicted instance level instances: $\mathbf{y}_c^k$

```
/* Iterative Algorithm                                                    */
```
1   $G_{u,\mathbf{y}_u}^k(\mathbf{y}_c) = F_{u,\mathbf{y}_u}^k(\boldsymbol{\theta}_c)$
2   **repeat**
3   **for** $v \in \mathcal{N}_u$ **do**
4       $H_{u,v}^{k,n-1}(\mathbf{y}_c) = \sum_{u,v \in \mathcal{N}_u} \left(G_{u,\mathbf{y}_u}^{k,n-1}(\mathbf{y}_c) - G_{v,\mathbf{y}_v}^{k,n-1}(\mathbf{y}_c) \right)^2$.
5       $G_{u,\mathbf{y}_u}^{k,n}(\mathbf{y}_c) = G_{u,\mathbf{y}_u}^{k,n-1}(\mathbf{y}_c) + \frac{1}{H_{u,v}^{k,n-1}(\mathbf{y}_c)+\delta} \exp\left(-I_{u,v}\right)$
6   **until** $G_{u,\mathbf{y}_u}^{k,n}(\mathbf{y}_c)$ *has coverged*
```
/* Greedily select highest scoring non-overlapping proposal              */
```
7   $Y \leftarrow \phi$
8   **for** $j \leftarrow \{1, \ldots, C\} \wedge \mathbf{a}^{(j)} = 1$ **do**
9     $Y_j \leftarrow \phi$
10    $R_j \leftarrow sort(G_{u,\mathbf{y}_u}^{k,n}(\mathbf{y}_c))$
11   **for** $i \in 1, \ldots, P$ **do**
12      $Y_j \leftarrow r_i$
13      $R_j \leftarrow R_j - r_i$
14   **for** $l \in R_j \wedge \frac{r_i \cap r_l}{r_l} > t$ **do**
15        $R_j \leftarrow R_j - r_l$
16    $Y \leftarrow Y_j$
17 **return** $\mathbf{y}_c^k = Y$

Here,

$$Q^k(\mathbf{y}_c) = \begin{cases} 0 & \text{if } \forall j \in \{1, \ldots, C\} \text{ s.t. } \mathbf{a}^{(j)} = 1, \\ & \exists i \in \mathcal{R} \text{ s.t. } \mathbf{y}^{(i)} = j, \\ -\infty & \text{otherwise.} \end{cases} \qquad (4)$$

Given the scoring function in Eq. (3), we compute the $k-$th sample of the conditional network as,

$$\mathbf{y}_c^k = \arg\max_{\mathbf{y} \in \mathcal{Y}} S^k(\mathbf{y}_c). \qquad (5)$$

Observe that in Eq. (5), the arg max is computed over the entire output space $\mathcal{Y}$. A naïve brute force algorithm is therefore not feasible. We design an efficient greedy algorithm that selects the highest scoring non-overlapping proposal. The inference algorithm is described in Algorithm 1.

3.3 Prediction Distribution

The task of the supervised instance segmentation model is to predict the instancemask given an image. We employ Mask R-CNN [18] for this task. As predictions for each of the regions in the Mask R-CNN is computed independently, we can view the output of the Mask R-CNN as the following fully factorized distribution,

$$\Pr_p(\mathbf{y} \mid \mathbf{x}; \boldsymbol{\theta}_p) = \prod_{i=1}^{R} \Pr(\mathbf{y}_i \mid \mathbf{r}_i, \mathbf{x}_i; \boldsymbol{\theta}_p). \tag{6}$$

Here, R are the set of bounding box regions proposed by the region proposal network and $\mathbf{r}_i$ are its corresponding region features. The term $\mathbf{y}_i$ is the corresponding prediction for each of the bounding box proposals. We call the above distribution a *prediction distribution* and the Mask R-CNN a *prediction network*.

4 Learning Objective

Given the weakly supervised data set $\mathcal{W}$, our goal is to learn the parameters of the prediction and the conditional distribution, $\boldsymbol{\theta}_p$ and $\boldsymbol{\theta}_c$ respectively. We observe that the task of both the prediction and the conditional distribution is to predict the instance segmentation mask. Moreover, the conditional distribution utilizes the extra information in the form of image-level annotations. Therefore, it is expected to produce better instance segmentation masks. Leveraging the task similarity between the two distribution, we would like to bring the two distribution close to each other. Inspired by the work of [4,5,8,22], we design a joint learning objective that can minimize the dissimilarity coefficient [33] between the prediction and the conditional distribution. In what follows, we briefly describe the dissimilarity coefficient before applying it to our setting.

Dissimilarity Coefficient: The dissimilarity coefficient between any two distributions $\Pr_1(\cdot)$ and $\Pr_2(\cdot)$ is determined by measuring their diversities. Given a task-specific loss function $\Delta(\cdot, \cdot)$, the diversity coefficient between the two distribution $\Pr_1(\cdot)$ and $\Pr_2(\cdot)$ is defined as the expected loss between two samples drawn randomly from the two distributions respectively. Formally,

$$DIV_\Delta(\Pr_1, \Pr_2) = \mathbb{E}_{\mathbf{y}_1 \sim \Pr_1(\cdot)} \left[\mathbb{E}_{\mathbf{y}_2 \sim \Pr_2(\cdot)} [\Delta(\mathbf{y}_1, \mathbf{y}_2)] \right]. \tag{7}$$

If the model brings the two distributions close to each other, we could expect the diversity $DIV_\Delta(\Pr_1, \Pr_2)$ to be small. Using this definition, the dissimilarity coefficient is defined as the following Jensen difference,

$$\begin{aligned} DISC_\Delta(\Pr_1, \Pr_2) = {}&DIV_\Delta(\Pr_1, \Pr_2) - \gamma DIV_\Delta(\Pr_2, \Pr_2) \\ &- (1 - \gamma) DIV_\Delta(\Pr_1, \Pr_1), \end{aligned} \tag{8}$$

where, $\gamma = [0, 1]$. In our experiments, we use $\gamma = 0.5$, which results in dissimilarity coefficient being symmetric for the two distributions.

4.1   Task-Specific Loss Function:

The dissimilarity coefficient objective requires a task-specific loss function. To this end, we use the multi-task loss defined by Mask R-CNN [17] as,

$$\Delta(\mathbf{y}_1, \mathbf{y}_2) = \Delta_{\text{cls}}(\mathbf{y}_1, \mathbf{y}_2) + \Delta_{\text{box}}(\mathbf{y}_1, \mathbf{y}_2) + \Delta_{\text{mask}}(\mathbf{y}_1, \mathbf{y}_2). \tag{9}$$

Here, Δ_{cls} is the classification loss defined by the log loss, Δ_{box} is the bounding box regression loss defined as the smooth-L1 loss, and Δ_{mask} is the segmentation loss for the mask defined by pixel-wise cross entropy, as proposed by [17].

Note that the conditional network outputs the segmentation region $\mathbf{y}$, where there are no bounding box coordinates predicted. Therefore, for the conditional network, only Δ_{cls} and Δ_{mask} is active as the gradients for Δ_{box} is 0. For the prediction network, all three components of the loss functions are active. We construct a tight bounding box around the pseudo segmentation label, which acts as a pseudo bounding box label for Mask R-CNN.

4.2   Learning Objective for Instance Segmentation:

We now specify the learning objective for instance segmentation using the dissimilarity coefficient and the task-specific loss function defined above as,

$$\boldsymbol{\theta}_p^*, \boldsymbol{\theta}_c^* = \arg \min_{\boldsymbol{\theta}_p, \boldsymbol{\theta}_c} DISC_\Delta \left(\Pr_p(\boldsymbol{\theta}_p), \Pr_c(\boldsymbol{\theta}_c) \right). \tag{10}$$

As discussed in Sect. 3.2, modeling the conditional distribution directly is difficult. Therefore, the corresponding diversity terms are computed by stochastic estimators from K samples y_c^k of the conditional network. Thus, each diversity term is written as[1],

$$DIV_\Delta(\Pr_p, \Pr_c) = \frac{1}{K} \sum_{k=1}^K \sum_{\mathbf{y}_p^{(i)}} \Pr_p(\mathbf{y}_p^{(i)}; \boldsymbol{\theta}_p) \Delta(\mathbf{y}_p^{(i)}, \mathbf{y}_c^k), \tag{11a}$$

$$DIV_\Delta(\Pr_c, \Pr_c) = \frac{1}{K(K-1)} \sum_{\substack{k,k'=1 \\ k' \neq k}}^K \Delta(\mathbf{y}_c^k, \mathbf{y}_c^{k'}), \tag{11b}$$

$$DIV_\Delta(\Pr_p, \Pr_p) = \sum_{\mathbf{y}_p^{(i)}} \sum_{\mathbf{y'}_p^{(i)}} \Pr_p(\mathbf{y}_p^{(i)}; \boldsymbol{\theta}_p) \Pr_p(\mathbf{y'}_p^{(i)}; \boldsymbol{\theta}_p) \Delta(\mathbf{y}_p^{(i)}, \mathbf{y'}_p^{(i)}) \tag{11c}$$

Here, $DIV_\Delta(\Pr_p, \Pr_c)$ measures the cross diversity between the prediction and the conditional distribution, which is the expected loss between the samples of the two distribution. Since $\Pr_p$ is a fully factorized distribution, the expectation of its output can be trivially computed. As $\Pr_c$ is not explicitly modeled, we draw K different samples to compute its required expectation.

---

[1] Details in the supplementary material.

5   Optimization

As the parameters of the two distribution, θ_p and θ_c are modeled by a neural network, it is ideally suited to be minimized by stochastic gradient descent. We employ a block coordinate descent strategy to optimize the two sets of parameters. The algorithm proceeds by iteratively fixing the prediction network and training the conditional network, followed by learning the prediction network for a fixed conditional network.

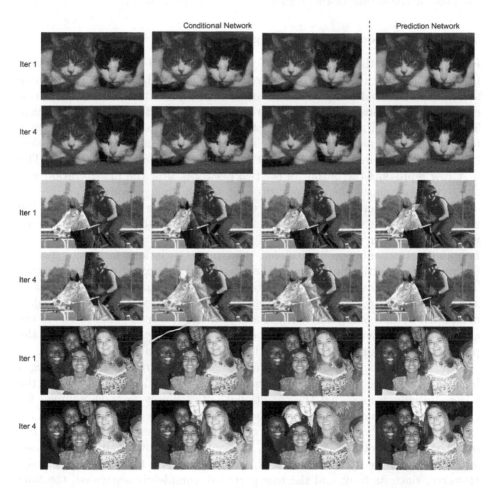

Fig. 2. Examples of the predictions from the conditional and prediction networks for three different cases of varying difficulty. Columns 1 through 3 are different samples from the conditional network. For each case, its first row shows the output of the two networks after the first iteration and its second row represents the output of the two networks after the fourth (final) iteration. Each instance of an object is represented by different mask color. Best viewed in color. (Color figure online)

The iterative learning strategy results in a fully supervised training of each network by using the output of the other network as the pseudo label. This allows us to readily use the algorithms developed in Mask R-CNN [17] and Discrete DISCO Nets [7]. Note that, as the conditional network obtains samples over the arg max operator in Eq. (5), the objective (10) for the conditional network is non-differentiable. However, the scoring function $S^k(\mathbf{y}_c)$ in Eq. (3) itself is differentiable. This allows us to use the direct loss minimization strategy [16,36] developed for computing estimated gradients over the arg max operator [7,27]. We provide the details of the algorithm in the supplementary.

5.1 Visualization of the Learning Process

Figure 2 provides the visualization of the output of the two networks for the first and the final iterations of the training process. The first three columns are the three output samples of the conditional distribution. Note that in our experiments, we output 10 samples corresponding to 10 different noise samples. The fourth column shows the output of the prediction distribution. The output for the prediction network is selected by employing a non-maximal suppression (NMS) with its score threshold kept at 0.7, as is the default setting in [17]. The first row represents the output of the two networks after the first iteration and the second row shows their output after the fourth (final) iteration.

The first case demonstrates an easy example where two cats are present in the image. Initially, the conditional distribution samples the segmentation proposals which do not cover the entire body of the cat but still manages to capture the boundaries reasonably well. However, due to the variations in these samples, the prediction distribution learns to better predict the extent of the cat pixels. This, in turn, encourages the conditional network to generate a better set of samples. Indeed, by the fourth iteration, we see an improvement in the quality of samples by the conditional network and they now cover the entire body of the cat, thereby improving the performance. As a result, we can see that finally the prediction network successfully learns to segment the two cats in the image.

The second case presents a challenging scenario where a person is riding a horse. In this case, the person is occluding the front and the rear parts of the horse. Initially, we see that the conditional network only provides samples for the most discriminative region of the horse - its face. The samples generated for the person class, though not accurate, covers the entire person. We observe that over the subsequent iterations, we get an accurate output for the person class. The output for the horse class also expands to cover its front part completely. However, since its front and the rear parts are completely separated, the final segmentation could not cover the rear part of the horse.

The third case presents another challenging scenario where there are multiple people present. Four people standing in front and two are standing at the back. Here, we observe that initially, the conditional network fails to distinguish between the two people standing in the front-left of the image and fails to detect persons standing at the back. The samples for the third and the fourth persons standing in front-center and front-right respectively are also not accurate. Over the iterations, the conditional network improves its predictions for the four people standing in front and also sometimes detect the people standing at the back. As a result, prediction network finally detects five of the six people in the image.

6 Experiments

6.1 Data Set and Evaluation Metric

Data Set: We evaluate our proposed method on Pascal VOC 2012 segmentation benchmark [12]. The data set consists of 20 foreground classes. Following previous works [1,13,18,20], we use the augmented Pascal VOC 2012 data set [14], which contains 10, 582 training images.

From the augmented Pascal VOC 2012 data set, we construct two different weakly supervised data sets. The first data set is where we retain only the image-level annotations. For the second data set, we retain the bounding box information along with the image-level label. In both the data sets, the pixel-level labels are discarded.

Evaluation Metric: We adopt the standard evaluation metric for instance segmentation, mean average precision (mAP) [15]. Following the same evaluation protocol from other competing approaches, we report mAP with four intersection over union (IoU) thresholds, denoted by mAP_k^r where k denotes the different values of IoU and $k = \{0.25, 0.50, 0.70, 0.75\}$.

6.2 Initialization

We now discuss various strategies to initialize our conditional network for different levels of weakly supervised annotations.

Image Level Annotations: Following the previous works on weakly supervised instance segmentation from image-level annotations [1,23,43], we use the Class Activation Maps (CAMs) to generate the segmentation seeds for each image in the training set. Specifically, like [1,23,43], we rely on the Peak Response Maps (PRM) [42] to generate segmentation seeds that identify the salient parts of the objects. We utilize these seeds as pseudo segmentation labels to initially train our conditional network. We also filter the MCG [3] segmentation proposal such that each selected proposal has at least a single pixel overlap with the PRM segmentation seeds. This helps us reduce the number of segmentation proposals needed thereby reducing the memory requirement. Once the initial training for the conditional network is over, we proceed with the iterative optimization strategy, described in Sect. 5.

Bounding Box Annotations For the weakly supervised data set where bounding box annotations are present, we filter the MCG [3] segmentation proposals such that only those who have a high overlap with the ground-truth bounding boxes are retained. The PRM [42] segmentation seeds are also pruned such that they are contained within each of the bounding box annotations.

6.3   Comparison with Other Methods

We compare our proposed method with other state-of-the-art weakly supervised instance segmentation methods. The mean average precision (mAP) over different IoU thresholds are shown in Table 1. Compared with the other methods, our proposed framework achieves state-of-the-art performance for both image-level and the bounding box labels. We also study the effect of using a different conditional network architecture based on ResNet-50 and ResNet-101. This is shown in the table as 'Ours (ResNet-50)' and 'Ours (ResNet 101)' respectively. Our main result employs a U-Net based architecture for the conditional network and is presented by 'Ours' in the table. The implementation details and the details of the alternative architecture are presented in the supplementary. The encoder-decoder architecture of the U-Net allows us to learn better features. As a result, we observe that our method which adopts U-Net architecture for the conditional network consistently outperforms the one which adopts a ResNet based architecture. In Table 1, observe that our approach performs particularly well for the higher IoU thresholds ($mAP^r_{0.70}$ and $mAP^r_{0.75}$) for both the image-level and the bounding-box labels. This demonstrates that our model can predict the instance segments most accurately by respecting the object boundaries. The per-class quantitative and qualitative results for our method is presented in the supplementary material.

Table 1. Evaluation of instance segmentation results from different methods with varying level of supervision on Pascal VOC 2012 *val* set. The terms $\mathcal{F}$, $\mathcal{B}$, and $\mathcal{I}$ denotes a fully supervised approach, methods that uses the bounding box labels, and methods that uses the image-level labels respectively. Our prediction network results when using a ResNet based conditional network is presented as 'Ours (ResNet-*) and the results of the prediction network using a U-Net based conditional network is presented as 'Ours'.

Method	Supervision	Backbone	$mAP^r_{0.25}$	$mAP^r_{0.50}$	$mAP^r_{0.70}$	$mAP^r_{0.75}$
Mask R-CNN [17]	$\mathcal{F}$	R-101	76.7	67.9	52.5	44.9
PRN [42]	$\mathcal{I}$	R-50	44.3	26.8	–	9.0
IAM [43]	$\mathcal{I}$	R-50	45.9	28.8	–	11.9
OCIS [10]	$\mathcal{I}$	R-50	48.5	30.2	–	14.4
Label-PEnet [13]	$\mathcal{I}$	R-50	49.1	30.2	–	12.9
WISE [23]	$\mathcal{I}$	R-50	49.2	41.7	–	23.7
IRN [1]	$\mathcal{I}$	R-50	–	46.7	–	23.5
Ours (ResNet-50)	$\mathcal{I}$	R-50	59.1	49.7	29.2	27.1
Ours	$\mathcal{I}$	R-50	**59.7**	**50.9**	**30.2**	**28.5**
SDI [20]	$\mathcal{B}$	R-101	–	44.8	–	17.8
BBTP [18]	$\mathcal{B}$	R-101	**75.0**	**58.9**	30.4	21.6
Ours (ResNet-101)	$\mathcal{B}$	R-101	73.1	57.7	33.5	31.2
Ours	$\mathcal{B}$	R-101	73.8	58.2	**34.3**	**32.1**

Table 2. Evaluation of the instance segmentation results for the various ablative settings of the conditional distribution on Pascal VOC 2012 data set

$mAP^r_{0.25}$			$mAP^r_{0.50}$			$mAP^r_{0.75}$		
U	U+P	U+P+H	U	U+P	U+P+H	U	U+P	U+P+H
57.9	59.1	59.7	47.6	49.9	50.9	23.1	26.9	28.5

6.4 Ablation Experiments

Effect of the Unary, the Pairwise and the Higher Order Terms. We study the effect of the conditional distributions unary, pairwise and the higher order terms have on the final output in Table 2. We use the terms U, U+P, and U+P+H to denote the settings where only the unary term is present, both the unary and the pairwise terms are present and all three terms are present in the conditional distribution. We see that unary term alone performs poorly across the different IoU thresholds. We argue that this is because of the bias of the unary term for segmenting only the most discriminative regions. The pairwise term helps allay this problem and we observe a significant improvement in the results. This is specially noticeable for higher IoU thresholds that require more accurate segmentation. The higher order term helps in improving the accuracy by ensuring that correct samples are generated by the conditional distribution.

Table 3. Evaluation of the instance segmentation results for the various ablative settings of the loss function's diversity coefficient terms on Pascal VOC 2012 data set

Method mAP^r_k	Pr_p, Pr_c (proposed)	PW_p, Pr_c	Pr_p, PW_c	PW_p, PW_c
$mAP^r_{0.25}$	59.7	59.5	57.3	57.2
$mAP^r_{0.50}$	50.9	50.3	46.9	46.6
$mAP^r_{0.75}$	28.5	27.7	23.4	23.0

Effect of the Probabilistic Learning Objective. To understand the effect of explicitly modeling the two distributions (Pr_p and Pr_c), we compare our approach with their corresponding pointwise network. In order to sample a single output from our conditional network, we remove the self-diversity coefficient term and feed a zero noise vector (denoted by PW_c). For a pointwise prediction network, we remove its self-diversity coefficient. The prediction network still outputs the probability of each proposal belonging to a class. However, by removing the self-diversity coefficient term, we encourage it to output a peakier distribution (denoted by PW_p). Table 3 shows that both the diversity coefficient term is important for maximum accuracy. We also note that modeling uncertainty over the pseudo label generation model by including the self-diversity in the conditional network is relatively more important. The self-diversity coefficient in the conditional network enforces it to sample a diverse set of outputs which helps in dealing with the difficult cases and in avoiding overfitting during training.

7 Conclusion

We present a novel framework for weakly supervised instance segmentation. Our framework efficiently models the complex non-factorizable, annotation consistent and boundary aware conditional distribution that allows us to generate accurate pseudo segmentation labels. Furthermore, our framework provides a joint probabilistic learning objective for training the prediction and the conditional distributions and can be easily extendable to different weakly supervised labels such as image-level and bounding box annotations. Extensive experiments on the benchmark Pascal VOC 2012 data set has shown that our probabilistic framework successfully transfers the information present in the image-level annotations for the task of instance segmentation achieving state-of-the-art result for both image-level and bounding box annotations.

Acknowledgements. This work is partly supported by DST through the IMPRINT program. Aditya Arun is supported by Visvesvaraya Ph.D. fellowship.

References

1. Ahn, J., Cho, S., Kwak, S.: Weakly supervised learning of instance segmentation with inter-pixel relations. In: CVPR (2019)
2. Ahn, J., Kwak, S.: Learning pixel-level semantic affinity with image-level supervision for weakly supervised semantic segmentation. In: CVPR (2018)
3. Arbeláez, P., Pont-Tuset, J., Barron, J., Marques, F., Malik, J.: Multiscale combinatorial grouping. In: CVPR (2014)
4. Arun, A., Jawahar, C.V., Kumar, M.P.: Learning human poses from actions. In: BMVC (2018)
5. Arun, A., Jawahar, C., Kumar, M.P.: Dissimilarity coefficient based weakly supervised object detection. In: CVPR (2019)
6. Bearman, A., Russakovsky, O., Ferrari, V., Fei-Fei, L.: What's the point: semantic segmentation with point supervision. In: Leibe, B., Matas, J., Sebe, N., Welling, M. (eds.) ECCV 2016. LNCS, vol. 9911, pp. 549–565. Springer, Cham (2016). https://doi.org/10.1007/978-3-319-46478-7_34
7. Bouchacourt, D.: Task-Oriented Learning of Structured Probability Distributions. Ph.D. thesis, University of Oxford (2017)
8. Bouchacourt, D., Kumar, M.P., Nowozin, S.: DISCO nets: dissimilarity coefficients networks. In: NIPS (2016)
9. Chen, L.C., Hermans, A., Papandreou, G., Schroff, F., Wang, P., Adam, H.: Masklab: instance segmentation by refining object detection with semantic and direction features. In: CVPR (2018)
10. Cholakkal, H., Sun, G., Khan, F.S., Shao, L.: Object counting and instance segmentation with image-level supervision. In: CVPR (2019)
11. Dai, J., He, K., Sun, J.: Boxsup: exploiting bounding boxes to supervise convolutional networks for semantic segmentation. In: CVPR (2015)

12. Everingham, M., Van Gool, L., Williams, C.K., Winn, J., Zisserman, A.: The pascal visual object classes (voc) challenge. IJCV **88**, 303–338 (2010). https://doi.org/10.1007/s11263-009-0275-4

13. Ge, W., Guo, S., Huang, W., Scott, M.R.: Label-PEnet: sequential label propagation and enhancement networks for weakly supervised instance segmentation. In: ICCV (2019)

14. Hariharan, B., Arbeláez, P., Bourdev, L., Maji, S., Malik, J.: Semantic contours from inverse detectors. In: ICCV (2011)

15. Hariharan, B., Arbeláez, P., Girshick, R., Malik, J.: Simultaneous detection and segmentation. In: Fleet, D., Pajdla, T., Schiele, B., Tuytelaars, T. (eds.) ECCV 2014. LNCS, vol. 8695, pp. 297–312. Springer, Cham (2014). https://doi.org/10.1007/978-3-319-10584-0_20

16. Hazan, T., Keshet, J., McAllester, D.A.: Direct loss minimization for structured prediction. In: NIPS (2010)

17. He, K., Gkioxari, G., Dollár, P., Girshick, R.: Mask R-CNN. In: ICCV (2017)

18. Hsu, C.C., Hsu, K.J., Tsai, C.C., Lin, Y.Y., Chuang, Y.Y.: Weakly supervised instance segmentation using the bounding box tightness prior. In: NeurIPS (2019)

19. Huang, Z., Wang, X., Wang, J., Liu, W., Wang, J.: Weakly-supervised semantic segmentation network with deep seeded region growing. In: CVPR (2018)

20. Khoreva, A., Benenson, R., Hosang, J., Hein, M., Schiele, B.: Simple does it: weakly supervised instance and semantic segmentation. In: CVPR (2017)

21. Kohl, S., et al.: A probabilistic u-net for segmentation of ambiguous images. In: NIPS (2018)

22. Kumar, M.P., Packer, B., Koller, D.: Modeling latent variable uncertainty for loss-based learning. In: ICML (2012)

23. Laradji, I.H., Vazquez, D., Schmidt, M.: Where are the masks: instance segmentation with image-level supervision. In: BMVC (2019)

24. Li, Y., Qi, H., Dai, J., Ji, X., Wei, Y.: Fully convolutional instance-aware semantic segmentation. In: CVPR (2017)

25. Lin, D., Dai, J., Jia, J., He, K., Sun, J.: Scribblesup: scribble-supervised convolutional networks for semantic segmentation. In: CVPR (2016)

26. Liu, S., Qi, L., Qin, H., Shi, J., Jia, J.: Path aggregation network for instance segmentation. In: CVPR (2018)

27. Lorberbom, G., Gane, A., Jaakkola, T., Hazan, T.: Direct optimization through argmax for discrete variational auto-encoder. In: NeurIPS (2019)

28. Novotny, D., Albanie, S., Larlus, D., Vedaldi, A.: Semi-convolutional operators for instance segmentation. In: ECCV (2018)

29. Oh, S.J., Benenson, R., Khoreva, A., Akata, Z., Fritz, M., Schiele, B.: Exploiting saliency for object segmentation from image level labels. In: CVPR (2017)

30. Oquab, M., Bottou, L., Laptev, I., Sivic, J.: Is object localization for free?-weakly-supervised learning with convolutional neural networks. In: CVPR (2015)

31. Papandreou, G., Chen, L.C., Murphy, K., Yuille, A.: Weakly-and semi-supervised learning of a DCNN for semantic image segmentation. In: ICCV (2015)

32. Pinheiro, P.O., Collobert, R.: From image-level to pixel-level labeling with convolutional networks. In: CVPR (2015)

33. Rao, C.R.: Diversity and dissimilarity coefficients: a unified approach. Theor. Popul. Biol. **21**, 24–43 (1982)

34. Ronneberger, O., Fischer, P., Brox, T.: U-Net: convolutional networks for biomedical image segmentation. In: Navab, N., Hornegger, J., Wells, W.M., Frangi, A.F. (eds.) MICCAI 2015. LNCS, vol. 9351, pp. 234–241. Springer, Cham (2015). https://doi.org/10.1007/978-3-319-24574-4_28

35. Selvaraju, R.R., Cogswell, M., Das, A., Vedantam, R., Parikh, D., Batra, D.: Grad-cam: visual explanations from deep networks via gradient-based localization. In: CVPR (2017)
36. Song, Y., Schwing, A., Urtasun, R., et al.: Training deep neural networks via direct loss minimization. In: ICML (2016)
37. Tang, P., Wang, X., Bai, X., Liu, W.: Multiple instance detection network with online instance classifier refinement. In: CVPR (2017)
38. Tang, P., Wang, X., Wang, A., Yan, Y., Liu, W., Huang, J., Yuille, A.: Weakly supervised region proposal network and object detection. In: ECCV (2018)
39. Vernaza, P., Chandraker, M.: Learning random-walk label propagation for weakly-supervised semantic segmentation. In: CVPR (2017)
40. Wei, Y., Feng, J., Liang, X., Cheng, M.M., Zhao, Y., Yan, S.: Object region mining with adversarial erasing: a simple classification to semantic segmentation approach. In: CVPR (2017)
41. Zhou, B., Khosla, A., Lapedriza, A., Oliva, A., Torralba, A.: Learning deep features for discriminative localization. In: CVPR (2016)
42. Zhou, Y., Zhu, Y., Ye, Q., Qiu, Q., Jiao, J.: Weakly supervised instance segmentation using class peak response. In: CVPR (2018)
43. Zhu, Y., Zhou, Y., Xu, H., Ye, Q., Doermann, D., Jiao, J.: Learning instance activation maps for weakly supervised instance segmentation. In: CVPR (2019)

DA4AD: End-to-End Deep Attention-Based Visual Localization for Autonomous Driving

Yao Zhou, Guowei Wan, Shenhua Hou, Li Yu, Gang Wang, Xiaofei Rui,
and Shiyu Song[✉]

Baidu Autonomous Driving Technology Department (ADT), Beijing, China
{zhouyao,wanguowei,houshenhua,yuli01,wanggang29,
ruixiaofei,songshiyu}@baidu.com

Abstract. We present a visual localization framework based on novel
deep attention aware features for autonomous driving that achieves centimeter level localization accuracy. Conventional approaches to the visual
localization problem rely on handcrafted features or human-made objects
on the road. They are known to be either prone to unstable matching
caused by severe appearance or lighting changes, or too scarce to deliver
constant and robust localization results in challenging scenarios. In this
work, we seek to exploit the deep attention mechanism to search for
salient, distinctive and stable features that are good for long-term matching in the scene through a novel end-to-end deep neural network. Furthermore, our learned feature descriptors are demonstrated to be competent
to establish robust matches and therefore successfully estimate the optimal camera poses with high precision. We comprehensively validate the
effectiveness of our method using a freshly collected dataset with high-
quality ground truth trajectories and hardware synchronization between
sensors. Results demonstrate that our method achieves a competitive
localization accuracy when compared to the LiDAR-based localization
solutions under various challenging circumstances, leading to a potential
low-cost localization solution for autonomous driving.

1 Introduction

Localization is a fundamental task in a self-driving car system. To exploit high
definition (HD) maps as priors for robust perception and safe motion planning,
this requires the localization system to reach centimeter-level accuracy [1,3].

Despite many decades of research, building a long-term, precise and reliable
localization system using low-cost sensors, such as automotive and consumer-
grade GPS/IMU and cameras, is still an open-ended and challenging problem.
Compared to the LiDAR, cameras are passive sensors meaning that they are

Electronic supplementary material The online version of this chapter (https://
doi.org/10.1007/978-3-030-58604-1_17) contains supplementary material, which is
available to authorized users.

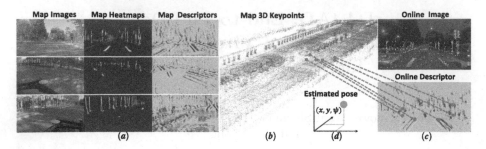

Fig. 1. The major steps of our proposed framework: (a) The heatmaps (middle) and descriptor maps (right) extracted by the local feature embedding module. (b) Map 3D keypoints are selected by the attentive keypoint selection module in accordance with the map heatmaps. (c) The neighboring keypoints in the map are projected onto the online image (top) given a set of candidate poses. The corresponding feature descriptors in the online image are found. (d) The optimal camera pose is estimated by evaluating the overall feature matching cost.

more susceptible to appearance changes caused by varying lighting conditions or changes in viewpoint. It is known that handcrafted point features (DIRD [25,27], FREAK [2,5], BRIEF [6,31] et al.) suffer from unreliable feature matching under large lighting or viewpoint change, leading to localization failure. Even when using recent deep features [12,21,49,64], local 3D-2D matching is prone to fail under strong visual changes in practice due to the lack of repeatability in the keypoint detector [18,46,47]. Another alternative to these methods is to leverage human-made objects, which encode appearance and semantics in the scene, such as lane [10,50] or sign [45] markings on the road [22,53], road curbs, poles [65] and so on. Those features are typically considered relatively stable and can be easily recognized as they are built by humans for specific purposes and also used by human drivers to aid their driving behavior. Nevertheless, those methods are only good for environments with rich human-made features but easily fail in challenging scenarios that lack them, for example, road sections with worn-out markings under poor maintenance, rural streets with no lane markings or other open spaces without clear signs. Furthermore, these carefully selected semantic signs or markings typically only cover a small area in an image. One obvious design paradox in a mainstream visual localization system is that it suffers from the absence of distinctive features, however, at the same time, it deliberately abandons rich and important information in an image by solely relying on these human-made features (Fig. 1).

In this work, titled "DA4AD" (deep attention for autonomous driving), we address the aforementioned problems by building a visual localization system that trains a novel end-to-end deep neural network (DNN) to extract learning-based feature descriptors, select attentive keypoints from map images, match them against online images and infer optimal poses through a differentiable cost volume. Inspired by prior works [13,41] that utilize the attention mechanism, our intuition is that we seek to effectively select a subset of the points in the map images as attentive keypoints. They are stable features in the scene and good for long-term matching. To this end, we first construct an image pyramid and train fully convolutional networks (FCN) to extract dense features from different scales on them independently. Using shared backbone networks, dense heatmaps from different scales are simultaneously estimated to explicitly evaluate the attention scores of these features for their capabilities in conducting robust feature matching under strong visual changes. To build a prior map, we process our map images and store the selected attentive keypoints, extracted features, and 3D coordinates into a database. The 3D coordinates are obtained from LiDAR scans which are only used for mapping. During the online localization stage, given a predicted prior vehicle pose as input, we query the nearest neighboring map image with selected keypoints in it from the database. We then sample a set of candidate poses around the prior pose. By projecting the 3D map keypoints onto the online image using each candidate pose, the matched 2D points in the online image can be found and their local features have been extracted accordingly. Finally, given these local feature descriptor pairs from both the online and map image as input, by evaluating overall feature matching cost across all the candidate poses, the optimal estimation can be obtained. More importantly, in this final feature matching step, we infer the unknown camera poses through a differentiable multi-dimensional matching cost volume in the solution space, yielding a trainable end-to-end architecture. Compared to other works [12, 13, 21, 49, 64] that learn deep feature descriptors, this architecture allows our feature representation and attention score estimation function to be trained jointly by backpropagation and optimized towards our eventual goal that is to minimize the absolute localization error. Furthermore, it bypasses the repeatability crisis in keypoint detectors in an efficient way. This end-to-end architecture design is the key to boost the overall performance of the system.

To summarize, our main contributions are:

- A novel visual localization framework for autonomous driving, yielding centimeter level precision under various challenging lighting conditions.
- Use of the attention mechanism and deep features through a novel end-to-end DNN which is the key to boost performance.
- Rigorous tests and benchmarks against several methods using a new dataset with high-quality ground truth trajectories and hardware camera, LiDAR, IMU timestamp synchronization.

2   Related Work

In the recent two decades, there has been a breakthrough in LiDAR-based localization technologies that has led to compelling performance [3, 28, 29, 35, 58, 61, 62]. However, camera-based solutions are particularly favored by car manufacturers and Tier 1 suppliers due to their low cost.

Structure Based. One important category of methods utilizes human-made structures in the environment. M. Schreiber et al. [50] localize the vehicle using a stereo camera and by matching curbs and lane segments in a map. D. Cui et al. [10,11] conversely detect consecutive lanes instead of lane segments and globally locate them by registering the lane shape with the map. Furthermore, K. Jo et al. [22] introduce an around-view monitoring (AVM) system and improve the localization performance by benefiting from the detected lane markings within it. A. Ranganathan et al. [45,63] propose to use signs marked on the road instead of the lane markings to localize the vehicles. J. K. Suhr et al. [53] further build a localization system using lane contours and road signs expressed by a minimum number of points solved in a particle filter framework. Y. Yu et al. [65] utilize line segments in the scene, such as lane markings, poles, building edges together with sparse feature points, and define a road structural feature (RSF) for localization.

Low-level Feature Based. Another category of methods employs low-level features. H. Lategahn et al. [26,27] detect salient 2D sparse points in the online image and matched with the queried 3D landmarks from the map using hand-crafted DIRD descriptors [25], and the 6 DoF poses are solved in a probabilistic factor graph. Since the number of successfully matched landmarks is crucial to the performance, H. Lategahn et al. [31] later propose to learn to select the most relevant landmarks to improve the overall long-term localization performance. Moving forward, [32] introduces linear SVM classifiers to recognize distinctive landmarks in the environment through a unsupervised mining procedure. Most recently, M. Bürki et al. [5] build a vision-based localization system with a classical 2D-3D correspondence detection-query-matching pipeline leveraging the FREAK [2] descriptor. Similar to us, LAPS-II [38,51] also utilizes the 3D structure and performs 6 DoF visual localization by first transforming RGB images to an illumination invariant color space and then finding the optimal vehicle poses by minimizing the normalized information distance (NID), which can still be considered as a handcrafted way to embed feature representations. Furthermore, [9,40,43,60] propose to localize their vehicles by generating numerous synthetic views of the environment rendered with LiDAR intensity, depth or RGB values, and comparing them to the camera images to find the optimal candidate by minimizing a handcrafted or learned cost. Recently, deep features [12,13,21,49,52,64] have been proposed to replace these traditional handcrafted ones. GN-Net [52] proposes to train deep features in a self-supervised manner (similar to us) with the newly proposed Gauss-Newton loss. The work most related to our approach is M. Dusmanu et al. [13]. It proposes a similar attentive *describe-and-detect* approach to us, but fails to integrate the feature descriptor and detector training process into a specific application task through an end-to-end DNN, which is the key to boost the performance.

Other recent attempts include DeLS-3D [59] that proposes to directly estimate the camera pose by comparing the online image with a synthetic view rendered with semantic labels given a predicted prior pose, and T. Caselitz [8] that localizes its self-position by matching reconstructed semi-dense 3D points from image features against a 3D LiDAR map. Similar to us, H. Germain et al. [18] proposes to only detect ("select" in our work) features in the reference image to bypass the repeatability crisis in the keypoint detection. A large body of literature [4,23,24,39,44,46,48,54–57] focuses on solving vision-based localization problems for other applications instead of the autonomous driving, which are not discussed in detail here.

3   Problem Statement

Our problem definition is similar to previous works [35,59], where the input to the localization system involves a pre-built map that encodes the memory of the environment in history, and a predicted coarse camera pose usually estimated by accumulating the localization estimation of the previous frame with the incremental motion estimation obtained from an IMU sensor. At the system initialization stage, this prior pose can be obtained using GPS, other image retrieval techniques or Wi-Fi fingerprinting. Our map representation contains 2D point features together with global 3D coordinates.

Therefore, given an online image, our task is to seek an optimal offset between the final and predicted pose by 3D-2D matching the features from the pre-built map to the ones from the online image. For better efficiency and robustness, we follow localization systems [29,35,58] for autonomous driving, and only the 2D horizontal and heading offset $(\Delta x, \Delta y, \Delta \psi)$ is estimated.

4   Method

There are three different stages in the system: (i) network training; (ii) map generation; (iii) online localization. Both the map generation and online localization can be considered as inferences of the trained network. The network architecture of the proposed framework in different stages is shown in Fig. 2.

4.1   Network Architecture

The overall architecture can be decomposed into three main modules: (i) local feature embedding (LFE); (ii) attentive keypoint selection (AKS); (iii) weighted feature matching (WFM). To seek the best performance, we may choose to use different algorithms or strategies in the same module when the system is in different stages. These choices are introduced in detail in Sect. 4.3, 4.4 and 4.5. The effectiveness of them is validated thoroughly in our experiments.

LFE Module. We seek to extract good local feature descriptors together with their relevance weights (attention scores) to our task represented as a heatmap in an image. Ideally, these extracted descriptors should be robust for matching under appearance changes caused by different lighting conditions or seasons. The attention scores should highlight reliable objects and avoid interferences and noises in the scene.

AKS Module. Despite the fact that our LFE module extracts dense features, similar to [13], we adopt a *describe-and-select* approach to select a set of keypoints that are good for long-term matching and save them in the map database.

WFM Module. Given 3D keypoints associated with their 2D feature descriptors from the map images and dense features extracted from the online image, the WFM module estimates the optimal pose by sampling a set of candidate poses around the prior pose and evaluating the matching cost given each candidate.

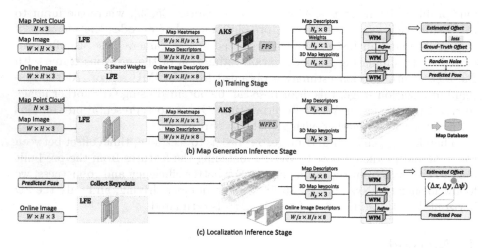

Fig. 2. The network architecture and system workflow of the proposed vision-based localization framework based on end-to-end deep attention aware features in three different stages: a) training; b) map generation; c) online localization.

4.2   System Workflow

Training. The training stage involves all the three modules, LFE, AKS, and WFM. First of all, given a predicted pose, its closest map image in the Euclidean distance is selected. Next, the LFE module extracts the dense features from both the online and map images, and the attention heatmap from the map image accordingly. Then the AKS module selects good features from the map image as the keypoints and their associated 3D coordinates are obtained from LiDAR point cloud projections. Finally, given these 3D keypoints, their feature descriptors, and corresponding attention scores as input, the WFM module seeks to find the optimal pose offset by searching in a 3D cost volume, and the optimal pose offset is compared with the ground truth pose to produce the training loss.

Map Generation. After training, there is a designated map generation step using a sub-portion of the network as shown in Fig. 2. To build the map and test the system, we did multiple trials of data collection on the same road. One of them is used for mapping. Given the LiDAR scans and the ground truth vehicle poses (see Sect. 5.1 for details), the global 3D coordinates of LiDAR points can be obtained readily. Note that the LiDAR sensors and ground truth poses are used for mapping purposes only. First, the map image pixels are associated with global 3D coordinates by projecting 3D LiDAR points onto the image, given the ground truth vehicle poses. Attention heatmaps and feature maps of different resolutions in the map image are then estimated by the LFE network inference. Next, a set of keypoints are selected for different resolutions in the pyramid in the AKS module. As a whole, we save keypoints together with their D-dimensional descriptors and 3D coordinates in the map database.

Online Localization. During the localization stage, feature maps of different resolutions in the online image are again estimated by the LFE network inference. We collect the keypoints with their feature descriptors and global 3D coordinates from the nearest map image given the predicted camera pose. Then these keypoints are projected onto the online image given the sampled candidate poses in the cost volume we built in the WFM module. Three feature matching networks of different resolutions cascade to achieve a coarse-to-fine inference and output the estimated vehicle pose.

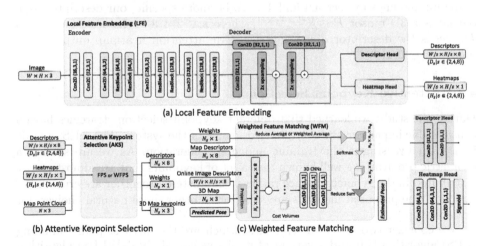

Fig. 3. The illustration of the network structure of the three main modules: (a) local feature embedding (LFE); (b) attentive keypoint selection (AKS); (c) weighted feature matching (WFM).

4.3   Local Feature Embedding

The same LFE module is used in all three different stages. We employ a network architecture similar to the feature pyramid network (FPN) introduced by T. Lin et al. [30] as shown in Fig. 3(a). With the lateral connections merging feature maps of the same spatial size from the encoder path to the decoder, the FPN can enhance high-level semantic features at all scales, thus harvesting a more powerful feature extractor. In our encoder, we have an FPN consisting of 17 layers that can be decomposed into four stages. The first stage consists of two 2D convolutional layers where the numbers in brackets are channel, kernel and stride sizes, respectively. Starting from the second stage, each stage consists of a 2D convolutional layer with stride size 2 and two residual blocks introduced in the ResNet [20]. Each residual block is composed of two 3×3 convolutional layers. In the decoder, after a 2D convolutional layer, upsampling layers are applied to hallucinate higher resolution features from coarser but semantically stronger features. Features of the same resolution from the encoder are merged to enhance these features in the decoder through the aforementioned lateral connections that element-wise average them. The outputs of the decoder are feature maps with different resolutions of the original image. They are fed into two different network heads as shown in the bottom right of Fig. 3, that are responsible for descriptor extraction and attention heatmap estimation, respectively. The feature descriptors are represented as D-dimensional vectors that are competent for robust matching under severe appearance changes caused by varying lighting or viewpoint conditions. The heatmap is composed of [0 - 1] scalars that are used as relevance weights in our attention-based keypoint selection and feature matching modules in Sect. 4.4 and 4.5. To be more specific, our descriptor map output is a 3D tensor $F \in \mathbb{R}^{\frac{H}{s} \times \frac{W}{s} \times D}$, where $s \in 2, 4, 8$ is the scale factor and $D = 8$ is the descriptor dimension size. Our attention heatmap output is an image $W \in [0, 1]^{\frac{H}{s} \times \frac{W}{s}}$.

4.4   Attentive Keypoint Selection

During the study, we learned that different keypoint selection strategies have a considerable impact on the overall performance of the system. The AKS module is used in two stages: the training and map generation. As we are solving a geometric problem, it's well known that a set of keypoints that are almost evenly distributed in the geometric space rather than clustered together are crucial. We find that the proposed methods are superior to other more natural choices, for example top-K.

We consider two selection strategies, which are the farthest point sampling (FPS) algorithm [14] and a variant of it, the weighted FPS (WFPS) algorithm as shown in Fig. 3(b). Given a set of selected points S and unselected Q, if we seek to iteratively select a new point $\hat{q}$ from Q, the FPS algorithm calculates

$$\hat{q} = \arg\max_{q \in Q}(\min_{s \in S}(d(q, s))). \tag{1}$$

In our WFPS algorithm, we instead calculate

$$\hat{q} = \arg\max_{q \in Q}(w(q) \min_{s \in S}(d(q, s))), \tag{2}$$

where $w(q)$ is the relevance attention weight of the query point q.

During the training stage, we aim to uniformly learn the attention scores of all the candidates, therefore it's necessary to have an efficient stochastic selection strategy. To this end, first of all, K candidate points are randomly selected and sent to the GPU cache. Next, we apply the FPS algorithm to select the keypoints among them. Interestingly, we find that a WFPS keypoint selection algorithm + a *weighted average* marginalization operation (introduced in Sect. 4.5) leads to catastrophic models. Our insight is that *weighted average* contributes as a positive feedback to the WFPS keypoint selection policy. A few good keypoints gain high weights rapidly, stopping others from being selected during the training, leading to a heatmap in where there are only a few clustered high weight points and of which the remaining part is simply empty. A WFPS keypoint + a *reduce average* marginalization operation (introduced in Sect. 4.5) is not a valid approach as the heatmap network can not be trained without effective incorporation of the attention weights.

During the map generation stage, we need an algorithm that can select good keypoints by effectively incorporating the trained attention weights. For this reason, again we first randomly selected K candidate points and then stick to the WFPS during map generation considering it as a density sampling function with the heatmap as probabilities.

In order to associate the 2D feature descriptors with 3D coordinates, we project 3D LiDAR points onto the image. Given the fact that not all image pixels are associated with LiDAR points, only the sparse 2D pixels with known 3D coordinates are considered as candidates, from which we select keypoints that are good for matching. Please refer to the supplemental materials for exact numbers of keypoints for different resolutions.

4.5   Weighted Feature Matching

Traditional approaches typically utilize a PnP solver [19] within a RANSAC [15] framework to solve the camera pose estimation problem given a set of 2D-3D correspondings. Unfortunately, these matching approaches including the outlier rejection step, are non-differentiable and thus prevent them from the feature and attention learning through backpropagation during the training stage. L^3-Net [35] introduced a feature matching and pose estimation method that leverages a differentiable 3D cost volume to evaluate the matching cost given the pose offset and the corresponding feature descriptor pairs from the online and map images.

In the following, we improve the original L^3-Net design by coming up with solutions to incorporate attention weights and making them effectively trainable. The network architecture is illustrated in Fig. 3(c).

Cost Volume. Similar to the implementation of L^3-Net [35], we build a cost volume $N_s \times n_x \times n_y \times n_\psi$, where N_s is the number of selected keypoints, n_x, n_y and n_ψ are the grid sizes in each dimension. To be more specific, given the predicted pose as the cost volume center, we divide its adjacent space into a three-dimensional grid evenly, denoted as $\{\Delta T = (\Delta x_i, \Delta y_j, \Delta \psi_k) | 1 \leq i \leq$

$n_x, 1 \leq j \leq n_y, 1 \leq k \leq n_\psi\}$. Nodes in this cost volume are candidate poses from which we desire to evaluate their corresponding feature pairs and find the optimal solution. By projecting the selected 3D keypoints in the map images onto the online images using each candidate pose, the corresponding local feature descriptors can be calculated by applying the bilinear interpolation on the descriptor map of the online image. Unlike the implementation of L^3-Net where it computes the element-wise $L2$ distance between both descriptors from the online and map images, we calculate the total $L2$ distance between them, bringing a single-dimensional cost scalar. The cost scalar is then processed by a three-layer 3D CNNs with a kernel of Conv3D(8,1,1)-Conv3D(8,1,1)-Conv3D(1,1,1), and the result is denoted as $P(p, \Delta T)$, where p is a keypoint out of N.

Marginalization. In the original implementation of L^3-Net, the regularized matching cost volume $N_s \times n_x \times n_y \times n_\psi$ is marginalized into a $n_x \times n_y \times n_\psi$ one across the keypoint dimension by applying a *reduce average* operation. Following [41], how to effectively incorporate the attention weights across all the keypoint features is the key to our success in the heatmap head training in the LFE module. Compared to the *reduce average* (no attention weight incorporation), the most straightforward solution to this is to use a *weighted average* operation replacing the *reduce average*. We choose to use *weighted average* for training as we use the FPS in the AKS module. We choose to use *reduce average* during the online localization stage and thoroughly evaluate the performance of the two different approaches in Sect. 5.3.

The remaining part that estimates the optimal offset $\Delta \hat{z}$ and its probability distribution $P(\Delta z_i)$ for $z \in \{x, y, \psi\}$ is identical to the design of L3-Net as shown in Fig. 3(c). Please refer to [35] for more details.

4.6 Loss

1) *Absolute Loss:* The absolute distance between the estimated offset $\Delta \hat{T}$ and the ground truth $\Delta T^* = (\Delta x^*, \Delta y^*, \Delta \psi^*)$ is applied as the first loss:

$$Loss_1 = \alpha \cdot (|\Delta \hat{x} - \Delta x^*| + |\Delta \hat{y} - \Delta y^*| + |\Delta \hat{\psi} - \Delta \psi^*|), \qquad (3)$$

where α is a balancing factor.

2) *Concentration Loss:* Besides the absolute loss above, the concentration of the probability distribution $P(\Delta z_i), z \in \{x, y, \psi\}$ also has a considerable impact on the estimation robustness. For this reason, the mean absolute deviation (MAD) of the probability distribution assuming the ground truth as the mean value is used as:

$$\sigma_z = \sum_i P(\Delta z_i) \cdot |\Delta z_i - \Delta z^*|, \qquad (4)$$

where $z \in \{x, y, \psi\}$. Accordingly, the second loss function is defined as $Loss_2 = \beta \cdot (\sigma_x + \sigma_y + \sigma_\psi)$.

3) *Similarity Loss:* In addition to geometry constrains, the corresponding 2D-3D keypoint pairs should have similar descriptors. Therefore, we define the third loss:

$$Loss_3 = \sum_p \max(\hat{P}(p) - C, 0), \tag{5}$$

where $\hat{P}(p)$ is the cost volume output from the 3D CNNs of the keypoint p, when we project the keypoint in the map using the ground truth pose onto the online image, find the corresponding point in the online image, and compute the descriptor distance between the pair. $C = 1.0$ is a constant.

5   Experiments

5.1   Apollo-DaoxiangLake Dataset

To evaluate the proposed method, we require a dataset with multiple trials of data collection of the same road over a long period of time containing aligned camera images and 3D LiDAR scans. To this end, we evaluated several public datasets [7,17,35,37,42,47]. The KITTI [16,17] and Ford Campus [42] datasets fail to enclose multiple trials of the same road. The NCLT dataset [7] is the closest one to our requirement, but unfortunately, we find that images are not well aligned with 3D LiDAR scans. The Oxford RobotCar dataset [37] doesn't provide ground truth trajectories with high confidence until the latest upgrade [36]. The Aachen Day-Night, CMU-Seasons and RobotCar-Seasons datasets [47] focus more on single-frame based localization, resulting in short trajectories lasting for only several seconds, incompatible for the application of autonomous driving. The Apollo-SouthBay dataset [34,35] doesn't release camera images.

Therefore, we recruited our mapping vehicles and built this new dataset, Apollo-DaoxiangLake. The cameras are hardware synchronized with the LiDAR sensor. That allows us to compensate for the rolling shutter and motion effects when we project 3D point clouds onto images, yielding precise alignment between 3D point clouds and image pixels. The ground truth poses are provided using high-end sensors through necessary post-processing solutions. We collected 9 trials of repetitive data within 14 weeks (Sep. to Dec.) over the same road adjacent to the Daoxiang Lake park in Beijing, China. In particular, our dataset includes different times of the day, for example, noon, afternoon, sunset, and seasonal changes, e.g., sunny, snowy days, and difficult circumstances, e.g. foggy lens, object occlusion, making it a challenging visual localization benchmark dataset. Some sample images are shown in Fig. 4. The data from the first trial on Sep. 18 is reserved for building the localization map. Please refer to the supplemental materials for more details about our dataset.

In our experiment, for simplicity, the input predicted poses are generated by extracting the inter-frame incremental motion from the trajectories estimated by the built-in GNSS/IMU integrated solution in NovAtel PwrPak7D-E1 with RTK disabled, and appending it to the localization output of our system at the previous frame, which is the same as the experimental setup of the LiDAR localization system in [29]. In practice, the incremental motion should be estimated by an inertial navigation system (INS).

5.2 Performances

Quantitative Analysis. Due to the fact that not all the methods can work properly in all circumstances in our dataset, we introduce an N/A ratio metric and allow the system to claim "results not available" under certain specific circumstances. Only the results from "available" frames are counted in the quantitative analysis of the localization accuracy. For our method, we monitor the variance of estimated probability vectors $P(\Delta z_i), z \in \{x, y, \psi\}$. We report the "unavailable" status when the variance is higher than a threshold. Our quantitative analysis includes horizontal and heading (yaw) errors with both RMS and maximum values. The horizontal errors are further decomposed to longitudinal and lateral directions. The percentages of frames where the system achieves better than thresholds are also shown in tables. To make a thorough evaluation, we compare the proposed approach with two methods, structure-based and feature-based.

i) Structure-based: Following [22,50], a map that contains line segments to represent the lane markings or curbs is used. 2D lane segments are extracted from online images and are matched against those in the map based on a particle filter framework. Objects, such as poles, are added to further improve the N/A ratio and longitudinal error. Similarly, only 3 DoF are estimated in this method. When there is no adequate detected or matched lane segments, the system reports the "unavailable" status.

ii) Feature-based: The latest work HF-Net [46] is included. When there is no sufficient matched inliers, the system reports the "unavailable" status. The original implementation of HF-Net includes global descriptors for coarse localization (image retrieval) and 6 DoF pose estimation using a PnP + RANSAC. To conduct a fairer comparison, we made necessary modifications including three parts: 1) We replaced its global retrieval with 10 neighboring images directly found using the prior pose. 2) The local 6-DoF pose estimation using a PnP is replaced with a PnP + bundle adjustment (BA) using the 3D-2D matches from 10 to 1 images (single camera) or 30 to 3 images (multi-cameras). 3) A 3 DoF BA across (x, y, yaw) dimensions is implemented. These modifications improve its performance as shown in Table 1. With regard to the feature descriptors which play an essential role during matching, we also present the experimental results using SIFT [33] in the HF-Net architecture.

In Table 1, we give a quantitative analysis of each method. The method labeled "(S)" uses only a single front camera, others use all three cameras. "HFNet[46]" is the original implementation with PnP +RANSAC which only works for single view. "HFNet++" is the method with our modifications to enhance the performance. "HFNet++SIFT" means that we use the SIFT descriptors in the HF-Net framework. It demonstrates that the localization performance of our proposed vision-based method is comparable to the latest LiDAR-based solution [58], achieving centimeter-level RMS error in both longitudinal and lateral directions. We also find that the LiDAR method [58] reaches its maximum error when the road surface is wet during snowy days. The low localization errors of our system demonstrate that our network can generalize decently

Table 1. Comparison with other methods. We achieve centimeter-level RMS errors in both longitudinal and lateral directions, which is comparable to the latest LiDAR-based solution [58]. Our overall performance, including the N/A rate and accuracy, is higher than both the structure-based and feature-based methods by a large margin.

Method	N/A (%)	Horizontal RMS/Max(m) 0.1/0.2/0.3(%)		Longitudinal RMS/Max(m)	Lateral RMS/Max(m)	Yaw RMS/Max(°) 0.1/0.3/0.6(%)
Struct-based (S)	91.0	0.244/2.669	20.5/49.5/71.3	0.218/**1.509**	0.076/2.533	0.151/4.218 42.1/89.7/99.0
HFNet[46] (S)	61.4	0.243/322.6	34.3/61.4/76.3	0.211/322.5	0.081/8.844	0.081/15.65 77.8/97.8/99.6
HFNet++(S)	79.8	0.213/6.049	30.4/59.0/76.6	0.186/2.341	0.074/6.004	0.079/16.03 74.5/98.3/99.8
HFNet++SIFT(S)	41.2	0.264/8.181	28.1/54.0/70.8	0.211/7.349	0.113/8.154	0.106/17.42 75.0/96.1/98.9
HFNet++	93.2	0.176/13.62	45.4/73.9/87.0	0.152/13.54	0.056/6.380	0.077/25.22 82.6/98.2/99.5
HFNet++SIFT	48.9	0.244/8.281	30.3/61.2/75.7	0.191/7.349	0.105/7.046	0.107/14.68 77.6/95.9/98.3
Ours (S)	95.4	0.123/3.119	61.7/83.6/91.9	0.106/3.074	0.043/1.787	0.070/**1.685** 80.5/97.4/99.4
Ours	**100.0**	**0.058/2.617**	**86.3/96.8/99.5**	**0.048**/2.512	**0.023/1.541**	**0.054**/3.208 **89.4/99.6/99.9**
LiDAR [58]	100.0	0.053/1.831	93.6/99.7/99.9	0.038/1.446	0.029/1.184	0.070/1.608 76.4/99.8/99.9

in varying lighting conditions. The system also boosts its performance by using all the three cameras. In addition, note our vast performance improvement over both the structure-based or feature-based methods. The structure-based baseline method achieves high lateral precision, which is crucial for autonomous driving. Compared to the traditional SIFT feature, the learning-based feature HF-Net demonstrates better performance. When the global descriptors fail to locate the vehicle in the ballpark, the original HF-Net [46] can produce significantly large localization errors as expected.

Run-time Analysis. We evaluated the runtime performance of our method with a GTX 1080 Ti GPU, Core i7-9700K CPU, and 16 GB Memory. The total end-to-end processing time per frame during online localization is 27 ms and 50 ms for single and three cameras, respectively. The pre-built map data size is about 10 MB/km.

5.3 Ablations and Visualization

Keypoint Selection and Marginalization. We carry out a series of comprehensive experiments to compare the different keypoint selection and dimension marginalization strategies we proposed in the AKS and WFM modules in Sect. 4 with the results shown in Table 2. "WFPS+Weighted" means that we choose the WFPS algorithm as our keypoint selection algorithm and the *weighted average* method in our WFM module during the online localization. Similarly, "Reduce" means we choose the *reduce average* in the WFM module. We note that using WFPS + *reduce average* outperforms others. In addition, the dramatic performance decline using FPS + *reduce average* which does not incorporate the estimated attention scores, proves the effectiveness of our proposed attention mechanism.

Table 2. Comparison with various keypoint selection and weighting strategies during the network inference. WFPS + *reduce average* achieves the best performance.

Method	N/A (%)	Horizontal		Longitudinal	Lateral	Yaw	
		RMS/Max(m)	0.1/0.2/0.3(%)	RMS/Max(m)	RMS/Max(m)	RMS/Max(°)	0.1/0.3/0.6(%)
WFPS+Weighted	99.9	0.063/**2.419**	83.4/96.5/99.3	0.051/**1.811**	0.026/2.095	0.056/**2.430**	88.3/99.5/99.8
WFPS+Reduce	**100.0**	**0.058**/2.617	**86.3/96.8/99.5**	**0.048**/2.512	**0.023/1.541**	**0.054**/3.208	**89.4/99.6/99.9**
FPS+Weighted	98.9	0.306/18.40	58.0/76.4/82.9	0.222/14.96	0.161/17.93	0.195/3.390	66.0/87.0/92.3
FPS+Reduce	98.1	0.135/6.585	69.7/85.1/90.5	0.109/4.643	0.055/6.151	0.105/3.287	76.3/93.4/97.3

Keypoint and Heatmap Visualization. To have better insights into the attention mechanism in our framework, we visualize the generated heatmaps together with the selected keypoints and the extracted feature descriptors in Fig. 4. Note the diverse lighting changes from noon to sunset, dramatic seasonal changes on tree leaves and snow on the ground, challenging circumstances caused by the foggy lens. Also interestingly, we find that the feature descriptors output by the network for dynamic objects, such as cars, are similar to the background. It implies both our learned feature maps and heatmaps suppress the influence of the dynamic objects in our localization task.

Fig. 4. Visualization of the camera images together with the generated heatmaps, feature maps, and keypoints. Note the dramatic visual differences between the online and map images and the various challenging circumstances in our dataset.

6   Conclusion

We have presented a vision-based localization framework designed for autonomous driving applications. We demonstrate that selecting keypoints based on an attention mechanism and learning features through an end-to-end DNN allows our system to find abundant features that are salient, distinctive and robust in the scene. The capability of full exploitation of these robust features enables our system to achieve centimeter-level localization accuracy, which is comparable to the latest LiDAR-based methods and substantially greater than other vision-based methods in terms of both robustness and precision. The strong performance makes our system ready to be integrated into a self-driving car, constantly providing precise localization results using low-cost sensors, thus accelerating the commercialization of self-driving cars.

Acknowledgments. This work is supported by Baidu Autonomous Driving Technology Department (ADT) in conjunction with the Apollo Project. Shufu Xie helped with the development of the lane-based method. Shirui Li and Yuanfan Xie helped with the sensor calibration. Shuai Wang, Lingchang Li, and Shuangcheng Guo helped with the sensor synchronization.

References

1. Baidu Apollo open platform. http://apollo.auto/
2. Alahi, A., Ortiz, R., Vandergheynst, P.: FREAK: fast retina keypoint. In: Proceedings of the IEEE Conference on Computer Vision and Pattern Recognition (CVPR), pp. 510–517. IEEE (2012)
3. Barsan, I.A., Wang, S., Pokrovsky, A., Urtasun, R.: Learning to localize using a LiDAR intensity map. In: Proceedings of the Conference on Robot Learning (CoRL), pp. 605–616 (2018)
4. Brahmbhatt, S., Gu, J., Kim, K., Hays, J., Kautz, J.: Geometry-aware learning of maps for camera localization. In: Proceedings of the IEEE Conference on Computer Vision and Pattern Recognition (CVPR) (2018)
5. Bürki, M., et al.: VIZARD: reliable visual localization for autonomous vehicles in urban outdoor environments. arXiv preprint arXiv:1902.04343 (2019)
6. Calonder, M., Lepetit, V., Strecha, C., Fua, P.: BRIEF: binary robust independent elementary features. In: Daniilidis, K., Maragos, P., Paragios, N. (eds.) ECCV 2010. LNCS, vol. 6314, pp. 778–792. Springer, Heidelberg (2010). https://doi.org/10.1007/978-3-642-15561-1_56
7. Carlevaris-Bianco, N., Ushani, A.K., Eustice, R.M.: University of Michigan North Campus long-term vision and LiDAR dataset. Int. J. Rob. Res. (IJRR) **35**(9), 1023–1035 (2015)
8. Caselitz, T., Steder, B., Ruhnke, M., Burgard, W.: Monocular camera localization in 3D LiDAR maps. In: Proceedings of the IEEE/RSJ International Conference on Intelligent Robots and Systems (IROS), pp. 1926–1931. IEEE (2016)
9. Chen, Y., Wang, G.: EnforceNet: monocular camera localization in large scale indoor sparse LiDAR point cloud. arXiv preprint arXiv:1907.07160 (2019)
10. Cui, D., Xue, J., Du, S., Zheng, N.: Real-time global localization of intelligent road vehicles in lane-level via lane marking detection and shape registration. In: Proceedings of the IEEE/RSJ International Conference on Intelligent Robots and Systems (IROS), pp. 4958–4964. IEEE (2014)
11. Cui, D., Xue, J., Zheng, N.: Real-time global localization of robotic cars in lane level via lane marking detection and shape registration. IEEE Trans. Intell. Transp. Syst. (T-ITS) **17**(4), 1039–1050 (2015)

12. DeTone, D., Malisiewicz, T., Rabinovich, A.: SuperPoint: self-supervised interest point detection and description. In: Proceedings of the IEEE Conference on Computer Vision and Pattern Recognition Workshops (CVPRW) (2018)
13. Dusmanu, Met al.: D2-Net: atrainable CNN for joint description and detection of local features. In: Proceedings of the IEEE Conference on Computer Vision and Pattern Recognition (CVPR) (2019)
14. Eldar, Y., Lindenbaum, M., Porat, M., Zeevi, Y.Y.: The farthest point strategy for progressive image sampling. IEEE Trans. Image Process. (TIP) **6**(9), 1305–1315 (1997)
15. Fischler, M.A., Bolles, R.C.: Random sample consensus: a paradigm for model fitting with applications to image analysis and automated cartography. Commun. ACM **24**, 381–395 (1981)
16. Geiger, A., Lenz, P., Stiller, C., Urtasun, R.: Vision meets robotics: the KITTI dataset. Int. J. Rob. Res. (IJRR) **32**(11), 1231–1237 (2013)
17. Geiger, A., Lenz, P., Urtasun, R.: Are we ready for autonomous driving? the KITTI vision benchmark suite. In: Proceedings of the IEEE Conference on Computer Vision and Pattern Recognition (CVPR), pp. 3354–3361. IEEE (2012)
18. Germain, H., Bourmaud, G., Lepetit, V.: Sparse-to-dense hypercolumn matching for long-term visual localization. In: Proceedings of the International Conference on 3D Vision (3DV), pp. 513–523. IEEE (2019)
19. Haralick, B.M., Lee, C.N., Ottenberg, K., Nölle, M.: Review and analysis of solutions of the three point perspective pose estimation problem. Int. J. Comput. Vis.(IJCV) **13**(3), 331–356 (1994)
20. He, K., Zhang, X., Ren, S., Sun, J.: Deep residual learning for image recognition. In: Proceedings of the IEEE Conference on Computer Vision and Pattern Recognition (CVPR), pp. 770–778 (2016)
21. He, K., Lu, Y., Sclaroff, S.: Local descriptors optimized for average precision. In: Proceedings of the IEEE Conference on Computer Vision and Pattern Recognition (CVPR) (2018)
22. Jo, K., Jo, Y., Suhr, J.K., Jung, H.G., Sunwoo, M.: Precise localization of an autonomous car based on probabilistic noise models of road surface marker features using multiple cameras. IEEE Trans. Intell. Transp. Syst. **16**(6), 3377–3392 (2015)
23. Kendall, A., Grimes, M., Cipolla, R.: PoseNet: a convolutional network for real-time 6-DOF camera relocalization. In: Proceedings of the IEEE International Conference on Computer Vision (ICCV), pp. 2938–2946 (2015). https://doi.org/10.1109/ICCV.2015.336
24. Kendall, A., Cipolla, R., et al.: Geometric loss functions for camera pose regression with deep learning. In: Proceedings of the IEEE Conference on Computer Vision and Pattern Recognition (CVPR), vol. 3, p. 8 (2017)
25. Lategahn, H., Beck, J., Kitt, B., Stiller, C.: How to learn an illumination robust image feature for place recognition. In: Proceedings of the IEEE Intelligent Vehicles Symposium (IV), pp. 285–291. IEEE (2013)
26. Lategahn, H., Schreiber, M., Ziegler, J., Stiller, C.: Urban localization with camera and inertial measurement unit. In: Proceedings of the IEEE Intelligent Vehicles Symposium (IV), pp. 719–724. IEEE (2013)
27. Lategahn, H., Stiller, C.: Vision only localization. IEEE Trans. Intell. Transp. Syst. (T-ITS) **15**(3), 1246–1257 (2014)
28. Levinson, J., Montemerlo, M., Thrun, S.: Map-based precision vehicle localization in urban environments. In: Proceedings of the Robotics: Science and Systems (RSS), vol. 4, p. 1 (2007)

29. Levinson, J., Thrun, S.: Robust vehicle localization in urban environments using probabilistic maps. In: Proceedings of the IEEE International Conference on Robotics and Automation (ICRA), pp. 4372–4378 (2010)
30. Lin, T.Y., Dollár, P., Girshick, R., He, K., Hariharan, B., Belongie, S.: Feature pyramid networks for object detection. In: Proceedings of the IEEE Conference on Computer Vision and Pattern Recognition (CVPR), pp. 2117–2125 (2017)
31. Linegar, C., Churchill, W., Newman, P.: Work smart, not hard: recalling relevant experiences for vast-scale but time-constrained localisation. In: Proceedings of the IEEE International Conference on Robotics and Automation (ICRA), pp. 90–97. IEEE (2015)
32. Linegar, C., Churchill, W., Newman, P.: Made to measure: bespoke landmarks for 24-hour, all-weather localisation with a camera. In: Proceedings of the IEEE International Conference on Robotics and Automation (ICRA), pp. 787–794. IEEE (2016)
33. Lowe, D.G.: Distinctive image features from scale-invariant keypoints. Int. J. Comput. Vis. (IJCV) **60**(2), 91–110 (2004)
34. Lu, W., Wan, G., Zhou, Y., Fu, X., Yuan, P., Song, S.: DeepVCP: an end-to-end deep neural network for point cloud registration. In: Proceedings of the IEEE International Conference on Computer Vision (ICCV) (2019)
35. Lu, W., Zhou, Y., Wan, G., Hou, S., Song, S.: L3-Net: towards learning based LiDAR localization for autonomous driving. In: Proceedings of the IEEE Conference on Computer Vision and Pattern Recognition (CVPR), pp. 6389–6398 (2019)
36. Maddern, W., Pascoe, G., Gadd, M., Barnes, D., Yeomans, B., Newman, P.: Real-time kinematic ground truth for the Oxford robotcar dataset. arXiv preprint arXiv:2002.10152 (2020)
37. Maddern, W., Pascoe, G., Linegar, C., Newman, P.: 1 year, 1000 km: the Oxford RobotCar dataset. Int. J. Rob. Res. (IJRR) **36**(1), 3–15 (2017)
38. Maddern, W., Stewart, A.D., Newman, P.: LAPS-II: 6-DoF day and night visual localisation with prior 3D structure for autonomous road vehicles. In: Proceedings of the IEEE Intelligent Vehicles Symposium (IV), pp. 330–337. IEEE (2014)
39. Naseer, T., Burgard, W.: Deep regression for monocular camera-based 6-DoF global localization in outdoor environments. In: Proceedings of the IEEE/RSJ International Conference on Intelligent Robots and Systems (IROS), pp. 1525–1530 (2017)
40. Neubert, P., Schubert, S., Protzel, P.: Sampling-based methods for visual navigation in 3D maps by synthesizing depth images. In: Proceedings of the IEEE/RSJ International Conference on Intelligent Robots and Systems (IROS), pp. 2492–2498. IEEE (2017)
41. Noh, H., Araujo, A., Sim, J., Weyand, T., Han, B.: Large-scale image retrieval with attentive deep local features. In: Proceedings of the IEEE International Conference on Computer Vision (ICCV), pp. 3456–3465 (2017)
42. Pandey, G., McBride, J.R., Eustice, R.M.: Ford campus vision and LiDAR data set. Int. J. Rob. Res. (IJRR) **30**(13), 1543–1552 (2011)
43. Pascoe, G., Maddern, W., Newman, P.: Direct visual localisation and calibration for road vehicles in changing city environments. In: Proceedings of the IEEE International Conference on Computer Vision Workshops (ICCVW), pp. 9–16 (2015)
44. Radwan, N., Valada, A., Burgard, W.: VLocNet++: deep multitask learning for semantic visual localization and odometry. IEEE Rob. Autom. Lett. (RA-L) **3**(4), 4407–4414 (2018)

45. Ranganathan, A., Ilstrup, D., Wu, T.: Light-weight localization for vehicles using road markings. In: Proceedings of the IEEE/RSJ International Conference on Intelligent Robots and Systems (IROS), pp. 921–927. IEEE (2013)
46. Sarlin, P.E., Cadena, C., Siegwart, R., Dymczyk, M.: From coarse to fine: robust hierarchical localization at large scale. In: Proceedings of the IEEE Conference on Computer Vision and Pattern Recognition (CVPR) (2019)
47. Sattler, T., et al.: Benchmarking 6-DoF outdoor visual localization in changing conditions. In: Proceedings of the IEEE Conference on Computer Vision and Pattern Recognition (CVPR), pp. 8601–8610 (2018)
48. Sattler, T., Zhou, Q., Pollefeys, M., Leal-Taixe, L.: Understanding the limitations of CNN-Based absolute camera pose regression. In: Proceedings of the IEEE Conference on Computer Vision and Pattern Recognition (CVPR) (2019)
49. Savinov, N., Seki, A., Ladicky, L., Sattler, T., Pollefeys, M.: Quad-networks: unsupervised learning to rank for interest point detection. In: Proceedings of the IEEE Conference on Computer Vision and Pattern Recognition (CVPR) (2017)
50. Schreiber, M., Knöppel, C., Franke, U.: Laneloc: lane marking based localization using highly accurate maps. In: Proceedings of the IEEE Intelligent Vehicles Symposium (IV), pp. 449–454. IEEE (2013)
51. Stewart, A.D., Newman, P.: LAPS-localisation using appearance of prior structure: 6-DOF monocular camera localisation using prior pointclouds. In: Proceedings of the IEEE International Conference on Robotics and Automation (ICRA), pp. 2625–2632. IEEE (2012)
52. von Stumberg, L., Wenzel, P., Khan, Q., Cremers, D.: GN-Net: the Gauss-Newton loss for multi-weather relocalization. IEEE Rob. Autom. Lett. 5(2), 890–897 (2020)
53. Suhr, J.K., Jang, J., Min, D., Jung, H.G.: Sensor fusion-based low-cost vehicle localization system for complex urban environments. IEEE Trans. Intell. Transp. Syst. (T-ITS) 18(5), 1078–1086 (2016)
54. Taira, H., et al.: InLoc: indoor visual localization with dense matching and view synthesis. In: Proceedings of the IEEE Conference on Computer Vision and Pattern Recognition (CVPR) (2018)
55. Toft, C., et al.: Semantic match consistency for long-term visual localization. In: Proceedings of the European Conference on Computer Vision (ECCV) (2018)
56. Valada, A., Radwan, N., Burgard, W.: Deep auxiliary learning for visual localization and odometry. In: Proceedings of the IEEE International Conference on Robotics and Automation (ICRA), pp. 6939–6946 (2018). https://doi.org/10.1109/ICRA.2018.8462979
57. Walch, F., Hazirbas, C., Leal-Taixe, L., Sattler, T., Hilsenbeck, S., Cremers, D.: Image-based localization using LSTMs for structured feature correlation. In: Proceedings of the IEEE International Conference on Computer Vision (ICCV), pp. 627–637 (2017)
58. Wan, G., et al.: Robust and precise vehicle localization based on multi-sensor fusion in diverse city scenes. In: Proceedings of the IEEE International Conference on Robotics and Automation (ICRA), pp. 4670–4677 (2018)
59. Wang, P., Yang, R., Cao, B., Xu, W., Lin, Y.: DeLS-3D: deep localization and segmentation with a 3D semantic map. In: Proceedings of the IEEE Conference on Computer Vision and Pattern Recognition (CVPR) (2018)
60. Wolcott, R.W., Eustice, R.M.: Visual localization within LiDAR maps for automated urban driving. In: Proceedings of the IEEE/RSJ International Conference on Intelligent Robots and Systems (IROS), pp. 176–183. IEEE (2014)

61. Wolcott, R.W., Eustice, R.M.: Fast LiDAR localization using multiresolution Gaussian mixture maps. In: Proceedings of the IEEE International Conference on Robotics and Automation (ICRA), pp. 2814–2821 (2015)
62. Wolcott, R.W., Eustice, R.M.: Robust LiDAR localization using multiresolution gaussian mixture maps for autonomous driving. Int. J. Rob. Res. (IJRR) **36**(3), 292–319 (2017)
63. Wu, T., Ranganathan, A.: Vehicle localization using road markings. In: Proceedings of the IEEE Intelligent Vehicles Symposium (IV), pp. 1185–1190. IEEE (2013)
64. Yi, K.M.Y., Trulls, E., Lepetit, V., Fua, P.: LIFT: learned invariant feature transform. In: Proceedings of the European Conference on Computer Vision (ECCV) (2016)
65. Yu, Y., Zhao, H., Davoine, F., Cui, J., Zha, H.: Monocular visual localization using road structural features. In: Proceedings of the IEEE Intelligent Vehicles Symposium Proceedings (IV), pp. 693–699. IEEE (2014)

Visual-Relation Conscious Image Generation from Structured-Text

Duc Minh Vo[1(✉)] and Akihiro Sugimoto[2]

[1] The Graduate University for Advanced Studies, SOKENDAI, Tokyo, Japan
vmduc@nii.ac.jp
[2] National Institute of Informatics, Tokyo, Japan
sugimoto@nii.ac.jp

Abstract. We propose an end-to-end network for image generation from given structured-text that consists of the visual-relation layout module and stacking-GANs. Our visual-relation layout module uses relations among entities in the structured-text in two ways: comprehensive usage and individual usage. We comprehensively use all relations together to localize initial bounding-boxes (BBs) of all the entities. We use individual relation separately to predict from the initial BBs relation-units for all the relations. We then unify all the relation-units to produce the visual-relation layout, i.e., BBs for all the entities so that each of them uniquely corresponds to each entity while keeping its involved relations. Our visual-relation layout reflects the scene structure given in the input text. The stacking-GANs is the stack of three GANs conditioned on the visual-relation layout and the output of previous GAN, consistently capturing the scene structure. Our network realistically renders entities' details while keeping the scene structure. Experimental results on two public datasets show the effectiveness of our method.

1 Introduction

Generating photo-realistic images from text descriptions (T2I) is one of the major problems in computer vision. Besides having a wide range of applications such as intelligent image manipulation, it drives research progress in multimodal learning and inference across vision and language [1–3].

The GANs [4] conditioned on unstructured text description [5–9] show remarkable results in T2I. Stacking such conditional GANs has shown even more ability of progressively rendering a more and more detailed entity in high resolution [6,9]. However, in more complex scenarios where sentences are with many entities and relations, their performance is degraded. This is because they use

---

The authors are thankful to Zehra Hayırcı for her valuable comments on this work.

Electronic supplementary material The online version of this chapter (https://doi.org/10.1007/978-3-030-58604-1_18) contains supplementary material, which is available to authorized users.

A. Vedaldi et al. (Eds.): ECCV 2020, LNCS 12373, pp. 290–306, 2020.
https://doi.org/10.1007/978-3-030-58604-1_18

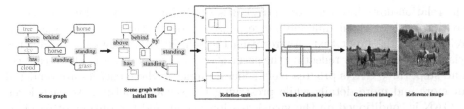

Fig. 1. Overall framework of our method. Given a structured-text (scene graph), our method predicts initial BBs for entities using all relations together, next takes individual relation one by one to infer a relation-unit for the relation, then unifies all the relation-units to produce visual-relation layout. Finally, the layout is converted to an image. Color of each entity BB corresponds to that in the scene graph. Red dotted arrow means the individual usage of relations. (Color figure online)

only entity information in given text descriptions for rendering a specific entity, leading to a poor layout of multiple entities in generated images.

In the presence of multiple entities, besides the details of each entity, how to localize all the entities so that they reflect given relations becomes crucial for better image generation. Indeed, recent work [1, 10–12] show the effectiveness of inferring the scene layout first from given text descriptions. Johnson+ [1], Li+ [10], and Ashual+ [11] use structured-text, i.e., scene graphs [2], first to construct a scene layout by predicting bounding boxes and segmentation masks for all entities, then convert it to an image. Hong+ [12] constructs a semantic layout, a scene structure based on object instances, from input text descriptions and converts the layout into an image. However, those mentioned methods [1, 10–12] aggregate all relations in which each entity is involved, and then localize all entities' bounding-boxes at the same time. As a result, the predicted bounding-boxes do not preserve the relations among entities well. Localizing entities faithfully by preserving their relations given in text descriptions is desired.

We leverage advantages of the pyramid of GANs and inferring the scene layout, proposing a GAN-based model for T2I where our network steps further in relation usage by employing not only all available relations together but also individual relation separately. We refer the former usage of relations as *comprehensive* while the latter as *individual*. Our network has two steps: (1) inferring from input the *visual-relation layout*, i.e., localized bounding-boxes for all the entities so that each of which uniquely corresponds to each entity and faithfully preserves relations between the entities, and (2) progressively generating coarse-to-fine images with the pyramid of GANs, namely stacking-GANs, conditioned on the visual-relation layout. The first step takes the comprehensive usage of relations first to generate initial bounding-boxes (BBs) for entities as in [1, 10–12], and then takes the individual usage to predict a relation-unit for each *subject–predicate–object* relation where all the relations in the input are extracted through its scene graph [2]. Each relation-unit consists of *two* BBs that participate in the relation: one for a "subject" entity and one for an "object" entity. Since one entity may participate in multiple relations, we then unify all the relation-units into refined (entity) BBs (including their locations and sizes) so that each of them uniquely corresponds to one entity while keeping their relations in the input text. Aggregating the refined BBs allows us to infer the visual-relation layout reflecting the scene structure given in the text. In the second step, three GANs progressively generate images where entities are rendered in more and more details while preserving the scene structure. At each level, a GAN is conditioned on the visual-relation layout and the output of previous GAN. Our network is trained in a fully end-to-end fashion.

The main contribution of our proposed method is our introduction to the individual usage of *subject–predicate–object* relations for localizing entity bounding-boxes, so that our proposed *visual-relation layout* surely preserves the visual relations among entities. In addition, we stack and condition GANs on the visual-relation layout to progressively render realistic detailed entities that keep their relations even from complex text descriptions. Experimental results on COCO-stuff [13] and GENOME [14] demonstrate outperformances of our method against state-of-the-arts. Figure 1 shows the overall framework of our proposed method.

2   Related Work

Recent GAN-based methods have shown promising results on T2I [1,5,6,8,9,12, 15]. They, however, struggle to faithfully reproduce complex sentences with many entities and relations because of the gap between text and image representations.

To overcome the limitation of GANs conditioned on text descriptions, a two-step approach was proposed where inference of the scene layout as an intermediate representation between text and image is followed by using the layout to generate images [1,10–12]. Since the gap between the intermediate representation and image is smaller than that of text and image, this approach generates more realistic images. Zhao+ [16] and Sun+ [17] propose a combination of ground-truth (GT) layout and entity embeddings to generate images. Hong+ [12] infers a scene layout by feeding text descriptions into a LSTM. More precisely, they use a LSTM to predict BBs for all entities independently, then employ a bi-directional conv-LSTM to generate entity shapes from each predicted BB without using any relation. The function of the bi-directional conv-LSTM used here is just the putting-together. They then combine the layout with text embeddings obtained from the pre-trained text encoder [7], and use a cascade refinement network (CRN) [18] for generating images.

Johnson+ [1], Li+ [10], and Ashual+ [11] employ a scene graph [2] to predict a layout and then condition CRN [18] on the layout. The graph convolution network (GCN) used in these methods aggregates available relations of all the entities together along the edges of the scene graph. Namely, only the comprehensive usage of relations is employed. Consequently, individual relation information is lost at the end of GCN because of the averaging operation on entity embeddings. Averaging entity embeddings means mixing different relations in which a single entity is involved, resulting in failure of retaining individual relation information. Different from [1], [10] retrieves entity appearances from a pre-defined

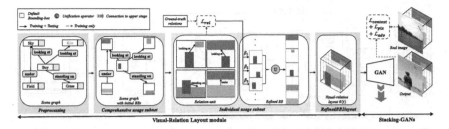

Fig. 2. Our proposed network model consisting of the visual-relation layout module and the Stacking-GANs.

tank while [11] adds entity appearances to the layout before feeding it to the generation part. The layout in [1,10–12] is constructed through only the comprehensive usage of relation among entities for BBs' localization, leading poor scene structure as a whole even if each entity is realistically rendered.

Our main difference from the aforementioned methods is to construct the visual-relation layout using *subject–predicate–object* relations between entities extracted from an input structured-text not only comprehensively but also individually. Recursively conditioning stacking-GANs on our constructed visual-relation layout enables us to progressively generate coarse-to-fine images that consistently preserve the scene structure given in texts.

3   Proposed Method

Our method is decomposed into two steps: (1) inferring the visual-relation layout $\theta(t)$ from structured-text description t, and (2) generating an image from the visual-relation layout, namely $\hat{I} = G(\theta(t))$. To this end, we design an end-to-end network with two modules: the visual-relation layout module and the stacking-GANs (Fig. 2). We train the network in a fully end-to-end manner.

3.1   Visual-Relation Layout Module

The visual-relation layout module constructs the visual-relation layout $\theta(t)$ from a given structured-text description t (Fig. 3) where t is assumed to be converted into a scene graph [2], i.e., the collection of *subject–predicate–object*'s. After the pre-processing on converting t to its scene graph, the comprehensive usage subnet in this module predicts initial BBs for all the entities in t by aggregating all available relations together through GCN ("comprehensive usage"). The individual usage subnet takes each *subject–predicate–object* relation from the scene graph one by one and select the pair of initial BBs involved in the relation (predicate): one for "subject" entity and one for "object" entity. The subnet then adjusts the location and size of the pair of initial BBs using the relation ("individual usage") to have a relation-unit for the relation. Since one entity may participate in multiple relations, it next unifies relation-units so that each

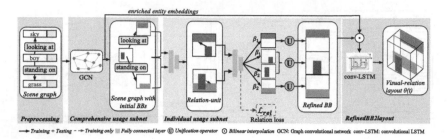

Fig. 3. Details of visual-relation layout module. This figure illustrates the prediction for two *subject–predicate–object* relations.

entity uniquely has a single BB (called refined BB) that is further adjusted in location and size using weights learned from all the participating relations. The RefinedBB2layout subnet constructs the visual-relation layout by aggregating all the refined BBs together using conv-LSTM.

Preprocessing. Similar to [1], we convert the structured-text t to its scene graph (E, P) where $E \subseteq \mathcal{C}$ and $P \subseteq \mathcal{C} \times \mathcal{R} \times \mathcal{C}$. $\mathcal{C}$ and $\mathcal{R}$ are the set of categories and the set of relations given in a dataset. An edge of (E, P) is associated with one *subject–predicate–object*. It is directed and represented by (e^s, p, e^o) with entities $e^s, e^o \in E$ and predicate $p \in \mathcal{R}$ (s and o indicate subject and object).

Like [1], we use a learned embedding layer to produce the entity embedding with the size of $1 \times |\mathcal{C}|$ and the predicate embedding with the size of $1 \times |\mathcal{R}|$ for any of all the entities and predicates appearing in (E, P). Any entity embedding is associated with a single default BB presented by $[x, y, w, h] \in [0,1]^4$ where x is the *left coordinate*, y is the *top coordinate*, w is the *width*, and h is the *height*. We set $x = y = 0$ and $w = h = 1$ as default. This process ensures that all the entities appear in the image. In practice, we concatenate the default BB and its associated entity embedding to produce the vector with the size of $1 \times (|\mathcal{C}| + 4)$.

Comprehensive Usage Subnet. This subnet applies the comprehensive usage to predict a single initial BB for each entity appearing in t as in [1,10–12]. This subnet gives us initial locations and sizes of entities and they do not necessarily satisfy the relations given in t.

In order to aggregate all information along the edges in the scene graph, we employ GCN [1]. Our GCN is mostly identical to [1] with a modification that produces 388 outputs instead of 384 not only to enrich entity/predicate embeddings as in [1,10,11] but also to infer initial BBs. We do not use the average pooling layer on top of GCN to retain individual relation information.

For each edge k of (E, P), the triplet (e_k^s, p_k, e_k^o) and two default BBs with the size of $1 \times (|\mathcal{C}| + |\mathcal{R}| + |\mathcal{C}| + 8)$ are processed to give enriched $e_k'^s$, p_k', and $e_k'^o$ embeddings with the size of 1×128 each, separately, and a pair of initial BBs (one for "subject" and one for "object") with the size of 1×4 each.

Individual Usage Subnet. Since the initial BBs of the entities do not always satisfy the relations given in t, we adjust their locations and sizes using each relation separately. For each relation, we select a pair of initial BBs corresponding to the "subject" and "object" involved in the relation, and adjust the locations and sizes of the pair of BBs using the relation to have a relation-unit for the relation consisting of *two* BBs for "subject" and "object" entities in the relation. This process causes the situation where multiple BBs correspond to the same entity, as different relations may involve same entities in common. We thus move to focus on each entity to unify its corresponding BBs into a single BB (called refined BB) where we use weights learned to retain all the relations. Accordingly, the function of this subnet is two-fold: relation-unit prediction using individual relation separately and unification of multiple BBs corresponding to the same entity into a single refined BB. The subnet is built upon two fully-connected layers followed by a ReLU layer [19] producing 512 and 8 outputs.

For each edge k of scene graph (E, P), its enriched embeddings and its corresponding pair of initial BBs with the size of $1 \times 392 (= 128+4+128+128+4)$ are fed into this subnet to infer relation-unit (b_k^s, b_k^o) with the size of 1×8. Each BB $(b_k^s$ or $b_k^o)$ in the relation-unit is associated with enriched embedding either $e_k'^s$ or $e_k'^o$, respectively for "subject" or "object". We remark that the total number of obtained BBs is $|\{b_k^s, b_k^o\}| = 2 \times |P|$, which is in general larger than $|E|$.

To encourage the refined BB of each entity to keep its involved relations, we use the relation loss $\mathcal{L}_{rel}$ (Sect. 3.3) in a supervised manner. This is because $\mathcal{L}_{rel}$ indicates the degree of retaining the involved relations in terms of relation-unit.

For entity $e_i \in E$, let $B_i = \{B_{i\nu}\}$ denote the set of its corresponding BBs (appearing in different relation-units) and $\beta_i = \{\beta_{i\nu}\}$ be the set of their weights. We define the refined BB: $\hat{B}_i = \frac{\sum_{\nu=1}^{|B_i|} \{(1+\beta_{i\nu}) \times B_{i\nu}\}}{\sum_{\nu=1}^{|B_i|} (1+\beta_{i\nu})}$.

Each weight in β_i is obtained from the outputs of the softmax function in the relation auxiliary classifier using the relation loss $\mathcal{L}_{rel}$.

At the beginning of training, relation-units cannot exactly reproduce their involved relations. Their weights thus tend to be close to *zero*, leading $\hat{B}_i$ above almost similar to the simple average. Our refined BBs may be close to those of [1,10,11] at the beginning of training yet they keep their relations thanks to their weights. As training proceeds, the contribution of the relation-units retaining relations consistent with text t to the refined BB gradually increases. As a result, the location and size of the refined BB are continuously altered to keep relations consistent with t.

For entity e_i, its embeddings that are associated with $\{B_{i\nu}\}$'s over ν are averaged. In this way, we obtain the set of refined BBs $\{\hat{B}_i\}$ and their associated embeddings for all the entities in E. We remark that $|\{\hat{B}_i\}| = |E|$.

If all the initial BBs completely keep their relations, the individual usage subnet works as the averaging operator as in [1,10,11] and our visual-relation layout is similar to the layout by [1,10,11]. In practice, however, the comprehensive usage of relations cannot guarantee to completely keep the relations. Our individual usage subnet plays the role of adjusting all the BBs in location and size to keep their relations as much as possible using each relation separately.

RefinedBB2layout Subnet. In order to construct the visual-relation layout, we aggregate all the refined BBs and transfer them from the bounding-box domain to the image domain. This process should meet two requirements: (i) each entity in the image should be localized and resized to match its individual refined BB, and (ii) each entity should appear in the image even if some refined BBs overlap with each other. To this end, we design *refinedBB2layout* subnet as a learnable network rather than the putting-together operation. We build this subnet using a conv-LSTM [20] with the 5 hidden states each outputting 128 channels.

For $\hat{B}_i$ of entity e_i, we first convert it to the binary mask with the size of $64 \times 64 \times 128$ whose element is 1 if and only if it is contained in $\hat{B}_i$, 0 otherwise. Then, we reshape its associated embedding from 1×128 to $1 \times 1 \times 128$. Finally, the reshaped embedding is wrapped to $\hat{B}_i$ using the bilinear interpolation [21] for the layout of entity e_i ($64 \times 64 \times 128$). To produce $\theta(t)$, we feed the sequence of entity layouts into the *refinedBB2layout* subnet. The size of $\theta(t)$ is $64 \times 64 \times 128$.

3.2 Stacking-GANs

We condition three GANs, namely stacking-GANs, on $\theta(t)$ to progressively generate coarse-to-fine images with the size of $n \times n \times 3$ ($n = 64, 128, 256$). Each GAN is identical to CRN [18]. Parameters are not shared by any GANs.

The first GAN generator receives the layout $\theta(t)$ and a standard Gaussian distribution noise as input while the others receive the bilinear upsampled [21] layout $\theta(t)$ and the output of the last refinement layer from the previous GAN. The discriminators receive an image-layout pair as their inputs. Each pair is either a real sample or a fake sample. A real sample consists of a real image and a real layout while a fake one consists of a predicted layout and a generated or real image. These samples not only encourage the GAN to improve the quality of generated images but also give the helpful feedback to the layout predictor.

3.3 Loss Function

Relation Loss: $\mathcal{L}_{\text{rel}}$ is a cross entropy between relation-units and their GT relations that is obtained by a relation auxiliary classifier. The classifier is built upon two fully-connected layers producing 512 and $|\mathcal{R}|$ outputs. The first layer is followed by a ReLU layer while the second one ends with the *softmax* function.

For each edge k of (E, P), its relation-unit and involved embeddings, i.e., $e_k'^s$, b_k^s, $e_k'^o$, and b_k^o, are concatenated in this order to have an input vector of 1×264. We then feed this vector into the relation auxiliary classifier to obtain the probability distribution w_k of the relations over $\mathcal{R}$. w_k is a vector of $1 \times |\mathcal{R}|$ and contains all the predicates $p_k \in \mathcal{R}$. We first obtain the *index* of predicate p_k $\in \mathcal{R}$. Since the order of predicates in w_k is the same as that in $\mathcal{R}$, the value at *index* in w_k is the weight of p_k, which is used as the weight of the relation-unit (b_k^s, b_k^o) in the individual usage subnet. Note that the weight of a relation-unit is used for the weight of both b_k^s and b_k^o involved in the relation-unit.

The relation loss is defined as: $\mathcal{L}_{\text{rel}} = -\sum_{k=1}^{|P|}\sum_{\nu'=1}^{|\mathcal{R}|} p_k[\nu']\log(w_k[\nu'])$. Minimizing the relation loss encourages relation-units to adjust their locations and sizes to meet the "predicate" relation. This is because the relation reflects the relative spatial locations among its associated relation-units.

Pixel Loss: $\mathcal{L}_{\text{pix}} = ||I - \hat{I}||_2$, where I is the ground-truth image and $\hat{I}$ is a generated image. The $\mathcal{L}_{\text{pix}}$ is useful for keeping the quality of generated images.

Contextual Loss [22]: $\mathcal{L}_{\text{context}} = -\log(CX(\Phi^l(I), \Phi^l(\hat{I})))$, where $\Phi^l(\cdot)$ denotes the feature map extracted from layer l of perceptual network Φ, and $CX(\cdot)$ is the function that computes the similarity between image features. $\mathcal{L}_{\text{context}}$ is used to learn the context of an image since refined BBs may lose the context such as missing pixel information or the size of entity.

Adversarial Loss [4]: $\mathcal{L}_{\text{adv}}$ encourages the stacking-GANs to generate realistic images. Since the discriminator also receives the real/predicted layout as its input, the $\mathcal{L}_{\text{adv}}$ is helpful in training the visual-relation layout module as well.

In summary, we jointly train our network in an end-to-end manner to minimize: $\mathcal{L} = \lambda_1\mathcal{L}_{\text{rel}} + \lambda_2\mathcal{L}_{\text{pix}} + \lambda_3\mathcal{L}_{\text{context}} + \sum_{i=1}^{3}\lambda_4\mathcal{L}_{\text{adv}i}$, where λ_i are hyperparameters. We compute $\mathcal{L}_{\text{adv}}$ at each level in the stacking-GANs, while $\mathcal{L}_{\text{pix}}$ and $\mathcal{L}_{\text{context}}$ are computed at the third GAN.

4 Experiments

4.1 Dataset and Compared Methods

Dataset. We conducted experiments on challenging COCO-stuff [13] and Visual GENOME [14] datasets, which have complex descriptions with many entities and relations in diverse context. We followed [1] to pre-process all the datasets: $|\mathcal{C}| = 171$ and $|\mathcal{R}| = 6$ (COCO-stuff [13]), and $|\mathcal{C}| = 178$ and $|\mathcal{R}| = 45$ (GENOME [14]).

Compared Methods. We employed Johnson+ [1] as the baseline (64×64). To factor out the influence of image generator, we replaced the CRN in [1] by our stacking-GANs to produce higher resolution images (128×128 and 256×256). We also compared our method with Hong+ [12], Zhang+ [6], Xu+ [9], Li+ [10], Ashual+ [11], Zhao+ [16], and Sun+ [17]. We reported the results in the original papers whenever possible. For the methods that released at least one reference pre-trained model [23] and [24], we trained authors' provided codes (Zhang+ [6] and Xu+ [9]) on GENOME dataset.

Evaluation Metrics. We use the inception score (IS) [25], and Fréchet inception distance (FID) [26] to evaluate the overall quality of generated images (implemented in [27,28]). We also use four metrics to evaluate the layout: the entity recall at IoU threshold ($R@\tau$), the relation IoU ($rIoU$), the relation score (RS) [29], and the BB coverage. To evaluate the relevance of generated images and input text descriptions, we use the image caption metrics: $BLEU$ [30], $METEOR$ [31], and $CIDEr$ [32]. For the diversity of generated images, we use the diversity score [33] (implemented in [34]).

To evaluate how much the predicted layout is consistent with the ground-truth (GT), we measure the agreement in size and location between predicted (i.e., refined) and GT BBs using the entity recall at IoU threshold: $R@\tau = |\{i \mid IoU(\hat{B}_i, GT_i) \geq \tau\}|/N$, where $\hat{B}_i$ and GT_i are predicted and GT BBs for entity e_i, $N = \min(|\{\hat{B}_i\}|, |\{GT_i\}|)$ (we always observed $|\{\hat{B}_i\}| = |\{GT_i\}|$), τ is a IoU threshold, and $IoU(\cdot)$ denotes Intersection-over-Union metric. Note that we used only the BBs that exist in both $\{\hat{B}_i\}$ and $\{GT_i\}$ to compute $R@\tau$.

We also evaluate the predicted layout using *subject–predicate–object* relations. For each *subject–predicate–object* relation, we computed the IoU of the predicted "subject" BB and its corresponding GT, and that for the "object". We then multiplied the two IoUs to obtain the IoU for the relation. $rIoU$ is the average over all the *subject–predicate–object* relations.

We use the relation score (RS) [29] for COCO-stuff to evaluate the compliance of geometrical relation between predicted BBs. For each edge k of scene graph (E, P), we define $score(\hat{B}_k^s, \hat{B}_k^o) = 1$ if and only if the relative location between $\hat{B}_k^s$ and $\hat{B}_k^o$ satisfies the relation p_k, 0 otherwise. $RS = \sum_{k=1}^{|P|} score(\hat{B}_k^s, \hat{B}_k^o)/|P|$.

To evaluate how much BBs cover the area of the whole image, we compute the coverage of predicted BBs over the image area: $coverage = \bigcup_{i=1}^{|E|} \hat{B}_i/(\text{image area})$.

We note that $R@\tau$ and $rIoU$ consider the consistency between predicted BBs and GT BBs, and RS and *coverage* are independent of GT BBs. In other words, $R@\tau$ and $rIoU$ evaluate absolute locations of BBs while RS (and *coverage* as well to some extent) does semantic relations. Therefore, they together effectively evaluate the layout in a wide range of aspects.

4.2   Implementation and Training Details

We optimized our model (built in PyTorch [35]) using the Adam optimizer with the recommended parameters [36] and the batch size of 16 for 500 epochs. We used VGG-19 [37] pre-trained on ImageNet as Φ, and $l = conv4\_2$ to compute $\mathcal{L}_{context}$. Each model took about one week for training on a PC with GTX1080Ti × 2 while testing time was less than 0.5 s per structured-text input.

We trained the model except for the pre-processing in the end-to-end manner where we set $\lambda_1 = \lambda_2 = \lambda_3 = \lambda_4 = 1$, and do not pre-train each individual subset, meaning that we do not use any ground-truth BBs to train the visual-relation layout. The layout predictor receives signals not only directly from the relation loss but also from the other losses. In an early stage of the training, the rendering part cannot generate reasonable images because the quality of BBs is poor. This means the signals from losses are strong, leading to quick convergence of the layout predictor. As the training proceeds, the layout predictor properly works, and the rendering part gradually becomes better. $\mathcal{L}_{rel}$, at that time, keeps the layout predictor stable and more accurate.

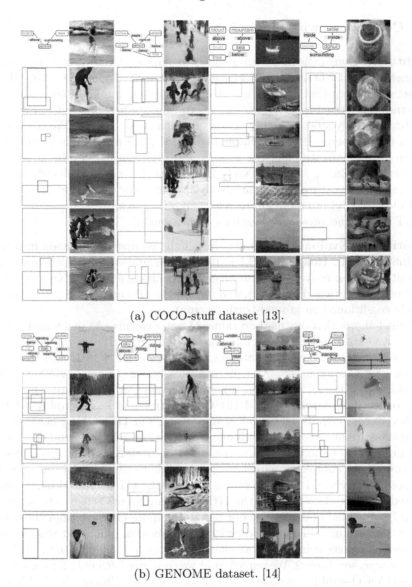

(a) COCO-stuff dataset [13].

(b) GENOME dataset. [14]

Fig. 4. Visual comparison on COCO-stuff and GENOME. For each example, we show the scene graph and reference image at the first row. From second to the last rows, we show the layouts and images generated by our method (256 × 256), Johnson+ [1] (64 × 64), Zhang+ [6] (256 × 256), Xu+ [9] (256 × 256), and Ashual+ [11] (256 × 256, COCO-stuff only, GT layout). The color of each entity BB corresponds to that in the scene graph. Zoom in for best view.

4.3   Comparison with State-of-the-Arts

Qualitative Evaluation. Figure 4 shows examples of the results obtained by our method and SOTAs [1,6,9,11] on COCO-stuff [13] and GENOME [14] datasets. It shows that the generated images by our method successfully preserve the scene structure given in text descriptions, indicating that our proposed visual-relation layouts are highly consistent with those of GTs. We see that the results by Johnson+ [1] have reasonable layouts, however, their layouts failed to keep all relations well and the visual impression of their results is not good. The results by Zhang+ [6] and Xu+ [9] are clear in (entities) details but they lose the scene structure (some entities disappear). The results by Ashual+ [11] (COCO-stuff only) are more impressive than ours to some extent, however, they use GT layout and pre-defined entities' appearances.

Quantitative Evaluation. We classify all the compared methods into three: (A) Johnson+ [1], Hong+ [12], Li+ [10], and Ashual+ [11] (which firstly infer a layout and then convert it to an image), (B) Zhang+ [6] and Xu+ [9] (which are directly conditioned on texts), and (C) Zhao+ [16] and Sun+ [17] (which are directly conditioned on ground-truth layouts).

Table 1 shows that our method (almost) outperforms (A) in IS and FID on both COCO-stuff and GENOME. In comparison with (B), our method achieves the best in FID on both the datasets, the best on GENOME and the second best on COCO-stuff in IS. Xu+ [9] achieves better IS on COCO-stuff than us because (i) Xu+ [9] focuses on generating images in good human perception based on entity information and (ii) COCO-stuff has less complex relations, in other words, layouts may be less important. On GENOME, however, text descriptions are more complex with many entities and relations, and their results are degraded due to poor layouts as seen later in Table 2. Table 1 also shows that the scores of our completed model are comparable to those of (C), meaning that our (predicted) visual-relation layout is close to the GT layout. When replacing the predicted layout by the GT (the 17th row), our results achieve the same level with (C). We thus conclude that our method is more effective than the others.

Next, we evaluated how the scene structure given in input text was preserved in generated images using $R@\tau$ (we changed τ from 0.3 to 0.9 by 0.2), $rIoU$, RS, and *coverage*, see Table 2. We remark that we computed RS only for COCO-stuff because COCO-stuff has geometrical relations only. For Zhang+ [6] and Xu+ [9], we employed Faster-RCNN [38] to estimate their predicted BBs of entities where we set the number of generated BBs to be the number of entities in an image. We note that the number of predicted BBs by ours or Johnson+ [1] was always the same with the number of entities in an image.

Table 2 shows that our method performs best, indicating that our predicted BBs more precisely agree with those in relation (location and size) of entities given in texts than the compared methods. To be more specific, $rIoU$'s in Table 2 show that our predicted BBs more successfully retain the relations of entities than the other methods. This observation is also supported by RS on COCO-stuff. Moreover, our method outperforms the others in *coverage* and achieves

Table 1. Comparison of the overall quality using *IS* and *FID*. From the 4th to the 16th rows: group (A) and (B) (the best in blue; the second best in red). From the 17th to the 19th rows: group (C) (**bold** indicates the best). Scores inside the parentheses indicate those reported in the original papers.

	IS ⇑						FID ⇓					
Dataset	COCO-stuff [13]			GENOME [14]			COCO-stuff [13]			GENOME [14]		
Image size	64 × 64	128 × 128	256 × 256	64 × 64	128 × 128	256 × 256	64 × 64	128 × 128	256 × 256	64 × 64	128 × 128	256 × 256
Ours w/o individual usage	7.02 ± 0.19	8.12 ± 0.41	9.95 ± 0.31	5.48 ± 0.16	5.66 ± 0.26	5.91 ± 0.41	63.28	59.52	55.21	72.42	72.02	71.49
Ours w/o weighted unifcation	7.10 ± 0.27	8.64 ± 0.37	10.49 ± 0.41	5.99 ± 0.22	6.61 ± 0.31	7.32 ± 0.37	61.89	57.20	49.16	69.37	60.89	57.18
Ours w/o refinedBB2layout	7.23 ± 0.20	8.70 ± 0.35	10.50 ± 0.37	6.11 ± 0.25	6.93 ± 0.29	7.87 ± 0.33	57.68	53.81	46.55	67.65	58.54	54.45
Ours w/o $\mathcal{L}_{pix}$	7.29 ± 0.17	9.26 ± 0.31	11.36 ± 0.40	6.05 ± 0.15	8.26 ± 0.27	8.66 ± 0.36	56.81	51.02	43.18	70.18	60.02	58.63
Ours w/o $\mathcal{L}_{context}$	7.56 ± 0.11	9.68 ± 0.33	11.47 ± 0.42	6.37 ± 0.16	8.41 ± 0.22	8.97 ± 0.31	50.89	47.22	40.10	68.20	56.39	53.75
Ours w/o $\mathcal{L}_{adv}$	7.31 ± 0.19	9.47 ± 0.34	11.41 ± 0.47	6.30 ± 0.19	8.39 ± 0.20	8.96 ± 0.39	56.24	50.87	41.05	68.34	57.23	53.86
Ours (completed model)	9.20 ± 0.32	12.01 ± 0.40	14.20 ± 0.45	7.97 ± 0.30	9.24 ± 0.41	11.75 ± 0.43	35.12	29.12	27.39	58.37	50.19	36.79
Johnson+ [1]	(6.70 ± 0.10)	7.13 ± 0.24	7.25 ± 0.47	(5.50 ± 0.10)	5.72 ± 0.33	5.81 ± 0.37	67.99	65.23	64.19	73.39	69.48	68.42
Hong+ [12]		(11.46 ± 0.09)										
Li+ [10]	(9.40 ± 0.20)			(7.30 ± 0.20)								
Ashual+ [11]	(7.90 ± 0.20)	(10.40 ± 0.40)	(14.50 ± 0.70)				(65.30)	(75.40)	(81.00)			
Zhang+ [6]	7.79 ± 0.32	8.49 ± 0.52	10.62 ± 0.19	6.35 ± 0.16	6.44 ± 0.25	7.39 ± 0.38	87.21	85.37	78.19	108.68	86.17	77.95
Xu+ [9]	11.78 ± 0.14	19.11 ± 0.28	25.89 ± 0.47	6.38 ± 0.22	6.88 ± 0.32	8.20 ± 0.35	50.06	43.98	34.48	96.40	83.39	72.11
Ours with GT layout	10.36 ± 0.41	13.73 ± 0.59	14.78 ± 0.65	8.87 ± 0.57	10.04 ± 0.45	12.03 ± 0.37	30.98	27.74	26.32	45.63	40.96	**27.33**
Zhao+ [16] (GT layout)	(9.10 ± 0.10)			(8.10 ± 0.10)								
Sun+ [17] (GT layout)	(9.80 ± 0.20)	(13.80 ± 0.40)		(8.70 ± 0.40)	(11.10 ± 0.60)		(34.31)	(29.65)		(34.75)	(29.36)	
GT	16.25 ± 0.38	25.89 ± 0.47	32.61 ± 0.69	13.92 ± 0.42	21.43 ± 1.03	31.22 ± 0.65						

Table 2. Comparison of the scene structure using $R@\tau$, $rIoU$, RS, and *coverage* (larger is better; the best in **bold**).

Dataset	COCO-stuff [13]							GENOME [2]					
Metric	$R@\tau$				$rIoU$	RS	*coverage*	$R@\tau$				$rIoU$	*coverage*
	0.3	0.5	0.7	0.9			GT = 98.24	0.3	0.5	0.7	0.9		GT = 77.10
Ours w/o individual usage	61.45	43.22	29.71	20.05	0.2652	53.48	94.96	26.48	14.29	11.90	9.81	0.1264	50.07
Ours w/o weighted unification	61.76	45.28	30.22	20.51	0.2795	56.27	95.07	29.57	18.22	13.76	10.80	0.1501	56.77
Ours (completed model)	**65.34**	**49.01**	**35.87**	**23.61**	**0.3186**	**68.23**	**97.19**	**35.00**	**23.12**	**16.34**	**13.40**	**0.1847**	**71.13**
Johnson+ [1]	59.75	42.53	29.23	19.89	0.2532	51.20	94.82	28.13	17.17	12.30	10.47	0.1485	52.28
Zhang+ [6]	37.81	20.50	10.64	7.76	0.0824	30.72	60.15	18.38	10.84	8.11	5.82	0.0643	40.07
Xu+ [9]	21.39	10.71	8.15	5.83	0.0671	31.97	52.76	16.02	9.33	7.66	5.15	0.0579	36.82

Table 3. Comparison using caption generation metrics on COCO-stuff (larger is better; the best in blue). Scores inside the parentheses indicate those reported in [12].

Method	$BLEU-1$	$BLEU-2$	$BLEU-3$	$BLEU-4$	$METEOR$	CIDEr
Ours	0.561	0.352	0.217	0.139	0.157	0.325
Johnson+ [1] Hong+ [12]	0.531 (0.541)	0.321 (0.332)	0.183 (0.199)	0.107 (0.122)	0.141 (0.154)	0.238 (0.367)
Zhang+ [6]	0.417	0.214	0.111	0.062	0.095	0.078
Xu+ [9]	0.450	0.251	0.157	0.087	0.105	0.251
GT	0.627 (0.678)	0.434 (0.496)	0.287 (0.349)	0.191 (0.243)	0.191 (0.228)	0.367 (0.802)

Table 4. Comparison using diversity score [33] (the best in blue; the second best in red). Scores are inside the parentheses indicates those in the original papers.

Method	COCO-stuff [13]	GENOME [2]
Ours (64×64)	0.36 ± 0.10	0.39 ± 0.09
Ours (128×128)	0.45 ± 0.12	0.49 ± 0.07
Ours (256×256)	0.52 ± 0.09	0.56 ± 0.06
Johnson+ [1]	0.29 ± 0.10	0.31 ± 0.08
Ashual+ [11]	(0.67 ± 0.05)	—
Zhao+ [16]	(0.15 ± 0.06)	(0.17 ± 0.09)
Sun+ [17]	(0.40 ± 0.09)	(0.43 ± 0.09)

comparable levels with the ground-truth BBs. These indicate that our visual-relation layout is well-structured. Our method thus has even better ability of rendering more realistic images with multiple entities since the faithful scene structure and more BB coverage (i.e., entity information) are achieved. Note that the observation that the *coverage*'s on COCO-stuff are better than those on GENOME explains the reason why generated images on COCO-stuff are better in IS and FID than those on GENOME.

Next, we use the image caption task to evaluate how the generated image is relevant to its input text. We follow [12] to report scores on COCO-stuff [13], see Table 3. Note that we evaluated on COCO-stuff only since the pre-trained image caption model on GENOME is not available. We also note that all the scores on the ground-truth dataset in [12] are higher than our re-computation. Table 3 shows that our method outperforms the others [1,6,9,12] on $BLEU$, $METEOR$ and comparable to [12] on $CIDEr$. We thus conclude that our method performs more consistently with input texts than the others.

Finally, we show the diversity score of generated images in Table 4. Overall, our scores are higher than Johnson+ [1], Zhao+ [16], and Sun+ [17] on both

COCO-stuff and GENOME, and comparable to Ashual+ [11] on COCO-stuff. Moreover, along with our stacking-GANs, our scores become better and better. These scores also support the efficacy of our method.

We note that the number of (trainable) parameters in our model is about 41M which is comparable with Johnson+ [1] (28M), Zhang+ [6] (57M), and Xu+ [9] (23M), and significantly smaller than Ashual+ [11] (191M).

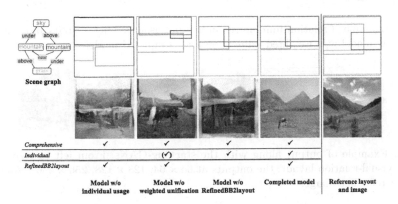

Fig. 5. Example of layouts and generated images by the ablation models. For each model, the 1st row shows the layout, the 2nd row shows the generated image. All images are at 256 × 256 resolution.

4.4 Ablation Study

We evaluated ablation models, see the first block of Tables 1 and 2: ours w/o individual usage denotes the model dropping the individual usage subnet; ours w/o weighted unification denotes the replacement of refining BBs with just averaging in the individual usage subnet; ours w/o refinedBB2layout denotes the replacement by just putting all entity layouts together in constructing the visual-relation layout. Figure 5 illustrates a typical output example of the ablation models. We note that model w/o comprehensive usage is not applicable since all the other subnets in our visual-relation layout module need the output by the comprehensive usage subnet.

The 4th and 5th rows of Tables 1 and 2 confirm the importance of the individual usage subnet. We also see the necessity of our learnable weights in refining BBs because model w/o weighted unification performs better than model w/o individual usage. We may conclude that the relation-unit prediction and the weighted unification together bring gain to our performance.

From Fig. 5, we visually observe that the layout by the model w/o individual usage does not successfully reflect relations. This observation is applicable to the model w/o weighted unification as well. As a result, both the models generated images in poorer quality than our complete model. The relation-units are in

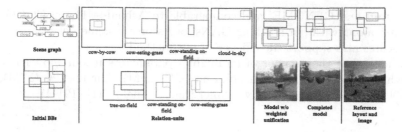

Fig. 6. Example of relation-units in the individual usage subnet; layouts and generated images by model w/o weighted unification and completed model.

Fig. 7. Example of output along with the stacking-GANs. From left to right, scene graph, visual-relation layout, the outputs at 64×64, 128×128, 256×256 resolutions, and the reference image.

diversity: entity BBs can be various in size and location because of multiple relations (see Fig. 6, for example), and thus simply averaging BBs corresponding to the same entity does not successfully retain the entity relations. The individual usage of relations is important for more consistent layout with input text.

The 6th row in Table 1 shows the significance of the refinedBB2layout. Complex descriptions with many entities and relations tend to produce overlapped BBs. The model w/o refinedBB2layout cannot necessarily produce all the entities in the layout, generating poor images.

We also evaluated the necessity of each term of the loss function through comparing our completed model with models dropping one term each: model w/o $\mathcal{L}_{\text{pix}}$, model w/o $\mathcal{L}_{\text{context}}$, and model w/o $\mathcal{L}_{\text{adv}}$ (we dropped each term in the loss function (Sect. 3.3) except for stacking-GANs). From the 2nd block of Table 1, we see that the absence of any term degrades the quality of generated images. This indicates that all the loss terms indeed contribute to performance.

Finally, we see that along with the stacking of GANs, our method progressively generates better images in terms of IS and FID (Table 1). We observe that at 64×64 resolution, generated images tend to be blurred and lose some details while the details of images are improved as the resolution becomes higher (the best result is obtained at 256×256 resolution) (see Fig. 7 as an example). We also confirmed that the visual-relation layouts of generated images at any resolutions are the same and highly consistent with texts.

When we replaced CRN in [1] with our stacking-GANs for 128×128 and 256×256 resolutions to factor out the influence of image generators, we see that the improvement of [1] on IS and FID along the resolution is worse than that of our model (the 10th and the 11th rows of Table 1). This indicates that better layout significantly improves the performance of the final image generation and also confirms clearer contribution of our proposed visual-relation layout module.

5   Conclusion

We proposed a GAN-based end-to-end network for text-to-image generation where entity relations are comprehensively and individually used to infer a visual-relation layout. We also conditioned the stacking-GANs on the visual-relation layout to generate high-resolution images. Our layout preserves the scene structure more precisely than the layout by SOTAs.

References

1. Johnson, J., Gupta, A., Fei-Fei, L.: Image generation from scene graphs. In: CVPR (2018)
2. Johnson, J., Krishna, R., Stark, M., Li, J., Bernstein, M., Fei-Fei, L.: Image retrieval using scene graphs. In: CVPR (2015)
3. Li, Y., Ouyang, W., Zhou, B., Wang, K., Wang, X.: Scene graph generation from objects, phrases and region captions. In: ICCV (2017)
4. Goodfellow, I., et al.: Generative adversarial nets. In: NIPS (2014)
5. Reed, S., Akata, Z., Yan, X., Logeswaran, L., Schiele, B., Lee, H.: Generative adversarial text-to-image synthesis. In: ICML (2016)
6. Zhang, H., et al.: StackGAN: text to photo-realistic image synthesis with stacked generative adversarial networks. In: ICCV (2017)
7. Reed, S., Akata, Z., Lee, H., Schiele, B.: Learning deep representations of fine-grained visual descriptions. In: CVPR (2016)
8. Dong, H., Yu, S., Wu, C., Guo, Y.: Semantic image synthesis via adversarial learning. In: ICCV (2017)
9. Xu, T., et al.: AttnGAN: fine-grained text to image generation with attentional generative adversarial networks. In: CVPR (2018)
10. Li, Y., Ma, T., Bai, Y., Duan, N., Wei, S., Wang, X.: PasteGAN: a semi-parametric method to generate image from scene graph. In: CVPR (2019)
11. Ashual, O., Wolf, L.: Specifying object attributes and relations in interactive scene generation. In: ICCV (2019)
12. Hong, S., Yang, D., Choi, J., Lee, H.: Inferring semantic layout for hierarchical text-to-image synthesis. In: CVPR (2018)
13. Caesar, H., Uijlings, J., Ferrari, V.: COCO-stuff: thing and stuff classes in context. In: CVPR (2018)
14. Krishna, R., et al.: Visual genome: connecting language and vision using crowd-sourced dense image annotations. Int. J. Comput. Vis. **123**, 32–73 (2017). https://doi.org/10.1007/s11263-016-0981-7
15. Reed, S., Akata, Z., Mohan, S., Tenka, S., Schiele, B., Lee, H.: Learning what and where to draw. In: NIPS (2016)
16. Zhao, B., Meng, L., Yin, W., Sigal, L.: Image generation from layout. In: CVPR (2019)
17. Wei, S., Tianfu, W.: Image synthesis from reconfigurable layout and style. In: ICCV (2019)

18. Chen, Q., Koltun, V.: Photographic image synthesis with cascaded refinement networks. In: ICCV (2017)
19. Nair, V., Hinton, G.E.: Rectified linear units improve restricted Boltzmann machines. In: ICML (2010)
20. Shi, X., Chen, Z., Wang, H., Yeung, D.Y., Wong, W., Woo, W.: Convolutional LSTM network: a machine learning approach for precipitation nowcasting. In: NIPS (2015)
21. Jaderberg, M., Simonyan, K., Zisserman, A., Kavukcuoglu, K.: Spatial transformer networks. In: NIPS (2015)
22. Mechrez, R., Talmi, I., Zelnik-Manor, L.: The contextual loss for image transformation with non-aligned data. In: Ferrari, V., Hebert, M., Sminchisescu, C., Weiss, Y. (eds.) Computer Vision – ECCV 2018. LNCS, vol. 11218, pp. 800–815. Springer, Cham (2018). https://doi.org/10.1007/978-3-030-01264-9_47
23. https://github.com/hanzhanggit/StackGAN-Pytorch
24. https://github.com/taoxugit/AttnGAN
25. Salimans, T., et al.: Improved techniques for training GANs. In: NIPS (2016)
26. Heusel, M., Ramsauer, H., Unterthiner, T., Nessler, B., Hochreiter, S.: GANs trained by a two time-scale update rule converge to a local Nash equilibrium. In: NIPS (2017)
27. https://github.com/openai/improved-gan/tree/master/inception_score
28. https://github.com/bioinf-jku/TTUR
29. Tripathi, S., Bhiwandiwalla, A., Bastidas, A., Tang, H.: Using scene graph context to improve image generation. In: CVPRW (WiCV) (2019)
30. Papineni, K., Roukos, S., Ward, T., Zhu, W.J.: BLEU: a method for automatic evaluation of machine translation. In: ACL (2002)
31. Lavie, A., Agarwal, A.: METEOR: an automatic metric for MT evaluation with improved correlation with human judgments. In: ACL (2005)
32. Vedantam, R., Zitnick, C.L., Parikh, D.: CIDEr: consensus-based image description evaluation. In: CVPR (2015)
33. Zhang, R., Isola, P., Efros, A.A., Shechtman, E., Wang, O.: The unreasonable effectiveness of deep features as a perceptual metric. In: CVPR (2018)
34. https://github.com/richzhang/PerceptualSimilarity
35. https://pytorch.org/
36. Kingma, D.P., Welling, M.: Auto-encoding variational Bayes. In: ICLR (2014)
37. Simonyan, K., Zisserman, A.: Very deep convolutional networks for large-scale image recognition. In: ICLR (2015)
38. Ren, S., He, K., Girshick, R., Sun, J.: Faster R-CNN: towards real-time object detection with region proposal networks. In: NIPS (2015)

Patch-Wise Attack for Fooling Deep Neural Network

Lianli Gao[1], Qilong Zhang[1], Jingkuan Song[1], Xianglong Liu[2],
and Heng Tao Shen[1(✉)]

[1] Center for Future Media and School of Computer Science and Engineering,
University of Electronic Science and Technology of China, Chengdu, China
[2] Beihang University, Beijing, China
qilong.zhang@std.uestc.edu.cn, shenhengtao@hotmail.com

Abstract. By adding human-imperceptible noise to clean images, the resultant adversarial examples can fool other unknown models. Features of a pixel extracted by deep neural networks (DNNs) are influenced by its surrounding regions, and different DNNs generally focus on different discriminative regions in recognition. Motivated by this, we propose a patch-wise iterative algorithm – a black-box attack towards mainstream normally trained and defense models, which differs from the existing attack methods manipulating pixel-wise noise. In this way, without sacrificing the performance of white-box attack, our adversarial examples can have strong transferability. Specifically, we introduce an amplification factor to the step size in each iteration, and one pixel's overall gradient overflowing the ϵ-constraint is properly assigned to its surrounding regions by a project kernel. Our method can be generally integrated to any gradient-based attack methods. Compared with the current state-of-the-art attacks, we significantly improve the success rate by 9.2% for defense models and 3.7% for normally trained models on average. Our code is available at https://github.com/qilong-zhang/Patch-wise-iterative-attack

Keywords: Adversarial examples · Patch-wise · Black-box attack · Transferability

1 Introduction

In recent years, Deep neural networks (DNNs) [9,10,15,16,30,31] have made great achievements. However, the adversarial examples [32] which are added with human-imperceptible noise can easily fool the state-of-the-art DNNs to give unreasonable predictions. This raises security concerns about those machine learning algorithms. In order to understand DNNs better and improve its robustness to avoid future risks [6], it is necessary to investigate the defense models, and meanwhile the generation of adversarial examples, e.g., [38].

Electronic supplementary material The online version of this chapter (https://doi.org/10.1007/978-3-030-58604-1_19) contains supplementary material, which is available to authorized users.

ⓒ Springer Nature Switzerland AG 2020
A. Vedaldi et al. (Eds.): ECCV 2020, LNCS 12373, pp. 307–322, 2020.
https://doi.org/10.1007/978-3-030-58604-1_19

Various attack methods have been proposed in these years. One of the most popular branches is gradient-based algorithms. For this branch, existing methods can be generally classified as single-step attacks and iterative attacks. In general, iterative attacks perform better than single-step attacks in the white-box setting. But in the real world, attackers usually cannot get any information about the target model, which is called the black-box setting. In this case, single-step attacks always have a higher transferability than iterative attacks at the cost of poor performance of substitute models. To sum up, the essential difference between the two sub-branches is the number of iterations. Iterative attacks require multiple iterations to obtain the final perturbation noise, and hence there is a risk of getting stuck in the local optimum during the iterations, reducing the transferability. While single-step attack methods only update once, which is easy to underfit but really improve the generalizability.

Moreover, with the development of attack methods, several adversarial examples have been applied to the physical world [6,12,20,29,33]. This has raised public concerns about AI security. Consequently, a lot of defense methods are proposed to tackle this problem. Lin et al. [18] propose defensive quantization method to defend adversarial attacks while maintain the efficiency. Guo et al. [8] use bit-depth reduction, JPEG compression [4], total variance minimization [26], and image quilting [5] to preprocess inputs before they are feed to DNNs. Tram èr et al. [34] use ensemble adversarial training to improve the robustness of models. Furthermore, Xie et al. [36] add feature denoising module into adversarial training, and the resultant defense models demonstrate greater robustness in both white-box and black-box attack settings. To generate more effective adversarial examples, it is necessary to study the properties of intrinsic classification logic of the DNNs. Here we use class activation mapping [39] to analyze it. Zhou et al. [39] observed that the discriminative regions always vary across predicted labels. Recent research [3] also showed that different models focus on different discriminative regions in recognition, and the defense models generally focus on larger discriminative regions than the normally trained models. The discriminative regions are often clustered together, as shown in Fig. 1. Therefore, only adding pixel-wise noise may hinder the transferability of adversarial examples across different DNNs. Based on these observations, we argue that in addition to reducing the responsiveness of the ground-truth regions while activating the regions of any other categories, crafting perturbation with the characteristic of aggregation in the above-discussed regions is also important. To that end, we study the advantages and disadvantages of single-step and iterative attacks [3,7,14], and we argue that linear nature of DNNs [7] does exist to some extent. Therefore we amplify step size with a fixed factor to analyze the effect of step size on transferability. Besides, we rethink the weakness of direct clipping operation which discards partial gradient information. To alleviate this problem, we reuse the cut noise and apply a heuristic project strategy to reduce the side effects of direct clipping as well as generating patch-wise noise. Finally, combined with the fast sign gradient method, we propose the **Patch-wise Iterative Fast Gradient Sign Method (PI-FGSM)** to generate strongly transferable adversarial

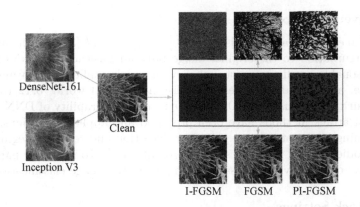

Fig. 1. We show the adversarial examples generated by FGSM [7], I-FGSM [14] and our method PI-FGSM for Inception V3 model [31] respectively. The maximum perturbation ϵ is limited to 16. On the left side of the figure, we use Inception V3 [31] and DenseNet-161 [10] to show the Gradient-weighted Class Activation Mapping (Grad-CAM) [28] of the ground-truth label, and on the right side of the figure, we divide it into three parts. **Top row**: the adversarial noise patch map (we define it in Sect. 3.2.1). **Middle row**: the adversarial noise. **Bottom row**: the adversarial examples. Our PI-FGSM can generate adversarial noise which has the same clustering property as the activation map and also well covers the different discriminative regions.

examples. The visualization results in Fig. 1 also demonstrate our approach. Compared with other methods, the noise generated by our PI-FGSM has obvious aggregation characteristics and can better cover varied discriminative regions of different DNNs. Our major contributions can be summarized as: 1) We propose a novel patch-wise attack idea named PI-FGSM. Compared with existing methods manipulating pixel-wise noise, our approach can have the advantage of both single-step and iterative attacks, i.e., improving the transferability without sacrificing the performance of the substitute model. 2) Technically, based on the mature gradient-based attack pipeline, we adopt an amplification factor and project kernel to generate more transferable adversarial examples by patch-wise noise. Our method can be generally integrated to any iteration-based attack methods; and 3) Extensive experiments on ImageNet show that our method significantly outperforms the state-of-the-art methods, and improves the success rate by 9.2% for defense models and 3.7% for normally trained models on average in the black-box setting.

2   Related Work

In this section, we briefly analyze the exiting adversarial attack methods, from the perspectives of classification of adversarial examples, attack setting, and ensemble strategy.

2.1 Adversarial Examples

Adversarial examples are first discovered by Szegedy *et al.* [32], which only added subtle perturbation to the original image but can mislead the DNNs to make an unreasonable prediction with unbelievably high confidence. To make matters worse, adversarial examples also exist in physical world [6,12,13], which raises security concerns about DNNs. Due to the vulnerability of DNNs, a large number of attack methods have been proposed and applied to various fields of deep learning in recent years, e.g., object detection and semantic segmentation [35], embodied agents [19], and speech recognition [1]. To make our paper more focused, we only analyze adversarial examples in the image classification task.

2.2 Attack Settings

In this section, we describe three common attack settings. The first is the white-box setting where the adversary can get the full knowledge of the targeted models, thus obtaining accurate gradient information to update adversarial examples. The second is the semi-black-box setting where the output of the targeted model is available but model parameters are still unknown. For example, Papernot *et al.* [24] train a local model with many queries to substitute for the target model. Ilyas *et al.* [11] propose the variant of NES [27] to generate adversarial examples with limited queries. The rest is the black-box setting, where the adversary generally cannot access the target model and adversarial examples are usually generated for substitute models without exception. That is why transferability plays a key role in this setting. Recently, the black-box attack is a hot topic and many excellent works have been proposed. Xie *et al.* [37] apply random transformations to the input images at each iteration to improve transferability. Dong *et al.* [2] propose a momentum-based iterative algorithm to boost adversarial attacks. Besides, the adversarial examples which are crafted by their translation-invariant attack method [3] can evade the defenses with effect. However, the above works cannot generate powerful patch-wise noise because they generally take valid gradient information into account. In this paper, our goal is crafting efficient patch-wise noise to improve the transferability of adversarial examples in the black-box setting.

2.3 Ensemble Strategy

There are two well-known but totally different strategies for this topic. One strategy uses an ensemble of legitimate examples to update only one universal adversarial perturbation. Moosavi-Dezfooli *et al.* [23] propose an iterative attack method to generate such perturbations which cause almost all images sampled from the data distribution to be misclassified. Another strategy uses an ensemble of models to get a better estimate of the gradient information. Liu *et al.* [21] propose novel ensemble-based approaches that attacking multiple models to generate adversarial examples. In this way, the adversarial examples are less likely to get stuck in the local optimum of any specific model, thus improving transferability.

3   Methodology

In this section, we describe our algorithm in detail. Let x^{clean} denote a clean example without any perturbation and y denote the corresponding ground-truth label. We use $f(x)$ to denote the prediction label of DNNs, and x^{noise} to denote the human-imperceptible perturbation. The adversarial example $x^{adv} = x^{clean} + x^{noise}$ is visually indistinguishable from x^{clean} but misleads the classifier to give a high confidence of a wrong label. In this paper, we focus on untargeted black-box attack, i.e., $f(x^{adv}) \neq y$. And the targeted version can be simply derived. To measure the perceptibility of adversarial perturbations, we follow previous works [2,3,37] and use l_∞-norm here. Namely, we set the max adversarial perturbation ϵ, i.e., we should keep $||x^{clean} - x^{adv}||_\infty \leq \epsilon$. To generate our adversarial examples, we should maximize the cross-entropy loss $J(x^{adv}, y)$ of the substitute models. Our goal is to solve the following constrained optimization problem:

$$\arg \max_{x^{adv}} J(x^{adv}, y), \qquad s.t. \ ||x^{clean} - x^{adv}||_\infty \leq \epsilon. \qquad (1)$$

Due to the black-box setting, the adversary does not allow to analytically compute the target models' gradient $\nabla J(x, y)$. In the majority of cases, they use the information of substitute models (i.e., official pre-trained models) to generate adversarial examples. Therefore, it is very important to improve the transferability of adversarial examples so that they still fool the black-box models successfully.

3.1   Development of Gradient-Based Attack Methods

In this section, we give a brief introduction of some excellent works which are based on the gradient sign method.

- *Fast Gradient Sign Method (FGSM)*: Goodfellow *et al.* [7] argue that the vulnerability of DNN is their linear nature. Consequently they update the adversarial example by:

$$x^{adv} = x^{clean} + \epsilon \cdot sign(\nabla_x J(x^{clean}, y)). \qquad (2)$$

  where $sign(\cdot)$ indicates the sign operation.
- *Iterative Fast Gradient Sign Method (I-FGSM)*: Kurakin *et al.* [14] use a small step size α to iteratively apply the gradient sign method multiple times. This method can be written as:

$$x_{t+1}^{adv} = Clip_{x^{clean}, \epsilon} \{x_t^{adv} + \alpha \cdot sign(\nabla_x J(x_t^{adv}, y))\}. \qquad (3)$$

  where $Clip_{x^{clean}, \epsilon}$ denotes element-wise clipping, aiming to restrict x^{adv} within the l_∞-bound of x^{clean}.

- *Momentum Iterative Fast Gradient Sign Method (MI-FGSM)*: Dong *et al.* [2] use momentum term to stabilize update directions. It can be expressed as:

$$g_{t+1} = \mu \cdot g_t + \frac{\nabla_x J(x_t^{adv}, y)}{||\nabla_x J(x_t^{adv}, y)||_1}, \quad x_{t+1}^{adv} = x_t^{adv} + \alpha \cdot sign(g_{t+1}). \quad (4)$$

where g_t is cumulative gradient, and μ is the decay factor.
- *Diverse Input Iterative Fast Gradient Sign Method (DI²-FGSM)*: Xie *et al.* [37] apply diverse input patterns to improve the transferability of adversarial examples. With the replacement of Eq. (3) by:

$$x_{t+1}^{adv} = Clip_{x^{clean}, \epsilon}\{x_t^{adv} + \alpha \cdot sign(\nabla_x J(D(x_t^{adv}), y))\}. \quad (5)$$

where $D(x)$ is random transformations to the input x. For simplicity, we use DI-FGSM later.
- *Translation-Invariant Attack Method*: Dong *et al.* [3] convolve the gradient with the pre-defined kernel W to generate adversarial examples which are less sensitive to the discriminative regions of the substitute model. For TI-FGSM, it is only updated in one step:

$$x^{adv} = x^{clean} + \epsilon \cdot sign(W * \nabla_x J(x_t^{adv}, y)). \quad (6)$$

and TI-BIM is its iterative version.

3.2 Patch-Wise Iterative Fast Gradient Sign Method

In this section, we elaborate our method in details. We first introduce our motivations in Sect. 3.2.1 and Sect. 3.2.2. In Sect. 3.2.3, we will describe our solution.

3.2.1 Patch Map

Natural images are generally made up of smooth patches [22] and the discriminative regions are usually focused on several patches of them. However, as demonstrated in Fig. 1, different DNNs generally focus on different discriminative regions, but these regions usually contain clustered pixels instead of scattered ones. Besides, Li et al. [17] have demonstrated that regionally homogeneous perturbations are strong in attacking defense models, which is especially helpful to learn transferable adversarial examples in the black-box setting. For this reason, we believe that noises with the characteristic of aggregation in these regions are more likely to attack successfully because they perturb more significant information. To better view the adversarial noise x^{noise}, we take the absolute value of x^{noise} to define its patch map x^{map}[1], which is done by:

$$x^{map} = |x^{noise}| \times \frac{256}{\epsilon}. \quad (7)$$

As shown in Fig. 1, compared with the patch map of I-FGSM, and FGSM, our PI-FGSM can generate the noise with more obvious aggregation characteristics.

---

[1] Pixel values of a valid image are in [0, 255]. If the values are more than 255, they will be modified into 0 for "uint8" type, to give better contrast.

3.2.2   Box Constraint

To the best of our knowledge, almost all iterative gradient-based methods apply *projected gradient descent* to ensure the perturbation within the box. Although this method can improve the generalization of adversarial examples to some extent [23], it also has certain limitations. Let us take the dot product $D(\cdot)$ as an example:

$$D(x_t^{adv}) = wx_t^{adv} + b, \qquad\qquad D'(x_t^{adv}) = w. \qquad (8)$$

where w denotes a weight vector and b denotes the bias. Then we add a noise αw to update x_t^{adv}:

$$D(Clip_{x^{clean},\epsilon}\{x_t^{adv} + \alpha w\}) \approx D(x_t^{adv}) + \alpha_2 w^2. \qquad (9)$$

If $x_t^{adv} + \alpha w$ excess the ϵ-ball of original image x^{clean}, the result is Eq. (9). Obviously, $\alpha_2 < \alpha$ due to element-wise clipping operation. If we adopt this strategy directly, we will waste some of the gradient information and change the input unexpectedly.

3.2.3   Our Method

From the above analysis, we observe that adding noise in a patch-wise style will have better transferability than the pixel-wise style. Also, the element-wise clipping operation of existing gradient-based attack methods will lose part of the gradient information and lead to unexpected changes. Therefore, we propose our method, which follows the mature gradient-based attack pipeline and tackles the above issues simultaneously.

To the best of our knowledge, many recent iterative attack methods [2,3,37] set step size $\alpha = \epsilon/T$, where T is the total number of iterations. In such a setting, we do not need the element-wise clipping operation, and the adversarial examples can finally reach the ϵ bound of x^{clean}. This seems like a good way to get around the above problem of direct clipping, but we notice that single-step attacks often outperform iterative attacks in the black-box setting. To study the transferability with respect to the step size setting, we make a tradeoff between single large step and iterative small step by setting it to $\epsilon/T \times \beta$, where β is an amplification factor.

The results in Fig. 2 show that iterative approaches with a large amplification factor will help to avoid getting stuck in poor local optimum, thus demonstrating a stronger attack towards black-box models. One possible reason is that attacks with an amplification factor increase each element's value of the resultant perturbation, thus providing a higher probability of misclassification due to the linear assumption of Goodfellow *et al.* [7]. However, simply increasing the step size does not get around the disadvantages of direct clipping operation, because the excess noise would be eliminated.

Therefore, we propose a novel heuristic project strategy to solve this problem. Our inspiration comes from Rosen Project Gradient Method [25]: by projecting

---

Algorithm 1: PI-FGSM

> **Input** : The cross-entropy loss function J of our substitute models;
> iterations T; L_∞ constraint ϵ; project kernel W_p; amplification
> factor $\beta(\geq 1)$; project factor γ; a clean image x^{clean} (Normalized to
> [-1,1]) and the corresponding groud-truth label y;
>
> **Output**: The adversarial example x^{adv};

1 Initialize cumulative amplification noise a_0 and cut noise C to 0;

2 $x_0^{adv} = x^{clean}$;

3 **for** $t \leftarrow 0$ **to** T **do**

4   Calculate the gradient $\nabla_x J(x_t^{adv}, y)$;

5      $a_{t+1} = a_t + \beta \cdot \frac{\epsilon}{T} \cdot sign(\nabla_x J(x_t^{adv}, y))$;   // Update a_{t+1}

6   **if** $\|a_{t+1}\|_\infty \geq \epsilon$ **then**

7        $C = clip(|a_{t+1}| - \epsilon, 0, \infty) \cdot sign(a_{t+1})$;

8        $a_{t+1} = a_{t+1} + \gamma \cdot sign(W_p * C)$;

9   **else**

10       $C = 0$;

11   **end**

12     $x_{t+1}^{adv} = Clip_{x^{clean}, \epsilon}\{x_t^{adv} + \beta \cdot \frac{\epsilon}{T} \cdot sign(\nabla_x J(x_t^{adv}, y)) + \gamma \cdot sign(W_p * C)\}$;

13     $x_{t+1}^{adv} = clip(x_{t+1}^{adv}, -1, 1)$;   // Finally clip x_{t+1}^{adv} into [-1,1]

14 **end**

15 Return $x^{adv} = x_T^{adv}$;

---

the gradient direction when the iteration point is on the edge of the feasible region, the method ensures the iteration point remains within the feasible region after updating. However, performing this method is a little complex and needs additional computational cost. Hence we take a heuristic strategy to apply this idea: just projecting the excess noise into the surrounding field. We argue that the part of the noise vector which is more easy to break ϵ-ball limitation has a higher probability of being in the highlighted area of discriminative regions. Our strategy can simply reuse the noise to increase the degree of aggregation in these regions without additional huge computational cost.

The integration of patch-wise iterative algorithm and fast gradient sign method (PI-FGSM) is summarized in Algorithm 1. Firstly, in line 5, we need to get the cumulative amplification noise a_t. After amplification operation, if L_∞-norm of a_t exceeds the threshold ϵ, we update the cut noise C by:

$$C = clip(|a_{t+1}| - \epsilon, 0, \infty) \cdot sign(a_{t+1}). \tag{10}$$

where $|\cdot|$ denotes the absolute operation. Finally, unlike other methods, we add an additional project term before restricting the L_∞-norm of the perturbations. Note that we do not abandon the clipping operation. Instead, we just reuse the cut noise to alleviate the disadvantages of direct clipping, thus increasing the aggregation degree of noise patches. More specifically, we update the adversarial examples by:

$$x_{t+1}^{adv} = Clip_{x^{clean}, \epsilon}\{x_t^{adv} + \beta \cdot \frac{\epsilon}{T} \cdot sign(\nabla_x J(x_t^{adv}, y)) + \gamma \cdot sign(W_p * C)\}. \tag{11}$$

where W_p is a special uniform project kernel of size $k_w \times k_w$, and $sign(W_p * C)$ is cut noise's "feasible direction". In this paper, we simply define W_p as:

$$W_p[i,j] = \begin{cases} 0, & i = \lfloor k_w/2 \rfloor, j = \lfloor k_w/2 \rfloor. \\ 1/(k_w^2 - 1), & else. \end{cases} \tag{12}$$

We also test other types of kernels actually, e.g., Gaussian kernel. However, experiment results show that there are no significant difference (only ∼1%). Besides, the uniform kernel does not need extra parameters. Therefore we choose it finally.

4 Experiment

4.1 Setup

Following the previous works [2,3], we also do our experiments on ImageNet-compatible dataset[2], which contains 1000 images and is used for NIPS 2017 adversarial competition. We choose eleven models to do these experiments. For normally trained models, we consider Inception V3 (Inc-v3) [31], Inception V4 (Inc-v4) [30], Inception-ResNet V2 (IncRes-v2) [30] ResNet152 V2 (Res-152) [9] and DenseNet 161 (Dense-161) [10]. For defense models, we include three ensemble adversarial trained models: Inc-v3$_{ens3}$, Inc-v3$_{ens4}$ and IncRes-v2$_{ens}$ [34], and three more robust models from [37]: ResNet152 Baseline (Res152$_B$), ResNet152 Denoise (Res152$_D$), ResNeXt101 DenoiseAll (ResNeXt$_{DA}$) [36]. For the sake of simplicity, we use NT to denote normally trained models, EAT to denote ensemble adversarial trained models and FD to denote feature denoising defense models (include Res152$_B$). Noted that the reported success rate of FD has subtracted the ratio of clean images that are predicted incorrectly by FD. In addition, PI-FGSM can be easily combined with other attack methods (e.g., DI-FGSM [37]). To make the abbreviation unambiguous, we use the first character to denote the corresponding method. For instance, DPI-FGSM means the integration of DI-FGSM with PI-FGSM.

In our experiment, we set equal weight when attacking an ensemble of models. The maximum perturbation ϵ is set to 16. The iteration T is set to 10 for all iterative methods. For iterative methods without our amplification factor, the step size is $\epsilon/T = 1.6$. For MI-FGSM, we set the decay factor $\mu = 1.0$; for TI-FGSM and TI-BIM, we set the kernel size $k = 15$; and for DI-FGSM, we set the transformation probability $p = 0.7$.

4.2 Amplification Factor

In this section, we calculate the success rate of different amplification factors, which are varied from 1 to 10. The results are shown in Fig. 2. In general, a larger

---

[2] https://github.com/tensorflow/cleverhans/tree/master/examples/
nips17_adversarial_competition/dataset.

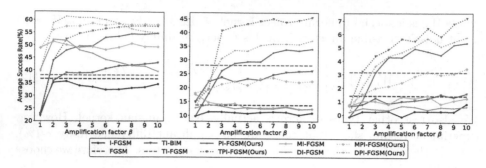

Fig. 2. The average success rate(%) of non-targeted attacks in different amplification factor β setting. The adversarial examples are crafted for Inc-v3 by FGSM, I-FGSM, MI-FGSM, TI-BIM, TI-FGSM, DI-FGSM, PI-FGSM and their combined versions respectively. **Left Column**: The result of NT, including Inc-v4, Res-152, IncRes-v2 and Dense-161 but except Inc-v3; **Middle Column**: The result of EAT, including Inc-v3$_{ens3}$, Inc-v3$_{ens4}$ and IncRes-v2$_{ens}$; **Right Column**: The result of FD, including ResNeXt$_{DA}$, Res152$_B$ and Res152$_D$.

amplification factor does improve performance. Moreover, we observe that when the amplification factor is large enough, further increasing it will not bring significant improvement and may even reduce the transferability of some attacks. For example, it is better not to use large amplification factor for DI-FGSM, because this method applies random transformations to the input images. If we set the amplification factor too large, the adversarial examples may deviate from the global optimum. In addition, a larger amplification factor has no obvious effect for MI-FGSM, which also proves that the momentum term can stabilize the update directions and avoid getting stuck in a poor local optimum. For our method, as the amplification factor increases, the success rate will increase rapidly and outperform other approaches soon. If we set $\beta = 1$, PI-FGSM degrades to I-FGSM because the cut noise has no effect anymore in this setting. By comparing the growth curves of I-FGSM and PI-FGSM, we observe that our heuristic project strategy can improve the transferability by a large margin, which fully validates the effectiveness of our method. We also examine the influence of amplification factor on the combined methods and show the results in Fig. 2. It can be observed that the optimal amplification factor of combined methods is usually between the best β of the two methods. If one of these methods' performance is negatively correlated with the amplification factor, then the combination with our method may not perform well (i.e., MPI-FGSM vs. EAT). In our experiments, the project factor γ is set to $\epsilon/T \cdot \beta$ in most cases, therefore we only focus on the amplification factor in this ablation study, specific parameter settings will be given in the later experiments.

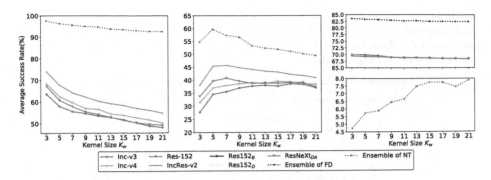

Fig. 3. The average success rate(%) of non-targeted attacks in different kernel size settings. The adversarial examples are crafted for different substitute models respectively, e.g., Inc-v3 (blue solid line). **Left Column**: The results of *NT*, including Inc-v3, Inc-v4, Res-152, IncRes-v2 and Dense-161; **Middle Column**: The results of *EAT*, including Inc-v3$_{ens3}$, Inc-v3$_{ens4}$ and IncRes-v2$_{ens}$; **Right Column**: The results of *FD*, including ResNeXt$_{DA}$, Res152$_B$ and Res152$_D$. (Color figure online)

4.3 Project Kernel Size

In fact, the function of the project kernel is to generate patch-wise noise. As shown in Fig. 1, the noise patch map of PI-FGSM is larger and regular than others. The results in Fig. 2 also demonstrate the effectiveness of our proposed method. However, The size of the kernel W_p play an important role for transferability. From Fig. 3, we find the optimal size of project kernel is different for NT, EAT and FD:

- When transferring to NT, 3×3 kernel is the best. Larger kernel size always decreases the transferability in the black-box setting.
- When transferring to EAT, 7×7 kernel can improve the transferability obviously. But if we keep increasing the size, the success rate grows slowly and even gets worse.
- When transferring to FD, if adversarial examples are generated for FD, 3×3 kernel is the best. And if we use NT to attack against FD, 21×21 is slightly better.

Considering the difference between the NT, EAT and FD, we use 3×3 kernel to attack against NT, 7×7 for EAT and 21×21 for FD if adversarial examples are crafted for NT. Also, we use 3×3 kernel to fool FD if adversarial examples are generated for FD.

4.4 Attacks vs. Normally Trained Models

In this section, we focus on the vulnerability of NT. we set $\beta = 10$ ($\gamma = 16$) for PI-FGSM and MPI-FGSM, and $\beta = 2.5, \gamma = 2$ for DMPI-FGSM and DPI-FGSM. We compare PI-FGSM with FGSM, I-FGSM, MI-FGSM, DI-FGSM to

Table 1. The success rate(%) of non-targeted attacks against NT. The leftmost column models are substitute models ("*" indicates white-box attack), the adversarial examples are crafted for them by FGSM, I-FGSM, MI-FGSM, DI-FGSM, PI-FGSM, and their combined versions respectively.

	Attacks	Inc-v3	Inc-v4	Res-152	IncRes-v2	Dense-161
Inc-v3	FGSM	80.9*	38.0	33.1	33.9	41.4
	I-FGSM	100.0*	29.6	19.4	20.3	20.7
	MI-FGSM	100.0*	54.1	43.5	50.9	45.8
	DI-FGSM	99.8*	54.2	32.1	43.6	30.4
	PI-FGSM(Ours)	100.0*	58.6	45.0	51.3	61.7
	MPI-FGSM(Ours)	100.0*	63.0	50.6	60.0	59.0
	DPI-FGSM(Ours)	100.0*	73.1	51.2	67.4	55.9
	DMI-FGSM	99.9*	78.9	63.9	75.6	60.7
	DMPI-FGSM(Ours)	100.0*	81.8	63.4	77.1	63.7
Inc-v4	FGSM	45.4	75.1*	35.1	35.8	45.4
	I-FGSM	43.3	100.0*	25.5	25.3	24.7
	MI-FGSM	71.2	100.0*	52.4	59.0	51.2
	DI-FGSM	66.6	100.0*	39.8	50.4	33.2
	PI-FGSM(Ours)	70.7	100.0*	50.9	54.9	65.8
	MPI-FGSM(Ours)	77.3	100.0*	56.5	63.7	64.3
	DPI-FGSM(Ours)	84.3	100.0*	57.6	70.6	61.8
	DMI-FGSM	89.0	100.0*	70.8	80.2	67.7
	DMPI-FGSM(Ours)	90.4	100.0*	70.6	82.2	70.0
Res-152	FGSM	41.4	36.4	82.3*	32.0	45.1
	I-FGSM	30.7	24.7	99.5*	16.9	23.7
	MI-FGSM	56.1	51.0	99.5*	47.9	50.2
	DI-FGSM	60.0	56.5	99.2*	49.3	43.1
	PI-FGSM(Ours)	63.3	54.4	99.7*	50.6	67.4
	MPI-FGSM(Ours)	68.8	62.5	99.7*	59.9	69.0
	DPI-FGSM(Ours)	81.0	77.2	99.6*	75.0	71.6
	DMI-FGSM	82.2	79.4	99.3*	74.8	72.0
	DMPI-FGSM(Ours)	86.1	83.4	99.5*	82.0	75.2
IncRes-v2	FGSM	45.9	39.2	35.7	68.3*	45.6
	I-FGSM	48.2	38.3	25.5	100.0*	27.0
	MI-FGSM	77.6	68.4	57.0	100.0*	57.1
	DI-FGSM	70.2	66.1	47.9	99.2*	42.0
	PI-FGSM(Ours)	76.1	68.8	58.2	99.9*	69.8
	MPI-FGSM(Ours)	80.2	75.5	63.8	100.0*	70.3
	DPI-FGSM(Ours)	87.2	83.4	65.0	99.7*	69.2
	DMI-FGSM	86.8	85.6	76.5	99.1*	70.9
	DMPI-FGSM(Ours)	92.2	89.0	77.1	99.6*	74.7

verify the effectiveness of our method. Moreover, we also test the performance of the combination of different methods, e.g., MPI-FGSM. It should be noted that we do not consider TI-BIM or TI-FGSM [3] here, because they focus more on attacking the defense models.

The results are shown in Table 1. To sum up, compared with other attacks, our PI-FGSM can improve the success rate by **3.7%** on average, and when we attack against Dense-161[3], transferability can be increased by up to **17.2%**. This is because our perturbation patches have the property of aggregation, thus reducing the impact of resizing. In particular, if we integrate PI-FGSM into

---
[3] Input size need to be [224,224,3], therefore we need resize adversarial examples whose size is [299,299,3].

Table 2. The success rate(%) of non-targeted attacks against EAT. The top row models are substitute models, we use them to generate adversarial examples by FGSM, I-FGSM, DI-FGSM, MI-FGSM, TI-FGSM, PI-FGSM and their combined versions respectively.

Attacks	Inc-v3			Inc-v4			Res-152			IncRes-v2		
	Inc-v3$_{ens3}$	Inc-v3$_{ens4}$	IncRes-v2$_{ens}$	Inc-v3$_{ens3}$	Inc-v3$_{ens4}$	IncRes-v2$_{ens}$	Inc-v3$_{ens3}$	Inc-v3$_{ens4}$	IncRes-v2$_{ens}$	Inc-v3$_{ens3}$	Inc-v3$_{ens4}$	IncRes-v2$_{ens}$
FGSM	16.8	15.8	8.3	16.6	17.2	9.1	21.4	19.4	11.4	18.6	17.5	11.2
I-FGSM	11.7	12.1	5.5	11.8	13.0	6.6	13.0	13.3	6.7	13.7	13.3	8.2
MI-FGSM	21.9	21.1	10.5	24.7	23.7	13.2	27.0	24.9	15.9	31.9	29.1	20.7
DI-FGSM	15.0	16.2	7.1	14.7	17.7	8.4	21.6	21.1	12.9	19.3	20.2	12.7
TI-FGSM	30.8	30.6	22.7	30.2	31.3	23.2	36.6	36.1	29.5	36.3	36.0	30.4
PI-FGSM(Ours)	**39.3**	**39.5**	**28.8**	**40.3**	**41.8**	**31.4**	**43.0**	**45.0**	**34.9**	**46.4**	**48.4**	**42.4**
TPI-FGSM(Ours)	49.1	50.2	36.5	49.6	51.7	38.5	51.5	51.4	43.3	59.2	60.3	56.5
DPI-FGSM(Ours)	40.9	41.6	31.2	43.4	46.0	33.8	47.9	48.5	41.4	48.8	50.4	45.8
DTMI-FGSM	50.7	50.3	39.5	**54.0**	54.2	**42.9**	59.5	58.4	53.1	65.4	63.8	**62.9**
DTPI-FGSM(Ours)	**51.5**	**53.1**	**40.0**	52.2	**54.7**	41.7	**65.3**	**64.5**	**56.3**	**70.0**	**67.7**	62.3

other attack methods such as DMI-FGSM, we can get a much better result. For instance, the adversarial examples generated for IncRes-v2 by DMPI-FGSM can fool Inc-v3 on **92.2%** images in the black-box setting which also demonstrates the vulnerability of NT.

4.5   Attacks vs. Defense Models

Our approach is especially effective for defense models. In this experiment, we use EAT [34] and FD [36] to examine the transferability and we do not integrate the momentum term into our proposed PI-FGSM because it may hinder the performance.

Here we study the single-model attacks firstly. In this case, we set $\beta = 10$ ($\gamma = 16$), and the results are shown in Table 2. Compared with TI-FGSM, the average success rate of our method is improved by about **9.0%**. In particular, if we use DTPI-FGSM to attack IncRes-v2, **70.0%** adversarial examples can fool Inc-v3$_{ens}$. Noted that the results of Table 2 are not our best parameter setting, because the best kernel size for a single-model attack is not the same. Here we just set the $k_w = 7$ to keep the experimental parameters consistent.

The transferability can be greatly improved when the adversarial examples are crafted for an ensemble of models at the same time [21]. It is because this strategy can prevent adversarial examples from falling into a local optimum of any specific model. In this case, we set $\beta = 5$ ($\gamma = 8$) and the result are shown in Table 3. Compared with MI-FGSM, our proposed PI-FGSM improves the performance by about **9.6%** on average. Furthermore, compared with DTMI-FGSM [3] which takes momentum into account, our DTPI-FGSM still outperform it.

Furthermore, when using Inc-v3 to attack against FD, we are surprised to find that sometimes I-FGSM even perturbs misclassified images into correctly classified ones (See Fig. 2). This may be due to the significant difference in decision boundaries between the NT and FD. Since FD are very robust, and the transferability largely depends on the substitute models. To make our proposed PI-FGSM more convincing, we generate adversarial examples for ResNeXt$_{DA}$, Res152$_B$, Res152$_D$ and an ensemble of them respectively. In this case, we set

Table 3. The success rate(%) of non-targeted attacks. We use an ensemble of Inc-v3, Inc-v4, Res-152, and IncRes-v2 to generate our adversarial examples by FGSM, I-FGSM, MI-FGSM, DI-FGSM, TI-FGSM, PI-FGSM, and their combined versions respectively.

	Inc-v3$_{ens3}$	Inc-v3$_{ens4}$	IncRes$_{ens}$	ResNeXt$_{DA}$	Res152$_B$	Res152$_D$
FGSM	27.1	24.0	13.5	3.1	1.4	2.2
I-FGSM	26.2	25.2	16.0	0.7	0.8	0.4
MI-FGSM	51.9	49.3	32.9	2.8	1.8	2.2
DI-FGSM	40.5	38.5	25.6	1.2	1.5	1.2
TI-FGSM	39.3	38.9	31.5	6.1	3.7	3.0
PI-FGSM(Ours)	**61.0**	**62.8**	**51.3**	**8.7**	**8.5**	**6.0**
TPI-FGSM(Ours)	79.6	81.4	74.0	11.5	10.5	9.4
DPI-FGSM(Ours)	66.7	68.5	58.7	9.0	7.4	6.4
DTMI-FGSM	81.2	81.1	76.6	6.1	5.5	4.8
DTPI-FGSM(Ours)	**89.3**	**89.2**	**83.4**	**11.7**	**10.6**	**10.4**

Table 4. The average success rate(%) of non-targeted attacks. The top row models are substitute models ("*" indicates white-box attack). We use ResNeXt$_{DA}$, Res152$_B$, Res152$_D$ and an ensemble of them to generate adversarial examples by FGSM, I-FGSM, DI-FGSM, TI-FGSM, MI-FGSM, PI-FGSM, and their combined versions respectively.

Attacks	ResNeXt$_{DA}$	Res152$_B$	Res152$_D$	ResNeXt$_{DA}$	Res152$_B$	Res152$_D$	ResNeXt$_{DA}$	Res152$_B$	Res152$_D$	ResNeXt$_{DA}$	Res152$_B$	Res152$_D$
	ResNeXt$_{DA}$			Res152$_B$			Res152$_D$			Ensemble		
DI-FGSM	58.3*	34.4	33.3	33.5	57.3*	32.5	34.7	34.8	56.8*	67.0*	66.8*	65.9*
TI-FGSM	66.7*	44.5	44.6	46.9	69.8*	44.3	48.6	46.6	65.3*	63.8*	62.1*	63.1*
FGSM	67.2*	45.7	45.0	47.5	71.3*	45.4	49.2	46.3	68.4*	67.2*	67.1*	65.7*
DTMI-FGSM	72.1*	51.0	52.3	52.4	74.0*	49.1	54.4	51.8	69.8*	69.6*	68.3*	65.4*
DMI-FGSM	72.5*	50.3	50.8	49.8	76.0*	48.3	51.7	48.9	72.2*	71.7*	71.9*	71.3*
MTI-FGSM	72.6*	50.1	52.1	51.8	77.7*	49.7	53.5	51.2	73.8*	70.6*	71.3*	68.4*
MI-FGSM	79.0*	54.0	54.4	56.6	81.5*	55.0	57.1	54.8	78.5*	75.3*	77.1*	75.7*
I-FGSM	81.6*	55.1	55.9	56.8	83.7*	55.9	57.7	55.8	82.5*	78.9*	79.6*	79.8*
PI-FGSM(Ours)	**86.9***	**62.0**	**60.8**	**62.0**	**88.1***	**61.9**	**62.7**	**62.4**	**86.6***	**84.8***	**82.5***	**83.2***

$\beta = 2.5, \gamma = 1$. In Table 4, we sort these methods in an ascending order. As we can observe, our approach is superior to other methods by a large margin for both the white-box and black-box settings. However, existing methods' performance is even worse than I-FGSM, which is a basic iterative method. It also reminds us that when attacking several robust defense models, simply combining with different methods may not be effective.

5   Conclusions

Here we propose a novel patch-wise iterative algorithm – a black-box attack towards mainstream normally trained and defense models, which differs from the existing attack methods manipulating pixel-wise noise. With this approach, our adversarial perturbation patches in discriminative regions will be larger, thus generating more transferable adversarial examples against both normally trained and defense models. Compared with state-of-the-art attacks, extensive experiments have demonstrated the extraordinary effectiveness of our attack. Besides, our method can be generally integrated to any gradient-based attack methods. Our approach can serve as a baseline to help generating more transferable adversarial examples and evaluating the robustness of various deep neural networks.

Acknowledgments. This work is supported by the Fundamental Research Funds for the Central Universities (Grant No. ZYGX2019J073), the National Natural Science Foundation of China (Grant No. 61772116, No. 61872064, No. 61632007, No. 61602049), The Open Project of Zhejiang Lab (Grant No. 2019KD0AB05).

References

1. Cissé, M., Adi, Y., Neverova, N., Keshet, J.: Houdini: fooling deep structured prediction models. CoRR abs/1707.05373 (2017)
2. Dong, Y., et al.: Boosting adversarial attacks with momentum. In: CVPR (2018)
3. Dong, Y., Pang, T., Su, H., Zhu, J.: Evading defenses to transferable adversarial examples by translation-invariant attacks. In: CVPR (2019)
4. Dziugaite, G.K., Ghahramani, Z., Roy, D.M.: A study of the effect of JPG compression on adversarial images. CoRR abs/1608.00853 (2016)
5. Efros, A.A., Freeman, W.T.: Image quilting for texture synthesis and transfer. In: SIGGRAPH (2001)
6. Eykholt, K., et al.: Robust physical-world attacks on deep learning visual classification. In: CVPR (2018)
7. Goodfellow, I.J., Shlens, J., Szegedy, C.: Explaining and harnessing adversarial examples. In: ICLR (2015)
8. Guo, C., Rana, M., Cissé, M., van der Maaten, L.: Countering adversarial images using input transformations. In: ICLR (2018)
9. He, K., Zhang, X., Ren, S., Sun, J.: Deep residual learning for image recognition. In: CVPR (2016)
10. Huang, G., Liu, Z., van der Maaten, L., Weinberger, K.Q.: Densely connected convolutional networks. In: CVPR (2017)
11. Ilyas, A., Engstrom, L., Athalye, A., Lin, J.: Black-box adversarial attacks with limited queries and information. In: Dy, J.G., Krause, A. (eds.) Proceedings of the 35th International Conference on Machine Learning, ICML (2018)
12. Komkov, S., Petiushko, A.: AdvHat: real-world adversarial attack on ArcFace face ID system. CoRR abs/1908.08705 (2019)
13. Kurakin, A., Goodfellow, I.J., Bengio, S.: Adversarial examples in the physical world. In: ICLR (2017)
14. Kurakin, A., Goodfellow, I.J., Bengio, S.: Adversarial machine learning at scale. In: ICLR (2017)
15. Li, X., et al.: Learnable aggregating net with diversity learning for video question answering. In: Proceedings of the 27th ACM International Conference on Multimedia, pp. 1166–1174 (2019)
16. Li, X., et al.: Beyond RNNs: positional self-attention with co-attention for video question answering. In: Proceedings of the AAAI Conference on Artificial Intelligence, vol. 33, pp. 8658–8665 (2019)
17. Li, Y., Bai, S., Xie, C., Liao, Z., Shen, X., Yuille, A.L.: Regional homogeneity: towards learning transferable universal adversarial perturbations against defenses. CoRR abs/1904.00979 (2019)

18. Lin, J., Gan, C., Han, S.: Defensive quantization: when efficiency meets robustness. In: ICLR (2019)
19. Liu, A., et al.: Spatiotemporal attacks for embodied agents. In: ECCV (2020)
20. Liu, A., Wang, J., Liu, X., Cao, b., Zhang, C., Yu, H.: Bias-based universal adversarial patch attack for automatic check-out. In: ECCV (2020)
21. Liu, Y., Chen, X., Liu, C., Song, D.: Delving into transferable adversarial examples and black-box attacks. In: ICLR (2017)
22. Mahendran, A., Vedaldi, A.: Understanding deep image representations by inverting them. In: CVPR (2015)
23. Moosavi-Dezfooli, S., Fawzi, A., Fawzi, O., Frossard, P.: Universal adversarial perturbations. In: CVPR (2017)
24. Papernot, N., McDaniel, P.D., Goodfellow, I.J., Jha, S., Celik, Z.B., Swami, A.: Practical black-box attacks against machine learning. In: Karri, R., Sinanoglu, O., Sadeghi, A., Yi, X. (eds.) AsiaCCS (2017)
25. Rosen, J.: The gradient projection method for nonlinear programming. Part I. Linear constraints. J. Soc. Ind. Appl. Math. **8**, 181–217 (1960)
26. Rudin, L.I., Osher, S., Fatemi, E.: Nonlinear total variation based noise removal algorithms. Physica D: Nonlinear Phenom. **60**(1-4), 259–268 (1992)
27. Salimans, T., Ho, J., Chen, X., Sutskever, I.: Evolution strategies as a scalable alternative to reinforcement learning. CoRR abs/1703.03864 (2017)
28. Selvaraju, R.R., Cogswell, M., Das, A., Vedantam, R., Parikh, D., Batra, D.: Grad-CAM: visual explanations from deep networks via gradient-based localization. In: ICCV (2017)
29. Sharif, M., Bhagavatula, S., Bauer, L., Reiter, M.K.: Accessorize to a crime: real and stealthy attacks on state-of-the-art face recognition. In: SIGSAC (2016)
30. Szegedy, C., Ioffe, S., Vanhoucke, V., Alemi, A.A.: Inception-v4, inception-ResNet and the impact of residual connections on learning. In: AAAI (2017)
31. Szegedy, C., Vanhoucke, V., Ioffe, S., Shlens, J., Wojna, Z.: Rethinking the inception architecture for computer vision. In: CVPR (2016)
32. Szegedy, C., et al.: Intriguing properties of neural networks. In: ICLR (2014)
33. Thys, S., Ranst, W.V., Goedemé, T.: Fooling automated surveillance cameras: adversarial patches to attack person detection. In: CVPR Workshops (2019)
34. Tramèr, F., Kurakin, A., Papernot, N., Goodfellow, I.J., Boneh, D., McDaniel, P.D.: Ensemble adversarial training: attacks and defenses. In: ICLR (2018)
35. Xie, C., Wang, J., Zhang, Z., Zhou, Y., Xie, L., Yuille, A.L.: Adversarial examples for semantic segmentation and object detection. In: ICCV (2017)
36. Xie, C., Wu, Y., van der Maaten, L., Yuille, A.L., He, K.: Feature denoising for improving adversarial robustness. In: CVPR (2019)
37. Xie, C., et al.: Improving transferability of adversarial examples with input diversity. In: CVPR (2019)
38. Xu, K., et al.: Interpreting adversarial examples by activation promotion and suppression. CoRR abs/1904.02057 (2019)
39. Zhou, B., Khosla, A., Lapedriza, À., Oliva, A., Torralba, A.: Learning deep features for discriminative localization. In: CVPR (2016)

Feature Pyramid Transformer

Dong Zhang[1], Hanwang Zhang[2], Jinhui Tang[1(✉)], Meng Wang[3],
Xiansheng Hua[4], and Qianru Sun[5]

[1] School of Computer Science and Engineering, Nanjing University of Science
and Technology, Nanjing, China
{dongzhang,jinhuitang}@njust.edu.cn
[2] Nanyang Technological University, Singapore, Singapore
hanwangzhang@ntu.edu.sg
[3] Hefei University of Technology, Hefei, China
eric.mengwang@gmail.com
[4] Damo Academy, Alibaba Group, Hangzhou, China
xiansheng.hxs@alibaba-inc.com
[5] Singapore Management University, Singapore, Singapore
qianrusun@smu.edu.sg

Abstract. Feature interactions across space and scales underpin modern visual recognition systems because they introduce beneficial visual contexts. Conventionally, spatial contexts are passively hidden in the CNN's increasing receptive fields or actively encoded by non-local convolution. Yet, the non-local spatial interactions are not across scales, and thus they fail to capture the non-local contexts of objects (or parts) residing in different scales. To this end, we propose a fully active feature interaction across both space and scales, called Feature Pyramid Transformer (FPT). It transforms any feature pyramid into another feature pyramid of the same size but with richer contexts, by using three specially designed transformers in self-level, top-down, and bottom-up interaction fashion. FPT serves as a generic visual backbone with fair computational overhead. We conduct extensive experiments in both instance-level (*i.e.*, object detection and instance segmentation) and pixel-level segmentation tasks, using various backbones and head networks, and observe consistent improvement over all the baselines and the state-of-the-art methods (Code is open-sourced at https://github.com/ZHANGDONG-NJUST).

Keywords: Feature pyramid · Visual context · Transformer · Object detection · Instance segmentation · Semantic segmentation

1 Introduction

Modern visual recognition systems stand in context. Thanks to the hierarchical structure of Convolutional Neural Network (CNN), as illustrated in Fig. 1 (a),

Electronic supplementary material The online version of this chapter (https://doi.org/10.1007/978-3-030-58604-1_20) contains supplementary material, which is available to authorized users.

A. Vedaldi et al. (Eds.): ECCV 2020, LNCS 12373, pp. 323–339, 2020.
https://doi.org/10.1007/978-3-030-58604-1_20

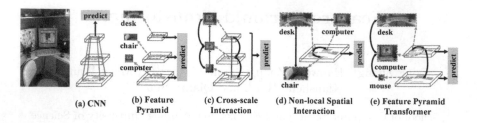

Fig. 1. The evolution of feature interaction across space and scale in feature pyramid for visual context. Transparent cubes: feature maps. Shaded `predict`: task-specific head networks. The proposed Feature Pyramid Transformer is inspired by the evolution.

contexts are encoded in the gradually larger receptive fields (the green dashed rectangles) by pooling [14,19], stride [30] or dilated convolution [37]. Therefore, the prediction from the last feature map is essentially based on the rich contexts—even though there is only one "feature pixel" for a small object, *e.g.*, `mouse`, its recognition will be still possible, due to the perception of larger contexts, *e.g.*, `table` and `computer` [11,29].

Scale also matters—the `mouse` recognition deserves more feature pixels, not only the ones from the last feature map, which easily overlooks small objects. A conventional solution is to pile an *image pyramid* for the same image [1], where the higher/lower levels are images of lower/higher resolutions. Thus, objects of different scales are recognized in their corresponding levels, *e.g.*, `mouse` in lower levels (high resolution) and `table` in higher levels (low resolution). However, the image pyramid multiplies the time-consuming CNN forward pass as each image requires a CNN for recognition. Fortunately, CNN offers an in-network *feature pyramid* [39], *i.e.*, lower/higher-level feature maps represent higher/lower-resolution visual content without computational overhead [25,28]. As shown in Fig. 1 (b), we can recognize objects of different scales by using feature maps of different levels, *i.e.*, small objects (`computer`) are recognized in lower-levels and large objects (`chair` and `desk`) are recognized in higher-levels [16,22,24].

Sometimes the recognition—especially for *pixel-level* labeling such as semantic segmentation—requires to combine the contexts from multiple scales [5,44]. For example in Fig. 1 (c), to label pixels in the frame area of the `monitor`, perhaps the local context of the object itself from lower levels is enough; however, for the pixels in the screen area, we need to exploit both of the local context and the global context from higher levels, because the local appearance of `monitor` screen is close to `TV` screen, and we should use scene context such as `keyboard` and `mouse` to distinguish between the two types.

The spirit of the above non-local context is recently modeled in a more explicit and active fashion—as opposed to the above passive feature map pile—by using the non-local convolution [34] and self-attention [3,33]. Such spatial feature interaction is expected to capture the reciprocal co-occurring patterns of multiple objects [16,41]. As shown in Fig. 1 (d), it is more likely that there is

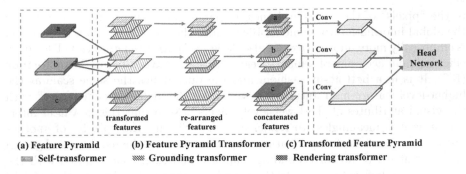

(a) Feature Pyramid   (b) Feature Pyramid Transformer   (c) Transformed Feature Pyramid
▓ Self-transformer   ⧗ Grounding transformer   ▨ Rendering transformer

Fig. 2. Overall structure of our proposed FPT network. Different texture patterns indicate different feature transformers, and different color represents feature maps with different scales. "Conv" denotes a 3×3 convolution with the output dimension of 256. Without loss of generality, the top/bottom layer feature maps has no rendering/grounding transformer.

a `computer` on the `desk` rather than on `road`, thus, the recognition of either is helpful to the other.

The tale of context and scale should continue, and it is our key motivation. In particular, we are inspired by the omission of the cross-scale interactions (Fig. 1 (c)) in the non-local spatial interactions (Fig. 1 (d)). Moreover, we believe that the non-local interaction *per se* should happen in the corresponding scales of the interacted objects (or parts), but not just in one uniform scale as in existing methods [33,34,41]. Figure 1 (e) illustrates the expected non-local interactions across scales: the low-level `mouse` is interacting with the high-level `computer`, which is interacting with `desk` at the same scale.

To this end, we propose a novel feature pyramid network called **Feature Pyramid Transformer** (FPT) for visual recognition, such as instance-level (*i.e.*, object detection and instance segmentation) and pixel-level segmentation tasks. In a nutshell, as illustrated in Fig. 2, the input of FPT is a feature pyramid, and the output is a transformed one, where each level is a *richer* feature map that encodes the non-local interactions across space and scales. Then, the feature pyramid can be attached to any task-specific head network. As its name implies, FPT's interaction adopts the transformer-style [3,33]. It has the neat *query, key* and *value* operation (cf. Sect. 3.1) that is shown effective in selecting informative long-range interaction, which tailors our goal: non-local interaction at proper scales. In addition, the computation overhead (cf. Sect. 4.1) can be alleviated by using TPUs like any other transformer models [18].

Our technical contributions, as illustrated in the FPT breakdown in Fig. 2, are the designs of three transformers: 1) **Self-Transformer** (ST). It is based on the classic non-local interaction within the same level feature map [34], and the output has the same scale as its input. 2) **Grounding Transformer** (GT). It is in a top-down fashion, and the output has the same scale as the lower-level feature map. Intuitively, we ground the "concept" of the higher-level feature maps to the "pixels" of the lower-level ones. In particular, as it is unnecessary to use the global information to segment objects, and the context within a local region is empirically more informative, we also design a *locality-constrained* GT for both efficiency and accuracy of semantic segmentation. 3) **Rendering Transformer** (RT). It is in a bottom-up fashion, and the output has the same scale as the higher-level feature map. Intuitively, we render the higher-level "concept" with the visual attributes of the lower-level "pixels". Note that this is a *local* interaction as it is meaningless to render an "object" with the "pixels" of another distant one. The transformed feature maps of each level (the red, blue and green) are re-arranged to its corresponding map size and then concatenated with the original map, before feeding into the conv-layer that resize them to the original "thickness".

Extensive experiments show that FPT can greatly improve conventional detection/segmentation pipelines by the following absolute gains: 1) 8.5% box-AP for object detection and 6.0% mask-AP for instance segmentation over baseline on the MS-COCO [23] *test-dev*; 2) for semantic segmentation, 1.6% and 1.2% mIoU on Cityscapes [7] and PASCAL VOC 2012 [9] test sets, respectively; 1.7% and 2.0% mIoU on ADE20K [45] and LIP [12] validation sets, respectively.

2   Related Work

FPT is generic to apply in a wide range of computer vision tasks. This paper focuses on two instance-level tasks: object detection, instance segmentation, and one pixel-level task: semantic segmentation. Object detection aims to predict a bounding box for each object and then assigns the bounding box a class label [29], while instance segmentation is additionally required to predict a pixel-level mask of the object [13]. Semantic segmentation aims to predict a class label to each pixel of the image [26].

Feature Pyramid. The in-network feature pyramid (*i.e.*, the Bottom-up Feature Pyramid (BFP) [22]) is one of the most commonly used methods, and has been shown useful for boosting object detection [25], instance segmentation [24] and semantic segmentation [43]. Another popular method of constructing feature pyramid uses feature maps of the scale while processing the maps through pyramidal pooling or dilated/atrous convolutions. For example, atrous spatial pyramid pooling [5] and pyramid pooling module [14,44] leverages output feature maps of the last convolution layer in the CNN backbone to build the four-level feature pyramid, in which different levels have the same resolution but different information granularities. Our approach is based on the existing BFP (for the instance-level) and unscathed feature pyramid [27] (for the pixel-level). Our contribution is the novel feature interaction approach.

Feature Interaction. An intuitive approach to the cross-scale feature interaction is gradually summing the multi-scale feature maps, such as Feature Pyramid Network (FPN) [22] and Path Aggregation Network (PANet) [24]. In particular, both FPN and PANet are based on BFP, where FPN adds a top-down path to propagate semantic information into low-level feature maps, and PANet adds a bottom-up path augmentation on the basis of FPN. Another approach is to concatenate multi-scale feature maps along the channel dimension. The specific examples for semantic segmentation are DeepLab [4] and pyramid scene parsing network [44]. Besides, a more recent work proposed the ZigZagNet [20] which exploits the addition and convolution to enhance the cross-scale feature interaction. Particularly, for the within-scale feature interaction, some recent works exploited non-local operation [34] and self-attention [33] to capture the co-occurrent object features in the same scene. Their models were evaluated in a wide range of visual tasks [16,38,41,48]. However, we argue that the non-local interaction performed in just one uniform scale feature map is not enough to represent the contexts. In this work, we aim to conduct the non-local interaction *per se* in the corresponding scales of the interacted objects (or parts).

3 Feature Pyramid Transformer

Given an input image, we can formally extract a feature pyramid, where the fine-/coarse-grained feature maps are in low/high levels, respectively. Without loss of generality, we express a low-level fine-grained feature map as $\mathbf{X}^f$ and a high-level coarse-grained feature map as $\mathbf{X}^c$. **Feature Pyramid Transformer** (FPT) enables features to interact across space and scales. It specifically includes three transformers: self-transformer (cf. Sect. 3.2), grounding transformer (cf. Sect. 3.3) and rendering transformer (cf. Sect. 3.4). The transformed feature pyramid is in the same size but with richer contexts than the original.

3.1 Non-local Interaction Revisited

A typical non-local interaction [34] operates on *queries*(Q), *keys*(K) and *values*(V) within a single feature map $\mathbf{X}$, and the output is the transformed version $\tilde{\mathbf{X}}$ with the same scale as $\mathbf{X}$. This non-local interaction is formulated as:

$$
\begin{aligned}
\textbf{Input:} \quad & \mathbf{q}_i, \mathbf{k}_j, \mathbf{v}_j \\
\textbf{Similarity:} \quad & s_{i,j} = F_{sim}(\mathbf{q}_i, \mathbf{k}_j) \\
\textbf{Weight:} \quad & w_{i,j} = F_{nom}(s_{i,j}) \\
\textbf{Output:} \quad & \tilde{\mathbf{X}}_i = F_{mul}(w_{i,j}, \mathbf{v}_j),
\end{aligned}
\tag{1}
$$

where $\mathbf{q}_i = f_q(\mathbf{X}_i) \in$ Q is the ith *query*; $\mathbf{k}_j = f_k(\mathbf{X}_j) \in$ K and $\mathbf{v}_j = f_v(\mathbf{X}_j) \in$ V are the jth *key/value* pair; $f_q(\cdot)$, $f_k(\cdot)$ and $f_v(\cdot)$ denote the *query*, *key* and *value* transformer functions [3,33], respectively. $\mathbf{X}_i$ and $\mathbf{X}_j$ are the ith and j^{th} feature positions in $\mathbf{X}$, respectively. F_{sim} is the similarity function (default as *dot product*); F_{nom} is the normalizing function (default as *softmax*); F_{mul} is the weight aggregation function (default as *matrix multiplication*); and $\tilde{\mathbf{X}}_i$ is the ith feature position in the transformed feature map $\tilde{\mathbf{X}}$.

3.2   Self-Transformer

Self-Transformer (ST) aims to capture the co-occurring object features on one feature map. As illustrated in Fig. 3 (a), ST is a modified non-local interaction [34] and the output feature map $\hat{\mathbf{X}}$ has the same scale as its input $\mathbf{X}$. A main difference with [33,34] is that we deploy the Mixture of Softmaxes (MoS) [35] as the normalizing function F_{mos}, which turns out to be more effective than the standard *Softmax* [41] on images. Specifically, we first divide $\mathbf{q}_i$ and $\mathbf{k}_j$ into $\mathcal{N}$ parts. Then, we calculate a similarity score $s_{i,j}^n$ for every pair, *i.e.*, $\mathbf{q}_{i,n}$, $\mathbf{k}_{j,n}$, using F_{sim}. The MoS-based normalizing function F_{mos} is as follows:

$$F_{mos}(s_{i,j}^n) = \sum_{n=1}^{\mathcal{N}} \pi_n \frac{\exp(s_{i,j}^n)}{\sum_j \exp(s_{i,j}^n)}, \tag{2}$$

where $s_{i,j}^n$ is the similarity score of the nth part. π_n is the nth aggregating weight that is equal to $Softmax(\mathbf{w}_n^T \bar{\mathbf{k}})$, where $\mathbf{w}_n$ is a learnable linear vector for normalization and $\bar{\mathbf{k}}$ is the arithmetic mean of all positions of $\mathbf{k}_j$. Based on F_{mos}, we then can reformulate Eq. 1 to elaborate our proposed ST as follows:

$$
\begin{aligned}
\textbf{Input:} \quad & \mathbf{q}_i, \mathbf{k}_j, \mathbf{v}_j, \mathcal{N} \\
\textbf{Similarity:} \quad & s_{i,j}^n = F_{sim}(\mathbf{q}_{i,n}, \mathbf{k}_{j,n}) \\
\textbf{Weight:} \quad & w_{i,j} = F_{mos}(s_{i,j}^n) \\
\textbf{Output:} \quad & \hat{\mathbf{X}}_i = F_{mul}(w_{i,j}, \mathbf{v}_j),
\end{aligned}
\tag{3}
$$

where $\hat{\mathbf{X}}_i$ is the ith transformed feature position in $\hat{\mathbf{X}}$.

3.3   Grounding Transformer

Grounding Transformer (GT) can be categorized as a top-down non-local interaction [34], which grounds the "concept" in the higher-level feature maps $\mathbf{X}^c$ to the "pixels" in the lower-level feature maps $\mathbf{X}^f$. The output $\hat{\mathbf{X}}^f$ has the same scale as $\mathbf{X}^f$. Generally, image features at different scales extract different semantic or contextual information or both [39,43]. Moreover, it has been empirically shown that the negative value of the *euclidean distance* F_{eud} is more effective in computing the similarity than *dot product* when the semantic information of two feature maps is different [42]. So we prefer to use F_{eud} as the similarity function, which is expressed as:

$$F_{eud}(\mathbf{q}_i, \mathbf{k}_j) = -||\mathbf{q}_i - \mathbf{k}_j||^2, \tag{4}$$

where $\mathbf{q}_i = f_q(\mathbf{X}_i^f)$ and $\mathbf{k}_j = f_k(\mathbf{X}_j^c)$; $\mathbf{X}_i^f$ is the ith feature position in $\mathbf{X}^f$, and $\mathbf{X}_j^c$ is the jth feature position in $\mathbf{X}^c$. We then replace the similarity function in Eq. 3 with F_{eud}, and get the formulation of the proposed GT as follows:

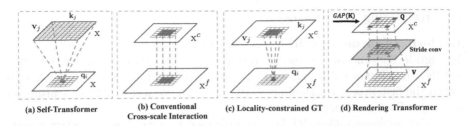

Fig. 3. Self-Transformer (ST), Conventional Cross-Scale Interaction in existing methods, Locality-constrained Grounding Transformer (GT), and Rendering Transformer. The red grid in low-level is a *query* position; grids in high-level are the *key* and the *value* positions (within a local square area in (b)); **Q** are the high-level feature maps, **K** and **V** are the low-level feature maps. Grey square is the down-sampled **V**.

$$
\begin{aligned}
\textbf{Input:} \quad & \mathbf{q}_i, \mathbf{k}_j, \mathbf{v}_j, \mathcal{N} \\
\textbf{Similarity:} \quad & s_{i,j}^n = F_{eud}(\mathbf{q}_{i,n}, \mathbf{k}_{j,n}) \\
\textbf{Weight:} \quad & w_{i,j} = F_{mos}(s_{i,j}^n) \\
\textbf{Output:} \quad & \hat{\mathbf{X}}_i^f = F_{mul}(w_{i,j}, \mathbf{v}_j),
\end{aligned}
\tag{5}
$$

where $\mathbf{v}_j = f_v(\mathbf{X}_j^c)$; $\hat{\mathbf{X}}_i^f$ is the ith transformed feature position in $\hat{\mathbf{X}}^f$. Based on Eq. 5, each pair of $\mathbf{q}_i$ and $\mathbf{k}_j$ with a closer distance will be given a larger weight as in [33,34]. Compared to the results of *dot product*, using F_{eud} brings clear improvements in the top-down interactions[1].

In feature pyramid, high-/low-level feature maps contain much global/local image information. However, for semantic segmentation by cross-scale feature interactions, it is unnecessary to use global information to segment two objects in an image. The context within a local region around the *query* position is empirically more informative. That is why the conventional cross-scale interaction (*e.g.*, summation and concatenation) is effective in existing segmentation methods [4,44]. As shown in Fig. 3 (b), they are essentially the implicit local style. However, our default GT is the global interaction.

Locality-Constrained Grounding Transformer. We therefore introduce a *locality-constrained* version of GT called Locality-constrained GT (LGT) for semantic segmentation, which is an explicit local feature interaction. As illustrated in Fig. 3 (c), each $\mathbf{q}_i$ (*i.e.*, the red grid on the low-level feature map) interacts with a portion of $\mathbf{k}_j$ and $\mathbf{v}_j$ (*i.e.*, the blue grids on the high-level feature map) within the local square area where the center coordinate is the same with $\mathbf{q}_i$ and the side length is *square_size*. Particularly, for positions of $\mathbf{k}_j$ and $\mathbf{v}_j$ that exceed the index, we use 0 value instead.

---

[1] More details are given in *Section A* of the supplementary.

3.4   Rendering Transformer

Rendering Transformer (RT) works in a bottom-up fashion, aiming to render the high-level "concept" by incorporating the visual attributes in the low-level "pixels". As illustrated in Fig. 3 (d), RT is a *local* interaction where the *local* is due to the fact that it is meaningless to render an "object" with the features or attributes from another distant one.

In our implementation, RT is not performed by pixel but the entire feature maps. Specifically, the high-level feature map is defined as $\mathbf{Q}$; the low-level feature map is defined as $\mathbf{K}$ and $\mathbf{V}$. To highlight the rendering target, the interaction between $\mathbf{Q}$ and $\mathbf{K}$ is conducted in a channel-wise attention manner [6]. $\mathbf{K}$ first computes a weight $\mathbf{w}$ for $\mathbf{Q}$ through Global Average Pooling (GAP) [21]. Then, the weighted $\mathbf{Q}$ (*i.e.*, $\mathbf{Q}_{att}$) goes through a 3×3 convolution for refinement [36]. $\mathbf{V}$ goes through a 3×3 convolution with stride to reduce the feature scale (the gray square in Fig. 3 (d)). Finally, the refined $\mathbf{Q}_{att}$ and the down-sampled $\mathbf{V}$ (*i.e.*, $\mathbf{V}_{dow}$) are summed-up, and processed by another 3×3 convolution for refinement. The proposed RT can be formulated as follows:

$$
\begin{aligned}
\textbf{Input:} \quad & \mathbf{Q}, \mathbf{K}, \mathbf{V} \\
\textbf{Weight:} \quad & \mathbf{w} = GAP(\mathbf{K}) \\
\textbf{Weight Query:} \quad & \mathbf{Q}_{att} = F_{att}(\mathbf{Q}, \mathbf{w}) \\
\textbf{Down-sampled Value:} \quad & \mathbf{V}_{dow} = F_{sconv}(\mathbf{V}) \\
\textbf{Output:} \quad & \hat{\mathbf{X}}^{c} = F_{add}(F_{conv}(\mathbf{Q}_{att}), \mathbf{V}_{dow}),
\end{aligned}
\tag{6}
$$

where $F_{att}(\cdot)$ is an *outer product* function; $F_{sconv}(\cdot)$ is a 3×3 stride convolution, in particular, where $stride = 1$ if the scales of $\mathbf{Q}$ and $\mathbf{V}$ are equal; $F_{conv}(\cdot)$ is a 3×3 convolution for refinement; $F_{add}(\cdot)$ is the feature map summation function with a 3×3 convolution; and $\hat{\mathbf{X}}^{c}$ denotes the output feature map of RT.

3.5   Overall Architecture

We build specific FPT networks for tackling object detection [16,22], inatance segmentation [13,24], and semantic segmentation [5,44]. Each FPT network is composed of four components: a backbone for feature extraction; a feature pyramid construction module; our proposed FPT for feature transformer; and a task-specific head network. In the following, we detail the proposed architectures.

FPT for Object Detection and Instance Segmentation. We follow [22,24] to deploy the ResNet as the backbone, and pre-train it on the ImageNet [8]. BFP [22] is used as the pyramid construction module. Then the proposed FPT is applied to BFP, for which the number of divided parts of $\mathcal{N}$ is set to 2 for ST and 4 for GT[2]. Then, the transformed feature maps (by FPT) are concatenated with the original maps along the channel dimension. The concatenated maps go through a 3×3 convolution to reduce the feature dimension into 256. On the

---

[2] More details are given in *Section B* of the supplementary.

top of the output feature maps, we apply the head networks for handling specific tasks, *e.g.*, the Faster R-CNN [29] head for object detection and the Mask R-CNN [13] head for instance segmentation. To enhance the feature generalization, we apply the DropBlock [10] to each output feature map. We set the drop block size as 5 and the feature keep probability as 0.9.

FPT for Semantic Segmentation. We use dilated ResNet-101 [37] as the backbone (pre-trained on the ImageNet) following [5,40]. We then apply the Unscathed Feature Pyramid (UFP) as the feature pyramid construction module, which basically contains a pyramidal global convolutional network [27] with the internal kernel size of 1, 7, 15 and 31, and each scale with the output dimension of 256. Then, the proposed FPT (including LGT) is applied to UFP with the same number of divided parts $\mathcal{N}$ as in the instance-level tasks. In particular, the *square_size* of LGT is set to 5. On the top of the transformed feature pyramid, we apply the semantic segmentation head network, as in [5,41]. We also deploy the DropBlock [10] on the output feature maps with the drop block size as 3 and the feature keep probability as 0.9.

4 Experiments

Our experiments were conducted on three interesting and challenging tasks: *i.e.*, instance-level object detection and segmentation, and pixel-level semantic segmentation. In each task, we evaluated our approach with careful ablation studies, extensive comparisons to the state-of-the-arts and representative visualizations.

4.1 Instance-Level Recognition

Dataset. Experiments on object detection and instance segmentation were conducted on MS-COCO 2017 [23] which has 80 classes and includes 115k, 5k and 20k images for training, validation and test, respectively.

Backbone. In the ablation study, ResNet-50 [15] was used as the backbone. To compare to state-of-the-arts, we also employed ResNet-101 [15], Non-local Network (NL-ResNet-101) [34], Global Context Network (GC-ResNet-101) [2] and Attention Augmented Network (AA-ResNet-101) [17] as the backbone networks.

Setting. As in [22,24], the backbone network was pre-trained on the ImageNet [8], then the whole network was fine-tuned on the training data while freezing the backbone parameters. For fair comparisons, input images were resized into 800 pixels/1,000 pixels for the shorter/longer edge [20].

Training Details. We adopted SGD training on 8 GPUs with the Synchronized Batch Norm (SBN) [40]. Each mini-batch involved one image per GPU and 512 Region of Interest (ROI) per image. The positive-to-negative ratio was set to 1 : 3. The weight decay and momentum were set to 0.0001 and 0.9, respectively. For object detection, the learning rate was 0.05 in the first 80k iterations, and 0.005 in the remaining 20k iterations. For instance segmentation, the learning rate was

332 D. Zhang et al.

Table 1. Ablation study on MS-COCO 2017 val set [23]. "BFP" is Bottom-up Feature Pyramid [22]; "ST" is Self-Transformer; "GT" is Grounding Transformer; "RT" is Rendering Transformer. Results on the left and right of the dashed are of bounding box detection and instance segmentation.

BFP	ST	GT	RT	AP		AP$_{50}$		AP$_{75}$		AP$_S$		AP$_M$		AP$_L$		Params	GFLOPs
✓	✗	✗	✗	31.6	29.9	54.1	50.7	35.9	34.7	16.1	14.2	32.5	31.6	48.8	48.5	34.6 M	172.3
✓	✓	✗	✗	32.0	30.6	54.9	51.4	36.9	35.5	16.5	15.1	34.0	32.1	49.1	49.7	55.0 M	248.2
✓	✗	✓	✗	35.1	33.9	55.2	52.4	38.1	37.7	17.4	16.9	36.3	33.3	50.3	51.7	63.9 M	265.1
✓	✗	✗	✓	34.7	33.1	55.5	52.0	37.5	37.7	17.0	15.3	36.6	34.9	52.0	52.1	39.8 M	187.9
✓	✓	✓	✗	35.7	34.6	55.7	54.1	38.3	37.9	18.0	17.4	36.5	34.0	52.1	50.5	82.5 M	322.9
✓	✓	✗	✓	35.9	34.4	56.8	55.1	38.8	38.0	19.1	17.9	37.0	34.8	53.1	52.2	61.2 M	256.7
✓	✗	✓	✓	36.9	35.1	56.6	54.5	38.2	38.5	18.8	17.7	37.7	35.3	54.3	53.2	69.6 M	281.6
✓	✓	✓	✓	**38.0**	**36.8**	**57.1**	**55.9**	**38.9**	**38.6**	**20.5**	**18.8**	**38.1**	**35.3**	**55.7**	**54.2**	88.2 M	346.2
improvements				↑ 6.4	↑ 6.9	↑ 3.0	↑ 5.2	↑ 3.0	↑ 3.9	↑ 4.4	↑ 4.6	↑ 5.6	↑ 3.7	↑ 6.9	↑ 5.7		

Table 2. Ablation study of SBN [40] and DropBlock [10] on the MS-COCO 2017 val set [23]. Results on the left and right of dashed lines are respectively for bounding box detection and instance segmentation.

FPT	SBN	DropBlock	AP		AP$_{50}$		AP$_{75}$		AP$_S$		AP$_M$		AP$_L$	
✓	✗	✗	37.2	35.9	56.0	54.3	37.7	36.9	19.0	17.2	37.7	34.8	53.1	51.3
✓	✓	✗	37.8	36.5	56.7	55.2	38.4	38.2	19.6	18.0	37.9	35.1	54.0	52.1
✓	✗	✓	37.5	36.2	56.5	54.8	38.0	37.3	19.5	17.8	37.8	35.0	53.8	51.9
✓	✓	✓	**38.0**	**36.8**	**57.1**	**55.9**	**38.9**	**38.6**	**20.5**	**18.8**	**38.1**	**35.3**	**55.7**	**54.2**

0.05 for the first 120k iterations, and 0.005 in the remaining 40k iterations. An end-to-end region proposal network was used to generate proposals, as in [34].

Comparison Methods. We compared our FPT to the state-of-the-art cross-scale feature pyramid interactions including FPN [22], Bottom-up Path Aggregation (BPA) in PANet [24], and Bi-direction Feature Interaction (BFI) in ZigZagNet [20]. We also reported the experimental results of using the Augmented Head (AH) [24] and Multi-scale Training (MT) [24], where the AH specifically includes the adaptive feature pooling, fully-connected fusion, and heavier head.

Metrics. We evaluated the model performance using the standard Average Precision (AP), AP$_{50}$, AP$_{75}$, AP$_S$, AP$_M$ and AP$_L$.

Ablation Study. Our ablation study aims to (1) evaluate the performance of three individual transformers (in our FPT) and combinations, for which the base pyramid method BFP [22] is the baseline (in Table 1), and (2) investigate the effects of SBN [40] and DropBlock [10] on our FPT (in Table 2).

Comparing to the Baseline. Table 1 show that three transformers bring consistent improvements over the baseline. For example, ST, GT and RT respectively brings 0.4%, 3.5% and 3.1% improvements for the bounding box AP in object detection. The improvements are higher as 0.7%, 4.0% and 3.2% for the mask AP in instance segmentation. The gain by ST is not as much as the gains

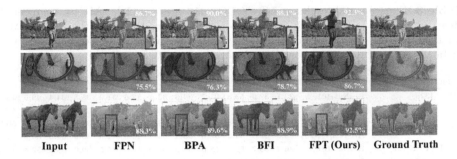

Fig. 4. Visualization results in instance segmentation. The red rectangle highlights the better predicted area of FPT. Samples are from MS-COCO 2017 validation set [23]. The value on each image represents the corresponding segmentation mIoU.

by the other two transformers. An intuitive reason is that, compared to self-interaction (*i.e.*, ST), the cross-scale interactions (*i.e.*, GT and RT) capture more diverse and richer inter-object contexts to achieve better object recognition and detection performances, which is consistent with the conclusion of instance-level recognition works [46,47]. The middle blocks in Table 1 show that the combination of transformers improves the performance over individuals in most of cases. In particular, the full combination of ST, GT and RT results the best performance, *i.e.*, 38.0% bounding box AP (6.4% higher than BFP) on object detection and 36.8% mask AP (6.9% higher than BFP) on instance segmentation.

Effects of SBN and DropBlock. Table 2 shows that both SBN and DropBlock improve the model performance. Their combination yields 0.8% AP improvement for object detection, and 0.9% AP improvement for instance segmentation.

Model Efficiency[3] We reported the model Parameters (Params) and GFLOPs with the Mask R-CNN [13]. Adding +ST/+GT/+RT to the baseline respectively increase Params by $0.59\times/0.85\times/0.15\times$ (with mask AP improvements of 0.7%/4.0%/3.2%). Correspondingly, GFLOPs are increased by $0.44\times$, $0.54\times$ and $0.09\times$. Compared to related works [20,22,34], these are relatively fair overheads on average.

Comparing to the State-of-the-Arts. Table 3 show that applying the cross-scale interaction methods, *e.g.*, FPN [22], BPA [24], BFI [20] and FPT, results consistent improvements over the baseline [22]. In particular, our FPT achieves the highest gains, *i.e.*, 8.5% AP in object detection and 6.0% mask AP in instance segmentation, with ResNet-101 [15]. Besides, the consistent improvements are also achieved on the stronger NL-, GC- and AA- ResNet-101, and validate that BFP+FPT can generalize well to stronger backbones, which make more senses in *the age of results*[4]. Two bottom blocks in Table 3 show that adding efficient training strategies such as AH, MT, and both (denoted as "[all]") to BFP+FPT yields

---

[3] More details are given in the *Section C* **of the supplementary.**.
[4] More results are given in *Section D* of the supplementary.

334   D. Zhang et al.

Table 3. Experimental results on MS-COCO 2017 *test-dev* [23]. "AH" is Augmented Head, and "MT" is Multi-scale Training [24]; "all" means that both the AH and MT are used. Results on the left and right of the dashed are of bounding box detection and instance segmentation. "-" means that there is no reported result in its paper.

Methods	Backbone	AP		AP$_{50}$		AP$_{75}$		AP$_S$		AP$_M$		AP$_L$	
BFP [22]	ResNet-101	33.1	32.6	53.8	51.7	34.6	33.3	12.6	11.4	35.3	34.4	49.5	48.9
	NL-ResNet-101	34.4	33.7	54.3	53.6	35.8	33.9	15.1	13.7	37.1	36.0	50.7	49.7
	GC-ResNet-101	35.0	34.2	55.8	54.1	36.5	35.3	14.8	13.9	38.6	37.3	50.9	50.5
	AA-ResNet-101	33.8	32.8	54.2	52.3	35.4	33.8	13.0	12.3	35.5	34.5	50.0	49.0
BFP+FPN [22]	ResNet-101	36.2	35.7	59.1	58.0	39.0	37.8	18.2	15.5	39.0	38.1	52.4	49.2
BFP+BPA [24]	ResNet-101	37.3	36.3	60.4	59.0	39.9	38.3	18.9	16.3	39.7	39.0	53.0	50.5
BFP+BFI [20]	ResNet-101	39.5	-	-	-	-	-	-	-	-	-	-	-
BFP+FPT	ResNet-101	41.6	38.6	60.9	58.2	44.0	43.3	23.4	19.0	41.5	39.2	53.1	50.8
	NL-ResNet-101	42.0	39.5	62.1	60.7	46.5	45.4	25.1	20.8	42.6	41.0	53.7	53.0
	GC-ResNet-101	42.5	**40.3**	62.0	61.0	46.1	45.8	**25.3**	21.1	42.7	**41.8**	53.1	52.7
	AA-ResNet-101	42.1	40.1	61.5	60.1	46.5	45.2	25.2	20.6	42.6	41.2	53.5	52.0
BFP+FPT [AH]	ResNet-101	41.1	40.0	62.0	59.9	46.6	45.5	24.2	20.5	42.1	41.0	53.3	52.5
BFP+FPT [MT]	ResNet-101	41.2	39.8	62.1	60.1	46.0	45.1	24.1	20.9	41.9	40.8	53.2	51.9
BFP+FPN [22] [all]	ResNet-101	37.9	36.3	59.6	58.8	40.1	39.1	19.5	16.7	41.0	40.3	53.5	51.1
BFP+BPA [24] [all]	ResNet-101	39.0	37.7	60.8	59.4	41.7	40.1	20.2	18.5	41.5	40.1	54.1	52.4
BFP+BFI [20] [all]	ResNet-101	40.1	38.2	61.2	60.0	42.6	42.4	21.9	19.6	42.4	40.8	54.3	52.5
BFP+FPT [all]	ResNet-101	**42.6**	**40.3**	**62.4**	**61.1**	**46.9**	**45.9**	24.9	**21.3**	**43.0**	41.2	**54.5**	**53.3**

performance boosts. For example, BFP+FPT [all] achieves a higher bounding box AP and the same mask AP, compared to the best performance of BFP+FPT (with stronger GC-ResNet-101). Besides, BFP+FPT [all] achieves the average 1.5% AP in object detection and 2.1% mask AP in instance segmentation (over BFP+BFI) using ResNet-101, which further verifies the robust plug-and-play ability of our FPT. The visualization results in instance segmentation are given in Fig. 4. Compared to other feature interaction methods, the results of FPT show more precise predictions for both small (*e.g.*, bottle) and large objects (*e.g.*, bicycle). Moreover, it shows the gracile parts in the object (*e.g.*, the horse legs) are also well predicted using our FPT.

4.2 Experiments on Pixel-Level Recognition

Dataset. Our pixel-level segmentation experiments were conducted on four benchmarks: (1) *Cityscapes* [7] contains 19 classes, and includes 2,975, 500 and 1,525 images for training, validation and test, respectively; (2) *ADE20K* [45] has 150 classes, and uses 20k, 2k, and 3k images for training, validation and test, respectively; (3) *LIP* [12] contains 50,462 images with 20 classes, and includes 30,462, 10k and 10k images for training, validation and test, respectively; (4) *PASCAL VOC 2012* [9] contains 21 classes, and includes 1,464, 1,449 and 1,456 images for training, validation and test, respectively.

Backbone. We used dilated ResNet-101 [37] as the backbone as in [41].

Setting. We first pre-trained the backbone network on the ImageNet [8], then fine-tuned the whole network on the training data while fixing the parameters

Table 4. Ablation study on the Cityscapes validation set [7]. "LGT" is Locality-constrained Grounding Transformer; "RT" is Rendering Transformer; "ST" is Self-Transformer. "+" means building the method on the top of UFP.

Methods	Tra.mIoU	Val.mIoU	Params	GFLOPs
UFP [27]	86.0	79.1	71.3 M	916.1
UFP+ST [27]	86.9	80.7	91.2 M	948.4
UFP+LGT [27]	86.5	80.3	102.8 M	1008.3
UFP+RT [27]	86.3	80.1	77.4 M	929.3
UFP+LGT+ST [27]	87.2	80.9	121.3 M	1052.6
UFP+RT+ST [27]	87.0	80.8	96.2 M	985.2
UFP+LGT+RT [27]	86.6	80.4	107.0 M	1014.8
UFP+LGT+ST+RT [27]	**87.4**	**81.7**	127.2 M	1063.9
the improvement	↑ **1.4**	↑ **2.6**		

Table 5. Comparisons with state-of-the-art on test sets of Cityscapes [7] and PASCAL VOC 2012 [9], validation sets of ADE20K [45] and LIP [12]. Results in this table refer to mIoU; "-" means that there is no reported result in its paper. The best and **second best** models under each setting are marked with corresponding formats.

Methods	Backbone	Cityscapes	ADE20K	LIP	PASCAL VOC 2012
Baseline	ResNet-101	65.3	40.9	42.7	62.2
CFNet [41]	ResNet-101	80.6	44.9	54.6	84.2
AFNB [48]	ResNet-101	81.3	45.2	-	-
HRNet [31]	HRNetV2-W48	81.6	44.7	**55.9**	**84.5**
OCNet [38]	ResNet-101	81.7	**45.5**	54.7	84.3
GSCNN [32]	Wide-ResNet-101	82.8	-	55.2	-
PPM [44]+OC [38]	ResNet-101	79.9	43.7	53.0	82.9
ASPP [5]+OC [38]	ResNet-101	80.0	44.1	53.3	82.7
UFP [27]+OC [38]	ResNet-101	80.6	44.7	54.5	83.2
PPM [44]+FPT	ResNet-101	80.4(↑ **0.5**)	44.8(↑ **1.1**)	54.2(↑ **1.2**)	83.2(↑ **0.3**)
ASPP [5]+FPT	ResNet-101	80.7(↑ **0.7**)	45.2(↑ **1.1**)	54.4(↑ **1.1**)	83.1(↑ **0.4**)
UFP [27]+FPT	ResNet-101	**82.2**(↑ **1.6**)	45.9(↑ **1.2**)	56.2(↑ **1.7**)	85.0(↑ **1.8**)

of backbone as in [40]. Before input, we cropped the image into 969 × 969 for *Cityscapes*, 573 × 573 for *LIP*, and 521 × 521 for *PASCAL VOC 2012*. Because images in ADE20K are of various sizes, we cropped the shorter-edge images to an uniform size $\{269, 369, 469, 569\}$ as that in [38].

Training Details. We followed [38] to use the learning rate scheduling $lr = baselr \times (1 - \frac{iter}{total_{iter}})^{power}$. On *Cityscapes*, *LIP* and *PASCAL VOC 2012*, the base learning rate was 0.01, and the power is 0.9. The weight decay and momentum were set to 0.0005 and 0.9, respectively. On *ADE20K*, the base learning rate was 0.02 and the power was 0.9. The weight decay and momentum were 0.0001 and 0.9, respectively. We trained models on 8 GPUs with SBN [40]. The model was trained for 120 epochs on *Cityscapes* and *ADE20K*, 50 on *LIP*, and 80 on

336   D. Zhang et al.

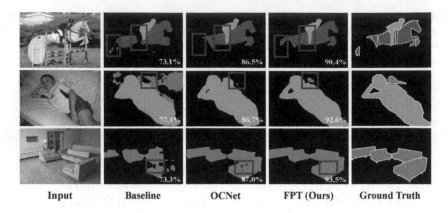

Input   **Baseline**   **OCNet**   **FPT (Ours)**   **Ground Truth**

Fig. 5. Visualization results. Samples are from the validation set of *PASCAL VOC 2012* [9]. The value on each image represents the corresponding segmentation mIoU.

PASCAL VOC 2012. For data augmentation, the training images were flipped left-right and randomly scaled between a half and twice as in [41].

Comparison Methods. Our FPT was applied to the feature pyramids constructed by three methods: UFP [27], PPM [14,44] and ASPP [5]. Based on each of these methods, we compared our FPT to the state-of-the-art pixel-level feature pyramid interaction method, *i.e.*, Object Context Network (OCNet) [38].

Metrics. We used the standard mean Intersection of Union (mIoU) as a uniform metric. We showed the results of ablation study by reporting the mIoU of training set (*i.e.*, Tra.mIoU) and validation set (*i.e.*, Val.mIoU) on the *Cityscapes*.

Ablation Study. Results are given in Table 4. Applying our transformers (*i.e.*, +ST, +LGT and +RT) to UFP respectively achieves the improvements of 0.9%, 0.5% and 0.3% Tr.mIoU, and the more impressive 1.6%, 1.2% and 1.0% Val.mIoU. Moreover, any component combinations of our transformers yields concretely better results than individual ones. Our best model achieves 1.4% and 2.6% improvements (over UFP) for Tr.mIoU and Val.mIoU, respectively.

Model Efficiency. In Table 4, we reported the model Params and GFLOPs. It is clear that using our transformers increases a fair computational overhead. For example, +ST, +LGT and +RT respectively add Params 0.28×, 0.44× and 0.09×, and increase GFLOPs by 0.04×, 0.10× and 0.01×, compared to UFP.

Comparing to the State-of-the-Arts. From Table 5, we can observe that our FPT can achieve a new state-of-the-art performance over all the previous methods based on ResNet-101. It obtains improvements as 1.6%, 1.2%, 1.7% and 1.8% mIoU on *Cityscapes* [7], *ADE20K* [45], *LIP* [12] and *PASCAL VOC 2012* [9], respectively. Besides, compared to OCNet, FPT obtains gain by 0.9%, 1.1%, 1.3% and 0.8% mIoU in these four datasets on average. In Fig. 5, we provide the qualitative results[5]. Compared to the baseline [27] and OCNet [38], results of FPT show more precise segmentation for smaller and thinner objects, e.g., the guardrail, person's leg and bird. Moreover, FPT can also achieve more integrated segmentation on some larger objects, e.g., the horse, person and sofa.

5   Conclusion

We proposed an efficient feature interaction approach called FPT, composed of three carefully-designed transformers to respectively encode the explicit self-level, top-down and bottom-up information in the feature pyramid. Our FPT does not change the size of the feature pyramid, and is thus *generic* and easy to plug-and-play with modern deep networks. Our extensive quantitative and qualitative results on three challenging visual recognition tasks showed that FPT achieves consistent improvements over the baselines and the state-of-the-arts, validating its high effectiveness and strong application capability.

Acknowledgements. We'd like to thank all the anonymous reviewers for their constructive comments. This work was partially supported by the National Key Research and Development Program of China under Grant 2018AAA0102002, the National Natural Science Foundation of China under Grant 61925204, the China Scholarships Council under Grant 201806840058, the Singapore Ministry of Education (MOE) Academic Research Fund (AcRF) Tier 1 grant, and the NTU-Alibaba JRI.

References

1. Adelson, E.H., Anderson, C.H., Bergen, J.R., Burt, P.J., Ogden, J.M.: Pyramid methods in image processing. RCA Eng. **29**(6), 33–41 (1984)
2. Cao, Y., Xu, J., Lin, S., Wei, F., Hu, H.: GCNet: non-local networks meet squeeze-excitation networks and beyond. In: ICCV (2019)
3. Carion, N., Massa, F., Synnaeve, G., Usunier, N., Kirillov, A., Zagoruyko, S.: End-to-end object detection with transformers. In: ECCV (2020)
4. Chen, L.C., Papandreou, G., Kokkinos, I., Murphy, K., Yuille, A.L.: DeepLab: semantic image segmentation with deep convolutional nets, atrous convolution, and fully connected CRFs. TPAMI **40**(4), 834–848 (2017)
5. Chen, L.C., Papandreou, G., Schroff, F., Adam, H.: Rethinking atrous convolution for semantic image segmentation. arXiv (2017)
6. Chen, L., et al.: SCA-CNN: spatial and channel-wise attention in convolutional networks for image captioning. In: CVPR (2017)
7. Cordts, M., et al.: The cityscapes dataset for semantic urban scene understanding. In: CVPR (2016)
8. Deng, J., Dong, W., Socher, R., Li, L.J., Li, K., Fei-Fei, L.: ImageNet: a large-scale hierarchical image database. In: CVPR (2009)
9. Everingham, M., Eslami, S.A., Van Gool, L., Williams, C.K., Winn, J., Zisserman, A.: The pascal visual object classes challenge: a retrospective. IJCV **111**(1), 98–136 (2015)

---

[5] More visualization results are given in the *Section E* of the supplementary.

10. Ghiasi, G., Lin, T.Y., Le, Q.V.: DropBlock: a regularization method for convolutional networks. In: NeurIPS (2018)
11. Girshick, R.: Fast R-CNN. In: ICCV (2015)
12. Gong, K., Liang, X., Zhang, D., Shen, X., Lin, L.: Look into person: self-supervised structure-sensitive learning and a new benchmark for human parsing. In: CVPR (2017)
13. He, K., Gkioxari, G., Dollár, P., Girshick, R.: Mask R-CNN. In: ICCV (2017)
14. He, K., Zhang, X., Ren, S., Sun, J.: Spatial pyramid pooling in deep convolutional networks for visual recognition. TPAMI 37(9), 1904–1916 (2015)
15. He, K., Zhang, X., Ren, S., Sun, J.: Deep residual learning for image recognition. In: CVPR (2016)
16. Hu, H., Gu, J., Zhang, Z., Dai, J., Wei, Y.: Relation networks for object detection. In: CVPR (2018)
17. Irwan, B., Barret, Z., Ashish, V., Jonathon, S., Quoc, V.L.: Attention augmented convolutional networks. In: ICCV (2019)
18. Jouppi, N.P., et al.: In-datacenter performance analysis of a tensor processing unit. In: ISCA (2017)
19. Lazebnik, S., Schmid, C., Ponce, J.: Beyond bags of features: spatial pyramid matching for recognizing natural scene categories. In: CVPR (2006)
20. Lin, D., et al.: ZigzagNet: fusing top-down and bottom-up context for object segmentation. In: CVPR (2019)
21. Lin, M., Chen, Q., Yan, S.: Network in network. In: ICLR (2014)
22. Lin, T.Y., Dollár, P., Girshick, R., He, K., Hariharan, B., Belongie, S.: Feature pyramid networks for object detection. In: CVPR (2017)
23. Lin, T.-Y., et al.: Microsoft COCO: common objects in context. In: Fleet, D., Pajdla, T., Schiele, B., Tuytelaars, T. (eds.) ECCV 2014. LNCS, vol. 8693, pp. 740–755. Springer, Cham (2014). https://doi.org/10.1007/978-3-319-10602-1_48
24. Liu, S., Qi, L., Qin, H., Shi, J., Jia, J.: Path aggregation network for instance segmentation. In: CVPR (2018)
25. Liu, W., et al.: SSD: single shot multibox detector. In: Leibe, B., Matas, J., Sebe, N., Welling, M. (eds.) ECCV 2016. LNCS, vol. 9905, pp. 21–37. Springer, Cham (2016). https://doi.org/10.1007/978-3-319-46448-0_2
26. Long, J., Shelhamer, E., Darrell, T.: Fully convolutional networks for semantic segmentation. In: CVPR (2015)
27. Peng, C., Zhang, X., Yu, G., Luo, G., Sun, J.: Large kernel matters-improve semantic segmentation by global convolutional network. In: CVPR (2017)
28. Redmon, J., Divvala, S., Girshick, R., Farhadi, A.: You only look once: Unified, real-time object detection. In: CVPR (2016)
29. Ren, S., He, K., Girshick, R., Sun, J.: Faster R-CNN: towards real-time object detection with region proposal networks. In: NeurIPS (2015)
30. Springenberg, J.T., Dosovitskiy, A., Brox, T., Riedmiller, M.: Striving for simplicity: the all convolutional net. In: ICLR (2015)
31. Sun, K., et al.: High-resolution representations for labeling pixels and regions. arXiv (2019)
32. Takikawa, T., Acuna, D., Jampani, V., Fidler, S.: Gated-SCNN: gated shape CNNs for semantic segmentation. In: ICCV (2019)
33. Vaswani, A., et al.: Attention is all you need. In: NeurIPS (2017)
34. Wang, X., Girshick, R., Gupta, A., He, K.: Non-local neural networks. In: CVPR (2018)
35. Yang, Z., Dai, Z., Salakhutdinov, R., Cohen, W.W.: Breaking the softmax bottleneck: a high-rank RNN language model. In: ICLR (2018)

36. Yu, C., Wang, J., Peng, C., Gao, C., Yu, G., Sang, N.: Learning a discriminative feature network for semantic segmentation. In: CVPR (2018)
37. Yu, F., Koltun, V.: Multi-scale context aggregation by dilated convolutions. In: ICLR (2016)
38. Yuan, Y., Wang, J.: OCNET: object context network for scene parsing. arXiv (2018)
39. Zeiler, M.D., Fergus, R.: Visualizing and understanding convolutional networks. In: Fleet, D., Pajdla, T., Schiele, B., Tuytelaars, T. (eds.) ECCV 2014. LNCS, vol. 8689, pp. 818–833. Springer, Cham (2014). https://doi.org/10.1007/978-3-319-10590-1_53
40. Zhang, H., et al.: Context encoding for semantic segmentation. In: CVPR (2018)
41. Zhang, H., Zhang, H., Wang, C., Xie, J.: Co-occurrent features in semantic segmentation. In: CVPR (2019)
42. Zhang, Y., Hare, J., Prügel-Bennett, A.: Learning to count objects in natural images for visual question answering. In: ICLR (2018)
43. Zhang, Z., Zhang, X., Peng, C., Xue, X., Sun, J.: ExFuse: enhancing feature fusion for semantic segmentation. In: Ferrari, V., Hebert, M., Sminchisescu, C., Weiss, Y. (eds.) ECCV 2018. LNCS, vol. 11214, pp. 273–288. Springer, Cham (2018). https://doi.org/10.1007/978-3-030-01249-6_17
44. Zhao, H., Shi, J., Qi, X., Wang, X., Jia, J.: Pyramid scene parsing network. In: CVPR (2017)
45. Zhou, B., Zhao, H., Puig, X., Fidler, S., Barriuso, A., Torralba, A.: Scene parsing through ADE20K dataset. In: CVPR (2017)
46. Zhou, Y., Zhu, Y., Ye, Q., Qiu, Q., Jiao, J.: Weakly supervised instance segmentation using class peak response. In: CVPR (2018)
47. Zhu, L., Wang, T., Aksu, E., Kamarainen, J.K.: Portrait instance segmentation for mobile devices. In: ICME (2019)
48. Zhu, Z., Xu, M., Bai, S., Huang, T., Bai, X.: Asymmetric non-local neural networks for semantic segmentation. In: ICCV (2019)

MABNet: A Lightweight Stereo Network Based on Multibranch Adjustable Bottleneck Module

Jiabin Xing, Zhi Qi$^{(\boxtimes)}$, Jiying Dong, Jiaxuan Cai, and Hao Liu

National ASIC System Engineering Research Center,
Southeast University, Nanjing, China
{xingjumping,101011256,213140498,213161230,nicky_lh}@seu.edu.cn

Abstract. Recently, end-to-end CNNs have presented remarkable performance for disparity estimation. But most of them are too heavy to resource-constrained devices, because of enormous parameters necessary for satisfactory results. To address the issue, we propose two compact stereo networks, MABNet and its light version MABNet_tiny. MABNet is based on a novel Multibranch Adjustable Bottleneck (MAB) module, which is less demanding on parameters and computation. In a MAB module, feature map is split into various parallel branches, where the depthwise separable convolutions with different dilation rates extract features with multiple receptive fields however at an affordable computational budget. Besides, the number of channels in each branch is adjustable independently to tradeoff computation and accuracy. On SceneFlow and KITTI datasets, our MABNet achieves competitive accuracy with fewer parameters of 1.65M. Especially, MABNet_tiny reduces the parameters 47K by cutting down the channels and layers in MABNet.

Keywords: Stereo matching · Disparity estimation · Multibranch adjustable bottleneck module · Compact networks

1 Introduction

Disparity estimation from a stereo pair of images provides depth information which is a significant cue for many computer vision applications, such as autonomous driving [19], 3D reconstruction [32] and augmented reality [1]. These applications usually run on mobile devices or embedded platforms, including drones [20], smart phones and vehicles. These resource-constrained devices prefer the stereo system with low power consumption and small memory footprint. Besides, stereo system has to be of low latency and high accuracy to ensure the safety and the comfort, especially in autonomous driving. However, in order to achieve high accuracy, we have to design complex model with a large number of parameters and floating-point-operations (FLOPs), which conflicts the energy efficiency required by resource-constrained devices. In this paper, we propose two lightweight end-to-end stereo networks to tradeoff computation and accuracy,

© Springer Nature Switzerland AG 2020
A. Vedaldi et al. (Eds.): ECCV 2020, LNCS 12373, pp. 340–356, 2020.
https://doi.org/10.1007/978-3-030-58604-1_21

namely MABNet and its light version MABNet_tiny. They have fewer parameters and FLOPs thus are more suitable to be deployed on embedded devices.

In general, traditional stereo matching pipeline consists of four steps: matching cost calculation, cost aggregation, disparity computation and disparity refinement [12]. It computes the matching cost within a finite window, with the limitation of dealing with the large texture-less areas, occlusions and repeating textures. The accuracy and speed of traditional stereo matching methods are still unable to meet the actual application requirements.

With the rapid development of deep convolutional neural networks (CNNs), people proposed many learning-based stereo methods to overcome the limitation of traditional methods. MC-CNN [44] first introduced CNNs in stereo to calculate the matching cost by comparing image patches, and proved the great potential of CNNs. Gradually, it replaced some of the aforementioned steps of the traditional stereo pipeline. CCNN [28] and PBCP [31] estimate confidence by CNNs, while LRCR [16] and RecResNet [3] train CNNs to refine the disparity. Learning-based stereo methods improve the accuracy but have to take more time to process.

Inspired by the successes of end-to-end neural networks in optical flow computation [8], object detection and semantic segmentation [2,5], CNNs have replaced the total traditional stereo matching pipeline. The first end-to-end stereo network is DispNet [24] proposed in 2016. DispNet achieves competitive accuracy with MC-CNN [44] on KITTI dataset [10,26] but runs 100× faster on GPU. It utilizes encoder-decoder architecture which extracts unary features from a stereo pair of images by 2D CNNs, correlates the features and then restores the original resolution by consecutive deconvolutions. CRL [27], iResNet [21], MADNet [34] encode similarity into feature channels by this feature correlation method. However, their results loss the real geometric context and have to improve accuracy at the expense of more parameters in filters. Instead of simply correlating features, some networks, such as GC-Net [17], PSMNet [4], GA-Net [45] and AMNet [9], correlate features at different disparity levels to build a 4D cost volume and aggregate cost by 3D CNNs. They have fewer parameters but take a longer time because of more operations in 3D CNNs.

Although end-to-end CNNs show superior performance in stereo, it is challenging to deploy end-to-end stereo networks on practical devices with limited resource due to their enormous parameters and excessive FLOPs. People pay too much attention to the high accuracy, constructing more complex networks. For example, in comparison with GC-Net [17], GA-Net-deep [45] reduced three-pixel-error (3PE) from 2.87% to 1.81% on KITTI2015 [26] but doubling the number of parameters and runtime. In contrast to previous works, we focus on the model size and feasibility of implementation on hardware and manage to build as compact as possible stereo networks on the precondition of guaranteeing precision.

We propose a lightweight bottleneck module constructed by depthwise separable convolutions [7] with fewer parameters and FLOPs than standard convolutions. In addition, in order to compensate the accuracy loss, it incorporates standard convolution and dilated convolution [13] with different dilation rates by split-transform-merge strategy [41], and uses channel shuffle operation [46] to promote the information communication between different groups. We name the bottleneck module as Multibranch Adjustable Bottleneck (MAB) module since it has several branches with different dilation rates and adjustable scale factors. As for 3D MAB module, we factorize a standard 3D convolution into disparity-wise convolution and spatial convolution to further reduce parameters and FLOPs. Details of our 2D and 3D MAB modules are described in Sect. 3.1. Based on the 2D and 3D MAB modules, we design our compact stereo networks MABNet and MABNet_tiny. MABNet with 1.65M parameters achieves 2.41% three-pixel-error (3PE) on KITTI2015, while MABNet_tiny 47 K parameters achieves 3.88% 3PE.

2 Related Work

There have been several concurrent works pushing towards learning-based stereo in different directions, such as high accuracy, low latency and strong self-adaption. In this paper, we are concerned with lightweight end-to-end stereo networks, which is prone to be applied on embedded devices instead of GPUs. Some works optimize the GPU to process neural network more efficiently and faster, or improve the neural network to adapt the operation mode of GPU. They speed up the stereo networks on GPU, but have fewer substantive benefit on the high energy efficient implementation on embedded devices than reducing model size.

Different from them, StereoDRNet [33] devoted to reducing FLOPs. Based on PSMNet [4], it improved the feature extraction module by vortex pooling [40], and proposed a novel cost filtering network with fewer FLOPs to aggregate cost. PDSNet [35], an applications-friendly deep stereo, designed a novel bottleneck module, drastically reducing the memory footprint in inference. It also proposed sub-pixel cross-entropy loss combined with a MAP estimator, making the system applicable to different disparity ranges without retraining. Besides, LWSM [43] utilized group convolution and dilated convolution to build upon an enhancement block which has low computation complexity and memory consumption. Their accuracy is competitive with classical end-to-end stereo networks, but their models are smaller obviously.

Furthermore, there are more compact models, such as StereoNet [18] and AnyNet [38]. StereoNet [18] achieved real-time performance by using a very low-resolution cost volume, reducing the parameters by an order of magnitude in comparison with PDSNet [35] or LWSM [43]. AnyNet [38] is a tiny stereo network with 40 K parameters by the aid of U-Net [29] and SPNet [22]. It can process 1242×375 resolution images within a range of 10–35 FPS on an NVIDIA Jetson TX2 module. However, due to excessive compression, both of StereoNet and AnyNet's accuracy drop severely.

In comparison with prior models on the approximate order of magnitude, our MABNet and MABNet_tiny achieve a noticeable improvement in accuracy. Moreover, our models with fewer parameters and FLOPs are easier to be deployed on embedded devices. The detailed experimental data is given in the Sect. 4.3.

3   Proposed Network

As the foundation of our networks, Multibranch Adjustable Bottleneck (MAB) module is introduced firstly, including the structure and the advantage. Then we provide an overview. In each part of its introduction, we describe the difference between MABNet_tiny and the origin MABNet.

3.1   Multibranch Adjustable Bottleneck (MAB) Module

Most prior works, such as PSMNet [4], StereoDRNet [33] and GA-Net [45], utilized ResNet block [11] (see Fig. 1) to design their feature extraction backbone, leading to oversized models. Recently, there have been more compact and more accurate networks, such as MobileNet [14,30], SqueezeNet [15] and ShuffleNet [23,46]. They are used or referenced in different fields, showing great performance. Besides for classification, FastDepth [39] adopted MobileNet [14,30] to design an encoder-decoder architecture for monocular depth estimation, while ESPNet [25] used techniques in compact CNNs to build a network for semantic segmentation. Driven by the successful experience, we designed Multibranch Adjustable Bottleneck (MAB) module, as shown in Fig. 2 and Fig. 3.

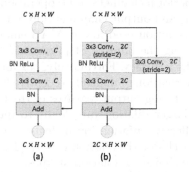

Fig. 1. ResNet block in PSMNet [4] does not apply ReLU after summation. (a)ResNet block with *stride*=1. (b)ResNet block with *stride*=2.

We adopt split-transform-merge strategy [33] to design our MAB module. Firstly, a 2D MAB module (see Fig. 2(a)) equally splits the input into two subblocks by channel split operation [23]. Then, the first subblock is fed into three parallel branches to generate features. The corresponding scale factors λ_i in Fig. 2 and Fig. 3 controls the number of channels for input feature maps in these branches separately. Generally, the first layer projects a high dimension feature map onto a low dimension space via a pointwise convolution. Then a depthwise

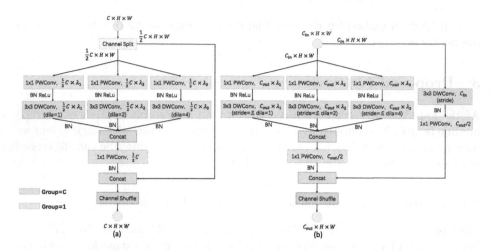

Fig. 2. (a)2D MAB module with $size_{in}=size_{out}$ ($stride$=1 and $C_{in} = C_{out} = C$). (b)2D MAB module with $size_{in} \neq size_{out}$ (($stride = S$) $\neq 1$ or $C_{in} \neq C_{out}$). PWConv: pointwise convolution. DWConv: depthwise convolution. $\lambda_i=\{\lambda_1,\lambda_2\,\lambda_3\}$.

convolution [6] with a certain dilation rate extracts features. The three branches with dilation rates of $\{1,2,4\}$ grab multilevel context information. Next, we combine the outputs of three branches along channel dimension, followed by another pointwise convolution to merge them. Finally, we concatenate it with another subblock of input, then perform channel shuffle operation proposed in ShuffleNet [23,46] to make the input and output channels fully related.

Although dilated convolution used in our MAB enlarges the effective receptive field without increasing the number of parameters, it may cause gridding artifact [37] sacrificing the accuracy. Fortunately, our multibranch structure not only contains context information of multiple receptive fields but also diminishes gridding artifact through fusing output features of the three branches. Furthermore, considering that larger dilation rate leads to more paddings (filling in zeros) which fades the effective information in feature maps and increases computational cost, we finally choose the dilation rate as $\{1,2,4\}$ in 2D MAB module. In Sect. 4.2, we prove the choice by ablation studies.

In addition, features with different receptive fields benefit the depth estimation of different scenes. Usually, large dilation rate learns coarse-grained relationship, such as houses, cars and roads, helpful for disparity estimation in background. On the contrary, small dilation rate needs more convolutions to get the same receptive field, and learns more fine-grained information, like windows, wheels and traffic lights. In Sect. 4.2, we research the best proportional relationship between the three scale factors and a reasonable receptive field in outputs.

Unlike the Fig. 2(a), the subfigure of Fig. 2(b) exhibits another 2D MAB module when $stride \neq 1$ or $C_{in} \neq C_{out}$. In the (b) module used to downsample,

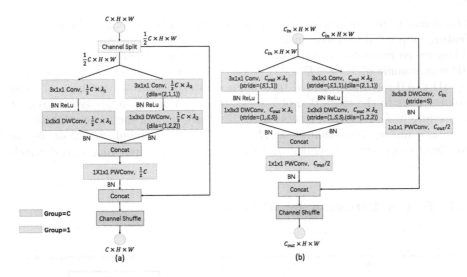

Fig. 3. (a)3D MAB module with $size_{in}=size_{out}$ ($stride=1$ and $C_{in} = C_{out} = C$). (b)3D MAB module with $size_{in} \neq size_{out}$ (($stride = S) \neq 1$ or $C_{in} \neq C_{out}$). PWConv: pointwise convolution. DWConv: depthwise convolution. $\lambda_i=\{\lambda_1,\lambda_2\}$.

we skip the channel split operation, but concatenate the input as a residual to the result through a shortcut connection.

Besides the 2D MAB, we also implement two kinds of computational efficient 3D MAB modules, as shown in Fig. 3. Inspired by the spatial and temporal convolutions in 3D CNNs [36,42] for video recognition, we factorize a standard 3D convolution into two stages, namely disparity-wise convolution and spatial convolution. The disparity-wise convolution plays the same role as the first pointwise convolution in 2D MAB module. Meanwhile, the resolution of 3D MAB in cost aggregation is smaller than that of 2D MAB in feature extraction, asking 3D MAB for fewer paddings. Therefore, 3D MAB deletes the branches with dilation rate=4 and remains only two branches, which also reduce computation.

Fig. 4. Architecture overview of MABNet and MABNet_tiny.

3.2   MABNet Overview

As shown in Fig. 4, our stereo matching pipeline consists of four classical steps. Firstly, the stereo pair of images each with the size of $3 \times H \times W$ are fed to two weight-sharing feature extractors respectively. The resolution of each output feature map is reduced to a quarter of the original input image as $C \times \frac{1}{4}H \times \frac{1}{4}W$. Then we correlate the two feature maps at different disparity levels to build a 4D cost volume of $2C \times \frac{1}{4}D \times \frac{1}{4}H \times \frac{1}{4}W$. Next, the cost volume is aggregated by 3D MAB modules followed by a bilinear interpolation to upsample the cost volume back to the resolution of $1 \times D \times H \times W$. Finally, we apply a regression procedure in D dimension to obtain the disparity map of the same resolution as the input images. Note that C, D, H and W denote the number of channels, the maximum disparity, the height and the weight of the input image respectively in the paper.

3.3   Feature Extraction by 2D MAB

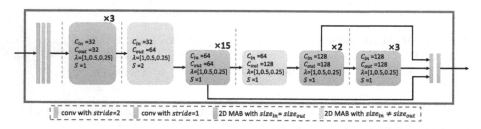

Fig. 5. Feature extraction in MABNet. ×2, ×3 and ×15 represent the number of repetitions. $\lambda=[\lambda_1,\lambda_2,\lambda_3]$. The height of the rectangle is proportional to the resolution of the output feature maps.

The schematic diagram of the feature extraction in MABNet and the parameters for each 2D MAB are presented in Fig. 5. We first use three cascaded 3×3 convolution filters, where the first filter has a stride of 2, downsampling the input image. Next, four groups of 2D MAB modules extract further features. The number of 2D MAB modules in the four groups are {3,16,3,3} individually, generating the output feature maps of {32,64,128,128} channels respectively. The outputs of the last three groups are concatenated to form a unary feature map of 320 channels. Finally, through two convolution layers, we fuse the 320-channel feature map to a cost volume of 32 channels then output it. Instead of using four groups of 2D MAB modules, MABNet_tiny uses only three groups of {4,8,4} modules corresponding {8,16,32} channels, and gives a cost volume of 8 channels by fusing the outputs of the last two groups.

3.4   Cost Volume

After the feature extraction, we get the left and right feature maps, both with the size of $C \times \frac{1}{4}H \times \frac{1}{4}W$. As illustrated in Fig. 6, following GC-Net [17], we form a 4D cost volume of $2C \times \frac{1}{4}D \times \frac{1}{4}H \times \frac{1}{4}W$ by concatenating left feature map with their corresponding right feature map at different disparity levels, rather than concatenating a bulk of right feature maps at the end of the entire group of left feature maps. Specifically, when a $\frac{1}{4}H \times \frac{1}{4}W$ feature map of left feature builds a $\frac{1}{4}D \times \frac{1}{4}H \times \frac{1}{4}W$ cost, the data stays at the original position. But the corresponding right feature map shifts to the right sequentially with the necessary trimming and padding.

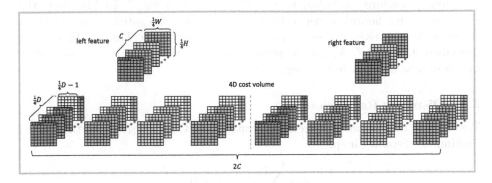

Fig. 6. Illustration of cost volume building. The colored parts represent data in feature maps, while the white parts in the illustration of 4D cost volume represent data filled with 0. (Color figure online)

3.5   Cost Aggregation by 3D MAB

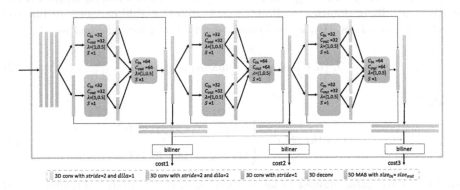

Fig. 7. Cost aggregation in MABNet.

At cost aggregation stage, instead of stacking standard hourglass (encoder-decoder) architecture proposed in PSMNet [4], we design a novel multibranch hourglass, a bit similar to split-transform-merge structure. MABNet takes the advantage of the three successive hourglass networks, as shown in Fig. 7. In each hourglass network, a combination of four parallel branches and a 3D MAB module encodes information with different receptive fields. The encoded information is upsampled back to the same size as the input image by two 3D deconvolutions and one bilinear interpolation. The two outputs in the first layer of each hourglass network are concatenated and added to the output of first 3D deconvolution through a short path to compensate the loss of features during the encoding procedure, as linked by the blue arrows in Fig. 7. In MABNet, the three successive hourglass networks generate three aggregated costs and three training losses ($Loss_1$, $Loss_2$, and $Loss_3$) correspondingly. The loss function is described in Sect. 3.7. As for the simplification of MABNet_tiny, we keep only one hourglass network in cost aggregation.

3.6   Disparity Regression

We employ the disparity regression proposed in GC-Net [17] to estimate the continuous disparity map:

$$\hat{d} = \sum_{d=0}^{D_{max}} d \times \sigma\left(-c_d\right) \tag{1}$$

where the estimation disparity $\hat{d}$ denotes the sum of each disparity d weighted by its probability. And the probability is calculated from the cost volume $-c_d$ via the softmax operation $\sigma\left(\cdot\right)$.

3.7   Training Loss

During training, we adopt smooth L1 loss to measure the difference between the output of MABNet and the ground truth. L1 loss is robust but nondifferentiable at disparity discontinuities, while L2 loss is differentiable everywhere but too sensitivity to outliers. Hence, we formulate smooth L1 loss, defined as

$$L\left(d,\hat{d}\right) = \frac{1}{N}\sum_{i=1}^{N} smooth_{L_1}\left(d_i - \hat{d}_i\right) \tag{2}$$

in which

$$smooth_{L_1}\left(x\right) = \begin{cases} 0.5x^2, & if\ \left|x\right| < 0.5 \\ \left|x\right| - 0.5, & otherwise \end{cases} \tag{3}$$

where N is the total number of labeled pixels, $\hat{d}_i$ is the predicted disparity and d_i is the ground-truth disparity. Similar to PSMNet [4], the total training loss is calculated as the weighted summation of the three losses. The total training loss L_{total} in MABNet is defined as

$$L_{total} = 0.5 \times Loss_1 + 0.7 \times Loss_2 + Loss_3. \tag{4}$$

Because MABNet_tiny uses just one hourglass network, its L_{total} equals to $Loss_1$.

4   Experiments

In this section, we evaluate our MABNet on SceneFlow, KITTI2012 and KITTI2015 stereo datasets. We first introduce the datasets and the experiment settings. Then we present ablation studies to compare different models with different parameter configurations. Finally, we compare the proposed stereo networks with other state-of-the-art published methods.

4.1   Implementation Details

Datasets. SceneFlow [24] is a large-scale synthetic dataset with 35454 stereo pairs for training and 4370 stereo pairs for testing, all being of 540×960 resolution. It provides dense disparity maps as ground truth. We use the end-point error (EPE) as the evaluation metric, which means the average absolute disparity error in pixels.

Unlike SceneFlow, KITTI is a real-world dataset with street views from a driving car, consisting of KITTI2012 [10] and KITTI2015 [26]. KITTI2012 contains 194 training stereo pairs with semi-dense ground truth disparities acquired using a LIDAR sensor and 195 testing stereo pairs without ground truth disparities, both of which are of 376×1240 resolution. KITTI2015 contains 200 training stereo pairs and 200 testing stereo pairs. Since there is no ground truth disparity in testing set, we divide the whole training data into a training set (80%) and a validation set (20%) in our ablation studies. Finally, we submit the results to the KITTI online benchmark to evaluate our models. Note that KITTI consider a pixel to be correctly estimated if the disparity end-point error is <3 pixels or <5%. The percentage of erroneous pixels (3PE) is the evaluation metric for KITTI dataset.

Experiment Settings. We implement our stereo networks in PyTorch and train them by Adam optimizer with β_1=0.9 and β_2=0.999 on four Nvidia RTX 2080Ti. During training, we crop the input image to size 256×512 randomly and perform color normalization to process all of them. Besides, we fix the batch size to 8 and set the maximum disparity D_{max} to 192.

4.2   Ablation Studies

In the proposed MAB module, the number of branches, scale factors are adjustable. Through the following ablation studies, we want to figure out the impact of the parameter configuration to the accuracy of MABNet. Basically, a larger number of branches and higher scale factors lead to more expensive computational demand while not necessarily a better accuracy of the stereo network. We performed two sets of experiments in MABNet to decide the proper parameter configuration in 2D and 3D MAB modules. Each model was evaluated on SceneFlow and KITTI2015. For SceneFlow dataset, we trained the model from scratch for 10 epochs with learning rate=0.001. For KITTI2015, there are only

160 training stereo pairs and 40 validation stereo pairs, making models susceptible to over-fitting. Thus, we used the pretrained SceneFlow model and finetuned
it for 300 epochs. The learning rate of this fine-tuning began at 0.001 for first
200 epochs, then drops to 0.0001 for remaining 100 epochs. Finally, we computed
EPE on the SceneFlow test set and the percentage of 3PE on the KITTI 2015
validation set.

Different Numbers of Branches in 2D MAB Module. To figure out the
best choice for the number of branches in 2D MAB module, we did four experiments in MABNet with the fixed scale factors as 0.5 both in 2D and 3D MAB
modules. The reason we only did experiments with 2D MAB is because the number of branches in 3D MAB can be inferred from the results about 2D MAB.
And adding a branch in 3D MAB will greatly increase FLOPs, which is time
and resources consuming. In the experiments, λ_1, λ_2 and λ_3 are the scale factor
in the branch with $dila=1$, $dila=2$ and $dila=4$ respectively. Besides, we added
the $4th$ branch with $dila=8$ and λ_4.

Table 1. Evaluation of MABNet with different numbers of branches in 2D MAB
module. λ_1, λ_2, λ_3 and λ_4 are scale factors in 2D MAB. FLOPs represent floating-point-
operations in processing a stereo pair of 256×512, including convolution, activation
function and batch normalization.

Branches	λ_1	λ_2	λ_3	λ_4	Parameters	FLOPs	SceneFlow(EPE)	KITTI2015(3PE)
1	0.5	–	–	–	1.525 M	188.26 G	1.072	3.236%
2	0.5	0.5	–	–	1.573 M	189.16 G	1.111	3.349%
3	0.5	0.5	0.5	–	1.621 M	190.07 G	**1.056**	**3.174%**
4	0.5	0.5	0.5	0.5	1.669 M	190.97 G	1.588	3.225%

The results listed in Table 1 show that setting three branches in 2D MAB is
the most reasonable case. As for experiments with one and two branches, they
do not extract enough multilevel features, causing lower accuracy than that
with three branches. As for the experiment with four branches, although it has
features with more level at the cost of more parameters and FLOPs, its result
is comparatively unacceptable especially when tested on Sceneflow [24] which
contains lots of pictures of monkey and flying objects. As mentioned in Sect. 3.1,
larger dilation rate in the additional branch leads to more paddings, fading
the effective information in feature maps. On the other hand, larger dilation
rate good for the estimation of background disparity contains scanty foreground
information. Therefore, the experiment with four branches yields a worse depth
estimation.

Different Scale Factors in MAB Module. After determining the number
of branches, we further explored the proportional relationship between the three

scale factors. Similar to 2D MAB, λ_1, λ_2 in 3D MAB are the scale factors in the branches with $dila=1$ and $dila=2$ respectively. To narrow the search space, we constrained the λ_i to be $\frac{1}{2^n}$ ($n=0,1,2$), which ensured that the number of output channels was an integer and greater than 1. Besides, we only performed experiments on SceneFlow since KITTI validation dataset has too few samples to get regular results.

We first carry out the experiments with fixed λ in 3D MAB module as 0.5 and 0.25. The results about 2D MAB modules in Table 2 proves that λ_1 had positive impact on the accuracy but λ_3 had opposite effect. Therefore, we empirically fixed the scale factors of 2D MAB in the next three experiments in Table 3, trying to explore the importance of λ_i in 3D MAB. We found that the configuration of {1,0.5,0.25,0.5,0.25} gives the best result.

Table 2. Evaluation of MABNet with different scale factors in 2D MAB module.

2D MAB			3D MAB		Parameters	SceneFlow (EPE)
λ_1	λ_2	λ_3	λ_1	λ_2		
0.25	0.5	0.5	0.5	0.25	1.591 M	1.107
0.5	0.5	0.5	0.5	0.25	1.615 M	1.072
1	0.5	0.5	0.5	0.25	1.663 M	1.041
0.5	**0.25**	0.5	0.5	0.25	1.591 M	1.075
0.5	**0.5**	0.5	0.5	0.25	1.615 M	1.072
0.5	**1**	0.5	0.5	0.25	1.663 M	1.073
0.5	0.5	**0.25**	0.5	0.25	1.591 M	1.091
0.5	0.5	**0.5**	0.5	0.25	1.615 M	1.072
0.5	0.5	**1**	0.5	0.25	1.663 M	1.161

Table 3. Evaluation of MABNet with different scale factors in 3D MAB modules.

2D MAB			3D MAB		Parameters	SceneFlow (EPE)
λ_1	λ_2	λ_3	λ_1	λ_2		
1	0.5	0.25	0.25	0.5	1.639 M	1.127
1	0.5	0.25	0.5	0.25	1.639 M	0.987
1	0.5	0.25	0.5	0.5	1.645 M	1.006
1	0.5	0.25	1	0.5	1.655 M	0.994

4.3 Evaluations on Benchmarks

We evaluated our MABNet and MABNet_tiny on SceneFlow and KITTI to prove the effectiveness of our MAB module. Unlike ablation studies, we increased the number of trainings to 20 epochs for SceneFlow and 600 epochs for KITTI. For SceneFlow, the learning rate was 0.001 initially, 0.0005 for $16th$-$18th$ epoch and 0.0001 for $19th$-$20th$. For KITTI, we used the pretrained SceneFlow model in $15th$ epoch. The learning rate was 0.001 initially, 0.0005 for $300th$-$399th$ epoch, 0.0002 for $400th$-$499th$ epoch and 0.0001 for $500th$-$600th$ epoch.

According to the online KITTI2015 leaderboard, as shown in Table 4, in comparison with other models on the approximate order of magnitude, our compact models with fewer parameters achieves competitive accuracy. Especially, MABNet_tiny improves the accuracy significantly over StereoNet and AnyNet. We obtain the same observation through the experimental results on KITTI2012 and SceneFlow, illustrated in Table 5.

Table 4. Evaluation results on KITTI2015 benchmark. The percentages of erroneous pixels for non-occluded (Noc) and all (All) pixels in background (D1-bg), foreground (D1-fg) and all areas (D1-all) are reported. Note that AnyNet [38] is tested on the Nvidia Jetson TX2 GPU computing module.

Method	All(%)			Noc(%)			Parameters	Runtime
	D1-bg	D1-fg	D1-all	D1-bg	D1-fg	D1-all		
GC-Net [17]	2.21	6.16	2.87	2.02	5.58	2.61	3.5 M	0.9 s
PSMNet [4]	1.86	4.62	2.32	1.71	4.31	2.14	5.2 M	0.41 s
PDSNet [35]	2.29	4.05	2.58	2.09	3.68	2.36	2.2 M	0.5 s
LWSM [43]	1.86	5.35	2.44	1.69	4.68	2.18	1.8 M	0.24 s
MABNet	1.89	5.02	2.41	1.74	4.59	2.21	1.65 M	0.38 s
StereoNet [18]	4.30	7.45	4.83	–	–	–	360 K	0.015 s
AnyNet [38]	–	–	6.20	–	–	–	40 K	0.0973 s
MABNet_tiny	3.04	8.07	3.88	2.80	7.28	3.54	47 K	0.11 s

Table 5. Evaluation results on KITTI2012 and SceneFlow benchmark. The percentages of erroneous pixels (Out) and the average end-point errors (Avg) for both non-occluded (Noc) and all (All) pixels are reported on KITTI2012. The error threshold is set to 2.

Method	KITTI2012				SceneFlow (EPE)
	Out-Noc(%)	Out-All(%)	Avg-Noc(px)	Avg-all(px)	
GC-Net [17]	2.71	3.46	0.6	0.7	2.51
PSMNet [4]	2.44	3.01	0.5	0.6	1.09
PDSNet [35]	3.82	4.65	0.9	1.0	1.12
LWSM [43]	2.48	3.17	0.5	0.6	0.8
MABNet	2.43	3.02	0.5	0.5	0.797
StereoNet [18]	4.91	6.02	0.8	0.9	1.101
MABNet_tiny	4.45	5.27	0.7	0.8	1.663

As shown in Table 6, compared with PSMNet [4] and StereoNet [18], the proposed MABNet and MABNet_tiny that have much less network parameters do not exhibit the advantage of running time on the platform of GPU. We discover that the depthwise convolutions involved in the 2D and 3D MAB modules cannot perform efficiently on GPUs. Because the procedure of a convolution is similar to a general matrix multiplication (GEMM) operation, before which GPU must perform an im2col operation, transforming the input 3D data into a 2D matrix. Therefore, a depthwise convolution needs to repeat the im2col and GEMM operation C times because it has C groups of feature map, while a standard convolution needs only once in2col operation. Since the number of parameters influences the memory access cost [46], as well as the number of FLOPs determines the number of multiply-and-accumulate (MAC) operations, we believe MABNet and its light version should achieve superior efficiency on the other hardware flatforms, like embedded DNN accelerators for edge devices.

Table 6. Evaluation results of FLOPs for processing a stereo pair of 256×512, including convolution, activate function and batch normalization.

Method	PSMNet [4]	MABNet	StereoNet [18]	MABNet_tiny
FLOPs	257.01 G	190.75 G	14.08 G	6.60 G
Runtime	0.41 s	0.38 s	0.015 s	0.11 s

5   Conclusions

We propose the MAB module which can extract features with multiple receptive fields and is adjustable in the number of channels in each branch. Moreover, we are looking forward to applying the MAB module to more fields, such as object detection, semantic segmentation and classification. Based on the MAB module, we propose two lightweight stereo network MABNet and its light version MABNet_tiny. Experimental results on SceneFlow and KITTI demonstrate the effectiveness of the MAB module, MABNet and MABNet_tiny. More importantly, our models with few parameters and low computational complexity are easy to be deployed on resource-constrained devices.

Acknowledgement. This research was supported by the Key Science and Technology Projects in Jiangsu Province (Grant No. BE2018002-2) and the National Nature Foundation of China (Grant No.61974024).

References

1. Alhaija, H.A., Mustikovela, S.K., Mescheder, L., Geiger, A., Rother, C.: Augmented reality meets computer vision: efficient data generation for urban driving scenes. Int. J. Comput. Vis. **126**(9), 961–972 (2018)

2. Badrinarayanan, V., Kendall, A., Cipolla, R.: Segnet: a deep convolutional encoder-decoder architecture for image segmentation. IEEE Trans. Pattern Anal. Mach. Intell. **39**(12), 2481–2495 (2017)
3. Batsos, K., Mordohai, P.: Recresnet: a recurrent residual CNN architecture for disparity map enhancement. In: 2018 International Conference on 3D Vision (3DV), pp. 238–247. IEEE (2018)
4. Chang, J.R., Chen, Y.S.: Pyramid stereo matching network. In: Proceedings of the IEEE Conference on Computer Vision and Pattern Recognition, pp. 5410–5418 (2018)
5. Chen, L.C., Papandreou, G., Kokkinos, I., Murphy, K., Yuille, A.L.: Semantic image segmentation with deep convolutional nets and fully connected crfs. arXiv preprint arXiv:1412.7062 (2014)
6. Chollet, F.: Xception: deep learning with depthwise separable convolutions. In: Proceedings of the IEEE Conference on Computer Vision and Pattern Recognition, pp. 1251–1258 (2017)
7. Denton, E.L., Zaremba, W., Bruna, J., LeCun, Y., Fergus, R.: Exploiting linear structure within convolutional networks for efficient evaluation. In: Advances in Neural Information Processing Systems, pp. 1269–1277 (2014)
8. Dosovitskiy, Aet al.: Flownet: Llarning optical flow with convolutional networks. In: Proceedings of the IEEE International Conference on Computer Vision, pp. 2758–2766 (2015)
9. Du, X., El-Khamy, M., Lee, J.: Amnet: deep atrous multiscale stereo disparity estimation networks. arXiv preprint arXiv:1904.09099 (2019)
10. Geiger, A., Lenz, P., Urtasun, R.: Are we ready for autonomous driving? the kitti vision benchmark suite. In: 2012 IEEE Conference on Computer Vision and Pattern Recognition, pp. 3354–3361. IEEE (2012)
11. He, K., Zhang, X., Ren, S., Sun, J.: Deep residual learning for image recognition. In: Proceedings of the IEEE Conference on Computer Vision and Pattern Recognition, pp. 770–778 (2016)
12. Hirschmuller, H.: Stereo processing by semiglobal matching and mutual information. IEEE Trans. Pattern Anal. Mach. Intell. **30**(2), 328–341 (2007)
13. Holschneider, M., Kronland-Martinet, R., Morlet, J., Tchamitchian, P.: A real-time algorithm for signal analysis with the help of the wavelet transform. In: Combes, J.M., Grossmann, A., Tchamitchian, P. (eds.) Wavelets, inverse problems and theoretical imaging, pp. 286–297. Springer, Heidelberg (1990). https://doi.org/10.1007/978-3-642-75988-8_28
14. Howard, A.G., et al.: Efficient convolutional neural networks for mobile vision applications. arXiv preprint ArXiv:1704.0486 (2017)
15. Iandola, F.N., Han, S., Moskewicz, M.W., Ashraf, K., Dally, W.J., Keutzer, K.: Squeezenet: Alexnet-level accuracy with $50\times$ fewer parameters and < 0.5 mb model size. arXiv preprint arXiv:1602.07360 (2016)
16. Jie, Z., et al.: Left-right comparative recurrent model for stereo matching. In: Proceedings of the IEEE Conference on Computer Vision and Pattern Recognition, pp. 3838–3846 (2018)
17. Kendall, A., et al.: End-to-end learning of geometry and context for deep stereo regression. In: Proceedings of the IEEE International Conference on Computer Vision, pp. 66–75 (2017)
18. Khamis, S., Fanello, S., Rhemann, C., Kowdle, A., Valentin, J., Izadi, S.: Stereonet: guided hierarchical refinement for real-time edge-aware depth prediction. In: Proceedings of the European Conference on Computer Vision (ECCV), pp. 573–590 (2018)

19. Lee, K.J., et al.: A 502-gops and 0.984-mw dual-mode intelligent adas soc with real-time semiglobal matching and intention prediction for smart automotive black box system. IEEE J. Solid-State Circ. **52**(1), 139–150 (2016)

20. Li, Z., et al.: 3.7 a 1920 × 1080 30fps 2.3 tops/w stereo-depth processor for robust autonomous navigation. In: 2017 IEEE International Solid-State Circuits Conference (ISSCC), pp. 62–63. IEEE (2017)

21. Liang, Z., et al.: Learning for disparity estimation through feature constancy. In: Proceedings of the IEEE Conference on Computer Vision and Pattern Recognition, pp. 2811–2820 (2018)

22. Liu, S., De Mello, S., Gu, J., Zhong, G., Yang, M.H., Kautz, J.: Learning affinity via spatial propagation networks. In: Advances in Neural Information Processing Systems, pp. 1520–1530 (2017)

23. Ma, N., Zhang, X., Zheng, H.T., Sun, J.: Shufflenet v2: practical guidelines for efficient cnn architecture design. In: Proceedings of the European Conference on Computer Vision (ECCV), pp. 116–131 (2018)

24. Mayer, N., et al.: A large dataset to train convolutional networks for disparity, optical flow, and scene flow estimation. In: Proceedings of the IEEE Conference on Computer Vision and Pattern Recognition, pp. 4040–4048 (2016)

25. Mehta, S., Rastegari, M., Caspi, A., Shapiro, L., Hajishirzi, H.: Espnet: efficient spatial pyramid of dilated convolutions for semantic segmentation. In: Proceedings of the European Conference on Computer Vision (ECCV), pp. 552–568 (2018)

26. Menze, M., Heipke, C., Geiger, A.: Joint 3D estimation of vehicles and scene flow. ISPRS Ann. Photogram. Remote Sens. Spat. Inf. Sci. **2**, 1–8 (2015)

27. Pang, J., Sun, W., Ren, J.S., Yang, C., Yan, Q.: Cascade residual learning: a two-stage convolutional neural network for stereo matching. In: Proceedings of the IEEE International Conference on Computer Vision Workshops, pp. 887–895 (2017)

28. Poggi, M., Mattoccia, S.: Learning from scratch a confidence measure. In: BMVC (2016)

29. Ronneberger, O., Fischer, P., Brox, T.: U-Net: convolutional networks for biomedical image segmentation. In: Navab, N., Hornegger, J., Wells, W.M., Frangi, A.F. (eds.) MICCAI 2015. LNCS, vol. 9351, pp. 234–241. Springer, Cham (2015). https://doi.org/10.1007/978-3-319-24574-4_28

30. Sandler, M., Howard, A., Zhu, M., Zhmoginov, A., Chen, L.C.: Mobilenetv 2: Inverted residuals and linear bottlenecks. In: Proceedings of the IEEE Conference on Computer Vision and Pattern Recognition, pp. 4510–4520 (2018)

31. Seki, A., Pollefeys, M.: Patch based confidence prediction for dense disparity map. In: BMVC, vol. 2, p. 4 (2016)

32. Shen, S.: Accurate multiple view 3D reconstruction using patch-based stereo for large-scale scenes. IEEE Trans. Image Process. **22**(5), 1901–1914 (2013)

33. Szegedy, C., et al.: Going deeper with convolutions. In: Proceedings of the IEEE Conference on Computer Vision and Pattern Recognition, pp. 1–9 (2015)

34. Tonioni, A., Tosi, F., Poggi, M., Mattoccia, S., Stefano, L.D.: Real-time self-adaptive deep stereo. In: Proceedings of the IEEE Conference on Computer Vision and Pattern Recognition, pp. 195–204 (2019)

35. Tulyakov, S., Ivanov, A., Fleuret, F.: Practical deep stereo (pds): toward applications-friendly deep stereo matching. In: Advances in Neural Information Processing Systems, pp. 5871–5881 (2018)

36. Wang, H., Lin, J., Wang, Z.: Design light-weight 3D convolutional networks for video recognition temporal residual, fully separable block, and fast algorithm. arXiv preprint arXiv:1905.13388 (2019)

37. Wang, P., et al.: Understanding convolution for semantic segmentation. In: 2018 IEEE Winter Conference on Applications of Computer Vision (WACV), pp. 1451–1460. IEEE (2018)
38. Wang, Y., et al.: Anytime stereo image depth estimation on mobile devices. In: 2019 International Conference on Robotics and Automation (ICRA), pp. 5893–5900. IEEE (2019)
39. Wofk, D., Ma, F., Yang, T.J., Karaman, S., Sze, V.: Fastdepth: fast monocular depth estimation on embedded systems. In: 2019 International Conference on Robotics and Automation (ICRA), pp. 6101–6108. IEEE (2019)
40. Xie, C.W., Zhou, H.Y., Wu, J.: Vortex pooling: improving context representation in semantic segmentation. arXiv preprint arXiv:1804.06242 (2018)
41. Xie, S., Girshick, R., Dollár, P., Tu, Z., He, K.: Aggregated residual transformations for deep neural networks. In: Proceedings of the IEEE Conference on Computer Vision and Pattern Recognition, pp. 1492–1500 (2017)
42. Xie, S., Sun, C., Huang, J., Tu, Z., Murphy, K.: Rethinking spatiotemporal feature learning: speed-accuracy trade-offs in video classification. In: Proceedings of the European Conference on Computer Vision (ECCV), pp. 305–321 (2018)
43. Xu, X., Hou, Y., Wang, P., Jiang, Z., Li, W.: Light weight stereo matching via deep extraction and integration of low and high level information. In: 2019 IEEE International Conference on Multimedia and Expo (ICME), pp. 320–325. IEEE (2019)
44. Žbontar, J., LeCun, Y.: Stereo matching by training a convolutional neural network to compare image patches. J. Mach. Learn. Res. **17**(1), 2287–2318 (2016)
45. Zhang, F., Prisacariu, V., Yang, R., Torr, P.H.: Ga-net: guided aggregation net for end-to-end stereo matching. In: Proceedings of the IEEE Conference on Computer Vision and Pattern Recognition, pp. 185–194 (2019)
46. Zhang, X., Zhou, X., Lin, M., Sun, J.: Shufflenet: an extremely efficient convolutional neural network for mobile devices. In: Proceedings of the IEEE Conference on Computer Vision and Pattern Recognition, pp. 6848–6856 (2018)

Guided Saliency Feature Learning for Person Re-identification in Crowded Scenes

Lingxiao He$^{(\boxtimes)}$ and Wu Liu$^{(\boxtimes)}$

JD AI Research, Beijing, People's Republic of China
{helingxiao3,liuwu1}@jd.com
https://air.jd.com

Abstract. Person Re-identification (Re-ID) in crowed scenes is a challenging problem, where people are frequently partially occluded by objects and other people. However, few studies have provided flexible solutions to re-identifying people in an image containing a partial occlusion body part. In this paper, we propose a simple occlusion-aware approach to address the problem. The proposed method first leverages a fully convolutional network to generate spatial features. And then we design a combination of a pose-guided and mask-guided layer to generate saliency heatmap to further guide discriminative feature learning. More importantly, we propose a new matching approach, called Guided Adaptive Spatial Matching (GASM), which expects that each spatial feature in the query can find the most similar spatial features of a person in a gallery to match. Especially, We use the saliency heatmap to guide the adaptive spatial matching by assigning the foreground human parts with larger weights adaptively. The effectiveness of the proposed GASM is demonstrated on two occluded person datasets: Crowd REID (51.52%) and Occluded REID (80.25%) and three benchmark person datasets: Market1501 (95.31%), DukeMTMC-reID (88.12%) and MSMT17 (79.52%). Additionally, GASM achieves good performance on cross-domain person Re-ID. The code and models are available at: https://github.com/JDAI-CV/fast-reid/blob/master/projects/CrowdReID.

Keywords: Person re-identification · Guided saliency feature learning · Guided adaptive spatial matching

1 Introduction

Person re-identification (Re-ID) has achieved significant improvement both in academic and industrial society in the past two years, making it widely used in many real-world scenarios, such as train station, airport, etc. However, two urgent yet challenging problems of person Re-ID in crowded scenes are still not well addressed. One major issue that challenges this task is the ubiquitous pedestrian occlusion by each other. For instance, as shown in Fig. 1, the captured person is occluded by a partial body of the front person, making it difficult to track

© Springer Nature Switzerland AG 2020
A. Vedaldi et al. (Eds.): ECCV 2020, LNCS 12373, pp. 357–373, 2020.
https://doi.org/10.1007/978-3-030-58604-1_22

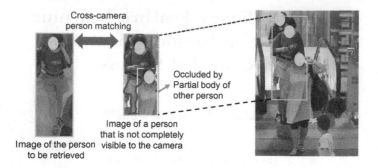

Fig. 1. Illustration of the person Re-ID in crowed scenes. Here, the Re-ID system aims to recognize the person within the red region. The captured person by the surveillance operator is occluded by the partial body of the front person.

her movement. Another major issue that challenges this task is cross-camera person image matching because of unpredictable dynamic background-bias under different cameras. From this perspective, person Re-ID in crowded scenes has attracted significant research attention as the demand for identification using images captured by video surveillance systems has been rapidly growing.

Most existing person Re-ID [9,11] approaches fail to identify a person when the body region is severely occluded by the partial body of the other person. To match an occluded person image, most of the attention-based approaches [10,18,25] (see in Fig. 2(a)) enforce the output features to mainly focus on the foreground human bodies. Our observations show that the attention-based approach can only eliminate the influence of background, but fail to remove the partial body of another person. Some other approaches [8,15,21] proposed a two-stream network as shown in Fig. 2(b), which consists of an appearance map extraction stream and a body part heatmap extraction stream. Following the two streams, a part-aligned feature map was obtained by a bilinear mapping of the corresponding local appearance and body part descriptors. But it inevitably requires more inference time to obtain the body part heatmap and fails to generate accurate body part heatmap under heavily occluded by the partial body of the other person in crowded scenes.

In this paper, we propose a towards accurate camera-aware person Re-ID framework that can re-identify a person occluded by a partial person's body as shown in Fig. 2(c). First, we utilize a fully convolutional neural network to produce spatial feature maps that contains the features of the person's body occlusion person body (partial body of another person) and background. To guarantee the extracted feature with less contamination of background and occlusion person body, we design a mask layer combined with a pose layer to predict the saliency heatmap. In particular, The predictive power of the saliency heatmap for the mask layer and pose layer are respectively learned from large human segmentation and pose estimation models. And then we obtain the discriminative feature by a bilinear mapping of the spatial feature map and the saliency heatmap.

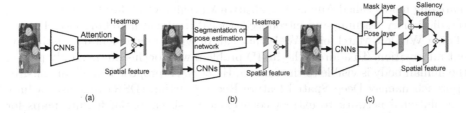

Fig. 2. (a) Attention-based approach (b) Two-stream approach (c) Our approach.

Finally, we develop an adaptive spatial matching method, which expects that each spatial feature in the query can find the most similar spatial feature of a person in a gallery to match. To achieve the more accurate matching, We also use the saliency heatmap to guide the spatial matching by assigning the person body with larger weights and the occlusion body and background with smaller weights to overcome the occlusion and background problem. Remarkably, the model improves the performance of cross-camera Re-ID by eliminating background-bias. The main contributions of our work are summarized as follows:

- We propose a novel saliency feature learning network that integrates Re-ID feature learning, human segmentation and pose estimation in a unified framework, which can effectively address person re-identification under severe occlusion in crowded scenes. Our approach does not rely on any external cues during the inference term.
- We propose guide adaptive spatial matching for person Re-ID, which can address person image misalignment problem and is flexible to arbitrary-sized person images.
- The proposed saliency feature presentation framework effectively eliminates dynamic background-bias, which helps to improve cross-domain person Re-ID.
- Experimental results demonstrate that the proposed approach achieves impressive results on multiple occlusion datasets including new Crowd REID and Occluded REID. It exceeds some occluded Re-ID approaches by more than 15% in terms of rank-1 accuracy. Besides, the proposed method achieves competitive results on multiple benchmark datasets including Market1501 [27], DukeMTMC-reID [30], MSMT17 [29].

2 Related Work

Occluded Person Re-identification. Occluded/Partial person Re-ID [2,16] has become an emerging problem in video surveillance. To address this problem. Part-based models are considered as a solution to occluded person Re-ID. A local-to-local matching strategy is employed to handle occlusions and cases where the target is partially out of camera's view. Zheng *et al.* [28] proposed a local-level matching model called Ambiguity-sensitive Matching Classifier (AMC) based on the dictionary learning and introduced a local-to-global matching model called Sliding Window Matching (SWM) that can provide complementary spatial layout information. To address the Re-ID problem with occlusion, *i.e.*, only part of the human body is visible to the camera, He *et al.* [4] proposed an alignment-free approach namely Deep Spatial feature Reconstruction (DSR) that uses a fully convolutional network to extract corresponding-sized spatial feature maps for the incomplete person images, and then exploits the reconstruction error based on sparse coding to avoid explicit alignment. Furthermore, a Foreground-aware Pyramid Reconstruction (FPR) [6] scheme also tries to remove the influence of background and scale various. Sun *et al.* introduce a Visibility-aware Part Model (VPM) [22] to extract stripe-level features, thus addressing the spatial misalignment in the incomplete images. Luo *et al.* [13] proposed STNReID that combines a spatial transformer network (STN) and a re-id network for partial re-id Besides, the Pose-Guided Feature Alignment (FGFA) [14] utilizes the pose landmarks to mine discriminative part information to address the occlusion noise. Although these methods mentioned above can solve the occlusion problem to some extent, it cannot deal with the situation where a person is partially occluded by a partial body of another person. To this end, we propose a guided saliency feature learning model that can effectively classify background and partial occlusion body, and then incorporate adaptive spatial matching to address occlusion problem in crowded scenes.

Person Re-identification. The attention mechanism is usually utilized in many human-centric video analysis applications [5,12], such as ReID, to extract more discriminative features. Si *et al.* [18] proposed a dual attention mechanism, in which both intra-sequence and inter-sequence attention strategies are used for feature refinement and feature-pair alignment, respectively. Chen *et al.* proposed an Attentive but Diverse Network (ABD-Net) [1], which integrates spatial-channel attention modules and diversity regularizations throughout the entire network to extract more discriminative features. Zhou *et al.* [32] introduce a novel consistent attention regularizer between feature representation layers to learn foreground-aware feature maps. Besides, most of the person Re-ID approaches leverage external cues such as human mask and human pose estimation to enhance feature representation. In some mask-guided models, mask as an external cue helps to remove the background clutters in pixel-level and only contain body shape information. Song *et al.* [19] introduced the binary segmentation masks to construct the synthetic RGB-Mask pairs as inputs, then they design a mask-guided contrastive attention model (MGCAM) [19] to learn features separately from the body and background regions. Kalayeh *et al.* [8] proposed a person re-identification model that integrated human semantic parsing in person re-identification. Pose-guided models utilize pose estimation information as an external cue in person Re-ID to reduce the part misalignment problem. Each key part can be well located using person landmarks. Su *et al.* [20] proposed a Pose-driven Deep Convolutional (PDC) model to learn improved feature extractors and matching models from end-to-end, PDC can explicitly leverage

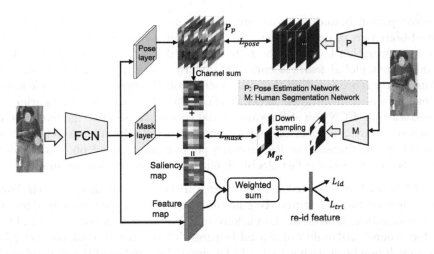

Fig. 3. Architecture of the proposed guided saliency feature learning. The backbone consists of a fully convolutional network (FCN), a mask layer and a pose layer. FCN is used to extract spatial features. The mask layer and pose layer are used to predict the mask-guided heatmap and pose-guided heatmap. And then saliency features are obtained by a bilinear mapping of the feature map and the saliency heatmap.

the human part cues to alleviate the pose variations. Suh *et al.* [21] proposed a two-stream network that consisted of an appearance map extraction stream and body part map extraction stream. And then a part-aligned feature map is obtained by a bilinear mapping of the corresponding local appearance and body part descriptors. Although mask-guided and pose-guided approaches can achieve satisfying performance, they extremely rely on accurate segmentation model and pose estimation model. Also, these existing approaches are two-stream structure so that the computation cost of these approaches is rather extensive during the inference term.

3 Proposed Approach

In this section, we elaborate on the proposed guided saliency feature learning for the occluded person re-identification approach. We first introduce the entire network architecture. After that, we will introduce the training of our model. Finally, we will explain saliency adaptive spatial matching.

3.1 Architecture of the Proposed Model

The architecture of the proposed Re-ID model is shown in Fig. 3. Structurally, it consists of a full convolutional neural network (FCN), a mask layer and a pose layer. We now introduce them one by one.

FCN. In the crowded scenes, the target person to re-identify is provided with person detection bounding boxes by a human detector. As shown in Fig. 1, the detected person bounding boxes are coarse, often containing background and partial body part of occlusion person. Conventional neural networks involving a feature aggregation layer like the fully connected layer or average pooling layer would output global features contaminated by background and occlusion. To obtain better representation that only focuses on the person to be re-identified, we use a fully convolutional network (FCN) as the backbone for spatial feature extraction. FCN can still retain spatial coordinate so that the background, occlusion features, and person features are extracted without interference with each other. We discard the last average pooling layer based on ResNet-50 to implement FCN, and the last Resblock outputs the spatial feature map.

Mask Layer. The extracted spatial features are often contaminated by the background and occlusion features. To guarantee the following person spatial feature are less contamination from the background, we design a mask layer to obtain the foreground probability of spatial features. The designed mask layer consists of a convolution layer with a $1 \times 1 \times d$ (d denotes the number of the channel of the output feature map, and d = 2048 in our model) convolution kernel. The output spatial features pass the mask layer to generate a correspondingly-size mask-guided heatmap, and the size of each mask-guided heatmap is $W \times H$, where W and H denote the width and the height of output feature map, respectively.

Pose Layer. The detected person may be occluded by other partial bodies of other persons, resulting in that only mask-guided heatmap unable to distinguish between persons to be identified or occlusion persons. Therefore, we also design a pose layer to predict the C human keypoints heatmap $(C = 13)$[1] that can only focus on the identified person. The pose layer consists of a convolution layer with 13 $1 \times 1 \times 2048$ kernels. Likewise, the output spatial features pass the pose layer to generate a correspondingly-size pose-guided heatmap, and the size of each pose-guided heatmap is $W \times H \times C$.

Pose-guided heatmap only focuses on human keypoints, the weights around person keypoints are relatively large while the weights beyond person keypoints are relatively small. As for Mask-guided heatmap, it only focuses on the person part, but it cannot address partial occlusion body contamination. Therefore, pose-guided heatmap combined with mask-guided heatmap can output a more accurate saliency heatmap for further guiding following feature learning and adaptive spatial matching.

3.2   Guided Saliency Feature Learning

In this section, we now explain the training strategy for learning saliency features. As shown in Fig. 3, four loss functions are used to optimize the whole Re-ID model.

Mask-Guided Loss. We design a mask layer to classify the spatial features of the background and foreground person. We treat this problem as a probabilistic

---

[1] Head, Left-shoulder, Right-shoulder, Left-elbow, Right-elbow, Left-wrist, Right-wrist, Left-hip, Right-hip, Left-knee, Right-knee, Left-ankle, Right-ankle.

Input Image   Pose heatmap

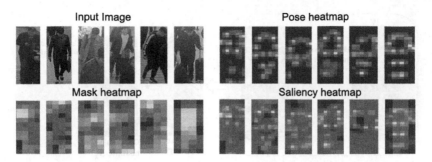

Mask heatmap   Saliency heatmap

Fig. 4. Example results of source image, pose heatmap, mask heatmap and saliency heatmap.

prediction problem. To generate a mask-guided heatmap, we use the semantic segmentation model PSPNet [26] trained with COCO dataset to guide the mask layer to predict the mask-guided heatmap $\mathbf{M}_p \in \mathbb{R}^{W \times H}$. Let $\mathbf{M}_{gt}$ generated by PSPNet with downsampling operation be the ground truth human mask of width W and height H. Our aim is to regress the $\mathbf{M}_p$ with regard to $\mathbf{M}_{gt}$. Therefore, the training objective of mask layer is a pixel-wise regression:

$$\mathcal{L}_{mask} = ||\mathbf{M}_p - \mathbf{M}_{gt}||_F \tag{1}$$

Pose-Guided Loss. The predicted mask-guided heatmap can only distinguish between backgrounds and persons, but is unable to distinguish between persons to be identified and partial body of other persons. Therefore, we want to design a pose layer to classify the spatial features of the person and partial body. The human pose estimation model CenterNet [33] (visualized human joints are shown in Fig. 4) is used to guide the pose layer to predict the pose-guided heatmap. Keypoint types included 13 human joints in human pose estimation. Let $\mathbf{P}_p \in \mathbb{R}^{W \times H \times 13}$ and $\mathbf{P}_g t \in \mathbb{R}^{W \times H \times 13}$ be predicted pose-guided heatmap by the pose layer and the generated ground truth pose heatmap by CenterNet with downsampling operation, respectively. Our aim is to use $\mathbf{P}_p$ to regress $\mathbf{P}_{gt}$. Therefore, the training objective of the pose layer is a pixel-wise regression:

$$\mathcal{L}_{pose} = ||\mathbf{P}_p - \mathbf{P}_{gt}||_F \tag{2}$$

And then, we use channel sum operation to obtain the final pose-guided heatmap $\mathbf{P}_p$.

The two complementary mask-guided heatmap and pose-guided heatmap are fused to obtain saliency heatmap to predict more accurate saliency person coordinate information.

Triplet Loss and Identification Loss. Our person re-identification model simply aggregates the output spatial feature map using the saliency heatmap. By using the weighted sum operation, the network finally generates a 2048-D global saliency feature representation. To train the network, we pass it to a

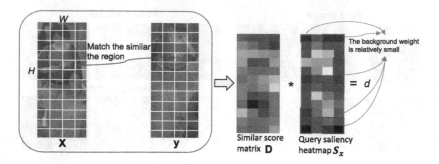

Fig. 5. Illustration of guided adaptive spatial matching. Here, each spatial feature in the query can find the most similar spatial feature of a person in a gallery to match. The saliency heatmap can refine the final matching result.

multi-class classification objective with softmax cross-entropy loss L_{id}. To obtain a more compact feature representation, we also use a metric learning objective with triplet loss L_{tri} to train the network.

The final loss function is a weighted sum of all the losses defined above: L_{mask} and L_{pose} are complementary to predict the saliency person heatmap. L_{id} and L_{tri} to preserve identity discrimination.

$$\mathcal{L} = \lambda_{mask}\mathcal{L}_{mask} + \lambda_{pose}\mathcal{L}_{pose} + \mathcal{L}_{id} + \mathcal{L}_{tri} \tag{3}$$

We set $\lambda_{mask} = 0.05$ and $\lambda_{pose} = 0.1$ in our experiments.

3.3   Guided Adaptive Spatial Matching

At present, Euclidean distance is used to match global features. However, such coarse matching is hard to solve the misalignment problem. The saliency adaptive spatial matching (SASM) is a more refined matching method, which can solve the misalignment to some extent. Given a pair of person images I_x (query) and I_y (gallery), Corresponding spatial feature maps $\mathbf{x} \in \mathbb{R}^{W \times H \times d}$ and $\mathbf{y} \in \mathbb{R}^{W \times H \times d}$ are inferred by FCN, where W, H and d denote the height, the width and the number of the channel of spatial feature map. $\mathbf{x}_{h,w} \in \mathbb{R}^{1 \times 1 \times d}$ represents a local spatial feature corresponding to a local region of a source image. As shown in Fig. 5, $\mathbf{x}_{w,h}$ attempt to search similar local spatial feature in $\mathbf{y}$ to match, and then outputs the similar score $d_{w,h}$. For $W \times H$ spatial features in $\mathbf{x}$, we can calculate the similarity score of each spatial feature $\mathbf{x}_{w=1,h=1}^{W,H}$ with regard to $\mathbf{y}$. The similar score matrix can be defined as $\mathbf{D}$.

However, it suffers from an obvious limitation: since $\mathbf{x}$ contains the background and partial occlusion body features, the spatial matching scores are inaccurate. To alleviate the problem, we want to reduce the influence of background and partial occlusion body by assigning their matching scores small weights, while enhancing the effect of foreground person by assigning these matching scores large weights adaptively. Therefore, we use the generated saliency heatmap to guide adaptive spatial matching for further improving the Re-ID performance. Given a query image I_x, the pose layer and mask layer as introduced above output the saliency heatmap $\mathbf{S}_x$. Then the saliency heatmap $\mathbf{S}_x$ can be used to guide the adaptive spatial matching. We perform weight sum operation over the spatial matching matrix $\mathbf{D}$ and saliency heatmap $\mathbf{S}_x$. Then the final guided adaptive spatial matching (GASM) distance d of I_x and I_y can be defined as

$$d = \sum_{h=1}^{H} \sum_{w=1}^{W} \mathbf{D}^{h,w} * \mathbf{S}_x^{h,w} \tag{4}$$

Also, the global matching distance provides the complementary matching information to GASM by average weighting operation.

4 Experiments

In this section, we first verify the effectiveness of our proposed approach for the task of occluded person Re-ID on two occluded person Re-ID dataset: Crowd REID and Occluded REID [7], and then experiment on three person Re-ID benchmarks: Market1501 [27], DukeMTMC-reID [30], and MSMT17 [24] to show its generalizability. Also, we verify the advantage of our proposed approach for the task of cross-domain person Re-ID. Finally, we perform the parameter analysis to investigate the influence of the separated pose layer and mask layer.

4.1 Experiment Settings

Implementation Details. Our implementation is based on the publicly available code of PyTorch. All models are trained and tested on Linux with P40 GPUs. In the training term, all training images are re-scaled to 384×128. For batch hard triplet loss function, one batch consists of 16 subjects, and each subject has 4 different images. We train the overall network with 120 epochs, We use the Adam optimizer with the base learning rate initialized to 10^{-4}, then decayed to 10^{-5}, 10^{-6} after 40, 90 epochs, respectively.

Evaluation Protocol. We employ the standard metrics as in most person Re-ID literature namely the cumulative matching curve (CMC) and the mean Average Precision (mAP).

4.2 Datasets

Crowd REID is a newly created, which is specifically designed for person Re-ID in crowded scenes. The dataset is collected in a train station by 11 surveillance cameras. The dataset is very challenging because most of the person images in these images to be identified are occluded by the partial body of other persons. The examples of occlusion persons in the Crowd REID dataset are shown in Fig. 6(a). To evaluate this dataset, 2,412 images of 835 identities are used as the gallery set and 845 images of 605 identities are used as the gallery set.

(a)   (b)

Fig. 6. (a) Example of person images in the crowd REID dataset, the person to be identified are occluded by partial bodies of other persons such as head-shoulder or half body. (b) Example of person images in the Occluded dataset, the person images are occluded by static objects such as tree, car, and umbrella, etc.

Occluded REID is an occluded person dataset captured by mobile cameras, consisting of 2,000 images of 200 occluded persons (see Fig. 6(b)). Each identity has 5 full-body person images and 5 occluded person images with different viewpoints, backgrounds and different types of severe occlusions.

Market1501 has 12,936 training and 19.732 testing images with 1,501 identities in total from 6 cameras. Deformable Part Model (DPM) is used as the person detector. We follow the standard training and evaluation protocols in [27] where 751 identities are used for training and the remaining 750 identities for testing.

DukeMTMC-reID is the subset of Duke Dataset [17], which consists of 16,522 training images from 702 identities, 2,228 query images and 1,7,661 gallery images from other identities. It provides manually labeled person bounding boxes. Here, we follow the setup in [30].

MSMT17 is the current largest available person Re-ID dataset, consisting of 126,441 images of 4,101 identities captured by 12 outdoor cameras and 3 indoor cameras. We follow the training-testing split of [24]. MSMT17 is significantly more challenging than market1501 and DukeMTMC-reID due to more complex collected scenes, different weather conditions (morning, noon, afternoon).

Table 1. Performance comparison on Crowd REID and Occluded REID using Market1501, DukeMTMC and MSMT17 training datasets, respectively.

Method	Crowd REID rank-1 (mAP)			Occluded REID rank-1 (mAP)		
	Market1501	DukeMTMC	MSMT17	Market1501	DukeMTMC	MSMT17
PCB [23]	14.1 (13.4)	20.3 (17.5)	32.7 (26.6)	41.3 (38.9)	47.5 (42.4)	56.2 (47.5)
MaskReID [15]	14.3 (13.7)	21.7 (19.8)	37.2 (31.2)	26.8 (25.0)	44.2 (38.1)	54.2 (51.2)
PABR [21]	24.3 (21.7)	26.5 (23.7)	41.6 (36.8)	67.1 (55.4)	-	-
DSR [4]	28.8 (26.7)	30.3 (27.3)	48.7 (43.3)	72.8 (62.8)	-	-
FPR [6]	30.2 (29.9)	32.6 (30.3)	50.7 (45.8)	78.3 (68.0)	-	-
self-attention	22.3 (23.2)	-	-	67.4 (55.8)	-	-
Baseline	16.7 (16.4)	26.6 (24.3)	44.0 (41.2)	60.2 (57.0)	66.1 (60.2)	74.6 (69.2)
GASM	32.4 (31.1)	35.8 (31.8)	51.5 (47.1)	74.5 (65.6)	76.5 (67.8)	80.3 (73.2)

4.3   Occluded Person Re-identification

The designed person Re-ID model is respectively trained with Market1501, DukeMTMC-reID, and MSMT17 datasets, and tested on Crowd REID and Occluded REID datasets. Therefore, it is a cross-domain setting. Firstly, we compare our GASM against existing person Re-ID approaches including a part-based model PCB [23], a mask-guided Re-ID model MaskReID [15] and pose-guided Re-ID model PABR [21]. Besides, we also compare our GASM against partial person Re-ID approaches DSR [4] and FPR [6]. For PCB, MaskReID, PABR, DSR, and FPR, we follow their original parameter settings. Besides, we compare our proposed GASM against the baseline model based on ResNet-50.

Table 1 respectively shows the experimental results on Crowd REID and Occluded REID datasets. It is noted that: (1) The proposed GSAM achieves stable results regardless of different training datasets and different testing datasets. Clear gaps are shown between our proposed GASM and these state-of-the-art, which suggests that GSAM is very solid to address the occlusion problem; (2) The proposed GASM outperforms AMC-SWM, PCB, MaskReID, SPReID, PABR, DSR and FPR on Crowd REID dataset. Such a result justifies the fact that GASM can reduce the influence of the partial body of other persons, making the network only focus on foreground person part; (3) The gap between GASM and AMC-SWM, PCB are significant on the two datasets. Compared to PCB: GASM increases from 14.1% to 32.4% and from 41.3% to 74.5% at rank-1 accuracy on Crowd REID and Occluded REID when we use Market1501 dataset to train the model. The results suggest that it is difficult to address occlusion problem since it fuses both occlusion/background part feature and human part feature to the final feature.; (4) PABR and FPR achieve comparable results (24.3%, 67.1% and 30.2%, 78.3% at rank-1 accuracy) on the two datasets because pose estimation heatmaps used in PABR and foreground-aware network can alleviate the influence the background; (5) GASM performs better than MaskReID due to eliminating the background-bias is not conducive to person Re-ID; (6) Although MaskReID and PABR are well suited for addressing occlusion problem, they depend on external models such segmentation network and pose estimation network during the inference. Therefore, the forward inference is inefficient.

As discussed above, GASM is an occlusion-aware approach that can both address background-bias, occlusion object, and occlusion partial body by assigning them small weights. Furthermore, GSAM is an adaptive local matching approach that can address misalignment person image.

4.4   Non-occluded Person Re-identification

We also experiment on non-occluded person datasets: Market1501, DukeMTMC-reID, and MSMT17 to test the generalizability of our proposed approach.

Results on Market1501. Comparisons between GSAM and 11 state-of-the-art: PCB [23], MasKReID [15], SPReID [8], PABR [21], DSR [4] and FPR [6], OSNet [31], ABDNet [1], CAR [32] and P^2-Net [3]. We only conduct a single query experiment. The results are shown in Table 2, which suggests that the

Table 2. Performance comparison on Market1501, DukeMTMC and MSMT17 datasets.

Method	Market1501	DukeMTMC	MSMT17
PCB [23]	92.3 (77.4)	81.8 (66.1)	-
PCB+RPP [23]	93.8 (81.6)	83.3 (69.2)	-
SPReID [8]	92.5 (81.3)	83.3 (68.8)	-
MaskReID [15]	90.0 (75.3)	-	-
PABR [21]	90.2 (76.0)	82.1 (64.2)	-
OSNet [31]	94.8 (84.9)	88.6 (73.5)	78.7 (52.9)
ABDNet [21]	95.6 (88.3)	89.0 (78.6)	82.3 (60.8)
CAR [32]	96.1 (84.7)	86.3 (73.1)	-
P^2-Net [3]	95.2 (85.6)	86.5 (73.1)	-
DSR [4]	94.7 (85.8)	88.1 (77.1)	-
FPR [6]	95.4 (86.6)	88.6 (78.4)	-
Baseline	94.8 (83.4)	87.3 (73.7)	77.3 (49.4)
GASM	95.3 (84.7)	88.3 (74.4)	79.5 (52.5)

proposed GSAM achieves competitive performance on all evaluation criteria. It is noted that: (1) The gaps between our results and baseline model (ResNet-50+Triplet loss + softmax cross-entropy loss) are significant: GASM increases from 94.8% to 95.3% at rank-1 accuracy and from 83.4% to 84.7% at mAP accuracy, which fully suggests that guided adaptive spatial matching is more effective than only using global feature matching. GASM can reduce the influence of background for cross-camera person Re-ID; (2) Benefit from guided saliency feature learning based on external human segmentation model and pose estimation model, GSAM can reduce the influence of background. Besides, adaptive spatial matching effectively addresses the misalignment problem; (3) Contributed by exacting human semantic parsing and pose estimation, SPReID, PABR, and P^2-Net achieves the competitive accuracy. However, SPReID, PABR, and P^2-Net rely on excellent human segmentation model and pose estimation during the inference term. GASM place a huge advantage over these mask-guided and pose-guided approaches since it does not depend on external cue models during the inference term; (4) Although attention-based approaches OSNet, ABDNet and CAR improve the performance of person Re-ID, only using self-attention mechanism easily result in unstable of these methods due to partial body occlusion.

Results on DukeMTMC-reID. Person Re-ID results on DukeMTMC-reID are given in Table 2. This dataset is challenging because the person bounding box size varies drastically across different camera views, which naturally suits the proposed GASM. We report the results of PCB, MasKReID, SPReID, PABR, DSR, FPR, OSNet, ABDNet, CAR and P^2-Net. The results show that GASM achieves 88.1% at rank-1 accuracy and 74.4% mAP accuracy. Besides, GASM

Table 3. Performance comparison on Cross-domain person Re-ID.

Method	M→D	M→MS	D→M	D→MS	MS→M	MS→D
Baseline	54.3 (34.8)	22.2 (7.5)	61.6 (29.6)	26.8 (8.7)	64.7 (43.3)	64.6 (33.8)
GASM	56.4 (36.5)	27.8 (9.5)	67.2 (34.8)	32.8 (10.4)	68.4 (49.1)	68.3 (35.8)

beats the spatial feature reconstruction method DSR by 0.3% at the rank-1 accuracy. However, GASM performs worse than FPR due to pyramid pooling used in FPR can cope with scale variations to some extent.

Results on MSMT17. Very few methods report the result on this dataset since it is recently released. Except for PCB, MasKReID, SPReID, PABR, other comparison methods have reported the result on MSMT17. The results show that the proposed GASM yields comparable results both at the rank-1 and mAP metrics.

As discussed above, GASM can achieve competitive performance on the three benchmark datasets. Referring to the results of occluded person Re-ID experimental result, our proposed GASM can both address occluded person Re-ID and non-occluded person Re-ID. Since these three datasets are collected in non-crowded scenes, it cannot show its superiority.

4.5 Cross-domain Person Re-identification

To verify the effectiveness of GASM in cross-domain person Re-ID, we conduct several cross-domain Re-ID experiments including M→D, M→MS, D→M, D→MS, MS→M and MS→D (M→D means that train model with Market1501 and test model with DukeMTMC-reID). More remarkable, we train a model using source-domain dataset, and then directly test on target-domain dataset without extra processing like finetuning and GAN on target-domain dataset. We only compare our proposed GASM against a baseline model (the baseline model is based on ResNet-50). Table 3 shows the results of cross-domain Re-ID. It is noted that GASM has lager superiority for cross-domain testing, improving rank-1 accuracy by 2.1%, 5.6%, 5.6%, 6.0%, 3.7% and 3.7% for M→D, M→MS, D→M, D→MS, MS→M and Ms→D, respectively. Such results also suggest that GASM improves the performance of cross-domain Re-ID by guided saliency feature learning. It is well known that the differences between different datasets mainly come from background, content, and camera parameters, GASM is capable of eliminating the background-bais to further improve the performance of person Re-ID.

In summary, we provide a good baseline for cross-domain person Re-ID and unsupervised person Re-ID.

4.6 Ablation Study

In this subsection, we aim to thoroughly analyze the effectiveness of each component in our Guided Saliency Feature Learning framework. Four different networks

Table 4. The performance of person Re-ID using different components.

Market1501 train	Market1501	DukeMTMC	MSMT17	Crowd REID	Occluded REID
Baseline	94.8 (83.8)	54.3 (34.8)	22.18 (7.5)	16.7 (16.4)	60.2 (57.0)
+mask	94.5 (84.1)	55.3 (35.2)	27.1 (9.3)	32.2 (30.4)	74.1 (64.3)
+pose	95.1 (84.3)	56.1 (35.7)	26.1 (9.0)	30.0 (30.4)	74.5 (65.6)
+pose, +mask	95.3 (84.7)	56.4 (36.5)	79.5 (52.5)	32.4 (31.1)	74.5 (56.6)
DukeMTMC train	Market1501	DukeMTMC	MSMT17	Crowd REID	Occluded REID
Baseline	61.6 (29.6)	87.3 (73.68)	26.8 (8.7)	26.6 (24.3)	66.1 (60.2)
+mask	65.6 (32.8)	87.8 (72.4)	31.5 (9.9)	32.2 (28.7)	75.5 (68.5)
+pose	67.2 (33.8)	87.9 (73.9)	32.5 (10.2)	34.3 (31.1)	75.4 (67.4)
+pose, +mask	67.2 (34.2)	88.1 (74.2)	32.8 (10.4)	35.8 (31.8)	76.5 (67.8)
MSMT17 train	Market1501	DukeMTMC	MSMT17	Crowd REID	Occluded REID
Baseline	64.6 (33.8)	64.7 (43.3)	77.3 (49.4)	44.0 (41.2)	74.6 (69.2)
+mask	67.9 (35.5)	67.9 (47.7)	79.3 (51.7)	50.9 (47.4)	78.9 (72.0)
+pose	67.2 (34.5)	67.7 (47.5)	78.5 (51.7)	50.4 (47.0)	78.4 (72.9)
+pose, +mask	68.2 (35.9)	68.3 (49.1)	79.7 (52.5)	51.5 (47.1)	80.3 (73.1)

including FCN + average pooling (baseline), FCN + pose layer, FCN + mask layer, and FCN + pose layer + mask + layer are designed, and test on occluded datasets and three benchmark datasets, respectively. Besides, we also conduct cross-domain person Re-ID experiments using the four networks.

Table 4 shows the experimental results using Market1501, DukeMTMC-reID and MSMT17. We find the results on three datasets are similar, FCN + pose layer + mask layer outperforms better than other three designed networks on different tasks because pose-guided heatmap combined with mask-guided heatmap can output more accurate saliency heatmap. Pose-guided heatmap only focuses on human keypoints, the weights around person keypoints are relatively large while the weights beyond person keypoints are relatively small. As for Mask-guided heatmap, it only focuses on the person part, but it cannot address partial occlusion body contamination. It is also noted that: (1) FCN + average pooling performs worse than other three networks on different tasks due to failing to address occlusion and background; (2) Mask-guided heatmap and pose-guided heatmap are complementary, mask-guided heatmap helps to find the person part but cannot address partial body occlusion; pose-guided heatmap helps to find the person to be identified but fails to address every part of person image. In summary, the two modules work well together to occluded person Re-ID, non-occluded person Re-ID and cross-domain person Re-ID.

5   Conclusion

We have proposed a novel approach called Guided Adaptive Spatial Matching to person Re-ID in crowded scenes. The proposed method design a pose-guided layer and mask-guide layer to learn the saliency heatmap to further guide feature learning. Besides, we proposed a novel matching approach called Guided Adaptive Spatial Matching (GASM) where each spatial feature in the query can find the most similar spatial features of a person in a gallery to match. Remarkably, saliency heatmap used in spatial matching can solve partial body occlusion and eliminate background-bais. Experimental results on Crowd REID and Occluded REID dataset validate that GSAM can address the occlusion problem. Besides, GSAM also shows its advantage in cross-domain by eliminating background-bais. Additionally, the proposed method is also competitive on the benchmark person datasets.

Acknowledgement. Special thanks to Xingyu Liao who support our experiments, and thanks to FastReID: https://github.com/JDAI-CV/fast-reid [5] that provides with codebase for GASM. This work is partially supported by Beijing Academy of Artificial Intelligence (BAAI).

References

1. Chen, T., et al.: ABD-NET: attentive but diverse person re-identification. In: Proceedings of the IEEE International Conference on Computer Vision (CVPR) (2019)
2. Fan, X., Luo, H., Zhang, X., He, L., Zhang, C., Jiang, W.: SCPNet: spatial-channel parallelism network for joint holistic and partial person re-identification. In: Jawahar, C.V., Li, H., Mori, G., Schindler, K. (eds.) ACCV 2018. LNCS, vol. 11362, pp. 19–34. Springer, Cham (2019). https://doi.org/10.1007/978-3-030-20890-5_2
3. Guo, J., Yuan, Y., Huang, L., Zhang, C., Yao, J.G., Han, K.: Beyond human parts: dual part-aligned representations for person re-identification. In: Proceedings of the IEEE International Conference on Computer Vision (ICCV) (2019)
4. He, L., Liang, J., Li, H., Sun, Z.: Deep spatial feature reconstruction for partial person re-identification: Alignment-free approach. In: Proceedings of the IEEE Conference on Computer Vision and Pattern Recognition (CVPR), pp. 7073–7082 (2018)
5. He, L., Liao, X., Liu, W., Liu, X., Cheng, P., Mei, T.: FastReID: a pytorch toolbox for general instance re-identification. arXiv preprint arXiv:2006.02631 (2020)
6. He, L., Wang, Y., Liu, W., Zhao, H., Sun, Z., Feng, J.: Foreground-aware pyramid reconstruction for alignment-free occluded person re-identification. In: Proceedings of the IEEE International Conference on Computer Vision (ICCV) (2019)
7. Jiaxuan Zhuo, Zeyu Chen, J.L.G.W.: Occluded person re-identification. In: IEEE International Conference on Multimedia and Expo (ICME) (2018)
8. Kalayeh, M.M., Basaran, E., Gökmen, M., Kamasak, M.E., Shah, M.: Human semantic parsing for person re-identification. In: Proceedings of the IEEE Conference on Computer Vision and Pattern Recognition (CVPR), pp. 1062–1071 (2018)
9. Li, S., Liu, X., Liu, W., Ma, H., Zhang, H.: A discriminative null space based deep learning approach for person re-identification. In: International Conference on Cloud Computing and Intelligence Systems (CCIS) (2016)
10. Li, W., Zhu, X., Gong, S.: Harmonious attention network for person re-identification. In: Proceedings of the IEEE Conference on Computer Vision and Pattern Recognition (CVPR) (2018)
11. Liu, W., Zhang, C., Ma, H., Li, S.: Learning efficient spatial-temporal gait features with deep learning for human identification. Neuroinformatics **16**(3–4), 457–471 (2018)
12. Long, X., Gan, C., De Melo, G., Wu, J., Liu, X., Wen, S.: Attention clusters: purely attention based local feature integration for video classification. In: Proceedings of the IEEE Conference on Computer Vision and Pattern Recognition (CVPR) (2018)

13. Luo, H., Jiang, W., Fan, X., Zhang, C.: STNReID: deep convolutional networks with pairwise spatial transformer networks for partial person re-identification. IEEE Trans. Multimed. (T-MM) (2020)
14. Miao, J., Wu, Y., Liu, P., Ding, Y., Yang, Y.: Pose-guided feature alignment for occluded person re-identification. In: Proceedings of the IEEE International Conference on Computer Vision (ICCV) (2019)
15. Qi, L., Huo, J., Wang, L., Shi, Y., Gao, Y.: MaskReID: a mask based deep ranking neural network for person re-identification. arXiv preprint arXiv:1804.03864 (2018)
16. Ren, M., He, L., Li, H., Liu, Y., Sun, Z., Tan, T.: Robust partial person re-identification based on similarity-guided sparse representation. In: Chinese Conference on Biometric Recognition (CCBR) (2017)
17. Ristani, E., Solera, F., Zou, R., Cucchiara, R., Tomasi, C.: Performance measures and a data set for multi-target, multi-camera tracking. In: Hua, G., Jégou, H. (eds.) ECCV 2016. LNCS, vol. 9914, pp. 17–35. Springer, Cham (2016). https://doi.org/10.1007/978-3-319-48881-3_2
18. Si, J., et al.: Dual attention matching network for context-aware feature sequence based person re-identification. arXiv preprint arXiv:1803.09937 (2018)
19. Song, C., Huang, Y., Ouyang, W., Wang, L.: Mask-guided contrastive attention model for person re-identification. In: Proceedings of the IEEE Conference on Computer Vision and Pattern Recognition (CVPR), pp. 1179–1188 (2018)
20. Su, C., Li, J., Zhang, S., Xing, J., Gao, W., Tian, Q.: Pose-driven deep convolutional model for person re-identification. In: IEEE International Conference on Computer Vision (ICCV), pp. 3980–3989 (2017)
21. Suh, Y., Wang, J., Tang, S., Mei, T., Lee, K.M.: Part-aligned bilinear representations for person re-identification. arXiv preprint arXiv:1804.07094 (2018)
22. Sun, Y., et al.: Perceive where to focus: Learning visibility-aware part-level features for partial person re-identification. In: Proceedings of the IEEE Conference on Computer Vision and Pattern Recognition (CVPR) (2019)
23. Sun, Y., Zheng, L., Yang, Y., Tian, Q., Wang, S.: Beyond part models: person retrieval with refined part pooling. arXiv preprint arXiv:1711.09349 (2017)
24. Wei, L., Zhang, S., Gao, W., Tian, Q.: Person transfer GAN to bridge domain gap for person re-identification. In: Proceedings of the IEEE Conference on Computer Vision and Pattern Recognition (CVPR) (2018)
25. Xu, J., Zhao, R., Zhu, F., Wang, H., Ouyang, W.: Attention-aware compositional network for person re-identification. In: Proceedings of the IEEE Conference on Computer Vision and Pattern Recognition (CVPR) (2018)
26. Zhao, H., Shi, J., Qi, X., Wang, X., Jia, J.: Pyramid scene parsing network. In: Proceedings of the IEEE Conference on Computer Vision and Pattern Recognition (CVPR) (2017)
27. Zheng, L., Shen, L., Tian, L., Wang, S., Wang, J., Tian, Q.: Scalable person re-identification: a benchmark. In: IEEE Conference on Computer Vision and Pattern Recognition (CVPR) (2015)
28. Zheng, W.S., Li, X., Xiang, T., Liao, S., Lai, J., Gong, S.: Partial person re-identification. In: IEEE International Conference on Computer Vision (ICCV) (2015)
29. Zheng, Z., Zheng, L., Yang, Y.: Pedestrian alignment network for large-scale person re-identification. arXiv preprint arXiv:1707.00408 (2017)
30. Zheng, Z., Zheng, L., Yang, Y.: Unlabeled samples generated by GAN improve the person re-identification baseline in vitro. In: Proceedings of the IEEE Conference on Computer Vision and Pattern Recognition (CVPR), pp. 3754–3762 (2017)

31. Zhou, K., Yang, Y., Cavallaro, A., Xiang, T.: Omni-scale feature learning for person re-identification. In: Proceedings of the IEEE International Conference on Computer Vision (ICCV) (2019)
32. Zhou, S., Wang, F., Huang, Z., Wang, J.: Discriminative feature learning with consistent attention regularization for person re-identification. In: Proceedings of the IEEE International Conference on Computer Vision (ICCV) (2019)
33. Zhou, X., Wang, D., Krähenbühl, P.: Objects as points. arXiv preprint arXiv:1904.07850 (2019)

Asymmetric Two-Stream Architecture for Accurate RGB-D Saliency Detection

Miao Zhang[1], Sun Xiao Fei[1], Jie Liu[1], Shuang Xu[1], Yongri Piao[1(✉)],
and Huchuan Lu[1,2]

[1] Dalian University of Technology, Dalian, China
{miaozhang,yrpiao,lhchuan}@dlut.edu.cn,
{xiaofeisun,1605721375,sxu1997}@mail.dlut.edu.cn
[2] Pengcheng Lab, Shenzhen, China
https://github.com/OIPLab-DUT/ATSA

Abstract. Most existing RGB-D saliency detection methods adopt symmetric two-stream architectures for learning discriminative RGB and depth representations. In fact, there is another level of ambiguity that is often overlooked: if RGB and depth data are necessary to fit into the same network. In this paper, we propose an asymmetric two-stream architecture taking account of the inherent differences between RGB and depth data for saliency detection. First, we design a flow ladder module (FLM) for the RGB stream to fully extract global and local information while maintaining the saliency details. This is achieved by constructing four detail-transfer branches, each of which preserves the detail information and receives global location information from representations of other vertical parallel branches in an evolutionary way. Second, we propose a novel depth attention module (DAM) to ensure depth features with high discriminative power in location and spatial structure being effectively utilized when combined with RGB features in challenging scenes. The depth features can also discriminatively guide the RGB features via our proposed DAM to precisely locate the salient objects. Extensive experiments demonstrate that our method achieves superior performance over 13 state-of-the-art RGB-D approaches on the 7 datasets. Our code will be publicly available.

Keywords: Saliency detection · Flow ladder · Depth attention

1 Introduction

Salient object detection, which involves identifying the visually interesting regions, is a well-researched domain of computer vision. It serves as an essential pre-processing step for various visual tasks such as image retrieval [7,15,17,28], visual tracking [2,20,38], object segmentation [12,39,40,42,43], object recognition [10,36,37], and therefore makes an important contribution towards sustainable development.

S. X. Fei and J. Liu—Denotes equal contributions.

© Springer Nature Switzerland AG 2020
A. Vedaldi et al. (Eds.): ECCV 2020, LNCS 12373, pp. 374–390, 2020.
https://doi.org/10.1007/978-3-030-58604-1_23

A majority of existing works [21,26] for saliency detection focus on operating RGB images. While RGB-based saliency detection methods have achieved great success, appearance features in RGB data are less predictive to some challenging scenes, such as multiple or transparent objects, similar foreground and background, complex background, low-intensity environment, etc.

The depth cue has the preponderance of discriminative power in location and spatial structure, which has been proved beneficial to accurate saliency prediction [35]. Moreover, the paired depth data for RGB natural images are widely available with the advent of depth sensors, e.g., Kinect and Lytro Illum. Consequently, using depth information gains growing interests in saliency detection.

Most RGB-D-based methods utilize symmetric two-stream architectures for extracting RGB and depth features [4,6,18,32]. However, we observe that while RGB data contain more information such as color, texture, contour, as well as limited location, grayscale depth data provide more information such as spatial structure and 3D layout. In consequence, a symmetric two-stream network may overlook the inherent differences of RGB and depth data. Asymmetric architectures have been adopted in few works to extract RGB and depth features, taking the differences between two modalities into account. Zhu et al. [48] present an architecture composed of a master network for processing RGB values, and a subnetwork making full use of depth cues, which incorporates depth-based features into the master network via direct concatenation. Zhao et al. [46] incorporate the contrast prior to enhance the depth maps and then

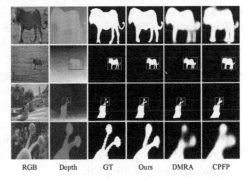

RGB   Depth   GT   Ours   DMRA   CPFP

Fig. 1. The comparison of predicted maps between our method and two top-ranking RGB-D-based methods on salient objects details, i.e., DMRA [32], CPFP [46]. The 1st row and the 4th row are the enlarged images of the red box area of the middle two rows, which show superior performance of our method on saliency details

integrate them into the RGB stream for saliency detection. However, simple fusion strategies like direct concatenation or summation are less adaptive to locate the salient objects due to myriad possibilities of salient objects positions in the real world. Overall, these above methods overlook the fact that depth cue contributes differently to the salient object prediction in various scenes. Furthermore, existing RGB-D methods inevitably suffer from detail information loss [16,41] for adopting strides and pooling operations in the RGB and depth streams. An intuitive solution is to use skip-connections [22] or short-connections [21] for reconstructing the detail information. Although these strategies have brought satisfactory improvements, they remain restrictive to predict the complete structures with fine details.

Building on the above observation, we strive to take a further step towards the goal of accurate saliency detection with an asymmetric two-stream model. **The primary challenge** towards this goal is how to effectively extract rich global context information while preserving local saliency details. **The second challenge** is how to effectively utilize the discriminative power of depth features to guide the RGB features for locating salient objects accurately.

To confront these challenges, we propose an asymmetric two-stream architecture as illustrated in Fig. 2. Concretely, our contributions are:

- We design a flow ladder module (FLM) and a lightweight depth network (DepthNet) with a small model size of 6.7MB. Instead of adopting skip-connections or short-connections, our FLM can effectively extract local detail information (see Fig. 1) and global context information through a local-global evolutionary fusion flow for accurate saliency detection.
- We propose a novel depth attention module (DAM) to ensure that the depth features can effectively guide the RGB features by using the discriminative power of depth cues. Its effectiveness has been experimentally verified (see Table 4).
- Furthermore, we conduct extensive experiments on 7 datasets and demonstrate that our method achieves consistently superior performance over 13 state-of-the-art RGB-D approaches in terms of 4 evaluation metrics. Numerically, our approach reduces the MAE performance by nearly 33% on DUT-RGBD dataset. In addition, our method minimizes the model size by 33% compared with the existing minimum method (PDNet) and achieves Top-2 running speed of 46 FPS.

2   Related Work

RGB-D Saliency Detection. Although many RGB-based saliency detection methods have achieved appealing performance [16,29,33,44,45,47], they may not accurately detect the salient area because the appearance features in RGB data are less predictive when encountering with some complex scenes, such as low-contrast scenes, transparent objects, foreground sharing similar contents with background, multiple objects, and complex backgrounds. With the advent of consumer-grade depth cameras such as Kinect cameras, light field cameras and lidars, depth cues with a wealth of geometric and structural information is widely used in salient object detection (SOD).

Existing RGB-D saliency detection methods can be generally classified into two categories: **Traditional methods** [8,9,11,24,31,35,49,50]. Ren *et al.* [35] propose a two-stage RGB-D saliency detection framework using the validity of global priors. Lang *et al.* [24] introduce the depth prior into the saliency detection model to improve detection performance. Desingh *et al.* [11] use a non-linear regression to combine the RGB-D saliency detection model with the RGB model to measure the saliency values. **CNNs-based methods** [4–6,18,32,34,46,48]. To better mine salient information in challenging scenes, some CNNs-based methods combine depth information with RGB information for more accurate

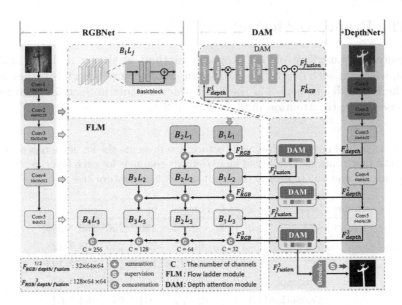

Fig. 2. The overall architecture of our proposed approach. Our asymmetric architecture consists of three parts, i.e., the RGBNet, the DAM and the lightweight DepthNet. The RGBNet includes a VGG-19 backbone and a flow ladder module. For depth stream, we also employ the same backbone of the RGBNet. The black arrows represent the information flows

results. Practices and theories that lead to symmetric two-stream architectures which extract RGB and depth representations equally have been studied for a long time [4–6,18,32]. Han *et al.* [18] design a symmetric architecture for fusing the deep representations of depth and RGB views automatically to obtain the final saliency map. Chen *et al.* [6] utilize two-stream CNNs-based models for introducing cross-model interactions in multiple layers by direct summation. Recently, several asymmetric architectures are proposed for processing different data types [46,48]. Zhao *et al.* [46] use the enhanced depth information as an auxiliary cue and adopt a pyramid decoding structure to obtain more accurate salient regions.

Because of the inherent differences between RGB and depth information, classic symmetric two-stream architectures and simple fusion strategies may work their ways down to inaccurate prediction. Besides, the strides and pooling operations adopted in existing RGB-D-based methods for downsampling inevitably result in information loss. To address the above-mentioned issues, in this work, we design an asymmetric network and ably fuse RGB and depth information by a depth attention mechanism for precise saliency detection.

3   The Proposed Method

The overall architecture of our proposed method is shown in Fig. 2. In this section, we begin with describing the overall architecture in Sect. 3.1, then introduce the DepthNet in Sect. 3.2, the flow ladder module in Sect. 3.3, and finally the proposed depth attention module in Sect. 3.4.

Table 1. Details of our DepthNet architecture, k represents the kernel, s represents the stride, chns represents the number of input/output channels for each layer, p represents the padding, in and out represent the input and output feature size

Name	Layer	k	s	p	chns	in	out
Conv1	*1	3	1	1	3/64	256 * 256	256 * 256
	Maxpool	-	2	-	64/64	256 * 256	128 * 128
Conv2	*1	3	1	1	64/128	128 * 128	128 * 128
	Maxpool	-	2	-	128/128	128 * 128	64 * 64
	Transition1	3	1	1	128/32	64 * 64	64 * 64
Conv3	*4	3	1	1	32/32	64 * 64	64 * 64
		3	1	1	32/32	64 * 64	64 * 64
Conv4	*4	3	1	1	32/32	64 * 64	64 * 64
		3	1	1	32/32	64 * 64	64 * 64
	Transition2	3	1	1	32/128	64 * 64	64 * 64
Conv5	*4	3	1	1	128/128	64 * 64	64 * 64
		3	1	1	128/128	64 * 64	64 * 64

3.1   The Overall Architecture

Considering that most RGB-D-based methods utilizing symmetric two-stream architectures overlook the inherent differences between RGB and depth data, we propose an asymmetric two-stream architecture, as illustrated in Fig. 2. Our two-stream architecture includes a lightweight depth stream and a RGB stream with a flow ladder module, namely DepthNet and RGBNet, respectively. As for the depth stream, we design a lightweight architecture as shown in Table 1. Then the extracted depth features are fed into the RGB stream through a depth attention mechanism (DAM, see Fig. 3) to generate complementary features with affluent information of location and spatial structure. For the RGB stream, we adopt the commonly used architecture VGG-19 as our baseline. Based on this baseline, we propose a novel flow ladder module (FLM) to preserve the detail information as well as receive global location information from representations of other vertical parallel branches in an evolutionary way, which benefits locating salient regions and achieves considerable performance gains.

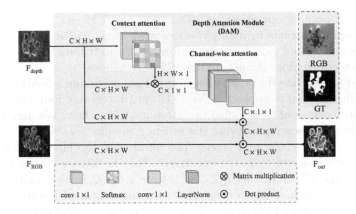

Fig. 3. Illustration of the depth attention module (DAM). The images above F_{out} are the corresponding original RGB image and ground truth

3.2 DepthNet

Compared with RGB data which contains richer color and texture information, depth cues focus on spatial location information. A large number of parameters in a complex depth extraction network are redundant, thus we consider that is unnecessary to process depth data with a complex network as large as RGBNet. In addition, the ablation experiments on symmetric and asymmetric architectures in Sect. 4.3 also confirm our claim. As illustrated in Fig. 2, we adopt a detail-transfer architecture for the depth stream (see Table 1 for detailed specification) and take the original depth maps as input. Our DepthNet transfers detail information in the whole architecture to capture fine spatial details. Considering the differences between RGB and depth data, numerous redundant channels of depth features are unnecessary. Therefore, we prune the number of feature channels to 32 in Conv3, 4 and 128 in final Conv, which further achieves a more lightweight DepthNet with a model size of 6.7MB.

3.3 RGBNet

Deeper networks are able to extract richer high-level information such as location and semantic information, but strides and pooling operations widely used in existing RGB-D-based methods may cause detail information loss, such as boundary, small object, for saliency detection. A straightforward solution to this issue is combining the low-level features with the high-level features by skip-connections [22]. However, the low-level features take a less discriminative and predictive power for complex scenes, which has trouble contributing to accurate saliency detection. Hence, we design a novel RGBNet consisting of a VGG backbone for fair comparison and a flow ladder model to preserve the local detail information by constructing four detail-transfer branches and fuse the global location information in an evolutionary way. In order to fit our task, we truncate the last three fully-connected layers and maintain the five convolution blocks as well as all pooling operations of VGG-19. The FLM can preserve the resolution of representations in multiple scales and levels, ensuring that the local detail information and global location information contribute to the precision of saliency detection. More details are described as follows.

In order to alleviate the detail information loss, we design a flow ladder model (FLM). This module is applied in VGG-19 and integrates four detail-transfer branches in the way of local-global evolutionary fusion flow. We design **detail-transfer branches** for preserving the saliency details. As shown in Fig. 2, the first two branches consist of 3 layers. The number of the layers in the 3rd and 4th branch is decreased to 2, 1, respectively. Specifically, we simply denote the jth layer of the ith branch as B_iL_j, $i\epsilon[1,4], j\epsilon[1,3]$. B_iL_j is composed of four *basicblocks* [19], each of which consists of two convolutional layers as shown in the top of Fig. 2. Our FLM consists of 4 evolved detail-transfer branches. Instead of adopting strides and pooling operations, our FLM preserves the resolution of representations with more details in each branch by employing convolutional operations with 1 * 1 stride.

We design a novel **local-global evolutionary fusion flow** for integrating multi-scale local and global features extracted from detail-transfer branches. Each branch receives rich information from other vertical parallel representations through our local-global evolutionary fusion flow. In this way, rich global context representations are generated while more local saliency details are preserved. Specifically, the representations of the deeper branches are fused into the shallower branches by upsampling and summation operations as well as the representations of the shallower branches are fused into the deeper branches by downsampling and summation operations as shown in the FLM of Fig. 2. Through the evolution between different branches (shown in Fig. 2), the local detail information and the global context information are effectively combined, which benefits the precision of saliency detection. The whole fusion process is described as the following equations:

$$B_iL_j = \begin{cases} trans(Conv2) & i=1, j=1 \\ trans(Conv(i+1)) & i=j+1, j\epsilon[1,3] \\ \sum_{n=1}^{j} f(B_nL_{j-1}) & i\epsilon[1,j], j\epsilon[2,3] \end{cases} \tag{1}$$

$$F_{RGB}^j = \sum_{n=1}^{j+1} f(B_nL_j) \quad j\epsilon[1,2], \tag{2}$$

$$F_{RGB}^3 = cat(f(B_nL_3)) \quad n\epsilon[1,4], \tag{3}$$

where B_i and L_j denote the ith branch and j^{th} layer, respectively. $f(\cdot)$ denotes $n-i$ times up-sampled when $n > i$ and $i-n$ times down-sampled when $n < i$. And when n is equal to i, $f(\cdot)$ means no operation. $Conv(i)$ means the output features of the ith Conv block in VGG-19 and $trans(\cdot)$ is operated by a convolutional layer to realize the transformation of the number of channels. $cat(\cdot)$ denotes concatenating all features together. The final output of our LFM namely F_{RGB}^3 is a concatenation of multi-scale features extracted from four branches. In

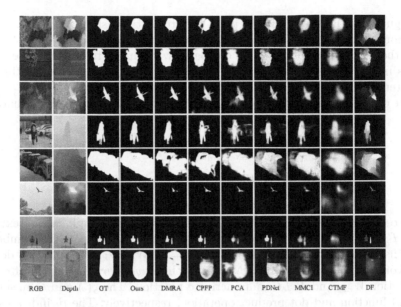

RGB   Depth   GT   Ours   DMRA   CPFP   PCA   PDNet   MMCI   CTMF   DF

Fig. 4. Comparisons of ours with state-of-the-art CNNs-based methods. Those methods are top ranking ones in quantitative evaluation. Obviously, our results are more consistent with the ground truths (GT), especially in complex scenes

conclusion, the features with local and global information are transferred to the parallel branches in an evolutionary way. Our proposed LFM can not only alleviate the object detail information loss but also effectively integrate multi-scale and multi-level features for precise saliency prediction.

3.4 Depth Attention Module

Changes in statistics of object positions in the real world makes linear fusion strategies of RGB and depth data less adaptive to complex scenes. To take full advantage of the depth cues with the discriminative power in location and spatial structure, we design a depth attention module to adaptively fuse the RGB and depth representations as shown in Fig. 3. Firstly, the depth features contain abundant spatial and structural information. We utilize the context attention block which contains a 1 * 1 convolutional layer W_k and a softmax function for extracting the salient location cues more precisely, instead of applying simple fusion like summation or concatenation. Then a matrix multiplication operation is adopted to aggregate all location features together to generate attention weights of each channel i (*i.e.*, α_i) for capturing pixel-wise spatial dependencies. Moreover, the degree of response to the salient regions varies between features of different channels. Thus we adopt a channel-wise attention block which contains two 1 * 1 convolutional layers W_c and a LayerNorm function to capture the interdependencies between channels, and further achieves a weighted depth feature β. Then we adopt dot product operation to fuse β into the RGB stream, which helps guide the RGB features at pixel-level to distinguish the foreground and background thoroughly. Furthermore, the ablation experiments in Sect. 4.3 also verify the effectiveness of our DAM compared with simple fusion. And the visual results in Fig. 6(b) also prove that the salient regions are emphasized through the attention mechanism.

The details of these three blocks can be formulated as the following equations:

$$\alpha_i = \sum_{j=1}^{N_p} \frac{e^{W_k F_d^j}}{\sum_{m=1}^{N_p} e^{W_k F_d^m}} F_d^j, \tag{4}$$

$$\beta_i = \varsigma(W_{c2} ReLU(LN(W_{c1}\alpha_i)) \odot F_d), \tag{5}$$

$$F_{fusion} = \varsigma(F_{RGB} \odot \beta), \tag{6}$$

where α_i denotes the weight of the ith channel to obtain the global context features. F_d^j means the jth position in depth feature F_{depth}. N_p is the number of positions in the depth feature map (e.g., $N_p = H \cdot W$). W_k, W_{c1} and W_{c2} denote $1 * 1$ convolutional operations. LN denotes the $LayerNorm$ operation after the convolution W_{c1}, and $ReLU$ is an activate function. The $\varsigma(\cdot)$ and $\odot$ mean the sigmoid function and dot product operation, respectively. The β_i indicates the depth pixel-wise attention map of ith channel of F_{RGB}. F_{RGB} and F_{fusion} represent the input RGB feature and the output feature of the DAM, respectively. The F_{fusion} can be calculated as a DAM output with much more effective depth-induced context-aware attention features. Furthermore, experiments in Sect. 4.3 show that our DAM is capable of fusing depth features discriminatively and filtering out features which are guided by depth cues in mistake.

As illustrated in Fig. 3, the inputs of our DAM are F_{RGB}^i and F_{Depth}^i extracted from our LFM and DepthNet, respectively, $i = 1, 2, 3$. At the end, a simple decoder is adopted for supervision. The decoder module contains two bilinear upsample functions, each of which is followed by 3 convolutional layers. The total loss L can be represented as:

$$L = l_f\{Decoder(F_{fusion}^3); gt\}, \tag{7}$$

where F_{fusion}^3 represents the output fusion feature of the third DAM and gt means the ground-truth map. The cross-entropy loss l_f can be computed as:

$$l_f\{\hat{y}; y\} = ylog\hat{y} + (1 - y)log(1 - \hat{y}), \tag{8}$$

where y and $\hat{y}$ denote the saliency ground-truth map and the predicted map, respectively.

4 Experiments

4.1 Dataset

We perform our experiments on 7 public RGB-D datasets for fair comparisons, i.e., NJUD [23], NLPR [31], RGBD135 [8], STEREO [30], LFSD [27], DUT-RGBD [32], SSD [25]. We split those datasets as [4,6,18] to guarantee fair comparisons. We randomly select 800 samples from DUT-RGBD, 1485 samples from

Table 2. Quantitative comparisons of E-measure (E_γ), S-measure (S_λ), F-measure (F_β) and MAE (M) on 7 widely-used RGB-D datasets. The best three results are shown in **boldface**, *bolditalic*, *italic* fonts respectively. From top to bottom: the latest CNNs-based RGB-D methods and traditional RGB-D methods

Method	Years	Backbone	DUT-RGBD E_γ↑	S_λ↑	F_β↑	M↓	NJUD E_γ↑	S_λ↑	F_β↑	M↓	NLPR E_γ↑	S_λ↑	F_β↑	M↓	SSD E_γ↑	S_λ↑
Ours	-	VGG-19	**0.948**	**0.918**	**0.920**	**0.032**	**0.921**	**0.901**	**0.893**	**0.040**	**0.945**	**0.907**	**0.876**	**0.028**	**0.901**	**0.860**
CPFP [46]	CVPR19	VGG-16	0.814	0.749	0.736	0.099	*0.906*	0.878	*0.877*	*0.053*	*0.924*	*0.888*	0.822	*0.036*	0.832	0.807
DMRA [32]	ICCV19	VGG-19	*0.927*	*0.888*	*0.883*	*0.048*	0.908	*0.886*	0.872	*0.051*	*0.942*	*0.899*	*0.855*	*0.031*	*0.892*	*0.857*
MMCI [6]	PR19	VGG-16	0.855	0.791	0.753	0.113	0.878	0.859	0.813	0.079	0.871	0.855	0.729	0.059	0.860	0.814
TANet [5]	TIP19	VGG-16	0.866	0.808	0.779	*0.093*	0.893	0.878	0.844	0.061	0.916	0.886	0.795	0.041	0.879	0.839
PDNet [48]	ICME19	VGG-16	0.861	0.799	0.757	0.112	0.890	*0.883*	0.832	0.062	0.876	0.835	0.740	0.064	0.813	0.802
PCA [4]	CVPR18	VGG-16	0.858	0.801	0.760	0.100	0.896	0.877	0.844	0.059	0.916	0.873	0.794	0.044	*0.883*	*0.843*
CTMF [18]	TCyb17	VGG-16	*0.884*	*0.834*	*0.792*	0.097	0.864	0.849	0.788	0.085	0.869	0.860	0.723	0.056	0.837	0.776
DF [34]	TIP17	-	0.842	0.730	0.748	0.145	0.818	0.735	0.744	0.151	0.838	0.769	0.682	0.099	0.802	0.742
MB [49]	CAIP17	-	0.691	0.607	0.577	0.156	0.643	0.534	0.492	0.202	0.814	0.714	0.637	0.089	0.633	0.499
CDCP [50]	ICCV17	-	0.794	0.687	0.633	0.159	0.751	0.673	0.673	0.181	0.785	0.724	0.591	0.114	0.714	0.604
DCMC [9]	SPL16	-	0.712	0.499	0.406	0.243	0.796	0.703	0.715	0.167	0.684	0.550	0.328	0.196	0.790	0.706
NLPR [31]	ECCV14	-	0.767	0.568	0.659	0.174	0.722	0.530	0.625	0.201	0.772	0.591	0.520	0.119	0.726	0.562
DES [8]	ICIMCS14	-	0.733	0.659	0.668	0.280	0.421	0.413	0.165	0.448	0.735	0.582	0.583	0.301	0.383	0.341

Table 3. Continuation of Table 2

Method	Years	Backbone	SSD F_β↑	M↓	STEREO E_γ↑	S_λ↑	F_β↑	M↓	LFSD E_γ↑	S_λ↑	F_β↑	M↓	RGBD135 E_γ↑	S_λ↑	F_β↑	M↓
Ours	-	VGG-19	**0.827**	**0.050**	**0.921**	**0.897**	**0.884**	**0.039**	**0.905**	**0.865**	**0.862**	**0.064**	**0.952**	**0.907**	**0.885**	**0.024**
CPFP [46]	CVPR19	VGG-16	0.725	0.082	0.897	0.871	0.827	*0.054*	0.867	0.828	0.813	*0.088*	0.927	*0.874*	0.819	*0.037*
DMRA [32]	ICCV19	VGG-19	*0.821*	*0.058*	*0.920*	*0.886*	*0.868*	*0.047*	*0.899*	*0.847*	*0.849*	0.075	*0.945*	*0.901*	*0.857*	*0.029*
MMCI [6]	PR19	VGG-16	0.748	0.082	0.890	0.856	0.812	0.080	0.840	0.787	0.779	0.132	0.899	0.847	0.750	0.064
TANet [5]	TIP19	VGG-16	0.767	*0.063*	*0.911*	0.877	*0.849*	0.060	0.845	0.801	0.794	0.111	0.916	0.858	0.782	0.045
PDNet [48]	ICME19	VGG-16	0.716	0.115	0.903	0.874	0.833	0.064	*0.872*	*0.845*	*0.824*	0.109	0.915	0.868	0.800	0.050
PCA [4]	CVPR18	VGG-16	*0.786*	0.064	0.905	*0.880*	0.845	0.061	0.846	0.800	0.794	0.112	0.909	0.845	0.763	0.049
CTMF [18]	TCyb17	VGG-16	0.709	0.100	0.870	0.853	0.786	0.087	0.851	0.796	0.781	0.120	0.907	0.863	0.765	0.055
DF [34]	TIP17	-	0.709	0.151	0.844	0.763	0.761	0.142	0.841	0.786	0.810	0.142	0.801	0.685	0.566	0.130
MB [49]	CAIP17	-	0.414	0.219	0.693	0.579	0.572	0.178	0.631	0.538	0.543	0.178	0.798	0.661	0.588	0.102
CDCP [50]	ICCVW17	-	0.524	0.219	0.801	0.727	0.680	0.149	0.737	0.658	0.634	0.199	0.806	0.706	0.583	0.119
DCMC [9]	SPL16	-	0.551	0.200	0.838	0.745	0.761	0.150	0.842	0.754	0.815	0.155	0.674	0.470	0.228	0.194
NLPR [31]	ECCV14	-	0.073	0.500	0.781	0.567	0.716	0.179	0.742	0.558	0.708	0.211	0.850	0.577	*0.857*	0.097
DES [8]	ICIMCS14	-	0.684	0.168	0.451	0.473	0.223	0.417	0.475	0.440	0.228	0.415	0.786	0.627	0.689	0.289

NJUD and 700 samples from NLPR for training. The remaining images in these 3 datasets and other 4 datasets are all for testing to verify the generalization ability of saliency models. To prevent overfitting, we additionally augment the training set by flipping, cropping and rotating those images.

4.2 Experimental Setup

Evaluation Metrics. To comprehensively evaluate various methods, we adopt 4 evaluation metrics including F-measure (F_β) [1], mean absolute error (M) [3], S-measure (S_λ) [13], E-measure (E_γ) [14]. Specifically, the F-measure can evaluate the performance integrally. The M represents the average absolute difference between the saliency map and ground truth. The S-measure which is recently proposed can evaluate the structural similarities. The E-measure can jointly capture image level statistics and local pixel matching information.

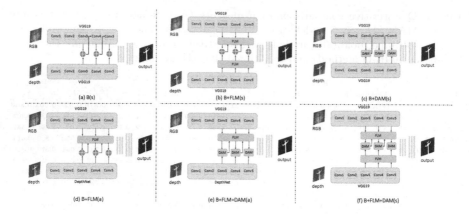

Fig. 5. Illustration of the six ablation experiments

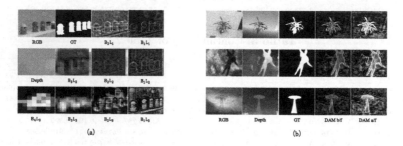

Fig. 6. (a) The visualization of the feature maps in FLM. The B_iL_j presents the output features of corresponding block in Fig. 2. (b) Visualization of the effectiveness of the DAM. The 4th (DAM b/f) and the 5th columns (DAM a/f) show the feature maps before and after adopting DAM, respectively

Implementation Details. Our method is implemented with pytorch toolbox and trained on a PC with GTX 2080Ti GPU and 16 GB memory. The input images are uniformly resized to 256 * 256. The momentum, weight decay, batch-size and learning rate of our network are set as 0.9, 0.0005, 2 and 1e-10, respectively. During training, we use softmax entropy loss described in Sect. 3.4 and the network converges after 60 epochs with mini-batch size 2.

4.3   Ablation Analysis

Effect of FLM. We adopt the commonly two-stream VGG-19 network fused by direct summation as our baseline(denoted as 'B[s]' shown in Fig. 5(a)). In order to verify the effectiveness of FLM, we employ the FLM in both the RGB and depth streams ('B+FLM[s]' shown in Fig. 5(b)). The experimental results of (a) and (b) in Table 4 clearly demonstrate that our FLM obtains impressive performance gains. Moreover, as shown in Fig. 7, we can note that after employing FLM, the saliency maps achieve sharper boundaries as well as finer structures.

Table 4. Ablation analysis on 7 datasets. The [s] and [a] following the modules represent the symmetric and asymmetric architectures, respectively. Obviously, each component of our architecture can achieve considerable accuracy gains. (a), (b), (c), (d), (e), (f) represent the modules indexed by the corresponding letters in Fig. 5

Components	Index	Modules	DUT-RGBD $F_\beta\uparrow$	$M\downarrow$	NJUD $F_\beta\uparrow$	$M\downarrow$	NLPR $F_\beta\uparrow$	$M\downarrow$	STEREO $F_\beta\uparrow$	$M\downarrow$	LFSD $F_\beta\uparrow$	$M\downarrow$	RGBD135 $F_\beta\uparrow$	$M\downarrow$	SSD $F_\beta\uparrow$	$M\downarrow$
FLM	(a)	B[s]	0.822	0.068	0.810	0.071	0.766	0.050	0.816	0.068	0.812	0.088	0.794	0.044	0.749	0.080
	(b)	B+FLM[s]	0.911	0.035	0.893	0.040	0.872	0.029	0.881	0.041	0.858	0.064	0.882	0.025	0.836	0.048
DAM	(a)	B[s]	0.822	0.068	0.810	0.071	0.766	0.050	0.816	0.068	0.812	0.088	0.794	0.044	0.749	0.080
	(c)	B+DAM[s]	0.839	0.059	0.811	0.064	0.799	0.041	0.818	0.061	0.817	0.087	0.822	0.037	0.738	0.082
	(d)	B+FLM[a]	0.909	0.034	0.886	0.041	0.870	0.029	0.879	0.041	0.870	0.060	0.882	0.025	0.825	0.052
	(e)	B+FLM+DAM[a]	0.920	0.032	0.893	0.040	0.876	0.028	0.884	0.039	0.862	0.064	0.885	0.024	0.827	0.050
Asymmetric	(b)	B+FLM[s]	0.911	0.035	0.893	0.040	0.872	0.029	0.881	0.041	0.858	0.064	0.882	0.025	0.836	0.048
	(d)	B+FLM[a]	0.909	0.034	0.886	0.041	0.870	0.029	0.879	0.041	0.870	0.060	0.882	0.025	0.825	0.052
	(f)	B+FLM+DAM[s]	0.920	0.033	0.895	0.040	0.890	0.025	0.891	0.038	0.863	0.066	0.876	0.026	0.834	0.052
	(e)	B+FLM+DAM[a]	0.920	0.032	0.893	0.040	0.876	0.028	0.884	0.039	0.862	0.064	0.885	0.024	0.827	0.050

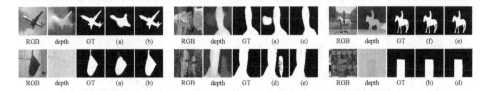

Fig. 7. Visual comparisons of ablation analyses. (a), (b), (c), (d), (e), (f) represent the visual results of the experiments indexed by the corresponding letters in Fig. 5

Furthermore, for effectively analyzing the working mechanism of FLM module, we visualized the output features of each block in FLM. As shown in Fig. 6(a), we can see that the branch 4 and branch 3 extract the global location information while the branch 2 and branch 1 preserve more local detail information. This benefits from the evolutionary process of salient regions with finer details.

Effect of DAM. We conduct contrast experiments for verifying the effectiveness of our DAM on both symmetric and asymmetric architectures. In terms of symmetric architecture, we replace simple summation with DAM on our baseline (denoted as 'B+DAM[s]', as shown in Fig. 5(c)). From the results of (a) and (c) in Table 4 we can see that the MAE is reduced by 18% on NLPR dataset after employing DAM, which intuitively verifies the effect of DAM. Meanwhile, the corresponding visual results in Fig. 7 also illustrate that our DAM can fuse depth features discriminatively and filter out features which are guided by depth cues in mistake. On the other hand, we employ FLM in the RGB stream and replace the VGG-19 backbone with DepthNet in the depth stream (denoted as 'B+FLM[a]', as shown in Fig. 5(d)). And we adopt DAM on 'B+FLM[a]' for verifying the effect of DAM on asymmetric architecture (denoted as 'B+FLM+DAM[a]' shown in Fig. 5(e)). The comparison results of (d) and (e) in Table 4 demonstrate the effectiveness of DAM on asymmetric architecture over all datasets. Additionally, we visualized the feature maps of our two-stream asymmetric architecture (before and after adopting DAM). As shown in Fig. 6(b), we can see that the salient regions are emphasized after adopting DAM, which significantly improves our detection accuracy.

Effect of Asymmetric Architecture. In order to illustrate the effectiveness of adopting asymmetric architecture, we compare the results of (b) and (d) in Fig. 5. Furthermore, for fair comparison, we adopt our FLM and DAM on the two-stream symmetric network (denoted as 'B+FLM+DAM[s]', as shown in Fig. 5(f)). As we can see from Table 4 (Asymmetric), the asymmetric architecture achieves considerable performance compared with symmetrical architecture, but has a small size. Specifically, the asymmetric architecture tremendously minimizes the model size by 47% (128.9 MB vs. 244.4 MB). Based on the above observation, we consider that is unnecessary to utilize large network as RGBNet for extracting features and we can replace it with a more lightweight network.

4.4 Comparison with State-of-the-Art

Considering that most of the existing approaches are based on VGG network, we adopt VGG as our backbone for fair comparisons. And We compare our model with 13 RGB-D based salient object detection models including 8 CNNs-based methods: CPFP [46], DMRA [32], MMCI [6], TANet [5], PDNet [48], PCA [4], CTMF [18], DF [34], and 5 traditional methods: MB [49], CDCP [50], DCMC [9], NLPR [31], DES [8]. For fair comparisons, the results of the competing methods are generated by authorized codes or directly provided by authors.

Quantitative Evaluation. Tables 2 and 3 show the validation results in terms of 4 evaluation metrics on 7 datasets. As we can see, our model achieves significant outperformance over all other methods. It is noted that our approach outperforms all other methods by a dramatic margin on datasets DUT-RGBD, NJUD and RGBD135, which are considered as more challenging datasets due to the large number of complex scenes like similar foreground and background, low-contrast and transparent object. It further indicates that our model can be generalized to various challenging scenes.

Qualitative Evaluation. We also visually compare our method with the most representative methods as shown in Fig. 4. From those results, we can observe that our saliency maps are closer to the ground truths. For instance, other methods have trouble in distinguishing salient objects in complex environments such as cluttered background (see the 1th row), while ours can precisely identify the whole object and exquisite details. And our model can locate and detect the entire salient object with sharp details more accurately than others in more challenging scenes such as low-contrast (see the 2nd - 3rd rows), transparent object (see the 8th row), multiple objects and small object (see the 5th - 7th rows). Those results further verify the effectiveness and robustness of our proposed model.

Table 5. Complexity comparisons on two datasets. The best three results are shown in **boldface**, *bolditalic*, *italic* fonts respectively

Methods	Size ↓	FPS ↑	DUT-RGBD		NLPR	
			F_β ↑	M ↓	F_β ↑	M ↓
PCA	533.6 MB	15	0.760	0.100	0.794	0.044
TANet	951.9 MB	14	0.779	*0.093*	0.795	0.041
MMCI	929.7 MB	19	0.753	0.113	0.729	0.059
PDNet	*192* MB	19	0.757	0.112	0.740	0.064
CPFP	278 MB	6	0.736	0.099	*0.822*	*0.036*
CTMF	826 MB	**50**	*0.792*	0.097	0.723	0.056
DMRA	*238.8* MB	*22*	*0.883*	*0.048*	*0.855*	*0.031*
Ours	**128.9 MB**	*46*	0.920	0.032	0.876	0.028

Complexity Evaluation. We compare the model size and execution time of our method with other 7 representative models, as shown in Table 5. It can be seen that our method achieves Top-1 model size and Top-2 FPS. To be specific, the model size of our architecture is only 128.9 MB which is 2/3 of the existing minimum model size (PDNet). Compared with the best performing method DMRA, our architecture tremendously minimizes the model size by 46% and boosts the FPS by 109%. Besides, we achieve a high running speed with 46 Frame Per Second (FPS) compared with the representative approaches.

5   Conclusion

In this paper, we propose an asymmetric two-stream architecture taking account of the inherent differences between RGB and depth data for saliency detection. For the RGB stream, we introduce a flow ladder module (FLM) for effectively extracting rich global context information while preserving local saliency details. And we design a lightweight DepthNet for depth stream with a small model size of 6.7MB. Besides, we propose a depth attention module (DAM) ensuring that the depth cues can discriminatively guide the RGB features for precisely locating salient objects. Our approach significantly advances the state-of-the-art methods over the widely used datasets and is capable of precisely capturing salient regions in challenging scenes.

Acknowledgement. This work was supported by the Science and Technology Innovation Foundation of Dalian (2019J12GX034), the National Natural Science Foundation of China (61976035), and the Fundamental Research Funds for the Central Universities (DUT19JC58, DUT20JC42).

References

1. Achanta, R., Hemami, S.S., Estrada, F.J., Süsstrunk, S.: Frequency-tuned salient region detection. In: CVPR, pp. 1597–1604 (2009)

2. Borji, A., Frintrop, S., Sihite, D.N., Itti, L.: Adaptive object tracking by learning background context. In: CVPR, pp. 23–30 (2012). https://academic.microsoft.com/paper/2158535435

3. Borji, A., Sihite, D.N., Itti, L.: Salient object detection: a benchmark. In: Fitzgibbon, A., Lazebnik, S., Perona, P., Sato, Y., Schmid, C. (eds.) ECCV 2012. LNCS, vol. 7573, pp. 414–429. Springer, Heidelberg (2012). https://doi.org/10.1007/978-3-642-33709-3_30

4. Chen, H., Li, Y.: Progressively complementarity-aware fusion network for RGB-D salient object detection. In: CVPR, pp. 3051–3060 (2018)

5. Chen, H., Li, Y.: Three-stream attention-aware network for RGB-D salient object detection. TIP 28(6), 2825–2835 (2019)

6. Chen, H., Li, Y., Su, D.: Multi-modal fusion network with multi-scale multi-path and cross-modal interactions for RGB-D salient object detection. PR 86, 376–385 (2019)

7. Cheng, M.M., Hou, Q.B., Zhang, S.H., Rosin, P.L.: Intelligent visual media processing: When graphics meets vision. JCST 32(1), 110–121 (2017). https://academic.microsoft.com/paper/2571295082

8. Cheng, Y., Fu, H., Wei, X., Xiao, J., Cao, X.: Depth enhanced saliency detection method. In: ICIMCS, pp. 23–27 (2014)

9. Cong, R., Lei, J., Zhang, C., Huang, Q., Cao, X., Hou, C.: Saliency detection for stereoscopic images based on depth confidence analysis and multiple cues fusion. SPL 23(6), 819–823 (2016)

10. Dai, J., Li, Y., He, K., Sun, J.: R-FCN: object detection via region-based fully convolutional networks. In: NIPS, pp. 379–387 (2016). https://academic.microsoft.com/paper/2407521645

11. Desingh, K., K, M.K., Rajan, D., Jawahar, C.V.: Depth really matters: improving visual salient region detection with depth. In: BMVC (2013)

12. Donoser, M., Urschler, M., Hirzer, M., Bischof, H.: Saliency driven total variation segmentation. In: ICCV, pp. 817–824 (2009). https://academic.microsoft.com/paper/2546160422

13. Fan, D.P., Cheng, M.M., Liu, Y., Li, T., Borji, A.: Structure-measure: a new way to evaluate foreground maps. In: ICCV, pp. 4558–4567 (2017). https://academic.microsoft.com/paper/2963868681

14. Fan, D.P., Gong, C., Cao, Y., Ren, B., Cheng, M.M., Borji, A.: Enhanced-alignment measure for binary foreground map evaluation. In: IJCAI, pp. 698–704 (2018)

15. Fan, D.P., Wang, J., Liang, X.M.: Improving image retrieval using the context-aware saliency areas. AMM 734, 596–599 (2015). https://academic.microsoft.com/paper/2090323693

16. Feng, M., Lu, H., Ding, E.: Attentive feedback network for boundary-aware salient object detection. In: CVPR, pp. 1623–1632 (2019). https://academic.microsoft.com/paper/2948510860

17. Gao, Y., Wang, M., Tao, D., Ji, R., Dai, Q.: 3-D object retrieval and recognition with hypergraph analysis. TIP 21(9), 4290–4303 (2012). https://academic.microsoft.com/paper/2068078373

18. Han, J., Chen, H., Liu, N., Yan, C., Li, X.: CNNs-based RGB-D saliency detection via cross-view transfer and multiview fusion. TSMC 48(11), 3171–3183 (2018)

19. He, K., Zhang, X., Ren, S., Sun, J.: Deep residual learning for image recognition. In: CVPR, pp. 770–778 (2016)

20. Hong, S., You, T., Kwak, S., Han, B.: Online tracking by learning discriminative saliency map with convolutional neural network. In: ICML, pp. 597–606 (2015). https://academic.microsoft.com/paper/1854404533

21. Hou, Q., Cheng, M.M., Hu, X., Borji, A., Tu, Z., Torr, P.H.S.: Deeply supervised salient object detection with short connections. CVPR. **41**, 815–828 (2017)
22. Hou, Q., Cheng, M.M., Hu, X., Borji, A., Tu, Z., Torr, P.H.S.: Deeply supervised salient object detection with short connections. TPAMI **41**(4), 815–828 (2019). https://academic.microsoft.com/paper/2569272946
23. Ju, R., Ge, L., Geng, W., Ren, T., Wu, G.: Depth saliency based on anisotropic center-surround difference. In: ICIP, pp. 1115–1119 (2014)
24. Lang, C., Nguyen, T.V., Katti, H., Yadati, K., Kankanhalli, M., Yan, S.: Depth matters: influence of depth cues on visual saliency. In: Fitzgibbon, A., Lazebnik, S., Perona, P., Sato, Y., Schmid, C. (eds.) ECCV 2012. LNCS, vol. 7573, pp. 101–115. Springer, Heidelberg (2012). https://doi.org/10.1007/978-3-642-33709-3_8
25. Li, G., Zhu, C.: A three-pathway psychobiological framework of salient object detection using stereoscopic technology. In: ICCVW, pp. 3008–3014 (2017). https://academic.microsoft.com/paper/2766315367
26. Li, G., Yu, Y.: Deep contrast learning for salient object detection. In: CVPR, pp. 478–487 (2016)
27. Li, N., Ye, J., Ji, Y., Ling, H., Yu, J.: Saliency detection on light field. PAMI **39**(8), 1605–1616 (2017)
28. Liu, G., Fan, D.: A model of visual attention for natural image retrieval. In: ISCC-C, pp. 728–733 (2013). https://academic.microsoft.com/paper/2314707829
29. Liu, N., Han, J.: DHSNet: deep hierarchical saliency network for salient object detection. In: CVPR, pp. 678–686 (2016)
30. Niu, Y., Geng, Y., Li, X., Liu, F.: Leveraging stereopsis for saliency analysis. In: CVPR, pp. 454–461 (2012)
31. Peng, H., Li, B., Xiong, W., Hu, W., Ji, R.: RGBD salient object detection: a benchmark and algorithms. In: Fleet, D., Pajdla, T., Schiele, B., Tuytelaars, T. (eds.) ECCV 2014. LNCS, vol. 8691, pp. 92–109. Springer, Cham (2014). https://doi.org/10.1007/978-3-319-10578-9_7
32. Piao, Y., Ji, W., Li, J., Zhang, M., Lu, H.: Depth-induced multi-scale recurrent attention network for saliency detection. In: ICCV (2019)
33. Qin, X., Zhang, Z., Huang, C., Gao, C., Dehghan, M., Jagersand, M.: BASNet: boundary-aware salient object detection. In: CVPR, pp. 7479–7489 (2019). https://academic.microsoft.com/paper/2961348656
34. Qu, L., He, S., Zhang, J., Tian, J., Tang, Y., Yang, Q.: RGBD salient object detection via deep fusion. TIP **26**(5), 2274–2285 (2017)
35. Ren, J., Gong, X., Yu, L., Zhou, W., Yang, M.Y.: Exploiting global priors for RGB-D saliency detection. In: CVPRW, pp. 25–32 (2015)
36. Ren, S., He, K., Girshick, R., Sun, J.: Faster R-CNN: towards real-time object detection with region proposal networks. TPAMI **39**(6), 1137–1149 (2017). https://academic.microsoft.com/paper/639708223
37. Ren, Z., Gao, S., Chia, L.T., Tsang, I.W.H.: Region-based saliency detection and its application in object recognition. TCSVT **24**(5), 769–779 (2014). https://academic.microsoft.com/paper/2055180303
38. Smeulders, A.W.M., Chu, D.M., Cucchiara, R., Calderara, S., Dehghan, A., Shah, M.: Visual tracking: an experimental survey. TPAMI **36**(7), 1442–1468 (2014). https://academic.microsoft.com/paper/2126302311
39. Wang, W., Shen, J., Porikli, F.: Saliency-aware geodesic video object segmentation. In: CVPR, pp. 3395–3402 (2015)
40. Wang, W., Shen, J., Sun, H., Shao, L.: Video co-saliency guided co-segmentation. TCSVT **28**(8), 1727–1736 (2018). https://academic.microsoft.com/paper/2887503470

41. Wu, R., Feng, M., Guan, W., Wang, D., Lu, H., Ding, E.: A mutual learning method for salient object detection with intertwined multi-supervision. In: CVPR, pp. 8150–8159 (2019). https://academic.microsoft.com/paper/2962680827

42. Zhang, M., et al.: LFNet: light field fusion network for salient object detection. IEEE Trans. Image Process. **29**, 6276–6287 (2020)

43. Zhang, M., Li, J., Ji, W., Piao, Y., Lu, H.: Memory-oriented decoder for light field salient object detection. In: NeurIPS 2019: Thirty-third Conference on Neural Information Processing Systems, pp. 898–908 (2019)

44. Zhang, P., Wang, D., Lu, H., Wang, H., Ruan, X.: Amulet: aggregating multi-level convolutional features for salient object detection. In: ICCV, pp. 202–211 (2017). https://academic.microsoft.com/paper/2963032190

45. Zhang, X., Wang, T., Qi, J., Lu, H., Wang, G.: Progressive attention guided recurrent network for salient object detection. In: CVPR (2018)

46. Zhao, J.X., Cao, Y., Fan, D.P., Cheng, M.M., Li, X.Y., Zhang, L.: Contrast prior and fluid pyramid integration for RGBD salient object detection. In: CVPR, pp. 3927–3936 (2019)

47. Zhao, R., Ouyang, W., Li, H., Wang, X.: Saliency detection by multi-context deep learning. In: CVPR, pp. 1265–1274 (2015)

48. Zhu, C., Cai, X., Huang, K., Li, T.H., Li, G.: PDNet: prior-model guided depth-enhanced network for salient object detection. In: ICME (2019)

49. Zhu, C., Li, G., Guo, X., Wang, W., Wang, R.: A multilayer backpropagation saliency detection algorithm based on depth mining. In: CAIP, pp. 14–23 (2017)

50. Zhu, C., Li, G., Wang, W., Wang, R.: An innovative salient object detection using center-dark channel prior. In: ICCVW, pp. 1509–1515 (2017)

Explaining Image Classifiers Using Statistical Fault Localization

Youcheng Sun[1]([⊠])[iD], Hana Chockler[2][iD], Xiaowei Huang[3][iD],
and Daniel Kroening[4][iD]

[1] Queen's University Belfast, Belfast, Northern Ireland
youcheng.sun@qub.ac.uk
[2] King's College London, London, England
[3] University of Liverpool, Liverpool, England
[4] University of Oxford, Oxford, England

Abstract. The black-box nature of deep neural networks (DNNs) makes
it impossible to understand *why* a particular output is produced, creating demand for "Explainable AI". In this paper, we show that statistical fault localization (SFL) techniques from software engineering deliver
high quality explanations of the outputs of DNNs, where we define an
explanation as a minimal subset of features sufficient for making the
same decision as for the original input. We present an algorithm and
a tool called DEEPCOVER, which synthesizes a ranking of the features
of the inputs using SFL and constructs explanations for the decisions
of the DNN based on this ranking. We compare explanations produced
by DEEPCOVER with those of the state-of-the-art tools GradCAM, LIME,
SHAP, RISE and Extremal and show that explanations generated by DEEP-
COVER are consistently better across a broad set of experiments. On a
benchmark set with known ground truth, DEEPCOVER achieves 76.7%
accuracy, which is 6% better than the second best Extremal.

Keywords: Deep learning · Explainability · Statistical fault
localization · Software testing

1 Introduction

Deep neural networks (DNNs) are increasingly used in place of traditionally
engineered software in many areas. DNNs are complex non-linear functions with
algorithmically generated (and not engineered) coefficients, and therefore are
effectively "black boxes". They are given an input and produce an output, but the
calculation of these outputs is difficult to explain [26]. The goal of *explainable AI*
is to create artifacts that provide a rationale for why a neural network generates
a particular output for a particular input. This is argued to enable stakeholders
to understand and appropriately trust neural networks.

A typical use-case of DNNs is classification of highly dimensional inputs,
such as images. DNNs are multi-layered networks with a predefined structure

A. Vedaldi et al. (Eds.): ECCV 2020, LNCS 12373, pp. 391–406, 2020.
https://doi.org/10.1007/978-3-030-58604-1_24

that consists of layers of neurons. The coefficients for the neurons are determined by a training process on a data set with given classification labels. The standard criterion for the adequacy of training is the accuracy of the network on a separate validation data set. This criterion is clearly only as comprehensive as the validation data set. In particular, this approach suffers from the risk that the validation data set is lacking an important instance [36]. Explanations provide additional insight into the decision process of a neural network [9,23].

In traditional software development, SFL measures have a substantial track record of helping engineers to debug sequential programs [19]. These measures rank program locations by counting the number of times a particular location is visited in passing and in failing executions for a given test suite and applying statistical formulae. The ranked list is presented to the engineer. The main advantage of SFL measures is that they are comparatively inexpensive to compute. There are more than a hundred of measures in the literature [33]. Some of the most widely used measures are Zoltar, Ochiai, Tarantula and Wong-II [8,14,21,34].

Our Contribution. We propose to apply the concept of *explanations* introduced by Halpern and Pearl in the context of *actual causality* [11]. Specifically, we define an explanation as a subset of features of the input that is *sufficient* (in terms of explaining the cause of the outcome), *minimal* (i.e., not containing irrelevant or redundant elements), and *not obvious*.

Using this definition and SFL measures, we have developed **DeepCover** – a tool that provides explanations for DNNs that classify images. DEEPCOVER ranks the pixels using four well-known SFL measures (Zoltar, Ochiai, Tarantula and Wong-II) based on the results of running test suites constructed from random mutations of the input image. DEEPCOVER then uses this ranking to efficiently construct an approximation of the explanation (as explained below, the exact computation is intractable).

We compare the quality of the explanations produced by DEEPCOVER with those generated by the state-of-the-art tools GradCAM, LIME, SHAP, RISE and Extremal in several complementary scenarios. First, we measure the size of the explanations as an indication of the quality of the explanations. To complement this setup, we further apply the explanation tools to the problem of weakly supervised object localization (WSOL). We also create a "chimera" benchmark, consisting of images with a known ground truth. DEEPCOVER exhibits consistently better performance in these evaluations. Finally, we investigate the use of explanations in a DNN security application, and show that DEEPCOVER successfully identifies the backdoors that trigger Trojaning attacks.

2   Related Work

There is a large number of methods for explaining DNN decisions. Our approach belongs to a category of methods that compute local perturbations. Such methods compute and visualize the important features of an input instance to explain the corresponding output. Given a particular input, LIME [27] samples the neighborhood of this input and creates a linear model to approximate the model's local behavior; owing to the high computational cost of this approach, the ranking uses super-pixels instead of individual pixels. In [4], the natural distribution of the input is replaced by a user-defined distribution and the Shapley Value method is used to analyze combinations of input features and to rank their importance. In [3], the importance of input features is estimated by measuring the flow of information between inputs and outputs. Both the Shapley Value and the information-theoretic approaches are computationally expensive. In RISE [25], the importance of a pixel is computed as the expectation over all local perturbations conditioned on the event that the pixel is observed. More recently, the concept of "extreme perturbations" has been introduced to improve the perturbation analysis by the Extremal algorithm [6].

On the other hand, gradient-based methods only need one backward pass. GradCAM [29] passes the class-specific gradient into the final convolutional layer of a DNN to coarsely highlight important regions of an input image. In [30], the activation of each neuron is compared with some reference point, and its contribution score for the final output is assigned according to the difference. The work of [4,18,27,30] is similar: an approximation of the model's local behavior using a simpler linear model and an application of the Shapley Value theory to solve this model.

Our algorithm for generating explanations is inspired by the statistical fault localization (SFL) techniques in software testing [19] (see Sect. 3.2 for an overview). SFL measures have the advantage of being simple and efficient. They are widely used for localizing causes of software failures. Moreover, there are single-bug optimal measures [15] that guarantee that the fault is localized when it is the single cause for the program failure. While it is not always possible to localize a single best feature to explain a DNN image classifier, single-bug optimal measures often perform well even when there is more than one fault in the program [16]. From the software engineering perspective, our work can be regarded as applying SFL techniques for diagnosing the neural network's decision. This complements recent works on the testing and validation of AI [20,22,31,32], for which a detailed survey can be found in [13].

3   Preliminaries

3.1   Deep Neural Networks (DNNs)

We briefly review the relevant definitions of deep neural networks. Let $f : \mathcal{I} \to \mathcal{O}$ be a deep neural network $\mathcal{N}$ with N layers. For a given input $x \in \mathcal{I}$, $f(x) \in \mathcal{O}$ calculates the output of the DNN, which could be, for instance, a classification label. Images are among the most popular inputs for DNNs, and in this paper we focus on DNNs that classify images. Specifically, we have

$$f(x) = f_N(\ldots f_2(f_1(x; W_1, b_1); W_2, b_2) \ldots; W_N, b_N) \tag{1}$$

where W_i and b_i for $i = 1, 2, \ldots, N$ are learnable parameters, and $f_i(z_{i-1}; W_{i-1}, b_{i-1})$ is the layer function that maps the output of layer $(i - 1)$, i.e., z_{i-1}, to the input of layer i. The combination of the layer functions yields a highly complex behavior, and the analysis of the information flow within a DNN is challenging. There is a variety of layer functions for DNNs, including fully connected layers, convolutional layers and max-pooling layers. Our algorithm is independent of the specific internals of the DNN and treats a given DNN as a black box.

3.2 Statistical Fault Localization (SFL)

Statistical fault localization techniques (SFL) [19], have been widely used in software testing to aid in locating the causes of failures of programs. SFL techniques rank program elements (e.g., statements or assignments) based on their *suspiciousness scores*. Intuitively, a program element is more suspicious if it appears in failed executions more frequently than in correct executions (the exact formulas for ranking differ). Diagnosis of the faulty program can then be conducted by manually examining the ranked list of elements in descending order of their suspiciousness until the culprit for the fault is found.

The SFL procedure first executes the program under test using a set of inputs. It records the program executions together with a set of Boolean flags that indicate whether a particular element was executed by the current test. The task of a fault localization tool is to compute a ranking of the program elements based on the values of these flags. Following the notation in [19], the suspiciousness score of each program statement s is calculated from a set of parameters $\langle a_{ep}^s, a_{ef}^s, a_{np}^s, a_{nf}^s \rangle$ that give the number of times the statement s is executed (e) or not executed (n) on passing (p) and on failing (f) tests. For instance, a_{ep}^s is the number of tests that passed and executed s.

A large number of measures have been proposed to calculate the suspiciousness scores. In Eq. 2 we list the most widely used ones [8,14,21,34]; those are also the measures that we use in our ranking procedure.

$$\text{Ochiai:} \quad \frac{a_{ef}^s}{\sqrt{(a_{ef}^s + a_{nf}^s)(a_{ef}^s + a_{ep}^s)}} \tag{2a}$$

$$\text{Tarantula:} \quad \frac{\frac{a_{ef}^s}{a_{ef}^s + a_{nf}^s}}{\frac{a_{ef}^s}{a_{ef}^s + a_{nf}^s} + \frac{a_{ep}^s}{a_{ep}^s + a_{np}^s}} \tag{2b}$$

$$\text{Zoltar:} \quad \frac{a_{ef}^s}{a_{ef}^s + a_{nf}^s + a_{ep}^s + \frac{10000 a_{nf}^s a_{ep}^s}{a_{ef}^s}} \tag{2c}$$

$$\text{Wong-II:} \quad a_{ef}^s - a_{ep}^s \tag{2d}$$

There is no single best measure for fault localization. Different measures perform better on different applications, and best practice is to use them together.

4   What Is an Explanation?

An explanation of an output of an automated procedure is essential in many areas, including verification, planning, diagnosis and the like. A good explanation can increase a user's confidence in the result. Explanations are also useful for determining whether there is a fault in the automated procedure: if the explanation does not make sense, it may indicate that the procedure is faulty. It is less clear how to define what a *good* explanation is. There have been a number of definitions of explanations over the years in various domains of computer science [2,7,24], philosophy [12] and statistics [28]. The recent increase in the number of machine learning applications and the advances in deep learning led to the need for *explainable AI*, which is advocated, among others, by DARPA [9] to promote understanding, trust, and adoption of future autonomous systems based on learning algorithms (and, in particular, image classification DNNs). DARPA provides a list of questions that a good explanation should answer and an epistemic state of the user after receiving a good explanation. The description of this epistemic state boils down to *adding useful information* about the output of the algorithm and *increasing trust* of the user in the algorithm.

In this paper, we are loosely adopting the definition of explanations by Halpern and Pearl [11], which is based on their definition of actual causality [10]. Roughly speaking, they state that a good explanation gives an answer to the question *"why did this outcome occur"*, which is similar in spirit to DARPA's informal description. As we do not define our setting in terms of actual causality, we omit the parts of the definition that refer to causal models and causal settings. The remaining parts of the definition of explanation are:

1. an explanation is a *sufficient* cause of the outcome;
2. an explanation is a *minimal* such cause (that is, it does not contain irrelevant or redundant elements);
3. an explanation is *not obvious*; in other words, before being given the explanation, the user could conceivably imagine other explanations for the outcome.

In image classification using DNNs, the non-obviousness holds for all but extremely trivial images. Translating 1) and 2) into our setting, we get the following definition.

Definition 1. *An explanation in image classification is a minimal subset of pixels of a given input image that is sufficient for the DNN to classify the image, where "sufficient" is defined as containing only this subset of pixels from the original image, with the other pixels set to the background colour.*

We note that (1) the explanation cannot be too small (or empty), as a too small subset of pixels would violate the sufficiency requirement, and (2) there can be multiple explanations for a given input image.

The precise computation of an explanation in our setting is intractable, as it is equivalent to the earlier definition of explanations in binary causal models, which is DP-complete [5]. A brute-force approach of checking all subsets of pixels of the input image is exponential in the size of the image. In Sect. 5 we describe an efficient linear-time approach to computing an approximation of an explanation and argue that for practical purposes, this approximation is sufficiently close to an exact explanation as defined above.

5   SFL Explanation for DNNs

We propose a *black-box explanation technique* based on statistical fault localization. In traditional software development, SFL measures are used for ranking program elements that cause a failure. In our setup, the goal is different: we are searching for an explanation of why a particular input to a given DNN yields a particular output; our technique is agnostic to whether the output is correct. We start with describing our algorithm on a high level and then present the pseudo-code and technical details.

Generating the Test Suite. SFL requires test inputs. Given an input image x that is classified by the DNN $\mathcal{N}$ as $y = \mathcal{N}[x]$, we generate a set of images by *randomly mutating* x. A *legal mutation* masks a subset of the pixels of x, i.e., sets these pixels to the background color. The DNN computes an output for each mutant; we annotate it with "y" if that output matches that of x, and with "$\neg y$" to indicate that the output differs. The resulting test suite $T(x)$ of annotated mutants is an input to the DEEPCOVER algorithm.

Ranking the Pixels of x. We assume that the original input x consists of n pixels $\mathcal{P} = \{p_1, \ldots, p_n\}$. Each test input $t \in T(x)$ exhibits a particular spectrum for the pixel set, in which some pixels are the same as in the original input x and others are masked. The presence or masking of a pixel in x may affect the output of the DNN.

We use SFL measures to rank the set of pixels of x by slightly abusing the notions of passing and failing tests. For a pixel p_i of x, we compute the vector $\langle a_{ep}^i, a_{ef}^i, a_{np}^i, a_{nf}^i \rangle$ as follows:

- a_{ep}^i is the number of mutants in $T(x)$ labeled y in which p_i is not masked;
- a_{ef}^i is the number of mutants in $T(x)$ labeled $\neg y$ in which p_i is not masked;
- a_{np}^i is the number of mutants in $T(x)$ labeled y in which p_i is masked;
- a_{nf}^i is the number of mutants in $T(x)$ labeled $\neg y$ in which p_i is masked.

Once we construct the vector $\langle a_{ep}^i, a_{ef}^i, a_{np}^i, a_{nf}^i \rangle$ for every pixel, we apply the SFL measures discussed in Sect. 3.2 to rank the pixels of x for their importance regarding the DNN's output (the importance corresponds to the suspiciousness score computed by SFL measures).

Constructing an Explanation. An explanation is constructed by iteratively adding pixels to the set in the descending order of their ranking (that is, we start with the highest-ranked pixels) until the set becomes sufficient for the DNN to classify the image. This set is presented to the user as an explanation.

Algorithm 1. SFL Explanation for DNNs

INPUT: DNN $\mathcal{N}$, image x, SFL measure M
OUTPUT: a subset of pixels $\mathcal{P}^{exp}$

1: $T(x) \leftarrow test\_inputs\_gen(\mathcal{N}, x)$
2: **for** each pixel $p_i \in \mathcal{P}$ **do**
3:     calculate $a_{ep}^i, a_{ef}^i, a_{np}^i, a_{nf}^i$ from $T(x)$
4:     $value_i \leftarrow M(a_{ep}^i, a_{ef}^i, a_{np}^i, a_{nf}^i)$
5: **end for**
6: $pixel\_ranking \leftarrow$ pixels in $\mathcal{P}$ from high $value$ to low
7: $\mathcal{P}^{exp} \leftarrow \emptyset$
8: **for** each pixel $p_i \in pixel\_ranking$ **do**
9:     $\mathcal{P}^{exp} \leftarrow \mathcal{P}^{exp} \cup \{p_i\}$
10:    $x^{exp} \leftarrow$ mask pixels of x that are **not** in $\mathcal{P}^{exp}$
11:    **if** $\mathcal{N}[x^{exp}] = \mathcal{N}[x]$ **then**
12:        **return** $\mathcal{P}^{exp}$
13:    **end if**
14: **end for**

5.1 SFL Explanation Algorithm

We now present our algorithms in detail. Algorithm 1 starts by calling procedure $test\_inputs\_gen$ to generate the set $T(x)$ of test inputs (Line 1). It then computes the vector $\langle a_{ep}^i, a_{ef}^i, a_{np}^i, a_{nf}^i \rangle$ for each pixel $p_i \in \mathcal{P}$ using $T(x)$ (Lines 2–5). Next, the algorithm computes the ranking of each pixel according to the specified measure M (Line 6). Formulas for measures are as in Eq. (2a)–(2d). The pixels are sorted in descending order of their ranking (from high $value$ to low $value$).

From Line 7 onward in Algorithm 1, we construct a subset of pixels $\mathcal{P}^{exp}$ to explain $\mathcal{N}$'s output on this particular input x as follows. We add pixels to $\mathcal{P}^{exp}$, while $\mathcal{N}$'s output on $\mathcal{P}^{exp}$ does not match $\mathcal{N}[x]$. This process terminates when $\mathcal{N}$'s output is the same as on the whole image x. Finally, $\mathcal{P}^{exp}$ is returned as the explanation. At the end of this section we discuss why $\mathcal{P}^{exp}$ is not a precise explanation according to Definition 1 and argue that it is a good approximation (coinciding with a precise explanation in most cases).

As the quality of the ranked list computed by SFL measures inherently depends on the quality of the test suite, the choice of the set $T(x)$ of mutant images plays an important role in our SFL explanation algorithm for DNNs. While it is beyond the scope of this paper to identify the best set $T(x)$, we propose an effective method for generating $T(x)$ in Algorithm 2. The core idea of Algorithm 2 is to balance the number of test inputs annotated with "y" (that play the role of the passing traces) with the number of test inputs annotated with "$\neg y$" (that play the role of the failing traces). Its motivation is that, when applying fault localisation in software debugging, the rule of thumb is to maintain a balance between passing and failing cases.

The fraction σ of the set of pixels of x that are going to be masked in a mutant is initialized by a random or selected number between 0 and 1 (Line 2)

Algorithm 2. *test_inputs_gen($\mathcal{N}, x$)*

INPUT: DNN $\mathcal{N}$, image x (with n pixels)
OUTPUT: test suite $T(x)$
PARAMETERS: σ, ϵ, test suite size m

1: $T(x) \leftarrow \emptyset$
2: $\sigma \leftarrow$ sample in the range $(0, 1)$
3: **while** $|T(x)| < m$ **do**
4:      $x' \leftarrow$ randomly select and mask $\sigma \cdot n$ pixels in x
5:      $T(x) \leftarrow T(x) \cup \{x'\}$
6:      **if** $\mathcal{N}[x'] \neq \mathcal{N}[x]$ **then**
7:          $\sigma \leftarrow \max\{\sigma - \epsilon, 0\}$
8:      **else**
9:          $\sigma \leftarrow \min\{\sigma + \epsilon, 1\}$
10:     **end if**
11: **end while**
12: **return** $T(x)$

---

and is later updated at each iteration according to the decision of $\mathcal{N}$ on the previously constructed mutant. In each iteration of the algorithm, a randomly chosen set of $(\sigma \cdot n)$ pixels in x is masked and the resulting new input x' is added to $T(x)$ (Lines 4–5). Roughly speaking, if a mutant is not classified with the same label as x, we decrease the fraction of masked pixels by a pre-defined small number ϵ; if the mutant is classified with the same label as x, we increase the fraction of masked pixels by the same ϵ.

5.2   Relationship Between $\mathcal{P}^{exp}$ and Definition 1

Recall that Definition 1 requires an explanation to be *sufficient, minimal,* and *not obvious* (see Sect. 4). As we argued above, the non-obviousness requirement holds for all but very simple images. It is also easy to see that $\mathcal{P}^{exp}$ is sufficient, since this is a stopping condition for adding pixels to this set (Line 11 in Algorithm 1).

The only condition that might not hold is minimality. The reason for possible non-minimality is that the pixels of x are added to the explanation in the order of their ranking, with the highest-ranking pixels being added first. It is therefore possible that there is a high-ranked pixel that was added in one of the previous iterations, but is now not necessary for the correct classification of the image (note that the process of adding pixels to the explanation stops when the DNN successfully classifies the image; this, however, shows minimality only with respect to the order of addition of pixels). We believe that the redundancy resulting from our approach is likely to be small, as higher-ranked pixels have a larger effect on the DNN's decision. In fact, even if our explanation is, strictly speaking, not minimal, it might not be a disadvantage, as it was found that humans prefer explanations with some redundancy [35].

Another advantage of our algorithm is that its running time is linear in the size of the set $T(x)$ and the size of the image, hence it is much more efficient than the brute-force computation of all explanations as described in Sect. 4 (and in fact, any algorithm that computes a precise explanation, as the problem is intractable). One hypothetical advantage of the enumeration algorithm is that it can produce all explanations; however, multiple explanations do not necessarily provide better insight into the decision process.

6   Experimental Evaluation

We have implemented the SFL explanation algorithm for DNNs presented in Sect. 5 in the tool DEEPCOVER[1]. We now present the experimental results. We tested DEEPCOVER on a variety of DNN models for ImageNet and we compare DEEPCOVER with the most popular and most recent work in AI explanation: LIME [27], SHAP [18], GradCAM [29], RISE [25] and Extremal [6].[2]

6.1   Experimental Setup

We configure the heuristic test generation in Algorithm 2 with $\sigma = \frac{1}{5}$ and $\epsilon = \frac{1}{6}$, and the size m of the test set $T(x)$ is 2,000. These values have been chosen empirically and remain the same through all experiments. It is possible that they are not appropriate for all input images, and that for some inputs increasing m or tuning σ and ϵ produces a better explanation. All experiments are run on a laptop with a 3.9 GHz Intel i7-7820HQ and 16 GB of memory.

6.2   Are the Explanations from DeepCover Useful?

Figure 1 showcases representative output from DEEPCOVER on the Xception model. We can say that explanations are indeed useful and meaningful. Each subfigure in Fig. 1 provides the original input and the output of DEEPCOVER. We highlight misclassifications and counter-intuitive explanations in red. One of the more interesting examples is the "cowboy hat"image. Although Xception labels the input image correctly, an explanation produced by DEEPCOVER indicates that this decision is not based on the correct feature (the hat in the image), but on the face, which is an unexpected feature for the label 'cowboy hat'. While this image was not, technically speaking, misclassified, the explanation points to a flaw in the DNN's reasoning. The "wool" and "whistle" are two misclassifications by Xception, and the explanations generated by DEEPCOVER can help us to understand why the misclassification happens: there are similarities between the features that are used for the correct and the incorrect labels.

---

[1] https://github.com/theyoucheng/deepcover.

[2] LIME version 0.1.33; SHAP version 0.29.1; GradCAM, RISE and Extremal are from https://github.com/facebookresearch/TorchRay (commit 6a198ee61d229360a3def59 0410378d2ed6f1f06).

'cowboy hat'   'dog'   'numbfish'   'sheep'

'hare'   'mushroom'   'wool'   'turnstile'

'langur'   'whistle'   'unicycle'   'fire engine'

'traffic light'   'ballpoint'   'bolo tie'   'projector'

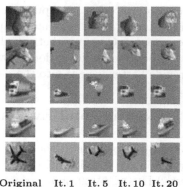

Original   It. 1   It. 5   It. 10   It. 20

Fig. 1. Input images and explanations from DEEPCOVER for Xception (red labels highlight misclassification or counter-intuitive explanations) (Color figure online)

Fig. 2. Explanations of the DNN at different training stages: the 1st column are the original images and the subsequent columns give the explanations for a particular training iteration (CIFAR-10 validation data set)

Furthermore, we apply DEEPCOVER after each training iteration to the intermediate DNN. In Fig. 2 we showcase some representative results at different stages of the training. Overall, as the training procedure progresses, explanations of the DNN's decisions focus more on the "meaningful" part of the input image, e.g., those pixels contributing to the interpretation of image (see, for example, the progress of the training reflected in the explanations of DNN's classification of the first image as a 'cat'). This result reflects that the DNN is being trained to learn features of different classes of inputs. Interestingly, we also observed that the DNN's feature learning is not always monotonic, as demonstrated in the bottom row of Fig. 2: after the 10th iteration, explanations for the DNN's classification of an input image as an 'airplane' drift away from the intuitive parts of the input towards pixels that may not fit human interpretation (we repeated the experiments multiple times to minimize the uncertainty because of the randomization in our SFL algorithm). The explanations generated by DEEPCOVER may thus be useful for assessing the adequacy of the DNN training: they allow us to check, whether the DNN is aligned with the developer's intent during training. Additionally, the results in Fig. 2 satisfy the "sanity" requirement postulated in [1]: the explanations from DEEPCOVER evolve when the model parameters change during the training.

6.3   Comparison with the State-of-the-art

We compare DEEPCOVER with state-of-the-art DNN explanation tools. The DNN is VGG16 and we randomly sample 1,000 images from ILSVRC2012 as inputs. We evaluate the effect of highly ranked features by different methods following an addition/deletion style experiment [6,25].

An explanation computed by Algorithm 1 is a subset $\mathcal{P}^{exp}$ of top-ranked pixels out of the set $\mathcal{P}$ of all 224×224 pixels that is sufficient for the DNN to classify the image correctly. We define the size of the explanation as $\frac{|\mathcal{P}^{exp}|}{|\mathcal{P}|}$. We use the size of an explanation as a proxy for its quality.

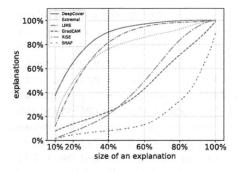 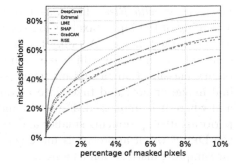

Fig. 3. Comparison in the size of generated explanations by different tools

Fig. 4. Misclassification vs percentage of masked pixels for different tools

Figure 3 compares DEEPCOVER and its competitors with respect to the size of the generated explanations. The position on the x-axis is the size of the explanation, and the position on the y-axis gives the accumulated percentage of explanations: that is, all generated explanations with smaller or equal size.

The data in Fig. 3 suggests that explanations based on SFL ranking are superior in terms of their size. For example, nearly 40% of the DNN inputs can be explained via DEEPCOVER using no more than 10% of the total input pixels, which is two times as good as the second best explanation method EXTREMAL.

We quantify the degree of redundancy in the generated explanations as follows. We mask pixels following the ranking generated by the different methods until we obtain a different classification. The smaller the number of pixels that have to be masked, the more important the highest-ranked features are. We present the number of pixels changed (normalized over the total number of pixels) in Fig. 4. Again, DEEPCOVER dominates the others. Using DEEPCOVER's ranking, the classification is changed after masking no more than 2% of the total pixels in 60% of the images. To achieve the same classification outcomes, the second best method EXTREMAL requires changing 4% of the total number of pixels, and that is twice the number of pixels needed by DEEPCOVER.

Discussion. We have refrained from using human judges to assess the quality of the explanations, and instead use size as a proxy measure to quantify the quality of explanation. However, a smaller explanation is not necessarily a better explanation—in fact, "people have a preference for explanations with some redundancy" [35]. We therefore complement our evaluation with further experiments. Figure 5 gives the results of using the explanations for the weakly supervised object localization (WSOL). We measure the intersection of union (IoU) between the object bounding box and the equivalent number of top-ranked pixels. The IoU is a standard measure of success in object detection and a higher IoU is better. The results confirm again that the top-ranked pixels from DEEPCOVER perform better than those generated by other tools.

Comparison with Rise. The RISE tool generates random masks and calculates a ranking of the input pixels using the expected confidence of the classification of the masked images. A rank of a pixel p by RISE depends only on the confidence of the images in which p is unmasked. By contrast, DEEPCOVER uses a binary classification (a mutant image is either classified the same as the original image or not) and takes into account both the images where p is masked and where it is unmasked. Figures 3 and 4 demonstrate that DEEPCOVER outperforms RISE, producing smaller and more intuitive explanations. Furthermore, the DEEPCOVER approach is more general and does not depend on a particular sampling distribution as long as its mutant test suite is balanced (Sect. 5.1). Moreover, the DEEPCOVER approach is less sensitive to the size of the mutant test suite (Fig. 6). When the size of the test suite decreased from 2,000 to 200, the size of the generated explanation only increased by 3% of the total pixels on average.

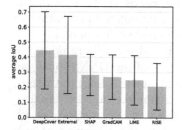

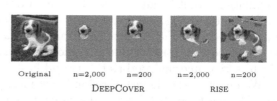

Original   n=2,000   n=200   n=2,000   n=200
DEEPCOVER   RISE

Fig. 5. Results for weakly supervised object localisation

Fig. 6. Explanations for the 'Welsh springer spaniel' by DEEPCOVER and RISE with varying number of samples (i.e. n)

Next, we present a synthetic benchmark (Sect. 6.4) and a security application (Sect. 6.5).

6.4   Generating "ground Truth" with a Chimera Benchmark

The biggest challenge in evaluating explanations for DNNs (and even for human decision making) is the lack of the *ground truth*. Human evaluations of the explanations remain the most widely accepted measure, but are often subjective. In

Fig. 7. Examples of embedding the red panda (Color figure online)

Table 1. IoUs between the embedded red panda and the highest ranked pixels for four different tools

	IoU ≥ 0.5	IoU ≥ 0.6	IoU ≥ 0.7
DeepCover	**76.7%**	**54.9%**	9.8%
Extremal	70.7%	21.5%	2.2%
RISE	55.8%	42.9%	**25.7%**
GradCAM	0%	0%	0%

the experiment we describe below, we synthesize a *Chimera benchmark*[3] by randomly superimposing a "red panda" explanation (a part of the image of the red panda) onto a set of randomly chosen images. The benchmark consists of 1,000 composed (aka "Chimera") images that retain the "red panda" label when using both the MobileNet and the VGG16 classifiers. Figure 7 gives several examples of the Chimera images. The rationale is that if such an image is indeed classified as "red panda" by the DNN, then the explanation of this classification must be contained among the pixels we have superimposed onto the original image.

For each image from the Chimera benchmark, we rank its pixels using DeepCover and other tools. We then check whether any of their top-π highest ranked pixels are part of the "red panda". In Table 1, we measure the IoU (intersection of union) between the ground truth explanation and the top-π highest ranked pixels, where π ranges from 1% to 100%. Assuming that an IoU ≥ 0.5 is a successful detection, DeepCover successfully detects the ground truth planted in the image in 76.7% of the total cases and it is 6% better than the second best Extremal. The benefit provided by DeepCover is even more substantial when requiring 0.6 IoU. Overall, the results in Table 1 are consistent with the addition/deletion experiment (Figs. 3 and 4) and the WSOL experiment (Fig. 5), with DeepCover topping the list. Interestingly, when RISE succeeds to find the explanation, it seems to localize it better (with IoU ≥ 0.7). GradCAM fails to detect the embedded red panda in all cases. These observations support the hypothesis that a benchmark like Chimera is a good approximation for ground truth, and helps us to compare algorithmic alternatives.

6.5 Trojaning Attacks

The authors of [17] say that a DNN is "trojaned" if it behaves correctly on ordinary input images but exhibits malicious behavior when a "Trojan trigger" is part of the input. Thus, we can treat this trigger as a ground truth explanation for the Trojaned behavior of the DNN. We have applied DeepCover to identify the embedded trigger in the input image for the Trojaned VGG Face [17]. The result is illustrated in Fig. 8. This use case suggests that there is scope for the application of DeepCover in DNN security.

---

[3] The benchmark images are publicly available at http://www.roaming-panda.com/.

Fig. 8. Applying DEEPCOVER to Trojaning attacks on VGG Face. The Trojan trigger is the square shape in the lower right corner of the image; the DEEPCOVER explanation for the Trojan behaviour is on the right.

When applying DEEPCOVER to the Trojaned data set in [17], the top 8% highest ranked pixels have an average IoU value of 0.6 with the Trojan trigger. According to DEEPCOVER, the Trojaning output for each input is caused by a small part of its embedded trigger. This black-box discovery by DEEPCOVER is consistent with and further optimizes the theory of DNN Trojaning [17]. Finally, as many as 80% of the (ground truth) Trojan triggers are successively localized (with IoU $\geq$ 0.5) by only $\pi = 8\%$ of the pixels top-ranked by DEEPCOVER. DEEPCOVER is thus very effective.

6.6 Threats to Validity

In this part, we highlight several threats to the validity of our evaluation.
Lack of Ground Truth. We have no ground truth for evaluating the generated explanations for Xception on ImageNet images, hence we use the size of an explanation as a proxy. We have the ground truth for the Chimera images of red panda (Fig. 7) and for the Trojaning attacks (Fig. 8), and the results support our claims of the high quality of DEEPCOVER explanations.

Selection of SFL Measures. We have only evaluated four SFL measures (Ochiai, Zoltar, Tarantula and Wong-II). There are hundreds more such measures, which may reveal new observations.

Selection of Parameters When Generating Test Inputs. When generating the test suite $T(x)$, we empirically configure the parameters in the test generation algorithm. The choice of parameters affects the results of the evaluation and they may be overfitted.

7 Conclusions

This paper advocates the application of statistical fault localization (SFL) for the generation of explanations of the output of neural networks. Our definition of explanations is inspired by actual causality, and we demonstrate that we can efficiently compute a good approximation of a precise explanation using a lightweight ranking of features of the input image based on SFL measures. The algorithm is implemented in the tool DEEPCOVER. Extensive experimental results demonstrate that DEEPCOVER consistently outperforms other explanation tools and that its explanations are accurate when compared to ground truth (that is, the explanations of the images have a large overlap with the explanation planted in the image).

References

1. Adebayo, J., Gilmer, J., Muelly, M., Goodfellow, I., Hardt, M., Kim, B.: Sanity checks for saliency maps. In: Advances in Neural Information Processing Systems, pp. 9505–9515 (2018)
2. Chajewska, U., Halpern, J.Y.: Defining explanation in probabilistic systems. In: Uncertainty in Artificial Intelligence (UAI), pp. 62–71. Morgan Kaufmann (1997)
3. Chen, J., Song, L., Wainwright, M., Jordan, M.: Learning to explain: an information-theoretic perspective on model interpretation. In: International Conference on Machine Learning (ICML), vol. 80, pp. 882–891. PMLR (2018)
4. Datta, A., Sen, S., Zick, Y.: Algorithmic transparency via quantitative input influence: theory and experiments with learning systems. In: Security and Privacy (S&P), pp. 598–617. IEEE (2016)
5. Eiter, T., Lukasiewicz, T.: Complexity results for explanations in the structural-model approach. Artif. Intell. **154**(1–2), 145–198 (2004)
6. Fong, R., Patrick, M., Vedaldi, A.: Understanding deep networks via extremal perturbations and smooth masks. In: International Conference on Computer Vision (ICCV), pp. 2950–2958. IEEE (2019)
7. Gärdenfors, P.: Knowledge in Flux. MIT Press, Cambridge (1988)
8. Gonzalez-Sanchez, A.: Automatic error detection techniques based on dynamic invariants. M.S. thesis, Delft University of Technology, The Netherlands (2007)
9. Gunning, D.: Explainable artificial intelligence (XAI) - program information. Defense Advanced Research Projects Agency (2017). https://www.darpa.mil/program/explainable-artificial-intelligence
10. Halpern, J.Y., Pearl, J.: Causes and explanations: a structural-model approach. Part I: causes. Br. J. Philos. Sci. **56**(4), 843–887 (2005)
11. Halpern, J.Y., Pearl, J.: Causes and explanations: a structural-model approach. Part II: explanations. Br. J. Philos. Sci. **56**(4), 889–911 (2005)
12. Hempel, C.G.: Aspects of Scientific Explanation. Free Press, New York (1965)
13. Huang, X., et al.: A survey of safety and trustworthiness of deep neural networks: verification, testing, adversarial attack and defence, and interpretability. Comput. Sci. Rev. **37**, 100270 (2020)
14. Jones, J.A., Harrold, M.J.: Empirical evaluation of the Tarantula automatic fault-localization technique. In: Proceedings of ASE, pp. 273–282. ACM (2005)
15. Landsberg, D., Chockler, H., Kroening, D., Lewis, M.: Evaluation of measures for statistical fault localisation and an optimising scheme. In: Egyed, A., Schaefer, I. (eds.) FASE 2015. LNCS, vol. 9033, pp. 115–129. Springer, Heidelberg (2015). https://doi.org/10.1007/978-3-662-46675-9_8
16. Landsberg, D., Sun, Y., Kroening, D.: Optimising spectrum based fault localisation for single fault programs using specifications. In: Russo, A., Schürr, A. (eds.) FASE 2018. LNCS, vol. 10802, pp. 246–263. Springer, Cham (2018). https://doi.org/10.1007/978-3-319-89363-1_14
17. Liu, Y., et al.: Trojaning attack on neural networks. In: Network and Distributed System Security Symposium (NDSS). The Internet Society (2018)

18. Lundberg, S.M., Lee, S.I.: A unified approach to interpreting model predictions. In: Advances in Neural Information Processing Systems, pp. 4765–4774 (2017)

19. Naish, L., Lee, H.J., Ramamohanarao, K.: A model for spectra-based software diagnosis. ACM TOSEM **20**(3), 11 (2011)

20. Noller, Y., Păsăreanu, C.S., Böhme, M., Sun, Y., Nguyen, H.L., Grunske, L.: HyDiff: hybrid differential software analysis. In: Proceedings of the International Conference on Software Engineering (ICSE) (2020)

21. Ochiai, A.: Zoogeographic studies on the soleoid fishes found in Japan and its neighbouring regions. Bull. Jpn. Soc. Sci. Fish. **22**, 526–530 (1957)

22. Odena, A., Olsson, C., Andersen, D., Goodfellow, I.: TensorFuzz: debugging neural networks with coverage-guided fuzzing. In: International Conference on Machine Learning, pp. 4901–4911 (2019)

23. Olah, C., et al.: The building blocks of interpretability. Distill **3**, e10 (2018)

24. Pearl, J.: Probabilistic Reasoning in Intelligent Systems. Morgan Kaufmann, Burlington (1988)

25. Petsiuk, V., Das, A., Saenko, K.: RISE: randomized input sampling for explanation of black-box models. In: British Machine Vision Conference (BMVC). BMVA Press (2018)

26. Rahwan, I., et al.: Machine behaviour. Nature **568**(7753), 477 (2019)

27. Ribeiro, M.T., Singh, S., Guestrin, C.: Why should I trust you? Explaining the predictions of any classifier. In: Knowledge Discovery and Data Mining (KDD), pp. 1135–1144. ACM (2016)

28. Salmon, W.C.: Four Decades of Scientific Explanation. University of Minnesota Press, Minneapolis (1989)

29. Selvaraju, R.R., Cogswell, M., Das, A., Vedantam, R., Parikh, D., Batra, D.: Grad-CAM: visual explanations from deep networks via gradient-based localization. In: International Conference on Computer Vision (ICCV), pp. 618–626. IEEE (2017)

30. Shrikumar, A., Greenside, P., Kundaje, A.: Learning important features through propagating activation differences. In: International Conference on Machine Learning (ICML), vol. 70, pp. 3145–3153. PMLR (2017)

31. Sun, Y., Wu, M., Ruan, W., Huang, X., Kwiatkowska, M., Kroening, D.: Concolic testing for deep neural networks. In: Proceedings of the 33rd ACM/IEEE International Conference on Automated Software Engineering, ASE, pp. 109–119 (2018)

32. Sun, Y., Zhou, Y., Maskell, S., Sharp, J., Huang, X.: Reliability validation of learning enabled vehicle tracking. In: International Conference on Robotics and Automation (ICRA). IEEE (2020)

33. Wong, W.E., Gao, R., Li, Y., Abreu, R., Wotawa, F.: A survey on software fault localization. IEEE TSE **42**(8), 707–740 (2016)

34. Wong, W.E., Qi, Y., Zhao, L., Cai, K.: Effective fault localization using code coverage. In: Computer Software and Applications Conference (COMPSAC), pp. 449–456 (2007)

35. Zemla, J.C., Sloman, S., Bechlivanidis, C., Lagnado, D.A.: Evaluating everyday explanations. Psychon. Bull. Rev. **24**(5), 1488–1500 (2017). https://doi.org/10.3758/s13423-017-1258-z

36. Ziegler, C.: A Google self-driving car caused a crash for the first time. The Verge (2016). https://www.theverge.com/2016/2/29/11134344/google-self-driving-car-crash-report

Deep Graph Matching via Blackbox Differentiation of Combinatorial Solvers

Michal Rolínek[1(✉)], Paul Swoboda[2], Dominik Zietlow[1], Anselm Paulus[1], Vít Musil[3], and Georg Martius[1]

[1] Max Planck Institute for Intelligent Systems, Tübingen, Germany
michal.rolinek@tue.mpg.de
[2] Max Planck Institute for Informatics, Saarbrücken, Germany
[3] Università degli Studi di Firenze, Florence, Italy
https://github.com/martius-lab/blackbox-deep-graph-matching

Abstract. Building on recent progress at the intersection of combinatorial optimization and deep learning, we propose an end-to-end trainable architecture for deep graph matching that contains unmodified combinatorial solvers. Using the presence of heavily optimized combinatorial solvers together with some improvements in architecture design, we advance state-of-the-art on deep graph matching benchmarks for keypoint correspondence. In addition, we highlight the conceptual advantages of incorporating solvers into deep learning architectures, such as the possibility of post-processing with a strong multi-graph matching solver or the indifference to changes in the training setting. Finally, we propose two new challenging experimental setups.

Keywords: Deep graph matching · Keypoint correspondence · Combinatorial optimization

1 Introduction

Matching discrete structures is a recurring theme in numerous branches of computer science. Aside from extensive analysis of its theoretical and algorithmic aspects [9,26], there is also a wide range of applications. Computer vision, in particular, is abundant of tasks with a matching flavor; optical flow [4,49,50], person re-identification [25,45], stereo matching [12,36], pose estimation [11,25], object tracking [39,57], to name just a few. Matching problems are also relevant in a variety of scientific disciplines including biology [28], language processing [40],

Fig. 1. Example keypoint matchings of the proposed architecture on SPair-71k.

Electronic supplementary material The online version of this chapter (https://doi.org/10.1007/978-3-030-58604-1_25) contains supplementary material, which is available to authorized users.

A. Vedaldi et al. (Eds.): ECCV 2020, LNCS 12373, pp. 407–424, 2020.
https://doi.org/10.1007/978-3-030-58604-1_25

bioinformatics [19], correspondence problems in computer graphics [43] or social network analysis [35].

Particularly, in the domain of computer vision, the matching problem has two parts: **extraction of local features** from raw images and **resolving conflicting evidence** e.g. multiple long-term occlusions in a tracking context. Each of these parts can be addressed efficiently in separation, namely by deep networks on the one side and by specialized purely combinatorial algorithms on the other. The latter requires a clean abstract formulation of the combinatorial problem. Complications arise if concessions on *either* side harm performance. Deep networks on their own have a limited capability of *combinatorial generalization* [6] and purely combinatorial approaches typically rely on fixed features that are often suboptimal in practice. To address this, many *hybrid* approaches have been proposed.

In case of *deep graph matching* some approaches rely on finding suitable differentiable relaxations [60,62], while others benefit from a tailored architecture design [23,27,59,64]. What all these approaches have in common is that they compromise on the combinatorial side in the sense that the resulting "combinatorial block" would not be competitive in a purely combinatorial setup.

In this work, we present a novel type of end-to-end architecture for semantic keypoint matching that **does not make any concessions on the combinatorial side** while maintaining strong feature extraction. We build on recent progress at the intersection of combinatorial optimization and deep learning [56] that allows to seamlessly embed **blackbox implementations** of a wide range of combinatorial algorithms into deep networks in a **mathematically sound** fashion. As a result, we can leverage heavily optimized graph matching solvers [52,53] based on dual block coordinate ascent for Lagrange decompositions.

Since the combinatorial aspect is handled by an expert algorithm, we can focus on the rest of the architecture design: building representative graph matching instances from visual and geometric information. In that regard, we leverage the recent findings [23] that large performance improvement can be obtained by correctly incorporating relative keypoint locations via SplineCNN [22].

Additionally, we observe that correct matching decisions are often simplified by leveraging global information such as viewpoint, rigidity of the object or scale (see also Fig. 1). With this in mind, we propose a natural **global feature attention mechanism** that allows to adjust the weighting of different node and edge features based on a global feature vector.

Finally, the proposed architecture allows a stronger post-processing step. In particular, we use a multi-graph matching solver [52] during evaluation to jointly resolve multiple graph matching instances in a consistent fashion.

On the experimental side, we achieve state-of-the-art results on standard keypoint matching datasets Pascal VOC (with Berkeley annotations [8,20]) and Willow ObjectClass [14]. Motivated by lack of challenging standardised benchmarks, we additionally propose two new experimental setups. The first one is the evaluation on SPair-71k [38] a high-quality dataset that was recently released in the context of *dense image matching*. As the second one, we suggest to drop the common practice of keypoint pre-filtering and as a result force the future methods to address the presence of keypoints without a match.

The contributions presented in this paper can be summarized as follows.

1. We present a novel and conceptually simple **end-to-end trainable architecture** that seamlessly incorporates a state-of-the-art combinatorial graph matching solver. In addition, improvements are attained on the feature extraction side by processing global image information.
2. We introduce two new experimental setups and suggest them as future benchmarks.
3. We perform an extensive evaluation on existing benchmarks as well as on the newly proposed ones. Our approach reaches higher matching accuracy than previous methods, particularly in more challenging scenarios.
4. We exhibit further advantages of incorporating a combinatorial solver:
   (i) possible post-processing with a multi-graph matching solver,
   (ii) an effortless transition to more challenging scenarios with unmatchable keypoints.

2   Related Work

Combinatorial Optimization Meets Deep Learning. The research on this intersection is driven by two main paradigms.

The first one attempts to improve combinatorial optimization algorithms with deep learning methods. Such examples include the use of reinforcement learning for increased performance of branch-and-bound decisions [5,25,30] as well as of heuristic greedy algorithms for NP-Hard graph problems [7,17,29,32].

The other mindset aims at enhancing the expressivity of neural nets by turning combinatorial algorithms into differentiable building blocks. The work on differentiable quadratic programming [3] served as a catalyzer and progress was achieved even in more discrete settings [21,37,58]. In a recent culmination of these efforts [56], a "differentiable wrapper" was proposed for *blackbox implementations* of algorithms minimizing a linear discrete objective, effectively allowing free flow of progress from combinatorial optimization to deep learning.

Combinatorial Graph Matching. This problem, also known as the quadratic assignment problem [33] in the combinatorial optimization literature, is famous for being one of the practically most difficult NP-complete problems. There exist instances with less than 100 nodes that can be extremely challenging to solve with existing approaches [10]. Nevertheless, in computer vision efficient algorithmic approaches have been proposed that can routinely solve sparse instances with hundreds of nodes. Among those, solvers based on Lagrangian decomposition [53,54,65] have been shown to perform especially well, being able to quickly produce high quality solutions with small gaps to the optimum. Lagrange decomposition solvers split the graph matching problem into many small subproblems linked together via Lagrange multipliers. These multipliers are iteratively

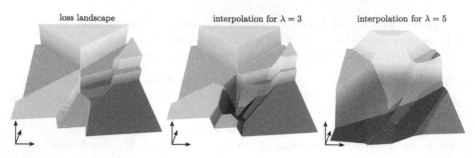

Fig. 2. Differentiation of a piecewise constant loss resulting from incorporating a graph matching solver. A two-dimensional section of the loss landscape is shown (left) along with two differentiable interpolations of increasing strengths (middle and right).

updated in order to reach agreement among the individual subproblems, typically with subgradient based techniques [48] or dual block coordinate ascent [51].

Graph matching solvers have a rich history of applications in computer vision. A non-exhaustive list includes uses for finding correspondences of landmarks between various objects in several semantic object classes [54,55,66], for estimating sparse correspondences in wide-displacement optical flow [2,54], for establishing associations in multiple object tracking [13], for object categorization [18], and for matching cell nuclei in biological image analysis [28].

Peer Methods. Wider interest in deep graph matching was ignited by [62] where a fully differentiable graph matching solver based on spectral methods was introduced. While differentiable relaxation of quadratic graph matching has reappeared [60], most methods [27,59,61] rely on the Sinkhorn iterative normalization [1,47] for the linear assignment problem or even on a single row normalization [23]. Another common feature is the use of various graph neural networks [6,34,44] sometimes also in a cross-graph fashion [59] for refining the node embeddings provided by the backbone architecture. There has also been a discussion regarding suitable loss functions [59,61,62]. Recently, nontrivial progress has been achieved by extracting more signal from the available geometric information [23,64].

3   Methods

3.1   Differentiability of Combinatorial Solvers

When incorporating a combinatorial solver into a neural network, differentiability constitutes the principal difficulty. Such solvers take continuous inputs (vertex and edge costs in our case) and return a discrete output (an indicator vector of the optimal matching). This mapping is piecewise constant because a small change of the costs typically does not affect the optimal matching. Therefore, the gradient exists almost everywhere but is equal to zero. This prohibits any gradient-based optimization.

A recent method proposed in [56] offers a mathematically-backed solution to overcome these obstacles. It introduces an efficient "implicit interpolation" of the solver's mapping while still treating the solver as a blackbox. In end effect, the intact solver is executed on the forward pass and as it turns out, only one other call to the solver is sufficient to provide meaningful gradient information during the backward pass.

Specifically, the method of [56] applies to *solvers* that solve an optimization problem of the form

$$w \in \mathbb{R}^N \mapsto y(w) \in Y \subset \mathbb{R}^N \quad \text{such that} \quad y(w) = \arg\min_{y \in Y} w \cdot y, \qquad (1)$$

where w is the continuous input and Y is *any* discrete set. This general formulation covers large classes of combinatorial algorithms that include the shortest path problem, the traveling salesman problem and many others. As will be shown in the subsequent sections, graph matching is also included in this definition.

If L denotes the final loss of the network, the suggested gradient of the piecewise constant mapping $w \mapsto L(y(w))$ takes the form

$$\frac{dL(y(w))}{dy} := \frac{y(w_\lambda) - y(w)}{\lambda}, \qquad (2)$$

in which w_λ is a certain modification of the input w depending on the gradient of L at $y(w)$. This is in fact the *exact gradient* of a piecewise linear interpolation of $L(y(w))$ in which a hyperparameter $\lambda > 0$ controls the interpolation range as Fig. 2 suggests.

It is worth pointing out that the framework does not require any *explicit* description of the set Y (such as via linear constraints). For further details and mathematical guarantees, see [56].

3.2 Graph Matching

The aim of graph matching is to find an assignment between vertices of two graphs that minimizes the sum of local and geometric costs.

Let $G_1 = (V_1, E_1)$ and $G_2 = (V_2, E_2)$ be two directed graphs. We denote by $\mathbf{v} \in \{0,1\}^{|V_1||V_2|}$ the indicator vector of matched vertices, that is $\mathbf{v}_{i,j} = 1$ if a vertex $i \in V_1$ is matched with $j \in V_2$ and $\mathbf{v}_{i,j} = 0$ otherwise. Analogously, we set $\mathbf{e} \in \{0,1\}^{|E_1||E_2|}$ as the indicator vector of matched edges. Obviously, the vector $\mathbf{e}$ is fully determined by the vector $\mathbf{v}$. Further, we denote by $\text{Adm}(G_1, G_2)$ the set of all pairs $(\mathbf{v}, \mathbf{e})$ that encode a valid matching between G_1 and G_2.

Given two cost vectors $c^v \in \mathbb{R}^{|V_1||V_2|}$ and $c^e \in \mathbb{R}^{|E_1||E_2|}$, we formulate the graph matching optimization problem as

$$\text{GM}(c^v, c^e) = \arg\min_{(\mathbf{v}, \mathbf{e}) \in \text{Adm}(G_1, G_2)} \{c^v \cdot \mathbf{v} + c^e \cdot \mathbf{e}\}. \qquad (3)$$

Algorithm 1. Forward and Backward Pass

function FORWARDPASS(c^v, c^e)	**function** BACKWARDPASS($\nabla L(\mathbf{v}, \mathbf{e})$, λ)
$\quad$ $(\mathbf{v}, \mathbf{e}) := \mathbf{GraphMatching}(c^v, c^e)$	$\quad$ **load** $(\mathbf{v}, \mathbf{e})$ and (c^v, c^e)
$\quad$ // Run the solver	$\quad$ $(c^v_\lambda, c^e_\lambda) := (c^v, c^e) + \lambda \nabla L(\mathbf{v}, \mathbf{e})$
$\quad$ **save** $(\mathbf{v}, \mathbf{e})$ and (c^v, c^e)	$\quad$ // Calculate modified costs
$\quad$ // Needed for backward pass	$\quad$ $(\mathbf{v}_\lambda, \mathbf{e}_\lambda) := \mathbf{GraphMatching}(c^v_\lambda, c^e_\lambda)$
$\quad$ **return** $(\mathbf{v}, \mathbf{e})$	$\quad$ // One more call to the solver
	$\quad$ **return** $\frac{1}{\lambda}(\mathbf{v}_\lambda - \mathbf{v}, \mathbf{e}_\lambda - \mathbf{e})$

It is immediate that GM fits the definition of the solver given in (1). If $L = L(\mathbf{v}, \mathbf{e})$ is the loss function, the mapping

$$(c^v, c^e) \mapsto L\big(\mathrm{GM}(c^v, c^e)\big) \tag{4}$$

is the piecewise constant function for which the scheme of [56] suggests

$$\nabla\Big(L\big(\mathrm{GM}(c^v, c^e)\big)\Big) := \frac{1}{\lambda}\big[\mathrm{GM}(c^v_\lambda, c^e_\lambda) - \mathrm{GM}(c^v, c^e)\big], \tag{5}$$

where the vectors c^v_λ and c^e_λ stand for

$$c^v_\lambda = c^v + \lambda \nabla_\mathbf{v} L\big(\mathrm{GM}(c^v, c^e)\big) \quad \text{and} \quad c^e_\lambda = c^e + \lambda \nabla_\mathbf{e} L\big(\mathrm{GM}(c^v, c^e)\big), \tag{6}$$

where $\nabla L = (\nabla_\mathbf{v} L, \nabla_\mathbf{e} L)$. The implementation is listed in Algorithm 1

In our experiments, we use the Hamming distance between the proposed matching and the ground truth matching of vertices as a loss. In this case, L does not depend on $\mathbf{e}$ and, consequently, $c^e_\lambda = c^e$.

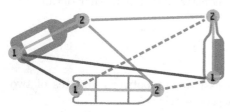

Fig. 3. Cycle consistency in multi-graph matching. The partial matching induced by light and dark green edges prohibits including the dashed edges. (Color figure online)

A more sophisticated variant of graph matching involves more than two graphs. The aim of multi-graph matching is to find a matching for every pair of graphs such that these matchings are consistent in a global fashion (i.e. satisfy so-called cycle consistency, see Fig. 3) and minimize the global cost. Although the framework of [56] is also applicable to multi-graph matching, we will only use it for post-processing.

3.3 Cost Margin

One disadvantage of using Hamming distance as a loss function is that it reaches its minimum value zero even if the ground truth matching has only fractionally lower cost than competing matchings. This increases sensitivity to distribution shifts and potentially harms generalization. The issue was already observed in [42], where the method [56] was also applied. We adopt the solution proposed in [42], namely the *cost margin*. In particular, during training we increase the unary costs that correspond to the ground truth matching by $\alpha > 0$, i.e.

$$\overleftrightarrow{c^v}_{i,j} = \begin{cases} c^v_{i,j} + \alpha & \text{if } \mathbf{v}^*_{i,j} = 1 \\ c^v_{i,j} & \text{if } \mathbf{v}^*_{i,j} = 0 \end{cases} \quad \text{for } i \in V_1 \text{ and } j \in V_2, \tag{7}$$

where $\mathbf{v}^*$ denotes the ground truth matching indicator vector. In all experiments, we use $\alpha = 1.0$.

3.4 Solvers

Graph Matching. We employ a dual block coordinate ascent solver [53] based on a Lagrange decomposition of the original problem. In every iteration, a dual lower bound is monotonically increased and the resulting dual costs are used to round primal solutions using a minimum cost flow solver. We choose this solver for its state-of-the-art performance and also because it has a highly optimized publicly available implementation.

Multi-graph Matching. We employ the solver from [52] that builds upon [53] and extends it to include additional constraints arising from cycle consistency. Primal solutions are rounded using a special form of permutation synchronization [41] allowing for partial matchings.

3.5 Architecture Design

Our end-to-end trainable architecture for keypoint matching consists of three stages. We call it BlackBox differentiation of Graph Matching solvers (BB-GM).

1. *Extraction of visual features.* A standard CNN architecture extracts a feature vector for each of the keypoints in the image. Additionally, a global feature vector is extracted.
2. *Geometry-aware feature refinement.* Keypoints are converted to a graph structure with spatial information. Then a graph neural network architecture is applied.

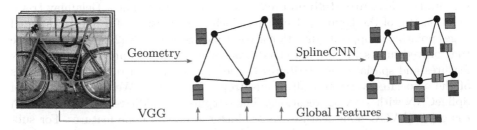

Fig. 4. Extraction of features for a single image. Keypoint locations and VGG features are processed by a SplineCNN and a global feature vector is produced.

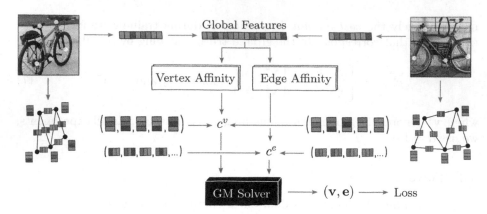

Fig. 5. Construction of combinatorial instance for keypoint matching.

3. *Construction of combinatorial instance.* Vertex and edge similarities are computed using the graph features and the global features. This determines a graph matching instance that is passed to the solver.

The resulting matching $\mathbf{v}$ is compared to the ground truth matching $\mathbf{v}^*$ and their Hamming distance $L(\mathbf{v}) = \mathbf{v} \cdot (1 - \mathbf{v}^*) + \mathbf{v}^* \cdot (1 - \mathbf{v})$ is the loss function to optimize.

While the first and the second stage (Fig. 4) are rather standard design blocks, the third one (Fig. 5) constitutes the principal novelty. More detailed descriptions follow.

Visual Feature Extraction. We closely follow previous work [23,59,62] and also compute the outputs of the `relu4_2` and `relu5_1` operations of the VGG16 [46] network pre-trained on ImageNet [16]. The spatially corresponding feature vector for each keypoint is recovered via bi-linear interpolation.

An image-wide global feature vector is extracted by max-pooling the output of the final VGG16 layer, see Fig. 4. Both the keypoint feature vectors and the global feature vectors are normalized with respect to the L^2 norm.

Geometric Feature Refinement. The graph is created as a Delaunay triangulation [15] of the keypoint locations. Each edge consists of a pair of directed edges pointing in opposite directions. We deploy SplineCNN [22], an architecture that proved successful in point-cloud processing. Its inputs are the VGG vertex features and spatial edge attributes defined as normalized relative coordinates of the associated vertices (called anisotropic in [23,24]). We use two layers of SplineCNN with MAX aggregations. The outputs are additively composed with the original VGG node features to produce the refined node features. For subsequent computation, we set the edge features as the differences of the refined node features. For illustration, see Fig. 4.

Matching Instance Construction. Both source and target image are passed through the two described procedures. Their global features are concatenated to one global feature vector g. A standard way to prepare a matching instance (the unary costs c^v) is to compute the inner product similarity (or affinity) of the vertex features $c_{i,j}^v = f_s^v(i) \cdot f_t^v(j)$, where $f_s^v(i)$ is the feature vector of the vertex i in the source graph and $f_t^v(j)$ is the feature vector of the vertex j in the target graph, possibly with a learnable vector or a matrix of coefficient as in [59].

In our case, the vector of "similarity coefficients" is produced as a weighted inner product

$$c_{i,j}^v = \sum_k f_s^v(i)_k \, a_k \, f_t^v(j)_k, \tag{8}$$

where a is produced by a one-layer NN from the global feature vector g. This allows for a gating-like behavior; the individual coordinates of the feature vectors may play a different role depending on the global feature vector g. It is intended to enable integrating various global semantic aspects such as rigidity of the object or the viewpoint perspective. Higher order cost terms c^e are calculated in the same vein using edge features instead of vertex features with an analogous learnable affinity layer. For an overview, see Fig. 5.

4   Experiments

We evaluate our method on the standard datasets for keypoint matching Pascal VOC with Berkeley annotations [8,20] and Willow ObjectClass [14]. Additionally, we propose a harder setup for Pascal VOC that avoids keypoint filtering as a preprocessing step. Finally, we report our performance on a recently published dataset SPair-71k [38]. Even though this dataset was designed for a slightly different community, its high quality makes it very suitable also in this context. The two new experimental setups aim to address the lack of difficult benchmarks in this line of work.

In some cases, we report our own evaluation of DGMC [23], the strongest competing method, which we denote by DGMC*. We used the publicly available implementation [24].

Runtime. All experiments were run on a single Tesla-V100 GPU. Due to the efficient C++ implementation of the solver [51], the computational bottleneck of the entire architecture is evaluating the VGG backbone. Around 30 image pairs were processed every second.

Hyperparameters. In all experiments, we use the exact same set of hyperparameters. Only the number of training steps is dataset-dependent. The optimizer in use is Adam [31] with an initial learning rate of 2×10^{-3} which is halved four times in regular intervals. Learning rate for finetuning the VGG weights is multiplied with 10^{-2}. We process batches of 8 image pairs and the hyperparameter λ from (2) is consistently set to 80.0. For remaining implementation details, the full code base will be made available.

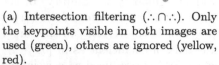

(a) Intersection filtering (∴∩∴). Only the keypoints visible in both images are used (green), others are ignored (yellow, red).

(b) Inclusion filtering (∴⊂∴). For any source image (left), only the targets (right) containing all the source keypoints are used.

Fig. 6. Keypoint filtering strategies. The image pair in (a) would not occur under inclusion filtering (b) because the different perspectives lead to incomparable sets of keypoints. Intersection filtering is unaffected by viewpoints. (Color figure online)

Table 1. Impact of filtering strategies on test accuracy (%) for DGMC [23] on Pascal VOC. Classes with drastic differences are highlighted.

Filter																					Mean
∴∩∴	50.4	67.6	70.7	70.5	87.2	85.2	82.5	74.3	46.2	69.4	69.9	73.9	73.8	65.4	51.6	98.0	73.2	69.6	94.3	89.6	73.2±0.5
∴⊂∴	45.5	66.6	54.5	67.8	87.2	86.4	85.6	73.2	38.5	67.3	86.9	64.9	78.9	60.3	61.5	96.8	68.7	93.5	93.6	85.0	73.1±0.4

Image Pair Sampling and Keypoint Filtering. The standard benchmark datasets provide images with annotated keypoints but do not define pairings of images or which keypoints should be kept for the matching instance. While it is the designer's choice how this is handled during training it is imperative that only one pair-sampling and keypoint filtering procedure is used at test time. Otherwise, the change in the distribution of test pairs and the corresponding instances may have unintended effects on the evaluation metric (as we demonstrate below), and therefore hinder fair comparisons.

We briefly describe two previously used methods for creating evaluation data, discuss their impact, and propose a third one.

Keypoint intersection (∴ ∩ ∴). Only the keypoints present in both source and target image are preserved for the matching task. In other words, all outliers are discarded. Clearly, any pair of images can be processed this way, see Fig. 6a.

Keypoint inclusion (∴⊂∴). Target image keypoints have to include all the source image keypoints. The target keypoints that are not present in the source image are then disregarded. The source image may still contain outliers. Examples in which both target and source images contain outliers such as in Fig. 6b, will not be present.

When keypoint inclusion filtering is used on evaluation, some image pairs are discarded, which introduces some biases. In particular, pairs of images seen from different viewpoints become underrepresented, as such pairs often have uncomparable sets of visible keypoints, see Fig. 6. Another effect is a bias towards a higher number of keypoints in a matching instance which makes the matching

Table 2. Keypoint matching accuracy (%) on Pascal VOC using standard intersection filtering ($\therefore \cap \therefore$). For GMN [62] we report the improved results from [59] denoted as GMN-PL. DGMC* is [23] reproduced using $\therefore \cap \therefore$. For DGMC* and BB-GM we report the mean over 5 restarts.

Method	aero	bike	bird	boat	bottle	bus	car	cat	chair	cow	table	dog	horse	mbike	person	plant	sheep	sofa	train	tv	Mean
GMN-PL	31.1	46.2	58.2	45.9	70.6	76.5	61.2	61.7	35.5	53.7	58.9	57.5	56.9	49.3	34.1	77.5	57.1	53.6	83.2	88.6	57.9
PCA-GM [59]	40.9	55.0	65.8	47.9	76.9	77.9	63.5	67.4	33.7	66.5	63.6	61.3	58.9	62.8	44.9	77.5	67.4	57.5	86.7	90.9	63.8
NGM+ [60]	50.8	64.5	59.5	57.6	79.4	76.9	74.4	69.9	41.5	62.3	68.5	62.2	62.4	64.7	47.8	78.7	66.0	63.3	81.4	89.6	66.1
GLMNet [27]	52.0	67.3	63.2	57.4	80.3	74.6	70.0	72.6	38.9	66.3	77.3	65.7	67.9	64.2	44.8	86.3	69.0	61.9	79.3	91.3	67.5
CIE$_1$-H [61]	51.2	69.2	70.1	55.0	82.8	72.8	69.0	74.2	39.6	68.8	71.8	70.0	71.8	66.8	44.8	85.2	69.9	65.4	85.2	92.4	68.9
DGMC* [23]	50.4	67.6	70.7	70.5	87.2	85.2	82.5	74.3	46.2	69.4	69.9	73.9	73.8	65.4	51.6	**98.0**	73.2	69.6	94.3	89.6	73.2 ± 0.5
BB-GM	**61.5**	**75.0**	**78.1**	**80.0**	**87.4**	**93.0**	**89.1**	**80.2**	**58.1**	**77.6**	**76.5**	**79.3**	**78.6**	**78.8**	**66.7**	97.4	**76.4**	**77.5**	**97.7**	**94.4**	**80.1 ± 0.6**

Table 3. F1 score (%) for Pascal VOC keypoint matching without filtering ($\therefore \cup \therefore$). As a reference we report an ablation of our method where the solver is forced to match all source keypoints, denoted as BB-GM-Max. BB-GM-Multi refers to using the multi-graph matching solver with cycle consistency [52] with sets of 5 images at evaluation. The reported statistics are over 10 restarts. The last row displays the percentage of unmatched keypoints in the test-set pairs.

Method	aero	bike	bird	boat	bottle	bus	car	cat	chair	cow	table	dog	horse	mbike	person	plant	sheep	sofa	train	tv	Mean
BB-GM-Max	35.5	68.6	46.7	36.1	85.4	58.1	25.6	51.7	27.3	51.0	46.0	46.7	48.9	58.9	29.6	93.6	42.6	35.3	70.7	79.5	51.9 ± 1.0
BB-GM	42.7	**70.9**	57.5	46.6	**85.8**	64.1	51.0	63.8	42.4	63.7	47.9	61.5	**63.4**	69.0	46.1	94.2	**57.4**	39.0	**78.0**	82.7	61.4 ± 0.5
BB-GM-Multi	**43.4**	70.5	**61.9**	**46.8**	84.9	**65.3**	**54.2**	**66.9**	44.9	**67.5**	**50.8**	**66.8**	63.3	**71.0**	46.1	**96.1**	56.5	**41.3**	73.4	**83.4**	**62.8 ± 0.5**
Unmatched (%)	22.7	4.9	30.6	29.1	2.7	23.8	40.8	26.4	17.3	25.1	21.2	27.4	26.8	16.6	22.1	6.7	36.7	27.5	31.7	14.0	22.7

task more difficult. While the effect on mean accuracy is not strong, Table 1 shows large differences in individual classes.

Another unsatisfactory aspect of both methods is that label information is required at evaluation time, rendering the setting quite unrealistic. For this reason, we **propose to evaluate without any keypoint removal**.

Unfiltered keypoints ($\therefore \cup \therefore$). For a given pair of images, the keypoints are used without any filtering. Matching instances may contain a different number of source and target vertices, as well as outliers in both images. This is the most general setup.

4.1 Pascal VOC

The Pascal VOC [20] dataset with Berkeley annotations [8] contains images with bounding boxes surrounding objects of 20 classes. We follow the standard data preparation procedure of [59]. Each object is cropped to its bounding box and scaled to 256×256 px. The resulting images contain up to 23 annotated keypoints, depending on the object category.

The results under the most common experimental conditions ($\therefore \cap \therefore$) are reported in Table 2 and we can see that BB-GM outperforms competing approaches.

All Keypoints. We propose, see Sect. 4, to preserve all keypoints ($\therefore \cup \therefore$). Matching accuracy is no longer a good evaluation metric as it ignores false positives. Instead, we report F1-Score, the harmonic mean of precision and recall.

Since the underlying solver used by our method also works for partial matchings, our architecture is applicable out of the box. Competing architectures rely on either the Sinkhorn normalization or a softmax and as such, they are hardwired to produce maximal matchings and do not offer a simple adjustment to the unfiltered setup. To simulate the negative impact of maximal matchings we provide an ablation of BB-GM where we modify the solver to output maximal matchings. This is denoted by BB-GM-Max.

In addition, we report the scores obtained by running the multi-graph matching solver [52] as post-processing. Instead of sampling pairs of images, we sample sets of 5 images and recover from the architecture the costs of the $\binom{5}{2} = 10$ matching instances. The multi-graph matching solver then searches for globally optimal set of consistent matchings. The results are provided in Table 3.

Note that sampling sets of 5 images instead of image pairs does not interfere with the statistics of the test set. The results are therefore comparable.

4.2   Willow ObjectClass

The Willow ObjectClass dataset contains a total of 256 images from 5 categories. Each category is represented by at least 40 images, all of them with consistent orientation. Each image is annotated with the same 10 distinctive category-specific keypoints, which means there is no difference between the described keypoint filtering methods. Following standard procedure, we crop the images to the bounding boxes of the objects and rescale to 256×256 px.

Multiple training strategies have been used in prior work. Some authors decide to train only on the relatively small Willow dataset, or pretrain on Pascal VOC and fine-tune on Willow afterward [59]. Another approach is to pretrain on Pascal VOC and evaluate on Willow without fine-tuning, to test the transfer-ability [60]. We report results for all different variants, following the standard procedure of using 20 images per class when training on Willow and excluding the classes *car* and *motorbike* from Pascal VOC when pre-training, as these images overlap with the Willow dataset. We also evaluated the strongest competing approach DGMC [23] under all settings.

The results are shown in Table 4. While our method achieves good performance, we are reluctant to claim superiority over prior work. The small dataset size, the multitude of training setups, and high standard deviations all prevent statistically significant comparisons.

4.3   SPair-71k

We also report performance on SPair-71k [38], a dataset recently published in the context of dense image matching. It contains $70,958$ image pairs prepared from Pascal VOC 2012 and Pascal 3D+. It has several advantages over the

Table 4. Keypoint matching accuracy (%) on Willow ObjectClass. The columns Pt and Wt indicate training on Pascal VOC and Willow, respectively. Comparisons should be made only within the same training setting. For HARG-SSVM [14] we report the comparable figures from [59]. Twenty restarts were carried out.

Method	Pt	Wt	Face	Motorbike	Car	Duck	Bottle
HARG-SSVM [59]	x	✓	91.2	44.4	58.4	55.2	66.6
GMN-PL [59,62]	✓	x	98.1	65.0	72.9	74.3	70.5
	✓	✓	99.3	71.4	74.3	82.8	76.7
PCA-GM [59]	✓	x	100.0	69.8	78.6	82.4	95.1
	✓	✓	100.0	76.7	84.0	93.5	96.9
CIE [61]	✓	x	99.9	71.5	75.4	73.2	97.6
	✓	✓	100.0	90.0	82.2	81.2	97.6
NGM [60]	x	✓	99.2	82.1	84.1	77.4	93.5
GLMNet [27]	✓	✓	100.0	89.7	93.6	85.4	93.4
DGMC* [23]	✓	x	98.6 ± 1.1	69.8 ± 5.0	84.6 ± 5.2	76.8 ± 4.3	90.7 ± 2.4
	x	✓	100.0 ± 0.0	98.5 ± 1.5	98.3 ± 1.2	90.2 ± 3.6	98.1 ± 0.9
	✓	✓	100.0 ± 0.0	98.8 ± 1.6	96.5 ± 1.6	93.2 ± 3.8	99.9 ± 0.3
BB-GM	✓	x	100.0 ± 0.0	95.8 ± 1.4	89.1 ± 1.7	89.8 ± 1.7	97.9 ± 0.7
	x	✓	100.0 ± 0.0	99.2 ± 0.4	96.9 ± 0.6	89.0 ± 1.0	98.8 ± 0.6
	✓	✓	100.0 ± 0.0	98.9 ± 0.5	95.7 ± 1.5	93.1 ± 1.5	99.1 ± 0.4

Table 5. Keypoint matching accuracy (%) on SPair-71k grouped by levels of difficulty in the viewpoint of the matching-pair. Statistics is over 5 restarts.

Method	Viewpoint difficulty			All
	Easy	Medium	Hard	
DGMC*	79.4 ± 0.2	65.2 ± 0.2	61.3 ± 0.5	72.2 ± 0.2
BB-GM	**84.8 ± 0.1**	**73.1 ± 0.2**	**70.6 ± 0.9**	**78.9 ± 0.4**

Pascal VOC dataset, namely higher image quality, richer keypoint annotations, difficulty annotation of image-pairs, as well as the removal of the ambiguous and poorly annotated *sofas* and *dining tables*.

Again, we evaluated DGMC [23] as the strongest competitor of our method. The results are reported in Table 5 and Table 6. We consistently improve upon the baseline, particularly on pairs of images seen from very different viewpoints. This highlights the ability of our method to resolve instances with conflicting evidence. Some example matchings are presented in Fig. 1 and Fig. 7.

4.4 Ablations Studies

To isolate the impact of single components of our architecture, we conduct various ablation studies as detailed in the supplementary material. The results on Pascal VOC are summarized in Tab. S1.

420   M. Rolínek et al.

Table 6. Keypoint matching accuracy (%) on SPair-71k for all classes.

Method	✈	🚲	🐦	🚤	🍾	🚌	🚗	🐱	🪑	🐄	🐎	🐕	🏍	🧍	🌿	🐑	🚂	🖥	Mean
DGMC*	54.8	44.8	80.3	70.9	65.5	90.1	78.5	66.7	66.4	73.2	66.2	66.5	65.7	59.1	98.7	68.5	84.9	98.0	72.2 ± 0.2
BB-GM	**66.9**	**57.7**	**85.8**	**78.5**	**66.9**	**95.4**	**86.1**	**74.6**	**68.3**	**78.9**	**73.0**	**67.5**	**79.3**	**73.0**	**99.1**	**74.8**	**95.0**	98.6	**78.9 ± 0.4**

Fig. 7. Example matchings from the SPair-71k dataset.

5 Conclusion

We have demonstrated that deep learning architectures that integrate combinatorial graph matching solvers perform well on deep graph matching benchmarks.

Opportunities for future work now fall into multiple categories. For one, it should be tested whether such architectures can be useful outside the designated playground for deep graph matching methods. If more progress is needed, two major directions lend themselves: (i) improving the neural network architecture even further so that input costs to the matching problem become more discriminative and (ii) employing better solvers that improve in terms of obtained solution quality and ability to handle a more complicated and expressive cost structure (e.g. hypergraph matching solvers).

Finally, the potential of building architectures around solvers for other computer vision related combinatorial problems such as MULTICUT or MAX-CUT can be explored.

References

1. Adams, R.P., Zemel, R.S.: Ranking via sinkhorn propagation (2011)
2. Abu Alhaija, H., Sellent, A., Kondermann, D., Rother, C.: GraphFlow – 6D large displacement scene flow via graph matching. In: Gall, J., Gehler, P., Leibe, B. (eds.) GCPR 2015. LNCS, vol. 9358, pp. 285–296. Springer, Cham (2015). https://doi.org/10.1007/978-3-319-24947-6_23
3. Amos, B., Kolter, J.Z.: OptNet: differentiable optimization as a layer in neural networks. In: International Conference on Machine Learning. ICML 2017, pp. 136–145 (2017)
4. Baker, S., Scharstein, D., Lewis, J.P., Roth, S., Black, M.J., Szeliski, R.: A database and evaluation methodology for optical flow. Int. J. Comput. Vision **92**(1), 1–31 (2011). https://doi.org/10.1007/s11263-010-0390-2
5. Balcan, M., Dick, T., Sandholm, T., Vitercik, E.: Learning to branch. In: International Conference on Machine Learning. ICML 2018, pp. 353–362 (2018)
6. Battaglia, P., et al.: Relational inductive biases, deep learning, and graph networks. arXiv preprint arXiv:1806.01261 (2018)
7. Bello, I., Pham, H., Le, Q.V., Norouzi, M., Bengio, S.: Neural combinatorial optimization with reinforcement learning. In: International Conference on Learning Representations, Workshop Track. ICLR 2017 (2017)
8. Bourdev, L., Malik, J.: Poselets: Body part detectors trained using 3D human pose annotations. In: IEEE International Conference on Computer Vision. ICCV 2009, pp. 1365–1372 (2009)
9. Burkard, R., Dell'Amico, M., Martello, S.: Assignment Problems. Society for Industrial and Applied Mathematics, Philadelphia (2009)
10. Burkard, R.E., Karisch, S.E., Rendl, F.: QAPLIB-a quadratic assignment problem library. J. Global Optim. **10**(4), 391–403 (1997). https://doi.org/10.1023/A:1008293323270
11. Cao, Z., Simon, T., Wei, S.E., Sheikh, Y.: Realtime multi-person 2D pose estimation using part affinity fields. In: IEEE Conference on Computer Vision and Pattern Recognition. CVPR 2017 (2017)
12. Chang, J.R., Chen, Y.S.: Pyramid stereo matching network. In: IEEE Conference on Computer Vision and Pattern Recognition. CVPR 2018, pp. 5410–5418 (2018)
13. Chen, H.T., Lin, H.H., Liu, T.L.: Multi-object tracking using dynamical graph matching. In: Proceedings of the 2001 IEEE Computer Society Conference on Computer Vision and Pattern Recognition. CVPR 2001, vol. 2, pp. II-II. IEEE (2001)
14. Cho, M., Alahari, K., Ponce, J.: Learning graphs to match. In: IEEE International Conference on Computer Vision. ICCV 2013 (2013)
15. Delaunay, B.: Sur la sphere vide. Izv. Akad. Nauk SSSR Otdelenie Matematicheskii i Estestvennyka Nauk **7**, 793–800 (1934)
16. Deng, J., Dong, W., Socher, R., Li, L.J., Li, K., Fei-Fei, L.: ImageNet: a large-scale hierarchical image database. In: IEEE Conference on Computer Vision and Pattern Recognition. CVPR 2009, pp. 248–255 (2009)

17. Deudon, M., Cournut, P., Lacoste, A., Adulyasak, Y., Rousseau, L.-M.: Learning heuristics for the TSP by policy gradient. In: van Hoeve, W.-J. (ed.) CPAIOR 2018. LNCS, vol. 10848, pp. 170–181. Springer, Cham (2018). https://doi.org/10.1007/978-3-319-93031-2_12

18. Duchenne, O., Joulin, A., Ponce, J.: A graph-matching kernel for object categorization. In: 2011 International Conference on Computer Vision, pp. 1792–1799. IEEE (2011)

19. Elmsallati, A., Clark, C., Kalita, J.: Global alignment of protein-protein interaction networks: a survey. IEEE/ACM Trans. Comput. Biol. Bioinform. **13**(4), 689–705 (2016)

20. Everingham, M., Van Gool, L., Williams, C., Winn, J., Zisserman, A.: The pascal visual object classes (VOC) challenge. Int. J. Comput. Vision **88**(2), 303–338 (2010). https://doi.org/10.1007/s11263-009-0275-4

21. Ferber, A., Wilder, B., Dilkina, B., Tambe, M.: Mipaal: Mixed integer program as a layer. arXiv preprint arXiv:1907.05912 (2019)

22. Fey, M., Eric Lenssen, J., Weichert, F., Müller, H.: SplineCNN: fast geometric deep learning with continuous b-spline kernels. In: IEEE Conference on Computer Vision and Pattern Recognition. CVPR 2018, pp. 869–877 (2018)

23. Fey, M., Lenssen, J.E., Morris, C., Masci, J., Kriege, N.M.: Deep graph matching consensus. In: International Conference on Learning Representations. ICLR 2020 (2020)

24. Fey, M., Lenssen, J.E., Morris, C., Masci, J., Kriege, N.M.: Deep graph matching consensus. https://github.com/rusty1s/deep-graph-matching-consensus (2020). Commit: be1c4c

25. Gasse, M., Chételat, D., Ferroni, N., Charlin, L., Lodi, A.: Exact combinatorial optimization with graph convolutional neural networks. In: Advances in Neural Information Processing Systems. NIPS 2019, pp. 15554–15566 (2019)

26. Grohe, M., Rattan, G., Woeginger, G.J.: Graph similarity and approximate isomorphism. In: 43rd International Symposium on Mathematical Foundations of Computer Science (MFCS 2018). Leibniz International Proceedings in Informatics (LIPIcs), vol. 117, pp. 20:1–20:16 (2018)

27. Jiang, B., Sun, P., Tang, J., Luo, B.: GLMNet: graph learning-matching networks for feature matching. arXiv preprint arXiv:1911.07681 (2019)

28. Kainmueller, D., Jug, F., Rother, C., Myers, G.: Active graph matching for automatic joint segmentation and annotation of *C. elegans*. In: Golland, P., Hata, N., Barillot, C., Hornegger, J., Howe, R. (eds.) MICCAI 2014. LNCS, vol. 8673, pp. 81–88. Springer, Cham (2014). https://doi.org/10.1007/978-3-319-10404-1_11

29. Khalil, E., Dai, H., Zhang, Y., Dilkina, B., Song, L.: Learning combinatorial optimization algorithms over graphs. In: Advances in Neural Information Processing Systems. NIPS 2017, pp. 6348–6358 (2017)

30. Khalil, E.B., Bodic, P.L., Song, L., Nemhauser, G., Dilkina, B.: Learning to branch in mixed integer programming. In: AAAI Conference on Artificial Intelligence. AAAI 2016, pp. 724–731 (2016)

31. Kingma, D.P., Ba, J.: Adam: a method for stochastic optimization. In: International Conference on Learning Representations. ICLR 2014 (2014)

32. Kool, W., van Hoof, H., Welling, M.: Attention, learn to solve routing problems! In: International Conference on Learning Representations. ICLR 2019 (2019)

33. Lawler, E.L.: The quadratic assignment problem. Manag. Sci. **9**(4), 586–599 (1963)

34. Li, Y., Zemel, R., Brockschmidt, M., Tarlow, D.: Gated graph sequence neural networks. In: International Conference on Learning Representations. ICLR 2016 (2016)

35. Liu, L., Cheung, W.K., Li, X., Liao, L.: Aligning users across social networks using network embedding. In: International Joint Conference on Artificial Intelligence. IJCAI 2016, pp. 1774–1780 (2016)
36. Luo, W., Schwing, A.G., Urtasun, R.: Efficient deep learning for stereo matching. In: IEEE Conference on Computer Vision and Pattern Recognition. CVPR 2016, pp. 5695–5703 (2016)
37. Mandi, J., Demirovic, E., Stuckey, P.J., Guns, T.: Smart predict-and-optimize for hard combinatorial optimization problems. arXiv preprint arXiv:1911.10092 (2019)
38. Min, J., Lee, J., Ponce, J., Cho, M.: SPair-71k: a large-scale benchmark for semantic correspondance. arXiv preprint arXiv:1908.10543 (2019)
39. Nam, H., Han, B.: Learning multi-domain convolutional neural networks for visual tracking. arXiv preprint arXiv:1510.07945 (2015)
40. Niculae, V., Martins, A., Blondel, M., Cardie, C.: SparseMAP: differentiable sparse structured inference. In: International Conference on Machine Learning. ICML 2018, pp. 3799–3808 (2018)
41. Pachauri, D., Kondor, R., Singh, V.: Solving the multi-way matching problem by permutation synchronization. In: Advances in Neural Information Processing Systems. NIPS 2013, pp. 1860–1868 (2013)
42. Rolínek, M., Musil, V., Paulus, A., Vlastelica, M., Michaelis, C., Martius, G.: Optimizing ranking-based metrics with blackbox differentiation. In: Conference on Computer Vision and Pattern Recognition. CVPR 2020, pp. 7620–7630 (2020)
43. Sahillioğlu, Y.: Recent advances in shape correspondence. Vis. Comput. **36**(8), 1705–1721 (2019). https://doi.org/10.1007/s00371-019-01760-0
44. Scarselli, F., Gori, M., Tsoi, A.C., Hagenbuchner, M., Monfardini, G.: The graph neural network model. Trans. Neur. Netw. **20**(1), 61–80 (2009)
45. Schroff, F., Kalenichenko, D., Philbin, J.: FaceNet: a unified embedding for face recognition and clustering. In: IEEE Conference on Computer Vision and Pattern Recognition. CVPR 2015, pp. 815–823 (2015)
46. Simonyan, K., Zisserman, A.: Very deep convolutional networks for large-scale image recognition. arXiv preprint arXiv:1409.1556 (2014)
47. Sinkhorn, R., Knopp, P.: Concerning nonnegative matrices and doubly stochastic matrices. Pac. J. Math. **21**, 343–348 (1967)
48. Storvik, G., Dahl, G.: Lagrangian-based methods for finding MAP solutions for MRF models. IEEE Trans. Image Process. **9**(3), 469–479 (2000)
49. Sun, D., Roth, S., Black, M.J.: A quantitative analysis of current practices in optical flow estimation and the principles behind them. Int. J. Comput. Vis. **106**(2), 115–137 (2014). https://doi.org/10.1007/s11263-013-0644-x
50. Sun, D., Yang, X., Liu, M.Y., Kautz, J.: PWC-Net: CNNs for optical flow using pyramid, warping, and cost volume. In: IEEE Conference on Computer Vision and Pattern Recognition. CVPR 2018, June 2018
51. Swoboda, P., Kuske, J., Savchynskyy, B.: A dual ascent framework for Lagrangean decomposition of combinatorial problems. In: IEEE Conference on Computer Vision and Pattern Recognition. CVPR 2017, pp. 1596–1606 (2017)
52. Swoboda, P., Mokarian, A., Theobalt, C., Bernard, F., et al.: A convex relaxation for multi-graph matching. In: IEEE Conference on Computer Vision and Pattern Recognition. CVPR 2019, pp. 11156–11165 (2019)
53. Swoboda, P., Rother, C., Alhaija, H.A., Kainmüller, D., Savchynskyy, B.: A study of Lagrangean decompositions and dual ascent solvers for graph matching. In: IEEE Conference on Computer Vision and Pattern Recognition. CVPR 2016, pp. 7062–7071 (2016)

54. Torresani, L., Kolmogorov, V., Rother, C.: A dual decomposition approach to feature correspondence. IEEE Trans. Pattern Anal. Mach. Intell. **35**(2), 259–271 (2013)
55. Ufer, N., Ommer, B.: Deep semantic feature matching. In: IEEE Conference on Computer Vision and Pattern Recognition. CVPR 2017, pp. 6914–6923 (2017)
56. Vlastelica, M., Paulus, A., Musil, V., Martius, G., Rolínek, M.: Differentiation of blackbox combinatorial solvers. In: International Conference on Learning Representations. ICLR 2020 (2020)
57. Wang, L., Ouyang, W., Wang, X., Lu, H.: Visual tracking with fully convolutional networks. In: IEEE International Conference on Computer Vision. ICCV 2015, pp. 3119–3127 (2015)
58. Wang, P.W., Donti, P., Wilder, B., Kolter, Z.: SATNet: bridging deep learning and logical reasoning using a differentiable satisfiability solver. In: International Conference on Machine Learning, pp. 6545–6554 (2019)
59. Wang, R., Yan, J., Yang, X.: Learning combinatorial embedding networks for deep graph matching. In: IEEE International Conference on Computer Vision. ICCV 2019, pp. 3056–3065 (2019)
60. Wang, R., Yan, J., Yang, X.: Neural graph matching network: learning Lawler's quadratic assignment problem with extension to hypergraph and multiple-graph matching. arXiv preprint arXiv:1911.11308 (2019)
61. Yu, T., Wang, R., Yan, J., Li, B.: Learning deep graph matching with channel-independent embedding and Hungarian attention. In: International Conference on Learning Representations. ICLR 2020 (2020)
62. Zanfir, A., Sminchisescu, C.: Deep learning of graph matching. In: Conference on Computer Vision and Pattern Recognition. CVPR 2018, pp. 2684–2693 (2018)
63. Zhang, Y., Hare, J., Prügel-Bennett, A.: Learning representations of sets through optimized permutations. arXiv preprint arXiv:1812.03928 (2018)
64. Zhang, Z., Lee, W.S.: Deep graphical feature learning for the feature matching problem. In: IEEE International Conference on Computer Vision. ICCV 2019 (2019)
65. Zhang, Z., Shi, Q., McAuley, J., Wei, W., Zhang, Y., van den Hengel, A.: Pairwise matching through max-weight bipartite belief propagation. In: IEEE Conference on Computer Vision and Pattern Recognition. CVPR 2016 (2016)
66. Zhou, F., la Torre, F.D.: Factorized graph matching. In: IEEE Conference on Computer Vision and Pattern Recognition. CVPR 2012, pp. 127–134 (2012)

Video Representation Learning by Recognizing Temporal Transformations

Simon Jenni$^{(\boxtimes)}$ ⓘ, Givi Meishvili ⓘ, and Paolo Favaro ⓘ

University of Bern, Bern, Switzerland
{simon.jenni,givi.meishvili,paolo.favaro}@inf.unibe.ch

Abstract. We introduce a novel self-supervised learning approach to learn representations of videos that are responsive to changes in the motion dynamics. Our representations can be learned from data without human annotation and provide a substantial boost to the training of neural networks on small labeled data sets for tasks such as action recognition, which require to accurately distinguish the motion of objects. We promote an accurate learning of motion without human annotation by training a neural network to discriminate a video sequence from its temporally transformed versions. To learn to distinguish non-trivial motions, the design of the transformations is based on two principles: 1) To define clusters of motions based on time warps of different magnitude; 2) To ensure that the discrimination is feasible only by observing and analyzing as many image frames as possible. Thus, we introduce the following transformations: forward-backward playback, random frame skipping, and uniform frame skipping. Our experiments show that networks trained with the proposed method yield representations with improved transfer performance for action recognition on UCF101 and HMDB51.

Keywords: Representation learning · Video analysis · Self-supervised learning · Unsupervised learning · Time dynamics · Action recognition

1 Introduction

A fundamental goal in computer vision is to build representations of visual data that can be used towards tasks such as object classification, detection, segmentation, tracking, and action recognition [11,26,39,41]. In the past decades, a lot of research has been focused on learning directly from single images and has done so with remarkable success [17,18,38]. Single images carry crucial information about a scene. However, when we observe a temporal sequence of image frames, *i.e.*, a video, it is possible to understand much more about the objects and the scene. In fact, by moving, objects reveal their shape (through a change in the

Electronic supplementary material The online version of this chapter (https://doi.org/10.1007/978-3-030-58604-1_26) contains supplementary material, which is available to authorized users.

© Springer Nature Switzerland AG 2020
A. Vedaldi et al. (Eds.): ECCV 2020, LNCS 12373, pp. 425–442, 2020.
https://doi.org/10.1007/978-3-030-58604-1_26

occlusions), their behavior (how they move due to the laws of Physics or their inner mechanisms), and their interaction with other objects (how they deform, break, clamp etc.). However, learning such information is non trivial. Even when labels related to motion categories are available (such as in action recognition), there is no guarantee that the trained model will learn the desired information, and will not instead simply focus on a single iconic frame and recognize a key pose or some notable features strongly correlated to the action [40].

To build representations of videos that capture more than the information contained in a single frame, we pose the task of learning an accurate model of motion as that of learning to distinguish an unprocessed video from a temporally-transformed one. Since similar frames are present in both the unprocessed and transformed sequence, the only piece of information that allows their discrimination is their temporal evolution. This idea has been exploited in the past [12,28,29,33,50] and is also related to work in time-series analysis, where dynamic time warping is used as a distance for temporal sequences [20].

In this paper, we analyze different temporal transformations and evaluate how learning to distinguish them yields a representation that is useful to classify videos into meaningful action categories. Our main finding is that the most effective temporal distortions are those that can be identified only by observing the largest number of frames. For instance, the case of substituting the second half of a video with its first half in reverse order, can be detected already by comparing just the 3 frames around the temporal symmetry. In contrast, distinguishing when a video is played backwards from when it is played forward [50] may require observing many frames. Thus, one can achieve powerful video representations by using as pseudo-task the classification of temporal distortions that differ in their long-range motion dynamics. Towards this goal, we investigate 4 different temporal transformations of a video, which are illustrated in Fig. 1:

1. **Speed**: Select a subset of frames with uniform sub-sampling (*i.e.*, with a fixed number of frames in between every pair of selected frames), while preserving the order in the original sequence;
2. **Random**: Select a random permutation of the frame sequence;
3. **Periodic**: Select a random subset of frames in their natural (forward) temporal order and then a random subset in the backward order;
4. **Warp**: Select a subset of frames with a random sub-sampling (*i.e.*, with a random number of frames in between every pair of selected frames), while preserving the natural (forward) order in the original sequence.

We use these transformations to verify and illustrate the hypothesis that learning to distinguish them from one another (and the original sequence) is useful to build a representation of videos for action recognition. For simplicity, we train a neural network that takes as input videos of the same duration and outputs two probabilities: One is about which one of the above temporal transformations the input sequence is likely to belong to and the second is about identifying the correct speed of the chosen **speed** transformation.

In the Experiments section, we transfer features of standard 3D-CNN architectures (C3D [44], 3D-ResNet [16], and R(2+1)D [45]) pre-trained through the

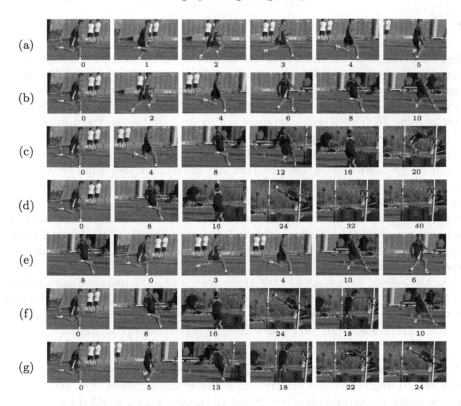

Fig. 1. Learning from Temporal Transformations. The frame number is indicated below each image. (a)–(d) `Speed` transformation by skipping: (a) 0 frames, (b) 1 frame, (c) 3 frames, and (d) 7 frames. (e) `Random`: frame permutation (no frame is skipped). (f) `Periodic`: forward-backward motion (at the selected speed). (g) `Warp`: variable frame skipping while preserving the order.

above pseudo-task to standard action recognition data sets such as UCF101 and HMDB51, with improved performance compared to prior works. We also show that features learned through our proposed pseudo-task capture long-range motion better than features obtained through supervised learning. Our project page https://sjenni.github.io/temporal-ssl provides code and additional experiments.

Our contributions can be summarized as follows: 1) We introduce a novel self-supervised learning task to learn video representations by distinguishing temporal transformations; 2) We study the discrimination of the following novel temporal transformations: **speed**, **periodic** and **warp**; 3) We show that our features are a better representation of motion than features obtained through supervised learning and achieve state of the art transfer learning performance on action recognition benchmarks.

2   Prior Work

Because of the lack of manual annotation, our method belongs to self-supervised learning. Self-supervised learning appeared in the machine learning literature more than 2 decades ago [2,7] and has been reformulated recently in the context of visual data with new insights that make it a promising method for representation learning [9]. This learning strategy is a recent variation on the unsupervised learning theme, which exploits labeling that comes for "free" with the data. Labels could be easily accessible and associated with a non-visual signal (for example, ego-motion [1], audio [35], text and so on), but also could be obtained from the structure of the data (e.g., the location of tiles [9,34], the color of an image [27,53,54]) or through transformations of the data [14,21,22]. Several works have adapted self-supervised feature learning methods from domains such as images or natural language to videos: Rotation prediction [23], Dense Predictive Coding [15], and [43] adapt the BERT language model [8] to sequences of frame feature vectors.

In the case of videos, we identify three groups of self-supervised approaches: 1) Methods that learn from videos to represent videos; 2) Methods that learn from videos to represent images; 3) Methods that learn from videos and auxiliary signals to represent both videos and the auxiliary signals (e.g., audio).

Temporal Ordering Methods. Prior work has explored the temporal ordering of the video frames as a supervisory signal. For example, Misra et al. [33] showed that learning to distinguish a real triplet of frames from a shuffled one yields a representation with temporally varying information (e.g., human pose). This idea has been extended to longer sequences for posture and behavior analysis by using Long Short-Term Memories [5]. The above approaches classify the correctness of a temporal order directly from one sequence. An alternative is to feed several sequences, some of which are modified, and ask the network to tell them apart [12]. Other recent work predicts the permutation of a sequence of frames [28] or both the spatial and temporal ordering of frame patches [6,24]. Another recent work focuses on solely predicting the arrow of time in videos [50]. Three concurrent publications also exploit the playback speed as a self-supervision signal [4,10,52]. In contrast, our work studies a wider range of temporal transformations. Moreover, we show empirically that the temporal statistics extent (in frames) captured by our features correlates to the transfer learning performance in action recognition.

Methods Based on Visual Tracking. The method of Wang and Gupta [48] builds a metric to define similarity between patches. Three patches are used as input, where two patches are matched via tracking in a video and the third one is arbitrarily chosen. Tracking can also be directly solved during training, as shown in [46], where color is used as a supervisory signal. By solving the task of coloring a grey-scale video (in a coherent manner across time), one can automatically learn how to track objects. Visual correspondences can also be learned by exploiting cycle-consistency in time [49] or by jointly performing region-level localization and fine-grained matching [29]. However, although trained on videos, these methods have not been used to build video representations or evaluated on action recognition.

Methods Based on Auxiliary Signals. Supervision can also come from additional signals recorded with images. For example, videos come also with audio. The fact that the sounds are synchronized with the motion of objects in a video, already provides a weak supervision signal: One knows the set of possible sounds of visible objects, but not precisely their correspondence. Owens *et al.* [36] show that, through the process of predicting a summary of ambient sound in video frames, a neural network learns a useful representation of objects and scenes. Another way to learn a similar representation is via classification [3]: A network is given an image-sound pair as input and must classify whether they match or not. Korbar *et al.* [25] build audio and video representations by learning to synchronize audio and video signals using a contrastive loss. Recently, [37] use multi-modal data from videos also in a contrastive learning framework. Several methods use optical flow as a supervision signal. For example, Wang *et al.* [47] extract motion and appearance statistics. Luo *et al.* [32] predict future atomic 3D flows given an input sequence, and Gan *et al.* [13] use geometry in the form of flow fields and disparity maps on synthetic and 3D movies. Optical flow is also used as input for video representation learning or filtering of the data [50]. Conversely, we do not make use of any auxiliary signals and learn video representations solely from the raw RGB frames.

3   Learning Video Dynamics

Recent work [47] showed how a careful learning of motion statistics led to a video representation with excellent transfer performance on several tasks and data sets. The learning of motion statistics was made explicit by extracting optical flow between frame pairs, by computing flow changes, and then by identifying the region where a number of key attributes (*e.g.*, maximum magnitude and orientation) of the time-averaged flow-change occurred. In this work, we also aim to learn from motion statistics, but we focus entirely our attention on the temporal evolution without specifying motion attributes of interest or defining a task based on appearance statistics. We hypothesize that these important aspects could be implicitly learned and exploited by the neural network to solve the lone task of discriminating temporal transformations of a video. Our objective is to encourage the neural network to represent well motion statistics that require a long-range observation (in the temporal domain). To do so, we train the network to discriminate videos where the image content has been preserved, but not the temporal domain. For example, we ask the network to distinguish a video

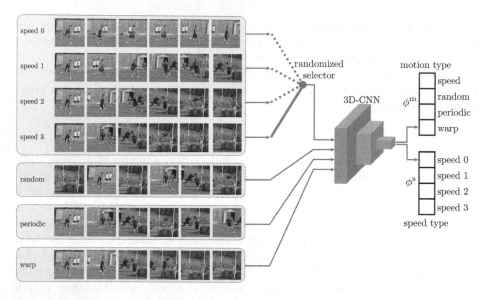

Fig. 2. Training a 3D-CNN to distinguish temporal transformations. In each mini-batch we select a video speed (out of 4 possible choices), *i.e.*, how many frames are skipped in the original video. Then, the 3D-CNN receives as input mini-batch a mixture of 4 possible transformed sequences: `speed` (with the chosen frame skipping), `random`, `periodic` and `warp`. The network outputs the probability of which motion type a sequence belongs to and the probability of which speed type the speed-transformed sequence has.

at the original frame rate from when it is played 4 times faster. Due to the laws of Physics, one can expect that, in general, *executing* the same task at different speeds leads to different motion dynamics compared to when a video is just *played* at different speeds (*e.g.*, compare marching vs walking played at a higher speed). Capturing the subtleties of the dynamics of these motions requires more than estimating motion between 2 or 3 frames. Moreover, these subtleties are specific to the moving object, and thus they require object detection and recognition.

In our approach, we transform videos by sampling frames according to different schemes, which we call *temporal transformations*. To support our learning hypothesis, we analyze transformations that require short- (*i.e.*, temporally local) and long-range (*i.e.*, temporally global) video understanding. As will be illustrated in the Experiments section, short-range transformations yield representations that transfer to action recognition with a lower performance than long-range ones.

3.1 Transformations of Time

Figure 2 illustrates how we train our neural network (a 3D-CNN [44]) to build a video representation (with 16 frames). In this section, we focus on the inputs to the network. As mentioned above, our approach is based on distinguishing different temporal transformations. We consider 4 fundamental types of transformations: Speed changes, random temporal permutations, periodic motions and temporal warp changes. Each of these transformations boils down to picking a sequence of temporal indices to sample the videos in our data set. $\mathcal{V}_\kappa^\tau \subset \{0, 1, 2, \dots\}$ denotes the chosen subset of indices of a video based on the transformation $\tau \in \{0, 1, 2, 3\}$ and with speed κ.

Speed ($\tau = 0$): In this first type we artificially change the video frame rate, *i.e.*, its playing speed. We achieve that by skipping a different number of frames. We consider 4 cases, **Speed 0, 1, 2, 3** corresponding to $\kappa = 0$, 1, 2, 3 respectively, where we skip $2^\kappa - 1$ frames. The resulting playback speed of **Speed** κ is therefore 2^κ times the original speed. In the generation of samples for the training of the neural network we first uniformly sample $\kappa \in \{0, 1, 2, 3\}$, the playback speed, and then use this parameter to define other transformations. This sequence is used in all experiments as one of the categories against either other speeds or against one of the other transformations below. The index sequence $\mathcal{V}_\kappa^0$ is thus $\rho + [0, 1 \cdot 2^\kappa, 2 \cdot 2^\kappa, \dots, 15 \cdot 2^\kappa]$, where ρ is a random initial index.

Random ($\tau = 1$): In this second temporal transformation we randomly permute the indices of a sequence without skipping frames. We fix $\kappa = 0$ to ensure that the maximum frame skip between two consecutive frames is not too dissimilar to other transformations. This case is used as a reference, as random permutations can often be detected by observing only a few nearby frames. Indeed, in the Experiments section one can see that this transformation yields a low transfer performance. The index sequence $\mathcal{V}_0^1$ is thus $\rho + \text{permutation}([0, 1, 2, \dots, 15])$. This transformation is similar to that of the pseudo-task of Misra *et al.* [33].

Periodic ($\tau = 2$): This transformation synthesizes motions that exhibit approximate periodicity. To create such artificial cases we first pick a point $2 \cdot 2^\kappa < s < 13 \cdot 2^\kappa$ where the playback direction switches. Then, we compose a sequence with the following index sequence: 0 to s and then from $s - 1$ to $2s - 15 \cdot 2^\kappa$. Finally, we sub-sample this sequence by skipping $2^\kappa - 1$ frames. Notice that the randomization of the midpoint s in the case of $\kappa > 0$ yields pseudo-periodic sequences, where the frames in the second half of the generated sequence often do not match the frames in the first half of the sequence. The index sequence $\mathcal{V}_\kappa^2$ is thus $\rho + [0, 1 \cdot 2^\kappa, 2 \cdot 2^\kappa, \dots, \bar{s} \cdot 2^\kappa, (\bar{s} - 1) \cdot 2^\kappa + \delta, \dots, (2\bar{s} - 15) \cdot 2^\kappa + \delta])$, where $\bar{s} = \lfloor s/2^\kappa \rfloor$, $\delta = s - \bar{s} \cdot 2^\kappa$, and $\rho = \max(0, (15 - 2\bar{s}) \cdot 2^\kappa - \delta)$.

Warp ($\tau = 3$): In this transformation, we pick a set of 16 ordered indices with a non-uniform number of skipped frames between them (we consider sampling any frame so we let $\kappa = 0$). In other words, between any of the frames in the generated sequence we have a random number of skipped frames, each chosen independently from the set $\{0, \dots, 7\}$. This transformation creates a warping of the temporal dimension by varying the playback speed from frame to frame. To construct the index sequence $\mathcal{V}_0^3$ we first sample the frame skips $s_j \in \{0, \ldots, 7\}$ for $j = 1, \ldots, 15$ and set $\mathcal{V}_0^3$ to $\rho + [0, s_1, s_1 + s_2, \ldots, \sum_{j=1}^{15} s_j]$.

3.2 Training

Let ϕ denote our network, and let us denote with ϕ^m (motion) and ϕ^s (speed) its two softmax outputs (see Fig. 2). To train ϕ we optimize the following loss

$$-\mathrm{E}_{\kappa \sim \mathcal{U}[0,3], p \in \mathcal{V}_\kappa^0, q \in \mathcal{V}_0^1, s \in \mathcal{V}_\kappa^2, t \in \mathcal{V}_0^3, x} \Big[\log \big(\phi_0^m (x_p) \, \phi_1^m (x_q) \, \phi_2^m (x_s) \, \phi_3^m (x_t) \big) \Big] \quad (1)$$
$$-\mathrm{E}_{\kappa \sim \mathcal{U}[0,3], p \in \mathcal{V}_\kappa^0, x} \Big[\log \big(\phi_\kappa^s (x_p) \big) \Big]$$

where x is a video sample, the sub-index denotes the set of frames. This loss is the cross entropy both for motion and speed classification (see Fig. 2).

3.3 Implementation

Following prior work [47], we use the smaller variant of the C3D architecture [44] for the 3D-CNN transformation classifier in most of our experiments. Training was performed using the AdamW optimizer [31] with parameters $\beta_1 = 0.9, \beta_2 = 0.99$ and a weight decay of 10^{-4}. The initial learning rate was set to $3 \cdot 10^{-4}$ during pre-training and $5 \cdot 10^{-5}$ during transfer learning. The learning rate was decayed by a factor of 10^{-3} over the course of training using cosine annealing [30] both during pre-training and transfer learning. We use batch-normalization [19] in all but the last layer. Mini-batches are constructed such that all the different coarse time warp types are included for each sampled training video. The batch size is set 28 examples (including all the transformed sequences). The speed type is uniformly sampled from all the considered speed types. Since not all the videos allow a sampling of all speed types (due to their short video duration) we limit the speed type range to the maximal possible speed type in those examples. We use the standard pre-processing for the C3D network. In practice, video frames are first resized to 128×171 pixels, from which we extract random crops of size 112×112 pixels. We also apply random horizontal flipping of the video frames during training. We use only the raw unfiltered RGB video frames as input to the motion classifier and do not make use of optical flow or other auxiliary signals.

4 Experiments

Datasets and Evaluation. In our experiments we consider three datasets. Kinetics [55] is a large human action dataset consisting of 500K videos. Video clips are collected from YouTube and span 600 human action classes. We use the training split for self-supervised pre-training. UCF101 [41] contains 13K video clips spanning 101 human action classes. HMDB51 [26] contains 5K videos belonging to 51 action classes. Both UCF101 and HMDB51 come with three pre-defined train and test splits. We report the average performance over all splits for

Table 1. Ablation experiments. We train a 3D-CNN to distinguish different sets of temporal transformations. The quality of the learned features is evaluated through transfer learning for action recognition on UCF101 (with frozen convolutional layers) and HMDB51 (with fine-tuning of the whole network).

Pre-training signal	Speed Loss	UCF101 (conv frozen)	HMDB51 (conv fine-tuned)
Action Labels UCF101	–	60.7%	28.8%
Speed	YES	49.3%	32.5%
Speed + Random	NO	44.5%	31.7%
Speed + Periodic	NO	40.6%	29.5%
Speed + Warp	NO	43.5%	32.6%
Speed + Random	YES	55.1%	33.2%
Speed + Periodic	YES	56.5%	36.1%
Speed + Warp	YES	55.8%	36.9%
Speed + Random + Periodic	NO	47.4%	30.1%
Speed + Random + Warp	NO	54.8%	36.6%
Speed + Periodic + Warp	NO	50.6%	36.4%
Speed + Random + Periodic	YES	60.0%	37.1%
Speed + Random + Warp	YES	60.4%	39.2%
Speed + Periodic + Warp	YES	59.5%	39.0%
Speed + Random + Periodic + Warp	NO	54.2%	34.9%
Speed + Random + Periodic + Warp	YES	60.6%	38.0%

transfer learning experiments. We use UCF101 train split 1 for self-supervised pre-training. For transfer learning experiments we skip 3 frames corresponding to transformation **Speed 2**. For the evaluation of action recognition classifiers in transfer experiments we use as prediction the maximum class probability averaged over all center-cropped sub-sequences for each test video. More details are provided in the supplementary material.

Understanding the Impact of the Temporal Transformations. We perform ablation experiments on UCF101 and HMDB51 where we vary the number of different temporal transformations the 3D-CNN is trained to distinguish. The 3D-CNN is pre-trained for 50 epochs on UCF101 with our self-supervised learning task. We then perform transfer learning for action recognition on UCF101 and HMDB51. On UCF101 we freeze the weights of the convolutional layers and train three randomly initialized fully-connected layers for action recognition. This experiment treats the transformation classifier as a fixed video feature extractor. On HMDB51 we fine-tune the whole network including convolutional layers on the target task. This experiment therefore measures the quality of the network initialization obtained through self-supervised pre-training. In both cases we again train for 50 epochs on the action recognition task. The results of the ablations are summarized in Table 1. For reference we also report the performance of network weights learned through supervised pre-training on UCF101.

We observe that when considering the impact of a single transformation across different cases, the types **Warp** and **Speed** achieve the best transfer performance. With the same analysis, the transformation **Random** leads to the worst transfer performance on average. We observe that **Random** is also the easiest transformation to detect (based on training performance – not reported). As can be seen in Fig. 1(e) this transformation can lead to drastic differences between consecutive frames. Such examples can therefore be easily detected by only comparing pairs of adjacent frames. In contrast, the motion type **Warp** can not be distinguished based solely on two adjacent frames and requires modelling long range dynamics. We also observe that distinguishing a larger number of transformations generally leads to an increase in the transfer performance. The effect of the **speed** type classification is quite noticeable. It leads to a very significant transfer performance increase in all cases. This is also the most difficult pseudo task (based on the training performance – not reported). Recognizing the speed of an action is indeed challenging, since different action classes naturally exhibit widely different motion speeds (*e.g.*, "applying make-up" vs. "biking"). This task might often require a deeper understanding of the physics and objects involved in the video. Notice also that our pre-training strategy leads to a better transfer performance on HMDB51 than supervised pre-training using action labels. This suggests that the video dynamics learned through our pre-training generalize well to action recognition and that such dynamics are not well captured through the lone supervised action recognition.

Transfer to UCF101 and HMDB51. We compare to prior work on self-supervised video representation learning in Table 2. A fair comparison to much of the prior work is difficult due to the use of very different network architectures and training as well as transfer settings. We opted to compare with some commonly used network architectures (*i.e.*, C3D, 3D-ResNet, and R(2+1)D) and re-implemented two prior works [33] and [23] using C3D. We performed self-supervised pre-training on UCF101 and Kinetics. C3D is pre-trained for 100 epochs on UCF101 and for 15 epoch on Kinetics. 3D-ResNet and R(2+1)D are both pre-trained for 200 epochs on UCF101 and for 15 epochs on Kinetics. We fine-tune all the layers for action recognition. Fine-tuning is performed for 75 epochs using C3D and for 150 epochs with the other architectures. When pre-training on UCF101 our features outperform prior work on the same network architectures. Pre-training on Kinetics leads to an improvement in transfer in all cases.

Table 2. Comparison to prior work on self-supervised video representation learning. Whenever possible we compare to results reported with the same data modality we used, *i.e.*, unprocessed RGB input frames. * are our reimplementations.

Method	Ref	Network	Train dataset	UCF101	HMDB51
Shuffle& Learn [33]	[33]	AlexNet	UCF101	50.2%	18.1%
O3N [12]	[12]	AlexNet	UCF101	60.3%	32.5%
AoT [50]	[50]	VGG-16	UCF101	78.1%	–
OPN [28]	[28]	VGG-M-2048	UCF101	59.8%	23.8%
DPC [15]	[15]	3D-ResNet34	Kinetics	75.7%	35.7%
SpeedNet [4]	[4]	S3D-G	Kinetics	81.1%	48.8%
AVTS [25] (RGB+audio)	[25]	MC3	Kinetics	85.8%	56.9%
Shuffle& Learn [33]*	–	C3D	UCF101	55.8%	25.4%
3D-RotNet [23]*	–	C3D	UCF101	60.6%	27.3%
Clip Order [51]	[51]	C3D	UCF101	65.6%	28.4%
Spatio-Temp [47]	[47]	C3D	UCF101	58.8%	32.6%
Spatio-Temp [47]	[47]	C3D	Kinetics	61.2%	33.4%
3D ST-puzzle [24]	[24]	C3D	Kinetics	60.6%	28.3%
Ours	–	C3D	UCF101	<u>68.3%</u>	<u>38.4%</u>
Ours	–	C3D	Kinetics	**69.9%**	**39.6%**
3D ST-puzzle [24]	[24]	3D-ResNet18	Kinetics	65.8%	33.7%
3D RotNet [23]	[23]	3D-ResNet18	Kinetics	66.0%	37.1%
DPC [15]	[15]	3D-ResNet18	Kinetics	68.2%	34.5%
Ours	–	3D-ResNet18	UCF101	<u>77.3%</u>	<u>47.5%</u>
Ours	–	3D-ResNet18	Kinetics	**79.3%**	**49.8%**
Clip Order [51]	[51]	R(2+1)D	UCF101	<u>72.4%</u>	30.9%
PRP [52]	[52]	R(2+1)D	UCF101	72.1%	<u>35.0%</u>
Ours	–	R(2+1)D	UCF101	**81.6%**	**46.4%**

Long-Range vs Short-Range Temporal Statistics. To illustrate how well our video representations capture motion, we transfer them to other pseudo-tasks that focus on the temporal evolution of a video. One task is the classification of the synchronization of video pairs, *i.e.*, how many frames one video is delayed with respect to the other. A second task is the classification of two videos into which one comes first temporally. These two tasks are illustrated in Fig. 3. In the same spirit, we also evaluate our features on other tasks and data sets and we report the results at our project page https://sjenni.github.io/temporal-ssl.

For the synchronization task, two temporally overlapping video sequences x_1 and x_2 are separately fed to the pre-trained C3D network to extract features $\psi(v_1)$ and $\psi(v_2)$ at the conv5 layer. These features are then fused through $\psi(v_1) - \psi(v_2)$ and fed as input to a randomly initialized classifier consisting of three fully-connected layers trained to classify the offset between the two sequences. We consider random offsets between the two video sequences in the range -6 to $+6$. For the second task we construct a single input sequence by sampling two

Fig. 3. Time-Related Pseudo-Tasks. (a) Synchronization problem: The network is given two sequences with a time delay (4 frames in the example) and a classifier is trained to determine the delay. (b) The before-after problem: The network is given two non-overlapping sequences, and it needs to determine which comes first (the bottom sequence after the top one in the example).

non-overlapping 8 frame sub-sequences x_{i1} and x_{i2}, where x_{i1} comes before x_{i2}. The network inputs are then either (x_{i1}, x_{i2}) for class "before" or (x_{i2}, x_{i1}) for the class "after". We reinitialize the fully-connected layers in this case as well.

Table 3. Time-Related Pseudo-Tasks. We examine how well features from different pre-training strategies can be transferred to time-related tasks on videos. As tasks we consider the synchronization of two overlapping videos and the temporal ordering of two non-overlapping videos. We report the accuracy on both tasks on the UCF101 test set and also report Mean Absolute Error (MAE) for the synchronization task. * are our reimplementations.

Method	Sync.		Before-After
	Accuracy	MAE	Accuracy
Action labels (UCF101)	36.7%	<u>1.85</u>	66.6%
3D-RotNet [23]*	28.0%	2.84	57.8%
Shuffle& Learn [33]*	<u>39.0%</u>	1.89	<u>69.8%</u>
Ours	**42.4%**	**1.61**	**76.9%**

In Table 3 we compare the performance of different pre-training strategies on the time-related pseudo-tasks. We see that our self-supervised features perform better at these tasks than supervised features and other self-supervised features, thus showing that they capture well the temporal dynamics in the videos.

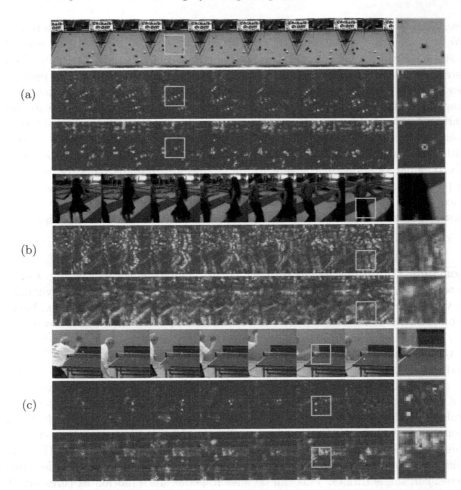

Fig. 4. Visualization of active pixels. The first row in each block corresponds to the input video. Rows two and three show the output of our adaptation of Guided Backpropagation [42] when applied to a network trained through self-supervised learning and supervised learning respectively. In all three cases we observe that the self-supervised network focuses on image regions of moving objects or persons. In (a) we can also observe how long range dynamics are being detected by the self-supervised model. The supervised model on the other hand focuses a lot on static frame features in the background.

Visualization. What are the attributes, factors or features of the videos that self-supervised and supervised models are extracting to perform the final classification? To examine what the self-supervised and supervised models focus on, we apply Guided Backpropagation [42]. This method allows us to visualize which part of the input has the most impact on the final decision of the model. We slightly modify the procedure by subtracting the median values from every frame of the gradient video and by taking the absolute value of the result. We visualize the pre-trained self-supervised and supervised models on several test samples from UCF101. As one can see in Fig. 4, a model pre-trained on our self-supervised task tends to ignore the background and focuses on persons performing an action and on moving objects. Models trained with supervised learning on the other hand tend to focus more on the appearance of foreground and background. Another observation we make is that the self-supervised model identifies the location of moving objects/people in past and future frames. This is visible in row number 2 of blocks *(a)* and *(c)* of Fig. 4, where the network tracks the possible locations of the moving ping-pong and billiard balls respectively. A possible explanation for this observation is that our self-supervised task only encourages the learning of dynamics. The appearance of non-moving objects or static backgrounds are not useful to solve the pretext task and are thus ignored.

Learning Dynamics vs. Frame Features. The visualizations in Fig. 4 indicate that features learned through motion discrimination focus on the dynamics in videos and not so much on static content present in single frames (*e.g.*, background) when compared to supervised features. To further investigate how much the features learned through the two pre-training strategies rely on motion, we performed experiments where we remove all the dynamics from videos. To this end, we create input videos by replicating a single frame 16 times (resulting in a still video) and train the three fully-connected layers on conv5 features for action classification on UCF101. Features obtained through supervised pre-training achieve an accuracy of 18.5% (vs. 56.5% with dynamics) and features from our self-supervised task achieve 1.0% (vs. 58.1%). Although the setup in this experiment is somewhat contrived (since the input domain is altered) it still illustrates that our features rely almost exclusively on motion instead of features present in single frames. This can be advantageous since motion features might generalize better to variations in the background appearance in many cases.

Nearest-Neighbor Evaluation. We perform an additional quantitative evaluation of the learned video representations via the nearest-neighbor retrieval. The features are obtained by training a 3D-ResNet18 network on Kinetics with our pseudo-task and are chosen as the output of the global average pooling layer, which corresponds to a vector of size 512. For each video we extract and average features of 10 temporal crops. To perform the nearest-neighbor retrieval, we first normalize the features using the training set statistics. Cosine similarity is used as the metric to determine the nearest neighbors. We follow the evaluation proposed by [6] on UCF101. Query videos are taken from test split 1 and all the videos of train split 1 are considered as retrieval targets. A query is considered correctly classified if the k-nearest neighbors contain at least one video of the correct class (*i.e.*, same class as the query). We report the mean accuracy for different values of k and compare to prior work in Table 4. Our features achieve state-of-the-art performance.

Table 4. Video Retrieval Performance on UCF101. We compare to prior work in terms of k-nearest neighbor retrieval accuracy. Query videos are taken from test split 1 and retrievals are computed on train 1. A query is correctly classified if the query class is present in the top-k retrievals. We report mean retrieval accuracy for different values of k.

Method	Network	Top1	Top5	Top10	Top20	Top50
Jigsaw [34]	AlexNet	19.7	28.5	33.5	40.0	49.4
OPN [28]	AlexNet	19.9	28.7	34.0	40.6	51.6
Büchler *et al.* [6]	AlexNet	25.7	36.2	42.2	49.2	59.5
Clip order [51]	R3D	14.1	30.3	40.0	51.1	66.5
SpeedNet [4]	S3D-G	13.0	28.1	37.5	49.5	65.0
PRP [52]	R3D	22.8	38.5	46.7	55.2	69.1
Ours	3D-ResNet18	**26.1**	**48.5**	**59.1**	**69.6**	**82.8**

5   Conclusions

We have introduced a novel task for the self-supervised learning of video representations by distinguishing between different types of temporal transformations. This learning task is based on the principle that recognizing a transformation of time requires an accurate model of the underlying natural video dynamics. This idea is supported by experiments that demonstrate that features learned by distinguishing time transformations capture video dynamics more than supervised learning and that such features generalize well to classic vision tasks such as action recognition or time-related task such as video synchronization.

Acknowledgements. This work was supported by grants 169622&165845 of the Swiss National Science Foundation.

References

1. Agrawal, P., Carreira, J., Malik, J.: Learning to see by moving (2015)
2. Ando, R., Zhang, T.: A framework for learning predictive structures from multiple tasks and unlabeled data. JMLR **6**, 1817–1853 (2005)
3. Arandjelovic, R., Zisserman, A.: Look, listen and learn. In: 2017 IEEE International Conference on Computer Vision (ICCV), pp. 609–617. IEEE (2017)
4. Benaim, S., et al.: Speednet: learning the speediness in videos. In: Proceedings of the IEEE/CVF Conference on Computer Vision and Pattern Recognition, pp. 9922–9931 (2020)

5. Brattoli, B., Büchler, U., Wahl, A.S., Schwab, M.E., Ommer, B.: Lstm self-supervision for detailed behavior analysis. In: Proceedings of the IEEE Conference on Computer Vision and Pattern Recognition (CVPR), vol. 2 (2017)
6. Büchler, U., Brattoli, B., Ommer, B.: Improving spatiotemporal self-supervision by deep reinforcement learning. arXiv preprint arXiv:1807.11293 (2018)
7. Caruana, R., de Sa, V.R.: Promoting poor features to supervisors: some inputs work better as outputs. In: NIPS (1996)
8. Devlin, J., Chang, M.W., Lee, K., Toutanova, K.: Bert: pre-training of deep bidirectional transformers for language understanding. arXiv preprint arXiv:1810.04805 (2018)
9. Doersch, C., Gupta, A., Efros, A.A.: Unsupervised visual representation learning by context prediction. In: ICCV (2015)
10. Epstein, D., Chen, B., Vondrick, C.: Oops! predicting unintentional action in video. In: Proceedings of the IEEE/CVF Conference on Computer Vision and Pattern Recognition, pp. 919–929 (2020)
11. Everingham, M., Zisserman, A., Williams, C., Van-Gool, L.: The pascal visual object classes challenge. In: VOC (2006)
12. Fernando, B., Bilen, H., Gavves, E., Gould, S.: Self-supervised video representation learning with odd-one-out networks. In: 2017 IEEE Conference on Computer Vision and Pattern Recognition (CVPR), pp. 5729–5738. IEEE (2017)
13. Gan, C., Gong, B., Liu, K., Su, H., Guibas, L.J.: Geometry guided convolutional neural networks for self-supervised video representation learning. In: Proceedings of the IEEE Conference on Computer Vision and Pattern Recognition, pp. 5589–5597 (2018)
14. Gidaris, S., Singh, P., Komodakis, N.: Unsupervised representation learning by predicting image rotations. In: International Conference on Learning Representations (2018). https://openreview.net/forum?id=S1v4N2l0-
15. Han, T., Xie, W., Zisserman, A.: Video representation learning by dense predictive coding. In: Proceedings of the IEEE International Conference on Computer Vision Workshops (2019)
16. Hara, K., Kataoka, H., Satoh, Y.: Can spatiotemporal 3D CNNs retrace the history of 2D CNNs and imagenet? In: Proceedings of the IEEE conference on Computer Vision and Pattern Recognition, pp. 6546–6555 (2018)
17. He, K., Gkioxari, G., Dollár, P., Girshick, R.: Mask r-cnn. In: Proceedings of the IEEE International Conference on Computer Vision, pp. 2961–2969 (2017)
18. He, K., Zhang, X., Ren, S., Sun, J.: Deep residual learning for image recognition. In: Proceedings of the IEEE Conference on Computer Vision and Pattern Recognition, pp. 770–778 (2016)
19. Ioffe, S., Szegedy, C.: Batch normalization: accelerating deep network training by reducing internal covariate shift. arXiv preprint arXiv:1502.03167 (2015)
20. Iwana, B.K., Uchida, S.: Time scrics classification using local distance-based features in multi-modal fusion networks. Pattern Recogn. **97**, 107024 (2020). https://doi.org/10.1016/j.patcog.2019.107024, http://www.sciencedirect.com/science/article/pii/S0031320319303279
21. Jenni, S., Favaro, P.: Self-supervised feature learning by learning to spot artifacts. In: Proceedings of the IEEE Conference on Computer Vision and Pattern Recognition, pp. 2733–2742 (2018)
22. Jenni, S., Jin, H., Favaro, P.: Steering self-supervised feature learning beyond local pixel statistics. In: Proceedings of the IEEE/CVF Conference on Computer Vision and Pattern Recognition, pp. 6408–6417 (2020)

23. Jing, L., Yang, X., Liu, J., Tian, Y.: Self-supervised spatiotemporal feature learning via video rotation prediction. arXiv preprint arXiv:1811.11387 (2018)
24. Kim, D., Cho, D., Kweon, I.S.: Self-supervised video representation learning with space-time cubic puzzles. In: Proceedings of the AAAI Conference on Artificial Intelligence, vol. 33, pp. 8545–8552 (2019)
25. Korbar, B., Tran, D., Torresani, L.: Cooperative learning of audio and video models from self-supervised synchronization. In: Advances in Neural Information Processing Systems, pp. 7763–7774 (2018)
26. Kuehne, H., Jhuang, H., Garrote, E., Poggio, T., Serre, T.: HMDB: a large video database for human motion recognition. In: Proceedings of the International Conference on Computer Vision (ICCV) (2011)
27. Larsson, G., Maire, M., Shakhnarovich, G.: Colorization as a proxy task for visual understanding. In: Proceedings of the IEEE Conference on Computer Vision and Pattern Recognition, pp. 6874–6883 (2017)
28. Lee, H.Y., Huang, J.B., Singh, M., Yang, M.H.: Unsupervised representation learning by sorting sequences. In: Proceedings of the IEEE International Conference on Computer Vision, pp. 667–676 (2017)
29. Li, X., Liu, S., De Mello, S., Wang, X., Kautz, J., Yang, M.H.: Joint-task self-supervised learning for temporal correspondence. In: Advances in Neural Information Processing Systems, pp. 317–327 (2019)
30. Loshchilov, I., Hutter, F.: Sgdr: Stochastic gradient descent with warm restarts. arXiv preprint arXiv:1608.03983 (2016)
31. Loshchilov, I., Hutter, F.: Fixing weight decay regularization in adam. arXiv preprint arXiv:1711.05101 (2017)
32. Luo, Z., Peng, B., Huang, D.A., Alahi, A., Fei-Fei, L.: Unsupervised learning of long-term motion dynamics for videos. In: Proceedings of the IEEE Conference on Computer Vision and Pattern Recognition, pp. 2203–2212 (2017)
33. Misra, I., Zitnick, C.L., Hebert, M.: Shuffle and learn: unsupervised learning using temporal order verification. In: Leibe, B., Matas, J., Sebe, N., Welling, M. (eds.) ECCV 2016. LNCS, vol. 9905, pp. 527–544. Springer, Cham (2016). https://doi.org/10.1007/978-3-319-46448-0_32
34. Noroozi, M., Favaro, P.: Unsupervised learning of visual representations by solving jigsaw puzzles. In: Leibe, B., Matas, J., Sebe, N., Welling, M. (eds.) ECCV 2016. LNCS, vol. 9910, pp. 69–84. Springer, Cham (2016). https://doi.org/10.1007/978-3-319-46466-4_5
35. Owens, A., Efros, A.A.: Audio-visual scene analysis with self-supervised multisensory features. In: The European Conference on Computer Vision (ECCV) (2018)
36. Owens, A., Wu, J., McDermott, J.H., Freeman, W.T., Torralba, A.: Ambient sound provides supervision for visual learning. In: Leibe, B., Matas, J., Sebe, N., Welling, M. (eds.) ECCV 2016. LNCS, vol. 9905, pp. 801–816. Springer, Cham (2016). https://doi.org/10.1007/978-3-319-46448-0_48
37. Patrick, M., Asano, Y.M., Fong, R., Henriques, J.F., Zweig, G., Vedaldi, A.: Multi-modal self-supervision from generalized data transformations. arXiv preprint arXiv:2003.04298 (2020)
38. Redmon, J., Divvala, S., Girshick, R., Farhadi, A.: You only look once: unified, real-time object detection. In: Proceedings of the IEEE Conference on Computer Vision and Pattern Recognition, pp. 779–788 (2016)
39. Russakovsky, O., et al.: Imagenet large scale visual recognition challenge. Int. J. Comput. Vis. **115**(3), 211–252 (2015). https://doi.org/10.1007/s11263-015-0816-y

40. Schindler, K., Van Gool, L.: Action snippets: how many frames does human action recognition require? In: 2008 IEEE Conference on Computer Vision and Pattern Recognition, pp. 1–8. IEEE (2008)
41. Soomro, K., Zamir, A.R., Shah, M.: Ucf101: a dataset of 101 human actions classes from videos in the wild. arXiv preprint arXiv:1212.0402 (2012)
42. Springenberg, J.T., Dosovitskiy, A., Brox, T., Riedmiller, M.: Striving for simplicity: the all convolutional net (2014)
43. Sun, C., Baradel, F., Murphy, K., Schmid, C.: Contrastive bidirectional transformer for temporal representation learning. arXiv preprint arXiv:1906.05743 (2019)
44. Tran, D., Bourdev, L., Fergus, R., Torresani, L., Paluri, M.: Learning spatiotemporal features with 3d convolutional networks. In: Proceedings of the IEEE International Conference on Computer Vision, pp. 4489–4497 (2015)
45. Tran, D., Wang, H., Torresani, L., Ray, J., LeCun, Y., Paluri, M.: A closer look at spatiotemporal convolutions for action recognition. In: Proceedings of the IEEE Conference on Computer Vision and Pattern Recognition, pp. 6450–6459 (2018)
46. Vondrick, C., Shrivastava, A., Fathi, A., Guadarrama, S., Murphy, K.: Tracking emerges by colorizing videos. In: Proceedings of the ECCV (2018)
47. Wang, J., Jiao, J., Bao, L., He, S., Liu, Y., Liu, W.: Self-supervised spatio-temporal representation learning for videos by predicting motion and appearance statistics. In: Proceedings of the IEEE Conference on Computer Vision and Pattern Recognition, pp. 4006–4015 (2019)
48. Wang, X., Gupta, A.: Unsupervised learning of visual representations using videos. In: Proceedings of the IEEE International Conference on Computer Vision, pp. 2794–2802 (2015)
49. Wang, X., Jabri, A., Efros, A.A.: Learning correspondence from the cycle-consistency of time. In: Proceedings of the IEEE Conference on Computer Vision and Pattern Recognition, pp. 2566–2576 (2019)
50. Wei, D., Lim, J., Zisserman, A., Freeman, W.T.: Learning and using the arrow of time. In: Proceedings of the IEEE Conference on Computer Vision and Pattern Recognition, pp. 8052–8060 (2018)
51. Xu, D., Xiao, J., Zhao, Z., Shao, J., Xie, D., Zhuang, Y.: Self-supervised spatiotemporal learning via video clip order prediction. In: Proceedings of the IEEE Conference on Computer Vision and Pattern Recognition, pp. 10334–10343 (2019)
52. Yao, Y., Liu, C., Luo, D., Zhou, Y., Ye, Q.: Video playback rate perception for self-supervised spatio-temporal representation learning. In: Proceedings of the IEEE/CVF Conference on Computer Vision and Pattern Recognition, pp. 6548–6557 (2020)
53. Zhang, R., Isola, P., Efros, A.A.: Colorful image colorization. In: Leibe, B., Matas, J., Sebe, N., Welling, M. (eds.) ECCV 2016. LNCS, vol. 9907, pp. 649–666. Springer, Cham (2016). https://doi.org/10.1007/978-3-319-46487-9_40
54. Zhang, R., Isola, P., Efros, A.A.: Split-brain autoencoders: unsupervised learning by cross-channel prediction. In: Proceedings of the IEEE Conference on Computer Vision and Pattern Recognition, pp. 1058–1067 (2017)
55. Zisserman, A., et al.: The kinetics human action video dataset. ArXiv (2017)

Unsupervised Monocular Depth Estimation for Night-Time Images Using Adversarial Domain Feature Adaptation

Madhu Vankadari[1]([envelope]), Sourav Garg[2], Anima Majumder[1], Swagat Kumar[1,3], and Ardhendu Behera[3]

[1] TATA Consultancy Services, Bangalore, India
{madhu.vankadari,anima.majumder}@tcs.com
[2] Queensland University of Technology, Brisbane, Australia
s.garg@qut.edu.au
[3] Edge Hill University, Ormskirk, UK
{swagat.kumar,beheraa}@edgehill.ac.uk

Abstract. In this paper, we look into the problem of estimating per-pixel depth maps from unconstrained RGB monocular *night-time* images which is a difficult task that has not been addressed adequately in the literature. The state-of-the-art day-time depth estimation methods fail miserably when tested with night-time images due to a large domain shift between them. The usual photometric losses used for training these networks may not work for night-time images due to the absence of uniform lighting which is commonly present in day-time images, making it a difficult problem to solve. We propose to solve this problem by posing it as a domain adaptation problem where a network trained with day-time images is adapted to work for night-time images. Specifically, an encoder is trained to generate features from night-time images that are indistinguishable from those obtained from day-time images by using a PatchGAN-based adversarial discriminative learning method. Unlike the existing methods that directly adapt depth prediction (network output), we propose to adapt *feature maps* obtained from the encoder network so that a pre-trained day-time depth decoder can be directly used for predicting depth from these *adapted features*. Hence, the resulting method is termed as "Adversarial Domain Feature Adaptation (ADFA)" and its efficacy is demonstrated through experimentation on the challenging Oxford night driving dataset. To the best of our knowledge, this work is a first of its kind to estimate depth from unconstrained night-time monocular RGB images that uses a completely unsupervised learning process. The modular encoder-decoder architecture for the proposed ADFA method allows us to use the encoder module as a feature extractor which can be used in many other applications. One such application is demonstrated where the features obtained from our adapted encoder network are shown to outperform other state-of-the-art methods in a visual place recognition problem, thereby, further establishing the usefulness and effectiveness of the proposed approach.

S. Kumar will like to thank NVIDIA GPU Grant Program for their support.

© Springer Nature Switzerland AG 2020
A. Vedaldi et al. (Eds.): ECCV 2020, LNCS 12373, pp. 443–459, 2020.
https://doi.org/10.1007/978-3-030-58604-1_27

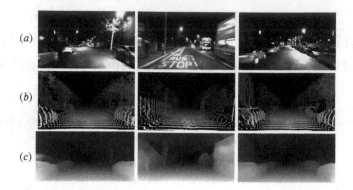

Fig. 1. The depth predictions of the proposed method on Oxford Night driving images. Top to bottom: (a) Input RGB night-time image. (b) Corresponding ground truth depth map generated from the LIDAR points. (c) The depth predictions using the proposed method

1   Introduction

Estimating depth from RGB images is a challenging problem which finds applications in a wide range of fields such as augmented reality [30], 3D reconstruction [16], self-driving cars [19], place recognition [11], etc. The recent success of deep learning methods has spurred the research in this field leading to the creation of several new benchmarks that now outperform traditional methods which rely on handcrafted features and exploit camera geometry and/or camera motion for depth and pose estimation from monocular or stereo sequence of images (video). These learning methods can be broadly classified into two categories: supervised and unsupervised. The supervised learning methods [7,10] necessitate explicit availability of ground truth information (Laser or LiDAR range data) which may not always be feasible in many real-world scenarios. This is overcome by the unsupervised methods [5,39,42] that harness the spatial and/or temporal consistency present in image sequences to extract the underlying geometry to be used as the implicit supervision signal required for training the models. Many of these methods were shown to provide very impressive results on several popular datasets such as KITTI [15] and Cityscapes [9] containing only day-time images. In contrast, there are a very few works that aim to solve the night-time depth estimation problem, which is comparatively more challenging owing to factors such as low visibility and non-uniform illumination arising from multiple (street lights, traffic lights) and possibly, moving light sources (car headlights). For instance, authors in [22] exploit the inherent motion component in burst shot (several successive shots with varying camera settings, also known as "auto-bracketing") to estimate depth from images taken under low-light condition. Similarly, Zhu et al. [43] present a deep learning based method for estimating motion flow, depth and pose from images obtained from event cameras that return a time-stamped event tuple whenever a change in pixel intensity is detected. In another work, Kim et al. [24] propose a deep network for estimating depth from thermal images taken during the night time. To the best of our knowledge, there is no reported work that addresses the problem of estimating depth and pose directly from a single ordinary RGB monocular night-time image. The deep learning models trained on day-time monocular [42] or stereo images [5] fail miserably on night-time images due to the inherent large domain shift between these images. The domain shift refers to the change from day-time conditions (well-lit and uniform illumination) to night-time conditions comprising low illumination/visibility with non-uniform illumination caused by unpredictable appearance and disappearance of multiple point-light sources (e.g., street lamps or car headlights, etc.).

One possible solution will be to apply image-to-image translation methods, such as Cycle-GAN [44] or MUNIT [21], to map night-time images to day-time images and then use a pre-trained day-time depth model to estimate depth from these translated images. Some of these image translation techniques have been used in the context of night-time images. For instance, the authors in [2] use night-to-day image translation for solving the place recognition problem required for localization. Similarly, authors in [4,40] explore image translation techniques to generate synthetic labeled data to reduce the requirement of real-world images for training depth estimation models. Many of these models trained on simulated images do not generalize well to natural images due to the inherent domain shift and hence, employ several domain adaptation techniques to improve their applicability to real-world situations [4,31,40]. These approaches have several limitations. For instance, many of these methods use two different deep networks - one for image translation and another for depth estimation, making it computationally heavy and with possibly, inferior performance due to the cascading error effect of using two models in a cascade. Since the image translation module is trained independent of the depth network module, it may not learn depth-specific attributes required for preserving structural information during image translation. This may, in turn, introduce artifacts which might not be understood by the depth estimation module leading to poor depth prediction for the input night-time image. Secondly, it is difficult to generate synthetic night-time images that can capture all the vagaries of real-world night conditions as one can observe in the Synthia dataset [33]. Many of the simulated night-time images in this dataset appear almost like day-time images and using them for night-time depth prediction may not give desired results. Finally, these methods have been applied so far to day-time images for depth estimation.

In this paper, we propose a PatchGAN-based domain adaptation technique for estimating depth from monocular night images by using a single encoder-decoder type deep network model. Specifically, an encoder network is trained to generate night-time *features* which are indistinguishable from those obtained from day-time images. This is achieved by using an adversarial discriminative learning [36] that uses day-time encoded features as the reference. These adapted night features could then be used directly with a decoder network pre-trained on day-time images for depth estimation. Since the domain *features* are adapted through adversarial learning, this method is termed as *"Adversarial Domain Feature Adaptation (ADFA)"* method to distinguish it from other methods that attempt to adapt depth predictions directly [4,31,40]. PatchGAN networks [23, 37] have been shown to provide superior performance compared to conventional GANs by capturing high frequency local structural information and hence, form a natural choice of GAN architecture for the proposed method.

The resulting outcome of our approach is shown qualitatively in Fig. 1. We are able to obtain reliable depth maps shown in Fig. 1(c) from monocular night-time images shown in Fig. 1(a). This is also evident from the interpolated ground-truth depth maps obtained from the LIDAR point clouds as shown in Fig. 1(b). The efficacy of the proposed approach is demonstrated by applying it to the challenging Oxford night-time driving dataset [29]. The modular encoder-decoder architecture provides the flexibility of using the encoder module as a feature extractor to extract or select useful features from input images. Such feature extractors are used in several applications such as pose estimation [18], Visual Place Recognition (VPR) [11,12], object detection [41] and segmentation [6]. We demonstrate one such application where the adapted features obtained from our encoder module are shown to provide superior place recognition accuracy compared to other state-of-the-art feature representations available in the literature.

In short, the main contributions made in this paper may be summarized as follows:

- We propose a novel PatchGAN-based domain *feature* adaptation method for estimating depth from unconstrained monocular night-time RGB images, which is considered to be more difficult compared to day-time images. To the best of our knowledge, this is the first instance where adversarial discriminative domain feature adaptation is being used for estimating depth from unconstrained night-time monocular RGB images and this may act as a stepping-stone for future research in this field.
- We also propose an image translation-based method for night-time depth estimation by using a combination of an image translating network (e.g. Cycle-GAN [44]) and a standard day-time depth estimation network (such as [18]) in cascade. This serves to highlight the difficulties involved in such methods and hence, provides a strong motivation in favour of the proposed work.
- The usefulness and effectiveness of our method is further established by demonstrating that the features obtained using the proposed ADFA method outperform other state-of-the-art feature representations in a visual place recognition problem.

Rest of this paper is organized as follows. The proposed method is described in the next section. The experimental evaluation of our approach on various datasets is discussed in Sect. 3. The concluding remarks and future scope of this work is presented in Sect. 4. Our code will be made available at https://github.com/madhubabuv/NightDepthADFA.

2   Proposed Method

We propose to solve the depth estimation problem for night-time images by posing it as a domain adaption problem in which a model pre-trained on day-time

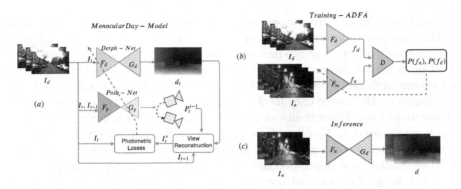

Fig. 2. Architectural overview of the proposed method. (a) The monocular day-model consists of a Depth-Net (F_d, G_d) and a Pose-Net (F_p, G_p) to predict per-pixel depth-map d_t and 6-DoF pose P_t^{t-1}, respectively. The day-model is trained using photometric losses calculated from images reconstructed from view-reconstruction module. (b) A new encoder F_n takes a night-time image I_n and predicts f_n. The f_n features are adapted to look-like day features f_d using adversarial learning with a Patch-GAN based discriminator D. The red dotted line is drawn to indicate modules trained using back propagation.(c) Finally, the new-encoder F_n and the day depth-decoder G_d are used together to predict depth for night-time images (Color figure online)

images is adapted to work for night-time images as well. The overall approach is shown in Fig. 2. It consists of three steps. First, an encoder-decoder type deep network model (F_d, G_d) is trained on day-time images to estimate depth directly from RGB images by using one of the existing methods as in [17,18,37,39,42]. This is shown in Fig. 2(a). The second step involves training a new image encoder F_n with night-time images using adversarial discriminative learning that uses F_d as the generator. This is shown in Fig. 2(b). The third and the final step involves using the new encoder F_n in conjunction with the day-time decoder G_d for estimating depth directly from night-time images as shown in Fig. 2(c).

The above three components of the proposed ADFA method are described in detail in the following subsections.

2.1 Learning F_d and G_d from Day-Time Images

Estimating depth from monocular day-time images is an active field of research where deep learning methods have been applied successfully and several new benchmarks have been reported in the literature [5,7,10,27,28,37,39,42]. These deep networks have an encoder-decoder type architecture as shown in Fig. 2(a). Such an architecture allows us to decompose the entire pipeline into two sub-networks, one for encoding (or extracting) features from input images and another for mapping these features to depth information. In unsupervised methods, the image reconstruction error is used as the loss function for training the entire model thereby avoiding the necessity of having the explicit ground truth depth information. The images are reconstructed by using spatial and/or temporal cues obtained from stereo or monocular sequence of images. The methods that use only temporal cues (such as optical flow) incorporate an additional network to estimate pose or ego motion required for image reconstruction [39,42]. The Depth-Net as shown in Fig. 2(a) is composed of a series of convolutional and deconvolutional layers with different filter sizes. Given a monocular daytime image I_d, the image encoder F_d generates, say, L number of convolutional feature maps with different shapes and sizes, one from each layer. This feature map is represented as $F_d(I_d) = f_d = \{f_d^i\}$, $i = 1, 2, \ldots, L$, where L is the total number of convolutional layers used in the image encoder. These feature maps are then passed to a depth-decoder G_d to predict per-pixel depth map $\mathcal{D}$ of the input image I_d. One can use any of the existing methods (supervised or unsupervised) to learn the functions F_d and G_d. In this work, we have used the state-of-the art depth-net model [18] as our F_d and G_d which are trained on the day-time monocular images. Since only monocular sequence of images are used for training, an additional pose network is required to estimate ego motion of the camera required for reconstructing images in the temporal domain. The encoder network F_d is used to train a new encoder F_n for night-images using an adversarial learning as explained in the next section.

2.2   Learning F_n Using Night-Time Images

Once the day-time image encoder F_d and depth decoder G_d are learned, our objective is to learn an image encoder F_n that can generate the features maps f_n from a night-time image I_n which are indistinguishable from the day-time feature maps f_d obtained from the day-time encoder F_d. There is no direct supervision signal available for computing the loss function from f_d and f_n as the input day and night images are *unpaired*. Here, the term *unpaired* means that these two images are not taken at the same time or at the same place. The encoder F_n is trained to reduce the distance between the distributions of day and night feature spaces by using an adversarial training approach proposed in [36]. In this approach, the image encoder F_n acts as a *generator* trying to generate feature maps from a night image I_n, which look similar to the day-time feature maps f_d obtained from a day-time image I_d using a day-time encoder F_d. These generated features maps are then evaluated by a *discriminator* network D that tries not to get fooled by the generator by assigning correct labels to them. In this way, the generator learns to generate day-like feature maps from the night-time images by playing a zero-sum min-max game with the discriminator.

Unlike a regular GAN discriminator which assigns a single scalar value for a given input, a patch-based discriminator [23] assigns a grid of $m \times n$ scalar values for a given feature map. Each value of this grid is a probability ranging from 0 (night) to 1 (day) and it corresponds to a patch of the input feature map. This allows the discriminator to evaluate the input feature maps locally thereby, providing superior distinguishing ability compared to normal GAN discriminators. In addition, the patch-based discriminators are fully convolutional and hence, are computationally much faster compared to the other discriminator models that use fully-connected layers along with the convolutional layers [37].

Instead of training a single discriminator network on the feature maps obtained from the final convolutional layer of the image encoder as is done in [31,36], we train multiple discriminators, one for each layer of the encoder network to constrain the solution space further. Hence, the proposed multi-stage patch-based discriminator is composed of L number of discriminators where each discriminator D_i, takes feature maps (f_n^i, f_d^i) obtained from the i−th convolutional layer of the encoder networks (F_n, F_d) as input. This multi-stage discriminator is shown to provide superior domain adaptation performance which will be discussed later in the experiments section.

2.3   Training Losses

The proposed method is an unsupervised learning approach which neither uses any explicit ground truth nor paired day-night image examples to calculate losses for training. Instead, we entirely rely on adversarial losses calculated using the discriminator module. The loss functions to learn F_n and D can be expressed as follows:

$$\mathcal{L}_{GAN}(F_n, D) = \min_{F_n} \max_{D} V(F_n, D) = \mathbb{E}_{f_d \sim F_d(I_d)}[\log(D(f_d))]$$
$$+ \mathbb{E}_{f_n \sim F_n(I_n)}\left[\log(1 - D(f_n))\right] \tag{1}$$

$$\min_{F_n} L_{F_n}(F_n, D, I_n) = \frac{1}{L}\sum_{i=1}^{L} - \mathbb{E}_{f_n \sim F_n(I_n)}\left[\sum_{m,n}\log\left[D_i(f_n^i)\right]_{m,n}\right] \tag{2}$$

$$\min_{D} L_D(F_d, F_n, D, I_d, I_n) = \frac{1}{L}\sum_{i-1}^{L} - \mathbb{E}_{f_d \sim F_d(I_d)}\left[\sum_{m,n}\log\left[D_i(f_d^i)\right]_{m,n}\right]$$
$$- \mathbb{E}_{f_n \sim F_n(I_n)}\left[\sum_{m,n}\log\left(1 - \left[D_i(f_n^i)\right]_{m,n}\right)\right] \tag{3}$$

The details about our experimental setup and various experiments conducted are explained in the following section.

3   Experiments and Results

In this section, we provide various experimental results to establish the efficacy of the proposed method for estimating depth from night-time monocular RGB images. We use the publicly available Oxford Robotcar dataset [29] for evaluating the performance of our method. This dataset is used to perform two sets of experiments. The first experiment is carried out to analyze the depth estimation performance of the proposed method while the second experiment is performed to demonstrate the flexibility of using the encoder for solving a Visual Place Recognition (VPR) problem. The overview of dataset used and the details of experiments performed are described next in this section.

3.1   Oxford Robotcar Dataset: Training and Testing Data Setup

Oxford RobotCar dataset [29] is a popular outdoor-driving dataset comprising of images collected during different seasons, weather conditions and at different timings of day and night. The data collection is carried out over a period of one year by setting cameras in all the four directions. The images captured from the front-view stereo cameras are of resolution 1280×960. We have used the left images of the front stereo-camera (Bumblebee XB3) data from the sequences captured on 2014-12-16-18-44-24 for night-time and 2014-12-09-13-21-02 for day-time images for depth estimation. The training is performed on the images from the first 5 splits of the day and night-time sequences after cropping the car-hood from the images and downscaling them to 256×512. The static images where the car has stopped at signals are not considered for the experiments and thus, the total number of images left for training is close to 20,000. We have randomly sampled a total of 498 images for testing from the 6th split of night-driving sequence.

For VPR, we have used day and night sequences as 2014-12-09-13-21-02 and 2014-12-10-18-10-50 respectively from the Oxford Robotcar dataset, where the query (night) sequence is different from that used in the network training. We only used the first 6000 *stereo-left* image frames from each of these traverses which were uniformly sub-sampled using the GPS data to maintain consecutive frame distance of approximately 2 m. The day traverse is used as the reference traverse against which each of the query (night) image representations is compared with Euclidean distance to retrieve the best match. The night images do not overlap geographically with the night data used for training the model employed for feature extraction for VPR experiments. The evaluation is done using the GPS data by calculating the recall rate for the localization radius varying between 0 to 100 m. Here, recall rate is defined as the ratio of correctly matched images within the given radius of localization to the total number of query images.

3.2   Experimental Setup

The proposed method is implemented using TensorFlow [1]. The network is trained for 40 epochs using a GTX 1080 Alienware-R4 laptop. The learning rate is initially set to 0.0001, then it is reduced by half after $3/5^{th}$ of the total iterations and finally, it is further reduced by half after $4/5^{th}$ of the total iterations. Leaky Relu [38] is used as an activation function in all the layers, except in disparity prediction layers. The predicted disparity is normalized to have the maximum disparity as 30% of the input image width by using sigmoid as activation function while learning the day-time depth estimation model. The network is trained using the Adam [25] optimizer. Two major experimental studies, one for depth estimation and another for visual place recognition, are carried out under extreme photometric variations using the Oxford dataset [29]. Both the experimental studies along with the qualitative and quantitative analyses are presented below.

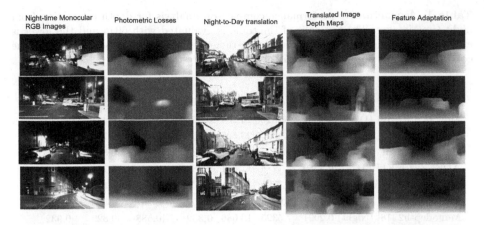

Fig. 3. A qualitative comparison of predicted depth-maps with different experiments. The first column shows the night-time images which are provided as input to different networks. The second column shows the output depth images obtained using photometric losses. As one can observe, these methods fail to maintain the structural layout of the scene. The third column shows the output of an image-translation network (Cycle-GAN) which are then applied to a day-depth estimation network to obtain depth-maps as shown in the fourth column. These are slightly better compared to the previous case but it introduces several artifacts which degrade the depth estimation in several cases. The last column shows the predictions using the proposed ADFA approach. As one can see, the proposed method provides better predictions compared to these methods and is capable of preserving structural attributes of the scene to a greater extent

3.3 Study 1: Depth Evaluation

In this study, we perform several experiments to establish the efficacy of our proposed method for estimating depth from monocular night-time images. The summary of these experiments is provided in Table 1. The first row of this table shows the outcome of our first experiment where we train a monocular version of Monodepth2 [18] network on Oxford day-time images and then, test it on Oxford night-time images. As expected, the day-time trained model performs poorly on night-time images because of the inherent domain shift present between day-time and night-time images. The second row shows the outcome of another experiment where the same network is trained on the Oxford night-time images and then, tested on a different set of night-time images (test-split). The performance in this case is better than the first experiment but still not good enough as the presence of temporal intensity gradient makes it difficult to use the existing photometric losses for training the network. The third row of this table shows the outcome of yet another experiment where we use image translation for depth estimation. In this approach, we use Cycle-GAN [44] for translating night-time Oxford images into day-time images and then use a day-time trained Monodepth2 model for estimating depth from these translated images. The performance of this approach is similar to the above methods (worse in terms of

Table 1. A quantitative performance comparison analysis for depth estimation from night-time images. The top split of the table is evaluated with 60 m and the lower is evaluate with 40 m as the maximum depth-range. Higher value is better for the blue color labeled cells and lower value is better for the rest

Method	Error Metric ↓				Accuracy Metric ↑		
	Abs Rel	Sq Rel	RMSE	logRMSE	$\delta < 1.25$	$\delta < 1.25^2$	$\delta < 1.25^3$
Monodepth2 [18] (Day)	0.7221	11.5155	14.253	0.663	0.252	0.467	0.644
Monodepth2 [18] (Night)	0.3990	38.8965	23.596	0.408	0.482	0.760	0.894
Cycle-GAN [44]	0.7587	12.7944	13.681	0.663	0.277	0.503	0.688
ADFA (with KITTI)	0.3589	5.1174	11.611	0.384	0.424	0.730	0.914
ADFA (with Oxford)	**0.2327**	**3.783**	**10.089**	**0.319**	**0.668**	**0.844**	**0.924**
Monodepth2 [18] (Day)	0.6108	6.9513	9.945	0.592	0.267	0.502	0.695
Monodepth2 [18] (Night)	0.2921	7.5395	10.686	0.332	0.588	0.829	0.932
Cycle-GAN [44]	0.6497	7.9346	9.521	0.596	0.298	0.546	0.740
ADFA (with KITTI)	0.2984	3.2349	7.801	0.328	0.495	0.833	0.942
ADFA (with Oxford)	**0.2005**	**2.5750**	**7.172**	**0.278**	**0.735**	**0.883**	**0.942**

'Abs Rel' metric and better in terms of 'RMSE' metric) indicating that image translation is not adequate for solving the night-time depth estimation problem. Moreover, it is a computationally expensive method that uses two independent networks in cascade unlike the above methods that use only one network for this task. We now apply our proposed ADFA method to adapt the depth model used in the first experiment above and the outcome is shown in the fifth row of this table. As one can see, it provides significant improvement over the previous three approaches, thereby establishing the superiority of our approach. In this case, day-time encoder-decoder pair (F_d, G_d) and night-time encoder (F_n) are trained using images from Oxford dataset and then tested using night-time images from the same dataset. We also perform another experiment where the day-time encoder-decoder network (F_d, G_d) is trained on the KITTI dataset, but the night-time encoder (F_n) is trained and then tested on night-time Oxford images. The corresponding result is shown in the fourth row and is labeled as 'ADFA (with KITTI)'. While its performance is worse than ADFA (Oxford), it is better than all other methods mentioned above. It is worth to mention that this is an extreme case of domain adaption where not only there is a domain variation from day to night, but also a place variation from KITTI to Oxford. It only demonstrates the resilience of our approach whose performance degrades gracefully in the face of this extreme domain variation. Even though Monodepth2 [18] model has been used as our base network architecture for providing the above performance analysis, ADFA is a generic approach which could be applied to any other deep network model with similar effect.

A qualitative performance comparison of these methods is shown in Fig. 3. The first column shows the input night-time images selected randomly from the test set. The second column shows the depth estimation results obtained by using methods such as Monodepth2 [18] that use photometric losses for training.

Table 2. Ablation study to determine the number of day-encoder convolutional layers to be used during the adversarial learning. The best performance is achieved by skipping the first two layers (without cnv-1,2) features

Method	Abs Rel	Sq Rel	RMSE	logRMSE
Full conv layers	0.2071	2.8971	7.619	0.282
without cnv-1	0.2038	2.7908	7.461	0.280
without cnv-1,2	**0.2005**	**2.575**	**7.172**	**0.278**
without cnv-1,2,3	0.2260	2.574	7.283	0.300

The third column shows the images obtained after image translation by using methods such as Cycle-GAN [44]. The fourth column shows the depth map obtained from these translated images by a pre-trained day-time depth network. We can clearly see that image translation introduces several artifacts leading to poor depth estimation results. The last column shows the depth prediction results obtained by using our proposed ADFA method. One can clearly notice the improvements achieved through our proposed domain feature adaptation method.

The front LMS laser sensor data with INS data is used to prepare the ground-truth needed for testing images using the official code-base released with the dataset. The maximum depth range is set to 60m in the first half of the Table 1 and changed to 40 m in the second half. The scale is calculated using the ground-truth depth data, as it is done in [39, 42]. In addition, an ablation study is carried out to determine the optimal number of night-time encoder F_n layers to be constrained for the best performance and the results are shown in Table 2. We observed that a model trained by skipping the first two layers of the day-encoder gives the best-performance and the same model is used to report the final results.

To the best of our knowledge, the proposed work is the first attempt at solving the depth estimation problem for unconstrained night-time monocular images for which no priors are available in the literature. However, there are some cases, shown in the Fig. 4, where the model is observed to provide poor or failed prediction results. Some of the failure cases include night-time images with very low-illumination conditions, blurred image regions and saturated regions (bright light spots). It is also difficult for our method to deal with small and narrow structures such as traffic poles. The failure case with low-illuminated night-time images could be due to the absence of such extreme conditions in day-time images on which the day encoder-decoder model is trained. The problems associated with small structures could be dealt by incorporating some semantic information (if available) into the training data. These limitations will provide a fertile ground for further research in this field.

Fig. 4. Failure cases of the proposed depth prediction approach. The model is not able to predict accurate depth for blurred image regions, traffic signal poles and very low illuminated regions of the image

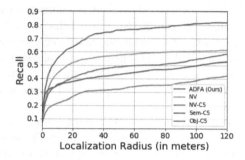

Fig. 5. Visual Place Recognition Performance Benchmark: It can be observed that the feature representations derived from our depth encoder perform the best as compared to other approaches

3.4 Study 2: Visual Place Recognition: Day Versus Night

The depth estimation network trained using our proposed approach is able to learn appearance-robust features within the encoder. This is particularly useful for visual place recognition under significant appearance variations, for example, day versus night. The state-of-the-art VPR methods use deep-learnt representations either based on end-to-end training [3,8,32] or indirectly derived from the internal layer representations [2,14,35]. For the performance benchmark presented in this section, we directly compare the convolutional features based image representations, extracted from different networks. In this way, the repeatability of activation patterns across day and night appearance conditions can be directly evaluated.

Figure 5 shows the performance comparison among different place representation methods. This includes flattened *conv*5 representations from four different networks trained on different tasks: *Ours-C5* uses the encoder output from our proposed network, trained to predict depth for night-time images; *NV-C5* uses VGG [34] based NetVLAD [3], trained for place recognition; *Obj-C5* uses ResNet50 [20], trained for object recognition; and *Sem-C5* uses the encoder output of RefineNet [26] which is based on ResNet101 [20] and trained for dense

Fig. 6. Qualitative Results: For night time query images (top row), Ground Truth (GT) match (second row) and matches obtained from different methods are displayed (subsequent rows) including successful matches using our proposed representation (third row)

semantic segmentation. The latter has also been effectively used for state-of-the-art place recognition descriptor LoST [13]. The flattened *conv*5 representations expect a similar viewpoint between the compared pairs of images; for sake of completion, we also include a viewpoint-invariant representation in our comparisons: NetVLAD as *NV* which uses 4096-dimensional descriptors. It can be observed that the feature representations based on our depth encoder perform the best. While there is a significant margin in performance for the flattened *conv*5 comparisons, the proposed representation also outperforms the end-to-end learnt viewpoint-invariant NetVLAD representation.

Figure 6 shows qualitative results for visual place recognition under significant appearance variations. The first row shows four query images captured under night time conditions; their corresponding Ground Truth (GT) day-time image matches are shown in the second row. In subsequent columns, image matches obtained through different representation methods are displayed with the third row comprising successful matches based on our proposed representation. The incorrect matches using other methods in the first column seem to indicate a bias in their selection based on the presence of a vehicle in the query image. In the second row, it can be observed that most of the retrieved matches comprise buildings viewed from far with an oblique viewpoint, however, only the proposed representation is able to obtain the correct match. We believe that learning to predict depth per pixel for night time imagery enables the latent representations to be more robust to perceptual aliasing caused by appearance variations. Moreover, our proposed depth-estimation network is trained in a completely unsupervised manner, where other vision-based tasks like object recognition and semantic segmentation would require labeled night-time data if they were to be used for extracting appearance-invariant image representations for place recognition.

4   Conclusions and Future Scope

This paper discusses the problem of estimating depth from night-time images, which suffers from poor visibility, non-uniform and unpredictable variation in illumination arising from multiple and possibly, moving light sources. The problem is tackled by applying a patchGAN-based domain adaptation technique that allows an encoder to adapt the *features* obtained from the night-time images to acquire the attributes of day-time features so that a decoder trained on day-time images could be directly used for estimating depth from these adapted features. The proposed novel approach is completely unsupervised as it does not necessitate the availability of either explicit ground truth signals (obtained from range sensors) or implicit supervision signals obtained from multi-view (spatial/temporal) images. Unlike many of the existing methods, the proposed method also does not require generating simulated data which is considerably difficult for night-time images. The efficacy of the proposed approach is demonstrated through extensive analyses on the challenging Oxford RobotCar dataset. Its usefulness is also demonstrated through its application to a visual place recognition problem where the feature representation obtained from our depth encoder is shown to outperform those obtained from the existing state-of-the-art methods. The proposed approach has some limitations which will form the scope for future investigations. As shown in Fig. 4, our method can not deal with saturated regions (bright lights), very low illuminated regions and thin structures, such as traffic signal poles. This could be solved to some extent by incorporating semantic information in the learning process. Secondly, instead of learning two separate encoders - one for day-time images and the other for night-time images, it would be good to have one encoder model which could be trained to learn context-specific features which are unique to different styles rather than image-specific features. These context-specific features could then provide the necessary semantics to deal with the above failure cases.

References

1. Abadi, M., et al.: TensorFlow: a system for large-scale machine learning. In: OSDI, vol. 16, pp. 265–283 (2016)
2. Anoosheh, A., Sattler, T., Timofte, R., Pollefeys, M., Van Gool, L.: Night-to-day image translation for retrieval-based localization. In: 2019 International Conference on Robotics and Automation (ICRA), pp. 5958–5964. IEEE (2019)

3. Arandjelovic, R., Gronat, P., Torii, A., Pajdla, T., Sivic, J.: NetVLAD: CNN architecture for weakly supervised place recognition. In: Proceedings of the IEEE Conference on Computer Vision and Pattern Recognition, pp. 5297–5307 (2016)

4. Atapour-Abarghouei, A., Breckon, T.P.: Real-time monocular depth estimation using synthetic data with domain adaptation via image style transfer. In: Proceedings of the IEEE Conference on Computer Vision and Pattern Recognition, pp. 2800–2810 (2018)

5. Babu, V.M., Das, K., Majumdar, A., Kumar, S.: UnDEMoN: unsupervised deep network for depth and ego-motion estimation. In: Proceedings of the IEEE/RSJ International Conference on Intelligent Robots and Systems (IROS), pp. 1082–1088. IEEE (2018)

6. Badrinarayanan, V., Kendall, A., Cipolla, R.: SegNet: a deep convolutional encoder-decoder architecture for image segmentation. IEEE Trans. Pattern Anal. Mach. Intell. **39**(12), 2481–2495 (2017)

7. Cao, Y., Wu, Z., Shen, C.: Estimating depth from monocular images as classification using deep fully convolutional residual networks. IEEE Trans. Circuits Syst. Video Technol. **28**(11), 3174–3182 (2018)

8. Chen, Z., et al.: Deep learning features at scale for visual place recognition. In: 2017 IEEE International Conference on Robotics and Automation (ICRA), pp. 3223–3230. IEEE (2017)

9. Cordts, M., et al.: The cityscapes dataset for semantic urban scene understanding. In: Proceedings of the IEEE Conference on Computer Vision and Pattern Recognition, pp. 3213–3223 (2016)

10. Eigen, D., Puhrsch, C., Fergus, R.: Depth map prediction from a single image using a multi-scale deep network. In: Advances in Neural Information Processing Systems, pp. 2366–2374 (2014)

11. Garg, S., et al.: Look no deeper: recognizing places from opposing viewpoints under varying scene appearance using single-view depth estimation. arXiv preprint arXiv:1902.07381 (2019)

12. Garg, S., Harwood, B., Anand, G., Milford, M.: Delta descriptors: change-based place representation for robust visual localization. IEEE Robotics and Automation Letters **5**(4), 5120–5127 (2020)

13. Garg, S., Suenderhauf, N., Milford, M.: Lost? Appearance-invariant place recognition for opposite viewpoints using visual semantics. In: Proceedings of Robotics: Science and Systems XIV (2018)

14. Garg, S., Sünderhauf, N., Milford, M.: Semantic-geometric visual place recognition: a new perspective for reconciling opposing views. Int. J. Rob. Res. (2019)

15. Geiger, A., Lenz, P., Stiller, C., Urtasun, R.: Vision meets robotics: the KITTI dataset. Int. J. Rob. Res. **32**(11), 1231–1237 (2013)

16. Geiger, A., Ziegler, J., Stiller, C.: StereoScan: dense 3D reconstruction in real-time. In: IEEE Intelligent Vehicles Symposium, Baden-Baden, Germany, June 2011

17. Godard, C., Mac Aodha, O., Brostow, G.J.: Unsupervised monocular depth estimation with left-right consistency. In: 2017 IEEE Conference on Computer Vision and Pattern Recognition (CVPR), pp. 6602–6611. IEEE (2017)

18. Godard, C., Mac Aodha, O., Firman, M., Brostow, G.: Digging into self-supervised monocular depth estimation. arXiv preprint arXiv:1806.01260 (2018)

19. Handa, A., Whelan, T., McDonald, J., Davison, A.J.: A benchmark for RGB-D visual odometry, 3D reconstruction and SLAM. In: 2014 IEEE International Conference on Robotics and automation (ICRA), pp. 1524–1531. IEEE (2014)

20. He, K., Zhang, X., Ren, S., Sun, J.: Deep residual learning for image recognition. In: Proceedings of the IEEE Conference on Computer Vision and Pattern Recognition, pp. 770–778 (2016)
21. Huang, X., Liu, M.-Y., Belongie, S., Kautz, J.: Multimodal unsupervised image-to-image translation. In: Ferrari, V., Hebert, M., Sminchisescu, C., Weiss, Y. (eds.) ECCV 2018. LNCS, vol. 11207, pp. 179–196. Springer, Cham (2018). https://doi.org/10.1007/978-3-030-01219-9_11
22. Im, S., Jeon, H.G., So Kweon, I.: Robust depth estimation from auto bracketed images. In: Proceedings of the IEEE Conference on Computer Vision and Pattern Recognition, pp. 2946–2954 (2018)
23. Isola, P., Zhu, J.Y., Zhou, T., Efros, A.A.: Image-to-image translation with conditional adversarial networks. In: 2017 IEEE Conference on Computer Vision and Pattern Recognition (CVPR), pp. 5967–5976. IEEE (2017)
24. Kim, N., Choi, Y., Hwang, S., Kweon, I.S.: Multispectral transfer network: unsupervised depth estimation for all-day vision. In: Thirty-Second AAAI Conference on Artificial Intelligence (2018)
25. Kingma, D.P., Ba, J.: Adam: a method for stochastic optimization. arXiv preprint arXiv:1412.6980 (2014)
26. Lin, G., Milan, A., Shen, C., Reid, I.: RefineNet: multi-path refinement networks for high-resolution semantic segmentation. In: IEEE Conference on Computer Vision and Pattern Recognition (CVPR), vol. 1, p. 3 (2017)
27. Luo, C., et al.: Every pixel counts++: joint learning of geometry and motion with 3D holistic understanding. arXiv preprint arXiv:1810.06125 (2018)
28. Luo, Y., et al.: Single view stereo matching. In: Proceedings of the IEEE Conference on Computer Vision and Pattern Recognition, pp. 155–163 (2018)
29. Maddern, W., Pascoe, G., Linegar, C., Newman, P.: 1 year, 1000 km: the Oxford RobotCar dataset. Int. J. Rob. Res. **36**(1), 3–15 (2017)
30. Marchand, E., Uchiyama, H., Spindler, F.: Pose estimation for augmented reality: a hands-on survey. IEEE Trans. Visual Comput. Graphics **22**(12), 2633–2651 (2016)
31. Nath Kundu, J., Krishna Uppala, P., Pahuja, A., Venkatesh Babu, R.: AdaDepth: unsupervised content congruent adaptation for depth estimation. In: Proceedings of the IEEE Conference on Computer Vision and Pattern Recognition, pp. 2656–2665 (2018)
32. Radenović, F., Tolias, G., Chum, O.: Fine-tuning CNN image retrieval with no human annotation. IEEE Trans. Pattern Anal. Mach. Intell. **41**(7), 1655–1668 (2018)
33. Ros, G., Sellart, L., Materzynska, J., Vazquez, D., Lopez, A.M.: The SYNTHIA dataset: a large collection of synthetic images for semantic segmentation of urban scenes. In: Proceedings of the IEEE Conference on Computer Vision and Pattern Recognition, pp. 3234–3243 (2016)
34. Simonyan, K., Zisserman, A.: Very deep convolutional networks for large-scale image recognition. arXiv preprint arXiv:1409.1556 (2014)
35. Sünderhauf, N., Shirazi, S., Dayoub, F., Upcroft, B., Milford, M.: On the performance of convnet features for place recognition. In: 2015 IEEE/RSJ International Conference on Intelligent Robots and Systems (IROS), pp. 4297–4304. IEEE (2015)
36. Tzeng, E., Hoffman, J., Saenko, K., Darrell, T.: Adversarial discriminative domain adaptation. In: Proceedings of the IEEE Conference on Computer Vision and Pattern Recognition, pp. 7167–7176 (2017)

37. Vankadari, M., Kumar, S., Majumder, A., Das, K.: Unsupervised learning of monocular depth and ego-motion using conditional PatchGANs. In: Proceedings of the Twenty-Eighth International Joint Conference on Artificial Intelligence, IJCAI 2019, pp. 5677–5684. International Joint Conferences on Artificial Intelligence Organization, July 2019. https://doi.org/10.24963/ijcai.2019/787

38. Xu, B., Wang, N., Chen, T., Li, M.: Empirical evaluation of rectified activations in convolutional network. arXiv preprint arXiv:1505.00853 (2015)

39. Yin, Z., Shi, J.: GeoNet: unsupervised learning of dense depth, optical flow and camera pose. In: Proceedings of the IEEE Conference on Computer Vision and Pattern Recognition (CVPR), vol. 2 (2018)

40. Zhao, S., Fu, H., Gong, M., Tao, D.: Geometry-aware symmetric domain adaptation for monocular depth estimation. In: Proceedings of the IEEE Conference on Computer Vision and Pattern Recognition, pp. 9788–9798 (2019)

41. Zhao, Z.Q., Zheng, P., Xu, S.T., Wu, X.: Object detection with deep learning: a review. IEEE transactions on neural networks and learning systems **30**(11), 3212–3232 (2019)

42. Zhou, T., Brown, M., Snavely, N., Lowe, D.G.: Unsupervised learning of depth and ego-motion from video. In: CVPR (2017)

43. Zhu, A.Z., Yuan, L., Chaney, K., Daniilidis, K.: Unsupervised event based learning of optical flow, depth, and egomotion. In: Proceedings of the IEEE Conference on Computer Vision and Pattern Recognition, pp. 989–997 (2019)

44. Zhu, J.Y., Park, T., Isola, P., Efros, A.A.: Unpaired image-to-image translation using cycle-consistent adversarial networks. In: 2017 IEEE International Conference on Computer Vision (ICCV) (2017)

Variational Connectionist Temporal Classification

Linlin Chao[✉], Jingdong Chen, and Wei Chu

Ant Financial Services Group, Hangzhou, China
{chulin.cll,jingdongchen.cjd}@antgroup.com
weichu.cw@alibaba-inc.com

Abstract. Connectionist Temporal Classification (CTC) is a training criterion designed for sequence labelling problems where the alignment between the inputs and the target labels is unknown. One of the key steps is to add a blank symbol to the target vocabulary. However, CTC tends to output spiky distributions since it prefers to output blank symbol most of the time. These spiky distributions show inferior alignments and the non-blank symbols are not learned sufficiently. To remedy this, we propose variational CTC (Var-CTC) to enhance the learning of non-blank symbols. The proposed Var-CTC converts the output distribution of vanilla CTC with hierarchy distribution. It first learns the approximated posterior distribution of blank to determine whether to output a specific non-blank symbol or not. Then it learns the alignment between non-blank symbols and input sequence. Experiments on scene text recognition and offline handwritten text recognition show Var-CTC achieves better alignments. Besides, with the enhanced learning of non-blank symbols, the confidence scores of model outputs are more discriminative. Compared with the vanilla CTC, the proposed Var-CTC can improve the recall performance by a large margin when the models maintain the same level of precision.

Keywords: Connectionist Temporal Classification · Scene text recognition · Handwritten text recognition

1 Introduction

Connectionist Temporal Classification (CTC) [4] is a training criterion designed for sequence labelling problems where the alignments between the inputs and the target labels are unknown. It has gained widespread traction from its successful use in tasks such as speech recognition [5,7,24], text recognition [6,30], sign language recognition [2], video segmentation [13] and so on. It is proven to be effective in sequence recognition tasks.

CTC works by adding an extra blank symbol to target vocabulary and maximizing the probabilities of all possible alignments. The added blank symbol represents outputting either a specific non-blank symbol or not. With the added blank symbol, the outputs over all timesteps are aligned to multiple paths, which

A. Vedaldi et al. (Eds.): ECCV 2020, LNCS 12373, pp. 460–476, 2020.
https://doi.org/10.1007/978-3-030-58604-1_28

consists of labels and blanks. The CTC-based training is then to sum up probabilities of all the corresponding paths and maximize them. However, the distribution of blank and non-blank symbols in the training data is unbalanced. This is because: 1) blank is almost added into every training data to make paths; 2) compared with the non-blank, the positions of blanks in paths are more flexible, which leads to more blanks are added. The unbalanced distribution leads to the model prefers output blank most of the time, which is known as the CTC spiky distribution problem [4, 24, 28]. As shown in Fig. 1, the outputs of the characters in label sequence only exist in only a few timesteps. The spiky distributions show inferior alignments [28]. The learning of non-blank symbols is not sufficient, which is suppressed by the added blank.

In this paper, we try to enhance the learning of non-blank symbols by proposing the variational CTC (Var-CTC). The Var-CTC approximates the posterior distribution of blank using a learned inference network. It is fit with variational inference [16] technique to improve the training bound. In the proposed Var-CTC, the influence of the unbalanced distribution for non-blank symbols is relieved. This is because the distributions of blank and non-blank symbols are not belonging to the same one. Var-CTC first learns the approximated posterior distribution of blank to determine whether to output a label or not. Then it learns to determine to output which label. This hierarchy output of Var-CTC is similar to the classification branch in objection detection [26], where the first hierarchy determines the background and non-background category and the second hierarchy determines the object category.

Besides, we find the confidence scores of the CTC model's predictions in text recognition are not discriminative enough. Confidence scores are important for practical use, as we want the model's predictions can achieve the desired precision and recall at the same time. Having a reliable confidence score is crucial for real world applications of OCR. As far as we know, the confidence score based evaluation has never been compared. In this paper, we add the confidence score based evaluation for model comparisons. We find the proposed Var-CTC can improve the Precision-Recall performance significantly.

The main contributions of this paper can be summarized as follows: (1) Variational inference for CTC is first introduced, which converts output distribution of vanilla CTC with hierarchy distribution; (2) The confidence scores of CTC based models on text recognition are analyzed. We show why the confidence score is not discriminative enough by case study and Precision-Recall curve; (3) With the enhanced learning of non-blank symbols, the proposed Var-CTC can improve the recall by a large margin while maintain the same level precision.

2 Related Work

CTC has been explored extensively in sequence recognition tasks, like text recognition [6, 30], speech recognition [4, 5, 7] and so on. A relevant and recent work to ours is the EnEs-CTC [20]. EnEs-CTC proposes a maximum conditional entropy based regularization method to penalize spiky distributions. The penalization

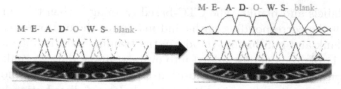

Fig. 1. (Better viewed in color). Visualization of the output distributions for CTC (left) and Var-CTC (right). For Var-CTC, we visualize two distributions, where the bottom one denotes $P(classes|blank, img) * P(blank|img)$ and the top one denotes $P(classes|img)$. The classes in this case represents the characters in label sequence "MEADOWS". (Color figure online)

operation enables the model to explore more paths for the sequence alignments, which improves the learning of the non-blank symbols. In contrast to them, our work improves the learning of non-blank symbols by changing the output distribution to hierarchy distribution. The hierarchy distribution relieves the influence of the unbalance problem, which is more thoroughly.

For large scale speech recognition, [32] introduces and evaluates Sampled CTC to speed up CTC training. Two sampling methods are proposed to sample the blank outputs, which are heuristic. Once the blank is sampled, the other parameters can be optimized by minimizing cross entropy objective. Our proposed Var-CTC can also sample the blank output. While the sampling procedure is guided by the approximated posterior distribution, which is end-to-end learnable. GTC [12] tries to learn better alignment with an attention decoder as a guidance for CTC training while this paper focuses on the underfitting for non-blanks in vanilla CTC.

Besides, [3] modifies the CTC by fusing focal loss with it and thus makes the model to attend to the low-frequent samples at training stage. The proposed method tries to solve the class unbalance problem of Chinese optical character recognition. Compared to them, our work try to solve the unbalance problem between blank and non-blank symbols rather then unbalance among non-blank symbols. For weakly-supervised action labelling in video, [13] introduces the extended CTC framework to enforce the consistency of all possible paths with frame to frame visual similarities. However, computing the visual similarities between consecutive frames is expensive.

Meanwhile, CTC based model for scene text recognition has achieved relative high recognition accuracy on several benchmark datasets. These models are often evaluated by sequence accuracy [20,30]. The confidence score is important but never analyzed. In this paper, we add the confidence score based performance as an evaluation criterion.

2.1 Methodology

Before proceeding, we define our mathematical notations. The input feature sequence is represented as $X = \{x^1, x^2, x^3, ..., x^T\}$, where T is the sequence

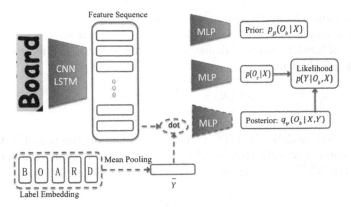

Fig. 2. The probabilistic graphical model of our proposed method. Dotted lines represent the calculation of the approximate posterior distribution. X and Y represent feature sequence and label sequence respectively. O_b represents whether to output a label or not at each timestep. $p(O_c|X)$ represents the categorical distribution for elements in label sequence Y, which does not contain blank.

length, and x^i is a vector representation in $\mathbb{R}^d$. The target label sequence is represented as $Y = \{y^1, y^2, ..., y^{T^y}\}$. T^y represents the length of target label sequence, which is no greater than T. The elements of label sequence come from the target vocabulary A. The blank symbol is represented as "$-$". The extended vocabulary $A \cup \{-\}$ is represented as A^*. The model output is represented as O and it contains blank output sequence O_b and non-blank output sequence O_c. o^t represents the output at timestep t.

2.2 Connectionist Temporal Classification

Given feature sequence X and label sequence Y, CTC learns the alignment without employing the frame level alignment information. The blank symbol "$-$" is added to the target label vocabulary for two reasons. Firstly, it separates the repeated label in the label sequence. Secondly, it is used as label for unlabeled data. At every timestep, the softmax function normalizes the outputs to get the distribution from x^t to A^*.

The complete sequence of outputs is then used to define a distribution over all possible alignments, where each possible alignment is named as a path π. The path π is composed by labels in Y and blanks. Assuming the outputs at each timestep to be independent of those at other timesteps, the probability of one particular path π can be calculated as:

$$p(\pi|X) = \prod_{t=1}^{T} p(o_{\pi^t}^t|x^t).$$

$$(1)$$

where π^t represents the label at the timestep t for path π. CTC then defines a many-to-one mapping function F. The mapping function F maps the paths to the label sequence by first merging the consecutive same labels into one and then discards the blanks. For example $F(a, -, a, b, -) = F(a, a, -, a, b) = aab$. The probability of label Y can be calculated as an aggregation of the probabilities of all possible CTC paths:

$$p(Y|X) = \sum_{\pi \in F^{-1}(Y)} p(\pi|X). \tag{2}$$

For CTC based models, the CTC is usually applied on the top of bidirectional recurrent neural networks (RNNs) [29] with Long Short Term Memory (LSTM) cells [11]. The RNNs can be trained to maximize the following objective function:

$$L(Y) = \log p(Y|X). \tag{3}$$

Unbalanced Distribution Between Blank and Non-blanks. Based on the mapping function F, blanks are inserted to label sequence to make paths. Blank can exist in almost every training data as long as the sequence length T is greater than label length T^y. Besides, the positions of blanks in paths are more flexible compared to non-blank symbols, which makes the unbalanced problem worse. The unbalanced distribution between blank and non-blank symbols leads to the non-blank symbols are not aligned to the input feature sequence sufficiently. This also means the model is underfitting the non-blanks.

2.3   Variational Connectionist Temporal Classification

As the unbalanced distribution between blank and non-blank symbols in CTC is inevitable, computing the distributions of blank and non-blank symbols separately may reduce the influence. So we propose to change the unified distribution to hierarchy distribution. Specifically, we put forward the following objective:

$$L(Y) = \log p(Y|X) = \log \sum_{O_b} p(O_b|X)p(Y|O_b, X). \tag{4}$$

The Eq. 4 shows the model first determines the blank, then outputs the non-blanks. The blank outputs determine the alignment paths between label and input sequence, which is vital for the unsupervised alignments. Given the posterior distribution of blank $(p(O_b|X, Y))$, the model should learn the alignment for non-blanks better. Thus, we propose to approximate the posterior of blank instead of learning the likelihood $(p(O_b|X))$. With the help of variational inference optimization strategy, we try to optimize the evidence lower bound (ELBO) [16] of $L(Y)$. In this paper, we define the ELBO as the Var-CTC loss. It is defined as:

$$L_{var-ctc}(Y) = E_{q_\psi(O_b|X,Y)}[\log p(Y|O_b, X)] - KL(q_\psi(O_b|X,Y)||p_\beta(O_b|X)). \tag{5}$$

It is composed of three different terms, likelihood $p(Y|O_b, X)$, prior $p_\beta(O_b|X)$ and posterior $q_\psi(O_b|X, Y)$. These three terms can be parameterized by three different layers, like multilayer perceptrons (MLPs) and RNN. Figure 2 shows the schematic diagram of the Var-CTC based model. For parameter efficiency, we utilize the MLP to represent the posterior and prior distributions in this paper. These three terms are described below:

Likelihood. Given the approximate posterior for blanks, the likelihood aggregates the probabilities of all possible paths. Different with the vanilla CTC, at each timestep, the categorical distribution form x^t to A^* is calculated as:

$$p(o^t|o_b^t, x^t) = \begin{cases} q_\psi(o_b^t|x^t, Y), & \text{if } o^t = \text{``\_''}, \\ p(o_c^t|x^t) \cdot (1 - q_\psi(o_b^t|x^t, Y)), & \text{otherwise}, \end{cases} \tag{6}$$

where $p(o_c^t|x^t) = softmax(x^t W_c)$ is the class distribution over all non-blank symbols in the vocabulary. $W_c \in \mathbb{R}^{d \times |A|}$ is the matrix parameter.

Once we get the output possibilities at each timestep, the function F maps the paths to sequence output like CTC. During inference time when the label sequence is not available, the prior term is used to replace posterior approximator to output the blank distribution.

Prior. The prior $p_\beta(O_b|X)$ is formulated as a sequence of Bernoulli distributions. Given feature sequence, it computes the distribution of blank at all the timesteps. For efficiency, we directly convert the feature at every timestep to distributions with one feed-forward layer. It is computed as follows:

$$p_\beta(o_b^t|x^t; \beta) = \sigma(x^t w_p), \tag{7}$$

where $\sigma(\cdot)$ is the sigmoid function with $w_p \in \mathbb{R}^d$ being vector parameter.

Approximate Posterior. The posterior distribution $q_\psi(O_b|X, Y)$ follows the similar architecture as the prior. The main difference lies in the fact that posterior approximator is aware of the label sequence Y, therefore outputting more accurate distributions. In order to incorporate the label sequence, we embed each symbol in vocabulary to a random initialized vector. These embeddings are learned with other parameters in the network together. For a particular label sequence, we get the label representation $\bar{Y}$ by mean pooling operation on time axis. The posterior is then computed as follows:

$$q_\psi(o_b^t|x^t, Y; \psi) = \sigma((f(x^t) \circ \bar{Y})w_a), \tag{8}$$

where function f is one feed-forward layer and it converts dimension of x^t to the same dimension of $\bar{Y}$. The $\circ$ denotes the Hadamard product. $w_a \in \mathbb{R}^d$ is the vector parameter.

Optimization. The loss function has two terms, which can be optimized jointly. The first term in Eq. 5 is motivated to get the target label based on blank distribution. Optimizing this term can also help the approximate posterior to obtain accurate blank output distribution. The second term is the KL-divergence between the prior distribution and the approximated posterior distribution, which is motivated to push the prior distribution towards the posterior distribution. The values of $q_\psi(O_b|X,Y)$ can be directly utilized to compute $p(Y|O_b,X)$ based on the forward-backward algorithm [4] and the mapping function F in vanilla CTC. Thus, the distributions $q_\psi(O_b|X,Y)$ and $p(Y|O_b,X)$ in the first term can be optimized based on the forward-backward algorithm like the vanilla CTC loss. The second term is the KL divergence between two distributions. The gradients of the second term can also be calculated analytically. So the loss can be optimized with any gradient based optimization algorithm.

The O_b can also be modeled as discrete values similar to the Sampled CTC [32]. It means their values are sampled binary values based on q_ψ. In this way, as O_b is not differentiable with respect to q_ψ, the REINFORCE algorithm [33] can be used to tackle this problem. One advantage of this modeling way is it can speed up the training process since the forward-backward algorithm is not needed. The disadvantage is that variance reduction technique for the REINFORCE based optimization should be considered. We leave this line for future work.

Complexity Analysis. The time complexity of CTC and Var-CTC forward-backward dynamic programming is $O(T)$. Compared to CTC, the mainly added computation is the posterior distribution, which is also $O(T)$. Since the forward and backward variable are kept for gradient computing, the space complexity of CTC and Var-CTC is $O(TT^y)$.

3   Experimental Results

In our experiments, two tasks are employed to evaluate the effectiveness of Var-CTC, including handwritten text recognition and scene text recognition. Besides, we also try to directly maximize the marginal likelihood $p(Y|X) = \sum_{O_b} p(O_b|X)p(Y|O_b,X)$ using only the prior and likelihood model following [8], which enables us to understand the superiority of introducing an approximate posterior. We call this objective as Mml-CTC.

3.1   Scene Text Recognition

Convolutional Recurrent Neural Network (CRNN) [30] is utilized as the feature extraction network. We compare our method with CRNN-CTC [30] and CRNN-EnEs-CTC [20] models. All models have the same feature extraction network.

Evaluation Metrics. There are two evaluation metrics in this experiment. The first one is the sequence accuracy, which is in accordance with the experiments setup of [20,30]. Sequence accuracy means the percentage of test images that are recognized totally correct.

The second one is the Precision-Recall curve. The confidence score is computed based on the greedy decode method. Greedy decode is the widely used decode method in scene text recognition [20,30]. It decodes the outputs by choosing the most feasible path, which is the concatenation of the most probable labelling for every timestep. The confidence score corresponding to this path is calculated as:

$$p(\pi^*|x) = \prod_{i=1}^{T} \max p(o^t|x^t).\tag{9}$$

Previous studies evaluate the model on benchmark datasets on the resized images. For example, both [20,30] resize the test images to 100×32. Thus, we plot the Precision-Recall curves based on the resized images.

Datasets. We train our models with the large scale synthetic dataset Synth90K [14] and test on four real-world benchmark datasets following [20,30]. Synth90K contains 8 million training images and 1 million test images. All the images are generated by a synthetic data engine using a 90k word dictionary. These four real-world test datasets are ICDAR 2003 (IC03) [21], ICDAR 2013 (IC13) [17], IIIT5kword (IIIT5K) [25] and Street View Text (SVT) [15]. IC03 test set consists of 251 full scene images and 860 cropped image patches containing words. IC13 extends IC03 and contains 1015 cropped word images from real scenes. In the experiments, only words with alphanumeric characters and at least three characters are considered. There are 860 and 857 test images are utilized for IC03 and IC13 respectively. IIIT5k contains 3,000 cropped word images downloaded from Google Image Search. SVT contains 647 word images cropped from 249 street-view images. The images are collected from Google Street View.

In the experiment, we use the 8 million training images of Synth90K as the training data and the 1 million test images as the validation data. The maximum iteration step is 1,600,000, which is roughly 50 epochs. We validate the models every 10 K iterations on the validation set. The best models are picked based on the sequence accuracy performance on the validation set.

Implementation Details. We use Tensorflow [1] to implement all the models. Our Tensorflow based implementation has two differences compared to the implementation of [30]. The first one is the different padding way in the third and fourth maximum pooling layers. We use the 0×0 padding in Tensorflow compared to 0×1 padding in Pytorch[1]. The second difference is that we add dropout [10] with probability 0.1 after convolutional layers except the first and the last ones. Because we find dropout improves performances. In order to accelerate the training process, all the images are resized to 100×32.

We take the outputs of the last BLSTM layer as feature sequence for the input image. In Var-CTC, the dimension of label embedding is set to 50. In order to prevent overfitting, we also add dropout with probability 0.5 for the pooled label embedding. We use Adam [18] to train all the models with batch size set to 256. The learning rate is fixed at 0.001 for the CTC and Mml-CTC based models. For Var-CTC based model, we set the learning rate to 0.0005.

Comparison Results. The sequence accuracy comparisons are shown in Table 1. Compared to the CRNN-CTC model [30], our implementation shows clear improvements on all the four datasets, which are 0.3%, 2.9%, 1.2% and 0.8%

---

[1] Tensorflow does not support 0×1 padding for MaxPooling operation.

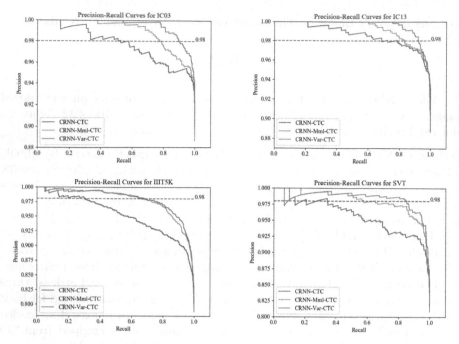

Fig. 3. Precision-Recall curves on four real-world datasets. The red dotted line is used to indicate the precision value equals to 98%. (Color figure online)

Table 1. Comparisons of SeqAcc on the four real-world datasets.

Method	IC03	IC13	IIIT5K	SVT
CRNN-CTC [30]	89.4	86.7	78.2	80.8
CRNN-EnEs-CTC [20]	**92.0**	**90.6**	**82.0**	80.6
CRNN-CTC(ours)	89.7	89.6	79.4	81.6
CRNN-Mml-CTC	88.6	89.4	81.3	**81.8**
CRNN-Var-CTC	90.0	88.7	78.7	80.8

Table 2. Comparisons of recall performances when all the models maintain 98% precision on the four real-world datasets.

Method	IC03	IC13	IIIT5K	SVT
CRNN-CTC	58.0	78.5	30.2	34.3
CRNN-Mml-CTC	78.5	83.2	**68.7**	57.7
CRNN-Var-CTC	**90.3**	**92.1**	66.4	**85.1**

respectively. The improvements mainly come from the added dropout operation in our implementation. Compared to the CRNN-EnEs-CTC model, our implementation does not show advantage on sequence accuracy performance.

The comparison between CRNN-Mml-CTC and CRNN-CTC (ours) shows that the CRNN-Mml-CTC model improves 1.9% and 0.2% on IIIT5K and SVT respectively. And it also shows that CRNN-Mml-CTC brings down the sequence accuracy with 0.7% and 0.2% on IC03 and IC13 respectively. While the CRNN-Var-CTC achieves the best performance on IC03 dataset compared to the CTC and Mml-CTC models, it has no advantage for the other three datasets. We can conclude the proposed Mml-CTC objective is comparable with vanilla CTC loss and the Var-CTC loss has slightly inferior performance when evaluating sequence accuracy.

The Precision-Recall curves of the compared models on the four datasets are shown in Fig. 3. The comparison results also show Mml-CTC and Var-CTC have clear improvements compared to the vanilla CTC and Var-CTC gets the best performances. These means the proposed Var-CTC and Mml-CTC perform better in average precision (AP). We also compare the recall performances when the models maintain 98% precision. The comparison results are shown in Table 2. Under the same condition, the Var-CTC can improve the recall with 31.7%, 13.6%, 36.2% and 50.8% respectively. In practical use, the proposed Var-CTC can recall more samples compared the vanilla CTC.

Table 3. Comparisons with attention based model.

Method	SeqAcc	AP	Recall@Precision=98%
ASTER [31]	**86.21**	98.37	69.84
CTC	82.37	98.01	67.57
Mml-CTC	83.83	98.59	77.21
Var-CTC	81.65	**98.64**	**81.92**

Comparison with Attention Based Method. We compare our proposed methods with ASTER [31]. ASTER is an attention based model and its well-trained models are public available. We take the same experiment setup of ASTER. The only difference is that all our CTC based models only utilize the ResNet based backbone, without the Spatial Transformer [15] based thin-plate spline (TPS) transformation network. There are seven testing datasets in ASTER. Due to limited space, we replace Precision-Recall curve with AP metric and the comparison in Table 3 is based on collection of all the seven datasets. The comparison results also show Var-CTC has the best AP or Precision-Recall performance, especially the recall performance at a high precision level.

3.2 Offline Handwritten Text Recognition

To verify the generalization capability of our method, we further evaluate our method on offline handwritten text recognition. Compared to scene text recognition, offline handwritten text recognition problem is highly complicated and challenging to solve. In the experiment, we follow the experiment setup of [34].

Datasets. The public handwritten datasets IAM [23] is used in this experiment. IAM is a handwritten text dataset, with 647 writers. It is partitioned into writer-independent training, validation and test partitions, where each partition contains 46945, 7554 and 20306 correctly segmented words respectively.

Evaluation Metrics. Three metrics are used to evaluate the handwritten text recognition model. The first two are the Character Error Rate (CER) and the Word Error Rate (WER). CER is defined as the Levenstein distance between the predicted and real character sequence of the word. WER denotes the percentage of words improperly recognized. For CER and WER, small values indicate better performance. The last metric is the Precision-Recall curve. We also use greedy decoding to decode the outputs. The confidence score of each word is computed based on Eq. 9.

Implementation Details. Different with the experiment in scene text recognition, we use a 25-layer residual network [9] as convolutional feature extractor. As IAM is much smaller than Synth90K, we stop the training at 20k iterations. The other setups are the same with scene text recognition task. We name the feature extraction network as ResNet to distinguish the CRNN in scene text recognition experiment.

Comparison Results. The comparison results are shown in Table 4 and Fig. 4. We also compare our method with the state-of-the-art approaches [34]. For WER and CER metrics, the proposed Var-CTC has no advantage compared to the vanilla CTC. However, for Precision-Recall curve metric, the proposed Var-CTC and Mml-CTC show strong performances compared to vanilla CTC.

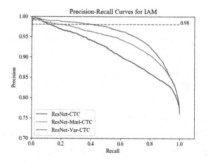

Table 4. Comparisons of WER and CER on IAM.

Method	WER	CER
zhang2019sequence [34]	**22.2**	**8.5**
ResNet-CTC	23.8	9.53
ResNet-Mml-CTC	23.6	9.35
ResNet-Var-CTC	24.0	9.52

Fig. 4. Precision-Recall curve performance comparisons on IAM.

3.3   Further Analysis

We first analyze the learning signals of non-blanks to check whether their learning is enhanced. Then we analyze whether the enhanced learning lead to a better alignment, especially for the non-blanks. We try to explain the reason for the improved Precision-Recall curve performance. The badcase analysis and the label embedding visualization for Var-CTC are also included in this part. At last, we give the exact comparisons of the space and time for the proposed models. All these analysises are based on scene text recognition task.

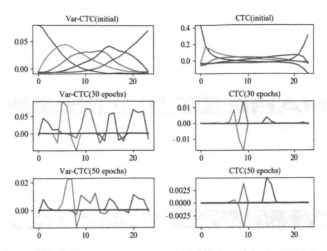

Fig. 5. The evolution of gradient signals for non-blank symbols. The input image is the first example in Fig. 6. The horizontal axis denotes the position in the image and colors represent different labels.

Gradient Signal Analysis. Figure 5 shows one example about the evolution of gradient signals for non-blank symbols. The experiment is based on the Synth5K [20] dataset. Synth5K is a small dataset with 5 K training data sampled randomly from Synth90K. Both the Var-CTC and CTC based models predict correctly for the chosen case. We can observe four points from the comparisons. Firstly, at the initial training stage, the gradient signals for Var-CTC are less than the CTC model; Secondly, the gradient signals of the CTC model decay much more quickly than the Var-CTC model; Thirdly, the gradients of CTC model quickly focus to several isolated points; At last, in the middle (30 epochs) and late (50 epochs) training periods, the gradients of Var-CTC are much greater than the CTC model. From the comparison, we can see the learning of non-blank symbols in Var-CTC model is more stable and sufficient.

Alignment Analysis. We depict the output distributions of six examples for CTC and Var-CTC based models in Fig. 6. The figure shows both the outputs of the two models are spiky, where blank dominates the outputs. We also depict the second hierarchy outputs for Var-CTC model. All the six examples show the distribution of $p(o_c^t|x^t)$ aligns to the corresponding non-blanks sufficiently, even for the cases with irregular shapes. The alignment visualization can be explained by the gradient signal visualization in Fig. 5, which is better learning signal leads to better alignment.

Confidence Score Analysis. We can also find the reason why the confidence score of the CTC model is not discriminative enough. The "SHARE" example in Fig. 6 shows there are two successive timesteps that the CTC model is aligned to the label "A". At the first timestep, it outputs "A" with probability close to 1.0. While at the successive timestep the model outputs "A" with probability close

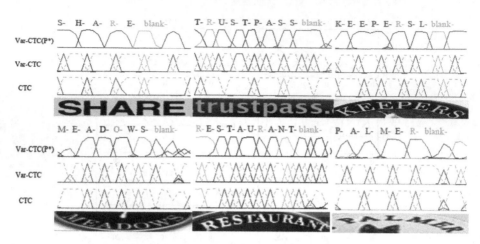

Fig. 6. Outputs visualizations of six examples. P^* represents the second hierarchy outputs $(p(o_c^t|x^t)$ in Eq. 6.

to 0.3 and blank with probability close to 0.7. It shows there is ambiguity at the second timestep between "A" and blank. Although the "SHARE" example is a clear and easy to recognize image visually, the confidence score of it keeps close to some hard examples (for example, the third example in Fig. 6). For the CTC model, the prediction confidence score of "SHARE" is less than "KEEPERS".

The "TRUSTPASS" example in Fig. 6 shows both the CTC and Var-CTC are influenced by the image content after the second "S". However, for this wrong decision, the CTC model still outputs a high level confidence score at the last timestep, which is close to probability 1.0. While the Var-CTC model is not sure which character it looks like and output character with low confidence score. As these cases show, the confidence score of the CTC model is not discriminative enough. It is difficult to set the threshold in practical use. And the proposed Var-CTC can relieve this problem with the improved confidence score.

Table 5. Error analysis for the IIIT5K datasets.

Method	Replace	Delete	Insert
CRNN-CTC	49%	14%	37%
CRNN-Var-CTC	40%	19%	41%

Error Analysis. We roughly classify the prediction errors into three types based on the sequence lengths of the labels and predictions. These three types are "Replace", "Delete" and "Insert". "Replace" means element in the label sequence is replaced by other symbols in the prediction sequence. "Insert" means the model predicts extra symbols compared to the label. We can see the blank outputs contribute more to the "Delete" and "Insert" types as those two types show segmentation error exists. The alignments between non-blank symbols and image contribute more about the "Replace" type. Table 5 shows the error analysis on IIIT5K datasets. Compared with the CTC model, the ratio of the "Replace" error is declined for the Var-CTC model. This proves the alignments of the non-blank symbols are improved. The statistics also shows the approximate posterior of blank should be improved.

Label Embedding Visualization. We visualize the label embeddings learned by Var-CTC in Fig. 7. For better visualization, we do not show the embeddings of 26 letters in English alphabet. The learned embeddings nicely reflect the clustering structures among the characters (the "6", "8" and "9" have similar shapes). It means the added label embedding has positive effect to the model learning, which can explain the superiority of Var-CTC compared to Mml-CTC.

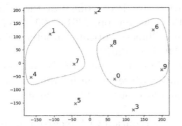

Table 6. Comparisons of parameters and FLOPS.

Model	#Parameters	#FLOPS
CRNN-CTC	8,720,165	17,436,510
CRNN-Mml-CTC	8,720,165	17,436,511
CRNN-Var-CTC	8,747,765	17,491,816

Fig. 7. Visualization of the label embeddings learned by Var-CTC using t-SNE [22]. Only the 10 number characters are shown.

Space and Time Comparisons. Table 6 lists the exact number of parameters and FLOPS for models in Sect. 3.1. All the MLPs in Fig. 2 are one layer in our implementation and they are used to transform features to the desired dimensions. Mml-CTC has exactly the same number of parameters with CTC. Compared to Mml-CTC, Var-CTC adds the approximated posterior. The table shows Var-CTC adds extra 0.3% more parameters and 0.3% more FLOPS compared to CTC, which is neglectable.

4 Conclusion

We proposed the variational CTC to improve CTC for enhancing the learning of the non-blank symbols. The proposed Var-CTC first determines whether to output a specific label or not and then learns the alignment of the non-blank symbols with the input feature sequence. With the hierarchy output, the influence of imbalanced distribution between blank and non-blanks is relieved. With the enhanced learning of non-blanks, our model can output more reliable confidence scores, which is important in practical use. Experiments on scene text recognition and offline handwritten text recognition tasks show the proposed Var-CTC improves the Precision-Recall curve performances significantly. Under the same condition, the Var-CTC can improve the recall performance with a large margin on four five-world benchmark datasets. Qualitative analysis also shows the effectiveness of the proposed method. As for future work, we plan to try variational inference techniques such as [19, 27] to improve the approximate posterior distributions.

References

1. Abadi, M., et al.: TensorFlow: a system for large-scale machine learning. In: 12th USENIX Symposium on Operating Systems Design and Implementation (OSDI 2016), pp. 265–283 (2016)
2. Cui, R., Liu, H., Zhang, C.: Recurrent convolutional neural networks for continuous sign language recognition by staged optimization. In: Proceedings of the IEEE Conference on Computer Vision and Pattern Recognition, pp. 7361–7369 (2017)
3. Feng, X., Yao, H., Zhang, S.: Focal CTC loss for Chinese optical character recognition on unbalanced datasets. Complexity **2019**, 1–11 (2019)
4. Graves, A., Fernández, S., Gomez, F., Schmidhuber, J.: Connectionist temporal classification: labelling unsegmented sequence data with recurrent neural networks. In: Proceedings of the 23rd International Conference on Machine Learning, pp. 369–376. ACM (2006)
5. Graves, A., Jaitly, N.: Towards end-to-end speech recognition with recurrent neural networks. In: International Conference on Machine Learning, pp. 1764–1772 (2014)
6. Graves, A., Liwicki, M., Fernández, S., Bertolami, R., Bunke, H., Schmidhuber, J.: A novel connectionist system for unconstrained handwriting recognition. IEEE Trans. Pattern Anal. Mach. Intell. **31**(5), 855–868 (2008)
7. Graves, A., Mohamed, A.R., Hinton, G.: Speech recognition with deep recurrent neural networks. In: 2013 IEEE International Conference on Acoustics, Speech and Signal Processing, pp. 6645–6649. IEEE (2013)
8. Guu, K., Pasupat, P., Liu, E.Z., Liang, P.: From language to programs: bridging reinforcement learning and maximum marginal likelihood. arXiv preprint arXiv:1704.07926 (2017)
9. He, K., Zhang, X., Ren, S., Sun, J.: Deep residual learning for image recognition. In: Proceedings of the IEEE Conference on Computer Vision and Pattern Recognition, pp. 770–778 (2016)
10. Hinton, G.E., Srivastava, N., Krizhevsky, A., Sutskever, I., Salakhutdinov, R.R.: Improving neural networks by preventing co-adaptation of feature detectors. arXiv preprint arXiv:1207.0580 (2012)
11. Hochreiter, S., Schmidhuber, J.: Long short-term memory. Neural Comput. **9**(8), 1735–1780 (1997)
12. Hu, W., Cai, X., Hou, J., Yi, S., Lin, Z.: GTC: guided training of CTC towards efficient and accurate scene text recognition. In: AAAI, pp. 11005–11012 (2020)
13. Huang, D.A., Fei-Fei, L., Niebles, J.C.: Connectionist temporal modeling for weakly supervised action labeling. In: Leibe, B., Matas, J., Sebe, N., Welling, M. (eds.) ECCV 2016. LNCS, vol. 9908, pp. 137–153. Springer, Cham (2016). https://doi.org/10.1007/978-3-319-46493-0_9

14. Jaderberg, M., Simonyan, K., Vedaldi, A., Zisserman, A.: Synthetic data and artificial neural networks for natural scene text recognition. arXiv preprint arXiv:1406.2227 (2014)
15. Jaderberg, M., Simonyan, K., Zisserman, A., et al.: Spatial transformer networks. In: Advances in Neural Information Processing Systems, pp. 2017–2025 (2015)
16. Jordan, M.I., Ghahramani, Z., Jaakkola, T.S., Saul, L.K.: An introduction to variational methods for graphical models. Mach. Learn. **37**(2), 183–233 (1999)
17. Karatzas, D., et al.: ICDAR 2013 robust reading competition. In: 2013 12th International Conference on Document Analysis and Recognition, pp. 1484–1493. IEEE (2013)
18. Kingma, D.P., Ba, J.: Adam: a method for stochastic optimization. arXiv preprint arXiv:1412.6980 (2014)
19. Kingma, D.P., Welling, M.: Auto-encoding variational bayes. arXiv preprint arXiv:1312.6114 (2013)
20. Liu, H., Jin, S., Zhang, C.: Connectionist temporal classification with maximum entropy regularization. In: Advances in Neural Information Processing Systems, pp. 831–841 (2018)
21. Lucas, S.M., et al.: Icdar 2003 robust reading competitions: entries, results, and future directions. IJDAR **7**(2–3), 105–122 (2005)
22. van der Maaten, L., Hinton, G.: Visualizing data using t-SNE. J. Mach. Learn. Res. **9**, 2579–2605 (2008)
23. Marti, U.V., Bunke, H.: The IAM-database: an english sentence database for offline handwriting recognition. Int. J. Doc. Anal. Recogn. **5**(1), 39–46 (2002)
24. Miao, Y., Gowayyed, M., Metze, F.: EESEN: end-to-end speech recognition using deep RNN models and WFST-based decoding. In: 2015 IEEE Workshop on Automatic Speech Recognition and Understanding (ASRU), pp. 167–174. IEEE (2015)
25. Mishra, A., Alahari, K., Jawahar, C.: Scene text recognition using higher order language priors (2012)
26. Redmon, J., Divvala, S., Girshick, R., Farhadi, A.: You only look once: unified, real-time object detection. In: Proceedings of the IEEE Conference on Computer Vision and Pattern Recognition, pp. 779–788 (2016)
27. Rezende, D.J., Mohamed, S.: Variational inference with normalizing flows. arXiv preprint arXiv:1505.05770 (2015)
28. Sak, H., et al.: Learning acoustic frame labeling for speech recognition with recurrent neural networks. In: 2015 IEEE International Conference on Acoustics, Speech and Signal Processing (ICASSP), pp. 4280–4284. IEEE (2015)
29. Schuster, M., Paliwal, K.K.: Bidirectional recurrent neural networks. IEEE Trans. Signal Process. **45**(11), 2673–2681 (1997)
30. Shi, B., Bai, X., Yao, C.: An end-to-end trainable neural network for image-based sequence recognition and its application to scene text recognition. IEEE Trans. Pattern Anal. Mach. Intell. **39**(11), 2298–2304 (2016)
31. Shi, B., Yang, M., Wang, X., Lyu, P., Yao, C., Bai, X.: ASTER: an attentional scene text recognizer with flexible rectification. IEEE Trans. Pattern Anal. Mach. Intell. **41**, 2035–2048 (2018)

32. Variani, E., Bagby, T., Lahouel, K., McDermott, E., Bacchiani, M.: Sampled connectionist temporal classification. In: 2018 IEEE International Conference on Acoustics, Speech and Signal Processing (ICASSP), pp. 4959–4963. IEEE (2018)
33. Williams, R.J.: Simple statistical gradient-following algorithms for connectionist reinforcement learning. Mach. Learn. **8**(3–4), 229–256 (1992)
34. Zhang, Y., Nie, S., Liu, W., Xu, X., Zhang, D., Shen, H.T.: Sequence-to-sequence domain adaptation network for robust text image recognition. In: Proceedings of the IEEE Conference on Computer Vision and Pattern Recognition, pp. 2740–2749 (2019)

End-to-end Dynamic Matching Network for Multi-view Multi-person 3D Pose Estimation

Congzhentao Huang[✉], Shuai Jiang, Yang Li, Ziyue Zhang, Jason Traish, Chen Deng, Sam Ferguson, and Richard Yi Da Xu

University of Technology Sydney, Sydney, Australia
congzhentao.huang@student.uts.edu.au

Abstract. As an important computer vision task, 3d human pose estimation in a multi-camera, multi-person setting has received widespread attention and many interesting applications have been derived from it. Traditional approaches use a 3d pictorial structure model to handle this task. However, these models suffer from high computation costs and result in low accuracy in joint detection. Recently, especially since the introduction of Deep Neural Networks, one popular approach is to build a pipeline that involves three separate steps: (1) 2d skeleton detection in each camera view, (2) identification of matched 2d skeletons and (3) estimation of the 3d poses. Many existing works operate by feeding the 2d images and camera parameters through the three modules in a cascade fashion. However, all three operations can be highly correlated. For example, the 3d generation results may affect the results of detection in step 1, as does the matching algorithm in step 2. To address this phenomenon, we propose a novel end-to-end training scheme that brings the three separate modules into a single model. However, one outstanding problem of doing so is that the matching algorithm in step 2 appears to disjoint the pipeline. Therefore, we take our inspiration from the recent success in Capsule Networks, in which its Dynamic Routing step is also disjointed, but plays a crucial role in deciding how gradients are flowed from the upper to the lower layers. Similarly, a dynamic matching module in our work also decides the paths in which gradients flow from step 3 to step 1. Furthermore, as a large number of cameras are present, the existing matching algorithm either fails to deliver a robust performance or can be very inefficient. Thus, we additionally propose a novel matching algorithm that can match 2d poses from multiple views efficiently. The algorithm is robust and able to deal with situations of incomplete and false 2d detection as well.

Keywords: 3d human pose estimation · End-to-end · Multi-view multi-person · Dynamic matching

Electronic supplementary material The online version of this chapter (https://doi.org/10.1007/978-3-030-58604-1_29) contains supplementary material, which is available to authorized users.

A. Vedaldi et al. (Eds.): ECCV 2020, LNCS 12373, pp. 477–493, 2020.
https://doi.org/10.1007/978-3-030-58604-1_29

1 Introduction

3d human pose estimation is a fundamental problem in computer vision. It can be applied to various applications such as human-computer interactions, augmented reality and video surveillance. Due to the availability of increasingly sophisticated datasets, and more and more powerful deep learning models, researchers have made significant progress in this area using deep convolutional neural networks (CNNs). While 3d pose estimation research into a single human under monocular or multi-camera settings has made remarkable advances, fewer works have studied 3d pose estimation of multiple humans, which is a significantly more challenging problem to address. This is primarily due to the occurrences of frequent and sometimes severe occlusions when multiple people are involved. These difficulties have been further exacerbated by the lack of labeling for identifying corresponding people under a multi-view setting.

Despite these difficulties, there are two main reasons why multi-view multi-person 3d pose estimations will become mainstream research. First, models involving multiple people are more generic in many real-world applications compared to those for a single human, such as in supermarkets and factories. Secondly, using multi-cameras, the pose estimation can be made more robust than using a monocular camera due to the multiplied information available from different views, such as when dealing with occlusions.

The methodology for multi-view multi-person 3d pose estimation in many existing studies includes two steps. The first is to predict 2d poses in each view individually using off-the-shelf 2d models [6,9,22]. The second is to aggregate these 2d poses and generate their 3d counterpart. One typical idea is to use the so-called 3d Pictorial Structures model (3DPS), which directly generates 3d human poses by exploring an ample state space of all possible human key points or human body parts in 3d space [3,20]. However, this method lacks efficiency due to the enormous state space needed for exploration.

In contrast to the above two-step models, a recent direction is to use a matching algorithm that identifies matched 2d skeletons from multiple views before the estimation for 3d poses [10]. If the matching algorithm is perfect, the subsequent 3d pose estimation for multiple people can be regarded as multiple 3d pose estimation for a single person. Thus the accuracy will be significantly improved. However, the matching algorithm may make mistakes or even fail. Once a reliable skeleton matching is established, we can then build an effective model in which its pipeline consists of three separate steps: (1) detect 2d skeletons in each camera view, (2) identify matched skeletons and (3) estimate the 3d pose.

An intuitive approach is, of course, to train each of these steps/modules independently. During testing, we can feed the 2d images and camera parameters through these trained modules one by one. However, all of the three operations are highly correlated in both directions of the pipeline. How individual poses are extracted in step 1 will undoubtedly influence the 3d pose estimation result in step 3. The reverse is also true: any adjustments that occur in the 3d estimation in step 3 will ultimately affect the way in which the detection should be carried out in step 1. Therefore, it is essential that the information can be back-propagated in reverse order through step 3 to step 1.

At the same time, when the parameters of the detection module in step 1 are not trained properly, especially during the early stage of the training, the matching algorithm in step 2 may fail to identify the matched skeletons and catastrophically impact the 3d estimation result in step 3. The traditional one-directional pipeline approach will not improve the parameters of step 1 as each module works independently while having an end-to-end training mechanism allows the model to keep improving the parameters of each step as a result.

However, there is still one bottleneck when we carry out this design. The matching algorithm in step 2 makes the pipeline discontinuous, i.e., it is not a smooth function in which we can back-propagate the changes in parameters freely. However, we can reconcile this with inspiration from Capsule Networks [14,26]. In CapsNet, the Dynamic Routing step decides how lower layer capsules are fed to their immediate upper layer, either by agreement or expectation-maximization (EM) clustering. In our work, the matching algorithm in step 2 acts in a very similar fashion to the Dynamic Routing. It also decides the feed-forward paths in which information flows from step 1 to step 3, i.e., we apply our matching algorithm to dynamically route/match the poses. This justification and analogy makes our end-to-end approach highly appropriate and is the central theme of our paper.

As one may appreciate, in this end-to-end training mechanism, the dynamic matching step plays a pivotal role. Hence it is vital that we also improve upon the existing works in this area. To this end, we additionally propose a novel matching algorithm which can match multiple 2d poses from multiple views efficiently. The algorithm is robust and can handle situations where there is incomplete and false 2d detection.

In summary, the main contributions of our work are stated below:

- We propose a novel end-to-end training scheme for multi-view multi-person 3d pose estimation. Different from training independent modules separately, our model back-propagates the gradients from the last 3d estimation step to the first 2d detection step, so as to significantly improve the efficiency, robustness and accuracy on 3d pose estimation.
- We propose a multi-view 2d human pose dynamic matching algorithm. This could dynamically match the corresponding 2d poses detected in multiple views for each person involved. The approach does not require the exact number of people in the scene and can handle cases where false detection and severe occlusions exist.
- Experiments on the Shelf and Campus datasets demonstrate that our proposed model outperforms the state-of-the-art methods with respect to both efficiency and accuracy.

2 Related Work

In this section, we review the literature related to the techniques of this paper.

2.1 Single-View 2D Pose Estimation

Single person pose estimation predicts 2d keypoints of the human body in one RGB image. Many existing deep learning-based methods have achieved amazing results [7,15,22] since DeepPose [28] was proposed, which was the first method to use deep neural networks for pose estimation.

For multi-person 2d pose estimation, current state-of-the-art solutions can be divided into two categories. The first category is called the "top-down methods" [9,12,17]. It uses an object detection method to detect all the people in the image and sends them separately to a single 2d pose detector to obtain their corresponding 2d poses. In [17], the authors constructed a fully connected graph from a set of detected joint candidates of each person in an image and resolved the joint-to-person association and outlier detection by using integer linear programming. [12] proposed a framework with three components for pose estimation which can extract a high-quality single person region from an inaccurate bounding box. In [9], a two-part network structure was proposed where GlobalNet localizes the "simple" keypoints and the RefineNet deals with the "hard" keypoints. The second category, "bottom-up methods", jointly labels part detection candidates and associates them with individuals by a matching algorithm [6,16,23]. The authors in [6] mapped the relationship between keypoints into part affinity fields (PAFs), then clustered detected keypoints into different 3d human poses. [23] interpreted the problem of distinguishing different people in an image as an Integer Linear Programming problem and partitioned part detection candidates into identity clusters. On the basis of [23], the authors in [16] used a stronger part detectors based on ResNet [13] and image-dependent pairwise scores, vastly improving the run time by using an incremental optimization approach.

In our work, we choose the "top-down methods" for their higher accuracy. We adopt the Cascaded Pyramid Network (CPN) [9] as the 2d pose estimator backbone.

2.2 Multi-view 3D Pose Estimation

Instead of estimating with a single image, multi-view 3d pose estimation methods require image inputs from multiple views, which are believed to obtain better 3d pose estimation than using a monocular camera. Most previous efforts had focused on single person estimation [19,27]. Traditional methods [1,4,5] used 2d pose estimation captured by calibrated cameras to predict 3d poses by point triangulation or 3DPS. Recent works have begun to adopt deep neural networks in this area and have delivered significant achievements. For example, in [18], a volumetric triangulation approach was proposed to project the feature maps produced by 2d pose estimators into 3d volumes, which were then used to predict 3d poses. There are also self-supervised approaches that predict 3d poses separately in different camera views and minimize the distance between pairwise 3d poses after rotating to the same view [8,21,25].

As for multi-view multi-person 3d pose estimation, 3DPS is the most widely used approach [2,3,20]. It predicts 3d keypoints or 3d body parts by exploring

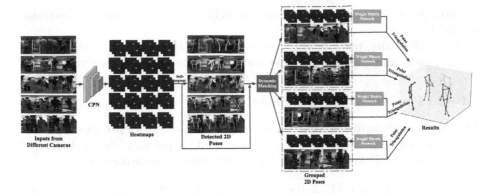

Fig. 1. The framework of our proposed model. First, the images I are input into the 2d human keypoints detector backbone, which is based on CPN [9], to get the heatmaps h. Next, we apply soft-argmax on h to get the corresponding 2d human poses y. Then, we feed both h and y into the dynamic matching module which groups them by identities and automatically determines the number of groups. After that, the heatmaps are sent into a network to get the weight matrices. Last, each cluster is sent to a weight-sharing 3d pose estimator to get the final results Y.

an ample state space and the candidates in the state space are generated by the grid sampling. With the 2d priors given by the 2d detector, the 3d pose can be generated through the maximum likelihood estimation. Recent work [10] has proposed a model to combine person re-identification (re-id) [29, 30] and epipolar geometry to match the pose, followed by the prediction of 3d poses using 3DPS. The shortcoming of this approach is that the speed of the person re-id model is relatively slow, which causes efficiency problems. On the contrary, our approach is efficient on multi-view multi-person 3d pose estimation, which benefits from our novel matching algorithm.

3   Method

In this section, we demonstrate our proposed end-to-end 3d pose estimation model in detail. The scenario assumes there are synchronized video streams from multiple cameras with known parameters, and all cameras capture the same scene with one or more people in it from different views. The goal is to estimate the 3d positions of the keypoints of these people. Note that the exact number of people in the scene is not required.

The inputs of the model are cropped 2d human images from all cameras in the same frame. The images, denoted by I, are cropped by using bounding boxes from either available off-the-shelf 2d human bounding box detectors or ground truths. $I = \{I_n^c | c = 1, 2, \ldots, C, n = 1, 2, \ldots, N_c\}$ where I_n^c is the nth image in the cth view, C is the number of views and N_c is the number of detected bounding boxes in the cth view. The outputs, denoted by Y, are the 3d keypoints of all detected people in the scene. The overview architecture of our model is illustrated in Fig. 1.

In the following text, we will demonstrate the 2d pose estimator backbone, dynamic matching algorithm and 3d pose estimation module respectively.

3.1 2d Pose Estimator Backbone

The 2d pose estimator backbone f_p with trainable weights θ_p consists of GlobalNet and RefineNet. The GlobalNet predicts all keypoints while the RefineNet justifies the "hard" keypoints. The backbone outputs the heatmaps:

$$h_n^c = f_p\left(I_n^c; \theta_p\right), c = 1, 2, \ldots, C, n = 1, 2, \ldots, N_c. \tag{1}$$

The next step is to estimate the 2d positions. To keep the gradient flow, we use soft-argmax instead of argmax to the heatmaps across spatial axes:

$$g_{n,j}^c = e^{h_{n,j}^c} / \left(\int_{q \in \Omega} e^{h_{n,j}^c(q)}\right), \tag{2}$$

where $h_{n,j}^c$ denotes the heatmap of the jth keypoint of the nth detected person in the cth view and Ω denotes the domain of the heatmap. Then the 2d coordinates of the estimated joint $y_{n,j}^c$ is the integration of all locations q in the domain, weighted by their corresponding probabilities (we use y_n^c to denote the 2d coordinates of all keypoints of the nth detected person in the cth view):

$$y_{n,j}^c = \int_{q \in \Omega} q * g_{n,j}^c(q). \tag{3}$$

3.2 Dynamic Matching

A matching algorithm is to group 2d poses from different views with people's identities so as to connect the 2d pose detection and 3d pose estimation. It is a challenging task due to several reasons. First of all, there are sizable errors in the estimated 2d poses which can significantly influence the matching accuracy. The second reason is that the number of people in the scene is unknown, which means one cannot cluster these 2d poses to centers like what k-means does. Furthermore, the matching itself is hard to be cycle-consistent. For example, 2d poses y_1^1 and y_1^2 are matched, so do y_1^1 and y_1^3, but y_1^2 and y_1^3 are not matched.

Different from previous methods which compute the matching score for 2d poses, we propose a new matching algorithm that creates a 3d pose subspace first and recursively finds matched 3d poses in this subspace. It resolves both the efficiency and cycle-consistent problems simultaneously. This newly proposed matching algorithm is illustrated in Fig. 2.

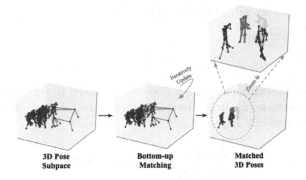

Fig. 2. Overview of the our matching algorithm

3d Pose Subspace Construction. To construct the 3d pose subspace, we first enumerate all possible pairs of 2d poses from different views. For each pair of 2d poses, we apply the traditional point triangulation to generate the corresponding 3d pose. All generated 3d poses compose a 3d pose subspace containing a small quantity of correct 3d poses (i.e., matched 2d poses) and a large quantity of incorrect 3d poses. For each pair of 2d keypoints $y_{n,j}^c$ and $y_{m,j}^d$, $c \neq d$, we can get the coefficient matrices for their corresponding homogeneous 3d vectors:

$$A_{n,j}^c = \begin{bmatrix} y_{n,j}^c \\ 1 \end{bmatrix} \times P_c, \qquad A_{m,j}^d = \begin{bmatrix} y_{m,j}^d \\ 1 \end{bmatrix} \times P_d, \tag{4}$$

where P_c and P_d are the projection matrices of cameras c and d respectively. Thus, the 3d point $\tilde{Y}_{(c_n,d_m),j}$ can be obtained by solving the following linear system:

$$\begin{bmatrix} A_{n,j}^c \\ A_{m,j}^d \end{bmatrix} \cdot \begin{bmatrix} \tilde{Y}_{(c_n,d_m),j} \\ 1 \end{bmatrix} = 0. \tag{5}$$

We use $\tilde{Y}_{(c_n,d_m)}$ to denote the calculated 3d pose given 2d poses y_n^c and y_m^d. The number of 3d poses constructed is

$$T = \sum_{c=1}^{C} N_c \sum_{d=c+1}^{C} N_d. \tag{6}$$

Bottom-Up Matching. After the construction of 3d pose subspace, we now need to pick out the correct 3d poses. The idea we distinguish the correct 3d poses with incorrect ones is that, the correct 3d poses are almost always calculated by 2d poses belonging to the same person. For example, if a person is captured by four cameras, we will detect four 2d poses which are used to construct six 3d poses, and these 3d poses are almost always very similar to each other, i.e. their distances are very small. Therefore, if the distance between a pair of 3d poses is sufficiently small, their corresponding 2d poses are regarded as a match.

We use the euclidean distance as the measurement between pairwise 3d poses $\tilde{Y}_{(c_n,d_m)}$ and $\tilde{Y}_{(c'_p,d'_q)}$:

$$E(\tilde{Y}_{(c_n,d_m)}, \tilde{Y}_{(c'_p,d'_q)}) = \|\tilde{Y}_{(c_n,d_m)} - \tilde{Y}_{(c'_p,d'_q)}\|_F, \tag{7}$$

where $\|\cdot\|$ is the Frobenius norm. Since we do not need to calculate the distance between 3d poses coming from the same views (i.e. $c = c'$ and $d = d'$), the number of distances calculated is

$$|D| = \sum_{c=1}^{C} \sum_{d=c+1}^{C} (T - N_c N_d) \cdot N_c N_d/2. \tag{8}$$

where D denotes the set of distances between all possible pairwise 3d poses and $|\cdot|$ here is the cardinality.

In order to efficiently obtain all matches, we propose a bottom-up matching algorithm. Suppose the matching result is stored in a set $S = \{s_k | k = 1, 2, \dots\}$ where s_k is a subset which contains the indices of 2d poses belonging to the same person. We initialize S as an empty set and update it by iterations. In each iteration, we first find the minimal distance in D, denoted by $D_{\min}$ which relates to two 3d poses generated by four 2d poses (three if one of them is shared by both pairs), say $y_{n_1}^{c_1}$, $y_{n_2}^{c_2}$, $y_{m_1}^{d_1}$ and $y_{m_2}^{d_2}$, and their corresponding indices can be denoted by a set of view-image pairs $V = \{(c_1, n_1), (c_2, n_2), (d_1, m_1), (d_2, m_2)\}$. Next, we find a subset s_k^* in S which contains any of the indices in V. If no subset is found, we add an empty set $s_k^* = \{\}$ into S. This finding process is referred as $F(S, V)$. Then we update s_k^* by $s_k^* = s_k^* \cup V$. Note that an index will be dropped if s_k^* has already contained another index from the same view. After the update, $D_{\min}$ will be removed from D. We repeat the above steps until $D_{\min} > \rho$ where ρ is a predefined threshold. The complete bottom-up matching algorithm is presented in Algorithm 1.

Algorithm 1. Bottom-up matching algorithm

Input: D, ρ
Output: S

1: *InitializeS* $\leftarrow \emptyset$
2: $D_{\min} \leftarrow \min(D)$
3: **while** $D_{\min} < \rho$ **do**
4:      $\{(c_1, n_1), (c_2, n_2), (d_1, m_1), (d_2, m_2)\} \leftarrow D_{\min}$
5:      $V \leftarrow \{(c_1, n_1), (c_2, n_2), (d_1, m_1), (d_2, m_2)\}$
6:      $s_k^* \leftarrow F(S, V) \cup V$
7:      $D \leftarrow D \setminus D_{\min}$
8:      $D_{\min} \leftarrow \min(D)$

Through the matching algorithm we can get the resultant $S = \{s_1, s_2, \dots, s_K\}$ where K is the estimated number of people in the scene. It

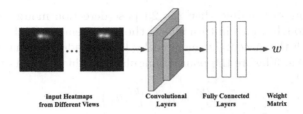

Fig. 3. The structure of the weight matrix network

is determined automatically by the algorithm. According to the indices in s_k we can select the 2d poses and heatmaps of the kth person and group them together:

$$y^{(k)}, h^{(k)} = G\left(y, h, s_k\right), k \in [1, K], \tag{9}$$

where y and h are the 2d poses and heatmaps for all people from all views, and function $G(\cdot)$ does the operations of both selection and grouping. Each group of 2d poses and heatmaps will be sent to the subsequent module for 3d pose estimation.

This dynamic matching module plays a similar role as the dynamic routing (especially the EM routing) in CapsNet. The difference between them is that the dynamic routing integrates the features from lower capsules by using weighted summation, while our dynamic matching clusters the 2d poses and corresponding heatmaps without any value changes.

Note that the proposed dynamic matching requires at least three views of the scene, which can be inferred form Eq. (8). When there are only two views, $|D|$ in Eq. (8) becomes 0, which invalidates the whole matching algorithm. Therefore, for this special case of two views, we use auxiliary approaches such as the above mentioned person re-id and epipolar geometry.

3.3   3D Pose Estimation

Given the grouped 2d poses and heatmaps of each person, we can reconstruct their 3d poses in several ways. The point triangulation described previously is one of them. However, we are now using the 2d keypoints from all views instead of a pair of views, and the corresponding linear system becomes:

$$A_j^{(k)} \cdot \begin{bmatrix} Y_j^{(k)} \\ 1 \end{bmatrix} = 0, \tag{10}$$

where $A_j^{(k)}$ is a matrix concatenating the homogeneous 3d vectors of all views for the $j$the keypoint of the kth person.

The point triangulation is an efficient 3d pose estimation algorithm with strong theoretical supports but often produces imprecise 3d poses if there are erroneous detection of 2d poses. The reason is that the coordinates of different keypoints are computed separately. This phenomenon can occur quite frequently at the beginning of training when the 2d pose detection module has not been trained well enough, which in turn affects the improvements of the 2d detection.

To deal with the inaccuracy, inspired by [18], we add a learnable module f_w illustrated in Fig. 3 before the point triangulation, which accepts the heatmaps as inputs:

$$w_j^{(k)} = f_w\left(h_j^{(k)}; \theta_w\right). \tag{11}$$

The output $w_j^{(k)}$ is a weight matrix which is in the same size of $A_j^{(k)}$. We add it to Eq. (10) and have

$$\left(w_j^{(k)} \circ A_j^{(k)}\right) \cdot \begin{bmatrix} Y_j^{(k)} \\ 1 \end{bmatrix} = 0, \tag{12}$$

The original module in [18] predicts a scalar weight for each view denoting how important the keypoints of a view will be. However, scalar weights cannot reflect the details of importance. For example, if a detected keypoint is inaccurate on the horizontal axis but very accurate on the vertical axis, scalar weights have to balance their importance and there will be no difference of importance if we switch the accuracy for both axes. Therefore, we propose to use a weight matrix instead of a scalar weight to better learn the importance so that the accuracy of point triangulation can be further improved.

3.4 Loss Function

Our loss function contains two parts, the 2d reprojection loss and the 3d mean square error (MSE) loss. The reason we add the 2d reprojection loss is that, if we only use the 3d MSE loss, there would be infinite points that have the same loss value but target at the 3d ground truth in different directions. The 2d reprojection loss can indicate the correct direction by constraining projected 2d poses from different views.

The 3d MSE loss between the estimated 3d pose and 3d ground truth is defined as:

$$L_{\text{mse}}^{3d} = \sum_{k=1}^{K} \frac{1}{|Y^{(k)}|} \|Y^{(k)} - Y_{gt}^{(k)}\|_F^2. \tag{13}$$

The 2d reprojection loss between the reprojected 2d pose from the computed 3d pose and the detected 2d pose from backbone is defined as:

$$L_{\text{repj}}^{2d} = \sum_{k=1}^{K} \sum_{c=1}^{C} \frac{1}{|y_c^{(k)}|} \|\tilde{y}_c^{(k)} - y_c^{(k)}\|_F^2, \tag{14}$$

where

$$\tilde{y}_c^{(k)} = \left[p_1 \cdot \begin{bmatrix} Y_k \\ 1 \end{bmatrix} \middle/ p_3 \cdot \begin{bmatrix} Y_k \\ 1 \end{bmatrix}, p_2 \cdot \begin{bmatrix} Y_k \\ 1 \end{bmatrix} \middle/ p_3 \cdot \begin{bmatrix} Y_k \\ 1 \end{bmatrix}\right], \tag{15}$$

and

$$P_c = \begin{bmatrix} p_1 & p_2 & p_3 \end{bmatrix}^T. \tag{16}$$

Thus, the total loss of our model is defined as:

$$L = L_{\mathrm{mse}}^{\mathrm{3d}} + \alpha L_{\mathrm{repj}}^{\mathrm{2d}}, \tag{17}$$

where α is a weight coefficient.

4 Experiments

4.1 Datasets

We conduct experiments on two standard datasets for multi-view multi-person 3d human pose estimation.

Shelf [2]: The Shelf dataset is one of the public 3d multi-person human pose datasets in multi-view setting. It consists of 3200 frames from 5 synchronized cameras along with the 2d pose annotations and 3d pose ground truth derived by pose triangulation. There are 4 human subjects interacting with each other in a small room. All 3200 frames are split into an evaluation set (frame 300–600) and a training set (other frames).

Campus [2]: The Campus dataset contains three human subjects interacting with each other in an outdoor environment. The scene is captured by three calibrated cameras. The dataset consists of 2000 frames and is divided into an evaluation set (frame 350–470, frame 650–750) and a training set (other frames).

For the evaluation protocol, we use the percentage of correctly estimated parts (PCP@0.5) to measure the model performance, which is the most commonly adopted in this area [2,10].

4.2 Implementation Details

As for the data preprocessing, we crop the images with bounding boxes estimated by an off-the-shelf 2d human detector, Yolo [24]. The 2d pose detection backbone is the same as [9] with pretrained weights, which outputs heatmaps and connects to a soft-argmax function to obtained the 2d poses. The dynamic matching module is implemented according to Algorithm 1. The 3d pose estimator consists of two convolutional layers and three fully-connected layers. The weight coefficient α in the loss function is set to 2. We choose the Adam optimizer with a learning rate of 10^{-6} which reduces by a decay factor of 10 in each epoch. The training set and evaluation set are kept the same as described in the datasets.

4.3 Ablation Study

Our first experiment is to verify the effectiveness of different settings for our model through the ablation study on the Shelf dataset.

End-to-end Vs Multi-step Architecture. Our model is end-to-end and can predict the 3d poses from 2d human images as a whole. An alternative is to divide the model into three consecutive steps which deal with the 2d pose detection, matching and 3d pose estimation separately. We compare these two architectures and the results are presented in Table 1.

Table 1. The PCP@0.5 performance of the alternative multi-step model and our end-to-end model on the Shelf dataset. They are using the same 2d pose detection backbone, matching algorithm, 3d pose estimator and loss function.

	Actor 1	Actor 2	Actor 3	Average
Multi-step	98.12	95.16	96.77	96.67
End-to-end (ours)	**98.75**	**96.22**	**97.20**	**97.39**

From the table, we can see that the performance of our end-to-end model is better than the multi-step model for all three people in the scene. The average improvement is 0.72. This demonstrates that the end-to-end model is more capable of learning the features of human poses which refines the 2d pose detection with gradients flowing back from the overall loss function.

Matching Method. Given the 2d poses obtained from the 2d detection module, we propose a novel matching algorithm to group the 2d poses and heatmaps by identities. There are two existing matching methods in the literature, the person re-id and epipolar geometry. The former finds matches by using the re-id appearance matrix as confidence scores, while the latter uses epipolar geometry affinity matrix as the confidence scores. The comparison between these three matching methods is shown in Table 2.

Table 2. Comparison of matching methods including the person re-id, epipolar geometry and our algorithm on the Shelf dataset over the PCP@0.5 and time cost. All three methods use the same 2d pose detector and 3d pose estimator.

	Actor 1	Actor 2	Actor 3	Average	Time (s)
Person re-id	97.62	93.72	95.69	95.68	6.73
Epipolar geometry	97.28	91.76	91.27	93.44	**0.64**
Our method	**98.75**	**96.22**	**97.20**	**97.39**	0.96

The results show that our matching method achieves the best performance among the three, with average improvements of 1.71 and 3.95. The time cost of person re-id is the highest while that of epipolar geometry is the lowest. Our matching method is slightly slower than epipolar geometry, but still much faster than person re-id. This experiment demonstrates that our matching algorithm is robust and efficient. The reason is that both person re-id and epipolar geometry use 2d information, thus there may be cases where the poses of different people result in a larger confidence score than those of the same person because of the angle of camera views or imprecise 2d detection. On the contrary, our method finds the matches in the 3d pose subspace directly, which leverages the information inequality between the 2d and 3d spaces and makes our method more robust and insensitive to imprecise or even incorrect 2d poses.

3d Pose Estimation Method. As described in the method section, we use the point triangulation with a learnable weight matrix to estimate 3d poses. Alternatives include the sole point triangulation or the original learnable triangulation network [18]. We compare these two methods with ours and the result is presented in Table 3.

Table 3. Performance of our 3d pose reconstruction method compared with the point triangulation and learnable triangulation on the Shelf dataset. They are implemented with the same 2d pose detection backbone and dynamic matching.

	Actor 1	Actor 2	Actor 3	Average
Point triangulation	98.05	91.17	92.78	94.00
Learnable triangulation	98.64	95.83	96.91	97.13
Our method	**98.75**	**96.22**	**97.20**	**97.39**

We can see from the table that our method outperforms the other two methods by 3.39 and 0.26 respectively in average. This demonstrates that (1) the 3d poses estimated by point triangulation is not accurate enough, (2) adding learnable scalar weights can significant improve the performance and (3) using a learnable weight matrix instead of the scalar weights can further improve the model's robustness.

4.4   Comparison with Previous Works

We compare our model with existing state-of-the-art models for multi-view multi-person 3d pose estimation on both datasets. The models compared are:

- Belagiannis et al. [2], the first one applying the 3DPS to 3d pose estimation for multiple humans.
- Belagiannis et al. [3], an improved version of their previous work.
- Ershadi-Nasab et al. [11], an extension of the 3DPS.
- Dong et al. [10], which uses person re-id and geometry methods to match 2d poses.

Table 4. Comparison of multi-view multi-person 3d pose estimation models on the Shelf and Campus datasets under PCP@0.5. All results are obtained from the original papers except for the (*) which only provides the average performance (in the parentheses) and its results on body parts presented here are from our own experiments using the authors' published code.

Shelf dataset		Head	Torso	Upper Arms	Lower Arms	Upper Legs	Lower Legs	All parts	Average
Belagiannis et al. [2]	Actor 1	89.30	90.20	72.16	60.59	37.12	70.61	66.05	71.39
	Actor 2	72.10	92.80	80.11	44.20	46.30	71.80	64.97	
	Actor 3	94.66	96.35	91.00	89.00	45.80	94.50	83.16	
Belagiannis et al. [3]	Actor 1	96.29	100.00	82.24	66.67	43.17	86.07	75.26	77.51
	Actor 2	78.95	100.00	82.58	47.37	50.00	78.95	69.67	
	Actor 3	98.00	100.00	93.15	92.30	56.50	97.00	87.59	
Ershadi-Nasab et al. [11]	Actor 1	98.27	97.34	92.57	83.33	95.94	96.83	93.29	87.99
	Actor 2	63.05	94.61	78.33	33.38	95.30	93.45	75.85	
	Actor 3	98.15	94.12	94.43	89.82	97.41	96.34	94.83	
Dong et al. [10]*	Actor 1	88.17	100.00	99.82	99.28	99.82	100.00	98.60	96.76 (96.90)
	Actor 2	97.30	100.00	98.65	71.62	100.00	100.00	93.78	
	Actor 3	94.41	100.00	95.96	96.27	100.00	100.00	**97.89**	
Our model	Actor 1	88.89	100.00	99.82	99.46	100.00	100.00	**98.75**	**97.39**
	Actor 2	100.00	100.00	100.00	81.08	100.00	100.00	**96.22**	
	Actor 3	90.06	100.00	95.65	95.96	95.96	99.38	97.20	
Campus dataset		Head	Torso	Upper Arms	Lower Arms	Upper Legs	Lower Legs	All parts	Average
Belagiannis et al. [2]	Actor 1	93.62	49.94	82.85	77.80	86.23	91.39	82.01	75.79
	Actor 2	97.40	41.13	90.36	39.65	73.87	89.02	72.43	
	Actor 3	81.26	69.67	77.58	61.84	83.44	70.27	73.72	
Belagiannis et al. [3]	Actor 1	96.55	93.10	96.55	86.21	93.10	96.55	93.45	84.49
	Actor 2	98.24	48.82	97.35	42.94	75.00	89.41	75.65	
	Actor 3	93.20	85.44	89.81	74.76	91.75	76.21	84.37	
Ershadi-Nasab et al. [11]	Actor 1	97.31	94.16	96.83	87.48	93.67	97.27	94.18	90.56
	Actor 2	98.73	95.41	94.12	78.98	98.94	95.34	92.89	
	Actor 3	95.36	84.37	93.16	70.34	88.36	81.38	84.62	
Dong et al. [10]*	Actor 1	100.00	100.00	97.96	89.80	100.00	100.00	97.55	95.85 (96.30)
	Actor 2	97.88	100.00	100.00	67.72	100.00	100.00	93.33	
	Actor 3	99.28	99.28	98.91	89.86	97.46	97.83	96.67	
Our model	Actor 1	100.00	100.00	98.98	90.82	100.00	100.00	**97.96**	**96.71**
	Actor 2	99.47	100.00	100.00	74.34	100.00	100.00	**94.81**	
	Actor 3	100.00	100.00	99.64	90.58	97.10	97.46	**97.39**	

For the Campus dataset, since the number of views is insufficient to generate enough 3d pose candidates, we use person re-id and epipolar geometry as auxiliaries in our matching algorithm. The comparison results are shown in Table 4.

On both datasets our model surpasses the state-of-the-art methods in almost all cases. The average performance of our model is 97.39 and 96.71 respectively with improvements of 0.63 and 0.86 comparing with the second best model (0.49 and 0.41 improvements if compared with the results from their paper). It is noteworthy that, the performance of existing models on the lower arms of Actor 2 in Shelf dataset is quite low, while ours achieves 81.08 with a huge improvement of 9.46. We notice that there exists a large quantity of occlusions in this case, which means our model can better handle occlusions than others in a multi-person setting.

5   Conclusion

In this paper, we have proposed a novel end-to-end dynamic matching network for multi-view multi-person 3d pose estimation. Different from previous studies, the end-to-end scheme of our work enables the gradients to flow back from the 3d pose estimation module to the 2d pose detection backbone. A bottom-up dynamic matching algorithm is proposed to group the 2d poses and heatmaps by identities so as to connect the 2d pose detector and the 3d pose estimator. The algorithm is efficient and robust and able to automatically determine the number of people in the scene. The ablation study verified the effectiveness of each part of our model and the experimental results on the Shelf and Campus datasets demonstrate that our proposed model is superior to the state-of-the-art models with respect to accuracy, robustness and efficiency.

References

1. Amin, S., Andriluka, M., Rohrbach, M., Schiele, B.: Multi-view pictorial structures for 3D human pose estimation. In: Bmvc. vol. 2, p. 7. Citeseer (2013)
2. Belagiannis, V., Amin, S., Andriluka, M., Schiele, B., Navab, N., Ilic, S.: 3D pictorial structures for multiple human pose estimation. In: Proceedings of the IEEE Conference on Computer Vision and Pattern Recognition, pp. 1669–1676 (2014)
3. Belagiannis, V., Amin, S., Andriluka, M., Schiele, B., Navab, N., Ilic, S.: 3D pictorial structures revisited: multiple human pose estimation. IEEE Trans. Pattern Anal. Mach. Intell. **38**(10), 1929–1942 (2015)
4. Bergtholdt, M., Kappes, J., Schmidt, S., Schnörr, C.: A study of parts-based object class detection using complete graphs. Int. J. Comput. Vis. **87**(1–2), 93 (2010). https://doi.org/10.1007/s11263-009-0209-1
5. Burenius, M., Sullivan, J., Carlsson, S.: 3D pictorial structures for multiple view articulated pose estimation. In: Proceedings of the IEEE Conference on Computer Vision and Pattern Recognition, pp. 3618–3625 (2013)
6. Cao, Z., Simon, T., Wei, S.E., Sheikh, Y.: Realtime multi-person 2D pose estimation using part affinity fields. In: Proceedings of the IEEE Conference on Computer Vision and Pattern Recognition, pp. 7291–7299 (2017)
7. Carreira, J., Agrawal, P., Fragkiadaki, K., Malik, J.: Human pose estimation with iterative error feedback. In: Proceedings of the IEEE Conference on Computer Vision and Pattern Recognition, pp. 4733–4742 (2016)
8. Chen, X., Lin, K.Y., Liu, W., Qian, C., Lin, L.: Weakly-supervised discovery of geometry-aware representation for 3D human pose estimation. In: Proceedings of the IEEE Conference on Computer Vision and Pattern Recognition, pp. 10895–10904 (2019)
9. Chen, Y., Wang, Z., Peng, Y., Zhang, Z., Yu, G., Sun, J.: Cascaded pyramid network for multi-person pose estimation. In: Proceedings of the IEEE Conference on Computer Vision and Pattern Recognition, pp. 7103–7112 (2018)

10. Dong, J., Jiang, W., Huang, Q., Bao, H., Zhou, X.: Fast and robust multi-person 3D pose estimation from multiple views. In: Proceedings of the IEEE Conference on Computer Vision and Pattern Recognition, pp. 7792–7801 (2019)
11. Ershadi-Nasab, S., Noury, E., Kasaei, S., Sanaei, E.: Multiple human 3D pose estimation from multiview images. Multimedia Tools Appl. **77**(12), 15573–15601 (2017). https://doi.org/10.1007/s11042-017-5133-8
12. Fang, H.S., Xie, S., Tai, Y.W., Lu, C.: RMPE: regional multi-person pose estimation. In: Proceedings of the IEEE International Conference on Computer Vision, pp. 2334–2343 (2017)
13. He, K., Zhang, X., Ren, S., Sun, J.: Deep residual learning for image recognition. In: Proceedings of the IEEE Conference on Computer Vision and Pattern Recognition, pp. 770–778 (2016)
14. Hinton, G.E., Sabour, S., Frosst, N.: Matrix capsules with EM routing. In: International Conference on Learning Representations (2018)
15. Huang, S., Gong, M., Tao, D.: A coarse-fine network for keypoint localization. In: Proceedings of the IEEE International Conference on Computer Vision, pp. 3028–3037 (2017)
16. Insafutdinov, E., Pishchulin, L., Andres, B., Andriluka, M., Schiele, B.: DeeperCut: a deeper, stronger, and faster multi-person pose estimation model. In: Leibe, B., Matas, J., Sebe, N., Welling, M. (eds.) ECCV 2016. LNCS, vol. 9910, pp. 34–50. Springer, Cham (2016). https://doi.org/10.1007/978-3-319-46466-4_3
17. Iqbal, U., Gall, J.: Multi-person pose estimation with local joint-to-person associations. In: Hua, G., Jégou, H. (eds.) ECCV 2016. LNCS, vol. 9914, pp. 627–642. Springer, Cham (2016). https://doi.org/10.1007/978-3-319-48881-3_44
18. Iskakov, K., Burkov, E., Lempitsky, V., Malkov, Y.: Learnable triangulation of human pose. arXiv preprint arXiv:1905.05754 (2019)
19. Joo, H., et al.: Panoptic studio: a massively multiview system for social motion capture. In: Proceedings of the IEEE International Conference on Computer Vision, pp. 3334–3342 (2015)
20. Joo, H., et al.: Panoptic studio: a massively multiview system for social interaction capture. IEEE Trans. Pattern Anal. Mach. Intell. **41**(1), 190–204 (2017)
21. Kocabas, M., Karagoz, S., Akbas, E.: Self-supervised learning of 3D human pose using multi-view geometry. arXiv preprint arXiv:1903.02330 (2019)
22. Newell, A., Yang, K., Deng, J.: Stacked hourglass networks for human pose estimation. In: Leibe, B., Matas, J., Sebe, N., Welling, M. (eds.) ECCV 2016. LNCS, vol. 9912, pp. 483–499. Springer, Cham (2016). https://doi.org/10.1007/978-3-319-46484-8_29
23. Pishchulin, L., et al.: DeepCut: joint subset partition and labeling for multi person pose estimation. In: Proceedings of the IEEE Conference on Computer Vision and Pattern Recognition, pp. 4929–4937 (2016)
24. Redmon, J., Farhadi, A.: YOLOv3: an incremental improvement. arXiv preprint arXiv:1804.02767 (2018)
25. Rhodin, H., et al.: Learning monocular 3D human pose estimation from multi-view images. In: Proceedings of the IEEE Conference on Computer Vision and Pattern Recognition, pp. 8437–8446 (2018)
26. Sabour, S., Frosst, N., Hinton, G.E.: Dynamic routing between capsules. In: Advances in Neural Information Processing Systems, pp. 3856–3866 (2017)
27. Song, Y., Morency, L.P., Davis, R.: Multimodal human behavior analysis: learning correlation and interaction across modalities. In: Proceedings of the 14th ACM International Conference on Multimodal Interaction, pp. 27–30. ACM (2012)

28. Toshev, A., Szegedy, C.: DeepPose: human pose estimation via deep neural networks. In: Proceedings of the IEEE Conference on Computer Vision and Pattern Recognition, pp. 1653–1660 (2014)
29. Zhong, Z., Zheng, L., Cao, D., Li, S.: Re-ranking person re-identification with k-reciprocal encoding. In: Proceedings of the IEEE Conference on Computer Vision and Pattern Recognition, pp. 1318–1327 (2017)
30. Zhong, Z., Zheng, L., Zheng, Z., Li, S., Yang, Y.: Camera style adaptation for person re-identification. In: Proceedings of the IEEE Conference on Computer Vision and Pattern Recognition, pp. 5157–5166 (2018)

Orderly Disorder in Point Cloud Domain

Morteza Ghahremani[1]([✉])(ID), Bernard Tiddeman[1](ID), Yonghuai Liu[2](ID),
and Ardhendu Behera[2](ID)

[1] Department of Computer Science, Aberystwyth University,
Aberystwyth, Wales, UK
{mog9,bpt}@aber.ac.uk
[2] Department of Computer Science, Edge Hill University, Lancashire, UK
{liuyo,beheraa}@edgehill.ac.uk

Abstract. In the real world, out-of-distribution samples, noise and distortions exist in test data. Existing deep networks developed for point
cloud data analysis are prone to overfitting and a partial change in test
data leads to unpredictable behaviour of the networks. In this paper,
we propose a smart yet simple deep network for analysis of 3D models
using 'orderly disorder' theory. Orderly disorder is a way of describing
the complex structure of disorders within complex systems. Our method
extracts the deep patterns inside a 3D object via creating a dynamic link
to seek the most stable patterns and at once, throws away the unstable
ones. Patterns are more robust to changes in data distribution, especially
those that appear in the top layers. Features are extracted via an innovative cloning decomposition technique and then linked to each other
to form stable complex patterns. Our model alleviates the vanishing-
gradient problem, strengthens dynamic link propagation and substantially reduces the number of parameters. Extensive experiments on challenging benchmark datasets verify the superiority of our light network
on the segmentation and classification tasks, especially in the presence
of noise wherein our network's performance drops less than 10% while
the state-of-the-art networks fail to work.

Keywords: Point cloud · Deep neural network · Orderly disorder ·
Segmentation · Classification

1 Introduction

Object classification and semantic segmentation of 3D models are foundations
of numerous computer vision applications like autonomous driving and robot
manipulation. Thus far, a considerable number of convolutional neural networks
(CNNs) have been developed for such tasks [1–6] and in most cases they yield
promising results, especially when the distributions of test and train datasets
are similar. However, 3D models in the real world contain out-of-distribution
samples, different samplings, noise and distortions that significantly influence
their performance. Figure 1 shows a few examples of wrong classification in the
presence of noise.

© Springer Nature Switzerland AG 2020
A. Vedaldi et al. (Eds.): ECCV 2020, LNCS 12373, pp. 494–509, 2020.
https://doi.org/10.1007/978-3-030-58604-1_30

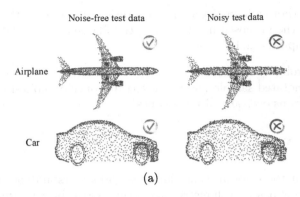

Noise-free test data   Noisy test data

Airplane

Car

(a)

Fig. 1. Classification results of most existing networks highly depend on the distribution of training and test data. A partial change in the distribution of test data by adding Gaussian noise $\mathcal{N}(0, 0.02)$ leads to misclassification.

Using a large number of parameters for modeling and training results in overfitting and exponentially growing computational cost. It also renders the networks to being more data-driven which makes them unable to work under a small change in the point set. Although several works [7–9] show less tendency towards overfitting, their performance is highly dependent on the samples. Most models are susceptible to irregular samples and work only under certain conditions. Meanwhile, developing highly accurate, robust and fast models for the processing of 3D data is demanded by many practical applications like autonomous driving.

Our studies have shown that patterns of an object represent the structural information of that object and remain almost unchanged under different samplings of the data and so are a more stable basis on which to build classification and segmentation algorithms. In this paper, we propose a novel cloning technique aiming at extraction of the stable patterns from an object. Such features can efficiently improve the network's performance. Our robust network is the first successful attempt to tackle and to investigate classification and segmentation under irregular samplings of point cloud data. Additionally, it needs a relatively low number of parameters so it is fast and less prone to overfitting. The key contributions of this paper are as follows:

- We design a robust deep neural network whose performance is not significantly affected by data grid, thus it is invulnerable to noise, out-of-distribution samples and distortions.
- The proposed model mitigates the problem of distance saturation in KNN-based models.
- The architecture of the proposed network allows the user to go deeper and deeper without the problem of vanishing-gradient. This scheme is capable of analysis of highly complex objects.

– We provide thorough empirical and theoretical analysis on the stability and efficiency of the proposed method using the 3D benchmark datasets: Model-Net and ShapeNet [2, 10].

In order to be robust to undesirable factors, our pattern-based network does not require any annotated samples, and it just trains once on noise-free point cloud data and then runs over any distorted ones[1].

2   Related Work

Deep learning methods for 3D shape analysis and understanding can be broadly divided into view-based, volumetric and point cloud-based categories. View-based techniques [3, 4, 11] map 3D models into 2D view scenes and then employ image-based CNNs for further analysis. Self-occlusions and information loss often occur during mapping. Volumetric methods [1, 2, 12–14] quantize the input 3D models into a regular grid before applying 3D CNNs. Loss of resolution, high memory and computational demands are the main limitations of voxelization.

Instead of converting or mapping 3D models into other domains, they can be analyzed in the point cloud domain directly. Due to the impressive results of PointNet [5], most studies have been devoted to learning directly in the point cloud domain. Since PointNet does not consider the local pattern of a given 3D point cloud, PointNet++ [15] was proposed, which uses a hierarchical application of PointNet to multiple subsets of a 3D point cloud. Inspired by DenseNet [16], DensePoint [17] was introduced that learns a dense contextual representation for point cloud processing via a deep hierarchy architecture. Exploitation of other aspects of local structure with PointNet are also reported in [6, 18]. Superpoint [19] partitions the point cloud into geometrical homogeneous elements and then a graph convolution network is applied to such local elements. The main drawback of these methods is their lack of shape awareness. More precisely, such methods do not explicitly model the local spatial layout of points. To this end, several works have been developed [9, 20–22] that capture the spatial layout of a point cloud by learning a high-level relation expression among 3D points.

Although the approach of explicitly modeling the relation improves the segmentation results, isolating high-level relation features from low-level ones may not strengthen relation propagation, subsequently there is a vanishing-gradient problem [16]. The appropriate distance or neighbour count parameter to use in the KNN-based networks [9, 17, 20] is often obtained via trial-and-error, which is saturated at a certain number of neighbours and even drastically drops by increasing the number of neighbours or neighbourhood radius. This aspect of such networks is not favorable, especially in dense 3D models.

Another main weakness of the existing networks that makes them impractical for real world data is their vulnerability to noise, distortions and out-of-distribution sampling schemes. Robustness is a key property that allows applying the same model to different irregular point clouds. Enriching the training step

---

[1] Supplementary materials are available at https://github.com/mogvision/pattern-net.

with annotated data, like adding noise, distortions etc., is not a straightforward solution to the above problem. This is because increasing the volume of input data with annotated samples makes the training convergence difficult to achieve. Additionally, a large-scale input data renders a high number of parameters, resulting in overfitting. Hence there is interest in developing CNNs that work efficiently under disparity between the training and test data.

3   Proposed Pattern-Wise Network

The goal is to establish and learn a deep neural network that converts an input point cloud $P = \{p_m \in \mathbb{R}^d, m = 1, ..., M\}$ into a set of segmentation labels $\Gamma_s = \{\gamma_s \in \mathbb{R}, s = 1, ..., S\}$ or a set of classification labels $\Gamma_c = \{\gamma_c \in \mathbb{R}, c = 1, ..., C\}$. Here, M is the total number of 3D points and d is the dimension of the point set that can be represented as a set of 3D coordinates plus other measured features like color, normal vectors etc. $p_m = \{coordinate : (x_m, y_m, z_m), color : (r_m, g_m, b_m), normal : (N_m^x, N_m^y, N_m^z)\}$. In this paper, we just consider the 3D coordinates and extension of the network over color and normal is straightforward. The output of the network for segmentation tasks is a vector of labels $\gamma_s \in \{1, ..., S\}$, where S is the number of segmentation labels. Likewise, for the classification task, 3D points are labelled as $\gamma_c \in \{1, ..., C\}$ with C classes.

3.1   Network Properties

A segmentation/classification network for a point set must meet the following four requirements [5,15,23]:

Property i (*Permutation Invariant*): It states that segmentation/classification scores must be invariant to changes in the order of 3D points. Unlike pixels in images or voxels in volumetric grids, 3D point cloud has no order and due to its irregular format, the network must be invariant to the order of points.

Property ii (*Transformation Invariant*): The labels/classifications of points must not be varied by their changes in rotation, scale and translation.

Property iii (*Points Relations*): In the point cloud, the relation between points is determined by their distance from each other. The distance metrics could be Euclidean distance, Manhattan distance, cosine distance, etc. Points in the point cloud are not isolated and their neighbours make a meaningful subset that can be measured by an appropriate metric.

Property iv (*Robustness*): The segmentation parts or classification labels of points must not be varied under different samplings. In practice, the distribution of test data is not close to that of the training data. Additionally, presence of out-of-distribution samples, noise and distortions in test data is inevitable so point cloud networks must be robust to the irregular samples.

The above properties are the backbone of our network.

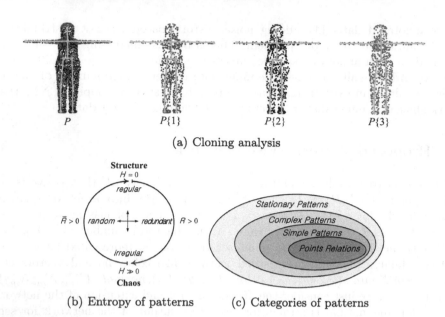

(a) Cloning analysis

(b) Entropy of patterns   (c) Categories of patterns

Fig. 2. (a) P is the input point set which is constituted of three subsets shown in blue ($P\{1\}$), black ($P\{2\}$) and red ($P\{3\}$). The abstract/structural information (solid green lines) remains unchanged across different samplings. (b) Entropy of patterns with different characteristics. (c) Categorization of potential patterns inside a rigid/non-rigid object in point clouds. (Color figure online)

3.2   Network Architecture

The orderly disorder theory was introduced in physics [24,25] and it refers to a way of describing the complex structure of disorders within complex systems. Unpredictable disorders could occur just under external disturbances not because of internal reasons. Ordered/predictable disorders may not be seen by human vision and this increases the ambiguity between the predictable and unpredictable disorders. However, the entropy metric could give us the degree of chaos inside a complex structure. Chaos theory has been well studied in mathematics, behavioral science, management, sociology etc. With the success of CNNs in solving high-order problems, our aim is to deeply analyze the links between points in the given point cloud.

For a rigid/non-rigid 3D object in the given point cloud, the location of points may change under different sampling operations, external disturbances etc. but its abstract information does not vary. Such abstract information can be named as *stationary* information and they are predictable while *non-stationary* information refers to those features that do not obey a regular pattern and under different conditions show different behaviours. The best way is to encode a 3D object by its stationary patterns which always show predictable behaviour. Contrary to stationary patterns, the behaviour of non-stationary patterns is completely unpredictable. For example, the minor details of a 3D model can vary under various samplings but its skeleton remains unchanged (Fig. 2(a)). Thus, we can claim that the classification score of a 3D object must not be varied under changes in the density and distribution of points if the number of points is sufficiently large, i.e.

$$\Gamma_{[p_1,...,p_N]} = \Gamma_{[p_1,...,p_M]} \quad if \quad N < M \ \& \ N \gg 1. \tag{1}$$

In other words, if our observation of an object is sufficiently large, then few sample variations must not change the label of the enquiry object. Let's assume $M = LN$ for a sufficiently large N, where L is a positive integer. According to Eq. 1, we can say that

$$\Gamma_{[p_1,...,p_N]} = \Gamma_{[p_{(l-1)N+1},...,p_{lN}]}, \quad \forall l \in \{2,...,L\}. \tag{2}$$

One possible solution to the above equation is to decompose the input point cloud P into L levels via a random down-sampling operator in such a way that all L point subsets $P\{l\}, l \in \{1,...,L\}$, are completely different while their overall schemes/abstracts are similar to each other. Under these conditions, Eq. 2 is asserted. If we apply a random down-sampling operator to point cloud P that provides

$$P\{l\} \cap P\{j\} = \emptyset \quad \forall l, j \in \{1,...,L\} \ \& \ l \neq j, \tag{3}$$

$$\bigcup_{l=1}^{L} P\{l\} = P, \tag{4}$$

$$H(P\{l\}) \simeq H(P\{j\}) \quad \forall l, j \in \{1,...,L\} \ \& \ l \neq j, \tag{5}$$

then we can assert that all the L point subsets have similar *stationary* structures/patterns. In Eq. 5, 'H' denotes the entropy of each subset and this equation assures that all the subsets have approximately similar information content. If R denotes the entropy of redundant/predictable patterns in a point cloud set and similarly, the entropy of random/less-redundant/unpredictable ones is denoted by $\overline{R}$, then the entropy H of each subset is equal to

$$H(P\{l\}) = R(P\{l\}) + \overline{R}(P\{l\}), \quad \forall l \in \{1,...,L\}. \tag{6}$$

The entropy of redundant patterns is close to zero and the large part of the overall entropy 'H' is assigned to unpredictable patterns $\overline{R}$. Possible values of entropy for patterns with different characteristics is depicted in Fig. 2(b). It is worth noting that the *randomness* of the down-sampling operator ensures that each point subset includes all parts/organs of an object. We name this strategy as 'cloning decomposition' and an example is illustrated in Fig. 2(a), where all the point subsets of the given 3D object share approximately similar structures across multiple decomposed levels while none of them shares identical

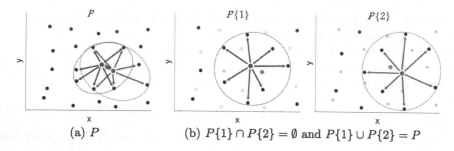

(a) P (b) $P\{1\} \cap P\{2\} = \emptyset$ and $P\{1\} \cup P\{2\} = P$

Fig. 3. An example of how the proposed cloning decomposition can successfully remedy chaos in the given point cloud. For better visualisation, axis 'z' was set to 0. (a) Conventional KNN-based networks yield asymmetric, complex, and dissimilar patterns for two adjacent points; (b) The cloning decomposition technique increases the probability of extracting symmetric, simple, and similar patterns.

3D samples. Overall, the feature space of an object could be categorized into a number of undesirable non-stationary patterns in which the patterns are chaotic and a series of stationary patterns, wherein complex and simple patterns are learnt from orderly stable relations (Fig. 2(c)).

The simplified point subsets can markedly help the network to extract stationary patterns, enhancing robustness as stated by **Property iv** above. An illustrative example is depicted in Fig. 3. This example aims at drawing the KNN responses (here, $K = 7$) of two adjacent points. According to Fig. 3(a), conventional KNN-based networks rely heavily on the density of 3D points and also they may not find reliable neighbours as the radius of the neighbourhood for an enquiry point depends on the density and distribution of the point cloud data. The proposed technique decomposes the given point cloud in Fig. 3(a) into two subsets via Eqs. 3–5. As shown in Fig. 3(b), it could provide similar patterns for a complex point cloud. The radius of the neighbourhood for both the blue and the red points is almost equal. As will be discussed later, this strategy efficiently helps the network not to be saturated with its K nearest neighbours while keeping the radius of the neighbourhood reasonable.

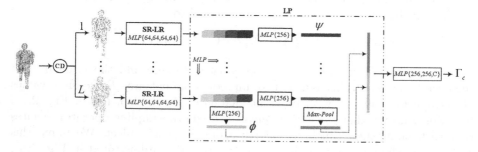

Fig. 4. Proposed network architecture for classification of point cloud data.

The proposed network is depicted in Fig. 4. The framework has four main layers including cloning decomposition (CD), searching relations (SR), learning relations (LR) and linkage patterns (LP) layers. In the following, we detail the functionality of each layer.

- **Cloning Decomposition (CD) Layer**: Image acquisition is often made under various conditions that directly affect quality and quantity of 3D models and subsequently, their point cloud samples. This layer decomposes the input object points into multiple subsets via Eqs. 3–5. Since high-level patterns are directly deduced from the low-level ones, this layer plays a key role in the extraction of reliable patterns. Cloning analysis reduces the number of parameters, alleviates the vanishing-gradient problem and improves the convergence pace.
- **Searching Relations (SR) Layer:** The task of this layer is to search all possible links between the feature vectors (or equivalently potential *low-level* patterns) according to **Property iii** above. This is done via the KNN algorithm in the Hilbert space. Instead of using the Euclidean space dominantly employed by most existing deep networks, we use a Hilbert kernel. Given two low-/high-level feature vectors X and Y, a measure/relation of similarity between them in the Euclidean space can be expressed as

$$\mathcal{E}(X, Y) = ||X||_2^2 + ||Y||_2^2 - 2 < X, Y >, \tag{7}$$

while the Hilbert kernel yields

$$\mathcal{H}(X, Y) = 2\big(1 - < \frac{X}{||X||_2}, \frac{Y}{||Y||_2} > \big). \tag{8}$$

In the above equations, the angle brackets denote an inner product operator. The Hilbert kernel emphasizes the cross-similarity while the self-similarity remains the same, i.e. unit. Unlike the Euclidean space that is biased by self-similarity, the Hilbert space just considers the cross-similarity between enquiry feature vectors and thus, it is expected that it can find reliable relations between feature vectors.

- **Learning Relations (LR) Layer:** This layer seeks and learns potential relations between all input feature vectors via a convolution kernel followed by a batch normalization operator. A max pooling operator is then applied to the outputs to obtain the global feature of the input features. The max pooling is a symmetric function that guarantees that the extracted features are permutation-invariant, as stated by **Property i** above. The combination of the convolution kernel, batch normalization and max pooling operators is often called multi-layer perceptron (MLP) [5].
- **Linkage Patterns (LP) Layer:** This layer comprises several MLP operators and its aim is to aggregate the relations across all the subsets and extract the most stable patterns from them. All the subsets have different samples and the LP layer is applied to the patterns for extracting the common ones. Such patterns carry stationary information of the object and they are robust to irregular samples and density.

Now, we detail the proposed pattern-based CNN (hereafter it is abbreviated as Pattern-Net) for the classification and segmentation of given point clouds.

3.3   Classification and Segmentation Networks

In the classifier model depicted in Fig. 4, the input point cloud data is first decomposed into 'L' subsets via the cloning technique described in the previous section. Inside each subset, relations between each query point and its neighbours is sought by the KNN algorithm. This is done by applying four MLPs $\{64, 64, 64, 64\}$ to each cloning subset. Similar to KNN-based networks [9,20,26], we compute K nearest neighbour responses of edges emanating from the enquiry feature point and stack them with the enquiry feature point. The KNN algorithm is considerably affected by the density of points. If the 3D model is sparse, then the best K responses will lie within a large volume neighbourhood while such responses in a high density model may fall into a small radius (Fig. 3(a)). Moreover, adjacent points in high density 3D samples would share similar KNN responses and this makes the network data-dependent. In other words, the network may fail to work for test point cloud data with different samplings from the training data. This problem can be seen in almost all KNN-based networks which here is solved by the cloning layer. In the proposed model, the LP layer finds the most repeated relations across different subsets and then labels them as stable patterns. Even in the presence of changes in point coordinates, the patterns remain approximately unchanged as we consider overall behaviour of a group of points rather than the exact behaviour of each point.

Each cloning subset yields a description vector of length 256 and they are called cloning description vectors $\psi_l, l \in \{1, ..., L\}$. All the L cloning description vectors are arranged in a matrix Ψ. An MLP is applied to all cube features over all the subsets to yield a global description vector ϕ, shown in light green in the figure. Here, the goal is to make each cloning description vector ψ_l similar to the global one ϕ as much as possible. If we consider a linear relationship between the cloning and global description vectors, i.e. $\phi = \Psi\omega$, then the estimated coefficients ω can be computed by the Moore-Penrose inverse, i.e. $\omega = \Psi^\dagger \phi = (\Psi^T \Psi)^{-1}\Psi^T \phi$. Parameter ω determines the contribution of each cloning vector in the resultant global vector. The deviation of ω elements should approach zero if all the cloning description vectors are completely similar to the global one. We add this term into the loss function:

$$L(\theta) = \underbrace{-\frac{1}{n}\sum_{i=1}^{n}\sum_{c=1}^{C} y_{ic} \log p_{ic}}_{classification\ loss} + \lambda \underbrace{\sigma(\Psi^\dagger \phi)}_{linear\ mapping\ loss} \tag{9}$$

In the above equation, the first term is the categorical cross-entropy function for computing the loss of the predicted labels and the second term enforces the

Table 1. Classification accuracy in percentage (%) on ModelNet40 ('-': unknown)

Method	Input	Avg. classes	Overall
PointNet [5]	1k-xyz	86.0	89.2
PointNet++ [15]	5k-xyz	-	91.9
PointCNN [23]	1k-xyz	88.1	92.2
ECC [27]	1k-xyz	83.2	87.4
DGCNN [20]	2k-xyz	90.7	93.5
SO-Net [26]	2k-xyz	88.7	90.9
DensePoint [17]	1k-xyz	-	93.2
RS-CNN [9]	1k-xyz	-	93.6
	1k-xyz	90.3	92.9
Pattern-Net	2k-xyz	90.7	93.6
	4k-xyz	**90.8**	**93.9**

network to yield zero standard deviation for weights obtained by the linear mapping between the cloning and global description vectors. λ is a predetermined constant, whose value is determined by the smoothing label's value in the one-hot encoded y_{ic}. Finally, p_{ic} is a scaled (softmax) logits. The Moore-Penrose pseudo-inverse can be simply implemented by singular value decomposition (SVD) [28]. The ultimate cloning vector is obtained by applying a max-pooling operator to the cloning vectors. The resulting vector is aggregated with the global vector to yield the description vector for the given point set which is of length 512. Finally, the description vector is fed into three MLPs $\{256, 256, C\}$, configured for classification. The resultant description vector is also used in segmentation. For this task, four MLPs $\{64,64,64,64\}$ are applied to the input data to extract low- and high-level features. They are then concatenated with the description vector to encode each point. Similar to the classification task, three MLPs $\{256, 256, S\}$ are employed for segmentation. The drop-rate of all decoding MLPs except the last one is fixed at 0.5.

4   Experimental Results

We have evaluated Pattern-Net on the ModelNet40 dataset [2] for the classification task. It contains 12311 meshed CAD models from 40 categories. Similar to the other work, 9843 models were used for training and the rest for testing and the models were normalized to a unit sphere. Each model is uniformly sampled from the mesh faces in 1k, 2k and 4k samples. During the training step, the points are augmented by randomly rotating, scaling and translating for being transformation invariant (**Property ii** above). The quantitative comparisons with the state-of-the-art point-based methods are presented in Table 1. Our method for 1k and 2k points is on par with the other methods and gives the best result for 4k points.

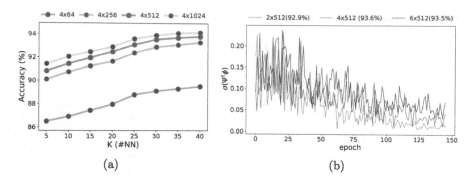

Fig. 5. (a) Influence of parameter K and number of points on the classification accuracy. (b) Linear mapping loss for different cloning levels (#cloning levels×#points).

Table 2. Classification accuracy in percentage (%) on ModelNet40 in the presence of noise $[2k - xyz + \mathcal{N}(0, \sigma)]$

Method	$\mathcal{N}(0, 0.02)$	$\mathcal{N}(0, 0.05)$	$\mathcal{N}(0, 0.08)$	$\mathcal{N}(0, 0.1)$	$\mathcal{N}(0, 0.15)$
PointCNN	78.7	40.8	18.6	10.5	4.7
DGCNN	92.9	69.1	29.9	11.4	4.2
SO-Net	70.6	35.4	11.9	9.8	5.8
Pattern-Net (4×512)	**93.5**	**92.4**	**89.1**	**84.2**	**32.6**

Unlike the existing methods, where the performance is quickly saturated by a specific number of points, our network is saturated slowly as can be seen in Fig. 5(a). For a fixed number of decomposed levels, an increase in the number of points improves the classification accuracy. There is also a direct link between the accuracy and parameter K in KNN. Tuning parameter K in the KNN-based networks is not straightforward and it is often obtained by trial-and-error. According to the figure, further increasing K yields better results but the performance increase slows down after $K = 30$. In order to make a balance between computational time and performance, parameter K was set to 30 throughout this study.

A suitable value for the number of cloning levels relies on the number of input points, parameter K and the convergence of Eq. 9. As shown in Fig. 5(b), the rate of convergence is reduced by increasing cloning numbers and the network requires more epochs to find similar patterns between different cloning levels. However, lower mapping loss does not guarantee high accuracy as the loss equation is constituted of two terms including the mapping loss and the classification loss. Our experiment shows that {3, 4, 5} cloning levels often yield good results. In Table 1, this parameter was set to 4.

As mentioned previously, the ability to tolerate noise is a necessity for robust and practical deep learning methods. In the following experiment, we added zero-mean white Gaussian noise with different standard deviation values $\mathcal{N}(0, \sigma)$ to

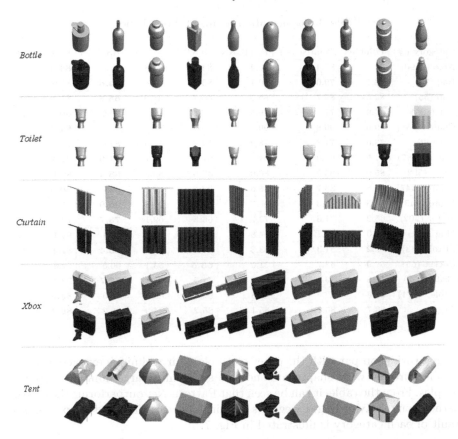

Fig. 6. Classification results on ModelNet40 with added Gaussian noise $\mathcal{N}(0, 0.05)$. First 10 shapes shown are for each query, with the first line for our Pattern-Net and the second line for DGCNN. The misclassified objects are highlighted in red. (Color figure online)

the test samples. The classification accuracy results are reported in Table 2 and a part of results is depicted in Fig. 6. The table shows that our networks can tolerate noise up to $\mathcal{N}(0, 0.1)$ while the state-of-the-art methods failed to work. The drop is less than 10% for $\mathcal{N}(0, 0.1)$, which is impressive.

Segmentation of Given Point Clouds: Segmentation of point cloud data is one of the popular 3D tasks. We carried out this experiment on the ShapeNet benchmark [10] and followed the data split in [5]. ShapeNet contains 16881 models of 16 categories and they are labelled in 50 parts in total. Like [10], the Intersection-over-Union (IoU) of a shape is computed by averaging the IoUs of different parts in that shape, and the IoU of each category is obtained by averaging the IoUs of all the shapes belonging to that category. The results are summarized in Table 3. When the training set is small, the performance of

Table 3. Segmentation results (%) on ShapeNet

Category (#)	PointNet	PointNet++	PointCNN	DGCNN	SO-Net	RS-CNN	Pattern-Net
Areo (2690)	83.4	82.4	82.4	84.0	82.8	83.5	**84.3**
Bag (76)	78.7	79.0	80.1	83.4	77.8	**84.8**	81.0
Cap (55)	82.5	87.7	85.5	86.7	88.0	**88.8**	87.4
Car (898)	74.9	77.3	79.5	77.8	77.3	79.6	**80.1**
Chair (3758)	89.6	90.8	90.8	90.6	90.6	91.2	**91.4**
Ear (69)	73.0	71.8	73.2	74.7	73.5	**81.1**	79.7
Guitar (787)	91.5	91.0	91.3	91.2	90.7	**91.6**	91.4
Knife (392)	85.9	85.9	86.0	87.5	83.9	**88.4**	88.1
Lamp (1547)	80.8	83.7	85.0	82.8	82.8	86.0	**86.3**
Laptop (451)	95.3	95.3	95.7	95.7	94.8	**96.0**	95.8
Motor (202)	65.2	71.6	73.2	66.3	69.1	**73.7**	72.1
Mug (184)	93.0	94.1	94.8	**94.9**	94.2	94.1	94.1
Pistol (283)	81.2	81.3	83.3	81.1	80.9	**83.4**	82.2
Rocket (66)	57.9	58.7	51.0	**63.5**	53.1	60.5	62.4
Skate (152)	72.8	76.4	75.0	74.5	72.9	**77.7**	72.4
Table (5271)	80.6	82.6	81.8	82.6	83.0	83.6	**83.9**
Avg.	83.7	85.1	85.1	85.2	84.9	86.2	**86.4**

our network is on par with the other methods. Our technique extracts common deep features between shapes so it needs a sufficiently large number of training samples. From the table, it can be seen that Pattern-Net outperforms the existing methods on relatively large categories like airplane, car, chair and lamp. A sample result of each category is illustrated in Fig. 7.

Table 4. Complexity of different methods for point cloud classification task

Method	PointNet++	PointCNN	DGCNN	SO-Net	RS-CNN	DensePoint	Pattern-Net
#params	1.48M	8.2M	11.8M	11.5M	1.41M	670k	**399k**

Complexity Analysis: Table 4 reports the complexity of Pattern-Net as well as those of the existing techniques for the classification task. The number of input points was set to 1024. Thanks to the cloning decomposition, our technique needs less than 0.4M parameters which is much lower than 670k of DensePoint. This characteristic of our method is more appealing for real-time applications like mobile robotics and autonomous driving.

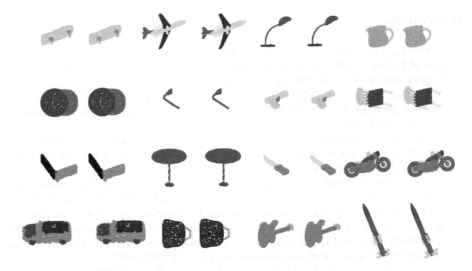

Fig. 7. Segmentation results on ShapeNet. First shape of each category is selected, where the left shape stands for the ground truth and the right one for our Pattern-Net.

5   Conclusions

In this study, we have proposed a novel technique for efficiently learning stationary patterns in the given point clouds, which is less susceptible to noise, distortions and overfitting. It is also invariant to changes in translation, rotation and scale. The key idea is to decompose the point cloud into multiple subsets with similar structural information. Then we enforce the network to learn stable patterns. Compared with noise that is order-less with unpredictable behaviour, natural objects have complex structures accompanied with irregularities in some parts due to the external disturbances. Informative patterns could be successfully extracted if the level of randomness and uncertainty is diminished. Unpredictable disorders cause inaccurate representation of given objects and this concept is known as 'orderly disorder' theory. To this end, we have proposed the cloning decomposing technique. Since our network learns just stable patterns, it is less prone to overfitting, which means it needs to train only once and can then run over a variety of data (e.g. different noise and sampling patterns). This method could provide a promising direction for robust representation of point cloud data.

Acknowledgements. The authors gratefully acknowledge the HPC resources provided by Supercomputing Wales (SCW) and Aberystwyth University. M. Ghahremani acknowledges his AberDoc and President scholarships awarded by Aberystwyth University. Y. Liu and A. Behera are partially supported by BBSRC grant BB/R02118X/1 and UKIERI-DST grant CHARM (DST UKIERI-2018-19-10) respectively.

References

1. Maturana, D., Scherer, S.: VoxNet: a 3D convolutional neural network for real-time object recognition. In: 2015 IEEE/RSJ International Conference on Intelligent Robots and Systems (IROS), pp. 922–928. IEEE (2015)
2. Wu, Z., et al.: 3D ShapeNets: a deep representation for volumetric shapes. In: Proceedings of the IEEE Conference on Computer Vision and Pattern Recognition, pp. 1912–1920 (2015)
3. Su, H., Maji, S., Kalogerakis, E., Learned-Miller, E.: Multi-view convolutional neural networks for 3D shape recognition. In: Proceedings of the IEEE International Conference on Computer Vision, pp. 945–953 (2015)
4. Qi, C.R., Su, H., Nießner, M., Dai, A., Yan, M., Guibas, L.J.: Volumetric and multi-view CNNs for object classification on 3D data. In: Proceedings of the IEEE Conference on Computer Vision and Pattern Recognition, pp. 5648–5656 (2016)
5. Qi, C.R., Su, H., Mo, K., Guibas, L.J.: PointNet: deep learning on point sets for 3D classification and segmentation. In: Proceedings of the IEEE Conference on Computer Vision and Pattern Recognition, pp. 652–660 (2017)
6. Guerrero, P., Kleiman, Y., Ovsjanikov, M., Mitra, N.J.: PCPNet learning local shape properties from raw point clouds. Comput. Graph. Forum 37(2), 75–85 (2018)
7. Zhi, S., Liu, Y., Li, X., Guo, Y.: LightNet: a lightweight 3D convolutional neural network for real-time 3D object recognition. In: 3DOR (2017)
8. Ma, C., An, W., Lei, Y., Guo, Y.: BV-CNNs: binary volumetric convolutional networks for 3D object recognition. In: BMVC, p. 4 (2017)
9. Liu, Y., Fan, B., Xiang, S., Pan, C.: Relation-shape convolutional neural network for point cloud analysis. In: Proceedings of the IEEE Conference on Computer Vision and Pattern Recognition, pp. 8895–8904 (2019)
10. Yi, L., et al.: A scalable active framework for region annotation in 3D shape collections. ACM Trans. Graph. (TOG) 35(6), 1–12 (2016)
11. Wang, C., Pelillo, M., Siddiqi, K.: Dominant set clustering and pooling for multi-view 3D object recognition. arXiv preprint arXiv:1906.01592 (2019)
12. Riegler, G., Ulusoy, A.O., Geiger, A.: OctNet: learning deep 3D representations at high resolutions. In: Proceedings of the IEEE Conference on Computer Vision and Pattern Recognition, pp. 3577–3586 (2017)
13. Tatarchenko, M., Dosovitskiy, A., Brox, T.: Octree generating networks: efficient convolutional architectures for high-resolution 3D outputs. In: Proceedings of the IEEE International Conference on Computer Vision, pp. 2088–2096 (2017)
14. Klokov, R., Lempitsky, V.: Escape from cells: deep KD-networks for the recognition of 3D point cloud models. In: Proceedings of the IEEE International Conference on Computer Vision, pp. 863–872 (2017)
15. Qi, C.R., Yi, L., Su, H., Guibas, L.J.: PointNet++: deep hierarchical feature learning on point sets in a metric space. In: Advances in Neural Information Processing Systems, pp. 5099–5108 (2017)
16. Huang, G., Liu, Z., Van Der Maaten, L., Weinberger, K.Q.: Densely connected convolutional networks. In: Proceedings of the IEEE Conference on Computer Vision and Pattern Recognition, pp. 4700–4708 (2017)
17. Liu, Y., Fan, B., Meng, G., Lu, J., Xiang, S., Pan, C.: DensePoint: learning densely contextual representation for efficient point cloud processing. In: Proceedings of the IEEE International Conference on Computer Vision, pp. 5239–5248 (2019)

18. Shen, Y., Feng, C., Yang, Y., Tian, D.: Mining point cloud local structures by kernel correlation and graph pooling. In: Proceedings of the IEEE Conference on Computer Vision and Pattern Recognition, pp. 4548–4557 (2018)
19. Landrieu, L., Simonovsky, M.: Large-scale point cloud semantic segmentation with superpoint graphs. In: Proceedings of the IEEE Conference on Computer Vision and Pattern Recognition, pp. 4558–4567 (2018)
20. Wang, Y., Sun, Y., Liu, Z., Sarma, S.E., Bronstein, M.M., Solomon, J.M.: Dynamic graph CNN for learning on point clouds. ACM Trans. Graph. (TOG) **38**(5), 146 (2019)
21. Xu, Q.: Grid-GCN for fast and scalable point cloud learning. arXiv preprint arXiv:1912.02984 (2019)
22. Zhang, Z., Hua, B.-S., Rosen, D.W., Yeung, S.-K.: Rotation invariant convolutions for 3D point clouds deep learning. In: 2019 International Conference on 3D Vision (3DV), pp. 204–213. IEEE (2019)
23. Atzmon, M., Maron, H., Lipman, Y.: Point convolutional neural networks by extension operators. arXiv preprint arXiv:1803.10091 (2018)
24. Peters, E.E.: Chaos and Order in the Capital Markets: A New View of Cycles, Prices, and Market Volatility. Wiley (1996)
25. Davood, S.S.: Orderly disorder in modern physics. Int. Lett. Chem. Phys. Astron. **48**, 163–172 (2015)
26. Li, J., Chen, B.M., Lee, G.H.: SO-Net: self-organizing network for point cloud analysis. In: Proceedings of the IEEE Conference on Computer Vision and Pattern Recognition, pp. 9397–9406 (2018)
27. Simonovsky, M., Komodakis, N.: Dynamic edge-conditioned filters in convolutional neural networks on graphs. In: Proceedings of the IEEE Conference on Computer Vision and Pattern Recognition, pp. 3693–3702 (2017)
28. Brake, D.A., Hauenstein, J.D., Schreyer, F.-O., Sommese, A.J., Stillman, M.E.: Singular value decomposition of complexes. SIAM J. Appl. Algebra Geom. **3**(3), 507–522 (2019)

Deep Decomposition Learning for Inverse Imaging Problems

Dongdong Chen$^{(\boxtimes)}$ and Mike E. Davies

School of Engineering, University of Edinburgh, Edinburgh, UK
{d.chen,mike.davies}@ed.ac.uk

Abstract. Deep learning is emerging as a new paradigm for solving inverse imaging problems. However, the deep learning methods often lack the assurance of traditional physics-based methods due to the lack of physical information considerations in neural network training and deploying. The appropriate supervision and explicit calibration by the information of the physic model can enhance the neural network learning and its practical performance. In this paper, inspired by the geometry that data can be decomposed by two components from the null-space of the forward operator and the range space of its pseudo-inverse, we train neural networks to learn the two components and therefore learn the decomposition, *i.e.* we explicitly reformulate the neural network layers as learning range-nullspace decomposition functions with reference to the layer inputs, instead of learning unreferenced functions. We empirically show that the proposed framework demonstrates superior performance over recent deep residual learning, unrolled learning and nullspace learning on tasks including compressive sensing medical imaging and natural image super-resolution. Our code is available at https://github.com/edongdongchen/DDN.

Keywords: Decomposition learning · Physics · Inverse problems

1 Introduction

We consider a linear inverse problem of the form:

$$\mathbf{y}_\epsilon = \mathbf{H}\mathbf{x} + \epsilon, \tag{1}$$

where the goal is to recover the unknown signal $\mathbf{x} \in \mathbb{R}^D$ from the noisy measurement $\mathbf{y}_\epsilon \in \mathbb{R}^d$ with typical dimension $D \gg d$, and $\mathbf{H} : \mathbb{R}^D \to \mathbb{R}^d$ is the forward operator which models the response of the acquisition device or reconstruction system, while $\epsilon \in \mathbb{R}^d$ represents the measurement noise intrinsic to the acquisition process.

Inverse problems have wide applications in computer vision, medical imaging, optics, radar, and many other fields. The forward operator $\mathbf{H}$ in (1) could represent various inverse problems, from *e.g.* an identity operator for image denoising,

© Springer Nature Switzerland AG 2020
A. Vedaldi et al. (Eds.): ECCV 2020, LNCS 12373, pp. 510–526, 2020.
https://doi.org/10.1007/978-3-030-58604-1_31

to convolution operators for image deblurring, random sensing matrices for compressive sensing (CS), filtered subsampling operators for super-resolution (SR), (undersampled) Fourier transform for magnetic resonance imaging (MRI) and the (subsampled) Radon transform in computed tomography (CT). The inverse problems in (1) are often noisy and ill-posed since the operator $\mathbf{H}$ has a nontrivial null space. Such under-determined systems are extremely difficult to solve and the solutions are very sensitive to the input data. The classical approach for solving them have traditionally been model-based [4,9], which typically aim to regularize the solutions by constraining them to be consistent with prior knowledge about the signal and usually can only be solved iteratively.

More recently, due to the powerful representation learning and transformation ability, deep neural networks (DNN) have emerged as a new paradigm for inverse problems. The community has already taken significant steps in this direction, with deep neural networks being successfully applied to a wide variety of inverse problems [25]. For example, [5,48] use a fully connected feedfoward neural network for image denoisng and inpainting. [12,22] learn end-to-end mappings between $\mathbf{y}_\epsilon$ and $\mathbf{x}$ with vanilla convolutional neural networks (CNN). [24,51] further use CNNs with residual blocks [17] and skip connections to improve the neural network performance. [20,28,36] learn downsampling and upsampling feature maps with encoder-decoder CNNs. [8,50] use autoencoders for learning new representations for $\mathbf{x}$ and $\mathbf{y}_\epsilon$ to solve the inverse problems. [47] use CNN as a prior and train with early stopping criteria to recover a single image from its observation. [33] use CNN to perform denoising-based approximate message passing. [31,46] unfold the model-based optimizations with DNN. [3,34] use generative models for natural images to recover images from Gaussian measurements.

However, the DNN itself in the above deep learning-based approaches often lack the guarantees of traditional physics-based methods as they are purely data-driven and learning-based. In addition, the designing of DNNs is usually complicated and has poor intuitive interpretation when they are decoupled from the inverse problem of interest. Furthermore, it is a commonly held belief in the inverse problems community that using the physics is preferable to relying solely on data [30,41]. This raises a number of questions: is a purely data-driven neural network the best way to solve an inverse problem? Does physical information facilitate neural networks to find a better inverse problem solution? How should one best make use of the prior physical (acquisition) information? All of these above questions inspire us to think about whether the introduction of physical information in neural networks would be beneficial to the training of deep learning methods to better solve inverse problems.

We present *Deep Decomposition learning Network* (DDN) as a way of using physics to reconstruct image from its measurement $\mathbf{y}_\epsilon$ ($\epsilon \neq 0$). Relying on the range-nullspace decomposition of data and the recent null-space learning [30,41], also known as affine projected network in [44], we propose to use two sets of neural network layers to separately capture the residuals lying on the range of $\mathbf{H}^\dagger$ and the nullspace of $\mathbf{H}$. By incorporating the two learned residuals with the pseudo-inverse input, the proposed framework DDN is able to recover a plausible image and preserve data consistency with respect to the measurements $\mathbf{y}_\epsilon$.

Decomposition learning can be used with various inverse imaging problems. In this paper, we follow a compressive sensing magnetic resonance fingerprinting (CS-MRF) reconstruction task [10,27]: reconstructing brain MR images sequence from highly undersampled and noisy Fourier space data. We show that the DDN outperforms recent related deep learning methods including deep residual learning [20] which is physics-free, deep nullspace learning [30,41,44] which neglected the noise component, and deep unrolled learning [15,16,38] which retained the undesirable iterative nature of model-based systems. We also performed an ablation study on the natural image super-resolution (SR) task, and the results show that simultaneous learning of two residuals is outperforming the way that does not use physics or only learn one of the residuals. Finally, all the experiments demonstrate that decomposition learning can facilitate the generalization of the deep neural network for inverse problems.

2 Background

2.1 Deep Learning for the Inverse Problem

Depending on whether the physical acquisition information with respect to $\mathbf{H}$ is used during DNN training and testing, we divide the deep learning approaches into two categories: *Physics-free* and *Physics-engaged*.

Physics-Free. The DNN aims to learn a direct mapping from $\mathbf{y}_\epsilon$ (or its projection, e.g. $\mathbf{H}^\dagger \mathbf{y}_\epsilon$) to $\mathbf{x}$ without exploiting the knowledge of $\mathbf{H}$ at any point in the training or testing process (with the exception of the input). The general principle is that, given enough training data, we should be able to design a proper DNN to learn everything we need to know about $\mathbf{H}$ to successfully estimate $\mathbf{x}$ directly. The success of this approach is likely to depend on the complexity of the forward operator $\mathbf{H}$. However, it has been observed to work well for numerous computer vision tasks, such as denoising and inpainting [48], superresoluion [12] and deblurring [23,49]. The DNN can be trained by a sole least squares loss [20,28,48] or a combination of least squares loss and auxiliary losses such as adversarial loss [23,24,37,43]. In general, this approach requires large quantities of training data because it is required to not only learn the geometry of the image space containing $\mathbf{x}$, but also aspects of $\mathbf{H}$. Hence, an interesting question is how hard (relatively) are each of these components to learn and how important is it to incorporate $\mathbf{H}$ into the learning process. When the forward problem is too complex such that it can not be incorporated into the DNN model it will always be necessary to go Physics-free. Finally, since direct estimation using a DNN for solving inverse problems is essentially a form of regression, there is a potential generalization issue with such physic-free DNN approaches.

Physics-Engaged. The most widely used strategy considering physics of $\mathbf{H}$ in deep learning approaches is through a model-based approach, in which one or more pretrained DNNs are used within a more traditional iterative physics-engaged model-based framework such as [4,9]. As mentioned before, the inverse problem (1) typically boils down to solving an optimisation problem broadly of the following form:

$$\arg\min_{\mathbf{x}} f(\mathbf{x}) + \lambda\phi(\mathbf{x}), \tag{2}$$

where the first term $f(\mathbf{x})$ aims to enforce data fidelity, *e.g.* f could be the MSE between $\mathbf{Hx}$ and $\mathbf{y}_\epsilon$, while the regularizer ϕ allows us to insert knowledge onto the solution $\mathbf{x}$, and $\lambda \in \mathbb{R}^+$ controls the strength of the regularization. Typically there is no closed-form solution to (2) and it usually needs to be solved iteratively. This has led to the following proposed uses for pretrained DNNs: (i) use DNN to replace the proximal operator associated with $\phi(\mathbf{x})$ in a proximal gradient algorithm [15,16,38], (ii) use DNN to replace the gradient $\nabla\phi$ in an unrolled optimization method [7,31,46], (iii) directly replace the regularizer ϕ with DNN [26,39], (iv) use DNN as a generative model to generate $\mathbf{x}$ from a latent code that needs to be estimated [3,42]. These iterative methods are Physics-engaged, as they actually use the regularizer along with the forward model and observation by minimizing the disparity between the oracle and its reconstruction.

As an exception to the above physics-engaged deep learning approaches, there have been some recent studies aimed at explicitly using $\mathbf{H}$-related information during the DNN training process in an end-to-end manner. For example, [30, 41] explicitly learn the nullspace component of $\mathbf{x}$ with respect to $\mathbf{H}$. However, this separate nullspace learning does not deal with the presence of noise in the input nor with situations where no nullspace exists. Another interesting direction presented in [11] considers a Neumann series expansion of linear operators to approximate the inverse mapping of (2). However, this requires the network to precondition and store the results of each iteration in order to accumulate the approximate Neumann series to solve the inverse problem.

In this paper, inspired by the nullspace method of [30,41,44], we explore the possibility of a more flexible end-to-end neural network structure that is capable of exploiting both the range and null space structures of the inverse problem. Before discussing the proposed method, let us briefly recall the Range-Nullspace decomposition of data.

2.2 Range-Nullspace ($\mathcal{R}$-$\mathcal{N}$) Decomposition

Given a linear forward operator $\mathbf{H} \in \mathbb{R}^{d \times D}$ and its right pseudo inverse $\mathbf{H}^\dagger \in \mathbb{R}^{D \times d}$, which satisfies $\mathbf{HH}^\dagger = \mathbf{I}_d$, it holds that $\mathbb{R}^D = \mathcal{R}(\mathbf{H}^\dagger) \oplus \mathcal{N}(\mathbf{H})$, which implies that for any sample $\forall \mathbf{x} \in \mathbb{R}^D$ there exists two unique elements $\mathbf{x}^+ \in \mathcal{R}(\mathbf{H}^\dagger)$ and $\mathbf{x}^\perp \in \mathcal{N}(\mathbf{H})$ such that $\mathbf{x} = \mathbf{x}^+ + \mathbf{x}^\perp$. Therefore we define the following range-nullspace ($\mathcal{R}$-$\mathcal{N}$) decomposition,

Definition 1. *$\mathcal{R}$-$\mathcal{N}$ Decomposition: Let $\mathcal{P}_r \triangleq \mathbf{H}^\dagger \mathbf{H}$ be the operator that projects the sample $\boldsymbol{x}$ from sample domain to the range of $\mathbf{H}^\dagger$, and denote by $\mathcal{P}_n \triangleq (\mathbf{I}_D - \mathbf{H}^\dagger \mathbf{H})$ the operator that projects $\boldsymbol{x}$ to the null space of $\mathbf{H}$. Then $\forall \boldsymbol{x} \in \mathbb{R}^D$, there exists the unique decomposition:*

$$\boldsymbol{x} = \mathcal{P}_r(\boldsymbol{x}) + \mathcal{P}_n(\boldsymbol{x}), \tag{3}$$

where we will call $\mathcal{P}_r(x)$ and $\mathcal{P}_n(x)$ the r-component and n-component of x, respectively.

Remark 1. In this paper we will only focus on the above decomposition. However, we comment that in principle the pseudo-inverse, $\mathbf{H}^\dagger$, could be replaced by any general right inverse of $\mathbf{H}$ in the above decomposition which might provide added flexibility in certain inverse problems.

Thus, the task of solving an inverse problem is to find these two components $\mathcal{P}_r(\mathbf{x})$ and $\mathcal{P}_n(\mathbf{x})$ based on the observed data, $\mathbf{y}_\epsilon$. The simple linear estimator to solve this problem is to use the approximation:

$$\mathbf{x}^* = \mathbf{H}^\dagger \mathbf{y}_\epsilon. \tag{4}$$

This estimator enjoys global and exact data-consistency, *i.e.* $\mathbf{H}\mathbf{x}^* \equiv \mathbf{y}_\epsilon$, which is an important consideration when solving inverse problems [30]. However, comparing (4) with (3) we can see that this is achieved by simply setting the nullspace component to zero: $\mathcal{P}_n(\mathbf{H}^\dagger \mathbf{y}_\epsilon) = 0$. In general this provides a poor solution for ill-posed problems. Thus it is necessary to further estimate the missing component $\mathcal{P}_n(\mathbf{x})$. Such an estimator is necessarily nonlinear.

Nullspace Learning. Recently, [30,41,44] explored the use of a neural network $\mathcal{G}$ to feed a refined backprojection $\mathcal{G}(\mathbf{H}^\dagger \mathbf{y}_\epsilon)$ to the null-space projection operator $\mathcal{P}_n$, then the reconstruction in (4) is reformulated as

$$\mathbf{x}^* = \mathbf{H}^\dagger \mathbf{y}_\epsilon + \mathcal{P}_n(\mathcal{G}(\mathbf{H}^\dagger \mathbf{y}_\epsilon)), \tag{5}$$

where the network $\mathcal{G}$ is suggested to be trained by minimizing the error between $\mathbf{x}$ and $\mathbf{x}^*$. Note the solution (5) enjoys global data consistency, *i.e.* $\mathbf{H}\mathbf{x}^* \equiv \mathbf{y}_\epsilon$. However, the solution (5) unfortunately, only works for the noise-free situation, and does not allow any denoising in the range $\mathcal{R}(\mathbf{H}^\dagger)$. Indeed, (5) can only denoise in the nullspace and the denoising ability is therefore worst-case bounded by $\|\epsilon\|/\|\mathbf{H}\|$ since $\|\mathbf{H}(\mathbf{x} - \mathbf{x}^*)\| = \|\epsilon\|$. The noise may further limit the ability to predict the null space component from the noisy measurements. Although it is reminiscent of decoupling the neural network denoiser from the inverse problem, it does not benefit from this since the training needs to be tailored to the task [38], which will be confirmed in our experiments.

3   Deep Decomposition Learning

Inspired by nullspace learning [30,41,44] we aim to remove the range space denoising deficiency while still exploiting the nullspace property. Let us consider the case $\epsilon \neq 0$ in (1) which is more practical. By the $\mathcal{R}$-$\mathcal{N}$ decomposition (3), it holds that $\mathbf{x}$ can be exactly recovered by,

$$\mathbf{x} = \mathbf{H}^\dagger \mathbf{y}_\epsilon - \mathbf{H}^\dagger \epsilon + \mathcal{P}_n(\mathbf{x}). \tag{6}$$

However, as mentioned before, in the scenario of the inverse problem, both the oracle image $\mathbf{x}$ and the noise term ϵ in (6) are still unknown and need to be recovered.

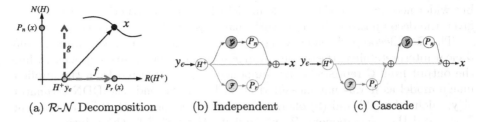

Fig. 1. Decomposition learning (a) and its two corresponding network architectures in (b) and (c). Decomposition learning trains neural network to recovery the range component $\mathcal{P}_r(\mathbf{x}) = \mathbf{H}^\dagger\mathbf{Hx}$ and nullspace component $\mathcal{P}_n(\mathbf{x}) = \mathbf{x} - \mathcal{P}_r(\mathbf{x})$ of oracle image $\mathbf{x}$ from its coarse reconstruction $\mathbf{H}^\dagger\mathbf{y}_\epsilon$. The residuals between $\mathbf{H}^\dagger\mathbf{y}_\epsilon$ and $\mathcal{P}_r(\mathbf{x})$ and $\mathcal{P}_n(\mathbf{x})$ are recovered by $f = \mathcal{P}_r(\mathcal{F})$ and $g = \mathcal{P}_n(\mathcal{G})$ respectively, where $\mathcal{F}$ and $\mathcal{G}$ are two sets of neural layers need to train. Different from direct learn the residual between $\mathbf{x}$ and $\mathbf{H}^\dagger\mathbf{y}_\epsilon$ without using physics, $\mathbf{x}$ is instead reconstructed by $\mathbf{H}^\dagger\mathbf{y}_\epsilon + f + g$ in a decomposition learning mechanism. This method enables physics to engage in neural network training and testing and generate more physics plausible reconstruction.

We address this problem by using two neural networks and introducing the decomposition learning framework (illustrated in Fig. 1a). Instead of hoping a single neural network will directly fit a desired underlying mapping between $\mathbf{H}^\dagger\mathbf{y}_\epsilon$ and $\mathbf{x} = \mathcal{P}_r(\mathbf{x}) + \mathcal{P}_n(\mathbf{x})$, we explicitly let two networks, denoted by $\mathcal{F}$ and $\mathcal{G}$ fit the two mappings from $\mathbf{H}^\dagger\mathbf{y}_\epsilon$ to the residual r-component $\mathcal{P}_r(\mathbf{x}) - \mathbf{H}^\dagger\mathbf{y}_\epsilon$ and the n-component $\mathcal{P}_n(\mathbf{x})$, respectively. In particular, the output of $\mathcal{F}$ should be bounded by the magnitude of noise ϵ, while $\mathcal{G}$ should be a smooth, *i.e.* a Lipschitz continuous neural network, since $\mathcal{G}$ is essentially a nullspace network, which does not need to be strongly bounded but should be regularized in order to get reasonable generalization. Therefore, the oracle $\mathbf{x}$ is decomposed as the sum of a linear component $\mathbf{H}^\dagger\mathbf{y}_\epsilon$ (the input), a bounded residual component $\mathcal{P}_r \circ \mathcal{F} \in \mathcal{R}(\mathbf{H}^\dagger)$ and a smooth n-component $\mathcal{P}_n \circ \mathcal{G} \in \mathcal{N}(\mathbf{H})$.

We consider two versions of DDN estimators. First, we define an independent connection architecture (Fig. 1b) estimator $\mathcal{A}_i$ using the $\mathcal{R}$-$\mathcal{N}$ decomposition,

$$\mathcal{A}_i(\mathbf{y}_\epsilon) \triangleq \mathbf{H}^\dagger\mathbf{y}_\epsilon + \mathcal{P}_r(\mathcal{F}(\mathbf{H}^\dagger\mathbf{y}_\epsilon)) + \mathcal{P}_n(\mathcal{G}(\mathbf{H}^\dagger\mathbf{y}_\epsilon)). \tag{7}$$

where there are no interactions between $\mathcal{F}$ and $\mathcal{G}$.

An alternative (but essentially equivalent) mapping $\mathcal{A}_c$ from $\mathbf{y}_\epsilon$ to $\mathbf{x}$ which is related to (7) uses a cascade of networks (Fig. 1c), *i.e.* first denoising with $\mathcal{F}$, then feeding the denoised $\mathbf{H}^\dagger\mathbf{y}_\epsilon + \mathcal{P}_r(\mathcal{F}(\mathbf{H}^\dagger\mathbf{y}_\epsilon))$ into $\mathcal{G}$ such that:

$$\mathcal{A}_c(\mathbf{y}_\epsilon) \triangleq \mathbf{H}^\dagger\mathbf{y}_\epsilon + \mathcal{P}_r(\mathcal{F}(\mathbf{H}^\dagger\mathbf{y}_\epsilon)) + \mathcal{P}_n(\mathcal{G}(\mathbf{H}^\dagger\mathbf{y}_\epsilon + \mathcal{P}_r(\mathcal{F}(\mathbf{H}^\dagger\mathbf{y}_\epsilon)))). \tag{8}$$

Intuitively (8) is preferable since it is no more complex than the independent network topology and provides the nullspace network $\mathcal{G}$ with a range denoised input, thereby reducing the learning burden needed to be done by $\mathcal{G}$. Our experiments also verified the cascade connections typically perform better than the independent one. Note that the independent model is by its nature a shallower but wider network than the cascade model which by construction is deeper, but given the decomposition both networks have essentially the same complexity.

The $\mathcal{R}$-$\mathcal{N}$ decomposition learning gives the outputs of the two networks $\mathcal{F}$ and $\mathcal{G}$ clear interpretability: the output from $\mathcal{F}$ estimates the noise component, while the output from $\mathcal{G}$ represents the component that is inferred from the implicit image model as it was not measured at all by $\mathbf{y}_\epsilon$. Second, the DDN estimator $\mathcal{A}(\mathbf{y}_\epsilon)$ defined in (7) and (8) offers the ability to denoise both the r-component $\mathcal{P}_r(\mathbf{x})$ and the n-component $\mathcal{P}_n(\mathbf{x})$, and if $\|\mathbf{H}\mathcal{F}\| \leq \|\epsilon\|$, the solution enjoys a relaxed notion of data-consistency (in the spirit of the discrepancy principle popular in inverse problems), which convergences to exact data consistency when $\|\mathbf{H}\mathcal{F} - \epsilon\| \to 0$, that makes the deep learning solutions more physically plausible. Finally, in the cascade architecture (Fig. 1c) we calculate $\mathcal{P}_r(\mathcal{F})$ first. If we had cascaded $\mathcal{P}_n(\mathcal{G}(\mathbf{H}^\dagger\mathbf{y}_\epsilon)) + \mathbf{H}^\dagger\mathbf{y}_\epsilon$ first we would have lost the $\mathcal{R}$-$\mathcal{N}$ decomposition as the input to $\mathcal{F}$ would live in the full space. The input to $\mathcal{G}$ would also have range noise, as in the independent architecture, thereby increasing the training burden on $\mathcal{G}$ network.

3.1   Training Strategy

Let $\mathbf{X} = \{(\mathbf{y}_\epsilon^{(i)}, \mathbf{x}^{(i)})\}_{i=1}^N$ denote a training set of N samples, where $\mathbf{x}^{(i)}$ and $\mathbf{y}_\epsilon^{(i)}$ are the clean oracle signal and its noisy measurement given by (1). Denote by $\ell(x, y)$ the loss function, which measures the discrepancy between x and y. In this paper we used ℓ_2 to compute ℓ. Given an estimator $\mathcal{A}$, we jointly training $\mathcal{F}$ and $\mathcal{G}$ by solving a single optimization program,

$$\min_{\mathcal{F},\mathcal{G}} \ell_{\text{emp}}(\mathcal{A}) + \lambda_1\phi_1(\mathcal{F}) + \lambda_2\phi_2(\mathcal{G}), \tag{9}$$

where the first term $\ell_{\text{emp}}(\mathcal{A}) \triangleq \frac{1}{N}\sum_{\mathbf{y}_\epsilon^{(i)},\mathbf{x}^{(i)}\in\mathbf{X}} \ell(\mathcal{A}(\mathbf{y}_\epsilon^{(i)}), \mathbf{x}^{(i)})$ is $\mathcal{A}$'s empirical loss associated with the training set $\mathbf{X}$ and serves the data-fidelity, and $\mathcal{A}$ take the form either in (7) or in (8). In this paper, we set $\phi_1(\mathcal{F}) = \sum_{i=1}^N \ell(\mathbf{H}\mathcal{F}(\mathbf{H}^\dagger\mathbf{y}_\epsilon^{(i)}), \epsilon^{(i)})$ in order to encourage the data discrepancy term to be small. We then set ϕ_2 as the weight decay term to control the Lipschitz of the network [41] and to encourage good generalization [21]. It worth noting we can flexibly define different ϕ_1 and ϕ_2 for $\mathcal{F}$ and $\mathcal{G}$ to impose the desired boundedness and smoothness conditions, such that to tune the networks to their specific tasks.

Due to the decomposition $\mathbf{x} = \mathcal{P}_r(\mathbf{x}) + \mathcal{P}_n(\mathbf{x})$ in the independent architecture there are no interactions between the respective targets of $\mathcal{F}$ and $\mathcal{G}$, therefore one can decouple (9) into two independent sub-optimizations to train $\mathcal{F}$ and $\mathcal{G}$ separately, i.e. $\min_{\mathcal{F}}(\mathcal{P}_r(\mathcal{F}), \mathcal{P}_r(\mathbf{X})) + \lambda_1\phi_1$ and $\min_{\mathcal{G}}(\mathcal{P}_n(\mathcal{G}), \mathcal{P}_n(\mathbf{X})) + \lambda_2\phi_2$. While joint training and decoupled training are theoretically equivalent, in practice, the decoupled training enjoys more intuitive interpretability, and it is easier to control $\mathcal{F}$ and $\mathcal{G}$ each to achieve better convergence results. However, the joint training is slightly more efficient than the decoupled because the networks can be trained simultaneously. Accordingly we use the cascade architecture as our DDN in our experiments and jointly train it using (9).

3.2   The Relationship to Other Work

In the noise-free case ($\epsilon = 0$), the decomposition learning (6) reduces naturally to vanilla nullspace learning (5). Thus a DDN can be regarded as a generalized nullspace network. While in the noisy case, one might be tempted to consider adopting a separate generic denoiser to preprocess the measurements $\mathbf{y}_\epsilon$. However, such denoisers are typically built in a manner decoupled from the inverse problem of interest, therefore to train a nullspace network with such denoised measurements could amplify the reconstruction error, causing more inconsistent results [38]. In contrast, the denoising process in the DDN is not decoupled from the inverse problem but integrated into a unified learning model. The experiments show this not only improves the quality of the results but in addition, helps the model's generalization. Note DDN is different from the recent heuristic decomposition network [35] which broadly separates the image into structure part and detail part. In contrast, we identify the natural $\mathcal{R}$-$\mathcal{N}$ decomposition induced by $\mathbf{H}$ that also allows us to select appropriate loss functions for the different components.

Our decomposition learning can also be regarded as a special gated neural network. To be specific, if we rewrite (7) as

$$\mathcal{A} = \mathbf{T}\mathcal{F}(\mathbf{z}) + (\mathbf{I} - \mathbf{T})\mathcal{G}(\mathbf{z}) + \mathbf{z}, \tag{10}$$

where $\mathbf{z} = \mathbf{H}^\dagger \mathbf{y}_\epsilon$, $\mathbf{T} = \mathbf{H}^\dagger \mathbf{H}$, it can be seen the output of $\mathcal{F}$ and $\mathcal{G}$ are gated in terms of $\mathbf{T}$ and $\mathbf{I} - \mathbf{T}$. The importance of the two components is determined by the physics in terms of $\mathbf{H}^\dagger \mathbf{H}$. This is different from previous gated networks such as [18,45] in which the model is gated by some bounded numerical function such as a sigmoid or hardlim which are not typically related to the physics of the forward model or its inverse. Our method can also be regarded as a generalized residual learning [17], *i.e.* we decompose the residual $\mathcal{A} - \mathbf{z}$ into two components in $\mathcal{R}(\mathbf{H}^\dagger)$ and $\mathcal{N}(\mathbf{H})$ with more explicit interpretability. In particular, in the absence of the nullspace $\mathcal{N}(\mathbf{H})$ or in the case $\mathbf{H} = \mathbf{I}$ such that $\mathcal{P}_r = \mathbf{I}$ and $\mathcal{P}_n = 0$, *i.e.* there is no nullspace learning, $\mathcal{G}$ will be irrelevant and only $\mathcal{F}$ will be learnable, and the decomposition learning will be reduced to a non-gated neural network and equivalent to the standard residual learning.

Remark 2. A key aspect of the DDN framework is access to the projection operators $\mathcal{P}_n$ and $\mathcal{P}_r$. The complexity will depend on how easy it is to approximate $\mathbf{H}^\dagger$, or another left inverse. While many computer vision problems admit an easily computable inverse, such as: deblurring, inpainting and the ones considered in this paper - compressed sensing and super-resolution, for more general inverse problems this approximation is more challenging and may even be unstable. However, it is possible to approximate $\mathbf{z} = \mathbf{H}^\dagger \mathbf{y}$ by a regularized linear operator, e.g. $\arg\min_{\mathbf{z}} \|\mathbf{y} - \mathbf{H}\mathbf{z}\|^2 + \lambda\|\mathbf{z}\|^2$. Here we can leverage the wealth of literature in inverse problems dedicated to efficiently computing this, e.g. using preconditioned conjugate gradient solvers, etc. *Unrolled* physics-engaged deep learning solutions [15,16,38] also solve a similar optimization problem but with an integrated complex DNN regularizer, and therefore resort to slower proximal first

Table 1. Four DNN solvers $\mathcal{A}$ that use different mechanisms for using physics to solve inverse problems. Note the residual learning is physic-free and $\text{Prox}_{\mathbf{H}}$ is the proximal operator in proximal gradient descent optimization.

Mechanism	Residual learning	Unrolled learning	Nullspace learning	Decomposition learning
Formulation	$\mathcal{A} = \mathbf{I} + \mathcal{G} \circ \mathcal{F}$	$\text{Prox}_{\mathbf{H}} \leftarrow \mathcal{G} \circ \mathcal{F}$	$\mathcal{A} = \mathbf{I} + \mathcal{P}_n(\mathcal{G} \circ \mathcal{F})$	$\mathcal{A} = \mathbf{I} + \mathcal{P}_r(\mathcal{F}) + \mathcal{P}_n(\mathcal{G})$

order methods. In contrast, the DDN allows us to separate the DNN mappings from this optimization. For such challenging problems we doubt whether a similar complexity physics-free solution would be competitive.

4   Experiments

We designed our experiments to address the following questions:

- *Does the proposed deep decomposition learning help the neural network produce superior results on different inverse problem tasks? Does the DDN enjoy better generalization?*
- *Which training strategy, e.g. jointly or decoupled, is best for training the DDN? Which connection type, e.g. the independent or cascade one, is better?*
- *How important is each component $\mathcal{P}_r(\mathcal{F})$ and $\mathcal{P}_n(\mathcal{G})$ to DDN?*

To do that, we validate the effectiveness of our proposed decomposition learning on the inverse problems of compressive sensing MR fingerprinting (CS-MRF) [10,27] reconstruction and natural images super-resolution. While our focus is mostly on CS-MRF, the SR experiments are included to shed some light on the ablation analysis.

4.1   Implementation

Our goal here is not to explore the potential designs of the neural networks, $\mathcal{F}$ and $\mathcal{G}$, but the usage of physics in the neural network. Therefore, we use a simple four layers CNN as $\mathcal{F}$ and directly apply UNet [40], which is commonly used in the field of image reconstruction [16,20,47], as $\mathcal{G}$. In particular, all the layers in $\mathcal{F}$ are with 3×3 kernels where the first three layers undergo ReLU activation and the 2nd and 3rd layers were followed by batch normalization and ReLU activation, and a fixed number of c, 64, 64, c feature maps for each layer where c is the number of input channels. We compare the proposed *decomposition learning* (DDN) with *residual learning* (ResUnet, [20]), *unrolled learning* (NPGD, [31]) and *nullspace learning* (NSN, [32,41]). The above different mechanisms are summarized in Table 1. We build NPGD with a fixed 3 recurrent steps [31]. It is important to note that we keep the base neural network topology and the number of parameters the same for both our DDN and the competitors.

We quantify the image reconstruction quality using Normalized MSE (NMSE), Peak Signal to Noise Ratio (PSNR), *i.e.* $\text{PSNR} = 10 \log_{10}(255/\text{MSE})^2$, and generalization error (GE)-the difference between the expected loss and the training loss, is evaluated by $\text{GE}(\mathcal{A}) = |\ell(\mathcal{A}, \mathcal{X}_{\text{test}}) - \ell(\mathcal{A}, \mathcal{X}_{\text{train}})|$ where $\ell(\mathcal{A}, \mathcal{X})$ denotes the loss evaluated over the data $\mathcal{X}$. We used ADAM to optimize the DDN and tuned the λ_1 and λ_2 for specific inverse problems. All networks used $\mathbf{H}^\dagger \mathbf{y}_\epsilon$ as the input, were implemented in PyTorch, and trained on NVIDIA 2080Ti GPUs.

4.2   CS-MRF Reconstruction

Magnetic Resonance Fingerprinting (MRF) [27] recently emerged to accelerate the acquisition of tissues' quantitative MR characteristics include T_1, T_2, off-resonance frequency, etc. The compressive sensing MRF (CS-MRF) [10] is typically involves two goals, reconstructing a reasonable MR fingerprint (multi-coil sensitivities, $i.e.$ MR images sequence) $\mathbf{x}$ from its undersampled k-space measurement $\mathbf{y}_\epsilon$, and at the same time using pattern recognition techniques such as dictionary matching [27] or neural networks [6,13,14], to query the corresponding quantitative map $\mathbf{m}$, such that achieve quantification of MRI. Accordingly, the data acquisition of CS-MRF can be boiled down to $\mathbf{y}_\epsilon = \mathbf{H}(\mathbf{x}) + \epsilon$ where the forward operator $\mathbf{H}$ consists a Fourier transformation $\mathcal{F}$ followed by a per-frame and time-varying subsampling operator $\mathcal{S}$, $i.e.$ $\mathbf{H} = \mathcal{S} \circ \mathcal{F}$. For the simplicity, we use the Cartesian sampling as example and now $\mathbf{H}^\dagger = \mathcal{F}^{-1} \circ \mathcal{S}^\top$.

Note that $\mathbf{x}$ can be generated by the Bloch equation using its tissue property/parameters map $\mathbf{m}$, thus predicting $\mathbf{m}$ from $\mathbf{x}$ is another inverse problem and is nonlinear. Recent studies show that this nonlinear inverse problem $\mathbf{x} \to \mathbf{m}$ can be effectively solved by neural networks [6,13,14]. Here we mainly focus on the inverse problem $\mathbf{y}_\epsilon \to \mathbf{x}$, $i.e.$ recover $\mathbf{x}$ from its noisy measurement $\mathbf{y}_\epsilon$. We then use the UNet-based network [13] that pre-trained on the clean oracle MRF images to predict the tissue property map $\mathbf{m}$ for a given MRF image $\mathbf{x}$.

Dataset. We use the simulated human brain MRF dataset in [6]. The ground truth parametric tissue property maps are collected from 8 volunteers (2k slices) using MAGIC [29] quantitative MRI protocol with Cartesian sampling. These parametric maps are then used to simulate MRF acquisition using the Fast imaging with Steady State Precession (FISP) [19] protocol and Cartesian sampling. In particular, we set the dimension reduced 10 channel MRF image $\mathbf{x}$ with scale $D = 200 \times 200$, the compression ratio is $d/D = 1/40$, and the noise level $\sigma_\epsilon = 0.01$. In order to evaluate the generalization ability of different methods under the extreme case that $scarce$ labelled anatomical quantitative MRI datasets that are available for training, small numbers of samples from the first 7 patients are randomly picked for training, $e.g.$ $N = 100, 50, 10$ in our experiments and 20 slices from the last volunteer are picked for the test.

Table 2. Comparison results on CS-MRF reconstruction task.

	IT	X (NMSE$\times 10^{-2}$/GE)			T_1 (PSNR dB)		
	(sec)	$N = 100$	$N = 50$	$N = 10$	$N = 100$	$N = 50$	$N = 10$
ResUnet [20]	0.005	0.62/0.027	0.743/0.069	1.119/0.164	17.10 ± 2.64	17.80 ± 1.93	15.18 ± 1.49
NPGD [31]	0.15	0.58/0.024	0.980/0.118	1.689/0.255	18.05 ± 2.02	15.49 ± 1.47	13.67 ± 1.31
NSN [41]	0.04	0.57/0.031	0.740/0.068	1.119/0.159	18.49 ± 2.39	18.03 ± 1.65	15.25 ± 1.53
DDN	0.06	0.51/0.019	0.711/0.062	1.056/0.139	18.92 ± 2.04	18.06 ± 1.54	15.90 ± 1.49

Comparison Results. Table 2 reports the inferring time (IT), NMSE and GE for the reconstruction of MRF images and the PSNRs for the tissue maps prediction results. Due to space limitation, we only list the PSNR results of T_1 here. Figure 2a and Fig. 2b show the reconstruction of a test MRF image $\mathbf{x}$'s first channel and $\mathbf{x}$'s T_1 map prediction, respectively. In summary, we make three key findings.

First, DDN obtained the best reconstruction results and the best generalization ability in all cases (Table 2). When training with fewer training samples *e.g.* 50 and 10, NSN and NPGD perform better than NPGD. This demonstrates that a neural network that improperly-trained using a few samples is not suitable as a proximal operator. ResUnet is more stable than NPGD because the former does not need to be used in another optimization algorithm which is irrelevant to the neural network training.

Second, let τ denotes the number of times a particular model accesses the physical model (*e.g.* $\mathbf{H}$, $\mathbf{H}^\dagger$). Clearly, $\tau_{\text{ResUnet}} = 0$, $\tau_{\text{NSN}} = 2$, $\tau_{\text{DDN}} = 2 \times \tau_{\text{NSN}} = 4$ and $\tau_{\text{NPGD}} = 2 \times 3 = 6$ since NPGD needs to access both $\mathbf{H}$ and $\mathbf{H}^\top$ in a proximal gradient descent iteration. As can be seen, the inferring time of ResUnet is very short due to its essence of the pure physics-free model. Although NPGD requires longer inferring time (2.5 times DDN), it only performs well when training using 100 samples, *i.e.* fewer samples are not sufficient to train a good neural proximal operator [31,38]. This also shows the usage of physics $\mathcal{P}_r$ and $\mathcal{P}_n$ in the proposed decomposition learning is reasonable since it obtained best results within an acceptable inferring time.

Finally, when the ResUnet, NPGD and NSN are trained with 50 or 10 samples, there exist lots of artifacts in their reconstructions (see Fig. 2a and Fig. 2b). In contrast, DDN can stably output reasonable MRF image reconstructions and such that lead to a physics plausible prediction of T_1 map. This shows the use of decomposition learning can help improve the generalization ability of the neural network and alleviate the dependence of deep learning performance on large-volume training samples.

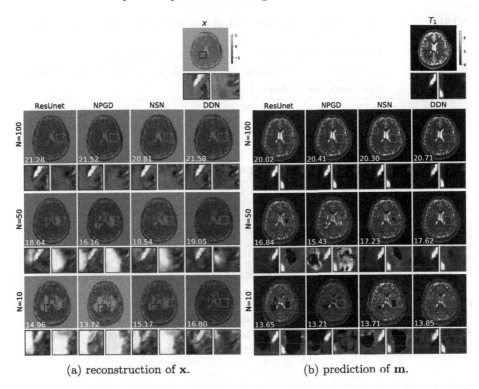

(a) reconstruction of **x**.   (b) prediction of **m**.

Fig. 2. (a) Reconstruction of MRF image **x** from its noisy measurement $\mathbf{y}_\epsilon$ ($\sigma_\epsilon = 0.01$) and (b) its corresponding T_1 map prediction. From top to bottom are the groundtruth x and m and their corresponding reconstructions by ResUnet [20], NPGD [31], NSN [41] and DDN (proposed) trained with 100, 50 and 10 sample, respectively.

4.3   Ablation Study

We are interested in studying (1) the impact of different training strategies (jointly/decoupled) and different connection types (independent/cascade) to DDN and (2) the importance of component $\mathcal{P}_r$ and $\mathcal{P}_n$ to DDN. To do that, we consider the Super-resolution (SR) task and train the models on the BSDS300 [1] and test on the benchmark dataset Set5 [2]. We super-resolve low-resolution (LR) images by a scale factor of 2. The LR images are formed by downsampling with bi-cubic anti-aliasing the HR images [12], and then corrupting them with Gaussian noise with a standard deviation $\sigma_\epsilon = 0.1$ (10% noise). The presence of anti-aliasing in the downsampling means that the bi-cubic upsampling operator is a reasonable approximation to $\mathbf{H}^\dagger$, and this is what we use in our DDN. Training is performed using 40×40 RGB image patches (LR). The quantitative results presented are then evaluated on the luminance (Y) channel. We *emphasize* that our goal here is not to achieve state-of-the-art performance on the SR task, but a simple scenario to study the behaviour of ablation analysis for decomposition learning.

Table 3. Comparison results of ablation study on image SR task ($\times 2$, $\sigma_\epsilon = 0.1$).

Metric	Training strategy study			Ablation study			
	Independent	Cascade		DDN_1	DDN_2	DDN_3	DDN_4
	Joint/Decoupled	Joint	Decoupled				
PSNR (dB)	26.15	26.30	26.38	22.31	20.95	25.82	26.30
GE (10^{-3})	1.24	1.26	1.24	1.75	1.41	1.83	1.26

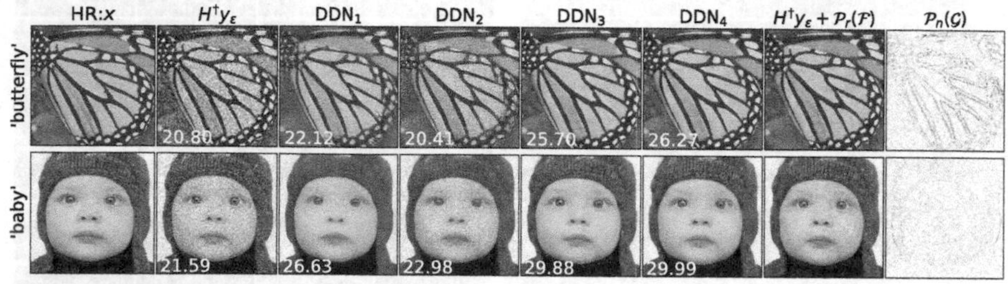

Fig. 3. Visualization of DDN with different specs on the SR task ($\times 2$, $\sigma_\epsilon = 0.1$). From the left to right are the oracle HR image $\mathbf{x}$, reconstructions by $\mathbf{H}^\dagger \mathbf{y}_\epsilon$, $\text{DDN}_1(\boxtimes\mathcal{P}_r,$ $\boxtimes\mathcal{P}_n)$, $\text{DDN}_2(\boxtimes\mathcal{P}_r, \boxdot\mathcal{P}_n)$, $\text{DDN}_3(\boxdot\mathcal{P}_r, \boxtimes\mathcal{P}_n)$, $\text{DDN}_4(\boxdot\mathcal{P}_r, \boxdot\mathcal{P}_n)$, and the r-component $\mathbf{H}^\dagger \mathbf{y}_\epsilon + \mathcal{P}_r(\mathcal{F})$ and n-component $\mathcal{P}_n(\mathcal{G})$ recovered by DDN_4.

Training Strategy Study. We trained DDN using different training strategies. The test results are reported in the Table 3 which demonstrates the cascade architecture always performs slightly better than the independent one in term of both PSNR and GE. Note that for the independent model the joint and decoupled training are exactly equivalent. We also find that $\mathcal{F}$ and $\mathcal{G}$ benefit from more iterations in the decoupled training, especially for very noisy cases. In contrast, joint training was observed to be more efficient. In all experiments, we therefore use the cascade architecture with joint training for the DDNs.

Importance of $\mathcal{P}_r$ and $\mathcal{P}_n$. We trained four DDN variants by different usages of $\mathcal{P}_r$ and $\mathcal{P}_n$: DDN_1 - deactivate both $\mathcal{P}_r$ and $\mathcal{P}_n$, DDN_2 - only use $\mathcal{P}_n$, DDN_3 - only use $\mathcal{P}_r$ and DDN_4 - use both $\mathcal{P}_r$ and $\mathcal{P}_n$. The statistics PSNRs and GEs of the reconstruction are listed in Table 3. Two reconstruction examples and the learnt r-component and n-component by DDN_4 are shown in Fig. 3. From the results, we have the following conclusions.

First, it can be seen that the DDN_4 achieves the best results which used both projectors $\mathcal{P}_r$ and $\mathcal{P}_n$. DDN_2 is essentially a nullspace network and performed poorly in the presence of noise, as in this scenario the denoising task plays a significant role in the inverse problem. DDN_1 is equivalent to residual learning and is purely learning-based and physics-free, it consistently provides better performance than DDN_2, but it has the higher GEs. This suggests that introducing physics into deep learning models can facilitate the neural network to enjoy better generalization for solving inverse problems.

Second, DDN$_3$ performs better than DDN$_1$ and DDN$_2$ but worse than DDN$_4$. It is because DDN$_3$ considers denoising by recovering the r-component of data but fails to learn the n-component. This demonstrates integrating $\mathcal{P}_r$ and $\mathcal{P}_n$ into the proposed decomposition learning allows the DDN to remove structural noise and to simultaneously accurately approximate the r-component $\mathcal{P}_r(\mathbf{x})$ (see the penultimate column in Fig. 3) and predict the n-component $\mathcal{P}_n(\mathbf{x})$ (see the last column in Fig. 3) from its noisy measurement. From the above discussions, we conclude that decomposition learning is well-principled, structurally simple, and highly interpretable.

Finally, we emphasize that given a linear forward operator $\mathbf{H}$, the decomposition learning naturally exists and is easy to define. One can plug the decomposition learning, into other existing specialized deep learning solvers for different inverse problems, with which we believe one could increase the performance limit of the deep learning solvers.

5   Conclusion

In this paper, we have proposed a deep decomposition learning framework for building an end-to-end and physics-engaged neural network solution for inverse problems. We have explicitly reformulated the neural network layers to learn range-nullspace decomposition functions with reference to the layer inputs, instead of learning unreferenced functions. We have shown that the decomposition networks not only produce superior results, but also enjoy good interpretability and generalization. We have demonstrated the advantages of decomposition learning on CS-MRF and image super-resolution examples. In future work, we will explore adapting the proposed deep decomposition learning to more challenging inverse problems such as tomographic imaging.

Acknowledgements. We thank Pedro Gómez, Carolin Prikl and Marion Menzel from GE Healthcare and Mohammad Golbabaee from Bath University for the quantitative anatomical maps dataset. DC and MD are supported by the ERC C-SENSE project (ERCADG-2015-694888).

References

1. Agustsson, E., Timofte, R.: NTIRE 2017 challenge on single image super-resolution: dataset and study. In: Proceedings of the IEEE Conference on Computer Vision and Pattern Recognition Workshops, pp. 126–135 (2017)
2. Bevilacqua, M., Roumy, A., Guillemot, C., Alberi-Morel, M.L.: Low-complexity single-image super-resolution based on nonnegative neighbor embedding (2012)
3. Bora, A., Jalal, A., Price, E., Dimakis, A.G.: Compressed sensing using generative models. In: Proceedings of the 34th International Conference on Machine Learning, vol. 70, pp. 537–546. JMLR.org (2017)

4. Boyd, S., Parikh, N., Chu, E., Peleato, B., Eckstein, J., et al.: Distributed optimization and statistical learning via the alternating direction method of multipliers. Found. Trends. Mach. Learn. **3**(1), 1–122 (2011)
5. Burger, H.C., Schuler, C.J., Harmeling, S.: Image denoising: Can plain neural networks compete with BM3D? In: 2012 IEEE Conference on Computer Vision and Pattern Recognition, pp. 2392–2399. IEEE (2012)
6. Chen, D., Golbabaee, M., Gómez, P.A., Menzel, M.I., Davies, M.E.: Deep fully convolutional network for MR fingerprinting. In: International Conference on Medical Imaging with Deep Learning (2019)
7. Chen, Y., Pock, T.: Trainable nonlinear reaction diffusion: a flexible framework for fast and effective image restoration. IEEE Trans. Pattern Anal. Mach. Intell. **39**(6), 1256–1272 (2016)
8. Cui, Z., Chang, H., Shan, S., Zhong, B., Chen, X.: Deep network cascade for image super-resolution. In: Fleet, D., Pajdla, T., Schiele, B., Tuytelaars, T. (eds.) ECCV 2014. LNCS, vol. 8693, pp. 49–64. Springer, Cham (2014). https://doi.org/10.1007/978-3-319-10602-1_4
9. Daubechies, I., Defrise, M., De Mol, C.: An iterative thresholding algorithm for linear inverse problems with a sparsity constraint. Commun. Pure Appl. Math. J. Iss. Courant Inst. Math. Sci. **57**(11), 1413–1457 (2004)
10. Davies, M., Puy, G., Vandergheynst, P., Wiaux, Y.: A compressed sensing framework for magnetic resonance fingerprinting. SIAM J. Imaging Sci. **7**(4), 2623–2656 (2014)
11. Davis, G., Greg, O., Rebecca, W.: Neumann networks for linear inverse problems in imaging. IEEE Trans. Comput. Imaging **6**, 328–343 (2019)
12. Dong, C., Loy, C.C., He, K., Tang, X.: Image super-resolution using deep convolutional networks. IEEE Trans. Pattern Anal. Mach. Intell. **38**(2), 295–307 (2015)
13. Fang, Z., et al.: Deep learning for fast and spatially-constrained tissue quantification from highly-accelerated data in magnetic resonance fingerprinting. IEEE Trans. Med. Imaging **38**(10), 2364–2374 (2019)
14. Golbabaee, M., Chen, D., Gómez, P.A., Menzel, M.I., Davies, M.E.: Geometry of deep learning for magnetic resonance fingerprinting. In: The 44th International Conference on Acoustics, Speech, and Signal Processing (ICASSP) (2019)
15. Gu, S., Timofte, R., Van Gool, L.: Integrating local and non-local denoiser priors for image restoration. In: 2018 24th International Conference on Pattern Recognition (ICPR), pp. 2923–2928. IEEE (2018)
16. Gupta, H., Jin, K.H., Nguyen, H.Q., McCann, M.T., Unser, M.: CNN-based projected gradient descent for consistent CT image reconstruction. IEEE Trans. Med. Imaging **37**(6), 1440–1453 (2018)
17. He, K., Zhang, X., Ren, S., Sun, J.: Deep residual learning for image recognition. In: Proceedings of the IEEE Conference on Computer Vision and Pattern Recognition, pp. 770–778 (2016)
18. Hochreiter, S., Schmidhuber, J.: Long short-term memory. Neural Comput. **9**(8), 1735–1780 (1997)
19. Jiang, Y., Ma, D., Seiberlich, N., Gulani, V., Griswold, M.A.: MR fingerprinting using fast imaging with steady state precession (FISP) with spiral readout. Magn. Reson. Med. **74**(6), 1621–1631 (2015)
20. Jin, K.H., McCann, M.T., Froustey, E., Unser, M.: Deep convolutional neural network for inverse problems in imaging. IEEE Trans. Image Process. **26**(9), 4509–4522 (2017)
21. Kawaguchi, K., Kaelbling, L.P., Bengio, Y.: Generalization in deep learning. arXiv preprint arXiv:1710.05468 (2017)

22. Kulkarni, K., Lohit, S., Turaga, P., Kerviche, R., Ashok, A.: ReconNet: non-iterative reconstruction of images from compressively sensed measurements. In: Proceedings of the IEEE Conference on Computer Vision and Pattern Recognition, pp. 449–458 (2016)
23. Kupyn, O., Budzan, V., Mykhailych, M., Mishkin, D., Matas, J.: DeblurGAN: blind motion deblurring using conditional adversarial networks. In: Proceedings of the IEEE Conference on Computer Vision and Pattern Recognition, pp. 8183–8192 (2018)
24. Ledig, C., et al.: Photo-realistic single image super-resolution using a generative adversarial network. In: Proceedings of the IEEE Conference on Computer Vision and Pattern Recognition, pp. 4681–4690 (2017)
25. Lucas, A., Iliadis, M., Molina, R., Katsaggelos, A.K.: Using deep neural networks for inverse problems in imaging: beyond analytical methods. IEEE Signal Process. Mag. **35**(1), 20–36 (2018)
26. Lunz, S., Öktem, O., Schönlieb, C.B.: Adversarial regularizers in inverse problems. In: Advances in Neural Information Processing Systems, pp. 8507–8516 (2018)
27. Ma, D., et al.: Magnetic resonance fingerprinting. Nature **495**(7440), 187–192 (2013)
28. Mao, X., Shen, C., Yang, Y.B.: Image restoration using very deep convolutional encoder-decoder networks with symmetric skip connections. In: Advances in Neural Information Processing Systems, pp. 2802–2810 (2016)
29. Marcel, W., AB, S.: New technology allows multiple image contrasts in a single scan. GESIGNAPULSE.COM/MR SPRING, pp. 6–10 (2015)
30. Mardani, M., et al.: Deep generative adversarial networks for compressed sensing automates MRI. IEEE Trans. Med. Imaging **38**(1), 167–179 (2019)
31. Mardani, M., et al.: Neural proximal gradient descent for compressive imaging. In: Advances in Neural Information Processing Systems, pp. 9573–9583 (2018)
32. Meinhardt, T., Moller, M., Hazirbas, C., Cremers, D.: Learning proximal operators: using denoising networks for regularizing inverse imaging problems. In: Proceedings of the IEEE International Conference on Computer Vision, pp. 1781–1790 (2017)
33. Metzler, C., Mousavi, A., Baraniuk, R.: Learned D-AMP: principled neural network based compressive image recovery. In: Advances in Neural Information Processing Systems, pp. 1772–1783 (2017)
34. Mousavi, A., Patel, A.B., Baraniuk, R.G.: A deep learning approach to structured signal recovery. In: 2015 53rd Annual Allerton Conference on Communication, Control, and Computing (Allerton), pp. 1336–1343. IEEE (2015)
35. Pan, J., et al.: Learning dual convolutional neural networks for low-level vision. In: Proceedings of the IEEE Conference on Computer Vision and Pattern Recognition, pp. 3070–3079 (2018)
36. Pathak, D., Krahenbuhl, P., Donahue, J., Darrell, T., Efros, A.A.: Context encoders: feature learning by inpainting. In: Proceedings of the IEEE Conference on Computer Vision and Pattern Recognition, pp. 2536–2544 (2016)
37. Quan, T.M., Nguyen-Duc, T., Jeong, W.K.: Compressed sensing MRI reconstruction using a generative adversarial network with a cyclic loss. IEEE Trans. Med. Imaging **37**(6), 1488–1497 (2018)
38. Rick Chang, J., Li, C.L., Poczos, B., Vijaya Kumar, B., Sankaranarayanan, A.C.: One network to solve them all-solving linear inverse problems using deep projection models. In: Proceedings of the IEEE International Conference on Computer Vision, pp. 5888–5897 (2017)
39. Romano, Y., Elad, M., Milanfar, P.: The little engine that could: Regularization by denoising (red). SIAM J. Imaging Sci. **10**(4), 1804–1844 (2017)

40. Ronneberger, O., Fischer, P., Brox, T.: U-Net: convolutional networks for biomedical image segmentation. In: Navab, N., Hornegger, J., Wells, W.M., Frangi, A.F. (eds.) MICCAI 2015. LNCS, vol. 9351, pp. 234–241. Springer, Cham (2015). https://doi.org/10.1007/978-3-319-24574-4_28
41. Schwab, J., Antholzer, S., Haltmeier, M.: Deep null space learning for inverse problems: convergence analysis and rates. Inverse Prob. **35**(2), 025008 (2019)
42. Shah, V., Hegde, C.: Solving linear inverse problems using GAN priors: an algorithm with provable guarantees. In: 2018 IEEE International Conference on Acoustics, Speech and Signal Processing (ICASSP), pp. 4609–4613. IEEE (2018)
43. Shaham, T.R., Dekel, T., Michaeli, T.: SinGAN: learning a generative model from a single natural image. In: Proceedings of the IEEE International Conference on Computer Vision, pp. 4570–4580 (2019)
44. Sønderby, C.K., Caballero, J., Theis, L., Shi, W., Huszár, F.: Amortised map inference for image super-resolution. arXiv preprint arXiv:1610.04490 (2016)
45. Srivastava, R.K., Greff, K., Schmidhuber, J.: Training very deep networks. In: Advances in Neural Information Processing Systems, pp. 2377–2385 (2015)
46. Sun, J., Li, H., Xu, Z., et al.: Deep ADMM-Net for compressive sensing MRI. In: Advances in Neural Information Processing Systems, pp. 10–18 (2016)
47. Ulyanov, D., Vedaldi, A., Lempitsky, V.: Deep image prior. In: Proceedings of the IEEE Conference on Computer Vision and Pattern Recognition, pp. 9446–9454 (2018)
48. Xie, J., Xu, L., Chen, E.: Image denoising and inpainting with deep neural networks. In: Advances in Neural Information Processing Systems, pp. 341–349 (2012)
49. Xu, L., Ren, J.S., Liu, C., Jia, J.: Deep convolutional neural network for image deconvolution. In: Advances in Neural Information Processing Systems, pp. 1790–1798 (2014)
50. Zeng, K., Yu, J., Wang, R., Li, C., Tao, D.: Coupled deep autoencoder for single image super-resolution. IEEE Trans. Cybern. **47**(1), 27–37 (2015)
51. Zhang, K., Zuo, W., Chen, Y., Meng, D., Zhang, L.: Beyond a Gaussian denoiser: residual learning of deep CNN for image denoising. IEEE Trans. Image Process. **26**(7), 3142–3155 (2017)

FLOT: Scene Flow on Point Clouds Guided by Optimal Transport

Gilles Puy[1(✉)], Alexandre Boulch[1], and Renaud Marlet[1,2]

[1] valeo.ai, Paris, France
{gilles.puy,alexandre.boulch,renaud.marlet}@valeo.com
[2] ENPC, Paris, France

Abstract. We propose and study a method called FLOT that estimates
scene flow on point clouds. We start the design of FLOT by noticing
that scene flow estimation on point clouds reduces to estimating a permutation matrix in a perfect world. Inspired by recent works on graph
matching, we build a method to find these correspondences by borrowing
tools from optimal transport. Then, we relax the transport constraints to
take into account real-world imperfections. The transport cost between
two points is given by the pairwise similarity between deep features
extracted by a neural network trained under full supervision using synthetic datasets. Our main finding is that FLOT can perform as well as
the best existing methods on synthetic and real-world datasets while
requiring much less parameters and without using multiscale analysis.
Our second finding is that, on the training datasets considered, most of
the performance can be explained by the learned transport cost. This
yields a simpler method, FLOT$_0$, which is obtained using a particular
choice of optimal transport parameters and performs nearly as well as
FLOT.

1 Introduction

Scene flow [38] is the 3D motion of points at the surface of objects in a scene. It
is one of the low level information for scene understanding, which can be useful,
e.g., in autonomous driving. Its estimation is a problem which has been studied
for several years using different modalities as inputs such as colour images, with,
e.g., variational approaches [1,45] or methods using piecewise-constant priors
[16,22,39], or also using both colour and depth as modalities [2,12,32].

In this work, we are interested in scene flow estimation on point clouds only
using 3D point coordinates as input. In this setting, [8] proposed a technique
based on the minimisation of an objective function that favours closeness of
matching points for accurate scene flow estimate and local smoothness of this
estimate. In [35], 2D occupancy grids are constructed from the point clouds and

Electronic supplementary material The online version of this chapter (https://
doi.org/10.1007/978-3-030-58604-1_32) contains supplementary material, which is
available to authorized users.

© Springer Nature Switzerland AG 2020
A. Vedaldi et al. (Eds.): ECCV 2020, LNCS 12373, pp. 527–544, 2020.
https://doi.org/10.1007/978-3-030-58604-1_32

given as input features to a learned background removal filter and a learned classifier that find matching grid cells. A minimisation problem using these grid matches is then proposed to compute a raw scene flow before a final refinement step. In [36], a similar strategy is proposed but the match between grid cells is done using deep features. In [3,47], the point clouds are projected onto 2D cylindrical maps and fed in a traditional CNN trained for scene flow estimation. In contrast, FLOT directly consumes point clouds by using convolutions defined for them. The closest related works are discussed in Sect. 2.

We split scene flow estimation into two successive steps. First, we find soft-correspondences between points of the input point clouds. Second, we exploit these correspondences to estimate the flow. Taking inspiration from recent works on graph matching that use optimal transport to match nodes/vertices in two different graphs [18,29,34], we study the use of such tools for finding soft-correspondences between points.

Our network takes as input two point clouds captured in the same scene at two consecutive instants t and $t + 1$. We extract deep features at each point using point cloud convolutions and use these features to compute a transport cost between the points at time t and $t+1$. A small cost between two points indicates a likely correspondence between them. In the second step of the method, we exploit these soft-correspondences to obtain a first scene flow estimate by linear interpolation. This estimate is then refined using a residual network. The optimal transport and networks' parameters are learned by gradient descent under full supervision on synthetic datasets.

Our main contributions are: (a) an optimal transport module for scene flow estimation and the study of its performance; (b) a lightweight architecture that can perform as well as the best existing methods on synthetic and real-world datasets with much less parameters and without using multiscale analyses; (c) a simpler method $FLOT_0$ obtained for a particular choice of the OT parameters and which achieves competing results with respect to the state-of-the-art methods. We arrive at this simplified version by noticing that most of the performance in FLOT are explained by the learned transport cost. We also notice that the main module of $FLOT_0$ can be seen as an attention mechanism. Finally, we discuss, in the conclusion, some limitations of FLOT concerning the absence of explicit treatment of occlusions in the scene.

2   Related Works

Deep Scene Flow Estimation on Point Clouds. In [4], a deep network is trained end-to-end to estimate rigid motion of objects in LIDAR scans. The closest related works where no assumption of rigidity is made are [11,15,40,46]. In [40], a parametric continuous convolution that operates on data lying on irregular structures is proposed and its efficiency is demonstrated on segmentation tasks and scene flow estimation. The method [15] relies on PointNet++ [30] and uses a new flow embedding layer that learns to mix the information of both point clouds to yield accurate flow estimates. In [11], a technique to perform sparse convolutions on a permutohedral lattice is proposed. This method allows the processing of large point clouds. Furthermore, it is proposed to fuse the information of both point clouds at several scales, unlike in [15] where the information is fused once at a coarse scale. In contrast, our method fuse the information once at the finest scale. Let us highlight that our optimal transport module is independent of the type of point cloud convolution. We choose PointNet++ but other convolution could be used. In [46], PWC-Net [33] is adapted to work on point clouds. The flow is estimated in a coarse-to-fine scale fashion showing improvement over the previous method. Finally, let us mention that recent works [25,46] address this topic using self-supervision. We however restrict ourselves to full supervision in this work.

Graph Matching by Optimal Transport. Our method is inspired by recent works on graphs comparison using optimal transport. In [18], the graph Laplacian is used to map a graph to a multidimensional Gaussian distribution that represents the graph structure. The Wasserstein distance between these distributions is then used as a measure of graph similarity and permits one to match nodes between graphs. In [27], each graph is represented as a bag-of-vectors (one vector per node) and the measure of similarity is the Wasserstein distance between these sets. In [29], a method building upon the Gromov-Wasserstein distance between metric-measure spaces [21] is proposed to compare similarity matrices. This method can be used to compare two graphs by, *e.g.*, representing each of them with a matrix containing the geodesic distances between all pairs of nodes. In [34], it is proposed to compare graphs by fusing the Gromov-Wassertsein distance with the Wasserstein distance. The former is used to compare the graph structures while the latter is used to take into account node features. In our work, we use the latter distance. A graph is constructed for each point cloud by connecting each point to its nearest neighbours. We then propose a method to train a network that extract deep features for each point and use these features to match points between point clouds in our optimal transport module.

Algorithm Unrolling. Our method is based on the algorithm unrolling technique which consists in taking an iterative algorithm, unrolling a fixed number of its iterations, and replacing part of the matrix multiplications/convolutions in these unrolled iterations by new ones trained specifically for the task to achieve. Several works build on this technique, such as [10,17,24,26] to solve linear inverse problems, or [5,14,20,41] in for image denoising (where the denoiser is sometimes used to solve yet another inverse problem). In this work, we unroll few iterations of the Sinkhorn algorithm and train the cost matrix involved in it. This matrix is trained so that the resulting transport plan provides a good scene flow estimate. Let us mention that this algorithm is also unrolled, *e.g.*, in [9] to train a deep generative network, and in [31] for image feature assignments.

3   Method

3.1   Step 1: Finding Soft-Correspondences Between Points

Let $p, q \in \mathbb{R}^{n \times 3}$ be two point clouds of the same scene at two consecutive instants t and $t + 1$. The vectors $p_i, q_j \in \mathbb{R}^3$ are the xyz coordinates of the ith and j^{th} points of p and q, respectively. The scene flow estimation problem on point clouds consists in estimating the scene flow $f \in \mathbb{R}^{n \times 3}$ where $f_i \in \mathbb{R}^3$ is the translation of p_i from t to $t + 1$.

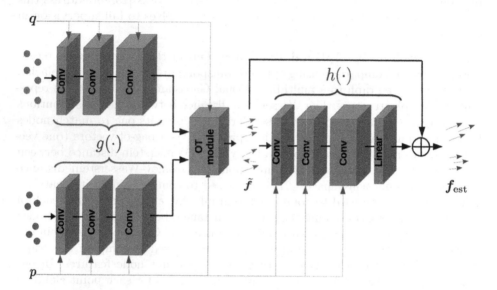

Fig. 1. The point clouds p and q go through g which outputs a feature for each input point. These features (black arrows) go in our proposed OT module where they are used to compute the pairwise similarities between each pair of points (p_i, q_j). The output of the OT module is a transport plan which informs us on the correspondences between the points of p and q. This information permits us to compute a first scene flow estimate $\tilde{f}$, which is refined by h to obtain f_{est}. The convolution layers (conv) are based on PointNet++ [30] but the OT module could accept the output of any other point cloud convolution. The dashed-blue arrows indicate that the point coordinates are passed to each layer to be able to compute convolutions on points.

Perfect World. We construct FLOT starting in the perfect world where $p + f = P q$, with $P \in \{0, 1\}^{n \times n}$ a permutation matrix. The role of FLOT is to estimate the permutation matrix P without the knowledge of f. In order to do so, we use tools from optimal transport. We interpret the motion of the points p_i as a displacement of mass between time t and $t + 1$. Each point in the first point cloud p is attributed a mass which we fix to n^{-1}. Each point q_j then receives

Input: cost matrix C; parameters $K, \lambda, \epsilon > 0$.
Output: transport plan T.
$\boldsymbol{a} \leftarrow 1n^{-1}$;
$\mathsf{U} \leftarrow \exp(- \mathsf{C}/\epsilon)$;
for $k = 1, \ldots, K$ **do**
$\quad \bigg|\; \boldsymbol{b} \leftarrow [(1n^{-1}) \oslash (\mathsf{U}^\intercal \boldsymbol{a})]^{\lambda/(\lambda+\epsilon)}$;
$\quad \bigg|\; \boldsymbol{a} \leftarrow [(1n^{-1}) \oslash (\mathsf{U}\, \boldsymbol{b})]^{\lambda/(\lambda+\epsilon)}$;
end
$\quad \mathsf{T} \leftarrow \mathrm{diag}(\boldsymbol{a})\, \mathsf{U}\, \mathrm{diag}(\boldsymbol{b})$;

Algorithm 1: Optimal transport module. The symbol $\oslash$ denote the element-wise division and multiplication, respectively.

the mass n^{-1} from $\boldsymbol{p}_i$ if $\boldsymbol{p}_i + \boldsymbol{f}_i = \boldsymbol{q}_j$, or, equivalently, if $\mathsf{P}_{ij} = 1$. We propose to estimate the permutation matrix P by computing a transport plan $\mathsf{T} \in \mathbb{R}^{n \times n}_+$ from $\boldsymbol{p}$ to $\boldsymbol{q}$ which satisfies

$$\mathsf{T} \in \underset{\mathsf{U} \in \mathbb{R}^{n \times n}_+}{\arg\min} \sum_{i,j=1}^{n} \mathsf{C}_{ij} \mathsf{U}_{ij} \quad \text{subject to} \quad \mathsf{U}\mathbf{1} = 1n^{-1} \text{ and } \mathsf{U}^\intercal\mathbf{1} = 1n^{-1}, \quad (1)$$

where $\mathbf{1} \in \mathbb{R}^n$ is the vector with all entries equal to 1, and $\mathsf{C}_{ij} \geqslant 0$ is the displacement cost from point $\boldsymbol{p}_i$ to point $\boldsymbol{q}_j$ [28]. Each scalar entry $\mathsf{T}_{ij} \geqslant 0$ of the transport plan T represents the mass that is transported from $\boldsymbol{p}_i$ to $\boldsymbol{q}_j$.

The first constraint in (1) imposes that the mass of each point $\boldsymbol{p}_i$ is entirely distributed over some of the points in $\boldsymbol{q}$. The second constraint imposes that each points $\boldsymbol{q}_j$ receives exactly a mass n^{-1} from some of the points $\boldsymbol{p}$. No mass is lost during the transfer. Note that in the hypothetical case where the cost matrix C would contain one zero entry per line and per column then the transport plan is null everywhere except on these entries and the mass constraints are immediately satisfied via a simple scaling of the transport plan. In this hypothetical situation, the mass constraints would be redundant for our application as it would have been enough to find the zero entries of C to estimate P. It is important to note the mass constraints play a role in the more realistic situation where "ambiguities" are present in C by ensuring that each point gives/receives a mass n^{-1} and that each point in $\boldsymbol{p}$ has a least one corresponding point in $\boldsymbol{q}$ and vice-versa.

We note that $n^{-1}\mathsf{P}$ satisfies the optimal transport constraints. We need now to construct C so that $\mathsf{T} = n^{-1}\mathsf{P}$.

Real World and Fast Estimation of T. In the real world, the equality $\boldsymbol{p} + \boldsymbol{f} = \mathsf{P}\boldsymbol{q}$ does not hold because the surfaces are not sampled at the same physical locations at t and $t + 1$ and because objects can (dis)appear due to occlusions. A consequence of these imperfections is that the mass preservation in (1) does not hold exactly: mass can (dis)appear. One solution to circumvent this issue is to relax the constraints in (1). Instead of solving (1), we propose to solve

$$\min_{U \in \mathbb{R}_+^{n \times n}} \left[\sum_{i,j=1}^n C_{ij}U_{ij} + \epsilon U_{ij} \left(\log U_{ij} - 1 \right) \right] + \lambda \, \mathrm{KL} \left(U\mathbf{1}, \frac{1}{n} \right) + \lambda \, \mathrm{KL} \left(U^\mathsf{T}\mathbf{1}, \frac{1}{n} \right),$$

$$(2)$$

where $\epsilon, \lambda \geq 0$, and KL denotes the KL-divergence. The term $U_{ij}(\log U_{ij} - 1)$ in (2) is an entropic regularisation on the transport plan. Its main purpose, in our case, is to allow the use of an efficient algorithm to estimate the transport plan: the Sinkhorn algorithm [7]. The version of this algorithm for the optimal transport problem (2) is derived in [6] and is presented in Algorithm 1. The parameter ϵ controls the amount of entropic regularisation. The smaller ϵ is, the sparser the transport plan is, hence finding sparse correspondences between p and q. The regularisation parameter λ adjust how much the transported mass deviates from the uniform distribution, allowing mass variation. One could let $\lambda \to +\infty$ to impose strict mass preservation.

Note that the mass regularisation is controlled by the power $\lambda/(\lambda+\epsilon)$ in Algorithm 1. This power tends to 1 when $\lambda \to +\infty$ to impose strict mass preservation and reaches 0 in absence of any regularisation. Instead of fixing the parameters ϵ, λ in advance, we let these parameters free and learn them by gradient descent along with the other networks' parameters.

We would like to recall that, in the perfect world, it is not necessary for the power $\lambda/(\lambda + \epsilon)$ to reach 1 to yield accurate results as the final quality is also driven by the quality of C. In a perfect situation where the cost would be perfectly trained with a bijective mapping already encoded in C by its zero entries, then any amount of mass regularisation is sufficient to reach accurate results. This follows from our remark at the end of the previous subsection but also from the discussion in the subsection below on the role of C and the mass regularisation. In a real situation, the cost is not perfectly trained and we expect the power $\lambda/(\lambda + \epsilon)$ to vary in the range of $(0, 1)$ after training, reaching values closer to 1 when trained in a perfect world setting and closer to 0 in presence of occlusions.

Learning the Transport Cost. An essential ingredient in (2) is the cost $C \in \mathbb{R}^{n \times n}$ where each entry C_{ij} encodes the similarity between p_i to point q_j. An obvious choice could be to take the Euclidean distance between each pair of points (p_i, q_j), i.e., $C_{ij} = \|p_i - q_j\|_2$, but this choice does not yield accurate results. In this work, we propose to learn the displacement costs by training a deep neural network $g : \mathbb{R}^{n \times 3} \to \mathbb{R}^{n \times c}$ that takes as input a point cloud and output a feature of size c for each input point. The entries of the cost matrix are then defined using the cosine distance between the features $g(p)_i, g(q)_j \in \mathbb{R}^c$ at points p_i and q_j, respectively:

$$C_{ij} = \left(1 - \frac{g(p)_i^\mathsf{T}\, g(q)_j}{\|g(p)_i\|_2 \, \|g(q)_j\|_2} \right) \cdot i_{\|\cdot\|_2 \leq d_{\max}} \left(p_i - q_j \right). \qquad (3)$$

The more similar the features $g(\boldsymbol{p})_i$ and $g(\boldsymbol{q})_j$ are, the less the cost of transporting a unit mass from $\boldsymbol{p}_i$ to $\boldsymbol{q}_j$ is. The indicator function

$$i_{\|\cdot\|_2 \leqslant d_{\max}} (\boldsymbol{p}_i - \boldsymbol{q}_j) = \begin{cases} 1 \text{ if } \|\boldsymbol{p}_i - \boldsymbol{q}_j\|_2 \leqslant d_{\max}, \\ +\infty \text{ otherwise}, \end{cases} \tag{4}$$

is used to prevent the algorithm to find correspondences between points too far away from each other. We set $d_{\max} = 10$ m.

In order to train the network g, we adopt the same strategy as, *e.g.*, in [9] to train generative models or in [31] for matching image features. The strategy consists in unrolling K iterations of Algorithm 1. This unrolled iterations constitute our OT module in Fig. 1. One can remark that the gradients can backpropagate through each step of this module and allow us to train g.

On the Role of C and of the Mass Regularisation. We gather in this paragraph the earlier discussions on the role of C and the mass regularisation. For the sake of the explanation, we come back in the perfect-world setting and consider (1). In this ideal situation, one could further dream that it is possible to train g perfectly such that C_{ij} is null for matching points, *i.e.*, when $\mathsf{P}_{ij} = 1$, and strictly positive otherwise. The transport plan would then satisfy $\mathsf{T} = n^{-1}\mathsf{P}$ with a null transport cost. However, one should note that the solution T would entirely be encoded in C up to a global scaling factor: the non-zero entries of T are at the zero entries of C. In that case, the mass transport constraints only adjust the scale of the entries in T. Such a perfect scenario is unlikely to occur but these considerations highlight that the cost matrix C could be exploited alone and could maybe be sufficient to find the appropriate correspondences between $\boldsymbol{p}$ and $\boldsymbol{q}$ for scene flow estimation. The mass transport regularisation plays a role in the more realistic case where ambiguities appears in C. The regularisation enforces, whatever the quality of C and with a "strength" controlled by λ, that the mass is distributed as uniformly as possible over all points. This avoids that some points in $\boldsymbol{p}$ are left with no matching point in $\boldsymbol{q}$, and vice-versa.

FLOT$_0$. FLOT$_0$ is a version of FLOT where only the cost matrix C is exploited to find correspondences between $\boldsymbol{p}$ and $\boldsymbol{q}$. This method is obtained when removing the mass transport regularisation in (2), *i.e.*, by setting $\lambda = 0$. In this limit, the "transport plan" satisfies

$$\mathsf{T} = \exp(-\,\mathsf{C}/\epsilon). \tag{5}$$

T is then used in the rest of the method as if it was the output of Algorithm 1.

3.2   Step 2: Flow Estimation from Soft-Correspondences

We obtained, in the previous step, a transport plan T that gives correspondences between the points of $\boldsymbol{p}, \boldsymbol{q}$. Our goal now is to exploit these correspondences to estimate the flow. As before, it is convenient to start in the perfect world and consider (1). In this setting, we have seen that $f = Pq - p$ and that, if g is well trained, we expect $n^{-1}P = T$. Therefore, an obvious estimate of the flow is

$$\tilde{f}_i = \sum_{j=1}^{n} P_{ij}\, q_j - p_i = \frac{1}{n^{-1}} \sum_{j=1}^{n} T_{ij}\, q_j - p_i = \frac{\sum_{j=1}^{n} T_{ij}\, q_j}{\sum_{j=1}^{n} T_{ij}} - p_i, \qquad (6)$$

where we exploited the fact that $\sum_{j=1}^{n} T_{ij} = n^{-1}$ in the last equality.

In the real world, the first equality in (6) does not hold. Yet, the last expression in (6) remains a sensible first estimation of the flow. Indeed, this computation is equivalent to computing, for each point p_i, a corresponding virtual point that is a barycentre of some points in q. The larger the transported mass T_{ij} from p_i to q_j is, the larger the contribution of q_j to this virtual point is. The difference between this virtual point and p_i gives an estimate of the flow f_i. This virtual point is a "guess" on the location of $p_i + f_i$ made knowing where the mass from p_i is transported in q.

However, we remark that the flow $\tilde{f}$ estimated in (6) is, necessarily, still imperfect as it is highly likely that some points in $p + f$ cannot be expressed as barycentres of the found corresponding points q. Indeed, some portion of objects visible in p might not visible any more in q due to the finite resolution in point cloud sampling. The flow in these missing regions cannot be reconstructed from q but has to be reconstructed using structural information available in p, relying on neighbouring information from the well sampled regions. Therefore, we refine the flow using a residual network:

$$f_{est} = \tilde{f} + h(\tilde{f}), \qquad (7)$$

where $h : \mathbb{R}^{n\times 3} \to \mathbb{R}^{n\times c}$ takes as inputs the estimated flow $\tilde{f}$ and uses convolutions defined on the point cloud p.

Let us finally conclude this section by highlighting the fact that, in the case of FLOT$_0$, (6) simplifies to

$$\tilde{f}_i = \frac{\sum_{j=1}^{n} \exp(-C_{ij}/\epsilon)\,(q_j - p_i)}{\sum_{j=1}^{n} \exp(-C_{ij}/\epsilon)}. \qquad (8)$$

On can remark that the OT module essentially reduces to an attention mechanism [37] in that case. The attention mechanism is thus a particular case of FLOT where the entropic regularisation ϵ plays the role of the softmax temperature. Let us mention that similar attention layers haved been showed effective in related problems such as rigid registration [42–44].

3.3 Training

The network's parameters, denoted by θ, and ϵ, γ are trained jointly under full supervision on annotated synthetic datasets of size L. Note that to enforce positivity of ϵ, γ, we learn their log values. A constant offset of 0.03 is applied to ϵ to avoid numerical instabilities in the exponential function during training.

The sole training loss is the ℓ_1-norm between the ground truth flow $\boldsymbol{f}$ and the estimated flow $\boldsymbol{f}_{\text{est}}$:

$$\min_{\theta} \frac{1}{3L} \sum_{l=1}^{L} \left\| \mathsf{M}^{(l)} \, (\boldsymbol{f}_{\text{est}}^{(\ell)} - \boldsymbol{f}^{(\ell)}) \right\|_1 , \tag{9}$$

where $\mathsf{M}^{(l)} \in \mathbb{R}^{n \times n}$ is a diagonal matrix encoding an annotated mask used to remove points where the flow is occluded.

We use a batchsize of 4 at $n = 2048$ and a batchsize of 1 at $n = 8192$ using Adam [13] and a starting learning rate of 0.001. The learning rate is kept constant unless specified in Sect. 4.

3.4 Similarities and Differences with Existing Techniques

A first main difference between FLOT and [11,15,46] is the number of parameters which is much smaller for FLOT (see Table 1). Another difference is that we do not use any downsampling and upsampling layers. Unlike [11,46], we do not use any multiscale analysis to find the correspondences between points. The information between point clouds is mixed only once, as in [15], but at the finest sampling resolution and without using skip connections between g and h.

We also notice that [11,15,46] rely on a MLP or a convnet applied on the concatenated input features to mix the information between both point clouds. The mixing function is learned and thus not explicit. It is harder to find how the correspondences are effectively done, *i.e.*, identify what input information is kept or not taken into consideration. In contrast, the mixing function in FLOT is explicit with only two scalars ϵ, λ adjusted to the training data and whose roles are clearly identified in the OT problem (2). The core of the OT module is a simple cross-correlation between input features, which is a module easy to interpret, study and visualise. Finally, among all the functions that the convnets/MLPs in [11,15,46] can approximate, it is unlikely that the resulting mixing function actually approximates the Sinkhorn algorithm, or an attention layer, after learning without further guidance than those of the training data.

4 Experiments

4.1 Datasets

As in related works, we train our network under full supervision using FlyingThings3D [19] and test it on FlyingThings3D and KITTI Scene Flow [22,23]. However, none of the datasets provide point clouds directly. This information needs to be extracted from the original data. There is at least two slightly different ways of extracting these 3D data, and we report results for both versions for a better assessment of the performance. The first version of the datasets are prepared[1] as in [11]. No occluded point remains in the processed point clouds. We

---

[1] Code and pretrained model available at https://github.com/laoreja/HPLFlowNet.

Table 1. Performance of FLOT on the validation sets of FT3D$_p$, FT3D$_s$, and FT3D$_o$ (top). Performance of FLOT measured at the output of the OT module, *i.e.*, before refinement by h, on FT3D$_p$ and FT3D$_s$ (bottom). The corresponding performance on FT3D$_o$ is in the supplementary material. We report average scores and, between parentheses, their standard deviations. Please refer to Sect. 4.3 for more details.

	Dataset	K	ϵ	$\lambda/(\lambda+\epsilon)$	EPE	AS	AR	Out.
With flow refinement		FLOT$_0$	0.03 (0.00)	0 (fixed)	0.0026 (0.0005)	99.56 (0.08)	99.69 (0.05)	0.44 (0.10)
	FT3D$_p$	1	0.03 (0.00)	0.70 (0.00)	0.0011 (0.0001)	99.83 (0.01)	99.89 (0.01)	0.17 (0.01)
		3	0.03 (0.00)	0.82 (0.00)	0.0009 (0.0001)	99.85 (0.01)	99.90 (0.01)	0.16 (0.01)
		5	0.03 (0.00)	0.88 (0.00)	0.0009 (0.0001)	99.84 (0.02)	99.90 (0.01)	0.17 (0.02)
		FLOT$_0$	0.03 (0.00)	0 (fixed)	0.0811 (0.0005)	50.32 (0.34)	83.08 (0.24)	52.15 (0.34)
	FT3D$_s$	1	0.03 (0.00)	0.64 (0.01)	0.0785 (0.0003)	50.91 (0.52)	83.67 (0.10)	51.73 (0.38)
		3	0.03 (0.00)	0.59 (0.00)	0.0786 (0.0010)	51.06 (0.95)	83.78 (0.35)	51.72 (0.76)
		5	0.03 (0.00)	0.56 (0.00)	0.0798 (0.0003)	49.77 (0.50)	83.39 (0.08)	52.58 (0.31)
		FLOT$_0$	0.03 (0.00)	0 (fixed)	0.1834 (0.0018)	21.94 (0.69)	52.79 (0.53)	77.19 (0.43)
	FT3D$_o$	1	0.03 (0.00)	0.50 (0.01)	0.1798 (0.0009)	22.01 (0.14)	53.39 (0.24)	76.77 (0.16)
		3	0.03 (0.00)	0.34 (0.00)	0.1797 (0.0014)	22.77 (0.53)	53.74 (0.54)	76.39 (0.43)
		5	0.03 (0.00)	0.35 (0.01)	0.1813 (0.0020)	22.64 (0.41)	53.58 (0.41)	76.52 (0.46)
No flow refinement		FLOT$_0$			0.0026 (0.0006)	99.59 (0.07)	99.70 (0.05)	0.42 (0.10)
	FT3D$_p$	1	*Same as above*		0.0010 (0.0001)	99.83 (0.01)	99.89 (0.01)	0.18 (0.01)
		3			0.0009 (0.0000)	99.85 (0.01)	99.90 (0.01)	0.16 (0.01)
		5			0.0010 (0.0001)	99.84 (0.03)	99.90 (0.01)	0.17 (0.02)
		FLOT$_0$			0.1789 (0.0004)	17.57 (0.07)	43.34 (0.08)	75.34 (0.07)
	FT3D$_s$	1	*Same as above*		0.1721 (0.0005)	18.24 (0.11)	44.64 (0.14)	74.54 (0.11)
		3			0.1764 (0.0003)	17.64 (0.07)	43.52 (0.10)	75.09 (0.07)
		5			0.1761 (0.0009)	17.68 (0.13)	43.60 (0.23)	75.07 (0.13)

denote these datasets FT3D$_s$ and KITTI$_s$. The second version of the datasets are the ones prepared[2] by [15] and denoted FT3D$_o$ and KITTI$_o$. These datasets contains points where the flow is occluded. These points are present at the input and output of the networks but are not taken into account to compute the training loss (9) nor the performance metrics, like in [15]. Further information about the datasets is in the supplementary material. Note that we keep aside 2000 examples from the original training sets of FT3D$_s$ and FT3D$_o$ as validation sets, which are used in Sect. 4.3.

4.2   Performance Metrics

We use the four metrics adopted in [11,15,46]: the end point error EPE; two measures of accuracy, denoted by AS and AR, computed with different thresholds on the EPE; a percentage of outliers also computed using a threshold on the EPE. The definition of these metrics is recalled in the supplementary material.

Let us highlight that the performance reported on KITTI$_s$ and KITTI$_o$ are obtained by using the model trained on FT3D$_s$ and FT3D$_o$, respectively without

---

[2] Code and datasets available at https://github.com/xingyul/flownet3d.

fine tuning. We do not adapt the model for any of the method. We nevertheless make sure that the xyz axes are in correspondence for all datasets.

4.3   Study of FLOT

We use FT3D$_s$, FT3D$_o$ and FT3D$_p$ to check what values the OT parameters ϵ, λ reach after training, to study the effect of K on the FLOT's performance and compare it with that of FLOT$_0$. FT3D$_p$ is exactly the same dataset as FT3D$_s$ except that we enforce $p + f = \mathsf{P}q$ when sampling the point to simulate the perfect world setting. The sole role of this ideal dataset is to confirm that the OT model holds in the perfect world, the starting point of our design.

For these experiments, training is done at $n = 2048$ for 40 epochs and takes about 9 h. Each model is trained 3 times starting from a different random draw of θ to take into account variations due to initialisation. Evaluation is performed at $n = 2048$ on the validation sets. Note that the n points are drawn at random also at validation time. To take into account this variability, validation is performed 5 different times with different draws of the points for each of the trained model. For each score and model, we thus have access to 15 values whose mean and standard deviation are reported in Table 1. We present the scores obtained before and after refinement by h.

First, we notice that $\epsilon = 0.03$ for all model after training. We recall that we applied a constant offset of 0.03 to prevent numerical errors occurring in Algorithm 1 in the exponential function when reaching to small value of ϵ. Hence, the entropic regularisation, or, equivalently, the temperature in FLOT$_0$, reaches its smallest possible value. Such small values favour sparse transport plans T, yielding sparse correspondences between p and q. An illustration of these sparse correspondences is provided in Fig. 2. We observe that the correspondences are accurate and that the mass is well concentrated around the target points, especially when these points are near corners of the object.

Second, the power $\lambda/(\lambda + \epsilon)$, which controls the mass regularisation, reaches higher values on FT3D$_p$ than FT3D$_o$. This is the expected behaviour as FT3D$_p$ contains no imperfection and FT3D$_o$ contains occlusions. The values reached on FT3D$_s$ are in between those reached on FT3D$_p$ than FT3D$_o$. This is also the expected behaviour as FT3D$_s$ is free of occlusions and the only imperfections are the different sampling of the scene as t and $t + 1$.

Third, on FT3D$_p$, FLOT reduces by 2 the EPE compared to FLOT$_0$, which nevertheless already yields good results. Increasing K from 1 to 3 further reduces the error and stabilises at $K = 5$. This validates the OT model in our the perfect world setting: the OT optimum and perfect world optimum coincide.

Fourth, on FT3D$_s$ and FT3D$_o$, the average scores are better for FLOT than FLOT$_0$, except for two metrics at $K = 5$ on FT3D$_s$. The nevertheless good performance of FLOT$_0$ indicates that most of it is due to the trained transport cost C. On FT3D$_s$ and FT3D$_o$, changing K from 1 to 3 has less impact on the EPE than on FT3D$_p$. We also detect a slight decrease of performance when increasing K from 3 to 5. The OT model (2) can only be an approximate model of the (simulated) real-world. The real-world optimum and OT optimum do not

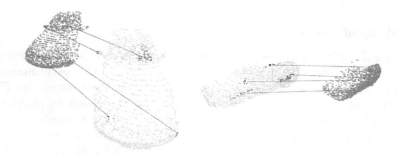

Fig. 2. Illustration of correspondences, found by FLOT ($K = 1$) trained on $n = 8192$ (see Sect. 4.4), between p and q in two different scenes of KITTI$_s$. We isolated one car in each of the scenes for better visualisation. The point cloud p captured at time t is represented in orange. The lines show the correspondence between a query point p_i and the corresponding point q_{j*} in q on which most the mass is transported: $j^* = \text{argmax}_j \, T_{ij}$. The colormap on q represents the values in T_i where yellow corresponds to 0 and blue indicates the maximum entry in T_i and show how the mass is concentrated around q_{j*}. (Color figure online)

Table 2. Performance on FT3D$_s$ and KITTI$_s$. The scores of FlowNet3D and HPLFlowNet are obtained from [11]. We also report the scores of PointPWC-Net available in [46], as well as those obtained using the official implementation[†]. Italic entries are for methods publicly available but not yet published at submission time.

Dataset	Method	EPE	AS	AR	Out.	Size (MB)
FT3D$_s$	FlowNet3D [15]	0.114	41.2	77.1	60.2	15
	HPLFlowNet [11]	0.080	61.4	85.5	42.9	77
	FLOT ($K = 1$)	**0.052**	**73.2**	**92.7**	**35.7**	**0.44**
	PointPWC-Net [46]	*0.059*	*73.8*	*92.8*	*34.2*	*30*
	PointPWC-Net[†]	*0.055*	*79.0*	*94.4*	*29.8*	*30*
KITTI$_s$	FlowNet3D [15]	0.177	37.4	66.8	52.7	15
	HPLFlowNet [11]	0.117	47.8	77.8	41.0	77
	FLOT ($K = 1$)	**0.056**	**75.5**	**90.8**	**24.2**	**0.44**
	PointPWC-Net [46]	*0.069*	*72.8*	*88.8*	*26.5*	*30*
	PointPWC-Net[†]	*0.067*	*78.5*	*90.6*	*22.8*	*30*

coincide. Increasing K brings us closer to the OT optimum but not necessarily always closer to the real-world optimum. K becomes an hyper-parameter that should be adjusted. In the following experiments, we use $K = 1$ or $K = 3$.

Finally, the absence of h has no effect on the performance on FT3D$_p$, with FLOT still performing better than FLOT$_0$. This shows that OT module is able to estimate accurately the ideal permutation matrix P on its own and that the residual network h is not needed in this ideal setting. However, h plays a important role on the more realistic datasets FT3D$_s$ and FT3D$_o$, with an EPE divided by around 2 when present.

4.4   Performance on FT3D$_s$ and KITTI$_s$

We compare the performance achieved by FLOT and the alternative methods on FT3D$_s$ and KITTI$_s$ in Table 2. We train FLOT using $n = 8192$ points, as in [11,46]. The learning rate is set to 0.001 for 50 epochs before dividing it by 10 and continue training for 10 more epochs.

The scores of FlowNet3D and HPLFlowNet are obtained directly from [11]. We report the scores of PointPWC-net available in [46], as well as the better scores we obtained using the associated code and pretrained model.[3] The model sizes are obtained from the supplementary material of [15] for FlowNet3D, and from the pretrained models provided by [11] and [46]. HPLFlowNet, PointPWC-Net and FLOT contain 19 M, 7.7 M, and 0.11 M parameters, respectively.

FLOT performs better than FlowNet3D and HPLFlowNet on both FT3D$_s$ and KITTI$_s$. FLOT achieves a slightly better EPE than PointPWC-Net on KITTI$_s$ and a similar one on FT3D$_s$. However, PointPWC-Net achieves better accuracy and has less outliers. FLOT is the method that uses the less trainable parameters (69 times less than PointPWC-Net).

We illustrate in Fig. 3 the quality of the scene flow estimation for two scenes of KITTI$_s$. We notice that FLOT aligns correctly all the objects. We also remark

Table 3. Performance on FT3D$_o$ and KITTI$_o$.

Dataset	Method	EPE	AS	AR	Out.
FT3D$_o$	FlowNet3D [15]	0.160	25.4	58.5	78.9
	FLOT$_0$	0.160	33.8	63.8	70.5
	FLOT ($K = 1$)	**0.156**	**34.3**	**64.3**	**70.0**
	FLOT ($K = 3$)	0.161	32.3	62.7	71.7
KITTI$_o$	FlowNet3D [15]	0.173	27.6	60.9	64.9
	FLOT$_0$	**0.106**	**45.3**	73.7	46.7
	FLOT ($K = 1$)	0.110	41.9	72.1	48.6
	FLOT ($K = 3$)	0.107	45.1	**74.0**	**46.3**

---

[3] Code and pretrained model available at https://github.com/DylanWusee/PointPWC.

Inputs p (orange) and q (blue)   Ground truth $p + f$ (orange) and input q (blue)

Estimated $p + \tilde{f}$ (orange) and input q (blue)   Refined $p + f_{\mathrm{est}}$ (orange) and input q (blue)

Inputs p (orange) and q (blue)   Ground truth $p + f$ (orange) and input q (blue)

Estimated $p + \tilde{f}$ (orange) and input q (blue)   Refined $p + f_{\mathrm{est}}$ (orange) and input q (blue)

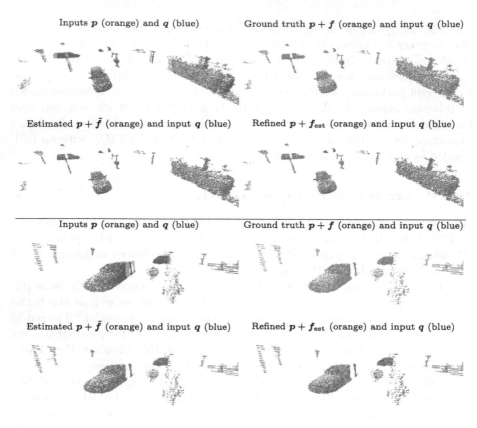

Fig. 3. Two scene from KITTI$_{\mathrm{s}}$ with input point clouds p, q along with the ground truth $p + f$, estimated $p + \tilde{f}$ and refined $p + f_{\mathrm{est}}$ using FLOT ($K = 1$) at $n = 8192$. (Color figure online)

that the flow $\tilde{f}$ estimated at the output of the OT module is already of good quality, even though the performance scores are improved after refinement.

4.5 Performance on FT3D$_{\mathrm{o}}$ and KITTI$_{\mathrm{o}}$

We present another comparison between FlowNet3D and FLOT using FT3D$_{\mathrm{o}}$ and KITTI$_{\mathrm{o}}$, originally used in [15]. We train FlowNet3D using the associated official implementation. We train FLOT and FLOT$_0$ on $n = 2048$ points using a learning rate of 0.001 for 340 epochs before dividing it by 10 and continue training for 60 more epochs.

The performance of both methods is reported in Table 3. We notice that FLOT and FLOT$_0$ achieve a better accuracy than FlowNet3D with an improvement of AS of 8.8 points on FT3D$_{\mathrm{o}}$ and 17.7 on KITTI$_{\mathrm{o}}$. The numbers of outliers are reduced by the same amount. FLOT at $K = 1$ performs the best with FLOT$_0$

close behind. On $KITTI_o$, the best performing model are those of $FLOT_0$ and FLOT at $K = 3$.

The reader can remark that the results of FlowNet3D are similar to those reported in [15] but worse on $KITTI_o$. The evaluation on $KITTI_o$ is done differently in [15]: the scene is divided into chunks and the scene flow is estimated within each chunk before a global aggregation. In the present work, we keep the evaluation method consistent with that of Sect. 4.4 by following the same procedure as in [11,46]: the trained model is evaluated by processing the full scene in one pass using n random points from the scene.

5   Conclusion

We proposed and studied a method for scene flow estimation built using optimal transport tools. It can achieves similar performance to that of the best performing method while requiring much less parameters. We also showed that the learned transport cost is responsible for most of the performance. This yields a simpler method $FLOT_0$, which performs nearly as well as FLOT.

We also noticed that the presence of occlusions affects the performance of FLOT negatively. The proposed relaxation of the mass constraints in Eq. (2) permits us to limit the impact of these occlusions on the performance but does not handle them explicitly. There is thus room for improvements by detecting, *e.g.*, by analysing the effective transported mass, and treating occlusions explicitly.

References

1. Basha, T., Moses, Y., Kiryati, N.: Multi-view scene flow estimation: a view centered variational approach. In: Conference on Computer Vision and Pattern Recognition, pp. 1506–1513. IEEE (2010)
2. Battrawy, R., Schuster, R., Wasenmller, O., Rao, Q., Stricker, D.: LiDAR-Flow: dense scene flow estimation from sparse lidar and stereo images. In: International Conference on Intelligent Robots and Systems, pp. 7762–7769. IEEE (2019)
3. Baur, S.A., Moosmann, F., Wirges, S., Rist, C.B.: Real-time 3D LiDAR flow for autonomous vehicles. In: Intelligent Vehicles Symposium, pp. 1288–1295. IEEE (2019)
4. Behl, A., Paschalidou, D., Donné, S., Geiger, A.: PointFlowNet: learning representations for rigid motion estimation from point clouds. In: Conference on Computer Vision and Pattern Recognition, pp. 7962–7971. IEEE (2019)
5. Chen, Y., Pock, T.: Trainable nonlinear reaction diffusion: a flexible framework for fast and effective image restoration. IEEE Trans. Pattern Anal. Mach. Intell. **39**(6), 1256–1272 (2017)
6. Chizat, L., Peyré, G., Schmitzer, B., Vialard, F.X.: Scaling algorithms for unbalanced transport problems. Math. Comput. **87**, 2563–2609 (2018)
7. Cuturi, M.: Sinkhorn distances: lightspeed computation of optimal transport. In: Burges, C.J.C., Bottou, L., Welling, M., Ghahramani, Z., Weinberger, K.Q. (eds.) Advances in Neural Information Processing Systems, pp. 2292–2300. Curran Associates, Inc. (2013)

8. Dewan, A., Caselitz, T., Tipaldi, G.D., Burgard, W.: Rigid scene flow for 3D LiDAR scans. In: International Conference on Intelligent Robots and Systems (IROS), pp. 1765–1770. IEEE (2016)
9. Genevay, A., Peyré, G., Cuturi, M.: Learning generative models with sinkhorn divergences. In: Storkey, A., Perez-Cruz, F. (eds.) International Conference on Artificial Intelligence and Statistics. Proceedings of Machine Learning Research, vol. 84, pp. 1608–1617. PMLR (2018)
10. Gregor, K., LeCun, Y.: Learning fast approximations of sparse coding. In: International Conference on Machine Learning, pp. 399–406 (2010)
11. Gu, X., Wang, Y., Wu, C., Lee, Y.J., Wang, P.: HPLFlowNet: hierarchical permutohedral lattice FlowNet for scene flow estimation on large-scale point clouds. In: Conference on Computer Vision and Pattern Recognition, pp. 3249–3258. IEEE (2019)
12. Hadfield, S., Bowden, R.: Kinecting the dots: particle based scene flow from depth sensors. In: International Conference on Computer Vision, pp. 2290–2295. IEEE (2011)
13. Kingma, D.P., Adam, J.B.: Adam : a method for stochastic optimization. In: International Conference on Learning Representations. arXiv.org (2015)
14. Liu, J., Sun, Y., Eldeniz, C., Gan, W., An, H., Kamilov, U.S.: RARE: image reconstruction using deep priors learned without ground truth. J. Sel. Top. Signal Process. **14**(6), 1088–1099 (2020)
15. Liu, X., Qi, C.R., Guibas, L.J.: FlowNet3D: learning scene flow in 3D point clouds. In: Conference on Computer Vision and Pattern Recognition, pp. 529–537. IEEE (2019)
16. Ma, W.C., Wang, S., Hu, R., Xiong, Y., Urtasun, R.: Deep rigid instance scene flow. In: Conference on Computer Vision and Pattern Recognition, pp. 3609–3617. IEEE (2019)
17. Mardani, M., et al.: Neural proximal gradient descent for compressive imaging. In: Bengio, S., Wallach, H., Larochelle, H., Grauman, K., Cesa-Bianchi, N., Garnett, R. (eds.) Advances in Neural Information Processing Systems, pp. 9573–9583. Curran Associates, Inc. (2018)
18. Maretic, H.P., Gheche, M.E., Chierchia, G., Frossard, P.: GOT: an optimal transport framework for graph comparison. In: Wallach, H., Larochelle, H., Beygelzimer, A., d'Alché-Buc, F., Fox, E., Garnett, R. (eds.) Advances in Neural Information Processing Systems, pp. 13876–13887. Curran Associates, Inc. (2019)
19. Mayer, N., et al.: A large dataset to train convolutional networks for disparity, optical flow, and scene flow estimation. In: Conference on Computer Vision and Pattern Recognition, pp. 4040–4048. IEEE (2016)
20. Meinhardt, T., Moller, M., Hazirbas, C., Cremers, D.: Learning proximal operators: using denoising networks for regularizing inverse imaging problems. In: International Conference on Computer Vision, pp. 1799–1808. IEEE (2017)
21. Mémoli, F.: Gromov-wasserstein distances and the metric approach to object matching. Found. Comput. Math. **11**(4), 417–487 (2011)
22. Menze, M., Heipke, C., Geiger, A.: Joint 3D estimation of vehicles and scene flow. In: ISPRS Workshop on Image Sequence Analysis (2015)
23. Menze, M., Heipke, C., Geiger, A.: Object scene flow. ISPRS J. Photogrammetry Remote Sens. **140**, 60–76 (2018)
24. Metzler, C., Mousavi, A., Baraniuk, R.: Learned D-AMP: principled neural network based compressive image recovery. In: Guyon, I., et al. (eds.) Advances in Neural Information Processing Systems, pp. 1772–1783. Curran Associates, Inc. (2017)

25. Mittal, H., Okorn, B., Held, D.: Just go with the flow: self-supervised scene flow estimation. In: Conference on Computer Vision and Pattern Recognition. IEEE (2020)
26. Mousavi, A., Baraniuk, R.G.: Learning to invert: signal recovery via deep convolutional networks. In: International Conference on Acoustics, Speech and Signal Processing, pp. 2272–2276. IEEE (2017)
27. Nikolentzos, G., Meladianos, P., Vazirgiannis, M.: Matching node embeddings for graph similarity. In: AAAI Conference on Artificial Intelligence, pp. 2429–2435 (2017)
28. Peyré, G., Cuturi, M.: Computational optimal transport: with applications to data science. Found. Trends Mach. Learn. **11**(5–6), 355–607 (2019)
29. Peyré, G., Cuturi, M., Solomon, J.: Gromov-Wasserstein averaging of kernel and distance matrices. In: Balcan, M.F., Weinberger, K.Q. (eds.) International Conference on Machine Learning, vol. 48, pp. 2664–2672. PMLR (2016)
30. Qi, C.R., Yi, L., Su, H., Guibas, L.J.: PointNet++: deep hierarchical feature learning on point sets in a metric space. In: Guyon, I., et al. (eds.) Advances in Neural Information Processing Systems, pp. 5099–5108. Curran Associates, Inc. (2017)
31. Sarlin, P.E., DeTone, D., Malisiewicz, T., Rabinovich, A.: SuperGlue: learning feature matching with graph neural networks. In: Conference on Computer Vision and Pattern Recognition. IEEE (2020)
32. Shao, L., Shah, P., Dwaracherla, V., Bohg, J.: Motion-based object segmentation based on dense RGB-D scene flow. Robot. Autom. Lett. **3**(4), 3797–3804 (2018)
33. Sun, D., Yang, X., Liu, M.Y., Kautz, J.: PWC-Net: CNNs for optical flow using pyramid, warping, and cost volume. In: Conference on Computer Vision and Pattern Recognition, pp. 8934–8943. IEEE (2018)
34. Titouan, V., Courty, N., Tavenard, R., Laetitia, C., Flamary, R.: Optimal transport for structured data with application on graphs. In: Chaudhuri, K., Salakhutdinov, R. (eds.) International Conference on Machine Learning, vol. 97, pp. 6275–6284. PMLR (2019)
35. Ushani, A.K., Wolcott, R.W., Walls, J.M., Eustice, R.M.: A learning approach for real-time temporal scene flow estimation from LIDAR data. In: International Conference on Robotics and Automation, pp. 5666–5673. IEEE (2017)
36. Ushani, A.K., Eustice, R.M.: Feature learning for scene flow estimation from LIDAR. In: Billard, A., Dragan, A., Peters, J., Morimoto, J. (eds.) Conference on Robot Learning. Proceedings of Machine Learning Research, vol. 87, pp. 283–292. PMLR (2018)
37. Vaswani, A., et al.: Attention is all you need. In: Guyon, I., et al. (eds.) Advances in Neural Information Processing Systems 30, pp. 5998–6008. Curran Associates, Inc. (2017)
38. Vedula, S., Baker, S., Rander, P., Collins, R., Kanade, T.: Three-dimensional scene flow. In: International Conference on Computer Vision, vol. 2, pp. 722–729. IEEE (1999)
39. Vogel, C., Schindler, K., Roth, S.: Piecewise rigid scene flow. In: International Conference on Computer Vision, pp. 1377–1384. IEEE (2013)
40. Wang, S., Suo, S., Ma, W.C., Pokrovsky, A., Urtasun, R.: Deep parametric continuous convolutional neural networks. In: Conference on Computer Vision and Pattern Recognition, pp. 2589–2597. IEEE (2018)
41. Wang, S., Fidler, S., Urtasun, R.: Proximal deep structured models. In: Lee, D.D., Sugiyama, M., Luxburg, U.V., Guyon, I., Garnett, R. (eds.) Advances in Neural Information Processing Systems, pp. 865–873. Curran Associates, Inc. (2016)

42. Wang, X., Jabri, A., Efros, A.A.: Learning correspondence from the cycle-consistency of time. In: Conference on Computer Vision and Pattern Recognition, pp. 2566–2576. IEEE (2019)

43. Wang, Y., Solomon, J.M.: Deep closest point: learning representations for point cloud registration. In: International Conference on Computer Vision, pp. 3522–3531. IEEE (2019)

44. Wang, Y., Solomon, J.M.: PRNet: self-supervised learning for partial-to-partial registration. In: Wallach, H., Larochelle, H., Beygelzimer, A., d'Alché-Buc, F., Fox, E., Garnett, R. (eds.) Advances in Neural Information Processing Systems, pp. 8814–8826. Curran Associates, Inc. (2019)

45. Wedel, A., Rabe, C., Vaudrey, T., Brox, T., Franke, U., Cremers, D.: Efficient dense scene flow from sparse or dense stereo data. In: Forsyth, D., Torr, P., Zisserman, A. (eds.) European Conference on Computer Vision, pp. 739–751. Springer, Heidelberg (2008). https://doi.org/10.1007/978-3-540-88682-2_56

46. Wu, W., Wang, Z., Li, Z., Liu, W., Fuxin, L.: PointPWC-Net: a coarse-to-fine network for supervised and self-supervised scene flow estimation on 3D point clouds. arXiv:1911.12408v1 (2019)

47. Zou, C., He, B., Zhu, M., Zhang, L., Zhang, J.: Learning motion field of LiDAR point cloud with convolutional networks. Pattern Recogn. Lett. **125**, 514–520 (2019)

Accurate Reconstruction of Oriented 3D Points Using Affine Correspondences

Carolina Raposo[1,2]([✉]) [ID] and Joao P. Barreto[1] [ID]

[1] Institute of Systems and Robotics, University of Coimbra, Coimbra, Portugal
{carolinaraposo,jpbar}@isr.uc.pt
[2] Perceive3D, Coimbra, Portugal

Abstract. Affine correspondences (ACs) have been an active topic of research, namely for the recovery of surface normals. However, current solutions still suffer from the fact that even state-of-the-art affine feature detectors are inaccurate, and ACs are often contaminated by large levels of noise, yielding poor surface normals. This article provides new formulations for achieving epipolar geometry-consistent ACs, that, besides leading to linear solvers that are up to 30× faster than the state-of-the-art alternatives, allow for a fast refinement scheme that significantly improves the quality of the noisy ACs. In addition, a tracker that automatically enforces the epipolar geometry is proposed, with experiments showing that it significantly outperforms competing methods in situations of low texture. This opens the way to application domains where the scenes are typically low textured, such as during arthroscopic procedures.

Keywords: Affine correspondences · Photoconsistency optimization · Tracking · Surface normal estimation

1 Introduction

Affine correspondences (ACs) encode important information about the scene geometry and researchers have been actively exploiting them for solving very different Computer Vision tasks, ranging from plane segmentation to the estimation of radial distortion parameters. In particular, Perdoch *et al.* [16] generate point correspondences from ACs for estimating the epipolar geometry, Bentolila and Francos [6] estimate the fundamental matrix from 3 ACs, Raposo and Barreto [18,20] use them to estimate the essential matrix and perform plane segmentation, Pritts *et al.* [17] retrieve distortion parameters from affine maps, and Hajder and Barath [9] accomplish planar motion estimation from a single AC. More recently, the estimation of affine transformations from two directions if the epipolar geometry is known has been proposed in [15].

Electronic supplementary material The online version of this chapter (https://doi.org/10.1007/978-3-030-58604-1_33) contains supplementary material, which is available to authorized users.

© Springer Nature Switzerland AG 2020
A. Vedaldi et al. (Eds.): ECCV 2020, LNCS 12373, pp. 545–560, 2020.
https://doi.org/10.1007/978-3-030-58604-1_33

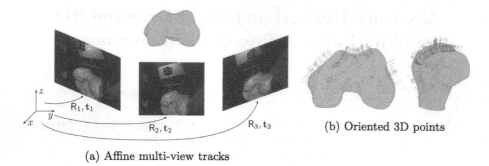

(a) Affine multi-view tracks   (b) Oriented 3D points

Fig. 1. a) A calibrated camera whose pose is known at all times observes a 3D scene from different viewpoints. ACs extracted across multiple frames are shown and identified with colors. b) For each multi-view track of affine maps, the proposed method provides an oriented 3D point, i.e., its 3D location and normal to the surface. Reconstructed 3D points are shown in black and red arrows represent normals. (Color figure online)

The fact that an AC encodes information about the normal to the surface has motivated a series of recent works to estimate normals from ACs when the epipolar geometry is known [2–4,7,8], with important applications in the fields of object detection, 3D registration and segmentation. In general terms, two families of algorithms exist: one that estimates the surface normal directly from the extracted ACs [2,4,8] and another that starts by correcting the AC to be consistent with the epipolar geometry and afterwards retrieves the normal [3,7]. All solutions in the second family of algorithms perform an initial correction of the point correspondence and afterwards modify the affine transformation. When considering highly textured scenes, this two-step process is reliable since point correspondences are usually accurate and it is the affine component that is significantly affected by noise. However, when working in low textured scenes, it cannot be assumed that point correspondences are known or can be corrected by triangulation [10] since accurate ones are difficult to extract, with methods typically yielding very sparse and inaccurate reconstructions.

This article provides new insights on how to solve the problem of obtaining 3D oriented points, i.e. 3D points augmented with the information about the surface normal, from ACs. In addition, schemes for the refinement and tracking of ACs based on photoconsistency that automatically enforce the epipolar constraints and that work well in situations of low texture are proposed. A valid alternative would be to formulate the problem using the plane equation to represent homographies. However, working directly with ACs enables the extracted affine regions to be used as the integration domain in photoconsistency. In the case of homographies, the optimal integration region depends on the scene geometry, which is unknown and not straightforward to determine.

Being able to obtain accurate and rich reconstructions of 3D oriented points in low-texture scenes greatly benefits several monocular vision algorithms. Examples include the reconstruction of indoor scenes, which are typically dominated by large low-textured planes, and the detection and 3D registration of objects with low texture. In particular, this would add significant value to the domain of arthroscopic procedures where obtaining 3D reconstructions of bone surface solely from the arthroscopic images is difficult mainly due to their inherent low texture [21]. In summary, the contributions are the following:

Fast Correction of ACs and Normal Estimation: Building on a recent study [20] that provides the relation between an AC and the epipolar geometry, we show how to write the AC as a function of only two unknown parameters (2 degrees of freedom (DoF)), in case the point correspondence is fixed, and three unknown parameters (3 DoF) otherwise, and propose fast linear solvers for enforcing noisy ACs to be consistent with the epipolar geometry. For the 2-DoF case, the multi-view solution comes in a straightforward manner. In addition, a fast linear solver for the estimation of normals from multiple frames is also presented.

Multi-view Refinement of ACs Consistent with the Epipolar Geometry: A fast method for multi-view photoconsistency refinement of the affine transformation of the AC that is the first to automatically enforce the epipolar geometry is proposed. Experiments show that it significantly improves the quality of the estimated normals, providing accurate oriented 3D points (Fig. 1).

Tracking of ACs Consistent with the Epipolar Geometry: We present the first formulation for correction of ACs to be consistent with the epipolar geometry that also corrects the point depth, avoiding the common two-step process [3] of fixing the point correspondence and the affine frame sequentially. Building on this formulation, a novel tracker that enables the accurate reconstruction of oriented 3D points in low textured scenes, outperforming a standard KLT tracker [1], is proposed.

2   Epipolar Geometry-Consistent ACs

Let $(\mathbf{x}, \mathbf{y}, \mathsf{A})$ be an affine correspondence (AC) such that the patches surrounding $\mathbf{x}$ and $\mathbf{y}$ are related by a non-singular 2×2 matrix A, with

$$\mathbf{x} = \begin{bmatrix} x_1 \ x_2 \end{bmatrix}^\mathsf{T}, \mathbf{y} = \begin{bmatrix} y_1 \ y_2 \end{bmatrix}^\mathsf{T}, \mathsf{A} = \begin{bmatrix} a_1 \ a_3 \\ a_2 \ a_4 \end{bmatrix}. \tag{1}$$

A point correspondence $(\mathbf{u}, \mathbf{v})$ in the patch is related by $\mathbf{v} = \mathsf{A}\mathbf{u} + \mathbf{b}$, with $\mathbf{b} = \mathbf{y} - \mathsf{A}\mathbf{x}$. As demonstrated in [20], an AC is consistent with the epipolar geometry if the following is verified:

$$\begin{bmatrix} x_1 y_1 & x_1 y_2 & x_1 & x_2 y_1 & x_2 y_2 & x_2 \ y_1 \ y_2 \ 1 \\ a_3 x_1 & a_4 x_1 & 0 & y_1 + a_3 x_2 & y_2 + a_4 x_2 & 1 \ a_3 \ a_4 \ 0 \\ y_1 + a_1 x_1 \ y_2 + a_2 x_1 & 1 & a_1 x_2 & a_2 x_2 & 0 \ a_1 \ a_2 \ 0 \end{bmatrix} \mathsf{E}(:) = \mathbf{0}, \tag{2}$$

with $\mathsf{D}(:)$ denoting the vectorization of matrix D by columns and E being the essential matrix.

From the relation $\mathbf{y} = A\mathbf{x} + \mathbf{b}$, Eq. 2 can be written as

$$M(E, \mathbf{x})\ [\mathbf{m}^\mathsf{T}\ \ 1]^\mathsf{T} = \mathbf{0}, \tag{3}$$

where M only depends on the essential matrix E and the point in the first image $\mathbf{x}$, and $\mathbf{m} = [A(:)^\mathsf{T}\ \ \mathbf{b}^\mathsf{T}]^\mathsf{T}$. By taking the null space of M, whose dimension is 3×7, a basis for the full AC $\underline{A} = [A\ \ \mathbf{b}]$ is obtained, and thus $\underline{A}$ can be written as a linear combination of this null space:

$$\underline{A}(:) = N_{6\times 4}\ [\underline{\alpha}^\mathsf{T}\ \ 1]^\mathsf{T}, \tag{4}$$

with $N_{6\times 4}$ being the matrix that is obtained by removing the last row of the null space matrix of $M_{3\times 7}$ and $\underline{\alpha}$ being the set of unknown parameters $\underline{\alpha}^\mathsf{T} = [\alpha_1\ \ \alpha_2\ \ \alpha_3]$. It comes in a straightforward manner that an AC $\tilde{\underline{A}}$ extracted from a pair of images can be corrected to an AC $\underline{A}$ that is consistent with the epipolar geometry by finding the solution $\underline{\alpha}^*$ to the system $N_{6\times 4}[\underline{\alpha}^{*\mathsf{T}}\ \ 1]^\mathsf{T} = \tilde{\underline{A}}(:)$ in the least-squares sense and afterwards computing $\underline{A} = N_{6\times 4}[\underline{\alpha}^{*\mathsf{T}}\ \ 1]^\mathsf{T}$.

As mentioned in the introduction, when extracting ACs in real scenarios, the level of noise present in the affine component is significantly larger than the one that affects the point correspondence. Thus, it may be desirable to assume that the point correspondence $(\mathbf{x}, \mathbf{y})$ is known, and only the affine component A is to be corrected to be consistent with the epipolar geometry. In this case, the problem is simplified since the two bottom equations of the system of Eqs. 2 can be written as

$$P(E, \mathbf{x}, \mathbf{y})\ [A(:)^\mathsf{T}\ \ 1]^\mathsf{T} = \mathbf{0}, \tag{5}$$

where P is a 2×5 matrix that only depends on the essential matrix E and the point correspondence $(\mathbf{x}, \mathbf{y})$. By taking the null space of P, the following is obtained

$$A(:) = Q_{4\times 3}[\alpha^\mathsf{T}\ \ 1]^\mathsf{T}, \tag{6}$$

where Q is the matrix that is obtained by removing the last row of the null space of P, having the following format

$$Q = \begin{bmatrix} q_1 & 0 & q_2 \\ 1 & 0 & 0 \\ 0 & q_1 & q_3 \\ 0 & 1 & 0 \end{bmatrix}. \tag{7}$$

In this case, the number of degrees of freedom (DoF) is 2, i.e., $\alpha = [\alpha_1\ \ \alpha_2]^\mathsf{T}$. The corrected AC is estimated similarly to the 3-DoF case.

2.1   Extension to the Multi-view Case

2-DoF Formulation. Consider a 3-view affine track consisting of two ACs $(\mathbf{x}, \mathbf{y}, A)$ and $(\mathbf{y}, \mathbf{z}, B)$ that relate patches in frames 1 and 2 and frames 2 and 3, respectively. By assuming that the point correspondences are fixed, it is possible to correct ACs A and B independently by performing as previously described.

However, a multi-view formulation for correcting one AC using information from more than two views simultaneously yields more accurate results [7].

This section proposes a new linear solver for accomplishing this task. Let $(\mathbf{x}, \mathbf{z}, \mathsf{C})$ be the AC that relates the patch in frame 1 surrounding $\mathbf{x}$ with the patch in frame 3 surrounding $\mathbf{z}$, so that $\mathsf{C} = \mathsf{BA}$. By representing each AC as in Eq. 6, i. e., $\mathsf{A}(:) = \mathsf{Q_A}[\alpha^{\mathsf{T}} \quad 1]^{\mathsf{T}}$, $\mathsf{B}(:) = \mathsf{Q_B}[\beta^{\mathsf{T}} \quad 1]^{\mathsf{T}}$ and $\mathsf{C}(:) = \mathsf{Q_C}[\gamma^{\mathsf{T}} \quad 1]^{\mathsf{T}}$, it is possible to write the unknown parameters β and γ as a function of α so that the latter can be estimated using the information from all three views:

$$
\begin{aligned}
\beta_1 &= \lambda_1\alpha_1 + \lambda_2\alpha_2/\lambda_3\alpha_1 + \lambda_4\alpha_2 \\
\beta_2 &= \lambda_5\alpha_1 + \lambda_6\alpha_2 + \lambda_7/\lambda_3\alpha_1 + \lambda_4\alpha_2 \\
\gamma_1 &= \lambda_8\alpha_1 + \lambda_9 \\
\gamma_2 &= \lambda_8\alpha_2 + \lambda_{10}
\end{aligned}
\tag{8}
$$

where $\lambda_i, i = 1, \ldots, 10$ are parameters that only depend on the known matrices $\mathsf{Q_A}$, $\mathsf{Q_B}$ and $\mathsf{Q_C}$.

Since the relationship between γ and α is linear, a linear system of equations relating ACs A and C with the unknown parameters α,

$$
\mathsf{L}[\alpha^{\mathsf{T}} \quad 1]^{\mathsf{T}} = [\mathsf{A}(:)^{\mathsf{T}} \quad \mathsf{C}(:)^{\mathsf{T}}]^{\mathsf{T}},
\tag{9}
$$

can be written, where

$$
\mathsf{L} = \begin{bmatrix} & \mathsf{Q_A} & \\ \lambda_8\mathsf{Q}_{\mathsf{C}}^{[1,2]} & \mathsf{Q_C}[\lambda_9 & \lambda_{10} & 1]^{\mathsf{T}} \end{bmatrix},
\tag{10}
$$

with $\mathsf{Q}_{\mathsf{C}}^{[1,2]}$ denoting columns 1 and 2 of matrix $\mathsf{Q_C}$. This formulation can be extended to more than 3 views in a straightforward manner by performing similarly for each new frame and stacking the new equations to the linear system 9.

3-DoF Formulation. Performing multi-view correction of ACs in the general case, i.e., when it is not assumed that the point correspondences are known and thus the full AC $\underline{\mathsf{A}}$ is accounted for, is possible but not as simple as described for the 2-DoF case. The reason for this is that, when attempting to follow a procedure analogous to the 2-DoF case, since point $\mathbf{y}$ is not known, it becomes impossible to directly obtain a representation of $\underline{\mathsf{B}}$ as in Eq. 4. However, $\mathbf{y}$ can be written as $\mathbf{y} = \underline{\mathsf{A}}[\mathbf{x}^{\mathsf{T}} \quad 1]^{\mathsf{T}}$, which, together with the null-space representations of ACs $\underline{\mathsf{A}}$ and $\underline{\mathsf{C}}$,

$$
\begin{aligned}
\underline{\mathsf{A}}(:) &= \mathsf{N}_{\underline{\mathsf{A}}} \; [\underline{\alpha}^{\mathsf{T}} \quad 1]^{\mathsf{T}} \\
\underline{\mathsf{C}}(:) &= \mathsf{N}_{\underline{\mathsf{C}}} \; [\underline{\gamma}^{\mathsf{T}} \quad 1]^{\mathsf{T}},
\end{aligned}
\tag{11}
$$

yields, after considerable algebraic manipulation[1], the following system of equations

$$
\mathsf{G} \, [\underline{\beta}^{\mathsf{T}} \; \underline{\gamma}^{\mathsf{T}}]^{\mathsf{T}} = \mathbf{g},
\tag{12}
$$

---

[1] We used MATLAB's symbolic toolbox for performing the algebraic manipulation. The MATLAB code for deriving all the equations in this section is provided as supplementary material.

where G and **g** depend on $\underline{\alpha}$. Unfortunately, this dependency precludes a linear system such as the one in Eq. 9 from being obtained, making this formulation significantly more complex than the 2-DoF one. One possibility for achieving AC correction in this case is to devise an iterative scheme for minimizing the Frobenius norm of the difference between the extracted and the corrected ACs. This could be done by starting with an initialization for $\underline{\alpha}$ obtained from the extracted AC $\underline{\tilde{A}}$, estimating β and γ using Eq. 12, retrieving the corrected ACs $\underline{A}$, $\underline{B}$ and $\underline{C}$ and iterating for every new estimation of $\underline{\alpha}$ until the sum of the squared Frobenius norms of the differences between the extracted and the corrected ACs is minimal. Generalization to an arbitrary number of views comes in a straightforward manner.

3   Multi-view Linear Estimation of Surface Normals

It is well known that the affine transformation A of an AC is the Jacobian of the homography in point **x** [11,12,20]. This result enables to relate the AC with the normal to the surface at the corresponding 3D point **X**, also enabling the latter to be estimated. Solutions for this problem, in the 2-view and multi-view cases, that formulate the problem in the 3D space have been proposed [2,4]. In this section we derive a simpler formulation that allows to build a linear solver for normal estimation in the multi-view case.

It has been shown in [20] that an AC $(\mathbf{x}, \mathbf{y}, A)$ induces a two-parameter family of homographies H that can be written up to scale as

$$H(\mathbf{j}; \mathbf{x}, \mathbf{y}, A) = \begin{bmatrix} A + \mathbf{y}\mathbf{j}^T & \mathbf{y} - (A + \mathbf{y}\mathbf{j}^T)\mathbf{x} \\ \mathbf{j}^T & 1 - \mathbf{j}^T\mathbf{x} \end{bmatrix}. \tag{13}$$

The equality $H(\mathbf{j}; \mathbf{x}, \mathbf{y}, A) = R + \mathbf{t}\mathbf{n}^T$, where $R, \mathbf{t}$ is the known rotation and translation between the cameras and **n** is the normal to be estimated, can be rewritten as $F[\mathbf{n}^T \; \mathbf{j}^T]^T = -R(:)$, with F being a 9×6 matrix that depends on $\mathbf{t}, \mathbf{x}, \mathbf{y}$ and A. By stacking the equations obtained for each view and solving the linear system, the multi-view estimation of **n** is accomplished.

Unlike in [2] where only the direction of the normal is recovered, this solver also provides the distance of the plane tangent to the surface, encoded in the norm of the normal vector. This extra information allows to reconstruct the 3D point by intersecting the back-projection rays of each camera with the plane.

4   Photoconsistency Optimization for Accurate Normals

Although there has been intensive research on affine region detectors [14,24], state-of-the-art methods still provide ACs that present high levels of noise [7]. Thus, in order to obtain accurate 3D oriented points, it does not suffice to correct the ACs to be consistent with the epipolar geometry. In this section, we propose two novel methods for photoconsistency error minimization that are based on the 2-DoF and 3-DoF formulations derived in Sect. 2. The first method works as an optimizer of ACs and is designed to work in scenes with texture, where point correspondences can be accurately extracted. The second method is a tracker as it only requires feature detection in one frame and performs tracking for every incoming frame. It handles situations of low texture by performing the tracking constrained by the epipolar geometry.

4.1 2-DoF Formulation

The refinement of the affine component of the ACs is formulated as a non-linear optimization problem whose cost function is the photoconsistency error, i.e., the sum of the squared error between a template T, considered as the patch from the first frame that encloses the affine region, and the second frame I. Given an initial estimate for the parameters to optimize $\mathbf{p}$, the goal is to iteratively compute the update parameters $\delta\mathbf{p}$ by minimizing the cost function [1]

$$\sum_{x \in \mathcal{N}} \left[\underbrace{\mathrm{I}(w(\mathbf{x}; \mathbf{p} + \delta\mathbf{p})) - \mathrm{T}(x)}_{E(\delta\mathbf{p})} \right]^2, \tag{14}$$

where w is the image warping function and $\mathcal{N}$ denotes the integration region.

The Efficient Second-order Minimization (ESM) alignment formulation [5,13] states that the incremental update $\delta\mathbf{p}$ which minimizes the error at each iteration is given, considering a second-order Taylor expansion approximation, by

$$\delta\mathbf{p} \approx - \left(\frac{J(\mathbf{0}) + J(\delta\mathbf{p})}{2} \right)^+ E(\mathbf{0}), \tag{15}$$

where the symbol $^+$ denotes the pseudoinverse and $J(\mathbf{i})$ is the Jacobian of the error $E(\mathbf{i})$, having as general formula

$$J(\mathbf{i}) = \frac{\partial E(\mathbf{i})}{\partial \mathbf{i}} = \frac{\partial \mathrm{I}\left(w\left(\mathbf{x}; \mathbf{p} + \mathbf{i}\right)\right)}{\partial \mathbf{i}}. \tag{16}$$

The Jacobian $J(\mathbf{0})$ evaluated using the current solution is given by

$$J(\mathbf{0}) = \frac{\partial \mathrm{I}\left(w\left(\mathbf{x}; \mathbf{p} + \mathbf{i}\right)\right)}{\partial \mathbf{i}} \bigg|_{\mathbf{i}=\mathbf{0}} = \frac{\partial \mathrm{I}(\mathbf{x}')}{\partial \mathbf{x}'} \bigg|_{\mathbf{x}'=w(\mathbf{x};\mathbf{p})} \frac{\partial w\left(\mathbf{x}; \mathbf{p} + \mathbf{i}\right)}{\partial \mathbf{i}} \bigg|_{\mathbf{i}=\mathbf{0}}. \tag{17}$$

The first term on the right-hand side of Eq. 17 is the gradient of the image warped at the current solution. The second term is the Jacobian of the warp function evaluated at $\mathbf{i} = \mathbf{0}$ which, using the formulations derived in Sect. 2, is easy to compute. For the sake of computational efficiency, we obtain the incremental update by solely considering $J(\mathbf{0})$, i.e., by computing $\delta\mathbf{p} = -J(\mathbf{0})^+ E(\mathbf{0})$, which is a valid approximation.

In the present case, where the point correspondence $(\mathbf{x}, \mathbf{y})$ is fixed, the unknown parameters $\mathbf{p}$ to be refined correspond to α in Eq. 6 and the warp function w transforms points $\mathbf{u}$ in the template into points $\mathbf{v}$ in the second image by an affine projection $\mathsf{H_A} = [\mathsf{A}(\mathsf{Q_A}, \mathbf{p}) \quad \mathbf{y} - \mathsf{A}(\mathsf{Q_A}, \mathbf{p})\mathbf{x}]$, where $\mathsf{A}(\mathsf{Q_A}, \mathbf{p})$ is the 2×2 matrix computed using $\mathsf{Q_A}$ and $\mathbf{p}$, as described in Sect. 2.

The extension to the multi-view case is obtained by writing the warp function that transforms points $\mathbf{u}$ in the template into points $\mathbf{w}$ in the third image as a function of the unknown parameters $\mathbf{p}$ using the relation between α and γ derived in Eq. 8. The Jacobian of this warp function is then computed, as well as the gradient of the third image warped at the current solution. By stacking the errors E and their Jacobians, obtained using frames 2 and 3, the update $\delta\mathbf{p}$ is computed using the information of the 3 frames simultaneously. By performing similarly for every incoming frame, the multi-view photoconsistency refinement of the affine transformation A is achieved.

4.2   3-DoF Formulation

The formulation for the case of 3 unknown parameters is analogous to the 2-DoF case, with the unknown parameters vector $\mathbf{p}$ corresponding to $\underline{\alpha}$ in Eq. 4, and the warp function being determined using matrix N. Since in this case the unknown parameters $\mathbf{p}$ allow to optimize both the affine component and the translation part, this formulation can be used as a tracker, with the affine features being extracted in the first frame for creating the templates to be tracked.

As previously explained, one drawback of this formulation is that, since it is not possible to obtain a linear relation between $\underline{\alpha}$ and $\underline{\gamma}$, as in the 2-DoF case, this formulation cannot be extended to the multi-view case in a straightforward manner. However, an alternative formulation for minimizing the cost function 14 can be devised using non-linear optimization algorithms such as Levenberg-Marquardt and the relation between $\underline{\alpha}$, $\underline{\beta}$ and $\underline{\gamma}$ derived in Eq. 12.

5   Experimental Validation

In this section, the proposed algorithms for AC correction, normal estimation, refinement of ACs using photoconsistency and tracking of affine regions are tested and compared with the state-of-the-art methods, both using synthetic data and real-world datasets. In all experiments using real data, affine covariant features are extracted with the Hessian Laplace detector [14,24] using the VLFeat library [25].

5.1   Synthetic Data

This experiment serves to compare the accuracy and computational efficiency of the two proposed linear solvers for correcting ACs and estimating normals with the state-of-the-art solutions [7] and [2], respectively.

The synthetic setup was generated as described in $[2,7]^2$, consisting of N cameras randomly located on the surface of a sphere of radius 5 and looking

---

[2] We thank the authors for kindly providing the source code.

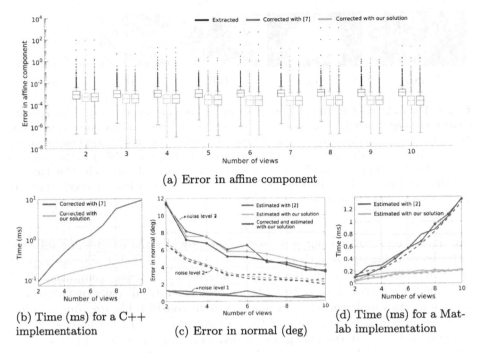

(a) Error in affine component

(b) Time (ms) for a C++
implementation

(c) Error in normal (deg)

(d) Time (ms) for a Mat-
lab implementation

Fig. 2. Comparison of the proposed multi-view solver for correcting ACs (a and b)
and the proposed multi-view method for normal estimation (c and d) with the state-
of-the-art alternatives [7] and [2], respectively. a) The proposed and competing methods
provide the same solutions when performing AC correction, with b) our method being
over an order of magnitude faster for $N > 5$ views. c) Similar results are obtained
by both methods, with [2] being slightly more accurate for $N > 6$ and the highest
noise level. Correcting the AC prior to estimating the surface normal is systematically
the best option. d) While our method scales well, having a nearly constant computational time for increasing number of views, [2] presents higher computational times
that increase approximately linearly with the number of views.

towards the origin of that sphere. Random oriented 3D points were generated
and projected onto the cameras, allowing the estimation of ground truth affine
maps and point locations. Zero-mean Gaussian noise with standard deviation
σ was added to the affine components. Figure 2 gives the comparison of our
solvers with the ones presented in [2,7], in terms of accuracy and computational
time. The ACs correction solvers are implemented in C++, while the normal
estimation algorithms are implemented in Matlab. The number of views N varies
from 2 to 10 and different noise levels are considered, by varying σ. Results were
obtained over 1000 trials.

Figure 2a shows the distribution of errors in the affine components of the
extracted ACs and of both the ACs corrected with the method proposed in [7]
and our approach. The error in the affine component is computed as the Frobenius norm of the difference between each AC 2×2 matrix and the ground truth

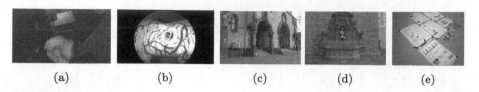

(a)	(b)	(c)	(d)	(e)

Fig. 3. Datasets used in the photoconsistency refinement experiment. The datasets consist of images acquired in very different scenes and the camera poses come from distinct sources, including detection of fiducial markers (a and b), application of an SfM pipeline (c and d) and GPS measurements (e). The high variability of the datasets evinces the large range of possible applications of the proposed approach. The datasets are identified in Fig. 4 by a) Bone model, b) Bone model arthro, c) herzjesu-p8, d) fountain-p11 and e) freiburg3.

one. It can be seen that our proposed solver provides the exact same solution as [7], while being significantly faster, as shown in Fig. 2b that it achieves a speed up of over $30\times$ for $N = 10$. While the solution in [7] involves computing SVD of a $2N \times C$-matrix, with C being the combination of all pairs of views, and performing two multiplications of matrices with considerable size, our solution solely requires the computation of the SVD of a $4(N - 1) \times 3$ matrix. As an example, for $N = 10$, the matrices sizes are 20×45 ([7]) vs 36×3 (ours). This difference in the solver results in a dramatic decrease in computational times. In addition, it can be seen that for the considered noise level ($\sigma = 1$) correcting the ACs always makes them closer to the ground truth ones.

In order to compare the performance of the multi-view normal estimation algorithm presented in [2] with our linear solver, we fed both algorithms with the noisy ACs and computed the angle between the obtained normals and the ground truth ones. Results are shown in Fig. 2c, where the angular errors of the normals estimated after correcting the ACs are also plotted. In this case, since the two solvers provide different solutions, we tested for different noise levels by considering $\sigma = 0.2, 1, 2$. It can be seen that although the solutions are not identical, they are very similar, demonstrating the effectiveness of our proposed linear solver. This result also confirms the findings reported in [7] that correcting the ACs before estimating the surface normal is beneficial in almost every case. Regarding the computational time, our solver is about $6.5\times$ faster than [2] for 10 views, and, unlike the latter, scales well for increasing number of views. The reason for this considerable speed up is that while the number of equations in our normal estimation solver is equal to $9(N - 1)$, the complexity of the one presented in [2] increases quadratically with N.

5.2   Photoconsistency Refinement

In this experiment we evaluate our proposed algorithm for optimizing ACs based on photoconsistency by considering 5 datasets of very different scenes for which dense 3D models exist, and containing images for which the cameras' poses are known, as well as their intrinsic calibrations. For each dataset, multi-view tracks

Table 1. Average times in ms of Matlab implementations of the proposed **Ref2DoF** method and **Ref4DoF**, for different number of views.

# views		2	3	4	5
Avg. time (ms)	**Ref2DoF**	19.7	39.7	62.0	103.6
	Ref4DoF	36.3	71.9	108.8	168.5

of affine maps were extracted and the ground truth 3D points and normals were obtained by intersecting the back-projection rays of the first camera with the 3D model, and retrieving both the point of intersection and the normal at that point. In order to enforce the epipolar geometry assumptions, for each multi-view track, the point was triangulated [10] and projected onto each camera, yielding correspondences that perfectly satisfy the epipolar geometry.

The considered datasets, described in Fig. 3, are the two sequences from the Strecha dataset [22] *fountain-p11* and *herzjesu-p8* with publicly available ground truth 3D point cloud, the sequence *freiburg3 nostructure texture far* from the RGB-D SLAM Dataset and Benchmark [23] and two other sequences we acquired similarly to what is described in [21]. In more detail, we considered a 3D printed model of a bone to which a fiducial with printed binary square patterns is attached and can be tracked, providing the camera pose for every frame. We acquired two sequences, one with a large-focal distance lens and another with an arthroscopic lens. For both sequences we undistorted the images before extracting ACs.

The proposed approach, referred to as **Ref2DoF**, is compared with 4 alternative methods: (1) estimating the normals directly from the extracted ACs, (2) correcting the ACs and afterwards estimating the normals, (3) performing a photoconsistency refinement using a 4-DoF formulation (referred to as **Ref4DoF**), where all 4 parameters of the affine transformation are considered as unknown parameters, and applying (1), and (4) performing (3) followed by (2).

Figure 4 shows the angular errors of the normals obtained by all 5 methods for the different datasets, and Table 1 gives the runtimes for **Ref2DoF** and **Ref4DoF**, for a varying number of views. Results show that although **Ref4DoF** significantly improves the quality of the estimated normals, it is always less accurate than our 2-DoF refinement algorithm, while also being considerably slower. In addition, it can be seen that, as expected, the improvement obtained by correcting the ACs is irrelevant when compared to the one achieved by a photoconsistency refinement. This experiment shows not only that refining ACs is crucial for achieving accurate 3D oriented points, but also that incorporating the constraints of the epipolar geometry into the refinement benefits both the accuracy and the computational efficiency. Figure 1b depicts some of the 3D oriented points obtained on the bone model dataset, where it can be visually confirmed that the normals are nearly perpendicular to the surface.

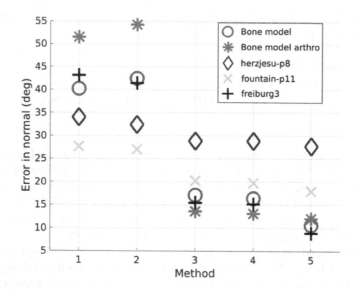

Fig. 4. Average errors in the normals estimated by 5 alternative methods, on the datasets described in Fig. 3. Methods 1 to 5 correspond to: (1) - estimating the normals directly from the extracted ACs; (2) - correcting the ACs and afterwards applying (1); (3) - **Ref4DoF** + (1); (4) - **Ref4DoF** + (2); (5) - **Ref2DoF**

5.3   Tracking

This final experiment serves to assess the performance of our proposed 3-DoF tracker (**Track3DoF**) under very challenging conditions of low texture, where existing solutions perform poorly. For this, we selected the sequence *freiburg3 nostructure notexture far* from the RGB-D SLAM Dataset and Benchmark [23] and extracted affine covariant features from the first frame. Figure 5a shows the frame with the point locations of the features. These features were tracked across 10 frames both using the proposed method **Track3DoF** and a formulation using 6 DoFs, referred to as **Track6DoF**, which is equivalent to a standard KLT affine tracker [1]. Figure 5b shows the obtained 3D oriented points by **Track3DoF**, as well as a green and a yellow planes. The green plane is obtained by finding the plane that best fits to the point cloud provided by the depth camera, and the yellow plane is obtained similarly from the reconstructed points. In order to quantitatively assess the quality of the oriented 3D points, we computed the angle between each obtained normal and the normals of both the green and the yellow planes, and the distance of each 3D point to both planes. Results are shown in Figs. 5c and 5d, and also include the errors obtained for **Track6DoF**, which were computed in a similar manner. It can be seen that 75% of the normals estimated by our method have an error below 20°, while for **Track6DoF** the value for the third quartile is 1.8× larger. Also, while our approach managed to successfully track 76% of the features, the 6-DoF formulation yielded only 64.8% of tracks with symmetric epipolar distance below 5 pix. In terms of computational time,

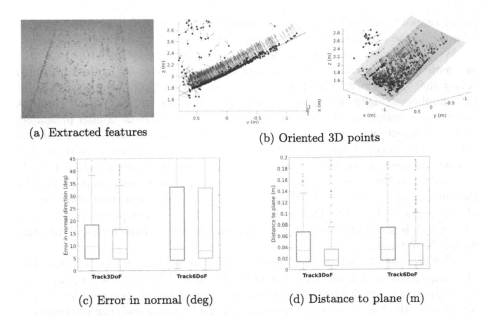

(a) Extracted features   (b) Oriented 3D points

(c) Error in normal (deg)   (d) Distance to plane (m)

Fig. 5. Experiment of tracking features in very low texture conditions. a) Affine features extracted from the first image to be tracked across multiple images. b) Oriented 3D points, represented as blue spheres with red arrows, reconstructed using the proposed **Track3DoF** method, with 76% of the features being correctly tracked. The obtained 3D points are fitted to a plane (yellow plane), as well as the ground truth 3D points provided in the dataset (green plane). Since the depth sensor presents non-negligible noise, we computed the errors in (c) the normals and in (d) the 3D point locations for both planes. Our method outperforms a standard 6-DoF affine KLT formulation (**Track6DoF**) that only successfully tracks 64.8% of the features and is 1.25× slower. (Color figure online)

our formulation is 1.25× faster, taking on average 45ms per tracklet in a Matlab implementation. In addition, we attempted to perform feature matching with the other frames in the dataset but, in this case, most retrieved correspondences were incorrect, and only 29% yielded a symmetric epipolar distance below 5 pix.

These experimental results confirm that including information about the epipolar geometry in the estimation of oriented 3D points significantly improves their quality. In particular, when working in very low textured situations, where feature matching algorithms fail and standard 6-DoF trackers perform poorly, our proposed solution is a viable alternative.

6   Conclusions and Future Work

We investigate the use of ACs in the tasks of normal estimation and reconstruction of oriented 3D points. Existing solutions still suffer from the low accuracy of affine detectors, yielding normals that are far from the ground truth. This paper proposes methods that greatly improve the quality of noisy ACs, being an advance in the literature on this subject and also having practical relevance.

We provide new, simpler representations for ACs consistent with the epipolar geometry. As a consequence, we obtain a multi-view AC correction linear solver that outperforms the state-of-the-art in terms of computational time for any number of views, reaching a speed up of $30\times$ for the case of 10 views. A novel linear solver for the multi-view estimation of normals is also presented, and experiments demonstrate that it is a valid faster alternative to the existing solvers. The novel simple representation of epipolar geometry-consistent ACs enables refinement schemes to be formulated as photoconsistency-based trackers, which, as demonstrated by the experimental results, significantly improve the quality of the extracted ACs. In addition, another important contribution of this paper is the new 3-DoF tracker that works in scenes presenting low texture, which is faster and accurately tracks more features than the standard affine 6-DoF KLT tracker.

The proposed 3-DoF tracker opens the way to applications in new domains. One important area where this type of tracker would be very useful is in surgical arthroscopic procedures, such as the reconstruction of the anterior cruciate ligament in the knee joint or the resection of the femoroacetabular impingement in the hip joint, where the access to the joint is made through two portals for inserting the arthroscopic camera and the surgical instruments. Existing solutions make use of instrumented touch probes for reconstructing bone surface and afterwards perform registration with a pre-operative model of the bone [21]. However, since the maneuverability inside the joint is limited, this procedure is often difficult. Also, existing image-based surface reconstruction procedures fail in providing acceptable results due to the very low texture of the bone surface. As future work, we intend to explore the possibility applying the new 3-DoF tracker to the arthroscopic images for the reconstruction of bone surface, which would then enable registration with the pre-operative model to be performed with schemes that make use of surface normals [19]. Additionally, we will further investigate how to perform multi-view photoconsistency refinement/tracking using the 3-DoF formulation in an efficient manner.

Acknowledgments. This work was funded by the Portuguese Science Foundation and COMPETE2020 program through project VisArthro (ref.: PTDC/EEIAUT/3024/2014). This paper was also funded by the European Union's Horizon 2020 research and innovation programme under grant agreement No 766850.

References

1. Baker, S., Matthews, I.: Lucas-kanade 20 years on: a unifying framework. Int. J. Comput. Vision **56**, 221–255 (2004). https://doi.org/10.1023/B:VISI.0000011205.11775.fd
2. Barath, D., Eichhardt, I., Hajder, L.: Optimal multi-view surface normal estimation using affine correspondences. IEEE Trans. Image Process. **28**(7), 3301–3311 (2019). https://doi.org/10.1109/TIP.2019.2895542

3. Barath, D., Matas, J., Hajder, L.: Accurate closed-form estimation of local affine transformations consistent with the epipolar geometry, pp. 11.1-11.12 (2016). https://doi.org/10.5244/C.30.11
4. Barath, D., Molnar, J., Hajder, L.: Novel methods for estimating surface normals from affine transformations. In: Braz, J., et al. (eds.) VISIGRAPP 2015. CCIS, vol. 598, pp. 316–337. Springer, Cham (2016). https://doi.org/10.1007/978-3-319-29971-6_17
5. Benhimane, S., Malis, E.: Homography-based 2D visual tracking and servoing. Int. J. Robot. Res. **26**(7), 661–676 (2007). https://doi.org/10.1177/0278364907080252
6. Bentolila, J., Francos, J.M.: Conic epipolar constraints from affine correspondences. Comput. Vis. Image Underst. **122**, 105–114 (2014). https://doi.org/10.1016/j.cviu.2014.02.004.   http://www.sciencedirect.com/science/article/pii/S1077314214000307
7. Eichhardt, I., Barath, D.: Optimal multi-view correction of local affine frames. In: BMVC (2019)
8. Eichhardt, I., Hajder, L.: Computer vision meets geometric modeling: multi-view reconstruction of surface points and normals using affine correspondences, October 2017. https://doi.org/10.1109/ICCVW.2017.286
9. Hajder, L., Barath, D.: Relative planar motion for vehicle-mounted cameras from a single affine correspondence, December 2019
10. Hartley, R.I., Sturm, P.: Triangulation. Comput. Vis. Image Underst. **68**(2), 146–157 (1997). https://doi.org/10.1006/cviu.1997.0547
11. Koser, K., Beder, C., Koch, R.: Conjugate rotation: parameterization and estimation from an affine feature correspondence. In: IEEE Conference on Computer Vision and Pattern Recognition, 2008. CVPR 2008, pp. 1–8, June 2008. https://doi.org/10.1109/CVPR.2008.4587796
12. Köser, K., Koch, R.: Differential spatial resection - pose estimation using a single local image feature. In: Forsyth, D., Torr, P., Zisserman, A. (eds.) ECCV 2008. LNCS, vol. 5305, pp. 312–325. Springer, Heidelberg (2008). https://doi.org/10.1007/978-3-540-88693-8_23
13. Mei, C., Benhimane, S., Malis, E., Rives, P.: Efficient homography-based tracking and 3-D reconstruction for single-viewpoint sensors. IEEE-TRO **24**(6), 1352–1364 (2008)
14. Mikolajczyk, K., et al.: A comparison of affine region detectors. Int. J. Comput. Vis. **65**, 2005 (2005)
15. Minh, N.L., Hajder, L.: Affine transformation from fundamental matrix and two directions. In: VISIGRAPP (2020)
16. Perdoch, M., Matas, J., Chum, O.: Epipolar geometry from two correspondences. In: 18th International Conference on Pattern Recognition (ICPR 2006), vol. 4, pp. 215–219, August 2006. https://doi.org/10.1109/ICPR.2006.497
17. Pritts, J., Kukelova, Z., Larsson, V., Chum, O.: Radially-distorted conjugate translations. In: 2018 IEEE/CVF Conference on Computer Vision and Pattern Recognition, pp. 1993–2001 (2017)
18. Raposo, C., Barreto, J.P.: πMatch: monocular vSLAM and piecewise planar reconstruction using fast plane correspondences. In: Leibe, B., Matas, J., Sebe, N., Welling, M. (eds.) ECCV 2016. LNCS, vol. 9912, pp. 380–395. Springer, Cham (2016). https://doi.org/10.1007/978-3-319-46484-8_23
19. Raposo, C., Barreto, J.P.: Using 2 point+normal sets for fast registration of point clouds with small overlap. In: 2017 IEEE International Conference on Robotics and Automation (ICRA), pp. 5652–5658, May 2017. https://doi.org/10.1109/ICRA.2017.7989664

20. Raposo, C., Barreto, J.P.: Theory and pratice of structure-from-motion using affine correspondences. In: Conference on Computer Vision and Pattern Recognition (CVPR) (2016)
21. Raposo, C., et al.: Video-based computer aided arthroscopy for patient specific reconstruction of the anterior cruciate ligament. In: Frangi, A.F., Schnabel, J.A., Davatzikos, C., Alberola-López, C., Fichtinger, G. (eds.) MICCAI 2018. LNCS, vol. 11073, pp. 125–133. Springer, Cham (2018). https://doi.org/10.1007/978-3-030-00937-3_15
22. Strecha, C., von Hansen, W., Van Gool, L., Fua, P., Thoennessen, U.: On benchmarking camera calibration and multi-view stereo for high resolution imagery. In: 2008 IEEE Conference on Computer Vision and Pattern Recognition, pp. 1–8, June 2008. https://doi.org/10.1109/CVPR.2008.4587706
23. Sturm, J., Engelhard, N., Endres, F., Burgard, W., Cremers, D.: A benchmark for the evaluation of RGB-D slam systems. In: IEEE-IROS, October 2012
24. Tuytelaars, T., Mikolajczyk, K.: Local invariant feature detectors: a survey. Found. Trends. Comput. Graph. Vis. 3, 177–280 (2008)
25. Vedaldi, A., Fulkerson, B.: VLFeat: an open and portable library of computer vision algorithms (2008). http://www.vlfeat.org/

Volumetric Transformer Networks

Seungryong Kim[1]([✉]), Sabine Süsstrunk[2], and Mathieu Salzmann[2]

[1] Department of Computer Science and Engineering, Korea University, Seoul, Korea
seungryong_kim@korea.ac.kr
[2] School of Computer and Communication Sciences, EPFL, Lausanne, Switzerland
{sabine.susstrunk,mathieu.salzmann}@epfl.ch

Abstract. Existing techniques to encode spatial invariance within deep convolutional neural networks (CNNs) apply the same warping field to all the feature channels. This does not account for the fact that the individual feature channels can represent different semantic parts, which can undergo different spatial transformations w.r.t. a canonical configuration. To overcome this limitation, we introduce a learnable module, the volumetric transformer network (VTN), that predicts channel-wise warping fields so as to reconfigure intermediate CNN features spatially and channel-wisely. We design our VTN as an encoder-decoder network, with modules dedicated to letting the information flow across the feature channels, to account for the dependencies between the semantic parts. We further propose a loss function defined between the warped features of pairs of instances, which improves the localization ability of VTN. Our experiments show that VTN consistently boosts the features' representation power and consequently the networks' accuracy on fine-grained image recognition and instance-level image retrieval.

Keywords: Spatial invariance · Attention · Feature channels · Fine-grained image recognition · Instance-level image retrieval

1 Introduction

Learning discriminative feature representations of semantic object parts is key to the success of computer vision tasks such as fine-grained image recognition [16,72], instance-level image retrieval [42,46], and people re-identification [35,74]. This is mainly because, unlike generic image recognition and retrieval [11,13], solving these tasks requires handling subtle inter-class variations.

A popular approach to extracting object part information consists of exploiting an attention mechanism within a deep convolutional neural network (CNN)

This work was supported in part by the Swiss National Science Foundation via the Sinergia grant CRSII5-180359. The work of S. Kim was supported by Institute for Information & communications Technology Planning & Evaluation (IITP) grant funded by the Korea government (MSIT) (No. 2020-0-00368, A Neural-Symbolic Model for Knowledge Acquisition and Inference Techniques).

A. Vedaldi et al. (Eds.): ECCV 2020, LNCS 12373, pp. 561–578, 2020.
https://doi.org/10.1007/978-3-030-58604-1_34

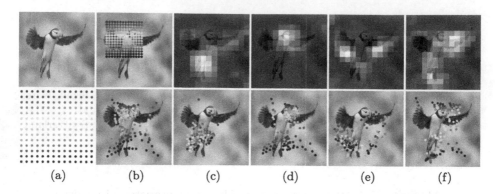

Fig. 1. Visualization of VTN: (a) input image and target coordinates for warping an intermediate CNN feature map, (b) source coordinates obtained using STNs [28] (top) and SSN [48] (bottom), and (c), (d), (e), and (f) four feature channels and samplers in VTN. Note that the colors in the warping fields represent the corresponding target coordinates. Unlike STNs [28] that applies the same warping field across all the feature channels, VTN maps the individual channels independently to the canonical configuration, by localizing different semantic parts in different channels.

[20,42,65,67]. While effective at localizing the discriminative parts, such an app-roach has limited ability to handle spatial variations due to, e.g., scale, pose and viewpoint changes, or part deformations, which frequently occur across different object instances [10,14,28]. To overcome this, recent methods seek to spatially warp the feature maps of different images to a canonical configuration so as to remove these variations and thus facilitate the subsequent classifier's task. This trend was initiated by the spatial transformer networks (STNs) [28], of which many variants were proposed, using a recurrent formalism [37], polar transforma-tions [12], deformable convolutional kernels [10], and attention based samplers [48,73]. All of these methods apply the *same* warping field to *all* the feature channels. This, however, does not account for the findings of [5,18,49], which have shown that the different feature channels of standard image classifiers typ-ically relate to different semantic concepts, such as object parts. Because these semantic parts undergo different transformations w.r.t. the canonical configu-ration, e.g., the wings of a bird may move while its body remains static, the corresponding feature channels need to be transformed individually.

In this paper, we address this by introducing a learnable module, the volu-metric transformer network (VTN), that predicts channel-wise warping fields. As illustrated by Fig. 1, this allows us to correctly account for the different transfor-mations of different semantic parts by reconfiguring the intermediate features of a CNN spatially and channel-wisely. To achieve this while nonetheless account-ing for the dependencies between the different semantic parts, we introduce an encoder-decoder network that lets information flow across the original fea-ture channels. Specifically, our encoder relies on a channel-squeeze module that aggregates information across the channels, while our decoder uses a channel-expansion component that distributes it back to the original features.

As shown in previous works [12, 28, 37, 69], training a localization network to achieve spatial invariance is challenging, and most methods [12, 28, 37, 69] rely on indirect supervision via a task-dependent loss function, as supervision for the warping fields is typically unavailable. This, however, does not guarantee that the warped features are consistent across different object instances. To improve the localization ability of the predicted warping fields, we further introduce a loss function defined between the warped features of pairs of instances, so as to encourage similarity between the representation of same-class instances while pushing that of different-class instances apart.

Our experiments on fine-grained image recognition [22, 32, 40, 64] and instance-level image retrieval [46], performed using several backbone networks and pooling methods, evidence that our VTNs consistently boost the features' representation power and consequently the networks' accuracy.

2   Related Work

Attention Mechanisms. As argued in [76], spatial deformation modeling methods [10, 28, 37, 48], including VTNs, can be viewed as hard attention mechanisms, in that they localize and attend to the discriminative image parts. Attention mechanisms in neural networks have quickly gained popularity in diverse computer vision and natural language processing tasks, such as relational reasoning among objects [4, 52], image captioning [67], neural machine translation [3, 61], image generation [68, 71], and image recognition [23, 63]. They draw their inspiration from the human visual system, which understands a scene by capturing a sequence of partial glimpses and selectively focusing on salient regions [27, 34].

Unlike methods that consider spatial attention [20, 42, 65, 67], some works [15, 23, 62, 70] have attempted to extract channel-wise attention based on the observation that different feature channels can encode different semantic concepts [5, 18, 49], so as to capture the correlations among those concepts. In those cases, however, spatial attention was ignored. While some methods [7, 65] have tried to learn spatial and channel-wise attention simultaneously, they only predict a fixed spatial attention with different channel attentions. More importantly, attention mechanisms have limited ability to handle spatial variations due to, e.g., scale, pose and viewpoint changes, or part deformations [10, 14, 28].

Spatial Invariance. Recent work on spatial deformation modeling seeks to spatially warp the features to a canonical configuration so as to facilitate recognition [10, 12, 28, 37, 48]. STNs [28] explicitly allow the spatial manipulation of feature maps within the network while attending to the discriminative parts. Their success inspired many variants that use, e.g., a recurrent formalism [37], polar transformations [12], deformable convolutional kernels [10], and attention based warping [48, 73]. These methods typically employ an additional network, called localization network, to predict a warping field, which is then applied to all the feature channels identically. Conceptually, this corresponds to using hard attention [20, 42, 65, 67], but it improves spatial invariance. While effective, this approach concentrates on finding the regions that are most discriminative across all the feature channels. To overcome this, some methods use multi-branches [28,72], coarse-to-fine schemes [16], and recurrent formulations [36], but they remain limited to considering a pre-defined number of discriminative parts, which restricts their effectiveness and flexibility.

Fine-Grained Image Recognition. To learn discriminative feature representations of object parts, conventional methods first localize these parts and then classify the whole image based on the discriminative regions. These two-step methods [6,25] typically require bounding box or keypoint annotations of objects or parts, which are hard to collect. To alleviate this, recent methods aim to automatically localize the discriminative object parts using an attention mechanism [8,16,36,48,51,58,72,73] in an unsupervised manner, without part annotations. However, these methods do not search for semantic part representations in the individual feature channels, which limits their ability to boost the feature representation power. Recently, Chen et al. [8] proposed a destruction and construction learning strategy that injects more discriminative local details into the classification network. However, the problem of explicitly processing the individual feature channels remains untouched.

Instance-Level Image Retrieval. While image retrieval was traditionally tackled using local invariant features [39,41] or bag-of-words (BoW) models [1,56], recent methods use deep CNNs [2,30,42,47,59,59] due to their better representation ability. In this context, the main focus has been on improving the feature representation power of pretrained backbone networks [21,33,55], typically by designing pooling mechanisms to construct a global feature, such as max-pooling (MAC) [59], sum-pooling (SPoC) [2], weighted sum-pooling (CroW) [30], regional max-pooling (R-MAC) [59], and generalized mean-pooling (GeM) [47]. These pooling strategies, however, do not explicitly leverage the discriminative parts, and neither do the methods [19,47] that have tried to fine-tune the pretrained backbone networks [21,33,55]. While the approach of [42] does, by learning spatial attention, it ignores the channel-wise variations. Taking such variations into account is the topic of this paper.

3   Volumetric Transformer Networks

3.1   Preliminaries

Let us denote an intermediate CNN feature map as $U \in \mathbb{R}^{H \times W \times K}$, with height H, width W, and K channels. To attend to the discriminative object parts and reduce the inter-instance spatial variations in the feature map, recent works [12,28,37,69] predict a warping field to transform the features to a canonical pose. This is achieved via a module that takes U as input and outputs the parameters defining a warping field $G \in \mathbb{R}^{H \times W \times 2}$ to be applied to U. The representation in the canonical pose is then obtained via a feature sampling mechanism, which, for every pixel i in the output representation, produces a warped feature such that $V(i) = U(i+G(i))$. As argued above, while this reduces

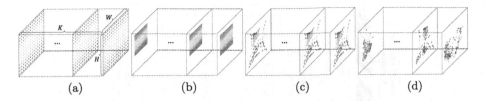

Fig. 2. Intuition of VTNs: (a) target coordinates for warping an intermediate CNN feature map and source coordinates obtained using (b) STNs [28], (c) SSN [48], and (d) VTNs, which predict channel-wise warping fields.

spatial variations and lets the network focus on discriminative image regions, the same warping field is applied across all the channels, without considering the different semantic meanings of these individual channels. Moreover, this does not explicitly constrain the warped features of different instances of the same class to be consistent.

3.2 Motivation and Overview

By contrast, our volumetric transformer network (VTN), which we introduce in the remainder of this section, encodes the observation that each channel in an intermediate CNN feature map acts as a pattern detector, i.e., high-level channels detect high-level semantic patterns, such as parts and objects [5,7,18,65], and, because these patterns can undergo different transformations, one should separately attend to the discriminative parts represented by the individual channels to more effectively warp them to the canonical pose. To achieve this, unlike existing spatial deformation modeling methods [10,28,37,48], which apply the same warping field to all the feature channels, as in Fig. 2(b), our VTN predicts channel-wise warping fields, shown in Fig. 2(d).

Concretely, a VTN produces a warping field $G_c \in \mathbb{R}^{H \times W \times 2}$ for each channel c. Rather than estimating the warping field of each channel independently, to account for dependencies between the different semantic parts, we design two modules, the channel squeeze and expansion modules, that let information flow across the channels. Furthermore, to improve the computational efficiency and localization accuracy, we build a group sampling and normalization module, and a transformation probability inference module at the first and last layer of VTN, respectively. To train the network, instead of relying solely on a task-dependent loss function as in [10,28,37,48], which may yield poorly-localized warping fields, we further introduce a loss function based on the distance between the warped features of pairs of instances, thus explicitly encouraging the warped features to be consistent across different instances of the same class.

3.3 Volumetric Transformation Estimator

Perhaps the most straightforward way to estimate channel-wise warping fields is to utilize convolutional layers that take the feature map U as input and output the warping fields $G = \{G_c\} \in \mathbb{R}^{H \times W \times 2 \times K}$. This strategy, however, uses

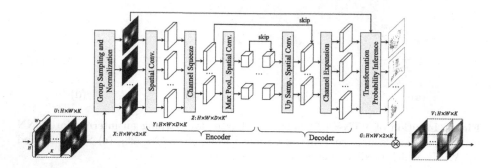

Fig. 3. VTN architecture. A VTN consists of a group sampling and normalization module, sequential spatial convolutions, channel squeeze and expansion modules, and a transformation probability inference module.

separate convolution kernels for each warping field G_c, which might be subject to overfitting because of the large number of parameters involved. As an alternative, one can predict each warping field G_c independently, by taking only the corresponding feature channel $U_c \in \mathbb{R}^{H \times W \times 1}$ as input. This, however, would fail to account for the inter-channel relationships, and may be vulnerable to outlier channels that, on their own, contain uninformative features but can yet be supported by other channels [18,29,71].

To alleviate these limitations, we introduce the channel squeeze and expansion modules, which yield a trade-off between the two extreme solutions discussed above. We first decompose the input feature map across the channel dimension, and apply a shared convolution to each of the K channels. We then combine the original feature channels into K' new channels by a channel-squeeze module, parameterized by a learned matrix W_{cs}, in the encoder and expand these squeezed feature channels into K channels by a channel-expansion module, parameterized by a learned matrix W_{ce}, in the decoder.

Formally, as depicted by Fig. 3, let us define an intermediate CNN feature map after a forward pass through an encoder as $Y = \mathcal{F}(U; W_{\mathrm{s}}) \in \mathbb{R}^{H \times W \times D \times K}$, where each feature channel is processed independently with spatial convolution parameters W_{s} shared across the channels, introducing an additional dimension of size D. We introduce a channel squeeze module, with parameters $W_{\mathrm{cs}} \in \mathbb{R}^{K \times K'}$, $K' < K$, applied to the reshaped $Y \in \mathbb{R}^{HWD \times K}$, whose role is to aggregate the intermediate features so as to output $Z = \mathcal{F}(Y; W_{\mathrm{cs}}) \in \mathbb{R}^{HWD \times K'}$, which can also be reshaped to $\mathbb{R}^{H \times W \times D \times K'}$. In short, this operation allows the network to learn how to combine the initial K channels so as to leverage the inter-channel relationships while keeping the number of trainable parameters reasonable. We then incorporate a channel expansion module, with parameters $W_{\mathrm{ce}} \in \mathbb{R}^{K' \times K}$, which performs the reverse operation, thereby enlarging the feature map $Z \in \mathbb{R}^{H \times W \times D \times K'}$ back into a representation with K channels. This is achieved through a decoder.

We exploit sequential spatial convolution and channel squeeze modules in the encoder, and sequential spatial convolution and channel expansion modules in the decoder. In our experiments, the volumetric transformation estimator consists of an encoder with 4 spatial convolution and channel squeeze modules followed by max-pooling, and a decoder with 4 spatial convolution and channel expansion modules followed by upsampling. Each convolution module follows the architecture Convolution-BatchNorm-ReLU [26].

Grouping the Channels. In practice, most state-of-the-art networks [21,24, 55] extract high-dimensional features, and thus processing all the initial feature channels as described above can be computationally prohibitive. To overcome this, we propose a group sampling and normalization module inspired by group normalization [66] and attention mechanisms [65]. Concretely, a group sampling and normalization module takes the feature map U as input and separates it into C groups following the sequential order of the channels. We then aggregate the features U_c in each group $c \in \{1, \ldots, C\}$ by using two pooling operations: $U_c^{\max} \in \mathbb{R}^{H \times W \times 1}$ and $U_c^{\text{avg}} \in \mathbb{R}^{H \times W \times 1}$, and concatenate them as $X_c \in \mathbb{R}^{H \times W \times 2}$, followed by group normalization without per-channel linear transform [66]. We then take the resulting $X = \{X_c\} \in \mathbb{R}^{H \times W \times 2 \times K}$ as input to the volumetric transformation estimator described above, instead of U.

Probabilistic Transformation Modeling. Unlike existing spatial deformation modeling methods [28,37] that rely on parametric models, e.g., affine transformation, VTNs estimate non-parametric warping fields, thus having more flexibility. However, regressing the warping fields directly may perform poorly because the mapping from the features to the warping fields adds unnecessary learning complexity. To alleviate this, inspired by [57,60], we design a probabilistic transformation inference module that predicts probabilities for warping candidates, instead of directly estimating the warping field. Specifically, we predict the probability $P_c(i, j)$ of each candidate $j \in N_i$ at each pixel i, and compute the warping field G_c by aggregating these probabilities as

$$G_c(i) = \sum_{j \in N_i} P_c(i, j)(j - i). \tag{1}$$

Furthermore, instead of predicting the probability $P_c(i, j)$ directly, we compute a residual probability and then use a softmax layer such that

$$P_c(i, j) = \Psi \left(\left(U_c^{\max}(j) + U_c^{\text{avg}}(j) + E_c(i, j) \right) / \beta \right), \tag{2}$$

where $E_c \in \mathbb{R}^{H \times W \times |N_i|}$ is the output of the volumetric transformation estimator whose the size depends on the number of candidates $|N_i|$. Note that $E_c(i, j)$ is a scalar because i denotes a spatial point over $H \times W$ and j indexes a point among all candidates. $\Psi(\cdot)$ is the softmax operator and β is a parameter adjusting the sharpness of the softmax output. At initialization, the network parameters are set to predict zeros, i.e., $E_c(i, j) = 0$, thus the warping fields are determined by candidate feature responses $U_c^{\max} + U_c^{\text{avg}}$, which provide good starting points. As training progresses, the network provides increasingly regularized warping fields. This is used as the last layer of the VTN.

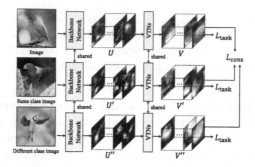

Fig. 4. Illustration of training VTNs using our consistency loss function. By simultaneously exploiting a sample from the same class and another sample from a different class, our consistency loss function improves the localization ability and the discriminative power of the intermediate features.

3.4 Loss Function

Similarly to existing deformation modeling methods [12,28,37,69], our network can be learned using only the final task-dependent loss function $\mathcal{L}_{\text{task}}$, without using ground-truth warping fields, since all modules are differentiable. This, however, does not explicitly constrain the warped features obtained from the predicted warping fields to be consistent across different object instances of the same class. To overcome this, we draw our inspiration from semantic correspondence works [31,50], and introduce an additional loss function modeling the intuition that the warped features of two instances of the same class should match and be similar. The simplest approach to encoding this consists of using a square loss between such features, which yields

$$\mathcal{L} = \sum_i \|V(i) - V'(i)\|^2, \tag{3}$$

where V and V' are the warped feature maps of two instances of the same class. Minimizing this loss function, however, can induce erroneous solutions, such as constant features at all the pixels. To avoid such trivial solutions, we use a triplet loss function [54,69] simultaneously exploiting a sample V' from the same class as V and another sample V'' from a different class. We then express our loss as

$$\mathcal{L}_{\text{cons}} = \sum_i \left[\|V(i) - V'(i)\|^2 - \|V(i) - V''(i)\|^2 + \alpha\right]_+, \tag{4}$$

where $\alpha > 0$ is a threshold parameter and $[\cdot]_+ = \max(\cdot, 0)$. Our loss function jointly encourages the instances' features from the same class to be similar, and the instances' features from different classes to be dissimilar. Together, this helps to improve the features' discriminative power, which is superior to relying solely on a task-dependent loss function, as in previous methods [12,28,37,69]. Note that our approach constitutes the first attempt at learning warping fields that generate consistent warped features across object instances. To train our VTNs, we then use the total loss $\mathcal{L}_{\text{total}} = \mathcal{L}_{\text{task}} + \lambda\mathcal{L}_{\text{cons}}$ with balancing parameter λ. Figure 4 depicts the training procedure of VTNs.

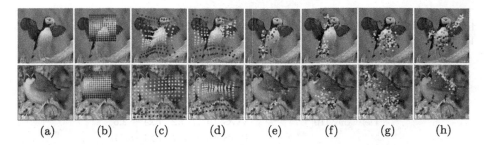

| (a) | (b) | (c) | (d) | (e) | (f) | (g) | (h) |

Fig. 5. Comparison of VTN warping fields with those of existing deformation modeling methods [28,48] on examples from CUB-Birds [64]: (a) input images and source coordinates obtained using (b) STNs [28], (c) SSN [48], (d) ASN [73], and (e), (f), (g), and (h) four feature channel samplers in VTNs. Points with the same color in different images are projected to the same point in the canonical pose. This shows that VTNs not only localize different semantic parts in different channels but identify the same points across different images.

3.5 Implementation and Training Details

In our experiments, we use VGGNet [55] and ResNet [21] backbones pretrained on ImageNet [11]. We build VTNs on the last convolution layers of each network. For fine-grained image recognition, we replace the 1000-way softmax layer with a k-way softmax layer, where k is number of classes in the dataset [22,32,40,64], and fine-tune the networks on the dataset. The input images were resized to a fixed resolution of 512×512 and randomly cropped to 448×448. We apply random rotations and random horizontal flips for data augmentation. For instance-level image retrieval, we utilize the last convolutional features after the VTNs as global representation. To train VTNs, we follow the experimental protocols of [19,47]. We set the hyper-parameters by cross-validation on CUB-Birds [64], and then used the same values for all experiments. We set the size of the transformation candidates $|N_i| = 11 \times 11$, the parameter $\beta = 10$, the number of groups $C = 32$, and the balancing parameter $\lambda = 1$. We also set the threshold parameter $\alpha = 20$ for VGGNet [55] and $\alpha = 30$ for ResNet [21], respectively, because they have different feature distributions. The source code is available online at our project webpage: http://github.com/seungryong/VTNs/.

4 Experiments

4.1 Experimental Setup

In this section, we comprehensively analyze and evaluate VTNs on two tasks: fine-grained image recognition and instance-level image retrieval. First, we analyze the influence of the different components of VTNs compared to existing spatial deformation modeling methods [10,28,48,73] and the impact of combining VTNs with different backbone networks [21,55] and second-order pooling strategies [9,17,35,36,38]. Second, we compare VTNs with the state-of-the-art

Table 1. Accuracy of VTNs compared to spatial deformation modeling methods on fine-grained image recognition benchmarks (CUB-Birds [64], Stanford-Cars [32], and FGVC-Aircraft [40]).

Methods	Backbone	[64]	[32]	[40]
Base	VGG-19	71.4	68.7	80.7
	ResNet-50	74.6	70.4	82.1
Def-Conv [10]	VGG-19	74.2	70.1	82.6
	ResNet-50	76.7	72.1	83.7
STNs [28]	VGG-19	72.1	69.2	81.1
	ResNet-50	76.5	71.0	81.2
SSN [48]	VGG-19	75.1	72.7	84.6
	ResNet-50	77.7	74.8	83.1
ASN [73]	VGG-19	76.2	74.1	82.4
	ResNet-50	78.9	75.2	85.7
VTNs wo/W_{cs}, W_{ce}	VGG-19	77.8	78.6	86.1
	ResNet-50	80.1	81.4	86.9
VTNs wo/Group	VGG-19	76.3	76.1	84.4
	ResNet-50	77.2	79.1	82.4
VTNs wo/T-Probability	VGG-19	78.1	79.7	84.9
	ResNet-50	79.0	80.4	85.1
VTNs wo/$\mathcal{L}_{cons}$	VGG-19	79.2	80.2	87.1
	ResNet-50	82.4	82.1	84.9
VTNs	VGG-19	80.4	81.9	87.4
	ResNet-50	**83.1**	**82.7**	**89.2**

methods on fine-grained image recognition benchmarks [22,32,40,64]. Finally, we evaluate them on instance-level image retrieval benchmarks [46].

4.2   Fine-Grained Image Recognition

Analysis of the VTN Components. To validate the different components of our VTNs, we compare them with previous spatial deformation modeling methods, such as STNs [28], deformable convolution (Def-Conv) [10], saliency-based sampler (SSN) [48], and attention-based sampler (ASN) [73] on fine-grained image recognition benchmarks, such as CUB-Birds [64], Stanford-Cars [32], and FGVC-Aircraft [40]. For the comparison to be fair, we apply these methods at the same layer as ours, i.e., the last convolutional layer. In this set of experiments, we utilize VGGNet-19 [55] and ResNet-50 [21] as backbone networks. As an ablation study, we evaluate VTNs without the channel squeeze and expansion modules, denoted by VTNs wo/W_{cs}, W_{ce}, without the group sampling and normalization module, denoted by VTNs wo/Group, and without the transformation probability inference module, denoted by VTNs wo/T-Probability. We further report the results of VTNs trained without our consistency loss function, denoted by VTNs wo/$\mathcal{L}_{cons}$.

Table 2. Accuracy of VTNs incorporated with second-order pooling methods on fine-grained image recognition benchmarks (CUB-Birds [64], Stanford-Cars [32], and FGVC-Aircraft [40]).

Methods	[64]	[32]	[40]
Base	74.6	70.4	82.1
BP [38]	80.2	81.5	84.8
CBP [17]	81.6	81.6	88.6
KP [9]	83.2	82.9	89.9
MPN-COV [36]	84.2	83.1	89.7
iSQRT-COV [35]	88.1	90.0	92.8
Base+**VTNs**	83.1	82.7	89.2
BP [38]+**VTNs**	84.9	84.1	90.6
CBP [17]+**VTNs**	85.2	84.2	91.2
KP [9]+**VTNs**	85.1	83.2	91.7
MPN-COV [36]+**VTNs**	86.7	88.1	90.6
iSQRT-COV [35]+**VTNs**	**89.6**	**93.3**	**93.4**

Table 3. Accuracy of VTNs compared to the state-of-the-art methods on fine-grained image recognition benchmarks (CUB-Birds [64], Stanford-Cars [32], and FGVC-Aircraft [40]).

Methods	Backbone	[64]	[32]	[40]
RA-CNN [16]	3×VGG-19	85.3	92.5	88.2
MA-CNN [72]	3×VGG-19	86.5	92.8	89.9
DFL-CNN [63]	ResNet-50	87.4	93.1	91.7
DT-RAM [36]	ResNet-50	87.4	93.1	91.7
MAMC [58]	ResNet-50	86.5	93.0	92.9
NTSN [58]	3×ResNet-50	87.5	91.4	93.1
DCL [8]	VGG-16	86.9	94.1	91.2
	ResNet-50	87.8	94.5	93.0
TASN [73]	VGG-19	86.1	93.2	–
	ResNet-50	87.9	93.8	–
[35]+TASN [73]	ResNet-50	89.1	–	–
DCL [8]+**VTNs**	ResNet-50	89.2	95.1	93.4
[35]+**VTNs**	ResNet-50	89.6	93.3	93.4
[35]+TASN [73]+**VTNs**	ResNet-50	**91.2**	**95.9**	**94.5**

The results are provided in Table 1 and Fig. 5. Note that all versions of our approach outperform the existing deformation modeling methods [10,28,48,73]. Among these versions, considering jointly spatial and channel-wise deformation fields through our squeeze and expansion modules improves the results. The group sampling and normalization and transformation probability inference modules also boost the results. Using the consistency loss function $\mathcal{L}_{cons}$ further

Table 4. Accuracy of VTNs compared to the state-of-the-art methods on iNaturalist-2017 [22].

Super class	ResNet [21]	SSN [48]	TASN [73]	[35]+**VTNs**
Plantae	60.3	63.9	66.6	**68.6**
Insecta	69.1	74.7	77.6	**79.1**
Aves	59.1	68.2	72.0	**72.9**
Reptilia	37.4	43.9	46.4	**48.1**
Mammalia	50.2	55.3	57.7	**60.6**
Fungi	62.5	64.2	70.3	**72.1**
Amphibia	41.8	50.2	51.6	**53.9**
Mollusca	56.9	61.5	64.7	**66.3**
Animalia	64.8	67.8	71.0	**73.2**
Arachnida	64.8	73.8	75.1	**78.2**
Actinopterygii	57.0	60.3	65.5	**68.4**
Chromista	57.6	57.6	62.5	**64.0**
Protozoa	78.1	79.5	79.5	**81.1**
Total	58.4	63.1	66.2	**68.2**

Table 5. Localization errors on CUB-Birds [64].

Methods	top-1 err	top-5 err
GoogLeNet+GAP [75]	59.00	–
VGGNet+ACoL [70]	54.08	43.49
ResNet+GCAM [53]	53.42	43.12
ResNet+STNs [28]+GCAM [53]	54.21	43.33
ResNet+**VTNs**+GCAM [53]	**52.18**	**41.76**

yields higher accuracy by favoring learning a warping to a consistent canonical configuration of instances of the same class and improving the discriminative power of the intermediate features.

Incorporating Second-Order Pooling Strategies. While our VTNs can be used on their own, they can also integrate second-order pooling schemes, such as bilinear pooling (BP) [38], compact BP (CBP) [17], kernel pooling (KP) [9], matrix power normalized covariance pooling (MPN-COV) [36], and iterative matrix square root normalization of covariance pooling (iSQRT-COV) [35], which yield state-of-the-art results on fine-grained image recognition. In this set of experiments, we use ResNet-50 [21] as backbone. As shown in Table 2, our VTNs consistently outperform the corresponding pooling strategy on its own, thus confirming the benefits of using channel-wise warped regions.

Comparison with the State-of-the-Art Methods. We also compare VTNs with the state-of-the-art fine-grained image recognition methods, such as RA-CNN [16], MA-CNN [72], DFL-CNN [63], DT-RAM [36], MAMC [58], NTSN [58],

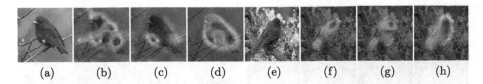

| | | | | | | | |
| (a) | (b) | (c) | (d) | (e) | (f) | (g) | (h) |

Fig. 6. Network visualization using Grad-CAM [53]: (a), (e) input images, (b), (f) ResNet-50 [21], (c), (g) ResNet-50 with STNs [28], and (d), (h) ResNet-50 with VTNs.

Table 6. Comparison of VTNs with the state-of-the-art methods on the $\mathcal{R}$Oxford and $\mathcal{R}$Paris benchmarks [46].

Methods	Medium		Hard	
	$\mathcal{R}$Oxf	$\mathcal{R}$Par	$\mathcal{R}$Oxf	$\mathcal{R}$Par
Pretr.+MAC [59]	41.7	66.2	18.0	44.1
Pretr.+SPoC [2]	39.8	69.2	12.4	44.7
Pretr.+CroW [30]	42.4	70.4	13.3	47.2
Pretr.+GeM [47]	45.0	70.7	17.7	48.7
Pretr.+R-MAC [59]	49.8	74.0	18.5	52.1
DELF [42,44,59]	67.8	76.9	43.1	55.4
[47]+GeM	64.7	77.2	38.5	56.3
[19]+R-MAC	60.9	78.9	32.4	59.4
[19]+R-MAC+STNs [28]	61.3	79.4	36.1	59.8
DELF [42,44,59]+**VTNs**	**69.7**	78.1	45.1	56.4
[47]+GeM+**VTNs**	67.4	80.5	**45.5**	57.1
[19]+R-MAC+**VTNs**	65.6	**82.7**	43.3	**60.9**

DCL [8], and TASN [73]. Since our VTN is designed as a generic drop-in layer that can be combined with existing backbones and pooling strategies, we report the results of VTNs combined with DCL [8], TASN [73], and iSQRT-COV [35], which are the top-performers on this task. As can be seen in Table 3, our method outperforms the state of the art in most cases. In Table 4, we further evaluate VTNs with iSQRT-COV [35] on iNaturalist-2017 [22], the largest fine-grained recognition dataset, on which we consistently outperform the state of the art.

Network Visualization. To analyze the feature representation capability of VTNs, we applied Grad-CAM (GCAM) [53], which uses gradients to calculate the importance of the spatial locations, to STN- and VTN-based networks. As shown in Fig. 6 and Table 5, compared to the ResNet-50 [21] backbone, STNs [28] only focus on the most discriminative parts, and thus discard other important parts. Unlike them, VTNs improve the feature representation power by allowing the networks to focus on the most discriminative parts represented by each feature channel.

Fig. 7. Visualization of warping fields of VTNs at each channel on some instances of the ROxford and RParis benchmarks [46]. VTNs not only localize different semantic parts in different channels but identify the same points across different images.

4.3   Instance-Level Image Retrieval

Finally, we evaluate our VTNs on the task of instance-level image retrieval using the ROxford and RParis benchmarks [46], which address some limitations of the standard Oxford-5K [44] and Paris-6K benchmarks [45], such as annotation errors, size of the dataset, and level of difficulty, and comprise 4,993 and 6,322 images, respectively. Following standard practice, we use the mean average precision (mAP) [44] for quantitative evaluation. We follow the evaluation protocol of [46], using two evaluation setups (*Medium* and *Hard*). As baselines, we use a pretrained ResNet-50 [21] backbone, followed by various pooling methods, such as MAC [59], SPoC [2], CroW [30], R-MAC [59], and GeM [47]. We also evaluate deep local attentive features (DELF) [42] with an aggregated selective match kernel [59] and spatial verification [44] that learns spatial attention, and incorporate our VTNs into them. Furthermore, we report the results of end-to-end training techniques [19,47], and incorporate our VTNs on top of them. As evidenced by our significantly better results in Table 6, focusing on the most discriminative parts at each feature channel is one of the key to the success of instance-level image retrieval. Note that the comparison with STNs shows the benefits of our approach, which accounts for different semantic concepts across different feature channels and thus, even for rigid objects, is able to learn more discriminative feature representations than a global warping. Figure 7 visualizes some warping fields of VTNs.

5   Conclusion

We have introduced VTNs that predict channel-wise warping fields to boost the representation power of an intermediate CNN feature map by reconfiguring the features spatially and channel-wisely. VTNs account for the fact that the individual feature channels can represent different semantic information and require different spatial transformations. To this end, we have developed an encoder-decoder network that relies on channel squeeze and expansion modules to account for inter-channel relationships. To improve the localization ability of the predicted warping fields, we have further introduced a loss function defined between the warped features of pairs of instances. Our experiments have shown that VTNs consistently boost the features' representation power and consequently the networks' accuracy on fine-grained image recognition and instance-level image retrieval tasks.

References

1. Arandjelovic, R., Zisserman, A.: All about vlad. In: CVPR (2013)
2. Babenko, A., Lempitsky, V.: Aggregating deep convolutional features for image retrieval. In: ICCV (2015)
3. Bahdanau, D., Cho, K., Bengio, Y.: Neural machine translation by jointly learning to align and translate. In: ICLR (2015)
4. Battaglia, P.W., Pascanu, R., Lai, M., Rezende, D.J., Kavukcuoglu, K.: Interaction networks for learning about objects, relations and physics. In: NeurIPS (2016)
5. Bau, D., Zhou, B., Khosla, A., Oliva, A., Torralba, A.: Network dissection: quantifying interpretability of deep visual representations. In: CVPR (2017)
6. Berg, T., Liu, J., Lee, S.W., Alexander, M.L., Jacobs, D.W., Belhumeur, P.N.: Birdsnap: large-scale fine-grained visual categorization of birds. In: CVPR (2014)
7. Chen, L., et al.: SCA-CNN: spatial and channel-wise attention in convolutional networks for image captioning. In: CVPR (2017)
8. Chen, Y., Bai, Y., Zhang, W., Mei, T.: Destruction and construction learning for fine-grained image recognition. In: CVPR (2019)
9. Cui, Y., Zhou, F., Wang, J., Liu, X., Lin, Y., Belongie, S.: Kernel pooling for convolutional neural networks. In: CVPR (2017)
10. Dai, J., et al.: Deformable convolutional networks. In: ICCV (2017)
11. Deng, J., Dong, W., Socher, R., Li, L.J., Li, K., Fei-Fei, L.: ImageNet: a large-scale hierarchical image database. In: CVPR (2009)
12. Esteves, C., Allen-Blanchette, C., Zhou, X., Daniilidis, K.: Polar transformer networks. In: ICLR (2018)
13. Everingham, M., Eslami, S.M.A., Van Gool, L., Williams, C.K.I., Winn, J., Zisserman, A.: The pascal visual object classes challenge: a retrospective. IJCV **111**(1), 98–136 (2015)
14. Felzenszwalb, P.F., Girshick, R.B., McAllester, D., Ramanan, D.: Object detection with discriminative trained part based models. IEEE Trans. PAMI **32**(9), 1627–1645 (2010)
15. Fu, J., Liu, J., Tian, H., Fang, Z., Lu, H.: Dual attention network for scene segmentation. In: CVPR (2019)
16. Fu, J., Zheng, H., Mei, T.: Look closer to see better: recurrent attention convolutional neural network for fine-grained image recognition. In: CVPR (2017)
17. Gao, Y., Beijbom, O., Zhang, N., Darrell, T.: Compact bilinear pooling. In: CVPR (2016)
18. Gonzalez-Garcia, A., Modolo, D., Ferrari, V.: Do semantic parts emerge in convolutional neural networks? IJCV **126**(5), 476–494 (2018)
19. Gordo, A., Almazàn, J., Revaud, J., Larlus, D.: End-to-end learning of deep visual representations for image retrieval. IJCV **124**(2), 237–254 (2017)
20. Gregor, K., Danihelka, I., Graves, A., Rezende, D.J., Wierstra, D.: Draw: a recurrent neural network for image generation. In: ICML (2015)
21. He, K., Zhang, X., Ren, S., Sun, J.: Deep residual learning for image recognition. In: CVPR (2016)

22. Horn, G.V., et al.: The inaturalist species classification and detection dataset. In: CVPR (2018)
23. Hu, J., Shen, L., Sun, G.: Squeeze-and-excitation networks. In: CVPR (2018)
24. Huang, G., Liu, Z., Laurens, V.D.M., Weinberger, K.Q.: Densely connected convolutional networks. In: CVPR (2017)
25. Huang, S., Xu, Z., Tao, D., Zhang, Y.: Part-stacked CNN for fine-grained visual categorization. In: CVPR (2016)
26. Ioffe, S., Szegedy, C.: Batch normalization: accelerating deep network training by reducing internal covariate shift. In: ICML (2015)
27. Itti, L., Koch, C., Niebur, E.: A model of saliency-based visual attention for rapid scene analysis. TPAMI 20(11), 1254–1259 (1998)
28. Jaderberg, M., Simonyan, K., Zisserman, A., Kavukcuoglu, K.: Spatial transformer networks. In: NeurIPS (2015)
29. Jeong, J., Shin, J.: Training CNNs with selective allocation of channels. In: ICML (2019)
30. Kalantidis, Y., Mellina, C., Osindero, S.: Cross-dimensional weighting for aggregated deep convolutional features. In: Hua, G., Jégou, H. (eds.) ECCV 2016. LNCS, vol. 9913, pp. 685–701. Springer, Cham (2016). https://doi.org/10.1007/978-3-319-46604-0_48
31. Kim, S., Min, D., Jeong, S., Kim, S., Jeon, S., Sohn, K.: Semantic attribute matching networks. In: CVPR (2019)
32. Krause, J., Stark, M., Deng, J., Fei-Fei, L.: 3D object representations for fine-grained categorization. In: CVPR (2015)
33. Krizhevsky, A., Sutskever, I., Hinton, G.E.: Imagenet classification with deep convolutional neural networks. In: NeurIPS (2012)
34. Larochelle, H., Hinton, G.E.: Learning to combine foveal glimpses with a third-order boltzmann machine. In: NeurIPS (2010)
35. Li, P., Xie, J., Wang, Q., Zuo, W.: Towards faster training of global covariance pooling networks by iterative matrix square root normalization. In: CVPR (2018)
36. Li, Z., Yang, Y., Liu, X., Zhou, F., Wen, S., Xu, W.: Dynamic computational time for visual attention. In: ICCVW (2017)
37. Lin, C.H., Lucey, S.: Inverse compositional spatial transformer networks. In: CVPR (2017)
38. Lin, T.Y., RoyChowdhury, A., Maji, S.: Bilinear CNN models for fine-grained visual recognition. In: ICCV (2015)
39. Lowe, D.G.: Distinctive image features from scale-invariant keypoints. IJCV 60(2), 91–110 (2004)
40. Maji, S., Kannala, J., Rahtu, E., Blaschko, M., Vedaldi, A.: Fine-grained visual classification of aircraft. Technical report (2013)
41. Mikolajczyk, K., Schmid, C.: A performance evaluation of local descriptors. TPAMI 27(10), 1615–1630 (2005)
42. Noh, H., Araujo, A., Sim, J., Weyand, T., Han, B.: Large-scale image retrieval with attentive deep local features. In: ICCV (2017)
43. Paszke, A., et al.: Automatic differentiation in pytorch (2017)
44. Philbin, J., Chum, O., Isard, M., Sivic, J., Zisserman, A.: Object retrieval with large vocabularies and fast spatial matching. In: CVPR (2007)
45. Philbin, J., Chum, O., Isard, M., Sivic, J., Zisserman, A.: Lost in quantization: improving particular object retrieval in large scale image databases. In: CVPR (2008)
46. Radenovič F., Iscen, A., Tolias, G., Avrithis, Y., Chum, O.: Revisiting oxford and paris: large-scale image retrieval benchmarking. In: CVPR (2018)

47. Radenovič F., Tolias, G., Chum, O.: Fine-tuning CNN image retrieval with no human annotation. TPAMI **41**(7), 1655–1668 (2019)
48. Recasens, A., Kellnhofer, P., Stent, S., Matusik, W., Torralba, A.: Learning to zoom: a saliency-based sampling layer for neural networks. In: ECCV (2018)
49. Ren, S., He, K., Girshick, R., Sun, J.: Faster r-cnn: towards real-time object detection with region proposal networks. In: NeurIPS (2015)
50. Rocco, I., Arandjelović, R., Sivic, J.: End-to-end weakly-supervised semantic alignment. In: CVPR (2018)
51. Rodriguez, P., Gonfaus, J.M., Cucurull, G., Xavierroca, F., Gonzalez, J.: Attend and rectify: a gated attention mechanism for fine-grained recovery. In: ECCV (2018)
52. Santoro, A., et al.: A simple neural network moduel for relational reasoning. In: NeurIPS (2017)
53. Selvaraju, R.R., Cogswell, M., Das, A., Vedantam, R.: Grad-cam: visual explanations from deep networks via gradient-based localization. In: ICCV (2017)
54. Simo-Serra, E., Trulls, E., Ferraz, L., Kokkinos, I., Fua, P., Moreno-Noguer, F.: Discriminative learning of deep convolutional feature point descriptors. In: ICCV (2015)
55. Simonyan, K., Zisserman, A.: Very deep convolutional networks for large-scale image recognition. In: ICLR (2015)
56. Sivic, J., Zisserman, A.: Video google: a text retrieval approach to object matching in videos. In: ICCV (2003)
57. Sun, K., Xiao, B., Liu, D.: Deep high-resolution representation learning for human pose estimation. In: CVPR (2019)
58. Sun, M., Yuan, Y., Zhou, F., Ding, E.: Multi-attention multi-class constraint for fine-grained image recognition. In: ECCV (2018)
59. Tolias, G., Avrithis, Y., Jégou, H.: Image search with selective match kernels: aggregation across single and multiple images. IJCV **116**(3), 247–261 (2016)
60. Tompson, J., Goroshin, R., Jain, A., LeCun, Y., Bregler, C.: Efficient object localization using convolutional networks. In: CVPR (2015)
61. Vaswani, A., et al.: Attention is all you need. In: NeurIPS (2017)
62. Wang, F., et al.: Residual attention network for image classification. In: CVPR (2017)
63. Wang, Y., Morariu, V.I., Davis, L.S.: Learning a discriminative filter bank within a CNN for fine-grained recognition. In: CVPR (2018)
64. Welinder, P., et al.: Caltech-ucsd birds 200. Technical report, CNS-TR-2010-001, California Institute of Technology (2010)
65. Woo, S., Park, J., Lee, J.Y., Kweon, I.S.: Cbam: convolutional block attention module. In: ECCV (2018)
66. Wu, Y., He, K.: Group normalization. In: ECCV (2018)
67. Xu, K., et al.: Show, attend and tell: neural image caption generation with visual attention. In: ICML (2015)
68. Xu, T., et al.: Attngan: fine-grained text to image generation with attentional generative adversarial networks. In: CVPR (2018)
69. Yi, K.M., Trulls, E., Lepetit, V., Fua, P.: LIFT: learned invariant feature transform. In: Leibe, B., Matas, J., Sebe, N., Welling, M. (eds.) ECCV 2016. LNCS, vol. 9910, pp. 467–483. Springer, Cham (2016). https://doi.org/10.1007/978-3-319-46466-4_28
70. Zhang, H., et al.: Context encoding for semantic segmentation. In: CVPR (2018)
71. Zhang, H., Goodfellow, I., Metaxas, D., Odena, A.: Self-attention generative adversarial networks. In: ICML (2019)

72. Zheng, H., Fu, J., Mei, T., Luo, J.: Learning multi-attention convolutional neural network for fine-grained image recognition. In: ICCV (2017)
73. Zheng, H., Fu, J., Zha, Z.J., Luo, J.: Looking for the devil in the details: learning trilinear attention sampling network for fine-grained image recognition. In: CVPR (2019)
74. Zheng, L., Shen, L., Tian, L., Wang, S., Wang, J., Tian, Q.: Scalable person re-identification: a benchmark. In: ICCV (2015)
75. Zhou, B., Khosla, A., Lapedriza, A., Oliva, A., Torralba, A.: Learning deep features for discriminative localization. In: CVPR (2016)
76. Zhu, X., Cheng, D., Zhang, Z., Lin, S., Dai, J.: An empirical study of spatial attention mechanisms in deep networks. In: ICCV (2019)

360° Camera Alignment via Segmentation

Benjamin Davidson$^{(\boxtimes)}$, Mohsan S. Alvi, and João F. Henriques

Disperse.io, London, UK
{ben,mohsan,joao}@disperse.io

Abstract. Panoramic 360° images taken under unconstrained conditions present a significant challenge to current state-of-the-art recognition pipelines, since the assumption of a mostly upright camera is no longer valid. In this work, we investigate how to solve this problem by fusing purely geometric cues, such as apparent vanishing points, with learned semantic cues, such as the expectation that some visual elements (e.g. doors) have a natural upright position. We train a deep neural network to leverage these cues to segment the image-space endpoints of an imagined "vertical axis", which is orthogonal to the ground plane of a scene, thus levelling the camera. We show that our segmentation-based strategy significantly increases performance, *reducing errors by half*, compared to the current state-of-the-art on two datasets of 360° imagery. We also demonstrate the importance of 360° camera levelling by analysing its impact on downstream tasks, finding that incorrect levelling severely degrades the performance of real-world computer vision pipelines.

1 Introduction

The ability of 360° (or spherical) imaging to record an entire scene with a single capture makes them a powerful tool, both for machine perception and for rapidly documenting entire scenes. For example, 360° imaging has been used to record crime scenes where it is vital to image the entire scene for evidence [32], to easily create Virtual Reality (VR) videos with minimal cost [24], and is perhaps most widely recognized in its role in creating Google Street View [12]. Arrays of cameras that can be composed into a full 360° image or video are also important in mobile applications with critical safety requirements, such as self-driving cars [1]. With the availability of inexpensive 360° capture devices, and the growth of VR headsets, there is an increased demand for techniques to automatically analyse and process spherical images.

The recent successes of computer vision, with deep learning playing a key role in the state-of-the-art object detectors [22], segmentation [30], camera pose estimation [20] and many others, seem to indicate that the same techniques should be directly applicable to 360° images. However, there are specific difficulties associated with this modality that need to be addressed. One common problem

---

Electronic supplementary material The online version of this chapter (https://doi.org/10.1007/978-3-030-58604-1_35) contains supplementary material, which is available to authorized users.

A. Vedaldi et al. (Eds.): ECCV 2020, LNCS 12373, pp. 579–595, 2020.
https://doi.org/10.1007/978-3-030-58604-1_35

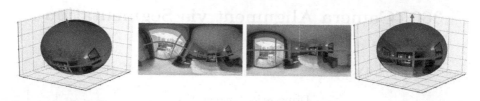

Fig. 1. Illustration of the problem of levelling spherical images. From left to right: a spherical image captured at a tilted angle relative to the sky (red arrow), with the horizon line shown in blue; its 2D representation (equirectangular image), with heavy distortions due to the rotation; the same image, undistorted by our system; the aligned spherical image in 3D. (Color figure online)

for spherical images is a misalignment between the camera frames' ground plane and the world frames' ground plane (see Fig. 2).

This misalignment makes automatically processing spherical images more challenging than it needs to be. For example, training a spherical object detector on misaligned images would require the network to learn a representation which was invariant to rotations away from the vertical axis [15]. In contrast to this, if all images are level (upright), the representation could be sensitive to these rotations, simplifying the task to be learned [11] (Fig. 1).

The ground-plane alignment that we focus on estimates 2° of freedom (DOF) (roll and pitch), and must be contrasted to general camera pose estimation, which estimates 6 DOF (translation and rotation in 3D) [20]. Ground-plane alignment can be performed *with a single image*, by using simple cues (e.g. vertical walls, ground or sky/ceiling positions). Differently, 6D camera pose estimation requires extra reference images [14,19,20], making it much less applicable.

Aligning spherical images to the ground is also an important pre-processing step for downstream tasks (we demonstrate this empirically in Sect. 3). State-of-the-art object detectors, and segmentation networks are trained and evaluated on upright equirectangular images [8,37,38], and do not work under arbitrary rotations. Similarly, human visual recognition also degrades quickly with extreme rotations [33], and there are classification problems that are impossible to solve under arbitrary rotations (the canonical example being the distinction between the digits 9 and 6). Ground-plane alignment can also make pose estimation more robust, as estimating the pose of a levelled image requires two fewer DOF [28].

At a high level, our method estimates the axis orthogonal to the ground (vertical axis) by segmenting the unit sphere (where each point corresponds to a different direction) into likely candidates. We leverage a state-of-the-art segmentation network [30], by exploiting the fact that the unit sphere can be mapped to a 2D image via the equirectangular transform (Sect. 2.1). The network is trained to segment the sphere into those directions likely to correspond to the vertical axis.

In addition to the novel segmentation formulation of this problem, we propose to combine the strengths of both geometrical methods and learning-based methods. Geometrical methods, such as those based on detecting and accumulating

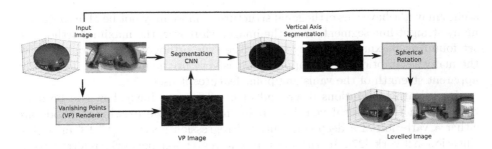

Fig. 2. Overview of the proposed method. We train a convolutional network to produce a segmentation of an equirectangular image, using vanishing point features as extra geometric information. The output segmentation encodes the endpoints of the vertical axis, which we use to orient the image upright.

votes for locations of vanishing points (VP) [10,21,37], are very accurate, but brittle under noise and uncertainty. Learning-based methods are less accurate but very robust. We combine both, by incorporating a residual stream that propagates information about VP likelihoods, and this way informs our segmentation network with precise geometrical information.

By leveraging the power of feature engineering with state-of-the-art segmentation techniques, our method is the most accurate to date. We compare our method with the two most recent automatic alignment methods Deep360Up [18] and Coarse2Fine [27]. We demonstrate improved performance on the Sun360 dataset [35], as well a new dataset of construction images that we collected.

1.1 Related Work

Ground plane alignment is related to pose estimation [14,19,20], as described in Sect. 1. Another related line of work is rotation invariant (or equivariant) networks [15,34], which aims to make models more robust and predictable w.r.t. rotations, and is complementary to our method. We aim instead to predict and undo the effect of a single global rotation, with a semantically-defined reference (the ground plane).

The classical solution to ground plane alignment has been to extract the straight line segments from an image, and use these to estimate a vanishing point in the direction of the vertical axis [10,21,37]. These methods rely on what are known as the Manhattan or Atlanta world assumptions [4,25], which assert that the scene that has been captured will contain some orthogonal structure, given the tendency in human construction to build at right angles. It must be remarked that this assumption does not always hold in practice. One typical way to extract this orthogonal structure is to determine the direction in which all straight lines in an image are pointing, and have each line vote on vanishing point directions [37], in a manner similar to the Hough transform [7] (c.f. Sect. 2.3). The orthogonal directions of the scene can then be found by looking for the three orthogonal directions which together have the most votes. However, many scenes may not have this orthogonal structure, and we may not be able to extract many straight line segments from the image. Moreover, the maximal orthogonal set found by maximisation may not be the true orthogonal directions. Due to the many assumptions of this approach, it is very brittle in practice, despite the apparent strength of the vanishing point features it uses.

Deep learning solutions to ground plane alignment have shown to be more robust than the classical vanishing point methods. The existing methods are either a variation of a deep convolutional regression network [17,18] or a classification network [27]. In the most recent regression network, referred to as Deep360Up, the vertical direction (pointing upwards) is output directly from a DenseNet [16], which is trained using the logarithm of the hyperbolic cosine between the estimated and ground truth vertical directions [18]. The most accurate and recent deep approach has been to use a *coarse to fine* classification network [27]. This approach, referred to as Coarse2Fine, classifies the pitch and roll of an image as belonging to a 10° bin (coarse), thus adjusting the image to be within ±5°, and then classifying the adjusted image to be within a 1° bin (fine). Another standard feature of such solutions is to generate training data from already levelled images (which we discuss in Sect. 2.4). Though these methods have once again demonstrated the power of deep networks, we show in Sect. 3 that the proposed segmentation approach is more accurate.

A related line of work is to propose network architectures that directly work with spherical images, for example for classification and detection [3], or for segmentation and depth prediction [31]. Our levelling method can alleviate any upright-world assumptions in these works, as well as standard networks, and is thus complementary.

2   Methods

Our approach can broadly be split into three stages: calculating the vanishing points, segmenting the image, and processing the segmentation into a single vertical direction. Before describing our method in detail, we provide some background on equirectangular images and some useful operations.

2.1   Background on Equirectangular Images

An equirectangular image is a planar representation of an image on the sphere, where height and width correspond respectively to latitude and longitude. The explicit transformation (denoted p) between pixel coordinates (x, y) and spherical coordinates (λ, ϕ) is straightforward:

$$p : \mathbb{R}^2 \to \mathbb{S}^2, \quad p(x, y) = \left(\frac{\pi y}{h}, 2\pi - \frac{\pi x}{w} \right) = (\lambda, \phi) \tag{1}$$

where w and h are the dimensions in pixels. Note that this is an invertible transformation and so we can move from the image to the sphere and vice-versa. Using p we will frequently refer to an equirectangular image as being on the sphere,

Fig. 3. An example equirectangular image, and its corresponding projection on the faces of a cube. Note the many curved lines in the equirectangular image, which become straight in the corresponding cube face.

by which we mean the projection of the image to the sphere. Furthermore we can map spherical to Cartesian coordinates and vice versa using the spherical to cartesian transformation: $f(\lambda, \phi) = (\cos(\phi)\sin(\lambda), \sin(\phi)\sin(\lambda), \cos(\lambda))$. We can use these transformations to rotate an equirectangular image I_{src} to create another image I_{dst} of different orientation, by rotating the sphere. Starting from a point x_{dst} in the pixel space of I_{dst} we project x_{dst} to the sphere $p(x_{\mathrm{dst}})$, and rotate the sphere with a rotation matrix $R \in SO(3)$. Note that R represents an arbitrary rotation in 3D space, with an axis of rotation not necessarily corresponding to latitude or longitude. Doing so gives the following relationship between coordinate systems:

$$y_{\mathrm{src}} = Rf(p(x_{\mathrm{dst}})) \qquad (2)$$

After this transformation we project back to image space: $x_{\mathrm{src}} = p^{-1}(f^{-1}(y_{\mathrm{src}}))$. The transformation of image coordinates x_{dst} to x_{src} allows us to re-sample an image I_{src} to create I_{dst}, for example by bilinear interpolation [15]. As can be seen in Eq. (2), we may rotate the image so that we have an equirectangular image of any orientation, which we will use to generate training data for our segmentation network.

Another subtle but important aspect about equirectangular images is how to extract straight line segments visible within the scene. Straight lines in the scene do not in general map to straight lines in an equirectangular image (see Fig. 3). To recover straight lines from an equirectangular image, we need to convert it to one or more perspective images. We cover the full 360° view with perspective views, corresponding to 6 cube faces (see Fig. 3). Each one is produced by rendering the sphere (with the mapped texture) from 6 different points-of-view, at right angles. This "cube mapping" is commonly used in computer graphics to render far-away scenes [26]. This allows using unmodified line segment detectors.

2.2 Segmentation Framework

Our method is based on a convolutional neural network optimised for segmentation, with side-information about vanishing points as input to an attention module. The output of our network is a binary segmentation of the original equirectangular image, which by applying the pixel to spherical transform p may be thought of as a segmentation of the sphere into background and likely directions for the vertical axis. Specifically, we segment all points on the sphere which are within 5° of the north or south pole, where the poles are taken relative to camera coordinates (see Fig. 2 for an example segmentation). By embedding all useful inputs and outputs in a 2-dimensional space, we can leverage highly successful 2D segmentation networks, and allow predictions to be based on both geometric and semantic cues (i.e., vanishing points and poses of distinctive objects in images).

Network Architecture. The base architecture that we use is the Gated-Shape CNN (GSCNN) [30]. The GSCNN is a fully convolutional network, designed to utilise side information about object boundaries to improve its performance on semantic segmentation tasks. It consists of a backbone feature extractor, in our case InceptionV3 [29], an ASPP (atrous spatial pyramid pooling) layer, and the shape stream. The shape stream in the original work accepts image gradients and intermediate backbone features as inputs, and outputs a single channel feature image. The output shape stream features are then combined with other backbone features in the ASPP layer to generate a dense feature map of the same resolution as the input image.

Our architecture modifies GSCNNs so that it would be more informative to call the shape stream the *vanishing point stream*, as we replace image gradients with the vanishing point image V (see Sect. 2.3). The reasoning behind this is that V is a feature that is highly informative w.r.t. the vertical axis, and we would like to let the network exploit this source of information. Also, feeding V to the network in this manner allows us to use a pre-trained backbone network, which would not be possible by just concatenating V to the channels of the image. Using a GSCNN enabled us to introduce information relating to vanishing points, whilst also retaining the ability to use pre-trained backbones.

2.3   Vanishing Point Image

Vanishing points have proven to be a strong geometric cue for many computer vision tasks, including ground plane alignment [10]. In many scenes a horizon line is visible, or orthogonal structures such as the corners of buildings. These structures are useful for determining the vertical axis, and can be emphasised by calculating vanishing points (see Fig. 4). Moreover, these features can be computed directly from images, with no learning required. This makes them excellent features for our purpose.

To build the vanishing point image in Fig. 4 we extract all of the straight lines in the scene and use each line to vote on vanishing directions. The first step of this process is to project the equirectangular image to the 6 cube faces (Fig. 3, right) and extract line segments from each face. To extract the line segments we use Canny edge detection combined with a probabilistic Hough transform [2,9]. We then convert each line segment to a plane, defined by the line endpoints, and the origin of the sphere. Let n be the normal vector to this plane. We use n

Fig. 4. An equirectangular image and the corresponding vanishing point image (Sect. 2.3). The 6 regions highlighted in red are areas which have received a large number of votes. Note that each highly-voted region corresponds to one face of the approximately cuboid room (the four walls, floor and ceiling). (Color figure online)

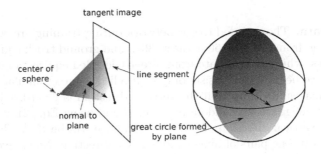

Fig. 5. Illustration of how to calculate vanishing point features from line segments in a cube face. We can see that every point on the great circle formed by intersecting the plane and the sphere will be orthogonal to the normal vector. Therefore, every point in this circle receives a vote. In practice the 2D surface of the sphere is discretised (Sect. 2.1), and every bin within some threshold distance of this circle receives a vote.

to vote for vanishing point locations, by voting for all directions on the sphere which are orthogonal to n. Geometrically this means all points on the great circle defined by the intersection of the plane and sphere receive a vote. In practice we split the sphere into $h \times w$ bins by projecting each pixel in an equirectangular image I to the sphere and then voting via

$$V^n_{h_0,w_0} = \begin{cases} 1 & |n \cdot f(p(I_{h_0,w_0}))| < \lambda_{\text{vanishing}} \\ 0 & \text{otherwise} \end{cases}. \tag{3}$$

We calculate a normal vector n for every line segment and accumulate votes by summing $V = \sum_n V^n$. Finally we normalise V to be an intensity image with values in the range of $[0, 255]$. High values will correspond to probable vanishing points, which have many line segments pointing towards them, and will assist our network in finding the vertical axis (Fig. 5).

2.4 Training Method

To train our network, we use a weighted generalised dice loss [5] on uniformly distributed points on the sphere. This is in contrast to the original GSCNN work which utilises auxiliary and regularising losses [30], and which have no direct analogue in our setting. We chose to use the generalised dice loss as this has been shown to perform well in situations where there are large class imbalances between foreground and background classes [5]. This is a concern in our setting, since vanishing points are sparse.

We do not compute the loss directly on the 2D segmentation image, as this would over-sample the polar regions, thus disproportionately weighing vertical directions near them. Instead, we select points that are uniformly distributed around the sphere, and project these into the equirectangular segmentation, and ground truth. Finally, we interpolate the values of each projected point to construct y and $\hat{y}$.

Training Data. The data fed to our network during training are equirectangular images (e.g. from the Sun360 dataset [36]), and ground truth equirectangular segmentations, which we generate from already levelled equirectangular images. The dataset we begin with consists only of levelled equirectangular images. For all of these images, we know that the vertical direction is $z = (0, 0, 1)$. By rotating a levelled image with a random rotation R and using Eq. (2), we know that the resulting vertical direction of the rotated image will be $R^{-1}z$. From this we can generate training pairs of image and vertical direction. Now, given a vertical direction, it is simple to construct a binary equirectangular segmentation. Let u be the generic vertical direction for some image and I an equirectangular image. After applying $f \circ p$ to all pixel values in I, we can consider the i, j^{th} pixel as sitting at $x_{i,j}$ on the sphere in $\mathbb{R}^3$. Our segmentation $s_{i,j}$ is 1 where $|u \cdot x_{i,j}| > \lambda_{seg}$ and 0 otherwise, which means that we consider pixels that project near to the vertical axis as foreground (1) and all others as background (0). Rotating level images whilst keeping track of the vertical axis allows us to construct many pairs of image and segmentation from a single levelled image.

To actually generate our dataset we compute n_{rot} rotations which will place the vertical axis uniformly around the sphere, and then apply a small offset rotation. Performing these almost uniform rotations avoids using the same n_{rot} rotations for every image, whilst ensuring that the directions completely cover the sphere (c.f. Appendix A). Note there are infinitely many rotations placing the vertical direction at a specific point (by rolling around the vertical axis). We incorporate this rotation online during training, as the rotation can be represented via rolling the equirectangular image along its width axis.

Even when using high quality interpolation methods, we cannot avoid rotational artifacts appearing in the rotated images, which can adversely impact generalization performance. This relatively subtle issue will be discussed in Sect. 3.

2.5 Test-Time Prediction

Once we have an equirectangular segmentation, we can extract a vertical direction by selecting the most probable connected component and taking its centroid

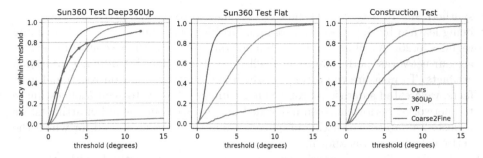

Fig. 6. Accuracy evaluation on the test splits of 3 datasets. From left to right: Sun360 with the same artificial rotations as used by Deep360up [18], Sun360 without rotation, and the construction dataset (Sect. 3.3). We report the accuracy over different angular thresholds, for 4 methods: ours, vanishing points (VP, a purely geometric method), and 2 state-of-the-art deep learning methods (360Up and Coarse2Fine). Our method significantly outperforms others on images without artificial rotations (center and right).

as the vertical direction. Given such a centroid c and Eq. (1) we recover the vertical direction via $p(c) \in \mathbb{S}^2$. While this is a simple computer vision operation, for completeness we describe it fully in Appendix A (Fig. 6).

Test-Time Augmentation. The final stage of our approach is an optional test time augmentation, which may rotate an image and rerun the segmentation. Let u be a candidate vertical direction obtained after running a single forward pass of the network. If the image was already close to level, *i.e.* u is close to $z = (0, 0, 1)$, then we rotate the images pitch by 20° and rerun the entire inference and post-processing steps to get a new u'. The reason for this is that, if the image is already close to level, the vanishing point features for the vertical axis are close to the points of most distortion: $\pm z$. Following this, we rotate u' back 20° and take the resulting vector as the vertical direction.

Testing Data. We collected a test set of unlevelled images, where the vertical direction has been calculated manually. To calculate the vertical direction manually two vertical lines, vertical in the world frame, are manually identified, which allows us to construct a plane parallel to the ground plane, by computing the normals as in Sect. 2.3. This plane parallel to the ground trivially gives us the vertical axis, as the axis orthogonal to the plane. By ensuring we use unrotated test images, we avoid data leakage due to rotational artifacts present in the images (see Sect. 3).

3 Experiments

We trained and tested our methods on three datasets: the Sun360 dataset, a synthetic dataset of noise, and a dataset of construction images. Training on synthetically rotated Sun360 images can lead to rotational artifacts (Sect. 3.2) being learned by the network, a common problem with similar synthetic training regimes [6,23]. As all images in the Sun360 dataset are level, we could only evaluate our networks' performance on levelled images without introducing rotational artifacts. To measure the extent to which the network relies on rotational artifacts, we created a dataset of rotated noise images. Lastly, to accurately estimate the networks' performance on unlevelled images, without the aid of artifacts, we collected a dataset consisting of images which were not level, and for which the vertical direction was known.

In the following experiments, we compare our method with that of Deep360Up [18] and a baseline vanishing point (VP) method based on [38]. We made use of the publicly available Deep360Up implementation. When possible we also report the performance of the Coarse2Fine [27] approach, by testing on the same test set. On the Sun360 dataset we also show the importance of the vanishing point stream, by removing it from the network and observing a reduced performance.

Finally, we demonstrate the importance of levelling images for downstream tasks by training a segmentation network on levelled and unlevelled images. We make use of our implementation of the original GSCNN work as the segmentation network, and the dataset from [13].

3.1 Sun360 Dataset

This dataset consists of 30,000 levelled images, and we use a 80-10-10 split for training, validation and test. As all images in this dataset are already level, we cannot test on any images which do not contain rotational artifacts. To account for this, we evaluated the network on the original, level, images as well as rotated images. We report performance on 3 subsets of data: the unrotated level test set (referred to as Test Flat), the unrotated validation set, and a rotated validation set where all vertical directions are in the upper-hemisphere. To compare our method with both Deep360Up and Coarse2Fine we also report results on a synthetically rotated test set, referred to as Test Deep360Up, consisting of 17,825 images that were used to evaluate both methods in the original works.

The accuracy of our method as well as the brittleness of the classical vanishing point method is shown in Table 1. Our approach is the most accurate on both the level and synthetically rotated test sets, when considering a threshold of at least 2°. The Coarse2Fine approach does achieve a higher accuracy than our method when considering a 1° threshold, but then falls off to be the lowest out of all considered deep learning methods, at larger thresholds. A possible explanation for this dropoff is that the Coarse2Fine approach solves the problem in two stages: first adjusting the image to be within 10° of level, and then refining this adjusted image to be within 1°. Therefore, if the initial estimation is incorrect, the network can never recover the true vertical direction. In contrast, our method is completely end-to-end, and so we do not depend on the output of a previous stage, giving a more robust approximation. Here we also demonstrate the importance of the vanishing point stream, as removing it significantly reduces

Table 1. Performance for different subsets of the Sun360 dataset (see text for details). We report the percentage of images for which the vertical axis is correctly estimated within a threshold of $x°$.

		Percentage of estimated axes within $x°$							
Dataset	Method	1°	2°	3°	4°	5°	7.5°	10°	12°
Val rotated	Ours	**25.1**	**60.5**	**80.5**	**90.3**	**94.7**	**97.5**	**98.1**	**98.4**
	Ours (no VP)	20.9	45.6	57.0	74.4	90.2	96.5	97.4	97.8
	Deep360Up	4.9	17.6	34.8	54.7	70.1	91.0	95.7	97.5
	VP	0.2	0.7	1.2	1.5	1.7	2.2	2.5	2.8
Val flat	Ours	**34.7**	**78.8**	**92.4**	**96.4**	**97.9**	**99.0**	**99.3**	**99.4**
	Ours (no VP)	0.3	1.0	2.9	67.0	97.0	98.9	**99.3**	**99.4**
	Deep360Up	9.8	20.5	33.3	45.5	58.8	81.4	93.2	97.1
	VP	0.5	2.8	5.1	7.3	9.4	12.9	16.0	17.6
Test Deep360	Ours	19.7	**53.6**	**75.5**	**87.2**	**92.6**	**97.1**	**98.2**	**98.4**
	Ours (no VP)	7.5	23.5	40.3	55.9	68.2	87.1	94.8	97.4
	Deep360Up	7.1	24.5	43.9	60.7	74.2	91.9	96.6	97.9
	Coarse2Fine	**30.9**	51.7	65.9	74.1	79.1	NA	NA	91.0
	VP	0.3	0.9	1.6	2.1	2.5	3.3	3.8	4.2
Test flat	Ours	**34.0**	**78.4**	**92.4**	**96.2**	**97.8**	**98.8**	**99.3**	**99.4**
	Ours (no VP)	0.4	1.3	3.1	63.9	96.5	98.6	99.0	99.2
	Deep360Up	10.2	22.5	35.3	48.2	60.1	82.3	93.4	97.3
	VP	0.3	2.5	6.1	8.8	11.0	14.1	16.7	18.5

performance. The poor performance of the vanishing point method is explained by the nature of the Sun360 dataset, which consists of mostly natural scenes (eg. forests), and therefore does not satisfy the Manhattan world assumption.

3.2 Noise Dataset

As we synthetically rotate images during training, it was crucial to ensure the network was not "cheating", i.e. simply using visual artifacts induced by synthetic rotations to solve the problem, and not learning high-level cues that generalize to images with real rotations. Deep networks are very efficient at finding the simplest solution to a problem, and the existence of shortcuts is a prevalent problem in unsupervised learning, for example taking advantage of boundary effects [23, Sect. 4.2] or chromatic aberrations of lenses [6, Sect. 3.1].

We demonstrate empirically that, in fact, a network can invert a rotation on *pure noise* successfully. To do this, we generated images of random (white) noise, rotated them, and used them to train both our method and the Deep360Up method. We found that in both cases the network could learn to undo the transformation. This highlights the need for an unrotated test set to be sure of the network's performance at test time. Note that we generated a new random noise

Fig. 7. Visualisation of automatically levelled validation images: proposed method (top), Deep360Up (middle), and the misaligned counterparts (bottom row).

image at each training and validation step, meaning that this was not a result of over-fitting, as every image the network saw was different. For Deep360Up, we observed the average angular error in this case to be around 5°, and for our method we saw the generalised dice loss fall to 0.04. Both indicate that the network was able to significantly beat chance using only rotational artifacts (Fig. 7).

3.3   Construction Dataset

To ensure our network was actually solving the problem at hand, we collected a dataset of images from construction sites where we had the raw capture, and the vertical axis of the raw capture. This dataset consists of 10,054 images where we use a 90–10 split for training and validation, and 1006 images for testing. The imbalance in the number of images for training and validation compared to testing images is due to the nature of the data collection process: the training and validation images were already rotated to be level; in contrast, the testing data was gathered manually and consisted of the original capture, which in many cases was not level. This permitted us to test our approach on unlevelled images, that did not contain rotational artifacts. A total of 9365 distinct locations were captured from 16 construction sites, with no overlap in locations between the training and testing data. 48.7% of images were within 3° of level, and 90% were within 12° of level, see Fig. 8 for typical example scenes from this dataset. Again, our method was considerably more accurate than existing state-of-the-art techniques. Table 2 shows that our approach is the most accurate on all datasets, achieving 98% of estimates within 5° for the test set.

Note that the performance of the vanishing point method on the construction data is significantly better than when applied to the Sun360 data. This can be explained due to the construction dataset consisting of rooms that satisfy the Manhattan world assumption, in contrast to the Sun360 dataset.

Table 2. Performance for different subsets of the construction dataset (see text for details). We report the percentage of images for which the vertical axis is correctly estimated within a threshold of $x°$.

Dataset	Method	\multicolumn{8}{c}{Percentage of estimated axes within $x°$}
		1°	2°	3°	4°	5°	7.5°	10°	12°
Val. rotated	Ours	**23.1**	**59.0**	**79.2**	**88.2**	**93.2**	**96.4**	**97.2**	**97.5**
	Deep360Up	3.0	12.1	27.4	42.7	58.3	82.5	91.6	95.7
	VP	4.2	13.4	22.3	28.9	33.3	38.9	41.6	43.0
Val. flat	Ours	**25.3**	**66.3**	**87.4**	**93.5**	**96.0**	**97.9**	**98.3**	**98.7**
	Deep360Up	12.4	25.3	39.6	50.8	61.5	82.4	93.5	96.7
	VP	2.8	11.6	25.7	39.1	47.4	60.8	68.6	73.2
Test	Ours	**26.9**	**67.3**	**88.6**	**95.0**	**97.5**	**99.4**	**99.7**	**99.7**
	Deep360Up	9.0	29.3	49.2	62.1	73.0	88.5	94.2	96.2
	VP	4.9	15.1	27.9	38.1	46.7	62.4	70.5	74.9

3.4 Downstream Segmentation Task

To illustrate the importance of levelling images for downstream tasks we trained several segmentation models using the dataset in [13], which consists of 666 images from the Sun360 dataset, for which the authors have added segmentation labels for 15 classes. As all images in the Sun360 dataset are already level, we created a rotated segmentation dataset by randomly rotating each image so that its vertical direction was at most 45° away from level. We also constructed a levelled dataset by applying our method to the rotated images, using the estimated rotations to level the images and their annotations. In total we used these 3 datasets: original, rotated, and levelled, to train 3 segmentation models.

The segmentation models consist of our own implementation of GSCNNs. Our training regime followed the original work [30] except that we trained for 100 epochs. After training each model, we then evaluated the mean IOU on the original, rotated, and levelled validation sets, consisting of 100 images.

Table 3. Downstream task performance (mean IOU, in percentages) on different subsets of data (Sect. 3.4). For each model we highlight the *worst* performance in bold.

		\multicolumn{3}{c}{Evaluation dataset}
		Original	Levelled	Rotated
Training dataset	Original	40.1	40.0	**26.7**
	Levelled	42.5	42.0	**31.4**
	Rotated	43.0	42.7	**39.1**

Table 3 shows that all models performed the worst on the rotated dataset, even the model trained specifically on rotated images. This drop in performance

Original   Rotated   Levelled

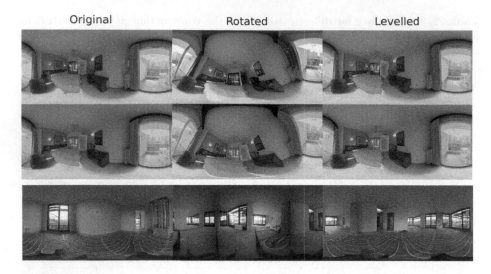

Fig. 8. Top row: Qualitative results for the downstream task of semantic segmentation (Sect. 3.4). Middle row: Ground truth. The model performs well on the original images (left), but significantly worse on rotated images (center). Levelling with our method (right) recovers the performance. This highlights the importance of levelling for realistic downstream tasks. Bottom row: Example scenes from the construction dataset.

is particularly striking for models trained on levelled images, with drops of 13.3% and 10.6% for the model trained on the original dataset and levelled dataset respectively. This highlights a significant problem for many 360° processing methods, which have been trained and evaluated on levelled images. These methods may not generalise well at test time where images may not be level. Our method solves this problem as can be seen in Table 3, where the automatically levelled images achieve close to the same performance as the original, levelled dataset.

4   Conclusion

In this paper, we presented the most accurate auto-alignment method to date, developed by combining state-of-the-art segmentation methods with classical vanishing point features. We have demonstrated that care needs to be taken when generating training data to avoid data leakage. Moreover, we have demonstrated that casting the vertical axis estimation problem as a segmentation problem results in improved performance, whilst using standard segmentation techniques.

One issue with our approach is that we make the assumption that the vertical direction is already in the upper hemisphere. Though this is a reasonable assumption given how images are captured (where such misalignment is rarely an issue), and the availability of onboard sensors to roughly align an image, we could remedy this problem by instead segmenting the image into three classes:

up, down and background. Doing so would allow us to calculate a vertical axis as before, but then use the up or down label to vote for the up direction. Future work could also try directly regressing the location of the vertical direction following the segmentation. We leave this for future work as it would require a considerable modification of the proposed framework.

References

1. Caesar, H., et al.: nuScenes: a multimodal dataset for autonomous driving. arXiv preprint arXiv:1903.11027 (2019)
2. Canny, J.: A computational approach to edge detection. IEEE Trans. Pattern Anal. Mach. Intell. **PAMI-8**(6), 679–698 (1986). https://doi.org/10.1109/TPAMI.1986.4767851
3. Coors, B., Condurache, A.P., Geiger, A.: SphereNet: learning spherical representations for detection and classification in omnidirectional images. In: The European Conference on Computer Vision (ECCV), September 2018
4. Coughlan, J.M., Yuille, A.L.: The manhattan world assumption: regularities in scene statistics which enable Bayesian inference. In: Leen, T.K., Dietterich, T.G., Tresp, V. (eds.) Advances in Neural Information Processing Systems 13, pp. 845–851. MIT Press (2001). http://papers.nips.cc/paper/1804-the-manhattan-world-assumption-regularities-in-scene-statistics-which-enable-bayesian-inference.pdf
5. Davidson, B., et al.: Automatic cone photoreceptor localisation in healthy and stargardt afflicted retinas using deep learning. Sci. Rep. **8**(1), 7911 (2018). https://doi.org/10.1038/s41598-018-26350-3
6. Doersch, C., Gupta, A., Efros, A.A.: Unsupervised visual representation learning by context prediction. In: The IEEE International Conference on Computer Vision (ICCV), December 2015
7. Duda, R.O., Hart, P.E.: Use of the hough transformation to detect lines and curves in pictures. Commun. ACM **15**(1), 11–15 (1972). https://doi.org/10.1145/361237.361242
8. Fernandez-Labrador, C., Fácil, J.M., Pérez-Yus, A., Demonceaux, C., Guerrero, J.J.: PanoRoom: from the sphere to the 3D layout. CoRR abs/1808.09879 (2018). http://arxiv.org/abs/1808.09879
9. Galamhos, C., Matas, J., Kittler, J.: Progressive probabilistic Hough transform for line detection. In: Proceedings. 1999 IEEE Computer Society Conference on Computer Vision and Pattern Recognition (Cat. No PR00149), vol. 1, pp. 554–560, June 1999. https://doi.org/10.1109/CVPR.1999.786993
10. Gallagher, A.C.: Using vanishing points to correct camera rotation in images. In: The 2nd Canadian Conference on Computer and Robot Vision. (CRV 2005), pp. 460–467, May 2005. https://doi.org/10.1109/CRV.2005.84
11. Gidaris, S., Singh, P., Komodakis, N.: Unsupervised representation learning by predicting image rotations. In: ICLR 2018 (2018)
12. Google: Google Street View product page (2007). https://www.google.com/streetview/. Accessed Mar 2020
13. Guerrero-Viu, J., Fernandez-Labrador, C., Demonceaux, C., Guerrero, J.J.: What's in my Room? Object recognition on indoor panoramic images. arXiv e-prints arXiv:1910.06138, October 2019
14. Hartley, R., Zisserman, A.: Multiple View Geometry in Computer Vision, 2nd edn. Cambridge University Press, Cambridge (2003)

15. Henriques, J.F., Vedaldi, A.: Warped convolutions: efficient invariance to spatial transformations. In: Proceedings of the 34th International Conference on Machine Learning, vol. 70, pp. 1461–1469. JMLR. org (2017)

16. Huang, G., Liu, Z., van der Maaten, L., Weinberger, K.Q.: Densely connected convolutional networks. In: 2017 IEEE Conference on Computer Vision and Pattern Recognition (CVPR), pp. 2261–2269, July 2017. https://doi.org/10.1109/CVPR. 2017.243

17. Jeon, J., Jung, J., Lee, S.: Deep upright adjustment of 360 panoramas using multiple roll estimations. In: Jawahar, C., Li, H., Mori, G., Schindler, K. (eds.) Computer Vision - ACCV 2018, pp. 199–214. Springer International Publishing, Cham (2019)

18. Jung, R., Lee, A.S.J., Ashtari, A., Bazin, J.: Deep360Up: a deep learning-based approach for automatic VR image upright adjustment. In: 2019 IEEE Conference on Virtual Reality and 3D User Interfaces (VR), pp. 1–8, March 2019. https://doi. org/10.1109/VR.2019.8798326

19. Kendall, A., Grimes, M., Cipolla, R.: PoseNet: a convolutional network for real-time 6-DOF camera relocalization. In: Proceedings of the IEEE International Conference on Computer Vision, pp. 2938–2946 (2015)

20. Lee, M., Fowlkes, C.C.: CeMNet: self-supervised learning for accurate continuous ego-motion estimation. In: Proceedings of the IEEE Conference on Computer Vision and Pattern Recognition Workshops (2019)

21. Lezama, J., von Gioi, R.G., Randall, G., Morel, J.: Finding vanishing points via point alignments in image primal and dual domains. In: 2014 IEEE Conference on Computer Vision and Pattern Recognition, pp. 509–515, June 2014. https://doi. org/10.1109/CVPR.2014.72

22. Liu, W., et al.: SSD: single shot MultiBox detector. In: Leibe, B., Matas, J., Sebe, N., Welling, M. (eds.) ECCV 2016. LNCS, vol. 9905, pp. 21–37. Springer, Cham (2016). https://doi.org/10.1007/978-3-319-46448-0_2

23. Noroozi, M., Favaro, P.: Unsupervised learning of visual representations by solving Jigsaw puzzles. In: Leibe, B., Matas, J., Sebe, N., Welling, M. (eds.) ECCV 2016. LNCS, vol. 9910, pp. 69–84. Springer, Cham (2016). https://doi.org/10.1007/978-3-319-46466-4_5

24. O'Sullivan, B., Alam, F., Matava, C.: Creating low-cost 360-degree virtual reality videos for hospitals: a technical paper on the dos and don'ts. J. Med. Internet Res. **20**(7), e239–e239 (2018).https://doi.org/10.2196/jmir.9596, https://www. ncbi.nlm.nih.gov/pubmed/30012545, 30012545[pmid]

25. Schindler, G., Dellaert, F.: Atlanta world: an expectation maximization framework for simultaneous low-level edge grouping and camera calibration in complex man-made environments. In: Proceedings of the 2004 IEEE Computer Society Conference on Computer Vision and Pattern Recognition, 2004. (CVPR 2004). vol. 1, p. I, June 2004. https://doi.org/10.1109/CVPR.2004.1315033

26. Sellers, G., Wright, R.S., Haemel, N.: OpenGL Superbible: Comprehensive Tutorial and Reference, 7th edn. Addison-Wesley Professional, Boston (2015)

27. Shan, Y., Li, S.: Discrete spherical image representation for CNN-based inclination estimation. IEEE Access **8**, 2008–2022 (2020). https://doi.org/10.1109/ACCESS. 2019.2962133

28. Sweeney, C., Flynn, J., Nuernberger, B., Turk, M., Höllerer, T.: Efficient computation of absolute pose for gravity-aware augmented reality. In: 2015 IEEE International Symposium on Mixed and Augmented Reality. pp. 19–24, September 2015. https://doi.org/10.1109/ISMAR.2015.20

29. Szegedy, C., Vanhoucke, V., Ioffe, S., Shlens, J., Wojna, Z.: Rethinking the inception architecture for computer vision. In: 2016 IEEE Conference on Computer Vision and Pattern Recognition (CVPR). IEEE, June 2016. https://doi.org/10.1109/cvpr.2016.308, https://doi.org/10.1109%2Fcvpr.2016.308

30. Takikawa, T., Acuna, D., Jampani, V., Fidler, S.: Gated-SCNN: Gated shape CNNs for semantic segmentation. In: The IEEE International Conference on Computer Vision (ICCV), October 2019

31. Tateno, K., Navab, N., Tombari, F.: Distortion-aware convolutional filters for dense prediction in panoramic images. In: The European Conference on Computer Vision (ECCV), September 2018

32. Trombka, J.I., et al.: Crime scene investigations using portable, non-destructive space exploration technology. Forensic Sci. Int. **129**(1), 1–9 (2002).https://doi.org/10.1016/S0379-0738(02)00079-8,http://www.sciencedirect.com/science/article/pii/S0379073802000798

33. Wallraven, C., Schwaninger, A., Schuhmacher, S., Bülthoff, H.: View-based recognition of faces in man and machine: re-visiting inter-extra-ortho, vol. 2525, pp. 651–660, November 2002. https://doi.org/10.1007/3-540-36181-2_65

34. Weiler, M., Hamprecht, F.A., Storath, M.: Learning steerable filters for rotation equivariant CNNs. In: Proceedings of the IEEE Conference on Computer Vision and Pattern Recognition, pp. 849–858 (2018)

35. Xiao, J., Ehinger, K.A., Oliva, A., Torralba, A.: Recognizing scene viewpoint using panoramic place representation. In: 2012 IEEE Conference on Computer Vision and Pattern Recognition, pp. 2695–2702, June 2012. https://doi.org/10.1109/CVPR.2012.6247991

36. Xiao, J., Ehinger, K., Oliva, A., Antonio, T.: Recognizing scene viewpoint using panoramic place representation. In: Proceedings of 25th IEEE Conference on Computer Vision and Pattern Recognition (2012)

37. Xu, J., Stenger, B., Kerola, T., Tung, T.: Pano2CAD: room layout from a single panorama image. In: 2017 IEEE Winter Conference on Applications of Computer Vision (WACV), pp. 354–362, March 2017. https://doi.org/10.1109/WACV.2017.46

38. Zhang, Y., Song, S., Tan, P., Xiao, J.: PanoContext: a whole-room 3D context model for panoramic scene understanding. In: Fleet, D., Pajdla, T., Schiele, B., Tuytelaars, T. (eds.) Computer Vision - ECCV 2014, pp. 668–686. Springer International Publishing, Cham (2014)

A Novel Line Integral Transform for 2D Affine-Invariant Shape Retrieval

Bin Wang[1,2](✉) and Yongsheng Gao[1]

[1] Griffith University, Nathan, QLD 4111, Australia
{bin.wang,yongsheng.gao}@griffith.edu.au
[2] Nanjing University of Finance & Economics, Nanjing 210023, China

Abstract. Radon transform is a popular mathematical tool for shape analysis. However, it cannot handle affine deformation. Although its extended version, trace transform, allow us to construct affine invariants, they are less informative and computational expensive due to the loss of spatial relationship between trace lines and the extensive repeated calculation of transform. To address this issue, a novel line integral transform is proposed. We first use binding line pairs that have the desirable property of affine preserving as a reference frame to rewrite the diametrical dimension parameters of the lines in a relative manner which make them independent on affine transform. Along polar angle dimension of the line parameters, a moment-based normalization is then conducted to degrade the affine transform to similarity transform which can be easily normalized by Fourier transform. The proposed transform is not only invariant to affine transform, but also preserves the spatial relationship between line integrals which make it very informative. Another advantage of the proposed transform is that it is more efficient than the trace transform. Conducting it one time can allow us to achieve a 2D matrix of affine invariants. While conducting the trace transform once only generates a single feature and multiple trace transforms of different functionals are needed to derive more to make the descriptors informative. The effectiveness of the proposed transform has been validated on two types of standard shape test cases, affinely distorted contour shape dataset and region shape dataset, respectively.

Keywords: Shape analysis · Affine distortions · Affine invariants · Radon transform · Trace transform

1 Introduction

Shape analysis is an active research area in the computer vision and pattern recognition community and has a large body of potential applications such as human activity recognition [28], target tracking [29], medical image retrieval [30], etc. The object images captured by the camera are generally subject to various deformations. One of the typical distortions is perspective transform which occurs on the situation of the pictures of the objects are taken under arbitrary

© Springer Nature Switzerland AG 2020
A. Vedaldi et al. (Eds.): ECCV 2020, LNCS 12373, pp. 596–611, 2020.
https://doi.org/10.1007/978-3-030-58604-1_36

orientations. The computer vision systems are also expected to effectively handle the recognition of perspective distorted shapes. Under certain circumstance like the distance between the camera and the object being far enough, or the thick of the object being very small that can be approximated a plane, the perspective transform can be well approximated by affine transformation [20, 31]. In this paper, we focus on recognizing shapes distorted by affine transform.

Conducting line integrals over the image plane and transform the image function to another 2D function of line parameters (θ, λ) is an effective way for shape analysis. This is one of the significant applications of the well-known Radon transform [1]. The main appealing characteristics of the Radon transform is that it benefits extracting feature of the inner structure of the object and the image function of the object can be fully reconstructed from its Radon transform.

Numerous efforts have been made on extracting invariant shape features from Radon transform for object recognition [32–36]. However, these methods can only handle similarity transform (translation, rotation and scaling) which is a kind of shape-preserving transformation and is a subset of larger affine group. Although affine transform is line-preserving, the complex behaviours of the line integrals of the image function make the affine transform challenging to extract affine invariants from the domain of the line integral transform.

Trace transform [37] is a generalized version of the Radon transform. It extends the line integral to any 1D functional along lines (termed trace functional). So, various functionals used will derive different trace transform. However, trace transform is still sensitive to affine transform because the functionals used along the line can not yield invariants. To achieve affine invariants, Petrou and Kadyrov [5] propose to further conduct diametrical functionals along the dimension of λ and circus functionals along the dimension of θ. It is worth noting that in this method, a set of functionals including a trace functional, a diametrical functionals and a circus functionals can only generate one invariant feature. So, to make the shape descriptors informative, many triples of functionals have to be developed for yielding more affine invariants. However, it is very difficult to find appropriate triple of functionals to constructing the desirable invariants and the expensive computational cost also make it not suitable for real applications.

In this paper, we propose a novel integral transform that can effectively and efficiently handle affine-distorted shapes. The proposed transform has the following advantages over the trace transform: (1) It is much more discriminative than the trace-transform based method [5]. The later uses diametrical functionals and circus functionals to achieve affine invariants which cannot preserve the information of diametrical dimension and circus dimension of the trace lines. While the proposed transform perfectly preserves it; (2) It has the higher efficiency to yield affine invariants than the trace transform. Conducting it one time can allow us to achieve a group of shape invariants. While conducting the trace transform once only generates a single feature and multiple trace transforms of different functionals are needed to derive more to make the descriptors informative; (3) The features obtained by the proposed transform has a physical interpretation, while the features obtained from the trace transform generally has no clearly physical meaning.

2   Related Work

The existing affine shape analysis methods can be categorized into two groups. One is contour based methods which represent the object boundary as ordered points or parameterized curves. The other is region based methods which attempt to generate affine invariants from the whole shape region.

A large body of methods have made attempts to model the silhouette of the shape for characterizing the behavior of the shapes that are subject to affine transform. The popular ideas of them model the silhouette as a parameterized curve. Then some mathematical tools can be used for analysis the geometric properties. The earlier work [20] applied Fourier transform to the affine-length parameterized boundary description for eliminating its dependency on the affine transformation. Various wavelet transforms with different wavelet basis functions are also utilized to generate affine shape invariants [22,23].

B-spline is a kind of continuous curve representation which make it very suitable for shape analysis. Wang and Teoh [18] modeled the shape contour using B-spline to construct the Curvature Scale Space (CSS) image for affine invariant shape matching. Huang and Cohen [17] proposed a fast algorithm for estimating the B-spline control points and used a new class of weighted B-spline curve moments to handle the affine transformation between curves. Various algebraic curve models such as quartic implicit polynomials [16] and conic curve [19] were proposed for extracting affine or perspective invariants. Zuliani et al. [10] used the area, centroid, and covariance of the domain enclosed by the curve to normalize the shape for removing the effect of affine transform.

There are also many methods treating the silhouette of the shape as a sequence of order points to construct shape descriptors or building corresponding to matching shapes. Mai et al. [13] represented shape as a sequence of chained edge points and proposed to project one shape onto the subspace spanned by the other. The two shapes are then matched by minimizing a subspace projection error. This method has a clear physical interpretation and works very fast for estimating the affine transform. Jia et al. [14] developed a new projective invariant, the characteristic number (CN) whose values is calculated on a series of five sample points along the shape contour. With the sample intervals varying, a coarse to fine strategy is developed for capturing both the global geometry described by projective invariants and the local contextual information. Xue et al. [25] proposed a fuzzy algorithm for aligning shapes under affine transform. This algorithm can efficiently estimate the point correspondence and the relevant affine parameters. Recently, Bryner et al. [7,8] presented a contour-based shape analysis framework based on Riemannian geometry that is invariant to affine transform and re-parameterization of contours. Three shape space, landmark-affine, curve-affine and landmark projective are studied in their work.

Different from the contour based methods, the region based shape analysis approaches characterize shape considering all the pixels over the shape domain.

Moment invariants are the popular region based shape descriptors. In the earlier work, Flusser and Suk [12] introduced affine moment invariants for object recognition. Heikkilä [21] used the second and higher order moments of the image points for both recognition and alignment under affine transform. The advantage of this method is that it does not require to know any point correspondences in advance. Yang and Cohen [26] proposed a framework for deriving a class of new global affine invariants based on a novel concept of cross-weighted moments with fractional weights.

Besides the moment descriptors, many recent works developed various strategies for region based shape recognition and matching. Domokos et al. [15] proposed a novel parametric estimation of affine deformations for planar shapes. Instead of finding the correspondences between the landmarks of the template shape and target shape for computing the affine parametric, they treat the affine parametric estimation as a solution of polynomial equations in which all the information available in the input image is used. More recently, Ruiz et al. [24] proposed a fast and accurate affine canonicalization method for recognizing and matching planar shapes. Different from many shape analysis methods which extract invariant features for recognition, this work attempts to produce multiple canonical versions of the shape for provides a common reference frame for accurate shape comparison.

The works that are most relevant to our research in this paper are various transform based methods. Ruiz et al. [11] proposed a multiscale autoconvolution (MSA) transform based on a probabilistic interpretation of the image function. The MSA transform is a 2D function derived from the shape image function which can present infinitely many affine invariant features by varying its two variable. So, it can be directly applied for shape recognition. The trace transform is a generalization of the Radon transform. Petrou and Kadyrov [5] proposed to conduct several trace functionals on the original image function firstly to obtain the same number of trace transforms of the image function, then for each available trace transform, several diametrical functionals are used to transform them to the same number of 1D functions of directional angle of line. The affine invariants are finally achieved by further performing circus functionals to the available 1D functions. The number of the available affine invariant features is the number of the combinations of the used three types of functionals. It can be directly used for shape recognition and its theory can be extended for affine parametric estimation [27]. Recently, Zhang and Chu [38] developed a ray projection transform and apply it for recovering a geometric transformation and an affine lighting change between two objects.

3   Affine Theory of Line Integral

Given a 2D function $f(\mathrm{x})$ and a straight line ℓ with equation $\lambda - \overrightarrow{\theta}^T \mathrm{x} = 0$, where $\overrightarrow{\theta} = (cos\theta, sin\theta)^T$ is a unit vector in the direction of the normal to the line ℓ, and $\mathrm{x} = (x, y)^T \in \mathbb{R}^2$ denote the coordinates of a point of the line ℓ. The integral of the function $f(\mathrm{x})$ over the line ℓ can be mathematically expressed as

$$\Re_f(\lambda, \theta) = \int f(\mathbf{x})\delta(\lambda - \overrightarrow{\theta}^T\mathbf{x})d\mathbf{x}, \tag{1}$$

where $\delta(\cdot)$ denotes a Dirac delta function. Through the line integral, the function $f(\mathbf{x})$ is transformed into another 2D function $\Re_f(\lambda, \theta)$ of line parameters (λ, θ) (in the later sections, we directly use the parameters (λ, θ) to denote a line). This is the well-known Radon transform [1] that has been widely applied for image analysis. In this section, we study the behavior of the line integral of the function $f(\mathbf{x})$ under affine transform.

An affine transform $\mathcal{H} = \mathcal{H}(A, s)$ can be defined as $\mathbf{x}' = A\mathbf{x} + s$, where A is a 2×2 nonsingular real matrix and $s \in \mathbb{R}^2$. Using it, a function $f(\mathbf{x})$ can be transformed to another function $g(\mathbf{x}) = f(A^{-1}\mathbf{x} - A^{-1}s)$. The relationship between their Radon transformed versions, $\Re_f(\lambda, \theta)$ and $\Re_g(\lambda, \theta)$, can be deduced as

$$\begin{aligned}
\Re_g(\lambda, \theta) &= \int g(\mathbf{x})\delta(\lambda - \overrightarrow{\theta}^T\mathbf{x})d\mathbf{x} \\
&= \int f(A^{-1}\mathbf{x} - A^{-1}s)\delta(\lambda - \overrightarrow{\theta}^T\mathbf{x})d\mathbf{x}.
\end{aligned} \tag{2}$$

Let $\mathbf{y} = A^{-1}\mathbf{x} - A^{-1}s$, Eq. (2) can be rewritten as

$$\Re_g(\lambda, \theta) = |det(A)| \int f(\mathbf{y})\delta(\lambda - \overrightarrow{\theta}^T s - (A^T\overrightarrow{\theta})^T\mathbf{y})d\mathbf{y}. \tag{3}$$

Note that the vector $A^T\overrightarrow{\theta}$ is a transformed version of the vector $\overrightarrow{\theta}$ and may not be a unit vector. Here, we use the scaling property [2] of the Dirac delta function, that is $\delta(\alpha x) = |\alpha|^{-1}\delta(x)$ for $\alpha \neq 0$, to normalize it and Eq. (3) can be rewritten as

$$\Re_g(\lambda, \theta) = \frac{|det(A)|}{\left\| A^T\overrightarrow{\theta} \right\|} \int f(\mathbf{y})\delta \left(\frac{\lambda}{\left\| A^T\overrightarrow{\theta} \right\|} - \frac{\overrightarrow{\theta}^T s}{\left\| A^T\overrightarrow{\theta} \right\|} - \frac{(A^T\overrightarrow{\theta})^T}{\left\| A^T\overrightarrow{\theta} \right\|}\mathbf{y} \right) d\mathbf{y}, \tag{4}$$

where $\|\cdot\|$ denotes the length of the vector. Defining following functions of variable θ:

$$\epsilon(\theta) = \frac{|det(A)|}{\left\| A^T\overrightarrow{\theta} \right\|}, \zeta(\theta) = \frac{1}{\left\| A^T\overrightarrow{\theta} \right\|}, \eta(\theta) = -\frac{\overrightarrow{\theta}^T s}{\left\| A^T\overrightarrow{\theta} \right\|},$$

and

$$\rho(\theta) = \left\langle A^T\overrightarrow{\theta} \right\rangle, \tag{5}$$

where $\langle\cdot\rangle$ denotes the direction angle of the vector, we then have

$$\begin{aligned}
\Re_g(\lambda, \theta) &= \epsilon(\theta) \int f(\mathbf{y}) \, \delta \left(\zeta(\theta) \cdot \lambda + \eta(\theta) - \overrightarrow{\rho(\theta)}^T\mathbf{y} \right) d\mathbf{y} \\
&= \epsilon(\theta) \cdot \Re_f(\zeta(\theta) \cdot \lambda + \eta(\theta), \rho(\theta)).
\end{aligned} \tag{6}$$

The above equation indicates the following effects of the affine transform $\mathcal{H}(A, s)$ on the line integral of the function $f(\mathbf{x})$: (1) its amplitude is scaled by $\epsilon(\theta)$; (2)

its parameter λ is scaled by $\zeta(\theta)$ and shifted by $\eta(\theta)$, and (3) its parameter θ is transformed to be $\rho(\theta)$.

Let the inverse transform of $\mathcal{H}(A, s)$ be $\mathcal{H}^{-1}(A^{-1}, -A^{-1}s)$. The inverse transformed versions $\epsilon^{-1}(\theta)$, $\zeta^{-1}(\theta)$, $\eta^{-1}(\theta)$, and $\rho^{-1}(\theta)$ of the functions $\epsilon(\theta)$, $\zeta(\theta)$, $\eta(\theta)$, and $\rho(\theta)$ can be defined by replacing A and s appeared in the Eq. (5) with A^{-1} and $-A^{-1}s$, respectively. From Eq. (6), we can also conclude that when a line (λ, θ) is subject to the affine transform $\mathcal{H}(A, s)$, it will become the line $(\zeta^{-1}(\theta) \cdot \lambda + \eta^{-1}(\theta), \rho^{-1}(\theta))$. In the next section, we will use the affine theories of the line and line integral under affine transform to construct a novel line integral transform for affine shape analysis.

4   The Proposed Line Integral Transform

A shape is defined as region D that is a subset of pixels in the image plane $\mathbb{R}^2$ [3]. The shape image function $f(\mathbf{x})$ can then be defined an indicator function $f(\mathbf{x}) = 1$ if $x \in D$ and $f(\mathbf{x}) = 0$ otherwise.

4.1   Binding Line Pair and Its Affine Property

Using the line integral $\Re_f(\lambda, \theta)$ of the function $f(\mathbf{x})$, we define a 1D function of the variable θ as

$$\sigma_f(\theta) = arg\min_{\lambda} \{\Re_f(\lambda, \theta) > 0\}. \tag{7}$$

Then for an angle $\theta \in [0, 2\pi]$, we can uniquely derive a line pair $(\sigma_f(\theta), \theta)$ and $(-\sigma_f(\theta + \pi), \theta)$. It can be easily concluded that they have the following relationships with the shape region D:

$$\exists x \in D, \sigma_f(\theta) - \vec{\theta}^T \mathbf{x} = 0. \tag{8}$$

and

$$\forall x \in D, \sigma_f(\theta) \leq \vec{\theta}^T \mathbf{x} \leq -\sigma_f(\theta + \pi). \tag{9}$$

The Eq. (8) and Eq. (9) indicate that the shape region D is located between the line pair $(\sigma_f(\theta), \theta)$ and $(-\sigma_f(\theta + \pi), \theta)$ and has at least one intersection point with them which also means that the shape region D is bound by the line pair. We term the line $(\sigma_f(\theta), \theta)$ and $(-\sigma_f(\theta+\pi), \theta)$ as binding line pair. An example of binding line pair is presented in Fig. 1.

Now, we analysis the property of the binding line pair under the affine transform $\mathcal{H}(A, s)$. According to Eq. (7), we can conclude that the function $\sigma_f(\theta)$ has the following relationship with the function $\sigma_g(\theta)$:

$$\sigma_f(\theta) = \frac{\sigma_g(\rho^{-1}(\theta)) - \eta^{-1}(\theta)}{\zeta^{-1}(\theta)}. \tag{10}$$

Under the affine transform $\mathcal{H}(A, s)$, the line $(\sigma_f(\theta), \theta)$ is transformed to be the line $(\zeta^{-1}(\theta) \cdot \sigma_f(\theta) + \eta^{-1}(\theta), \rho^{-1}(\theta))$ which can be rewritten as

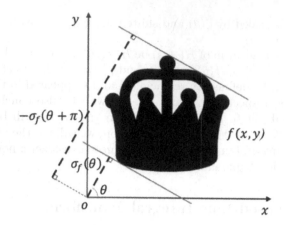

Fig. 1. An example of a binding line pair for a shape (marked in green color). (Color figure online)

$(\sigma_g(\rho^{-1}(\theta)), \rho^{-1}(\theta))$ in terms of Eq. (10). Therefore, we can conclude that the affine transformed version of a binding line of the shape is the binding line of the affine transformed version of the shape. Note that the parameters $(-\sigma_f(\theta+\pi), \theta)$ and the parameters $(\sigma_f(\theta+\pi), \theta+\pi)$ represent the same line. Thus, another binding line $(-\sigma_f(\theta+\pi), \theta)$ also keeps its binding property under the affine transform. A graphical illustration of this property is shown in Fig. 2.

Fig. 2. An example to indicate the binding line pairs (marked by the same color for each) having the property of being affine transform preserved, i.e. the affine transformed version of a binding line pair of the shape is the binding pair of the affine transformed version of the shape.

4.2   The Proposed Transform

Given an image function $f(\mathbf{x})$ and a direction angle $\theta \in [0, 2\pi)$, a binding line pair $(\sigma_f(\theta), \theta)$ and $(-\sigma_f(\theta+\pi), \theta)$ can be calculated. The distance between them is $-\sigma_f(\theta+\pi) - \sigma_f(\theta)$. The line that has equal distance to the binding line pair, i.e., the center line, can be represented as $((\sigma_f(\theta) - \sigma_f(\theta+\pi))/2, \theta)$. Taking the center line and the binding line $(\sigma_f(\theta), \theta)$ as the reference lines, each line that is located between them can be then uniquely represented as the parameter form of $(\Gamma_f(\mu, \theta), \theta)$. Where $\theta \in [0, 2\pi]$ is the direction angle of the line which is also the direction angle of the reference lines and the parameter $\Gamma_f(\mu, \theta)$ is a 2D function of the variables (μ, θ) defined by

$$\Gamma_f(\mu, \theta) = \frac{\sigma_f(\theta) - \sigma_f(\theta + \pi)}{2} - \mu \cdot \frac{-\sigma_f(\theta + \pi) - \sigma_f(\theta)}{2}, \tag{11}$$

where $\mu \in [0, 1]$ is the ratio of the distance between the line with the reference line $(\sigma_f(\theta), \theta)$ to the distance between the two reference lines, $(\sigma_f(\theta), \theta)$ and $((\sigma_f(\theta) - \sigma_f(\theta + \pi))/2, \theta)$.

Let the parameter θ vary from 0 to 2π and the parameter μ vary from 0 to 1, all the lines that go through the shape region D can then be available to form a line set denoted by

$$\{(\Gamma_f(\mu, \theta), \theta) : \mu \in [0, 1], \theta \in [0, 2\pi]\}. \tag{12}$$

We integral the shape image function $f(\mathbf{x})$ over each line in the above set and obtain a novel integral transform for the function $f(\mathbf{x})$ as follows:

$$\Psi_f(\mu, \theta) = \Re_f(\Gamma_f(\mu, \theta), \theta). \tag{13}$$

which is a 2D function of the parameters $\mu \in [0, 1]$ and $\theta \in [0, 2\pi]$.

The proposed transform $\Psi_f(\mu, \theta)$ has the following property under the affine transform $\mathcal{H} = \mathcal{H}(A, s)$ of the shape image function $f(\mathbf{x})$:

$$\Psi_g(\mu, \theta) = \epsilon(\theta) \cdot \Psi_f(\mu, \rho(\theta)). \tag{14}$$

Comparing the above equation with Eq. (6), we can find the difference between the proposed transform with the Radon transform under affine transform as follows: the first parameter λ for the Radon transform embeds the parameters of affine transform, while the first parameter μ for the proposed transform is independent of the affine transform. However, Eq. (14) also indicates that the second parameter θ and the amplitude of the proposed transform still encode the affine transform parameters. Since the parameter μ of the proposed transform is independent of the affine transform, we fix it and rewrite the function $\Psi_f(\mu, \theta)$ as the function $\Psi_f^\mu(\theta)$ which has only one variable θ. Delimited by the function $\Psi_f^\mu(\theta)$, a region W_f^μ can be derived and mathematically defined as

$$W_f^\mu = \left\{ w \in \mathbb{R}^2 : \exists \theta \in [0, 2\pi] \wedge \exists r \in [0, 1] \, such\,that \, w = (r \cdot \Psi_f^\mu(\theta)) \overrightarrow{\theta} \right\}. \tag{15}$$

Similarly, a region W_g^μ that is delimited by the function $\Psi_g^\mu(\theta)$ can be defined by replacing f with g in Eq. (15). We are interested in the relationship between the available regions W_f^μ and W_g^μ. For any $w' \in W_g^\mu$, there exists $w \in W_f^\mu$ such that

$$w' = |det(A)|A^{-T}w. \tag{16}$$

and on the other hand, for any $w \in W_f^\mu$, there exists $w' \in W_g^\mu$ which also makes Eq. (16) hold, where A^{-T} denotes the transpose matrix of A^{-1}. Therefore, we can deduce that the region W_f^μ and the region W_g^μ are correlated by the affine transform $\mathcal{H}' = \mathcal{H}'(|det(A)|A^{-T}, 0)$. This is a desirable property which allows us to use their respective second-order geometric moment to derive a transformation for reducing the relation between them from an affinity into a similarity. Similar ideas can be found in [4,5].

For the region W_f^μ, we construct its second-order geometric moment matrix as

$$M_f^\mu = \int_{W_f^\mu} w w^T dw. \tag{17}$$

Similarly, the second-order geometric moment matrix M_g^μ for the region W_g^μ can be available. For the integration expression of calculating the moment matrix M_g^μ, by making following changes: the variable $w' = |det(A)|A^{-T}w$, the derivative $dw' = |det(A)|dw$, and the integration region $W_g^\mu \to M_f^\mu$, we can easily deduce that

$$M_g^\mu = |det(A)|^3 A^{-T} M_f^\mu A^{-1}. \tag{18}$$

which indicates the relationship between the moment matrix M_f^μ and the moment matrix M_g^μ. Define $M^{1/2}$ as any matrix that satisfies $(M^{1/2})(M^{1/2})^T = M$. Since $det(M) > 0$, the $M^{1/2}$ can be always achieved. It can be calculated by using an eigenvalue method [5,6]. Let $\Delta_f = (M_f^\mu)^{1/2}$ and $\Delta_g = (M_g^\mu)^{1/2}$, we accordingly achieve $M_f^\mu = \Delta_f \Delta_f^T$ and $M_g^\mu = \Delta_g \Delta_g^T$. Using the matrices Δ_f and Δ_g, we can produce a transformation matrix as

$$E = \Delta_g^{-1}(|det(A)|A^{-T})\Delta_f. \tag{19}$$

Then we have

$$EE^T = \Delta_g^{-1}(|det(A)|A^{-T})\Delta_f \Delta_f^T(|det(A)|A^{-1})\Delta_g^{-T}. \tag{20}$$

Using Eq. 18, the above equation can be rewritten as

$$\begin{aligned} EE^T &= |det(A)|^{-1}\Delta_g^{-1}M_g^\mu \Delta_g^{-T} \\ &= |det(A)|^{-1}\Delta_g^{-1}\Delta_g \Delta_g^T \Delta_g^{-T} \\ &= |det(A)|^{-1}I. \end{aligned} \tag{21}$$

where I is an identity matrix. The above equation indicates that E is a similarity matrix which encodes the relation of the matrices A, Δ_f and Δ_g. According to Eq. (21), the transform matrix E can be denoted by $E = \alpha R_{\theta_0}$ for $det(E) > 0$ and $E = \alpha \tilde{R}_{\theta_0}$ for $det(E) < 0$, where $\alpha = |det(A)|^{-1/2}$ play the role of scale factor, R_{θ_0} and $\tilde{R}_{\theta_0}$ are

$$R_{\theta_0} = \begin{bmatrix} cos\theta_0 & -sin\theta_0 \\ sin\theta_0 & cos\theta_0 \end{bmatrix} \tag{22}$$

and

$$\tilde{R}_{\theta_0} = \begin{bmatrix} cos\theta_0 & sin\theta_0 \\ sin\theta_0 & -cos\theta_0 \end{bmatrix} \tag{23}$$

which can transform a vector $\overrightarrow{\theta}$ to be $\overrightarrow{\theta + \theta_0}$ and $\overrightarrow{\theta_0 - \theta}$ respectively. It is worth noting that for Eq. (19), since $det(\Delta_f) > 0$ and $det(\Delta_g) > 0$ [5,6], $det(E)$ takes the same sign as $det(A)$. While $det(A) < 0$ indicates that besides the scaling, rotation and shearing, the affine transform with the affine matrix A also includes a mirror transform.

We have now obtained the matrices Δ_f and Δ_g, they are then be used to normalize the function $\Psi_f^\mu(\theta)$ and its affine-transform version $\Psi_g^\mu(\theta)$ respectively. We first normalize the function $\Psi_f^\mu(\theta)$ as

$$\dot{\Psi}_f^\mu(\theta) = \frac{1}{\left\| \Delta_f \overrightarrow{\theta} \right\|} \Psi_f^\mu\left(\left\langle \Delta_f \overrightarrow{\theta} \right\rangle \right). \tag{24}$$

Similarly, the normalized version of $\Psi_g^\mu(\theta)$ is defined as $\dot{\Psi}_g^\mu(\theta)$. The relationship between them can be achieved as

$$\dot{\Psi}_g^\mu(\theta) = \alpha \cdot \dot{\Psi}_f^\mu(\theta - \theta_0) \quad for \quad det(A) > 0, \tag{25}$$

and

$$\dot{\Psi}_g^\mu(\theta) = \alpha \cdot \dot{\Psi}_f^\mu(\theta_0 - \theta) \quad for \quad det(A) < 0. \tag{26}$$

which indicate that the normalized versions $\dot{\Psi}_f^\mu(\theta)$ and $\dot{\Psi}_g^\mu(\theta)$ are only correlated by a similarity transform. The Eq. (26) also indicates that when the affine transform includes a mirror transform, the original function $\dot{\Psi}_f^\mu(\theta)$ is also subject to an additional mirror transform.

Also, we can see that for any $\mu \in [0, 1]$, its corresponding 1D function $\dot{\Psi}_f^\mu(\theta)$ for the shape f only suffers from scaling, translation and mirror distortions when the shape f is subject to affine transform. In the former section, we fix the variable μ for the convenience of presenting the details of the proposed transform. Now, we set it free and rewrite the 1D function $\dot{\Psi}_f^\mu(\theta)$ to a 2D function $\dot{\Psi}_f(\mu, \theta)$. Obviously, the affine transform makes the 2D function $\dot{\Psi}_f(\mu, \theta)$ occur only shifting and mirror effects on the dimension of θ and a scaling of the amplitude of the function.

4.3   Affine Invariants

Here we apply the proposed transform $\dot{\Psi}_f(\mu, \theta)$ to affine invariant shape recognition. As discussed in the former section, the transform $\dot{\Psi}_f(\mu, \theta)$ is only subject to a shifting and a mirror transform on the dimension of θ and a scaling on the amplitude of the function. So, it is very easy to remove these effects from the proposed transform. To do so, we apply the 1D Fourier transform to the dimension of θ against the proposed transform $\dot{\Psi}_f(\mu, \theta)$. Assume that $\dot{\Psi}_f(\mu_i, \theta_j)$, $i = 1, ..., k$ and $j = 1, ..., N$ is the digital form of the proposed transform $\dot{\Psi}_f(\mu, \theta)$, where K and N are the number of the points uniformly sampled from the range $[0,1]$ and the range $[0,2\pi]$ respectively. Then we obtain a matrix of size $K \times N$. For each row of the matrix, we perform discrete 1D Fourier transform against it and keep the magnitudes of Fourier coefficients. According to the theory of Fourier transform, the shifting and mirror effects are removed from the transform $\dot{\Psi}_f(\mu_i, \theta_j)$. As for the scaling effect, we normalize each row of the matrix using its respective 0th-order Fourier coefficient. Then we obtain a completely affine invariant version of the transform $\dot{\Psi}_f(\mu_i, \theta_j)$ which can be directly utilized for shape recognition. The dissimilarity between two shapes can be measured by calculating the L1 norm between their transforms $\dot{\Psi}(\mu_i, \theta_j)$.

5   Experimental Results and Discussions

To examine the feasibility and effectiveness of the proposed method on shape retrieval, we perform the proposed method on two groups of shape image datasets: (1) Contour shape dataset in which each shape is enclosed by a single silhouette and no content is contained inside, and (2) Region shape dataset in which each sample has several separated regions or its whole region is though enclosed by a single silhouette, it also contain some contents inside which usually have complex structure. For all the experiments, we uniformly sample 18 values from the range $[0,1]$ and 180 values from the range $[0,2\pi]$ for conducting the proposed transform.

To quantify the retrieval performance of the algorithms, the standard metric for information retrieval, knee-point score [7,8], is used in our experiments. For any query shape Q_i, calculate the distances of all the dataset samples to it and rank them to a sequence in ascending order. Let H be the number of all the dataset samples and V_i be the number of the relevant ones to the query shape Q_i in the dataset. For each integer number $1 \leq h \leq H$, count the number $v_{i,h}$ of the relevant samples of the top k best matches in the sequence. Then for the given query Q_i, its precision and recall at the top h best matches are defined as

$$p_{i,h} = \frac{v_{i,h}}{h} \quad and \quad r_{i,h} = \frac{v_{i,h}}{V_i}, \tag{27}$$

respectively. We calculate their average values over all the queries Q_i. In our experiments, each sample from the dataset is taken in turn as a query. So, there are a total of H queries. When $V_i = h$, precision and recall will take the same value which is termed knee-point score as measurement [7,8].

Multiview Curve Database (MCD): To evaluate the performance of the algorithms on recognizing the curved shapes in presence of affine distortion, Zuliani et al. [10] chose 40 samples from the MPEG-7 CE-1 contour shape dataset [9] with each selected from one shape class. Each of them is then printed on a white paper and 7 pictures are taken to it from different view angles using a digital camera. Another 7 images are achieved by randomly rotating and reflecting the available seven samples. So, there are a total of $40 \times 14 = 560$ samples in the MCD which consists of MPEG-7 shapes that are affected by natural perspective

Table 1. The retrieval accuracy on the MCD dataset

Algorithm	Knee-point score (%)
Affine-invariant elastic metric [7]	90.00*
Hierarchical projective invariant contexts [14]	88.14*
Subspace approach [13]	90.15
Affine-invariant curve matching [10]	80.00*
Affine moment invariants [12]	66.01
Mutiscale Autoconvolution (MSA) [11]	71.84
Affine invariant features from the Trace transform [5]	80.08
Proposed method	**97.07**

* *The results from the original papers.*

skew due to the manner of extracting from real images. Some typical samples from the MCD are shown in Fig. 3. This dataset is publicly available and has been used as test case in many works [7,10,14].

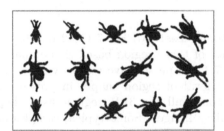 

Fig. 3. Part of typical samples in the dataset MCD. Left: the 14 affine-distorted insect shapes, right: the 14 affine-distorted camel shapes.

To make a fair comparison, we choose those approaches which are particularly designed for affine shape recognition. Three region based methods, including Trace transform based method [5], Multiscale autoconvolution (MSA) [11] and Affine moment invariants [12] which are state-of-the-arts descriptors for affine shape recognition, are used as benchmarks in our experiments. Since the template sample of the shapes in MCD database are from the MPEG-7 CE-1 dataset which is a contour based test case, four recently published contour based methods including Affine-invariant elastic metric [7], Hierarchical projective invariant contexts [14], subspace approach [13] and Affine-invariant curve matching [10] are selected as benchmarks for a wide comparison. All of them take the MCD dataset as the test case in their experiments. The Knee-point scores of the proposed method together with the benchmark methods are summarized in Table 1. It can be seen that the proposed method achieves 97.07% of retrieval accuracy which is about 17% higher than the Trace transform based method [5] and much more than the other two region based methods [12] and [11]. While compare with the other four contour based methods which generally perform better on the contour based test case than those region based methods, the proposed method still achieves more than about 7% of retrieval accuracy than them.

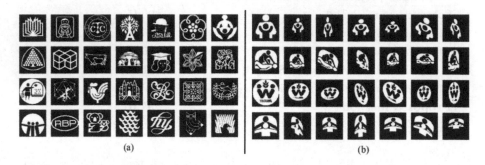

Fig. 4. Example samples from the MPEG CE-2 database which consists of 3101 region shape images. (a) Some typical samples that are used as gallery images. (b) Some typical images that are used as queries, where for each row, the top left one is template shape and the remaining ones are part of its various perspective transformed versions.

MPEG-7 CE-2 Perspective Transform Test: MPEG-7 CE-2 database is developed for evaluating the performance of those region based shape analysis methods. Here, we perform the MPEG-7 CE-2 perspective test to validate the effectiveness of the proposed on the retrieval of region shapes in presence of perspective transform. In this test protocol, all the 3101 region-based shape images in the database are used as gallery images (Some typical samples are shown in Fig. 4(a)). Among them, 330 images of 30 classes with 11 images in each class are labeled as queries for the retrieval experiment. In each query class, one image is the original shape, and the other ten images are its perspective transformed versions (Example images are shown in Fig. 4(b)). As can be seen that different from the CE-1 shapes, the CE-2 samples usually have complex interior structures and some samples have even separate shape regions.

In our experiments, we follow the protocol of the CE-2 perspective transform test. Since the contour based shape recognition methods used in the former experiments can not handle region shapes, we only compare the proposed method with the other three region based methods. The knee-point scores for all the compared methods are summarized in Table 2. It can be seen that the proposed method achieved an accuracy of 97.49%, much higher than those of all the benchmarks (2.48% higher than the second best approach), on retrieving shapes with various perspective transformations. As can be seen that on the CE-2 perspective test, the proposed method keeps the best retrieval performance over the benchmark methods. The encouraging experimental results demonstrate the effectiveness of the proposed transform in describing shapes in presence of perspective transform and its superior discriminability over the existing region based methods on handling the shapes with complex interior structures.

Table 2. The retrieval accuracy for the MPEG-7 CE-2 perspective test

Algorithm	Knee-point score (%)
Affine moment invariants [12]	42.53
Mutiscale Autoconvolution (MSA) [11]	62.09
Affine invariant features from the Trace transform [5]	95.01
Proposed method	**97.49**

6 Conclusions

A novel line integral transform has been presented for affine-invariant shape recognition. It is a 2D function which is not only invariant to affine transform, but also preserves the spatial relationship between the line integrals which makes it more discriminative than those shape descriptors from the trace transform. In additional, the proposed method is more efficient than the trace transform. In the proposed method, a 2D matrix of affine invariants can be generated by conducting the proposed transform once. While conducting the trace transform once can only generate a single feature and multiple times of transforms should be performed make shape descriptors discriminative. The proposed transform has been tested on the standard affinely distorted contour shape database and region shape database and compared with the state-of-the-art shape descriptors that are designed for affine shape analysis. The encouraging experimental results showed that the proposed method is effective for affine shape recognition.

Acknowledgement. This work was supported in part by the Australian Research Council (ARC) under Discovery Grant DP140101075 and the Natural Science Foundation of China under Grant 61372158.

References

1. Deans, S.R.: The Radon Transform and Some of Its Applications. Wiley, New York (1983)
2. Strichartz, R.: A Guide to Distribution Theory and Fourier Transforms. CRC Press, Boca Raton (1994)
3. Hong, B., Soatto, S.: Shape matching using multiscale integral invariants. IEEE Trans. Pattern Anal. Mach. Intell. 37(1), 151–160 (2015)
4. Baumberg, A.: Reliable feature matching across widely separated views. In: Proceedings of the IEEE Conference on Computer Vision and Pattern Recognition, vol. 1, pp. 774–781 (2000)
5. Petrou, M., Kadyrov, A.: Affine invariant features from the trace transform. IEEE Trans. Pattern Anal. Mach. Intell. 26(1), 30–44 (2004)
6. Golub, G.H., Van Loan, C.F.: Matrix Computations, 3rd edn. Johns Hopkins University Press, Baltimore (1996)
7. Bryner, D., Srivastava, A., Klassen, E.: Affine-invariant, elastic shape analysis of planar contours. In: Proceedings of the IEEE Conference on Computer Vision Pattern Recognition, pp. 390–397 (2012)

8. Bryner, D., Klassen, E., Le, H., Srivastava, A.: 2D affine and projective shape analysis. IEEE Trans. Pattern Anal. Mach. Intell. **36**(5), 998–1011 (2014)
9. Latecki, L.J., Lakamper, R., Eckhardt, T.: Shape descriptors for no-rigid shapes with a single closed contour. In: Proceedings of the IEEE Conference on Computer Vision Pattern Recognition, vol. 1, pp. 424–429 (2000)
10. Zuliani, M., Bhagavathy, S., Manjunath, B.S., Kenney, C.: Affine-invariant curve matching. In: Proceedings of the IEEE International Conference on Image Processing (2004)
11. Rahtu, E., Salo, M., Heikkila, J.: Affine invariant pattern recognition using multiscale autoconvolution. IEEE Trans. Pattern Anal. Mach. Intell. **27**(6), 908–918 (2005)
12. Flusser, J., Suk, T.: Pattern recognition by affine moment invariants. Pattern Recogn. **26**(1), 167–174 (1993)
13. Mai, F., Chang, C., Hung, Y.S.: A subspace approach for matching 2D shapes under affine distortions. Pattern Recogn. **44**(2), 210–221 (2011)
14. Jia, Q., Fan, X., Liu, Y., Li, H., Luo, Z., Guo, H.: Hierarchical projective invariant contexts for shape recognition. Pattern Recogn. **52**(52), 358–374 (2016)
15. Domokos, C., Kato, Z.: Parametric estimation of affine deformations of planar shapes. Pattern Recogn. **43**(3), 569–578 (2010)
16. Tarel, J., Wolovich, W., Cooper, D.B.: Covariant-conics decomposition of quartics for 2D shape recognition and alignment. J. Math. Imaging Vis. **19**(3), 255–273 (2003). https://doi.org/10.1023/A:1026285105653
17. Huang, Z., Cohen, F.S.: Affine-invariant B-spline moments for curve matching. IEEE Trans. Image Process. **5**(10), 1473–1480 (1996)
18. Wang, Y., Teoh, E.K.: 2D affine-invariant contour matching using B-spline model. IEEE Trans. Pattern Anal. Mach. Intell. **29**(10), 1853–1858 (2007)
19. Srestasathiern, P., Yilmaz, A.: Planar shape representation and matching under projective transformation. Comput. Vis. Image Underst. **115**(11), 1525–1535 (2011)
20. Arbter, K., Snyder, W.E., Burkhardt, H., Hirzinger, G.: Application of affine-invariant Fourier descriptors to recognition of 3-D objects. IEEE Trans. Pattern Anal. Mach. Intell. **12**(7), 640–647 (1990)
21. Heikkilä, J.: Pattern matching with affine moment descriptors. Pattern Recogn. **37**(9), 1825–1834 (2004)
22. Khalil, M.I., Bayoumi, M.M.: A dyadic wavelet affine invariant function for 2D shape recognition. IEEE Trans. Anal. Mach. Intell. **23**(10), 1152–1164 (2001)
23. Rube, I.E., Ahmed, M., Kamel, M.S.: Wavelet approximation-based affine invariant shape representation functions. IEEE Trans. Pattern Anal. Mach. Intell. **28**(2), 323–327 (2006)
24. Ruiz, A., Lopez-de-Teruel, P.E., Fernandez-Maimo, L.: Efficient planar affine canonicalization. Pattern Recogn. **72**, 236–253 (2017)
25. Xue, Z., Shen, D., Teoh, E.K.: An efficient fuzzy algorithm for aligning shapes under affine transformations. Pattern Recogn. **34**(6), 1171–1180 (2001)
26. Yang, Z., Cohen, F.S.: Cross-weighted moments and affine invariants for image registration and matching. IEEE Trans. Pattern Anal. Mach. Intell. **21**(8), 804–814 (1999)
27. Kadyrov, A., Petrou, M.: Affine parameter estimation from the trace transform. IEEE Trans. Pattern Anal. Mach. Intell. **28**(10), 1631–1645 (2006)
28. Wang, Y., Huang, K., Tan, T.: Human activity recognition based on R transform. In: CVPR, pp. 1–8 (2007)

29. Andriluka, M., Roth, S., Schiele, B.: People-tracking-by-detection and people-detection-by-tracking. In: Proceedings of the IEEE Conference on Computer Vision and Pattern Recognition (CVPR) (2008)
30. Korn, P., Sidiropoulos, N.D., Faloutsos, C., Siegel, E.L., Protopapas, Z.: Fast and effective retrieval of medical tumor shapes. IEEE Trans. Knowl. Data Eng. **10**(6), 889–904 (1998)
31. Suk, T., Flusser, J.: Affine moment invariants generated by graph method. Pattern Recogn. **44**(9), 2047–2056 (2011)
32. Chen, Y.W., Chen, Y.Q.: Invariant description and retrieval of planar shapes using Radon composite features. IEEE Trans. Signal Process. **56**(10), 4762–4771 (2008)
33. Hjouj, F., Kammler, D.W.: Identification of reflected, scaled, translated, and rotated objects from their Radon projections. IEEE Trans. Image Process. **17**(3), 301–310 (2008)
34. Tabbone, S., Wendling, L., Salmon, J.: A new shape descriptor defined on the Radon transform. Comput. Vis. Image Underst. **102**(1), 42–51 (2006)
35. Hoang, T.V., Tabbone, S.: The generalization of the R-transform for invariant pattern representation. Pattern Recogn. **45**(6), 2145–2163 (2012)
36. Hasegawa, M., Tabbone, S.: Amplitude-only log Radon transform for geometric invariant shape descriptor. Pattern Recogn. **47**(2), 643–658 (2014)
37. Kadyrov, A., Petrou, M.: The trace transform and its applications. IEEE Trans. Pattern Anal. Mach. Intell. **23**(8), 811–828 (2001)
38. Zhang, Y., Chu, C.H.: IEEE Trans. Pattern Anal. Mach. Intell. **33**(3), 446–458 (2011)

Explanation-Based Weakly-Supervised Learning of Visual Relations with Graph Networks

Federico Baldassarre[(⊠)], Kevin Smith, Josephine Sullivan,
and Hossein Azizpour

KTH - Royal Institute of Technology, Stockholm, Sweden
{fedbal,ksmith,sullivan,azizpour}@kth.se

Abstract. Visual relationship detection is fundamental for holistic image understanding. However, the localization and classification of (subject, predicate, object) triplets remain challenging tasks, due to the combinatorial explosion of possible relationships, their long-tailed distribution in natural images, and an expensive annotation process.

This paper introduces a novel weakly-supervised method for visual relationship detection that relies on minimal image-level predicate labels. A graph neural network is trained to classify predicates in images from a graph representation of detected objects, implicitly encoding an inductive bias for pairwise relations. We then frame relationship detection as the *explanation* of such a predicate classifier, i.e. we obtain a complete relation by recovering the subject and object of a predicted predicate.

We present results comparable to recent fully- and weakly-supervised methods on three diverse and challenging datasets: HICO-DET for human-object interaction, Visual Relationship Detection for generic object-to-object relations, and UnRel for unusual triplets; demonstrating robustness to non-comprehensive annotations and good few-shot generalization.

1 Introduction

Visual perception systems, built to understand the world through images, are not only required to identify objects, but also their interactions. Visual relationship detection aims at forming a holistic representation by identifying triplets in the form (subject, predicate, object). Subject and object are localized and classified instances such as a cat or a boat, and predicates include actions such as *pushing*, spatial relations such as *above*, and comparatives such as *taller than*.

In recent years, we have witnessed unprecedented development in various forms of object recognition; from classification to detection, segmentation, and

---

Electronic supplementary material The online version of this chapter (https://doi.org/10.1007/978-3-030-58604-1_37) contains supplementary material, which is available to authorized users.

A. Vedaldi et al. (Eds.): ECCV 2020, LNCS 12373, pp. 612–630, 2020.
https://doi.org/10.1007/978-3-030-58604-1_37

person push motorcycle   person wear helmet   person drive motorcycle   person wear helmet

Fig. 1. Weakly-supervised relationship detection: detecting all $\langle$subj, pred, obj$\rangle$ triplets by training only on weak image-level predicate annotations {*push, wear, drive*}

pose estimation. Yet, the higher-level visual task of inter-object interaction recognition remains unsolved, mainly due to the combinatorial number of possible interactions w.r.t. the number of objects. This issue not only complicates the inference procedure, but also complicates data collection – the cost of gathering and annotating data that spans a sufficient set of relationships is enormous. In this work, we propose a novel inference procedure that requires minimal labeling thereby making it easier and cheaper to collect data for training.[1]

Consider the problem of adding a predicate category to a small vocabulary of 20 objects. A single predicate could introduce up to 20^2 new relationship categories, for which samples must be collected and models should be trained. Moreover, we know that the distribution of naturally-occurring triplets is long-tailed, with combinations such as *person ride dog* rarely appearing [29]. This exposes standard training methods to issues arising from extreme class imbalance. These challenges have prompted modern techniques to take a compositional approach [15,24,29,34] and to incorporate visual and language knowledge [24,29,31], improving both training and generalization.

Although some progress has been made towards recognition of rare triplets, successful methods require training data with exhaustive annotation and localization of $\langle$subj, pred, obj$\rangle$ triplets. This makes weakly-supervised learning a promising research direction to mitigate the costs and errors associated with data collection. Nonetheless, we identified only two weakly-supervised works tackling general visual relation detection [30,48], both requiring image-level triplet annotation. In this work, we use an even weaker setup for visual relationship detection that relies only on *image-level predicate* annotations (Fig. 1).

To achieve that, we decompose a probabilistic description of visual relationship detection into the subtasks of object detection, predicate classification and retrieval of localized relationship triplets. Due to considerable progress in object detection, we focus on the last two and use existing pre-trained models for object detection. For predicate classification, we use graph neural networks operating on a graph of object instances, encoding a strong inductive bias for object-object relations. Finally, we use backward explanation techniques to attribute the graph network's predicate predictions to pairs of objects in the input.

---

[1] PyTorch implementation, data and experiments: github.com/baldassarreFe/ws-vrd.

Contributions. The main contributions of this work are threefold:
I) We tackle visual relation detection using a weaker form of label, i.e. *image-level predicate annotations* only, which reduces data collection cost, is more robust to non-exhaustive annotations, and helps generalization w.r.t. rare/unseen triplets.
II) We propose a novel explanation-based weakly-supervised approach for relationship detection. We believe this is the first work to *(a)* use weakly-supervised learning beyond object/scene recognition, and *(b)* employ explanation techniques on graph networks as the *key component* of a relationship detection pipeline.
III) Despite using weaker supervision, we show comparable results to state-of-the-art methods with stronger labels on several visual relation benchmarks.

2   Related Works

We are interested in weakly-supervised learning of visual relations. We achieve this by employing graph network explanation techniques. In this section, we cover the related papers corresponding to the different aspects of our work.

Visual Relationship Detection. Visual relation detection involves identifying groups of objects that exhibit semantic relations, in particular (subject, predicate, object) triplets. Relations are usually either comparative attributes/relative spatial configurations [12] which are useful for referral expression [26] and visual question answering [17], or, inter-object interactions [39] which is crucial for scene understanding. Due to the importance of human-centered image recognition for various applications, many of such works focus on human-object interactions [6,7,15,34,46,51].

Visual relation detection has been initially tackled by considering the whole relationship triplet as a single-phrase entity [39]. However, this approach comes with high computational costs and data inefficiency due to the combinatorial space of possible phrases. It is therefore important to devise methods that improve data efficiency and better generalize to rare or unseen relations.

Most modern works take a compositional approach [15,24,29–31,34], where objects and predicates are modelled in their own right, which enables better and more efficient generalization. Leveraging language through construction of priors, text embeddings, or joint textual-visual embeddings has also been shown to improve generalization [24,29,31]. The recent work of Peyre *et al.* [29] deals with the combinatorial growth of relation triplets using visual-language analogies. While this approach generalizes well to unseen combinations of seen entities, it adopts a fully-supervised training procedure that demands a considerable amount of annotated triplets for training.

In contrast, our approach improves data efficiency by only requiring image-level predicate labels, and instead learning relation triplets through weakly-supervised learning. Our non-reliance on the subject/object entities, in turn, improves generalization to unseen relations as, importantly, we do not require subject/object entities to appear in the training set.

Weakly-Supervised Learning. Weakly-supervised learning is generally desirable since it reduces the need for costly annotations. It has already proven effective for various visual recognition tasks including object detection [5,28], semantic segmentation [10,20], and instance segmentation [14,52]. Relationship detection can benefit from weakly-supervised learning even more than object/scene recognition, since the number of possible relation triplets grows quadratically with the number object categories. Despite this, weakly-supervised learning of visual relations has received surprisingly less attention than object-centric tasks.

Weakly-Supervised Learning of Visual Relations. The early work of Prest *et al.* [33], similar to our work, only requires image-level action labels. But Prest *et al.* focused on human-object interactions using part detectors, as opposed to general visual relationship detection. More recent works [30,48] learn visual relations in a weakly-supervised setup where triplets are annotated at the image level and not localized through bounding boxes. Peyre *et al.* [30] represents object pairs by their individual appearance as well as their relative spatial configuration. Then, they use discriminative clustering with validity constraints to assign object pairs to image-level labels. In [48], three separate pipelines are used, one for object detection, one for object-object relation classification and the third for object-object pair selection for each relation. The softmax output of the latter is then used as an attention mechanism over object pairs to account for the weak labels.

Both [30,48] work with non-localized triplets annotated at the image-level[2]. Our weaker supervision setup, by not requiring subject and object annotations, allows for potentially simpler, more general, and less costly construction of large training datasets using search engines or image captions. Furthermore, our method is based on object-centric explanations of graph networks, which sets it apart from previous works on weakly-supervised learning of visual relations.

Explanation Techniques. In mission-critical applications such as medical prognosis, a real-world deployment of trained AI systems require explanations of the predictions. Thus, many explanation techniques have been developed based on local approximation [37], game theory [25], or gradient propagation [2,41,50]. Recently, following the success of graph networks, explanation methods have been extended to those models as well [4,32,47]. We use graph networks to obtain image-level predicate predictions and then apply graph explanation techniques to obtain the corresponding subject and object in an unsupervised manner.

Explanation-Based Weakly-Supervised Learning. The idea of using explanations to account for weak labels has been previously used for object recognition. Class Activation Mapping (CAM) uses a specific architecture with

---

[2] It should be noted that [30] can be extended to work with only predicate annotations, using a new set of more relaxed constraints.

fully-convolutional layers and global average pooling to obtain object localization at the average pooling layer [50]. [52] extends this approach by backpropagating the maximum response of the CAM back to the image space for weakly-supervised instance segmentation. Grad-CAM [41] generalizes CAM and extends its applicability to a wider range of architectures by pushing the half-rectified gradient backward and using channel-wise average pooling to obtain location-wise importance. Similar to CAM, Grad-CAM is applied to ILSVRC [38] for weakly-supervised object localization. Finally, [14] develops a cascaded label propagation setup with conditional random fields and object proposals to obtain object instance segmentation from image-level predictions, using excitation back-propagation [49] for the backward pass. Our work is an extension to this line of research: we consider a more complicated application, namely visual relationship detection, and use explanation techniques on graph networks.

3   Method

Detecting visual relationships in an image consists in identifying triplets $\tau = \langle \text{subj}, \text{pred}, \text{obj} \rangle$ of subject, predicate and object. For example, *person drive car* or *tree next to building*. To formalize this, we denote the set of objects in an image by $\mathcal{O}$, where each object instance, i, has a corresponding bounding box b_i and is categorized as c_i according to a vocabulary of object classes $\{1 \ldots C\}$. Predicates belong to a vocabulary of predicate classes $\{1 \ldots K\}$ that include actions such as *eating*, spatial relations such as *next to* and comparative terms such as *taller than*.

With this notation, detecting visual relations from an image $\mathcal{I}$ corresponds to determining high-density regions of the following joint probability distribution:

$$P(\tau|\mathcal{I}) \triangleq P(c_{\text{subj}} = c_i, \; k_{\text{pred}} = k, \; c_{\text{obj}} = c_j, \; b_{\text{subj}} = b_i, \; b_{\text{obj}} = b_j \; |\mathcal{I}), \quad (1)$$

where c_{subj} and c_{obj} indicate resp. the class of the subject and the object, k_{pred} indicates the class of the predicate, b_{subj} and b_{obj} indicate resp. the location of the subject and the object, and $i, j = 1 \ldots |\mathcal{B}|$ index the bounding boxes.

To accommodate weakly-supervised learning, we propose the following approximate factorization based on object detection and predicate classification:

$$P(\tau|\mathcal{I}) =$$
$$P(c_{\text{subj}} = c_i|\mathcal{I}, b_{\text{subj}} = b_i)P(c_{\text{obj}} = c_j|\mathcal{I}, b_{\text{obj}} = b_j) \qquad \text{object detection} \quad (2)$$
$$P(k_{\text{pred}} = k|\mathcal{I}) \qquad \text{predicate classification} \quad (3)$$
$$P(b_{\text{subj}} = b_i, b_{\text{obj}} = b_j|\mathcal{I}, k_{\text{pred}} = k) \qquad \text{likelihood of a pair} \quad (4)$$
$$P(c_{\text{subj}} = c_i, c_{\text{obj}} = c_j|k_{\text{pred}} = k). \qquad \text{prior over relations} \quad (5)$$

For Eq. 2, we use an object detection pipeline to localize and classify objects in an image. The two terms, then, refer to the confidence scores assigned by the object detector to the subject and object of the relationship (Sect. 3.1).

Equation 3 corresponds to a predicate classifier that predicts the presence of predicate k in the image. This component only relies on image-level predicate annotations during training, and does not explicitly attribute its predictions to pairs of input objects. However, by carefully designing the architecture of the predicate classifier, we introduce a strong inductive bias towards objects and relations, which we can later exploit to recover $\langle subj, pred, obj \rangle$ triplets (Sect. 3.2).

Given a certain predicate k, Eq. 4 recovers the likelihood of object pairs to be the semantic subject and object of that predicate. In other words, we wish to identify *all* possible (subj, obj) pairs by their likelihood Eq. 4 w.r.t. a given predicate. Therefore, we use an explanation technique to compute unnormalized scores that associate predicates to pairs of objects (Sect. 3.3).

Term 5, which we refer to as *prior over relationships*, represents the co-occurrence of certain classes as subjects or objects of a predicate, and the directionality of such relationship. For instance, it can indicate that *(person, truck)*, with *person* as the subject, is a more likely pair for *drive* than *(fork, sandwich)*. As such, this term is optional, and excluding it would be the same as assuming a uniform prior. However, this term assumes great importance in a weakly-supervised setup, since isolated predicate labels provide no clue on the directionality of the relation between subject and object (Sect. 3.4).

3.1 Object Detection

We use an object detection module to extract a set of objects $\mathcal{O}$ from a given image $\mathcal{I}$. We describe each object bounding box by the visual appearance features and the classification scores obtained from the detector. These objects will then be used to classify the predicates present in $\mathcal{I}$ and, later on, serve as targets for explanations that identify relevant relationship triplets. Similar to the weakly-supervised setup of Peyre *et al.* [30] we assume the availability of pre-trained object detectors [36] as there is substantial progress in that field.

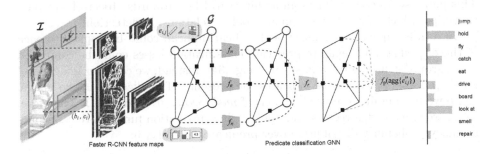

Fig. 2. A graph neural network (GNN) trained to classify the predicates depicted in a scene. Object detections extracted through Faster R-CNN are represented as a fully-connected graph. The GNN classifier aggregates local information across nodes and produces an image-level predicate prediction. The input representation and architecture implicitly encode an inductive bias for pairwise relationships

3.2 Predicate Classification

Predicate classification as described in Eq. 3 is a mapping from image to predicate(s) and as such does not necessarily require an understanding of objects. Thus, a simple choice for the classifier would be a convolutional neural network (CNN) trained on image-level predicate labels, e.g. ResNeXt [44]. However, the raw representation of images as pixels does not explicitly capture the compositional nature of the task. Instead, we introduce a strong inductive bias towards objects and relationships in both the data representation and the architecture. Specifically, the module is implemented as a graph neural network (GNN) with architecture similar to [40], that takes as input a graph representation of the image $\mathcal{G} = (\mathcal{O}, \mathcal{E})$, aggregates information by passing messages over the graph, and produces image-level predicate predictions. This design choice allows us to later explain the predictions in terms of objects, rather than raw pixels.

Each node in the image graph represents an object $i \in \mathcal{O}$ with its spatial and visual features extracted by the object detector, which together we denote as the tuple $n_i = (n_i^s, n_i^v)$. The image graph is built as fully-connected and therefore impartial to relations between objects. Directed edges $i \rightarrow j$ are placed between every pair of nodes, excluding self loops, resulting in $|\mathcal{O}|^2 - |\mathcal{O}|$ edges.

Node n_i and edge $e_{i,j}$ representations are first transformed through two small networks f_n and f_e:

$$n'_i = f_n(n_i) \tag{6}$$
$$e'_{i,j} = f_e(e_{i,j}). \tag{7}$$

Then, a relational function f_r aggregates local information by considering pairs of nodes and the edge connecting them:

$$e''_{i,j} = f_r(n'_i,\ e'_{i,j},\ n'_j). \tag{8}$$

This pairwise function induces an architectural bias towards object-object relationships, which hints at the ultimate goal of relationship detection.

In a fully-supervised scenario, a classification head could be applied to each of the $e''_{i,j}$ edges and separate predicate classification losses could be computed using ground-truth pairwise labels $p_{i,j}$, e.g. [34]. Instead, we consider image-level labels $p \in \{0,1\}^K$, where p_k indicates the presence of predicate k in the image, e.g. p would contain 1s at the locations of *push, wear, drive* for Fig. 1. Therefore, we aggregate all edge vectors and apply a final prediction function that outputs a binary probability distribution over predicates as in Eq. 3:

$$y = f_p\left(\text{agg}\left\{e''_{i,j}\right\}\right) \in [0,1]^K, \tag{9}$$

where *agg* is a permutation-invariant pooling function such as *max, sum* or *mean*.

Designed as such, the graph-based predicate classifier can be trained by minimizing the binary cross entropy between predictions and ground-truth labels:

$$\mathcal{L} = -\sum_{k=1}^{K} \left\{ p_k \log(y_k) + (1 - p_k)\log(1 - y_k) \right\}. \tag{10}$$

input   wear 74%   above 74%

Fig. 3. Grad-CAM heatmap visualization of a ResNet predicate classifier. Ground-truth annotations contain *person wear jacket* and *person above snowboard*, but it would be hard to identify subjects and objects from the pixel-level explanation.

3.3   Explanation-Based Relationship Detection

Once the predicate classifier is trained, we wish to use it to detect complete relationship triplets ⟨subj, pred, obj⟩. This is where the relational inductive bias introduced for the predicate classifier plays a key role. In fact, had the predicate classifier been a simple CNN, we would only be able to attribute its predictions to the input pixels, e.g. through sensitivity analysis [3] or Grad-CAM [41]. Figure 3 shows an example of Grad-CAM explanations obtained for a ResNeXt architecture [44] trained for predicate classification on the Visual Relationship Detection dataset (see appendix B.3). While it is possible to guess which areas of the image are relevant for the predicted predicate, it is undoubtedly hard to identify a distinct (subj, obj) pair from the pixel-wise heatmaps.

Thanks to the GNN architecture of the previous module, we can instead attribute predicate predictions to the nodes of the input graph, evaluating the importance of *objects* rather than *pixels*. We can then consider all pairs of nodes representing the candidate subject and object of a predicate of interest, score them with a backward explanation procedure and select the top-ranking triplets.

Specifically, we apply *sensitivity analysis* [3] to compute the relevance of a node (r_i^k) and of an edge ($r_{i,j}^k$) with respect to a predicate k:

$$r_i^k = \left\| \frac{\partial y_k}{\partial \boldsymbol{n}_i} \right\|_1 \qquad \text{single-object relevance} \qquad (11)$$

$$r_{i,j}^k = \left\| \frac{\partial y_k}{\partial \boldsymbol{e}_{i,j}} \right\|_1 \qquad \text{object-pair relevance} \qquad (12)$$

We experimented with different ways to compute these relevances, including gradient × input, max(gradient × input, 0), and the L1, L2 norms, but no significant differences were noticed on the validation set.

The product of these relevances is then used as a proxy for the unnormalized likelihood of a subject-object pair given a predicate (Eq. 4):

$$P(b_{\text{subj}} = b_i, b_{\text{obj}} = b_j | k_{\text{pred}} = k) \propto r_i^k \cdot r_{i,j}^k \cdot r_j^k. \qquad (13)$$

Rather than computing this quantity for every predicate and for every pair of objects, we limit the search to the N top-scoring predicates, reducing the number of candidates from $K(|\mathcal{O}|^2 - |\mathcal{O}|)$ to $N(|\mathcal{O}|^2 - |\mathcal{O}|)$ relationships. A Big O complexity that scales as $|\mathcal{O}|^2$ might seem unappealing, yet with $|\mathcal{O}| < 30$ we could process batches of 128 image graphs in a single pass (Fig. 4).

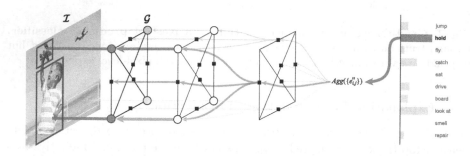

Fig. 4. Relationship detection through explanation. A predicate prediction is *explained* by attributing it to the pair of objects in the input that are most relevant for it, effectively recovering a full relationship triplet in the form $\langle \text{subj}, \text{pred}, \text{obj} \rangle$

3.4   Prior over Relationships

Learning to detect $\langle \text{subj}, \text{pred}, \text{obj} \rangle$ relations using image-level predicate labels is inherently ill-defined. Consider the task of learning a new predicate, e.g. *squanch*. By observing a sufficient number of labeled images, we could learn that two specific objects are often in a *squanch* relationship. However, we would not be able to determine which should be the subject and which the object, i.e. the direction of such relation, without semantic knowledge about the new word (can things be *squanchier than* others? can objects *squanch* each other?).

Equation 5 represents the belief over which categories can act as subject and objects of a certain predicate. In fully- or weakly-supervised scenarios, where $\langle \text{subj}, \text{pred}, \text{obj} \rangle$ triplets are available during training, a relationship detector would learn such biases directly from data. Our graph-based predicate classifier, trained only image-level predicate annotations, can indeed learn to recognize object-object relations and to assign high probability to meaningful pairs (Eq. 13), but neither the training signal nor the inductive biases contain hints about directionality. In fact, the relevance $r_{i,j}^k$ is in no way constrained to represent the relationship that has i as subject and j as object, even though Eq. 8 considers the edge $i \rightarrow j$. Thus the explanation (Eq. 13) for *hold* might score both *person hold pencil* and its semantic opposite *pencil hold person* equally.

Previous work [24] use `word2vec` [27] embeddings of $\langle \text{subj}, \text{pred}, \text{obj} \rangle$ triplets from the training set to form a semantically-grounded prior. Instead, we compute a simple frequency-based prior $\text{freq}(c_i, c_j | k)$ over a small validation set, to avoid including exclusive relationship information from the training set (app. C.3).

4   Experiments

In this section, we test our weakly-supervised method for visual relationship detection on three different datasets, each one presenting specific challenges and different evaluation metrics. Before discussing the individual experiments, we provide further implementation details about the object detection, predicate classification and visual relationship explainer modules. Additional experiments and ablation studies can be found in appendix C.

4.1   Setup

Object Detection. Our object detection module is based on the `detectron2` [43] implementation of Faster R-CNN [36]. Given an object i and its bounding box b_i, either from the ground-truth annotations or detected by Faster R-CNN, we use RoIALIGN [16] to pool a $256 \times 7 \times 7$ feature volume $\boldsymbol{n}_i^v$ from the pyramid of features [22] built on top of a ResNeXt-101 backbone [44]. Furthermore, we compute a feature vector $\boldsymbol{n}_i^s$ that represents the spatial configuration of b_i. Specifically, the tuple of spatial and visual features $\boldsymbol{n}_i = (\boldsymbol{n}_i^s, \boldsymbol{n}_i^v)$ is defined as:

$$\boldsymbol{n}_i^s = \left[\frac{w_i}{h_i}, \frac{h_i}{w_i}, \frac{w_i h_i}{WH} \right] \qquad \text{spatial features} \qquad (14)$$

$$\boldsymbol{n}_i^v = \text{RoIALIGN}\left(\text{FPN}(\mathcal{I}), b_i\right), \qquad \text{visual features} \qquad (15)$$

where (w_i, h_i) and (W, H) represent width and height of the box b_i and of the image $\mathcal{I}$ respectively, FPN is the feature pyramid network used to extract visual features from the whole image, and RoIALIGN is the pooling operation applied to the feature pyramid to extract features relative to the box b_i.

Edge attributes $\boldsymbol{e}_{i,j}$ are chosen to represent the spatial configuration of the pair of objects they connect:

$$\boldsymbol{e}_{i,j} = \left[\frac{\|\boldsymbol{x}_j - \boldsymbol{x}_i\|}{\sqrt{WH}}, \; \sin(\angle_{ij}), \; \cos(\angle_{ij}), \; \text{IoU}(b_j, b_i), \; \frac{w_j h_j}{w_i h_i} \right], \qquad (16)$$

where $\boldsymbol{x}_i \in \mathbb{R}_+^2$ is the center of b_i, $\angle_{ij}$ is the angle between $\boldsymbol{x}_j - \boldsymbol{x}_i$ and the positive horizontal axis, and IoU is the intersection over union of the two boxes.

Predicate Classifier. At training time, the input of the predicate classifier described in Sect. 3.2 is a fully-connected graph of ground-truth objects. During inference, we apply the object detector and build a graph with all objects having confidence score of 30% or more. For each dataset, the hyperparameters of the GNN-based predicate classifier are selected on a validation split of 15% training images. The following values apply to the HICO-DET dataset, more details about the hyperparameter space are available in appendix B.2.

The input node function f_n is implemented as i) a $2 \times (\text{CONV} + \text{RELU})$ network applied to $\boldsymbol{n}^v$, where the convolutional layers employ 256 kernels of size

3×3 each, and ii) a LINEAR + RELU operation that transforms n^s into a 1024-vector. The input edge functions f_e consist of a LINEAR + RELU operation that outputs a 1024-vector of transformed edge features. The relational function f_r in Eq. 8 is implemented as a LINEAR + RELU operation where the features of two nodes and of the directed edge between them are concatenated at the input. The output of f_r is a 1024-vector for each ordered pair of nodes. For all datasets, the aggregation function in Eq. 9 is element-wise max, and f_p is a LINEAR + SIGMOID operation that outputs a $K-$vector of binary probabilities.

We train the weights of the predicate classifier by minimizing the loss in Eq. 10 with the Adam optimizer [19] with 10^{-3} initial learning rate and 10^{-5} weight decay. During training, we track `recall@5`, i.e. the fraction of ground-truth predicates retrieved among the top-5 confident predictions for an image. We let the optimization run on batches of 128 graphs for 18 epochs, at which point the classifier achieves 94% recall on a validation split.

Relationship Detector. The explanation-based relationship detection algorithm described in Sect. 3.3 does not have many hyperparameters. We tried i) whether to multiply the gradient with the input when computing relevances, ii) which norm to use between L1, L2 and max(L1,0), and iii) the number N of top-scoring predicates whose gradient is traced back to the input to identify relevant triplets. As observed in [8], optimizing these parameters on the whole training set would violate the premise of weakly-supervised learning by accessing fully-labeled data. Therefore, we employ once again the 15% validation split used to optimize the classifier, assuming that in a real-world scenario it should always be possible to manually annotate a small subset of images for validation purposes. The best choice of N for all datasets was found to be 10, while the other two parameters seem to have little effect on performance.

4.2 HICO-DET

The Humans Interacting with Common Objects (HICO-DET) dataset contains $\sim 50K$ exhaustively annotated images of *human-object interactions* (HOI), split into $\sim 40K$ train and $\sim 10K$ test images [6,7]. The subject of a relationship is always *person*, the 117 predicates cover a variety of human-centric actions (e.g. *cook, wash, paint*), and the 80 objects categories are those defined as `thing_classes` in MS-COCO [23]. We can therefore use the pre-trained object detector from [43], of which we report performances in appendix A.1.

The nature of this dataset allows us to embed the relationship prior in the graph itself. A fully-connected graph encodes a uniform prior, i.e. no preference about subject-object pairs, while a sparse graph containing only edges from humans to objects encodes a bias towards *human-object interactions*.

The metric for this dataset is the 11-point interpolated mean Average Precision (mAP) [11] computed over the 600 human-object interaction classes of the dataset [6]. The following criteria should be met for a detected triplet to match with a ground-truth triplet: a) subject, predicate and object categories match, and b) subject boxes overlap with IoU > .5, and c) object boxes overlap with IoU > .5, and d) the ground-truth triplet was not matched with a previously-considered detected triplet. Table 1 reports mAP for the standard splits of HICO-DET[6]: all 600 human-object interactions, 138 rare triplets, and 462 non-rare triplets (10 or more training samples). We compare with various fully-supervised baselines including the original HO-RCNN from [6] and the method from [29] that uses semantic and visual analogies to improve detection of rare and unseen triplets. Despite the weaker supervision signal, the strong inductive bias towards pairwise relationships allows our explanation method to achieve higher mAP for both the uniform and human-object priors (Fig. 5).

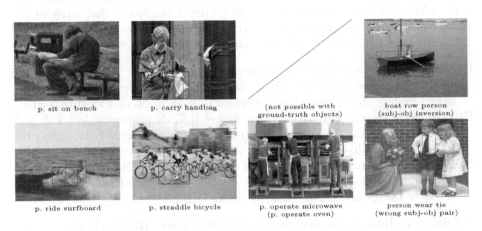

Fig. 5. Relationship detection on HICO-DET. Top row uses GT objects, bottom row uses Faster R-CNN objects. Left to right: correct relationship detection, correct but missing ground-truth, incorrect due to object misdetection, incorrect detection (selected predictions of our model using a uniform relationship prior)

Table 1. Mean Average Precision on the HICO-DET dataset. The choice of relationship prior embedded in the graph is indicated in parentheses

	Full (600)	Rare (138)	Non-rare (462)
Fully supervised			
Chao [6]	7.81	5.37	8.54
InteractNet [15]	9.94	7.16	10.77
GPNN [34]	13.11	9.34	14.23
iCAN [13]	14.84	10.45	16.15
Analogies [29]	19.40	14.60	20.90
Weakly supervised			
Ours (uniform)	24.25	20.23	25.45
Ours (human-object)	28.04	24.63	29.06

4.3   Visual Relationship Detection Dataset

The Visual Relationship Detection dataset (VRD) contains ~5000 annotated images, split into ~4000 train and ~1000 test images [18,24]. The 70 predicates in this dataset include both verbs and spatial relationships, e.g. *carry, next to*. The 100 object categories cover both well spatially-defined objects such as *bottle* and concepts like *sky* and *road*, that are harder to localize. For this set of objects there is no ready-to-use object detector, therefore we finetune a `detectron2` model using annotations from the training set (details in appendix A.2).

The standard metric for VRD [24] is `recall@x` i.e. fraction of ground-truth triplets retrieved among the x top-ranked detections [1]. Here, recall is preferred over mAP since it does not penalize the retrieval of triplets that exist in the image, but are missing in the ground-truth. Criteria for true positive in VRD follow those of HICO-DET, and are used in the following settings [24]:

Predicate detection: objects for the image graph come from ground-truth annotations,allowing to test the explanation-based retrieval of relationships under perfect object detection conditions (classification and localization).

Phrase detection: objects come from Faster R-CNN proposals, but IoU > .5 is evaluated on the union box of subject and object, effectively localizing the entire relationship as a single image region, or *visual phrase* [39].

Relationship detection: objects come from Faster R-CNN proposals, subject and object boxes are required to individually overlap with their corresponding boxes in the ground-truth (same as HICO-DET).

As shown in Table 2, our method achieves recall scores R@100 close to a fully-supervised baseline [24], despite the weaker training signal. By analyizing the top 100 predictions of a model with uniform prior, we often observed the coappearance of a relationship and its semantic opposite, e.g. *person drive car* and *car drive person*, which possibly "wastes" half of the top-x detection due to incorrect directionality (corroborated by the gap between R@50 and R@100 of ours-uniform). Importantly, moving from a uniform to a frequency-based prior almost doubles R@50, which highlights the importance of the relationship prior in connection with our method. We expect that including a stronger prior, e.g. based on natural-language embeddings of objects and predicates, would further improve detection of semantically-correct relationships.

The test set of VRD contains a triplets that never occur during training and can be used to evaluate zero-shot generalization. As shown in Table 3, our method performs on a par with other methods that use stronger annotations and explicitly improve generalization through language embeddings [24] or visual analogy transformations [29]. Expectedly, the freq-based prior computed on the validation set does not improve recall of unseen triplets. To verify importance of this term, we show that a simple prior with access to a few zero-shot triplets readily improves recall. Clearly, peeking at the test set is not correct practice, but serves

Table 2. Recall at 50 and 100 on the VRD dataset. Comparison of fully- and weakly-supervised methods. The choice of relationship prior is indicated in parentheses

| | GT objects | | R-CNN objects | | | |
| | Predicate det. | | Phrase det. | | Relation. det. | |
	R@50	R@100	R@50	R@100	R@50	R@100
Fully supervised						
Visual Phrases [39]	0.9	1.9	0.04	0.07	–	–
Visual [24]	3.5	3.5	0.7	0.8	1.0	1.1
Visual+Language [24]	47.9	47.9	16.2	17.0	13.9	14.7
Sup. PPR-FCN [48]	47.4	47.4	19.6	23.2	14.4	15.7
Peyre [30]	52.6	52.6	17.9	19.5	15.8	17.1
Weakly sup. (subj, pred, obj)						
PPR-FCN [48]	–	–	6.9	8.2	5.9	6.3
Peyre [30]	46.8	46.8	16.0	17.4	14.1	15.3
Weakly sup. (predonly)						
Ours (uniform)	27.3	47.1	6.8	13.0	5.3	8.4
Ours (frequentist)	43.0	57.4	14.8	20.2	10.6	13.2

as a proxy for what could be achieved by improving this term, e.g. via incorporating language or visual analogies. The next experiment better demonstrates the generalization of our method to unseen triplets.

4.4   Unusual Relations Dataset

The Unusual Relations dataset (UnRel) is an evaluation-only collection of $\sim$1000 images, which shares the same vocabulary as VRD and depicts rarely-occurring relationships [30]. For relationship detection methods trained on $\langle$subj, pred, obj$\rangle$ triplets, this dataset represents a benchmark for zero-shot retrieval of triplets not seen during training. E.g. our predicate classifier trained on VRD has clearly encountered *hold* during training, but never in *person hold plane* (Fig. 2).

In Table 4 we report mAP over the 76 unusual triplets of UnRel. We follow the evaluation setup of [30]: the test set of VRD is mixed in to act as distractor, up to 500 candidate triplets per image are retained, and they are matched if $IoU > .3$. Since the average number of detected objects per image is small, $\sim$4 we increase the number of top-scoring predicates considered in the explanation step to $N = 50$. Differently from [29,30], we use obj. detection scores for ranking triplets, and we do not introduce a *no-interaction* predicate. Compared to recall, mAP is less affected by unseen triplets and the prior from VRD results effective.

Table 3. Zero-shot recall on the VRD dataset: triplets from the test set that are never seen during training. The choice of relationship prior is indicated in parentheses

| | GT objects | | R-CNN objects | | | |
| | Predicate det. | | Phrase det. | | Relation. det. | |
	R@50	R@100	R@50	R@100	R@50	R@100
Fully supervised						
Visual [24]	3.5	3.5	0.7	0.8	1.0	1.1
Visual+Language [24]	8.5	8.5	3.4	3.8	3.1	3.5
Peyre 2017 [30]	21.6	21.6	6.8	7.8	6.4	7.4
Weakly sup. (subj, pred, obj)						
Peyre 2017 [30]	19.0	19.0	6.9	7.4	6.7	7.1
Weakly sup. (predonly)						
Ours (uniform)	13.7	29.2	3.8	6.5	2.8	4.6
Ours (VRD freq.)	13.5	28.2	4.4	6.4	3.3	4.6
Ours (Zero freq.)	20.5	37.0	4.7	8.2	4.0	6.4

Table 4. Mean average precision on UnRel with VRD as a distractor

| | GT objects | R-CNN objects | | |
	Predicate	Phrase	Subj. only	Relationship
Fully supervised				
Peyre 2017 [30]	62.6	14.1	12.1	9.9
Analogies [29]	63.9	17.5	15.9	13.4
Weakly sup. (subj, pred, obj)				
Peyre 2017 [30]	58.5	13.4	11.0	8.7
Weakly sup. (predicate only)				
Ours (uniform)	70.9	19.8	18.1	14.9
Ours (frequency)	70.6	20.0	18.3	15.1

5   Conclusion

We considered the task of learning visual relationship detection with weak image-level predicate labels. While this makes learning significantly harder, it enables collecting datasets that are more representative of possible relations without suffering from combinatorial scaling of search queries and annotation cost.

Using pretrained object detectors, strong inductive bias via graph networks, backward explanations, and a direction prior, we showed that it is possible to achieve results on par with recent works that benefit from stronger supervision.

An issue with predicate-only annotation is the lack of directional information, which can only be provided using auxiliary sources such as language. While we mitigated this issue through a simple frequentist prior, an important future direction is to solve it in a principled way. For instance, one can annotate a subset of images with unlocalized image-level triplets, only to disambiguate the direction of the relations. Note that, since such a dataset does not have to be exhaustively annotated for all triplets, the collection cost would be negligible.

Finally, another interesting direction is to study the proposed explanation-based weakly-supervised method in other domains such as situation recognition [21], video recognition [45], segmentation [35], chemistry [9] and biology [42].

Acknowledgements. Funded by Swedish Research Council project 2017-04609 and by Wallenberg AI, Autonomous Systems and Software Program (WASP).

References

1. Alexe, B., Deselaers, T., Ferrari, V.: Measuring the objectness of image windows. IEEE Trans. Pattern Anal. Mach. Intell. **34**(11), 2189–2202 (2012)
2. Bach, S., Binder, A., Montavon, G., Klauschen, F., Müller, K.R., Samek, W.: On pixel-wise explanations for non-linear classifier decisions by layer-wise relevance propagation. PloS one **10**(7), e0130140 (2015)
3. Baehrens, D., Schroeter, T., Harmeling, S., Kawanabe, M., Hansen, K., MÃžller, K.R.: How to explain individual classification decisions. J. Mach. Learn. Res. **11**(Jun), 1803–1831 (2010)
4. Baldassarre, F., Azizpour, H.: Explainability techniques for graph convolutional networks. In: International Conference on Machine Learning (ICML) Workshops, 2019 Workshop on Learning and Reasoning with Graph-Structured Representations (2019)
5. Bilen, H., Vedaldi, A.: Weakly supervised deep detection networks. In: The IEEE Conference on Computer Vision and Pattern Recognition (CVPR) (2016)
6. Chao, Y.W., Liu, Y., Liu, X., Zeng, H., Deng, J.: Learning to detect human-object interactions. In: 2018 IEEE Winter Conference on Applications of Computer Vision (WACV), pp. 381–389. IEEE (2018)
7. Chao, Y.W., Wang, Z., He, Y., Wang, J., Deng, J.: Hico: a benchmark for recognizing human-object interactions in images. In: Proceedings of the IEEE International Conference on Computer Vision, pp. 1017–1025 (2015)
8. Choe, J., Oh, S.J., Lee, S., Chun, S., Akata, Z., Shim, H.: Evaluating weakly supervised object localization methods right. arXiv preprint arXiv:2001.07437 (2020)
9. Do, K., Tran, T., Venkatesh, S.: Graph transformation policy network for chemical reaction prediction. In: Proceedings of the 25th ACM SIGKDD International Conference on Knowledge Discovery & Data Mining, pp. 750–760 (2019)
10. Durand, T., Mordan, T., Thome, N., Cord, M.: Wildcat: weakly supervised learning of deep convnets for image classification, pointwise localization and segmentation. In: Proceedings of the IEEE Conference on Computer Vision and Pattern Recognition, pp. 642–651 (2017)
11. Everingham, M., Van Gool, L., Williams, C.K., Winn, J., Zisserman, A.: The pascal visual object classes (voc) challenge. Int. J. Comput. Vis. **88**(2), 303–338 (2010)
12. Galleguillos, C., Rabinovich, A., Belongie, S.: Object categorization using co-occurrence, location and appearance. In: 2008 IEEE Conference on Computer Vision and Pattern Recognition, pp. 1–8. IEEE (2008)
13. Gao, C., Zou, Y., Huang, J.B.: ican: Instance-centric attention network for human-object interaction detection (2018)

14. Ge, W., Guo, S., Huang, W., Scott, M.R.: Label-penet: sequential label propagation and enhancement networks for weakly supervised instance segmentation. In: Proceedings of the IEEE International Conference on Computer Vision, pp. 3345–3354 (2019)
15. Gkioxari, G., Girshick, R., Dollár, P., He, K.: Detecting and recognizing human-object interactions. In: Proceedings of the IEEE Conference on Computer Vision and Pattern Recognition, pp. 8359–8367 (2018)
16. He, K., Gkioxari, G., Dollár, P., Girshick, R.: Mask r-cnn. In: Proceedings of the IEEE International Conference on Computer Vision, pp. 2961–2969 (2017)
17. Johnson, J., Hariharan, B., van der Maaten, L., Fei-Fei, L., Lawrence Zitnick, C., Girshick, R.: Clevr: a diagnostic dataset for compositional language and elementary visual reasoning. In: Proceedings of the IEEE Conference on Computer Vision and Pattern Recognition, pp. 2901–2910 (2017)
18. Johnson, J., et al.: Image retrieval using scene graphs. In: Proceedings of the IEEE Conference on Computer Vision and Pattern Recognition, pp. 3668–3678 (2015)
19. Kingma, D.P., Ba, J.: Adam: A method for stochastic optimization. arXiv preprint arXiv:1412.6980 (2014)
20. Lee, J., Kim, E., Lee, S., Lee, J., Yoon, S.: Ficklenet: weakly and semi-supervised semantic image segmentation using stochastic inference. In: Proceedings of the IEEE Conference on Computer Vision and Pattern Recognition, pp. 5267–5276 (2019)
21. Li, R., Tapaswi, M., Liao, R., Jia, J., Urtasun, R., Fidler, S.: Situation recognition with graph neural networks. In: Proceedings of the IEEE International Conference on Computer Vision, pp. 4173–4182 (2017)
22. Lin, T.Y., Dollár, P., Girshick, R., He, K., Hariharan, B., Belongie, S.: Feature pyramid networks for object detection. In: Proceedings of the IEEE Conference on Computer Vision and Pattern Recognition, pp. 2117–2125 (2017)
23. Lin, T.Y., et al.: Microsoft COCO: common objects in context. In: Fleet, D., Pajdla, T., Schiele, B., Tuytelaars, T. (eds.) ECCV 2014. LNCS, vol. 8693, pp. 740–755. Springer, Cham (2014). https://doi.org/10.1007/978-3-319-10602-1_48
24. Lu, C., Krishna, R., Bernstein, M., Fei-Fei, L.: Visual relationship detection with language priors. In: Leibe, B., Matas, J., Sebe, N., Welling, M. (eds.) ECCV 2016. LNCS, vol. 9905, pp. 852–869. Springer, Cham (2016). https://doi.org/10.1007/978-3-319-46448-0_51
25. Lundberg, S.M., Lee, S.I.: A unified approach to interpreting model predictions. In: Guyon, I., et al. (eds.) Advances in Neural Information Processing Systems, vol. 30, pp. 4765–4774. Curran Associates, Inc. (2017)
26. Mao, J., Huang, J., Toshev, A., Camburu, O., Yuille, A.L., Murphy, K.: Generation and comprehension of unambiguous object descriptions. In: Proceedings of the IEEE Conference on Computer Vision and Pattern Recognition, pp. 11–20 (2016)
27. Mikolov, T., Chen, K., Corrado, G., Dean, J.: Efficient estimation of word representations in vector space. arXiv preprint arXiv:1301.3781 (2013)
28. Oquab, M., Bottou, L., Laptev, I., Sivic, J.: Is object localization for free?-weakly-supervised learning with convolutional neural networks. In: Proceedings of the IEEE Conference on Computer Vision and Pattern Recognition, pp. 685–694 (2015)
29. Peyre, J., Laptev, I., Schmid, C., Sivic, J.: Detecting unseen visual relations using analogies. In: Proceedings of the IEEE International Conference on Computer Vision, pp. 1981–1990 (2019)
30. Peyre, J., Sivic, J., Laptev, I., Schmid, C.: Weakly-supervised learning of visual relations. In: Proceedings of the IEEE International Conference on Computer Vision, pp. 5179–5188 (2017)

31. Plummer, B.A., Mallya, A., Cervantes, C.M., Hockenmaier, J., Lazebnik, S.: Phrase localization and visual relationship detection with comprehensive image-language cues. In: Proceedings of the IEEE International Conference on Computer Vision, pp. 1928–1937 (2017)
32. Pope, P.E., Kolouri, S., Rostami, M., Martin, C.E., Hoffmann, H.: Explainability methods for graph convolutional neural networks. In: Proceedings of the IEEE Conference on Computer Vision and Pattern Recognition, pp. 10772–10781 (2019)
33. Prest, A., Schmid, C., Ferrari, V.: Weakly supervised learning of interactions between humans and objects. IEEE Trans. Pattern Anal. Mach. Intell. **34**(3), 601–614 (2011)
34. Qi, S., Wang, W., Jia, B., Shen, J., Zhu, S.C.: Learning human-object interactions by graph parsing neural networks. In: Proceedings of the European Conference on Computer Vision (ECCV), pp. 401–417 (2018)
35. Qi, X., Liao, R., Jia, J., Fidler, S., Urtasun, R.: 3D graph neural networks for RGBD semantic segmentation. In: Proceedings of the IEEE International Conference on Computer Vision, pp. 5199–5208 (2017)
36. Ren, S., He, K., Girshick, R., Sun, J.: Faster r-cnn: Towards real-time object detection with region proposal networks. In: Advances in Neural Information Processing Systems, pp. 91–99 (2015)
37. Ribeiro, M.T., Singh, S., Guestrin, C.: "why should I trust you?": explaining the predictions of any classifier. In: Proceedings of the 22nd ACM SIGKDD International Conference on Knowledge Discovery and Data Mining, San Francisco, CA, USA, 13–17 August 2016, pp. 1135–1144 (2016)
38. Russakovsky, O., et al.: Imagenet large scale visual recognition challenge. Int. J. Comput. Vis. **115**(3), 211–252 (2015)
39. Sadeghi, M., Farhadi, A.: Recognition using visual phrases. In: Proceedings of the 2011 IEEE Conference on Computer Vision and Pattern Recognition, pp. 1745–1752 (2011)
40. Santoro, A., et al.: A simple neural network module for relational reasoning. In: Advances in Neural Information Processing Systems, pp. 4967–4976 (2017)
41. Selvaraju, R.R., Cogswell, M., Das, A., Vedantam, R., Parikh, D., Batra, D.: Grad-cam: visual explanations from deep networks via gradient-based localization. In: Proceedings of the IEEE International Conference on Computer Vision, pp. 618–626 (2017)
42. Tsubaki, M., Tomii, K., Sese, J.: Compound-protein interaction prediction with end-to-end learning of neural networks for graphs and sequences. Bioinformatics **35**(2), 309–318 (2019)
43. Wu, Y., Kirillov, A., Massa, F., Lo, W.Y., Girshick, R.: Detectron2 (2019). https://github.com/facebookresearch/detectron2
44. Xie, S., Girshick, R., Dollár, P., Tu, Z., He, K.: Aggregated residual transformations for deep neural networks. In: Proceedings of the IEEE Conference on Computer Vision and Pattern Recognition, pp. 1492–1500 (2017)
45. Yan, S., Xiong, Y., Lin, D.: Spatial temporal graph convolutional networks for skeleton-based action recognition. In: Thirty-second AAAI Conference on Artificial Intelligence (2018)
46. Yao, B., Fei-Fei, L.: Modeling mutual context of object and human pose in human-object interaction activities. In: 2010 IEEE Computer Society Conference on Computer Vision and Pattern Recognition, pp. 17–24. IEEE (2010)
47. Ying, Z., Bourgeois, D., You, J., Zitnik, M., Leskovec, J.: Gnnexplainer: Generating explanations for graph neural networks. In: Advances in Neural Information Processing Systems, pp. 9240–9251 (2019)

48. Zhang, H., Kyaw, Z., Yu, J., Chang, S.F.: Ppr-fcn: weakly supervised visual relation detection via parallel pairwise r-fcn. In: Proceedings of the IEEE International Conference on Computer Vision, pp. 4233–4241 (2017)
49. Zhang, J., Bargal, S.A., Lin, Z., Brandt, J., Shen, X., Sclaroff, S.: Top-down neural attention by excitation backprop. Int. J. Comput. Vis. **126**(10), 1084–1102 (2018)
50. Zhou, B., Khosla, A., Lapedriza, A., Oliva, A., Torralba, A.: Learning deep features for discriminative localization. In: Proceedings of the IEEE Conference on Computer Vision and Pattern Recognition, pp. 2921–2929 (2016)
51. Zhou, P., Chi, M.: Relation parsing neural network for human-object interaction detection. In: Proceedings of the IEEE International Conference on Computer Vision, pp. 843–851 (2019)
52. Zhou, Y., Zhu, Y., Ye, Q., Qiu, Q., Jiao, J.: Weakly supervised instance segmentation using class peak response. In: Proceedings of the IEEE Conference on Computer Vision and Pattern Recognition, pp. 3791–3800 (2018)

Guided Semantic Flow

Sangryul Jeon[1], Dongbo Min[2], Seungryong Kim[3], Jihwan Choe[4],
and Kwanghoon Sohn[1(✉)]

[1] Yonsei University, Seoul, South Korea
{cheonjsr,khsohn}@yonsei.ac.kr
[2] Ewha Womans University, Seoul, South Korea
dbmin@ewha.ac.kr
[3] Korea University, Seoul, South Korea
seungryong_kim@korea.ac.kr
[4] Samsung, Suwon, South Korea
jihwan.choe@samsung.com

Abstract. Establishing dense semantic correspondences requires dealing with large geometric variations caused by the unconstrained setting
of images. To address such severe matching ambiguities, we introduce
a novel approach, called guided semantic flow, based on the key insight
that sparse yet reliable matches can effectively capture non-rigid geometric variations, and these confident matches can guide adjacent pixels
to have similar solution spaces, reducing the matching ambiguities significantly. We realize this idea with learning-based selection of confident
matches from an initial set of all pairwise matching scores and their
propagation by a new differentiable upsampling layer based on moving
least square concept. We take advantage of the guidance from reliable
matches to refine the matching hypotheses through Gaussian parametric
model in the subsequent matching pipeline. With the proposed method,
state-of-the-art performance is attained on several standard benchmarks
for semantic correspondence.

Keywords: Dense semantic correspondence · Matching confidence ·
Moving least square

1 Introduction

Finding pixel-level correspondences across *semantically* similar images facilitates
a variety of computer vision applications, including non-parametric scene parsing [22,30,52], image manipulation [10,26,51], visual localization [41,47], and to
name a few.

Classical approaches for dense correspondence take *visually* similar images
taken under constraint settings, such as 1D epipolar line for stereo matching [43,

Electronic supplementary material The online version of this chapter (https://
doi.org/10.1007/978-3-030-58604-1_38) contains supplementary material, which is
available to authorized users.

A. Vedaldi et al. (Eds.): ECCV 2020, LNCS 12373, pp. 631–648, 2020.
https://doi.org/10.1007/978-3-030-58604-1_38

50] and 2D small motion for optical flow estimation [1,9]. Contrarily, semantic correspondence has no such constraints on the input image pairs except that two images describe the same object or scene category, posing additional challenges due to large appearance and geometric intra-class variations. Recent state-of-the-art methods [17,19,20,23,26,28,39–41,44] have attempted to address these challenges by carefully designing convolutional neural networks (CNNs) that mimic the classical matching pipeline [36]: feature extraction, similarity score computation, and correspondence estimation.

(a) image pair   (b) guidance displacements   (c) our result

Fig. 1. Visualization of our intuition: (a) image pair, (b) selected confident matches, and (c) warped image using the correspondences from our method. The proposed method, *guided semantic flow*, establishes reliable dense semantic correspondences by leveraging the guidance from confident matches to reduce matching ambiguities.

Since no viewpoint constraint is imposed on the source and target images, the search space for each pixel on the source image have to be defined with all pixels of the target image. However, searching over the full set of pairwise matching candidates inevitably increases the uncertainty in the matching pipeline, especially in the presence of non-rigid deformations and repetitive patterns.

One possible approach to this issue is to design additional modules that can vote for plausible transformation candidates from the full set of pairwise matches [17,39–41,44]. Following the pioneering work of [39], several methods [40,44] attempted to directly regress an image-level global transformation (*e.g.* affine or thin plate spline) between images. However, all matching scores are equally treated regardless of how confident they are, thus these approaches are inherently vulnerable to inaccurate matching scores that are often produced under severe intra-class variations. Without the need of global geometry, some methods [17,41] recently proposed to identify locally consistent matches by analyzing neighborhood consensus patterns. They down-weight ambiguous matches by assessing the confidence of matching scores, but this is performed only with a hand-crafted criterion (*e.g.* mutual consistency) that may often produces high confidence scores even for unconfident pixels.

Alternatively, similar to stereo matching and optical flow estimation [9,50], one can simply discard ambiguous matches by constraining the search space within a predefined local region centered at the querying pixel [20,26], but these approaches disregard the possibility of non-local matches that often appear across the semantically similar images. To address this issue, dilation technique [49] was utilized in [23], but the number of ambiguous matches increases at the same time. Some methods alleviated this by limiting the search space based on the heuristic matching cues, *e.g.* computing the discrete argmax [28] or starting with an image-level global transformation [19] estimated from a full set of pairwise similarity scores. However, such heuristics are often violated under large intra-class variations where the feature representations are quite inconsistent to measure accurate matching similarity or non-rigid geometric deformations that cannot be modeled with a global transformation model.

In this paper, we propose a novel approach, dubbed as *guided semantic flow*, that reliably infers dense semantic correspondence fields under large intra-class variations, as illustrated in Fig. 1. Our key idea is based on two observations: sparse yet reliable matches can effectively capture non-rigid geometric variations, and these confident matches can guide the adjacent pixels to have similar solution spaces, reducing the matching ambiguities significantly. Our method realizes this idea through three different modules consisting of pruning, propagation, and matching. We first select confident matches from a complete set of pairwise matching candidates through deep networks, and then propagate their reliable information to invalid neighborhoods through a new differentiable upsampling layer inspired by moving least square (MLS) approach [42]. Lastly, dense correspondence fields are reliably inferred from the refined correlation volume by constraining the search space with Gaussian parametric model that is centered at the interpolated displacement vector. Experimental results on various benchmarks demonstrate the effectiveness of the proposed model over the latest methods for dense semantic correspondence.

2 Related Works

Stereo Matching and Optical Flow Estimation. There have been numerous efforts on reducing the matching ambiguitiy for classical dense correspondence problems, *i.e.* stereo matching and optical flow estimation.

Based on the seminal work of PatchMatch [2], the randomized search scheme has been utilized and extended in numerous literature thanks to its effectiveness in pruning the search space [7,15,16]. Another popular idea is to leverage the spatial pyramid of an image, naturally imposing the hierarchical smoothness constraint in a coarse-to-fine manner [5,38,45]. Also, in order to enhance matching scores, recent approaches for depth estimation [35,37] additionally exploit sparse yet reliable measurements retrieved from an external source (*e.g.* LiDAR). However, since these approaches are tailored to the specific problem constraints such as epipolar geometry and relatively small motion, they are not directly applicable to the semantic correspondence task where two images may have large variations in terms of appearance and geometry.

Semantic Correspondence. Most conventional methods for semantic correspondence that use hand-crafted features and regularization terms [22,30,32] have provided limited performance due to a low discriminative power. Recent state-of-the-art approaches have used deep CNNs to extract their features [11,

25,27] and/or spatially regularize correspondence fields in an end-to-end manner [19,23,39,44].

To deal with large geometric deformations, several approaches [17,39–41,44] first computed similarity scores with respect to all possible pairwise matching candidates and then predicted the semantic correspondence through deep networks. As a pioneering work, Rocco et al. [39,40] estimates a global geometric model such as an affine and thin plate spline (TPS) transformation through CNN architecture mimicking the traditional matching pipeline. Seo et al. [44] proposed an offset-aware correlation kernel to put more attention to reliable similarity scores. Without the need of global geometric model, Rocco et al. [41] proposed to identify sets of spatially consistent matches by analyzing neighborhood consensus patterns. Huang et al. [17] extended this architecture by leveraging context-aware semantic representation to further resolve local ambiguities.

Rather than considering all possible matching candidates, some methods [19,20,23,26,28] constrain matching candidates within pre-defined local regions, like stereo matching and optical flow approaches [9,50]. In [20,23,26], locally-varying affine transformation fields are iteratively estimated within locally constrained cost volume. More recently, Lee et al. [28] proposed to leverage a kernel soft argmax function to deal with multi-modal distribution within a correlation volume.

The most relevant method to ours is [19] that utilizes intermediate results from the previous level to constrain the search space of the current level in a coarse-to-fine manner. However, they start with the global affine transformation estimation that often fails to capture reliable matches under large geometric variations with non-rigid transformation.

3   Problem Statement

Let us denote *semantically* similar source and target images as I^s and I^t, respectively. The objective is to establish a two dimensional correspondence field $\tau_i = [u_i, v_i]^T$ between the two images that is defined for each pixel $i = [i_\mathbf{x}, i_\mathbf{y}]^T$ in I^s.

Analogously to the classical matching pipeline [36], this objective involves first extracting dense feature maps from I^s and I^t, denoted by $F^s, F^t \in \mathbb{R}^{h \times w \times d}$ where (h, w) denotes the spatial resolution of the image, and d the dimensionality of feature. Then, given two dense feature maps, a correlation volume C is computed by encoding the similarity as cosine distance:

$$C_{ij}(F^s, F^t) = \langle F_i^s, F_j^t \rangle / \|F_i^s\|_2 \|F_j^t\|_2 \tag{1}$$

where i and j indicate the individual feature position in the source and target images, respectively.

In this stage, several methods [17,39–41,44] construct a full correlation volume C^f considering a set of all possible matching candidates $\mathcal{J}_i^f$, such that

$$\mathcal{J}_i^f = \{j | j_\mathbf{x} \in [1, ..., w], j_\mathbf{y} \in [1, ..., h]\}. \tag{2}$$

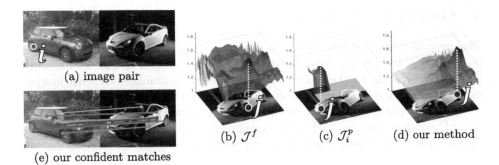

(a) image pair

(b) $\mathcal{J}^f$ (c) $\mathcal{J}_i^p$ (d) our method

(e) our confident matches

Fig. 2. (a) Given an image pair and a reference pixel i, we visualize its corresponding match ($j = \operatorname{argmax}_l(C_{il})$) and correlation score map (C_{il}), computed with: (b) matching candidates $\mathcal{J}^f$ [17,39–41,44], (c) matching candidates $\mathcal{J}_i^p$ [19,20,23,26,28], and (d) the proposed method. (e) Our key observation is that sparse yet reliable matches can guide the adjacent pixels to have similar solution spaces, reducing matching ambiguities significantly.

Note that $\mathcal{J}_i^f$ is independent to pixel i and identical for all i pixels. However, as exemplified in Fig. 2 (a), the similarity scores in C^f are not guaranteed to be accurate due to inconsistent feature representations under large semantic variations. To address this, several approaches [39,40,44] design an additional module that can vote for the transformation candidates by regressing an image-level single transformation, but they treat the matching scores of all pixels evenly regardless of their confidence. While some methods [17,41] alleviate this by filtering the correlation volume with mutual consistency constraint, they assess the confidences based on a simple criterion such as maximum normalization which may lack the robustness that is attainable with deep CNNs.

Meanwhile, as shown in Fig. 2(b), some approaches [19,20,23,26,28] construct a partial correlation volume C^p by constraining the search space of each reference pixel i as the restricted local region $\mathcal{N}_k$ centered at the pixel k on the target image. Formally, denoting the pixel k that is dependent on pixel i as $k(i)$, the constrained matching candidates $\mathcal{J}_i^p$ can be defined as

$$\mathcal{J}_i^p = \{j | j \in \mathcal{N}_{k(i)}\}. \tag{3}$$

The center of the local region, $k(i)$, is determined in various ways; as a reference pixel i itself ($k(i) = i$) [20,23,26] or by finding the matching cues from the fully constructed correlation volume through applying the discrete argmax function [28] ($k(i) = \operatorname{argmax}_j(C_{ij}^f)$) or estimating an image-level coarse transformation $\tau^g(C^f)$ [19] ($k(i) = i + \tau_i^g(C^f)$). However, as exemplified in Fig. 2(b), these approaches often fail to constrain the search space correctly under the large intra-class variations where the feature representations between two input images are quite inconsistent to measure accurate matching scores or complex geometric deformations cannot be modeled with a global affine transformation model.

4   Guided Semantic Flow

The proposed method leverages guidance cues from the confident matches to
generate reliable likelihood matching hypotheses, as illustrated in Fig. 2(c).
Unlike the existing methods that alleviate matching ambiguities with inaccu-
rately assessed matching confidences [17,41] or with the heuristically constrained
search spaces [19,20,23,26,28], we address this issue with a learning-based selection of confident matches and their propagation, reducing matching ambiguities
significantly while maintaining the robustness to large geometric variations.

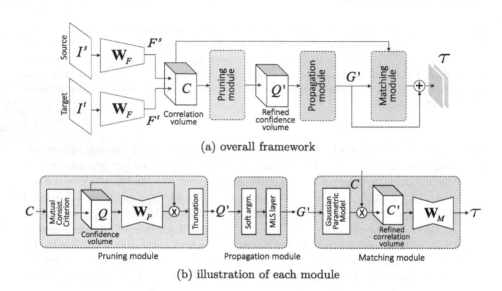

(a) overall framework

(b) illustration of each module

Fig. 3. (a) Our overall framework consists of pruning, propagation, and matching modules. (b) The pruning module takes a full correlation volume C as an input and predicts pairwise confidence scores Q' from it by retaining confident matches and rejecting
ambiguous ones with the parameters $\mathbf{W}_P$. The propagation module converts this volume Q' into a dense guidance map G' in a fully differentiable manner. The matching
module refines the initial correlation volume C with the guidance map G' and then
estimates a dense correspondence field τ with the pararmeters $\mathbf{W}_M$.

4.1   Network Architecture

The proposed method consists of three modules as illustrated in Fig. 3: *pruning
module* that estimates the confidence probability volume Q', *propagation module*
that converts the confidence probability volume into a guidance displacement
map G', and *matching module* that refines the initial correlation volume and
estimates dense correspondence fields τ from it.

To extract convolutional feature maps of source and target images, the input
images are passed through the shared feature extraction networks with param-
eters $\mathbf{W}_F$ such that $F = \mathcal{F}(I; \mathbf{W}_F)$ where $\mathcal{F}$ denotes a feed-forward operation.

The initial correlation volume C^f is then constructed considering all possible pairwise matching candidates, following (1) and (2), to consider the large intra-class geometric deformations.

Pruning Module. To establish an initial set of confidence probabilities over all pairwise matches, we adopt a differentiable mutual consistency criterion [17,41], such that

$$Q_{ij} = \frac{(C_{ij})^2}{\max_i C_{ij} \cdot \max_j C_{ij}} \tag{4}$$

where Q_{ij} equals one if and only if the match between i and j satisfies the mutual consistency constraint, and becomes smaller than 1 otherwise. Recent works [17,41] utilized this confidence volume Q to filter their similarity scores C (e.g. $Q \cdot C$), but the confidence of each pixel is assessed only with the handcrafted criterion as in (4), thus often producing a high confidence score even for an unconfident pixel as exemplified in Fig. 4(a).

In this work, we propose to refine the initial confidence volume with the pruning networks that consist of an encoder-decoder style architecture and a sigmoid function, yielding a value in $(0,1)$ to suppress false positives, as exemplified in Fig. 4(b). Formally, the refined confidence probability volume Q' can be obtained by

$$Q'_{ij} = T(Q_{ij} \cdot [\mathcal{F}(Q; \mathbf{W}_P)]_{ij}, \rho) \tag{5}$$

where $\mathbf{W}_P$ is the parameters of the pruning networks and $T(\cdot, \rho)$ is a truncation function that discards a probability lower than a threshold ρ to retain only confident matches, such that $T(X,\rho) = X$ if $X > \rho$ and $T(X,\rho) = 0$ otherwise.

It should be noted that several works have also attempted to find the reliable correspondences from the full pairwise similarity scores by thresholding [40], the correspondence consistency [19], or learning with the probabilisitic model [20]. However, these constraints are used in the loss functions only as a supervision for training their deep networks, and are not explicitly used to refine the correlation volume.

Propagation Module. Taking the refined confidence volume Q' as an input, our propagation module first extracts the displacement vectors of the confident matches that can guide nearby ambiguous ones to have similar solution space. Specifically, given a set of the collected confident pixels $\mathcal{S} = \{i| \sum_j Q'_{ij} \neq 0\}$, our propagation module converts the confidence volume Q' into 2-dimensional displacement map G through a soft argmax layer [21], such that

$$G_i = \begin{cases} \sum_j j \cdot \exp(Q'_{ij})/\sum_l \exp(Q'_{il}) - i, & \text{if } i \in \mathcal{S} \\ \text{invalid}, & \text{otherwise.} \end{cases} \tag{6}$$

The displacement map G can then be used to constrain the plausible search range from all possible matching candidates, but this guidance is valid only for confident pixels ($i \in \mathcal{S}$). To guide the search space of the invalid pixels

(a) image pair   (b) confident matches in Q (c) confident matches in Q'

Fig. 4. The effectiveness of the pruning networks: (a) matches that satisfy the mutual consistency criterion (*i.e.* $Q_{ij} = 1$), and (b) matches from the refined confidence volume Q' (*i.e.* $Q'_{ij} > \rho$). Our pruning networks effectively suppress the false positive confidence matches that often occur at ambiguous regions.

($i \notin \mathcal{S}$) with the help of confident pixels, we attempted to interpolate the sparse displacement map G using the existing bilinear upsampler of [18]. However, this cannot be directly realized since the confident matches in $\mathcal{S}$ are sparsely and irregularly distributed in the spatial dimension. In this work, we introduce a new differentiable upsampling layer that interpolates the sparse displacement map G into a dense guidance map G'. Concretely, inspired by moving least square approach [42], the displacement vector G'_i at a pixel i can be computed with a spatially-varying weight function w as

$$G'_i = \sum_{s \in \mathcal{S}} G_s \cdot w(s - i) / \sum_{s \in \mathcal{S}} w(s - i) \tag{7}$$

where $w(z) = \exp(-||z||^2/2c_P{}^2)$ is formed with a coefficient c_P. The differentiability of this operator G'_i with respect to G_i can be easily derived similar to [18].

Matching Module. With a favor of densely interpolated guidance displacements G', we refine the initial correlation volume C by maintaining only the similarity scores of highly probable matches. To be specific, we compute the refined correlation volume C' by modulating the original volume C with Gaussian parametric model centered at the guidance displacement vector G':

$$C'_{ij} = \exp(-(j - G'_i)^2/2c_M{}^2) \cdot C_{ij} \tag{8}$$

where c_M adjust the distribution of Gaussian model. Unlike the existing methods [19,20,23,26,28] that constrain the search space with simple heuristics, our method leverages the reliable information propagated from the confident matches to effectively deal with large intra-class geometric variations.

With the resulting uni-modal likelihood hypotheses where matching ambiguities are significantly reduced, we subsequently formulate matching networks to regress residual displacements at sub-pixel level, facilitating fine-grained localization. The final dense correspondence field τ is computed as

$$\tau_i = G'_i + [\mathcal{F}(C'; \mathbf{W}_M)]_i \tag{9}$$

where $\mathbf{W}_M$ is the parameters of our matching networks.

4.2   Objective Functions

To overcome the limitation of insufficient training data for semantic correspondence, our matching networks are learned using weak image-level supervision in a form of matching image pairs. Additionally, we expedite the learning process by allowing only the gradients of the foreground pixels to be backpropagated within object masks of the source and target images, similar to [19, 23, 24, 28].

Pruning Networks. To train the pruning networks with the parameter $\mathbf{W}_P$, we define a novel loss function that consists of silhouette consistency loss and geometry consistency loss, such that

$$\mathcal{L}_P = \mathcal{L}_{\text{sil}} + \lambda \mathcal{L}_{\text{geo}} \tag{10}$$

where λ is the weighting parameter.

With the intuition that local structures between source and target image features should be similar at the correct confident correspondences, we encourage the pruning networks to automatically discard the matches that do not satisfy the following local geometry consistency constraint

$$\mathcal{L}_{\text{geo}} = \sum_{i \in \mathcal{S}} \sum_{l \in \mathcal{N}_i} ||F_l^s - [G' \circ F^t]_l||_F^2 \tag{11}$$

where $\mathcal{N}_i$ is a local window centered at the pixel i, $\circ$ is a warping operator, and $|| \cdot ||_F^2$ denotes Frobenius norm. By aggregating the contextual information of $\mathcal{N}_i$ through the parameters $\mathbf{W}_P$, we can predict more accurate confidence scores than the handcrafted criterion of (4) that relies only on the pixel-level similarity scores.

Additionally, we formulate the silhouette consistency loss that encourages the refined confidence volume Q' to lie within the silhouette of the initial volume Q:

$$\mathcal{L}_{\text{sil}} = \sum_{\{i,j\} \in \mathcal{S}^*} |\log(Q'_{ij}/Q_{ij})| \tag{12}$$

where $\mathcal{S}^* = \{i, j | Q_{ij} > \rho\}$, hence Q'_{ij}/Q_{ij} becomes $[\mathcal{F}(Q; \mathbf{W}_P)]_{ij}$. Note that similar loss function is used in the object landmark detection literature [46] to encourage the landmarks to lie within the silhouette of the object of interest.

Matching Networks. Thanks to the guidance displacements G', most of geometric deformations are already resolved, and thus computing the residual transformation field $\mathcal{F}(C'; \mathbf{W}_M)$ with the weakly-supervised loss function of [23] is tractable, such that

$$\mathcal{L}_M = \sum_i -\log(P_i(\tau)) \tag{13}$$

where $P(\tau)$ is the softmax matching probability defined with a local neighborhood $\mathcal{M}_i$ as

$$P_i(\tau) = \frac{\exp(< F_i^s, [\tau \circ F^t]_i >)}{\sum_{l \in \mathcal{M}_i} \exp(< F_i^s, [\tau \circ F^t]_l >)}. \tag{14}$$

This objective allows us to consider both positive and negative samples by maximizing the similarity score at the correct transformation while minimizing the scores of remaining candidates within local neighborhood $\mathcal{M}_i$.

Final Objective Function. We additionally utilize L_1 regularization loss $\mathcal{L}_{sm}$ for the spatial smootheness in the final correspondence field τ [26,28]. A final objective is defined as a weighted summation of the presented three losses:

$$\mathcal{L}_{final} = \lambda_P \mathcal{L}_P + \lambda_M \mathcal{L}_M + \lambda_{sm} \mathcal{L}_{sm}. \tag{15}$$

4.3   Training Details

Inspired by recent works on finding good matches for wide-baseline stereo [4,34], we first freeze the network parameters $\mathbf{W}_F$, $\mathbf{W}_M$ and learn the pruning networks $\mathbf{W}_P$ only with the gradients from $\mathcal{L}_P$. This allows the pruning networks to be converged stably by fixing the values Q of silhouette consistency loss (12). In second stage, we train the whole networks in an end-to-end manner with $\mathcal{L}_{final}$ where the properly selected confident matches from the pruning networks boost the convergence of the feature extraction and matching networks by providing well-defined negative samples within the neighborhood $\mathcal{M}_i$ of matching loss (14).

Following [20,26,40], this two-stage learning procedure first utilizes synthetically generated image pairs, by applying random synthetic transformations to a single image of PASCAL VOC 2012 segmentation dataset [8] using the split in [28]. Then, our networks are finetuned with semantically similar image pairs from PF-PASCAL dataset [12] using the split in [40].

5   Experimental Results

5.1   Implementation Details

For feature extraction, we used two CNNs as main backbone networks; ImageNet [6]-pretrained ResNet 101 [14] and PASCAL VOC 2012 [8]-pretrained SFNet [28], where activations are sampled at 'conv4-23' and 'conv5-3'. The activations adapted from 'conv5-3' are upsampled using bilinear interpolation. We denote these backbone networks in the following evaluations as "Ours w/ResNet" and "Ours w/SFNet". We set threshold ρ to 0.9, the variances $\{c_P, c_M\}$ to $\{7, 5\}$, and Referring to the ablation study of [23], the radius of local window $\mathcal{M}_i$ is set to 5. More details about the implementation and the performance analysis with respect to the hyper-parameters are provided in the supplemental material.

5.2   Results

PF-WILLOW and PF-PASCAL Dataset. PF-WILLOW dataset [11] includes 10 object sub-classes with 10 keypoint annotations for each image, providing 900 image pairs. PF-PASCAL dataset [12] contains 1,351 image pairs over

20 object categories with PASCAL keypoint annotations [3]. Following the split in [13,40], we used only 300 testing image pairs for the evaluation. We used a common metric of the percentage of correct keypoint (PCK) by computing the distance between flow-warped keypoints and the ground-truth ones [31]. The warped keypoints are determined to be correct if they lie within $\alpha \cdot \max(h, w)$ pixels from the ground-truth keypoints for $\alpha \in [0, 1]$, where h and w are the height and width of either an image (α_{img}) or an object bounding box (α_{bb}). PCK with α_{bb} is more stringent metric than that of α_{img} [33]. In line with the previous works, we used α_{bb} for PF-WILLOW [11] and α_{img} for PF-PASCAL [12].

Table 1. Matching accuracy compared to state-of-the-art correspondence techniques on PF-WILLOW dataset [11], PF-PASCAL dataset [12], and Caltech-101 dataset [29]. Results of [13,39–41,44] are borrowed from [33].

Methods		PF-PASCAL (PCK@α_{img})			PF-WILLOW (PCK@α_{bb})			Caltech-101	
		$\alpha = 0.05$	$\alpha = 0.1$	$\alpha = 0.15$	$\alpha = 0.05$	$\alpha = 0.1$	$\alpha = 0.15$	LT-ACC	IoU
Unsupervised	CNNgeo [39]	41.0	69.5	80.4	36.9	69.2	77.8	0.79	0.56
	A2Net [44]	42.8	70.8	83.3	36.3	68.8	84.4	0.80	0.57
Fully supervised	SCNet [13]	36.2	72.2	82.0	38.6	70.4	85.3	0.79	0.51
	HPF [33]	60.1	84.8	92.7	45.9	74.4	85.6	0.87	0.63
Weakly supervised	CNNinlier [40]	49.0	74.8	84.0	37.0	70.2	79.9	0.85	0.63
	NCNet [41]	54.3	78.9	86.0	33.8	67.0	83.7	0.85	0.60
	RTNs [23]	55.2	75.9	85.2	41.3	71.9	86.2	0.86	0.65
	SFNet [28]	50.0	78.7	88.9	37.5	71.1	88.5	0.88	0.67
	SAMNet [26]	60.1	80.2	86.9	–	–	–	–	–
	DCCNet [17]	–	82.3	–	43.6	73.8	86.5	–	–
	Ours w/ResNet	62.8	84.5	93.7	47.0	75.8	88.9	0.88	0.69
	Ours w/SFNet	65.6	87.8	95.9	49.1	78.7	90.2	0.89	0.69

The average PCK scores are summarized in Table 1 showing that our model ("Ours w/ResNet") exhibits a competitive performance to the latest weakly-supervised and even fully-supervised techniques for semantic correspondence, demonstrating the benefits of generating highly probable hypotheses based on the confident matches. When combined with sophisticate CNN features ("Ours w/SFNet"), the outstanding performance was attained.

Caltech-101 Dataset. We also evaluated our method on Caltech-101 dataset [29] which provides the images of 101 object categories with ground-truth object masks. For the evaluation, we used the 1,515 image pairs used in [13,40], *i.e.* 15 image pairs for each object category. Compared to other datasets described above, the Caltech-101 dataset [29] enable us to evaluate the performances under more general settings with the image pairs from more diverse classes. Following the experimental protocol in [22], the matching accuracy was evaluated with two metrics: the label transfer accuracy (LT-ACC), and the intersection-over-union (IoU) metric.

In Table 1, our method achieves a competitive performance compared to state-of-the-art methods in terms of both LT-ACC and IoU metrics. In particular, our results show better performances with significant margins compared to the methods [39–41, 44] that consider all possible matching scores.

This reveals the effectiveness of the proposed pruning and propagation modules where only reliable information is propagated and leveraged to reduce the matching ambiguity.

(a) image pair and our result   (b) RTNs [23], NCNet [41], SFNet [28]

Fig. 5. Qualitative results of the semantic alignment on the testing pair of SPair-71k benchmark [33]: (a) input image pairs and warped source images using correspondences obtained from our method, and (b) warped source images from state-of-the-art-methods; (left) RTNs [23], (middle) NCNet [41], (right) SFNet [28].

SPair-71k Benchmark. The evaluation was also performed on the SPair-71k benchmark [33] that includes 70,958 image pairs of 18 object categories from PASCAL 3D+ [48] and PASCAL VOC 2012 [8], providing 12,234 pairs for testing. This benchmark is more challenging than other datasets [11, 12, 29] for semantic correspondence evaluation, as it covers significantly large variations of 4 factors as shown in Table 2. For the evaluation metric, we used the PCK setting the threshold with respect to the object bounding box to $\alpha_{bb} = 0.1$.

Table 2. Matching accuracy compared to the state-of-the-art techniques on SPair-71k benchmark [33]. Difficulty levels of viewpoints and scales are labeled 'easy', 'medium', and 'hard', while those of truncation and occlusion are indicated by 'none', 'source', 'target', and 'both'. The performances are evaluated by fixing the levels of other variations as 'easy' and 'none'. Results of [39–41,44] are borrowed from [33].

Methods	Viewpoint			Scale			Truncation				Occlusion				All
	easy	medi	hard	easy	medi	hard	none	src	tgt	both	none	src	tgt	both	
CNNgeo [39]	25.2	10.7	5.9	22.3	16.1	8.5	21.1	12.7	15.6	13.9	20.0	14.9	14.3	12.4	18.1
A2Net [44]	27.5	12.4	6.9	24.1	18.5	10.3	22.9	15.2	17.6	15.7	22.3	16.5	15.2	14.5	20.1
CNNinlier [40]	29.4	12.2	6.9	25.4	19.4	10.3	24.1	16.0	18.5	15.7	23.4	16.7	16.7	14.8	21.1
NCNet [41]	34.0	18.6	12.8	31.7	23.8	14.2	29.1	22.9	23.4	21.0	29.0	21.1	21.8	19.6	26.4
RTNs [23]	34.8	18.2	11.7	33.4	24.7	14.3	30.1	20.9	22.7	20.5	28.8	19.5	20.9	18.8	25.7
HPF [33]	35.6	20.3	15.5	33.0	26.1	15.8	31.0	24.6	24.0	23.7	30.8	23.5	22.8	21.8	28.2
Ours w/ResNet	40.6	22.3	17.8	39.5	30.1	18.7	37.0	28.7	27.1	27.7	36.4	27.8	27.5	23.7	33.5
Ours w/SFNet	**42.1**	**25.7**	**20.1**	**42.3**	**34.0**	**20.8**	**39.8**	**31.1**	**30.0**	**29.9**	**38.8**	**29.3**	**28.3**	**26.9**	**36.1**

Table 2 reports the quantitative performance with respect to different levels of four variation factors. The qualitative results are visualized in Fig. 5. As shown in Table 2 and Fig. 5, our results have shown highly improved performances qualitatively and quantitatively compared to the state-of-the-art techniques on all variation factors. In contrast to the methods [23,28] that cannot capture large geometric variations due to the simple heuristics used to constrain the search space, a large PCK gain for difficult image pairs in Table 2 indicates that our method is effective especially in the presence of severe appearance and shape variations thanks to the guidance by the confident matches learned from all matching candidates. Though the performance was evaluated only on the sparsely annotated keypoints provided from the benchmark, the qualitative results in Fig. 5 indicates that the objective measure can be significantly boosted if dense ground-truth annotations are given for evaluation.

5.3 Ablation Study

Lastly, we conducted an ablation study on different modules and losses in our model of "Ours w/ResNet" evaluating on the testing image pairs of SPair-71k benchmark [33].

Network Architecture. We report the quantitative assessment when one of our modules is removed from the network architecture in Table 3(a) in terms of average PCK at $\alpha_{bb} = 0.1$. Interestingly, the guidance displacement map G', which is the result obtained with only the pruning and propagation modules, already outperforms state-of-the-art methods by a large margin as shown in Table 2. The performance degradation due to the lack of the pruning or propagation modules highlights the importance of the learning-based selection of confident matches and the MLS layer. Figure 6 shows the intermediate results of our method.

Training Loss. To validate the effectiveness of the utilized losses, we examined the performance of our model when learned with different loss functions. In Table 3(b), the first three rows compare the performances for the variants of the pruning networks. The performance gain from 25.1 to 28.5 with respect to $\mathcal{L}_{geo}$ indicates the effectiveness of imposing local geometry consistency constraint by aggregating the contextual information. On the other hand, with respect to $\mathcal{L}_{sil}$, the degraded performance from 28.5 to 24.3 demonstrates the importance of regularizing the refined confidence scores to be similar with the initial ones, so that the retained confident matches also satisfy mutual consistency.

Table 3. Ablation study on the testing pairs of SPair-71k benchmark [33] for (a) different components and (b) different loss functions. Note that, in (a), when the 'MLS layer' in the propagation module is removed, the refined correlation volume C' is computed by applying Gaussian parametric model only on the confident pixels[a].

Pruning $(Q \to Q')$	MLS layer $(G \to G')$	Matching $(C, G' \to \tau)$	PCK $(\alpha_{bb} = 0.1)$
✓	✓	✗	29.3
✓	✗	✓	26.8
✗	✓	✓	25.1
✓	✓	✓	**33.5**

(a) network architecture

$\mathcal{L}_{sil}$	$\mathcal{L}_{geo}$	$\mathcal{L}_M$	$\mathcal{L}_{sm}$	Training stage	PCK
–	✓	–	–	1st	24.3
✓	–	–	–	1st	25.1
✓	✓	–	–	1st	28.5
✓	✓	✓	✓	only 2nd	30.2
✓	✓	✓	✓	1st & 2nd	**33.5**

(b) training loss

$$^a C'_{ij} = \begin{cases} \exp(-(j - G_i)^2/2c_M{}^2) \cdot C_{ij}, & \text{if } i \in \mathcal{S} \\ C_{ij}, & \text{otherwise.} \end{cases}$$

(a) confident matches in Q' (b) matching result with G' (c) matching result with τ

Fig. 6. The visualization of the intermediate results: (a) source and target images, (b) the selected confident matches Q', (c) matching results with the guidance displacements G', and (d) matching results with the final correspondence fields τ.

The last two rows in Table 3(b) reveal the effect of the used two-stage learning process. The performance drop from 33.5 to 30.2 by removing the first stage highlights that the properly selected confident matches from the pruning networks can boost the convergence of our training by allowing only well-defined matching candidates to be utilized during the second stage.

6   Conclusion

We presented a novel framework, guided semantic flow, that reliably infers dense semantic correspondences under large appearance and spatial variations. Taking advantage of the reliable information of confident matches, we effectively handle severe non-rigid geometric deformations and reduce matching ambiguities. The outstanding performance was validated through extensive experiments on various benchmarks.

Acknowledgements. This research was supported by Next-Generation Information Computing Development Program through the National Research Foundation of Korea(NRF) funded by the Ministry of Science and ICT (NRF2017M3C4A7069370).

References

1. Baker, S., Scharstein, D., Lewis, J., Roth, S., Black, M.J., Szeliski, R.: A database and evaluation methodology for optical flow. Int. J. Comput. Vision **92**(1), 1–31 (2011)
2. Barnes, C., Shechtman, E., Finkelstein, A., Goldman, D.B.: PatchMatch: a randomized correspondence algorithm for structural image editing. ACM Trans. Graph. (ToG) **28**, 24 (2009)
3. Bourdev, L., Malik, J.: Poselets: body part detectors trained using 3D human pose annotations. In: 2009 IEEE 12th International Conference on Computer Vision, pp. 1365–1372. IEEE (2009)
4. Brachmann, E., et al.: DSAC-differentiable RANSAC for camera localization. In: Proceedings of the IEEE Conference on Computer Vision and Pattern Recognition, pp. 6684–6692 (2017)
5. Chang, J.R., Chen, Y.S.: Pyramid stereo matching network. In: Proceedings of the IEEE Conference on Computer Vision and Pattern Recognition, pp. 5410–5418 (2018)
6. Deng, J., Dong, W., Socher, R., Li, L.J., Li, K., Fei-Fei, L.: ImageNet: a large-scale hierarchical image database. In: 2009 IEEE Conference on Computer Vision and Pattern Recognition, pp. 248–255. IEEE (2009)
7. Duggal, S., Wang, S., Ma, W.C., Hu, R., Urtasun, R.: DeepPruner: learning efficient stereo matching via differentiable PatchMatch. In: The IEEE International Conference on Computer Vision (ICCV), October 2019
8. Everingham, M., Van Gool, L., Williams, C.K., Winn, J., Zisserman, A.: The pascal visual object classes (VOC) challenge. Int. J. Comput. Vision **88**(2), 303–338 (2010)
9. Fischer, P., et al.: FlowNet: learning optical flow with convolutional networks. In: ICCV (2015)
10. HaCohen, Y., Shechtman, E., Goldman, D.B., Lischinski, D.: Non-rigid dense correspondence with applications for image enhancement. ACM Trans. Graph. (TOG) **30**(4), 70 (2011)
11. Ham, B., Cho, M., Schmid, C., Ponce, J.: Proposal flow. In: Proceedings of the IEEE Conference on Computer Vision and Pattern Recognition, pp. 3475–3484 (2016)
12. Ham, B., Cho, M., Schmid, C., Ponce, J.: Proposal flow: semantic correspondences from object proposals. IEEE Trans. PAMI **40**(7), 1711–1725 (2018)

13. Han, K., et al.: SCNet: learning semantic correspondence. In: ICCV (2017)
14. He, K., Zhang, X., Ren, S., Sun, J.: Deep residual learning for image recognition. In: Proceedings of the IEEE Conference on Computer Vision and Pattern Recognition, pp. 770–778 (2016)
15. Heise, P., Klose, S., Jensen, B., Knoll, A.: PM-Huber: PatchMatch with Huber regularization for stereo matching. In: Proceedings of the IEEE International Conference on Computer Vision, pp. 2360–2367 (2013)
16. Hu, Y., Song, R., Li, Y.: Efficient coarse-to-fine PatchMatch for large displacement optical flow. In: Proceedings of the IEEE Conference on Computer Vision and Pattern Recognition, pp. 5704–5712 (2016)
17. Huang, S., Wang, Q., Zhang, S., Yan, S., He, X.: Dynamic context correspondence network for semantic alignment. In: The IEEE International Conference on Computer Vision (ICCV), October 2019
18. Jaderberg, M., Simonyan, K., Zisserman, A., et al.: Spatial transformer networks. In: Advances in Neural Information Processing Systems, pp. 2017–2025 (2015)
19. Jeon, S., Kim, S., Min, D., Sohn, K.: PARN: pyramidal affine regression networks for dense semantic correspondence. In: Ferrari, V., Hebert, M., Sminchisescu, C., Weiss, Y. (eds.) ECCV 2018. LNCS, vol. 11210, pp. 355–371. Springer, Cham (2018). https://doi.org/10.1007/978-3-030-01231-1_22
20. Jeon, S., Min, D., Kim, S., Sohn, K.: Joint learning of semantic alignment and object landmark detection. In: The IEEE International Conference on Computer Vision (ICCV), October 2019
21. Kendall, A., et al.: End-to-end learning of geometry and context for deep stereo regression. In: Proceedings of the International Conference on Computer Vision (ICCV) (2017)
22. Kim, J., Liu, C., Sha, F., Grauman, K.: Deformable spatial pyramid matching for fast dense correspondences. In: Proceedings of the IEEE Conference on Computer Vision and Pattern Recognition, pp. 2307–2314 (2013)
23. Kim, S., Lin, S., Jeon, S., Min, D., Sohn, K.: Recurrent transformer networks for semantic correspondence. In: Advances in Neural Information Processing Systems (2018)
24. Kim, S., Min, D., Ham, B., Jeon, S., Lin, S., Sohn, K.: FCSS: fully convolutional self-similarity for dense semantic correspondence. In: CVPR (2017)
25. Kim, S., Min, D., Ham, B., Lin, S., Sohn, K.: FCSS: fully convolutional self-similarity for dense semantic correspondence. IEEE Trans. Pattern Anal. Mach. Intell. 41, 581–595 (2018)
26. Kim, S., Min, D., Jeong, S., Kim, S., Jeon, S., Sohn, K.: Semantic attribute matching networks. In: Proceedings of the IEEE Conference on Computer Vision and Pattern Recognition, pp. 12339–12348 (2019)
27. Kim, S., Min, D., Lin, S., Sohn, K.: DCTM: discrete-continuous transformation matching for semantic flow. In: ICCV (2017)
28. Lee, J., Kim, D., Ponce, J., Ham, B.: SFNet: learning object-aware semantic correspondence. In: Proceedings of the IEEE Conference on Computer Vision and Pattern Recognition, pp. 2278–2287 (2019)
29. Li, F.F., Fergus, R., Perona, P.: One-shot learning of object categories. IEEE Trans. PAMI 28(4), 594–611 (2006)
30. Liu, C., Yuen, J., Torralba, A.: SIFT Flow: dense correspondence across scenes and its applications. IEEE Trans. Pattern Anal. Mach. Intell. 33(5), 978–994 (2010)
31. Long, J.L., Zhang, N., Darrell, T.: Do convnets learn correspondence? In: Advances in Neural Information Processing Systems, pp. 1601–1609 (2014)

32. Lu, J., Li, Y., Yang, H., Min, D., Eng, W., Do, M.N.: PatchMatch filter: edge-aware filtering meets randomized search for visual correspondence. IEEE Trans. PAMI **39**(9), 1866–1879 (2017)
33. Min, J., Lee, J., Ponce, J., Cho, M.: Hyperpixel flow: semantic correspondence with multi-layer neural features. In: The IEEE International Conference on Computer Vision (ICCV), October 2019
34. Moo Yi, K., Trulls, E., Ono, Y., Lepetit, V., Salzmann, M., Fua, P.: Learning to find good correspondences. In: Proceedings of the IEEE Conference on Computer Vision and Pattern Recognition, pp. 2666–2674 (2018)
35. Park, K., Kim, S., Sohn, K.: High-precision depth estimation with the 3D lidar and stereo fusion. In: 2018 IEEE International Conference on Robotics and Automation (ICRA), pp. 2156–2163. IEEE (2018)
36. Philbin, J., Chum, O., Isard, M., Sivic, J., Zisserman, A.: Object retrieval with large vocabularies and fast spatial matching. In: 2007 IEEE Conference on Computer Vision and Pattern Recognition, pp. 1–8. IEEE (2007)
37. Poggi, M., Pallotti, D., Tosi, F., Mattoccia, S.: Guided stereo matching. In: Proceedings of the IEEE Conference on Computer Vision and Pattern Recognition, pp. 979–988 (2019)
38. Ranjan, A., Black, M.J.: Optical flow estimation using a spatial pyramid network. In: Proceedings of the IEEE Conference on Computer Vision and Pattern Recognition, pp. 4161–4170 (2017)
39. Rocco, I., Arandjelović, R., Sivic, J.: Convolutional neural network architecture for geometric matching. In: CVPR (2017)
40. Rocco, I., Arandjelović, R., Sivic, J.: End-to-end weakly-supervised semantic alignment. In: Proceedings of the IEEE Conference on Computer Vision and Pattern Recognition, pp. 6917–6925 (2018)
41. Rocco, I., Cimpoi, M., Arandjelović, R., Torii, A., Pajdla, T., Sivic, J.: Neighbourhood consensus networks. In: Advances in Neural Information Processing Systems, pp. 1658–1669 (2018)
42. Schaefer, S., McPhail, T., Warren, J.: Image deformation using moving least squares. ACM Trans. Graph. (TOG) **25**, 533–540 (2006)
43. Scharstein, D., Szeliski, R.: A taxonomy and evaluation of dense two-frame stereo correspondence algorithms. Int. J. Comput. Vision **47**(1–3), 7–42 (2002)
44. Seo, P.H., Lee, J., Jung, D., Han, B., Cho, M.: Attentive semantic alignment with offset-aware correlation kernels. In: Ferrari, V., Hebert, M., Sminchisescu, C., Weiss, Y. (eds.) ECCV 2018. LNCS, vol. 11208, pp. 367–383. Springer, Cham (2018). https://doi.org/10.1007/978-3-030-01225-0_22
45. Sun, D., Yang, X., Liu, M.Y., Kautz, J.: PWC-Net: CNNs for optical flow using pyramid, warping, and cost volume. In: Proceedings of the IEEE Conference on Computer Vision and Pattern Recognition, pp. 8934–8943 (2018)
46. Suwajanakorn, S., Snavely, N., Tompson, J.J., Norouzi, M.: Discovery of latent 3D keypoints via end-to-end geometric reasoning. In: Advances in Neural Information Processing Systems, pp. 2059–2070 (2018)
47. Taira, H., et al.: Is this the right place? Geometric-semantic pose verification for indoor visual localization. In: The IEEE International Conference on Computer Vision (ICCV), October 2019
48. Xiang, Y., Mottaghi, R., Savarese, S.: Beyond PASCAL: a benchmark for 3D object detection in the wild. In: IEEE Winter Conference on Applications of Computer Vision, pp. 75–82. IEEE (2014)
49. Yu, F., Koltun, V.: Multi-scale context aggregation by dilated convolutions. In: ICLR (2016)

50. Zbontar, J., LeCun, Y.: Stereo matching by training a convolutional neural network to compare image patches. JMLR **17**(1), 2287–2318 (2016)
51. Zhang, B., et al.: Deep exemplar-based video colorization. In: Proceedings of the IEEE Conference on Computer Vision and Pattern Recognition, pp. 8052–8061 (2019)
52. Zhou, T., Jae Lee, Y., Yu, S.X., Efros, A.A.: FlowWeb: joint image set alignment by weaving consistent, pixel-wise correspondences. In: Proceedings of the IEEE Conference on Computer Vision and Pattern Recognition, pp. 1191–1200 (2015)

Document Structure Extraction Using Prior Based High Resolution Hierarchical Semantic Segmentation

Mausoom Sarkar[1](✉), Milan Aggarwal[1], Arneh Jain[2], Hiresh Gupta[2],
and Balaji Krishnamurthy[1]

[1] Media and Data Science Research Labs, Adobe, San Jose, USA
msarkar@adobe.com
[2] Adobe Experience Cloud, San Jose, USA

Abstract. Structure extraction from document images has been a long-standing research topic due to its high impact on a wide range of practical applications. In this paper, we share our findings on employing a hierarchical semantic segmentation network for this task of structure extraction. We propose a prior based deep hierarchical CNN network architecture that enables document structure extraction using very high resolution (1800×1000) images. We divide the document image into overlapping horizontal strips such that the network segments a strip and uses its prediction mask as prior for predicting the segmentation of the subsequent strip. We perform experiments establishing the effectiveness of our strip based network architecture through ablation methods and comparison with low-resolution variations. Further, to demonstrate our network's capabilities, we train it on only one type of documents (Forms) and achieve state-of-the-art results over other general document datasets. We introduce our new human-annotated forms dataset and show that our method significantly outperforms different segmentation baselines on this dataset in extracting hierarchical structures. Our method is currently being used in Adobe's AEM Forms for automated conversion of paper and PDF forms to modern HTML based forms.

Keywords: Documents structure extraction · Hierarchical semantic segmentation · High resolution semantic segmentation

1 Introduction

Semantic structure extraction for documents has been explored in various works [16,17,47,49]. The task is important for applications such as document

---

M. Aggarwal, A. Jain and H. Gupta—Equal contributions.

Electronic supplementary material The online version of this chapter (https://doi.org/10.1007/978-3-030-58604-1_39) contains supplementary material, which is available to authorized users.

© Springer Nature Switzerland AG 2020
A. Vedaldi et al. (Eds.): ECCV 2020, LNCS 12373, pp. 649–666, 2020.
https://doi.org/10.1007/978-3-030-58604-1_39

650   M. Sarkar et al.

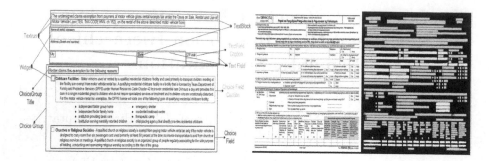

Fig. 1. (Left): Part of an example form that illustrates elements and structures at different levels of hierarchy. (Right): An illustrative dense form and lower elements segmentation mask predicted by our model. The TextRuns are marked in green and Widgets in yellow. (Color figure online)

retrieval, information extraction, and categorization of content. Document structure extraction is also a key step for digitizing documents to make them reflowable (automatically adapt to different screen sizes), which is useful in web-based services [1,13,22,36]. Organizations in domains such as govt services, finance, administration, and healthcare have many documents that they want to digitize. These industries which have been using paper or flat PDF documents would want to re-flow them into digitised version [36] (such as an HTML) so that they can be used on many devices with different form factors [1,13]. A large part of these documents are forms used to capture data. Forms are complex types of documents because, unlike regular documents, their semantic structure is dense and not dominated by big blobs[1] of structural elements like paragraphs, images.

To make paper or flat-pdf documents reflowable (see footnote 1), we need to extract its semantic structure at multiple levels of hierarchy. PDFs contain only low-level elementary structures such as text, lines. PDFs do not contain any metadata about other higher-order structures, and therefore, there is a need to retrieve such constructs. Much of previous work looks at regular documents comprising of coarse structural elements that span a large area in the document image, e.g., paragraphs, figures, lists, tables [30,41,49]. But, such studies leave out documents having the most complicated structures, i.e., forms. Forms have dense and intricate semantic structures, as shown in Fig. 1(right). In many forms, the structure is induced due to the presence of large empty areas, like in Fig. 2b. They also have a deeper hierarchy in structure as compared to other documents, as shown in Fig. 1(left). We build our method focusing on the hardest cases, i.e., form documents and show that this method generalizes well and establishes new-state-of-art across different document datasets.

To extract the hierarchical form structure, we identify several composite structures like *TextBlocks*, *Text Fields*, *Choice Fields*, *Choice Groups* that comprise of basic entities like *TextRuns* and *Widgets* as illustrated in Fig. 1(left).

---

[1] Please refer to supplementary for more visualisations.

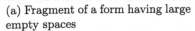

(a) Fragment of a form having large empty spaces

(b) Semantic structure induced around these empty spaces

Fig. 2. Fragment of a form document

We define a *TextRun* as a group of words present in a single line and *Widgets* as empty spaces provided to fill information in forms. A *TextBlock* is a logical block of self-contained text comprising of one or more *TextRuns*; a *Text Field* comprises of a group of one or more Widgets and a caption *TextBlock* describing the content to be filled in the field. *Choice Fields* are Boolean fields used for acquiring optional information. A *Choice Group* is a collection of such *Choice Fields* and an optional *Choice Group Title*, which is a *TextBlock* that describes instructions regarding filling the *Choice Fields*. Figure 1(left) illustrates different semantic structures present in a form document at different hierarchical levels.

We started with fully CNN (FCNNs) based segmentation network since they have been shown to perform well on natural images. However, we found that they perform poorly on form documents as shown in Experiments section. Even FCNNs [17,47,49] focusing on document structure extraction perform well at only extracting coarse structures in documents. They do not perform well at extracting closely spaced structures in form images. Since they process the entire image in a single forward pass, due to memory constraints, they downscale the original image before providing it as input to their model. Moreover, downscaling of input makes it difficult to disambiguate closely spaced structures, especially in dense regions and leads to merging of different structures. These gaps in current solutions became the motivation behind our current research. In this work, we propose a method to extract the lower-level elements like TextRuns and Widgets along with higher-order structures like Fields, ChoiceGroups, Lists, and Tables. Our key contributions can be summarised as:

- We propose a prior and sub-strips based segmentation mechanism to train a document segmentation model on very high resolution (1800×1000) images. Further, our network architecture does not require pre-training with Imagenet [8] or other large image datasets.
- We perform hierarchical semantic segmentation and show it leads to better structure extraction for forms. We also compare different variants of our approach to highlight the importance of shared hierarchical features.
- We propose bi-directional 1d dilated conv blocks to capture axis parallel dependency in documents and show it is better than equivalent 2d dilated conv blocks.

Fig. 3. HighRes model predicts a single choice group correctly. Two strips cut across group causing NoPrior model to split it since it did not have prior from previous strip. We train our model to predict crisp masks through convex hull.

- We introduce a new human-annotated Forms Image dataset, which contains bounding boxes of a complete hierarchy of semantic classes and all the structures present in the images.
- We compare our method with semantic segmentation baselines, including DeeplabV3+ (state of the art for semantic segmentation), which uses Imagenet pre-training, outperforming them significantly.

Our strip based segmentation helps to mitigate the memory limitation on GPU while training a neural network on high-resolution images. However, strip-based segmentation without prior can potentially fail to predict continuous semantic structures that span across multiple strips (Fig. 3). Hence we introduce a prior based strip segmentation, where each image strip's prediction is cached on the GPU and provided as prior concatenated with the input while predicting the segmentation mask of the subsequent strip. Structures that typically span a large area of a form or document like tables and lists could be processed at a lower resolution, but they significantly benefit from the 1D dilated conv network. The hierarchical 1D dilated conv network was introduced to train multi-level hierarchy segmentation together in a single network, so that it learns to predict consistent segmentation masks across these hierarchies [4,27].

Our method is currently being used in Adobe AEM Forms as Automated Form Conversion Service[2] enabling digitisation to modern HTML based forms.

2   Related Work

Document structure analysis started as heuristic-based methods [9,14,15,46] based on handcrafted features [24] for extracting paragraphs and graphics. Most of the recent deep-learning based approaches are based on fully-convolution neural network (FCN) [6,17,47,49] and avoid any heuristic-based approaches. These FCN's are trained to generate semantic segmentation [29] for the rasterized version of the document. FCNs have also been used to locate and recognize handwritten annotations in old documents [23]. [48] proposed a joint text detection and recognition model. They used a region proposal network which detects the beginnings of text lines, a line following model predicts a sequence of short

---

[2] https://docs.adobe.com/content/help/en/aem-forms-automated-conversion-service/using/introduction.html.

bounding boxes along the text-line, which is then used to extract and recognize the text. We employ our high resolution segmentation network to extract and disambiguate closely spaced textruns and textblocks from form images.

Table detection has been the key focus of some works like [2,16,17,26,37]. In [16], table region candidates were chosen based on some loose rules which were later filtered using a CNN. In [17], an FCN was proposed, having a multi-scale architecture which had two branches where one was dedicated to table segmentation while the other was used to find contours. After that, an additional CRF (Conditional Random Field) was used to refine the segmentation output further. We propose a multi-branch architecture to segment hierarchical structures that overlap in same region in a form. For tables, we compare our model with [17] on marmot dataset, one of the largest publicly available table evaluation dataset [10]. While there are other works [34,41] that perform table decomposition into rows and columns (which our model is capable of doing), we discuss table detection only in the scope of this paper. Other works like [45] introduced a large dataset of 5.5 million document labels focusing on detecting bounding boxes for figures using an Overfeat [42] network, trained over image embedding generated using ResNet-101.

It is evident that FCN based segmentation approaches have led to great advancement in document structure extraction. However, a few approaches have also tried other network architectures and input modalities such as text. [21,28] are some of the multi-modal approaches proposed to extract named entities from invoices. Other network architectures such as Graph Neural Networks (GNNs) have been explored in [35,39] for detecting tables in invoice documents and parsing table structure, respectively. In a related domain of document classification also, CNN based methods have been explored in recent times. [43] used them for document verification. Moreover, [50] proposed HAN to create sentence and document embedding in a hierarchical fashion using a multi-level attention mechanism. Document classification has also been explored using multi-modal models [3] by extracting visual and textual features from MobileNet [19] and FastText [5] respectively. These features are later on concatenated to learn a better classification model.

In domains such as biomedical imaging and remote sensing, semantic segmentation in high resolution has been explored. [53] uses past slice's mask along the z-axis as prior for the entire 2d cross-section and marks out the entire ROI. They convert prior masks into features by a separate net, which are used in decoding. In our approach, each strip prior is partially filled, and only the beginning of ROI is known. Also, we use the mask as prior with the image, which reduces model parameters. Similarly some works use tiles with context mask [20], but without prior [40,54]. However for documents, width length slices are required because most context is spread horizontally & tile-wise context passing would make it harder to understand context spread across the width. [25,33,38] do iterative refinement of segmentation with different strategies. However, our method does iterative prediction instead of refinement for getting HighRes masks.

Multi-modal Semantic segmentation has been proposed in [49] to extract figures, tables, lists, and several other types of document structures. A text embedding map for the entire page of the document image gets concatenated with the visual feature volume in a spatially coherent manner such that there is a pixel to text correspondence. We use their approach as one of our baselines on forms. We do not compare with object detection methods like [18] since we found they often merge close structures in dense documents and rather chose better segmentation baseline - DeepLabV3+ [7], which is the current state-of-the-art in semantic segmentation.

3   Methodology

In this section, we discuss our proposed model to extract various structures from documents like widgets, fields, textblocks, choice-groups etc. For documents, especially in the case of forms, the semantic structure extends extensively in both vertical and horizontal directions. For many structures such as widgets and fields, it may even extend to empty spaces in the input image requiring the model to predict objects in parts where there is no explicit visual signal. Also, the higher-level structures are composed of lower-level elements and it is necessary to make fine grained predictions at different levels. This leads to our motivation to use a hierarchical dilated 1D conv based semantic segmenter to capture long-range relationships and predict multiple masks at different hierarchies that are mutually consistent. Finally, to address the issue of dense text documents and forms, we modify the network input mechanism by enabling a tile stitching behavior in our network while performing segmentation to train it at higher resolutions.

3.1   Network Pipeline

We convert the RGB input image into grayscale and resize the grayscale image having height and width $(I_H \times I_W)$ to $(H \times w)$ such that I_W scales to w and I_H gets scaled by the same ratio, i.e., w/I_W. The resulting image is further cropped or padded with zeros to a size of $h \times w$. h is kept larger than H to accommodate elongated document images. We divide the input image into overlapping horizontal strips. Let S_h be strip height, O_h be overlap height between consecutive strips, $SegNet$ is our segmentation network, and $SegMsk$ denote segmentation mask. Following this notation, Algorithm 1 describes our method where the network predicts the segmentation mask of different strips in succession. Each strip's mask prediction uses the predicted mask for the previous strip as prior. We copy logits corresponding to all classes from segmentation output masks to prior mask having many channels with each channel dedicated to one class.

As stated earlier, we use a dilated 1D conv architecture to predict precise and uniform segmentation masks. Our network broadly comprises of three components, Image Encoder (IE), Context Encoder (CE), and Output Decoder (DE).

Algorithm 1: Stripwise, prior based image segmentation

---

1   **Input:** Image (Img) of size $h \times w$, strip height(S_h) and overlap height in-between strips(O_h)
2   **Output:** Segmentation mask ($OutMsk$) of size $h \times w$
    // Initialize $SegMsk, PriorMsk$ and $StripCount$
3   **for** $x \leftarrow 0$ **to** w, $y \leftarrow 0$ **to** S_h **do**
4 | $SegMsk[y, x] \leftarrow 0$,
5 | $PriorMsk[y, x] \leftarrow 0$,
6   **end**
7   $StripCount \leftarrow 1 + (h - S_h)/(S_h - O_h)$
    // Now process strips one by one
8   **for** $step \leftarrow 0$ **to** $StripCount$ **do**
       // Concat $SegMsk$ with $PriorMsk$
9   **for** $x \leftarrow 0$ **to** w, $y \leftarrow 0$ **to** S_h **do**
10 | $InpImg[y, x] \leftarrow Img[(S_h - O_h) * step + y, x] \parallel PriorMsk[y, x]$
11   **end**
       // Predict the segmentation mask and propagate the gradients
12      $SegMsk \leftarrow SegNet(InpImg)$
       // Copy overlapping area of the segmentation mask into prior mask
13   **for** $x \leftarrow 0$ **to** w, $y \leftarrow 0$ **to** O_h **do**
14 | $PriorMsk[y, x] \leftarrow SegMsk[S_h - O_h + y, x]$
15   **end**
       // Calculate the vertical offset for output
16      $y\_start \leftarrow (S_h - O_h) * step$
17      $v_h \leftarrow S_h$
18   **if** $step < StripCount - 1$ **then**
19 | $v_h \leftarrow S_h - O_h$
20   **end**
       // Collect prediction in $OutMsk$
21   **for** $x \leftarrow 0$ **to** w, $y \leftarrow 0$ **to** v_h **do**
22 | $OutMsk[y\_start + y, x] \leftarrow SegMsk[y, x]$
23   **end**
24   **end**

We concatenate a prior mask to each image strip and feed it into the Image Encoder (IE) to generate features at multiple granular levels. The final features of IE, are then processed through a dilated 1D conv based Context Encoder (CE), which generates features capturing contextual dependencies. All these sets of features from CE and IE is then passed to Output Decoder (DE) to generate segmentation masks for different semantic structure levels. We would now explain each of these modules in greater detail.

3.2 Network Architecture

Image Encoder. Figure 4 depicts the architecture of Image Encoder (IE) that comprises of multiple convolution layers, max-pooling layers. As shown in the figure, the first conv layer has 3×3 kernel with a 64 channel output. The parameters of the remaining layers are highlighted using the same notation. Each convolution layer has a stride of 1 unless specified, the third conv layer in Image Encoder has a stride of 2 and is denoted by "1/2" in the figure. Similarly, all the max-pooling layers have a stride of 2 by default. The output of these convolutions is passed on to the Context Encoder. We extract several intermediate features ($detail_1, detail_2, detail_3, detail_4$) from the Image Encoder that act as skip connections [31] and are used by the decoder.

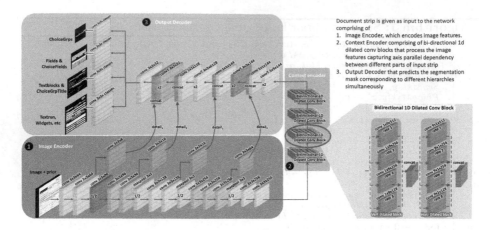

Fig. 4. Detailed overview of our network architecture.

Context Encoder. The context encoder (CE) is composed of four bidirectional 1D dilated conv blocks (BDB). Each BDB contains a vertical dilated block followed by a horizontal dilated block. The dilated blocks consist of four dilated conv layers [51] that work in parallel on the same feature volume at different dilation rates, as seen in Fig. 4. The BDB processes the feature volume in vertical direction, and subsequently, its outputs are processed in a horizontal direction. Each BDB's output is fed to the next BDB, and final output is fed to a CNN decoder to predict the segmentation mask at all levels of the hierarchy.

Output Decoder. The network consists of a single decoder that has multiple heads for generating segmentation maps for different levels in hierarchy. It up-samples it by passing it through a transposed convolution layer [32]. The up-sampled features are subsequently passed through another conv layer. Finally, these features are concatenated with another feature volume $detail_4$, obtained from Image Encoder. The decoder branch repeats the sequence of such operations multiple times, as shown in Fig. 4. Each convolution in the decoder branch has a stride of 1, and each transpose conv, depicted as convT in Fig. 4, has a stride of 2 by default. The different segmentation heads on the penultimate layer of the decoder are used to predict segmentation masks for different spatially overlapping classes like widget and fields. The first segmentation head predicts the lowest level of the semantic structure (TextRun and Widget), and the other segmentation heads output prediction corresponding to higher levels of hierarchy. Such a network design helps in segregating the classes according to hierarchy since the container groups, and their constituent classes are predicted in separate masks.

4 Experiments

4.1 Datasets

Forms Dataset: We used our rich hierarchical Forms Dataset[3] comprising of 52,490 human annotated Form images. These forms are from diverse domains such as automobile, insurance, finance, medical, government (court, military, administration). We employed annotators to annotate the form images to mark the bounding box of different structures in the form image and also asked them to mark the constituent elements that comes lower in the hierarchy for each structure. We split the dataset into 48,256 images for training and 3,234 images for validation. We used a separate set of 1,300 test images for the final evaluation of our model with the baselines and to perform ablation studies.

Marmot Dataset: We evaluate and compare our model trained on Forms Dataset on the Marmot Dataset [10]. This dataset is one of the largest publicly available Table evaluation dataset. It contains 2000 document images corresponding to an approximately equal number of English and Chinese documents.

RVL-CDIP: The dataset comprises of 400k greyscale images divided into 16 different classes. We select 518 images (mostly scanned) from invoice class annotated with table regions as done by [39] to evaluate and compare our framework on table detection.

ICDAR 2013: We also evaluate our approach on the table decomposition task on ICDAR 2013 dataset [11] where the goal is to decompose tabular regions into rows and columns. It comprises of two sets of pdfs - US and EU split. We extract the images from the pdfs with the corresponding ground truth for tables. We evaluate our model trained a) only on ICDAR datset and b) additional forms data, outperforming state of the art in both settings.

4.2 Implementation Details

We set $w = 1000$, $h = 1800$, $S_h = 600$, $O_h = 200$ for the *SegNet* model defined in Sect. 3. We slice the high resolution input image into 4 overlapping horizontal strips. All the convolution and deconvolution layers have ReLU activation. We train our model at a batch size of 32 on 8 Tesla V100 GPUs in parallel. We use AdaDeltaOptimizer [52] to train the parameters of our model with an exponentially decaying learning rate using 1×10^{-1} as the starting learning rate and a decay factor of 0.1. Please refer to Fig. 4 for specific configuration details of different network layers. To enable the network to predict concise masks, we use convex hull [12] to determine segmentation masks.

---

[3] A part of the dataset will be made available at https://github.com/flamingo-eccv/flamingo-data.

Table 1. Mean IoU of different ablation methods for several hierarchical form structures.

Structure → Model ↓	Text Run	Widget	Text Block	ChoiceGroup Title	Text Field	Choice Field	Choice Group
Lowresnet (ours)	89.31	82.17	88.49	69.03	81.93	65.85	72.61
NoPriorNet (ours)	91.46	84.79	89.88	78.89	86.19	79.42	80.14
2D-DilatedNet (ours)	91.63	85.91	89.71	79.1	87.34	81.95	81.11
Highresnet (ours)	**92.7**	**87.32**	**90.55**	**80.87**	**88.87**	**84.05**	**83.01**

Table 2. Precision-Recall numbers for the different hierarchical form structures on the different ablation models computed with an IoU threshold of 0.7.

Model → Structure ↓	Lowresnet			NoPriorNet			2D-DilatedNet			Highresnet		
	P	R	F1	P	R	F1	P	R	F1	P	R	F1
TextRun	72.8	55.0	62.6	79.1	66.9	72.5	80.0	66.7	72.7	**80.2**	**67.3**	**73.2**
Widget	52.8	51.8	52.3	69.2	70.6	69.9	71.0	71.5	71.2	**75.0**	**75.4**	**75.2**
TextBlock	51.0	45.6	48.2	69.6	71.6	70.6	68.6	70.4	69.5	**71.2**	**72.5**	**71.9**
Text Field	43.1	53.4	47.7	66.7	78.0	71.9	69.9	79.7	74.5	**73.4**	**82.5**	**77.7**
ChoiceGroup title	48.2	41.0	44.3	83.2	81.8	82.5	82.0	80.8	81.4	**85.0**	**84.9**	**84.9**
Choice Field	28.3	33.3	30.6	69.8	74.9	72.2	71.7	76.6	74.1	**77.7**	**81.5**	**79.6**
ChoiceGroup	26.5	33.1	29.4	32.5	43.8	37.3	34.4	43.6	38.5	**37.8**	**44.5**	**40.9**

4.3   Results

Model Evaluation and Ablation Studies

On Forms dataset, we train our high resolution model for predicting TextRuns, Widgets, TextBlocks, ChoiceGroup Titles, ChoiceFields, TextFields and Choice Groups such that its decoder predicts structures at various levels of hierarchy. The first hierarchy comprises of TextRuns and Widgets, the second comprises of TextBlocks and ChoiceGroup Titles, the third hierarchy comprises of TextFields and ChoiceFields while the fourth comprises of Choice Groups only. We add another class - Border, surrounding each structure and make the network predict this class to enable it to disambiguate different objects and generalise better. We refer to this network configuration as *Highresnet*. We perform ablations establishing gains from our high resolution segmentation network by comparing it with: 1) *Lowresnet* - a low resolution variation of *Highresnet* that takes input image at 792 resolution and predicts hierarchical segmentation masks for the entire image in a single forward pass; 2) *NoPriorNet* - A *Highresnet* variation where we divide the input image into horizontal strips with no overlap between consecutive strips. In this variant, the segmentation mask predicted for a strip is not given as prior for the subsequent strip prediction; 3) *2D-DilatedNet* - where the horizontal (vertical) 1d dilated conv layers in our network's context encoder

Table 3. Mean IoU comparison between our Lowresnet model and its variant. Lowresnet-1 to Lowresnet-4 are trained specifically for a single hierarchy only while $Lowresnet_{MD}$ comprises of shared encoder but separate decoders for different hierarchies in a single model.

Structure → Model ↓	Text Run	Widget	Text Block	ChoiceGroup Title	Text Field	Choice Field	Choice Group
Lowresnet-1 (ours)	87.75	80.11	–	–	–	–	–
Lowresnet-2 (ours)	–	–	87.42	63.95	–	–	–
Lowresnet-3 (ours)	–	–	–	–	80.8	63.07	–
Lowresnet-4 (ours)	–	–	–	–	–	–	70.55
$Lowresnet_{MD}$ (ours)	86.42	78.96	86.87	65.67	79.28	62.79	69.37
Lowresnet (ours)	**89.31**	**82.17**	**88.49**	**69.03**	**81.93**	**65.85**	**72.61**

are replaced with 2d dilated conv layers with exactly same dilation rates and kernel parameters (each 1×9 or 9×1 kernel is replaced with 3×3 kernel). We use pixel mean Intersection over Union (MIoU) to evaluate different models. We summarise MIoU of different ablations in Table 1. We also estimate object level recall and precision (Table 2) and compare with ablation methods. For this, we consider a predicted structure as correct match if the IoU of its predicted mask is above a threshold (0.7) with an expected structure mask. **Object-level extraction plays a crucial role in deciding the quality of final re-flow conversion. We, therefore, report these numbers to assess the performance of final structure extraction.**

Compare Highresnet with Lowresnet: It can be seen that by extracting hierarchical structure in high resolution, *Highresnet* is able to improve the MIoU scores significantly over all classes. Similar trend is observed for object level performance (Table 2 and Table 3).

Compare Highresnet with NoPriorNet: Adding predicted segmentation mask as prior while making prediction for subsequent strip in a page improves the MIoU scores. Further these improvements in MIoU leads to a significant and even better improvement in object extraction performance (Table 2 and 3).

Compare Highresnet with 2D-DilatedNet: It can be seen that using 1d dilated convs performs slightly better than 2d dilated convs (having same number of parameters) in terms of MIoU. However such improvements result in profound impact on object level performance.

Ablation on Importance of Detecting Hierarchies Simultaneously:
To analyse the importance of segmenting different hierarchical structures together, we consider different variants of our Lowresnet where we train 4 different models, one for each hierarchy separately: Lowresnet-1 for textruns and

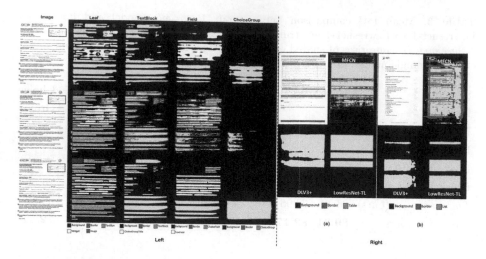

Fig. 5. Left: Visualisations showing segmentation masks predicted by DLV3+ (top row), MFCN (middle row), and our method *Highresnet* (bottom row) for a sample form image. Right: Visualisation of List and Table Segmentation masks on our model and baselines respectively: For each of the two images, MFCN, DLV3+ and Lowresnet-TL predictions are shown in top right, bottom left and bottom right subparts.

Table 4. Mean IoU comparison between the baseline methods and our model on different form structures.

Structure → Model ↓	Text Run	Widget	Text Block	ChoiceGroup Title	Text Field	Choice Field	Choice Group
DLV3+ NoImagenet	80.05	71.2	79.61	18.69	66.91	33.59	39.61
DLV3+ Imagenet	81.63	77.73	83.44	48.09	76.26	50.12	56.11
MFCN	77.81	47.58	71.33	29.76	39.55	28.1	35.43
Lowresnet (ours)	89.31	82.17	88.49	69.03	81.93	65.85	72.61
Highresnet (ours)	**92.7**	**87.32**	**90.55**	**80.87**	**88.87**	**84.05**	**83.01**

widgets, Lowresnet-2 for textblocks and choice group title, Lowresnet-3 for text fields and choice fields, and Lowresnet-4 for choice groups. For these variants we scale down the number of filters in each convolution layer by 2 so that the number of parameters in each variant is scaled down by 4. Since there are 4 such variants, together combined they have same number of parameters as our Lowresnet model. As can be seen in Table 3, the Lowresnet model has significantly better MIoU for all the structures compared with models trained for individual hierarchy levels. This shows that predicting hierarchical structures simultaneously results in better hierarchical features that benefit structures across the hierarchies (for instance, choice group title, choice field and choice group are inter-dependent). We further investigate this through training a variant $Lowresnet_{MD}$ which comprises of the same encoder as in Lowresnet but

Table 5. Comparison of precision-recall for the different hierarchical form structures between baseline and our method computed with an IoU threshold of 0.7. *CG Title - ChoiceGroup Title, **CG - ChoiceGroup

Model →	DLV3+ NoImagenet			DLV3+ Imagenet			MFCN			LowRes Net (ours)			HighRes Net (ours)		
Structure ↓	P	R	F1	P	R	F1	P	R	F1	P	R	F1	P	R	F1
TextRun	57.4	35.1	43.5	63.0	38.1	47.5	58.7	45.9	51.5	72.8	55.0	62.6	**80.2**	**67.3**	**73.2**
Widget	37.0	32.7	34.7	58.7	53.4	55.9	14.3	26.6	18.6	52.8	51.8	52.3	**75.0**	**75.4**	**75.2**
TextBlock	52.3	47.5	49.8	57.3	53.3	55.2	17.4	22.3	19.5	51.0	45.6	48.2	**71.2**	**72.5**	**71.9**
TextField	15.6	14.5	15.0	29.6	23.8	26.4	4.2	27.6	7.4	43.1	53.4	47.7	**73.4**	**82.5**	**77.7**
CG Title*	46.3	11.2	18.1	59.9	41.3	48.9	10.6	20.8	14.1	48.2	41.0	44.3	**85.0**	**84.9**	**84.9**
ChoiceField	22.0	14.8	17.7	31.8	23.5	27.0	8.9	19.5	12.2	28.3	33.3	30.6	**77.7**	**81.5**	**79.6**
CG**	4.5	6.8	5.4	14.2	19.4	16.4	1.3	6.0	2.2	26.5	33.1	29.4	**37.8**	**44.5**	**40.9**

Table 6. Comparison of MIoU, object level precision, recall, F1 scores of our method with the baselines for Table and List on Forms Dataset.

Model → Metric ↓	DLV3+ NoImagenet		DLV3+ Imagenet		MFCN		Lowresnet-TL	
	Table	List	Table	List	Table	List	Table	List
MIoU	69.9	55.7	77.9	65.1	48.1	22.1	**79.83**	**63.60**
P	20.6	17.4	35.2	29.8	4.09	1.49	**55.71**	**55.55**
R	50.0	26.5	60.4	38.4	59.375	23.67	**77.20**	**52.29**
F1	29.2	21.0	44.4	33.6	7.66	2.81	**62.89**	**53.73**

comprises of four different decoders corresponding to each hierarchy level. The encoder features are shared between different decoders in $Lowresnet_{MD}$. Each decoder has same architecture and parameters as in the decoder of Lowresnet. It can be seen in Table 3 that predicting hierarchical structures together at the last layer in Lowresnet is beneficial compared to having separate decoders in $Lowresnet_{MD}$, even though the latter has more number of trainable parameters. This is because the shared hierarchical features upto the last layer helps in predicting different structures better as compared to having independent features for different hierarchies through separate decoders.

Comparison with Baselines. We consider two baselines - DeepLabV3+ [7] (DLV3+), which is the state of the art for semantic segmentation tasks on natural images and Multimodal FCNN (MFCN) [49] designed for extracting several complex structures in documents. The baseline segmentation models segment the input image into a flattened hierarchy. To address this, we process output of penultimate layer of the baseline models through 4 separate FC layers to obtain hierarchical masks using data schema similar to *Highresnet*. We train baselines on RGB images at a resolution of 792×792 following an aspect ratio preserving

Table 7. Comparison of table detection precision-recall numbers on Marmot and RVL-CDIP datasets and table decomposition on ICDAR2013 dataset

Method (IoU)	Marmot English			Marmot Chinese			RVL-CDIP			ICDAR2013		
	P	R	F1	P	R	F1	P	R	F1	P	R	F1
MSMT-FCN (0.8)	**75.3**	70.0	72.5	**77.0**	76.1	**76.5**	–	–	–	–	–	–
MSMT-FCN (0.9)	47.0	45.0	45.9	49.3	49.1	49.1	–	–	–	–	–	–
Lowresnet-TL (0.8)	75.2	**72.2**	**73.7**	71.7	**77.4**	74.4	–	–	–	–	–	–
Lowresnet-TL (0.9)	**61.2**	**64.6**	**62.8**	62.3	70.5	66.1	–	–	–	–	–	–
GNN-Net [39] (0.5)	–	–	–	–	–	–	25.2	39.6	30.8	–	–	–
Lowresnet-TL (0.5)	–	–	–	–	–	–	**43.6**	**65.4**	**52.3**	–	–	–
Baseline [44] (0.5)	–	–	–	–	–	–	–	–	–	93.4	93.4	93.4
Lowresnet-TL (0.5)	–	–	–	–	–	–	–	–	–	93.9	94.3	94.1
+FormsData (0.5)	–	–	–	–	–	–	–	–	–	**94.7**	**95.7**	**95.2**

resize. For DLV3+, we train both with and without imagenet pre-trained weights for the Resnet-101 backbone variants. For MFCN, loss for different classes is scaled according to pixel area covered by elements of each class (calculated over the dataset) as described in their work. Table 4 compares the MIoU of our approach with baselines while Table 5 compares the object level F1 score. As can be seen, our model *Highresnet* significantly outperforms both baselines on all form structures. In particular, DLV3+ without imagenet pre-training performs poorly on segmenting different form structures. The pre-trained version performs much better but our Highresnet significantly outperforms it without requiring imagenet pre-training with large improvements in MIoU scores.

Figure 5(Left) illustrates segmentation masks predicted by different baseline methods, and our model on a sample form image (see footnote 1). Baseline methods merge different elements and hierarchical structures such as TextBlocks and Fields. In contrast, our model predicts crisp segmentation masks while extracting all such structures. For choice group, the baseline methods predict incomplete segmentation mask while our model captures long-range dependencies among its constituent elements and predict the complete mask.

Evaluation on Other Higher Order Constructs. In this section, we discuss the performance of our model at extracting other higher order structures like Lists and Tables. These structures are relatively more evident and span large regions in a page reducing the need to disambiguate them in high resolution. Consequently, we train a separate low resolution (792×792) version of our proposed network similar to *Lowresnet* which we refer to as *Lowresnet-TL* to predict these structures. In order to compare the performance of this network, we also train networks for the two baselines for extracting Tables and Lists simultaneously. Table 6 compares the MIoU of our method with the baseline models and the Fig. 5(Right) illustrates the network outputs for the task of Table and List segmentation. It can be seen that *Lowresnet-TL* significantly outperforms both the baselines, specifically it outperforms imagenet pre-trained DLV3+ while itself not requiring imagenet pre-training.

We also compare precision-recall of Table predictions of *Lowresnet-TL* on Marmot Dataset with previous best method – Multi-Scale Multi-Task FCN (*MSMT-FCN*) [17] in Table 7. It can be seen that *Lowresnet-TL* performs similar to *MSMT-FCN* for an IoU threshold of 0.8. However, *Lowresnet-TL* performs significantly better than *MSMT-FCN* for higher IoU threshold of 0.9 indicating our architecture is able to predict crisper predictions. On RVL-CDIP, our model outperforms GNN-Net [39] which is state of the art for table detection on this dataset. We also evaluate our method for task of table decomposition into rows an columns on ICDAR 2013 dataset and compare it against [44]. The numbers reported are average of precision, recall and F1 obtained for rows and columns as done by [44]. We train our model in two settings - one using ICDAR2013 data only (using same train-test split) and secondly by adding our forms data (105 tables). We apply post processing on network outputs where we filter row predictions based on area threshold and extend row mask horizontally to obtain completed row predictions and apply similar transformation for columns. As can be seen our method outperforms [44] (Table 7).

5   Conclusion

We propose a novel neural network training mechanism to extract document structure on very high resolution. We observe that higher resolution segmentation is beneficial for extracting structure, particularly on forms since they posses highly dense regions. We show that a single network hierarchical segmentation approach leads to better results on structure extraction task. In addition, we also show that 1D dilated conv based model captures long range contextual dependencies while segmenting different hierarchical constructs. Various ablation studies show the effectiveness of our high resolution segmentation approach and network architecture design. We compare our method with different semantic segmentation baselines outperforming them significantly on our Forms Dataset for several structures such as TextBlocks, Fields, Choice Groups etc. Additionally, our model trained on Forms Dataset outperforms prior art for table detection on Marmot and ICDAR 2013 dataset.

References

1. Alam, H., Rahman, F.: Web document manipulation for small screen devices: a review. In: Web Document Analysis Workshop (WDA) (2003)
2. Arif, S., Shafait, F.: Table detection in document images using foreground and background features. In: 2018 Digital Image Computing: Techniques and Applications (DICTA), pp. 1–8. IEEE (2018)
3. Audebert, N., Herold, C., Slimani, K., Vidal, C.: Multimodal deep networks for text and image-based document classification. arXiv preprint arXiv:1907.06370 (2019)
4. Baxter, J.: A bayesian/information theoretic model of learning to learn via multiple task sampling. Mach. Learn. **28**, 7–39 (1997). https://doi.org/10.1023/A: 1007327622663

5. Bojanowski, P., Grave, E., Joulin, A., Mikolov, T.: Enriching word vectors with subword information. Trans. Assoc. Comput. Linguist. **5**, 135–146 (2017)
6. Chen, L.C., Papandreou, G., Kokkinos, I., Murphy, K., Yuille, A.L.: Semantic image segmentation with deep convolutional nets and fully connected CRFs. arXiv preprint arXiv:1412.7062 (2014)
7. Chen, L.-C., Zhu, Y., Papandreou, G., Schroff, F., Adam, H.: Encoder-decoder with atrous separable convolution for semantic image segmentation. In: Ferrari, V., Hebert, M., Sminchisescu, C., Weiss, Y. (eds.) ECCV 2018. LNCS, vol. 11211, pp. 833–851. Springer, Cham (2018). https://doi.org/10.1007/978-3-030-01234-2_49
8. Deng, J., Dong, W., Socher, R., Li, L.J., Li, K., Fei-Fei, L.: ImageNet: a large-scale hierarchical image database. In: 2009 IEEE Conference on Computer Vision and Pattern Recognition, pp. 248–255. IEEE (2009)
9. Drivas, D., Amin, A.: Page segmentation and classification utilising a bottom-up approach. In: Proceedings of 3rd International Conference on Document Analysis and Recognition, vol. 2, pp. 610–614. IEEE (1995)
10. Fang, J., Tao, X., Tang, Z., Qiu, R., Liu, Y.: Dataset, ground-truth and performance metrics for table detection evaluation. In: 2012 10th IAPR International Workshop on Document Analysis Systems, pp. 445–449. IEEE (2012)
11. Göbel, M., Hassan, T., Oro, E., Orsi, G.: ICDAR 2013 table competition. In: 2013 12th International Conference on Document Analysis and Recognition, pp. 1449–1453. IEEE (2013)
12. Graham, R.L., Yao, F.F.: Finding the convex hull of a simple polygon. J. Algorithms **4**(4), 324–331 (1983)
13. Gupta, A., Kumar, A., Tripathi, V., Tapaswi, S., et al.: Mobile web: web manipulation for small displays using multi-level hierarchy page segmentation. In: Proceedings of the 4th International Conference on Mobile Technology, Applications, and Systems and the 1st International Symposium on Computer Human Interaction in Mobile Technology, pp. 599–606. ACM (2007)
14. Ha, J., Haralick, R.M., Phillips, I.T.: Document page decomposition by the bounding-box project. In: Proceedings of 3rd International Conference on Document Analysis and Recognition, vol. 2, pp. 1119–1122. IEEE (1995)
15. Ha, J., Haralick, R.M., Phillips, I.T.: Recursive XY cut using bounding boxes of connected components. In: Proceedings of 3rd International Conference on Document Analysis and Recognition, vol. 2, pp. 952–955. IEEE (1995)
16. Hao, L., Gao, L., Yi, X., Tang, Z.: A table detection method for PDF documents based on convolutional neural networks. In: 2016 12th IAPR Workshop on Document Analysis Systems (DAS), pp. 287–292. IEEE (2016)
17. He, D., Cohen, S., Price, B., Kifer, D., Giles, C.L.: Multi-scale multi-task FCN for semantic page segmentation and table detection. In: 2017 14th IAPR International Conference on Document Analysis and Recognition (ICDAR), vol. 1, pp. 254–261. IEEE (2017)
18. He, K., Gkioxari, G., Dollár, P., Girshick, R.: Mask R-CNN. In: Proceedings of the IEEE International Conference on Computer Vision, pp. 2961–2969 (2017)
19. Howard, A.G., et al.: MobileNets: efficient convolutional neural networks for mobile vision applications. arXiv preprint arXiv:1704.04861 (2017)
20. Januszewski, M., et al.: High-precision automated reconstruction of neurons with flood-filling networks. Nat. Methods **15**(8), 605–610 (2018)
21. Katti, A.R., et al.: Chargrid: towards understanding 2D documents. arXiv preprint arXiv:1809.08799 (2018)
22. Khemakhem, M., Herold, A., Romary, L.: Enhancing usability for automatically structuring digitised dictionaries (2018)

23. Kölsch, A., Mishra, A., Varshneya, S., Afzal, M.Z., Liwicki, M.: Recognizing challenging handwritten annotations with fully convolutional networks. In: 2018 16th International Conference on Frontiers in Handwriting Recognition (ICFHR), pp. 25–31. IEEE (2018)
24. Lebourgeois, F., Bublinski, Z., Emptoz, H.: A fast and efficient method for extracting text paragraphs and graphics from unconstrained documents. In: Proceedings of 11th IAPR International Conference on Pattern Recognition, Conference B: Pattern Recognition Methodology and Systems, vol. II, pp. 272–276. IEEE (1992)
25. Li, K., Hariharan, B., Malik, J.: Iterative instance segmentation. In: Proceedings of the IEEE Conference on Computer Vision and Pattern Recognition, pp. 3659–3667 (2016)
26. Li, X.H., Yin, F., Liu, C.L.: Page object detection from PDF document images by deep structured prediction and supervised clustering. In: 2018 24th International Conference on Pattern Recognition (ICPR), pp. 3627–3632. IEEE (2018)
27. Liu, X., Gao, J., He, X., Deng, L., Duh, K., Wang, Y.Y.: Representation learning using multi-task deep neural networks for semantic classification and information retrieval. In: Proceedings of the 2015 Conference of the North American Chapter of the Association for Computational Linguistics: Human Language Technologies, May–June 2015
28. Liu, X., Gao, F., Zhang, Q., Zhao, H.: Graph convolution for multimodal information extraction from visually rich documents. arXiv preprint arXiv:1903.11279 (2019)
29. Long, J., Shelhamer, E., Darrell, T.: Fully convolutional networks for semantic segmentation. In: Proceedings of the IEEE Conference on Computer Vision and Pattern Recognition, pp. 3431–3440 (2015)
30. Mao, S., Rosenfeld, A., Kanungo, T.: Document structure analysis algorithms: a literature survey. In: Document Recognition and Retrieval X, vol. 5010, pp. 197–207. International Society for Optics and Photonics (2003)
31. Mao, X., Shen, C., Yang, Y.B.: Image restoration using very deep convolutional encoder-decoder networks with symmetric skip connections. In: Advances in Neural Information Processing Systems, pp. 2802–2810 (2016)
32. Noh, H., Hong, S., Han, B.: Learning deconvolution network for semantic segmentation. In: Proceedings of the IEEE International Conference on Computer Vision, pp. 1520–1528 (2015)
33. Pinheiro, P., Collobert, R.: Recurrent convolutional neural networks for scene labeling. In: International Conference on Machine Learning, pp. 82–90 (2014)
34. Qasim, S.R., Mahmood, H., Shafait, F.: Rethinking table parsing using graph neural networks. CoRR abs/1905.13391 (2019). http://arxiv.org/abs/1905.13391
35. Qasim, S.R., Mahmood, H., Shafait, F.: Rethinking table parsing using graph neural networks. arXiv preprint arXiv:1905.13391 (2019)
36. Rahman, F., Alam, H.: Conversion of PDF documents into HTML: a case study of document image analysis. In: The Thrity-Seventh Asilomar Conference on Signals, Systems & Computers 2003, vol. 1, pp. 87–91. IEEE (2003)
37. Rastan, R., Paik, H.Y., Shepherd, J.: TEXUS: a unified framework for extracting and understanding tables in PDF documents. Inf. Process. Manag. **56**(3), 895–918 (2019)
38. Ren, M., Zemel, R.S.: End-to-end instance segmentation with recurrent attention. In: Proceedings of the IEEE Conference on Computer Vision and Pattern Recognition, pp. 6656–6664 (2017)
39. Riba, P., Dutta, A., Goldmann, L., Fornés, A., Ramos, O., Lladós, J.: Table detection in invoice documents by graph neural networks. In: ICDAR (2019)

40. Ronneberger, O., Fischer, P., Brox, T.: U-Net: convolutional networks for biomedical image segmentation. In: Navab, N., Hornegger, J., Wells, W.M., Frangi, A.F. (eds.) MICCAI 2015. LNCS, vol. 9351, pp. 234–241. Springer, Cham (2015). https://doi.org/10.1007/978-3-319-24574-4_28

41. Schreiber, S., Agne, S., Wolf, I., Dengel, A., Ahmed, S.: DeepDeSRT: deep learning for detection and structure recognition of tables in document images. In: 2017 14th IAPR International Conference on Document Analysis and Recognition (ICDAR), vol. 1, pp. 1162–1167. IEEE (2017)

42. Sermanet, P., Eigen, D., Zhang, X., Mathieu, M., Fergus, R., LeCun, Y.: OverFeat: integrated recognition, localization and detection using convolutional networks. arXiv preprint arXiv:1312.6229 (2013)

43. Sicre, R., Awal, A.M., Furon, T.: Identity documents classification as an image classification problem. In: Battiato, S., Gallo, G., Schettini, R., Stanco, F. (eds.) ICIAP 2017. LNCS, vol. 10485, pp. 602–613. Springer, Cham (2017). https://doi.org/10.1007/978-3-319-68548-9_55

44. Siddiqui, S.A., Khan, P.I., Dengel, A., Ahmed, S.: Rethinking semantic segmentation for table structure recognition in documents. In: 2019 International Conference on Document Analysis and Recognition (ICDAR), pp. 1397–1402. IEEE (2019)

45. Siegel, N., Lourie, N., Power, R., Ammar, W.: Extracting scientific figures with distantly supervised neural networks. In: Proceedings of the 18th ACM/IEEE on Joint Conference on Digital Libraries, pp. 223–232. ACM (2018)

46. Simon, A., Pret, J.C., Johnson, A.P.: A fast algorithm for bottom-up document layout analysis. IEEE Trans. Pattern Anal. Mach. Intell. **19**(3), 273–277 (1997)

47. Wick, C., Puppe, F.: Fully convolutional neural networks for page segmentation of historical document images. In: 2018 13th IAPR International Workshop on Document Analysis Systems (DAS), pp. 287–292. IEEE (2018)

48. Wigington, C., Tensmeyer, C., Davis, B., Barrett, W., Price, B., Cohen, S.: Start, follow, read: end-to-end full-page handwriting recognition. In: Ferrari, V., Hebert, M., Sminchisescu, C., Weiss, Y. (eds.) ECCV 2018. LNCS, vol. 11210, pp. 372–388. Springer, Cham (2018). https://doi.org/10.1007/978-3-030-01231-1_23

49. Yang, X., Yumer, E., Asente, P., Kraley, M., Kifer, D., Lee Giles, C.: Learning to extract semantic structure from documents using multimodal fully convolutional neural networks. In: Proceedings of the IEEE Conference on Computer Vision and Pattern Recognition, pp. 5315–5324 (2017)

50. Yang, Z., Yang, D., Dyer, C., He, X., Smola, A., Hovy, E.: Hierarchical attention networks for document classification. In: Proceedings of the 2016 Conference of the North American Chapter of the Association for Computational Linguistics: Human Language Technologies, pp. 1480–1489 (2016)

51. Yu, F., Koltun, V.: Multi-scale context aggregation by dilated convolutions. arXiv preprint arXiv:1511.07122 (2015)

52. Zeiler, M.D.: ADADELTA: an adaptive learning rate method. arXiv preprint arXiv:1212.5701 (2012)

53. Zheng, Q., Delingette, H., Duchateau, N., Ayache, N.: 3-D consistent and robust segmentation of cardiac images by deep learning with spatial propagation. IEEE Trans. Med. Imaging **37**(9), 2137–2148 (2018)

54. Zhu, X.X., et al.: Deep learning in remote sensing: a comprehensive review and list of resources. IEEE Geosci. Remote Sens. Mag. **5**(4), 8–36 (2017)

Measuring the Importance of Temporal Features in Video Saliency

Matthias Tangemann[1]([✉])(iD), Matthias Kümmerer[1](iD), Thomas S.A. Wallis[1,2](iD), and Matthias Bethge[1,2]

[1] University of Tübingen, Tübingen, Germany
{matthias.tangemann,matthias.kuemmerer,tom.wallis,matthias}@bethgelab.org
[2] Amazon Research, Tübingen, Germany

Abstract. Where people look when watching videos is believed to be heavily influenced by temporal patterns. In this work, we test this assumption by quantifying to which extent gaze on recent video saliency benchmarks can be predicted by a static baseline model. On the recent LEDOV dataset, we find that at least 75% of the explainable information as defined by a gold standard model can be explained using static features. Our baseline model "DeepGaze MR" even outperforms state-of-the-art video saliency models, despite deliberately ignoring all temporal patterns. Visual inspection of our static baseline's failure cases shows that clear temporal effects on human gaze placement exist, but are both rare in the dataset and not captured by any of the recent video saliency models. To focus the development of video saliency models on better capturing temporal effects we construct a meta-dataset consisting of those examples requiring temporal information.

Keywords: Gaze prediction · Saliency · Video · Temporal modelling · Model evaluation

1 Introduction

The human visual system processes information from the environment selectively. Several attention mechanisms limit the amount of information to be processed and thus enable efficient perception of the world (e.g., [9]). The most obvious form of attention is the shifting of gaze, which orients the high-resolution fovea towards areas of interest.

Modelling those gaze shifts is an important topic in computer vision. Predictive models of human gaze have the potential to advance our understanding of human visual attention, for example by aiding the development of hypotheses that can be tested with human subjects [7]. Besides their scientific usefulness, such models have various technical applications. They can be used for graphic

---

Electronic supplementary material The online version of this chapter (https://doi.org/10.1007/978-3-030-58604-1_40) contains supplementary material, which is available to authorized users.

A. Vedaldi et al. (Eds.): ECCV 2020, LNCS 12373, pp. 667–684, 2020.
https://doi.org/10.1007/978-3-030-58604-1_40

design [6], automated cropping, video compression [11] or other computer vision tasks (e.g., [48]).

Great progress has been made recently in predicting where people look in still images. With the use of pre-trained models the performance improved from 1/3 to more than 80% of explainable information explained (e.g., [25,27]). Since the human visual system developed in a dynamic environment, there is growing interest to also model human gaze on videos. Previous studies revealed that motion patterns are an important factor attracting visual attention [8,16,39]. All recent video gaze models therefore are based on temporal modeling components such as recurrent units or spatiotemporal convolutions to capture those dynamic patterns.

To which degree those temporal patterns influence human gaze on natural videos and to which degree the recent performance improvements in video gaze prediction can be attributed to capturing these effects, however, has not been evaluated thoroughly so far. With our work we aim at filling this gap, by providing a method to measure the influence of temporal patterns on human gaze. We construct a static baseline model that by design cannot capture temporal effects and compare its performance to a gold standard model estimating the total information in the ground truth gaze data. The performance difference to the gold standard then represents an upper bound to the influence of temporal effects on the respective dataset. Furthermore, by looking at the largest failure cases of our static baseline, we can identify situations in the dataset where human gaze is driven by temporal patterns. Evaluating gaze prediction models on those situations then lets us draw conclusions about the capabilities of models to predict temporal effects.

Applying this method to the recent LEDOV dataset [20] and state-of-the-art video gaze models we arrive at the following conclusions: (1) Human gaze placement on the videos contained in the LEDOV dataset is largely driven by spatial appearance. (2) Clearly identifiable temporal effects on human visual attention exist, but occur rarely in the videos considered. (3) We need to construct suitable video data sets to enable learning based models to capture temporal effects. Indeed, we show that all other recent video gaze models with the capacity for temporal modelling fail in the same situations as our restricted model.

We explicitly note that the main contribution of our work are above findings and the proposed evaluation method that we need to come to those findings, but not the static baseline model that is required for our analysis. Interestingly though, our baseline model outperforms state-of-the-art video gaze prediction models on the LEDOV and DIEM [34] datasets—despite deliberately ignoring all temporal information.

To enable other researches to apply our proposed evaluation method more easily, we collect a meta-benchmark from existing datasets that contains the situations requiring temporal information revealed by our analysis. The performance of new models on this meta-benchmark indicates how much an improved predictive performance can be attributed to better handling of temporal effects. We will make this meta-benchmark as well as our pre-trained baseline model publicly available.

2   Related Work

Substantial progress has been made on the task of gaze prediction for free viewing of images. While the influential model by Itti and Koch [18], inspired by Treisman and Gelade's feature integration theory [45], was devised to explain effects observed in visual search originally, it also achieved first successes in predicting where people look. Since then, more than 50 models have been proposed predicting probable gaze locations based on image content (for a recent comparison see, e.g., [12]). As in other areas of computer vision, the advent of deep learning gave rise to models greatly improving state-of-the-art performance [15,24,27,35,46]. DeepGaze II [27], the current state of the art model on the MIT Saliency Benchmark [5], captures 81% of the explainable information gain on that dataset (explainable information gain is an information-theoretic analogue of explainable variance, see [25] for details).

In contrast, gaze prediction for videos only recently attracted more attention. Several datasets and models have been developed, but neither a widely accepted benchmark nor an estimate of the amount of explainable information in those datasets exist. This makes an evaluation of the state of the field difficult.

Recently, two video gaze datasets have been introduced that are large enough to train deep neural network based models: LEDOV [20] and DHF1K [47]. More recently, Wang et al. also provided gaze recordings for video segmentation datasets [48]. The gaze recordings provided by Mathe and Sminichescu [32] for the Hollywood and UCF-Sports dataset are large enough for deep learning based approaches, but most of the subjects have not been recorded in the free-viewing setting. Several small datasets exists that provide high-quality recordings (e.g., DIEM [34], for an overview see [20]).

Starting with an extension of the Itti and Koch model to videos [16,17], several models predicting gaze specifically for videos have been proposed [10,13,14,30,38,40,41,51–53]. The performance of video gaze models has been greatly improved with the advent of deep learning. Bazzani et al. [3] trained a recurrent neural network based on features extracted from a spatiotemporal DNN predicting gaze using a mixture of Gaussians. The models by Wang et al. [47] and Wu et al. [50] pair convolutional LSTM units with an attention mechanism. Bak et al. [2] proposed a two-stream network using optical flow in parallel to RGB features. This two-stream approach has also been combined with convolutional LSTM units by [19,20] and with convolutional GRU and an attention mechanism by [28]. Linardos et al. [31] proposed a model based on an exponential moving average of frame-wise features. Very recently, [33] and [43] proposed spatio-temporal encoder-decoder networks for video gaze prediction.

3   Methods

The main objective of our work is to evaluate the influence of temporal patterns on human gaze. To that end, we propose a baseline model that cannot learn temporal patterns by design but predicts human gaze on videos solely relying on static appearance. This baseline model is then compared to a gold standard model as an estimate of the total information in the ground truth gaze data. The performance difference between those models represents an upper bound of the influence of temporal patterns on human gaze placement.

3.1   Center Bias

The center bias is an important lower baseline. It is obtained by blurring and normalizing a histogram of all gaze positions in the training set. As humans tend to look at the center of images [44] and videos are usually recorded such that interesting objects are in the middle of videos, there is a clear bias in the gaze data towards the center of the videos. The center bias therefore represents a prior distribution of gaze position independent of visual content. Predicting this spatial prior for every frame yields a lower baseline, comparable to the chance level performance in classification tasks.

The center bias is much stronger in the beginning of each video due to the subjects fixating the center of the screen before each trial. As described later, we ignore this effect by not evaluating on the first 15 frames and confirmed experimentally that a stationary center bias models the remaining data well. Furthermore, we optimized the blur size using a grid search.

3.2   Gold Standard Model

The maximal performance that gaze prediction models can achieve is limited by the consistency of the subjects and varies from frame to frame. We use a gold standard model [49] to measure the inter-subject variability of the gaze positions. The model predicts where each subject looked given the ground truth information from all other subjects on the same frame. This is done by blurring the gaze positions of all but one subject and performing leave-one-out cross validation. Moreover, the prediction of the gold standard model is mixed with a uniform distribution to handle outliers. The gold standard therefore predicts subjects to look where other subjects look with a high probability, and to randomly look anywhere on the image with a small probability defined by the mixing coefficient. The optimal blur size of the gaussian filter and the mixing weight of the uniform distribution are determined using a grid search.

A high gold standard performance indicates very consistent gaze locations across all subjects and vice versa. Therefore, the gold standard model yields an estimate of the maximal performance that can be achieved for every frame. All reported gold standard performances refer to the leave-one-subject-out performance.

3.3   Static Baseline Model

Our proposed evaluation method requires a static baseline model that cannot handle temporal effects by design. Initial experiments revealed that DeepGaze II [27], the current state-of-the-art model for images, achieves a very competitive performance when simply applied to videos frame-by-frame (see Sect. 4). However, this instantaneous model ignores delays due to the required processing in the human brain. This suggests a way to improve the DeepGaze II architecture for videos by averaging deep features over multiple recent video frames. Based on this approach, we propose a space-time separable variant of DeepGaze II using a temporal box filter as static baseline model (see Fig. 1), which we call *DeepGaze Mean Readout (DeepGaze MR)*.

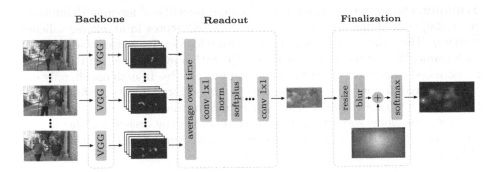

Fig. 1. Architecture of our static baseline model "DeepGaze MR": A feature representation is extracted from individual frames in a fixed size window using the VGG-19 network. A non-linear readout network transforms this representation into a priority map by first averaging the feature channels over time, and then applying a series of 1×1 convolutions. The resulting map is then resized, blurred, weighted by the center bias, and normalized to obtain the final prediction.

Input to our model is a fixed length window of consecutive frames, which is used to predict the gaze distribution on the last frame ("target frame") in this window. We use a window length of 16 frames, which was the optimal value found using a grid search (see supplement for details).

Backbone. Our model applies the VGG-19 network pretrained on Imagenet [42] to every frame individually and extracts the representation from the last convolutional layer (conv5_4) after the nonlinearity. We keep the parameters of the backbone fixed to prevent overfitting.

Readout. A non-linear readout network is used to transform the feature representation into a priority map of probable gaze locations. The readout network first averages the feature representation over time. A series of 1×1 pixel convolutions is then used to non-linearly combine the feature channels to the priority map. Layer Normalization [1] is used after all but the last convolutional layer to stabilize training. As non-linearity we use the softplus function, which is a smooth approximation of the commonly used ReLU and avoided units zeroing out early in training. We use three convolutional layers with 32, 32, and one channel, respectively. This optimal instantiation of the readout network has been found using a random search (see supplement for details).

Finalization. Finally, the output of the readout network is turned into the predicted probability distribution: First, the priority map is resized to the resolution of the input. It is then smoothed using a Gaussian with learnable standard deviation per x and y dimension. The logarithm of the center bias density from the training set is added to the map using a learnable weight, acting as a spatial prior. Finally, a softmax is applied to obtain the predicted spatial probability distribution of gaze locations.

Training. Our model is trained using maximum-likelihood learning (Kümmerer et al. [26] suggest that this allows for best metric scores in all classic saliency metrics). Thus, the loss function is the average log-density at gaze locations for each frame. We use the Adam optimizer [23] with a learning rate of 0.01, which is decreased by a factor of ten after one and five epochs. In each epoch, only one random target frame per video is used for training. Experiments confirmed, that this training scheme is sufficient for our model to converge.

Since our model averages features over time, it is by design not able to represent temporal patterns such as movements, or appearing and disappearing objects.

4   Experiments

In this section, we evaluate our baseline models described above on recent video gaze datasets. We then analyse the baseline predictions in comparison to state-of-the-art video gaze models to better understand the importance of temporal effects in video saliency.

The evaluation of gaze prediction models comes with challenges: different evaluation protocols and metrics typically lead to inconsistent model rankings. Building on recent work to better understand this evaluation process, we first describe and motivate the model evaluation approach used in this work.

4.1   Metrics

A large number of metrics exist that are used to evaluate gaze predictions (for a review see [4]). As typically used, these metrics give rise to inconsistent model rankings. Kümmerer et al. [26] proposed to adapt a probabilistic setting, i.e., to formulate models so that they predict spatial probability distributions, train them for log-likelihood and differentiate between predictions and derived saliency maps. In this way, consistent model ratings can be achieved.

We adopt this setting in our work, and use information gain (average log-likelihood per fixation compared to the center bias, [25]) as our primary metric.

To enable a comparison to models that did not use a probabilistic approach, we additionally evaluate the AUC [22], NSS [36], CC [21], KLDiv [29,37] and SIM [22] metrics to judge the performance of our model relative to state-of-the-art. To obtain an overall score for a model, the metrics are applied to the prediction for every frame individually, and then averaged first over frames and then over videos.

4.2 Datasets

The main dataset for this work is the LEDOV dataset [19]. It contains 538 short videos (11s on average) with eye tracking data of 32 subjects. The authors removed smooth pursuits and saccades and artificially stabilized fixations during their preprocessing, so this dataset does not allow to investigate the precise dynamics of individual gaze trajectories. However, the dataset covers the common factors driving human gaze placement sufficiently well to develop and compare models. All videos have been rescaled to 640×360px and resampled to 30 Hz. Models from other groups are evaluated using the resolutions and frame rates that the respective models have been trained on.

For additional analyses we are using the DIEM dataset [34] (84 videos, 66 subjects on average, mean duration 95.2 s). The videos have been padded to match the viewing conditions reported in the paper and rescaled to 640×480px.

The DHF1K dataset [47] is comparable in scope to LEDOV, but contains artifacts in the provided gaze maps. As those artifacts affect the model scores and make it impossible to properly evaluate the gold standard model, we excluded this dataset from our analysis. In the supplemental information we provide more details on this issue together with overall performance results which suggest that our conclusions are also valid for DHF1K.

For all datasets, the subject had to fixate the center of the screen before each trial. We do not evaluate models on the first 15 frames to ignore the centered gaze due to the experimental paradigm.

4.3 Performance Results

In Table 1, we show the performances of our baselines and other recent gaze models on LEDOV. Despite deliberately ignoring all temporal effects, DeepGaze MR performs very well and explains as much as 75% of the explainable information (as a comparison, the state-of-the-art for images on MIT1003 is 81%). Moreover, DeepGaze MR performs substantially better than DeepGaze II which confirms the effectiveness of our proposed adaptations. Interestingly, in AUC our model matches the gold standard performance, which might be due to the fact that AUC saturates very quickly. Furthermore, the AUC metric might suffer from the leave-one-subject-out cross validation applied in the gold standard.

We further compare the performances of our baselines to recent video gaze prediction models: The DeepVS model [19,20] allows the most direct comparison, as it was trained on the LEDOV dataset as well. ACLNet [47], SalEMA [31], TASED-Net [33] and STRA-Net [28] are recent video gaze models developed on the DHF1K dataset [47]. For all models, we used the published weights and adapted size and frame rate of the input videos to match the samples encountered in the respective model training. As the results in Table 1 show, DeepGaze MR clearly outperforms all evaluated previous state-of-the-art models on the LEDOV dataset across all metrics, despite being designed as a static baseline model.

Table 1. Performance comparison of recent gaze prediction models on the LEDOV dataset. The information gain can only be evaluated for models that predict a spatial probability distribution. All models have been applied using the published weights. TASED-NET, SalEMA, ACLNet and STRA-Net have been trained on the DHF1K dataset, DeepGaze II on SALICON and MIT1003.

LEDOV val

Model	IG	%	AUC	CC	KLDiv	NSS	SIM
Center bias	0	0	0.833	0.157	3.521	1.546	0.062
TASED-Net [33]	-	-	0.887	0.647	3.214	3.498	0.496
STRA-Net [28]	-	-	0.890	0.610	2.315	3.324	0.460
SalEMA [31]	-	-	0.890	0.596	2.573	3.331	0.466
ACLNet [47]	-	-	0.892	0.587	1.905	3.156	0.430
DeepVS [19]	-	-	0.894	0.397	2.445	3.098	0.210
DeepGaze II [27]	1.216	62.8	0.908	0.588	1.259	3.368	0.434
DeepGaze MR	**1.445**	**74.6**	**0.917**	**0.665**	**1.105**	**3.857**	**0.498**
Gold standard	1.961	100	0.917	-	-	4.992	-

LEDOV test

Model	IG	%	AUC	CC	KLDiv	NSS	SIM
Center bias	0	0	0.844	0.142	3.689	1.585	0.057
SalEMA [31]	-	-	0.897	0.590	2.377	3.152	0.465
TASED-Net [33]	-	-	0.897	0.650	2.965	3.361	0.505
ACLNet [47]	-	-	0.898	0.573	1.667	2.922	0.435
STRA-Net [28]	-	-	0.899	0.597	2.024	3.130	0.466
DeepVS [19]	-	-	0.903	0.394	2.398	3.081	0.218
DeepGaze II [27]	1.117	61.0	0.909	0.606	1.195	3.403	0.447
DeepGaze MR	**1.367**	**75.5**	**0.920**	**0.667**	**1.035**	**3.657**	**0.506**
Gold standard	1.810	100	0.920	-	-	4.676	-

Additionally, we evaluated the models on the DIEM dataset. The size of the dataset is rather small (84 videos), therefore we did not train but only evaluate the models on this dataset. As the results in Table 2 show, our model performs clearly better than all other video saliency methods on this dataset except TASED-Net [33]. Interestingly, the original DeepGaze II model for images performs even better than the variant adapted to videos.

The performances on DIEM are worse than those on LEDOV for two reasons. First, this dataset is much harder as the videos in this dataset contain much more temporal activity. Second, the domain gap to LEDOV is rather large, as DIEM contains cuts and many objects not present in LEDOV. The good performance of DeepGaze II on this dataset could therefore be explained by the much broader range of objects it has seen during training. Moreover, DeepGaze II is applied purely frame-by-frame, so it probably copes better with the many cuts in DIEM.

4.4   Analyzing Temporal Effects

In the following, we try to better understand the influence of temporal information on gaze placement. As motivated earlier, we use the information gain difference of the gold standard and DeepGaze MR as an estimator of the information that is not captured by our model. Since the model cannot learn temporal patterns by design, temporal effects on human gaze placement should result in large differences to the gold standard.

In Fig. 2 we plot the distribution of those differences grouped by video. The median remaining information is close to 0bit for roughly half of the videos in the validation set. This indicates that our static baseline model successfully predicts gaze positions on a large number of frames. However, the results also clearly show two kinds of failure cases: (1) There are some videos for which the average performance gap to the gold standard is large. For the first three videos in the plot, the median difference is almost 2bit. (2) For other videos there is a large number of outlier frames whose performance gap is much greater than for most of the other remaining frames in the video. As our model is not able to exploit temporal structure by design, they should include cases in which temporal patterns affect human gaze placement.

We analyze the found failure cases in more detail by visualizing them in Figs. 3 and 4. We plot the NSS scores of the models over time (bottom) and visualize the model log predictions at interesting frames (top, frame position indicated by dashed lines in the NSS plot). As SalEMA averages features and thus cannot handle temporal effects by design, we don't consider it in this case study. The figures reveal three common factors that strongly influence where people look and are difficult for all models:

Interactions between objects occur in several of the videos. Here, most subjects look at the interaction point, not at the objects themselves. This is clearly observable in Fig. 4b, when the child is feeding the giraffe or in Fig. 3a when the robot is grabbing objects.

Suddenly appearing objects have a very strong ability to attract human attention as well. As can be seen in Fig. 4a the shifting of the gaze to the appearing text is very consistent across all subjects. We assume that this effect can be observed with suddenly appearing objects in general, but cannot verify this hypothesis properly due to the small number of samples. A related effect is the appearing of the two persons due to the camera motion in Fig. 4d. They also clearly attract attention, however much less than the sudden appearing of the text in Fig. 4a.

Table 2. Performance comparison of recent gaze prediction models on the full DIEM dataset. Due to the small number of videos, none of the models has been trained on this dataset.

Model	DIEM						
	IG	%	AUC	CC	KLDiv	NSS	SIM
Center bias	0	0	0.892	0.436	1.511	2.053	0.341
DeepVS [19]	-	-	0.853	0.424	2.070	2.096	0.309
SalEMA [31]	-	-	0.911	0.576	1.743	2.987	0.465
STRA-Net [28]	-	-	0.914	0.595	1.975	3.069	0.477
TASED-Net [33]	-	-	0.914	**0.621**	2.098	**3.194**	**0.493**
ACLNet [47]	-	-	0.914	0.558	1.468	2.826	0.428
DeepGaze MR	0.660	43.1	0.920	0.602	1.091	3.116	0.471
DeepGaze II [27]	**0.674**	**44.0**	**0.926**	0.619	**1.058**	2.898	0.477
Gold standard	1.531	100	0.940	-	-	4.659	-

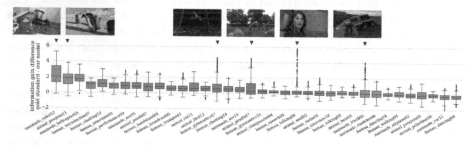

Fig. 2. Distribution of the unexplained information across frames in the LEDOV validation set (x-axis shows distinct videos). The remaining explainable information is estimated by the difference of our model to the gold standard in bit using the information gain metric. The videos marked are the largest failure cases of our model.

Movements of objects also clearly have the potential to change which parts of a scene are observed. In Fig. 4c, none of the subjects looks at the gymnast's arms or hands, but all are looking at his torso that is moving in the respective scene. This stands in contrast to most cases in which humans appear, where subjects tend to look at people's hands or faces. Also global camera movements seem to be able to shift people's gaze towards the side of the direction of the movement, as indicated in Fig. 4d. However the effect in this example is small and entangled with the appearing persons. A closer investigation would be necessary to address this effect.

The temporal effects described are compiled from the qualitative analysis of our model's largest failure cases. As their number is small, the list given is most likely not exhaustive. Moreover, it is not possible to reliably draw any general conclusions about the relative strengths of those effects. However, the cases presented clearly reveal the existence of such temporal effects and show

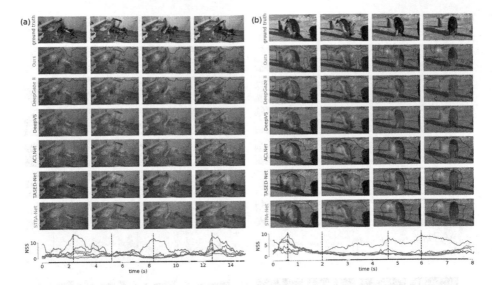

Fig. 3. Failure cases with a high average difference to the gold standard: **(a)** Most of the subjects look at the robot's hand while it puts a glass into a dishwasher. The models however distribute their prediction over the whole robot. **(b)** After roughly two seconds a small penguin becomes visible under the big penguin in the foreground, shifting the gaze of most subjects to the small penguin for the rest of the video. Markers on the x-axis of the NSS plots indicate frames that are part of our proposed meta-benchmark (see Sect. 4.5).

that they are not captured by all recent video gaze models that should have the capacity to model them.

4.5 Evaluating Temporal Modelling

The detailed analysis of the failure cases in the previous section showed that none of the considered models was able to correctly predict cases in which temporal information influences where people look. As our proposed method requires training and evaluating two baseline models, the hurdle to apply it is quite high. To facilitate applying our method to new models, we propose a principled new meta-benchmark consisting of those hard cases.

Our meta-dataset contains all frames of videos where our static baseline's information gain is at least 1bit worse than the gold standard (indicated by markers on the x-axis of the NSS plots in Figs. 3 and 4). We propose to run the models on the full videos, but only average the performances over the frames included in our meta-dataset. This evaluation scheme discards roughly 80% of the frames in LEDOV and 65% of the frames in DIEM. As our model cannot learn temporal effects by design, gaze on the discarded frames can be explained by spatial features. The performance on the remaining frames reflects the ability of models to handle cases in which temporal information is necessary much better than existing benchmarks.

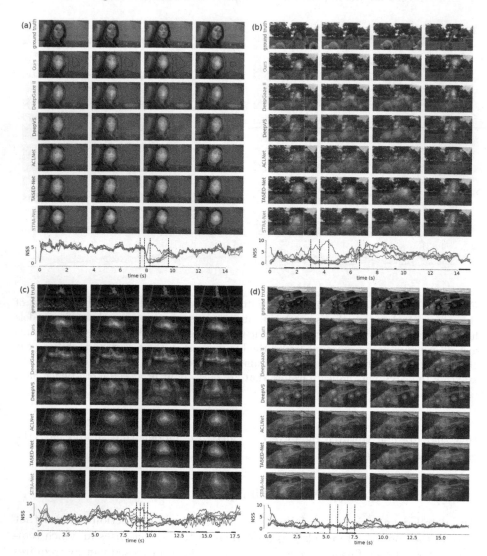

Fig. 4. Failure cases due to localized events: **(a)** A text suddenly appearing draws almost all attention for a short time, whereas the models predict people to mainly look at the person talking. **(b)** When a child is feeding a giraffe, the subjects' attention focuses at their interaction point and not at the giraffe's head that is looked at during the remainder of the video. **(c)** Gaze concentrates on the gymnast's torso during a swinging exercise, whereas other body parts are much less looked at. **(d)** Two persons enter the scene due to the movement of the camera, which temporarily attracts the attention of most of the subjects.

Table 3. Performance of state-of-the-art models on our proposed meta-benchmark, which discards frames in which the information gain of our model is more than 1bit less as the gold standard. As our model cannot exploit temporal patterns, the reported performances reflect the ability to handle cases in which temporal information is needed to predict where people look much better.

Model	Meta-Benchmark: LEDOV & DIEM						
	IG	%	AUC	CC	KLdiv	NSS	SIM
Center bias	0	0	0.853	0.274	2.580	1.679	0.195
DeepVS [19]	-	-	0.854	0.337	2.599	2.152	0.225
SalEMA [31]	-	-	0.887	0.477	2.584	2.596	0.394
STRA-Net [28]	-	-	0.889	0.497	2.681	2.658	0.39
ACLNet [47]	-	-	0.891	0.483	2.044	2.579	0.377
TASED-Net [33]	-	-	0.893	**0.583**	2.995	**2.855**	**0.430**
DeepGaze MR	0.528	24.2	0.898	0.454	1.568	2.458	0.365
DeepGaze II [27]	**0.787**	**36.1**	**0.908**	0.507	**1.420**	2.693	0.389
Gold Standard	2.182	100.0	0.948	-	-	5.093	-

In Table 3 we report the model performances on this meta-benchmark derived from LEDOV and DIEM. As indicated by our previous analysis, all models considered in this work perform poorly. As this benchmark was derived from failure cases of our model, the performance reduction of our model is disproportionally large. When using DeepGaze II as a baseline model, our model performs much better in this meta-benchmark (see supplement for details).

5 Discussion

Human gaze on dynamic stimuli such as videos is hypothesized to be strongly driven by temporal patterns in the stimuli, e.g., temporal popup and motion [8,16]. In this work, we measured the importance of temporal features in video saliency. To that end, we developed and analysed DeepGaze MR, a static baseline model predicting gaze positions on the LEDOV dataset, and compared it's performance to a gold standard model. DeepGaze MR is adapted from the successful DeepGaze II model for still images and is not able to learn temporal patterns by design. Nevertheless, our model outperforms previous state of the art with a large margin on the LEDOV dataset and captures 75% of the explainable information gain.

When we analyzed failure cases of our model, we found clear temporal effects that drove the subject's gaze such as sudden appearances and movements and, to a certain degree, also interactions. We found that the gold standard performance and therefore the consistency among subjects is very high in those cases. This confirms the hypothesis that temporal patterns are an important factor influencing human gaze placement.

Given this importance of temporal effects, we would expect a good video saliency model to predict human gaze in those cases well. While our model wasn't able to capture those effects by design, we found that all other models we tested consistently failed to capture those effects either. In particular, this is the case also for models like DeepVS, ACLNet, STRA-Net and TASED-Net that have explicitly been designed to capture temporal patterns.

We argue that the main reason for this shortcoming is a deficiency of the datasets used to train video saliency models. Temporal patterns in the videos can influence gaze placement in ways that are highly consistent over subjects (Fig. 4, see also [8,16]). However, these effects turn out to be rare compared to the influence of spatial patterns such as faces on gaze placement. We suppose that they are so rare that current state-of-the-art models do not benefit from investing modelling capacity into modelling them. This difficulty for learning-based approaches to handle rare, but important, events correctly is a general problem relevant for many fields. In autonomous driving, for example, it is crucial to handle rare events correctly, e.g. when children running onto the street.

Several aspects can contribute to tackling this issue: the model architecture, the loss function and the datasets.

Adding general temporal modelling components, as done by previous works on video saliency, has shown to be ineffective to learn temporal effects. However, our study reveals distinct temporal effects on human gaze. Models might benefit from adding modules that are explicitly designed to detect effects that we know to be relevant, such as appearing objects.

To evaluate models predicting gaze on videos, image-based metrics are typically applied per frame and averaged. As a result, some of the failure cases seen above do not substantially affect the overall model performance as those effects tend to be short compared to the whole video. This is opposed to our subjective impression of the clear failure of the model on those samples. A loss function that penalizes such failures more visibly would align the benchmark results better with human judgement.

We see the most fundamental need for improvement in the datasets. Obviously, one could explicitly collect and add cases of relevant temporal patterns to the training datasets. In particular, it would be possible to have multiple validation datasets tailored towards effects that might be considered relevant, such as appearing objects, motion and interactions. In this way, one can quantitatively judge how well new models incorporate effects that researchers consider relevant for understanding behaviour, but that are rare in the usual training datasets.

Finally, we introduced a meta-benchmark derived from existing datasets that allows to quantify the ability of models to handle those temporal effects much better: Instead of averaging performances over all frames, we only consider frames in which the information gain of our model is more than 1bit smaller than the gold standard. As our model cannot learn temporal patterns, only frames are discarded in which spatial information is sufficient. The low performance of existing models on this meta-dataset confirms our previous analysis. We will make a list of the frames we considered in this study available. In the future, our proposed benchmark could be improved by considering more datasets and by improving our spatial baseline model.

Acknowledgements. This work was supported by the German Federal Ministry of Education and Research (BMBF): Tübingen AI Center, FKZ: 01IS18039A and the Deutsche Forschungsgemeinschaft (DFG, German Research Foundation): Germany's Excellence Strategy – EXC 2064/1 – 390727645 and SFB 1233, Robust Vision: Inference Principles and Neural Mechanisms, TP 3, project number: 276693517. The authors thank the International Max Planck Research School for Intelligent Systems (IMPRS-IS) for supporting Matthias Tangemann.

References

1. Ba, J.L., Kiros, J.R., Hinton, G.E.: Layer Normalization. arXiv:1607.06450 [cs, stat], July 2016
2. Bak, C., Kocak, A., Erdem, E., Erdem, A.: Spatio-temporal saliency networks for dynamic saliency prediction. IEEE Trans. Multimed **20**(7), 1688–1698 (2018). https://doi.org/10.1109/TMM.2017.2777665
3. Bazzani, L., Larochelle, H., Torresani, L.: Recurrent mixture density network for spatiotemporal visual attention. In: ICLR 2017 (2017)
4. Borji, A., Itti, L.: State-of-the-art in visual attention modeling. IEEE Trans. Pattern Anal. Mach. Intell. **35**(1), 185–207 (2013). https://doi.org/10.1109/TPAMI.2012.89
5. Bylinskii, Z., et al.: MIT saliency benchmark. http://saliency.mit.edu/
6. Bylinskii, Z., et al.: Learning visual importance for graphic designs and data visualizations. In: Proceedings of the 30th Annual ACM Symposium on User Interface Software and Technology, UIST 2017, pp. 57–69. ACM, New York (2017). https://doi.org/10.1145/3126594.3126653
7. Cichy, R.M., Kaiser, D.: Deep neural networks as scientific models. Trends Cogn. Sci. **23**(4), 305–317 (2019). https://doi.org/10.1016/j.tics.2019.01.009
8. Dorr, M., Martinetz, T., Gegenfurtner, K.R., Barth, E.: Variability of eye movements when viewing dynamic natural scenes. J. Vis. **10**(10), 28–28 (2010). https://doi.org/10.1167/10.10.28
9. Eysenck, M.W., Keane, M.T.: Cognitive Psychology: A Student's Handbook, vol. 6. Psychology Press, London (2010)
10. Fang, Y., Lin, W., Chen, Z., Tsai, C.M., Lin, C.W.: A video saliency detection model in compressed domain. IEEE Trans. Circuits Syst. Video Technol. **24**(1), 27–38 (2014). https://doi.org/10.1109/TCSVT.2013.2273613
11. Guo, C., Zhang, L.: A novel multiresolution spatiotemporal saliency detection model and its applications in image and video compression. IEEE Trans. Image Process. **19**(1), 185–198 (2010). https://doi.org/10.1109/TIP.2009.2030969
12. He, S., Tavakoli, H.R., Borji, A., Mi, Y., Pugeault, N.: Understanding and visualizing deep visual saliency models. In: The IEEE Conference on Computer Vision and Pattern Recognition (CVPR), pp. 10206–10215, June 2019
13. Hossein Khatoonabadi, S., Vasconcelos, N., Bajic, I.V., Shan, Y.: How many bits does it take for a stimulus to be salient? In: The IEEE Conference on Computer Vision and Pattern Recognition (CVPR), pp. 5501–5510, June 2015

14. Hou, X., Zhang, L.: Dynamic visual attention: searching for coding length increments. In: Koller, D., Schuurmans, D., Bengio, Y., Bottou, L. (eds.) Advances in Neural Information Processing Systems 21, pp. 681–688. Curran Associates, Inc. (2009)

15. Huang, X., Shen, C., Boix, X., Zhao, Q.: SALICON: reducing the semantic gap in saliency prediction by adapting deep neural networks. In: The IEEE International Conference on Computer Vision (ICCV), pp. 262–270, December 2015

16. Itti, L.: Quantifying the contribution of low-level saliency to human eye movements in dynamic scenes. Visual Cogn. **12**(6), 1093–1123 (2005). https://doi.org/10.1080/13506280444000661

17. Itti, L., Koch, C.: Computational modelling of visual attention. Nat. Rev. Neurosci. **2**(3), 194–203 (2001). https://doi.org/10.1038/35058500

18. Itti, L., Koch, C., Niebur, E.: A model of saliency-based visual attention for rapid scene analysis. IEEE Trans. Pattern Anal. Mach. Intell. **20**(11), 1254–1259 (1998). https://doi.org/10.1109/34.730558

19. Jiang, L., Xu, M., Liu, T., Qiao, M., Wang, Z.: DeepVS: a deep learning based video saliency prediction approach. In: Ferrari, V., Hebert, M., Sminchisescu, C., Weiss, Y. (eds.) Computer Vision – ECCV 2018. LNCS, vol. 11218, pp. 625–642. Springer, Cham (2018). https://doi.org/10.1007/978-3-030-01264-9_37

20. Jiang, L., Xu, M., Wang, Z.: Predicting Video Saliency with Object-to-Motion CNN and Two-layer Convolutional LSTM. arXiv:1709.06316 [cs], September 2017

21. Jost, T., Ouerhani, N., von Wartburg, R., Müri, R., Hügli, H.: Assessing the contribution of color in visual attention. Comput. Vis. Image Underst. **100**(1–2), 107–123 (2005). https://doi.org/10.1016/j.cviu.2004.10.009

22. Judd, T., Durand, F., Torralba, A.: A benchmark of computational models of saliency to predict human fixations. MIT Technical report, January 2012

23. Kingma, D.P., Ba, J.: Adam: a method for stochastic optimization. In: ICLR 2015, May 2015

24. Kümmerer, M., Theis, L., Bethge, M.: Deep gaze I: boosting saliency prediction with feature maps trained on ImageNet. In: ICLR Workshops 2015, May 2015

25. Kümmerer, M., Wallis, T.S.A., Bethge, M.: Information-theoretic model comparison unifies saliency metrics. Proc. Natl. Acad. Sci. **112**(52), 16054–16059 (2015). https://doi.org/10.1073/pnas.1510393112

26. Kümmerer, M., Wallis, T.S.A., Bethge, M.: Saliency benchmarking made easy: separating models, maps and metrics. In: Ferrari, V., Hebert, M., Sminchisescu, C., Weiss, Y. (eds.) ECCV 2018. LNCS, vol. 11220, pp. 798–814. Springer, Cham (2018). https://doi.org/10.1007/978-3-030-01270-0_47

27. Kümmerer, M., Wallis, T.S., Gatys, L.A., Bethge, M.: Understanding low- and high-level contributions to fixation prediction. In: The IEEE International Conference on Computer Vision (ICCV), pp. 4799–4808, October 2017

28. Lai, Q., Wang, W., Sun, H., Shen, J.: Video saliency prediction using spatiotemporal residual attentive networks. IEEE Trans. Image Process. **29**, 1113–1126 (2020). https://doi.org/10.1109/TIP.2019.2936112

29. Le Meur, O., Baccino, T.: Methods for comparing scanpaths and saliency maps: strengths and weaknesses. Behav. Res. Methods **45**(1), 251–266 (2013). https://doi.org/10.3758/s13428-012-0226-9

30. Leborán, V., García-Díaz, A., Fdez-Vidal, X.R., Pardo, X.M.: Dynamic whitening saliency. IEEE Trans. Pattern Anal. Mach. Intell. **39**(5), 893–907 (2017). https://doi.org/10.1109/TPAMI.2016.2567391

31. Linardos, P., Mohedano, E., Nieto, J.J., O'Connor, N.E., Giro-i-Nieto, X., McGuinness, K.: Simple vs complex temporal recurrences for video saliency prediction. In: British Machine Vision Conference (BMVC), September 2019
32. Mathe, S., Sminchisescu, C.: Actions in the eye: dynamic gaze datasets and learnt saliency models for visual recognition. IEEE Trans. Pattern Anal. Mach. Intell. **37**(7), 1408–1424 (2015). https://doi.org/10.1109/TPAMI.2014.2366154
33. Min, K., Corso, J.J.: TASED-Net: temporally-aggregating spatial encoder-decoder network for video saliency detection. In: The IEEE International Conference on Computer Vision (ICCV), pp. 2394–2403, October 2019
34. Mital, P.K., Smith, T.J., Hill, R.L., Henderson, J.M.: Clustering of gaze during dynamic scene viewing is predicted by motion. Cogn. Comput. **3**(1), 5–24 (2011). https://doi.org/10.1007/s12559-010-9074-z
35. Pan, J., et al.: SalGAN: visual saliency prediction with generative adversarial networks. arXiv:1701.01081 [cs], January 2017
36. Peters, R.J., Iyer, A., Itti, L., Koch, C.: Components of bottom-up gaze allocation in natural images. Vision. Res. **45**(18), 2397–2416 (2005). https://doi.org/10.1016/j.visres.2005.03.019
37. Rajashekar, U., Cormack, L.K., Bovik, A.C.: Point-of-gaze analysis reveals visual search strategies. In: Human Vision and Electronic Imaging IX, vol. 5292, pp. 296–306. International Society for Optics and Photonics, June 2004. https://doi.org/10.1117/12.537118
38. Ren, Z., Gao, S., Chia, L.T., Rajan, D.: Regularized feature reconstruction for spatio-temporal saliency detection. IEEE Trans. Image Process. **22**(8), 3120–3132 (2013). https://doi.org/10.1109/TIP.2013.2259837
39. Rosenholtz, R.: A simple saliency model predicts a number of motion popout phenomena. Vision. Res. **39**(19), 3157–3163 (1999). https://doi.org/10.1016/S0042-6989(99)00077-2
40. Rudoy, D., Goldman, D.B., Shechtman, E., Zelnik-Manor, L.: Learning video saliency from human gaze using candidate selection. In: The IEEE Conference on Computer Vision and Pattern Recognition (CVPR), pp. 1147–1154, June 2013
41. Seo, H.J., Milanfar, P.: Static and space-time visual saliency detection by self-resemblance. J. Vis. **9**(12), 15–15 (2009). https://doi.org/10.1167/9.12.15
42. Simonyan, K., Zisserman, A.: Very deep convolutional networks for large-scale image recognition. In: ICLR 2015, May 2015
43. Sun, Z., Wang, X., Zhang, Q., Jiang, J.: Real-time video saliency prediction via 3d residual convolutional neural network. IEEE Access **7**, 147743–147754 (2019). https://doi.org/10.1109/ACCESS.2019.2946479
44. Tatler, B.W.: The central fixation bias in scene viewing: selecting an optimal viewing position independently of motor biases and image feature distributions. J. Vis. **7**(14), 4–4 (2007). https://doi.org/10.1167/7.14.4
45. Treisman, A.M., Gelade, G.: A feature-integration theory of attention. Cogn. Psychol. **12**(1), 97–136 (1980). https://doi.org/10.1016/0010-0285(80)90005-5
46. Vig, E., Dorr, M., Cox, D.: Large-scale optimization of hierarchical features for saliency prediction in natural images. In: The IEEE Conference on Computer Vision and Pattern Recognition (CVPR), pp. 2798–2805 (2014)
47. Wang, W., Shen, J., Guo, F., Cheng, M.M., Borji, A.: Revisiting video saliency: a large-scale benchmark and a new model. In: The IEEE Conference on Computer Vision and Pattern Recognition (CVPR), pp. 4894–4903, June 2018
48. Wang, W., et al.: Learning unsupervised video object segmentation through visual attention. In: The IEEE Conference on Computer Vision and Pattern Recognition (CVPR), pp. 3064–3074, June 2019

49. Wilming, N., Betz, T., Kietzmann, T.C., König, P.: Measures and limits of models of fixation selection. PLoS ONE **6**(9), e24038 (2011). https://doi.org/10.1371/journal.pone.0024038
50. Wu, X., Wu, Z., Zhang, J., Ju, L., Wang, S.: SalSAC: a video saliency prediction model with shuffled attentions and correlation-based ConvLSTM. In: Thirty-Fourth AAAI Conference on Artificial Intelligence. AAAI Press, February 2020
51. Zhang, L., Tong, M.H., Cottrell, G.W.: SUNDAy: saliency using natural statistics for dynamic analysis of scenes. In: Proceedings of the 31st Annual Meeting of the Cognitive Science Society, pp. 2944–2949. AAAI Press, Cambridge (2009)
52. Zhong, S.h., Liu, Y., Ren, F., Zhang, J., Ren, T.: Video saliency detection via dynamic consistent spatio-temporal attention modelling. In: Twenty-Seventh AAAI Conference on Artificial Intelligence. AAAI Press, July 2013
53. Zhou, F., Bing Kang, S., Cohen, M.F.: Time-mapping using space-time saliency. In: The IEEE Conference on Computer Vision and Pattern Recognition (CVPR), pp. 3358–3365, June 2014

Searching Efficient 3D Architectures
with Sparse Point-Voxel Convolution

Haotian Tang[1], Zhijian Liu[1(✉)], Shengyu Zhao[1,2], Yujun Lin[1], Ji Lin[1],
Hanrui Wang[1], and Song Han[1]

[1] Massachusetts Institute of Technology, Cambridge, USA
{zhijian,songhan}@mit.edu
[2] IIIS, Tsinghua University, Beijing, China

Abstract. Self-driving cars need to understand 3D scenes efficiently and
accurately in order to drive safely. Given the limited hardware resources,
existing 3D perception models are not able to recognize small instances
(*e.g.*, pedestrians, cyclists) very well due to the low-resolution voxelization and aggressive downsampling. To this end, we propose *Sparse Point-
Voxel Convolution (SPVConv)*, a lightweight 3D module that equips the
vanilla Sparse Convolution with the high-resolution point-based branch.
With negligible overhead, this point-based branch is able to preserve
the fine details even from large outdoor scenes. To explore the spectrum of efficient 3D models, we first define a flexible architecture design
space based on SPVConv, and we then present *3D Neural Architecture
Search (3D-NAS)* to search the optimal network architecture over this
diverse design space efficiently and effectively. Experimental results validate that the resulting SPVNAS model is fast and accurate: it outperforms the state-of-the-art MinkowskiNet by 3.3%, ranking 1st on the
competitive SemanticKITTI leaderboard*. It also achieves 8−23× computation reduction and 3× measured speedup over MinkowskiNet and
KPConv with higher accuracy. Finally, we transfer our method to 3D
object detection, and it achieves consistent improvements over the one-
stage detection baseline on KITTI.

1 Introduction

3D perception models have received increased attention as they serve as the eyes
of autonomous driving systems: *i.e.*, they are used to understand the semantics
of the scenes to parse the drivable area (*e.g.*, roads, parking areas). As the
safety of the passenger is the top priority of the self-driving cars, 3D perception
models are required to achieve *high accuracy and low latency*. Also, the hardware

---

H. Tang and Z. Liu—indicates equal contributions; order determined by a coin toss.
* https://competitions.codalab.org/competitions/20331#results.

Electronic supplementary material The online version of this chapter (https://
doi.org/10.1007/978-3-030-58604-1_41) contains supplementary material, which is
available to authorized users.

© Springer Nature Switzerland AG 2020
A. Vedaldi et al. (Eds.): ECCV 2020, LNCS 12373, pp. 685–702, 2020.
https://doi.org/10.1007/978-3-030-58604-1_41

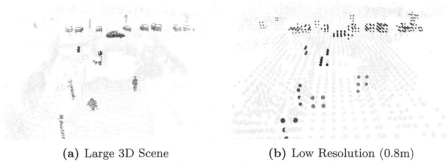

(a) Large 3D Scene   (b) Low Resolution (0.8m)

Fig. 1. Small instances (e.g., pedestrians and cyclists) are hard to be recognized at a low resolution (due to the coarse voxelization or the aggressive downsampling).

resources on the self-driving cars are tightly constrained by the form factor (since we do not want a whole trunk of workstations) and heat dissipation; therefore, it is crucial to design efficient 3D models with *low computational resource, e.g.,* memory.

Researchers have mainly exploited two 3D data representations: point cloud and rasterized voxel grids. As analyzed in Liu *et al.* [22], point-based methods [18,29,32] waste up to 90% of their time on structuring the irregular data, not on the actual feature extraction. On the other hand, voxel-based methods usually suffer from the low resolution: the resolution of dense voxels [22,25] is strictly constrained by the memory; the sparse voxels [6,9] require aggressive downsampling to achieve larger receptive field, leading to low resolution at deeper layers. With low resolution (see Fig. 1), multiple points or even multiple small objects may be merged into one grid and become indistinguishable. In this case, small instances (*e.g.*, pedestrians and cyclists) are at a disadvantage compared to large objects (*e.g.*, cars). Therefore, the effectiveness of previous 3D modules is discounted when the hardware resource is limited and resolution is low.

To tackle these problems, we propose a new 3D module, *Sparse Point-Voxel Convolution (SPVConv)* that introduces a low-cost high-resolution point-based stream to the vanilla Sparse Convolution, which helps to capture the fine details. On top of the new SPVConv module, we further present *3D Neural Architecture Search (3D-NAS)* to search an efficient network architecture. We refer our whole framework as *Sparse Point-Voxel Neural Architecture Search (SPVNAS)*. Fine-grained channel numbers in the search space allow us to explore efficient models; progressive depth shrinking is introduced for training SPVNAS with elastic depth stably. Experimental results validate that our model is fast and accurate: compared to MinkowskiNet, it improves the accuracy by 3.3% with lower latency. It also achieves **8–23×** computation reduction and **3×** measured speedup over MinkowskiNet and KPConv, while offering higher accuracy. We also transfer our method to KITTI for 3D object detection and achieve consistent improvements over previous one-stage detection baseline.

The contribution of this paper has three aspects:

1. We design a lightweight 3D module, SPVConv, that pays attention to both local fine details and neighborhood relationship. It boosts the accuracy on small objects, which used to be challenging under limited hardware resource.
2. We boost the efficiency of the module by 3D-NAS: a fine-grained search space offers model efficiency balanced against accuracy; the progressive shrinking gets rid of re-training from scratch and reduces deployment complexity over various hardware platform and conditions.
3. Our method outperforms all previous methods with a large margin and ranks 1st on the competitive SemanticKITTI leaderboard. It can also be transferred to the object detection task and achieve consistent improvements.

2   Related Work

2.1   3D Perception Models

Increased attention has been paid to 3D deep learning, which is important for LiDAR perception in autonomous driving. Previous research [5,25,31,53,61] relied on the volumetric representation and vanilla 3D convolution to process the 3D data. Due to the *sparse* nature of 3D representation, the *dense* volumetric representation is inherently inefficient and it also inevitably introduces information loss. Therefore, later research [29] proposes to directly learn on 3D point cloud representation using a symmetric function. To improve the neighborhood modeling capability, researchers define point-based convolutions on the geometric [18,24,32,41,44,45,55,56] or semantic [52] neighborhood. There are also 3D models tailored for specific tasks such as detection [27,28,30,36–38,57,59] and instance segmentation [11,14,15,58] built upon these primitives.

Recently, some research started to pay attention to efficient 3D deep learning primitives. Riegler *et al.* [34], Wang *et al.* [49,50] and Lei *et al.* [16] proposed to reduce the memory footprint of volumetric representation using octrees. Liu *et al.* [22] analyzed the efficiency bottleneck of point-based deep learning methods and proposed Point-Voxel Convolution. Graham *et al.* [9] and Choy *et al.* [6] proposed Sparse Convolution which accelerates the volumetric convolution by skipping non-activated regions.

2.2   Neural Architecture Search

Designing neural networks is highly challenging and time-consuming. To alleviate the burden of manually designing neural networks [13,23,35,60], researchers have introduced neural architecture search (NAS) to automatically design the neural network with high accuracy using reinforcement learning [63,64] and evolutionary search [19]. A new wave of research starts to design efficient models with neural architecture search [42,43,54], which is very important for the mobile deployment. However, conventional frameworks require high computation cost (typically 10^4 GPU hours) and considerable CO^2 emission [40]. To this end, researchers have proposed different techniques to reduce the computation cost (to 10^2 GPU hours), such as differentiable architecture search [20], path-level binarization [4], single-path one-shot sampling [10], and weight sharing [2,17,39,46]. Besides, neural architecture search has also been used in compressing and accelerating neural networks, such as pruning [3,12,21] and quantization [10,47,48,51]. Most of these methods are tailored for 2D visual recognition, which has many well-defined search spaces [33]. To the best of our knowledge, neural architecture search for 3D deep learning is under-studied. Previous research on VNAS [62] only focus on 3D medical image segmentation, which is not suitable for general-purpose 3D deep learning.

Table 1. Point-Voxel Convolution [22] is not suitable for large 3D scenes. If processing with sliding windows, the large latency is not affordable for real-time applications. If taking the whole scene, the resolution is too coarse to capture useful information.

	Input	Voxel Size (m)	Latency (ms)	Mean IoU
PVConv [22]	Sliding Window	0.05	35640	–
	Entire Scene	0.78	146	39.0
SPVConv (Ours)	Entire Scene	0.05	**85**	**58.8**

3   SPVConv: Designing Effective 3D Modules

We revisit two recent 3D modules: Point-Voxel Convolution [22] and Sparse Convolution [6] and analyze their bottlenecks. We observe that both of them suffer from information loss (caused by coarse voxelization or aggressive downsampling) when the memory is constrained. To this end, we introduce *Sparse Point-Voxel Convolution (SPVConv)*, to effectively process the large 3D scene (as in Fig. 2).

3.1   Point-Voxel Convolution: Coarse Voxelization

Liu *et al.* [22] proposed Point-Voxel Convolution where the 3D input are represented in high-resolution points and convolution is applied over low-resolution voxel grids. Specifically, the point-based branch transforms each point individually, and the voxel-based branch convolves over the voxelized input from the point-based branch.

PVCNN (which is built upon Point-Voxel Convolution) can afford the resolution of at most 128 in its voxel-based branch on a single GPU (with 12 GB of memory). For a large outdoor scene (with size of 100m×100m×10m), each voxel grid will correspond to a fairly large area (with size of 0.8m×0.8m×0.1m). In this case, the small instances (*e.g.*, pedestrians) will only occupy a few voxel grids (see Fig. 1). From such few points, PVCNN can hardly learn any useful information from the voxel-based branch, leading to a relatively low performance (see Table 1). Alternatively, we can process the large 3D scenes piece by piece so that each sliding window is of smaller scale. In order to preserve the fine-grained information, we found empirically that the voxel size needs to be at least lower than 0.05m. In this case, we have to run PVCNN once for each of the 244 sliding windows, which will take 35 seconds to process a single scene. Such a large latency is not affordable for most real-time applications (*e.g.*, autonomous driving).

3.2 Sparse Convolution: Aggressive Downsampling

Volumetric convolution has always been considered inefficient and prohibitive to be scaled up. Lately, researchers proposed Sparse Convolution [6,9] that skips the non-activated regions to significantly reduce the memory consumption. More specifically, it first finds all active synapses (denoted as *kernel map*) between the input and output points; it then performs the convolution based on this kernel map. In order to keep the activation sparse, it only considers these output points that also belong to the input point cloud.

As such, Sparse Convolution can afford a much higher resolution than the vanilla volumetric convolution. However, the network cannot be very deep due to the limited computation resource. As a result, the network has to downsample very aggressively in order to achieve a sufficiently large receptive field, which is very lossy. For example, the state-of-the-art MinkowskiNet [6] gradually applies four downsampling layers to the input point cloud, after which, the voxel size will be $0.05 \times 2^4 = 0.8$m. Similar to Point-Voxel Convolution, this resolution is too coarse to capture the small instances (see Fig. 3).

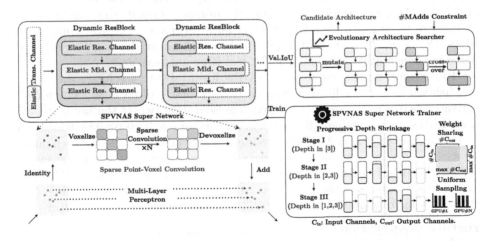

Fig. 2. Overview of SPVNAS: we first train a super network composed of SPVConv layers and supports elastic depth and width. Then, we perform computation-constrained 3D-NAS to obtain best candidate model.

3.3   Solution: Sparse Point-Voxel Convolution

In order to solve the problem of both modules, we present Sparse Point-Voxel Convolution as shown in Fig. 2. The point-based feature transformation branch **always** keeps high-resolution representation. The voxel-based branch applies Sparse Convolution to efficiently model over different receptive field size. Two branches communicate at negligible cost through sparse voxelization and devoxelization.

Our Sparse Point-Voxel Convolution operates on:

- sparse voxelized tensor representation $\boldsymbol{S} = \{(\boldsymbol{p}_m^s, \boldsymbol{f}_m^s), v\}$, where $\boldsymbol{p}_m^s = (\boldsymbol{x}_m^s, \boldsymbol{y}_m^s, \boldsymbol{z}_m^s)$ is the grid coordinates and $\boldsymbol{f}_m^s$ is the grid feature vector of m-th nonzero grid, v is the voxel size for one grid in the current layer;
- point cloud tensor representation $\boldsymbol{T} = \{(\boldsymbol{p}_k^t, \boldsymbol{f}_k^t)\}$, where $\boldsymbol{p}_k = (\boldsymbol{x}_k, \boldsymbol{y}_k, \boldsymbol{z}_k)$ is the point coordinates and $\boldsymbol{f}_k$ is point feature vector of k-th point.

Sparse Voxelization. We start from introducing the voxel-based neighborhood aggregation branch in Fig. 2. We first transform the high-resolution point cloud representation $\boldsymbol{T}$ to a sparse tensor $\boldsymbol{S}$ by sparse voxelization:

$$\hat{\boldsymbol{p}}_k^t = (\hat{\boldsymbol{x}}_k^t, \hat{\boldsymbol{y}}_k^t, \hat{\boldsymbol{z}}_k^t) = (\text{floor}(\boldsymbol{x}_k^t/v), \text{floor}(\boldsymbol{y}_k^t/v), \text{floor}(\boldsymbol{z}_k^t/v)), \tag{1}$$

$$\boldsymbol{f}_m^s = \frac{1}{N_m} \sum_{k=1}^{n} \mathbb{I}[\hat{\boldsymbol{x}}_k^t = \boldsymbol{x}_m^s, \hat{\boldsymbol{y}}_k^t = \boldsymbol{y}_m^s, \hat{\boldsymbol{z}}_k^t = \boldsymbol{z}_m^s] \cdot \boldsymbol{f}_k^t, \tag{2}$$

where $\mathbb{I}[\cdot]$ is the binary indicator of whether $\hat{\boldsymbol{p}}_k^t$ belongs to the voxel grid $\boldsymbol{p}_m^s$, and N_m is the normalization factor (*i.e.*, the number of points that fall in the m-th nonzero voxel grid). Such formulation, however, requires $\mathcal{O}(mn)$ complexity where $|\boldsymbol{S}| = m, |\boldsymbol{T}| = n$. With typical values of m, n at the order of 10^5, the naive implementation is impractical for real time applications.

To this end, we propose to use the GPU hash table to accelerate the sparse voxelization and devoxelization. Specifically, we first build a hash table for all activated points in the sparse voxelized representation (where the key is the 3D coordinates, and the value is the index in the sparse voxelized tensor), which can be finished in $\mathcal{O}(n)$ time. After that, we iterate over all points, and for each point, we use its coordinate as the key to query the corresponding index in the sparse voxelized representation. As the lookup over the hash table requires $\mathcal{O}(1)$ time in the worst case [26], this query step will in total take $\mathcal{O}(m)$ time. Therefore, the total time of coordinate indexing will be reduced from $\mathcal{O}(mn)$ to $\mathcal{O}(m + n)$.

Feature Aggregation. We then perform neighborhood feature aggregation on the sparse voxelized tensor using a sequence of Sparse Convolution residual blocks [6]. We parallelize the kernel map operation in Sparse Convolution (see Sect. 3.2) on GPU with the same hash table implementation in sparse voxelization, which offers 1.3× speedup over Choy *et al.*'s latest implementation. Both our method and the baseline have been upgraded to this accelerated implementation.

Sparse Devoxelization. With transformed neighborhood features and a sparse tensor representation, we hope to transform it back to the point-based representation so that information from both branches can be fused later. Similar to [22], we choose to interpolate a point's feature with its 8 neighbor voxel grids using trilinear interpolation instead of naive nearest interpolation.

Point Transformation and Feature Fusion. We directly apply MLP on each point to extract individual point features, and then fuse the outputs of two branches with an addition to combine the complementary information provided. Compared against Sparse Convolution, MLP layers only cost little computation overhead (4% in terms of #MACs) but introduce important fine details into the information flow.

4   3D-NAS: Searching Efficient 3D Architectures

Even with our module, designing an efficient neural network is still challenging. We need to carefully adjust the network architecture (*e.g.*, channel numbers and kernel sizes of all layers) to meet the constraints for real-world applications (*e.g.*, latency, energy, and accuracy). To this end, we introduce *3D Neural Architecture Search (3D-NAS)*, to automatically design efficient 3D models (as in Fig. 2).

4.1   Design Space

The performance of neural architecture search is greatly impacted by the design space quality. In our search space, we incorporate fine-grained channel numbers and elastic network depths; however, we do not support different kernel sizes.

Fine-grained Channel Numbers. The computation cost increases quadratically with the number of channels; therefore, the channel number selection has a large influence on the network efficiency. Most existing neural architecture frameworks [4] only support the coarse-grained channel number selection: *e.g.*, searching the expansion ratio of the ResNet/MobileNet blocks over a few (2–3) choices. In this case, only intermediate channel numbers of the blocks can be changed; while the input and output channel numbers will still remain the same. Empirically, we observe that this limits the variety of the search space. To this end, we enlarge the search space by allowing all channel numbers to be selected from a large collection of choices (with size of $O(n)$). This fine-grained channel number selection largely increase the number of candidates for each block: *e.g.*, from constant (2–3) to $\mathcal{O}(n^2)$ for a block with two consecutive convolutions.

Elastic Network Depths. We support different network depth in our design space. For 3D CNNs, reducing the channel numbers alone cannot achieve significant measured speedup, which is very different from the 2D CNNs. For example, by shrinking all channel numbers in MinkowskiNet [6] by 4× and 8×, the number of MACs will be reduced to 7.5 G and 1.9 G, respectively. However, although #MACs is drastically reduced, their measured latency on the GPU is very similar: 105 ms and 96 ms (measured on a single GTX 1080Ti GPU). This suggests that scaling down the number of channels cannot offer us with very efficient models, even though the number of MACs is very small. This might be because 3D modules are usually more memory-bounded than 2D modules; #MACs decreases quadratically with channel number, while memory decreases linearly. Motivated by this, we choose to incorporate the elastic network depth into our design space so that these layers with very small computation (and large memory cost) can be removed and merged into their neighboring layers.

Small Kernel Matters. Kernel sizes are usually included into the search space of 2D CNNs. This is because a single convolution with larger kernel size can be more efficient than multiple convolutions with smaller kernel sizes on GPUs. However, it is not the case for the 3D CNNs. From the computation perspective, a single 2D convolution with kernel size of 5 requires only 1.4× more MACs than two 2D convolutions with kernel sizes of 3; while a single 3D convolution with kernel size of 5 requires 2.3× more MACs than two 3D convolutions with kernel sizes of 3 (if applied to dense voxel grids). This larger computation cost makes it less suitable to use large kernel sizes in 3D CNNs. Furthermore, the computation overhead of 3D modules is also related to the kernel sizes. For example, Sparse Convolution [6,9] requires $\mathcal{O}(k^3n)$ time to build the kernel map, where k is the kernel size and n is the number of points, which indicates that its cost grows cubically with respect to the kernel size. Based on these reasons, we decide to keep the kernel size of all convolutions to be 3 and do not allow the kernel size to change in our search space. Even with the small kernel size, we can still achieve a large receptive field by changing the network depth, which can achieve the same effect as changing the kernel size.

4.2   Training Paradigm

Searching over a fine-grained design space is very challenging as it is impossible to train every sampled candidate network from scratch [42]. Motivated by Guo *et al.* [10], we incorporate all candidate networks into a single super network so that the total training cost can be reduced from $\mathcal{O}(n)$ to $\mathcal{O}(1)$: we train the super network once, and after that, each candidate network can be directly extracted from this super network with inherited weights.

Uniform Sampling. At each training iteration, we randomly sample a candidate network from the super network: randomly select the channel number for each layer, and then randomly select the network depth (*i.e.*the number of blocks to be used) for each stage. The total number of candidate networks to be sampled during training is very limited; therefore, we choose to sample different candidate networks on different GPUs and average their gradients at each step so that more candidate networks can be sampled. For 3D, this is more critical because the 3D datasets usually contain fewer training samples than the 2D datasets: *e.g.*20 K on SemanticKITTI [1] *vs.*1M on ImageNet [7].

Weight Sharing. As the total number of candidate networks is enormous, every candidate network will only be optimized for a small fraction of the total schedule. Therefore, uniform sampling alone is not enough to train all candidate networks sufficiently (*i.e.*, achieving the same level of accuracy as being trained from scratch). To this end, we adopt the weight sharing technique so that every candidate network can be optimized at each iteration even if it is not sampled. Specifically, given the input channel number C_{in} and output channel number C_{out} of each convolution layer, we simply index the first C_{in} and C_{out} channels from the weight tensor accordingly to perform the convolution [10]. For each batch normalization layer, we similarly crop the first c channels from the weight tensor based on the sampled channel number c. Finally, with the sampled depth d for each stage, we choose to keep the first d layers, instead of randomly sampling d of them. This ensures that each layer will always correspond to the same depth index within the stage.

Progressive Depth Shrinking. Suppose we have n stages, each of which has m different depth choices from 1 to m. If we sample the depth d_k for each stage k randomly, the expected total depth of the network will be

$$\mathbb{E}[d] = \sum_{k=1}^{n} \mathbb{E}[d_k] = n \times \frac{m+1}{2}, \tag{3}$$

which is much smaller than the maximum depth nm. Furthermore, the probability of the largest candidate network (with the maximum depth) being sampled is extremely small: m^{-n}. Therefore, the largest candidate networks are poorly trained due to the small possibility of being sampled. To this end, we introduce progressively shrinking the depth to alleviate this issue. We divide the training epochs into m segments for m different depth choices. During the kth training segment, we only allow the depth of each stage to be selected from $m - k + 1$ to m. This is essentially designed to enlarge the search space gradually so that these large candidate networks can be sampled more frequently.

4.3 Search Algorithm

After the super network is fully trained, we use evolutionary architecture search to find the best architectures under a certain resource constraint.

Resource Constraints. We use the number of MACs as the resource constraint. For the 3D CNNs, the number of MACs cannot be simply determined by the input size and network architecture: *e.g.*, Sparse Convolution only performs the computation over the active synapses; therefore, its computation is also related to the kernel map size, which is determined by the input sparsity pattern. To address this, we first estimate the average kernel map size over the entire dataset for each convolution layer, and we can then measure the number of MACs based on these statistics.

Evolutionary Search. We automate the architecture search with evolutionary algorithm [10]. We first initialize the starting population with n randomly sampled candidate networks. At each iteration, we evaluate all candidate networks in the population and select the k models with the highest accuracies (*i.e.*, the fittest individuals). The population for the next iteration is then generated with $(n/2)$ mutations and $(n/2)$ crossovers. For each mutation, we randomly pick one among the top-k candidates and alter each of its architectural parameters (*e.g.*, channel numbers, network depths) with a pre-defined probability; for each crossover, we select two from the top-k candidates and generate a new model by fusing them together randomly. Finally, the best model is obtained from the population of the last iteration. During the evolutionary search, we ensure that all the candidate networks in the population always meet the given resource constraint (otherwise, we will resample another candidate network until the resource constraint is satisfied).

5   Experiments

We conduct experiments on 3D semantic segmentation and 3D object detection for outdoor scenes. Benefit from our designed module (SPVConv) and neural architecture search framework (3D-NAS), our model (denoted as SPVNAS) consistently outperforms previous state-of-the-art methods with lower computation cost and measured latency (on an NVIDIA GTX1080Ti).

5.1   3D Scene Segmentation

We first evaluate our method on 3D semantic segmentation and conduct experiments on the large-scale outdoor scene dataset, SemanticKITTI [1]. This dataset contains 23,201 LiDAR point clouds for training and 20,351 for testing, and it is annotated from all 22 sequences in the KITTI [8] Odometry benchmark. We train all models on the entire training set and report the mean intersection-over-union (mIoU) on the official test set under the single scan setting. We provide more implementation details and experimental results in the appendix.

Results. As in Table 2, our SPVNAS outperforms the previous state-of-the-art MinkowskiNet [6] by **3.3%** in mIoU with 1.7× model size reduction, 1.5×

Table 2. Results of outdoor scene segmentation on SemanticKITTI: our SPVNAS outperforms the state-of-the-art MinkowskiNet with **2.7×** measured speedup.

	#Params (M)	#MACs (G)	Latency (ms)	Mean IoU
PointNet [29]	3.0	–	500	14.6
PointNet++ [32]	6.0	–	5900	20.1
PVCNN [22]	2.5	42.4	146	39.0
KPConv [45]	18.3	207.3	279	58.8
MinkowskiNet [6]	21.7	114.0	294	63.1
SPVNAS (Ours)	2.6	15.0	110	63.7
	12.5	73.8	259	**66.4**

computation reduction and 1.1× measured speedup. We further downscale our SPVNAS by setting the resource constraint to 15G MACs. This offers us with a much smaller model that outperforms MinkowskiNet by 0.6% in mIoU with **8.3×** model size reduction, **7.6×** computation reduction, and **2.7×** measured speedup. In Fig. 3, we also provide some qualitative comparisons between SPVNAS and MinkowskiNet: our SPVNAS has lower errors especially for small instances.

Table 3. Results of outdoor scene segmentation on SemanticKITTI: our SPVNAS outperforms the 2D projection-based DarkNets by more than **10%** in mIoU.

	#Params (M)	#MACs (G)	Latency (ms)	Mean IoU
DarkNet21Seg [1]	24.7	212.6	73	47.4
DarkNet53Seg [1]	50.4	376.3	102	49.9
SPVNAS (Ours)	1.1	8.9	89	**60.3**

We further compare our SPVNAS with 2D projection-based models in Table 3. With the smaller backbone (by removing the decoder layers), SPV-NAS outperforms DarkNets [1] by more than **10%** in mIoU with 1.2× measured speedup even though 2D convolutions are much better optimized by modern deep learning libraries. Furthermore, our SPVNAS achieves higher mIoU than KPConv [45], which is the previous state-of-the-art point-based model, with **17×** model size reduction, **23×** computation reduction and **3×** measured speedup.

5.2 3D Object Detection

We also evaluate our method on 3D object detection and conduct experiments on the popular outdoor scene dataset, KITTI [8]. We follow the generally adopted training-validation split, where 3,712 samples are used for training and 3,769 samples are left for validation. We report the mean average precision on the test split using the official evaluation code (with 40 recall positions) under 3D IoU theresholds of 0.7 for car, 0.5 for cyclist and pedestrian. We refer the readers to the appendix for additional results on the validation set.

Results. We compare our method against SECOND [57], the state-of-the-art single-stage model for 3D object detection. SECOND consists of a sparse encoder using 3D Sparse Convolutions and a region proposal network that performs 2D convolutions after projecting the encoded features to the bird's-eye view (BEV). We reimplement and retrain SECOND: our implementation already outperforms the results in the original paper [57]. As for our model, we only replace the 3D Sparse Convolutions in SECOND with our SPVConv while keeping all the other settings the same for fair comparison. As summarized in Table 4, our SPVCNN achieves significant improvement in cyclist detection, for which we argue that the high-resolution point-based branch carries more information for small instances.

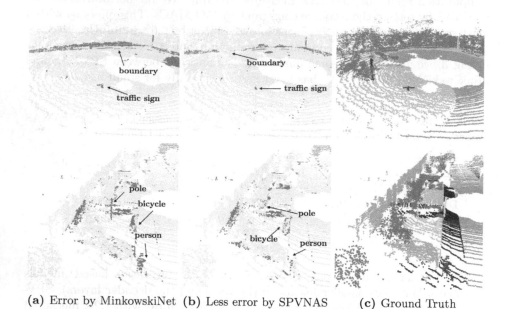

(a) Error by MinkowskiNet   (b) Less error by SPVNAS   (c) Ground Truth

Fig. 3. MinkowskiNet has a higher error recognizing small objects and region boundaries, while SPVNAS recognizes small objects better thanks to the high-resolution point-based branch.

Table 4. Results of outdoor object detection on KITTI: our SPVCNN outperforms SECOND in most categories especially for the cyclist.

	Car			Cyclist			Pedestrian		
	Easy	Mod	Hard	Easy	Mod	Hard	Easy	Mod	Hard
SECOND [57]	84.7	76.0	68.7	75.8	60.8	53.7	45.3	35.5	33.1
SECOND (Repro.)	87.5	77.9	74.4	76.0	59.7	52.9	49.1	**41.7**	**39.1**
SPVCNN (Ours)	**87.8**	**78.4**	**74.8**	**80.1**	**63.7**	**56.2**	**49.2**	41.4	38.4

6   Analysis

Our SPVNAS significantly outperforms the previous state of the art, MinkowskiNets with better efficiency. After carefully examining the per-class performance of both methods on the test split (Table 5), we find that SPVNAS has very large advantage (up to **25%**) on relatively small objects such as pedestrians and cyclists, which justifies our design of a high resolution point-based branch in SPVConv. In this section, we provide more detailed analysis on the effectiveness of SPVConv and also perform ablation experiments on our 3D-NAS pipeline to further explain the benefit of SPVNAS.

Table 5. Results of per-class performance on SemanticKITTI: SPVNAS has a large advantage on small objects, such as bicyclist and motorcyclist.

	Person	Bicycle	Bicyclist	Motorcycle	Motorcyclist
MinkowskiNet [6]	60.9	40.4	61.9	47.4	18.7
SPVNAS (Ours)	65.7	51.6	65.2	50.8	43.7
	(**+4.8**)	(**+11.2**)	(**+3.3**)	(**+3.4**)	(**+25.0**)

6.1 Sparse Point-Voxel Convolution

We analyze the effectiveness of SPVConv by comparing the *point* and *sparse-voxel* activations from the last SPVConv layer in SPVCNN. The model is trained on part of SemanticKITTI [1] training set with the ninth sequence left out for visualization. Specifically, we first calculate the norm of point/sparse voxel features from each point. Then, we rank the feature norms from both branches separately and define points with top 10% largest feature norm from each branch respectively as **activated** points of that branch. In Fig. 5 we show the top 50% activated points of the point-based branch with red color and all other points with gray color. Clearly, the point branch of our SPVCNN learns to attend to small objects such as pedestrians, cyclists, trunks and traffic signs. As a result, our method does achieve compelling performance on these small classes.

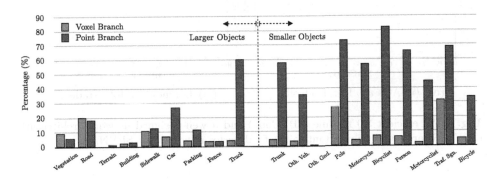

Fig. 4. Average percent of activated points on voxel/point branches from all 19 classes of SemanticKITTI [1] dataset: the point-branch attends to smaller objects as the red bar is much higher.

We also collect the statistics of class-wise averaged percentage for activated points from both point-based and sparse voxel-based branch in Fig. 4. On small objects, the percentage of activated points from the point-based branch is significantly higher than the sparse voxel-based branch. For some classes like the bicyclist, more than **80%** of its points are activated on the point branch, which validates that our observation in Fig. 5 is general.

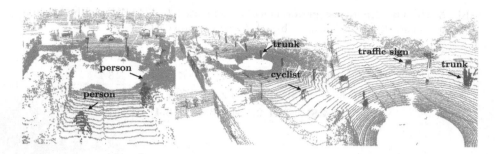

Fig. 5. The point-based branch learns to put its attention on small instances (*i.e.*, pedestrians, cyclists, traffic signs). Here, the points in red are the ones with the top 5% largest feature norm in the point-based branch. (Color figure online)

6.2 Architecture Search

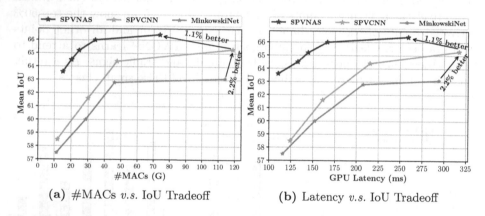

(a) #MACs *v.s.* IoU Tradeoff   (b) Latency *v.s.* IoU Tradeoff

Fig. 6. An efficient 3D module (SPVConv) and a well-designed network architecture (3D-NAS) are equally important to the final performance of our SPVNAS.

In Fig. 6 we show the MACs (Fig. 6a) and latency (Fig. 6b) tradeoff curves on SemanticKITTI [1]. Manually designed SPVCNN and MinkowskiNets with uniform channel shrinking are the baselines. Clearly, a better 3D module (SPVConv) and a well-designed network architecture contribute equally to the performance boost. Remarkably, the improvement over MinkowskiNets exceeds **6%** mIoU at 110 ms latency. We believe the improvement comes from the non-uniform channel scaling and depth selection in our 3D-NAS. In the original MinkowskiNets [6] or SPVCNN, 77% of the total MACs is concentrated on the upsampling stages. However, this ratio is reduced to 47% to 63% in 3D-NAS, making computation more balanced and downsampling stages more emphasized.

We also compare our evolutionary search method with random architecture search to prove that the succeed of 3D-NAS doesn't entirely come from the search space. As is shown in Fig. 7, random architecture search has poor sample efficiency in our search space: the best model at the 20th generation performs even worse than the best model in the 4th generation. In contrast, our evolutionary search is capable of progressively finding better architecture as iteration increases,

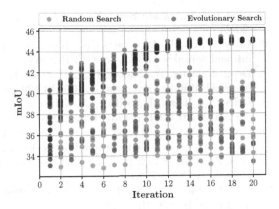

Fig. 7. Evolutionary Search has better sample efficiency comparing with Random Search.

and the final best architecture performs around 4% better than the best one in the first generation.

7 Conclusion

We present Sparse Point-Voxel Convolution (SPVConv), a novel module for efficient 3D deep learning, especially for small object recognition. With SPVCNN built upon the SPVConv module, we solve the problem that Sparse Convolution cannot always keep high resolution representation and that Point-Voxel Convolution doesn't scale up to large outdoor scenes. We then propose 3D-NAS, the first AutoML method for 3D scene understanding, to greatly improve the efficiency and performance of SPVCNN. Extensive experiments on outdoor 3D scene benchmarks demonstrates that SPVNAS models are lightweight, fast and powerful. We hope that this work will inspire more future research on efficient 3D deep learning model design.

Acknowledgement. We thank MIT Quest for Intelligence, MIT-IBM Watson AI Lab, Xilinx, Samsung for supporting this research. We also thank AWS Machine Learning Research Awards for providing the computational resource.

References

1. Behley, J., et al.: SemanticKITTI: a dataset for semantic scene understanding of LiDAR sequences. In: ICCV (2019)
2. Cai, H., Gan, C., Wang, T., Zhang, Z., Han, S.: Once for all: train one network and specialize it for efficient deployment. In: ICLR (2020)
3. Cai, H., et al.: AutoML for architecting efficient and specialized neural networks. IEEE Micro **40**(1), 75–82 (2019)
4. Cai, H., Zhu, L., Han, S.: ProxylessNAS: direct neural architecture search on target task and hardware. In: ICLR (2019)

5. Chang, A.X., et al.: ShapeNet: an information-rich 3D model repository. arXiv (2015)
6. Choy, C., Gwak, J., Savarese, S.: 4D spatio-temporal convNets: minkowski convolutional neural networks. In: CVPR (2019)
7. Deng, J., Dong, W., Socher, R., Li, L.J., Li, K., Fei-Fei, L.: ImageNet: a large-scale hierarchical image database. In: CVPR (2009)
8. Geiger, A., Lenz, P., Stiller, C., Urtasun, R.: Vision meets robotics: the KITTI dataset. IJRR **32**(11), 1231–1237 (2013)
9. Graham, B., Engelcke, M., van der Maaten, L.: 3D semantic segmentation with submanifold sparse convolutional networks. In: CVPR (2018)
10. Guo, Z., et al.: Single path one-shot neural architecture search with uniform sampling. In: ECCV (2020)
11. Han, L., Zheng, T., Xu, L., Fang, L.: OccuSeg: occupancy-aware 3D instance segmentation. In: CVPR (2020)
12. He, Y., Lin, J., Liu, Z., Wang, H., Li, L.J., Han, S.: AMC: autoML for model compression and acceleration on mobile devices. In: ECCV (2018)
13. Howard, A.G., et al.: MobileNets: efficient convolutional neural networks for mobile vision applications. arXiv (2017)
14. Jiang, L., Zhao, H., Shi, S., Liu, S., Fu, C.W., Jia, J.: PointGroup: dual-set point grouping for 3D instance segmentation. In: CVPR (2020)
15. Lahoud, J., Ghanem, B., Pollefeys, M., Oswald, M.R.: 3D instance segmentation via multi-task metric learning. In: ICCV (2019)
16. Lei, H., Akhtar, N., Mian, A.: Octree guided CNN with spherical kernels for 3D point clouds. In: CVPR (2019)
17. Li, M., Lin, J., Ding, Y., Liu, Z., Zhu, J.Y., Han, S.: GAN compression: efficient architectures for interactive conditional GANs. In: CVPR (2020)
18. Li, Y., Bu, R., Sun, M., Wu, W., Di, X., Chen, B.: PointCNN: convolution on $\mathcal{X}$-transformed points. In: NeurIPS (2018)
19. Liu, C., et al.: Progressive neural architecture search. In: ECCV (2018)
20. Liu, H., Simonyan, K., Yang, Y.: DARTS: differentiable architecture search. In: ICLR (2019)
21. Liu, Z., et al.: MetaPruning: meta learning for automatic neural network channel pruning. In: ICCV (2019)
22. Liu, Z., Tang, H., Lin, Y., Han, S.: Point-voxel CNN for efficient 3D deep learning. In: NeurIPS (2019)
23. Ma, N., Zhang, X., Zheng, H.T., Sun, J.: ShuffleNet v2: practical guidelines for efficient CNN architecture design. In: ECCV (2018)
24. Mao, J., Wang, X., Li, H.: Interpolated convolutional networks for 3D point cloud understanding. In: ICCV (2019)
25. Maturana, D., Scherer, S.: VoxNet: a 3D convolutional neural network for real-time object recognition. In: IROS (2015)
26. Pagh, R., Rodler, F.F.: Cuckoo hashing. J. Algorithms **51**(2), 122–144 (2001)
27. Qi, C.R., Chen, X., Litany, O., Guibas, L.J.: ImVoteNet: boosting 3D object detection in point clouds with image votes. In: CVPR (2020)
28. Qi, C.R., Litany, O., He, K., Guibas, L.J.: Deep hough voting for 3D object detection in point clouds. In: ICCV (2019)
29. Qi, C.R., Su, H., Mo, K., Guibas, L.J.: PointNet: deep learning on point sets for 3D classification and segmentation. In: CVPR (2017)
30. Qi, C.R., Liu, W., Wu, C., Su, H., Guibas, L.J.: Frustum pointNets for 3D object detection from RGB-D data. In: CVPR (2018)

31. Qi, C.R., Su, H., Niessner, M., Dai, A., Yan, M., Guibas, L.J.: Volumetric and multi-view CNNs for object classification on 3D data. In: CVPR (2016)
32. Qi, C.R., Yi, L., Su, H., Guibas, L.J.: PointNet++: deep hierarchical feature learning on point sets in a metric space. In: NeurIPS (2017)
33. Radosavovic, I., Johnson, J., Xie, S., Lo, W.Y., Dollar, P.: On network design spaces for visual recognition. In: ICCV (2019)
34. Riegler, G., Ulusoy, A.O., Geiger, A.: OctNet: learning deep 3D representations at high resolutions. In: CVPR (2017)
35. Sandler, M., Howard, A., Zhu, M., Zhmoginov, A., Chen, L.C.: MobileNetV2: inverted residuals and linear bottlenecks. In: CVPR (2018)
36. Shi, S., et al.: PV-RCNN: point-voxel feature set abstraction for 3D object detection. In: CVPR (2020)
37. Shi, S., Wang, X., Li, H.: PointRCNN: 3D object proposal generation and detection from point cloud. In: CVPR (2019)
38. Shi, S., Wang, Z., Shi, J., Wang, X., Li, H.: PV-RCNN: point-voxel feature set abstraction for 3D object detection. In: TPAMI (2020)
39. Stamoulis, D., et al.: Single-path NAS: designing hardware-efficient convNets in less than 4 hours. In: Brefeld, U., Fromont, E., Hotho, A., Knobbe, A., Maathuis, M., Robardet, C. (eds.) ECML PKDD 2019. LNCS (LNAI), vol. 11907, pp. 481–497. Springer, Cham (2020). https://doi.org/10.1007/978-3-030-46147-8_29
40. Strubell, E., Ganesh, A., McCallum, A.: Energy and policy considerations for deep learning in NLP. In: ACL (2019)
41. Su, H., et al.: SPLATNet: sparse lattice networks for point cloud processing. In: CVPR (2018)
42. Tan, M., et al.: MnasNet: platform-aware neural architecture search for mobile. In: CVPR (2019)
43. Tan, M., Le, Q.V.: EfficientNet: rethinking model scaling for convolutional neural networks. In: ICML (2019)
44. Tatarchenko, M., Park, J., Koltun, V., Zhou, Q.Y.: Tangent convolutions for dense prediction in 3D. In: CVPR (2018)
45. Thomas, H., Qi, C.R., Deschaud, J.E., Marcotegui, B., Goulette, F., Guibas, L.J.: KPConv: flexible and deformable convolution for point clouds. In: ICCV (2019)
46. Wang, H., et al.: HAT: hardware-aware transformers for efficient natural language processing. In: ACL (2020)
47. Wang, K., Liu, Z., Lin, Y., Lin, J., Han, S.: HAQ: hardware-aware automated quantization with mixed precision. In: CVPR (2019)
48. Wang, K., Liu, Z., Lin, Y., Lin, J., Han, S.: Hardware-centric autoML for mixed-precision quantization. Int. J. Comput. Vis. 128(8), 2035–2048 (2020). https://doi.org/10.1007/s11263-020-01339-6
49. Wang, P.S., Liu, Y., Guo, Y.X., Sun, C.Y., Tong, X.: O-CNN: octree-based convolutional neural networks for 3D shape analysis. SIGGRAPH 36(4), 1–11 (2017)
50. Wang, P.S., Liu, Y., Guo, Y.X., Sun, C.Y., Tong, X.: Adaptive O-CNN: a patch-based deep representation of 3D shapes. SIGGRAPH Asia 37(6), 1–11 (2018)
51. Wang, T., et al.: APQ: joint search for network architecture, pruning and quantization policy. In: CVPR (2020)
52. Wang, Y., Sun, Y., Liu, Z., Sarma, S.E., Bronstein, M.M., Solomon, J.M.: Dynamic graph CNN for learning on point clouds. SIGGRAPH 38(5), 1–12 (2019)
53. Wang, Z., Lu, F.: VoxSegNet: volumetric CNNs for semantic part segmentation of 3D shapes. TVCG (2019)
54. Wu, B., et al.: Fbnet: hardware-aware efficient convnet design via differentiable neural architecture search. In: CVPR (2019)

55. Wu, W., Qi, Z., Fuxin, L.: PointConv: deep convolutional networks on 3D point clouds. In: CVPR (2019)
56. Xu, Y., Fan, T., Xu, M., Zeng, L., Qiao, Y.: SpiderCNN: deep learning on point sets with parameterized convolutional filters. In: ECCV (2018)
57. Yan, Y., Mao, Y., Li, B.: SECOND: sparsely embedded convolutional detection. Sensors 18(10), 3337 (2018)
58. Yang, B., et al.: Learning object bounding boxes for 3D instance segmentation on point clouds. In: NeurIPS (2019)
59. Yang, Z., Sun, Y., Liu, S., Shen, X., Jia, J.: STD: sparse-to-dense 3D object detector for point cloud. In: ICCV (2019)
60. Zhang, X., Zhou, X., Lin, M., Sun, J.: ShuffleNet: an extremely efficient convolutional neural network for mobile devices. In: CVPR (2018)
61. Zhou, Y., Tuzel, O.: VoxelNet: end-to-end learning for point cloud based 3D object detection. In: CVPR (2018)
62. Zhu, Z., Liu, C., Yang, D., Yuille, A., Xu, D.: V-NAS: neural architecture search for volumetric medical image segmentation. In: 3DV (2019)
63. Zoph, B., Le, Q.V.: Neural architecture search with reinforcement learning. In: ICLR (2017)
64. Zoph, B., Vasudevan, V., Shlens, J., Le, Q.V.: Learning transferable architectures for scalable image recognition. In: CVPR (2018)

Towards Reliable Evaluation of Algorithms for Road Network Reconstruction from Aerial Images

Leonardo Citraro[✉], Mateusz Koziński, and Pascal Fua

Computer Vision Laboratory, École Polytechnique Fédérale de Lausanne (EPFL), Lausanne, Switzerland
{leonardo.citraro,mateusz.kozinski,pascal.fua}@epfl.ch

Abstract. Existing connectivity-oriented performance measures rank road delineation algorithms inconsistently, which makes it difficult to decide which one is best for a given application. We show that these inconsistencies stem from design flaws that make the metrics insensitive to whole classes of errors. This insensitivity is undesirable in metrics intended for capturing overall general quality of road reconstructions. In particular, the scores do not reflect the time needed for a human to fix the errors, because each one has to be fixed individually. To provide more reliable evaluation, we design three new metrics that are sensitive to all classes of errors. This sensitivity makes them more consistent even though they use very different approaches to comparing ground-truth and reconstructed road networks. We use both synthetic and real data to demonstrate this and advocate the use of these corrected metrics as a tool to gauge future progress.

1 Introduction

Reconstruction of road networks from aerial images is an old computer vision problem. It has been tackled almost since the inception of the field in the 1970s [4, 13, 26, 28]. Yet, it is still open and is addressed by many recent papers [5, 6, 9, 10, 19, 21–25, 33]. One pitfall however, is that the metrics used to gauge performance often prove to be inconsistent. It is not unusual for a method to perform well according to one popular metric and poorly according to another. Trusting to one single metric can therefore be misleading and can hamper progress.

This situation arises from the fact that assessing the quality of a road graph is hard. The quality assessment should not only depend on the spatial accuracy of the reconstructed road centerline but also on the topology of the network these centerlines form. The first is relatively easy to quantify while the second is much more difficult and there is no generally accepted way of doing it. This is because comparing the predicted topology to the ground truth one amounts

---

Electronic supplementary material The online version of this chapter (https://doi.org/10.1007/978-3-030-58604-1_42) contains supplementary material, which is available to authorized users.

A. Vedaldi et al. (Eds.): ECCV 2020, LNCS 12373, pp. 703–719, 2020.
https://doi.org/10.1007/978-3-030-58604-1_42

to solving a complex graph-matching problem for which no efficient algorithm exists. Current topology-aware metrics are therefore hand-crafted to perform a simplified comparison, with some constraints of the full graph-matching problem relaxed. They fall into three main categories: the metrics that compare the junctions, or road intersections, in the two graphs, ones that compare the lengths of the paths connecting random pairs of junctions, and ones that match small subgraphs. Unfortunately, as we will show, all these metrics correlate poorly with the number of topological discrepancies—missed road branches, unwarranted or missing connections—between the two graphs. This makes it hard to use them to reason about the number of mistakes present in a reconstruction and the cost of fixing them.

In this paper, we show that these inconsistencies arise from design flaws in currently popular metrics and propose ways to fix them. We incorporate these fixes into three topologically-aware metrics that capture a large range of errors and balance their contributions in the final score. We show that this makes them more consistent both with each other and with the number of topological discrepancies. Our contributions are therefore:

- An in-depth analysis of existing metrics that exposes their lack of sensitivity to certain types of errors and the resulting lack of consistency when using them to compare different algorithms.
- Three new measures free from this problem and that we advocate for future algorithm evaluation.

We make the code for computing our measures publically available. In the remainder of the paper, we first describe existing metrics and their shortcomings. We then introduce our new metrics and test them on synthetic and real data.

2   Existing Metrics

Road networks are often represented by graphs whose nodes have a double function. They serve as control points that enable modeling potentially curvy road segments and represent road intersections, and end points. Let us assume we are given a *predicted* graph and a *ground truth* graph, whose similarity we want to assess. Comparing these two networks that are similar, but not identical, is nontrivial. Doing this in a graph-theoretic way can be viewed as an NP-complete graph matching problem [30]. In this section, we review strategies commonly used to circumvent this problem.

One such approach is to first project the graphs to point clouds, by representing graph edges as sequences of closely spaced points, and then to evaluate the spatial overlap of these point clouds. Chamfer and Hausdorff measures may be employed to evaluate the sum and maximum of distances from each point in one set to its closest point in the second set. However, Chamfer and Hausdorff do not measure connectivity and are not sensitive to connectivity-oriented errors, like small gaps in roads, or predicting two closely spaced roads in place of a single real road. Such errors are common in road network reconstructions from aerial images, and that is why these metrics are typically not used to evaluate them.

Task-specific measures are used in some problems involving predicting graphs from images, but they do not generalize to the case of road networks. The DIA-DEM score [15], used for comparing reconstructions of neuronal morphologies, relies on the assumption that both graphs have tree-like topologies. The Rand index [2,14], used for comparing segmentations of neuronal cells in microscopy images, compares the presence or absence of connections between pixel pairs in the prediction and annotation. In road lane reconstruction [3,16,17,20], the evaluation involves comparing the number of predicted lanes to the number of the annotated ones. These comparisons are not well suited for city-scale road networks, which form a single connected component with thousands of loops.

In this paper, we focus specifically on metrics for evaluating connectivity of road networks reconstructed from aerial images. Several metrics have been developed for this purpose, and they can be classified into four main categories, depending on whether they are pixel-based, junction-based, path-based, or subgraph-based. We now review these four classes of existing metrics and argue that they *all* ignore particular type of errors.

2.1 Pixel-Based Metrics

Road delineation can be understood as foreground/background segmentation problem. The quality of the segmentation can be evaluated in terms of the *precision* $P = \frac{|TP|}{|PP|}$ and *recall* $R = \frac{|TP|}{|AP|}$, where PP is the set of pixels predicted to be foreground, AP is the set of pixel labeled as foreground, and TP = PP ∩ AP. When a single number is preferred, either the *intersection-over-union* IoU $= \frac{TP}{PP \cup AP}$, or the *f1-score* F1 $= 2/(\frac{1}{P} + \frac{1}{R})$ is used.

Correctness/Completeness/Quality (CCQ). To account for the fact that the position of the pixels estimated to be foreground might be slightly off, the definitions of precision and recall were relaxed in [29,32] to allow small shifts in pixel location. *correctness* is the relaxed precision, *completeness* the relaxed recall, and *quality* is the equivalent of intersection over union.

Discussion. **CCQ** is adequate to gauge segmentation quality but does not capture connectivity of the predicted road maps. This makes it insensitive to topological errors, for example, road breaks smaller than the allowed shift between the annotation and the prediction. We demonstrate this insensitivity experimentally in Sect. 4.1. The indifference of the pixel-based metrics to connectivity variations inspired the creation of the path- and junction-based metrics, described below.

2.2 Path-Based Metrics

The idea behind path-based metrics is that if two graphs are similar, so should paths connecting any pair of their nodes via a sequence of edges. Edges that appear in one graph and not in the other result in measurably different paths. There are two main ways to measure such differences.

*Too Long / Too Short (***TLTS***).* In [31], it was proposed to compare the length of the shortest path between randomly-chosen but corresponding pairs of nodes in the predicted and ground-truth networks. Here, and in the metrics that we describe below, the correspondences are found simply by randomly selecting a point in one graph and taking its closest point from the other graph. A path in the predicted graph is classified as *correct* if its length is within 5% of that of the path in the ground-truth graph, and as *too-long*, or *too-short* otherwise. A path is marked *infeasible* if its end points are not connected in the other network. The percentage of *correct* paths is used to assess the quality of a delineation and the other percentages serve to characterize the errors.

*Average Path Length Similarity (***APLS***).* The alternative to counting too long/short paths is aggregating path differences. This has been proposed first for evaluating road network reconstructions from GPS tracks [1,18] and, more recently, for image-based reconstructions [12], in the form of the Average Path Length Similarity score

$$1 - \frac{1}{|\mathcal{P}|} \sum_{(p^>,p^{est})\in\mathcal{P}} \min\left\{1, \frac{|l(p^>) - l(p^{est})|}{l(p^>)}\right\}, \tag{1}$$

where $p^>$ is a ground-truth path, p^{est} the corresponding predicted one and $l(.)$ denotes the path length. The set $\mathcal{P}$ is obtained by sampling pairs of points in one graph, retrieving the corresponding pairs in the other graph, and computing the shortest paths between them.

Discussion. **TLTS** and **APLS** are better at capturing topological differences than pixel-based scores, but they suffer from major flaws. Since both metrics rely on the comparison of the length of shortest paths, false positive roads that do not alter the length of these are completely neglected. Moreover, since paths are sampled independently, multiple paths from a graph can be compared to a single path in the other graph. This makes the scores insensitive to the errors made by predicting one road where many closely spaced roads exist and predicting more than one road where there is just one, as shown in Fig. 1.

2.3   Junction-Based Metric (JUNCT)

The path-based metrics capture the topological similarity indirectly. A more direct approach [5], is to compare the degree of corresponding nodes with at least three incident edges, called junctions. The correspondences are established greedily by matching closest nodes. For each ground-truth junction v that is matched to a predicted junction u, the per-junction recall $f_{v,correct}$ is taken to be the fraction of edges incident on v that are also captured around u. Similarly, the false discovery rate—one minus precision—$f_{u,error}$ is taken to be the fraction of edges incident on u that do not appear around v. For unmatched junctions, $f_{v,correct} = 0$ and $f_{u,error} = 1$, respectively. These per-junction scores are then aggregated

$$n_{\text{correct}} = \sum_{v \in \mathcal{V}} f_{v,\text{correct}} , \qquad\qquad n_{\text{error}} = \sum_{u \in \mathcal{U}} f_{u,\text{error}} ,$$

$$F_{\text{correct}} = \frac{n_{\text{correct}}}{|\mathcal{V}|} , \qquad \text{and} \qquad F_{\text{error}} = \frac{n_{\text{error}}}{n_{\text{error}} + n_{\text{correct}}} ,$$

where $|\mathcal{V}|$ is the number of ground-truth junctions.

Discussion. The main issue with **JUNCT** is that it only accounts for nodes with three or more incident edges. This disregards what happens at road end points and makes the metric insensitive to interruptions in predicted networks. In other words, a predicted network where all the roads are broken in the middle still receives a perfect score. Moreover, a node that lacks $k - 2$ out of its k incident edges is penalized more than any other, because it is no longer considered a junction. This amounts to saying that a road junction with only two correctly predicted incident roads is completely misclassified, a conclusion that is hard to justify. The top of Fig. 2 illustrates this problem: An edge is missing from a junction with three incident edges, which results in $n_{\text{correct}} = \frac{0}{3}$ instead of $\frac{2}{3}$.

2.4 Subgraph-Based Metric (SUBG)

In [7], it is suggested to compare the sets of locations accessible by traveling a predefined distance away from corresponding points in two graphs. To this end, a starting location is randomly selected in the ground truth network, and its closest point in the predicted network is identified. Then, local subgraphs are extracted by a breadth-first exploration of the graphs away from the starting locations. The computation of the score is based on spatial coincidence of 'control points' inserted at regular intervals to the subgraphs. A control point is considered to be matched, or a true positive, if it lies sufficiently close to a control point in the other network. Unmatched control points in the predicted, and annotated subgraphs are treated as false positives and false negatives, respectively. Sampling and matching of local subgraphs is repeated many times, and precision and recall are computed from the total counts of matched and unmatched control points.

Discussion. As the starting point is always sampled from the ground truth network, the false positive roads that are sufficiently far from any ground truth road are not covered by control points. In consequence, **SUBG** is not sensitive to such errors. Moreover, since multiple control points of the ground truth network can be matched to the same control point in the prediction, errors consisting in predicting just one instead of two closely spaced roads go unnoticed.

2.5 Summary

One might imagine that the metrics were deliberately designed to expose some errors and suppress the others in the interest of some specific application. However, no trace of such intentions can be found in the original publications. All the

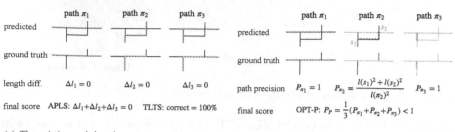

(a) The existing path length statistics **TLTS**, **APLS**. Both sampled paths (green) and their matches (cyan) overlap. As a result, the scores do not capture the difference between the networks.

(b) Our new path-based score (**OPT-P**). Paths do not overlap and the score captures the difference between the networks.

Fig. 1. A comparison of (a) the existing path-based statistics and (b) our new path score. Three paths are sampled from the predicted network (overlayed in green), and matched to the ground truth network (the matching chains are highlighted in cyan). The unmatched parts of the paths are highlighted in red. Removed parts of the networks are shown in dotted gray. See Sect. 2.2 for the definition of the **APLS** and **TLTS** and Sect. 3.1 for **OPT-P**. (Color figure online)

studied metrics were proposed for general-purpose evaluation of road network reconstructions, their insensitivity was never reported before, and seems to be an artifact of relaxing the underlying graph-matching problem to independent comparison of junctions, paths, and subgraphs. In many cases, the insensitivity is not immediately obvious from the design of the metric alone, and in Sect. 4.1 we propose a benchmark dataset for exposing it. In Sect. 3, we show that these flaws can be removed by careful metric design.

3   New Metrics

In Sect. 2, we identified weaknesses of existing metrics that make them insensitive to whole classes of errors, such as producing unwarranted breaks and spurious roads, or merging parallel but distinct roads. Here, we introduce new metrics that are sensitive to *all* these errors.

3.1   Path-Based Metric (OPT-P)

In Sect. 2.2 we argued that **TLTS** [31] and **APLS** [12] are insensitive to false positive predictions that do not affect the length of the shortest paths, for example, ones that run close to other predicted roads. We illustrate such a case in the left part of Fig. 1. We therefore introduce a new path-based metric **OPT-P**, not affected by this insensitivity. It involves computing R_P, which can loosely be interpreted as path recall, and P_P, which plays the role of path precision. In contrast to earlier metrics, we do not sample or match paths independently. Instead, we ensure that no two paths sampled from a graph share the same edges, and that any two sampled paths are matched to two disjoint sets of edges in the other graph. Moreover, when matching a pair of paths, we not only compare their lengths, as done in existing metrics, but also ensure that their trajectories run close in the image. This makes P_P sensitive to the types of false positive road predictions that the **TLTS** and **APLS** miss.

More precisely, we developed an iterative path sampling and matching scheme. To compute recall, we iteratively sample a path from the ground truth network and match it to the predicted network. Using the match, we compute our measure of connectivity as described in the next paragraph. We then remove the sampled path from the ground-truth network to ensure that no two paths share the same edges. We also remove the matched edges from the predicted network in order to guarantee that no edge from the predicted network is matched to two different paths. We iterate until one of the networks has no more edges. Figure 1 illustrates this process. Precision is computed similarly, but the roles of the networks are exchanged.

Matching a path π to a graph is performed using the Viterbi algorithm, and more details of this procedure can be found in the appendix. If possible, the path is projected to a chain of connected graph nodes. If the whole path cannot be matched to a single chain due to disconnections in the predicted graph, its subpaths are still matched to connected chains whenever possible. This matching induces a partitioning of the path π into a set of segments $\mathcal{S}(\pi)$, such that each $s \in \mathcal{S}(\pi)$ maps to a different chain. If the path π exists in the graph and has no disconnections, $\mathcal{S}(\pi)$ contains only one segment. In case of disconnections $|\mathcal{S}(\pi)| > 1$ and $|\mathcal{S}(\pi)| = 0$ if π does not exist in the graph.

To compute P_P and R_P, we use the matched segments $\mathcal{S}(\pi)$ to estimate the probability that a sub-path of π, with end points selected randomly and with uniform probability along π, is connected in the target network. The sub-path is connected in the target network only if its both end-points lie on the same path segment s. The probability of such event is $P_\pi = \frac{\sum_{s \in S} l(s)^2}{l(\pi)^2}$, where $l(.)$ denotes path length. Note that, if the matched path is entirely connected, then $|\mathcal{S}(\pi)| = 1$, and this probability is $P_\pi = 1$. When the matched path has disconnections, $|\mathcal{S}(\pi)| > 1$ and $P_\pi < 1$. We define path recall as the average of these probabilities over all paths $\pi \in \Pi$ sampled from the ground truth network $R_P = \frac{1}{|\Pi|} \sum_{\pi \in \Pi} P_\pi$. The path precision P_P is computed according to the same formula, but with paths sampled from the predicted network and matched to the ground truth one.

3.2   Junction-Based Metric (OPT-J)

As discussed in Sect. 2.3, the junction score **JUNCT** [5] is insensitive to road interruptions and excessively penalizes junctions that lack $k - 2$ out of k incident edges. To address these shortcomings, we propose a new junction score **OPT − J**, including the junction precision P_J and recall R_J. As for **JUNCT**, computing **OPT − J** involves matching feature nodes in the two networks and comparing the numbers of edges incident on them. Unlike in **JUNCT**, where the set of features comprises only junctions – nodes with at least three incident edges – we

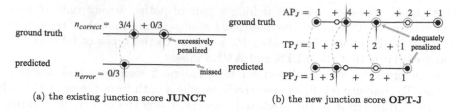

(a) the existing junction score **JUNCT**   (b) the new junction score **OPT-J**

Fig. 2. A comparison of the existing junction score (a) to our junction score (b). Feature points are marked as black dots, matches in green and unmatched features in red. For readability, we only consider the features on the horizontal lines, and assume the vertical lines continue indefinitely. Candidate and actual edge matches are depicted by hollow nodes. Unmatched hollow nodes are not penalized. See Sect. 2.3 for the definition of **JUNCT** and Sect. 3.2 for the definition **OPT-J**. (Color figure online)

use both junctions and endpoints as features. Moreover, we enable matching a feature of one graph not only to a feature of the other graph, but also to any point on its edge. This gives our metric the desired sensitivity to unwarranted road breaks and prevents excessively penalizing specific patterns of missing edges. Figure 2 illustrates the differences between **JUNCT** and **OPT − J**.

We denote a match by (i, j), where i belongs to the ground truth and j to the predicted graph, and both are features, or one of them is a feature, and the other is its closest point on an edge. We perform greedy matching with the cost of a match $c_{ij} = \alpha d_{ij} + |o_i - o_j|$, where o_i is the number of edges incident on i if i is a feature and by convention $o_i = 2$ if i is a point on an edge. d_{ij} is the distance between i and j. α is a parameter of the score. We only allow a feature to be matched once, but we do not constrain the number of features matched to a single edge. We only consider matches (i, j) such that i and j are within a predefined small distance $d^{\max}$.

We denote the set of matches M, the sets of unmatched ground truth features by F_{gt}^- and the set of unmatched predicted features by F_{est}^-. We estimate the number of true positive incident edges as $\mathrm{TP}_J = \sum_{(i,j)\in M} \min\{o_i, o_j\}$, the number of predicted edges as $\mathrm{PP}_J = \sum_{(i,j)\in M} o_j + \sum_{j\in F_{est}^-} o_j$, and the number of ground truth edges as $\mathrm{AP}_J = \sum_{(i,j)\in M} o_i + \sum_{i\in F_{gt}^-} o_i$. We compute the precision and recall as $P_J = \frac{\mathrm{TP}_J}{\mathrm{PP}_J}$ and $R_J = \frac{\mathrm{TP}_J}{\mathrm{AP}_J}$.

3.3   Subgraph-Based Metric (OPT-G)

In Sect. 2.4 we have exposed the lack of sensitivity of the local graph comparison **SUBG** [7] to false positive roads that are far away from ground truth roads and to errors involving missing one of several closely spaced roads. To remove this lack of sensitivity, we propose a new score **OPT-G**. Like **SUBG**, **OPT-G** is based on comparing sets of graph locations accessible by traveling a short distance in the graph from a randomly selected starting point. To prevent distinct roads that parallel each other closely from being matched to a single one in the

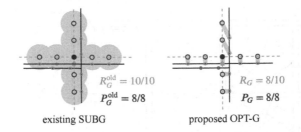

$R_G^{old} = 10/10$
$P_G^{old} = 8/8$

$R_G = 8/10$
$P_G = 8/8$

existing SUBG   proposed OPT-G

Fig. 3. The difference between the existing subgraph-based score **SUBG** and our subgraph-based score **OPT-G**. A single starting point is shown in both the predicted network (as filled blue circle) and the ground truth networks (as a filled green circle). The networks are drawn with dashed gray and solid black lines, respectively. All the control points in the ground truth network (hollow green circles) are within a matching distance (visualized with light blue disks) from the control points in the predicted network (hollow blue circles). This makes the existing score insensitive to the missing road. In our score, the matching is one-to-one (visualized by light blue lines). In result, some of the control points remain unmatched (marked in red), which gives the score sensitivity to the missing road. (Color figure online)

other graph, we force the matching to be one-to-one. In addition, unlike in the old score, we sample the starting points both in the ground-truth and predicted graphs, which makes the score sensitive to false positive, as shown in Fig. 3.

To compute the score, we iteratively sample a starting point in one of the graphs. We then find its closest point in the other graph. Using breadth-first graph traversal, we crop out subgraphs accessible by traveling a predefined distance from the starting points. Control points are inserted at equal intervals during the traversal. We then perform a one-to-one matching of control points from the two graphs by the Hungarian algorithm, with the cost of matching two points equal to the Euclidean distance between them. Only points within a predefined distance are matched. Calculation of the score is based on the number of matched and unmatched control points. We define subgraph-based precision as $P_G = \frac{TP_G}{PP_G}$ and subgraph-based recall as $R_G = \frac{TP_G}{AP_G}$, where TP_G is the total number of matched control points, PP_G is the number of control points in the predicted graph and AP_G is the number of control points in the ground truth graph.

4   Experiments

In this section, we first use synthetic data to compare the behavior of the current and new performance metrics. We will show that current ones are insensitive to certain types of errors, while ours capture all of them. We then evaluate all the metrics on real data and use them to compare state-of-the-art road reconstruction methods.

712   L. Citraro et al.

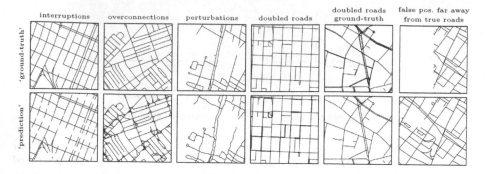

Fig. 4. Example pairs of road networks from the benchmark dataset.

4.1 Synthetic Data

We created a synthetic benchmark dataset from crops of road networks from [5]. Its purpose is to enable the analysis of the responses of the metrics to varying numbers of errors of a single type, for different types of errors.

We formed the dataset by duplicating the selected crops to emulate pairs of 'ground truth' and 'predicted' networks. We then perturbed the graphs by introducing a controlled number of errors that are representative of those encountered in practice.

- Interruptions: Unwarranted breaks in roads.
- Overconnections: Spurious additional roads connecting randomly selected pairs of points.
- Perturbations: displacing graph nodes from their true locations without disconnecting the roads.
- Doubled roads: Spurious copies of road segments shifted slightly and connected to the originals.
- Doubled roads-ground truth: Same as above, but the copies are added to the ground-truth, to emulate roads missing from the prediction.
- False positives far away from true roads: To simulate them, we removed part of the ground truth while keeping the prediction unchanged.

Figure 4 depicts example graphs from our dataset. As shown in Fig. 7, similar errors appear in real reconstructions. In Fig. 5, we plot the behavior of all the metrics as a function of the number of perturbations. If a metric is sensitive to a particular kind of error, the curve will exhibit a large slope. By contrast, if the metric is insensitive to that kind of error, the curve will be flat. Note that the curves for our new metrics are never flat, which indicates that are adequately sensitive to all the kinds of errors listed above. Unfortunately, this cannot be said of the existing metrics.

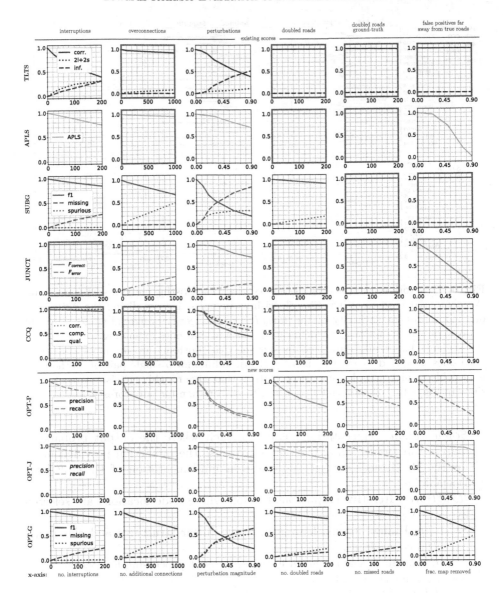

Fig. 5. Sensitivity of the existing and the new scores to different types of errors. The plots that exhibit lack of sensitivity are outlined in red. Our proposed metrics do not exhibit any of such insensitivity. See Sect. 4.1 for details. Best viewed in color.

4.2   Real Data

We now turn to the recent road delineation algorithms, and analyze their predictions for the publicly available Roadtracer [5] and DeepGlobe [11] datasets. To do so we used publicly available algorithms implementations, and ones whose authors kindly shared with us the delineation results:

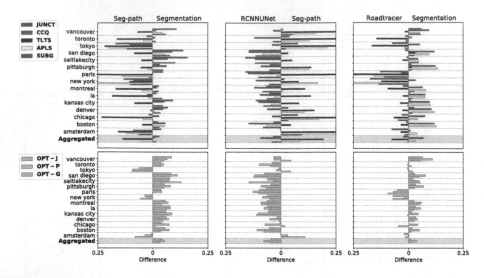

Fig. 6. This work was inspired by the observation that existing metrics are inconsistent. We compared road reconstruction algorithms in pairs, by visualizing the differences of their scores for each city of the *RoadTracer* test set.Bars extending to the right express preference for the first delineation method and ones extending to the left for the second. The results produced by our metrics (bottom) are far more consistent than ones produced by existing metrics (top). While, for a single pair of methods, it is possible to pick a triplet of existing metrics that give roughly consistent results, we show in Fig. 8 that their correlation is much weaker than for our scores.

- *Segmentation.* Segmentation-based approach where the output probability map is thresholded and skeletonized. We use the prediction provided in [5] for the Roadtracer dataset and our own implementation of UNet [27] for DeepGlobe.
- *RoadTracer.* Iterative graph construction where node locations are selected by a CNN [5].
- *Seg-Path.* Unified approach to segmenting linear structures and classifying potential connections. [24]
- *DeepRoad.* Image segmentation followed by post-processing focused at fixing missing connections [21].
- *RCNNUNet.* Recursive image segmentation with post-processing for graph extraction [33].
- *MultiBranch.* A recursive architecture co-trained in road segmentation and orientation estimation [6].
- *LinkNet.* An encoder-decoder architecture [8] co-trained in segmentation and orientation estimation [6].

Comparing Reconstruction Methods. A performance measure is meant to be used to compare methods and, ultimately, to decide which one is best. In this section, we show that this is difficult to do using existing metrics because they tend to

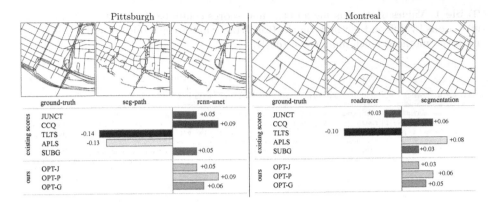

Fig. 7. Crops of a road network of (*left*) Pittsburgh and (*right*) Montreal and their reconstructions from aerial images. *Left*: Predictions by *seg-path* [24] and *rcnn-unet* [33]. *Right*: Predictions by *roadtracer* and *segmentation* both provided by [5] *Bottom*: Differences of the metrics for the two reconstructions.

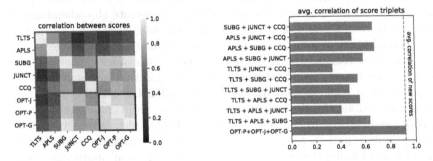

Fig. 8. Analysis of the correlations. *Left*: A matrix of correlations of the scores computed for the maps reconstructed by different methods on the roadtracer dataset. The correlation coefficients of the old scores are outlined in green, the correlation coefficients of the new scores in blue. *Right*: The average correlation of all possible existing score triplets (blue bars) against the average correlation of the three new scores (dashed red line). Our metrics show better correlation than the existing ones. (Color figure online)

return different rankings. By contrast, ours are far more consistent. To show this, we performed the following experiment.

For each individual metric, we computed the differences of the scores it returns for two different delineation methods in a specific city of the RoadTracer dataset. These differences are depicted in Fig. 6 by colored bars that extend to the left when the score of the first method is higher than that of the second and to the right otherwise. It is almost impossible to discern a clear pattern at the top of the figure where we plotted the bars corresponding to the existing metrics. By contrast, our metrics deliver a far clearer picture.

Table 1. Values of the existing and the new scores computed for road networks reconstructions by different methods on the RoadTracer and DeepGlobe datasets. Our scores rank the methods much more consistently.

dataset		Existing scores										New scores						
		CCQ			TLTS		APLS	JUNCT			SUBG	OPT-P			OPT-J			OPT-G
		corr.	comp.	qual.	corr.	2l+2s		F_{cor}	F_{err}	f1	f1	pre.	rec.	f1	pre.	rec.	f1	f1
RoadTracer	Roadtracer [5]	0.681	0.615	0.478	0.422	0.174	0.595	0.763	0.129	**0.812**	0.710	0.597	0.458	0.519	0.801	0.758	0.779	0.683
	Segmentation [5]	0.775	0.649	0.546	0.346	0.190	0.625	0.728	0.137	0.782	0.704	0.645	0.488	0.556	0.820	0.760	0.788	0.690
	Seg-path [24]	0.647	**0.755**	0.535	**0.483**	0.137	0.678	**0.925**	0.355	0.754	0.688	0.443	**0.581**	0.503	0.649	**0.882**	0.748	0.662
	DeepRoadMapper [21]	**0.842**	0.474	0.435	0.071	0.235	0.243	0.422	0.203	0.514	0.477	0.651	0.271	0.383	0.822	0.524	0.640	0.482
	RCNN-Unet [33]	0.830	0.719	**0.626**	0.291	0.353	0.594	0.723	**0.120**	0.790	0.729	**0.672**	0.510	**0.580**	**0.827**	0.759	**0.792**	**0.707**
DGlobe	*LinkNet* [6]	0.778	0.803	0.653	0.632	0.107	0.660	0.682	0.234	0.722	0.819	0.727	0.761	0.744	0.782	0.793	0.787	0.789
	MultiBranch [6]	**0.804**	**0.826**	**0.687**	**0.684**	0.101	0.699	0.734	0.185	**0.773**	**0.843**	**0.740**	**0.792**	**0.765**	**0.805**	0.810	**0.807**	**0.813**
	Segmentation [27]	0.545	**0.841**	0.495	**0.720**	0.138	0.618	**0.941**	0.542	0.616	0.787	0.520	**0.859**	0.648	0.582	**0.872**	0.698	0.724

A possible interpretation of this result is that some type of problems are encountered more often in specific cities. As the existing metrics are more sensitive to some kinds of errors than others, that would explain the discrepancies. This would not necessarily be an issue if the metrics were designed to measure different, possibly uncorrelated, qualities of interest. However, they are typically used as overall quality measures and to demonstrate the advantage of one method over the others. In this context their inconsistency *is* an issue, and the greater consistency of our proposed measures is a distinct advantage.

In Fig. 7, we visualize fragments of two predicted networks. The scores on the bottom of the figure show the comparison by the existing scores is inconclusive. As we have seen in the benchmark experiment, **APLS** and **TLTS** are insensitive to overconnections therefore they positively react to overconnected graphs as *seg-path* predictions. On the other hand, **OPT-P**, which is based on the same principle, takes spurious roads into account and agree with the other metrics. In term of cost of fixing the errors, an operator would spend more time removing spurious roads from *seg-path* than by adding the missing connection in *rcnn-unet*. More visual comparisons are provided in the supplementary material.

Correlation Analysis. In contrast to the consistency analysis we just discussed we now turn to compare correlations between the various metrics. On the left side of Fig. 8 we show the correlations between pairs of scores on the RoadTracer dataset and on the right side we compare the average correlation of all possible triplets of existing metrics to that of our three new scores. To evaluate the consistency of a score triplet, we average correlations for all pairs within the triplet. Either way, it can be seen that our metrics are far more correlated among themselves than any pair of triplet of the other ones.

Comparing State-of-the-Art Methods. We now use both existing and new metrics to compare state-of-the-art road reconstruction methods. As can be seen in Table 1, on the RoadTracer dataset, existing metrics favor *RoadTracer*, *RCN-NUNet*, or *Seg-Path*. By contrast, the proposed metrics consistently point to *RCNNUNet*. Moreover, all of them rank *Segmentation* second and *Seg-Path* and *RoadTracer* compete for the third place with very similar scores in all our metrics. As seen in the bottom part of Table 1 this also holds for the DeepGlobe data.

The existing scores are less inconsistent than for the RoadTracer dataset, with **TLTS** favoring segmentation while other scores prefer *MultiBranch*, but our metrics all agree on *MultiBranch*. Note also that precision- and recall-related scores for **OPT-J** and **OPT-P** show recurring patterns whereas **CCQ** and **JUNCT** do not.

5 Conclusion

We were surprised to discover that *all* the existing scores for evaluation of road network reconstructions suffer from design faults that make them insensitive to particular types of errors. Our experiments show that the concerns this rises about the reliability of evaluation by means of these scores are justifiable – one could overturn the results of a study by carefully selecting the score used for evaluation. We have demonstrated that correcting the flaws of the existing metrics leads to improved consistency – our three new metrics are much more coherent than the old ones, despite the fact that each of them is computed in a different way.

We have focused on road network reconstructions, but the proposed scores can be used for comparing any curvilinear networks.

Acknowledgments. This work was supported in part by the Swiss National Science Foundation.

References

1. Ahmed, M., Fasy, B., Hickmann, K., Wenk, C.: A path-based distance for street map comparison. ACM Trans. Spat. Algorithms Syst. **1**(1), 31–328 (2015)
2. Arganda-Carreras, I., et al.: Crowdsourcing the creation of image segmentation algorithms for connectomics. Front. Neuroanat. **9**, 142 (2015)
3. Bai, M., Máttyus, G., Homayounfar, N., Wang, S., Lakshmikanth, S., Urtasun, R.: Deep multi-sensor lane detection. In: CoRR abs/1905.01555 (2019)
4. Bajcsy, R., Tavakoli, M.: Computer recognition of roads from satellite pictures. IEEE Trans. Syst. Man Cybern. SMC **6**(9), 623–637 (1976)
5. Bastani, F., et al.: Roadtracer: automatic extraction of road networks from aerial images. In: Conference on Computer Vision and Pattern Recognition (2018)
6. Batra, A., Singh, S., Pang, G., Basu, S., Jawahar, C., Paluri, M.: Improved road connectivity by joint learning of orientation and segmentation. In: Conference on Computer Vision and Pattern Recognition, June 2019
7. Biagioni, J., Eriksson, J.: Inferring road maps from global positioning system traces: survey and comparative evaluation. Trans. Res. Rec. J. Trans. Res. Board **2291**(1), 61–71 (2012)
8. Chaurasia, A., Culurciello, E.: Linknet: exploiting encoder representations for efficient semantic segmentation. In: CoRR abs/1707.03718 (2017)
9. Cheng, G., Wang, Y., Xu, S., Wang, H., Xiang, S., Pan, C.: Automatic road detection and centerline extraction via cascaded end-to-end convolutional neural network. IEEE Trans. Geosci. Remote Sens. **55**(6), 3322–3337 (2017)

10. Chu, H., et al.: Neural turtle graphics for modeling city road layouts. In: International Conference on Computer Vision (2019)
11. Demir, I., et al.: DeepGlobe 2018: a challenge to parse the earth through satellite images. In: Conference on Computer Vision and Pattern Recognition, June 2018
12. Etten, A.V., Lindenbaum, D., Bacastow, T.: Spacenet: a remote sensing dataset and challenge series. CoRR abs/1807.01232 (2018)
13. Fischler, M., Tenenbaum, J., Wolf, H.: Detection of roads and linear structures in low-resolution aerial imagery using a multisource knowledge integration technique. Comput. Vis. Graph. Image Process. **15**(3), 201–223 (1981)
14. Funke, J., et al.: Large scale image segmentation with structured loss based deep learning for connectome reconstruction. IEEE Trans. Pattern Anal. Mach. Intell. **41**(7), 1669–1680 (2018)
15. Gillette, T., Brown, K., Ascoli, G.: The DIADEM metric: comparing multiple reconstructions of the same neuron. Neuroinformatics **9**, 233–245 (2011)
16. Homayounfar, N., Ma, W., Lakshmikanth, S., Urtasun, R.: Hierarchical recurrent attention networks for structured online maps. In: Conference on Computer Vision and Pattern Recognition, pp. 3417–3426 (2018)
17. Homayounfar, N., Ma, W., Liang, J., Wu, X., Fan, J., Urtasun, R.: DAGMapper: learning to map by discovering lane topology. In: International Conference on Computer Vision, October 2019
18. Karagiorgou, S., Pfoser, D.: On vehicle tracking data-based road network generation. In: Proceedings of the 20th International Conference on Advances in Geographic Information Systems, pp. 89–98 (2012)
19. Li, Y., Zhang, X., Chen, D.: CSRNet: dilated convolutional neural networks for understanding the highly congested scenes. In: Conference on Computer Vision and Pattern Recognition (2018)
20. Liang, J., Homayounfar, N., Ma, W., Wang, S., Urtasun, R.: Convolutional recurrent network for road boundary extraction. In: Conference on Computer Vision and Pattern Recognition, pp. 9512–9521 (2019)
21. Máttyus, G., Luo, W., Urtasun, R.: DeepRoadMapper: extracting road topology from aerial images. In: International Conference on Computer Vision, pp. 3458–3466 (2017)
22. Mnih, V.: Machine Learning for Aerial Image Labeling. Ph.D. thesis, University of Toronto (2013)
23. Mnih, V., Hinton, G.E.: Learning to detect roads in high-resolution aerial images. In: Daniilidis, K., Maragos, P., Paragios, N. (eds.) ECCV 2010. LNCS, vol. 6316, pp. 210–223. Springer, Heidelberg (2010). https://doi.org/10.1007/978-3-642-15567-3_16
24. Mosińska, A., Kozinski, M., Fua, P.: Joint segmentation and path classification of curvilinear structures. IEEE Trans. Pattern Anal. Mach. Intell. **42**(6), 1515–1521 (2020)
25. Mosińska, A., Marquez-Neila, P., Kozinski, M., Fua, P.: Beyond the pixel-wise loss for topology-aware delineation. In: Conference on Computer Vision and Pattern Recognition, pp. 3136–3145 (2018)
26. Quam, L.: Road tracking and anomaly detection. In: DARPA Image Understanding Workshop, pp. 51–55, May 1978
27. Ronneberger, O.: Invited talk: U-Net convolutional networks for biomedical image segmentation. Bildverarbeitung für die Medizin 2017. I, pp. 3–3. Springer, Heidelberg (2017). https://doi.org/10.1007/978-3-662-54345-0_3
28. Vanderbrug, G.: Line detection in satellite imagery. IEEE Trans. Geosci. Electron. **14**(1), 37–44 (1976)

29. Wang, S., et al.: Torontocity: seeing the world with a million eyes. In: International Conference on Computer Vision, pp. 3028–3036 (2017)

30. Wegener, I., Pruim, R.: Complexity Theory: Exploring the Limits of Efficient Algorithms. Springer-Verlag, Berlin (2005)

31. Wegner, J., Montoya-Zegarra, J., Schindler, K.: A higher-order CRF model for road network extraction. In: Conference on Computer Vision and Pattern Recognition, pp. 1698–1705 (2013)

32. Wiedemann, C., Heipke, C., Mayer, H., Jamet, O.: Empirical evaluation of automatically extracted road axes. Empirical Evaluation Techniques in Computer Vision, pp. 172–187. Citeseer, New Jersey (1998)

33. Yang, X., Li, X., Ye, Y., Lau, R.Y.K., Zhang, X., Huang, X.: Road detection and centerline extraction via deep recurrent convolutional neural network U-Net. IEEE Trans. Geosci. Remote Sens. **57**(9), 1–12 (2019)

Online Continual Learning Under Extreme Memory Constraints

Enrico Fini[1,2]([✉]), Stéphane Lathuilière[3], Enver Sangineto[1], Moin Nabi[2], and Elisa Ricci[1,4]

[1] University of Trento, Trento, Italy
enrico.fini@unitn.it
[2] SAP AI Research, Berlin, Germany
[3] LTCI, Télécom Paris, Institut Polytechnique de Paris, Palaiseau, France
[4] Fondazione Bruno Kessler, Trento, Italy

Abstract. Continual Learning (CL) aims to develop agents emulating the human ability to sequentially learn new tasks while being able to retain knowledge obtained from past experiences. In this paper, we introduce the novel problem of Memory-Constrained Online Continual Learning (MC-OCL) which imposes strict constraints on the memory overhead that a possible algorithm can use to avoid catastrophic forgetting. As most, if not all, previous CL methods violate these constraints, we propose an algorithmic solution to MC-OCL: Batch-level Distillation (BLD), a regularization-based CL approach, which effectively balances stability and plasticity in order to learn from data streams, while preserving the ability to solve old tasks through distillation. Our extensive experimental evaluation, conducted on three publicly available benchmarks, empirically demonstrates that our approach successfully addresses the MC-OCL problem and achieves comparable accuracy to prior distillation methods requiring higher memory overhead (Code available at https://github.com/DonkeyShot21/batch-level-distillation).

Keywords: Continual Learning · Online learning · Memory efficient

1 Introduction

A well-known problem in deep learning is the tendency of Deep Neural Networks (DNNs) to *catastrophically forget* the knowledge acquired from old tasks when learning a new task. Differently from humans, who have the natural ability to selectively retain knowledge obtained through past experience when facing a new problem or task, a DNN, trained on a given data distribution, tends to be drastically affected when new training data drawn from a different distribution are provided, losing the ability to solve the past task(s). *Continual Learning* (CL) [17] investigates this *stability-plasticity dilemma*: how can a DNN be adapted to solve a new task without losing the ability to deal with previously seen tasks?

Electronic supplementary material The online version of this chapter (https://doi.org/10.1007/978-3-030-58604-1_43) contains supplementary material, which is available to authorized users.

A. Vedaldi et al. (Eds.): ECCV 2020, LNCS 12373, pp. 720–735, 2020.
https://doi.org/10.1007/978-3-030-58604-1_43

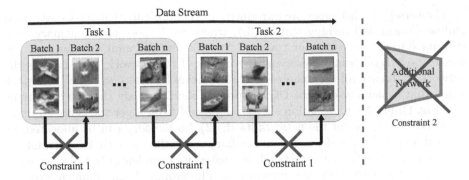

Fig. 1. Illustration of the proposed Memory-Constrained Online Continual Learning setting, where two constraints should be satisfied: (1) No information should be transferred between data batches and between tasks; (2) No memory can be allocated for auxiliary networks or network expansions.

Due to the relevance of its applications, in the last few years, the computer vision research community has put considerable effort into developing CL methods. Previous work in the field can be categorized according to the strategy used to mitigate catastrophic forgetting [17]. Replay-based methods [5,13,26,31], for instance, alleviate forgetting by storing old data or synthesizing virtual samples from the past. Parameter-isolation approaches [22,28] dedicate specific portions of the network parameters to each task. Finally, regularization-based methods [1,8,15,20] introduce additional regularization terms in the loss function to encourage the stability of the network with respect to the previous tasks. Specifically, regularization may be obtained using a distillation-like [12] approach or enforcing a prior on the model parameters. In the first case, the network is encouraged to keep the predictions consistent with respect to the old tasks [20]. Prior-based methods, on the other hand, estimate and store a prior on the parameter distribution which indicates the importance of each parameter with respect to the old tasks [15].

Online Learning (OL) studies optimization methods which can operate with a stream of data: learning goes on as the data are collected [9,17]. A typical application of OL are those scenarios in which training data cannot be stored (e.g., due to memory restrictions or data privacy concern). While classic OL assumes i.i.d. data sampling over a single task, in this paper we deal with *Online Continual Learning* (OCL), where data are provided with a sequential stream and the data distribution undergoes drastic changes when a new task is introduced. Previous works in this field [3,4] mainly focus on the task-free scenario, in which no task-boundary information is provided. However, the solutions they propose rely on either a buffer or a generator to replay data from previous time steps. On the one hand, the buffer-based solution violates a strict online regime, where training data from past time steps should be discarded. On the other hand, a generator network involves a big memory and computational overhead that needs to be allocated on purpose.

Conversely, in this paper, we introduce a novel problem, Memory-Constrained Online Continual Learning (MC-OCL), where we impose strict memory constraints during the course of training. Specifically, we want to minimize the memory overhead, while preserving the utility of the network. This implies the network to discard all the unnecessary information for inference. Specifically, we argue that a memory-efficient OCL approach should satisfy the two conditions (see Fig. 1): (1) No information should be passed from a generic time step s to time step $s + 1$, except the network itself; (2) No memory can be allocated for network expansions or dedicated as auxiliary networks. Note that constraint (1) does not only imply that each batch is treated independently but also excludes information pass through subsequent tasks. The proposed constraints are particularly relevant for those application scenarios in which the network is deployed on devices with small memory footprint (e.g. robots or smartphones) or in which past images cannot be stored due to privacy issues.

Currently, existing CL solutions cannot deal with the proposed MC-OCL scenario. In fact, replay-based methods [13,24,26] need to either explicitly store (part of the) training samples (violating constraint (1)) or to train an ad-hoc generator network (violating constraint (2)). Even regularization-based methods using distillation [8,20] either need to store the model output probabilities (violating constraint (1)) or task-specific networks (violating constraint (2)) in order to produce distillation information on the fly. Finally, parameter-isolation based methods [22,28] which select a subset of the network parameters for each task, assume that task-specific information (e.g. mask in [22]) can be transferred from different tasks and do not perform data stream processing on a mini-batch basis (violating constraint (1)).

In this paper, we propose a conceptually simple yet empirically powerful solution to the MC-OCL problem called Batch-level Distillation (*BLD*), in which distillation information is re-generated at each time step without violating constraint (1). Our approach is articulated into two main phases. In the first stage, the *warm-up*, data of the current batch are exploited to perform a first gradient descent step minimizing the cross-entropy loss over the new task classifier. The predictions of the old task classifiers are stored in a probability bank that is required in the second stage, referred to as *joint training*. In this stage, both the distillation and the new task learning are performed, adopting a dynamic weighting strategy that uses the gradient norm computed in the *warm-up* stage. We extensively evaluate the proposed solution on three widely-used benchmarks: MNIST [18], SVHN [23] and CIFAR10 [16]. Our results demonstrate that *BLD* achieves comparable accuracy to state of the art distillation methods despite the imposed memory constraints.

To summarize, our contributions are the following:

- We introduce a realistic yet challenging OCL setting which operates under extreme memory constraints (MC-OCL).
- We propose the notion of Batch-level Distillation (*BLD*) as a viable solution to the MC-OCL problem.

- An extensive empirical study is carried out which confirms the effective alleviation of forgetting despite the strict memory constraints.

2 Related Work

Over the past few years, Continual Learning [15,17] has received increased interest in computer vision. Indeed, CL is highly relevant for several applications. For instance, for object recognition it is very desirable to dispose of deep models which are able to recognize new object classes, while retaining their knowledge on the categories they have been originally trained for. Previous CL methods can be roughly categorized into three main groups [17]: regularization-based [1,8,15,20], parameter-isolation based [22,28] and replay-based [13,24,26] methods.

Data-focused regularization-based methods [8,20] develop from the idea of applying the distillation paradigm [12] to prevent catastrophic forgetting. One of the earlier approaches in this category is Learning without Forgetting (LwF) [20], where a distillation loss is introduced to preserve information of the original classes considering the output probabilities. LwF exploits data from the original classes during training when the classifier is trained to recognize novel categories. Recently, the concept of distillation has been extended to attention and segmentation maps [6,8].

Prior-focused regularization-based methods [1,15] consider the network parameter values as a source of knowledge to be transferred and operate by penalizing changes of parameters relevant for old tasks when learning on the new task. These approaches mostly differ in the way parameter relevance is computed. A prominent work in this category is Elastic Weight Consolidation (EWC) [15], where parameter update rules are obtained approximating the posterior as a Gaussian distribution. Differently, Aljundi et al. propose Memory Aware Synapses (MAS) [1], an approach that estimates the network weight importance using small perturbations of the parameters.

Parameter-isolation based approaches [22,28] address catastrophic forgetting by allocating specific model parameters to each task. For instance, in [22] a fixed architecture is considered and parts that are specific for some previous tasks are masked out while training on novel tasks. Rusu et al. [28] proposed Progressive Neural Networks (PNNs), a framework which transfers across sequences of tasks by retaining a pool of pre-trained models and learning connections in order to get useful features for the novel task.

Replay-based methods alleviate catastrophic forgetting by either storing [5, 13,26,31] or by artificially generating [24,29] images of previous tasks, often referred to as exemplars. Based on this idea Rebuffi et al. propose ICARL where a strategy to select exemplars in combination with a distillation loss is introduced. Subsequent works [7,31] further analyze exemplars selection strategies. Differently, other works [24,29,30] propose to employ generative networks to generate synthetic data of old tasks. However, these methods significantly depend on the network capacity and struggle to generate high-quality images.

Our approach belongs to the category of data-focused regularization-based methods, as it also attempts to counteract catastrophic forgetting through distillation. However, differently from previous methods we focus on an online setting where no information is passed through different tasks and batches.

Recently, few works in CL have considered an online CL setting [2–4,19]. However, they mostly focus on task-free continual learning, developing methodologies to automatically detect task boundaries and address the online learning problem benefiting from specific buffers. Our work develops with a different perspective as we aim to design an OCL framework maintaining memory requirements at minimum, thus assuming that no information is retained when processing the next batch in the data stream.

Finally, MER [27] and OML [14] are two recent meta-learning approaches to continual learning. However, the former needs a very large buffer (1k samples per task). On the other hand, OML, does not require any buffer, but works with very short tasks, while we use much larger datasets. Also, OML is based on an offline meta-pretraining, while we train the whole network from scratch.

3 Memory-Constrained Online Continual Learning

3.1 Problem and Notation

Without loss of generality, a typical CL scenario can be formalized assuming a set $\mathcal{T} = \{T_1, ..., T_n\}$ of n different tasks, where each task is characterized by a different joint probability distribution P_t of the raw images $x \in \mathcal{X}_t$ and the class labels $y \in \mathcal{Y}_t$. During time t, a new task T_t is presented to the DNN (see Fig. 2) and the goal is to learn T_t without catastrophically forgetting $T_1, ...T_{t-1}$. Note that not only the set of images $\mathcal{X}_t$ is task-specific, but so is the corresponding set of possible labels $\mathcal{Y}_t$. Following common practice in CL literature, we assume that the task-change event is known, and when a new task T_{t+1} arrives we ask the network to learn to classify the new images according to $\mathcal{Y}_{t+1}$, being simultaneously able to solve the old tasks.

In this paper, we assume that our classification network is composed of a backbone, the feature extractor Ψ, and multiple heads $\Phi = \{\phi_1, \ldots, \phi_n\}$, where the t-th head ϕ_t is composed of a linear classifier with a softmax activation which computes task-specific classification probabilities over $\mathcal{Y}_t$. In addition, ϕ_t also accepts an optional temperature parameter τ.

In the proposed MC-OCL setting the memory overhead must be kept at minimum. To fulfill this requirement we set several constraints. We impose that, when learning a new task T_t, the only memory overhead are the parameters of each task-specific classifier ϕ_t, while Ψ is shared over all the tasks and no other high-capacity network can be used to solve the CL problem (constraint (2)). In addition, it is reasonable to suppose that the complete dataset of the task cannot fit in memory. Consequently, standard batch training procedures consisting in observing several times each sample cannot be applied. Training must be addressed following an online formulation. More precisely, we assume that only a mini-batch of data $\mathcal{B}$ associated with task T_t is available at every

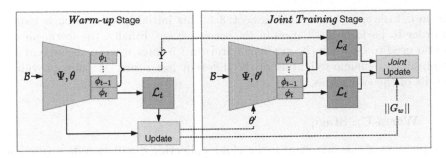

Fig. 2. Overview of *BLD*: considering the current batch $\mathcal{B}$, we proceed in two stages. In the *warm-up* stage, we perform a first gradient descent step minimizing the cross-entropy loss over the new task classifier. The predictions of the old task classifiers are stored in a probability bank. The *joint training* stage performs knowledge distillation to prevent forgetting, and new task learning employing a dynamic weighting strategy that uses the gradient norm computed in the *warm-up* stage.

time step. Importantly $\mathcal{B}$ contains only a few data (e.g., a few dozen images). This "mini-batch" based relaxation of the typical OL scenario [9] is commonly adopted in other COL settings [2]. Moreover, in our MC-OCL setting, every information, except the network parameters, must be discarded after processing each batch $\mathcal{B}$ (constraint (1)). $\mathcal{B}$ is used to update the network weights, but no explicit information can be stored or passed to the next batch processing step.

3.2   Batch-Level Distillation

In this section, we describe the proposed method, named Batch-level Distillation (*BLD*). Inspired by [20], we adopt a formulation based on knowledge distillation to mitigate catastrophic forgetting. Our distillation approach is composed of two main stages, both depending only on the current mini-batch data $\mathcal{B}$ which is sampled from the data distribution of the current task T_t and on the network parameters θ. The overall pipeline is illustrated in Fig. 2. The first stage, named *warm-up* stage, is introduced in order to enable the use of knowledge distillation in the second stage, named *joint training* stage.

The key idea of distillation for CL, is to use a regularization loss which prevents that the predictions of the old task classifiers are significantly modified when learning the new task. Since we only have available a mini-batch $\mathcal{B}$ of data, we propose to apply the distillation paradigm at the mini-batch level rather than at the dataset level. In other words, we enforce that, while learning the new task, the predictions of the old classifiers do not change much *between the beginning and the end of the current mini-batch processing*. This regularization and the new-task loss are optimized together in the *joint training* stage.

In order to use a distillation regularization, we need to estimate the predictions of the old task classifiers before updating the network parameters. This is the main purpose of the *warm-up* stage. In addition to computing the old task predictions, the *warm-up* stage also performs a first learning step by minimizing the new task loss. As detailed in Sect. 3.4, this initial learning step is required in order to perform distillation in the second stage. Finally, the *warm-up* stage is also used to estimate the gradient norm that is later used in the second stage to obtain a dynamic weighting of the different loss terms. We now provide the details of the two stages.

3.3 Warm-Up Stage

The purpose of this first stage is threefold: collecting distillation data (used only in the second stage), starting learning the new task on the current batch and estimate the norm of the new task loss. The details of the warm-up stage are provided in Algorithm 1.

Algorithm 1: *Warm-up* Stage

Input   : Current network (Ψ, Φ, θ), current batch $\mathcal{B}$ with labels $\mathbf{y}$,
            learning rate α_w, temperature τ

$\mathbf{v} = \Psi(\mathcal{B}; \theta)$ // feature extraction

$\hat{Y} = \varnothing$ // initialize empty probability bank

for $o \in \{1, ..., t-1\}$ // for every past task

   | $\hat{\mathbf{y}}^o = \phi_o(\mathbf{v}, \tau; \theta)$ // compute predictions

   | $\hat{Y} \leftarrow \hat{Y} \bigcup \{\hat{\mathbf{y}}^o\}$ // fill probability bank

end

$\mathcal{L}_t = H(\phi_t(\mathbf{v}; \theta), \mathbf{y})$ // compute warm-up loss

$G_w = \frac{\partial \mathcal{L}_t}{\partial \theta}$ // compute warm-up gradient

$\theta' = \theta - \alpha_w G_w$ // parameter update

return $\theta', \hat{Y}, \|G_w\|$

Specifically, let θ be the set of all the parameter values in Ψ and Φ. Considering an image $x_b \in \mathcal{B}$, we use the current feature extractor Ψ to get $\mathbf{v}_b = \Psi(x_b; \theta)$. We introduce the notation $\mathbf{v} = \{\mathbf{v}_b, 1 \leq b \leq |\mathcal{B}|\}$ to indicate all the images of the current batch, and we simply write $\mathbf{v} = \Psi(\mathcal{B}; \theta)$.

Then, we use these features to compute the predictions for the new images using the old task classifiers. More specifically, for each old task T_o, we estimate $\hat{\mathbf{y}}^o = \{\hat{\mathbf{y}}_b^o, 1 \leq b \leq |\mathcal{B}|\} = \phi_o(\mathbf{v}, \tau; \theta)$, where τ is the temperature of the softmax. These probability vectors are then appended to a probability bank $\hat{Y}$. At the end of the *warm-up* stage, $\hat{Y}$ will contain the predicted probabilities for every image of the batch according to every old classifier. This memory is later used for distillation in the second stage but it is released before receiving the next data batch. Since the number of classes is relatively small (hence, each $\hat{\mathbf{y}}_b^o$ is a low-dimensional vector), the memory required to store $\hat{Y}$ remains negligible compared to the memory space used by the batch of input images and the network parameters.

The previously computed features $\mathbf{v}$ are used also by the new-task classifier for computing the standard cross-entropy loss. Specifically, given the features $\mathbf{v}$

and their corresponding one-hot labels $\mathbf{y} \in \{0,1\}^{|\mathcal{B}| \times |\mathcal{Y}_t|}$, we use:

$$\mathcal{L}_t = H\left(\phi_t(\mathbf{v}; \theta), \mathbf{y}\right) = -\sum_{b=1}^{|\mathcal{B}|} \mathbf{y}_b \cdot \log \phi_t\left(\mathbf{v}_b; \theta\right). \tag{1}$$

Then, the gradient $G_w = \frac{\partial \mathcal{L}_t}{\partial \theta}$ is computed, and the parameters of the network are updated using the standard gradient descent. The warm-up stage also returns the norm of the gradient $\|G_w\|$, which is used for the parameter normalization in the second stage (*joint training* stage). In practice, since the norm of the gradient is computed layer-wise (see later), it can be obtained during the backward pass without storing the gradient of the whole network.

To conclude this stage, the memory used by the intermediate variables (e.g. $\mathbf{v}$ and θ) is released. At this point, the memory contains the parameters θ', the batch $\mathcal{B}$, the probability bank $\hat{Y}$ and the norm of the gradient $\|G_w\|$.

3.4 Joint Training Stage

We now provide the description of the joint training stage. The goal of this stage is to update the network parameters with respect to the new task while preserving the knowledge of the previous tasks. The details are provided in Algorithm 2.

Algorithm 2: *Joint Training* Stage

Input : Current network (Ψ, Φ, θ'), current batch $\mathcal{B}$ with labels $\mathbf{y}$, old task probability bank $\hat{Y}$, learning rate α_j, temperature τ, gradient-balancing factor λ, norms of the gradients $\|G_w\|$.

$\mathbf{v}' = \Psi(\mathcal{B}; \theta')$ // feature extraction
$\mathcal{L}_d = \sum_{o=1}^{t-1} H(\phi_o(\mathbf{v}', \tau; \theta'), \hat{y}^o)$ // compute distillation loss
$G_j = \frac{\partial \mathcal{L}_d}{\partial \theta'}$ // distillation gradient
$G_j \leftarrow \lambda \frac{\|G_w\|}{\|G_j\|} G_j$ // balance the distillation gradient
$\mathcal{L}_t = H(\phi_t(\mathbf{v}'; \theta'), \mathbf{y})$ // compute new task loss
$G_j \leftarrow G_j + \frac{\partial \mathcal{L}_t}{\partial \theta'}$ // accumulate new task gradient
$\theta'' = \theta' - \alpha_j G_j$ // parameter update
Return: θ''

Using the current batch $\mathcal{B}$ and the *updated* feature extractor $\Psi(\cdot; \theta')$, we get $\mathbf{v}' = \{\mathbf{v}'_b, 1 \le b \le |\mathcal{B}|\} = \Psi(\mathcal{B}; \theta')$. Note that the features $\mathbf{v}'$ are different from $\mathbf{v}$, computed in the *warm-up* stage, because of the parameter update in Algorithm 1. Then, we use the old-task classifiers ϕ_o (for every old tasks T_o) to predict the output probabilities using $\mathbf{v}'$. Following a distillation approach, we want that the predictions $\phi_o(\mathbf{v}', \tau; \theta')$ should not differ much from the initial values $\hat{y}^o \in \hat{Y}$. To measure this change in the predictions, we use a cross-entropy loss between the initial and current predicted probability distributions:

$$\mathcal{L}_d = \sum_{o=1}^{t-1} H(\phi_o(\mathbf{v}', \tau; \theta'), \hat{y}^o) = -\sum_{o=1}^{t-1} \sum_{b=1}^{|\mathcal{B}|} \hat{y}^o_b \log\left(\phi_o(\mathbf{v}'_b, \tau; \theta')\right). \tag{2}$$

It is worth noting that the distillation loss is used only in the *joint training* stage and not in the *warm-up* stage. The reason for this choice is that, in the *warm-up* stage, the distillation loss $\mathcal{L}_d$ would have a zero gradient since $\phi_o(\mathbf{v}'_b, \tau; \theta) = \phi_o(\mathbf{v}_b, \tau; \theta) = \hat{\mathbf{y}}^o_b$. Because of the first gradient descent step in the *warm-up* stage, we obtain non-null gradients for the distillation loss in the second stage. This observation mainly motivates our two-stage pipeline.

The distillation loss gradient is weighted using a normalization factor. Specifically, given the distillation gradient $G_j = \frac{\partial \mathcal{L}_d}{\partial \theta'}$ and the cross-entropy gradient norm $||G_w||$ computed in the warm-up stage, the gradient is multiplied by $\lambda \frac{||G_w||}{||G_j||}$. The intuition behind this normalization is that we want to balance the two gradients in a dynamic way while training. The parameter λ is a static parameter that adjusts the weight of the distillation and the cross-entropy gradients, accounting for the possible imbalance originated with the unconstrained *warm-up* update. Finally, we use the new-task classifier ϕ_t to compute the network predictions and its resulting cross-entropy loss $\mathcal{L}_t$. Assuming that the norm of the gradient of this loss does not change drastically between the two stages (i.e., $||G_w|| \simeq ||\frac{\partial \mathcal{L}_t}{\partial \theta'}||$), we can sum G_j with $\frac{\partial \mathcal{L}_t}{\partial \theta'}$ (all the gradient terms have a balanced contribution).

For sake of simplicity, we used above the notation $\frac{||G_w||}{||G_j||}$, which includes the gradients of all the layers of the network. In practice, we actually compute the norms separately for each layer, because in this way the memory cost can be kept extremely small and, empirically, we observed that this leads to a more stable training.

The *joint training* stage can be iterated several times. Empirically, we found iterating twice to be beneficial. Note that, in the second iteration of this stage, $\mathcal{L}_d$ and $\mathcal{L}_t$ are computed at the value θ'' obtained from the first iteration.

Before proceeding to the next batch, all the memory (including the probability bank $\hat{Y}$) is released, except for the parameters θ''.

3.5   Memory Efficient Data Augmentation

Data augmentation is a widely-used technique in CL. However, in the extreme memory constraint scenario, standard data augmentation procedures cannot be used since it would result in an important memory cost. We propose a specific data-augmentation procedure that is integrated in our *BLD* framework. We use a set of data augmentation techniques (e.g., image cropping, flip, rotation, color jittering etc.) in order to artificially populate $\mathcal{B}$. In the warm-up stage, when filling the probability bank $\hat{Y}$, we also store the transformation type (e.g. rotation) and possible parameters (e.g. angle). However, we do not store the transformed images. Consequently, the memory cost of data augmentation remains negligible with respect to the batch and network memory sizes. In the *joint training* stage, when computing the feature $\mathbf{v}'$, we read the transformation information stored together with the probability bank and use it to re-generate the transformed images. The transformed image is then provided as input to the feature extractor. In this way, we use the same data augmentation in the two stages without requiring to store all the augmented images.

4   Experiments

4.1   Experimental Protocol

Datasets. We measure the performance of the proposed solution to MC-OCL using accuracy on three publicly available and widely used datasets.

The MNIST [18] and SVHN [23] datasets are composed of images depicting digits. In our experiments, both datasets are split into different tasks with non-overlapping classes. We choose not to perform experiments on the permuted variant of MNIST, since it has been shown to be a poor benchmark for CL [10]. Some previous works [2,3,21] prefer to extract a small subset of the samples for training. Instead, consistently with the most prior art, we use all the training data available. This choice enables us to assess which methods are robust to a large number of gradient steps and which are not.

CIFAR10 [16] is also split into disjoint tasks as in [2,4], with the difference that, given the memory constraints we introduce, we cannot store any data and therefore we are unable to perform validation. Consequently, we use all the training samples for training.

For all datasets we split the data into 2 and 5 tasks, which generates subsets of 5 and 2 classes respectively. This enables finer behavioral analysis of the model with respect to short and long task sequences. The splits are performed randomly, but, for fairness, we run all methods on the same splits to minimize the bias that different splits could introduce in the evaluation.

Implementation Details. Throughout all experiments, regardless of the dataset and the number of tasks, we employ a ResNet18 [11] as a feature extractor. As per Sect. 3.2, on top of the feature extractor we use a classifier composed of a linear layer and a softmax. As soon as a new task starts, a new classifier is instantiated with randomly initialized weights and biases.

For all experiments that only require a single sweep through the data we train on batches composed of 20 images, randomly sampled from a task-specific subset of data. We found this batch size to be the right trade-off for our experiments, since it well approximates the online setup without preventing the model from properly learning new tasks. These batches are then transformed 50 times and forwarded into the network. The gradients generated by all losses are averaged over these transformations. Note that these operations do not require any additional memory, since the transformations can be applied right before the forward pass, without storing the augmented images, and gradients can be averaged in-place. For the details on this matter refer to Algorithm 1 and 2. In Pytorch [25] this can be implemented by calling `backward()` multiple times (one for each transformation) without performing any optimization steps in-between.

Two iterations are performed for every joint training stage, with learning rate α_j set to 10^{-4}, while the *warm-up* stage is performed only once with a learning rate $\alpha_w = 10^{-2} \cdot \alpha_j$. The parameter λ has a value of 2. For *offline LwF* [20], instead, batches contain 500 images each and only one transformation is computed per batch. Depending on the dataset and the number of tasks we train the model for a different number of epochs, ranging from 10 epochs for MNIST (5-tasks) to 120 epochs for CIFAR10 (2-task) with learning rate equal to 10^{-4}. For all the methods, we run each experiment 5 times and report the average accuracy. Note that our method (*BLD*) is trained using only one epoch.

4.2   Experimental Evaluation

Baselines. Our method can be accommodated among regularization-based methods, which in turn can be divided into prior-based and data-driven categories. However, we do not consider prior-based baselines such as EWC [15] as they have been shown to work poorly in the online setting [2], and do not satisfy the MC-OCL constraints. Instead, we include an extensive comparison with *LwF* [20], which is the most similar data-driven method to ours. Therefore, we consider the following reference baselines:

- *Finetune.* It trains continuously as the data for the new task is available without any attempt to avoid forgetting;
- *Batch-level L2*, denoted as *L2*, is a naïve baseline we devised specifically for CL with extreme memory constraints. For every incoming batch it saves a copy of the parameters before the model gets updated. Subsequently, it proceeds to update the network, first with a *warm-up* step, similar to the *warm-up* we perform for our method, and then with a series of joint steps. These joint steps are the result of the back-propagation of two losses: the cross-entropy loss with respect to the current task and the *L2* loss between current and previous parameters.
- *Offline LwF* [20] (upper-bound) trained using multiple passes through the data, sampled i.i.d.. We use a variable number of epochs, depending on the size and the complexity of the dataset, while the batch size is fixed.
- *Single-pass LwF* [20] is a modified version of *LwF*, in which only a single-pass through the data is performed. The distillation mechanism is implemented as in the original offline version. Note that, although each sample is only processed once, this variant can not be considered fully online because it still needs to compute the predictions for the whole task beforehand.

Results and Analysis. Table 1 shows the performance of the evaluated methods on MNIST, CIFAR10 and SVHN on the 2-task scenario. Looking at the results of the *Finetune* model, the difference in performance between the two tasks T0 and T1 shows that the *Finetune* model suffers from catastrophic forgetting. The difference is especially important in the case of the MNIST (18.8%) and CIFAR10 (25.2%) datasets. We observe that *L2* mitigates this catastrophic forgetting issue reaching a higher average accuracy in the three datasets, at the cost of a higher memory consumption. *BLD* consistently improves the performance over all the datasets. Our method, obtains better scores on the task T0 compared

Table 1. Final test accuracy on MNIST, CIFAR10 and SVHN with 2 tasks

Method		MNIST			CIFAR10			SVHN		
		T0	T1	Avg.	T0	T1	Avg.	T0	T1	Avg.
MC-OCL	*Finetune*	80.8	99.6	90.2	60.4	85.6	73.0	78.9	95.5	87.2
	L2	91.7	99.6	**95.7**	70.7	84.0	77.4	82.8	96.2	89.5
	BLD	89.6	99.5	94.5	70.0	86.0	**78.0**	88.2	96.2	**92.2**
Single-pass	*LwF*	98.2	99.7	98.9	75.7	85.8	80.7	91.5	95.6	93.5
Offline	*LwF*	99.5	99.8	99.7	89.6	93.0	91.3	93.9	96.3	95.1

to the *Finetune* baseline. For CIFAR10 and SVHN, we also observe that *BLD* outperforms *Finetune* on T1, possibly due to the fact that some information from T0 has been used to improve the performance on T1 (*forward-transfer*). Overall, *BLD* reaches the best performance in two datasets out of three. Only *L2* performs slightly better on MNIST but requiring much more memory.

When it comes to comparing to the offline baseline that can have access to each image several times, we observe that our method can bridge half of the gap between *Finetune* and the offline *LwF* on the MNIST and SVHN datasets. Interestingly, *BLD* is able to obtain results close to the *single-pass LwF* on the SVHN dataset even though the latter breaks constraint (1) of MC-OCL.

Concerning the 5-tasks experiments, results are reported in Table 2, 3 and 4 for the MNIST, CIFAR10 and SVHN datasets, respectively. Note that, for every method, we also report the memory overhead. More specifically, we report the memory storage that is required by every method while training on the current batch (*Intra-batch*), when switching between batches (*Inter-batch*) and for data storage in the case of non-online methods. We report memory in bytes.

Table 2. Final test accuracy on MNIST with 5 tasks

Method		MNIST						Memory overhead		
		T0	T1	T2	T3	T4	Avg.	Intra-batch	Inter-batch	Data storage
MC-OCL	*Finetune*	66.6	68.0	76.8	91.8	99.8	80.6	–	–	–
	L2	54.9	55.7	85.7	94.0	99.8	78.0	44.8 MB	–	–
	BLD	78.0	82.5	93.0	96.4	99.7	**89.9**	32 kB	–	–
Single-pass	*LwF*	98.2	99.4	98.5	99.8	99.8	99.1	384 kB	384 kB	2 MB
Offline	*LwF*	99.5	99.6	98.0	99.8	99.8	99.3	384 kB	384 kB	2 MB

In the three datasets, we again observe strong catastrophic forgetting in the case of the *Finetune* model. Again, *L2* prevents forgetting to some extent but it has a high intra-batch memory overhead since it requires to store a copy of the network parameters. Despite its lower memory overhead, our approach reaches

Table 3. Final test accuracy on CIFAR10 with 5 tasks

Method		CIFAR10						Memory overhead		
		T0	T1	T2	T3	T4	Avg.	Intra-batch	Inter-batch	Data storage
MC-OCL	*Finetune*	59.6	58.2	66.8	80.2	97.0	72.3	–	–	–
	L2	75.5	65.3	73.5	81.3	96.8	78.5	44.8 MB	–	–
	BLD	83.4	83.2	79.5	88.1	97.0	**86.2**	32 kB	–	–
Single-pass	*LwF*	81.2	83.6	81.1	88.5	96.5	86.2	320 kB	320 kB	36.8 MB
Offline	*LwF*	93.8	94.1	91.6	96.2	98.3	94.8	320 kB	320 kB	36.8 MB

Table 4. Final test accuracy on SVHN with 5 tasks

Method		SVHN						Memory overhead		
		T0	T1	T2	T3	T4	Avg.	Intra-batch	Inter-batch	Data storage
MC-OCL	*Finetune*	65.9	60.6	77.5	87.6	98.4	78.0	–	–	–
	L2	75.2	61.8	90.9	93.4	98.1	81.3	44.8 MB	–	–
	BLD	78.5	79.6	92.1	95.7	98.1	**88.8**	32 kB	–	–
Single-pass	*LwF*	78.9	91.5	94.3	95.6	98.2	91.7	469 kB	469 kB	-
Offline	*LwF*	97.7	97.8	97.2	98.7	98.9	98.1	469 kB	469 kB	47.2 MB

the best performance on the three datasets with a significant margin with respect to *L2* (+11.9%, 7.7% and 7.5%, respectively). This result is extremely interesting since it shows that *BLD* can prevent the network from drifting and forgetting even for longer sequences of tasks.

When it comes to offline methods, they both outperform our proposed method. Nevertheless, we observe that *BLD* reaches the same performance as *Single-pass LwF* on CIFAR10, which requires access to the complete training set of the current task. This requirement leads non-negligible data storage depending on the dataset (from 2 MB to 47 MB for SVHN). Note that, the data storage requirement grows linearly with the size of the dataset. In addition, we observe that both methods require an intra-batch memory overhead approximately ten times higher than our approach.

Ablation Study. We perform an in-depth ablation study to evaluate each component of the proposed method. In addition to the *Finetune* and the *L2* baselines described above, we compare with the following variants of our models: *Alternated*, a model that does not perform joint updates but simply alternates between a learning step on the new task and a distillation step, and *No-balancing*, a variant of our model that uses our two-stage approach but where the cross-entropy $\mathcal{L}_t$ and distillation $\mathcal{L}_d$ losses are not dynamically balanced. More precisely, this method is equivalent to our full model replacing $\frac{\|G_w\|}{\|G_j\|}$ with 1 in Algorithm 2. In Table 5, *Full* denotes the full model as described in Sect. 3.

Table 5. Ablation study on the CIFAR10 datatset with 2 and 5 tasks

(a) 2 tasks (5 classes each)

Method	T0	T1	Avg.
Finetune	60.4	85.6	73.0
L2	70.7	84.0	77.4
Alternated	57.8	85.8	71.8
No-balancing	61.4	86.3	73.8
Full	70.0	86.0	**78.0**

(b) 5 tasks (2 classes each)

Method	T0	T1	T2	T3	T4	AVG
Finetune	59.6	58.2	66.8	80.2	97.0	72.3
L2	75.5	65.3	73.5	81.3	96.8	78.5
Alternated	77.7	74.5	70.2	87.1	96.9	81.3
No-balancing	78.5	72.9	74.9	85.0	96.9	81.6
Full	83.4	83.2	79.5	88.1	97.0	**86.2**

The results of the ablation study are reported in Table 5. As previously observed, the *Finetune* model suffers from catastrophic forgetting. The forgetting problem is even clearer on the 5-task setting. As in previous experiments, *L2* helps preventing forgetting but breaks our proposed constraints. *Alternated* improves the performance on the 5-task setting but deteriorates on the 2-task setting, showing that naively alternating between new task learning and distillation is not enough in our challenging scenario. Conversely, we observe that the *No-balancing* model improves the performance with respect to *Finetune* in both settings. Note that, in the 2-task setting, *No-balancing* and the full model outperform *Finetune* on T1. This shows that our two-stage pipeline might produce some *forward transfer* from task T0 to T1. On the 5-task setting, the gain of *No-balancing* is more important (+9.3% with respect to *Finetune* and +0.9% with respect to *alternated*). Finally, using our dynamic gradient weighting with balancing leads to further improvement reaching the highest performance. The gain in performance is consistent over all the tasks and is especially clear for the first tasks. This ablation study experimentally confirms the importance of the two-stage approach and the dynamic gradient weighting.

5   Conclusions

In this paper we proposed setting that allows us to study continual learning under extreme memory constraints. More precisely, we impose two constraints: 1) No information is passed between batches and tasks; 2) No auxiliary network can be used. To tackle this setting that cannot be addressed by the current methods, we introduced Batch-level Distillation. Based on knowledge distillation, our approach proceeds in two stages where, first, we start learning the new task classifier and compute old classifier predictions, and then, we perform a joint training using both distillation and the new task loss. We evaluated our method on three publicly available datasets and show that *BLD* can efficiently prevent catastrophic forgetting. As future work, we plan to extend *BLD* to other problems such as image segmentation and object detection.

Acknowledgements. We acknowledge financial support from the European Institute of Innovation & Technology (EIT) and the H2020 EU project SPRING - Socially

Pertinent Robots in Gerontological Healthcare. This work was carried out under the "Vision and Learning joint Laboratory" between FBK and UNITN.

References

1. Aljundi, R., Babiloni, F., Elhoseiny, M., Rohrbach, M., Tuytelaars, T.: Memory aware synapses: learning what (not) to forget. In: Ferrari, V., Hebert, M., Sminchisescu, C., Weiss, Y. (eds.) ECCV 2018. LNCS, vol. 11207, pp. 144–161. Springer, Cham (2018). https://doi.org/10.1007/978-3-030-01219-9_9
2. Aljundi, R., et al.: Online continual learning with maximal interfered retrieval. In: NeurIPS, pp. 11849–11860 (2019)
3. Aljundi, R., Kelchtermans, K., Tuytelaars, T.: Task-free continual learning. In: CVPR (2019)
4. Aljundi, R., Lin, M., Goujaud, B., Bengio, Y.: Gradient based sample selection for online continual learning. In: NeurIPS (2019)
5. Castro, F.M., Marín-Jiménez, M.J., Guil, N., Schmid, C., Alahari, K.: End-to-end incremental learning. In: Ferrari, V., Hebert, M., Sminchisescu, C., Weiss, Y. (eds.) ECCV 2018. LNCS, vol. 11216, pp. 241–257. Springer, Cham (2018). https://doi.org/10.1007/978-3-030-01258-8_15
6. Cermelli, F., Mancini, M., Bulo, S.R., Ricci, E., Caputo, B.: Modeling the background for incremental learning in semantic segmentation. In: CVPR, pp. 9233–9242 (2020)
7. Chaudhry, A., Dokania, P.K., Ajanthan, T., Torr, P.H.S.: Riemannian walk for incremental learning: understanding forgetting and intransigence. In: Ferrari, V., Hebert, M., Sminchisescu, C., Weiss, Y. (eds.) ECCV 2018. LNCS, vol. 11215, pp. 556–572. Springer, Cham (2018). https://doi.org/10.1007/978-3-030-01252-6_33
8. Dhar, P., Singh, R.V., Peng, K.C., Wu, Z., Chellappa, R.: Learning without memorizing. In: CVPR (2019)
9. Duda, R.O., Hart, P.E., Stork, D.G.: Pattern Classification, 2nd edn. Wiley, New York (2000)
10. Farquhar, S., Gal, Y.: Towards robust evaluations of continual learning. arXiv preprint arXiv:1805.09733 (2018)
11. He, K., Zhang, X., Ren, S., Sun, J.: Deep residual learning for image recognition. In: CVPR, pp. 770–778 (2016)
12. Hinton, G., Vinyals, O., Dean, J.: Distilling the knowledge in a neural network. stat (2015)
13. Hou, S., Pan, X., Loy, C.C., Wang, Z., Lin, D.: Learning a unified classifier incrementally via rebalancing. In: CVPR (2019)
14. Javed, K., White, M.: Meta-learning representations for continual learning. In: NeurIPS, pp. 1820–1830 (2019)
15. Kirkpatrick, J., et al.: Overcoming catastrophic forgetting in neural networks. In: PNAS (2017)
16. Krizhevsky, A.: Learning multiple layers of features from tiny images. Technical report (2009)
17. Lange, M.D., et al.: Continual learning: a comparative study on how to defy forgetting in classification tasks. arXiv:1909.08383 (2019)
18. LeCun, Y., Cortes, C.: MNIST handwritten digit database (2010). http://yann.lecun.com/exdb/mnist/
19. Lee, S., Ha, J., Zhang, D., Kim, G.: A neural dirichlet process mixture model for task-free continual learning. In: ICLR (2020)

20. Li, Z., Hoiem, D.: Learning without forgetting. IEEE T-PAMI **40**(12), 2935–2947 (2017)
21. Lopez-Paz, D., Ranzato, M.: Gradient episodic memory for continual learning. In: NIPS (2017)
22. Mallya, A., Lazebnik, S.: PackNet: adding multiple tasks to a single network by iterative pruning. In: CVPR (2018)
23. Netzer, Y., Wang, T., Coates, A., Bissacco, A., Wu, B., Ng, A.Y.: Reading digits in natural images with unsupervised feature learning. In: NIPS (2011)
24. Ostapenko, O., Puscas, M., Klein, T., Jahnichen, P., Nabi, M.: Learning to remember: a synaptic plasticity driven framework for continual learning. In: CVPR (2019)
25. Paszke, A., et al.: Automatic differentiation in pytorch (2017)
26. Rebuffi, S.A., Kolesnikov, A., Sperl, G., Lampert, C.H.: iCaRL: incremental classifier and representation learning. In: CVPR (2017)
27. Riemer, M., et al.: Learning to learn without forgetting by maximizing transfer and minimizing interference. arXiv preprint arXiv:1810.11910 (2018)
28. Rusu, A.A., et al.: Progressive neural networks. arXiv preprint arXiv:1606.04671 (2016)
29. Shin, H., Lee, J.K., Kim, J., Kim, J.: Continual learning with deep generative replay. In: NeurIPS (2017)
30. Wu, C., Herranz, L., Liu, X., van de Weijer, J., Raducanu, B., et al.: Memory replay GANs: learning to generate new categories without forgetting. In: NeurIPS (2018)
31. Wu, Y., et al.: Large scale incremental learning. In: CVPR (2019)

Learning to Cluster Under Domain Shift

Willi Menapace[1(✉)], Stéphane Lathuilière[3], and Elisa Ricci[1,2]

[1] University of Trento, Trento, Italy
willi.menapace@gmail.com
[2] Fondazione Bruno Kessler, Trento, Italy
[3] LTCI, Télécom Paris, Institut Polytechnique de Paris, Palaiseau, France

Abstract. While unsupervised domain adaptation methods based on deep architectures have achieved remarkable success in many computer vision tasks, they rely on a strong assumption, i.e. labeled source data must be available. In this work we overcome this assumption and we address the problem of transferring knowledge from a source to a target domain when both source and target data have no annotations. Inspired by recent works on deep clustering, our approach leverages information from data gathered from multiple source domains to build a domain-agnostic clustering model which is then refined at inference time when target data become available. Specifically, at training time we propose to optimize a novel information-theoretic loss which, coupled with domain-alignment layers, ensures that our model learns to correctly discover semantic labels while discarding domain-specific features. Importantly, our architecture design ensures that at inference time the resulting source model can be effectively adapted to the target domain without having access to source data, thanks to feature alignment and self-supervision. We evaluate the proposed approach in a variety of settings (Code available at https://github.com/willi-menapace/acids-clustering-domain-shift), considering several domain adaptation benchmarks and we show that our method is able to automatically discover relevant semantic information even in presence of few target samples and yields state-of-the-art results on multiple domain adaptation benchmarks.

Keywords: Unsupervised learning · Domain adaptation · Deep clustering

1 Introduction

The astonishing performance of deep learning models in a large variety of applications must be partially ascribed to the availability of large-scale datasets with abundant annotations. Over the years, several solutions have been proposed to

---

Electronic supplementary material The online version of this chapter (https://doi.org/10.1007/978-3-030-58604-1_44) contains supplementary material, which is available to authorized users.

A. Vedaldi et al. (Eds.): ECCV 2020, LNCS 12373, pp. 736–752, 2020.
https://doi.org/10.1007/978-3-030-58604-1_44

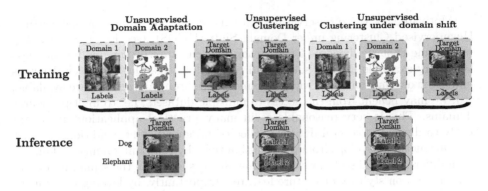

Fig. 1. In the Unsupervised Domain adaptation (UDA) setting, a model is trained combining labeled images from one or several source domains and unlabeled images from the target domain. In the unsupervised clustering setting, unlabeled images from the same domain are grouped into visually similar images. We introduce the Unsupervised Clustering under Domain Shift (UCDS) setting where we leverage unlabeled source domain data to improve target domain clustering.

avoid prohibitively expensive and time-consuming data labeling such as transfer learning [25] or domain adaptation [6] strategies. In particular, unsupervised domain adaptation (UDA) methods [2, 10, 16–18, 22, 26, 28, 41] leverage the knowledge extracted from labeled data of one (or multiple) source domain(s) to learn a prediction model for a different but related target domain where no labeled data are available. This strategy is illustrated in Fig. 1-left.

Over the last decade, increasing efforts have been devoted to develop deep architectures for UDA and promising results have been obtained in several applications such as object recognition [2, 17, 34], semantic segmentation [10], depth estimation [42], etc. While effective in many tasks, current UDA methods rely on a key assumption: annotations associated with data from the source domain(s) must be available. In this paper, we argue that this assumption may hinder the use of UDA in many practical applications. For instance, relaxing the constraints of disposing of labeled source data can broaden the applicability of knowledge transfer methods to tasks and scenarios where gathering annotations is challenging or even impossible (e.g. medical).

A possible alternative to supervised training is unsupervised clustering (Fig. 1-center). Clustering is a class of unsupervised learning methods that are designed to group images in such a way that images in the same group contain similar content. Recently, some works [4, 9, 12] have shown that appropriately designed deep architectures can be successfully used to discover clusters in a training set and perform representation learning. By opposition to UDA, clustering does not require any annotation. However, it relies on the assumption that all the data belongs to the same domain. If this condition is not fulfilled, clustering algorithms would tend to group data according to the visual style associated to their domain and not according to their semantic content.

Motivated by these observations, in this paper, we propose a new setting, Unsupervised Clustering under Domain Shift (UCDS), (see Fig. 1-right) where we assume that we dispose of data from different known domains but no class labels are available in both source and target domains. Our approach develops under the assumption that, while no annotations from source data are available, still we may benefit from the access to multiple datasets, i.e. to multiple source domains. This is very reasonable as in many practical applications it is very likely to dispose of several datasets collected under different conditions.

Our method develops from the intuition that, by combining multiple domains with different visual styles, we can obtain clusters based on the semantic content rather than on stylistic or texture features. Importantly, by leveraging multiple source domains, we show that the target domain can be clustered accurately even when target data is limited. Our method is organized in two steps. First, a novel multi-domain deep clustering model is learned which, by seamlessly combining domain-specific distribution alignment layers [2] and an information-theoretic loss permits to discover semantic categories across domains. In a subsequent step, target data are exploited to refine the learned clustering model by simultaneously matching source features distributions with domain-alignment layers and by maximizing the mutual information between the class assignments of pairs of perturbed samples. Recalling these elements, we name our algorithm ACIDS: Adaptive Clustering of Images under Domain Shift.

The major advantage of our two-stage pipeline is that it does not require source and target data to be available simultaneously. Consequently, our setting differs from classical UDA and unsupervised transfer learning scenarios [6,25] since only the source model is provided to the unlabeled target domain. Discarding the source data at adaptation time can broaden the applicability of our framework to tasks and scenarios that suffer from transmission or privacy issues. Our extensive experimental evaluation demonstrates that our approach successfully discovers semantic categories and outperforms state of the art unsupervised learning models on popular domain adaptation benchmarks: Office-31 [29], PACS [14] and Office-Home [37] dataset.

Contributions. To summarize, the main contributions of this work are: (i) We introduce a new setting, Unsupervised Clustering under Domain Shift (Fig. 1-right), where we learn a semantic predictor from unsupervised target samples leveraging from multiple unlabeled source domains; (ii) We propose an information-theoretic algorithm for unsupervised clustering that operates under domain shift. Our method successfully integrates the data-augmentation strategy typically used by deep clustering methods [12] within a feature alignment process; (iii) We evaluate our method on several domain adaptation benchmarks demonstrating that our approach can successfully discover semantic categories even in the presence of domain shift and with few target samples.

2   Related Works

In the following we review previous approaches on UDA, discussing both single source and multi-source methods. Since we propose a deep architecture for unsupervised learning under domain shift, we also review related work on deep clustering.

Domain Adaptation. Earlier UDA methods assume that only a single source domain is available for transferring knowledge. These methods can be roughly categorized into three main groups. The first category includes methods which align source and target data distributions by matching the distribution statistical moments of different orders. For instance, Maximum Mean Discrepancy, *i.e.* the distance between the mean of domain feature distributions, is considered in [17, 18, 36, 37], while second order statistics are used [22, 26, 33]. Domain alignment layers derived from batch normalization (BN) [11] or whitening transforms [31] are employed in [2, 16, 21, 28].

The methods in the second category learn domain-invariant representations considering an adversarial framework. For instance, in [7] a gradient reversal layer is used to learn domain-agnostic representations. Similarly, ADDA [35] introduces a domain confusion loss to align the source and the target domain feature distributions. The third category of methods consider a generative framework (i.e., GANs ([8]) to create synthetic source and/or target images. Notable works are CyCADA [10], I2I Adapt [23] and Generate To Adapt (GTA) [30]. Our method is related to previous works in the first category, as we also leverage domain-alignment layers to perform adaptation. However, we consider a radically different setting where no annotation is provided in the source domain and only the source model (and not the source data) is exploited at adaptation time.

While most previous works on UDA consider a single source domain, recently some works have shown that performance can be considerably improved by leveraging multiple datasets. For instance, in [21] multiple latent source domains are discovered and used for transferring knowledge. Recently, Deep Cocktail Network (DCTN) [40] introduce a distribution-weighted rule for classification which is combined with an adversarial loss. M^3SDA is described in [27]: it reduces the discrepancy between the multiple source and the target domains by dynamically aligning moments of their feature distributions.

Differently from these methods, ACIDS does not assume annotations in the source domain. One related work to ours is [20] where information from multiple source domains is exploited for constructing a domain-dependency graph and then used when the target data are made available. However, in [20] an entropy loss for target model adaptation is considered, which we experimentally observe is less effective than our proposal self-supervised loss. Our method is also related to recent domain generalization (DG) methods [1, 15]. In fact, similarly to DG, we also assume that source and target data are not simultaneously available. However, differently from DG, we make use of target data for model adaptation when they are available.

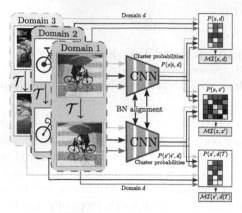 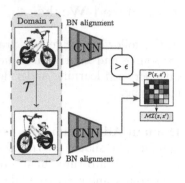

(a) Training on Sources   (b) Adaptation on Target

Fig. 2. Illustration of the ACIDS framework for UCDS. In the training stage (Fig. 2a), images are clustered by maximizing mutual information between the predictions from the original and transformed images. Domain alignment is addressed combining a Batch Normalization (BN) alignment technique with a novel mutual information minimizing formulation. In the adaptation phase (Fig. 2b), domain shift is handled by combining BN alignment with a specific mutual information maximization procedure.

Deep Clustering. Over the last few years, unsupervised representation learning has attracted considerable attention in the computer vision community. Self-supervised learning approaches mostly differ in the self-supervised losses used to learn feature representations. Notable examples are methods which derive indirect auxiliary supervision from spatial-temporal consistency [38], from solving jigsaw puzzles [24] or from colorization [13].

Recently, some studies have attempted to derive deep clustering algorithms which simultaneously discover groups in training data and perform representation learning. For instance, DEC [39] makes use of an autoencoder to produce a latent space where cluster centroids are learned. DAC [5] casts the clustering problem into pairwise-classification using a convolutional network to learn feature representations. In [4] DeepCluster, an iterative clustering procedure is devised which adopts k-means to learn representations and uses the subsequent assignments as supervision. Similarly, in [9] an end-to-end clustering approach is proposed where an encoder network is trained with an alternate scheme. Recently, Ji *et al.* propose Invariant Information Clustering (IIC) [12], where a deep network is learned with an information-theoretic criterion in order to output semantic labels, rather than high dimensional representations. Our approach is inspired by this method. However, we specifically address the problem of transferring knowledge from source to target domains.

3   Proposed Method

In this section, we introduce the proposed ACIDS fully unsupervised multi-source domain adaptation framework. The design of the source training framework is guided by two motivations. First, we need to take advantage of the different domains in order to obtain clusters that correspond to semantic labels rather than domain-specific image styles. Second, the network must learn image representations that can be transferred to any unknown target domain.

We assume to observe S source domains I_s composed of images, each depicting an object from C different object categories. In this work, we assume that C is known a priori but we do not dispose of image labels. We propose to learn image representations allowing to cluster source images according to the unknown category labels. Our goal is to adapt the representation learned on the source domains in order to predict labels on a target domain I_t. In this adaptation stage, we consider that we do not dispose of the images from $I_1, \ldots, I_S$. To this aim, we employ a deep neural network $\phi_\theta : I \to Z$ with parameters θ that predicts cluster assignments probabilities. To obtain network outputs $Z \in [0,1]^C$ that can be interpreted as probability vectors, ϕ_θ is terminated by a layer with a softmax activation function.

In Sect. 3.1 we describe the objective used to cluster source images. In order to ensure clustering based on semantic labels and not on domain-specific styles, we introduce in Sect. 3.2 a novel information-theoretic alignment mechanism based on the minimization of mutual information between domains and cluster assignments. Here, we also detail our batch normalization alignment layers that complement the framework. Adaptation on the target domain is described in Sect. 3.3.

3.1   Multi-domain Clustering with Mutual Information

Let $i \in I = \bigcup_{s=1}^{S} I_s$ be an image from the domain $d \in 1..S$. Both i and d are treated here as random variables. We consider that we dispose of a set of image transformations $\mathcal{T}$. After sampling a transformation $t \in \mathcal{T}$, we obtain a transformed version of the image i denoted as i'. Following the approach of [12], we train ϕ_θ in such a way that, first, it returns the same output for both i and i' and, second, it returns different outputs for different images. This double objective can be achieved by maximizing the mutual information between the predictions from i and i' with respect to the network parameters:

$$\max_{\theta} \mathcal{MI}(z, z') \tag{1}$$

where $z = \phi_\theta(x)$ and $z' = \phi_\theta(x')$ are the network cluster assignment predictions. To estimate the mutual information $\mathcal{MI}(z, z')$, we need to compute the joint probability of the cluster assignment $P_{cc'} = P(z=c, z'=c')$ where $c \in 1..C$ and $c' \in 1..C$ are all the possible cluster indexes. This probability is estimated by marginalization over the current batch. Let us assume to observe a batch composed of N unlabeled images $\{i_s^n\}_{n=1}^N \subset I_s$ from each of S source domains. We have:

$$P_{cc'} = P(z=c, z'=c') = \sum_{s=1}^{S} P(d=s)P(z=c, z'=c'|d=s)$$
$$= \frac{1}{SN} \sum_{s=1}^{S} \sum_{n=1}^{N} \phi_\theta(i_s^n) \cdot \phi_\theta(i_s^{n'})^\top \qquad (2)$$

Similarly, we estimate the marginal distribution:

$$P_c = P(z=c) = \frac{1}{S} \sum_{s=1,n=1}^{S \times N} \phi_\theta(i_s^n) \text{ and } P'_c = P(z=c') = \frac{1}{S} \sum_{s=1,n=1}^{S \times N} \phi_\theta(i_s^{n'}).$$

From these probability distributions, the mutual information loss is given by:

$$\mathcal{MI}(z, z') = \sum_{c=1}^{C} \sum_{c'=1}^{C} P_{cc'} \ln \frac{P_{cc'}}{P_c \cdot P_{c'}} \qquad (3)$$

3.2   Domain Alignment

Feature Alignment via Mutual Information Minimization. Training the network ϕ_θ only via the maximization of (3) may lead to solutions where input images are clustered according to the domain information rather than their semantics. To tackle this problem, feature distribution from the different domains should be aligned in such a way that the classifier cannot cluster images according to the domain. We propose to address this domain alignment problem by the combination of two complementary strategies.

First, we propose to formulate domain alignment as a mutual information optimization problem. The key idea of ACIDS alignment strategies is that cluster assignment z should be independent from the domain d of the input image. Consequently, the mutual information between the predicted label z and the image domain d must be minimal. To this aim, we estimate the joint probability distribution $P(z, d)$ by marginalization:

$$P(z, d) = \frac{1}{N} \sum_{s=1}^{S} \sum_{n=1}^{N} \mathbb{1}(s = d)\phi_\theta(i_s^n) \qquad (4)$$

Similarly to (3), we can estimate $\mathcal{MI}(z, d)$. Note that this mutual information loss leads to an extremely limited computation overhead compared to alternative solutions such as adversarial approaches.

Even though minimizing $\mathcal{MI}(z, d)$ enforces alignment between the domains, this formulation does not take advantage of the image transformation framework described in Sect. 3.1. In order to further use the potential of our data augmentation approach, we propose to use the transformed image to favor domain alignment. More specifically, for every transformation $t \in \mathcal{T}$, the cluster assignment z' should be independent from the domain d of the input image. In other words, the mutual information $\mathcal{MI}(z', d|t)$ should be minimized for every transformation t.

Here again, the mutual information $\mathcal{MI}(z', d|t)$ is computed via marginalization similarly to $\mathcal{MI}(z, z')$ and $\mathcal{MI}(z, d)$.

This mutual information minimization is both lightweight and efficient. Nevertheless, it acts only according to a top-down strategy, since alignment is imposed only on the output of the network and not in the early layers. Consequently, we propose to complement our framework with a feature alignment strategy based on batch normalization that acts all over the network.

Feature Alignment via Batch Normalization. We consider that the network ϕ_θ embeds Batch normalization (BN) layers. We adopt the idea of previous works [2,16,19] and perform domain adaptation by updating the BN statistics. The main assumption behind this strategy is that the domain-shift can be reduced by aligning the different source feature distributions to a Gaussian reference distribution. We consider that we observe S batches of images, one from each of the S source domains. Assuming a given BN layer, $\{x_s^n\}_{n=1}^N$ and $\{x_s^{n'}\}_{n=1}^N$ denote the features, corresponding to domain s, in input to the BN layer for each image and the transformed counterpart respectively. We compute the batch statistics for each domain separately:

$$\forall s \in \{1..S\}, \quad \hat{\mu}_s = \frac{1}{2m}\sum_{n=1}^N (x_s^n + x_s^{n'}) \quad \hat{\sigma}_s^2 = \frac{1}{2m}\sum_{n=1}^N [(x_s^n - \hat{\mu}_s)^2 + (x_s^{n'} - \hat{\mu}_s)^2] \quad (5)$$

For a given input x computed from an image of the domain s, the output of the normalization layer is computed as follows:

$$\hat{x} = \gamma \frac{x - \mu_s}{\sqrt{\sigma_s^2 + \epsilon}} + \beta \tag{6}$$

where γ and β are the usual affine transformation parameters of the BN layer, while $\epsilon \in \mathbb{R}$ is a constant introduced for numerical stability. Note that the affine transformation parameters are shared among the different domains. This strategy guarantees that every BN layer outputs feature distributions from every domain with a mean value equal to 0 and a variance equal to 1. The main advantage of ACIDS framework is twofold. First, it does not require any additional loss that would imply more hyper-parameter tuning to obtain good convergence. Second, adaptation on the target data can be performed without accessing the source data.

3.3 Training and Adaptation Procedures

Overall Objective Function. In the previous section, we detailed how we estimate three different mutual information terms. The term $\mathcal{MI}(z, z')$ must be maximized while $\mathcal{MI}(z, d)$ and $\mathcal{MI}(z', d|t)$ must be minimized. Consequently the total minimization objective function can be written:

$$\mathcal{L} = -\mathcal{MI}(z, z') + \mathcal{MI}(z, d) + \frac{1}{T}\sum_{t \in \mathcal{T}} \mathcal{MI}(z', d|t). \tag{7}$$

where T is that cardinality of $\mathcal{T}$.

Improving Stability. The computation of the mutual information $\mathcal{MI}(z, z')$ is based on the estimation of the marginal probability matrix $P_{cc'} \in \mathbb{R}^{C \times C}$. Following a standard SGD approach, this matrix is computed for every batch. However, estimating this full probability matrix from a small batch can be inaccurate when the number of classes C is high. In addition, increasing the batch size may lead to memory issues. Practically, we observed in our preliminary experiments, that a large batch size is critical to obtain satisfying convergence of the IIC model. In our context, the issue appears to be even stronger since the images originate from different domains. Our assumption is that the higher variance of the features, despite feature alignment, leads to gradients with higher variance and unstable training. To tackle this issue, we propose to robustify the estimation of the marginal probability matrices using a moving average strategy. Considering that $P_{cc'}$ is the matrix associated to the current batch, the mutual information in Eq. (3) is computed using $\tilde{P}_{cc'}$:

$$\tilde{P}_{cc'} = \alpha P_{cc'} + (1 - \alpha)\hat{P}_{cc'} \tag{8}$$

where $\hat{P}_{cc'}$ is the probability matrix $\tilde{P}_{cc'}$ estimated on the previous batch and α is a dynamic parameter. From a probabilistic point of view, this formulation can be understood as a stronger marginalization since the distribution is estimated considering in Eq. (2) not only on the N samples of the current batches but also the past batches. This estimation is correct under the assumption that the network ϕ_θ did not change too much in past SGD steps.

Adaptation to the Target Domain. At test time, we dispose of images from the target domain $\{i_\tau^n\}_{n=1}^{N_\tau} \in I_\tau$. However, we assume that we do not dispose anymore of the training data from the source domains. Adaptation is performed using two successive procedures. First, in order to align the feature distribution of the target data with the source distributions, we estimate the statistics of the inputs of each BN layer as in Eq. (5). The output of each BN layer is then computed according to Eq. (6). Second, our model is adapted using a variant of the mutual formulation used at training time and described in Sect. 3.1 computed only on the target domain I_τ. We argue that in an unsupervised setting it is beneficial to treat samples with high prediction confidence differently from the ones with low confidence [32]. The rationale is to drive low confidence predictions towards certainty represented by high confidence predictions while not altering the latter. We propose to treat images i_τ with a prediction confidence larger than a given threshold ϵ as fixed points whose output class prediction c must be replicated by the corresponding transformed image i_τ'. This differs from the mutual information approach employed in Sect. 3.1 where the output correspondence is achieved only implicitly and an incorrect class assignment to image i_τ' may negatively alter the prediction of i_τ as well, causing instability. We define:

$$\tilde{\phi}_\theta(i) = \begin{cases} \mathbb{1}(c = \arg\max \phi_\theta(i)) & \text{if } \max \phi_\theta(i) \geq \epsilon \\ \phi_\theta(i) & \text{otherwise} \end{cases}$$

Table 1. Ablation results on the PACS dataset: (i) training is performed on a single, merged source domain (ii) training performed on a single source domain, (iii) removed feature alignment via mutual information minimization, (iv) removed BN feature alignment + (iii); (v) no target adaptation, (vi) target adaptation using entropy instead of mutual information. Accuracy (%) on target domain.

Target domain:	A	C	P	S	Avg
Merged source (i)	23.6	32.8	31.2	28.2	29.0
Single source A (ii)	–	31.0	45.8	28.7	–
Single source C (ii)	31.0	–	42.5	35.0	–
Single source P (ii)	33.0	33.8	–	30.5	–
Single source S (ii)	25.0	30.2	37.2	–	–
w/o domain mi loss (iii)	27.4	24.3	50.9	23.0	31.4
w/o BN alignment (iv)	23.7	34.3	38.6	23.0	22.1
w/o target adaptation (v)	34.8	36.5	44.2	40.8	39.1
entropy target adaptation (vi)	29.2	36.6	29.7	41.0	34.1
ACIDS	**42.1**	**44.5**	**64.4**	**51.1**	**50.5**

$$P_{cc'} = \frac{1}{N} \sum_{n=1}^{N} \tilde{\phi}_\theta(i_\tau^n) . \phi_\theta(i_\tau^{n'})^\top \text{ and } P_c = P(z=c) = \sum_{n=1}^{N} \tilde{\phi}_\theta(i_\tau^n)$$

Then, we compute the mutual information term $\mathcal{MI}(z, z')$ in Eq. 3 using the newly defined $P_{cc'}$ and P_c. This newly defined mutual information loss no longer suffers from the wrong i_τ' prediction problem because the arg max operation stops gradient propagation in the high confidence predictions, fixing them and making the model focus on low confidence ones.

4   Experiments

In this section, we evaluate the effectiveness of ACIDS on three widely used domain adaptation datasets and perform an ablation study showing the importance of each component of our method.

Datasets. The PACS [14] dataset is a domain adaptation dataset composed of 9,991 images divided in 7 classes spanning 4 different domains: Photo (P), Art (A), Cartoon (C) and Sketch (S). The different domains of PACS represent a rich variety of visual characteristics, from natural images to sketches, which cause large semantic gaps and make it a challenging domain adaptation dataset.

The Office31 dataset [29] contains 4,110 images divided in 3 different domains and 31 classes, namely: Amazon (A), DSLR (D) and Webcam (W).

The Office-Home [37] dataset is a larger domain adaptation benchmark containing about 15,500 images belonging to 65 different classes across 4 domains:

Art (A), Clipart (C), Product (P), RealWorld (R). In addition to containing domains with a large variety of visual characteristics, the dataset presents the challenge of a large number of classes.

Evaluation Protocol. We perform multiple evaluations of our model, considering at each time one of the domains as the target and the remaining ones as the source domains. We train the model until convergence on all the sources. Then, the target domain becomes available and the source domains are discarded. At adaptation time we instantiate the domain-specific BN parameter for the target domain and perform their estimation using the newly available target images. This provides the starting point for the adaptation phase which proceeds until convergence on the target domain. In all our experiments we report the accuracy score computed on the target domain.

Implementation Details. We use a randomly initialized ResNet-18 as the backbone of our model. Following [12], we adopt an overclustering strategy that fosters the model to learn more discriminant features. Instead of using only a single head with a number of outputs equal to C, we add an auxiliary overclustering head with a larger number of outputs and train the two in alternating epochs. Joint training was also considered as an alternative, but performance was negatively affected. We use respectively 49, 155 and 130 output units in the auxiliary head for the PACS, Office-Home and Office31 datasets respectively. Moreover, in order to increase robustness to bad head initialization and facilitate convergence, we replicate both the standard and the overclustering head 5 times and compute the losses for the current batch on each of them, using the average loss as the optimization objective. Further implementation details are reported in supplementary material.

4.1 Ablation Study

In this section, we present the results of our ablation study evaluating the impact of each of the components of ACIDS. We produce different variations of our method obtained as follows: (i) Training is performed on a single source domain created by merging all the source domains; (ii) Training is performed only on a single source domain, while the others are discarded; (iii) The feature alignment via mutual information mechanism proposed in Sect. 3.2 is removed; (iv) Both the feature alignment via mutual information minimization mechanism and the Batch normalization feature alignment mechanism are removed, relying only on the mutual information clustering loss during training; (v) No target adaptation is performed; (vi) During adaptation the mutual information clustering loss is replaced by a prediction entropy maximization loss with threshold.

We report the quantitative results on the PACS dataset in Table 1. The ablation (iii) confirms the importance of using the mutual information loss for feature alignment during training. An analysis of the produced label assignments which we report in the supplementary material, in fact, shows that without this alignment mechanism the model produces clusters based on the domain rather than the underlying classes. The effect is that the network focuses more on learning style differences between domains rather than on semantic features, resulting in degraded performance. Removing also the BN feature alignment mechanism (iv) exacerbates the alignment problems, producing features that are not representative of the image's semantics. Moreover, training using only a single domain as the source (ii) shows a loss in performance with respect to multi-source training, highlighting that the model acquires stronger generalization capabilities when given information about the multiple sources. Furthermore, (i) shows that it is beneficial to instantiate different BN parameters for each source domain, otherwise, the domain shift between the multiple source domains would not be mitigated. Lastly, the proposed mutual information procedure for target adaptation outperforms the entropy-based target domain adaptation method (vi) which causes a degradation in time of the performance after a small gain in the first few epochs.

In the supplementary material we report an additional ablation on the α parameter introduced in Sect. 3.3.

4.2   Comparison with Other Methods

We now present a comparison of ACIDS against different baseline methods. We employ two popular deep clustering methods as the first baselines, namely IIC [12] and DeepCluster [4]. In both cases, we train the model using only the target data. The choice of IIC is motivated by its similarity to our method and by its state-of-the-art clustering performance [12]. For fairness, we make use of a ResNet-18 backbone on both methods and train them on the target domain. Besides, we introduce two variations of IIC that include source information: *IIC-Merge*: We train IIC on a dataset obtained by merging all the source and the target domain together; *IIC+DIAL*: Following [3], we insert domain-specific BN layers into IIC and jointly train on all source domains plus the target domain. We also compare our method with a continuous domain adaptation strategy used in [20] where we use ACIDS for training on the sources but adopt an entropy loss term for the target adaptation phase which is performed online. We also provide upper bounds for our method's performance given by SOTA domain adaptation algorithms using labeled source domains.

We report the performance of our method on the PACS dataset in Table 2. Our method performs substantially better than the DeepCluster and IIC baselines in the Art, Cartoon and Sketch domains with accuracy gains in the range from 2.3% to 4.9% with respect to IIC, while on the Photo domain our approach does not reach its performance. Moreover, our adaptation procedure outperforms the continuous domain adaptation baseline whose entropy loss does capture the semantic aspects given by our mutual information approach. The comparison with the upper bounds shows instead the obvious advantage of using supervision on the source domains. Due to the large difference of this setting with the proposed one, we omit these upper bounds from the successive evaluations.

Table 2. Comparison of the proposed approach with SOTA on the PACS dataset. Accuracy (%) on target domain. MS denotes multi source DA methods.

	Source supervision	C,P,S→A	A,P,S→C	A,C,S→P	A,C,P→S	Avg
DeepCluster [4]	✗	22.2	24.4	27.9	27.1	25.4
IIC [12]	✗	39.8	39.6	**70.6**	46.6	49.1
IIC-Merge [12]	✗	32.2	33.2	56.4	30.4	38.1
IIC [12] + DIAL [3]	✗	30.2	30.5	50.7	30.7	35.3
Continuous DA [20]	✗	35.2	34.0	44.2	42.9	39.1
ACIDS	✗	**42.1**	**44.5**	64.4	**51.1**	**50.5**
AdaBN [16]	✓	77.9	74.9	95.7	67.7	79.1
DIAL [3]	✓	87.3	85.5	97.0	66.8	84.2
DDiscovery [21] MS	✓	87.7	86.9	97.0	69.6	85.3
Jigsaw [1] MS	✓	84.9	81.07	98.0	79.1	85.7
AutoDIAL [2] MS	✓	90.3	90.9	97.9	79.2	89.6

Table 3. Comparison of the proposed approach with SOTA on the Office31 dataset. Accuracy (%) on target domain.

	D,W→A	A,W→D	A,D→W	Avg
DeepCluster [4]	19.6	18.7	18.9	19.1
IIC [12]	31.9	34.0	37.0	34.3
IIC-Merge [12]	29.1	**36.1**	33.5	32.9
IIC [12] + DIAL [3]	28.1	35.3	30.9	31.4
Continuous DA [20]	20.5	28.8	30.6	26.6
ACIDS	**33.4**	**36.1**	**37.5**	**35.6**

In Table 3 we report the performance of ACIDS on the Office31 dataset. The proposed approach achieves state of the art results, performing better than both DeepCluster and IIC on all domains with accuracy gains from 0.5% to 2.1% with respect to the strongest baseline.

Lastly, Table 4 shows the results obtained on the Office-Home dataset. The proposed approach performs significantly better than the DeepCluster baseline on each domain and performs better than IIC on the Clipart and Product domains. Similarly to the results on the PACS dataset, our target adaptation procedure performs better than the continuous domain adaptation strategy.

Table 4. Comparison of the proposed approach with SOTA on the Office-Home dataset. Accuracy (%) on target domain.

	C,P,R→A	A,P,R→C	A,C,R→P	A,C,P→R	Avg
DeepCluster [4]	8.9	11.1	16.9	13.3	12.6
IIC [12]	**12.0**	15.2	22.5	**15.9**	16.4
IIC-Merge [12]	11.3	13.1	16.2	12.4	13.3
IIC [12] + DIAL [3]	10.9	12.9	15.4	12.8	13.0
Continuous DA [20]	10.2	11.5	13.0	11.7	11.6
ACIDS	**12.0**	**16.2**	**23.9**	15.7	**17.0**

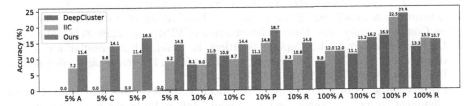

Fig. 3. Comparison of the proposed approach with SOTA on the Office-Home dataset in the limited target data scenario. Labels express the target domain (A,C,P or R) and the percentage of images used in the target domain.

4.3 Limited Target Data Scenario

One of the major advantages of ACIDS is the possibility of extracting semantic features from the source domains that directly transfer to the target domain. This makes it particularly suitable for the task of domain adaptation when few target samples are available. We repeat the same experiments of Sect. 4.2 on the Office-Home dataset where the source domains are not altered and we consider a target domain built by randomly sampling a given portion of images in each class of the original target domain. We show the numerical results in Fig. 3. We achieve a large performance boost compared to the baselines, in particular, we achieve an average 4.1% and 4.9% increase in accuracy with respect to IIC when 10% and 5% of the target images are available. Note that DeepCluster is not able to operate in the 5% scenario due to an insufficient number of target samples.

5   Conclusions

In this paper, we propose a novel domain adaptation setting and show it is possible to transfer knowledge from multiple source domains to a target domain when both sources and target data have no annotations. Our method makes use of a novel information-theoretic loss for feature alignment and couples it with domain-alignment layers to discover semantic labels from the source domains. When target data becomes available, we perform adaptation without requiring the availability of source data. We achieve state-of-the-art performance on three widely used domain adaptation datasets and show a clear advantage of the proposed approach under low target data conditions. Future works will consider the adaptation of the approach to the unsupervised segmentation scenario.

Acknowledgements. We acknowledge financial support from H2020 EU project SPRING - Socially Pertinent Robots in Gerontological Healthcare. This work was carried out under the "Vision and Learning joint Laboratory" between FBK and UNITN.

References

1. Carlucci, F.M., D'Innocente, A., Bucci, S., Caputo, B., Tommasi, T.: Domain generalization by solving jigsaw puzzles. In: Proceedings of the IEEE Conference on Computer Vision and Pattern Recognition (CVPR), pp. 2229–2238 (2019)
2. Carlucci, F.M., Porzi, L., Caputo, B., Ricci, E., Bulò, S.R.: Autodial: automatic domain alignment layers. In: Proceedings of the IEEE International Conference on Computer Vision (ICCV), pp. 5077–5085 (2017)
3. Carlucci, F.M., Porzi, L., Caputo, B., Ricci, E., Bulò, S.R.: Just dial: domain alignment layers for unsupervised domain adaptation. In: Image Analysis and Processing - International Conference on Image Analysis and Processing (ICIAP) 2017, pp. 357–369 (2017)
4. Caron, M., Bojanowski, P., Joulin, A., Douze, M.: Deep clustering for unsupervised learning of visual features. In: Ferrari, V., Hebert, M., Sminchisescu, C., Weiss, Y. (eds.) Computer Vision – ECCV 2018. LNCS, vol. 11218, pp. 139–156. Springer, Cham (2018). https://doi.org/10.1007/978-3-030-01264-9_9
5. Chang, J., Wang, L., Meng, G., Xiang, S., Pan, C.: Deep adaptive image clustering. In: IEEE International Conference on Computer Vision (ICCV), pp. 5880–5888 (2017)
6. Csurka, G.: Domain Adaptation in Computer Vision Applications. ACVPR, vol. 2. Springer, Cham (2017). https://doi.org/10.1007/978-3-319-58347-1
7. Ganin, Y., Lempitsky, V.: Unsupervised domain adaptation by backpropagation. In: Proceedings of the 32nd International Conference on International Conference on Machine Learning (ICML), vol. 37, pp. 1180–1189 (2015)
8. Goodfellow, I., et al.: Generative adversarial nets. In: Advances in Neural Information Processing Systems (NIPS), pp. 2672–2680 (2014)
9. Haeusser, P., Plapp, J., Golkov, V., Aljalbout, E., Cremers, D.: Associative deep clustering: training a classification network with no labels. In: Brox, T., Bruhn, A., Fritz, M. (eds.) GCPR 2018. LNCS, vol. 11269, pp. 18–32. Springer, Cham (2019). https://doi.org/10.1007/978-3-030-12939-2_2
10. Hoffman, J., et al.: CyCADA: cycle-consistent adversarial domain adaptation. In: Proceedings of the 35th International Conference on Machine Learning (ICML). Proceedings of Machine Learning Research, PMLR, 10–15 July 2018, vol. 80, pp. 1989–1998. http://proceedings.mlr.press/v80/hoffman18a.html
11. Ioffe, S., Szegedy, C.: Batch normalization: accelerating deep network training by reducing internal covariate shift. In: International Conference on Machine Learning (ICML), pp. 448–456 (2015)
12. Ji, X., Vedaldi, A., Henriques, J.F.: Invariant information clustering for unsupervised image classification and segmentation. In: IEEE/CVF International Conference on Computer Vision (ICCV), pp. 9864–9873 (2019)

13. Larsson, G., Maire, M., Shakhnarovich, G.: Learning representations for automatic colorization. In: Leibe, B., Matas, J., Sebe, N., Welling, M. (eds.) ECCV 2016. LNCS, vol. 9908, pp. 577–593. Springer, Cham (2016). https://doi.org/10.1007/978-3-319-46493-0_35

14. Li, D., Yang, Y., Song, Y.Z., Hospedales, T.M.: Deeper, broader and artier domain generalization. In: Proceedings of the IEEE International Conference on Computer Vision (ICCV), pp. 5542–5550 (2017)

15. Li, D., Zhang, J., Yang, Y., Liu, C., Song, Y.Z., Hospedales, T.M.: Episodic training for domain generalization. In: Proceedings of the IEEE International Conference on Computer Vision (ICCV), pp. 1446–1455 (2019)

16. Li, Y., Wang, N., Shi, J., Liu, J., Hou, X.: Revisiting batch normalization for practical domain adaptation. In: 5th International Conference on Learning Representations (ICLR). OpenReview.net (2017). https://openreview.net/forum?id=Hk6dkJQFx

17. Long, M., Cao, Y., Wang, J., Jordan, M.I.: Learning transferable features with deep adaptation networks. In: Proceedings of the 32nd International Conference on Machine Learning (ICML), vol. 37, pp. 97–105 (2015)

18. Long, M., Zhu, H., Wang, J., Jordan, M.I.: Deep transfer learning with joint adaptation networks. In: Proceedings of the 34th International Conference on Machine Learning (ICML), vol. 70, pp. 2208–2217 (2017)

19. Mancini, M., Karaoguz, H., Ricci, E., Jensfelt, P., Caputo, B.: Kitting in the wild through online domain adaptation. In: IEEE/RSJ International Conference on Intelligent Robots and Systems (IROS), October 2018

20. Mancini, M., Bulo, S.R., Caputo, B., Ricci, E.: AdaGraph: unifying predictive and continuous domain adaptation through graphs. In: Proceedings of the IEEE Conference on Computer Vision and Pattern Recognition (CVPR), pp. 6568–6577 (2019)

21. Mancini, M., Porzi, L., Rota Bulò, S., Caputo, B., Ricci, E.: Boosting domain adaptation by discovering latent domains. In: Proceedings of the IEEE Conference on Computer Vision and Pattern Recognition (CVPR), pp. 3771–3780 (2018)

22. Morerio, P., Cavazza, J., Murino, V.: Minimal-entropy correlation alignment for unsupervised deep domain adaptation. In: International Conference on Learning Representations (ICLR) (2018). https://openreview.net/forum?id=rJWechg0Z

23. Murez, Z., Kolouri, S., Kriegman, D., Ramamoorthi, R., Kim, K.: Image to image translation for domain adaptation. In: The IEEE Conference on Computer Vision and Pattern Recognition (CVPR), pp. 4500–4509, June 2018

24. Noroozi, M., Favaro, P.: Unsupervised learning of visual representations by solving jigsaw puzzles. In: Leibe, B., Matas, J., Sebe, N., Welling, M. (eds.) ECCV 2016. LNCS, vol. 9910, pp. 69–84. Springer, Cham (2016). https://doi.org/10.1007/978-3-319-46466-4_5

25. Pan, S.J., Tsang, I.W., Kwok, J.T., Yang, Q.: Domain adaptation via transfer component analysis. IEEE Trans. Neural Netw. **22**, 199–210 (2011)

26. Peng, X., Saenko, K.: Synthetic to real adaptation with generative correlation alignment networks. In: 2018 IEEE Winter Conference on Applications of Computer Vision (WACV), pp. 1982–1991 (2018)

27. Peng, X., Bai, Q., Xia, X., Huang, Z., Saenko, K., Wang, B.: Moment matching for multi-source domain adaptation. In: CVPR, pp. 1406–1415, October 2019

28. Roy, S., Siarohin, A., Sangineto, E., Bulo, S.R., Sebe, N., Ricci, E.: Unsupervised domain adaptation using feature-whitening and consensus loss. In: Proceedings of the IEEE Conference on Computer Vision and Pattern Recognition (CVPR), pp. 9463–9472 (2019)

29. Saenko, K., Kulis, B., Fritz, M., Darrell, T.: Adapting visual category models to new domains. In: Daniilidis, K., Maragos, P., Paragios, N. (eds.) ECCV 2010. LNCS, vol. 6314, pp. 213–226. Springer, Heidelberg (2010). https://doi.org/10.1007/978-3-642-15561-1_16

30. Sankaranarayanan, S., Balaji, Y., Castillo, C.D., Chellappa, R.: Generate to adapt: aligning domains using generative adversarial networks. In: CVPR (2018)

31. Siarohin, A., Sangineto, E., Sebe, N.: Whitening and coloring transform for GANs (2019). https://openreview.net/forum?id=S1x2Fj0qKQ

32. Sohn, K., et al.: FixMatch: simplifying semi-supervised learning with consistency and confidence (2020)

33. Sun, B., Saenko, K.: Deep CORAL: correlation alignment for deep domain adaptation. In: Hua, G., Jégou, H. (eds.) ECCV 2016. LNCS, vol. 9915, pp. 443–450. Springer, Cham (2016). https://doi.org/10.1007/978-3-319-49409-8_35

34. Tzeng, E., Hoffman, J., Darrell, T., Saenko, K.: Simultaneous deep transfer across domains and tasks. In: Proceedings of the IEEE International Conference on Computer Vision (ICCV), pp. 4068–4076 (2015)

35. Tzeng, E., Hoffman, J., Saenko, K., Darrell, T.: Adversarial discriminative domain adaptation. In: Proceedings of the IEEE Conference on Computer Vision and Pattern Recognition (CVPR), pp. 2962–2971 (2017)

36. Tzeng, E., Hoffman, J., Zhang, N., Saenko, K., Darrell, T.: Deep domain confusion: maximizing for domain invariance. arXiv preprint arXiv:1412.3474 (2014)

37. Venkateswara, H., Eusebio, J., Chakraborty, S., Panchanathan, S.: Deep hashing network for unsupervised domain adaptation. In: Proceedings of the IEEE Conference on Computer Vision and Pattern Recognition (CVPR), pp. 5018–5027 (2017)

38. Wang, X., He, K., Gupta, A.: Transitive invariance for self-supervised visual representation learning, pp. 1338–1347, October 2017. https://doi.org/10.1109/ICCV.2017.149

39. Xie, J., Girshick, R., Farhadi, A.: Unsupervised deep embedding for clustering analysis. In: Proceedings of the 33rd International Conference on International Conference on Machine Learning (ICML), ICML-2016, vol. 48, pp. 478–487 (2016)

40. Xu, R., Chen, Z., Zuo, W., Yan, J., Lin, L.: Deep cocktail network: multi-source unsupervised domain adaptation with category shift. In: Proceedings of the IEEE Conference on Computer Vision and Pattern Recognition (CVPR), pp. 3964–3973 (2018)

41. Zen, G., Sangineto, E., Ricci, E., Sebe, N.: Unsupervised domain adaptation for personalized facial emotion recognition. In: Proceedings of the 16th International Conference on Multimodal Interaction (2014)

42. Zhao, S., Fu, H., Gong, M., Tao, D.: Geometry-aware symmetric domain adaptation for monocular depth estimation. In: Proceedings of the IEEE Conference on Computer Vision and Pattern Recognition (CVPR), pp. 9788–9798 (2019)

Defense Against Adversarial Attacks via Controlling Gradient Leaking on Embedded Manifolds

Yueru Li, Shuyu Cheng, Hang Su[(✉)], and Jun Zhu[(✉)]

Deptartment of Computer Science and Technology, BNRist Center, Institute for AI, THBI Lab, Tsinghua University, Beijing 100084, China
{liyr18,chengsy18}@mails.tsinghua.edu.cn,
{suhangss,dcszj}@tsinghua.edu.cn

Abstract. Deep neural networks are vulnerable to adversarial attacks. Though various attempts have been made, it is still largely open to fully understand the existence of adversarial samples and thereby develop effective defense strategies. In this paper, we present a new perspective, namely gradient leaking hypothesis, to understand the existence of adversarial examples and to further motivate effective defense strategies. Specifically, we consider the low dimensional manifold structure of natural images, and empirically verify that the leakage of the gradient (w.r.t input) along the (approximately) perpendicular direction to the tangent space of data manifold is a reason for the vulnerability over adversarial attacks. Based on our investigation, we further present a new robust learning algorithm which encourages a larger gradient component in the tangent space of data manifold, suppressing the gradient leaking phenomenon consequently. Experiments on various tasks demonstrate the effectiveness of our algorithm despite its simplicity.

Keywords: Gradient leaking · DNNs · Adversarial robustness

1 Introduction

Deep neural networks (DNNs) have shown impressive performance in a variety of application domains, including computer vision [13], natural language processing [18] and cybersecurity [6]. However, it has been widely recognized that their predictions could be easily subverted by the adversarial perturbations that are carefully crafted and even imperceptible to human beings [27]. The vulnerability of DNNs to adversarial examples along with the design of appropriate countermeasures has recently drawn a wide attention.

Y. Li and S. Cheng—Equal contribution.

Electronic supplementary material The online version of this chapter (https:// doi.org/10.1007/978-3-030-58604-1_45) contains supplementary material, which is available to authorized users.

© Springer Nature Switzerland AG 2020
A. Vedaldi et al. (Eds.): ECCV 2020, LNCS 12373, pp. 753–769, 2020.
https://doi.org/10.1007/978-3-030-58604-1_45

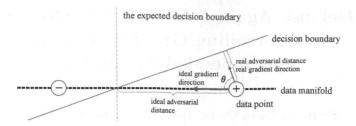

Fig. 1. An illustration of gradient leaking. If the manifold and decision boundaries are relatively flat, the robust distance in this case is approximately the order of $O(\cos(\theta))$ (θ is the angle between gradient direction and the tangent space) of the theoretical longest distance on the manifold.

Recent years have witnessed the development of many kinds of defense algorithms. However, it still remains a challenge to achieve robustness against adversarial attacks. For example, defenses based on input transformation or randomization usually give obfuscated gradients [1] and hence could be cracked by adaptive attacks. Defenses such as adversarial training [17] and controlling Lipschitz constants [20] will significantly decrease the gradient norm of the model loss function, which may sacrifice the accuracy on natural images. The difficulty in designing defense algorithms is partly due to the unclear reason for the existence and pervasiveness of adversarial examples. Though various attempts have been made including the linearity of the decision boundary [8], insufficiency of samples [25], the concentration property of high dimensional constraints [26] and the computational constraints [2], it is still an open question to explore the intrinsic mechanism of adversarial examples and design better defense algorithms.

In our paper, we analyze the existence of adversarial examples from the perspective of the data manifold, and propose a new hypothesis called *Gradient Leaking Hypothesis*. When analyzing the adversarial robustness at a given data point (which is classified correctly as class y), we focus on the *adversarial gradient*, i.e. the gradient of the objective function in untargeted attack such as the negative predicted likelihood function of class y. As is illustrated in Fig. 1, the ideal direction of adversarial gradient lies in (the tangent space of) the data manifold, so that only the necessary gradient to classify the dataset remains. However, through extensive analysis we find that in most normally trained models, the gradient points to a nearly perpendicular direction to the data manifold, resulting in the leakage of gradient information and weak robustness in adversarial attacks. In such cases, adversarial examples can be found outside of but very close to the data manifold. As shown in the figure, the perturbation norm of the adversarial is the order of $\cos(\theta)$ relative to that in the ideal case.

As the adversarial gradient is approximately perpendicular to the decision boundary between the original class and the class of the adversarial example, a more intuitive description of gradient leaking is that the decision boundary is nearly *parallel to* the data manifold, which implies vulnerability to adversarial attacks. To show its reason visually, we illustrate an inspiring example

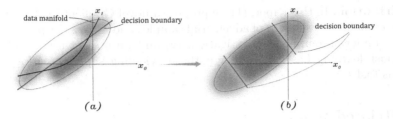

Fig. 2. An illustrative case when gradient leaking happens (a), and our method to train a robust classifier through preprocessing the dataset (b).

in Fig. 2(a). The data points are distributed in different colored regions corresponding to the different classes. We identify an approximate 1-dimensional data manifold shown as the black parabolic curve (we exaggerate the distance from data points to the manifold in the figure). The dataset is linearly separable shown as the purple line. However, it is nearly parallel to the data manifold, which does not correspond to a robust classifier. The adversary could perturb the data points in a perpendicular direction to the data manifold, suggesting that gradient leaking happens. We see that vulnerability to the adversarial attack is usually caused by some small-scale features (e.g., the direction perpendicular to the decision boundary in Fig. 2(a)) which are easily learned by the classifier since they might be highly correlated to the labels. This is also in line with recent studies such as [11] which demonstrate that adversarial examples can be attributed to the non-robust features useful for classification.

Based on the above analysis, we present a novel data preprocessing framework to reduce gradient leaking during training, thereby enhancing the adversarial robustness. We first make the data manifold flat by projecting the dataset to the PCA principal subspace to eliminate the small-scale features mentioned above. After that, we add independent noise in the normal space of the data manifold to enforce the classifier to learn a decision boundary nearly perpendicular to the data manifold. The result is illustrated in Fig. 2(b), in which we change the data distribution to learn a robust classifier that remains a high accuracy on the original dataset. Extensive experiments demonstrate that we can obtain a more robust model in image classification and face recognition tasks. By simply preprocessing images before training, we can achieve a 2–3 times improvement on the mean perturbation norm of adversarial examples under a powerful ℓ_2-BIM attack. Our algorithm is nearly orthogonal to other methods and can be easily integrated with them. As an example, we integrate our method with the Max-Mahalanobis center (MMC) loss training [19], and reach much higher robustness compared to the baseline MMC. The robustness of our obtained model is close to that of the model trained by adversarial training [17], yet with a much higher clean accuracy and much lower training time cost.

Contribution. In this paper, (1) we propose a novel Gradient Leaking Hypothesis to explain the existence of adversarial samples and analyze its possible mechanisms under an empirical investigation; (2) and we present a novel algorithm of robust learning based on our hypothesis, yielding superior performance in various tasks.

2   Related Work

[2] analyzes four opinions on adversarial samples. The authors point out that though robust models could exist, the requirement of robustness and computational efficiency might contradict in specific task. Our analysis and empirical evidence support the idea that there is a trade-off between "easiness to learn" and robustness. [25] claims that sampling complexity may be the reason for adversarial samples, but we point out that having more samples on the manifold may not help if the gradient leaking is not suppressed efficiently.

The authors in [7] analyze the geometric properties of DNN image classifiers in the input space. They show that DNNs learn connected classification regions, and the decision boundary in the vicinity of data points is flat along most directions. But they claim the results reflect the complex topological properties of classification regions. We believe that it could happen in spaces with simple topology (for example, homeomorphic to $\mathbb{R}^D$) caused by gradient leaking.

[11] points out that adversarial examples are highly related to the presence of non-robust features, which are brittle and incomprehensible to humans. They distill robust features from a robust model. Our work bridges the inherent geometry of data manifold and the robustness of features, and could be considered as developing a way to quantitatively study the reliance of classifier on these non-robust features, and using them to improve the robustness of DNNs.

The authors of [9] systematically suggest a framework of Gaussian noise randomization to improve robustness. They inject isotropic Gaussian noise, whose scale is trainable through solving the Min-Max optimization problem embedded with adversarial training, at each layer on either activation or weights. Our noise adding procedure could be seen as a variant considered as a subspace selection procedure to add Gaussian noise on the input.

Defense-GAN [24] shows that by projecting data points to lower-dimensional manifold during inference time, the classifier can be more robust. Their defense partially relies on obfuscated gradients [1] and is only tested on MNIST. By contrast, our method is applied to the training process, able to obtain a robust classifier used in a vanilla way, and more scalable to larger datasets.

3   Gradient Leaking Hypothesis

In this section, we first present the Gradient Leaking Hypothesis formally, and analyze its relationship with robustness empirically.

3.1   Preliminary

In general, the data points $\{x_i\}$ in a natural image dataset lie on a manifold $\mathbb{M}$ embedded in $\mathbb{R}^D$, which is called the *ambient space*. The intrinsic dimension of $\mathbb{M}$, n, is generally much lower than D. A **tangent space** of $\mathbb{M}$ on x (denoted as $T_x\mathbb{M}$) can be defined as

$$T_x\mathbb{M} := \left\{ v \Big| \exists \text{ differentiable curve } \gamma : [-\epsilon, \epsilon] \to \mathbb{M}, \gamma(0) = x, \ s.t. \ v = \frac{d\gamma}{dt}\Big|_{t=0} \right\},$$

which is a linear subspace of $\mathbb{R}^D$. Moreover, the **normal space** on x (denoted as $N_x\mathbb{M}$) is the orthogonal complement of the tangent space $T_x\mathbb{M}$.

3.2   Gradient Leaking

We now formally present the gradient leaking hypothesis. Without loss of generality, we consider a two-class classification problem. Typically, we want to learn a prediction function $h : \mathbb{R}^D \to [0,1]$ such that $h(x) = p(y = 1|x)$. Assuming that all the data points are on the manifold $\mathbb{M}$, then the restriction of h on $\mathbb{M}$ (denoted by $h|_\mathbb{M}(x)$) completely determines training loss and testing accuracy. In other words, if we have a function e defined on $\mathbb{R}^D$ such that $\forall x \in \mathbb{M}$, $e(x) = 0$, then $h + e$ shares the same training/testing statistics with h since they are the same on $\mathbb{M}$. However, the adversarial robustness of $h + e$ and h could be very different, since adversarial examples usually do not lie on the manifold $\mathbb{M}$. This is an ambiguity of the functions in $\mathbb{R}^D$, when they share the same values on $\mathbb{M}$.

Considering this ambiguity issue, we need to specify an extension of some given $h|_\mathbb{M}(x)$ to $\mathbb{R}^D$ for adversarial robustness. Specifically, the following is a desirable property suggesting adversarial robustness of an extension h:

$$\forall x \in \mathbb{M}, \nabla h(x) \in T_x\mathbb{M}, \tag{1}$$

which means that the prediction does not change if x is perturbed in a perpendicular direction of the manifold tangent space. Intuitively, the adversary cannot perform the attack successfully by only perturbing the input image away from the manifold. We note that the tangent component of $\nabla h(x)$ is indispensible to enable the value of $h(x)$ to vary on the manifold to classify the dataset, and hence intuitively, Eq. (1) describes an ideal case to maintain the accuracy while improving robustness.

In reality, however, the classifier is usually inclined to make its gradient nearly perpendicular to the tangent space of the data manifold. We call this phenomenon **gradient leaking**. Formally speaking, we propose *Gradient Leaking Hypothesis* as follows:

Let h denote the learned prediction function in typical machine learning tasks and $x \in \mathbb{M}$. If we decompose the gradient into the tangent space and normal space as $\nabla h(x) = v_\| + v_\perp$, where $v_\| \in T_x\mathbb{M}$ and $v_\perp \in N_x\mathbb{M}$, then $\|v_\|\| \ll \|v_\perp\|$.

The hypothesis suggests that even if h is a good classifier on the manifold $\mathbb{M}$, it may fail to be robust since it puts too much of its gradient in the normal space of the manifold. An geometric description of gradient leaking is that the hypersurface $\{x : h(x) = c\}$ for $c \in (0,1)$ is nearly parallel to the data manifold, while in the ideal case they should be perpendicular to each other. When $c = 0.5$, the hypersurface $\{x : h(x) = c\}$ is the decision boundary, so gradient leaking basically means that the decision boundary is along the data manifold.

An illustrating case when gradient leaking happens is shown in Fig. 3. The data manifold is the green sine-wave surface, in which the part above the blue surface is in one class, and the part below the blue surface is in the other class. The blue surface itself seems a natural choice to classify the two classes since it is nearly linear, but the classifier using it as the decision boundary is not a robust classifier, since we can change its prediction by perturbing the data point up or down slightly. This aligns with our gradient leaking hypothesis since the blue surface is nearly parallel to the data manifold. A more robust decision boundary should be perpendicular to the data manifold, but it must be wave-like as well, making it more difficult to learn in practice.

Intuitively, the non-robust classifier corresponding to the blue surface utilizes the direction of fluctuation of the data manifold, which could be rather small despite correlating with the true label well. We call such directions *small-scale features*, and call their opposite, the main spanning direction of the data manifold, *large-scale features*. Similar cases of gradient leaking happens in real datasets as well, since there exist such small-scale features like textures. We assume that in the learning procedure, the classifier would rely

Fig. 3. Illustration of the gradient leaking phenomenon. The green surface is the data manifold (all of the data points are on it), and the label is decided by whether the data point is above or below the blue surface. However, if the blue surface is chosen as the decision boundary, then gradient leaking occurs and the classifier is not robust. (Color figure online)

on the most discriminative dimensions, which may be small-scale but linear separable. We perform a data poisoning experiment on CIFAR10 (see Appendix E) to verify the hypothesis that the preference for small scale features may cause the classifier to be non-robust.

Our hypothesis can explain the limitation of the present methods. For example, the gradient regularization methods [12,23] or Lipschitz limited methods [5,15] assume that one could design a robust model by making the gradient norm smaller. Adversarial training [8] has shown a great performance which can reduce the gradient norm considerably. However, these methods do not distinguish between the tangent space and the normal space, and cannot preserve the useful gradient component in the tangent space while reducing that in the normal space. Our hypothesis suggests that to improve robustness, we should focus on the direction instead of the norm of the gradient. Moreover, simply increasing the number of training data points may not help much [4], because

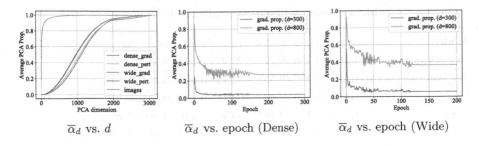

$\overline{\alpha}_d$ vs. d $\overline{\alpha}_d$ vs. epoch (Dense) $\overline{\alpha}_d$ vs. epoch (Wide)

Fig. 4. Average PCA proportion of the gradient on CIFAR10.

points sampled from the data manifold tell the classifier nothing about what its prediction should be outside of the manifold.

3.3   Empirical Study

In this section, we empirically show that the gradient leaking phenomenon widely exists in DNNs.

Evaluation Metric. To detect the gradient leaking phenomenon in the real scenario, it is expected that we can clearly recognize the tangent space and normal space on each point at a low cost, which demands an efficient way to represent the data manifold approximately. Among various choices, in this paper, we resort to the PCA subspace since it is convenient yet effective for manifold representation. Specifically, suppose the PCA eigenvectors are $\{v_1, v_2, ..., v_D\}$ in a descending order of corresponding eigenvalues, which is an orthogonal basis of the ambient space. We refer to the d-dimensional PCA (principal) subspace as spanned by $\{v_1, v_2, ..., v_d\}$, where $d \ll D$. We define an evaluation metric of gradient leaking, with the PCA principal subspace serving as an approximation to the local tangent space. For a data point x, suppose $g = \nabla f(x)$ is the adversarial gradient where f is some loss function w.r.t. the label of x. Then a larger proportion of g in the PCA subspace indicates less gradient leaking, which can be calculated as

$$\alpha_d(g) = \frac{\sum_{i=1}^{d}(g^\top v_i)^2}{\|g\|_2^2}. \tag{2}$$

We note that for $d_1 < d_2$, $0 \le \alpha_{d_1}(g) \le \alpha_{d_2}(g) \le 1$. By drawing a curve of $\alpha_d(g)$ to $d \in \{1, 2, ..., D\}$, complete information of g can be recovered.

Existence of Gradient Leaking Phenomenon. We conduct experiments on CIFAR10 ($D = 32 \times 32 \times 3 = 3072$) by training two different state-of-the-art network architectures, namely DenseNet [10] and Wide-ResNet [31]. We also conduct experiments on CASIA-WebFace, a dataset for face recognition, but leave the results to Appendix C due to space limitation. To evaluate the extent

Table 1. Statistics of 8 pretrained models on ImageNet.

Model	inc	res50	res152	vgg	ens	hgd	iat	iat-den	R^2
Accuracy	0.769	0.740	0.751	0.694	0.764	0.787	0.602	0.639	
1/Mean grad norm	0.115	0.197	0.157	0.272	0.264	0.248	1.535	1.743	0.904
$\overline{\alpha}_{400}$	0.011	0.020	0.021	0.018	0.037	0.014	0.145	0.152	**0.940**
$\overline{\alpha}_{1241}$	0.053	0.102	0.103	0.096	0.146	0.060	0.284	0.296	0.878
$\overline{\alpha}_{6351}$	0.333	0.449	0.465	0.628	0.559	0.314	0.588	0.612	0.319
Mean pert norm	0.199	0.190	0.306	0.262	1.084	0.540	1.952	2.332	–

of gradient leaking, we calculate the average PCA proportion of the gradient over the dataset as[1]

$$\overline{\alpha}_d \triangleq \frac{1}{N} \sum_{n=1}^{N} \alpha_d(\nabla f(x_n)). \tag{3}$$

We show the curve of $\overline{\alpha}_d$ vs. d at the last epoch in Fig. 4(a). It can be seen that the component of gradients in the PCA principal subspace is far less than the component of images in the same subspace, indicating that the model relies on small-scale features to classify, i.e. leaks gradient outside of the data manifold.

Meanwhile, we also explore the property of the adversarial perturbation direction here. We try to perturb the original input x such that the perturbed sample is misclassified, and find such smallest ℓ_2-perturbation $\delta(x)$ by the ℓ_2-BIM attack [14] implemented by Foolbox [21]. Then we calculate $\overline{\alpha}_d$ for $d = \{1, 2, ..., D\}$ in the same way except that $\nabla f(x_n)$ is replaced by $\delta(x_n)$, and draw the curve in the same figure. The PCA proportion of the gradient and the adversarial perturbation is almost identical, suggesting that the direction of adversarial samples could be seen as a first-order effect[2], hence reducing the gradient leaking phenomenon at data points should be a good option for improving the robustness.

Furthermore, we explore the trends of gradient leaking along the training process. For the training model, we plot $\overline{\alpha}_d$ to the training epochs for $d = 300$ and 800 in Fig. 4(b) on DenseNet and in Fig. 4(c) on Wide-ResNet[3]. At Epoch 0 (before training), gradient leaking is severe since the model has no knowledge of the data manifold then. At Epoch 1, the model leaks the least proportion of gradients since it learns to classify the data points in the data manifold during the first epoch. However, the gradient leaking becomes more and more notable in the remaining epochs. This validates our conjecture that small-scale features might be preferred by DNNs when they are discriminative and easy for classification. In the beginning of training, the models discover the data manifold and learn to classify with the large-scale features along the manifold. However, DNNs would

---

[1] We omit the dependence of the loss function f on the label of x_n.
[2] Though the distance may be affected by the non-linearity introduced by softmax.
[3] In CIFAR10, PCA with $d = 300$ and 800 preserve 96.85% and 99.40% of the energy of the image dataset respectively.

finally discover such small-scale features and use them to improve classification performance at the expense of robustness.

Gradient Leaking as an Indicator of Robustness. Having established that gradient leaking phenomenon exists when training typical neural architectures, we empirically study the relationship between the robustness and the tensity of gradient leaking. We note that the norm of the gradient might not be the best indicator of robustness, since that for example, an image with a rather small gradient norm could also have an adversarial example in its neighborhood.

We analyze 8 models trained on ImageNet, in which 4 are normally trained models ('inc': Inception-v3, 'vgg': VGG-16, 'res50': ResNet-v1-50, 'res152': ResNet-v2-152) and 4 are models which are intended to be robust ('ens': Inception-ResNet-v2 through ensemble adversarial training [28], 'hgd': An ensemble of networks with a high-level representation guided denoiser [16], 'iat': a ResNet-152 model through large-scale adversarial training [29], 'iat-den': the 'iat' model with feature-denoising layers [29]). We conduct the experiments on the first 1000 images in the validation set. The results are shown in Table 1. The d in $\overline{\alpha}_d$ is chosen as 400, 1241 and 6351 since they correspond to preserving 90%, 95% and 99% of the energy respectively after the images are projected to the PCA subspace. In the last column, we show the coefficient of determination R^2 of the linear regression which predicts the mean perturbation norm of the adversarial example we find by ℓ_2-BIM (the last row). Note that according to Fig. 1, the perturbation norm of adversarial examples should be approximately proportional to $\sqrt{\overline{\alpha}_d}$. We hence show R^2 w.r.t. $\sqrt{\overline{\alpha}_d}$ instead of $\overline{\alpha}_d$ here. We find that compared with the reciprocal of mean gradient norm, $\overline{\alpha}_{400}$ turns out to be a better indicator of the mean perturbation norm which represents adversarial robustness.[4]

Discussion. From the validation in the real scenario, we find that

1. Gradient leaking widely exists in DNNs. Considering that the PCA subspace can be much larger than the real data manifold, it might be worse than we already observed and be a reason for adversarial vulnerability.
2. Adversarial vulnerability is a first order phenomenon in the sense that the adversarial perturbation direction aligns with the gradient direction well.
3. During the training procedure, the gradients concentrate on main components at first, and then leak gradually, showing a clear dynamics of changing the gradients' direction to fit the small-scale features.
4. Small-scale features are preferred by DNNs. They could even generalize well on the testing dataset, but we need to reduce their effect in robustness-sensitive tasks.

---

[4] R^2 w.r.t. $\sqrt{\overline{\alpha}_{1241}}$ and $\sqrt{\overline{\alpha}_{6351}}$ deteriorate perhaps because the intrinsic dimension of the data manifold should be much smaller than 1241.

4   Adversarial Defenses

With our discussion above, making gradients lie in the tangent space of data manifold might be a central mission to construct a robust classifier. Hence, we propose to improve robustness by suppressing the gradient leaking phenomenon.

4.1   Making the Data Manifold Flat

To deal with gradient leaking, we consider modifying the training dataset to make the data manifold 'flat'. Taking Fig. 3 as an example, we propose to project the data manifold onto the blue surface, making the currently shown decision boundary invalid. It forces a model with sufficient expressive power to learn to classify with a more robust feature such as the coordinate along the blue surface (although the decision boundary could be more complicated).

Specifically, we propose to project the training dataset to its PCA principal subspace before training, so that the fluctuation of data manifold is partially eliminated. Note that in evaluation (Sect. 3.3), we consider the data manifold *as* the PCA hyperplane since they are similar in the large-scale stretching direction; however, they are very different in the training process as we mentioned above. Formally speaking, we project each data point x as[5]

$$x \leftarrow \sum_{i=1}^{d} \langle x, v_i \rangle v_i,$$

before training, where d is a hyperparameter representing the dimension of the PCA subspace, and $v_1, v_2, ..., v_d$ are the d principal eigenvectors. We note that we perform PCA projection during training process instead of during testing process, which suffices to improve robustness significantly. The time cost of computation of PCA principal eigenvectors is relatively small (see Appendix A).

4.2   Adding Noise in the Normal Space

A more direct way to suppress gradient leaking is to perform data augmentation so that the loss of the classifier would be large if the decision boundary is not perpendicular enough to the data manifold. The idea is best illustrated in Fig. 2. Figure 2(a) shows the original data distribution in which regions of two different colors represent two categories of data points. We recognize the black parabolic curve as the 1-D approximate data manifold. Figure 2(b) (approximately) shows that by adding noise independent of the label in the normal direction of the data manifold , the augmented data can force the classifier to learn a decision boundary that is perpendicular to the data manifold.

Adding noise in the normal space is in contrast to the previously introduced idea of flattening the data manifold. In Sect. 4.1, we actually did not impose constraints upon the classifier, but made it easier for it to learn the robust

---

[5] For clarity, we assume the dataset has been centralized so that $\bar{x} = \frac{1}{N} \sum_{n=1}^{N} x_n$ is 0.

Algorithm 1. Modifying training data for training robust models

---

Input: A training data point x; with the $N \times D$ training dataset $\mathbf{X} = [x_1, ..., x_N]^\top$, dimension d of PCA subspace, dimension m of the subspace to add noise, noise scale $c > 0$.

Output: Modified training data point x'.

1: Perform spectral decomposition on the covariance matrix $\mathbf{C} = \frac{1}{N}\sum_{n=1}^{N}(x_n - \bar{x})(x_n - \bar{x})^\top$ (where $\bar{x} = \frac{1}{N}\sum_{n=1}^{N} x_n$) as
$$\mathbf{C} = \sum_{i=1}^{D} \lambda_i v_i v_i^\top, \quad \lambda_1 \geq \lambda_2 \geq ... \geq \lambda_D;$$

2: Compute the components of $x - \bar{x}$ on $V = [v_1, v_2, ..., v_D]$ as
$$a \leftarrow V^\top(x - \bar{x});$$

3: Projecting x to the PCA subspace:
   For the ith component of a: $a_i \leftarrow 0, \quad$ for $\quad i = d+1, d+2, ..., D$;

4: Add noise:
$$a_i \leftarrow c\sqrt{\lambda_i}\xi_i, \quad \text{with} \quad \xi_i \overset{i.i.d.}{\sim} \mathcal{N}(0,1) \quad \text{for} \quad i = d+1, d+2, ..., d+m;$$

5: Reconstruction:
$$x' \leftarrow Va + \bar{x};$$

6: **return** x'.

---

decision boundary. Each of the two methods can be independently applied in theory. However, it is difficult to access the tangent space or the normal space in a general data manifold. But if we combine the two methods together, thanks to the fact that the dataset has been projected into a PCA hyperplane, we can access (a subspace of) the normal space easily by identifying it as the space spanned by remaining PCA eigenvectors orthogonal to the principal hyperplane.

Specifically, utilizing the PCA basis and combining with the method in Sect. 4.1, we modify the training data x as

$$x \leftarrow \sum_{i=1}^{d} \langle x, v_i \rangle v_i + \sum_{i=d+1}^{D} \sigma_i \xi_i v_i,$$

where $\xi_i \overset{i.i.d.}{\sim} \mathcal{N}(0,1)$ and $\{\sigma_i\}_{i=d+1}^{D}$ is a set of hyperparameters which could be set in a principled way. In this view, by adding label-irrelevant noise, we make the small-scale directions, i.e. $\{v_{d+1}, ..., v_D\}$ hardly utilized by the model for classification even if the decision boundary is highly non-linear, thus suppressing gradient leaking.

Contrast to former robust learning methods by randomization like [9] in which authors add isotropic Gaussian noise to weights or inputs of each layer, our method augments the dataset with Gaussian noise in the direction of PCA eigenvectors and in the specific subspace of small-scale features. To maximize the efficiency of injected noises, for a small value of integer m (e.g. $m = 10$), we set $\sigma_i = 0$ for all $i > d+m$ while setting σ_i to be a relatively large value for $d+1 \leq i \leq d+m$. With a subspace of lower dimension, the efficiency of noise sampling to cover the space could be much higher. Meanwhile, we find that this not only reduces the gradient component in the subspace spanned by $\{v_{d+1}, ..., v_{d+m}\}$ but also reduces the gradient components along other eigenvectors with small eigenvalues. A possible explanation is that by preventing the convolution kernel from being activated by some patterns, it will also drop other similar features (e.g. of similar frequency).

To summarize, we present our algorithm to preprocess the training data in Algorithm 1. Note that for $d + 1 \leq i \leq d + m$, we set $\sigma_i = c\sqrt{\lambda_i}$ which means that the scale of the ith dimension of the modified training dataset is c times larger than before.

5   Experiments

5.1   Primary Experiments

In this section, we apply our defense algorithm to improve the robustness upon the baseline training algorithm. We first present the experimental setup, and then report the quantitative results to demonstrate the effectiveness of our algorithm.

Experiment Setup
Dataset. We test our algorithms on two datasets, namely CIFAR10 (shown here) and CASIA-WebFace (see Appendix D).

Backbone Models. Same as in Sect. 3.3, namely DenseNet and Wide-ResNet.

Metric. We report the testing error rate on clean data (Err), the mean/median perturbation norm (Pert) that represents the robustness (higher is better), the mean gradient norm $\|g\|_2$ (Grad) (lower is better) and $\overline{\alpha}_d$ defined in Eq. (3) as relevant quantities of robustness (higher is better).

Attack Method. We perform ℓ_2-C&W attack [3] implemented in Foolbox 2.3.0 with default parameters, which is the strongest attack among the ones (including PGD [17], DDN [22], BIM and C&W) we have tested in Foolbox.

Experimental Results. We compare three different types of training methods, namely the ordinary training method ('ord'), our proposed algorithm ('noise') (with hyperparameters $c = 10$ and $m = 10$), and a degenerated version of our algorithm ('pca') by skipping the step of adding noise, i.e. Algorithm 1 without Line 4. In the testing phase (including robustness evaluation), we directly feed the original test image (without any preprocessing) into the trained models.

We report the experimental results in Table 2. The subscript of each method name refers to the dimension of PCA subspace d. With a suppression of utilization of small-scale features, our method consistently outperforms the ordinary models in terms of the robustness although there are different degrees of accuracy degeneration for clean images. It, from another side, provides an evidence

Table 2. CIFAR10 results of DenseNet and Wide-ResNet. The mean/median perturbation norm are in the 'Pert' column.

Method	DenseNet					Wide-ResNet				
	Err	Grad	$\overline{\alpha}_{300}$	$\overline{\alpha}_{800}$	Pert	Err	Grad	$\overline{\alpha}_{300}$	$\overline{\alpha}_{800}$	Pert
ord	**5.92**	0.248	0.040	0.273	0.090/0.085	**9.08**	0.195	0.056	0.352	0.113/0.100
pca$_{800}$	6.97	0.123	0.244	0.817	0.160/0.155	9.7	0.091	0.253	0.845	0.193/0.178
noise$_{800}$	8.82	0.140	0.460	0.988	0.208/0.192	10.49	0.076	0.512	**0.978**	0.251/0.233
pca$_{300}$	11.71	0.075	0.713	0.973	0.256/0.240	13.75	0.050	0.667	0.910	0.308/0.283
noise$_{300}$	16.53	**0.060**	**0.942**	**0.988**	**0.308/0.265**	19.09	**0.027**	**0.843**	0.881	**0.320/0.299**
trades	21.22	0.009	0.416	0.639	0.664/0.579	19.37	0.008	0.446	0.673	0.725/0.639

that the robust features are more difficult to learn and may not be that discriminative. To compare with the state-of-the-art method, we train TRADES [32], an adversarial-training method, on the two architectures and report the results in the table. Although there remains a gap of robustness (perturbation norm) between our method and TRADES, our improvement of robustness has been significant, with controllable and less deterioration of accuracy on clean data than TRADES. Moreover, in Sect. 5.2 we will propose a stronger defense by integrating our data preprocessing procedure into other defense algorithms.

The results also show that $\overline{\alpha}_d$ becomes larger as we reduce the dimension of d and add noise in the normal space, which is highly related to the improvement of robustness. They also provide a strong evidence that for normally trained models, the gradient component leaks in the normal space. Our results are in line with our theory that the projection of the gradient on the manifold is a more essential attribute of the classification function. For instance, the DenseNet model trained by noise$_{800}$ method has a higher gradient norm than pca$_{800}$ which should imply less robustness, but actually its average perturbation distance is higher than pca$_{800}$. This, however, aligns with the improvement of $\overline{\alpha}_{300}$ and $\overline{\alpha}_{800}$. The contradictory phenomenon cannot be explained without the insight of gradient leaking that the additional Gaussian noise on the normal space further suppresses gradient leaking. We also note that the $\overline{\alpha}_d$ value of TRADES, the most robust model among those listed in the table, is relatively small compared with $\overline{\alpha}_d$ of our methods. This is perhaps because our perspective of gradient leaking cannot address the issue of in-manifold robustness, and also because our PCA approximation of the data manifold is rather rough. Nevertheless, less gradient leaking still correlates with and promotes stronger robustness well.

5.2 Integration into Other Defense Algorithms

Our method is light-weight and can be naturally integrated with other defense methods. To further boost the robustness, we provide an exemplary result by integrating it with a recently proposed method of Max-Mahalanobis center (MMC) loss [19]. Roughly speaking, it proposes to replace the softmax cross-entropy (SCE) loss with MMC loss which acts upon the layer just before the logits layer.

Table 3. The experimental results using MMC loss on CIFAR10.

Attack	Training method	Clean	Untargeted				Targeted			
		$\epsilon = 0$	8	16	24	32	8	16	24	32
PGD$_{10}$	SCE	93.5	3.9	2.9	2.2	1.9	0.0	0.0	0.0	0.0
	MMC	92.5	25.6	11.7	5.9	3.7	45.5	29.2	20.2	14.2
	MMC-P-500	90.3	42.5	30.6	21.4	15.9	57.9	46.5	37.6	30.4
	MMC-P-300	87.9	43.9	33.4	25.5	20.6	56.5	46.6	38.9	32.7
	SCE-AT	84.0	50.5	20.9	11.2	8.7	68.2	36.5	14.6	4.3
	MMC-AT	83.3	54.2	40.1	35.1	30.8	63.2	50.8	44.2	39.3
PGD$_{50}$	SCE	93.5	3.8	3.1	2.3	1.8	0.0	0.0	0.0	0.0
	MMC	92.5	9.2	4.8	3.3	2.2	26.9	16.6	12.7	9.5
	MMC-P-500	90.3	24.9	15.1	11.3	9.1	41.4	30.3	26.6	22.9
	MMC-P-300	87.9	29.2	20.1	17.1	14.8	41.0	30.9	27.9	24.7
	SCE-AT	84.0	48.9	17.4	9.6	8.2	66.6	28.0	6.0	1.0
	MMC-AT	83.3	51.1	35.4	31.2	27.8	60.9	44.8	40.2	35.7

To further reduce gradient leaking, we preprocess our training data according to our algorithm before feeding them into the MMC training process, resulting in a even stronger defense denoted as MMC-P. We conduct experiments on CIFAR10 in which we simply project the dataset to 500/300-dimensional PCA subspace as the preprocessing procedure. We report results of MMC and MMC-P in Table 3. The robustness is evaluated using ℓ_∞ PGD attacks (see Appendix B for evaluation under ℓ_2 attacks) with different settings (targeted/untargeted, 10/50 iteration steps), and we show the natural accuracy ($\epsilon = 0$) and the robustness accuracy under attacks with different ℓ_∞ perturbation bounds $\epsilon = 8, 16, 24, 32$. In PGD$_{10}$, we adopt the step size $2, 3, 4, 5$ respectively for $\epsilon = 8, 16, 24, 32$; in PGD$_{50}$, we set the step size to 2 in all cases. We utilize the C&W loss [3] (instead of the ordinary cross-entropy loss) which constitutes a stronger attack, so the robustness accuracy we report is lower than that in [19].

We found despite that the MMC baseline is satisfactory, our proposed MMC-P outperforms the vanilla MMC by a large margin with a simple data preprocessing step. To compare with the state-of-the-art methods, we report the performance of MMC-AT (adversarial training (AT) [17] using MMC loss) proposed in [19], which is adversarially trained using 10-step targeted PGD attack under perturbation bound $\epsilon = 8$. We note that it is stronger than vanilla AT (i.e. SCE-AT in the table). Experimental results show that despite the remaining gap of robustness between MMC-P and MMC-AT, MMC-P is still a competitive defense compared with the state-of-the-art AT methods since it brings a satisfactory robustness performance with less sacrifice in accuracy on clean data. Meanwhile, MMC-P is more convenient to use, and much faster to train. The results demonstrate that our method can further boost the robustness performance of some well-developed methods by integrating with them naturally.

6   Conclusion and Future Work

We reveals a possible path named "gradient leaking" to explain the existence and properties of adversarial samples. We further develop a method to examine the gradient leaking phenomenon, analyze its relationship with existence of adversarial samples, and further propose a novel method to defend against adversarial attacks based on the hypothesis, which adopts the linear dimension reduction and randomization technique before training. It brings an explainable robustness improvement with little extra time cost.

In the future, the mechanism of gradient leakage still requires a theoretical explanation, which may include the aspects of learning methods, data distribution and network architecture. A better data manifold representation method from which the local tangent space can be identified, such as VAE and localized GAN as suggested in [30], may lead us to deeper understanding of data manifold, more accurate estimate of gradient leaking, and more impressive robustness improvement. Combining our methods with other defense algorithms and figuring out how they work together could also be a potential direction.

Acknowledgements. This work was supported by the National Key Research and Development Program of China (No. 2017YFA0700904), NSFC Projects (Nos. 61620106010, U19B2034, U1811461, U19A2081, 61673241), Tsinghua-Huawei Joint Research Program, a grant from Tsinghua Institute for Guo Qiang, Beijing Academy of Artificial Intelligence (BAAI), Tiangong Institute for Intelligent Computing, the JP Morgan Faculty Research Program, and the NVIDIA NVAIL Program with GPU/DGX Acceleration.

References

1. Athalye, A., Carlini, N., Wagner, D.: Obfuscated gradients give a false sense of security: circumventing defenses to adversarial examples. arXiv preprint arXiv:1802.00420 (2018)
2. Bubeck, S., Price, E., Razenshteyn, I.: Adversarial examples from computational constraints. arXiv preprint arXiv:1805.10204 (2018)
3. Carlini, N., Wagner, D.: Towards evaluating the robustness of neural networks. In: 2017 IEEE Symposium on Security and Privacy (sp), pp. 39–57. IEEE (2017)
4. Carmon, Y., Raghunathan, A., Schmidt, L., Liang, P., Duchi, J.C.: Unlabeled data improves adversarial robustness. arXiv preprint arXiv:1905.13736 (2019)
5. Cisse, M., Bojanowski, P., Grave, E., Dauphin, Y., Usunier, N.: Parseval networks: Improving robustness to adversarial examples. In: Proceedings of the 34th International Conference on Machine Learning, vol. 70, pp. 854–863. JMLR. org (2017)
6. Dahl, G.E., Stokes, J.W., Deng, L., Yu, D.: Large-scale malware classification using random projections and neural networks. In: 2013 IEEE International Conference on Acoustics, Speech and Signal Processing, pp. 3422–3426. IEEE (2013)
7. Fawzi, A., Moosavi-Dezfooli, S.M., Frossard, P., Soatto, S.: Empirical study of the topology and geometry of deep networks. In: The IEEE Conference on Computer Vision and Pattern Recognition (CVPR), June 2018
8. Goodfellow, I.J., Shlens, J., Szegedy, C.: Explaining and harnessing adversarial examples. arXiv preprint arXiv:1412.6572 (2014)

9. He, Z., Rakin, A.S., Fan, D.: Parametric noise injection: trainable randomness to improve deep neural network robustness against adversarial attack. In: Proceedings of the IEEE Conference on Computer Vision and Pattern Recognition, pp. 588–597 (2019)

10. Huang, G., Liu, Z., Van Der Maaten, L., Weinberger, K.Q.: Densely connected convolutional networks. In: Proceedings of the IEEE Conference on Computer Vision and Pattern Recognition, pp. 4700–4708 (2017)

11. Ilyas, A., Santurkar, S., Tsipras, D., Engstrom, L., Tran, B., Madry, A.: Adversarial examples are not bugs, they are features. arXiv preprint arXiv:1905.02175 (2019)

12. Jakubovitz, D., Giryes, R.: Improving DNN robustness to adversarial attacks using Jacobian regularization. In: Proceedings of the European Conference on Computer Vision (ECCV), pp. 514–529 (2018)

13. Krizhevsky, A., Sutskever, I., Hinton, G.E.: ImageNet classification with deep convolutional neural networks. In: Pereira, F., Burges, C.J.C., Bottou, L., Weinberger, K.Q. (eds.) Advances in Neural Information Processing Systems 25, pp. 1097–1105. Curran Associates, Inc. (2012). http://papers.nips.cc/paper/4824-imagenet-classification-with-deep-convolutional-neural-networks.pdf

14. Kurakin, A., Goodfellow, I., Bengio, S.: Adversarial machine learning at scale. arXiv preprint arXiv:1611.01236 (2016)

15. Li, Q., Haque, S., Anil, C., Lucas, J., Grosse, R., Jacobsen, J.H.: Preventing gradient attenuation in Lipschitz constrained convolutional networks. arXiv preprint arXiv:1911.00937 (2019)

16. Liao, F., Liang, M., Dong, Y., Pang, T., Hu, X., Zhu, J.: Defense against adversarial attacks using high-level representation guided denoiser. In: Proceedings of the IEEE Conference on Computer Vision and Pattern Recognition, pp. 1778–1787 (2018)

17. Madry, A., Makelov, A., Schmidt, L., Tsipras, D., Vladu, A.: Towards deep learning models resistant to adversarial attacks. arXiv preprint arXiv:1706.06083 (2017)

18. Mikolov, T., Chen, K., Corrado, G., Dean, J.: Efficient estimation of word representations in vector space. arXiv preprint arXiv:1301.3781 (2013)

19. Pang, T., Xu, K., Dong, Y., Du, C., Chen, N., Zhu, J.: Rethinking softmax cross-entropy loss for adversarial robustness. arXiv preprint arXiv:1905.10626 (2019)

20. Qian, H., Wegman, M.N.: L2-nonexpansive neural networks. arXiv preprint arXiv:1802.07896 (2018)

21. Rauber, J., Brendel, W., Bethge, M.: Foolbox: a Python toolbox to benchmark the robustness of machine learning models. arXiv preprint arXiv:1707.04131 (2017). http://arxiv.org/abs/1707.04131

22. Rony, J., Hafemann, L.G., Oliveira, L.S., Ayed, I.B., Sabourin, R., Granger, E.: Decoupling direction and norm for efficient gradient-based L2 adversarial attacks and defenses. In: Proceedings of the IEEE Conference on Computer Vision and Pattern Recognition, pp. 4322–4330 (2019)

23. Ross, A.S., Doshi-Velez, F.: Improving the adversarial robustness and interpretability of deep neural networks by regularizing their input gradients. In: Thirty-Second AAAI Conference on Artificial Intelligence (2018)

24. Samangouei, P., Kabkab, M., Chellappa, R.: Defense-GAN: protecting classifiers against adversarial attacks using generative models. arXiv preprint arXiv:1805.06605 (2018)

25. Schmidt, L., Santurkar, S., Tsipras, D., Talwar, K., Madry, A.: Adversarially robust generalization requires more data. In: Advances in Neural Information Processing Systems, pp. 5014–5026 (2018)

26. Shamir, A., Safran, I., Ronen, E., Dunkelman, O.: A simple explanation for the existence of adversarial examples with small hamming distance. arXiv preprint arXiv:1901.10861 (2019)
27. Szegedy, C., et al.: Intriguing properties of neural networks. arXiv preprint arXiv:1312.6199 (2013)
28. Tramèr, F., Kurakin, A., Papernot, N., Goodfellow, I., Boneh, D., McDaniel, P.: Ensemble adversarial training: attacks and defenses. arXiv preprint arXiv:1705.07204 (2017)
29. Xie, C., Wu, Y., van der Maaten, L., Yuille, A.L., He, K.: Feature denoising for improving adversarial robustness. In: The IEEE Conference on Computer Vision and Pattern Recognition (CVPR), June 2019
30. Yu, B., Wu, J., Ma, J., Zhu, Z.: Tangent-normal adversarial regularization for semi-supervised learning. In: Proceedings of the IEEE Conference on Computer Vision and Pattern Recognition, pp. 10676–10684 (2019)
31. Zagoruyko, S., Komodakis, N.: Wide residual networks. arXiv preprint arXiv:1605.07146 (2016)
32. Zhang, H., Yu, Y., Jiao, J., Xing, E.P., Ghaoui, L.E., Jordan, M.I.: Theoretically principled trade-off between robustness and accuracy. arXiv preprint arXiv:1901.08573 (2019)

Improving Optical Flow on a Pyramid Level

Markus Hofinger[2]([✉])[iD], Samuel Rota Bulò[1][iD], Lorenzo Porzi[1][iD],
Arno Knapitsch[1][iD], Thomas Pock[2][iD], and Peter Kontschieder[1][iD]

[1] Facebook, Zürich, Switzerland
[2] Graz University of Technology, Graz, Austria
{markus.hofinger,pock}@icg.tugraz.at

Abstract. In this work we review the coarse-to-fine spatial feature pyramid concept, which is used in state-of-the-art optical flow estimation networks to make exploration of the pixel flow search space computationally tractable and efficient. Within an individual pyramid level, we improve the cost volume construction process by departing from a warping- to a sampling-based strategy, which avoids ghosting and hence enables us to better preserve fine flow details. We further amplify the positive effects through a level-specific, loss max-pooling strategy that adaptively shifts the focus of the learning process on under-performing predictions. Our second contribution revises the gradient flow across pyramid levels. The typical operations performed at each pyramid level can lead to noisy, or even contradicting gradients across levels. We show and discuss how properly blocking some of these gradient components leads to improved convergence and ultimately better performance. Finally, we introduce a distillation concept to counteract the issue of catastrophic forgetting during finetuning and thus preserving knowledge over models sequentially trained on multiple datasets. Our findings are conceptually simple and easy to implement, yet result in compelling improvements on relevant error measures that we demonstrate via exhaustive ablations on datasets like Flying Chairs2, Flying Things, Sintel and KITTI. We establish new state-of-the-art results on the challenging Sintel and KITTI 2012 test datasets, and even show the portability of our findings to different optical flow and depth from stereo approaches.

1 Introduction

State-of-the-art, deep learning based optical flow estimation methods share a number of common building blocks in their high-level, structural design. These blocks reflect insights gained from decades of research in *classical* optical flow estimation, while exploiting the power of deep learning for further optimization of *e.g.* performance, speed or memory constraints [14,37,44]. Pyramidal representations are among the fundamental concepts that were successfully used in

Electronic supplementary material The online version of this chapter (https://doi.org/10.1007/978-3-030-58604-1_46) contains supplementary material, which is available to authorized users.

optical flow and stereo matching works like [3]. However, while pyramidal representations enable computationally tractable exploration of the pixel flow search space, their downsides include difficulties in the handling of large motions for small objects or generating artifacts when warping occluded regions. Another observation we made is that vanilla agglomeration of hierarchical information in the pyramid is hindering the learning process and consequently leading to reduced performance.

In this paper we identify and address shortcomings in state-of-the-art flow networks, with particular focus on improving information processing in the pyramidal representation module. For cost volume construction at a single pyramid level, we introduce a novel feature sampling strategy rather than relying on warping of high-level features to the corresponding ones in the target image. Warping is the predominant strategy in recent and top-performing flow methods [14,44] but leads to degraded flow quality for fine structures. This is because fine structures require robust encoding of high-frequency information in the features, which is sometimes not recoverable after warping them towards the target image pyramid feature space. As an alternative we propose *sampling* for cost volume generation in each pyramid level, in conjunction with the sum of absolute differences as a cost volume distance function. In our sampling strategy we populate cost volume entries through distance computation between features *without* prior feature warping. This helps us to better explore the complex and non-local search space of fine-grained, detailed flow transformations (see Fig. 1).

Using *sampling* in combination with a per-pyramid level *loss max-pooling* strategy further supports recovery of the motion of small and fast-moving objects. Flow errors for those objects can be attributed to the aforementioned warping issue but also because the motion of such objects often correlates with large and underrepresented flow vectors, rarely available in the training data. Loss max-pooling adaptively shifts the focus of the learning procedure towards under-performing flow predictions, without requiring additional information about the training data statistics. We introduce a loss max-pooling variant to work in hierarchical feature representations, while the underlying concept has been successfully used for dense pixel prediction tasks like semantic segmentation [30].

Our second major contribution targets improving the gradient flow *across* pyramid levels. Functions like cost volume generation depend on bilinear interpolation, which can be shown [19] to produce considerably noisy gradients. Furthermore, fine-grained structures which are only visible at a certain pyramid level, can propagate contradicting gradients towards the coarser levels when they move in a different direction compared to their background. Accumulating these gradients across pyramid levels ultimately inhibits convergence. Our proposed solution is as simple as effective: by using level-specific loss terms and smartly blocking gradient propagation, we can eliminate the sources of noise. Doing so significantly improves the learning procedure and is positively reflected in the relevant performance measures.

Fig. 1. Optical flow predictions from our model on images from Sintel and KITTI.

As minor contributions, we promote additional *flow cues* that lead to a more effective generation of the cost volume. Inspired by the work of [15] that used backward warping of the optical flow to enhance the upsampling of occlusions, we advance symmetric flow networks with multiple cues (like consistencies derived from forward-backward and reverse flow information, occlusion reasoning) to better identify and correct discrepancies in the flow estimates. Finally, we also propose *knowledge distillation* to counterfeit the problem of catastrophic forgetting in the context of deep-learning-based optical flow algorithms. Due to a lack of large training datasets, it is common practice to sequentially perform a number of trainings, first on synthetically generated datasets (like Flying Chairs2 and Flying Things), then fine-tuning on target datasets like Sintel or KITTI. Our distillation strategy (inspired by recent work on scene flow [18] and unsupervised approaches [20,21]) enables us to preserve knowledge from previous training steps and combine it with flow consistency checks generated from our network and further information about photometric consistency.

Our combined contributions lead to significant, cumulated error reductions over state-of-the-art networks like HD³ or (variants of) PWC-Net [2,15,37,44], and we set new state-of-the-art results on the challenging Sintel and KITTI 2012 datasets. We provide exhaustive ablations and experimental evaluations on Sintel, KITTI 2012 and 2015, Flying Things and Flying Chairs2, and significantly improve on the most important measures like *Out-Noc* (percentage of erroneous non-occluded pixels) and on *EPE* (average end-point-error) metrics.

2   Related Work

Classical Approaches. Optical flow has come a long way since it was introduced to the computer vision community by Lucas and Kanade [23] and Horn and Schunck [13]. Following these works, the introduction of pyramidal coarse-to-fine warping frameworks were giving another huge boost in the performance of optical flow computation [4,34] – an overview of non learning-based optical flow methods can be found in [1,9,35].

Deep Learning Entering Optical Flow. Many parts of the classical optical flow computations are well-suited for being learned by a deep neural network. Initial work using deep learning for flow was presented in [40], and was using a learned matching algorithm to produce semi-dense matches then refining them with a classical variational approach. The successive work of [29], whilst also relying on learned semi-dense matches, was additionally using an edge detector [7] to interpolate dense flow fields before the variational energy minimization. End-to-end learning in a deep network for flow estimation was first done in FlowNet [8]. They use a conventional encoder-decoder architecture, and it was trained on a synthetic dataset, showing that it still generalizes well to real world datasets such as KITTI [11]. Based on this work, FlowNet2 [16] improved by using a carefully tuned training schedule and by introducing warping into the learning framework. However, FlowNet2 could not keep up with the results of traditional variational flow approaches on the leaderboards. SpyNet [27] introduced spatial image pyramids and PWC-Net [36,37] additionally improved results by incorporating spatial feature pyramid processing, warping, and the use of a cost volume in the learning framework. The flow in PWC-Net is estimated by using a stack of flattened cost volumes and image features from a Dense-Net. In [15], PWC-Net was turned into an iterative refinement network, adding bilateral refinement of flow and occlusion in every iteration step. ScopeFlow [2] showed that improvements on top of [15] can be achieved simply by improving training procedures. In the work of [28], the group around [36] was showing further improvements on Kitti 2015 and Sintel by integrating the optical flow from an additional, previous image frame. While multi-frame optical flow methods already existed for non-learning based methods [6,10,41], they were the first to show this in a deep learning framework. In [44], the hierarchical discrete distribution decomposition framework HD^3 learned probabilistic pixel correspondences for optical flow and stereo matching. It learns the decomposed match densities in an end-to-end manner at multiple scales. HD^3 then converts the predicted match densities into point estimates, while also producing uncertainty measures at the same time. Devon [22] uses a sampling and dilation based deformable cost-volume, to iteratively estimate the flow at a fixed quarter resolution in each iteration. While they showed good results on clean synthetic data, the performance on real images from KITTI was sub-optimal, indicating that sampling alone may not be sufficient. We will show here, that integrating a direct sampling based approach into a coarse-to-fine pyramid together with LMP and Flow Cues can actually lead to very good results. Recently, Volumetric Correspondence Networks (VCN) [43] showed that the 4D cost volume can also be efficiently filtered directly without the commonly used flattening but using separable 2D filters instead.

Unsupervised Methods. Generating dense and accurate flow data for supervised training of networks is a challenging task. Thus, most large-scale datasets are synthetic [5,8,17], and real data sets remained small and sparsely labeled [25,26]. Unsupervised methods do not rely on that data, instead, those methods usually utilize the photometric loss between the original image in the warped, second image to guide the learning process [45]. However, the photometric loss does not work for occluded image regions, and therefore methods have been proposed to generate occlusion masks beforehand or simultaneously [24,42].

Distillation. To learn the flow values of occluded areas, DDFlow [20] is using a student-teacher network which distills data from reliable predictions, and uses these predictions as annotations to guide a student network. SelFlow [21] is built in a similar fashion but vastly improves the quality of the flow predictions in occluded areas by introducing a superpixel-based occlusion hallucination technique. They obtain state-of-the-art results when fine-tuning on annotated data after pre-training in a self-supervised setting. SENSE [18] tries to integrate optical flow, stereo, occlusion, and semantic segmentation in one semi-supervised setting. Much like in a multi-task learning setup, SENSE [18] uses a shared encoder for all four tasks, which can exploit interactions between the different tasks and leads to a compact network. SENSE uses pre-trained models to "supervise" the network on data with missing ground truth annotations using a distillation loss [12]. To couple the four tasks, a self-supervision loss term is used, which largely improves regions without ground truth (*e.g.* sky regions).

3   Main Contributions

In this section we review pyramid flow network architectures [36,44], and propose a set of modifications to the pyramid levels (§ 3.2) and their training strategy (§ 3.3), which work in a synergistic manner to greatly boost performance.

3.1   Pyramid Flow Networks

Pyramid flow networks (PFN) operate on pairs of images, building feature pyramids with decreasing spatial resolution using "siamese" network branches with shared parameters. Flow is iteratively refined starting from the top of the pyramid, each layer predicting an offset relative to the flow estimated at the previous level. For more details about the operations carried out at each level see § 3.2.

Notation. We represent multi-dimensional feature maps as functions $I_i^l : \mathcal{I}_i^l \to \mathbb{R}^d$, where $i = 1, 2$ indicates which image the features are computed from, l is their pyramid level, and $\mathcal{I}_i^l \subset \mathbb{R}^2$ is the set of pixels of image i at resolution l. We call *forward flow* at level l a mapping $F_{1\to 2}^l : \mathcal{I}_1^l \to \mathbb{R}^2$, which intuitively indicates where pixels in I_1^l moved to in I_2^l (in relative terms). We call *backward flow* the mapping $F_{2\to 1}^l : \mathcal{I}_2^l \to \mathbb{R}^2$ that indicates the opposite displacements. Pixel coordinates are indexed by u and v, *i.e.* $x = (x_u, x_v)$, and given $x \in \mathcal{I}_1^l$, we assume that $I_1^l(x)$ implicitly applies bilinear interpolation to read values from I_1^l at sub-pixel locations.

3.2   Improving Pyramid Levels in PFNs

Many PFNs [36,44] share the same high-level structure in each of their levels. First, feature maps from the two images are aligned using the coarse flow estimated in the previous level, and compared by some distance function to build a cost volume (possibly both in the *forward* and *backward* directions). Then,

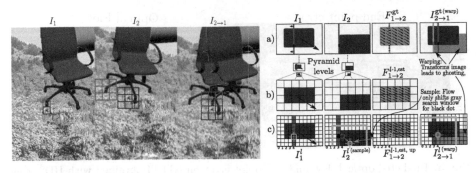

Fig. 2. Sampling vs. Warping. **Left**: Warping leads to image ghosting in the warped image $I_{2\to1}$; Also, neighbouring pixels in I_1 must share parts of their search windows in $I_{2\to1}$, while for sampling they are independently sampled from the original image I_2. **Right**: A toy example; a) Two moving objects: a red line with a black dot and a blue box. Warping with $F_{1\to2}^{gt}$ leads to ghosting effects. b) Zooming into lowest pyramid resolution shows loss of small details due to down-scaling. c) *Warping* I_2^l with the flow estimate from the coarser level leads to distortions in $I_{2\to1}^l$ (the black dot gets covered up). Instead, direct *sampling* in I_2^l with a search window(gray box) that is offset by the flow estimate avoids these distortions and hence leads to more stable correlations.

the cost volume is combined with additional information from the feature maps (and optionally additional "flow cues") and fed to a "decoder" subnet. This subnet finally outputs a residual flow, or a match density from which the residual flow can be computed. A separate loss is applied to each pyramid layer, providing deep supervision to the flow refinement process. In the rest of this section, we describe a set of generic improvements that can be applied to the pyramid layers of several state of the art pyramid flow networks.

Cost Volume Construction. The first operation at each level of most pyramid flow networks involves comparing features between I_1^l and I_2^l, conditioned on the flow $F_{1\to2}^{l-1}$ predicted at the previous level. In the most common implementation, I_2^l is warped using $F_{1\to2}^{l-1}$, and the result is cross-correlated with I_1^l. More formally, given I_2^l and $F_{1\to2}^{l-1}$, the warped image is given by $I_{2\to1}^l(x) = I_2^l(x + F_{1\to2}^{l-1}(x))$ and the cross-correlation is computed with:

$$V_{1\to2}^{\text{warp}}(x,\delta) = I_1^l(x) \cdot I_{2\to1}^l(x+\delta) = I_1^l(x) \cdot I_2^l(x + \delta + F_{1\to2}^{l-1}(x+\delta)), \quad (1)$$

where $\delta \in [-\Delta, \Delta]^2$ is a restricted search space and $\cdot$ is the vector dot product. This warping operation, however, suffers from a serious drawback which occurs when small regions move differently compared to their surroundings.

This case is represented in Fig. 2: A small object indicated by a red line moves in a different direction than a larger blue box in the background. As warping uses the coarse flow estimate from the previous level, which cannot capture fine-grained motions, there is a chance that the smaller object gets lost during the feature warping. This makes it undetectable in $I_{2\to1}^l$, even with an infinite

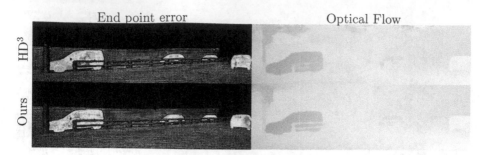

Fig. 3. Predicted optical flow and end point error on KITTI obtained with HD^3 from the model zoo (top) and our IOFPL version (bottom). Note how our model is better able to preserve small details.

cost volume range (CVr/CV-range) δ. To overcome this limitation, we propose a different cost volume construction strategy, which exploits direct sampling operations. This approach always accesses the original, undeformed features I_2^l, without loss of information, and the cross-correlation in Eq. (1) now becomes:

$$V_{1\to2}^{samp,Corr}(x,\delta) = I_1^l(x) \cdot I_2^l(x + \delta + F_{1\to2}^{l-1}(x)). \tag{2}$$

For this operator, the flow just acts as an offset that sets the center of the correlation window in the feature image I_2^l. Going back to Fig. 2, one can see that the sampling operator is still able to detect the small object, as it is also exemplified on real data in Fig. 3. In contrast to [22], our approach still uses the coarse to fine pyramid and hence doesn't require dilation in the cost volume for large motions. In our experiments we also consider a variant where the features are compared in terms of Sum of Absolute Differences (SAD) instead of a dot product:

$$V_{1\to2}^{samp,SAD}(x,\delta) = \|I_1^l(x) - I_2^l(x + \delta + F_{1\to2}^{l-1}(x))\|_1. \tag{3}$$

Loss Max Pooling. We apply a Loss Max-Pooling (LMP) strategy [30], also known as Online Hard Example Mining (OHEM), to our knowledge for the first time in the context of optical flow. In our experiments, and consistent with the findings in [30], we observe that LMP can help to better preserve small details in the flow. The total loss is the sum of a pixelwise loss ℓ_x over all $x \in \mathcal{I}_1$, but we optimize a weighted version thereof that selects a fixed percentage of the highest per-pixel losses. The percentage value α is best chosen according to the quality of the ground-truth in the target dataset. This can be written in terms of a loss max-pooling strategy as follows:

$$L = \max\left\{\sum_{x\in\mathcal{I}_1} w_x \ell_x \: : \: \|w\|_1 \leq 1, \|w\|_\infty \leq \frac{1}{\alpha|\mathcal{I}_1|}\right\}, \tag{4}$$

which is equivalent to putting constant weight $w_x = \frac{1}{\alpha|\mathcal{I}_1|}$ on the percentage of pixels x exhibiting the highest losses, and setting $w_x = 0$ elsewhere.

LMP lets the network focus on the more difficult areas of the image, while reducing the amount of gradient signals where predictions are already correct. To avoid focussing on outliers, we set the loss to 0 for pixels that are out of reach for the current relative search range Δ. For datasets with sparsely annotated ground-truth, like $e.g.$ KITTI [11], we re-scale the per pixel losses ℓ_x to reflect the number of valid pixels. Note that, when performing distillation, loss max-pooling is only applied to the supervised loss, in order to further reduce the effect of noise that survived the filtering process described in § 3.4.

3.3   Improving Gradient Flow Across PFN Levels

Our quantitatively most impacting contribution relates to the way we pass gradient information across the different levels of a PFN. In particular, we focus on the bilinear interpolation operations that we implicitly perform on I_2^l while computing Eqs. (1), (2) and (3). It has been observed [19] that taking the gradient of bilinear interpolation w.r.t. the sampling coordinates ($i.e.$ the flow $F_{1 \to 2}^{l-1}$ from the previous level in our case) is often problematic. To illustrate the reason, we restrict our attention to the 1-D case for ease of notation, and write linear interpolation from a function $\hat{f} : \mathbb{Z} \to \mathbb{R}$:

$$f(x) = \sum_{\eta \in \{0,1\}} \hat{f}(\lfloor x \rfloor + \eta) \left[(1 - \eta)(1 - \tilde{x}) + \eta \tilde{x} \right], \tag{5}$$

where $\tilde{x} = x - \lfloor x \rfloor$ denotes the fractional part of x. The derivative of the inter-polated function $f(x)$ with respect to x is:

$$\frac{df}{dx}(x) = \sum_{\eta \in \{0,1\}} \hat{f}(\lfloor x \rfloor + \eta)(2\eta - 1). \tag{6}$$

The gradient function $\frac{df}{dx}$ is discontinuous, for its value drastically changes as $\lfloor x \rfloor$ crosses over from one integer value to the next, possibly inducing strong noise in the gradients. An additional effect, specific to our case, is related to the issues already highlighted in § 3.2: since $F_{1 \to 2}^{l-1}$ is predicted at a lower resolution than level l operates at, it cannot fully capture the motion of smaller objects. When this motion contrasts with that of the background, the gradient w.r.t. $F_{1 \to 2}^{l-1}$ produced from the sampling at level l will inevitably disagree with that produced by the loss at level $l - 1$, possibly slowing down convergence.

While [19] proposes a different sampling strategy to reduce the noise issues discussed above, in our case we opt for a much simpler work around. Given the observations about layer disagreement, and the fact that the loss at $l - 1$ already provides direct supervision on $F_{1 \to 2}^{l-1}$, we choose to stop back-propagation of partial flow gradients coming from higher levels, as illustrated in Fig. 4.

Evidence for this effect can be seen in Fig. 5, where the top shows the development of the training loss for a Flying Chairs 2 training with an HD^3 model. The training convergence clearly improves when the partial flow gradient is stopped

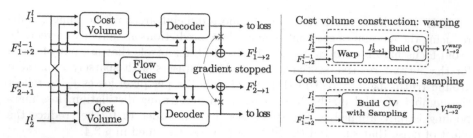

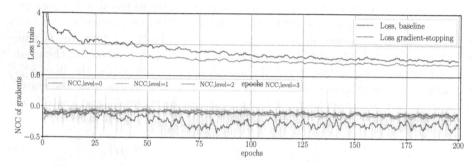

Fig. 4. Left: network structure – flow estimation per pyramid level; gradients are stopped at red cross; right: cost volume computation with sampling vs. warping. (Color figure online)

Fig. 5. Top: Loss of model decreases when the flow gradient is stopped; bottom: partial gradients coming from the current level loss and the next level via the flow show a negative Normalized Cross Correlation (NCC), indicating that they oppose each other.

between the levels (red cross in Fig. 4). On the bottom of the figure the Normalized Cross Correlation (NCC) between the partial gradient coming from the next level via the flow and the current levels loss is shown. On average the correlation is negative, indicating that for each level of the network the partial gradient that we decided to stop (red cross), coming from upper levels, points in a direction that opposes the partial gradient from the loss directly supervising the current level, thus harming convergence. Additional evidence of the practical, positive impact of our gradient stopping strategy is given in the experiment section § 4.2.

Further evidence on this issue can be gained by analyzing the parameters gradient variance [38] as it impacts the rate of convergence for stochastic gradient descent methods. Also the β-smoothness [33] of the loss function gradient can give similar insights. In the supplementary material (section § A) we provide further experiments that show that gradient stopping also helps to improve these properties, and works for stereo estimation and other flow models as well.

3.4   Additional Refinements

Flow Cues. As mentioned at the beginning of § 3.2, the decoder subnet in each pyramid level processes the raw feature correlations to a final cost volume or direct flow predictions. To provide the decoder with contextual information, it commonly [36, 44] also receives raw features (*i.e.* I_1^l, I_2^l for forward and backward flow, respectively). Some works [15, 17, 39] also append other cues, in the form of hand-crafted features, aimed at capturing additional prior knowledge about flow consistency. Such flow cues are cheap to compute but otherwise hard to learn for CNNs as they require various forms of non-local spatial transformations. In this work, we propose a set of such flow cues that provides mutual beneficial information, and perform very well in practice when combined with costvolume sample and LMP (see § 4.2). These cues are namely forward-backward flow warping, reverse flow estimation, map uniqueness density and out-of-image occlusions, and are described in detail in the supplementary material (§ B).

Fig. 6. Illustration of our data distillation process. Left to right: input image and associated KITTI ground truth, dense prediction from a Flying Things3D-trained network and pseudo-ground truth derived from it.

Knowledge Distillation. Knowledge distillation [12] consists in extrapolating a training signal directly from another trained network, ensemble of networks, or perturbed networks [31], typically by mimicking their predictions on some available data. In PFNs, distillation can help to overcome issues such as lack of flow annotations on *e.g.* sky, which results in cluttered outputs in those areas. Formally, our goal is to distill knowledge from a pre-trained master network (*e.g.* on Flying Chairs2 and/or Flying Things) by augmenting a student network with an additional loss term, which tries to mimic the predictions the master produces on the input at hand (Fig. 6, bottom left). At the same time, the student is also trained with a standard, supervised loss on the available ground-truth (Fig. 6, top right). In order to ensure a proper cooperation between the two terms, we prevent the distillation loss from operating blindly, instead enabling it selectively based on a number of consistency and confidence checks (refer to the supplementary material for details). Like for the ground-truth loss, the data distillation loss is scaled with respect to the valid pixels present in the pseudo ground-truth. The supervised and the distillation losses are combined into a total loss

$$\mathcal{L} = \alpha \mathcal{L}_S + (1 - \alpha)\mathcal{L}_D \tag{7}$$

with the scaling factor $\alpha = 0.9$. A qualitative representation of the effects of our proposed distillation on KITTI data is given in Fig. 7.

4 Experiments

We assess the quality of our contributions by providing a number of exhaustive ablations on Flying Chairs, Flying Chairs2, Flying Things, Sintel, Kitti 2012 and Kitti 2015. We ran the bulk of ablations based on HD^3 [44], *i.e.* a state-of-the-art, 2-frame optical flow approach. We build on top of their publicly available code and stick to default configuration parameters where possible, and describe and re-train the baseline model when deviating.

Fig. 7. Qualitative evaluation on KITTI, comparing the HD^3 modelzoo (left), our version with all contributions except distillation (center), and with distillation (right).

The remainder of this section is organized as follows. We provide i) in § 4.1 a summary about the experimental and training setups and our basic modifications over HD^3, ii) in § 4.2 an exhaustive number of ablation results for all aforementioned datasets by learning **only** on the Flying Chairs2 training set, and for all reasonable combinations of our contributions described in § 3, as well as ablations on Sintel, and iii) list and discuss in § 4.3 our results obtained on the Kitti 2012, Kitti 2015 and Sintel test datasets, respectively. In the supplementary material we further provide i) more technical details and ablation studies about the used *flow cues*, ii) smoothness and variance analyses for gradient stopping and its impact on depth from stereo or with a PWC baseline iii) ablations on extended search ranges for the cost volume, and iv) ablations on distillation.

4.1 Setup and Modifications over HD^3

We always train on 4xV100 GPUs with 32 GB RAM using PyTorch, and obtain additional memory during training by switching to In-Place Activated Batch-Norm (non-synchronized, Leaky-ReLU) [32]. We decided to train on Flying Chairs2 rather than Flying Chairs for our main ablation experiments, since it provides ground truth for both, forward and backward flow directions. Other modifications are experiment-specific and described in the respective sections.

Flow - Synthetic Data Pre-Training. Also the Flying Things dataset provides ground truth flow for both directions. We always train and evaluate on both flow directions, since this improves generalization to other datasets. We use a batch size of 64 to decrease training times and leave the rest of configuration parameters unchanged w.r.t. the default HD³ code.

Flow - Fine-Tuning on KITTI. Since both the Kitti 2012 and the Kitti 2015 datasets are very small and only provide forward flow ground truth, we follow the HD³ training protocol and join all KITTI training sequences for the final fine-tuning (after pre-training on Flying Chairs2 and Flying Things). However, we ran independent multi-fold cross validations and noticed faster convergence of our model over the baseline. We therefore perform early stopping after 1.6k (CVr±4)/1.4k (CVr±8) epochs, to prevent over-fitting. Furthermore, before starting the fine-tuning process of the pre-trained model, we label the KITTI training data for usage described in the knowledge distillation paragraph in § 3.4.

Flow - Fine-Tuning on Sintel. We only train on all the images in the *final* pass and ignore the *clean* images like HD³ for comparability. Also, we only use the forward flow ground truth since backward flow ground truth is unavailable. Although not favorable, our model can still be trained in this setting since we use a single, shared set of parameters for the forward and the backward flow paths. We kept the original 1.2k finetuning iterations for comparability, since our independent three-fold cross validation did not show signs of overfitting.

Table 1. Ablation results when training HD³ CVr ± 4 on Flying Chairs2 in comparison to the official model zoo baseline, our re-trained baseline and when adding all our proposed contributions. Results are shown on validation data for Flying Chairs2 and Flying Things (validation set used in the original HD³ code repository), and on the official training data for Sintel, Kitti 2012 and Kitti 2015, due to the lack of a designated validation split. (Highlighting **best** and second-best results).

Gradient Stopping	Sampling	Flow Cues	SAD	LMP	Flying Chairs2 EPE [1]	Flying Chairs2 Fl-all [%]	Flying Things EPE [1]	Flying Things Fl-all [%]	Sintel final EPE [1]	Sintel final Fl-all [%]	Sintel clean EPE [1]	Sintel clean Fl-all [%]	Kitti 2012 EPE [1]	Kitti 2012 Fl-all [%]	Kitti 2015 EPE [1]	Kitti 2015 Fl-all [%]
HD³ baseline model zoo					1.439	7.17	20.973	33.21	5.850	**14.03**	3.70	**8.56**	12.604	49.13	22.67	57.07
HD³ baseline – re-trained					1.422	6.99	17.743	26.72	6.273	15.24	3.90	10.04	8.725	34.67	20.98	50.27
✓	✗	✗	✗	✗	1.215	6.23	19.094	26.84	5.774	15.89	3.72	10.51	9.469	44.58	19.07	53.65
✓	✗	✗	✓	✗	1.216	6.24	16.294	26.25	6.033	16.26	3.43	9.98	7.879	43.92	17.97	51.14
✓	✓	✗	✗	✗	1.208	6.19	17.161	24.75	6.074	15.61	3.70	9.96	8.673	45.29	17.42	51.23
✓	✓	✓	✗	✗	1.186	6.16	19.616	28.51	7.420	15.99	3.61	9.39	**6.672**	**32.59**	16.23	47.56
✓	✓	✓	✓	✗	1.184	6.15	15.136	25.00	5.625	16.35	3.38	9.97	8.144	41.59	17.13	52.51
✓	✗	✗	✗	✓	1.193	6.02	44.068	40.38	12.529	17.85	5.48	10.95	8.778	42.37	19.08	51.13
✓	✓	✗	✗	✓	1.170	5.98	15.752	24.26	5.943	16.27	3.55	9.91	7.742	35.78	18.75	**49.67**
✓	✓	✓	✓	✓	**1.168**	**5.97**	14.458	23.01	5.560	15.88	3.26	9.58	6.847	35.47	16.87	49.93

4.2 Flow Ablation Experiments

Here we present an extensive number of ablations based on HD³ to assess the quality of all our proposed contributions. We want to stress that all results in

782   M. Hofinger et al.

Table 1 were obtained by **solely training on the Flying Chairs2 training set**. More specifically, we report error numbers (EPE and Fl-all; lower is better) and compare the original HD³ model zoo baseline against our own, retrained baseline model, followed by adding combinations of our proposed contributions. We report performance on the target domains validation set (Flying Chairs2), as well as on unseen data from different datasets (Flying Things, Sintel and KITTI), to gain insights on generalization behavior.

Our ablations show a clear trend towards improving EPE and Fl-all, especially on the target domain, as more of our proposed improvements are integrated. Due to the plethora of results provided in the table, we highlight some of them next. GRADIENT STOPPING is often responsible for a large gap w.r.t. to both baseline HD³ models, the original and our re-trained. Further, all variants with activated SAMPLING lead to best- or second-best results, except for Fl-all on Sintel. Flow Cues give an additional benefit when combined with SAMPLING but not with warping. Another relevant insight is that our full model using all contributions at the bottom of the table always improves on Fl-all compared to the variant with deactivated LMP. This shows how LMP is suitable to effectively reduce the number of outliers by focusing the learning process on the under-performing (and thus more rare) cases.

Table 2. Ablation results on Sintel, highlighting **best** and <u>second-best</u> results. Top: baseline and Flying Chairs2 & Flying Things pre-trained (P) models only. Bottom: results after additional fine-tuning (F) on Sintel.

FINE-TUNED PRETRAINED	GRADIENT STOPPING	SAMPLING	FLOW CUES	SAD	LMP	CV RANGE ±8	Flying Things EPE [1]	Fl-all	Sintel final EPE [1]	Fl-all	Sintel clean EPE [1]	Fl-all
HD³ baseline – re-trained							12.52	18.06%	13.38	16.23 %	3.06	6.39%
P	✓						7.98	13.41%	**4.06**	**10.62 %**	<u>1.86</u>	<u>5.11%</u>
P	✓	✓	✓	✓	✓		<u>7.06</u>	<u>12.29%</u>	<u>4.23</u>	<u>11.05 %</u>	2.20	5.41%
P	✓	✓	✓	✓	✓	✓	**5.77**	**11.48%**	4.68	11.40 %	**1.77**	**4.88%**
F							19.89	27.03%	(1.07)	(4.61 %)	1.58	4.67%
F	✓						<u>13.80</u>	<u>20.87%</u>	(0.84)	(3.79 %)	<u>1.43</u>	4.19%
F	✓	✓	✓	✓	✓		14.19	20.98%	(0.82)	(3.63 %)	<u>1.43</u>	<u>4.08%</u>
F	✓	✓	✓	✓	✓	✓	**11.80**	**19.12%**	(0.79)	(3.49 %)	**1.19**	**3.86%**

We provide additional ablation results on Flying Things and Sintel in Table 2. The upper half shows PRETRAINED (P) results obtained after training on Flying Chairs2 and Flying Things, while the bottom shows results after additionally FINE-TUNING (F) on Sintel. Again, there are consistent large improvements on the target domain currently trained on, i.e. (P) for Flying Things and (F) for Sintel. On the cross dataset validation there is more noise, especially for sintel final that comes with motion blur etc., but still always a large improvement over the baseline. After finetuning (F) the full model with CVr±8 shows much better performance on sintel and at the same time comparable performance on Flying Things to the original baseline model directly trained on Flying Things.

4.3   Optical Flow Benchmark Results

The following provides results on the official Sintel and KITTI test set servers.

Sintel. By combining all our contributions and by using a cost volume search range of ± 8, we set a new state-of-the-art on the challenging Sintel FINAL test set, improving over the very recent, best-working approach in [2] (see Table 3). Even by choosing the default search range of CVr± 4 as in [44] we still obtain significant improvements over the HD^3-ft baseline on training and test errors.

Kitti 2012 and Kitti 2015. We also evaluated the impact of our full model on KITTI and report test data results in Table 4. We obtain new state-of-the-art test results for EPE and Fl-all on Kitti 2012, and rank second-best at Fl-all on Kitti 2015. On both, Kitti 2012 and Kitti 2015 we obtain strong improvements on the training set on EPE and Fl-all. Finally, while on Kitti 2015 the recently published VCN [43] has slightly better Fl-all scores, we perform better on foreground objects (test Fl-fg 8.09 % vs. 8.66 %) and generally improve over the HD^3 baseline (Fl-fg 9.02 %). It is worth noting that all KITTI finetuning results are obtained after integrating knowledge distillation from § 3.4, leading to significantly improved flow predictions on areas where KITTI lacks training data (*e.g.* in far away areas including sky, see Fig. 7). We provide further qualitative insights and direct comparisons in the supplementary material (§ C).

Table 3. EPE scores on the Sintel test datasets. The appendix *-ft* denotes fine-tuning on Sintel.

METHOD	TRAINING		TEST	
	CLEAN	FINAL	CLEAN	FINAL
FlowNet2 [16]	2.02	3.14	3.96	6.02
FlowNet2-ft [16]	(1.45)	(2.01)	4.16	5.74
PWC-Net [36]	2.55	3.93	-	-
PWC-Net-ft [36]	(2.02)	(2.08)	4.39	5.04
SelFlow [21]	2.88	3.87	6.56	6.57
SelFlow-ft [21]	(1.68)	(1.77)	3.74	4.26
IRR-PWC-ft [15]	(1.92)	(2.51)	3.84	4.58
PWC-MFF-ft [28]	-	-	3.42	4.56
VCN-ft [43]	(1.66)	(2.24)	**2.81**	4.40
ScopeFlow [2]	-	-	3.59	4.10
Devon [22]	-	-	4.34	6.35
HD^3 [44]	3.84	8.77	-	-
HD^3-ft [44]	(1.70)	(1.17)	4.79	4.67
IOFPL-no-ft	2.20	4.32	-	-
IOFPL-ft	1.43	(0.82)	4.39	4.22
IOFPL-CVr8-no-ft	1.77	4.68	-	-
IOFPL-CVr8-ft	**1.19**	**(0.79)**	3.58	4.01

Table 4. EPE and Fl-all scores on the KITTI test datasets. The appendix *-ft* denotes fine-tuning on KITTI. Ours is IOFPL.

METHOD	KITTI 2012			KITTI 2015		
	EPE train	EPE test	Fl-noc [%] test	EPE train	Fl-all [%] train	Fl-all [%] test
FlowNet2 [16]	4.09	-	-	10.06	30.37	-
FlowNet2-ft [16]	(1.28)	1.8	4.82	(2.30)	8.61	10.41
PWC-Net [36]	4.14	-	-	10.35	33.67	-
PWC-Net-ft [36]	(1.45)	1.7	4.22	(2.16)	9.80	9.60
SelFlow [21]	1.16	2.2	7.68	(4.48)	-	14.19
SelFlow-ft [21]	(0.76)	1.5	6.19	(1.18)	-	8.42
IRR-PWC-ft [15]	-	-	-	(1.63)	5.32	7.65
PWC-MFF-ft [28]	-	-	-	-	-	7.17
ScopeFlow [2]	-	1.3	2.68	-	-	6.82
Devon [22]	-	-	6.99	-	-	14.31
VCN [43]	-	-	-	(1.16)	4.10	**6.30**
HD3F [44]	4.65	-	-	13.17	23.99	
HD3F-ft [44]	(0.81)	1.4	**2.26**	1.31	4.10	6.55
IOFPL-no-ft	2.52	-	-	8.32	20.33	-
IOFPL-ft	(0.73)	1.2	2.29	1.17	3.40	6.52
IOFPL-CVr8-no-ft	2.37	-	-	7.09	18.93	-
IOFPL-CVr8-ft	(0.76)	1.2	2.25	1.14	3.28	6.35

5   Conclusions

In this paper we have reviewed the concept of spatial feature pyramids in context of modern, deep learning based optical flow algorithms. We presented complementary improvements for cost volume construction at a single pyramid level, that i) departed from a warping- to a sampling-based strategy to overcome issues like handling large motions for small objects, and ii) adaptively shifted the focus of the optimization towards under-performing predictions by means of a loss max-pooling strategy. We further analyzed the gradient flow across pyramid levels and found that properly eliminating noisy or potentially contradicting ones improved convergence and led to better performance. We applied our proposed modifications in combination with additional, interpretable flow cue extensions as well as distillation strategies to preserve knowledge from (synthetic) pre-training stages throughout multiple rounds of fine-tuning. We experimentally analyzed and ablated all our proposed contributions on a wide range of standard benchmark datasets, and obtained new state-of-the-art results on Sintel and Kitti 2012.

Acknowledgements. T. Pock and M. Hofinger acknowledge that this work was supported by the ERC starting grant HOMOVIS (No. 640156).

References

1. Baker, S., Scharstein, D., Lewis, J.P., Roth, S., Black, M.J., Szeliski, R.: A database and evaluation methodology for optical flow. Int. J. Comput. Vis. **92**(1), 1–31 (2011). https://doi.org/10.1007/s11263-010-0390-2
2. Bar-Haim, A., Wolf, L.: ScopeFlow: dynamic scene scoping for optical flow. In: CVPR, June 2020
3. Bouguet, J.Y.: Pyramidal implementation of the Lucas Kanade feature tracker. Intel Corporation Microprocess. Res. Labs **5**(1–10), 4 (2000)
4. Brox, T., Bruhn, A., Papenberg, N., Weickert, J.: High accuracy optical flow estimation based on a theory for warping. In: ECCV (2004)
5. Butler, D.J., Wulff, J., Stanley, G.B., Black, M.J.: A naturalistic open source movie for optical flow evaluation. In: Fitzgibbon, A., et al. (eds.) European Conference on Computer Vision (ECCV), pp. 611–625. Part IV. LNCS 7577. Springer-Verlag, October 2012, The MPI Sintel Flow Dataset presented in this work uses a modified version of the Sintel movie copyright Blender Foundation, www.sintel.org
6. Chaudhury, K., Mehrotra, R.: A trajectory-based computational model for optical flow estimation. IEEE Trans. Robot. Autom. **11**(5), 733–741 (1995). https://doi.org/10.1109/70.466611
7. Dollár, P., Zitnick, C.L.: Structured forests for fast edge detection. In: (ICCV) (2013)
8. Dosovitskiy, A., et al.: FlowNet: learning optical flow with convolutional networks. In: IEEE International Conference on Computer Vision (ICCV) (2015). http://lmb.informatik.uni-freiburg.de/Publications/2015/DFIB15
9. Fortun, D., Bouthemy, P., Kervrann, C.: Optical flow modeling and computation. Comput. Vis. Image Underst. **134**(C), 1–21, May 2015. https://doi.org/10.1016/j.cviu.2015.02.008

10. Garg, R., Roussos, A., Agapito, L.: A variational approach to video registration with subspace constraints. Int. J. Comput. Vis. **104**(3), 286–314, September 2013. https://doi.org/10.1007/s11263-012-0607-7
11. Geiger, A., Lenz, P., Stiller, C., Urtasun, R.: Vision meets robotics: the KITTI dataset. IJRR **32**(11), 1231–1237 (2013)
12. Hinton, G.E., Vinyals, S., Dean, J.: Distilling the knowledge in a neural network. In: Deep Learning Workshop, NIPS (2014)
13. Horn, B.K.P., Schunck, B.G.: Determining optical flow. Artif. Intell. **17**, 185–203 (1981)
14. Hui, T.W., Tang, X., Loy, C.C.: A lightweight optical flow CNN - revisiting data fidelity and regularization. arXiv preprint arXiv:1903.07414 (2019). http://mmlab. ie.cuhk.edu.hk/projects/LiteFlowNet/
15. Hur, J., Roth, S.: Iterative residual refinement for joint optical flow and occlusion estimation. In: CVPR (2019)
16. Ilg, E., Mayer, N., Saikia, T., Keuper, M., Dosovitskiy, A., Brox, T.: FlowNet 2.0: evolution of optical flow estimation with deep networks. In: CVPR (2017). http:// lmb.informatik.uni-freiburg.de/Publications/2017/IMSKDB17
17. Ilg, E., Saikia, T., Keuper, M., Brox, T.: Occlusions, motion and depth boundaries with a generic network for disparity, optical flow or scene flow estimation. In: ECCV (2018)
18. Jiang, H., Sun, D., Jampani, V., Lv, Z., Learned-Miller, E., Kautz, J.: SENSE: a shared encoder network for scene-flow estimation. In: The IEEE International Conference on Computer Vision (ICCV), October 2019
19. Jiang, W., Sun, W., Tagliasacchi, A., Trulls, E., Yi, K.M.: Linearized multi-sampling for differentiable image transformation. In: ICCV, pp. 2988–2997 (2019)
20. Liu, P., King, I., Lyu, M.R., Xu, S.J.: DDFlow: learning optical flow with unlabeled data distillation. CoRR abs/1902.09145 (2019)
21. Liu, P., Lyu, M.R., King, I., Xu, J.: SelFlow: self-supervised learning of optical flow. In: CVPR (2019)
22. Lu, Y., Valmadre, J., Wang, H., Kannala, J., Harandi, M., Torr, P.: Devon: deformable volume network for learning optical flow. In: The IEEE Winter Conference on Applications of Computer Vision (WACV), March 2020
23. Lucas, B.D., Kanade, T.: An iterative image registration technique with an application to stereo vision. In: Proceedings of Imaging Understanding Workshop, pp. 4884–4893 (1981). http://cseweb.ucsd.edu/classes/sp02/cse252/lucaskanade81.pdf
24. Mac Aodha, O., Humayun, A., Pollefeys, M., Brostow, G.J.: Learning a confidence measure for optical flow. IEEE Trans. Pattern Anal. Mach. Intell. **35**(5), 1107–1120 (2013). https://doi.org/10.1109/TPAMI.2012.171
25. Menze, M., Heipke, C., Geiger, A.: Joint 3D estimation of vehicles and scene flow. In: ISPRS Workshop on Image Sequence Analysis (ISA) (2015)
26. Menze, M., Heipke, C., Geiger, A.: Object scene flow. ISPRS J. Photogrammetry Remote Sens. (JPRS) **140**, 60–76 (2018)
27. Ranjan, A., Black, M.J.: Optical flow estimation using a spatial pyramid network. In: 2017 IEEE Conference on Computer Vision and Pattern Recognition (CVPR), pp. 2720–2729, July 2017. https://doi.org/10.1109/CVPR.2017.291
28. Ren, Z., Gallo, O., Sun, D., Yang, M.H., Sudderth, E.B., Kautz, J.: A fusion approach for multi-frame optical flow estimation. In: IEEE Winter Conference on Applications of Computer Vision (2019)
29. Revaud, J., Weinzaepfel, P., Harchaoui, Z., Schmid, C.: Epicflow: Edge-preserving interpolation of correspondences for optical flow. CoRR (2015)

30. Rota Bulò, S., Neuhold, G., Kontschieder, P.: Loss max-pooling for semantic image segmentation. In: CVPR, July 2017
31. Bulò, S.R., Porzi, L., Kontschieder, P.: Dropout distillation. In: Proceedings of The 33rd International Conference on Machine Learning, Proceedings of Machine Learning Research. PMLR, 20–22 June 2016, New York, USA , vol. 48, pp. 99–107 (2016)
32. Rota Bulò, S., Porzi, L., Kontschieder, P.: In-place activated batchnorm for memory-optimized training of DNNs. In: (CVPR) (2018)
33. Santurkar, S., Tsipras, D., Ilyas, A., Mądry, A.: How does batch normalization help optimization? In: Proceedings of the 32nd International Conference on Neural Information Processing Systems. (NIPS 2018), pp. 2488–2498. Curran Associates Inc., Red Hook (2018)
34. Sun, D., Roth, S., Black, M.J.: Secrets of optical flow estimation and their principles. In: CVPR, pp. 2432–2439 (2010)
35. Sun, D., Roth, S., Black, M.J.: A quantitative analysis of current practices in optical flow estimation and the principles behind them. Int. J. Comput. Vis. **106**(2), 115–137 (2014). https://doi.org/10.1007/s11263-013-0644-x
36. Sun, D., Yang, X., Liu, M.Y., Kautz, J.: PWC-Net: CNNs for optical flow using pyramid, warping, and cost volume. In: CVPR (2018)
37. Sun, D., Yang, X., Liu, M.Y., Kautz, J.: Models matter, so does training: an empirical study of CNNs for optical flow estimation. IEEE Trans. Pattern Anal. Mach. Intell. (TPAMI) **42**(6), 1408–1423 (2020). https://doi.org/10.1109/TPAMI.2019.2894353 (to appear)
38. Wang, C., Chen, X., Smola, A.J., Xing, E.P.: Variance reduction for stochastic gradient optimization. In: Burges, C.J.C., Bottou, L., Welling, M., Ghahramani, Z., Weinberger, K.Q. (eds.) Advances in Neural Information Processing Systems 26, pp. 181–189. Curran Associates, Inc. (2013). http://papers.nips.cc/paper/5034-variance-reduction-for-stochastic-gradient-optimization.pdf
39. Wang, Y., Yang, Y., Yang, Z., Zhao, L., Wang, P., Xu, W.: Occlusion aware unsupervised learning of optical flow. In: CVPR, pp. 4884–4893 (2018). https://doi.org/10.1109/CVPR.2018.00513
40. Weinzaepfel, P., Revaud, J., Harchaoui, Z., Schmid, C.: DeepFlow: large displacement optical flow with deep matching. In: IEEE Intenational Conference on Computer Vision (ICCV), Sydney, Australia, December 2013. http://hal.inria.fr/hal-00873592
41. Werlberger, M., Trobin, W., Pock, T., Wedel, A., Cremers, D., Bischof, H.: Anisotropic Huber-L1 optical flow. In: Proceedings of the British Machine Vision Conference (BMVC), London, UK, September 2009 (to appear)
42. Yamaguchi, K., McAllester, D., Urtasun, R.: Efficient joint segmentation, occlusion labeling, stereo and flow estimation. In: ECCV (2014)
43. Yang, G., Ramanan, D.: Volumetric correspondence networks for optical flow. In: Advances in Neural Information Processing Systems 32, pp. 793–803. Curran Associates, Inc. (2019). http://papers.nips.cc/paper/8367-volumetric-correspondence-networks-for-optical-flow.pdf
44. Yin, Z., Darrell, T., Yu, F.: Hierarchical discrete distribution decomposition for match density estimation. In: CVPR (2019)
45. Yu, J.J., Harley, A.W., Derpanis, K.G.: Back to basics: unsupervised learning of optical flow via brightness constancy and motion smoothness. In: Computer Vision - ECCV 2016 Workshops, Part 3 (2016)

Author Index

Printed in the United States
By Bookmasters